DICTIONARY OF IRISH LITERATURE

DICTIONARY OF IRISH LITERATURE

Revised and Expanded Edition

A–L

ROBERT HOGAN, EDITOR-IN-CHIEF

ASSOCIATE EDITORS: Zack Bowen,
Richard Burnham, Mary Rose Callaghan,
Anne Colman, Peter Costello, William J. Feeney,
Maryanne Felter, James Kilroy, Bernard McKenna,
and Marguerite Quintelli-Neary

GREENWOOD PRESS
Westport, Connecticut • London

Library of Congress Cataloging-in-Publication Data

Dictionary of Irish literature / Robert Hogan, editor-in-chief ;
    associate editors, Zack Bowen . . . [et al.].—Rev. and expanded ed.
        p.   cm.
    Includes bibliographical references and index.
    ISBN 0–313–29172–1 (alk. paper : set).—ISBN 0–313–30175–1 (alk. paper : A-L).—
ISBN 0–313–30176–X (alk. paper : M-Z)
    1.   English literature—Irish authors—Dictionaries.   2. Ireland—
In literature—Dictionaries.   3. Irish literature—Dictionaries.
I.   Hogan, Robert Goode.   II.   Bowen, Zack R.
PR8706.D5   1996
820'.99415—dc20   95–50428

British Library Cataloguing in Publication Data is available.

Library of Congress Catalog Card Number: 95–50428
ISBN: 0–313–29172–1 (set)
        0–313–30175–1 (A-L)
        0–313–30176–X (M-Z)

First published in 1996

Greenwood Press, 88 Post Road West, Westport, CT 06881
An imprint of Greenwood Publishing Group, Inc.

Printed in the United States of America

The paper used in this book complies with the
Permanent Paper Standard issued by the National
Information Standards Organization (Z39.48–1984).

10   9   8   7   6   5   4   3   2   1

CONTENTS

CONTRIBUTORS

Jonathan Allison
University of Kentucky

Mary Ball
Dublin

Ivy Bannister
Dublin

John Barrett
University College, Dublin

Sheila Barrett
Dublin

Kate Bateman
Dublin

Jerry C. Beasley
University of Delaware

Paul Bew
Queen's University of Belfast

John Boyd
Belfast

Zack Bowen
University of Miami

Terence Brown
Trinity College, Dublin

Richard Burnham
Dominican College

Mary Rose Callaghan
Bray, Co. Wicklow

Anne Clune
Trinity College, Dublin

Anne Colman
*Institute of Irish Studies,
Queen's University, Belfast*

Evelyn Conlon
Dublin

Peter Costello
Dublin

Dennis Cotter, Jr.
Dublin

Jane Cunningham
Dublin

Kathleen Danaher
Wilmington, Delaware

John F. Deane
Dedalus Press

Seamus de Burca
Dublin

Celia de Fréine
Dublin

Tim Dennehy
Mullagh, Co. Clare

Alan Denson
Aberdeenshire

Barbara DiBernard
University of Nebraska

William G. Dolde
University of Iowa

Mary E. Donnelly
University of Miami

Aileen Douglas
Trinity College, Dublin

James Douglas
Bray, Co. Wicklow

Rachel Douglas
Bray, Co. Wicklow

Paul A. Doyle
Nassau Community College

Peter Drewniany
Germantown Academy

Seán Dunne

Grace Eckley

Owen Dudley Edwards
University of Edinburgh

Antony Farrell
Lilliput Press

Christopher Fauske
University of New Hampshire

William J. Feeney
Oak Park, Illinois

Maryanne Felter
Cayuga Community College

Deborah Fleming
Ashland University

John Wilson Foster
University of British Columbia

Jean Franks
Anaheim, California

Barbara Freitag
Dublin City University

Helmut E. Gerber

Priscilla Goldsmith
University of Delaware

Eamon Grennan
Vassar College

Christopher Griffin
Strayer College, Washington, D.C.

Patricia Boyle Haberstroh
La Salle University

Andrew Haggerty
Miami University

Jay L. Halio
University of Delaware

Jack Harte
Lucan Community College

Mark D. Hawthorne
James Madison University

Rüdiger Imhof
University of Wuppertal

K.P.S. Jochum
University of Bamburg

Fred Johnston
Galway

Richard M. Kain

Colbert Kearney
University College, Cork

A. A. Kelly
Lymington, Hampshire

Kevin Kerrane
University of Delaware

Frank Kersnowski
Trinity University

James Kilroy
Tulane University

Thomas Kinsella
County Wicklow

James Liddy
University of Wisconsin–Milwaukee

Nora F. Lindstrom

William J. Linn
University of Michigan–Dearborn

Victor Luftig
Brandeis University

M. Kelly Lynch
Babson College

J. B. Lyons
Royal College of Surgeons, Dublin

Dolores MacKenna
Dublin

Alf MacLochlainn
County Galway

Bryan MacMahon
Listowel, County Kerry

Michael McDonnell
Fairfield University

Patricia McFate

Nora McGuinness
University of California-Davis

Bernard McKenna
Middletown, Delaware

Sean McMahon
Derry

Donald McNamara
Catholic University of America

Andrew Marsh (John O'Donovan)

Augustine Martin
University College, Dublin

James H. Matthews

D.E.S. Maxwell
Belfast

Donald C. Mell
University of Delaware

Thomas F. Merrill
Sanibel, Florida

Liam Miller

Sven Eric Molin

Christopher Murray
University College, Dublin

Jerry H. Natterstad
Framingham State College

John Nemo

James Newcomer

Eilís Ní Dhuibhne
National Library of Ireland

Johann A. Norstedt
Virginia Tech

Micheál Ó hAodha
Dingle, County Kerry

Shawn O'Hare
Florida State University

Seamus O'Neill

Cóilín Owens
George Mason University

Christopher Penna
University of Delaware

Åke Persson
Sigturna International College of the Humanities, Uppsala

Richard Pine
Dublin

Raymond J. Porter

Victor Price

Kathleen A. Quinn
Queen's University, Belfast

Marguerite Quintelli-Neary
Winthrop University

Dorothy Robbie
Greystones, County Wicklow

Peter Robbie
Greystones, County Wicklow

Helen Ryan
Children's Literature Association of Ireland

Martin Ryan
Dublin

Ann Saddlemyer
University of Toronto

George Brandon Saul

N. A. Saunders
Convent of Mercy,
Callan, Co. Kilkenny

Bonnie Kime Scott
University of Delaware

Colin Smythe
Colin Smythe, Ltd.

Bruce Stewart
University of Ulster, Coleraine

Mary Helen Thuente
Indiana University/Purdue University,
Fort Wayne, Indiana

Alan Titley
St. Patrick's College, Drumcondra

Terence Winch
Smithsonian Institution

Terence de Vere White

PREFACE

A preliminary word seems necessary about the plan of this book.

The Introduction might really be titled "The Literary Uses of Ireland," for the principal characteristic of writing in Ireland is its Irishness. While this statement may seem obvious, it also is obvious that, since the Renaissance, nationality, as expressed in literature, has been increasingly diminished by internationality. For instance, the excellence of what D. H. Lawrence called "Classic American Literature" was considerably diluted by an international, and particularly an English, influence. The inimitable excellence of the nineteenth-century American authors Emerson, Thoreau, Poe, Hawthorne, Melville, and especially Walt Whitman appears to lie mainly in the extent to which they resisted that influence and allowed themselves to be receptive to their own native milieu. The triumphant progression of Russian literary masters in the nineteenth century, from Pushkin to Gogol to Tolstoy and Dostoyevsky, Turgenev, and Chekhov, certainly must be attributed to the backwardness, the provinciality, the isolation, and the ingrown "Russianness" of their society.

Irish society also, until the very recent past, remained surprisingly insulated from the modern world. Although in many ways pernicious, that isolation did have the effect of intensely focusing the attention of the Irish writer on the little world of his Four Green Fields. Even now, when Ireland is a much more outward-looking society, the effects remain dramatically evident. The Introduction, then, is an attempt to chart how the Irish writer used this narrow, but rich, subject matter—the landscape, the climate, the history, the manners, the morals, the customs of his native land.

The Introduction is not a capsule review of Ireland past and present, as any attempt to compress so much information into so little space would be to court superficiality with a vengeance. Rather, it deals with those facets of Ireland that the writers themselves have thought the most salient and that have appeared so constantly in their work. As a historical or sociological or even literary survey, the Introduction is too short and malproportioned to serve; but as a not wholly subjective view of how Ireland's writers have portrayed their country, and of what those writers have thought important, it may introduce the reader to at least the primary preoccupations of Irish literature.

In planning this dictionary, the most difficult editorial question to resolve has been how to treat literature written in the Irish language. Such literature is centuries-old and continues to be written even today. The range of that literature, from saga to satire, is broad indeed, and the quality of much of that literature is brilliant. However, the fortunes of the Irish language have been wedded to the fortunes of the Irish nation. As England's power waxed in Ireland, the old Irish culture waned and Irish as a living language progressively decayed. The year 1800 may be taken as symptomatic of the triumph of the English language in Ireland. In that year, the Act of Union abolished the separate Irish Parliament and included Irish representatives in Westminster. Irish, of course, was still spoken, but as the sole language it survived only in secluded rural pockets. An Irish language revival around the turn of the twentieth century was a harbinger of the secretly growing political revival that was to culminate in the Easter Rising of 1916, in the Irish Free State, and finally in an independent republic that comprised most of the island. However, political independence did not mean that the Irish language could be restored as the living language of the people. Ireland became nominally bilingual, but, despite great dedication and immense effort, it was impossible to go back.

Today, Irish alone is spoken in a few small sections of the country. The language is studied in the schools from an early age, and some modern books of merit have been written in Irish. Nevertheless, it remains true that the great works of modern Irish literature have been written in English. It is also lamentably true that the classic works of the Irish language are to be perceived, even by the Irish themselves, mainly through their influence on modern Irish writing in English. Whether in direct translation, adaptation, or even simply as a fecund source of allusion and inspiration, that influence is profound and pervasive, but it is an influence at one remove.

A dictionary of Irish literature assuredly must deal with writing in Irish. Apart from its own extraordinary merits, literature in Irish remains the bedrock foundation for much, if not most, modern Irish writing in English. Nevertheless, it seemed that this work must stress Irish writing in the English language. After all, W. B. Yeats, James Stephens, and James Joyce are the mirrors in which the entire world, including Ireland itself, sees reflected the old Ireland that was. Consequently, we have adopted a compromise by reprinting from the first edition the lengthy critical and historical survey of writing in Irish. This survey was written by the late Seamus O'Neill, himself a distinguished writer who published mainly in Irish. The survey of the most recent writing in Irish by Alan Titley has been written specially for this second edition; and both chapters are a most necessary preliminary to the bulk of the dictionary, which treats Irish writing in English.

The first edition of this book contained 470 entries on authors who wrote mainly in the English language. The entries contained biographical data, critical evaluation, and a bibliography. This edition contains about 1,000 such entries and about 200 short entries, mainly of very recent authors, which give only bibliographical and sometimes biographical information. Most of the new entries are devoted to the extraordinary number of new writers who have appeared in the Irish publishing explosion of the last fifteen years. However, the number of writers from the eighteenth and nineteenth centuries has been considerably expanded also.

The choice of authors to be included has been basically the decision of the editor, although he has availed himself of the oral suggestions of so many people and of the written opinions of so many more, that the final choice probably approaches a consensus. Most of the authors included are obvious choices, authors whose omission would have been ridiculous from the standpoint of either literature or history. The choice, however, of the most recent authors, those who appeared from 1980 to 1995, has been the most difficult, not only because there have been so many of them but also because one is too close to them to see clearly. I fully expect that the next fifteen years will witness the flowering of some reputations that seem at the moment unimpressive and whose authors I may not have included. I hasten to offer my mea culpas in advance. In the first edition I remarked that I fully expected to be asked, ''Why did you leave out the brilliant A_____ and include that poetaster X_____?'' My answer must still be the same: ''The reason is probably attributable to ignorance, bias, lack of taste, and human fallibility.''

Still and all, in this area of minimal excellence and excellent potential, there is no thoroughly satisfactory solution. One arbitrary solution adopted in the first edition was to limit the entries almost exclusively to authors who have published a book, no matter how slim. I have not entirely been able to keep to that criterion in this second, much expanded edition. Another arbitrary criterion was to lend a tolerant ear to new writers who are still establishing themselves. There are so many new writers that I fear I have not entirely been able to keep to that criterion either.

I have again included a few Irish writers—among them Congreve and Goldsmith and Sheridan and even George Darley—who hardly wrote of Ireland at all. My reasons are partly an intractable bias in their favor and partly pure chauvinism. A few foreign authors were included in the first edition, because of the rich and lasting contribution they had made to Irish literature. Such volumes as, for instance, Robin Flower's *The Western Island* or Richard Ellmann's *James Joyce* or J. P. Donleavy's *The Ginger Man* or J. G. Farrell's *Troubles* seem classics of Irish literature, and to have omitted their remarkable authors from this company would have been chauvinistic indeed. In this edition, the number of foreign authors has been somewhat expanded to include, for instance, from the nineteenth century, Trollope and Thackeray, and from the twentieth, Thomas Flanagan and Nina Fitzpatrick (even though a prestigious award to Fitzpatrick was withdrawn because she was not Irish).

I hope that no author of outstanding achievement has been omitted. However, that was what I wrongly hoped about the first edition, and I daresay that I am still wrong. If so, perhaps some other, and younger, editor will make amends at some future date.

The length of the alphabetical entries varies from about 25 words to about 10,000, and obviously the length of an entry implies some judgment about the author's work as it at present appears. However, this is only a very rough judgment, and the reader is cautioned not to regard Author A, who is discussed in 250 words, as one-sixth less admirable than Author B, who is discussed in 1,500. Also, the length of the articles has not entirely been my editorial judgment. There are many entries longer than my personal judgment of an author's worth might have allowed, and this is particularly so in the case of the recent writers. However, there is a received general critical opinion about the literary worth of nearly every author discussed here. Although I think that a good deal of contemporary Irish literary criticism is gushingly hyperbolic, it would be editorially arrogant to ignore it.

The Irish are, possibly with good reason, fond of the term ''begrudgery,'' which means a snidely vicious condemnation. This is not a begrudger's book. The authors of the individual entries have been chosen not only for their taste and knowledge but also for their enthusiasm about their author. Some few comments in this volume strike me as more book-blurbish than critical, but the glumness of much recent Irish writing may have affected my own aging and increasingly sour critical view, and so I have, of course, welcomed my commentators' enthusiasms. Some other comments—among them possibly a few of my own—are doubtless hard-hitting, but the reason, I trust, is not begrudgery, but judicious judgment, which must be the chief criterion for a volume such as this. As Richard Stanyhurst well remarked in 1584, ''I have no stomach for decrying anyone with stinging insults nor do I consider it to be in keeping with my dignity (insofar as it exists) to insinuate myself into the ear with bland, emollient words.''

The body of the dictionary also contains a handful of general articles on topics such as folklore and children's literature. At one time, I contemplated a larger number of these articles, which would deal with historical writing, travel writing, biographies, memoirs, journalism, broadcasting, and other endeavors whose best examples have strong claims to literary worth. After much consideration, however, I decided that comprehensive surveys of such fields would not only extend the book greatly but also dissipate its major impact by including much that was tangential or transitory. On the other hand, individual entries for major historians, political writers, editors, orators, journalists, and the like have been expanded. The dictionary also contains a number of entries for important organizations or publications, such as the Abbey Theatre, the Cuala Press, and *The Nation*.

The original entries from the first edition have been in every instance reconsidered, revised, corrected, and frequently expanded. In nearly all instances, the revision has been made by the original writer. However, since the first edition of this book, some of its most distinguished authors have died: Helmut Gerber, Richard M. Kain, Liam Miller, Sven Eric Molin, John Nemo, John O'Donovan ("Andrew Marsh"), Seamus O'Neill, Raymond J. Porter, George Brandon Saul, and Terence de Vere White. In every instance, their original entries seemed sound enough to stand, with only an occasional sentence or two appended to add significant new matter. In a few instances, I have not been able to contact the original writers, and often I have allowed those sound entries to stand also.

The particular articles have been signed by their authors, and any unsigned entries have been written by the general editor. Finally, a person's name or topic or organization followed by an asterisk has its own separate entry in the appropriate alphabetical place in the dictionary.

Perhaps a third to a half of this book consists of bibliographies. The bibliographies of specific writers or topics follow their individual entries. Most have been compiled by the author of the entry, although the editor is responsible for the bibliographical form of the citations and has frequently made additions and, occasionally, deletions. In the case of the important and complicated W. B. Yeats bibliography, however, the original compiler was deceased; and the revised and expanded bibliography has been entrusted to the leading authority, K.P.S. Jochum. The individual bibliographies list all of the author's significant work, and "significant work" has usually been taken to mean every individual book publication and the important fugitive material. In many instances, it has been possible to list practically everything an author is known to have written. However, in the case of an extremely important or prolific writer, such as Shaw or Yeats, a complete listing has been impossible. Even so, a diligent attempt has been made to list everything of primary or even secondary importance.

The individual bibliographies are divided into two sections. The first section lists the writer's works in the order in which they were published. Usually, American editions as well as British and Irish ones are listed. The second, and usually shorter, section lists the major critical, biographical, and bibliographical works about the writer and is arranged alphabetically by the last names of the authors, editors, or compilers. To conserve space, the name of the publisher has been shortened to its essential components: thus, Maunsel and Company appears simply as "Maunsel," the Dolmen Press simply as "Dolmen," and so on (though "Press" is retained in university presses). The subtitles of books have usually been retained.

Although the limitations of space and human energy have prevented an exhaustive or complete listing, I believe that these bibliographies as a whole constitute the most comprehensive listing of Irish literature that is in print or is likely to be in print for many years.

The Chronology of historical and literary events given at the end of the dictionary is intended not as a substitute for a basic grasp of Irish history and literature but as a simple chart for the neophyte traveler in moments of occasional bafflement. For more precise knowledge, the reader is directed to the excellent volumes of history and literary history cited in the general Bibliography. The latter is a concise listing of the best general books on Ireland, its geography, its climate, its history, its economics, its architecture, its customs, and, particularly, its literature.

A dictionary or an encyclopedia does not always have an index. This volume does, and I trust that the reader will quickly appreciate its utility. Irish literature has emerged from a small and close-knit society. One Irish wit remarked that a literary movement occurred when a number of writers lived in the same place and did not speak to each other. There is a deal of justice in that remark, but in Ireland the writers do always speak about each other. They also necessarily work together, and they inevitably influence one another. For instance, the most pervasive influence in modern Irish literature has been W. B. Yeats, who is discussed at considerable length in the entry by Richard M. Kain. However, Yeats was of crucial importance for the careers of scores of writers, and additional information about him appears throughout this book. To a lesser extent, that same point is valid for many other writers. Hence, judicious readers will not only read the article about the author they are interested in but also consult the Index for other citations.

To save space, there are no separate entries for individual works in the text, unless the author is unknown. Thus, a discussion of *Ulysses* or *Juno and the Paycock* will be found under the entries for their authors, Joyce and O'Casey. If the reader knows the work and not the author, he may quickly find a discussion of the work by referring to its title in the Index. An anonymous work like *The Táin,* which is not entered separately in the dictionary but is discussed in Seamus O'Neill's chapter on Gaelic literature, can also be located through use of the Index. The Index does not cite information from the bibliographies, but everything cited in the text proper—both in the introductory material and in the alphabetical entries—is noted.

Not every Irish author or magazine or literary society has been thought important enough to be accorded a separate listing in the body of the work. However, a glance at the Index will indicate that many of these individuals or organizations have been discussed somewhere in the dictionary. For instance, Richard Lovell Edgeworth is cited only in the Index but will be found briefly discussed in the entry on his very important daughter, Maria; the magazine *Threshold* is cited only in the Index but will be found in the entry on its parent organization, the Lyric Players Theatre of Belfast.

An editor of such a volume as this must feel like the captain of a ship manned by many and much more knowledgeable sailors than he. As I have that feeling quite strongly, I should like to mention my particular gratitude to the late Richard M. Kain, the late John O'Donovan, the late Seamus O'Neill, and the late

Sven Eric Molin, whose erudition, kindness, and generous labors contributed immensely to the first edition of this work. To Zack Bowen, Mary Rose Callaghan, William J. Feeney, and James Kilroy I am indebted for their continuing contributions, and to their names I must add those of Anne Colman, Peter Costello, Maryanne Felter, Bernard McKenna, Cóilín Owens, Marguerite Quintelli-Neary, and Alan Titley. To them and to a host of others, particularly to Mervyn Wall and to Lis Pihl, who called my attention to errors and omissions, my deepest and most abiding thanks.

Dr. Johnson said, "A man will turn over half a library to make one book." Of the half a library that was turned over in the making of this book, there were some volumes to which I constantly returned and to which every student of Irish literature must remain indebted. I have particularly in mind D. J. O'Donoghue's *The Poets of Ireland,* Stephen J. Brown's *Ireland in Fiction,* Richard Best's *Bibliography of Irish Philology* and its sequel, Patrick Rafroidi's *Irish Literature in English: The Romantic Period,* Brian McKenna's *Irish Literature, 1800–1875,* and *The Field Day Anthology* of Seamus Deane and others. I have constantly had recourse to the annual bibliographies printed by the Modern Language Association of America and to those in the *Irish University Review* and *Études Irlandaises;* and my copies of Anne M. Brady and Brian Cleeve's *A Biographical Dictionary of Irish Writers* and of Anne Owens Weekes's *Unveiling Treasures: The Attic Guide to the Published Works of Irish Women Literary Writers* have become well thumbed.

It was momentarily gratifying to hear that several Irish librarians referred to the first edition as "the bible." It was, however, a bible with missing pages. In correcting that edition, I was chagrined to discover more errors than I had thought possible to be there. I am certain that errors of fact have undoubtedly found their way in here also, and I will be most grateful if readers will bring them to my attention. I hope that this new edition might also be thought worthy enough to be termed a bible, for a bible has its "Revelations." Undoubtedly, this volume also has some heresies of opinion, and I am happy enough with them too. If they prove, finally, errors of judgment, let Time be the judge, for he is much more judicious than I and considerably less vulnerable.

Robert Hogan
Bray, Co. Wicklow
November 30, 1995

ACKNOWLEDGMENTS

For permission to quote published material, the editor and publisher gratefully make the following acknowledgments: to the Blackstaff Press for lines from Norman Dugdale's *Running Repairs.* Belfast: Blackstaff, 1983 and from Michael Foley's *The Go Situation.* Dundonald, N. I.: Blackstaff, 1982, and *Insomnia in the Afternoon.* Belfast: Blackstaff, 1994; to John and Patricia Coffey for various lines by Brian Coffey; to Colin Smythe, Ltd. for quotations from Austin Clarke's *Collected Poems;* to Anthony Cronin for lines from several poems; to the Dedalus Press for lines from Chris Agee's *In the New Hampshire Woods,* for lines from Padraig J. Daly, for lines from "Corc's Gold Vessel" and "Setting the Type" from Greg Delanty's *Southward,* for lines from Conleth Ellis's *Darkness Blossoming,* for lines from "Joyce Cycling to Oughterard and Vico" from John Ennis's *Down in the Deeper Helicon,* for lines from "During the Illness of Dolores Ibarruri" from John Jordan's *Collected Poems,* for lines from Hugh Maxton's *The Engraved Passion,* and for lines from *Personal Places* in Thomas Kinsella's Peppercanister volume; to Gill & Macmillan for lines from "After Love," "Goodbye," "Ploughman and Kestrel," and "West of Here" from Conleth Ellis's *Under the Stone;* to Graywolf Press and Eamon Grennan for lines from various poems: "A Closer Look" copyright 1989 by Eamon Grennan. Reprinted from *What Light There Is* with the permission of Graywolf Press, Saint Paul, Minnesota and "Breaking Point," "Sea Dog," "The Cave Painters" copyright 1991 by Eamon Grennan. Reprinted from *As If It Matters* with the permission of Graywolf Press, Saint Paul, Minnesota; to Faber and Faber Ltd for quotations from *Wintering Out, North, Station Island, The Haw Lantern,* and *Seeing Things* by Seamus Heaney, Faber and Faber Ltd; selections from *Selected Poems* 1966–1987 by Seamus Heaney. Copyright © 1990 by Seamus Heaney. Reprinted by permission of Farrar, Straus & Giroux, Inc.; selections from *Seeing Things* by Seamus Heaney. Copyright © 1991 by Seamus Heaney. Reprinted by permission of Farrar, Straus & Giroux, Inc.; to James Liddy for lines from *In a Blue Smoke;* to Michael Longley for lines from ''Letters'' and ''Wounds'' from *An Exploded View;* to Michael Longley and Wake Forest University Press: lines from ''Northern Lights'' and ''Laertes'' by Michael Longley are reprinted from *Gorse Fires* with the permission of Wake Forest University Press; to Martin Secker & Warburg Ltd; for Michael Longley, *Gorse Fires,* London: Martin Secker & Warburg Ltd; to The Lilliput Press for lines from ''Winter Landscape'' from Bryan Guinness's *On a Ledge;* to Roy McFadden and Chatto & Windus for lines from *The Garryowen.* London: Chatto & Windus, 1971; to Mercier Press for permission to use lines from Sigerson Clifford's ''The Boys of Barr na Sraide,'' Cork: Mercier, 1989; to Faber and Faber Ltd for *Quoof* and *Meeting the British* by Paul Muldoon, Faber and Faber Ltd; lines from ''Gathering Mushrooms'' from *Quoof,* ''Meeting the British,'' and ''7, Middagh Street'' from *Meeting the British* by Paul Muldoon are reprinted with the permission of Wake Forest University Press. To Richard Murphy for lines from *Sailing to an Island, High Island, The Price of Stone* and *The Mirror Wall;* to Máire Cruise O'Brien for lines from Sean MacEntee's *The Poems of John Francis MacEntee;* to Faber and Faber Ltd for *Seize the Fire, The Strange Museum* and *Liberty Tree* by Tom Paulin, Faber and Faber Ltd; to Dennis O'Driscoll for lines from ''Someone'' from his volume *Kist;* to R. Dardis Clarke, 21 Pleasants Street, Dublin 8, for lines from *Night and Morning* and *Ancient Lights* by Austin Clarke; to Salmon Publishing, Ltd., for lines of Nuala Archer from *Two Women, Two Shores* and from *The Hour of Pan Ama,* for lines of Roz Cowman from *The Goose Herd,* for lines of Rita Ann Higgins from *Goddess & Witch,* from *Witch in the Bushes,* and from *Philomena's Revenge,* and for lines of Desmond O'Grady from *Tipperary.* To Carcanet Press Limited, for permission to quote the remarks on Austin Clarke from Thomas Kinsella's *The Dual Tradition: An Essay on Poetry and Politics in Ireland* (1995). To Bloodaxe Books Ltd for permission to use material by Åke Persson.

DICTIONARY OF
IRISH LITERATURE

INTRODUCTION

Ireland is a small, wet island about four hours to the west of England if you travel by the mailboat from Holyhead to Dun Laoghaire. The island was not considered important enough to conquer by Julius Caesar, but ever since then it has been thrusting itself upon the world's notice. Indeed, despite its small size and population, its negligible mineral resources, and its minor strategic value in time of war, Ireland has taken up a remarkable amount of the world's attention.

The country's richest contribution to the world has been its emigrants. Otherwise, Ireland has been, until quite recently, mainly absorbed by itself. Sometimes it has seemed to assume that the world would find that subject equally interesting, and, despite moments of exasperation with that "most distressful country," the world usually has been interested and often fascinated.

Perhaps the reason is that there is an Irish Problem. One caustic thinker shrugged the matter off by remarking, "The Irish problem—there is always an Irish problem. It is the Irish." The Irish themselves would probably say that the problem is the outsiders. For centuries, they would point out, their little bit of heaven has been overrun by outsiders who have victimized, exploited, and oppressed the inhabitants. The oppressor may have been the Danes, the Normans, the English, or American blue jeans, hamburgers, vulgarity and affluence.

The world's view is somewhat similar: Ireland is an ideal; we regard its fields as greener, its virgins purer, and its poets wittier than any others anywhere ever were. It is the repository of whimsy, charm, and geniality, and yet. . . . And yet something diabolical is always going on in that little bit of heaven. The Potato Famines of the 1840s, to take but one example, were probably the most effective decimation of a race until Hitler turned his attention to the Jews. Perhaps the Irish decimation was even worse because it happened not by madness or any overt policy, but simply by the inability to cope, by incompetence, and by not caring enough. Then there have been all of the other diabolical instances—the assassinations, the wars, and the continuing petty turmoil that is a microcosm of the world's turmoil.

In our hearts we probably know that every place is a ravaged Eden, but in Ireland we seem to see more clearly our own plight, our own faults, and our own fate. Yet why do we see it there? Why has Wales or Finland or Iceland not so held the attention of the world? Why have there been so many memorable and resounding voices from this island, which today numbers only about 3.5 million souls in the Republic and a million and a half more in the North?

Any answer must be speculative and subjective, and this book attempts only part of an answer. That part is concerned with why Ireland has been blessed with such a proportionately startling number of extraordinary writers. In philosophy, music, painting, sculpture, architecture, and practically every branch of human endeavor, the Irish contribution to the wealth of the world's wisdom has been, as one would expect, minor. In literature, however, in decade after decade and in century after century, this small country has produced men like Swift and Burke and Berkeley, Sheridan and Goldsmith and Wilde, Shaw and Yeats and Joyce, Synge and Fitzmaurice, O'Casey and O'Flaherty, O'Connor and O'Faolain, Bowen and Behan and Beckett, and many, many others. This volume attempts to tell something about these Irish writers and their work, but this introductory essay will attempt to suggest something more—to suggest why there were so many who were so good.

The qualities that have formed the Irish writer are the qualities that have formed the Irish man. Among them are:

GEOGRAPHY AND CLIMATE

The effects of geography and climate upon Ireland have been crucial in its history, its economy, and the character of its people.

The landscape of Ireland is startlingly beautiful and extremely various. The weather is statistically, if not convincingly, temperate, but the perennially falling rain may at any moment be dissipated by the most dramatic appearance of blue sky to be seen anywhere in the world. The combination of mountain and bog, lake and lowland with a gentle climate and abundant rain has made the country most profitable for the growing of grass and the grazing of cattle. Hence, it has had a major effect upon the Irish economy. The combination of geography and climate upon people is perhaps even more important. Much of Ireland has a stark grandeur or a sensual beauty that can elevate or delight and that often does. However, the effect of the landscape is inevitably tempered by the weather. A good deal of the sombre and brooding character of the Irish landscape seems due to the quality of the light, to the constantly shifting and low-lying masses of clouds, and to the rain, the softly falling and ever-present rain. The psychic effect upon people must be subliminally schizophrenic—a depressed elevation, a dull delight briefly shot through with instants of manic joy. One might well argue that those are the tones of Irish literature.

One might almost say that those Irish novels that start off by describing a hot and sunny day usually turn out to be either exaggerations or simple entertainments. At any rate, one can say that descriptions of landscape in Irish literature impart not only the striking beauty of the country, but also even a spiritual overtone, an extra meaningfulness, much as landscape and weather, heath and storm, enrich the meaning of *King Lear.*

THE MEMORY OF THE DEAD

When a truce was called in the Anglo-Irish war in 1921, the Irish leader Eamon de Valera went to England to negotiate a final peace settlement with the English prime minister, Lloyd George. A story is told about de Valera then, which is too good to be true and yet too Irish to be basically wrong in anything but the facts. Someone asked after several days how negotiations were progressing, and the answer was that de Valera was rehearsing the historical background, and so far talks had progressed up to the Battle of Clontarf. That had occurred in the year 1014.

One Irish novel gives a quick sense of the city of Dublin merely by leaping from statue to statue—from Parnell to O'Connell, to Tom Moore, to Grattan, to Burke and Goldsmith, Davis, Tone, Emmet, and quite a few others.

And, of course, if one is extracting symptoms, there are the innumerable poems and ballads which still are read and sung about Owen Roe, Red Hugh, brave Patrick Sarsfield, bold Father Murphy, and young Roddy McCorley. Then for years there was the constant political evocation of the past—the stirring allusion to, the rousing quotation from, and the frequent reading of the works of Tone and Davis, of Mitchel's Jail Journal, of Pearse's essays and speeches. Perhaps the most dramatic, or at least the loudest, evocation of all was the memory of King Billy crossing the Boyne on the Glorious 12th of July, celebrated by the horrific cannonade of the Lambeg drums. Yet, the most quietly telling evocation of all was that until very modern times the cities, towns, and countryside changed little, and so the past was noticeably ever present; one lived in the middle of it.

Culturally, Irish legend and history have been, at least since the Literary Renaissance, a source of pride; politically, Irish history seems remembered as a grudge and a frustration. How deeply and how broadly the sense of history runs through the Irish population is conjectural, but one plausible conjecture would be that it runs more deeply and broadly than it does for Americans. In an ordinarily peaceful time, the great mass of the Irish population probably is rather oblivious to history, but this dormant memory may be readily roused by current events.

Until quite recently, the Irish politician has, by and large, used history rather differently than has the Irish writer. The politician has often evoked the glorious past either for the admiration of a nobility that has come to be invested in him or for the admiration of heroism in the face of a yet unredressed wrong. No matter that the nobility is tinged by a kind of madness, or the heroism by a kind of hatred, the appeal is to the people's admiration, and the appeal has often worked.

Many novels, stories, plays, and poems have espoused this public view of history, but few of them have been of much literary merit. When the serious writer has turned to historical subjects, his primary attitude has seemed less admiring than critical, satirical, or whimsical. Even a nominally patriotic poem of great power like Yeats' "Easter 1916" when read closely is a most ambiguous statement. There is admiration for nobility and heroism, but there is also the nagging speculation of whether the nobility and heroism may not in the end have been folly.

THE LAND

Until quite recently, the one great, pervasive, primary theme of both Irish life and literature has been the land. All of the other usual themes of both life and literature—religion, love, patriotism, individual aspiration—seem in Ireland to have been amalgamated with, or attached to, some facet of love for the land.

Perhaps the reason is that the dweller in Ireland, whether Firbolg or Celt, Dane or Norman, or even modern Ulster Presbyterian, always has had good reason to fear that his hold on the land was transitory and tenuous. All of recorded Irish history, down to the Northern troubles of the present, has seemed to revolve around the ineradicable, inescapable, perhaps even irresolvable question of who owns Ireland. The ramifications of this ever different, but always same, situation have been immense, intense, far-reaching, and deep-rooted. Politically, the question for centuries has occasioned invasion, war, rebellion, murder, and violence. Economically, for the small minority it has occasioned riches, cultivation, and absenteeism, and for the large majority, poverty, backwardness, and emigration. Agriculturally, it has been a national disaster, its most horrific embodiment being the Potato Famine when the land itself seemed the nemesis and not the prize.

But if to the Irish man the land was the ultimate glittering prize, to the Irish writer it has often seemed a curse. If the land could cause physical blight and death, it could also cause psychic blight and death. Some of the most powerful Irish plays and stories are those in which a person gives his soul wholly to the land. He may be deadened and animalized by it, as is the farmer in Patrick Kavanagh's poem *The Great Hunger;* he may sell his daughter for it, as occurs in Louis D'Alton's *Lovers Meeting* or John B. Keane's *Sive;* he may want it enough to murder for it, as the peasant does in T. C. Murray's *Birthright* or even in Keane's modern play *The Field.* To realistic writers, such as those above, an almost tragic pattern attaches to the theme of the land. A man so lusts for it that he struggles indomitably, hardens himself irremediably, and even casts off every other human tie or desire; but when he wins it, somehow, by death or by psychic death, he loses.

If the realistic writer most powerfully criticizes his countrymen's most in-grained desire, the romantic writer makes precisely the same criticism but makes it flippantly. The romantic writer long has idealized the landless man—even the tinker or the tramp. Even such a son of the cities as Sean O'Casey once referred to himself as a wandering road-minstrel. Synge's Nora in *The Shadow of the Glen* leaves her home to go wandering with a tramp. Colum's Conn Hourican leaves the land to his children and takes to the roads with his fiddle. Padraic Ó Conaire in reality left his office in London to wander the roads of Ireland and write short stories in Gaelic. From Synge's *Playboy* to the tinkers of Bryan MacMahon's *The Honey Spike,* there is this glorification of the shaughraun, with only an occasional demurrer like Colum's moving little poem "An Old Woman of the Roads."

Both the realistic writer and the romantic writer, however, seem deeply critical of the Irishman's love of the land, and in that criticism they may have touched the core of Ireland's tragedy. But perhaps the most tragic and ironic aspect of the love of the land is that the people who live on it are rapidly leaving it. M. J. Molloy's bittersweet play of 1953, *The Wood of the Whispering,* depicts a West nearly depleted of its young and inhabited mainly by the old and ec-centric. What Molloy wrote of more than forty years ago had already been going on for generations, and it is going on apace today.

(There is one other aspect of love for the land that should be touched on, and that is the love of the emigrant. In America or Australia, he usually has little or no hope of ever returning, and so his love for the land is entirely uncritical. Rather, he idealizes it, remembering it as better than it ever was. His nostalgia and also his money have had some economic and political effect at home. His nostalgia has had little literary effect, although it has been the basis for innu-merable poems and ballads. If these usually have been mawkishly sentimental, they have been none the less deeply felt.)

RELIGION

There is a traditional story in Ireland of how Oisin, the great, truculent hero of the Fianna, returned from the Land of Youth and met with St. Patrick. One fine, modern retelling of their conversations is Darrell Figgis' *The Return of the Hero,* which excellently contrasts the two utterly conflicting attitudes toward life. After many vicissitudes, the spiritual sons of St. Patrick seem finally to have triumphed in modern recorded history. And yet the triumph never has been quite total, as, indeed, the conflict never was quite thoroughgoing. It was the heroic spirit of Oisin that for centuries impelled the various armed and doomed rebellions, just as it was the same spirit that, in another way, impelled the Literary Renaissance.

For most of modern Irish history, the Roman Catholic Church has been iden-tified closely with the people. It was the church of the people, and its priests were as oppressed as the people and sometimes much worse off. Only in quite modern times, following the Catholic emancipation of the nineteenth century, the disestablishment of the Church of Ireland, and finally the severance of the tie with Britain, did the Irish Catholic Church become publicly accepted and secure. A symptom of how recent that change is may be noticed in many towns, such as Listowel in Kerry, where the Protestant Church is set proudly in the middle of the square and the Catholic Church is tucked unobtrusively off to one side. Nowadays, of course, the Protestant Church is most sparsely attended, a dramatic change which is well embodied in Jack White's play *The Last Eleven.*

With the formation of the Irish Free State, the Catholic Church established itself with a vengeance as a social and political force. Its favored position was written into the Irish Constitution, and that clause was only excised in the late 1970s. For the first fifty years of Irish self-government, then, the Catholic Church was probably the most powerful social force in the land. Its influence was so potent and so pervasive that it overtly or tacitly dominated every significant facet of Irish life. The government almost seemed the secular right arm of the church; and should a government, as it rarely did, oppose the views of the church, the government could be toppled. An example is the dissolution of the interparty government in 1951, after the church had opposed a mother-and-child care scheme proposed by Minister of Health Noel Browne.

How much government was a spokesman for the ecclesiastical position may be seen in various instances involving the arts. There was the rigorous book censorship which banned even innocuous references to sex (although it had no violent objections to violence). Among the thousands of books banned were many of little or no discernible merit, but the best of the banned read like a Who's Who of modern literature. The government film censorship acted with similar rigor; to take but one rather late example, *Anatomy of a Murder,* a popular courtroom melodrama of the early 1960s, was reduced to incomprehensibility when all shots of an uninhabited pair of women's panties were excised. There was also the legally unformulated but tacit censorship of the stage; one well-known example is the case of the director Alan Simpson who spent a night in Bridewell for producing Tennessee Williams' *The Rose Tattoo.* Perhaps just how enthusiastically the government supported the church's views may be seen in the Senate debates over the banning of Eric Cross's *The Tailor and Ansty* in the early 1940s. Today the remarks of the government opponents of the book seem almost satirically extravagant.

These well-known instances are merely a few among many, but they suggest a serious variance between the practices of the church and the opinions of the best writers. There was much bland popular literature that expressed the social attitudes of the church, as there was a good deal of popular hortatory literature to express the establishment political views. But the best work of the best writers either ignored the church or (as in the case of O'Casey) criticized it loudly.

It is curious that the establishment church of this century became so different from the outlawed church of the past. In the seventeenth and eighteenth centuries and much of the nineteenth century (perhaps until the Parnell split), the church had a remarkable sympathetic union with the people. After the establishment of Maynooth, the national seminary, in 1795 and the importation of Jansenistic teachers from France, the church grew more puritanical and identified ever more closely with the current political establishment. For one instance, in the Great Lockout of 1913, the workers of Dublin planned to send a shipload of their hungry children to England where they could be cared for. A line of priests barred the way on the docks, however, and the Dublin children returned to the starving tenements. In other words, when the church grew in power, it grew also to uphold power and often to diverge sharply from the opinions of many of its members.

Nevertheless, the power of the church over Irishmen, until the very recent period, has been enormous. Even when ecclesiastical opinion and popular aspiration were profoundly at odds—as they sometimes were in labor or in political struggles—the rift, though deep, was ignored by the people. Or, rather, the opinions of the church were ignored, but the church was not. In any case, the Catholic Church in Ireland became an intractable and inflexible body, bearing almost more resemblance to a fundamentalist sect in Alabama than to the Catholic Church in other European countries. The 1960s and 1970s, however, were marked by new affluence in Ireland, in the aftermath of Vatican II, and considerable upheaval in world Catholicism. As a result, the influence of the Church in Ireland seems to have waned, and its character seems to be changing.

The influence of the church upon literature generally has been to foster among the best writers an attitude of criticism and opposition. There was, of course, a morally innocuous and patriotically unctuous literature, typified perhaps at its impressive best by the novels of Kate O'Brien or the poems of Robert Farren. But, at the same time, there was the growth of an antiestablishment and frequently anticlerical literature, which contains much of the best of the most remarkable writing in modern Ireland. Probably, then, it is true to say that, if an intractable and puritanic church had not pushed the literary artist into opposition, there would be much less that is individual and exciting about modern Irish letters.

Today, when the church is a much less powerful force in society, how will literature be affected? Thus far, two stages are discernible. The first might be suggested by the all-too-brief career of the late John Feeney. Feeney was old enough to have been formed by the Jansenistic 1950s and young enough to have been a leader in the pale Irish version of the university students' revolt of the late 1960s. His career reflected that division. His punch-pulling, whitewashing biography of Archbishop McQuaid was balanced by a novel outspokenly condemning the establishment, as typified by the national television service; his several-year stint as editor of *The Catholic Standard* was balanced by a book of stories whose best pieces were strongly condemnatory of Catholic standards. The second stage might be typified by two older writers who have been exposed as people and as artists to England and America. In Brian Friel's play *Living Quarters* and in Thomas Murphy's play *Sanctuary Lamp,* the position of the modern church in Ireland is scathingly criticized by the failure of the priests in the plays to do what priests should do. As life often follows art, the 1990s saw the scandals of a bishop who was revealed to be but barely supporting his teenage son and of a priestly pedophile whose clerically protected activities helped to bring a government down. After such bizarre matters, the old hold of clericalism might, for better or worse, be growing less firm.

DRINK

The bellicose and drunken Irishman is as irritating a cliché as was once the allegation of the pig in every parlor. In the nineteenth century, the redoubtable Father Mathew led an extraordinary temperance crusade. Its effects long since have been largely dissipated, and it has been estimated that 10 percent of all personal spending in Ireland today is for drink.

Whether that be an exaggeration, to the observant onlooker it does seem to have some basis. A sociologist or psychologist would be needed to investigate the reasons for Irish drinking, but some reasons seem fairly obvious. Ireland has always been a poor country, and drink is a prime anodyne for the frustrations of poverty, hopelessness, and boredom. The effects of a drinking culture on the country are manifold and undoubtedly pernicious, especially in a psychological sense. The toleration, even the macho glamorization of drink, seems to hold a good deal of the country in the thrall of social adolescence.

For Irish literature, the importance of drink is unquestionable as well as, like drink itself, both invigorating and enervating. Some of the greatest comic scenes of Synge, O'Casey, Joyce, and Flann O'Brien have centered around drink, and merely to list the works in which drink is significant would be well-nigh impossible. While drink is only infrequently a central theme, it seems ubiquitous as a contributory theme, and generally a source of considerable excellence.

At the same time, the tales of increasingly sodden writers whose careers are pickled in alcohol are so numerous, that the figure of the drunken Irish genius has become a cliché. For the Irish writer, drink has been a magnificent theme, but all too often a source of personal destruction.

Nevertheless, even in this sensitive area, Ireland appears to be changing. In late 1994, the government of the day passed a drunk-driving law intended to bring Irish law more into conformity with European standards. Although there was great opposition from the Vintners' Association, which claimed that the effect would be the destruction of social life in rural areas, at this writing the law seems to have the support or at least the acquiescence of the bulk of the public.

SEX

Perhaps most great writing is in some way or another—and frequently centrally—about sex. Much literature in the Irish language, from the occasional ribaldry of *The Táin* to the inimitable *Midnight Court* of Brian Merriman is unashamedly sexual. Perhaps that fact may serve as one indicator that until modern times sex was more or less a nakedly normal part of Irish life.

Still, given the climate and geography, sex could not be too naked, for the simple reason that it usually was necessary to wear a fair amount of clothing. At the same time, economics, politics, and religion seemed to support each other mutually in inhibiting a free functioning of the sexual man. Economics may well have been the most inhibiting. Given the Irish way of life, the questions of who slept with whom and who married whom and how many children were born were of prime importance. People married carefully to remain solvent, and, when it was economic freedom versus sexual freedom, economic freedom usually won. For the mass of people, remaining solvent meant coming into a bit of land. That usually was impossible until the head of the household, the father, died or became feeble with age. Therefore, there were many late marriages, although most were prolific, perhaps partly for economic reasons again. The unfortunate younger sons tended either to emigrate or to become old bachelors, a situation reflected eloquently in M. J. Molloy's play *The Wood of the Whispering.* This situation lasted until the 1960s when the effect of relative prosperity and stronger influence from the outside world caused a gradual but considerable change.

Until recently, sex has been treated with reticence in literature. Of course, there are exceptions, the most notorious being for many years Joyce's *Ulysses.* The Catholic Church and the government, acting pretty much hand in glove, contrived to inhibit sexual expression in literature as in life. For many Irish, the effect of a sternly religious education was to extend sexual ignorance, distrust, and even antipathy well into adult years. For about the first thirty years of Irish self-government, a public puritanism was effective and thorough. The later plays of O'Casey are, among other things, simplistic satiric condemnations of this public puritanism.

In 1900, the realistic novels of George Moore were considered anathema. Thirty years later, little had changed; and when T. C. Murray in *Autumn Fire* tackled a theme bordering on incest, he had to treat the topic with a rigid dignity and a profound reticence altogether lacking in the American play *Desire under the Elms,* by Eugene O'Neill, which deals with the same situation. Since the 1960s, the Irish milieu has changed considerably, but even so the novels of the much admired John McGahern and Edna O'Brien, who dealt frankly but hardly luridly with sex, were initially banned. For that matter, one Irish short story twenty years ago has a character closely resembling O'Brien, who returns to her native village and is viciously raped, the moral apparently being, "That'll show her!"

Today, such a view seems anachronistic indeed, and today's Irish writer can write really about any topic and from just about any point of view. The euphemizing of sex in modern Irish literature is a thing of the past, and that would seem to be a good thing. The bad thing is that Irish literature reflects Irish life. Hugh Leonard can now refer to "the rape page" of the *Irish Times,* in which one or two of the stories are inevitably about incest. People wonder—is this another dismal symptom of Ireland having joined the modern world? Or was it always there and covered up?

VIOLENCE

In their popular entertainments and even their serious literature, Americans have a penchant for violence that periodically alarms even them. Although the Irish have not developed the more outré refinements of violence in their entertainments, they do have a similar tolerance for violence. Indeed, "tolerance" may be a less appropriate word than "admiration" or "glorification."

In any society, the active perpetrators of public violence are a minority, but private violence can seep into ordinary life and color opinions and attitudes. Corporal punishment in the schools and wife-beating in the homes are but two such ways; and, although the toleration of political violence waxes and wanes according to current circumstances, the potentiality for such a tolerance seems well prepared for in ordinary Irish life.

Public acts of violence have deep historical roots in Ireland. When a large majority of the population was politically, economically, socially, and culturally oppressed, any means of temporary or partial redress seemed admirable to them. For centuries, the Irish were in a weak and intolerable position, and they coped with it in two ways: by charming cunning and by covert violence. A play like Bernard Shaw's *John Bull's Other Island* is only one of innumerable reflections of the cunning guile; and the popular ballads and poems of Ireland offer hundreds of examples of the glorification of the violent hero, who stood up to the oppressors, although often dying in the attempt ("Whether on the scaffold high, or on battlefield we die . . .").

Some quite recent events also can suggest how deeply the admiration for violence runs in the Irish. In the 1960s, the country seemed to be basking in a new and uncharacteristic affluence, and the people seemed interested mainly in acquiring goods and in improving their lot in life. In 1966, the extensive and elaborate fifty-year commemorative celebrations of the Easter Rising seemed largely an empty public self-congratulation. Its rhetoric sounded hollow, and the memory of the glorious past irrelevant to the business of life. References to Ireland's lost fourth green field were lip service to a rather remote ideal, and what was relevant was tending one's own garden in the three green fields that remained.

Yet before the decade had ended, the civil rights movement in the North had become transformed into a political movement, and the smoldering ashes of nationalism once again had erupted into flames. In the South, some prominent government ministers were involved in a notorious public scandal for supplying guns to the IRA in the North. And for a time, before the subsequent years of cumulative assassination and outrage again disillusioned people, there seemed a resurgence of the old political fervor. However, twenty-five years of violence and more than 3,000 dead made the overwhelming mass of people in both the North and the South heartily sick of the situation and eagerly welcoming the IRA and Loyalist Paramilitary cease-fire of 1994. Nevertheless, despite the national disgust at twenty-five years of atrocity, torture, and murder, violence may yet retain some claim to respectability in people's minds. It is worth noting that after the cease-fire, Gerry Adams, chief spokesman and apologist for the IRA, was greeted on the steps of Leinster House by the Taoiseach and welcomed to Boston by Senator Kennedy and to the White House by President Clinton.

As violence has been an integral part of the Irishman's historical heritage, it predictably pervades his literature. To take but one extreme example, consider the poems and plays of W. B. Yeats. What could have been so totally unviolent as the early work of Yeats with its roses and *langours?* And who could have seemed so totally unviolent as the lissome young bard with the flowing tie and the lank lock of hair falling over his marble brow? Yet, as Yeats' work developed, it became harder, tougher, more dramatically combative. The images, the diction, even the rhythms of the late work, are both energetic and abrasive. At the same time, the poet personally grew ever bolder. His apologetic remark to the *Playboy* rioters of 1907 was, "It is the author of 'Cathleen ni Houlihan' who addresses you"; twenty years later, his first remark to *The Plough and the Stars* rioters was the inflammatory "You have disgraced yourselves again!"

From the brawls and ructions in Synge and Fitzmaurice, to the fist fights which conclude a Maurice Walsh entertainment, to the brutalities of an O'Flaherty political novel, and even to the abrasive content of many of the youngest poets and short story writers, violence is everywhere in Irish literature. It is a violence in both subject matter and diction. Synge, Yeats, Joyce, O'Casey, Samuel Beckett, and Flann O'Brien are merely the most distinctive Irish writers to have used words violently, but their uses have forced language from the traveled road of smooth convention into startling new directions. So if violence has been a political and social bane for Irish life, it has been also a major glory of Irish literature.

THE JUDGMENT OF SAINTS AND THE LANGUAGE OF SCHOLARS

The cliché that replaced the moronic Paddy of nineteenth-century *Punch* cartoons was the ebullient Wild Irish Boy. The first figure was an amiable Handy Andy idiot; the second is a brilliantly "cute" jackeen. The first figure talked with a charming and quaint stupidity; the second talks with a wild and profane wit. Either kind of talk has an intermittent, not totally tenuous, basis in reality, but neither cliché accords well with the reality of the Irish writer.

There are perhaps two types of Irish writer. There is the serious or affirmative Man with a Cause who has a mystic, an oratorical, or a whimsical fluency; he may be the young Yeats or the ever-young James Stephens; he may be the warmly passionate Padraic Pearse or the coolly passionate Conor Cruise

O'Brien. On the other hand, the frivolous or negative Man Disillusioned with Causes has a witty, destructive, and satirical eloquence; he may be the young Myles, the middle-aged Joyce, the old O'Casey, or the infinitely ancient Beckett.

Both types talk incessantly and eloquently, and the reasons for the talk seem social, economic, political, and even geographical and climatic. If one has no money, if one is politically impotent and socially scorned, and if the rain so frequently necessitates staying indoors, the major antidote to all of these frustrations is language. In ancient Ireland, language came to be so valued that complicated codes and techniques grew up around it. In historical times, language was one of the few free entertainments in an otherwise bleak world, and so good language was admired and remembered. In other words, a sense of rhetoric grew, and judgment developed.

The language of the affirmative writer painted a world better than the existing—whether the early, idealized, pre-Raphaelite embroideries of Yeats or Standish O'Grady's tumultuous language of heroism, or the neoclassic order of Burke or the whimsical fantasies of James Stephens. The language of the negative writer painted a world more extravagantly intolerable than even the existing—whether the savage, absurd reductions of Swift, or the mad caricatures of Flann O'Brien, or the depressing exaggerations of Samuel Beckett.

Exposed to this plethora of rhetoric, the Irishman became a connoisseur of language, a brutal but refreshingly unacademic literary critic. Even the huge sales of a bad volume of florid poems like *The Spirit of the Nation* does not refute the fact; it testifies to an enthusiasm for rhetoric so intense that it occasionally accepts fool's gold for the genuine article. But as many volumes of Great Irish Oratory suggest, the Irishman could genuinely admire the genuine. Emmet's speech from the dock was not admired solely for what it said, but also for how nobly it said it; and the dull writings of a merely noble man like John O'Leary have been little read.

Nevertheless, affirmative eloquence does invite enthusiasm and does tend to squelch discrimination. Fortunately, Irish literature is fuller of negative eloquence which demands niceties of judgment. To take the language of comedy as an example, we might note that all of the great Irish dramatists, save Wilde and Synge, write on various levels of language and that their plays cannot be fully appreciated unless that fact is perceived. *The Rivals* of Sheridan, for instance, has a satire on the language of romance in Lydia, on the language of sensibility in Faulkland, on pretensions to pedantry in Mrs. Malaprop, on contemporary slang in Bob Acres, on Irish bluster in Sir Lucius, and on the inadequacies of the language of rage in Sir Anthony. The play is as brilliant for its levels of language as it is for its abundant comic situations and striking caricatures. In fact, one zealous commentator has asserted that there are potentially 327 laughs in the play arising from the audience's apprehension that a character has misused language.

It has sometimes been stated that all of Shaw's characters talk like Shaw. Actually they do not; they only talk with Shaw's fluency and energy. (See

Pygmalion, see *John Bull,* see *Major Barbara,* see . . . etc.) It is really only a few writers, such as Wilde and Synge and the later O'Casey, who write in a uniform style, and they write to evoke admiration rather than to provoke criticism.

The same point of the Irishman's nice discrimination about language might be reinforced by noting how acutely the Irish have honed the destructive sub-genres of invective and gossip. The poet's curse, or even the enraged layman's curse, was considered a potent, a fearful, an ultimate weapon. It demanded the full resources of rhetoric, and it worked because those resources were widely appreciated. The language of gossip also, which pervades Irish literature and riddles Irish life, demands the utmost refinements and subtleties, and has a range stretching from the crudest scurrility to the gentlest (and most disemboweling) innuendo.

If this tradition of verbal dexterity and appreciation was originally motivated by frustration, it has long since become self-generated by narcissistic delight— hence lies, hence deceit, hence the most remarkable body of English literature in the world.

IRELAND IN THE MODERN WORLD

Most of the foregoing reflections are really applicable to a world that is fast disappearing. There are still pockets of the country that remain little changed, such as the Blue Stacks in Donegal, so ably described by the American Robert Bernen. But one may walk through a town in the Gaeltacht like Ranafest and not hear a word of Irish spoken and note the television antennas on every roof.

In 1960, it was only a minor satirical exaggeration to say that Ireland was lagging about fifty years behind the rest of the modern world. Today, it is an integral part of that world. The country wins the Eurovision Song Contest four years out of the last five. Rock performers like U2 or Sinead O'Connor are high on the charts in England and America. Movies by Jim Sheridan and Neil Jordan win Academy Awards. A novel by Pat McCabe is shortlisted for England's Booker Prize, and the next year a novel by Roddy Doyle wins it. In 1990 and 1994, the Irish soccer team reaches the finals of the World Cup, thereby causing national hysteria and almost total cessation of work and thereby making the team's English coach the most popular man in the country. (Sport, incidentally, would have been listed earlier among the national obsessions except that it has had little influence on Irish writers. One might, however, cite John B. Keane's play *The Man from Clare,* which does attack the obsession with sport as a kind of national sex-substitute that kept men harmlessly immature into early middle age.)

A less superficial symptom of the modernizing of Ireland may be seen in a set of figures released in October 1994 by the Central Statistics Office. As the *Irish Times* reported, "The birth rate for last year [1993] was not only the lowest on record but it has now fallen below the level needed to replace the population.'' In 1980, there were 74,400 births; in 1993, the number had declined to 49,456, a massive drop of one-third. Several reasons were advanced for this startling figure. The number of marriages in the Republic had declined from nearly 22,000 in 1980 to about 15,500 in 1993. Married couples had fewer children, while the number of extramarital births was about 9,600 or about a fifth of the total number. A growth in consumerism was cited as a significant factor, with people tending to spend more on the good things of life before settling down to start families. Of course, the availability of the once-outlawed condom was of major significance. James Plunkett's novel *The Circus Animals* treated the plight of a Catholic couple in the 1950s who yearned for a normal sex life but who could not afford to have more children. Their only recourse was to the vagaries of the "rhythm method" or to continence. The book was published in 1990, but it was an historical novel. By 1990, the sexual habits of the Irish had changed, changed utterly.

In 1986, there was a national referendum about allowing Irish people to divorce. It failed, but about a third of the voters favored divorce, a figure much higher than what might have been expected a generation earlier. In May 1995, a book entitled *Divorce? Facing the Issues of Marital Breakdown* estimated that from 1986 to 1991 there had been an increase of 48% in the number of marriages breaking down, or more than 3,500 legal separations in each of those years. A second national referendum on divorce was held in November 1995, and this time divorce slipped through by the wafer-thin majority of 50.28% of the votes cast.

Two other sobering symptoms of Irish modernity might be found in another *Irish Times* story of late September 1994, when the paper noted that there were "some 1,500 carriers of the [HIV] virus in Ireland" and that "the statistical probability is that there are many more who simply have not been tested." At the same time, it announced that "heroin abuse is more prevalent than ever before, at least in Dublin," and estimated that there were from 5,000 to 7,000 addicts in the city. From January 31 to May 9, 1995, there were twelve major finds of illegal drugs in Ireland, and their estimated total worth came to £29,473,000.

In yet another *Irish Times* story, of May 2, 1995, it was estimated that "The level of serious crime has . . . doubled in the past 20 years and almost quadrupled since the late 1960s." There has also been much ominous recent speculation that, if the Sinn Féin cease-fire became (as it did not) permanent, the graduates of the IRA would turn their interesting talents from political violence to the more lucrative possibilities of organized crime.

Finally, recent governments, particularly those of Fianna Fail, have gone on spending sprees and handouts for votes that entailed massive borrowing to finance the day-to-day running of the government. Without exaggeration, one may say that the national debt of Ireland, which is now approaching 30 billion pounds, is in terms of population comparable to that of Brazil. The country exists so much on handouts from the European Union that it is, in effect, one of the two or three banana republics of Europe.

At the same time, political venality and greed amazingly triumph over blatant political incompetence and mismanagement. . . . however, this is a book about literature; and so it is perhaps enough to say that the country no longer exactly resembles a little bit of heaven that fell from out the sky one day. But perhaps it did only in the minds of many who lived there and many more who reluctantly had to leave. Perhaps even now something of that happy delusion may continue to persist.

As Ireland prepares to enter the new century, it is probably important to reiterate that there is no such thing as the Irish race. Generations of invaders have become, like Behan's Monsewer, more Irish than . . . whoever the Irish were. What there is—simply—is an Irish attitude (which is quite different, indeed, from that caricature of it to be found in the second and third generations of the sea-divided Gael in Boston and New York). The Irish attitude requires that one have lived long enough in the island to be primarily and irrationally affected by its splendors and miseries. Perhaps, too, it finally requires that one reduce the world, as does the excellent *Irish Times,* to the rather unimportant topic of how the world affects Ireland. One blow-in writer, Constantine Fitzgibbon, in a novel about Michael Collins, managed to lug in the supporting characters of, among many others, T. E. Lawrence, Woodrow Wilson, and Lenin.

One cannot write fairly or objectively about the Irish attitude, for one slips unnoticed into the national rhetorical techniques of hyperbole and prevarication. And perhaps also into the snotty innuendo, the fulsome phrase, the empty alliteration. And, worse, into the self-adulation, the pique, the hatred, the remembrance of old hatred, the loathsome sentimentality, and all, all, all the other disgusting techniques of the Irish attitude. Indeed, it occurs to me that the only Irish rhetorical devices that this essay has missed have been wit, eloquence, and inventiveness.

In any event, wit and eloquence and all the rest produced such a rich and abundant literature. How much of the Irish attitude will persist into the new century and continue to produce such literature is perhaps too dismal a question to raise. But if the Irish attitude melds and disappears into the European or the modern, the world will be much the worse for it. One would bitterly regret it if Bonaparte O'Coonassa's last words proved to be true: "I do not think that my like will ever be there again!"

ROBERT HOGAN

GAELIC LITERATURE
Seamus O'Neill

The great German Celtic scholar Kuno Meyer described Gaelic literature as "the earliest voice from the dawn of West European civilization." The Romans had not brought Ireland within the empire, and consequently the native culture had not been overwhelmed by the Latin. With Christianity, however, came a knowledge of classical literature and the art of writing. As might have been expected, there was a tendency among the early Christian clerics to look askance at the vernacular and its lore as something barbaric and pagan, but from the first there were men among them who knew better. We have the two views represented in *The Life of Colmcille (Vita Sancti Columbae),* written by Adamnan, the ninth abbot of Iona. Adamnan, who wrote in Latin, apologizes to his readers for having to use the crude Irish forms of names of people and places. Nevertheless, he tells us a story about Colmcille which reveals that his great predecessor was indeed a lover of poetry and poets. According to the story, Colmcille was sitting one day on the bank of the River Boyle when a certain Irish bard came up to him and engaged him in conversation for a while. Then when he had proceeded on his way, the monks who were in Colmcille's company asked him why he did not ask the bard for a song. Colmcille replied that he could not do so because he knew the poor fellow was about to meet his death. Adamnan quotes this story as an example of the prescient power which he attributes to Colmcille, but it also shows that the saint used to invite wandering bards and minstrels to entertain him and his company. Little wonder, for he was himself a poet and champion of poets.

We have also a delightful story of how St. Patrick, as he was listening to one of the ancient tales, was suddenly troubled in his conscience for fear that he was wasting his time. But he was assured by his guardian angels not only that there was no harm in giving ear to the old stories, pagan though they were, but also that he should have them written down because they would serve to entertain future generations until the end of time.

That is what the Irish monks proceeded to do. They adapted the Latin alphabet to the Irish language, and they committed to manuscripts the traditional literature of their ancestors. The Irish epic, the *Táin Bó Cuailnge (Cattle Raid of Cooley),* for example, was first written down in the ninth century, but the story belongs to the La Tène period of civilization, perhaps about 100 B.C. The monks, however, did not confine their efforts to garnering the relics of the old civilization; they used the vernacular for all the purposes of life—for prayer and instruction, spiritual and secular, for histories and poetic composition and imaginative prose. A new, written literature developed. The *Cambrai Homily,* which generally is accepted as the oldest piece of writing in the Irish language, dating from the second half of the seventh century, is in itself a reminder of this great achievement of the monks.

While the Irish language and culture were cultivated in the monasteries, classical learning was not neglected. Latin was, of course, the language of divine office and the language which the peregrini used daily. It also was used for literary composition. Some of the most important contributions to medieval Latin literature were made by Irishmen. Existing side by side, it was inevitable that the two cultures should intertwine. A new system of Irish versification grew up under the influence of Latin metrics.

OLD IRISH POETRY

We may name four distinct periods in the history of Irish poetry: (1) a period of rhythmical alliterative verse, similar to the verse of Anglo-Saxon; (2) a period of syllabic verse; (3) the period of the amhrán or stressed meters; and (4) the modern period in which there has been much experimentation with different forms.

The first period of the sixth and seventh centuries is not very important. At any rate, not much of this kind of verse has come down to us. The examples are mostly apostrophes to warriors, such as:

> Fo-chén Conall, críde lícce,
> lóndbruth lóga, Lúchar éga,
> gúss flánd férge fo chích curad. . . .

> (Hail Conall, heart of stone,
> fierceness of a lynx, sheet of ice,
> blood-red fury of anger, under the breast of a warrior. . . .)

The second period begins in about the eighth century with the introduction of syllabic verse and lasts until the seventeenth century. A most intricate metrical system evolved during this time. Basically, the verse depended on the number of syllables in it, but in dán díreach (in perfect verse), subtle end-rhymes, internal rhymes, consonance, and alliteration were essential. The poet, however, could use looser forms of meter, called óglachas and brúilingeacht. Perfect rhyme existed between words of which the stressed vowels were identical, and all the consonants after the first stressed vowel of the same class and quality. The consonants were ranked in six classes according to kind. Thus, in syllabic meter, "mall" rhymed with "barr," "crann" with "am," "long" with "fonn." Imperfect rhyme consisted of identity of vowels, agreement of consonants in quality, but not in class, as in meas: leath; críoch: díon.

A great number of meters were devised, variation being achieved by changing the length of the verses and by manipulating the other necessary poetic artifices. The names of the most common meters were, perhaps, Rannaigheacht mhór, Rannaigheacht bheag, Deibhidhe, Séadna, Séadna mór, or Dian-mhidsheang.

As this metrical system developed, so did the subject matter of the verse. As might have been expected, the monks wrote religious verse, but as dwellers in rude beehive huts, they lived close to nature. Consequently, they were ever conscious of the physical world around them, and they have given us many nature poems of rare beauty. They delighted in the wonders of the sky, the sea, the forest, the song of the birds:

> A colonnade of trees looks down on me,
> A blackbird's lays sings to me;
> Above my lined booklet
> The trilling birds chant to me.
> In a grey mantle from the top of the bushes
> The cuckoo sings;
> Verily, may the Lord shield me!
> Well do I write under the greenwood.

Kuno Meyer pointed out that these nature poems do not contain elaborate or detailed descriptions of scenery, but rather create impressions which the poet conveys with a few swift significant strokes:

> My tidings for you: the stag bells,
> Winter snows, summer is gone.
>
> Wind high and cold, low the sun,
> Short his course, sea running high.
>
> Deep-red the bracken, its shape all gone,
> The wild-goose has raised his wonted cry.
>
> Cold has caught the wings of birds;
> Season of ice—these are my tidings.

Lines such as these remind us of Japanese *haiku.*

We have poems on every aspect of the monk's life: the joy of complete dedication to the Lord, the struggle with the flesh, the satisfaction of study, the occasional experience that enables us to see over a thousand years right into the anchorite's cell.

All alone in my little cell, without a single human
being along with me: such a pilgrimage would be
dear to me before going to meet death.

One monk made his cat immortal:

I and Pangur Bán, my cat,
'Tis a like task we are at;
Hunting mice is his delight,
Hunting words I sit all night.

'Gainst the wall he sets his eye
Full and fierce and sharp and sly;
'Gainst the wall of knowledge I
All my little wisdom try.

The terror inspired by the Viking raids is brought home to us in the quatrain

The wind is rough tonight,
It tosses the white mane of the waves;
I do not fear that the Irish sea will be crossed
By the fierce warriors from the North.

Although they certainly began the writing of the Irish language, the monks
were not the only poets in the country. Indeed, they were merely amateurs.
There existed a professional caste of poets from time immemorial, and if anything, they became more important with the introduction of written literature.
These were the filí, or the áes dána, who, usually being of aristocratic stock,
enjoyed many privileges. There were also the bards, but, although the word
"bard" is used in English to denote a Celtic poet, the bards were inferior to
the filí. "Bard dano; fer gin dliged foglama acht inntlicht fadesin" (A bard is
a man without proper learning, but intellect, nevertheless), says one of the law
tracts. To become a file, one had to spend several years at a school where poetry
was studied as a craft. The highest grade of file, the ollamh, studied for twelve
years. The filí were not merely poets in our sense of the term; they were also
chroniclers and keepers of the genealogies of their patrons, the great lords. Giolla
Bríghde Mac Con Midhe explained the importance of this function in a poem
in the thirteenth century:

Dá mbáidhtí an dán, a dhaoine,
gan seanchas, gan seanlaoidhe,
go bráth, acht athair gach fhir,
rachaidh cách gan a chluinsin.

(If poetry were to be suppressed, my people,
if we were without history, without ancient lays,
forever, but the father of each man,
every one will pass unheralded.)

As a result of this conception of the poet's task, the profession of poetry often became hereditary in certain families. Among these families might be mentioned the O'Higginses, the O'Clerys, the O'Dalys, and the Macawards.

OLD IRISH PROSE

The Ulster Cycle: *Táin Bó Cuailnge*

The ancient Irish epic, the *Táin Bó Cuailnge,* has come down to us in three recensions found in several manuscripts. The oldest recension is contained in Lebor na hUidre (LU), the Book of the Dun Cow, compiled at Clonmacnois; in the Yellow Book of Lecan (YBL); and in Egerton 1782. The second recension is contained in the Book of Leinster (LL), and the third in two late manuscripts.

The *Táin Bó Cuailnge* is the story of the great deeds of the central figure, Cuchulainn, especially in the war fought between the Ulaidh, the men of Ulster, and fir Erenn, the men of Ireland. While Cuchulainn is a mythical figure, and the tales of his exploits are fictional, the setting of the *Táin* is historical. That there was a powerful kingdom in Ulster with its capital at Eamhain Macha and that it was overthrown in the fourth or fifth century by attacks from the South are certain. The earthen rampart of Eamhain Macha (now called Navan Fort) can be seen to the present day near Armagh.

The *Táin* is the greatest of a large number of tales deriving from this era which are known as the Ulster Cycle. The *Táin* itself attracted a number of subsidiary tales called remscéla, or introductory tales, and iarscéla, or after-tales. Some of these are the remscéla of ''The Revealing of the Táin,'' ''The Debility of the Ulstermen,'' and ''The Cattle Driving of Fraech''; and the iarscéla of ''The Battle of Rosnaree,'' ''The Death of Cuchulainn,'' and ''The Phantom Chariot of Cuchulainn.''

The hold that the Cuchulainn saga took of the Irish imagination may perhaps be inferred from the fact that, when the German traveler Kohl visited Drogheda in the year 1843, he heard a storyteller recite the tragic story of the death of Cuchulainn's son, ''Aided Conlaoich.'' The same story was recorded by Séamus Ó Grianna in Donegal in 1915, and Yeats wrote a long poem and a play on the same theme.

The *Táin* is a typical tale of the ancient world, emphasizing the heroic deeds of the great warrior. Unlike the *Iliad,* the *Aeneid,* or *Beowulf,* however, it is told in prose, although interspersed with lyrics and verse duologues. Cuchulainn himself sets the tone of the tale when he exclaims, ''Acht ropa airdirc-se, maith lem ceni beinn acht óen-láa for domun'' (Provided that I be famous, I care not if I be only one day in the world). The *Táin,* then, depicts a civilization where the warrior is paramount, a world perhaps essentially like our own where the dividing line between civilization and savagery is very thin.

The most impressive episode of the *Táin* is the story of the fight to the death between Cuchulainn and Ferdiad. Cuchulainn had slain the best warriors that

Maeve and Ailill, queen and king of the Connaught men, had sent against him, and they were in despair of finding a man to match him. They sought the advice of their counselors, who said there was only one man fit to do battle with Cuchulainn; that was Ferdiad, son of Daman, son of Daire, the force that could not be withstood, the rock of destruction.

But Ferdiad and Cuchulainn were foster-brothers. They had learned the use of arms from Scathach, the female-warrior of Scotland. Maeve and Ailill sent messengers to Ferdiad, asking him to come to them, but he refused, knowing why they wanted him. Then Maeve sent poets and druids to satirize him, and for fear of their scorn he went with them. Maeve and Ailill rejoiced to see him and entertained him lavishly. Finnavair, the daughter of Ailill and Maeve, sat at his side. It was she who placed her hand on every cup that Ferdiad quaffed; it was she who gave him three kisses with every cup; it was she who gave him sweet-smelling apples over the bosom of her tunic, and said he was her lover and her choice of the men of the world.

Maeve promised Ferdiad that he should have Finnavair for his wife when he had destroyed Cuchulainn; but even this bait did not tempt him. He had no wish to kill the foster-brother he loved. Then Maeve taunted him. Cuchulainn had spoken truly, she said; he did not think much of Ferdiad as a champion. That jibe struck home, and at last Ferdiad consented to meet Cuchulainn.

They still point out the ford on the River Dee, earlier Nee, on which the town of Ardee stands and where according to tradition the combat between the two friends was fought. The name Ardee comes from the Irish "Áth Fhirdia," which means "the Ford of Ferdia." Cuchulainn came down to the north side of the ford, and Ferdiad was waiting on the south side. As Cuchulainn drove up, Ferdiad's servant described his chariot; and the fact that Cuchulainn often fought from a "carbad faebrach," a scythed chariot, as did the Gauls and Britons against the Romans, is one of the features of the *Táin* that helps us to determine the period in which the great deeds of the tale are supposed to take place.

THE COMBAT

"We are too long talking thus," said Ferdiad. "What arms shall we employ today?"

"You have the choice of arms today," answered Cuchulainn, "for it was you reached the ford first."

"Do you remember the feats of arms we used to practice with Scathach and Uatach and Aife?"

"I do, indeed."

"If you do, let's try them."

So they began to try their warrior skills. They buckled on their shields, and they took up their eight javelins, their eight swords, and their eight darts that flew to and fro between them like bees on a fine day. They made no cast that did not strike, and they continued to cast at each other from the twilight of morning till the midday. Although their aiming was excellent, their defense was equal to it, and neither succeeded in wounding the other.

"Let us rest from these feats," said Ferdiad, "for we cannot reach a decision with them."

"Let us rest," said Cuchulainn, and they gave their arms to their charioteers.

"What arms shall we employ today?" asked Ferdiad.

"Yours is the choice of arms till nightfall," replied Cuchulainn, "for you came first to the ford."

"Let us try our polished smooth hardened spears," said Ferdiad.

So they began to aim their spears at each other, and, although they parried skillfully, they hurled their spears with such deadliness that each of them wounded and reddened the other.

Then they rested from the fight, and they went towards each other in the ford, each of them putting his arms around the other's neck and giving him three kisses. They brought their horses to the same paddock that night, and their charioteers to the same fire, and the charioteers made a bed of fresh rushes for the wounded men. A band of leeches came who applied healing herbs to their cuts, gashes, and many wounds.

Cuchulainn lamented. He spoke these words:

"Oh, Ferdiad, if it be you,
Death awaits you, I am certain.
You fight your comrade for a shrew."
And Ferdiad replied:
"Cuchulainn, warrior brave,
Wisely has it been decreed,
Everyone must tread the path
That leads onward to the grave."

Then Cuchulainn called for the gae bolga. This weapon made a wound like a single spear going into the body, but it had thirty barbs and could only be removed from the body of a man by being cut out of it. Cuchulainn hurled the gae bolga at Ferdiad, and it passed through his iron apron so his every joint and every limb were filled with its barbs. Ferdiad said:

"Oh, Hound of great fame [Cuchulainn means the Hound of Culainn],
Unkind was that wound;
On you falls my blood,
On you falls the shame."

Then Cuchulainn rushed towards Ferdiad, clasped his two arms around him, and carried him northwards across the ford, so that it would be to the north of the ford that he should fall. And then a swoon came over Cuchulainn as he bent over Ferdiad.

The Book of Leinster version of the *Táin* is the fullest and most artistic that has come down to us. It is the conscious effort of a literary artist to give definitive form to the tale. With a good deal of justified self-assurance, he added a note at the end praying "a blessing on all such as dutifully recite the *Táin* as it stands here, and shall not give it any other form."

Nevertheless, a twelfth-century scribe described the *Táin* as containing "quaedam figmenta poetica, quaedam similia vero, quaedam non, quaedam ad delectationem stultorum" (some poetic fictions, some things like the truth, some things not, and some things for the delectation of fools). This judgment, to say the least, reflected a rather philistine approach to a great work of the imagination.

The Tragical Death of the Sons of Uisnech

The story of Deirdre and the Sons of Uisnech also belongs to the Ulster Cycle. It is one of the most tragic and beautiful of Irish stories and perhaps the best known of them all. It has been translated many times into English and other languages, and there are several dramatic versions of it. The most impressive version is that by Synge, although he errs a few times in putting into the mouth of King Conor language that would be more appropriate to a Connaught peasant.

Deirdre is a girl of singular beauty whom Conor has reared up for himself. But she falls in love with Naise, son of Uisnech, and she and Naise and his two brothers fly to Scotland to escape the king's wrath. When the warriors of Ulster protest that the sons of Uisnech should have to spend their lives in exile, Conor pretends to relent and invites them to return to Ireland with Deirdre, guaranteeing them safety. He breaks his bond, however, and has Naise and his brothers slaughtered and Deirdre seized. In Geoffrey Keating's version of the story (seventeenth century), she leaps from his chariot, strikes her head against a pillarstone, and dies. In the medieval version of the tale, she leaps into the grave after Naise and expires over his body. This is the ending which Synge chose.

In this tale, as in many other Irish prose tales, we have beautiful lyric passages, such as Deirdre's farewell to Scotland:

> Ionmhain tír an tír úd thoir,
> Alba go n-a hiongantaibh;
> > nocha dtiocfainn aisti i-le,
> > muna dtíosainn le Naoise.
>
> Gleann Dá Ruadh!
> mo-chean gach fear dana dual;
> > is binn guth cuaiche ar chraoibh chruim
> > ar an ndruim ós Gleann Dá Ruadh.

> (Dear the land, that land to the east,
> Scotland with its wonders;
> I would not have come from it here,
> Did I not come with Naoise.
>
> Glen Dá Ruadh!
> Hail to every man who is native there,

sweet the voice of the cuckoo on the bent branch,
on the ridge above Glen Dá Ruadh.)

Two other important cycles of tales are the Fenian, sometimes called the Ossianic, Cycle, and the Cycle of the Kings. To these some scholars would add a third, the so-called mythological cycle. But it can be argued that the *Táin* itself is basically a mythological tale. The principal character, Cuchulainn, is a mythological figure, being the offspring of Lugh, the Irish sun-god; it has been suggested that in the conflict of the bulls, around which the story is built, we have a motif from a pagan cult.

The Fenian Cycle

Like the Ulster Cycle, the Fenian Cycle has a central character, Finn mac Cumhaill, but he cuts a rather unstable figure. Unlike the Ulster tales, the Fenian Cycle is not bound to any particular historical era or place, although it certainly developed later than the Ulster Cycle. Tales of Finn and the Fianna continued to be composed and told almost down to our own day, and they were eventually to influence the whole of European literature. They supplanted almost entirely the Ulster tales in popularity. The reasons for this are, no doubt, that they possess a much greater variety of characters and lack the stark tragic quality of the Ulster cycle. There is also their romantic appeal. Finn and his companions live in a kind of Arcadia, spending their time hunting and feasting, although war sometimes interrupts the serenity of their existence.

The spirit of the Fenian tales is expressed in lines attributed to Oisin:

Mian mhic Cumhaill fá maith gnaoi
Éisteacht re faoidh Droma Deirg,
Codhladh fá shruth Easa Ruaidh,
Fiadh Gaillmhe na gcuan do sheilg.

Sgolaidheacht luin Leitreach Laoigh,
Tonn Rudhraighe ag buain re tráigh,
Dordán an daimh ó Mhaigh Mhaoin,
Búithre an laoigh ó Ghleann Dá Mhail.

In Róis ní Ógáin's translation:
(The desire of Cumhall's son of noble mien
Was to listen to the sound of Drumderg,
To sleep by the stream of Assaroe,
To hunt the deer of Galway of the bays.

The singing of the blackbird of Letterlee,
The wave of Rury striking the shore,
The belling of the stag from Magh Maoin,
The fawn's cry from Glen-da-Máil.)

In *Agallamh na Seanórach (The Colloquy of the Old Men)*, compiled towards the end of the twelfth century, we have a great collection of Fenian stories brought together in the form of a Dindsenchus or geographical guide. Caoilte mac Rónáin, who with Oísin is supposed to have survived the other heroes of the Fianna, journeys around Ireland with St. Patrick. At each place where they rest, Caoilte recalls for Patrick some heroic exploit of the Fianna in days gone by. But best known of all the Fenian tales is certainly "Tóraigheacht Dhiarmada agus Ghráinne" ("The Pursuit of Diarmaid and Grainne"). The story is famous because of its dramatic quality and because its chief characters are not mere legendary types but possess an individuality often associated with modern literature. Little wonder that Micheál Mac Liammóir turned it into a successful play, *Diarmuid agus Gráinne* (1928).

The story tells how Gráinne, the daughter of Cormac mac Airt, who is promised in marriage to Fionn, induces Diarmaid Ó Duibhne of the white teeth to carry her off. Fionn pursues the couple all over the country, but they succeed in escaping his wrath many times. To this day, hollows at the foot of many cromlechs or dolmens are pointed out as the beds of Diarmaid and Gráinne. At length Fionn catches up with them, but Aonghus an Bhrogha makes peace between them. But Fionn is not to be trusted. Diarmaid is wounded to the death by the boar of Ben Ghulban, but he may be saved by a drink of water from Fionn's hands. He implores Fionn to fetch a handful of water from a nearby spring. Fionn goes to the spring, but when returning with the water he thinks of Gráinne, and he allows the water to run through his fingers, and so Diarmaid dies.

Although the oldest extant manuscript copy of the story of Diarmaid and Gráinne is a rather late one of the seventeenth century, it is certain that the tale itself is much older. Many features of the story—the part played by Aonghus an Bhrogha, for example—show that it has its roots in the ancient mythology.

Other famous stories of the Fianna are "Cath Finntrágha" or The Battle of Ventry, "Bruildhean Chaorthainn" or The Hostel of the Rowan Tree, "Bodach an Chóta Lachtna" or The Clown of the Dun Coat, and "Cath Gabhra" or The Battle of Gabhra. The word "fian" is cognate with the Latin "vena" from which "venari," meaning "to hunt," is derived; in Ireland, however, the word came to mean a roving band of warriors. The Fenian tales became influenced by the Norse raids on Ireland, and the Fianna assume the position of a national army defending the country against the invaders. "Cath Finntrágha" is an account of how the Fianna repel the attack of the King of the World, who comes with a great fleet to Ventry. It is perhaps the most impressive of the stories in which the Fianna play this role of protecting their native land. Included in the story is the verse lament of Creidhe for her husband Caol, who is drowned in the waves while fighting against the foreigners. It is a very good example in Irish of the pathetic fallacy:

Géisidh cuan
ós buinne ruadh Rinn dá Bhárc,
bádhadh laoich Locha dhá Chonn
is eadh chaoineas tonn re trácht.

Truagh an gháir
do-ní tonn trágha re tráigh;
ó ro bháidh mh'fhear seaghda saor
is saoth liom a dhul 'na dháil.

(The harbor moans above the rushing stream
of Rinn da Bhárc,
the drowning of the warrior of Loch dhá Chonn
that is the lament of the wave against the strand.

Sad the cry the ebbing tide makes on the beach,
since it drowned my fine noble man,
my grief that he went near it.)

The Fenian literature comprises not only the prose tales, but a great number of poems as well. Lyrics like the one quoted above are found scattered throughout the tales, as are also an immense corpus of long narrative poems, or lays, as they are commonly known. These lays are contained principally in three collections: Duanaire Finn, which was compiled by three scribes in Louvain during the years 1626–1627 for Captain Sorley MacDonnell; the Book of the Dean of Lismore (Argyllshire), which was written there by the dean, Sir James McGregory, and his brothers during the years 1512–1526; and Leabhar na Finne, compiled from many sources by J. F. Campbell and first published in 1872. The Fenian lays became as popular in Gaelic-speaking Scotland as in Ireland. In Scotland, however, the Fenian tales often mingle with those of the Ulster Cycle, this, indeed, being a feature of MacPherson's Ossian.

Among the well-known Fenian lays are "Laoi na Seilge" or Lay of the Hunt, "Cath Chnoc an Áir" or Battle of the Hill of the Slaughter, "Laoi Oisín ar Thir na nÓg" or Lay of Oisin in the Land of Youth, "Laoi Chatha Gabhra" or Lay of the Battle of Gabhair, and "Tiomna Ghoill mhic Mhórna" or Will of Goll mac Morna. These poems celebrate the great deeds in battle of the champions of the Fianna, and express regret for their passing. Many of these poems also extol the outdoor life, supposed to have been lived by the Fianna, and the beauties of nature. In the "Agallamh Oisín agus Phádraig" ("Colloquy of Oisin and Patrick"), the aged Oisin recalls all these things in order to contrast the happy days in which the Fianna roamed the land with the narrow life Patrick was proposing:

I have heard music sweeter far
Than hymns and psalms of clerics are;
The blackbird's pipe on Letterlea,
The Dord Finn's wailing melody.

> The thrush's song of Glenna-Scál,
> The hound's deep bay at twilight's fall,
> The barque's sharp grating on the shore,
> Than cleric's chants delight me more.

"Laoi Oisín ar Thir na nÓg," which tells how Oisin went with the beautiful fairy maiden Niamh Cinn Óir to the Land of Youth, is one of enduring charm because it responds to a longing set deep in the human breast. It is this bitter-sweet romanticism which gives the Fenian Cycle its place in Gaelic literature and which spread its influence throughout Europe.

Ossian and the Romantic Movement

In 1760, a Dr. Blair published in Edinburgh *Fragments of Ancient Poetry, collected in the Highlands of Scotland, and translated from the Gaelic or Erse language.* The reputed collector was a Scottish schoolmaster named James Macpherson.

In 1762, Macpherson published *Fingal, an Ancient Epic Poem,* and in the next year, another epic, *Temora.* Macpherson brought out all of these poems as translations and attributed them to a Gaelic bard called Ossian. The poems of Ossian became the rage of the day and were translated into every major European language. Ossian was compared to Homer. Men of literature turned away from the arid classicism in which they had been schooled to delight in the naturalness, simplicity, and virtue of the primitive heroes of the Celtic past. It is said that Herder, the apostle of Romanticism in Germany, knew Ossian by heart. France was slower to succumb to the new movement, but was finally introduced to it by Madame de Staël and Chateaubriand during the time of the First Empire. Napoleon was an avid reader of Ossian and took a copy of the poems with him on his great campaigns, and even at the end to Saint Helena. His predilection for Ossian may perhaps be explained by the fact that he disliked the tragedies of Shakespeare, each one of which portrayed the fall of a great man. In any event, the heroic spirit of the Ossianic lays appealed to him, and he even had two Ossianic pictures painted for his chateau at Malmaison.

Macpherson's effusions were far from being translations from the original Gaelic poems and stories. Rather they are a hodgepodge of his own concoction with echoes of the Fenian and Ulster Cycles thrown together. Even the names of the warriors celebrated in them are not easily recognizable.

Nevertheless, Macpherson did a service to Gaelic literature by drawing attention to it and bringing many to study it seriously. Groups like the Scottish Highland Society and the Irish Ossianic Society were founded for that purpose. To the influence of Macpherson's Ossian may be attributed the publication in 1789 of Charlotte Brooke's *Reliques of Irish Poetry.* Unlike Macpherson, however, Brooke had a good knowledge of the language. She printed the original Gaelic poems with her translations alongside. The Irish Gaelic revival may be traced to her book.

The Cycle of the Kings

This cycle, as the title conveys, is concerned with kings. Sometimes the plural of the word "cycle" is used because in some of the stories the one king is the central figure. These tales are a mixture of fact and fiction, the creation of a world in which gods and men play a part. Few historians would deny that Cormac mac Airt and Niall of the Nine Hostages were historical figures, and it was natural that legends should grow up around such famous names. We know that the battle of Magh Rath was an historical event, and we actually know the year in which the battle was fought; but, although we should be thankful for the stories that were told about it, we would be unwise to regard them as the mere truth. Indeed, as far back as the ninth or tenth century, an Irish scribe went to the heart of this matter when he wrote: "And Suibhne Geilt having become mad is not a reason why the battle of Magh Rath is a triumph, but it is because of the stories and poems he left after him in Ireland." (Carney thinks this tale originated among the Britons of Strathclyde, but, strangely, he does not mention the traditions of Glannagalt, nor the possible origin of the Irish phrase "téighim le craobhachaibh" [I go mad; literally, I go among branches, as did Suibhne who lived in the trees].) "Buile Shuibhne" ("The Madness of Sweeney") is one of the most interesting, imaginative, and poetic of Irish tales. Incidentally, it inspired *At Swim-Two-Birds* by Flann O'Brien.

Among the most famous of the stories of the kings are "Cath Maighe Léana" or the Battle of Magh Lena, "Togail Bruidne Dá Derga" or the Destruction of Da Derga's Hostel, "Cath Maige Muccrime" or the Battle of Moy Muccruime, "Cath Crinna" or the Battle of Crinna, and "Fingal Rónáin" or the Kin-Slaying by Ronan. "Togail Bruidne Dá Derga" has an affinity with the Ulster Cycle, for several of the Ulster heroes appear in it. The story tells of the destruction of the bruidhean, the house or hostel of Da Derga, which was built over the River Dodder near Donnybrook; but the plot centers on the fate of the young king Conaire who is doomed because he unwittingly breaks his taboos or geasa. The relentless working out of these taboos lends the story its most tragic and most interesting aspect. The taboos show that the story reaches back into the dim beginnings of our civilization.

"Fingal Rónáin," which means "the murder of a kinsman by Rónán," is the story of the femme fatale who brings disaster to all those around her. The story has come down to us as little more than a synopsis, which was perhaps intended to be filled out by the storyteller.

The Mythological Cycle

The mythological cycle purports to give us an account of the early peoples who came to inhabit Ireland—the Nemedians, the Fomorians, the Firbolgs, the Tuatha Dé Danann, and others. We read also of their gods, such as the Dagda Mór, Lugh, Midir, and Angus. While most of these stories are invention, they do give a glimpse of the beliefs of pre-Christian Ireland. Indeed, it is clear that even after the coming of Christianity the people were loath to part entirely with the old gods. It was held that after a great battle at Teltown, the Tuatha Dé Danann retired into great mounds in the hills and valleys. In Irish the fairies are often referred to as "uaisle na gcnoc," or "the nobles of the hills," and a fairy mound is known as an "áit uasal," or a noble place. One of these great prehistoric figures was Balor of the Evil Eye, also called Balor Bailcbhéimneach and Balor na mBéimeann (of the Blows). Balor was the leader of the Fomorians and was defeated in a great battle, the second battle of Moytura, by Lugh Lámhfhada and his Tuatha Dé Danann. The strength of the tradition of this story is shown by the fact that it is told in Donegal to the present day. Balor was supposed to live on Tory Island and on the island Dún Bhalair, and Príosún Bhalair bears his name. At Cloughaneely they show the stone, Cloich Cheann Fhaolaidh, on which Balor beheaded Ceann Fhaolaidh.

"Tochmarc Étaine," or the successful wooing of Etain, is the most charming of the mythological stories. It is in itself a series of stories. Etain belongs to the Other World, but she weds a mortal king, Eochaidh Airem, who discovers her washing her hair in a stream. She is so beautiful that he falls in love with her immediately. "Never a maid fairer than she, or more worthy of love, was till then seen by the eyes of men; and it seemed to them that she must be one of those that have come from the fairy mounds." This blending of the magical world of the Sidhe with the physical world of mortals gives these stories their fascination.

The Immrama

The Immrama, or Voyages, form one of the most imaginative group of tales in the whole range of Irish literature. The immram is not a voyage of discovery in the ordinary sense of the term. The motif of these tales is the quest for the Other World, the Tír Tairngire, the land of promise, or Magh Mell or the plain of honey. Among the Immrama are "Immram Brain," "Immram Maíle Dúin," "Immram Snédgusa agus Maic Riagla," and "Immram Ua Corra." These tales date from the Old Irish period, and their origins are pagan.

In "Immram Brain" (Professor James Carney would see "Immram Brain" as a Christian allegory. Professor Myles Dillon does not accept that interpretation, which would remove from the story the pagan motif of the search for Magh Mell.) we meet Manannan mac Lir, the Celtic god of the ocean, who sings:

A n-as muir glan
don noi brainig i tá Bran,
is mag meld con n-imbud scoth
damsa i carput dá roth.

(What is a clear sea
to the leaky vessel in which Bran is,

is a plain of honey with many flowers
to me in my two-wheeled chariot.)

"Immram Maíle Dúin" tells of a voyage made by Máel Dúin and his companions in early Christian times, but in both conception and detail the story is
pagan. Máel Dúin visits many strange islands and meets with many strange
adventures. The story incorporates much from Oriental and classical mythology;
for example, we read of the Bridge of Difficulty, a Persian or Indian invention.
Lord Tennyson tried his hand at making an English metrical version of the
voyage of Máel Dúin (we have the story in Irish in both prose and verse), but,
as Eleanor Hull has stated, he failed to capture much of the style of the original,
taming it to suit Victorian taste. "Immram Maíle Dúin" was probably the model
for the Brendan legend.

"Immram Ua Corra," the voyage of the grandsons of Corra, supposedly
began in about the year 540 A.D. from the coast of Connaught. This story is
still remembered in the West. The Stag Rocks north of Aranmore off the Donegal Coast are called Na Mic Uí gCorra in Irish, for they are supposed to
represent the grandsons of Corra who were turned into stone for their crimes
and were destined to remain thus until the day of judgment.

When the spirit of extreme asceticism spread among the early Fathers of the
Irish Church, they began to seek lonely places and remote islands where they
could spend their lives as hermits far from the distractions of the world. Soon
stories were being told of the adventures of the monks on the sea, such as the
tale of Cormac Ó Liatháin's voyage northwards as recounted by Adamnan in
his life of Colmcille. In this way developed the "Navigatio Brendani," which
purports to be an account of St. Brendan's sea-wanderings but is actually a
skillful piece of fiction, having "Immram Máile Dúin" as its prototype. But as
the legend of St. Brendan's sea-wanderings was told first in Latin, it became
known throughout Europe and was translated into the major vernacular languages. It was eventually regarded as a record of fact and was an important
factor in inspiring the voyages of discovery of the fifteenth and sixteenth centuries. Consequently, the old Irish voyage tales have their place not merely in
literature, but also in history.

BARDIC POETRY

The Bardic schools flourished from the late sixth century to the seventeenth
century. Although, as we have seen, the bards were inferior in rank as poets to
the filí, the poetry of the filí is best known as bardic poetry, even though the
term *syllabic poetry* is also used for it. Bardic poetry does not in general conform
to our conception of poetry. It was not composed to create an original emotion
in the breast of the reader or listener, but rather to stir up one already there. A
vast number of bardic poems are no more than eulogies of princes and great
lords, their houses, and a recital of the glories of their ancestors. The bards laid

great stress on pride of ancestry—sometimes too much even for their patrons. When the poets came at Christmas to Turlough Luineach O'Neill with their usual genealogical encomiums, he told them bluntly that he would prefer to hear something about his own prowess. A great deal of bardic poetry is, therefore, dull, although it has some value for social and political historians.

The file was so tightly bound by the tradition of his craft—in meter, in language, and in subject—that for four centuries, from 1250 to 1650, hardly the slightest change or development is discernible in this type of official verse. While the charge of sterility against so much of bardic poetry cannot be gainsaid, it must be admitted that the obligations which the system imposed led not merely to the development of an extraordinary metrical skill, but also to the creation of a language of classical conciseness and dignity. These are compensations for the lack of originality in themes, which the student of bardic poetry comes to appreciate and often to marvel at. And, of course, despite the restraints of the bardic system, some genuine poets succeeded in leaving us some of the great works in Irish literature.

There were two periods in which the filí burst into verse of power and beauty, and both were periods of national recovery and hope. The first was in the thirteenth century when the native Irish were rolling back the tide of Norman invasion, and the second was in the sixteenth century. The chief poet of the earlier period was Giolla Bríghde Mac Con Midhe. Although he is most widely known as the author of the lament for Brian O'Neill, king of Ulster, who fell in the battle of Down in 1260, some of his greatest poems were inspired by Cathal Crobhdhearg who was leading a revival of the Gaelic kingship in Connaught. An inaugural ode to Cathal begins, "Tabhraidh chugam cruit mo ríogh" ("Bring to me the harp of my king"). He also wrote many poems for the O'Donnells and seems to have sojourned in Scotland, for he is called Albanach. He was a much-traveled man, and one of his most interesting poems was composed during a storm at sea: "A ghiolla ghabhas an stiúir" (O lad who takes the rudder).

Another poet who earned the epithet "Albanach" was Muireadhach Albanach Ó Dálaigh, who fled to Scotland because he had killed one of O'Donnell's stewards. Muireadhach, in a poem asking his patron's pardon, expresses his surprise that O'Donnell should be angry with him over the loss of a mere servant, a sentiment which shows that these filí were aristocrats writing for an aristocratic world. Ó Dálaigh was the author of "M'anam do sgar riomsa a-raoir" (I parted from my life last night), a touching elegy on the death of his wife. Like Giolla Bríghde Mac Con Midhe, he also wrote a poem at sea, addressing it to Cathal Crobhdhearg. As the vessel was in the Adriatic at the time, he may have been going on a pilgrimage to the Holy Land. In the end he returned to Ireland, was forgiven by O'Donnell, and entered a monastery. We have a poem, "A Mhuireadhaigh, meil do sginn" (O Murray grind your knife), which purports to describe Cathal and Muireadhach about to enter the Cistercians together. The poem is not regarded as authentic, even though both king and poet did take the habit. A number of devotional poems by Muireadhach are preserved in the Book of the Dean of Lismore. He was regarded as the chief poet of Scotland in his time, Ireland and Gaelic Scotland then sharing the same culture.

Donnchadh Mór Ó Dálaigh, a brother of Muireadhach, was the greatest of the religious poets, and the Four Masters describe him as a poet who never was and never shall be surpassed. He wrote many poems to the Blessed Virgin, many on the hollowness of life, and others on repentance. The most moving of his poems is the well-known "Truagh mo Thuras ar Loch Dearg" (Sorrowful my Pilgrimage to Loch Dearg). The poet making his pilgrimage was genuinely distressed that he could not feel true contrition for his sins:

> Yruagh mo thuras ar Loch Dearg,
> A Righ na gceall as no gclog,
> Do chaoineadh do chneadh's do chréacht
> 'S nach dtig déar thar mo rosg.

Seán Ó Faolain's translation of this poem captures the spare beauty of the original:

> Pity me on my pilgrimage to Loch Derg!
> O King of the churches and bells,
> bewailing your sores and your wounds,
> but not a tear can I squeeze from my eyes!

Donnchadh Mór Ó Dálaigh's poems became an integral part of Irish folk tradition. Douglas Hyde met a beggarman in Connaught who could recite many of them. His poems are also known in Donegal in our day. He died in 1244 A.D.

Another eminent poet of this family was Gofraidh Fionn Ó Dálaigh, most of whose poems were addressed to the earls of Desmond. Perhaps the best known of these poems is "Mór ar bhfearg riot, a rí Saxan" ("Great our anger with you, O king of the Saxons"), a poem composed in honor of Maurice Fitz-Maurice, second earl of Desmond. His poem "Mairg mheallas muirn an tsaoghail" was one of the most popular religious poems in Ireland for centuries. In the verses beginning, "Filí Éireann go haonteach," he celebrated the famous festival organized for all the poets of Ireland by O'Kelly of Hy Many during Christmas 1351.

Although the poets are sometimes accused of having been cynical and self-seeking and indifferent to the national welfare, they did their best in the sixteenth century to inspire the Irish chiefs in their last great struggle against the English. It was ironic that the bardic system was to produce its greatest poetry just when it and the civilization of which it was such a distinctive part were to be overthrown. Among the principal poets of this period were Tadhg Dall ÓhUiginn, Aonghus Fionn Ó Dálaigh, Aonghus mac Doighre Ó Dálaigh, Aonghus Ó Dálaigh, i.e., Aonghus na nAor, Eoghan Ruadh Mac an Bhaird, Tadhg mac Dáire Mac Bruaideadha, and Eochaidh Óh Eóghusa.

Tadhg Dall Óh Uiginn was probably the greatest master of the dán direach* that ever lived. His metrical skill and his command of the cultivated bardic language were superb. Most of his poems, however, were conventional in subject, consisting almost entirely of odes to chieftains. He does exhort the chieftains to unite in the common cause of their country, but there is little urgency or real passion in his verses. His poem on ''Inis Ceithleann,'' the residence of Maguire, gives us a picture of a household such as might have been lifted right out of the *Táin*.

> Buidhean cheard ag ceangal bhleidheadh,
> buidhean ghaibhneadh ag gléas arm;
> buidhean saor nách d'éanfonn uirre-
> néamhonn chaomh na mbuinne mbalbh.
>
> Géill dá ngabháil, géill dá léigean;
> laoich dá leigheas, laoich dá nguin;
> seóid dá síorchur inn is uadha-
> an síothbhru gh slinn cuanna cuir.

(A company of artificers binding vessels, a company of smiths preparing weapons, a company of wrights that were not from one land at work upon her—fair pearl of babbling streams.

Taking of hostages, releasing of hostages; healing of warriors, wounding of warriors; continual bringing in and giving out of treasure at the wondrous, smooth, comely, firm, castle.)

A love of nature has been a characteristic of the Celtic muse from earliest times, and the bardic poets, despite the artificiality of their training, were no exception in this respect. They knew the beauties of their country—the hills, the woods, and the streams. They appreciated, too, the use of place-names in verse. The opening stanza of ''Inis Ceithleann'' is a good example of this feature of their work:

> Mairg fhéagas ar Inis Ceithleann
> na gcuan n-éadrocht, na n-eas mbinn;

*''The rules of the Irish Classic Metres (which went under the generic name of *Dán Direach* or 'Straight Verse') required a break or suspension of the sense at the end of every second line, while each idea or thought of the poet must be completed within a quatrain. Hence there could be no carrying over of the sense from one stanza to another. Within these narrow limits the laws governing the construction of the verse were extraordinarily complicated, alliteration, rhyme, and number of syllables being all governed by precise laws. The result of this close attention to metrical exactitude is that a great number of the poems produced under this system are unimpassioned, sententious and mechanical. It would have been impossible for them to be otherwise; the wonder is, that they ever rise into true poetry at all.''—Eleanor Hull, *A Text Book of Irish Literature*. Vol. II (New York: AMS Press, 1900), p. 6.

guais dúinn, 'snach féadair a fágbháíl,
féagain an mhúir fádbháin fhinn.

(Alas for him who looks on Enniskillen, with its glistening bays and melodious
falls; it is perilous for us, since one cannot forsake it, to look upon the fair castle
with its shining sward.)

Despite the orthodoxy of Tadhg Dall's syllabic verse, among his poems are two
examples of the aisling or vision-poem, which was to become an important
political device in Irish poetry in the eighteenth century. Unlike the eighteenth-
century aisling, however, Tadhg Dall's vision, the beautiful lady who appears
to the poet, does not reveal herself at the end as the personification of Ireland.

Aonghus Fionn Ó Dálaigh was celebrated for his poems to the Blessed Virgin,
but they are inclined to be uninspired and uninspiring.

Aonghus mac Doighre Ó Dálaigh was poet to the O'Byrnes of Wicklow and
one of the greatest of the patriotic poets. His stirring address to the warriors of
Fiacha mac Aodha is said to have been composed before the battle of Glenmalure in which Fiacha defeated the Lord Justice. If it was, it was certainly
worthy of the occasion:

Dia libh, a laochruidh Gaoidhiol!
   ná cluintior claoiteacht oraibh;
riamh nior thuilliobhair masla
   a n-am catha iná cogaidh.

(God be with you, ye warriors of the Gael,
Let not subjugation be heard reported of you,
For infamy ye have never merited
In time of battle or war.—O'Grady's translation)

Aonghus na nAor was a satirist who was employed by the English to create
dissension among the leading Irish families. He finally paid for his treachery
with his life, for he was foolish enough to outrage the hospitality of his host
O'Meagher of Ikerrin in Tipperary, with the result that one of O'Meagher's
servants avenged the insult to his master by promptly cutting the bard's throat.
A fair example of his undoubted skill as a satirist is the quatrain:

Ní fhuil fearg nach dtéid ar gcúl
Acht fearg Chríost le cloinn Ghiobin,
Beag an t-iongnadh a mbeith mar tá
Ag fás in olc gach aon lá.

(There is no anger that does not abate,
but the anger of Christ with the Fitzgibbonses;
little wonder that they are as they are,
growing in evil every day.)

Eoghan Ruadh Mac an Bháird dedicated himself mostly to the service of the great Northern chiefs O'Donnell and O'Neill. Like Eochaidh Ó hEóghusa, he was in every sense a true poet. His elegiac address to Nuala O'Donnell weeping over the grave of her loved ones at Rome has the solemnity of "Venit summa dies et ineluctabile tempus/Dardaniae. Fuimus Troes, fuit Ilium et ingens/gloria Teucrorum" (the despairing cry of Panthus in Virgil's *Aeneid* at the fall of Troy, which says, in effect, Our last day is come, Troy is no more, and we and the great glory of the Trojans passed away.):

> Do shaoileamar, do shaoil sibh
> dál gcabhra ag macaibh Míleadh
> tres an dtriar tarla san uaigh
> ag triall ón mBanba mbeannfhuair.

(You thought and so did we that the Irish would get assistance through the three when they were leaving cool peaked Banba—the three who are now in the grave.)

This poem is well known to readers of English through Mangan's adaptation, "O, Woman of the Piercing Wail."

Tadhg mac Dáire Mac Bruaideadha was poet to the O'Briens of Thomond, and was responsible primarily for renewing the sterile controversy known as Iomarbhaidh na bhifledh, or the Contention of the Bards, about the respective merits of North and South. The folly of this academic debate had been made rather apparent by Lord Mountjoy's disastrous defeat of the Irish at Kinsale on Christmas day of 1601 and was aptly summed up by Flaithrí Ó Maoilchonaire in his lines:

> Lughaidh, Tadhg agus Torna,
> filí eólcha bhur dtalaimh,
> coin go niomad bhfeasa
> ag gleic fán easair fhalaimh.

(Lughaidh, Tadhg and Torna,
the learned poets of the land,
hounds with too much knowledge
wrangling over an empty kennel.)

Mac Bruaideadha addressed poems to his lord Donnchadh Ó Briain, fourth earl of Thomond. One of them—"Mo cheithre rainn duit, a Dhonnchaidh" or "My four verses are hereby dedicated to you, Donnchadh"—consists merely of time-worn maxims; however, his poem "A Mhacaoimh shéaas mo sheirc" (O maiden who rejects my love), has genuine feeling in it. As an old man, he met a violent death when he was hurled over a cliff by one of Cromwell's soldiers.

Eochaidh Ó hEóghusa was probably the greatest poet of this era. Despite the restrictions of the dán díreach, he was able to write poems of passion and imagination. His patron and master was Hugh Maguire, lord of Fermanagh and one of the bravest leaders in the war against Elizabeth. In the winter of 1600, Hugh O'Neill, then at the height of his power, marched into Munster, calling on the Munstermen to join him in what he knew to be a struggle for national survival. With him went Hugh Maguire. Safe at home in Fermanagh, Eochaidh Ó hEóghusa began to think of the hardships and dangers which his young master was undergoing during this winter campaign. Eochaidh composed a poem into which he poured his love for his young chief, his apprehension for his safety, and his dread of the outcome of the war for his country. It was a severe winter, and the very fierceness of the elements seemed to threaten disaster. A cloud of foreboding hung over the poet, and alas his fears were only too justified. Maguire was killed outside Cork in combat with Warham St. Leger, one of the English commissioners for Munster. St. Leger also fell in the conflict, but, as Cyril Falls, the British historian says, the death of St. Leger was small price to pay for the death of Hugh Maguire "who was one of the bravest and most determined of the rebel chiefs, and one of the most popular figures in Ulster."

Ó hEóghusa's poem begins:

> Fuar leam an oidhche-se d'Aodh!
> Cúis toirse truime a ciothbhraon,
> Mo thruaighe sein dar seise
> Neimh fhuaire na hoidhcheise.

Mangan's English version of this poem captures its air of impending doom:

> Where is my Chief my Master, this bleak night, mavrone!
> O, cold, cold, miserably cold is this bleak night for Hugh;
> Its showery, arrowy, speary sleet pierceth one through and through,
> Pierceth one to the very bone.

LOVE POEMS

Dánta Grádha, an anthology of Irish love poetry compiled by T. F. O'Rahilly, was first published in 1916. Most of the poems were composed in the sixteenth and seventeenth centuries, and some were from earlier times. As Robin Flower, then a lecturer in Irish in the University of London, said in the introduction, the subject of the poems was not the direct passion of the folk-singers or the high vision of the great poets. Rather, it was the learned and fantastic love of European tradition, the *amour courtois,* which was first shaped into art in Provence and found a home in all the languages of Christendom, wherever refined society and the practice of poetry met.

The poetry in O'Rahilly's anthology was that of high society in Ireland and in Scotland, as can be seen from the names of the authors of the poems in the volume: Gerald the Earl of Desmond, Manus O'Donnell prince of Tyrconnell, Piaras Ferriter, head of one of the chief families of Kerry, the earl and countess of Argyll, Duncan Campbell of Glenorquhy, "the good knight" who died at Flodden.

The first practitioner of this sophisticated type of verse was Gerald the Rhymer, fourth earl of Desmond and lord justice of Ireland in 1367. According to tradition, he disappeared in 1398 and sleeps under the waters of Loch Gur, whence he emerges every seven years to sweep over the lake. Piaras Ferriter, poet and soldier who was hanged at Killarney in 1653, may be said to have been the last and greatest exponent of the art.

These love poems are fanciful, extravagant, often ironic, and always elegant. As was common to this type of verse, the poet delights in describing the beauty of his mistress. One poet devotes a long poem to the praise of his favorite's hair, in this fashion:

> A bhean fuair an falachán
> do chiú ar fud do chiabh snáithmhin,
> ni as a bhfuighthear achmhasán,
> d'fholt Absolóin mic Dháibhidh.

> (All envious eyes amazing,
> Lady, your hair soft-waved
> Has cast into dispraising
> Absalon, son of David.—Robin Flower's translation)

But when the poet's compliments went unrequited, he could express himself in another mood:

> Ní bhfuighe mise bás duit,
> a bhean úd an chuirp mar ghéis;
> daoine leamha ar mharbhais riamh,
> ní hionann iad is mé féin.

> (For thee I shall not die,
> Woman of high fame and name,
> Foolish men thou mayest slay,
> I and they are not the same.)

THE RISE OF THE FOLK-POETS

With the defeat of the Irish at Kinsale in 1601 the Gaelic aristocratic order collapsed. The professional poets lost their patrons, the schools of poetry dissolved, and the classical meters and language were gradually abandoned. Irish began to be confined to the cabin, and the poets of the people came into their own. The folk-poets, like folk-poets everywhere, composed mostly songs, and their meter was the stressed or amhrán song meter.

The meters of the classical poets were syllabic and carried no regular stress. The new generation of poets sang songs of the sorrows of Éire and also songs of hope promising that help would come over the sea. While none of the poets could forget the calamity that had befallen their nation, they also sang of the sorrows and joys of everyday life. Love songs, laments, drinking songs, satire in plenty, and devotional verse have survived.

The poets who had been educated in the classical schools, and who had formed an important part of the Gaelic aristocratic civilization, looked with contempt on the new upstart, unskilled rhymers. Jack was now as good as his master. Innovators in the arts are never welcomed, but, to add insult to injury, the lot of the common people improved for a time after the Cromwellian plantation, and the poets of the old school found that boors were giving themselves airs. Dáibhí Ó Bruadair was one of these poets who resented the change. His life had covered most of the seventeenth century. He had lived through the Confederate wars (1642–1649), the Cromwellian massacres and plantations, the reigns of Charles II and James II, had seen the defeats of the Boyne and Aughrim, the complete overthrow of his country, and he had recorded it all in his poems. At the end of his days, he was reduced to utter poverty, going to the wood daily to cut faggots for his fire and seeking work as a laborer. Although he composed mostly in the new meters, Ó Bruadair used the archaic language of the classical schools. He expressed his chagrin at the way life had treated him, as follows:

IS MAIRG NACH FUIL NA DHUBHTHUATA

Is mairg nach fuil 'na dhubhthuata,
Ce holc duine 'na thuata,
Ionnas go mbeinn magcuarda
Idir na daoinibh duarca. . . .

A PITY I'M NOT A CHURL

A pity I'm not a mere churl,
Though it's no joke being a churl,
So that I'd be moving about
Like any common lout.

A pity I'm not a stammerer,
Among you, my good people,
For stammerers serve you well,
Since you know no better.

If I could only find a buyer,
I'd gladly sell my skill
Of culture, for some attire;
I'd let him have his fill.

Less value store of mind
Than dress of any gawk,
On learning all I spent
I'd have now on my back.)

HISTORY AND ANNALS

Professor E. C. Quiggin of Cambridge University, a Celtic scholar, claimed that "No people on the face of the globe have ever been more keenly interested in the past of their native country than the Irish." Many similar statements could be quoted. Certainly the amount of historical material, fanciful and genuine, genealogical and chronical, accumulated in Irish manuscripts is astonishing.

Eoin Mac Neill believed that the writing of Irish history began in the monastery of Bangor towards the end of the sixth century when a version of the Chronicle of Eusebius was compiled, which included what purported to be a synopsis of early Irish history. The author of this *Chronicon Eusebii* was probably Sinlan or Mo Shinu Moccu Min, abbot of Bangor, who died in 609 A.D. "But," says Kenney, "it was not until the ninth, and especially the tenth, eleventh and twelfth centuries, that this historical impulse acquired full momentum." Then, many of the filí seem to have turned their energies almost entirely to the task of transmuting the national folklore into a harmonized history. A twelfth-century text declares that "he is no file who does not synchronize and harmonize all the sagas." Scholars have noted that, although the country was divided politically into a large number of small states, the particular history of these states was never written. From the beginning, the history written was the history of Ireland.

In the brief space available here, it is impossible to give an adequate summary of the amount of historical writing we possess. However, inasmuch as until recently history has been regarded as a branch of literature, some account of it is necessary. It might be helpful to classify the material under the headings chronicles or annals, particular histories, biographies, and genealogies.

Annals

The practice of keeping or compiling annals, begun by Mo Shinu Moccu Min, continued until the overthrow of the old Gaelic civilization in the seventeenth century. Among the chief annals are the Annals of Tighernach, compiled in the monastery of Clonmacnois, in Latin and Irish, and continued down to 1178, although Tighearnach O Braein, whose name they bear, died in 1088. The Annals of Inisfallen were compiled in a monastery situated on the island of Inisfallen in the lower lake of Killarney. These annals cover the history of Ireland from the earliest times to the year 1326, the first part of the manuscript dating from about 1092. They are the chief source for the history of Munster in medieval times. The Annals of Ulster were compiled on Upper Loch Erne by Cathal Maguire, who died in 1498, but they were continued until 1604 by two other scribes. The title of these annals, given to them by Archbishop Ussher, is misleading, for they are not records of events in Ulster solely, although they do give prominence to Ulster affairs. Other annals are the Annals of Connacht,

the Psalter of Cashel, compiled in about 900 A.D., contained a corpus of genealogies, as many references to them show. Other collections that have survived are contained in the *Book of Leinster,* the *Book of Ballymote,* and the *Book of Genealogies,* compiled by the great antiquary Dubhaltach Mac FirBhisigh in 1650. This last is the largest collection of all, but there are many others. M. A. O'Brien has edited the pedigrees from the twelfth-century manuscripts kept in Oxford. While these genealogies may throw light on early Irish history, particularly on the history of the great septs and families, such compilations of names are scarcely the concern of the literary historian.

REFORMATION AND COUNTER-REFORMATION

The Tudor conquest of Ireland brought with it an attempt to force the Protestant religion on the people who clung to the old faith. The Irish language was to be employed towards this end. The first book in Irish to be printed in Ireland was the Protestant catechism, the *Caiticiosma lá Seaan Ó Kearnaigh,* in 1571. A font of type styled more after the Anglo-Saxon than the Irish script had been sent over from England by Elizabeth for the purpose. The catechism was followed by the New Testament translated by William Ó Domhnaill in 1602 and by the Book of Common Prayer in 1608. To counter the attempted reformation, the Irish set up colleges or seminaries on the Continent where priests were educated for the home mission. The Franciscans who had founded the college of St. Anthony at Louvain decided that they must produce Catholic books, and the first Catholic book to be printed in the Irish language was a catechism compiled by Bonaventura Ó Eodhasa, "a poor brother of the Order of Saint Francis," in 1611. The book was printed at Antwerp. After that, the friars acquired a press of their own, with a font of type based on the so-called Gaelic script, with *proprios characteres* as they claimed. This press issued a series of devotional works which were important not only in the struggle to maintain the Catholic religion in Ireland, but also in the history of Gaelic writing.

These writers wanted to get their message over to the people, and to do so they realized they must write in a language understood by the people, not in the learned jargon of the filí. With only two exceptions, they could not have written as the filí at any rate, for they had not been trained in the bardic schools. Hugh Caughwell, also called Aodh Mac Aingil (1571–1626), explained why he wrote in Irish in his introduction to his *Scáthán Shacramuinte na hAithridhe,* or The Mirror of the Sacrament of Penance, which he published in 1618. A native speaker of Irish and a Latinist of the first rank, he felt he had to apologize for attempting to write in his native tongue, so fast were the shackles of the filí on the language. He wrote: "Da n-abarthaoi gur dána dhúinn nidh do sgríobhadh a nGaoidhilg, snár shaothruigheamar innti; As í ár bhfeagra air sin, nách do mhúnadh Gaoidhilge sgríobhmaoid, acht do mhúnadh na h-aithridhe, agus as lór linn go dtuigfidhear sinn gé nach biadh ceart na Gaoidhilge againn" (If we were to be told that it was rash of us to write in Irish and that we had not cultivated it, our answer to that is that it is not to teach Irish that we write, but to teach penance, and we shall be satisfied if we are understood, although we might not have correct Irish).

Aodh Mac Aingil wrote beautifully clear, idiomatic Irish. He was the author of the delightful Christmas carol "Dia do bheatha, a Naoidhe naoimh!" ("Greetings to you, Holy Child!").

Many other devotional works were written by exiled Irish clerics during the seventeenth century, but from the purely literary point of view the most important was *Desiderius* by Flaithrí Ó Maolchonaire (1561–1629). This book, which began as a translation of a Catalan devotional work, ended up with more of Ó Maolchonaire in it than its Catalan author. Its principal distinction is its style. Flaithri Ó Maolchonaire, like Bonaventura Ó hEodhasa, belonged to a literary family and had studied in the bardic schools before entering the religious life. Consequently, he was a master of the learned language taught and used in them. But he realized that the highly artificial language of the schools would not serve the purpose he now had in mind. In the preface to his work, he states that he wished to express himself in Irish that was clear and intelligible, in a simple style for simple people. He could not, however, entirely suppress the effects of his early training; his grammar is inclined to be somewhat archaic, and his vocabulary literary, but this lends a dignity to his style which makes it one of the classics of Irish prose.

Desiderius was first published at Louvain in 1616. A new edition, edited by Thomas F. O'Rahilly, was issued by the Dublin Institute for Advanced Studies in 1955.

THE AISLING

As a result of the disaster of Kinsale, and of their failures in the Confederate War (1641–1649) and in the Williamite War (1688–1691), the old Irish were completely overthrown. Historians have called eighteenth-century Ireland the Protestant nation, for the Protestant planters possessed nine-tenths of the land, formed the government and Parliament, to neither of which any Catholic was admitted, controlled industry and the professions with the single exception of medicine, and enjoyed every privilege in the state. The Catholics, on the other hand, had no right in law. Their position was defined clearly by Lord Chancellor Bowes and Chief Justice Robinson, who laid it down from the bench "that the law does not suppose any such person to exist as an Irish Roman Catholic." Irish Catholics did exist, however, most of them in a lowly state.

The old Gaelic aristocratic society had perished, and with it went the profession of the filí. But poetry itself was not dead. Indeed, for a time at any rate, poetry freed from the shackles of pedantry blossomed into a new life. Poets now sang not to please a master, but to express their own hopes and fears, their own loves and hates, their own sorrows and joys. Love songs, for example, were no longer the conceits of the *amour courtois* but the outpouring of passion from the human heart, such as "Bean an Fhir Rua" ("The Red-haired Man's Wife") and "Moll Dubh an Ghleanna" ("Dark Moll of the Glen").

This is not to say that the poets could ignore or forget the downfall of their nation, a downfall in which they shared. Now poets were not an aristocratic caste, but poor hedge-schoolmasters who taught their informal classes out of doors, like Donncha Rua MacNamara, Peadar Ó Doirnín, and Eoghan Rua Ó Súilleabháin, or wandering minstrels like an Dall Mac Cuarta and Ó Reachtabhra, or common tradesmen and manual workers like the hackler Aodh Mhallaile, the fuller Maghnus Mhac Ardghaill, or the agricultural laborer Art Mac Cubhthaigh.

If the bardic schools were no more, schools or courts of poetry, as they were called, remained. Traditions of the old learning still survived. The hedge-schoolmaster poets were steeped in the history of their country, and many of them were first-rate Latinists. Donncha Rua Mac Conmara wrote an excellent Latin epitaph for his friend Tadhg Gaedhlach Ó Súilleabháin at the age of eighty. Tadhg Gaedhlach was himself well educated and was one of the most popular religious poets.

A new poetic convention arose in the eighteenth century, that of the political aisling, or vision-poem. Scholars are still in dispute about the origin of this aisling, some arguing that it is to be found in European literature. What is certain is that the vision-poem was not new to Gaelic literature. From earliest times we have stories in which Ireland is represented as a beautiful lady, and the myth of the lady from the síodh, the fairy-mound, uttering prophecies about the sovereignty of Éire is common. Only in the eighteenth century, however, did the aisling become a cult, especially with the Munster poets; its theme was the promise of the return of the Stuarts, or, as it has been derisively phrased, "Charly-over-the-waterism." We even know who started this fashion. It was Aodhgan Ó Raithille who composed the first political aisling when he led off with "Mac an Cheannuidhe." This poem is famous not merely because it is the first of these political vision-poems, but because of its excellence. It is a good example of the amhrán or stress meter, although it might be argued that its rhythm is too swift for its subject, as the poem does not end on a note of promise but of despair. The language is simple and direct, not excessively ornate and wordy as are his celebrated "Gile na Gile" ("Brightest of the Bright") and many of the aislingí by other poets. The opening stanzas of "Gile na Gile" read:

Gile na Gile do chonnarc ar slighe i n-uaigneas;
Criostal an chriostail a guirm-ruisc rinne-uaine;
Binneas an bhinnis a friotal nár chrion-ghruamdha;
Deirge as finne do fionnadh 'n-a gríos-ghruadhnaibh.

Caise na caise i ngach ruibe d'á buidhe-chuachaibh;
Bhaineas an ruithneadh de'n chruinne le rinn-scuabaibh,
Iorradh ba ghlaine na gloine ar a bruinn bhuacaigh,
Do geineadh ar gheineamhain di-se'san tír uachtraig.

Mangan's translation of these lines gives a very fair impression of the style of the original to the non-Gaelic reader:

> The brightest of the Bright met me on my path so lonely;
> The Crystal of all Crystals was her flashing dark-blue eye;
> Melodious more than music was her spoken language only;
> And glories were her cheeks, of a brilliant crimson dye.
>
> With ringlets above ringlets her hair in many a cluster
> Descended to the earth, and swept the dewy flower;
> Her bosom shone as bright as a mirror in its lustre;
> She seemed like some fair daughter of the Celestial Powers.

Ó Rathaille was born near Killarney in the second half of the seventeenth century, in a region where some of the old noble families had survived. These families were swept away after the Williamite Wars, and most of his poems are laments for them. Despite the undoubted sincerity of these laments and their felicity of diction and rhythm, they begin to pall after a time because of the monotony of theme and of approach. But this criticism cannot be applied to one of his poems which, in my opinion, is among the greatest in the language.

Ó Rathaille, old and poverty-stricken, lay down one night in his cabin at the mouth of Castlemaine Harbor. But, wearied as he was, he did not rest, for a storm raged outside. It was one of the nights when the great waves of Ireland could be heard moaning. According to the ancient writers, the three great waves of Ireland were Tonn Chlíodhna in Glandore Harbor, County Cork; Tonn Rudhraighe in Dundrum Bay, County Down; and Tonn Tuaidh Inbhir at the mouth of the Bann. These waves, it was believed, could be heard beating the strand, ag buain re traigh, when something momentous was to happen to Ireland. Tonn Tóime is also mentioned as a wave of fateful significance, and it was Tonn Tóime that would not let Ó Rathaille sleep. It kept reminding him of his own destitution and of the sad story of his country, and it inspired him to express his grief and chagrin in words that have the passion of great poetry. The poem has been translated into English by James Stephens, who addresses the wave by the name Tonn Clíodhna because, no doubt, of its more legendary allusion and its more musical sound than Tonn Tóime.

> O Wave of Cliona, cease thy bellowing!
> And let mine ears forget a while to ring
> At thy long, lamentable misery;
> The great are dead indeed, the great are dead;
> And I, in little time, will stoop my head
> And put it under, and will be forgot
> With them, and be with them, and thus be not.
>
> Ease thee, cease thy long keening, cry no more;
> End is, and here is end, and end is sore,
> And to all lamentations be there end;
> If I might come on thee, O howling friend,

Knowing that sails were drumming on the sea
Westward to Éire, and that help would be
Trampling for her upon a Spanish deck,
I'd ram thy lamentation down thy neck.

Other Munster poets of note were Seaghan (John) Clárach Mac Domhnaill (1691–1754), Eoghan Rua Ó Súilleabháin (1748–1784), Seán Óa Tuama (1708–1775), Seán Ó Coileáin (1754–1816?), Piaras Mac Gearailt (1709–1788?), Donnchadh Rua Mac Conmara (1715–1810), Tadhg Gaedhealach Ó Súilleabháin (died 1795), Brian Merrimann (c. 1747–1805), and Eibhlín Dubh Ní Chonaill (1743?–1800). Many other poets or writers of verse were living in Munster during this period, for Munster was one of the two great centers of literary activity in Ireland in the eighteenth century, the other being the eastern part of South Ulster, sometimes called Oriel.

Nearly all of these poets are sometimes called the Jacobite poets, for in their verses they expressed a desire for a Jacobite restoration, as did especially Eoghan Rua Ó Súilleabháin, Seaghan Clárach Mac Domhnaill, Piaras Mac Gearailt, and, of course, Aodhagán Ó Rathaille.

Eoghan Ruadh Ó Súilleabháin was, perhaps, the most popular of all these poets, earning for himself the sobriquet Eoghan an Bhéil Bhinn, or Owen of the Sweet Mouth. "Im'Leabaidh Aréir" and "Ceo Draoidheachta," two of his most frequently printed poems, are typical aislingí, but there is more poetry in his lullaby, said to have been composed for his own illegitimate child, for there is more imagination in it. In his endeavor to soothe the child to sleep, the poet promises him a host of precious things steeped in legend and magic—Cuchulainn's gae bolga, Naise's white shield, Failbhe or Fionn's swift steed, the Golden Fleece, the nectar Hebe served to Jupiter at the table of the gods, the pipe of Pan, and so on—a cornucopia of native and classical treasures. The only fault of the poem is its great length; a tendency towards prolixity is a characteristic of all these Munster poets.

Eoghan Ruadh led an adventurous and stormy life. He was by turns a farm laborer, hedge-schoolmaster, soldier, and sailor. By a strange turn of fate, he who sang of the return of the Stuarts fought against the French in a naval engagement under the English Admiral Rodney off Dominica in 1782. Moreover, as Rodney gained a great victory, Eoghan Ruadh composed an ode in English in his praise and was invited to recite it before him on the flagship. He did so, and Rodney was extremely pleased. Surely this was a strange honor for the poor wandering Jacobite poet in whose veins ran the best blood of Munster.

Seán Ó Tuama an Ghrinn, or Seán Ó Tuama of the wit, was an innkeeper and often presided over assemblies of poets at Croom and in Limerick. Over the door of his tavern in Mungret Street in Limerick was a notice which proclaimed that any brother bard was welcome to the hospitality of the house, even if he had not the price of a drink. This invitation seems to have been accepted only too readily, so that in the end poor Ó Tuama was ruined. He wrote the usual Jacobite songs, but he well merited his name as a fellow of fun, and he was ready with a drinking song, a love song, or a satire as the occasion demanded. Among his best known pieces are "Móirín Ní Chuilleannáin" ("Maureen O'Cullinane"), which is a vision-poem, "As duine mé dhíolas liún lá" ("I am a person who sells ale"), which is a drinking song, and "Bean na Cleithe Caoile" ("Woman of the Slender Wattle"), which is a satire on the cantankerous old woman to whom the over-generous poet became servant when he had fallen on evil days.

Seán Ó Coileáin is known primarily for his poem "Machtnamh an Duine Dhoilgheasaigh" ("The Melancholy Man's Meditation"), which is a lamentation over the destroyed abbey of Timoleague. The poem conveys the sadness and loneliness which the poet feels in the ancient ruins at night.

Piaras Mac Gearailt was the author of the rousing "Rosc Catha na Mumhan" ("The Munster Battle-Cry"), which is appropriately also called "Amhrán an Dóchais" ("The Song of Hope"). Hopeful it is, promising that the waves will soon carry a French fleet to free Ireland. It is impossible to render the wonderful word music of the refrain into English:

Measaim gur subhach don Mhumhain an fhuaim,
'S d'á maireann go dubhach de chrú na mbuadh,
Torann na dtonn le sleasaibh na long
Ag tarraing go teann 'nar gceann ar cuaird.

(I feel that the news is welcome to the province of Munster,
And to all who are eking out a miserable life:
The sound of the waves on the sides of the ships
Drawing boldly on a visit to us.)

What a strange twist of fortune that this song and the Orange song, "The Boyne Water," should be sung to the same air.

Donnchadh Rua Mac Conmara was famous as a schoolmaster. A pass from him was a qualification for admission to that lowly profession. He spent a year or more in Newfoundland, and it was probably there that he composed "Bánchnoic Éireann Óigh" ("The Fair Hills of Holy Ireland"), which is without doubt the most beautiful of all the many Irish songs of exile.

Tadhg Gaedhealach Ó Súilleabháin, the most popular of the Munster religious poets, wrote "Pious Miscellany" which has been printed many times. His devotional verses move one by their very intensity. The directness and intimacy of his address in "Duan Chroidhe Iosa" ("Poem on the Sacred Heart of Jesus") derive from the fervor of his faith. It is, perhaps, the most beautiful of his poems:

Gile mo chroidhe do Chroidhe-se a Shlanuightheoir,
As ciste mo chroidhe do Chroidhe-se d'fhaghail im' chomhair;
Ós follus gur líon do Chroidhe dom' ghvádh-sa, a Stóir,
I gcochall mo chroidhe do Chroidhe-se fág i gcomhad.

(You are the brightness of my heart, O Saviour,
Since it is my heart's desire to have Yours for mine;

And since it is clear that Your heart, my Dear, is filled with love for me,
Deep down in my heart leave Your heart in keeping.)

Brendan Behan quite rightly said that his own simple Catholicism went back to the Mass rock and to the poems of Tadhg Gaedhealach Ó Súilleabháin, not to the pious intellectualism of Newman and his ilk.

MERRIMAN

Brian Merriman was a Clareman who died in Limerick in 1805. In its death notice, the *General Advertiser and Limerick Gazette* for Monday, July 29, of that year, merely stated: "Died—On Saturday morning, in Old Clare-street, after a few hours' illness, Mr. Bryan Merryman, teacher of mathematics." Merriman is known for one poem, *Cúirt an Mheadhon Oidhche,* or *The Midnight Court.* Merriman, also called Brian Mac Giolla Meidhre and Brian MacConmara, stands apart from other Irish poets of his day because, as O'Rathaille said, "*Cúirt an Mheadhon Oidhche* is by far the most successful sustained effort in verse in Modern Irish." Merriman also seems to have stood apart in the physical sense, for there is little evidence that he had any contact with his fellow-poets. Some have claimed that he was the most original of the Irish poets, that his poem was a tour de force, being an attack on Irish Catholic puritanism as it was supposed to be practiced in the eighteenth century. An onslaught on the mores of the times it is, but, despite the enthusiasm of critics such as Piaras Béaslaí and Frank O'Connor who saw the poet as a kind of Irish Rousseau, O'Rathaille showed that the theme was used in many other Irish verses. O'Rathaille found the poem as conventional as anything in literature and its grossness as utterly repellent. O'Connor described the poem "as classical as the Limerick Custom House, and fortunately the Board of Works has not been able to get at it." Many English versions of the *Court* have been produced; the best by far, in my opinion, being that by Frank O'Connor.

Cúirt an Mheadhon Oidhche has been edited and translated into German by Ludwig Stern.

EIBHLÍN DUBH NÍ CHONAILL

Eibhlín Dubh Ní Chonaill was an aunt of Domhnall Ó Conaill, the Liberator. She composed "Caoineadh Airt Uí Laoghaire," a lament for her husband Art Ó Laoghaire who was shot by a British soldier in a feud originating in the penal law that a Catholic could not be the owner of a horse worth more than £5. Arthur O'Leary had such a horse, and, when offered five pounds for it by a Protestant landlord named Morrison, whom he had just beaten in a race, he scornfully rejected the offer. For Arthur O'Leary was not merely an Irish gentleman, but a brave soldier who had been a captain in the Imperial army. He challenged Morrison to a duel, which Morrison refused on the basis that he could not lower himself to fight a Papist. He then had O'Leary shot down at a distance. O'Leary's riderless horse galloped home. His wife, guessing what had happened, leaped into the saddle and found her husband lying dead beside a furze bush at Carriganima, with an old woman keening over him. She then began to compose her own lament, which is remarkable for its dramatic outpouring of grief. Strangely, the inscription on O'Leary's tomb is in English, and reads:

> Lo! Arthur O'Leary
> Generous, handsome, brave,
> Slain in his bloom, lies in this humble grave.

A few words which are not a bad summing up of the tragedy.

THE POETS OF ORIEL

As mentioned above, the only other region of Ireland that could compare with Munster for literary activity during the eighteenth century was South Ulster, an area which is sometimes called Oriel and which embraced South Down, South Armagh, much of Monaghan and Cavan, much of Louth, and even extended as far as Meath. The literary tradition survived in this region for the same reason as it did in Munster: namely, economic and social conditions were not as bad there as in Connaught and in western Ulster. Courts or schools of poetry still existed in Oriel into the early years of the nineteenth century, and the copying of manuscripts and the composition of occasional verse continued until the beginning of the twentieth century.

The chief poets of South Ulster in this period were Séamus Dall Mac Cuarta (died 1753); Peadar Ó Doirnín (died 1760); Art Mac Cubhthaigh or MacCooey in English (died probably in 1773); Pádraig Mac a Liondáin (died 1733); and Cathal Buídhe Mac Giolla Ghunna (died ca. 1756). Their death dates are known because it was the custom for the elegiast to recite the date. There were innumerable other minor poets in Ulster, some of whom composed beautiful songs but whose names must go unrecorded here.

Séamus Dall Mac Cuarta was probably the best lyric poet of his time. As he was blind from birth, he was given to introspection. Hence, much of his verse springs from his very heart and is not the product of convention as is so much of Gaelic composition.

One day Mac Cuarta heard a bird calling. It reminded him that spring had come and that the earth was about to clothe itself in finery again, finery which he would never see. His sorrow welled up in him into this lovely lyric:

> Fáilte don éan is binne ar an chraoibh,
> Labhras ar cheann na dtor le gréin,
> Damhsa is fada tuirse an tsaoil,
> Nach bhfeiceann í le teacht an fhéir.

So runs the first verse. I have translated the whole poem as follows:

WELCOME TO THE BIRD

Welcome to the bird, sweetest on the bough,
That sings aloft in the heat of the sun,
I see her not in the Spring of the year,
I nearly wish my life were done.

I hear her voice, tho' I do not see
The bird that men the cuckoo call,
A glimpse of her on the topmost branch
Would my very soul enthrall.

All those who behold the shapely bird,
And the land of Ireland north and south
The flowers blooming on every side,
For them it's easy to rejoice.
            The song
My sorrow that vision was never once granted to me!
That I might gaze in quiet on the foliage growing free,
I have no mind to be moving among the throng,
But sit here, near the bird, at the rim of the wood alone.

This poem was composed in a form called trí rann agus amhrán in Irish, three verses and a song, a form favored by the Ulster poets. It often saved them from the vice of longwindedness, so common among Gaelic poets. Another pathetic poem of Mac Cuarta is addressed to a young girl, Róis Ní Raghailligh, who sold stockings at fairs. On his way to a fair one day, the blind poet had the misfortune to fall into a stream, and, as he scrambled out, his bedraggled appearance caused some merriment to the onlookers. But the young girl took pity on him, brought him into the house, and dried his clothes. The poet thanked her in the best way he could—"A Chaoin Róis" ("O gentle Rose"):

Sé d'aon phóg
A d'fhág pian mhór
Agus creapaill ann mo cliabh.

(It was your single kiss
That left a great pain
And torment in my breast.)

In another poem, "Sgannradh an Daill" ("The Fright of the Blind Man") Mac Cuarta cries out in outraged despair when a low scoundrel steals his savings from him:

A dhaoine, nach truagh libh mé 'mo thruaill bocht ag éagcaoin,
Tá mé 'nocht faor ghruaim 's gan m'fhuasgailt ag aoinneach
Fa na hocht ngeinidh dheag do bhí mé a chúdach,
Gur fúaideadh go léir iad ón gcréatur gan súile.

(O, people, do you not pity me, a poor wretch lamenting,
I am tonight in gloom with no one to relieve me,
For the eighteen guineas which I had in my keeping
Have all been filched from the eyeless creature.)

This poem rises to a crescendo of fury.

In these poems, as in others such as "Toigh Chorr a' Chait" ("The House at Barrakit") and the "Mo Chead Mhairgneadh" ("My First Lament") Mac Cuarta speaks to us directly, at times in sorrow, at times with tenderness, at times in anger, and at times with such satisfaction that it becomes apparent that he is a true poet and not a mere versifier.

Peadar Ó Doirnín was a hedge-schoolmaster. Indeed, he died outside the little school he kept at Forkhill. The children who were playing thought he was sleeping, but when one of the older boys tried to awaken him, he found that the master "was sleeping in the sleep that would never be broke." Ó Doirnín had studied in Munster's poetry schools and was a superb artist in the Irish language. He is best known for his love song "Úr-Chnoc Chéin Mhic Cáinte" ("The freshly cultivated hill of Cian the Son of Cáinte"), which is sung to an air composed in this century by Peadar Ó Dubhda. An older air for it also exists. It must have been an easy task to set Ó Doirnín's words to music because no Irish poet has ever achieved greater musical effect than has Ó Doirnín in this song.

A chiúin-bhean tséimh na gcuachann péarlach,
Gluais liom féin ar ball beag,
Nuair bheas uaisle is cléir is tuataigh i néall,
Ina suan faoi éadaighe bána.

(O quiet, sweet-tempered lady of the pearly tresses,
Come along with me in a little while,
When the nobles, the clergy, and the lay folk will be deep
Asleep under white bedclothes.)

In Irish, the word-music is created by a marvelous interplay of assonance, by allowing the stress to fall on long vowels followed by liquid consonants, and by alternating iambic and trochaic rhythms in the succeeding verses. The sentiment of the poem is in keeping with the witchery of its music. The poet is calling on his loved one to steal away with him from the world of reality to Arcadia where they will live on mead and sweet fruits. They will find their Arcadia on "úr-Chnoc Chéin Mhic Cáinte," a hill not far from Dundalk, doubtless selected by Ó Doirnín for the musical quality of its name.

Art Mac Cubhthaigh (MacCooey) was born near Crossmaglen. He is the poet of the O'Neills of the Fews; in his poems he laments the fall of that great family and the destruction of their castle of Glasdrummond. Like the Munster poets,

had always been, the language of the cities and towns, although many people in the smaller towns knew Irish and spoke it when necessary. Because of the predominance of English in the towns among the commercial classes and in government, Irish was almost unknown to the printing press. The only books printed in Irish in the eighteenth century were a few catechisms and devotional works. The Franciscans' seventeenth-century effort to provide Catholics with a wide range of religious works had petered out. Some prose works, such as the County Down translation of the "Imitatio," were not printed until our own time. The Catholic Church sounded the death-knell of the ancient language of the country when it succumbed to the policy of anglicization in about midcentury. After the Forty Five, it was apparent to all that the Stuart cause was lost, and the Church began to take the view that there was no hope of a restoration of the old order in Ireland and that the Catholics had no alternative but to accept the rule of the Hanoverians. The adoption of the English language was a logical corollary to such a policy.

Despite the Penal Laws, the flood of Catholic devotional books issuing from the printing presses in Dublin in the eighteenth century was astonishing. Yet, in a list of seventy Catholic works printed and sold by a Dublin house in 1777, only three are in Irish, and two of them are elementary catechisms. As O'Rahilly says in his introduction to *Irish Dialects Past and Present,* "The climax came with the foundation by the British Government in 1795 of the Royal College of St. Patrick in Maynooth, for the education of the Catholic priesthood. In Maynooth College, English from the start held a position of complete supremacy, almost as if Trinity College had been taken as the model for the new institution. Henceforth, English becomes in effect the official language of the Church in Ireland." John O'Donovan, when touring County Down for the Ordnance Survey in order to collect the place-names, tells us that the young priests just out of Maynooth pretended not to know any Irish, although O'Donovan knew that most of them had not spoken a word of English until they were twelve years of age.

It is somewhat ironic, then, that the one Irish prose work of importance printed in the eighteenth century was a book of sermons by Bishop James Gallagher of the Diocese of Raphoe, later of Kildare and Leighlin. Gallagher's sermons were first published in Dublin in 1736. They were printed in English characters because the printers had no Gaelic type and because, as Gallagher himself says in his introduction which he wrote in English, "Our mother language, sharing so far the fate of her professors, is so far abandoned, and is so great a stranger in her native soil that scarce one in ten is acquainted with her characters." These sermons became the most widely known work in the Irish language. They have been printed at least twenty times and have been translated into English. As Canon Ulick J. Bourke, who edited an edition of the sermons in 1877 said, Gallagher's sermons spoke from every fireside in three provinces. They did so not only because so few books in Irish were available, but also because of the manner in which they were written. Gallagher himself described them as written "in an easy and familiar stile," and so they were, in the language of the people. Indeed, pedants censured the author for using English words in his text which were commonly heard on the lips of Irish speakers at the time. But the popularity of the sermons was not to be attributed to these causes only. Gallagher had style. Although he used the language the people understood, he used it with great skill. He was a master of the concrete image, and there is a freshness, an originality and charm about his writing which the Irish people were quick to recognize. He could write, "Ar maidin, adeirim, an Uair a fhosglus fuinneogauidh an lae, is cóir duinn fuinneoguidh ar nanama dfoscuilt, fo chomair grasa an Tiagherna, agus a ndrud naighe gach droch rúdn, agus gach cathuidh" (In the morning, I say, when the windows of day open, we should open the windows of our souls to let in the grace of the Lord, and shut them against every evil thought and temptation), or "Chuir me cul mo laimhe ris an tsaoghal" (I gave the back of my hand to the world).

Tomas Rua Ó Súilleabháin, the Kerry hedge-schoolmaster and poet, spoke of him as "Dochtuir áluinn Gallchobhair," or "the beautiful Doctor Gallagher." In Donegal, after hearing a good sermon, someone would say, "B'fhurasta aithne gur léigh sé an Dochtúir Ó Gallchobhair" (It was easy to see that he had read Dr. O Gallagher).

THE WEST

Dr. Gallagher was a Donegal man and, as far as can be ascertained, his sermons were written while he was bishop of Raphoe and was in hiding from the British authorities on the island of Inismacsaint in Lough Erne. Nonetheless, there was little literary activity in Donegal at this time. The bardic tradition had depended on the patronage of the chiefs of Tyrconnell, and, when they fell, the bardic order fell too. The Gaelic-speaking districts of Donegal were too poor to support poets and scholars such as we find in South Ulster and in Munster. The production of great books and the copying of manuscripts ceased, but a rich folklore still survived. Storytelling and the singing of Gaelic songs continued, and local poets still composed songs which were handed down traditionally. Therefore, West Donegal is one of the remaining districts of Ireland where the Irish language is the native tongue of the people. Unfortunately, it has disappeared entirely in South Ulster and almost entirely in Munster.

The same is true of Connaught. Douglas Hyde, in his *Literary History of Ireland,* wrote:

In Connacht during the eighteenth century the conditions of life were less favourable to poetry, the people were much poorer, and there was no influential class of native schoolmasters and scribes to perpetuate and copy Irish manuscripts, as there was all over Munster; consequently, the greater part of the minstrelsy of that province is hopelessly lost, and even the very names of its poets with the exception of Carolan, Netterville, Mac Cabe, Mac Govern, and a few more of the last century, and Mac Sweeny, Barrett, and Raftery of this century, have been lost. That there existed, however, amongst the natives of the province a most wide-spread love of song and poetry, even though most of their manuscripts have perished, is certain, for I have collected among them, not to speak of Ossianic lays, and other things, a volume of love poems and two volumes of religious songs, almost wholly taken from the mouths of the peasantry. This love of poetry and passion for song, which seems to be the indigenous birthright of every one born in an Irish-speaking district, promises to soon be a thing of the past, thanks, perhaps partly, to the apathy of the clergy, who in Connacht almost always preach in English, and partly to the dislike of the gentry to hear Irish spoken, but chiefly owing to the far-reaching and deliberate efforts of the National Board of Education to extirpate the national language (605–606).

Then came the Famine, which struck hardest in the Irish-speaking areas, for they were the poorest. Thousands died, hundreds of thousands fled the country, and the Irish language suffered accordingly. Indeed, for many it became associated with poverty and suffering, and its decline was greatly hastened. Any kind of literary composition in the language eventually petered out.

A few people, especially scholars and antiquaries, deplored the abandonment of the ancient language of Ireland. As explained earlier, Macpherson's "Ossian" stimulated interest in things Celtic, and cultured men and women began to study Irish literature and Irish music. Charlotte Brooke published her *Reliques of Irish Poetry* in 1789. In addition, a great harpers' festival was held in Belfast in 1792, at which Edward Bunting was employed to write down the airs played by the harpers; it may be said that the modern Irish revival can be traced to that time. Several societies for the study of the Irish language were founded: the Irish Ossianic Society, in 1853, devoted to the study and publication of Irish manuscripts; the Society for the Preservation of the Irish Language, in 1876; the Gaelic Union, in 1880; and the Gaelic League, the most important of all these societies, in 1893.

No other organization has had as great an effect on the cultural and political history of Ireland in our time as the Gaelic League. From the first, it attracted a support that none of the other language societies had enjoyed. The reason was principally that the Parnell split had created a disgust with politics among many young people, who turned from the tiresome wrangling of the politicians to the cultural nationalism of the Gaelic League. Other factors also favored the League. The Land Acts, from the great act of 1881 on, had raised the standard of living throughout the country, as a result of which the people now had some leisure for cultural interests. The league also benefited from a renewed interest in Celtic literature and civilization on the Continent. In 1853, Zeuss published his *Grammatica Celtica,* which laid the basis for the scientific study of Old Irish. The *Revue Celtique* was founded in 1870 by Henri Gaidoz and d'Arbois de Jubainville, and the *Zeitschrift für celtische Philologie,* in 1896 by Kuno Meyer and Ludwig Stern. In these journals and elsewhere, a long line of European scholars, especially German, contributed to our knowledge of Celtic literature and the Celtic past. The most famous of these were Rudolf Thurneysen, Kuno Meyer, Ernst Windisch, and Heinrich Zimmer. Therefore, the Gaelic League frequently argued that, if the Irish language was worthy of the attention of foreign scholars, it merited the attention of Irishmen. Thus a new generation of Irish scholars arose.

The Gaelic League differed from the antiquarian societies that preceded it in declaring that its aims were the preservation of Irish as the national language of Ireland and the extension of its use as a spoken tongue. Moreover, it would apply itself not merely to the study and publication of existing Gaelic literature, but also to the cultivation of a modern literature in the language. Even men such as Eoin Mac Neill, who was primarily a scholar and was one of the founders of the League, stressed the importance of the creation of a new literature in the language. He realized that the language had no chance of survival unless it could produce a modern literature to satisfy contemporary tastes. Thus, as the nineteenth century drew to a close, just when it seemed that the Irish language was doomed to extinction, men began to write it again.

Although much of the writing done in the early days of the League was amateurish, it would be wrong to state that this effort was merely artificial and therefore could not produce literature. Such a notion would derive from an ignorance of the cultural excitement which the Gaelic League stimulated in the nation.

P. S. O'Hegarty was correct when he wrote:

The language led inevitably to other things, to Irish music, Irish customs and traditions, Irish place-names, Irish territorial divisions, Irish history. It emphasized the separateness of Ireland as nothing else could; it brought with it national self-respect, a feeling of kinship with the past, the version of a persistent and a continuing tradition going back beyond human memory. Many a man and woman went casually, through curiosity, to a branch meeting, or to a concert, or a festival; and heard the language spoken, or heard Irish songs, or the Irish pipes, or a traditional air on the violin, and straightway found themselves gripped and held as if an old memory were being re-awakened; returned, and returned again, and finally became one with the others, reaching back to that Irish nation, Irish civilization, that was in the land ere ever the English came, and that was the motive force of the expressions of Irish separateness that had been made in English. The Gaelic League was not alone a re-discovery of the language, but a re-discovery of the Nation, a resurrection of the Gael.

That the Gaelic League inspired not only the writing anew of Irish, but also the creation of a new drama in English can be seen from the statement of their intentions drawn up by Lady Gregory, Edward Martyn, and W. B. Yeats when they founded the Irish Literary Theatre in 1899. "We propose," they said, "to have performed in Dublin in the spring of every year certain Celtic and Irish plays, which, whatever be their degree of excellence, will be written with a high ambition, and so build up a Celtic and Irish school of dramatic literature." The influence of the League can be gauged by the titles of the first plays presented by the new theatre. They were *The Countess Cathleen* by Yeats and *The Heather Field* by Martyn, which were staged in the Antient Concert Rooms, Brunswick Street, Dublin, in May 1899. Productions of the following year were *The Bend-*

ing of the Bough by George Moore, *Maeve* by Martyn, and *The Last Feast of the Fianna* by Alice Milligan. The third and last productions of the Irish Literary Theatre were *Diarmuid and Grania* by Yeats and George Moore and a play in the Irish language, *Casadh an tSúgáin,* or *The Twisting of the Rope,* by Douglas Hyde. These plays were presented in the Gaiety Theatre, Dublin, on October 21, 1901. *Casadh an tSúgáin* was the first play in Irish ever to be put on the boards of a theatre. It received far more favorable notices than the more pretentious play of Moore and Yeats, and still survives.

In 1895, the Gaelic League took over the *Gaelic Journal,* the organ of the Gaelic Union, and renamed it *Irisleabhar na Gaedhilge.* Over many years much good work, especially in scholarship and folklore, appeared in it. The League also founded the weekly paper *Fáinne an Lae* in 1898 and later, *An Claidheamh Soluis;* these papers were the propaganda sheets for the League and dealt with the topics of the day.

The first writer of importance to appear in modern Irish was Canon Peter O'Leary. Although he was advanced in age when, under the inspiration of the Gaelic League, he began to write, he produced a large number of works, mostly translations and adaptations from the older language and from Latin. He even tried his hand at rendering *Don Quixote* into Irish, although he emasculated it incredibly. In 1904, however, he put all lovers of the Irish language eternally in his debt when he published *Séadna.* This was a rather unsuccessful attempt to make a novel of a folktale, but *Séadna* consists of three hundred printed pages of the Irish that was spoken in West Cork when O'Leary was a boy. While the story may not stand up to the test to which a modern psychological novel is subjected, it contains descriptive passages and dialogue that are a delight. No wonder the book became a kind of bible with revivalists, especially in Munster: three hundred pages of the living language!

When the revival began, the question that arose was what kind of Irish should be written. This was a complicated question because three main dialects were still being spoken in the country—the Munster, the Connaught, and the Ulster. Some scholars argued for a common literary language as of yore and a return to the classical language of Keating. Others argued that Keating's Irish was too far removed from the spoken tongue of our time. The publication of *Séadna* put an end to the discussion. Henceforth, "caint na ndaoine," the language of the people, was written.

Despite the great importance of Canon O'Leary's work, it may be said that modern literature in Irish begins in the writings of Patrick Pearse and Padraic Ó Conaire. Pearse, who was born in Dublin and had learned Irish well, wrote short stories, mostly about children in Connaught. Though sometimes regarded as sentimental, the stories have an enduring charm because they capture the innocent world of childhood. Pearse also wrote a small number of poems which are among the most impressive pieces of poetry to appear in Irish in this century. Even if we did not know that "Fornocht Do Chonnaic Thu" ("Naked I Saw Thee") was autobiographical and prophetic, it would still be a great poem:

Fornocht do chonnac thu
A áille na háille,
Is do dhallas mo shúil
Ar eagla go stánfainn.

(Naked I saw thee,
O beauty of beauty,
And I blinded my eyes
For fear I should fail.

I heard thy music,
O melody of melody,
And I closed my ears
For fear I should falter.

I tasted thy mouth,
O sweetness of sweetness,
And I hardened my heart
For fear of my slaying.

I blinded my eyes,
And I closed my ears,
I hardened my heart,
And I smothered my desire.

I turned my back
On the vision I had shaped,
And to this road before me
I turned my face.

I have turned my face
To this road before me,
To the deed that I see
And the death I shall die.)

This translation, which is by Pearse himself, does scant justice to the original. It does not have the original's beauty of rhyme and assonance, nor its rhythm, nor its strength of imagery. "And I blinded my eyes / For fear I should fail" is a very weak rendering of "Is do dhallas mo shúil / Ar eagla go stánfain."

Padraic Ó Conaire (1883–1928) might be described as the first and only professional writer in modern Irish. He gave up a job in the British civil service to wander the roads of Ireland with a donkey and cart, and to earn his bread by writing in Irish. He was the first Gaelic writer to come under the influence of the Russians, and some say the first Irish writer. He wrote many short stories, one novel, and one short play. Most of his stories deal with characters who have suffered much, but he frequently lapses into melodrama, and his style sometimes reproduces some of the worst features of Victorian writing. However, he had the fertility of the truly creative writer, and through his Bohemian life, he became a legend in his lifetime. Fred Higgins wrote a very fine lament for him in

English, and there is a delightful statue by Albert Power of his leprechaun-like figure in Eyre Square, Galway.

The first two writers of note to appear in Ulster were the brothers Séamus and Seosamh Mac Grianna. Séamus (1891–1969) was the most prolific of modern Irish writers. Much of his later work was of little value, for he went on for years churning out short stories which were little more than anecdotes, and many of them rehashes of earlier pieces. Nevertheless, he produced many first-rate stories and some very readable autobiographical volumes. Séamus Mac Grianna (or Ó Grianna), who wrote under the pen name Máire, commanded the purest Irish written in this century. For that reason alone, his best books will always be read.

Seosamh Mac Grianna (1901–1990) was a more imaginative writer than his brother, but illness cut short his literary career. His best works are a picaresque autobiography and a novel set in his native Rannafast. He is also the author of two volumes of short stories, an account of some folk poets of Donegal, a narrative of a walking tour in Wales, some literary essays, and two worthless historical works.

The foundation of the Gaelic publishing firm of Sairséal and Dill, and of the Gaelic Book Club in 1947 gave fresh stimulus to writing in the language, and a new crop of writers sprang up. The government publishing agency An Gúm, set up by Ernest Blythe, was, despite many defects, of great assistance to Gaelic writers. Among them were poets, novelists, short story writers, dramatists, and historians. The standard of the work produced was high. In 1955, the periodical *Irish Writing* published a selection of short stories and poems translated from the modern Gaelic revival; I translated the stories, and Valentin Iremonger the poems. *The Times Literary Supplement* devoted an editorial to this issue of the journal on January 25, 1956. It stated in part: "Whether the native language can be restored is a matter of continual national controversy. . . . What is beyond dispute is the existence of a school of eager and imaginative writers and the gradual raising of critical standards." The writers who appeared in this selection were Padraic Ó Conaire, Séamus Mac Grianna, Seosamh Mac Grianna, Tarlach Ó hUid (1917–1990), Seán Ó Ríordáin (1916–1977), Máire Mhac an tSaoi (1922–   ), Máirtín Ó Direáin (1910–1988), and myself. Máirtín Ó Cadhain (1907–1970) did not contribute, although he was invited to do so. Ó Cadhain was probably the most robust of modern Gaelic writers, but he had little appreciation of form and was inclined towards the old Gaelic weakness of verbosity. It was an old jibe that Gaelic books used to be judged according to the number of difficult words in them.

The drama was slow to develop in Irish, for the older writers were not acquainted with the theater; they were storytellers. In recent years, several competent dramatists have appeared, among them Eoghan Ó Tuairisc (1919–1982), Seán Ó Tuama (1926–   ), and Críostóir Ó Floinn (1927–   ). Seán Ó Ríordáin, who died a short time ago, was the best of the modern poets, although Máirtín Ó Direáin, who writes a less sophisticated type of verse, was more prolific.

I am glad to say that a host of young poets is hard on his heels.

Despite the number of people writing in Irish at present, I am afraid that I must finish on a pessimistic note. As the statistics show, the Gaeltachta, the Irish-speaking districts, are fast disappearing. If they die, the language is dead, and no more literature will be written in it.

a chríoch sín

BIBLIOGRAPHY

Corkery, Daniel. *The Hidden Ireland.* Dublin: M. H. Gill, 1967.

de Blacam, Aodh. *Gaelic Literature Surveyed.* New York: Barnes & Noble, 1974. (With an added chapter on the twentieth century by Eoghan O'Hanluain.)

Flower, Robin. "Introduction," *Dánta Grádha.* Thomas F. O'Rahilly, ed. Cork: Cork University Press, 1926.

Hull, Eleanor. *A Text Book of Irish Literature.* Dublin: M. H. Gill, n.d.

Hyde, Douglas. *A Literary History of Ireland.* New York: Barnes & Noble, 1967.

Jackson, Kenneth Hurlstone. *A Celtic Miscellany.* Harmondsworth, Middlesex: Penguin, 1971.

Knott, Eleanor. "Introduction," *The Bardic Poems of Tadhg Dall Ó hUiginn.* Vol. I. Dublin: Irish Texts Society [1920], 1922.

Mangan, James Clarence. *The Poets and Poetry of Munster, with Poetical Translations by James Clarence Mangan.* 4th ed. Dublin: James Duffy, 1925.

Meyer, Kuno. *Selections from Ancient Irish Poetry.* London: Constable, 1911.

Murphy, Gerald. *Early Irish Lyrics.* Oxford: Clarendon Press, 1956.

———. *Saga and Myth in Ancient Ireland.* Dublin: Cultural Relations Committee, 1955.

O'Connor, Frank. *The Backward Glance.* London: Macmillan, 1967; published in America as *A Short History of Irish Literature.* New York: Capricorn Books, 1968.

O'Neill, Seamus, ed. *Irish Writing,* No. 33. Dublin: Trumpet Books, 1955.

Power, Patrick C. *A Literary History of Ireland.* Cork: Mercier, Press, 1969.

Quiggin, E. C. "Prolegomena to the Study of the Poetry of the Later Irish Bards, 1200–1500," *Encyclopaedia Britannica,* 11th ed.

CONTEMPORARY LITERATURE IN THE IRISH LANGUAGE
Alan Titley

In his essay on literature in the Irish language for the first edition of this book, Seamus O'Neill ends on a pessimistic note. He refers to the "fast disappearing" Gaeltachtaí or Irish-speaking areas and asserts, "If they die, the language is dead, and no more literature will be written in it." While this appears to be eminently sensible, it ignores one of the major premises on which all modern literature in the Irish language has been constructed.

When the Irish language "revival" began at the end of the last century, it was always seen as holding out an ideal for the entire country. Although the Gaeltachtaí were extremely important, the language did not exclusively belong to them. The language was a powerful force in repossessing consciousness and binding up historical wounds now openly recognized in most postcolonial criticism. The literature was to be an expression of this consciousness in all its plenitude, and so it has proved in the more than 100 years of modern Irish writing.

The theme of death and of an end to it all has been common in the Irish tradition since the seventeenth century. Yet to write in the Irish language is an act of hope, of defiance even, and an investment in the future. Anybody who writes now knows the odds, knows the reality, and yet goes on because he or she must go on, and because there always is a future if you want there to be. The amazing fact is that there are now more books produced every year in Irish than ever before; there have been more collections of poetry produced annually during the last twenty-five years than in any comparable period; there were more novels written in the 1980s than in any other decade; there are a greater range and variety and choice of material available than at any time in the entire long and venerable existence of the Irish literary tradition. There are many writers investing in the future, and they cannot all be wrong.

It was common in the decades from the Second World War until the 1970s to refer to a few major figures in Irish writing who dominated the landscape.

Máirtín Ó Cadhain was our colossus in prose, while poetry was ruled over by Seán Ó Ríordáin, Máirtín Ó Direáin, and Máire Mhac an tSaoi. Ó Cadhain died in 1970, leaving a long, intimidating shadow that was eventually escaped from by writers doing something entirely different. Seán Ó Ríordáin died in 1977; Máirtín Ó Direáin's best work was behind him by that time; and, while Máire Mhac an tSaoi is thankfully still writing, she is not seen as a model to follow because of the particularly personal and traditional nature of her craft.

Whatever else we might say of these major figures, we cannot argue that they constituted a movement. Some were modernizers, others more conservative, and a certain personal animosity and rivalry—as with all good literary castes—added their own spice. What happened in 1970, however, was a revolution. Unbidden, unheralded, and unexpectedly, a group of young poets started their own literary magazine in University College, Cork. It was initially a broadsheet but has since become the single most important poetry journal in Irish. The group of poets quickly became known as the *Innti* poets after the name of their publication. The idea was that of an undergraduate student, Michael Davitt. He edited the first edition, and apart from a few issues in the 1980s, he continued to be its editor until the present day. He quickly gathered around him like-minded spirits, and between them they have changed the face and the nature of Irish poetry in the last twenty-five years.

The initial impetus was probably just youth and the consequent search for a voice of one's own. Their energy and brashness were certainly fueled by the 1960s (which came a few years later in Ireland), and they seemed determined to bring life and fun back into poetry. The poets most associated with this movement, apart from Davitt himself, were Gabriel Rosenstock, Nuala Ní Dhomhnaill, and Liam Ó Muirthile. They traveled the country giving poetry readings and drawing large and enthusiastic crowds. They also read with English-language poets, which helped heal the divide that was often perceived to exist between the writers of the two languages. This gained a wider respect for the Irish tradition, which it had hitherto often been denied. Although each of these poets was considerably different, from the beginning a sense of a movement that these readings gave and their long association with *Innti* clouded their individual achievements for some years.

Michael Davitt, although the daddy of them all, was also the most revolutionary in experimentation. His early work throws the lot at the reader—lyrics, pastiche, satire, block poetry, concrete poetry, mantra poetry. His later work can occasionally still retain this element of structural surprise, but the newness is more likely to reside in a striking image, a painfully beautiful memory, a fistful of truth.

Gabriel Rosenstock's revolution consisted in bringing in the poetic winds and philosophical thoughts of faraway places with strange-sounding names to an Irish tradition whose horizons were generally bounded by home. This willingness to cast widely is reflected in his extremely successful project of translating the best of modern world poetry into Irish, which he has done with lyric facility.

Both Nuala Ní Dhomhnaill and Liam Ó Muirthile are more traditional, although that is a word that has to be tread on carefully. Nuala Ní Dhomhnaill struck an early alliance with the strong female characters of Irish mythology and folklore. This was no convenient ploy, but a deep psychic necessity. Although the force of her personality throbs from her work, we are always sensitive to the voices of traditions speaking through her. In Nuala, there is always something else happening apart from the words on the page. She has mined whatever is permanent and archetypal for the human being in the Irish tradition and made of it a poetry of passion and wonder.

Liam Ó Muirthile, on the other hand, is much more historical. The real people in his poetry are either those he knew or persons from history with whom he has an affinity. This gives his work, especially his later poetry, a wide public resonance that is often lacking in the work of his contemporaries. He may well be the better craftsman also. There is always the impression in a poem by Ó Muirthile of something carved, wrought, worked, turned, honed, shaped. It has an edge that cuts through to the mind.

The early success of *Innti* aided the flourishing of many other poets. Cathal Ó Searcaigh joined the readings at an early stage and developed a love lyricism that could join the best of native song with the American beats. In recent years, he has gone home to live in his native Donegal and sees himself as the poet of his own people. Michael Hartnett turned to writing in Irish after a successful career as an English-language poet. He was deeply influenced by the great seventeenth-century Irish poets of his own area in County Limerick and has also made miraculous English translations of them. His talent was always wild, unpredictable, and generous, and these traits are reflected in all his original work.

In some ways the last twenty-five years have belonged to the poets, if for no other reason than that prose was the dominant medium throughout the twentieth century until then. In this way, they appeared to be reclaiming the crown of the eighteenth and nineteenth centuries, when precious little else apart from poetry was composed in Irish. There are about ten anthologies of this poetry available since 1980 (some of them bilingual), and more books of poetry are published in Irish than any other single genre. From time to time, a lone frail voice is raised to say that this imbalance is unhealthy, but the answer must surely be for others to correct.

This has, however, been largely done. The 1970s were not a hugely successful time for creative prose, but both the 1980s and the 1990s have seen a resurgence. There was the popular *Lig Sinn i gCathú* (1976, *Lead Us Not into Temptation*) by Breandán Ó hEithir, which topped the best-seller lists in both languages for several weeks. This was partly due to the fact that it was a prizewinning novel, partly that it dealt with sex, booze, and growing up, partly that it was well marketed, and partly that the author was a well-known journalist and broadcaster. It proved, however, that Irish novels could sell well if they got the same hype as their counterparts in English. Ó hEithir's second novel, *Sionnach ar mo Dhuán* (1988, *A Fox on My Hook*), although better written, broader in scope, greater in ambition, more deeply layered, and more fully executed, did not enjoy the same success. It seemed for a while that a long, complex narrative was beyond the energy of many readers of Irish fed on lyric poems and bites of journalism. There was always a category of Irish readers who wanted their authors to be famous as long as their books were unread.

A similar neglect befell Dónal Mac Amhlaigh's *Deoraithe* (1986, *Exiles*), a novel that, more than any other, captured the life of the struggling Irish working class in 1950s England. I am not aware that anything like it has appeared in English. When we think of the drain of energy and talent that this scandalous emigration entailed, we wonder at the morality of writers anguishing over the petty pains of their own growing up, as if their suffering had cosmic consequences. Compared with the horror and vacuity and suffering of this forced emigration, adultery in Ardee or buggery in Ballybunnion seems a facile subject and an easy target. Mac Amhlaigh was the great documentor of this experience, of course, as he had shown in *Dialann Deoraí* (1960). But his novel is a massive imaginative re-creation in sweep and in detail of what it was like to be there. Not so much a slice as a chunk of life, with all the beef left in.

One could at least predict that there should be novels on growing up—yet again—or on exile—however rare—but nothing prepared Irish readers for the whirlwind of *Cuaifeach Mo Lon Dubh Buí* (1983) by an unknown and unsung twenty-one-year-old from Fermanagh called Séamas Mac Annaidh. This was a storm of a book, linking prehistoric myth with lexicographical seances, with student life in the Donegal Gaeltacht, with rock bands, with current politics, in a thin, wobbly, interweaving narrative that went everywhere and nowhere and beyond. Students were heard laughing while reading it in libraries, and dull, shiny-pated professors puzzled how they could fit it into their tight scheme of things between Pádraic Ó Conaire and Máirtín Ó Cadhain. It did not matter because it was a whale and a howl of a book whose energy was infectious and that presaged a great literary career for its author. Unfortunately, the follow-ups did not hit home as sharply. *Mo Dhá Mhicí* (1986) had some of the same madcap energy but a little dissipated, and *Rubble na Mickies* (1990) degenerated into the literary games beloved of postmodernist critics. At least this meant that literature in Irish could be anything it wanted to be and was not being written at the behest of any simple, easily defined agenda. It is a point of view difficult to hammer across when the market for books in Irish insists on sentimentality, slush, and slop. Many Irish-speakers might abhor Mac Annaidh because he was not "traditional" enough, and Anglo-Irishists despise him because he dared outside his preserve. This is the dilemma facing every writer in Irish today, whether to soup up the folksy bit for the national theme park or to write as if Irish were one of those languages that dealt with the whole world up and down and in and out, amen.

Pádraig Standún never had that problem. He writes for his own people, the local community of Connemara and the islands. They are his own people because he has been a priest among them for more than twenty years. He has written seven novels to date, all of which deal with the bleak realities of life in rural Ireland without sentimentality or romanticism. All in all, he is the best selling author in Irish, word for word and pound for pound. His initial novel, *Súil le Breith* (1983), may have had a certain scandalous success because of its theme of priest and lover and clash with authority, but his later works show that he is involved in every aspect of his community. The problem of priestly celibacy surfaces in *Cíocras* (1991), while lesbianism is the central concern of *Cion Mná* (1993). Outsiders' poking their knowing noses into rural mores fashions the plot of *Na hAnthropologicals* (1993), while *Stigmata* (1994) sets up a debate between superstition and real Christian morality. Pádraig Standún has admitted that his novels are simply a means of disseminating Christianity. His Christianity, however, is not always the stuff of conforming orthodoxy but is concerned with setting the oak of orthodoxy against the reed of bending life. Although his characters sometimes get bogged down in theological disputes that never took place in any bar or kitchen, they always retain enough life to demonstrate that they are people in books and not counters in those abstract journalistic debates that constitute intellectual life in Ireland. The real, although intangible, Dublin 4, of the *Sunday Independent,* of Democratic Left, of confused and degraded Blueshirts, of sneaking Unionist regarders, of gobblers-up of the considered trifles of state-classists, of every hie and hue—all these do not simply or even complicatedly exist in the world of Pádraig Standún. It is an Ireland bent to his own agenda, without a doubt, but it is not a stage construction, a tourist wish fulfillment, a John B. Keaney up-and-at-'em, bull-in-the-parlor romp in the fields or behind the haystacks. Whether his novels live or not, they are certainly far more than a documentary account of what it is like to live now in the butt-end of the twentieth century in a writhing Ireland neither here nor there. The point about Pádraig Standún is that he would be relevant to Ireland no matter which language he wrote in.

More parlous than this is the state of the short story. For many years touted as the Irish literary genre for excellence and boasting a pedigree exceeding that of Shergar and Master MacGrath, there has not been a great deal to shiver the timbers of all and sundry in the last twenty years. There has been the noted exception of Pádraic Breathnach, who, with at least six collections of short stories at the last count, is away ahead of the field in a prolixity of production tempered only by the spare beauty of his prose. He is a minimalist searching for the significant moment in the dross of everyday encounters. We would have said that he might have been influenced by Raymond Carver, only that he was writing before Carver. He has been criticized for going over the same ground again and again, but there is no real reason for ceasing to do something because it is being done well. His one attempt at a novel cannot really be counted a success, but it at least points up the fact that some writers are particularly suited to one genre rather than another.

Some writers have, of course, crossed the divide and written the prose of the long haul and the short gasp simultaneously. A recently much praised writer from the Kerry Gaeltacht is Pádraig Ó Cíobháin, who suddenly produced several novels and collections of short stories. He is important in that he continues the tradition of Gaeltacht writing while modernizing and expanding it. The first flush of Gaeltacht autobiographies in the 1920s and 1930s has indeed been followed by a second slush in the past ten years or so. Whereas the early books were delineating a way of life that was quickly vanishing, the new wave was largely a rip-off of the fame that they had earned. The publication of sentimental memoirs hardly helps the self-confidence of a community even if they do look good on the shelves of the latest interpretive center. Ó Cíobháin's stories, even if they are sometimes unwieldy and undisciplined, show a vibrancy beating within the heart of a community and an imagination confident in its own authenticity beyond special pleading and image.

So far I have been attempting to draw out some of the patterns of contemporary Irish writing and to mention some of the more important figures. There is still the clash, or at least the contrast, between the more "traditional" writing and the more "modernist"—even if, increasingly, these terms begin to mean less and less. There is writing for the Gaeltacht market, for the learners' market, for the learned market. But because of the nature of the Irish-speaking and Irish-reading public—much fractured, very loyal, often uncritical, subject to false dawns and new horizons every which year—it is necessarily true that a great part of the best writing in Irish consists of successful singletons. Because virtually nobody can make a living from writing exclusively in Irish, it is not surprising that we have a lot of one-book authors, many bad, some indifferent, but quite a few of excellent quality. These admit of no easy pattern but are, far and away, the biggest category of books in Irish. This element of anarchy is an important factor in keeping the life and excitement of the unexpected alive in the literature.

As I am the author of four novels, two collections of short stories, several plays, and some works of literary scholarship, it would be genuinely immodest of me not to mention myself. If my first novel, *Méirscrí na Treibhe* (1978, Tribal Scars), is bloated and soupy, and *Stiall Fhial Feola* (1980, A Fine Fillet of Flesh) amounts to Gothic schlock, *An Fear Dána* (1993, The Man of Letters) is, I like to think, a fine literary novel. It is an imaginative reconstruction of the life and times of a thirteenth-century bardic Irish poet who was banished to Scotland because of an admitted murder and later was involved in the Crusades. It is also a meditation on the Gaelic (Irish and Scottish) literary traditions seen through the mind of somebody who was there at its height. *Eiriceachtaí agus scéalta eile* (1987, Heresies and Other Stories) is a collection of which I would not still change a word, while *Fabhalscéalta* (1995, Fables) are short allegorical and parabolic pieces of a kind not attempted in Ireland before. Drama is a more tricky medium because theater in Ireland, whether in Irish or in English, depends on fat subsidies from the state. My own *Tagann Godot* (1991, Godot Turns Up), which, as one might expect, is a sequel to Beckett's play, was staged by the Abbey,* toured the country, was translated into other languages, and was produced outside Ireland. Many Irish writers would like to write for the stage, but the lack of outlets and the conservatism in the directing establishment inhibit the development of a vibrant theater in Irish.

The one most important development in writing in Irish during the last quarter of a century has been the appearance of real and committed literary and historical scholarship. Since the end of the last century, Irish literary and linguistic scholarship had been in thrall to the desiccated and, strange as it may seem, emasculated Germanic tradition. It is not that this tradition of meticulous philological exactitude does not have its place in the academies of arts; to hunt the origin of a word back through modern Irish to early modern, to classical, to middle, to old, to putative Celtic, to supposed Sanskrit, to reconstructed Indo-European to Cro-Magnon croaks and Neolithic grunts certainly has a kind of orgasmic excitement for some people. But to suppose that this is the *only* kind of Irish scholarship worth talking about, as has sometimes been argued, flies in the face of the normal intellectual discourse in other languages and cultures. Anybody studying Irish in the university in the 1960s would have had difficulty in finding any book of length and substance dealing with a writer or a genre or a theme or a topic in modern Irish literature. There were essays and articles and bits and pieces. Since then, however, there have been major studies of a literary kind of individual authors, of movements, of forms of literature, of philosophical reflection.

This reflective study of literature in Irish may be said to have begun with the American scholar Frank O'Brien's *Filíocht Ghaeilge na linne seo* (1968, Modern Irish Poetry). Although it is generally seen now as a deeply flawed work because of the author's lack of sympathy with, and, therefore, lack of understanding of, Seán Ó Riordáin, it paved the way for other kinds of literary scholarship beyond the merely philological. On the other hand, there has been no comparable study of Irish poetry since then, despite its flower and its bloom. Aisling Nic Dhonnchada has tackled the first generation of the modern short story in *An Gearrscéal sa Ghaeilge 1900–1940* (1981, The Irish Short Story, 1900–1940). Pádraig Ó Siadhail has examined the Irish theatrical movement with *Stair Drámaíocht na Gaeilge* (1993, A History of Irish Drama). I have treated comprehensively of the novel in *An tÚrscéal Gaeilge* (1991, The Irish Novel).

Individual authors have also received full frontal critical treatment. Sometimes this has been in the form of a literary biography, as in Seán Ó Coileáin's *Seán Ó Riordáin: Beatha agus Saothar* (1982, Seán Ó Riordáin: His Life and Work), which made excellent use of the subject's own diaries and papers. Elliptically told and drawn from a well of deep empathy, the author echoes Ó Riordáin's own prose style, which is one of the finest in modern Irish when it does not tend toward self-parody. Máirín Nic Eoin's *Eoghan Ó Tuairisc: Beatha agus Saothar* (1988, Eoghan Ó Tuairisc: His Life and World) is a more objective study of the bilingual novelist, dramatist, and poet who only belatedly began to get the recognition he deserved. These biographies dramatize not the choice between perfection of the life and perfection of the work, as is so often the case, but the profound artistic loneliness and frustration of the writer in Irish in his own country. They are case studies of the artist whose only way out is down. They point out yet again that, despite the clichés of the cosseted Irish writer (and this was a cliché that was never true), the lot of one who wrote in the native tongue would be either frustration or circumcised ambition. Pádraic Ó Conaire, the subject of two major biographies, died from drink and vagrancy at a scandalously early age; Seosamh Mac Grianna, who carried the hopes of Ulster into the gap, suffered mental breakdown and clamped up in silence to the end of his isolated days in the hospital; his brother Séamas took the state's shilling and contented himself with writing variations on the same romantic theme for half a century when the sharpness of his intellect and the acerbity of his style suggested he could have done much more; Seán Ó Riordáin degenerated into pastiche and personal isolation; Eoghan Ó Tuairisc fluctuated between anger and despair.

The only major writer so far who seems to have negotiated himself success-fully through this morass was Máirtín Ó Cadhain. He is the subject of Gearóid Denvir's *Cadhan Aonair* (1987), but this is much more a study of the writings than of the writer. It is a rich and lucid book dealing in microcriticism with a sustained flair. Denvir's is a liberal and engaged criticism that treats the writer, his words, and his intentions with the seriousness that they deserve.

A sign of the maturity of literary scholarship in Irish is that critics have now begun to engage in factious disputations about the nature of theory and its place in the examination of literature. Some of this credit must go to Breandán Ó Doibhlin, professor of French in St. Patrick's College, Maynooth, who intro-duced much Francophone thought into Irish studies in the 1960s. His criticism and the school that followed him introduced a discipline and seriousness into the reading of literature that are still with us. Maybe not inevitably, but certainly understandably, the more recent theoretical entanglements have cast their soupy darkness upon this intelligent discourse. Unfortunately for its lackeys, just as they began to put their roots down, it began to be discovered that they were being discarded elsewhere. The structuralism that is now as dead as a dolmen maintained a certain glassy sheen in Irish for a few years after its international decease, despite massive shots of institutional aids. This did not prevent others whoring after the certainty that only a theory can give and, even if it were never found, that still retains the attraction of the perfect ideal. No matter—a lively intellectual or even theoretical debate is now part of Irish writing. More inter-estingly, after the hand-me-down remnants of recycled French and American whacked-out ideas have been embarrassingly laid aside, there are signs that Irish critics are beginning to set down their own theories based on the particular circumstances of writing in Irish today.

Irish literary scholarship does not deal with Irish alone. No literature lives by self-referential, incestuous cross talk. An interesting and entirely successful de-velopment has been discourse on writers in other languages who have a connection with the Gaelic tradition. One of the most valuable is Máire Ní Annracháin's study of the contemporary Scottish poet Sorley Maclean, *Aisling agus Tóir: an slánú i bhfilíocht Shomhairle Mhic Gill-Eain* (1992). Apart from its intrinsic value as a work of meticulous criticism and its unusually sensitive use of theory, it is a landmark book in the reaccommodation of the Irish Gaelic and the Scottish Gaelic traditions. These traditions were sundered by the growth of sectarianism in religion and English-speaking political nationalism in politics. There is some hope that the writers and artists can reconstruct some of that valuable community of cultural interests.

Flann O'Brien or Myles na gCopaleen or Brian O'Nolan is best known internationally for his quirky, funny, and literary novels such as *At Swim-Two-Birds* or *The Dalkey Archive*. Like Brendan Behan or Patrick Pearse or Liam O'Flaherty, however, he also wrote in Irish. His classic novel, *An Béal Bocht* (The Poor Mouth), and its antecedents, along with his entire corpus of writing in Irish, are the subject of Breandán Ó Conaire's *Myles na Gaeilge* (1966). This is a book that hunts down to its lair in the Irish tradition just about every hint and echo and nuance in Myles na gCopaleen's work and is an indispensable study for anyone who wishes to know about his hard life and good times. In a different direction, Gréagóir Ó Dúill's literary biography of Sir Samuel Ferguson, *Samuel Ferguson: Beatha agus Saothar* (1993), uncovers the interest that this northern poet had in the Irish language and its literature and destroys the facile fiction of a one-strand, easily reducible Gaelic tradition.

Unlike English studies (until very recently), Irish literature was always perceived to be more than the sum of its poetry, fiction, and drama. It encompassed history and social studies and reflective prose just as well. Although, not surprisingly, most Irish people who engage in original research in any of these areas will publish their findings in English, there have been some contributions in Irish to the sum of human knowledge not available elsewhere. One example will suffice. Liam Ó Caithnia's *Stair na hIomána* (1980) is, ostensibly, close on a 1,000-page history of the game of hurling. But it is just as much a history of the pastimes and leisure of the common people of the country from the beginning of records to the present day. No other historian dealing in the social past has approached his depth of digging or his breadth of references. In the best tradition of feeling historians, he is a superb stylist who brings his subject to life and entices you to read on for the pleasure of the prose just as much as for the quality of his insight. Much valuable work has been done in other areas also, reinforcing my earlier assertion that there has never been a greater amount of material over a wider range of subjects by a bigger number of authors in the Irish language. Much trash and much dross, of course, but much also that is of immediate and of more permanent value.

Thus, it is not appropriate to finish on a gloomy note. It is true that the early expectation of a "revival" of the language throughout the country in one or two generations did not materialize. It is true that the Gaeltachtaí or Irish-speaking districts are thinner and more attenuated than ever before. But it is also true that more people claim to know the language than at any time since the state was founded. It is still the language of communities in various parts of the country and increasingly of networks of individuals and of families; it still receives a goodly measure of state support in ways that are satisfactory and unsatisfactory; and it is very unlikely that Irish polity will seriously abandon this support. What this simply means is that the language will not die like Manx or Cornish or Trumai or Tocharian. For the foreseeable future, it will live on as some people's native language, as others' first language of choice, as others' language of regular use, as others' language of occasions, and for others still as a shadowy presence that lies behind and beneath the English that they speak and read—and both speaking and reading are now part of any culture in the modern world. Irish writing has *never* been healthier.

Language lives in many ways. Even hitherto great world languages are now under assault from English being the dominant language of the United States. The echoes of the British Empire ensure that English literature is now also written in Africa, in the Caribbean, in India, and in the Far East. In most of these places, literature is also composed in the native languages for practical, artistic, sentimental, or political reasons. Ireland is no different. In the contemporary world, more and more people are free to choose their traditions from the long postmodern menu. For Irish people, the Irish language and its literature are a main course on that menu. The achievements of writers in Irish over the last twenty years show that it is well worth choosing.

O'Grady found the Gaelic tradition like a neglected antique dun with the doors barred. Listening, he heard from within the hum of an immense chivalry, and he opened the doors and the wild riders went forth to work their will.'' To which, W. B. Yeats added, albeit less poetically, ''I think it was his *History of Ireland, Heroic Period,* that started us all.''

What it started was this: in 1888, the Dublin firm of M. H. Gill published *Poems and Ballads of Young Ireland,* which included the work of most of the new poets—Yeats, T. W. Rollestan, John Todhunter, Katharine Tynan, Rose Kavanagh, and others. According to the knowledgeable Stephen Gwynn, this book ''announced the co-operative, concerted nature of the effort of the younger generation to give a new impulse to Irish poetry.'' In 1889, Yeats published *The Wanderings of Oisin,* which treated, although in rather Pre-Raphaelite fashion, an Irish legendary story. In 1891, at a meeting in Yeats' house in London, he, Rolleston, Todhunter, and others initiated what was to become in the next year the Irish Literary Society of London. In 1892, a sister organization, the National Literary Society, was formed in Dublin, and Douglas Hyde gave before it his influential lecture on ''The Necessity of De-Anglicising Ireland.'' In that same year, Yeats published his play *The Countess Cathleen.* In 1893, Hyde published his beautiful translations, *The Love Songs of Connacht,* and founded the Gaelic League for the propagation of the Irish language. In 1894, Yeats' book of folklore, *The Celtic Twilight,* gave a popular, if misleading, title to the whole movement. In the same year, he published another play, *The Land of Heart's Desire,* and it was produced in March in London with Todhunter's *A Comedy of Sighs.* In 1897, George Sigerson published his *Bards of the Gael and Gall.* In 1899, Hyde published his monumental *Literary History of Ireland,* and the Irish Literary Theatre made its first appearance. Called back to Ireland to assist in the production was George Moore, who did little for the Irish theater but who wrote some excellent stories to be translated into Irish by the Gaelic League. In that volume, *The Untilled Field,* may surely be seen the beginnings of realistic modern Irish prose fiction.

The impulses of the literary renaissance were two: to send Irish writers for their subjects either back to the mythical and historical Irish past or into the rural Irish present. Behind these impulses lay the assumption that the historic past and the rural present contained qualities that were both noble and indigenously Irish. Certainly, many earnest people made the further assumption that the past and the present could be merged and that thereby a cultural and a national revivification could be achieved. That assumption of dying but still reclaimable value underlay the folklore investigations of Hyde, Yeats, and Lady Gregory, all of whom thought that the virtues of the Celtic past were still to be discerned in the modern rural present. The further assumption, that ancient tradition and present rural virtue could be amalgamated and could transform the modern, Anglicized, town-bred Irishman, underlay much of the cultural fervor at the turn of the century.

Another issue was never quite faced. A literary work is composed of both matter and manner. To a certain extent, an Irish subject matter determined the Irish literary manner. Linguistically, certain Irish locutions and the faintly phonetic spelling of dialogue could bring a richness into the English. With Lady Gregory and particularly with John Synge, it even seemed for a while that a new style of writing was evolving; but Lady Gregory's Kiltartan style was rural, and Synge's style simply inimitable. Had W. B. Yeats known Irish, he might have become intrigued by the possibilities of adapting the intricate techniques of Irish verse to English. Yeats had no Irish, however, and he developed in his own very personal way. The writers who were followable and followed were more stylistically bland: Padraic Colum, Lennox Robinson, T. C. Murray.

Certain writers, such as Yeats, Synge, Joyce, O'Casey, and Beckett, finally developed remarkable stylistic strategies, but these strategies were hardly usable for anyone else. Until nearly the present, the Irishness of Irish literature resided in the primary business of an Irish subject matter and in the rich but dying difference of English as the Irish spoke it.

Even the subject matter, however, raised problems. Early in the century, a writer like Synge was sent by Yeats into the rural past of the Aran Islands, and a writer like Stephens, to a certain extent, followed Yeats into the past of legend. Yeats, though, was enamored of the Irish past more for the influence it might have upon his artistry than for patriotic reasons. Also, he was liable at any time to be diverted from his antiquarian predilections by theosophy or Noh drama or any of half a dozen other attractions. So, while Yeats' early work may have shown a vague direction, it did not map the road; a young Irish writer may have been startled to find his mentor not merely in another green field but in some distant, alien, chartreuse one. Yeats finally gave his primary allegiance to art rather than to Ireland, and that was probably his great gift to Irish literature and to those who would write it after him.

Lady Gregory, who had a more comic and prosaic mind than did Yeats, had a foot in both the past and the present. She wrote modern versions of the sagas in *Cuchulain of Muirthemne* and *Gods and Fighting Men* and treatments of recorded history in *Kincora* and *The White Cockade*. At the same time, her popular peasant comedies depicted in exaggerated fashion the quirks, if not always the virtues, of the rural present.

For some years, the countryside proved the strongest of Irish subjects; and quite early the staple of the Abbey Theatre repertoire became not the lyrical legendary past of Yeats but the realistic rural present of Padraic Colum, William Boyle, T. C. Murray, and Brinsley MacNamara. These writers were good enough to temper their realism with criticism, but to the purely patriotic Irish person, such as Arthur Griffith or Maud Gonne, it soon seemed that the celebration had become transformed into denigration and that a terrible ugliness was being born.

Influential patriotic journalists, such as Griffith and D. P. Moran, approved the use of the rural present as the basic subject matter for the national literature but did not want that subject matter in any way criticized. A national literature that did not basically celebrate the nation was to them, and probably to most

Irish people, anathema. The realistic stories of Moore and Joyce, therefore, obviously offered no direction either. They may have been among the most brilliant productions of the early literary renaissance, but they were much too highly critical of Irish life to be acceptable. Joyce's stories were even about city dwellers, and the city was for him "the centre of paralysis." If Dubliners were to be discussed in literature, it would have to be in the unrealistic and charming fashion of Stephens' *Charwoman's Daughter.* J. M. Synge did treat rural Ireland but was so critically inflammatory that his *Playboy of the Western World* incited the most famous theatrical protest of the century.

A considerable body of popular literature did develop, however, which celebrated the rural present and served the national cause by presenting the vision of Ireland that the nationalists wanted to propagate. Among such writers in the early years of the century were a gaggle of lady poets, such as Alice Milligan, Ethna Carbery, Moira O'Neill, and the legendary Lizzie Twigg. There was also a prolific group of prose writers, such as Rosa Mulholland, Alice Furlong, Seumas MacManus, and Victor O'D. Power. Most of their work was of scant literary worth, being characterized by rampant patriotism, broad humor, and circumspect piety. In any event, such writers were merely treating uncritically the same basic subject matter of Synge, Lady Gregory, and Colum, if not of Moore and Joyce.

Meanwhile, the historical or legendary past was attracting far fewer writers. Of course, a number of strong works with a historical background would be produced. Among novels, some that immediately leap to mind are Darrell Figgis's *The Return of the Hero,* Joseph O'Neill's *Wind from the North,* Eimar O'Duffy's *The Lion and the Fox,* and Liam O'Flaherty's *Famine.* On the whole, however, there were few fine works in this vein, and the attitude of many writers toward that past soon came to be more whimsical or satirical than celebrative. Not until the dramatic events of the 1916 Rising and the troubled years following it did Irish writers in any significant numbers return to Irish history for their subject matter. Then, as in the plays of O'Casey, the novels of O'Flaherty, and the stories of O'Faolain and O'Connor, that history was so recent as to be, in effect, contemporary.

The decade from the Great Lockout of 1913 to the end of the civil war in 1923 was such a dramatic time that it seemed unavoidable to writers as a subject matter, as well as much more urgent than the past of legend and history. At the same time, as many of those events occurred in the city, there was a slow shifting of literary interest from the countryside to an urban setting. Lennox Robinson and W. F. Casey turned to the town and the suburb. O'Faolain and O'Connor turned from the Old Woman of the Roads to the Young Men from the South. O'Casey and O'Flaherty, although both were capable of celebrating that Irish nostalgia that Paul Vincent Carroll called the Old Foolishness, turned to the Troubles and the tenements. Joyce's *Ulysses,* the most celebrated of all modern Irish works of fiction, is quintessentially urban.

The rural present was a tenacious subject matter, however, and an even more tenacious idea. The founding of the Irish Free State in 1922 enshrined a politically correct idea of Irishness, and the coming to power ten years later of de Valera's Fianna Fail ensured that this idea of a simple, rural, isolated society based on frugality, morality, and authority would dominate Irish life until 1960. This was a cultural, occasionally an economic, and, with Ireland's neutrality in World War II, a political isolation. De Valera might uphold Ireland's neutrality by going to the German Embassy to sign a Book of Condolence on the death of Hitler in 1945; and there was a certain truculent, even admirable independence about that deplorable act. However, in 1949 on the death of Ireland's first president, Douglas Hyde, he would not, as a good Catholic, enter the Protestant St. Patrick's Cathedral for the burial service. For a little while, isolation continued, and in 1951, the Costello government fell because a health scheme for mothers and children proposed to provide women with some information about sex. In these years, the subservience to a rigid authority and a puritanic morality had brought about a book censorship rather more right-wing than the Vatican's Index and containing at its fullest more than 15,000 banned volumes, among which was just about every modern Irish writer of note. As Behan sang, "Oh, me name is Brendan Behan; I'm the latest of the banned." The film censorship was, if anything, more rigorous—a fact made plain when that quintessential Irishman of the day, Joseph Holloway, was deputizing for the film censor and made a cut in *Snow White and the Seven Dwarfs.* The years from 1922 to 1960 were gray ones, and many fine writers were either stunted or warped by their milieu. One thinks particularly of the notable talents of Flann O'Brien, Patrick Kavanagh, and Behan. Many other writers simply left. Here the list is endless and distinguished: Yeats, AE, Stephens, Gogarty, O'Casey, O'Connor, Beckett, and many more.

In these years, from 1922 to 1960, it is perhaps small exaggeration to claim that the best and most eminent Irish writers were those whose voices were the most critical of Irish society. In 1922, Joyce published *Ulysses,* a novel too eminent to censor but too scathingly realistic to be sold above the counter. In 1926, the Abbey produced O'Casey's *The Plough and the Stars,* a play that seemed so critical of 1916 and, indeed, of Irish morality that it occasioned vehement patriotic protests in the theater; and Yeats, inaudible above the din, cried out, "You have disgraced yourselves again!" Not too many critical voices were audible in these years, but the best were eloquent: Yeats in poem and play and for a while in the Senate, O'Flaherty, O'Connor, Sean O'Faolain, and, later, Peadar O'Donnell in their magazine *The Bell,* Flann O'Brien, whose whimsy grew ever more sour, Patrick Kavanagh, whose criticism grew ever more shrill, Brendan Behan, whose escape from puritanic Ireland destroyed his talent and his life. Few of these writers were as savage as the now mild writer of Abbey comedies Brinsley MacNamara had once been in *The Valley of the Squinting Windows,* and few went as far as the ambivalent Paul Vincent Carroll did when he referred to rural Ireland as "a warping, killing, crookening rat-trap where the human mind and spirit are driven mad." But the best of Irish writers were taking a bleak and disillusioned view of the country, and it would not be long until

Mervyn Wall wrote *Leaves for the Burning,* and John McGahern wrote *The Barracks,* and William Trevor wrote "The Ballroom of Romance."

However, if there were fewer idealizations of Irish life, such as nostalgic Irish-Americans would enjoy, there were still some celebrations of it, among them the diverting entertainments of Maurice Walsh and the clearly observed and more serious novels of Francis MacManus. There were the beautiful, mournful plays of M. J. Molloy that celebrated the values of a rapidly disappearing past. There were talents, such as Mary Lavin's and James Plunkett's, that could develop even in a thin cultural soil.

Ireland's neutrality in World War II seems, in retrospect, the last stand of the Island of Saints and Scholars. By the late 1950s, it was abundantly clear that de Valera's attempt to preserve Ireland as an enclave of rural purities and historical integrities had not worked. The country was too poor economically to support, and too poor culturally to satisfy, many of its young people, and the emigration rate was soaring. When, about 1960, Sean Lemass's Fianna Fail government turned to woo the outside world and pursue a vigorous campaign of attracting foreign investment, the long-delayed transformation of Ireland into a modern state had begun. The archbishop of Dublin might return from Vatican II and firmly announce that nothing had changed, but in actuality everything was changing quickly, even in the Church.

Television antennas appeared on Dublin roofs, and people avidly watched the uncensorable British programs from across the Irish Sea. The country joined the United Nations, with an idealistic notion of being a neutral and temporizing force. Irish troops were part of the UN peacekeeping mission in the Congo, and an Irish writer was Dag Hammarskjold's man in Katanga. New buildings of an incongruous and ugly modernity appeared among the decaying Georgian buildings of the capital. For both economic and cultural reasons, young people fled from the countryside to the towns. Even the tide of emigration slowly receded and even turned. The tourist trade grew. In 1973, Ireland entered what was then called the Common Market.

All of this activity had an intense cultural and social effect on the country. Film censorship began to relax, and book censorship dwindled to such a trickle that in the 1970s John McGahern and Edna O'Brien were practically the only writers of note whose books were banned. In 1977, the banning of a book on family planning led to a court decision that probably administered the coup de grâce to literary censorship of serious work. A production in 1977 at the Gate Theatre of the English play *Equus,* with a naked boy and a naked girl on stage, occasioned neither a police raid nor, indeed, any protest whatsoever. People married earlier, traffic grew congested, the suburbs sprawled, and McDonald's ubiquitous hamburgers appeared on Grafton Street. Civil rights protests in the North spawned a resurgence of horrendous political violence that, although minuscule by the standards of Guatemala or Rwanda, only looked like dissipating more than a quarter of a century later. Social services increased, and so did government borrowing and the national debt. In the 1980s, dole queues lengthened, and by 1994 nearly 300,000 people were out of work. The drug culture became a major social problem. Irish people began to die of AIDS. About 4,000 Irishwomen every year had to go to England for their abortions. Muggings, murders, incest, and clerical interference with altar boys seemed the daily staple of news.

As Ireland became less Ireland and more a homogenized part of the modern world, Irish writing changed also. For the Irish writer of today, the new outward-looking Ireland has had an impact both on his subject matter and his technique. His subject matter is no longer, as it was at the beginning of the century, the celebration of national virtue. National virtue is celebrated by pop songs that win the Eurovision Song Contest and could have been written in America or Italy. Or it is celebrated with much national hysteria by appearances in the World Cup, the Irish team playing not Gaelic football but soccer.

During this period, important writers of an older generation continued to produce excellent work that reflected an Ireland that was past or passing. One thinks of much of the work of M. J. Molloy or of Bryan MacMahon, for instance, or of the recent novels of John B. Keane or of Hugh Leonard's memories of Dalkey as well as his admired play *Da* or of Brian Friel's *Aristocrats* or *Translations* or *Dancing at Lughnasa*.

Nevertheless, there has been a vital tradition in twentieth-century Irish writing that has been thoroughly modernist, experimental in technique, and, in the context of most Irish writing, shocking in content. Its Gogol's "Overcoat" was, of course, James Joyce's seminal modernist novel, *Ulysses*. Slowly, modernism made its inroads. Irish poets of the 1930s, such as Denis Devlin, Brian Coffey, and Thomas McGreevy, owed their allegiance to Pound and Eliot and not to Yeats. Denis Johnston's *The Old Lady Says "No!"* actually became a popular play, even though it owed more to the allusiveness of Pound and Eliot than it did to the Irish patriotic melodramas it mournfully parodied. Johnston might deny the influence of German Expressionism, but it was the strength, even though the Irish did not think so, of Sean O'Casey's *The Silver Tassie*. Flann O'Brien's *At Swim-Two-Birds* is Irish in its jokiness but thoroughly modernist in its technique. But, undoubtedly, the vastly influential Samuel Beckett, in his growing minimalist technique and in his increasingly bleak content, seemed the quintessential avant-garde reflector of the malaise of the modern world.

The growth of literary modernism was a slow one in Ireland, but by the 1990s it has certainly triumphed, and it has paralleled the growth and the triumph of an international, rather than a national, culture. Perhaps the change may be seen in the career of Austin Clarke, who began as the last inhabitant of the Celtic Twilight. Although Clarke never relinquished formalism of style (a style derived from some techniques of Gaelic verse, particularly assonance), his late poems showed him often as a caustic observer of a new Ireland he did not much like. The poets, novelists, and playwrights born in the 1960s and after have much more thoroughly, in loosened technique and liberated content, reflected their own world and its culture. In form, no modern Irish novelist deviates more from traditional plotting than John Banville, but few modern novelists are more admired. In content, the vital and squalid lives depicted by Roddy Doyle, Patrick McCabe, and Joseph O'Connor have made a powerful impact. A playwright like Tom MacIntyre, who can command comic eloquence, chooses drastically to diminish the number of words he uses; and several of his plays have been considered the most successfully experimental of recent years. Other playwrights, such as Tom Murphy, Frank McGuinness, and even Brian Friel, choose to diminish plot; and their plays are often basically talk. A few characters sit around for two hours, discuss the past, and, in lieu of action, occasionally joke, sing, or dance. Such plays as *The Gigli Concert, The Bird Sanctuary, Dancing at Lughnasa,* and even *Wonderful Tennessee* have been described as both masterly and eloquent. But perhaps the strongest break with Irish tradition may be seen in the practice of the poets. The most significant immediately post-Clarke poets were Thomas Kinsella, John Montague, and, in terms of popularity, Seamus Heaney. Their mode was free verse; and the poets who followed, such as Eavan Boland, Brendan Kennelly, and, to a lesser extent, Desmond O'Grady and Derek Mahon, worked also in free verse. The explosion of poetry that began in the 1980s is almost entirely in free verse. Rhyme may occasionally occur here and there, but anything approaching rhythmic regularity is rare. Modern Irish verse may often attain great strength from its diction, imagery, and metaphor, but the length of its lines and the shape of its stanzas are mainly determined by its content. Hence, the prototypical contemporary Irish poem, apart from its arbitrary line and stanza lengths, is virtually indistinguishable from prose. As the great Irish poet of the century, Yeats, was a formal virtuoso, the Irish poetry of the present really represents a nearly total about-face in Irish poetic tradition. One of Yeats' most quoted remarks was "Irish poets, learn your trade"; and one might surmise that, in his view, the poets of the present have not.

Although the jury is still out on the writing of the last twenty years, a tentative generalization or two might be made about it. The modern Irish writer seems to reflect the chaos and stress of modern-day Ireland with a disorganization of form and a pervasive glumness of view. This charge can hardly be made against some very popular writers like John B. Keane or Maeve Binchy, but it seems distinctly applicable to their more critically admired contemporaries. For them, the patron saint of modern Irish writing is not now Yeats; it is Samuel Beckett.

Despite that, there are a liveliness and an individuality about much modern Irish writing. One is sometimes tempted to think that there are also a new spuriousness and a new barbarousness and that writers have become less Irish as their world has. But in any event, modern Irish writers certainly now have their freedom, both of style and of subject. Perhaps, just as the turn-of-the-century writers hoped to effect an amalgamation of the traditional past with the present, some new revivifying merging may be found. One hopes it will not resemble the recent poem in which the speaker climbs to the top of Queen

Maeve's cairn and has so much admiration for heroic, big-bladdered Maeve that she enthusiastically urinates on it. In free verse. Whether this be a modern celebration of tradition or simply a fouling of one's nest is a question for a new generation of writers and readers to answer.

to Synge and Colum than were most of his contemporaries, was particularly successful in his dramatic reconstructions of a vanished Ireland in *The King of Friday's Men, The Paddy Pedlar,* and *The Wood of the Whispering.* The dominant lyrical note gives his best work an authenticity ranking with that of the folk dramatists of the earlier period.

Most of the best plays written in Ireland since the 1950s, whether staged at the Abbey or elsewhere, conform to the Abbey pattern. Although not all of the plays of Molloy, Macken, John B. Keane,* Brendan Behan, Brian Friel,* Eugene McCabe,* Thomas Kilroy,* and Thomas Murphy* are set in kitchens, tenements, or prisons, all are written within a naturalistic framework while making use of somewhat non-naturalistic dialogue, often with poetic overtones. Just as O'Casey took the Abbey play into the tenement, Behan took it behind prison walls in *The Quare Fellow* and into the brothel in *The Hostage.* Brian Friel, who is one of the most technically accomplished, living Irish playwrights, shows us the country boy setting off for America in *Philadelphia, Here I Come!,* and the Irish countrywoman coming home from the states in *The Loves of Cass Maguire.*

In 1966, the Irish government gave the Abbey an excellently designed and splendidly equipped modern theatre on the old site. Some critics expressed the opinion that giving such a theatre to the Abbey was akin to putting a Christian Dior creation on a barefooted Connemara colleen. Since 1966, however, the company has visited Florence, Vienna, Brussels, Paris, Edinburgh, Frankfurt, London, New York, Boston, Philadelphia, and Washington. And for the first time ever, the Abbey has brought plays in Irish to the Aran Islands and the Irish-speaking districts in the West.

In the early 1900s, the Abbey Players won rave notices from critics such as Max Beerbohm, C. E. Montague, and A. B. Walkley. The players and plays were a new phenomenon in the theatre. Today, the Abbey Company, no longer a source of novelty, is the inheritor and upholder of a tradition that must be redefined and revivified for each succeeding generation of theatre-goers. The prowess of many of the earlier players has to be taken more or less on trust. Most playgoers of today can only recall the work of Sara Allgood, Arthur Sinclair, Maire O'Neill, and W. G. Fay after each had passed his zenith; what they can and do enjoy is the work of the present company, many of whom have not reached even the meridian of their careers. But they have already proved themselves not only in the native repertoire, but also in their interpretations of Chekhov, Brecht, and Sophocles. This turn in the tide of the Abbey's fortunes, under directors such as Tómas Mac Anna and Hugh Hunt, will come as a surprise to those who have heard allegations that the theatre was dead or dying. But the fabulous invalid has made a remarkable recovery in spite of some of the ailments which might have killed a younger and less hardy patient.

The Abbey's dependence on adaptations in the 1970s was noted as indicative of a dearth of original plays, as also were a large number of revivals. However, as the Broadway critic Walter Kerr asked, "What is a revival?" In the Abbey

context, a revival is something brought back from the near-dead, like Boucicault's *The Shaughraun* or *Arrah na Pogue*. The term should not be applied to
plays from the Abbey repertoire that have proved successful decade after decade.
These would include not only such unchallenged masterpieces as *The Playboy
of the Western World* and *The Plough and the Stars* but at least a score of other
pieces that have earned a permanent place on the playbills of a national theatre.

During Joe Dowling's term as artistic director from 1977 to 1983, the Abbey's
small experimental theatre, the Peacock, saw the rise of a new school of playwrights, including J. Graham Reid,* Bernard Farrell,* Tom MacIntyre,* Frank
McGuinness,* Neil Donnelly,* Michael Harding,* Dermot Bolger,* and Sebastian Barry.* Some of the work of Farrell and McGuinness was also successful
on the larger Abbey stage.

Nevertheless, the work of an earlier generation of playwrights—particularly
Brian Friel, Tom Murphy, and Hugh Leonard*—has been the mainstay of the
Abbey repertoire since the 1970s. Also, John B. Keane,* who was once regarded
as a regional playwright, has been belatedly accepted as a writer whose work
should be seen regularly at the national theatre. The present decade was heralded
by the international acclaim of Friel's *Dancing at Lughnasa,* arguably the most
significant Abbey play since *The Plough and the Stars.* This success was all the
more significant for the Abbey, as regional ventures like the Field Day Company* based in Derry and the Druid Theatre* in Galway had staged important
new plays by Friel, Murphy, Thomas Kilroy,* and Seamus Heaney.* Even in
Dublin, the Project Theatre and the Passion Machine, which staged innovative
work by Paul Mercier* and Roddy Doyle,* now provide an alternative to the
Abbey and the Peacock as the home of original drama. Further, in the past
decade the Abbey has had to face the challenge of a revitalized Gate Theatre*
and competition from the Gaiety and Olympia Theatres, where former Abbey
successes are frequently staged without benefit of subsidy.

The Abbey has thus been compelled to redefine the role of a national theatre
in a changing Ireland. To a great extent, the theatre's problems are a microcosm
of those of a small country on the periphery of Europe, emerging from a postcolonial situation and trying to take its place as a modern state. Given the
support that a national theatre should command, the Abbey and its sister theatre,
the Peacock, are likely to remain the mecca of the aspiring playwright with
something to say, in tragic or comic vein, about the tensions and conflicts of
the day. It can draw on the strength of the regional and community theatres to
meet the challenges of the future while continuing to keep in its repertoire the
dramatic heritage of almost a century.

MICHEÁL Ó hAODHA

WORKS: Some of the early Abbey plays were published in two series by Maunsel in Dublin.
The first series of fifteen volumes included: J. M. Synge, *The Well of the Saints* (1905); Lady
Gregory, *Kincora* (1905); Padraic Colum *The Land* (1905); W. B. Yeats, *The Hour-Glass, Cathleen
Ni Houlihan, The Pot of Broth* (1905); W. B. Yeats, *The King's Threshold* (1905); W. B. Yeats,
On Baile's Strand (1905); William Boyle, *The Building Fund* (1905); Lady Gregory, *The White
Cockade* (1906?); Lady Gregory, *Spreading the News, The Rising of the Moon,* and Lady Gregory

and Douglas Hyde, *The Poorhouse* (1906); J. M. Synge, *The Playboy of the Western World* (1907); Thomas MacDonagh, *When the Dawn Is Come* (1908); Lennox Robinson, *The Cross Roads* (1909); Padraic Colum, *Thomas Muskerry* (1910); St. John G. Ervine, *Mixed Marriage* (1911). The plays in the second series were: Lady Gregory, *The Image* (1911); Lennox Robinson, *Patriots* (1912); Joseph Campbell, *Judgment* (1912); T. C. Murray, *Maurice Harte* (1912); Seumas O'Kelly, *The Bribe* (1912); George Fitzmaurice, *The Country Dressmaker* (1914); Edward McNulty, *The Lord Mayor* (1917); J. Bernard McCarthy, *Crusaders* (1918); Maurice Dalton, *Sable and Gold* (1922). In 1977, a New Abbey Theatre Series of plays was published by Proscenium Press of Newark, Delaware, and included P. J. O'Connor's *Patrick Kavanagh's Tarry Flynn*, W. J. White's *The Last Eleven* (1978), Frank O'Connor and Hugh Hunt's *The Invincibles* (1980), Wesley Burrowes's *The Becauseway* (1983), and Micheál Ó hAodha's *Seumas O'Kelly's The Weaver's Grave* (1984). REFERENCES: Blythe, Ernest. *The Abbey Theatre*. Dublin: National Theatre Society, Ltd., 1963; Boyd, Ernest A. *The Contemporary Drama of Ireland*. Dublin: Talbot, 1917/London: T. Fisher Unwin, 1918/Boston: Little Brown, 1928; Ellis-Fermor, Una. *The Irish Dramatic Movement*. London: Methuen, 1939/2d ed., 1954; Fay, Frank J. *Towards a National Theatre*. Robert Hogan, ed. Dublin: Dolmen, 1970; Fay, Gerard. *The Abbey Theatre, Cradle of Genius*. London: Hollis & Carter, 1958; Fay, W. G., & Carswell, Catherine. *The Fays of the Abbey Theatre*. London: Rich & Cowan, 1935/New York: Harcourt Brace, 1935; Flannery, James. *Miss Annie F. Horniman and the Abbey Theatre*. Dublin: Dolmen, 1970; French, Frances-Jane. *The Abbey Theatre Series of Plays*. Dublin: Dolmen, 1969. (Bibliography); Gregory, Lady Augusta. *Our Irish Theatre*. London & New York: Putnam's, 1913/2d ed., with added material, Gerrards Cross: Colin Smythe, 1970; Hogan, Robert. *After the Irish Renaissance*. Minneapolis: University of Minnesota Press, 1967/London: Macmillan, 1968; Hogan, Robert, with James Kilroy, Richard Burnham, & Daniel Poteet. *The Modern Irish Drama*. 6 vols. Dublin: Dolmen, 1975–1984/Newark: University of Delaware Press/Gerrards Cross: Colin Smythe, 1992; Holloway, Joseph. *Joseph Holloway's Abbey Theatre*. Robert Hogan & Michael J. O'Neill, eds. Carbondale: Southern Illinois University Press, 1967; *Joseph Holloway's Irish Theatre*. Robert Hogan & Michael J. O'Neill, eds. 3 vols. Dixon, Calif.: Proscenium, 1968–1970; Hunt, Hugh. *The Abbey: Ireland's National Theatre, 1904–1979*. Dublin: Gill & Macmillan/New York: Columbia University Press, 1979; Kavanagh, Peter. *The Story of the Abbey Theatre*. New York: Devin-Adair, 1950/Orono, Maine: National Poetry Foundation, University of Maine at Orono, 1984; McCann, Sean, ed. *The Story of the Abbey*. London: New English Library, 1967; Mac Liammóir, Micheál. *Theatre in Ireland*. 2d ed., with added material. Dublin: Cultural Relations Committee of Ireland, 1964; MacNamara, Brinsley. *Abbey Plays, 1899–1948*. Dublin: At the Sign of the Three Candles, 1949; Malone, Andrew E. *The Irish Drama*. London: Constable/New York: Scribner's, 1929/New York: Benjamin Blom, 1974; Maxwell, D.E.S. *A Critical History of Modern Irish Drama, 1891–1980*. Cambridge: Cambridge University Press, [1984]; Mikhail, E. H., ed. *The Abbey Theatre: Interviews and Recollections*. [Basingstoke & London]: Macmillan, [1988]; Nic Shiubhlaigh, Maire, & Kenny, Edward. *The Splendid Years*. Dublin: James Duffy, 1955; O'Connor, Frank. *My Father's Son*. London: Macmillan, 1968; Ó hAodha, Micheál. *Theatre in Ireland*. Totowa, N.J.: Rowman & Littlefield, 1975; Ó hAodha, Micheál. *Siobhán: A Memoir of an Actress*. [Dingle, Co. Kerry]: Brandon, [1994]; Robinson, Lennox. *Ireland's Abbey Theatre*. London: Sidgwick & Jackson, 1951/Port Washington, N.Y.: Kennikat, 1968; Robinson, Lennox, ed. *The Irish Theatre*. London: Macmillan, 1939/New York: Haskell House, 1971; Saddlemyer, Ann, ed. *Theatre Business: The Correspondence of the First Abbey Theatre Directors: William Butler Yeats, Lady Gregory and J. M. Synge*. Gerrards Cross: Colin Smythe, [1982]; Weygandt, Cornelius. *Irish Plays and Playwrights*. London: Constable/Boston & New York: Houghton Mifflin, 1913/Port Washington, N.Y.: Kennikat, 1966; Yeats, W. B., ed. *Beltaine*. London: Frank Cass, 1970; Yeats, W. B., ed. *Samhain*. London: Frank Cass, 1970.

ADAMS, GERRY (1948–   ), politician and writer. One of the most controversial figures of contemporary Irish politics, Gerry Adams was born on October 6, 1948, into a large family with a long tradition of involvement with the cause of radical republicanism. In *Falls Memories* (1982), an amalgam of personal reminiscence and local history, he recalls his childhood in Catholic, working-class West Belfast as basically happy: an "uneventful" time before this latest reeruption of the interminable Troubles. Educated at the local Christian Brothers school, Adams did not attend university, preferring instead to remain close to home during the civil rights disturbances of the late 1960s and early 1970s. He worked for a time as a barman but eventually devoted himself full-time to a life of political agitation and organization. Adams was arrested in 1972 and, after an interval of beatings and torture and a brief detention aboard a British prison ship, was sent to the notorious Long Kesh internment camp. While incarcerated, he wrote a series of columns for the republican newspaper *An Poblacht* under the pseudonym "Brownie"; these columns would later provide the basis for *Cage Eleven* (1990), a semifictionalized memoir of his prison experience. By the time of his release in 1977, Adam's prominence in the radical nationalist movement was assured. In 1983, he became president of Sinn Féin, the party commonly described as the political wing of the Provisional Irish Republican Army (IRA). Also in 1983, Adams was elected member of Parliament for West Belfast, an office he held until a narrow defeat in 1992. Since the early 1980s, Adams has been the best-known voice of hard-line opposition to the British presence in the six counties of Northern Ireland.

Adams' political position, as outlined most fully in *The Politics of Irish Freedom* (1986) and *A Pathway to Peace* (1988), is that political agitation and even armed resistance are a justifiable response to the cruelties of the "colonial" British presence in Ireland. For such a position to remain tenable, of course, Adams must continually lay claim to authenticity: both the authenticity of an interpretation of contemporary Northern Irish history as a history of British oppression and the authenticity of his claim to legitimately represent the society this history victimizes. This political necessity invariably permeates his more personal writings. In his volume of short stories, *The Street* (1992), Adams paints a portrait of a normal, vital—if sentimentalized—community fully capable of handling its own affairs on its own terms, yet always threatened by essentially foreign elements: never does Adams admit any doubt as to who is the native and who the invader. Some of the stories are set in a domestic and apparently apolitical space, such as in "Does He Take Sugar?," a send-up of the unconscious patronization of a teenager with Down's syndrome. The majority of the sketches, however, deal with the tangled politics of Northern Ireland directly. In "The Rebel," for example, a middle-aged mother becomes devoted to the "rebel" cause after a rude police sergeant refuses her permission to visit her son, arrested unjustly on a charge of "riotous behaviour." The potentially divisive choice to become politically active is shown to be one taken by a perfectly ordinary member of the community, not by a bloodthirsty fanatic. That it is the British who are ultimately at fault for threatening the well-being of the community Adams evokes is the point of "The Mountains of Mourne," in which a young Catholic working as temporary help for a delivery company experiences a brief but genuine connection with his partner, a middle-aged, working-class Protestant. Adams works to leave the reader with the impression that the differences between his Catholic narrator and his Protestant counterpart, deep as these are, would not be insurmountable were it not for the realities of life under colonialism.

The Street, then, is probably best read in the light of Adams' well-known political views; given its author, it would be difficult to read the book otherwise. *The Street,* like all of Adams' writings, asserts that sine qua non of radical political activity: authenticity. Whether or not one accepts Adam's claim will determine whether or not one sees him as the public face of a terrorist organization that cynically manipulates a climate of violence to its own ends or as the legitimate representative of an endangered community.

ANDREW HAGGERTY

WORKS: *Falls Memories: A Belfast Life.* Dingle, Co. Kerry: Brandon, 1982; *The Politics of Irish Freedom.* Dingle, Co. Kerry: Brandon, 1986; *A Pathway to Peace.* Dublin: Mercier, 1988; *Cage Eleven.* Dingle, Co. Kerry: Brandon, 1990; *The Street and Other Stories.* Dingle, Co. Kerry: Brandon, 1992; *Free Ireland: Towards a Lasting Peace.* Niwot, Colo.: Roberts Rinehart, 1994 (a reissue of *The Politics of Irish Freedom,* with an expanded and updated conclusion); *Selected Writings.* [Dingle]: Brandon, [1993]; *Free Ireland: Towards a Lasting Peace.* [Dingle, Co. Kerry]: Brandon, [1995]. REFERENCE: Kenna, Colm. *Gerry Adams: A Biography.* [Cork & Dublin]: Mercier, 1990.

AE (1867–1935), poet, painter, economist, and editor. AE is the pseudonym of George William Russell, who was a pivotal figure in the Irish Revival. His pen name was adopted from a proofreader's query, "AE—?" about an earlier pseudonym "Aeon," suggesting mankind's age-old, mysterious quest, his constant theme.

Born on April 10, 1867, in Lurgan, County Armagh, Russell moved to Dublin in 1878. At the Metropolitan School of Art, he met W. B. Yeats* and the theosophist Charles Johnston, both of whom confirmed his bent toward mystical speculation and identification with Ireland's spiritual mission. Yeats, a close associate for fifteen years, later became increasingly distant. Dublin's Theosophical Society and the Hermetic Society, however, gave Russell the first forum for his beliefs. From 1891 to 1897, he lived at the Theosophical Household with fellow believers, among them Violet North, whom he married in 1898. The Household's regimen included asceticism, meditation, and study of esoteric philosophy.

Meanwhile, he left a job with a local draper to work for the Irish Agricultural Organization Society, a cooperative sponsored by Sir Horace Plunkett, who also supported two influential journals which AE edited, *The Irish Homestead* (1905–1923) and *The Irish Statesman** (September 15, 1923–April 12, 1930). Journalism and travel through Ireland for the Society did not interfere with AE's steady outpouring of verse, constant activity as a painter, or his role as spokesman for the conscience of Ireland.

With publication of *Homeward: Songs by the Way* in 1894, AE was hailed as a poet equal to Yeats, an opinion soon revised as Yeats continued to develop and AE did not. *The Earth Breath and Other Poems* (1897) and *The Divine Vision and Other Poems* (1904) preceded his *Collected Poems* (1913), which underwent successive editions and enlargements. *Gods of War* (1915) was followed by four volumes published by Macmillan: *Voices of the Stones* (1925), *Vale and Other Poems* (1931), *The House of the Titans and Other Poems* (1934), and *Selected Poems* (1935).

AE's poetry is predominantly visionary. Trusting his intuitions and eschewing the meticulous craftmanship of Yeats, he was too often content with vague symbols, cloudy metaphors, and misty colors. These faults are found also in his painting and sometimes in his prose. *The Candle of Vision* (1918) and *Song and Its Fountains* (1932) present his beliefs.

Welcome exceptions to the prevailing monotony can be found. The metallic clarity of some lines suggests Yeats—for example: "The golden heresy of truth," "We are men by anguish taught," or "The Greece of Pericles is cold." Some poems echo folk themes; the most direct confront the tragedies of war. More surprising is the sly humor, a feature of his famed conversational ability. It emerges in the parodies printed in *Secret Springs of Dublin Song* (1918), written by several unnamed authors. AE's "S. O'. S" (Seumas O'Sullivan*) can be seen as self-mockery in its caricature of the Celtic Twilight. It opens with the line "Child, there are mists in my mind."

AE was active in the Irish Literary Society and in the early stirrings of the theatre. In 1902, his drama on the lengendary Deirdre was acclaimed as an evocation of Irish ideals. His delight in discovering new talent was exemplified by his edition of *New Songs* (1904) with works by Padraic Colum,* Seumas O'Sullivan, Eva Gore-Booth,* Thomas Keohler (1874–1942), Alice Milligan,* Susan Mitchell,* George Roberts (1873–1953), and Ella Young.*

To an unusual degree, Russell was both dreamer and planner, but when he spoke of the political upheavals of the time he was ignored, at great cost to Ireland. Speaking out with surprising force, he attacked "The Masters of Dublin" for their Lockout of 1913, which reduced thousands to abject poverty. In "Salutation," he celebrated the leaders of the 1916 Easter Rising. He scorned Ulster for its intransigence and attempted to conciliate England by serving briefly in the fruitless Convention of 1917–1918. He opposed the anti-Treaty Republicans but retired from politics by refusing in 1922 to become a member of the Irish Free State Senate, in which Yeats and Oliver Gogarty* served.

Much of AE's prose was ephemeral, but *The National Being* (1916) and two prose fantasies, *The Interpreters* (1922) and *The Avatars: A Futurist Fantasy* (1933), represent his thought, as does Monk Gibbon's* selection of prose, *The Living Torch* (1937) and Alan Denson's *Letters from AE* (1961).

Disillusioned by the decline of Irish culture and bereaved by the loss of his wife, AE retired to England in 1933. He had lectured in the United States in 1928 and 1930; a final trip, to advise Roosevelt's secretary of agriculture, Henry

A. Wallace, was cut short by fatal illness. He died at Bournemouth, England, on July 17, 1935.

At the zenith of his career, he was widely loved and regarded as a seer. Now he is an almost forgotten figure in the Irish scene, upstaged by Yeats, Joyce,* Synge,* and others. His facile talent achieved versatility at the expense of artistic perfection. Only a handful of poems and a cluster of anecdotes remain, but his historical importance is becoming more widely recognized.

RICHARD M. KAIN

WORKS: *Homeward Songs by the Way.* Dublin: Whaley, 1894; *The Earth Breath and Other Poems.* New York & London: John Lane, 1896; *The Nuts of Knowledge.* Dundrum: Dun Emer, 1903; *The Mask of Apollo and Other Stories.* London & New York: Macmillan, 1903; *The Divine Vision and Other Poems.* London & New York: Macmillan, 1904; *Some Irish Essays.* Dublin: Maunsel, 1906; *By Still Waters.* Dundrum: Dun Emer, 1906; *Deirdre.* Dublin: Maunsel, 1907; *Collected Poems.* London: Macmillan, 1913; *Gods of War, with Other Poems.* Dublin: Privately printed, 1915; *Imaginations and Reveries.* Dublin & London: Maunsel, 1915; *The National Being.* Dublin & London: Maunsel, 1916; *The Candle of Vision.* London: Macmillan, 1918; *The Interpreters.* London: Macmillan, 1922; *Voices of the Stones.* London: Macmillan, 1925; *Midsummer Eve.* New York: Crosby Gaige, 1928; *Enchantment and Other Poems.* New York: Fountain/London: Macmillan, 1930; *Vale and Other Poems.* London: Macmillan, 1931; *Song and Its Fountains.* London: Macmillan, 1932; *The Avatars.* London: Macmillan, 1933; *The House of Titans and Other Poems.* London: Macmillan, 1934; *Selected Poems.* London: Macmillan, 1935; *Some Passages from the Letters of AE to W. B. Yeats.* Dublin: Cuala, 1936; *The Living Torch.* Monk Gibbon, ed. London: Macmillan, 1937; *Letters from AE.* Alan Denson, ed. London: Abelard-Schuman, 1961. A collected edition is being published jointly by Colin Smythe in England and Humanities Press in the United States. Thus far, the first part has appeared: *Selections from the Contributions to The Irish Homestead,* Henry Summerfield, ed. 2 vols. Gerrard's Cross: Colin Smythe; Atlantic Highlands, N.J.: Humanities Press, 1978. REFERENCES: Davis, Robert B. *George William Russell ("AE").* Boston: Twayne, 1977; Denson, Alan. *Printed Writings of George W. Russell (AE): A Bibliography.* Evanston, Ill.: Northwestern University Press, 1961; Eglinton, John (W. K. Magee). *A Memoir of A. E.* London: Macmillan, 1937; Figgis, Darrell. *AE (George W. Russell): A Study of a Man and a Nation.* Dublin & London: Maunsel, 1916/Port Washington, N.Y.: Kennikat, 1970; Howarth, Herbert. *The Irish Writers 1880–1940.* London: Rockliff, 1958; Kain, Richard M., & O'Brien, James H. *George Russell (A.E.).* Lewisburg, Pa.: Bucknell University Press, 1976; Summerfield, Henry. *That Myriad-Minded Man: A Biography of G. W. Russell—"A. E."* Gerrards Cross: Colin Smythe/ Totowa, N.J. Rowman & Littlefield, 1975.

AGEE, CHRIS (1956–   ), poet. Chris Agee was born in San Francisco on January 18, 1956, of American parents. He attended Andover and Harvard, from which he received a B.A. in 1979. He then spent a year in France at the Université d'Aix-en-Provence. As an undergraduate at Harvard, he was particularly influenced by philosopher Roberto Unger and by poet and translator Robert Fitzgerald, who taught a popular course on Versification and who supervised Agee's thesis on W. H. Auden.

Agee initially traveled to Belfast as a research assistant for a Harvard professor of medical ethics, but he settled there in 1979, working as a lecturer in literacy at the Belfast Institute of Further and Higher Education. From 1985 to 1990, he gave annual lectures on literacy at the School of Education, Queen's University, and did graduate work at Queen's, receiving an M.A. in 1987 for a thesis on Irish poet Eugene Watters.* He has worked more recently as a tutor for the Open University in Northern Ireland and as adult education adviser for the Belfast branch of the University of East London. Since 1988, he has been a member of the Board of Directors of *Poetry Ireland.* He has traveled widely in Europe, the West Indies, Israel, and Mexico and in 1992 went to the Soviet Union to represent Ireland in a literary exchange.

His book *In the New Hampshire Woods* (1992) is divided into two parts: the first section, "North America," concerns his American experience, while his life in Ireland provides matter for the second. The landscapes and seascapes of section one are the New England coast, Block Island, and the backwaters of Squam Lake, near Holderness, New Hampshire. Agee has an acute eye for how light falls upon land and sea, by day and night. He is a poetic impressionist in his sensitivity to how the changing light can shape and transform the contours of things. Those artists of light, Monet, Rembrandt, and Hopper, all make an appearance in the poetry. Elsewhere, he finds the night sky "radiant/with archipelagoes of light." In some ways, he might be considered a poet of the environment and wilderness, and his poems evoke the minutest details of New Hampshire's flora and fauna.

There is a mystical undercurrent to many of these poems, as though some supernatural blessing flows beneath the surfaces of the astounding scenes of the poetry. Indeed, he has recently written that "an ancient Sufic term captures something of the ineffable undertow running through many of my poems: *baraka,* meaning both a 'blessing' and the 'breath of life' from which the evolutionary process unfolds." As this might suggest, an interest in Oriental religions merges with the poet's preoccupation with the natural environment: "I moored there for a noon plunge, innocent of the Buddha-smile of time." This is a very literary book, with allusions to Auden, Eliot, Frost, and Lowell, to name a few, though it is never stuffy, and the language is always charged and energetic. A poem about New England's whalers has the intensity of Lowell's evocation of the Quaker graveyard, as, for example, when Agee remembers "the imperial galleons and marauding whalers/doomed to the shipwreck of the eternal holocaust." Despite this poet's obvious erudition and his immersion in the traditions of modern lyric form, his voice is strongly his own.

It would be wrong to think of Agee as a passive recorder of natural beauty, because he is aware of the threatened environment in what he has called "the Age of Petrol," and his poems are sketched in the shadow of "the State/Juggernaut." Some of his poems attempt to deliver a fresh perception of places and cultures before the shock of colonization, whether in Ireland or Block Island. A recent poem, dedicated to the memory of Graham Bamford, who immolated himself against British policy in Bosnia, adopts a Gaelic diction to deliver the apprehension of genocide in a modern European nation: "Old Sarajevo! Tomorrow, the Shell-pump's sunny vista./Past *cre na cilla* the living debate the dead."

Now an Irish citizen, Agee lives in Belfast with his wife, Noirin McKinney, a well-known art critic and administrator, and son, Jacob.

JONATHAN ALLISON

WORKS: *In the New Hampshire Woods.* Dublin: Dedalus, 1992; "Old Sarajevo." In *Klaonica: Poems for Bosnia.* Newcastle upon Tyne: Bloodaxe, 1993; "The Sierra de Zacatecas." In *Toward Harmony.* Dublin: Dedalus, 1993; "Poetic Silence." In *Poetry Ireland* 40 (Winter 1993–1994). (Essay).

ALEXANDER, CECIL FRANCES (1818–1895), poet and hymnist. Alexander's first name, Cecil, is sometimes misrepresented as Cecilia, although she was called Fanny by her family and friends. She was born in 1818 in Dublin, Tyrone, the daughter of Major John Humphreys, a landowner in Tyrone and County Wicklow. Her mother was the former Elizabeth Reed. Most biographical accounts either omit her birth date or erroneously report it as 1825. Her daughter reveals that Cecil was six years older than her husband, a source of great concern to herself and her husband's family, so her birth date was reported to be seven years later during her life. The young Cecil Humphreys collaborated with Lady Harriet Howard, daughter of the earl of Wicklow, on a series of tracts, with Lady Howard being responsible for the prose sections and Cecil writing the poetry. Their brief partnership ended when Lady Harriet died of consumption. Both women were influenced by the Oxford movement. During a visit to her sister, Cecil met Dr. Hook, who edited her volume, *Verses for Holy Seasons,* and provided a "sane and masculine influence" on her, according to her husband's memoir. She later developed her talents as a hymnist, and her hymns for children were especially popular.

In October 1850, she married Rev. William Alexander of Termonamongan, diocese of Derry. He became archbishop of Armagh and, later, primate of Ireland, although she did not live to see him become primate. From their marriage until 1855, the Alexanders lived at Derg Lodge, in Termonamongan, and she wrote poetry and hymns extensively. In 1867, William was named archbishop of Derry and Raphoe, and their circle of friends included Dean Stanley, Mr. Lecky, and Matthew Arnold. She occasionally published under the pseudonyms of X? and C.F.A., and she died on October 12, 1895.

Alexander's poetry and hymns are pious and frequently intended to provide the reader with instructions on how to be a better Christian. Her best-known hymn, "There is a green hill far away," appeared in numerous hymnals. She was virtually unrivaled as a children's hymnist, with 546,000 copies of *Hymns for Little Children* printed in its first thirty years and sixty-two editions by 1884. There were fourteen editions of the *Moral Songs* poetry volume. Her meditative poems revolve around Old and New Testament subjects or the plight of children. There is little of the secular in her work, except for the memorial poems written to Mrs. Hemans, Southey, and the kaiser. Even when the topic is emigration, as an excerpt from "For Our Emigrants" demonstrates, she focuses on the religious aspects:

And let the Church that first did bless
    The Mother of our youth,
Go with us through the wilderness
    And hold the lamp of truth.

And let her words so sweet and strong
    In the old measure flow,
Lest we forget the cradle song
    That lulled us long ago.

Lest in the time that's far away,
    Estranged in heart and word,
Your children to our children say,
    "Ye serve not the same Lord."

ANNE COLMAN

WORKS: *Verses for Holy Seasons*. (1846). London: Bell & Daldy, 1858; *Hymns for Little Children*. (1848). Multiple editions; *The Lord of the Forest and His Vassels: An Allegory*. London, 1848; *Moral Songs*. (1849). Multiple editions; *Narrative Hymns for Village Schools*. 1854; *Poems of Subjects in the Old Testament*. 1854; *Hymns, Descriptive and Devotional*. 1858; *The Legend of the Golden Prayers, and Other Poems*. London: Bell & Daldy, 1859; *Easy Questions on the Life of Our Lord*. London: Griffith & Farren, 1891; *Hymns for Children*. London: Marcus Ward, [1894]; *Poems by Cecil Frances Alexander (C.F.A.)*. William Alexander, ed. London: Macmillan, 1896; *Selected Poems from William and Frances Alexander*. A. P. Graves, ed. London: Society for Promoting Christian Knowledge, 1930. REFERENCES: Alexander, Eleanor. *Primate Alexander: Archbishop of Armagh*. London: Edward Arnold, 1914; Alexander, William. "Memoir" in *Poems by Cecil Frances Alexander*. London: Macmillan, 1896; Lovell, Ernest W. O. *A Green Hill Far Away: The Life of Mrs. C. F. Alexander*. Dublin: Association for Promoting Christian Knowledge/London: S.P.C.K., 1970; Wallace, Valerie. *Mrs. Alexander: A Life of the Hymn-Writer, 1818–95*. Dublin: Lilliput, 1995.

ALEXANDER, MRS. *See* HECTOR, ANNIE FRENCH.

ALLEN, ALFRED (1925–   ), poet and farmer. Allen was born on January 24, 1925, at Clashenure House, Ovens, County Cork, where he still lives and farms. As a farmer, he has been generally outside the literary milieu and so formed his style largely by his own reading and study. Consequently, among Irish poets of the last quarter-century, he is one of the more committed to traditional form. He is capable of considerable awkwardness, but his rigid adherence to form gives some of his work a strength and even memorableness rarely paralleled in the more sophisticated and much better known work of his contemporaries Thomas Kinsella* and John Montague.* Allen seems a kind of masculine Emily Dickinson. His poetic vision is a direct pondering on the small physical world that immediately surrounds him or a personal reduction of the larger issues that he has read about in the world outside. The couplets of his first short collection, *Clashenure Skyline* (1970), are a somewhat incongruous form for his subject, but they are a form, and he frequently uses them with considerable effect. *Interrogations* (1975) is more miscellaneous than the cohering evocations of his own countryside in *Clashenure Skyline,* but it is also better work. The pieces range from those of personal emotion and commonsense comment to a series of literary character studies of figures from the Trojan War. Allen has published little in recent years, which is a pity in this day of ubiquitous vers libre.

WORKS: *Clashenure Skyline.* Dublin: Dolmen, 1970; *Interrogations.* Cork: Tower Books, [1975]; *Shades of a Rural Past.* [Cork: Tower Books, 1978].

ALLEN, FERGUS (ca. 1920–), novelist. Allen was born in London of an Irish father and an English mother. He grew up in Ireland, attending Quaker schools in Dublin and Waterford. He graduated from Trinity College, Dublin, in civil engineering and has lived in England, working in the civil service.

WORK: *The Brown Parrots of Providencia.* London & Boston: Faber, [1993].

ALLINGHAM, WILLIAM (1824–1889), poet. Because Allingham was so highly regarded in his lifetime and given his friendships with important figures such as Tennyson and Browning, his diary and letters are particularly rich sources of information on the period. His own verse reflects both the Romantics' pleasure in natural scenery and the less appealing Victorian tendency toward sentimentality and moralism.

Allingham was born on March 19, 1824, in Ballyshannon, County Donegal. Although a member of the Ascendancy, he came to know and sympathize with the farming class. He worked as a customs official most of his adult life, before assuming a career as a writer and editor. In his later years he lived in England, where he died, in Hampstead, on November 18, 1889.

Throughout his career, he maintained close connections with the London literary set. He dedicated his first book, *Poems* (1850), to Leigh Hunt. Later, as editor of *Fraser's Magazine,* he acquired considerable influence and developed lifelong friendships with Tennyson, Browning, Carlyle, and Rossetti. His diary, most often consulted for information about those better-known writers, is itself a piece of literary art, containing numerous keen and sensitive perceptions. Unlike many minor writers who mixed with great men of his time, he was not sycophantic; in conversations he regularly asserted his own convictions and disagreed frequently with such luminaries. One subject on which he repeatedly stood his ground was his quarrel with English policies toward Ireland, for he was a consistent anti-imperialist, although not quite an Irish nationalist. However, although Yeats* praised him as "the Poet of Ballyshannon," he is neither a regionalist nor a proponent of Irish independence.

More than his Dublin contemporary writers who extolled the virtues of Irish rural life, Allingham understood its realities, and his accurate descriptions of village life and of the natural landscape are the most successful aspects of his poetry. His knowledge of folk literature was extensive, reflecting contemporary interest in ballads and folktales. His collection *The Ballad Book* (1864), while not scholarly, reflects both the range of such poems and their lively appeal.

In the best of his poems, the long narrative *Laurence Bloomfield in Ireland*

(1864), his astute observations about contemporary political issues add substance to the sensitive and gentle descriptions that characterize his early works. Its subject is the land question, and it includes frank descriptions of the conflicts between landlords and tenants. The poem is long, possibly too long for the subject, but its scope allows Allingham to range widely in his topical comments, including reasonable discourse on the practice of evictions. Strong as were his convictions, his treatment of both landlords and tenants is judicious, and his affection for all parties is evident. There are even forceful and enjoyable bits of satire sprinkled throughout. This is Allingham's most thoroughly Irish poem, in that it best reveals his understanding and sympathy for the Irish peasants in their struggle to regain their land. Its directness and sense of urgency make it his best work.

Like his close friend Tennyson, Allingham attempted long narrative poems and even an historical drama, *Ashby Manor* (1883), but they are less successful because they tend toward prettiness and even sentimentality. At his best, Allingham was remarkably sensitive to subtle nuances of feeling. Compared with more politically committed contemporaries such as Davis* and Mangan,* Allingham's poetry lacks conviction and force, but in the broader scope of literary history it claims a secure place for its intelligence, freshness, and manifest sincerity. In his best work, *Laurence Bloomfield,* such exceptional qualities were combined with energetic expressions of social concern to achieve a level of rare artistry.

JAMES KILROY

WORKS: *Poems.* London: Chapman & Hall, 1850; *Day and Night Songs.* London: Routledge, 1854; *Peace and War.* London: Routledge, 1854; *The Music Master.* London: Routledge, 1855; *Laurence Bloomfield in Ireland.* London: Macmillan, 1864/reprint, New York: AMS, 1972; *Fifty Modern Poems.* London: Bell & Daldy, 1865; *In Fairyland. A Series of Pictures by Richard Doyle with a Poem by William Allingham.* London: Longmans, Green, 1870; *Songs, Ballads and Stories.* London: Bell, 1877; *Evil May-Day.* London: Stott, 1882. (Poetry); *Ashby Manor.* Oxford: Stott, 1882 (drama); *The Fairies.* London: De La Rue, 1883. (Poetry); *Blackberries.* London: Philip, 1884 (Poetry); *Rhymes for the Young Folk.* London: Cassell, 1887; *Irish Songs and Poems.* London: Reeves & Turner, 1887; *Flower Pieces and Other Poems.* London: Reeves & Turner, 1888; *Life and Phantasy.* London: Reeves & Turner, 1889. (Poetry); *Thought and Word, and Ashby Manor.* London: Reeves & Turner, 1890; *Laurence Bloomfield in Ireland.* Revised, London: Reeves & Turner, 1890; *Blackberries.* Revised. London: Reeves & Turner, 1890; *Varieties in Prose.* London: Longmans, Green, 1893. (Collected prose); *Sixteen Poems,* selected by William Butler Yeats. Dundrum: Dun Emer, 1905; *By the Way: Verses, Fragments, and Notes.* Helen Allingham, ed. London: Longmans, Green, 1912; *Poems,* selected & arranged by Helen Allingham. London: Macmillan, 1912; *The Poems of William Allingham.* John Hewitt, ed. Dublin: Dolmen, 1967; *William Allingham: A Diary.* Helen Allingham & Dollie Radford, eds. London: Macmillan, 1907/revised ed. by John Julius Norwich. London: Penguin, 1985.   REFERENCES: Allingham, Helen, & Williams, E. Baumer, eds. *Letters to William Allingham.* London: Longmans, 1911; Hill, George Birkbeck, ed. *Letters of Dante Gabriel Rossetti to William Allingham, 1854–1870.* London: Fisher Unwin, 1897; Lasner, Mark Samuels. "William Allingham: Some Uncollected Authors LVI." *Book Collector* 39 (Summer 1991): 174–204, & (Autumn 1991): 321–349; Lasner, Mark Samuels. *William Allingham: A Bibliographical Study.* Philadelphia: Holmes, 1993; O'Hegarty, Patrick S. *A Bibliography of William Allingham.* Dublin: Privately printed by Thom, 1945. Reprinted from *The Dublin Magazine* of January–March and July–September 1945; Warner, Alan. *William Allingham: An Introduction.* Dublin: Dolmen, 1971; Warner, Alan. *William Allingham.* Lewisburg, Pa.: Bucknell University Press, 1975; Warner, Alan. "William Allingham: Bibliographical Survey." *Irish Book Lore* 2 (1976): 303–307.

AMORY, THOMAS (1691?–1788), novelist. Amory was apparently the son of Councillor Amory, who accompanied William III to Ireland and who possessed considerable property in Clare. It is uncertain whether he was born in Ireland or born in England and taken to Ireland as a child. It seems that he did not attend Trinity College, Dublin, as he attested; and it is doubtful if he knew Swift,* as he also attested. In later years, he lived a secluded life in London and is said to have gone abroad only at dusk. He died on November 15, 1788, at the age of ninety-seven.

Of most interest among Amory's writings is his curious novel *The Life of John Buncle, Esq.* (1756, 1766), which was admired by Hazlitt and which Ian Campbell Ross believes "anticipates the work of Maria Edgeworth* and Sydney Owenson, Lady Morgan,* while remaining happily as free of the moral earnestness of the former as of the enervating sentiment of the latter." Although full of rambling footnotes about Irish history and of rhapsodic descriptions of landscape, the book is redeemed by the episodic and quasi-autobiographical adventures of the hero, who marries (on the briefest acquaintance) eight women and shortly buries them. As Hazlitt remarks, "The soul of Rabelais has passed into . . . Amory." Generally ignored in recent years, this volume has not lost its eccentric fascination.

WORKS: *Memoirs of Several Ladies of Great Britain. Interspersed with Literary Reflexions, and Accounts of Antiquities and Curious Things. In Several Letters.* London: John Noon, 1755; *The Life of John Buncle, Esq.; Containing Various Observations and Reflections, Made in Several Parts of the World. . . .* 2 vols. London: J. Noon, 1756, 1766/London: Routledge, 1904; *An Antiquarian Doctor's Sermon on an Antiquated Subject; Lately Found among the Sweepings of His Study. . . .* London: J. Johnson, 1768. REFERENCES: Hazlitt, William. "On John Buncle." *The Round Table* (1817); Ross, Ian Campbell. "Thomas Amory, *John Buncle,* and the Origins of Irish Fiction." *Éire-Ireland* 18 (Fall 1983): 71–85; Walters, John Cuming. "*John Buncle:* A Curio of Literature." Manchester: Skerratt & Hughes, 1919 (monograph).

ANDERSON, LINDA (1949–   ), novelist. Anderson was born in Belfast of a Protestant family, graduated from Queen's University in French and philosophy, and took a postgraduate diploma of education. She worked in the civil rights movement from 1968 but moved to England in 1972, where she worked first as a teacher and then at several low-paying jobs in order to have time to write. In addition to two novels, she has written some stories and plays.

Her second novel, *Cuckoo* (1986), is a curiously structured story about a young woman from Belfast who has an illegitimate black baby in England and moves in with a couple who have also just had a child. Their marriage is unhappy, and the heroine, Fran, has an affair with the lecturer husband. She does not fall out with his wife, however, but protests on Greenham Common and visits Stonehenge with her. Eventually, because of a blighted past, she moves out, lives on the dole, and continues her antinuclear protests. The story is told mainly from Fran's view, with occasional chapters from the wife's or the husband's view. A more conventional section in the center of the novel relates the heroine's youth, young womanhood, and failed first marriage in Belfast. The point of the book would seem to be one of idealism surviving the depressing incidents of a dreary life. There is considerable emphasis on sex, but the vigor—even violence—of the writing is not confined to four-letter words. Even without them, Anderson has an often powerful diction, with striking similes and images:

He [a hairdresser] lifted clumps of my hair with distaste as if it were some kind of striated dung.

The sickening exclusive power of marriage with its rings and photos, its rights and atrocities.

The dowdy, genderless creatures [slum dwellers] who scurry past, head down, fearing your hello like an assault.

I ran to the bathroom, everything in my stomach rising at the thought of the Last Day, rotting corpses flinging soil aside like blankets, standing up and stretching their white bones, the flesh hanging from them like defiled rags.

Indeed, the strength of the book is more in the writing than in the plotting or characterization.

WORKS: *To Stay Alive*. London: Bodley Head, 1984/as *We Can't All Be Heroes, You Know*. New Haven, Conn.: Ticknor & Fields, 1985; *Cuckoo*. London: Bodley Head, 1985/[Dingle]: Brandon, [1988].

ANDERSON, PARIS (fl. 1815–1837), novelist. A Paris Anderson served as a lieutenant in the Kilkenny militia in 1815, and a man of that name was living in Dublin in 1837. He seems to have been steeped in the lore of Kilkenny town, and his novel, *The Warden of the Marshes* (ca. 1840) is a historical piece with real local characters, such as Dame Alice Kyteler the witch. Stephen J. Brown remarks: "The author has built up his romance with much lore from archives and from legends, and describes carefully the manners, dress, etc. of the period. This is perhaps the chief interest of the book."

WORK: *The Warden of the Marshes*. Kilkenny: Printed at the Moderator Office, [ca. 1840].

ANSTER, JOHN [MARTIN] (1793–1867), translator and poet. Anster was born at Charleville, County Cork. He received a B.A. from Trinity College, Dublin, in 1816, was called to the Irish Bar in 1824, and received an LL.D. in 1825. His *Poems. With Some Translations from the German* (1819) contained a fragment of *Faust,* which was praised by Goethe. This encouraged Anster to produce the first complete translation in English (1835, 1864). Of it, Arthur Symons wrote, "John Anster besides writing some valueless verse of his own, did a translation of Goethe's 'Faust' which remains one of the best for lightness of touch on rhymes and rhythm.'' Anster's original verse is hardly as valueless as Symons suggested. Consider, for instance, the sonnet "If I Might Choose":

If I might choose where my tired limbs shall lie
When my task here is done, the oak's green crest
    Shall rise above my grave—a little mound,
Raised in some cheerful village cemetery.
And I could wish, that, with unceasing sound,
A lonely mountain rill was murmuring by—
    In music—through the long soft twilight hours.
And let the hand of her, whom I love best,
    Plant round the bright green grave those fragrant flowers
In whose deep bells the wild-bee loves to rest;
    And should the robin from some neighboring tree
Pour his enchanted song—oh! softly tread,
For sure, if aught of earth can soothe the dead,
    He still must love that pensive melody!

Milton it is not; valueless it is not either.

Anster was regius professor of civil law at Trinity from 1850 until his death in Dublin on June 9, 1867.

WORKS: *Ode to Fancy. With Other Poems.* Dublin: Milliken, 1815; *Lines on the Death of Her Royal Highness the Princess Charlotte of Wales.* . . . Dublin: R. Milliken/London: Longman, 1818. (Poetry pamphlet); *Poems. With Some Translations from the German.* Edinburgh: Blackwood/London: Cadell & Davies/Dublin: R. Milliken, 1819; tr., *Faustus, A Dramatic Mystery; The Bride of Corinth; The First Walpurgis Night.* London: Longman, 1835; *Xeniola. Poems including Translations from Schiller and de la Motte-Fouque.* Dublin: Milliken, 1837; *Introductory Lecture on the Study of the Roman Civil Law.* Dublin: Hodges & Smith, 1850; *Faustus, the Second Part, from the German of Goethe.* London: Longman, 1864; "German Literature at the Close of the Last Century and the Commencement of the Present" in *The Afternoon Lectures on Literature and Art.* . . . London: Bell & Daldy/Dublin: Hodges & Smith. 1864, pp. 151–195.

AOSDÁNA. Aosdána, which might be translated as "the artistic kind of person," is a government-sponsored group of Irish artists. It was largely the brainchild of Anthony Cronin* when he was cultural adviser to the Fianna Fail Taoiseach, Charles J. Haughey, and of Colm Ó Briain of the Arts Council. Its makeup and function are well described in a press release by the group in February 1993:

Aosdána was established by the Arts Council with the support of government in 1981. It was originally envisaged as attempting to address the neglect of many Irish artists including writers, painters, sculptors and composers who were contributing enormously to artistic and cultural life in Ireland but who did not have their contributions properly recognised. Additionally, many of our artists at the time were living in poor circumstances and Aosdána introduced a facility whereby artists can benefit from a subsidy (based on a means test) to allow them [to] work full-time at their art.

The membership of Aosdána is limited and there are now 150 members [more recently raised to 200]. Members must be of one of the creative artforms in literature, visual art or music. An artist becomes a member of Aosdána through an election process and for the next number of years no more than five members can be elected in any one year. At the moment of the 150 members 83 are in receipt of the annual subsidy (called a Cnuas) which is currently valued at £8,000 per annum. The Cnuas is tax-free under Section 2 of 1969 Finance Act which allows the income from the work of artists free of income tax.

The members may also elect as many as five of their number as Saoi (or someone eminent, a seer or wise man). The Saoithe thus far have included Samuel Beckett,* Sean O'Faolain,* Mary Lavin,* Benedict Kiely, and the painters Patrick Collins, Louis le Brocquy, and Tony O'Malley. Although not confined to literary artists, Aosdána has, in effect, taken over the function of the now-dormant Irish Academy of Letters.*

ARBUCKLE, JAMES (ca. 1700–1742), essayist, poet, and journalist. A native of Belfast, Arbuckle studied at the University of Glasgow, published in 1717 a poem called "Snuff," and was a friend of the Scottish poet Allan Ramsay. In Dublin, as "Hibernicus," he contributed to, and for a couple of years edited, James Carson's *Dublin Weekly Journal.* A Dublin broadside of 1725 or 1726 titled "The Printers Petition to the Poetical Senate Assembled in Grub-Street" lampoons his work as editor thusly:

> Arbuckle writes in's *Wee[k]ly Journal*
> How *Phoebus* rose and set diurnal,
> A motto takes from *Rome* or *Greece,*
> A venerable Frontispiece,
> He tells how forty Thousand Men
> Arose, and went to bed again,
> And mixes true News with what's Spurious,
> To please the Ignorant and the Curious.
> Yet after all this Stir and Pother,
> The *Journal* soon became BumFodder. . . .

He ceased to be editor on March 25, 1727, but his rather tedious "Hibernicus" papers were published in two volumes in London under the title of *Letters and Essays on Several Subjects Published in the Dublin Journal.* Robert Munter in *The History of the Irish Newspaper, 1685–1760* remarked that they "were written in a vigorous but unsubtle style, his obvious aim being to teach virtue in a way that the public could not possibly misunderstand." Such good intentions did not save him from considerable contemporary ridicule as in the broadsides "Wit upon Crutches, or, the Biter Bitten" and "The Last and Dying Words of D-n A-rb-kle, author of 'The Weekly Journal.' " He also wrote the short-lived periodical *The Tribune* in 1729, the authorship of which has occasionally been mistakenly attributed to Patrick Delany.* A poem entitled "A Funeral Apotheosis on the Tribunes," which celebrates the demise of *The Tribune* is attributed, probably wrongly, to Swift* by F. Elrington Ball. One of Arbuckle's own most effective poems, "Momus Mistaken," is, however, a defense of Swift. Despite much contemporary satire about him, Arbuckle is generally considered a significant force in developing the Irish newspaper. After 1729, he worked no more in journalism, and apparently he died intestate on January 16, 1742, and was then described in contemporary papers as a clerk in the Custom House and Quit Rent Office.

PRINCIPAL WORKS: "Snuff, a Poem" (Glasgow, 1717); "An Epistle to the Right Honourable Thomas Earl of Hadington, on the Death of Joseph Addison, Esq." (London, 1719); "Glotta, a Poem Humbly Inscribed to the Right Honourable the Marquess of Carnarvon" (Glasgow, 1721); with others, *A Collection of Letters and Essays on Several Subjects, Lately Publish'd in the Dublin Journal.* 2 vols. London, 1729/rpt., New York: Garland, 1970; *Hibernicus's Letters: or, a Philosophical Miscellany.* 2d ed. 2 vols. London, 1734; "Momus Mistaken: A Fable, Occasioned by the Publication of the Works of the Revd. Dr. Swift, D.S.P.D. in Dublin" (Dublin, 1735); "A Poem Inscribed to the Dublin Society" (Dublin, 1737). REFERENCES: "The Bibliographical Society of Ireland" [Report of a talk by T.P.C. Kirkpatrick] in *The Irish Book Lover,* 26 (May 1939): 103–104; Coleborne, Bryan. "James Arbuckle and Jonathan Swift: New Light on Swift's Biography" in *Studies in the Eighteenth Century,* 6, Colin Duckworth & Homer Le Grand, eds., published in *Eighteenth-Century Life,* 11, n.s. 1 (February 1987): 170–180; Woolley, James. "Arbuckle's 'Panegyrick' and Swift's Scrub Libel: The Documentary Evidence" in *Contemporary Studies of Swift's Poetry,* John Irwin Fisher & Donald C. Mell, eds. (Newark: University of Delaware Press, 1981), pp. 191–209; Woznak, John F. "James Arbuckle and the *Dublin Weekly Journal*" in *The Journal of Irish Literature* 22 (May 1993): 46–52.

ARCHDEACON, MATTHEW (1800?–1853?), fiction writer. Archdeacon was born in Castlebar, County Mayo, and was a teacher.

WORKS: *Connaught, A Tale of 1798.* Dublin: M. Archdeacon, 1830; *Everard: An Irish Tale of the XIXth Century.* 2 vols. Dublin: M. Archdeacon, 1835; *Legends of Connaught.* Dublin: J. Cumming, 1839; *The Priest-Hunter.* Dublin: J. Duffy, 1844. (Another edition of the same year has the title *Shawn na Soggarth; or, The Priest Hunter.*)

ARCHER, NUALA (1955–   ), poet and anthologist. Archer was born to Irish parents in Rochester, New York, on June 21, 1955. The family lived briefly in Canada, Costa Rica, and Ecuador before settling in Panama for most of the 1960s. Archer went to high school in Texas and received her B.A. in British and American literature from Wheaton College in Illinois, then studied Anglo-Irish literature at Trinity College, Dublin, in 1977–1978, and taught in Ireland and the United States while working toward her Ph.D., which she received in 1983 from the University of Wisconsin at Milwaukee. After graduation, she taught literature and writing and edited *The Midland Review* at Oklahoma State University until 1989; she then spent a year teaching in New Haven, Connecticut, at Yale and Albertus Magnus before being named director of the Poetry Center at Cleveland State University in 1992.

Irish women's writing, as a discernible category for study and discussion, may be said to date from Archer's winter 1986 special issue of *The Midland Review.* The volume collected the works of more than forty women writers, including a number of since-distinguished figures—such as Moya Cannon,* Roz

Cowman,* and Mary Dorcey*—who had not then published their first books. Archer's introduction acknowledged the precedent of Ruth Hooley's 1985 anthology of Northern Irish women's works, *The Female Line;* but here in the *Review* were, as Archer wrote, "women of the Republic of Ireland as well as of Northern Ireland, Catholic women, Protestant, Jewish, Atheist, married, single, separated, with and without children, old and young, dole-destitute and salaried, straight as well as lesbian women, native-born women, women who are returning from exile and/or emigration, as well as those women who have come from different countries, cultures and languages to make Ireland their home," women represented by their poetry, fiction, essays, and drama—all, Archer said, representing "a new vision, . . . new ways of life for Irish society as a whole." The principles of selection for subsequent anthologies of writing by Irishwomen have never matched Archer's breadth and generosity (and, indeed, Archer herself, a lesbian born and living abroad who has ventured into unusual forms like the prose poem, has rarely since been included or mentioned). Though published in journal rather than book form and in the United States rather than Ireland, Archer's collection might well claim the title of the most important anthology of new Irish writing to be published in the 1980s.

She described herself in the introduction as "both an immigrant and an emigrant," and Archer's most important poetic contribution has been to offer an aesthetic that derives joy and energy from that exiled condition. Medbh McGuckian* has attributed to Archer a "restless and often painful search for rootedness," but a more apt characterization might be Robin Becker's: Archer, she says, "has been developing a poetics to examine displacement—geographical, social, and sexual." "There is no need for a home," wrote Archer in "Riding Out a Storm," one of the poems in her 1981 *Whale on the Line.*

That first volume, which won the 1980 Irish Distillers/Patrick Kavanagh Award, features a series of poems focused on movement—"Passing By," "Rocking," "Walking"—in lines that seem nevertheless relatively uniform and restrained. But by the time of the poems Archer contributed to *Two Women, Two Shores, Poems by Medbh McGuckian and Nuala Archer* (1989), she had found a great variety of fluid, flexible poetic forms. Here she offers a wonderful linguistic self-reflexiveness, asking, in "Between Swilly and Sewanee," "Who is the mother of these words?" In one of the volume's three concluding poems, each written "From a Mobile Home," Archer says, "I wanted us / to slide down each worded knot toward / whatever joys so always and difficult / to express." The Joycean wordplay, lists of place-names, and meditations on exile in Archer's poems in this volume suggest that she has discovered a bountiful and itinerant sense of place.

"What kind of home?" Archer asks in "Here in Oklahoma," the answer to be generated only by displaced syllables: "Did I say I was so low and la? / So low and la? Did I say / so Lola and here in Oklahoma? . . . / Did I say Okla? / Oklahoma? Homa? Homa?" Archer's next book finds a comparable home in her childhood residence: *The Hour of Pan/Amá* (1992) shows her particularly interested in "the ellipses / between *Pa* and *Ma.*" Archer is a gifted photographer and painter, but the visual sensibility of *The Hour of Pan/Amá* is mostly cinematic, the book's perspective shifting rapidly to encompass, seemingly, every available visual sign. (One poem is entitled "%%%%%%.") The suggestion implicit in Archer's early works, that wordplay entails both heady freedom and great risk, is rendered more explicit here: "Weird Little Wordless Words" may sound like a title for light verse, but those words, though "like fresh-scented breath," turn out to be "soft lips, pagan clits, / responding to memory's tongue / transforming the debris / of incest into living flesh" are far from harmless. Archer's language of dislocation registers both great pain and as strong a faith as is to be found in contemporary Irish writing. In "Barbed Wire / Blessed / Thistle," she writes:

> with this noise,
> this blowing, this breathing, this lamp
> unto our barbed-wired feet burning brightly
> I bring back, with you & you & you, into
> the land of the living, the breathing books
> of our belonging. Together we call
> into being our every being.

VICTOR LUFTIG

WORKS: *Whale on the Line.* Dublin: Gallery, 1981; ed., *The Midland Review* 3 (Winter 1986) (a Contemporary Irish Women's Writing number); with Medbh McGuckian. *Two Women, Two Shores.* Baltimore: New Poets Series/Galway: Salmon, 1989; *The Hour of Pan/Amá.* Galway: Salmon, 1992; *Pan/Amá.* New York: Red Dust, 1992; *From a Mobile Home.* Dublin: Salmon, 1995.

ARMITAGE, MARIGOLD (1920s–   ), novelist. Eldest daughter of Sir Arthur Harris, Armitage was born on a Royal Air Force (RAF) station in Lincolnshire. After her marriage, she lived in Tipperary and Limerick but now lives in England.

WORKS: *A Long Way to Go: An Anglo-Irish Near-tragedy.* London: Faber, 1952/London: Robin Clark, 1989; *A Motley to the View.* London: Faber, 1961.

ARMSTRONG, GEORGE FRANCIS SAVAGE. *See* SAVAGE-ARMSTRONG, GEORGE FRANCIS.

ARNOLD, BRUCE (1936–   ), novelist, literary and political editor, art critic, and historian. Arnold was born in London on September 6, 1936, and educated at Kingham Hill School, Oxfordshire, and at Trinity College, Dublin (1957–1961), where he took an honors degree in modern languages (English and French).

He joined the *Irish Times* in November 1961 and was a staff journalist there until 1965, when he became freelance and worked as well for the *Irish Press,* the *Sunday Independent,* and *Hibernia.* He edited the *Dubliner,* a literary journal, and from 1962 to 1968 was correspondent for the *Guardian.* He wrote widely for other papers, journals, and periodicals in Britain and did much lecturing as well as radio and television work. In 1972, he joined the *Irish Independent* as political commentator and parliamentary correspondent. He wrote frequently on politics during the 1970s and early 1980s, twice winning an award for an outstanding contribution to journalism. In 1986, he became London editor of the *Irish Independent* before returning the following year to Dublin to become literary editor of the paper. His work in all three journalistic spheres—art, literature, and politics—continues, exemplifying in each an appropriate independence of judgment.

He is the author of the four novels of the Coppinger sequence: *A Singer at the Wedding* (1978), *The Song of the Nightingale* (1980), *The Muted Swan* (1981), and *Running to Paradise* (1983). Their picture of a youth and young manhood in the 1940s, 1950s, and 1960s is as valuable as social history as it is art. The "cold-eyed," motherless narrator's account of his time at Coppinger, of his relations with his sister, his preferred older brother, his father's women, and the outrageous but loved father, George, bears comparison with other romans-fleuves like Anthony Powell's *Music of Time* sequence and Waugh's *Sword of Honour.* The unnamed narrator is as much a slave to duty as W. S. Gilbert's Frederick and, in spite of humiliation, moral blackmail, and ingratitude, remains filial. The last novel of the tetralogy ends where the first began, with George's death, the lingering final illness being described in unsparing detail and stoic acceptance. The twenty-eight-year-old narrator, like his creator an art historian, can at last honorably relinquish his burden and face with equanimity the post-Camelot days after Dallas.

Other works by Arnold reflect his prevailing passions: *A Concise History of Irish Art* (1969); *Orpen: Mirror to an Age* (1969), a biography of the important Anglo-Irish painter Sir William Orpen (1878–1931); a shorter life of the same artist, *William Orpen* (1991), and *An Art Atlas of Britain and Ireland* in the same year. The year 1991 also saw *Mainie Jellet and the Modern Movement in Ireland,* an account of the Irish cubist abstract painter (1897–1944). His preoccupation with politics engendered *What Kind of Country* (1984), an account of Irish political life in the years 1963–1983; *Margaret Thatcher: A Study in Power* (1984), and *Haughey: His Life and Unlucky Deeds* (1993), an account of Ireland's most colorful prime minister. He published *The Scandal of* Ulysses, an anatomy of the publishing history of James Joyce's* most famous novel in 1991. It formed the subject matter of one of three films Arnold made. Others were *Images of Joyce* and *To Make It Live: Mainie Jellett 1897–1944.*

Married with three children, he is currently writing the authorized biography of the Irish artist Jack B. Yeats.*

SEAN McMAHON

WORKS: *A Concise History of Irish Art.* London: Thames & Hudson, 1959; *A Singer at the Wedding.* London: Hamish Hamilton, 1978. (Novel); *The Song of the Nightingale.* London: Hamish Hamilton, 1980. (Novel); *The Muted Swan.* London: Hamish Hamilton, 1981. (Novel); *Running to Paradise.* London: Hamish Hamilton, 1983. (Novel); *Orpen: Mirror to an Age.* London: Cape,

1981; *What Kind of Country.* London: Cape, 1984; *Margaret Thatcher: A Study in Power.* London: Hamish Hamilton, 1984; *An Art Atlas of Britain and Ireland.* London: Viking Penguin, 1991; *William Orpen.* Dublin: Town House, 1991; *The Scandal of* Ulysses. London: Sinclair Stevenson, 1991/New York: St. Martin's, 1992; *Mainie Jellett and the Modern Movement in Ireland.* London: Yale University Press, 1991/New York: Yale University Press, 1992; *Haughey: His Life and Unlucky Deeds.* London: HarperCollins, 1993. REFERENCE: Kiely, Benedict. "The Coppinger Novels of Bruce Arnold." *Hollins Critic* 21 (April 1984): 1–12.

ASHE, THOMAS (1770–1835), novelist and travel writer. Ashe was born in Glasnevin near Dublin, on July 15, 1770, the third son of a half-pay officer. He received a commission in the 83rd regiment of foot, but on its being shortly disbanded, he was sent to a countinghouse in Bordeaux. There he was briefly imprisoned for having wounded in a duel a man whose sister he had seduced. The wound proving not fatal, Ashe was released and returned to Dublin as secretary of the Diocesan and Endowed Schools Commission. Amassing debts, however, he resigned and retired to the Continent and spent several years in foreign travel, even as far afield as North and South America. Among his novels, *The Spirit of "The Book"; or, Memoirs of Caroline, Princess of Hasburgh* (1811), was popular enough to go through several editions and abridgements. Impoverished in his later years, he died in Bath on December 17, 1835.

WORKS: *Travels in America. . . .* 3 vols. London: Richard Phillips, 1808; *The Spirit of "The Book"; or, Memoirs of Caroline, Princess of Hasburgh.* 3 vols. London: Allen, 1811. (Novel); *The Liberal Critic.* 3 vols. London: B. & R. Crosby, 1812. (Novel); *A Commercial View and Geographical Sketch, of the Brasils in South America, and of the Island of Mediera.* London: Allen, 1812; *History of the Azores, or Western Islands.* London: Sherwood, Neely & Jones, 1813; *Memoirs and Confessions of Captain Ashe. . . .* 3 vols. London: Henry Colburn, 1814. (Autobiography); *The Soldier of Fortune.* 2 vols. London: Sherwood, Neely & Jones, 1816.

ASHTON, ROBERT (fl. ca. 1756), playwright. Ashton was the author of *The Battle of Aughrim; or, The Fall of M. St. Ruth* (1756), a play popular in Ireland for about 100 years and going through some twenty-four editions until 1839. Although written from the Orange point of view, Sarsfield was heroically depicted, and the play became immensely popular among Catholic audiences. In an 1841 edition, the editor, Rev. John Graham, says that the author was William Ashton, an eighteen-year-old student at Trinity College, Dublin. Stephen J. Brown, however, wonders if the author was not the Robert Aston who published several broadsides in 1725 and 1726, one of them "A Congratulatory Poem to Dean Swift.*"

WORK: *The Battle of Aughrim; or, The Fall of M. St. Ruth.* Dublin: W. Davis, 1756.

ATKINSON, JOSEPH (1743–1818), poet and dramatist. Atkinson was born in Dublin and became a captain in the army and secretary of the Ordnance Board. His plays were based on French sources, but *The Mutual Deception,* which he produced in Dublin, appeared also at the Haymarket. His poems sometimes describe Irish scenes, such as Killarney and Wicklow. However, Tom Moore,* who wrote his epitaph, also described him as "my old friend and bad brother poet."

WORKS: *Congratulatory Ode to General Sir William Howe, on His Return from America.* Dublin: James Hoey, 1778; *The Mutual Deception.* London: Dilly, 1785. (Comedy after Marivaux); *A Match for a Widow; or, The Frolics of Fancy.* London: Dilly, 1786. (Musical comedy after Patrat); *Killarny [sic].* Dublin: Thomas Ewing, 1790?/*Killarney.* Dublin: W. Porter, 1798; *Love in a Blaze.* Dublin: W. Porter, 1799. (Musical comedy after Lafont); *A Poetic Excursion.* Dublin: R. Milliken, 1818.

ATKINSON, SARA (1823–1893), writer on religious and historical subjects. Atkinson was born Sara Gaynor in Athlone on October 13, 1823. She married George Atkinson, part-owner of *The Freeman's Journal.* According to such friends as Katharine Tynan* and Rosa Mulholland, she was a sweet and pious lady much given to charitable good works. She died in Dublin on July 8, 1893.

Atkinson's life of Mary Aikenhead contains much out-of-the-way information about the Penal days and was commended by W.E.H. Lecky.* Her posthumous *Essays* contain lives of O'Curry, John Hogan, and John Henry Foley, as well as of St. Brigid, St. Fursey, and Dervorgilla. Today, however, her works probably are read only for their subject matter.

WORKS: *Mary Aikenhead,* by S. A. Dublin: Gill, 1875/2d ed., revised, 1882; *Essays,* with a memoir by Rosa Mulholland Gilbert. Dublin: Gill, 1895.

B

BALFOUR, MARY (ca. 1775–ca. 1820), poet and playwright. The date of Mary Balfour's birth is contested; as D. J. O'Donoghue* says she was "probably born on 24 January 1775," while other sources suggest that she was born as late as 1780 (O'Donoghue, p. 17). She was the daughter of a Protestant clergyman who had obtained his position through the assistance of the earl of Bristol. Following the death of her parents, she opened a school in Limavady and assumed the responsibility of caring for her younger sisters. She was living in Limavady when *Hope* was published in 1810. By 1813, she had moved to Belfast and had again opened a school, reportedly at the junction of Castle Place and Castle Street. Although the Belfast school was initially successful, it closed after a few years. Her melodrama *Kathleen O'Neill* was performed at the Belfast Theatre in 1814 and published anonymously in the same year. Mary Balfour died unmarried, around 1820, in Belfast. Biographical and critical information about her sometimes refers to her simply as Mary of Belfast. Her poetic translations from the Irish vary in their adherence to the original text, and she was known for writing English lyrics to old Irish airs.

ANNE COLMAN

WORKS: *Hope, a Poetical Essay; with Various Other Poems.* Belfast: Smyth & Lyons, 1810; *Kathleen O'Neil, A Grand National Melodrama.* Belfast: Archbold & Duncan, 1814. REFERENCE: O'Donoghue, D. J. *Poets of Ireland.* Dublin: Hodges Figgis/London: Henry Frowde, Oxford University Press, 1912.

BANIM, JOHN (1798–1842) and **BANIM, MICHAEL** (1796–1874), novelists. Born in Kilkenny on April 3, 1798, John Banim was the guiding force in shaping the O'Hara stories, a project completed with the close cooperation of his older brother Michael, who was born in Kilkenny on August 5, 1796. The brothers were given good educations by their father, a prosperous farmer and merchant, and very early their different temperaments received special training.

Michael, the more pragmatic, at first read for the bar, but later was forced to go into business to cover his father's losses; John, the more artistic, was sent in 1813 to Dublin, where he studied drawing at the Academy of the Royal Dublin Society. After returning to Kilkenny, John taught drawing and fell deeply in love. This brief but romantic attachment, cut short by the girl's death, was the turning point in his career, for he began to devote himself to literature.

After a long poem, "The Celt's Paradise" (February 1821), in which he drew upon his early familiarity with Irish mythology, John wrote an unsuccessful drama, *Turgesius,* and the successful *Damon and Pythias.* The latter was performed at Covent Garden on May 28, 1821, with Charles Kemble and William Charles Macready in the chief roles. After several unsuccessful tragedies drawing on non-Irish material, John suggested to his brother that they collaborate on a series of Irish tales in the style of Sir Walter Scott.

During the following decade, John and Michael, as the O'Hara Brothers, created the novels that earned John the title the Scott of Ireland. But success was bittersweet for both brothers. John, who had married in 1822, suffered from a progressive spinal disease that made him a cripple by 1829 and caused his death on August 13, 1842. Meanwhile, Michael, who had been a prosperous trader, lost his fortune in 1840–1841 through the failure of a merchant. Thereafter, he suffered delicate health while acting as postmaster for Kilkenny. He died in Booterstown on August 30, 1874, almost thirty-five years after his brother.

In their attempt in the 1820s to create a distinctive Anglo-Irish literature that would find a wide audience in England, John and Michael sought to make the Irish character sympathetic without falsifying it by excessive sentimentality. In their twenty-four volumes, they portrayed Irish cabin life as a mixture of rich humor and lawlessness often verging on violence and even brutality. Although their writing occasionally is marred by an attempt to capture Irish speech in outlandishly garbled phonetic transcriptions and by catering to the English audience's desire for supernatural thrills, they present a portrait of Irish life that is historical in scope and realistic in depth. The mature works of the O'Hara Brothers readily fall into three categories. First are novels that deal with life in the cabin supposedly as it was at the time. *The Nowlans* (1826), *The Mayor of Wind-Gap* (1835), and *Father Connell* (1842) are among the most realistic and best written of these novels. In each of the novels in this category, the brothers take pains to place the characters in a world that is carefully and fully (sometimes too fully) detailed. Hence, the stories are sharp vignettes of pre-Famine cabin life merged into the Banims' melodramatic treatment of murder, betrayal, seduction, and the like. Second are a large number of works that attempt to join realism and otherworldliness. These novels—among them *Crohoore of the Bill-Hook* (1825), *The Fetches* (1825), and *The Ghost Hunter and His Family* (1831)—seek to bring what the Banims conceived of as Irish otherworldliness and folklore into the framework of English realism. The resulting hybrid satisfies neither component, though this kind of fusion fascinated many readers. Third, and perhaps most significant, are the Banims' historical novels—*The Boyne Water* (1826), *The Croppy* (1828), and *The Denounced* (1830). In these novels, the brothers analyze the crucial historical events that had shaped Ireland as they understood it—the Williamite Wars, the Penal Age, and the Rebellion of 1798. Seeking in these events the causes for Ireland's problems in the 1820s, they wrote with maturity and insight.

While today largely forgotten, John and Michael Banim share an important niche in the development of the Anglo-Irish novel. Coming between Maria Edgeworth* and William Carleton,* they helped the Irish novel evolve from its focus on the Big House to an emphasis on the "mere Irish." They imitated Scott but had neither his richness of style nor his depth of insight. Nevertheless, in their limited way they helped to prepare the audience for Griffin* and Carleton, and began to give English readers a faithful picture of cabin life.

MARK D. HAWTHORNE

WORKS—by John Banim: "The Celt's Paradise." London: John Warren, 1821. (Poem); *Damon and Pythias.* London: John Warren, 1821. (Tragedy in five acts); *Revelations of the Dead Alive.* London: J. Simpkin & R. Marshall, 1824; *The Sergeant's Wife.* London: T. H. Lacy, [1824]. (Drama in two acts); *The Fetches.* London: Simpkin & Marshall, 1825. Vol. 2 of *Tales by the O'Hara Family; The Nowlans.* London: Colburn: 1826. Vols. 1 & 2 of *Tales by the O'Hara Family.* 2d Series; *The Anglo Irish of the XIXth Century.* 3 vols. London: Colburn, 1828; *The Denounced.* 3 vols. London: Colburn & Bentley, 1830; *The Smuggler.* 3 vols. London: Colburn & Bentley, 1831. by Michael Banim: *Crohoore of the Bill-Hook.* London: Simpkin & Marshall, 1825. Vol. 1 & part of Vol. 2 of *Tales by the O'Hara Family; The Croppy.* London: Colburn, 1828; *The Ghost-Hunter and His Family.* London: Smith, Elder, 1833; *The Mayor of Windgap.* 3 vols. London: Saunders & Otley, 1835; *The Town of the Cascade.* 2 vols. London: Chapman & Hall, 1864. by John and Michael in collaboration: *John Doe.* London: Simpkin & Marshall, 1825. Vol. 3 of *Tales by the O'Hara Family; Peter of the Castle.* London: Colburn, 1826. Vol. 3 of *Tales by the O'Hara Family.* 2d Series; *The Bit o' Writing and Other Tales.* 3 vols. London: Saunders & Otley, 1838; *Father Connell.* 3 vols. London: Newby & Boone, 1842. There is no full or scholarly edition of the Banims' novels, nor is there any definitive study of the attribution. The fullest collection is *The Works of the O'Hara Family,* collected by Michael Banim (New York: D. & J. Sadlier, 1869).   REFERENCES: Cahalan, J. M. *Great Hatred, Little Room: The Irish Historical Novel.* Syracuse: Syracuse University Press/Dublin: Gill & Macmillan, 1984; Cahalan, J. M. *The Irish Historical Novel: A Critical History.* Dublin: Gill & Macmillan, 1989; Flanagan, Thomas. *The Irish Novelists, 1800–1850.* New York: Columbia University Press, 1959; Hawthorne, Mark D. *John and Michael Banim ("the O'Hara Brothers").* Salzburg, Austria: Institut fur Englische Sprache und Literatur, 1975; Murray, Patrick Joseph. *The Life of John Banim . . . with Extracts from His Correspondence . . . Also, Selections from His Poems.* London: Lay, 1857; Sloan, Barry. *The Pioneers of Irish Fiction 1800–1850.* Gerrards Cross: Colin Smythe/Totowa, N.J.: Barnes & Noble, 1986.

BANNISTER, IVY (1951–   ), playwright and short story writer. Bannister was born in New York City on July 11, 1951, and received her B.A. from Smith College and her Ph.D. from Trinity College, Dublin. Several of her plays have received rehearsed readings at the Peacock and the Project, and others have been broadcast by RTÉ Radio. As a dramatist, she has received the O. Z. Whitehead Award, the Listowel Award, and the P. J. O'Connor Award. Her one published play thus far is *The Wilde Circus Show,* which treats of the early life of Oscar Wilde's* family by, in part, using the metaphor of various circus acts. Several of Bannister's plays utilize similar clever devices, such as two actresses in *The Rebel Countess* to portray Countess Markievicz. Rather in the manner of Hugh Leonard's* *Da,* one actress plays the mature countess, and the other the young one. Bannister's ideas, however, do not always disguise the problem of her plays often being static expositions rather than dramatic actions. Her often droll dialogue goes far to mitigate this flaw; and, indeed, her superb sense of comedy—except for the excellent Casimir de Markievicz in *The Rebel Countess*—is too little apparent in her plays.

Bannister has also been a prolific short story writer, and her well-crafted and often moving stories have received many awards—among them the Hennessy, the *IT*/Mills and Boon, the *Image*/Maxwell House, and the Francis MacManus. Her first collection, *Magician,* appeared in 1996.

WORKS: *The Wilde Circus Show. The Journal of Irish Literature* 19 (September 1990); *Magician.* [Dublin]: Poolbeg, [1996].

BANVILLE, JOHN (1945–   ), novelist, short story writer, and playwright. Banville, born in Wexford on December 8, 1945, was educated at Christian Brothers' schools and St. Peter's College in Wexford. He has worked in journalism since 1969 and has been literary editor of the *Irish Times* since 1988. He is married to Janet Durham, and they have two sons, Colm and Douglas. He lives in Howth, County Dublin. Banville has published a number of short stories in literary magazines and nine books of fiction. His adaptation of Heinrich von Kleist's *Der zerbrochene Krug* (The Broken Jug) was premiered in Dublin at the Peacock in June 1994. He is a member of Aosdána.*

Banville's first book, *Long Lankin* (1970), consists of nine short stories and the novella *The Possessed.* Thematically, the narratives have at least two aspects in common: they feature characters who are caught in the hell of a peculiar guilt, and in each a particular persona acts as the Long Lankin figure, intruding upon human relationships and severing them. Long Lankin was a mason in an old Scottish ballad ("Lamkin" in F. J. Child's *The English and Scottish Popular Ballads,* Vol. 2) who, seeking revenge for not having been paid by Lord Wearie, forces his way into the lord's castle and kills Wearie's wife and son. The narratives are grouped with respect to the age of the principal characters—childhood, adolescence, middle age—and the area of public life, recalling the organizing principle of Joyce's* *Dubliners. The Possessed* focuses on the "public life." Livia Gold, who punishes herself for the death of her small son, holds a very Irish party. Present at the party, in addition to characters from the stories, are Ben White, a writer, and his sister, Flora, for whom he has incestuous feelings. Their make-believe world has maimed them both, rendering it impossible for them to act without being bruised by reality. White acts as a catalyst for the others, each of whom is seeking to be cleansed. The novella is indebted to Joyce and, even more so, to the great Russian novelists, especially to Dostoevsky and his novel *The Devils* (1871), also known by the title of *The Pos-*

sessed. Long Lankin, above all on account of the novella (which Banville did not include in the revised edition of 1984), may have certain flaws as a result of Banville's thinking he was being sophisticated when he was not, but the book clearly marked the debut of a major writer.

The title of his first novel, *Nightspawn* (1971), involves a pun: "night spawn," "night's pawn," and "knight's pawn," heralding the ludic nature of the whole book. *Nightspawn* plays with literary conventions in order to show their exhaustive nature. *Nightspawn* is an inside-out novel, one of the very few metanovels to have come out of Ireland. Ben White tells of a coup d'état in Greece and his embroilment therein. White is a writer; in fact, he is Ben White of *The Possessed,* and he succeeds in working his account into a gripping thriller. But *Nightspawn* is anything but a straitlaced thriller; it is a parody of the narrative genre. Most scenes end in farce. Behind all the parodying, the playful turning upside-down of conventions and self-reflexive commenting, there lies a most serious intention: the age-old desire of the artist to express the things in their essence, to transfix beauty and truth. Like Beckett's* narrators, White permanently urges himself on "to express it all." But he fails, is bound to fail, because every artist must necessarily fail in this respect, beauty and truth defying his efforts.

A similar predicament underlies *Birchwood* (1973). The novel treats of the fall of the big house Birchwood and its inhabitants, the Godkins. Gabriel Godkin, the sole survivor of the family, searches among the madeleines of his memories for the sense of his life. He himself speaks of madeleines, thus slyly referring to Marcel Proust's masterwork *A la recherche du temps perdu.* Like Marcel in Proust's novel, Gabriel strives to come to terms with his life by writing it down in the form of a sustained narrative. Since Birchwood was a big house, what would be better than to employ the conventions of the big house novel? In his hands, though, these take a parodic turn, thus making it plain that they are ill equipped for getting at the truth. He exploits other genres (e.g., the Gothic, the picaresque), building up an intricate clockwork structure. But in the end, he feels constrained to acknowledge his failure. The "rosy grail," the symbol of beauty and truth, has eluded him. He has been only a wizard with words, a magician who has conjured up a world in which chaos, coincidences, sleight-of-hand, and dark laughter hold sway. Gabriel accepts this with Wittgensteinian despair, knowing that whereof he cannot speak thereof he must be silent.

Doctor Copernicus (1976), *Kepler* (1981), *The Newton Letter* (1982), and *Mefisto* (1986) make up Banville's "scientific" tetralogy. The first two novels chart the lives of the two famous astronomers, adhering faithfully to the historical facts. But *Copernicus* and *Kepler* are no historical novels in the strict sense; the historical reconstruction is just a means to a different end. Here, as in *The Newton Letter* and *Mefisto,* the main concern is with communicating a particular idea. Kepler and Copernicus are representatives of what *The Newton Letter* terms "those high cold heroes who renounced the world and human happiness to pursue the big game of the intellect.'' They sought to explain the world by means of unifying systems, gearing their whole lives toward that one goal. Finally, however, they are forced to accept that their theories are only supreme fictions, of great beauty and harmony, for which they have sacrificed their humaneness. It is not enough to spend one's life gazing at the stars; the most important thing is to live and establish genuine human relationships. Copernicus wants to *explain* the phenomena, no longer simply save them. Languishing away after an apoplectic stroke, he realizes that, in order to do so, he had to use language, the great falsifier, for words are not the thing themselves. Even more painfully, he becomes aware of never in his life having formed a true relationship with any human soul. ''[W]e *are* the truth. The world, and ourselves, this is the truth. There is no other,'' his brother, Andreas, tells him before Copernicus dies, and he accepts this insight with redemptive despair.

The historian in *The Newton Letter,* the third of Banville's ''cold heroes,'' has rented the lodge of a big house in the south of Ireland to put the finishing touches to his biography of Newton, yet another cold hero. He comes into contact with the people who live on the estate and dreams up horrid dramas around them that have no basis in fact, thus failing to see the tragedy that is playing itself out in real life. Although he contracts not to be known, he becomes embroiled in a love affair that is modeled on the central character constellation in Goethe's *Elective Affinities.* Furthermore, like Hugo von Hofmannsthal's Lord Chandos, he finds himself overwhelmed by the commonplace, that strangest of phenomena, and he gives up work on his book.

Gabriel Swan's Faustian efforts in *Mefisto* aim at accounting for the world in terms of numbers. But the chaos of life through which he is led by the Mephistophelian Felix defies him, and he decides to leave everything to chance. Yet, Gabriel is a cunning old fox. Like his namesake in *Birchwood,* he tells his own story and tells it in such a way that everywhere mirror-symmetries and parallelisms result. Thus, the novel's two parts correspond as far as characters and events are concerned; the opening is mirrored by the ending. The world of *Mefisto,* apart from being a negative version of Goethe's *Faust,* is indebted to recent ideas in computer mathematics and chaos theory (cf. fractals, binary patterns, palindromes, chaos turning into order and vice versa). In addition, this world is Mephistophelian, imbued by Nietzsche's dictum that God is dead. Man is denied redemption, because he lacks God's mercy.

The tetralogy investigates the scientific imagination and finds it closely related to the creative, artistic imagination. *The Book of Evidence* (1989) and *Ghosts* (1993), the first two novels in Banville's projected ''artistic'' trilogy, deal with how the imagination of the artist operates upon reality. Freddie Montgomery, in *The Book of Evidence,* murders a young woman who comes upon him while he is stealing a painting, a portrait of a Dutch woman, with which he is hopelessly infatuated. He is now in prison awaiting his trial; and, knowing that he will not be given a proper chance to explain his heinous deed, he writes his ''book of evidence.'' Essentially, though, this book represents an attempt to bring the young woman, whom he says he could kill because he did not imagine her vividly enough, back to life. The manner in which Freddie goes about his task is highly significant. While in prison, he has developed into an expert on seventeenth-century Dutch painting, and to a large extent he views the world with the eye of a painter. Moreover, he transfixes his own life and that of his victim by caging them in art, literature, and films, with a large number of intertextual echoes, the most telling ones being of Nabokov's *Lolita*. In fact, Freddie's narrative procedure is strongly reminiscent of Humbert Humbert's. He, too, makes amends by transfiguring his victim in a work of art. Again Nietzschean ideas, especially those on morals, permeate the book. But, above all, *The Book of Evidence* asks, What is there to express when life is apprehended through a particular kind of poetic imagination? Freddie's redemption, if redemption it is, lies in an acknowledgment of the disjunction that exists between the artistic and the commonplace world and the impossibility of ever bridging the gap.

If *The Book of Evidence* is, to a large extent, about the world as perceived by the artistic imagination, then *Ghosts* is about the world as *created* by the artistic imagination. After his release from prison (delineated in Part II), Freddie Montgomery has come to a penitential island. There are intertextual references to *Robinson Crusoe* and *The Tempest*. Freddie is seeking atonement for his callous crime; he feels compelled—as he puts it at the end of *The Book of Evidence*—to bring the woman he killed back to life, and he attempts to do so by weaving a narrative around a group of shipwrecked pleasure trippers who spend a couple of hours on the island. A little world is gradually coming into being, one characterized by absences and a state of suspension, like ghosts who belong to neither the world of the living nor the world of the dead. It is the world of art and a world grounded in art: the commedia dell'arte and the *fêtes galantes* paintings of Jean-Antoine Watteau (1684–1721), who figures as the artist Vaublin—in short, the world of romance and pastoral.

Freddie feels he has forfeited his sense of being through his crime, and he seeks to find himself again by restoring the life of the young woman. But in the course of his imaginative efforts, he learns that he has to imagine himself first before he can imagine the woman, impersonating himself in a work of art, much in the sense in which being can be attained through narrative: confessional autobiography in the vein of St. Augustine's *Confessions* and Rousseau's autobiographical writings. Freddie is after "pure existence," but that can be accomplished only in, and through, a work of the imagination, in the autonomous world of art within our world—a world that belongs to neither the living nor the dead. Significantly, Freddie's little world offers a negative variant of pastoral, a dark Arcadia. The golden world has forever been lost in a post-Nietzschean universe governed by chance and chaos.

The Newton Letter was filmed for Channel 4 television as *Reflections*. Among the awards Banville's books have won are the Allied Irish Banks Fiction Prize, the American-Irish Foundation Award, the James Tait Black Memorial Prize, and the Guardian Fiction Prize. In 1989, *The Book of Evidence* was short-listed for the Booker Prize and was awarded the first Guinness Peat Aviation Award; in Italian, as *La Spiegazione dei Fatti,* the book was awarded the 1991 Premio Ennio Plaiano. *Ghosts* was short-listed for the Whitbread Fiction Prize in 1993.

RÜDIGER IMHOF

WORKS: *Long Lankin.* London: Secker & Warburg, 1970/rev. ed., Dublin: Gallery, 1984; *Nightspawn.* London: Secker & Warburg/New York: Norton, 1971/Oldcastle, Co. Meath: Gallery, 1993; *Birchwood.* London: Secker & Warburg, 1973/New York: Norton, 1994; *Doctor Copernicus.* London: Secker & Warburg/New York: Norton, 1976; *Kepler.* London: Secker & Warburg, 1981/ Boston: Godine, 1983; *The Newton Letter.* London: Secker & Warburg, 1982/Boston: Godine, 1987; *Mefisto.* London: Secker & Warburg, 1986/Boston: Godine, 1989; *The Book of Evidence.* London: Secker & Warburg, 1989/New York: Scribners, 1990; *Ghosts.* London: Secker & Warburg/New York: Knopf, 1993; *Athena.* London: Secker & Warburg, 1995. REFERENCES: Brown, Terence. "Redeeming the Time: The Novels of John Banville" in J. Acheson, ed., *The British and Irish Novel since 1960.* New York: St. Martin's, 1991, pp. 159–173; Cornwell, Neil. *The Literary Fantastic. From Gothic to Postmodernism.* New York: London: Harvester/Wheatsheaf, 1990, pp. 172–184; Cronin, Gearoid. "John Banville and the Subversion of the Big House Novel" in J. Genet, ed., *The Big House in Ireland. Reality and Representation.* Dingle, Co. Kerry: Brandon, 1991, pp. 251–260; Imhof, Rüdiger. *John Banville. A Critical Introduction.* Dublin: Wolfhound, 1989; *Irish University Review* (special Banville issue) 11 (Spring 1981); Lysaght, Sean. "Banville's Tetralogy: The Limits of Mimesis" in *Irish University Review* 21 (Spring/Summer 1991): 82–100; McMinn, Joseph. *John Banville. A Critical Study.* Dublin: Gill & Macmillan, 1991; McMinn, Joseph. "Naming the World: Language and Experience in John Banville's Fiction." *Irish University Review* 23 (Autumn/Winter 1993): 183–196; Swann, Joseph. "Banville's Faust" in D. E. Morse, C. Bertha & I. Palffy, eds., *A Small Nation's Contribution to the World: Essays on Anglo-Irish Literature and Language.* Gerrards Cross: Colin Smythe/Debrecen: Lajos Kossuth University, 1993, pp. 148–160.

BANVILLE, VINCENT (1940–   ), novelist. Banville was born in Wexford and graduated from University College, Dublin, in 1961. He taught in Nigeria for five years and has since taught and worked as a literary journalist in Dublin. He is a brother of John Banville.* His Nigerian years are used to powerful effect in *An End to Flight* (1973), a novel published under the name of Vincent Lawrence. This novel about the civil war in Nigeria caused by the declaration of an independent state of Biafra, is a grisly account of cruelty, torture, and murder. The protagonist, Michael Painter, an Irishman teaching in Nigeria, sinks into an apathetic malaise of not caring enough about anyone or anything to make a decision, even a decision to leave his village when all of the other Europeans are evacuated. After viewing horror upon horror, he does finally attempt to save a wounded friend, who, nevertheless, dies. A year later, back in Dublin, when the war has about concluded, he has reverted from a momentary caring to the view of what does it, or anything, matter? This is a grim, disturbing, and powerful book.

More recently, Banville has written a series of successful Irish children's stories and embarked on a series of detective thrillers set in Dublin. *Death by Design* (1993) uses the Raymond Chandler template of a battered and cynical private investigator whose urban setting is simply Philip Marlowe's seedy Los Angeles transmuted to today's seedy Dublin. Like Chandler, Banville uses a flip and breezy style, full of sardonic quips and one-liners—not all as bad as "the anteroom was as deserted as a eunuch's jockstrap.'' There is little original here, but the books are a sour and professional entertainment.

PRINCIPAL WORKS: As Vincent Lawrence: *An End to Flight.* London: Faber, [1973]. As Banville: *Death by Design.* [Dublin]: Wolfhound, [1993]; *Death the Pale Rider.* [Dublin]: Poolbeg, [1995]; *Hennessy to the Rescue.* [Dublin]: Poolbeg, [1995]. (Juvenile fiction).

BARBER, MARY (ca. 1690–ca. 1757), poet. Estimates regarding Mary Barber's date of birth range from 1690 to 1712, with the earlier date being the more likely. She was the wife of Jonathan Barber, an English-born woollen-draper of Capel Street in Dublin. She had four children and began composing poetry "chiefly to form the Minds of my Children" (*Poems,* Preface). Her purpose was to assist her children with their education by versifying important precepts, thus promoting memorization. Her methods apparently worked, as one of her sons, Constantine, became president of the College of Surgeons. Rupert, another son, was a painter and engraver.

Writing and publishing her own work were not a reliable source of income for Mary Barber, although her *Poems on Several Occasions* (1734) was well received by the critics. Jonathan Swift* believed her to be the most talented woman poet of his circle. He aided her in publishing her own work and allowed her to publish his own *Polite Conversation* in 1738. Swift's work proved to be the greater financial success for Mary. She suffered from gout and rheumatism throughout her life and died around 1757, with speculation on the exact death date ranging from 1755 to 1757.

ANNE COLMAN

WORKS: *The Poetry of Mary Barber.* London: C. Rivington, 1734; *Poems on Several Occasions.* London: C. Rivington, 1734. REFERENCES: Carpenter, Andrew. "On a Manuscript of Poems Catalogued as by Mary Barber in the Library of T.C.D." *Hermathena* 109 (1969): 54–64; Ferguson, Oliver W. "The Authorship of 'Apollo's Edict.' " PMLA 70 (1955): 433–440; Lonsdale, Roger. *Eighteenth-Century Women Poets.* Oxford: Oxford University Press, 1989; O'Donoghue, D. J. *Poets of Ireland.* Dublin: Hodges Figgis/London: Henry Frowde, Oxford University Press, 1912; Tucker, Bernard. "Swift's 'Female Senate.' " *Irish Studies Review* 7 (Summer 1994): 7–10.

BARDWELL, LELAND (1928?–), poet and fiction writer. Born Leland Hone in India of Irish parents, Bardwell grew up in Leixlip, County Kildare. She was educated at Alexandra College, Dublin, but had to leave at sixteen to attend her dying mother. After living in London, she returned to Dublin in 1959 and began publishing. With Eilean Ni Chuilleanain,* Macdara Woods,* and Pearse Hutchinson,* she founded the literary magazine *Cyphers.* She has had six children, and she lives in County Sligo. She is a member of Aosdána.*

Her first novel, *Girl on a Bicycle* (1977), is short, sparely written, and concretely observed. Its plot—mainly a succession of fornications, drinking bouts, and subsequent vomitings—does not, however, so much conclude as simply stop. *That London Winter* (1981) is an ambling narrative with lots of dialogue and a large cast of not awfully realized characters. *The House* (1984) is a portrait of a Protestant family of the professional class and is a considerable advance in narrative control and in characterization. Some of the chapters are rather feck-lessly short; indeed, one is only three lines. Occasionally, the writing becomes a bit mannered or florid, as in "his skin is a furnace of desire." Nevertheless, it is finally a sad, a touching, and a successful book. *There We Have Been* (1989), on the other hand, is a short, depressing novel about people who are variously unhappy, retarded, violent, drunken, and nasty. Much of it is laid in a decayed farmhouse near the border, and typical descriptive adjectives are "rusty," "dusty," "wet," "damp," "sodden," and "hideous." Even the river is "a mass of noxious weeds with an unhealthy scum on the surface." Never-theless, in characterization and in structure, it at least equals the control of *The House* and is enormously better than her first two novels. In it, her world is much grottier than that, say, of William Trevor.* Unlike Trevor's better-crafted world, however, Bardwell's does have a few oases of good-heartedness.

Her poems tend to be clear, flip, and lively, but with no attempt at even the loose rhythm of free verse. With no sense of poetic form, the author depends chiefly on content and striking diction for her effect. Occasionally, she strains too much for effect and becomes simply curious. In *The Fly and the Bedbug* (1984), she describes barges lying deck-to-deck "like lesbians" or solicitors tearing the cloth of hospital chairs "[w]ith their ravenous backsides." *Dostoev-sky's Grave* (1991), a collection of new and selected poems, is no advance whatsoever, but typically breezy, sometimes arresting in diction, and sometimes silly. It cannot be judged as poetry or even prose poetry; it is just short pieces of writing. She has also written some unpublished plays.

WORKS: *The Mad Cyclist.* Dublin: New Writers', 1970. (Poetry); *Girl on a Bicycle.* Dublin: Co-op Books, 1977. (Novel); *That London Winter.* [Dublin]: Co-op Books, [1981]. (Novel); *The House.* [Dingle, Co. Kerry]: Brandon, [1984]. (Novel); *The Fly and the Bedbug.* [Dublin]: Beaver Row, [1984]. (Poetry); *Different Kinds of Love.* Dublin: Attic, 1987. (Short stories); *There We Have Been.* Dublin: Attic, 1989. (Novel); *Dostoevsky's Grave.* Dublin: Dedalus, 1991. (Poetry).

BARLOW, JANE (1857–1917), poet and novelist. Barlow was born at Clon-tarf, County Dublin, in 1857, and lived most of her life at Raheny. Her father was the Reverend J. W. Barlow, later vice-provost of Trinity College. She pub-lished much fugitive prose and verse before the appearance of her very popular *Bog-Land Studies* in 1892. This volume contains a series of narrative poems in dialect, often with a strong melodramatic or pathetic story. The meter is obtru-sive enough to charm the popular ear, and the dialogue has more "mushas, bedads, begorrahs and whishts" than ever occurred in the speech of even the quaintest peasant. Her prose fiction also deals with peasant life, but the style ranges uneasily from the rather stagey dialect to a stilted formality. She lacked the fine humor or redoubtable talents of Maria Edgeworth* or Somerville and Ross,* and her once popular work is now little read. She died in Bray on April 17, 1917.

WORKS: *History of a World of Immortals without God: Translated from an Unpublished Man-uscript in the Library of a Continental University, by Antares Skorpios* [pseud]. Dublin: William

McGee/London: Simpkin, Marshall, 1891; *Bog-Land Studies.* London: Unwin, 1892; 2d ed., enlarged, London: Hodder & Stoughton, 1893. (Verse); *Irish Idylls.* London: Hodder & Stoughton,
1892. (Stories); *The End of Elfintown.* London: Macmillan, 1894. (Verse); *Kerrigan's Quality.* London: Hodder & Stoughton/New York: Dodd, Mead, 1894. (Novel); *Maureen's Fairing, and Other Stories.* London: Dent/New York: Macmillan, 1895; *Strangers at Lisconnel, a Second Series of Irish
Idylls.* London: Hodder & Stoughton/New York: Dodd, Mead, 1895. (Stories); *Mrs. Martin's Company, and Other Stories.* London: J. M. Dent, 1896; *A Creel of Irish Stories.* London: Methuen, 1897/
New York: Dodd, Mead, 1898; *From the East to the West.* London: Methuen, 1898. (Stories); *From
the Land of the Shamrock.* New York: Dodd, Mead, 1900/London: Methuen, 1901. (Stories); *Ghost-
Bereft.* [London]: Smith, Elder, 1901. (Stories in verse); *At the Back of Beyond.* New York: Dodd,
Mead, 1902. (Stories); *The Founding of Fortunes.* London: Methuen, 1902. (Novel); *By Beach and
Bog-Land.* London: Unwin, 1905. (Stories); *Irish Neighbours.* London: Hutchinson, 1907. (Stories);
The Mockers and Other Verses. London: G. Allen, 1908; *Irish Ways.* London: G. Allen, 1909. (Sto-
ries); *Flaws.* London: Hutchinson, 1911. (Novel); *Mac's Adventures.* London: Hutchinson, 1911. (Sto-
ries); *Doings and Dealings.* London: Hutchinson, 1913; *Between Doubting and Daring.* Oxford: B. H.
Blackwell, 1916. (Verses); *In Mio's Youth.* London: Hutchinson, 1917. (Novel).

BARRETT, EATON STANNARD (1786–1820), satirist. Barrett was born in
Cork and graduated from Trinity College, Dublin, after which he studied law at
the Middle Temple, London. However, the short-lived Whig ministry of 1807,
of which Richard Brinsley Sheridan* was a minor member, called forth his
greatly popular satirical poem *All the Talents,* which gave the name by which
that government is still known. In 1808, Barrett founded a satirical mock-
newspaper called the *Comet.* There followed a long and lively series of bur-
lesques, parodies, and satires in prose and in verse, as well as his comedy of
1815, *My Wife! What Wife?* His short poem "Woman" showed, however, that
he could be effective also in a serious vein:

> Not she with traitorous kiss her Saviour stung,
> Not she denied Him with unholy tongue;
> She, while apostles shrank, could dangers brave,
> Last at the cross and earliest at the grave.

The satiric point of *All the Talents* has been blunted by time, but Barrett's
brilliant parodies of popular fiction, such as *The Heroine; or, Adventures of a
Fair Romance Reader* (1813), are as funny as ever. For instance:

But, alas! misfortunes are often gregarious, like sheep. For one night, when our heroine
had repaired to the chapel, intending to drop her customary tear on the tomb of her
sainted benefactress, she heard on a sudden,
  "Oh, horrid, horrible, and horridest horror!" the distant organ peal a solemn voluntary.
While she was preparing, in much terror and astonishment, to accompany it with her
voice, four men in masks rushed from among some tombs and bore her to a carriage,
which instantly drove off with the whole party. In vain she sought to soften them by
swoons, tears, and a simple little ballad; they sat counting murders and not minding her.

Barrett died in Glamorgan, Wales, on March 20, 1820.

WORKS: *All the Talents.* London: J. J. Stockdale, 1807. (Under the pseudonym of Polypus); *All
the Talents in Ireland.* London: J. J. Stockdale, 1807. (Under the pseudonym of Scrutator); *The

Rising Sun. 2 vols. London: Appleyards, 1807. (Under the pseudonym of Cervantès Hogg); *The Second Titan War; or, The Talents Buried under Portland-Isle.* London: H. Colburn, 1807. (Satirical poem); *The Comet.* London: J. J. Stockdale, 1808. (Satirical tracts in prose and verse); *The Mis-led General.* London: H. Oddy, 1808. (A "serio-comic, satiric, mock-heroic romance"); *The Setting Sun; or, Devil amongst the Placemen, to Which Is Added, a New Musical Drama; Being a Parody on* The Beggar's Opera. . . . 3 vols. London: Hughes, 1809. (Under the pseudonym of Cervantès Hogg); *The Tarantula; or, The Dance of Fools.* 2 vols. London: Hughes, 1809. (Prose); *Woman, a Poem.* London: Murray, 1810; *The Heroine; or, Adventures of a Fair Romance Reader.* 3 vols. London: Colburn, 1813/2d ed., with additions and alterations, published as *The Heroine; or, Adventures of Cherubina.* London: Colburn, 1814; *My Wife! What Wife?* London: C. Chapple, 1815. (Three-act comedy); *The Talents Run Mad; or, Eighteen Hundred and Sixteen.* London: Colburn, 1816. (Satirical poem); *Six Weeks at Long's by a Late Resident.* 3d ed. 3 vols. London: For the author, 1817.

BARRETT, SHEILA (1943–   ), fiction writer. Barrett was born in Dallas, Texas, on June 7, 1943. She obtained a B.A. at Vassar College and an M.A. at the University of Texas at Austin, where she met and married Irish academic John Barrett in 1968. In 1969, the couple returned to Dublin, where they brought up their six children. She now teaches creative writing at University College, Dublin, and has published a number of short stories. She was an Arlen House-Maxwell House winner in 1982 and won an *Image* magazine fiction award in 1989.

Her novel *Walk in a Lost Landscape* (1994) is set in an imaginary future and opens when a nuclear holocaust is about to devastate the world. The story is narrated by Maura O'Keefe, a schoolchild in Killiney Convent when it starts, but now of marriageable age. She has psychic gifts and likes to imagine the old times before her birth when the modern Volorail was called the Dart. The novel has a marvelous sense of place, and the atmosphere of oncoming chaos is skillfully suggested, as Maura flees with her artist mother and baby brother to a family cottage in the Midlands, where they survive the blast by using turf as insulation. Although Maura dreams about a river "made of knives," no one knows exactly what has happened in the outside world. Scrambled radio reports of lost cities come over the air. In Ireland, people sicken and die; everything is primitive. As law and order break down, marauding bands roam the countryside, and the family has to flee yet again, this time to Wicklow, where Maura's aunt is a nun. She and other characters hop to life, and there are many page-turning adventures, as Maura walks back across Ireland, looking for her kidnapped brother. The book is a great read and is written with a painter's eye for landscape. It works on several levels and would suit younger as well as older readers. It is a story about growing up and coming to terms with love and loss, an adventure, and a lament for a lost world. But Barrett's characters are survivors, so it is not finally gloomy.

                                                                                    MARY ROSE CALLAGHAN

WORK: *Walk in a Lost Landscape.* [Dublin]: Poolbeg, [1994].

BARRINGTON, SIR JONAH (ca. 1760–1834), memoirist and politician. Barrington was born at Knapton, near Abbeyleix, Queen's County, probably in 1760. He was educated at Trinity College, Dublin, admitted to the bar in 1788, and served in the Irish Parliament from 1790 until its dissolution by the Act of Union in 1800. Although he voted against the Act of Union, he was by no means a simple nationalist. He was appointed judge of the Admiralty Court in 1798 and knighted in 1807. To escape his creditors, he removed to France in about 1815, although he retained his office and emoluments. However, after it was discovered that he had misappropriated court funds, he was deprived of office in 1830.

Barrington's histories and memoirs are of great value to the political and social historian, and his three-volume *Personal Sketches* are a considerable charm and delight to the general reader. The Ireland he portrays is an intriguing mixture of civilization and barbarism, a world of raucous pranks, heavy drinking, hardy fighting (he had fought his duels, including an amusing one with Leonard McNally*), political intrigue, and tolerance for loutishness as well as appreciation of wit and good address. Barrington has given us some vivid sketches of important personalities of his time, such as John Philpot Curran, Wolfe Tone, and the immortal word-garbler Sir Boyle Roche. Since his complete *Sketches* suffer from excessive length, he is probably best read in the modern abridgment by Hugh B. Staples. He died in Versailles on April 8, 1834.

WORKS: *Personal Sketches of His Own Times*. 3 vols. London: Henry Colburn, & H. Colburn & R. Bentley, 1827–1832; *Historic Memoirs of Ireland.* 2 vols. London: R. Bentley for H. Colburn, 1833; *Rise and Fall of the Irish Nation.* Paris: G. G. Bennis, 1833; *The Ireland of Sir Jonah Barrington, Selections from His Personal Sketches.* Hugh B. Stapes, ed. Seattle & London: University of Washington Press, 1967/London: Owen, 1968.

BARRINGTON, MARGARET (1896–1982), novelist and short story writer. Barrington was the daughter of Richard Barrington, a district inspector of police in the Royal Irish Constabulary. She was born on May 10, 1896, at Malin, County Donegal, and was educated in the West of Ireland, at Alexandra College in Dublin, at a French school in Normandy, and at Trinity College, Dublin. She married the historian Edmund Curtis,* but the marriage was dissolved, and in 1926 she married Liam O'Flaherty,* from whom she separated in 1932, after having one child. In the 1930s, she lived in England, where she organized support for the republican side in the Spanish civil war, and she assisted refugees from Nazi Germany. In 1939, she published a novel, *My Cousin Justin*. Basically about a love triangle, the novel is not particularly successful in its modern scenes, especially those set in London. However, the initial section about an Irish rural childhood is beautifully evoked. After the Second World War broke out, she moved to West Cork and continued writing, both articles and short stories. She died on March 8, 1982, but later that year a collection of her stories, *David's Daughter, Tamar,* appeared. Introducing it, William Trevor* noted "her sharp, unique voice," but the stories are so varied in locale and mood and significance that it is difficult to discern one individuality behind them. What is constant, however, even in the thinner sketches, are a lean prose and a fine ability to dramatize. At least one of the stories, "Men Are Never God's Creatures," is a prime candidate for any anthology of the modern Irish short story.

WORKS: *My Cousin Justin*. London: Jonathan Cape, 1939; *David's Daughter, Tamar*. [Dublin]: Wolfhound, [1982].

BARRY, MICHAEL JOSEPH (1817–1889), poet. Barry was born in Cork and became an enthusiastic Young Irelander and a contributor to *The Dublin University Magazine,* to *The Nation,** and to *Punch.* His patriotic poems, such as "The Massacre at Drogheda," often have a jaunty and bouncing meter that is at odds with their content. His humorous verse is mildly better. For instance, this dialect version of an imaginary meeting between Queen Victoria and Louis Philippe of France in 1848:

> My dear Vic, ses he,
> I'm mighty sick, ses he,
> For I've cut my stick, ses he,
> Tarnation quick, ses he,
> From the divil's breeze, ses he,
> At the Tooleyrees, ses he;
> For the blackguards made, ses he
> A barricade, ses he.

Changing his politics later in life, he became a police magistrate in Dublin and died on January 23, 1889.

WORKS: *Ireland, As She Was, As She Is, and As She Shall Be*. Dublin: Duffy, 1845. (Nonfiction); ed., *The Songs of Ireland*. Dublin: Duffy, 1845; ed., *Echoes from Parnassus, Selected from the Original Poetry of the* Southern Reporter. Cork: *Southern Reporter, 1849*; *A Waterloo Commemoration for 1854. . . .* London: Orr/Dublin: McGlashan, 1854; *Lays of the War*. Cork: *Daily Reporter* Office, 1855; *Lays of the War and Miscellaneous Lyrics*. London: Longman, 1856; *The Pope and the Romagna*. Dublin: Hodges & Smith, 1860. (Nonfiction); *Irish Emigration Considered*. Cork, 1863. (Nonfiction); *Poems Addressed to Minnie*. Cork: Nash, 1867; *Six Songs of Beranger*. Dublin: Privately printed, 1871; as Bouillon de Garcon, *The Kishogue Papers*. London: Chapman & Hall, 1875; *Heinrich and Leonore*. Dublin: Hodges, Figgis, 1886.

BARRY, SEBASTIAN (1955–   ), poet, playwright, and novelist. Barry was born in Dublin in 1955, the son of Joan O'Hara, the actress, and the nephew of Mary O'Hara, the singer. He read English and Latin at Trinity College. From 1977 until 1985, he lived in France, England, Greece, and Switzerland. He has now returned to Ireland to live and write in Dublin. He has published three books of poetry: *The Water-Colourist* (1983), *The Rhetorical Town* (1985), and *Fanny Hawke Goes to the Mainland Forever* (1989). He has had five plays staged in Dublin: *The Pentagonal Dream* (Damer, 1986), *Boss Grady's Boys* (Peacock, 1989), which won the first BBC/Stewart Parker* Award, *Prayers of Sherkin* (Peacock, 1990), *White Woman Street* (Peacock and Bush Theatre, London, 1992), and *The Only True History of Lizzie Finn* (Abbey, 1995). His first novel, *Macker's Garden,* appeared in 1982; this was followed by two novellas, *Time out of Mind* and *Strappado Square* (1983); and his most recent full-length fiction is *The Engine of Owl-Light* (1987). He has also edited a collection of poems by younger poets from the Republic of Ireland, such as Dermot Bolger,* Aidan Mathews,* and Matthew Sweeney,* *The Inherited Boundaries* (1986); and he has written a book of fiction for younger readers, *Elsewhere: The Adventures of Belemus* (1985). In 1982, Barry was awarded an Arts Council Bursary for his creative writing; he was elected to Aosdána* in 1989; and he was Ansbacher writer-in-residence at the Abbey Theatre* in 1990 as well as an Abbey board member in 1990–1991.

Barry has been hailed as a genuinely significant new voice in modern Irish poetry. Only a few of his contemporaries show in their works as conspicuous an influence of classical precedents as he does. His first book of poems, *The Water-Colourist,* much in the sense of the eponymous painter, responds to the presence in his life of various family members who have, in varying ways, contributed to his encounter with life. Additionally, Barry celebrates places that have been an influence on him, exploring himself and others who have created the memories of his youth. *Fanny Hawke Goes to the Mainland Forever* is a book of journeys, undertaken, interrupted, or abandoned. It is about the necessity of embarking, but also of recognizing the possibility of discovering home in where you arrive. In this collection, as in the earlier *The Rhetorical Town* (especially in Part III, "The Room of Rhetoric"), he elucidates the use and power of language and thematizes the nature and function of poetry.

Macker's Garden features five boys who move through the garish pleasures and pressures of adolescence. They meet in the titular garden, steal a bicycle, and come upon a couple making love, whom they pelt with stones. In Part II, one boy brings his girlfriend, and another boy strikes up a relationship with her, thus sowing the seeds of discord. *Time Out of Mind* is set in Sligo in the 1930s. The bleak narrative charts the collapse of a marriage entered into too hastily. Mai Galligan and Jack Haugh are bound by a loveless union. Ignorance of one another and feelings of isolation and uprootedness that lead to alcoholism precipitate the destruction of love within the stifling confines of the new Irish middle class. *Strappado Square* represents a strange kind of fiction that blends the memoirs of one Jacques, in which the love and presence of Lena—student, teacher, and lover—are all-important, with, it would seem, his inchoate writings about a Monsieur Le Loüet. The outcome may be slightly too idiosyncratic for everyone's taste.

The Engine of Owl-Light represents an attempt at fabulation that relies for effect on split narrative. Basic to the book is one Moran, a sleeping giant, who, like Beckett's* Moran, is a compulsive storyteller. His stories are addressed to a woman called Moll, but they are likewise addressed to the narrator. In all there are six stories. The one about the last days of Oliver Conn, a petty thief, and his poet master Owl, who owes something to Moran, is written in a whimsically "foul" English, the raison d'être of which is hard to discern. There are, furthermore, accounts of a child haunted by his living father and of a mistaken sojourn in Lucerne of a neurotic man and a Swiss woman. A reincarnation of the giant Moran figures in certain adventures at Key West. These and the rest of the stories are told in distinctive styles that range from the meditative to the free-flowing. The novel may be seen as an effort to keep the Irish comic tradition alive.

Prayers of Sherkin is an empathic and evocative play set in the 1890s about the dwindling of a religious sect who came to Sherkin Island, off the southwest coast of Ireland, from Manchester in search of their "New Jerusalem." The arrival of Patrick Kirwin, Catholic lithographer from Cork city, in the neighboring town of Baltimore threatens the end of the sect but brings hope for the future to its last daughter. The piece highlights the moment at which ideology and doctrine are abandoned for the sake of survival. *Boss Grady's Boys,* set on a forty-acre hill farm on the Cork/Kerry border, centers around two brothers in their sixties arriving at a comic awareness of their personal predicament, with the author's keeping a precarious balance between ironic absurdity and unrestrained yearning.

RÜDIGER IMHOF

WORKS: *Macker's Garden.* Dublin: Co-op Books, 1982; *Time Out of Mind* and *Strappado Square.* Dublin: Wolfhound, 1983; *The Water-Colourist.* Mountrath, Portlaoise: Dolmen, 1983; *Elsewhere: The Adventures of Belemus.* Mountrath, Portlaoise: Dolmen, 1985; *The Rhetorical Town.* Mountrath, Portlaoise: Dolmen, 1985; ed., The *Inherited Boundaries: Younger Poets of the Republic of Ireland.* Mountrath, Portlaoise: Dolmen, 1986. (Poems by Thomas McCarthy, Aidan Carl Mathews, Harry Clifton, Dermot Bolger, Michael O'Loughlin, Matthew Sweeney, and Barry); *The Engine of Owl-Light.* Manchester: Carcanet, 1987; *Boss Grady's Boys.* Dublin: Raven Arts, 1989; *Fanny Hawke Goes to the Mainland Forever.* Dublin: Raven Arts, 1989; *Prayers of Sherkin and Boss Grady's Boys.* London: Methuen, 1991; *The Only True History of Lizzie Finn, Steward of Christendom, White Woman Street.* [London]: Methuen, [1995]. REFERENCES: Murray, Christopher. " 'Such a Sense of Home': The Poetic Drama of Sebastian Barry." *Colby Quarterly* 27 (December 1991): 242–247; Wallace, Arminta. "The Prodigious Sebastian Barry." *Irish Times* (November 17, 1990).

BATEMAN, COLIN

WORK: *Divorcing Jack.* London: HarperCollins, 1995. (Novel).

BAX, SIR ARNOLD [EDWARD TREVOR] (1883–1953), composer and man of letters. Although an eminent English composer, Bax under the pen name of Dermot O'Byrne was a determinedly Irish writer. He was born in London on November 8, 1883, and won prizes for composition and piano playing at the Royal Academy of Music. He wrote seven symphonies, some concertos, and some chamber music. He was knighted in 1937 and made Master of the King's Music in 1942.

In 1902, his reading of Yeats'* *The Wanderings of Oisin* so dazzled him that "the Celt within me stood revealed," and he enthusiastically adopted Ireland as his spiritual home and even became a friend of Pearse* and other 1916 leaders. He was an imitative poet, several poems being reminiscent of Yeats and his "Allurement" and "In Glencullen" suggesting Synge.* His "The Song of the Old Fiddler" is particularly close to Colum's* "Old Woman of the Roads" but does not wither in the least by the comparison. His best-known poem, "A Dublin Ballad—1916," was banned as seditious but has a fine control and a sour power.

His short stories and his play *Red Owen* are less successful, for he allows himself to fall into the most extravagant excesses of Synge-song. For instance:

It's not a man of my clan would be giving the lie to a guest, but I would take surety by sun and moon there's many a coloured rag of sweet music does be choking your throat this moment!

Or:

When I am seeing yourself in the dirty dawn and your two arms moving like the swaying branches of the mayblossom in the spring I think I'm looking on a gaudy angel from the doorpost of the Lord's House.

However, as one of his own characters remarked, "Maybe it's a poet he is with the soaring flame of curses hissing in his learned heart."

He became extern examiner for University College, Cork, and died in Cork on October 3, 1953. As Boylan notes, "The College has dedicated a room to his memory."

WORKS: As Dermot O'Byrne: *Seafoam and Firelight.* Hampstead: Orpheus Press, [1909?]. (Poems); *The Sisters, and Green Magic.* Hampstead: Orpheus Press, [1912]. (Poems); *Children of the Hills: Tales and Sketches of Western Ireland in the Old Time and the Present Day.* Dublin & London: Maunsel, [1913]; *Wrack and Other Stories.* Dublin: Talbot/London: T. Fisher Unwin, 1918; *Red Owen.* Dublin: Talbot, 1919. (Play); *Dermot O'Bryne: Poems by Arnold Bax.* Lewis Foreman, ed. London: Thames, 1979. As Arnold Bax: *Farewell, My Youth.* London: Longmans, 1943. (Reminiscences).

BECKETT, MARY (1926–   ), novelist and short story writer. Beckett was born in Belfast, Northern Ireland, to Sean and Catherine (Bryson) Beckett. She married Peter Gaffey in 1956 after teaching primary schools in Belfast for eleven years and stopped both writing and teaching for twenty years to raise five children. Her first collection of short stories, *A Belfast Woman* (1980) begins with tales that handle universal problems women face as they struggle to balance family relationships, personal economies, and moral values. Their dilemmas range from bearing a racially mixed child out of wedlock ("Theresa") to coping with a stagnating marriage and a mother-in-law's unfailingly sharp tongue ("Saints and Scholars"). However, as the stories progress, problems particular to women of Northern Ireland begin to dominate. Fergus's sister, in "Flags and Emblems," finds her brother's willingness to carry the Union Jack on celebration day, in order to please his wife, both sensitive and touching, if a bit disturbing to his own Catholic family. Helen of "The Master and the Bombs" is filled with consternation at her husband's ready confession to the storing of explosives in a school coal shed. Like many of Beckett's lonely women, she accepts the failure of her marriage and consoles herself with her children.

Bearing children annually or biannually is a fact of Irish Catholic life that Beckett does not ignore. In her acclaimed novel, *Give Them Stones* (1987), which won the Arts Award for Literature from Dublin's *Sunday Tribune,* Beckett articulates the ordeals of an Irish Catholic woman as she chronicles fifty years in the life of Martha Murtagh. Martha observes the unjust incarceration of her father during the Troubles of the 1920s; she and her husband are flooded out because their Catholic neighborhood is given no protection against the torrential spring rains; she is burned out of a home after refusing to contribute to Irish Republican Army (IRA) men who kneecapped a boy against her wall; and she witnesses the execution of her brother Danny, who had joined the IRA. Throughout these episodes, Martha strives to maintain dignity and normality in her life. As a young girl, she observes that her family pitched their voices high to get rid of their Belfast accents and that Catholics, by and large, were invisible in Northern literature. As a woman trying to raise four sons, Martha takes charge of her life by starting a small bake shop and announcing the unofficial beginning of a celibate life after the birth of her fourth child. From the burnings and shootings of 1935 to the barricades and Falls Road curfew of 1970, Martha endures the oppression of the politically disabled, and she grapples with restraints upon her gender, yet she never crumbles or gives up hope.

Beckett concludes her most recent collection of short stories, *A Literary Woman* (1990) with optimism again, despite the continuing troubles, pointing out that the dust, dirt, and pollution contribute to Belfast's legendary sunsets. In this series of ten tales, she cleverly develops a theme of secrecy and revelation, as an emotionally disturbed woman, Winifred Teeling, writes anonymous letters to assorted neighbors. She invents knowledge of homosexuality, thievery, and political conspiracy from mere glimpses into their lives. Teeling, epitomizing the child of the dysfunctional family, appears in the ninth and title story and is found dead in the tenth, yet her undefined presence in the first eight unifies the collection and bears out the maxim that "there are no secrets in Ireland." What her written warnings and threats of blackmail actually reveal, however, are character or relationship flaws that would otherwise have gone untreated. Jenny and Matt of "Sudden Infant Death" must deal with their guilt over the loss of a two-year-old child to drowning; Fiona and Fintan of "A Ghost Story" are forced to confront their class differences and manipulation of each other; and Kathleen of "Under Control" is driven to write a cathartic letter to a sister in England after a standoff with her rebellious daughter. Despite the evil forces that lurk about these troubled people, Beckett fashions the series of stories into an appeal for perseverance and hope. Maeve and Jeff O'Reilly of the final tale reminisce over family seaside holidays and find peace in the enduring quality of the moon. As a feminine symbol, the moon is a fitting endnote for Beckett, reinforcing her faith in woman and her ability to survive.

MARGUERITE QUINTELLI-NEARY

WORKS: *A Belfast Woman.* Dublin: Poolbeg, 1980/New York: William Morrow, 1989. (Short stories); *Give Them Stones.* Dublin: Poolbeg, 1987/London: Bloomsbury, 1987/New York: William Morrow, 1988/New York: Harper & Row, 1989. (Novel); *Orla Was Six.* Dublin: Poolbeg, [1989]. (Children's novel); *A Literary Woman.* London: Bloomsbury, 1990. (Short stories); *Orla at School.* [Dublin: Poolbeg], [1991]. (Children's novel); *A Family Tree.* [Dublin: Poolbeg], [1992]. (Children's novel). REFERENCE: Sullivan, Megan. "Mary Beckett: An Interview," *Irish Literary Supplement* 14 (Fall 1995): 10–12.

BECKETT, SAMUEL (1906–1989), novelist, playwright, poet, and winner of the Nobel Prize in literature. Beckett remains one of the twentieth century's most acclaimed and influential avant-garde writers. After he won the Nobel Prize in 1969, he also became one of the few extremely well known experimental writers. In the past forty years, the academic fascination with Beckett has come to rival that with Yeats* or Joyce.* Indeed, in 1990, one critic asserted, "By the year 2000 Beckett criticism will equal that of Wagner and Napoleon, who are the most written about personae in history."

He was born Samuel Barclay Beckett on April 13 or May 13, 1906, in Fox-rock, a fashionable southern suburb of Dublin, into a prosperous Protestant family. From 1920 to 1923, he attended Portora Royal School in Enniskillen, County Fermanagh, as had Oscar Wilde* before him. In October 1923, he entered Trinity College, Dublin. After a lackluster beginning, he distinguished himself in modern languages and received his B.A. in 1927. In 1928, he taught French for nine months at Campbell College in Belfast, and then for two years (1929–1930), he served as *lecteur* at the École Normale Supérieure in Paris.

While in Paris, he met his lifelong friend, the poet and art critic Thomas MacGreevy,* who introduced him to the English novelist Richard Aldington and, more importantly, to James Joyce. Joyce's later work was undoubtedly the single greatest literary influence on Beckett. He was not, as has sometimes been said, Joyce's paid secretary, but, as he himself has said, "like all his friends, I helped him. He was greatly handicapped because of his eyes. I did odd jobs for him, marking passages for him or reading to him, but I never wrote any of his letters." For some time, Beckett was closely involved with Joyce and his family, and he contributed the first essay in the collection of Joycean apologetics, *Our Exagmination Round His Factification for Incamination of Work in Progress.* He also published in the magazine *Transition.* His first separately printed piece, the poem *Whoroscope,* appeared in 1930 and was followed in 1931 by his short critical book *Proust.*

In the fall of 1930, Beckett returned to Dublin to serve as a lecturer in French at Trinity College. MacGreevy introduced him to Jack B. Yeats* whom he came to admire and revere, but in general Beckett's sojourns in Dublin, at this time and later, were such unhappy experiences that they made him acutely, physically ill;

his demanding mother was apparently much to blame. In December 1931, he received his M.A., and, after fleeing to the Continent, he resigned his lectureship.

Beckett's next twenty years were years of great difficulty for him. He lived in Paris, intermittently in London, and was often drawn back to Dublin by the demands of his family. He suffered a remarkable variety of physical ailments, many of them apparently psychosomatic and brought on by his having to return to Ireland from time to time.

In 1932, Beckett wrote a novel not published until after his death, called *Dream of Fair to Middling Women*. In parts, quite funny, it was a conventional avant-garde work that might have been written by any clever young intellectual, and it did not reflect the highly individual voice that Beckett was to fashion. In 1934, he published a collection of stories called *More Pricks than Kicks*, which considerably develops his bizarre sense of humor without entirely relinquishing its hold on the real world for the Beckettian one.

During World War II, Beckett was active in the French Resistance in Paris. In the fall of 1942, he was forced to flee from the Germans to Roussillon, a village in southeast France. There he remained until 1945, managing in the interim to write his novel *Watt*. After the war, in 1945, he received the Croix de Guerre for his work in the Resistance.

It was not until after the war that Beckett, now back in Paris, entered upon his most productive period. *Molloy,* which is perhaps his best novel, was begun in September 1947 and was finished in January 1948; like most of his best work, it was written in French. It was followed in 1948 by a kind of sequel, *Malone meurt* or *Malone Dies,* and then by his most famous play *En Attendant Godot* or *Waiting for Godot,* which was written between October 9, 1948, and January 29, 1949. In the fall of 1949 and the winter of 1950, he completed his trilogy of novels with *L'Innommable* or *The Unnamable.*

Early in 1953, *Waiting for Godot* was produced in Paris to immediate wide acclaim and equally wide bafflement. Subsequent productions of *Godot* in London and New York were similarly startling. The play became a topic for excited debate and made its author famous—partly because of the play's undoubted merit and partly because of its novelty. Theatre is a commercial and, therefore, conventional art. Audiences in the early 1950s were used to explicit and rather simple statements in plays. The most admired dramatists were Jean Paul Sartre, Christopher Fry, Arthur Miller, Tennessee Williams, and even T. S. Eliot, none of whom made particularly elusive theatrical statements. Here, however, was a work that offered the tantalizing ambiguity that the well-read had come to expect in the modern poem and novel. Hence, the play was warmly attacked, hotly defended, and feverishly discussed. The vogue of *Godot* not only established its author as important, but also cleared the way for a whole new wave of theatrical experiment—by Ionesco, Adamov, Pinter, and all of those writers who were to be classed as dramatists of the Absurd.

After *Godot,* Beckett's other major works began to be published; much of his subsequent effort was devoted to translating his own work from French into

English or from English into French. In 1956, however, he wrote what is probably his second best known play, *Fin de Partie* or *Endgame*. In the years after his Nobel Prize in 1969, he tended to write more plays than fiction. His pieces tended to become ever more brief, and the later plays tended to rely on only one character. In his last two decades, he became closely involved in the direction of his plays, attending rehearsals and demanding a strict interpretation of his intentions. As a director, he was probably as much a martinet as W. S. Gilbert, insisting even on an exact and prescribed stage movement.

In 1961, he married Suzanne Deschevaux-Dumesnil. He retained a flat in Paris but also kept a small country house at Ussy. He also spent extended periods in Morocco and Tunisia. His wife died in July 1989, and he died in Paris on December 22, 1989, and was buried in Montparnasse Cemetery.

Perhaps the greatest influences on Beckett as a writer have been Joyce, Ireland, and illness. Beckett met Joyce at an early and impressionable age. He was in his early twenties, and Joyce at that time was engaged in writing the most complicated experimental novel in the English or probably any other language. The enormous impact of Joyce and of *Finnegans Wake* made it impossible for Beckett to conceive of rich and meaningful writing as being conventional in form or realistic in view. So appreciative a Joycean could hardly be expected to embrace the methods of a Frank O'Connor* or Sean O'Faolain.*

Beckett's other major influences, Ireland and illness, seem quite interconnected. He has been afflicted with an astonishing array of ailments in his life, and often his worst symptoms seemed brought on by a return to Ireland. His catalogue of ills is so extensive and so painful that it brings to mind Pope's remark about "that long disease, my life." It also does much to explain his gallery of enfeebled, debilitated characters and his constant theme of life as a kind of incurable disease. The Beckett characters do not really exist in an identifiable Irish landscape, but they do seem refugees from that landscape. There are so many Irish overtones, faint Irish allusions, and Irish words and turns of speech, that the bleak Beckett landscape seems to be the Irish landscape after someone has dropped an H-bomb on it.

Beckett's works, then, represent experiments in form, which have been influenced by Joyce, illness, and Ireland; which depict an unrealistic world filled with repugnant and pointless details; and which make the point that the real world is repugnant and pointless. Such characteristics would seem unpromising indeed for the creation of works of art, but Beckett has three extraordinary qualities as an experimental writer. First, there is the ingenious, often comic objectification that he finds for his world-view. The details of *Molloy* and *Godot* and *Endgame* create a world as inimitable as the worlds of Lewis Carroll or William Faulkner. The details of such works are probably so engaging, so dourly droll, that to some extent they defeat the author's purpose. In his later, more austere works, he keeps a much tighter rein upon his comic invention.

Second, there is the quality of his prose which, phrase by phrase and sentence by sentence, has an utterly unJoycean simplicity and clarity. In *Finnegans Wake*,

Joyce is the great "accretor," piling nuance upon nuance, until the density of meaning defies conventional reading and demands translation. Beckett goes almost to the other extreme. His prose is always lucid and always fluent and never quirky or idiosyncratic, as the simple styles of Gertrude Stein or Ernest Hemingway sometimes become. Beckett's prose is always a clear mirror of his content.

Third, there is Beckett's attempt to wrench his form into an emphasis of his statement, and this attempt is both his most daring and least successful. One of the not always true "truisms" of aesthetics is that form should emulate, or at least emphasize, content. Certainly, form can sometimes do that, and one can cite innumerable successful examples in modern literature, from Walt Whitman on. However, a rigid form like the Shakespearean sonnet, for instance, suggests nothing except a certain pattern of reasoning; yet, into that form poets have poured a multitude of diverse meanings and emotions.

Beckett, by rigidly molding his form to his content, has at his most Beckettian broken the mold. Someone has said that *Waiting for Godot* is a play in which nothing happens twice. That same point can be made about many of Beckett's other works. The Moran portion of *Molloy* is basically a reprise of the Molloy portion. The second half of the play, entitled *Play*, repeats the first half verbatim, the only difference being that Beckett thinks the second half should be done more hesitantly. The "Dramaticule" *Come and Go* in its scant ten minutes repeats the same action three times. The play *Breath* in its thirty-five or forty seconds repeats its initial action in reverse. The only difference in these works is that Beckett succeeds in being boring in an ever shorter period of time.

"Boring," however, is too innocuous a word. As the Beckett world-view is of an intolerable existence which it is not worthwhile terminating, the appropriate Beckettian form is necessarily a worthless one, an anti-form. Such a form evokes neither emotion nor amusement; it passes the time at worst tediously and at best intolerably. Increasingly over the years, Beckett seems to have refined that form, to have stripped it of details, and to have made it more austere. He has used fewer words and even no words; he has used fewer actors, parts of actors, and even no actors.

There is no question that Beckett's form emulates his meaning; there is the question of how valid the effect of his form is upon an audience. In 1960, when the Irish actor Cyril Cusack consummately played *Krapp's Last Tape* as an afterpiece rather than as a curtain-raiser to Shaw's* *Arms and the Man,* he succeeded in half-emptying his theatre of an up-to-then highly appreciative audience. That may, of course, have been the effect Beckett wanted; the effect was not a dramatic one, but it certainly was memorable. Similarly, one may set off a cannon during a Shakespearean production at the Globe Theatre; and, when the theatre burns down, the effect is certainly memorable, even though the dramatic experiment has destroyed the form of the drama.

To a conventional or traditional view of what literature can do, it would seem that Beckett's most successful works are those in which he has been less Beckettian. In this view, the early works *Murphy, Molloy* and *Endgame,* and to some extent *Malone Dies* and *Godot* would appear to be those by which Beckett will be remembered. In these works, his subsequently stifled comic imagination is brilliantly apparent. While that comic imagination may work against the author's intention, it triumphantly works for the traditional methods of the artist.

WORKS: *Whoroscope.* Paris: Hours, 1930. (Poem); *More Pricks Than Kicks.* London: Chatto & Windus, 1934. (Stories); *Echo's Bones and Other Precipitates.* Paris: Europa, 1935. (Poems); *Murphy.* London: Routledge, 1938/translated into French by Beckett & Alfred Péron, Paris: Bordas, 1947. (Novel); *Molloy.* Paris: Editions de Minuit, 1951/translated into English by Beckett & Patrick Bowles, Paris: Merlin/Olympia, 1954/New York: Grove, 1955. (Novel); *Malone Meurt.* Paris: Editions de Minuit, 1951/translated into English as *Malone Dies* by Beckett, New York: Grove, 1956/ London: Calder & Boyars, 1958. (Novel); *En Attendant Godot.* Paris: Editions de Minuit, 1952/ translated into English as *Waiting for Godot* by Beckett, New York: Grove, 1954/London: Faber, 1956. (Play); *Watt.* Paris: Merlin/Olympia, 1953/New York: Grove, 1959/London: Calder & Boyars, 1961. (Novel); *L'Innommable.* Paris: Editions de Minuit, 1953/translated into English as *The Unnamable* by Beckett, New York: Grove, 1958. (Novel); *Nouvelles et Textes pour Rien.* Paris: Editions de Minuit, 1955/translated into English as *Stories and Texts for Nothing* by Beckett, New York: Grove, 1967/collected edition under the title of *No's Knife,* London: Calder & Boyars, 1966; *All That Fall.* London: Faber, 1957/New York: Grove, 1960/translated into French by Beckett and Robert Pinget as *Tous ceux qui tombent,* Paris: Editions de Minuit, 1957. (Radio play); *Fin de Partie.* Paris: Editions de Minuit, 1957/translated into English as *Endgame* by Beckett, New York: Grove, 1958/London: Faber, 1958. (Play); *Acte sans Paroles I.* Paris: Editions de Minuit, 1957 (together with *Fin de Partie*)/translated into English as *Act Without Words I* by Beckett, London: Faber, 1958 (together with *Endgame*)/in *Krapp's Last Tape and Other Dramatic Pieces,* New York: Grove, 1960; *From an Abandoned Work.* London: Faber, 1958/in *First Love and Other Stories,* New York: Grove, 1974/*Krapp's Last Tape.* London: Faber, 1959/New York: Grove, 1960/translated into French as *La dernière bande* by Beckett & Pierre Leyris, Paris: Editions de Minuit, 1959. (Play); *Embers.* London: Faber, 1959/in *Krapp's Last Tape and Other Dramatic Pieces,* New York: Grove, 1960; *Happy Days.* New York: Grove, 1961/London: Faber, 1962/translated into French as *Oh les beaux jours* by Beckett, Paris: Editions de Minuit, 1963. (Play); *Comment C'est.* Paris: Editions de Minuit, 1961/translated into English as *How It Is* by Beckett, New York: Grove; London: Calder & Boyars, 1966. (Novel); *Words and Music* in *Play and Two Short Pieces for Radio,* London: Faber, 1964/in *Cascando and Other Short Dramatic Pieces,* New York: Grove, 1969/translated into French as *Paroles et Musique* by Beckett, in *Comédie et Actes divers,* Paris: Editions de Minuit, 1966; *Play.* London: Faber, 1964/in *Cascando and Other Short Dramatic Pieces,* New York: Grove, 1967; *Imagination morte imaginez.* Paris: Editions de Minuit, 1965/translated into English as *Imagination Dead Imagine* by Beckett, London: Calder & Boyars, 1966/in *First Love and Other Shorts,* New York: Grove, 1974; *Bing.* Paris: Editions de Minuit, 1966/translated into English as *Ping* by Beckett, London: Calder & Boyars, 1967/in *First Love and Other Shorts,* New York: Grove Press; *Acte sans Paroles II* in *Comédie et Actes divers.* Paris: Editions de Minuit, 1966/translated into English as *Act Without Words II* by Beckett, in *Krapp's Last Tape and Other Dramatic Pieces,* New York: Grove, 1960/in *Eh Joe and Other Writings,* London: Faber, 1967; *Cascando in Comédie et Actes divers.* Paris: Editions de Minuit, 1966/translated into English as *Cascando* by Beckett, in *Cascando and Other Short Dramatic Pieces,* New York: Grove, [1968] in *Play and Two Short Pieces for Radio,* London: Faber, 1964; *Film in Cascando and Other Short Dramatic Pieces.* New York: Grove, [1968] in *Eh Joe,* London: Faber, 1967; *Eh Joe in Cascando and Other Short Dramatic Pieces.* New York: Grove, 1967/London: Faber, 1967/translated into French as *Dis Joe* by Beckett in *Comédie et Actes divers,* Paris: Editions de Minuit, 1966; *Assez.* Paris: Editions de Minuit, 1967, in *Têtes-Mortes*/translated into English as *Enough* by Beckett in *First Love and Other Shorts,* New York: Grove, 1974; *Mercier et Camier.* Paris: Editions de Minuit, 1970/translated into English as *Mercier and Camier* by Beckett, New York: Grove, 1974/London: Calder & Boyars, 1974. (Novel); *Premier Amour.* Paris: Editions de Minuit, 1970/translated into English as *First Love* in *First Love and Other Shorts,* New York: Grove, 1974; *The Collected Works of Samuel Beckett.* 19 vols. New York: Grove, 1970; *Le Depeupleur.* Paris. Editions de Minuit, 1971/translated into English as *The*

Lost Ones by Beckett, New York: Grove, 1972/London: Calder & Boyars, 1972; *Not I*. London: Faber, 1973/in *First Love and Other Shorts,* New York: Grove, 1974; *Fizzles.* New York: Grove, 1976; *Ends and Odds.* New York: Grove, 1976. (Contains *That Time, Not I, Footfalls, Radio I, Radio II, Theatre I, Theatre II,* and *Tryst*); *For to End Yet, and Other Fizzles.* London: Faber, 1977; *Four Novellas.* London: J. Calder, 1977; *Collected Poems in English and French.* London: J. Calder, 1977; *Companie.* Paris: Editions de Minuit, 1979/translated into English as *Company* by Beckett, New York: Grove, 1980; *Samuel Beckett: Krapp's Last Tape: A Theatre Workbook.* James Knowlson, ed. London: Brutus Books, [1980]; *Rockaby and Other Short Pieces.* New York: Grove, 1981. (Includes "Rockaby," "Ohio Impromptu," "All Strange Away," and "A Piece of Monologue"); *Three Plays by Samuel Beckett: What Where, Catastrophe, Ohio Impromptu.* New York: Grove, 1983; *Worstword Ho.* New York: Grove, [1983]; *Collected Poems 1930–1978.* London: John Calder, 1984; *Collected Shorter Prose 1945–1980.* London: J. Calder, [1984]; *Collected Shorter Plays.* New York: Grove Weidenfeld, [1984]; *Disjecta: Miscellaneous Writings and a Dramatic Fragment by Samuel Beckett.* Ruby Cohn, ed. New York: Grove, [1984]; *Happy Days: The Production Notebook of Samuel Beckett.* James Knowlson, ed. New York: Grove, [1985]; *As the Story Was Told.* London: J. Calder/New York: Riverrun, [1990]. (Prose); *Krapp's Last Tape.* Revised text, edited by James Knowlson. New York: Grove, 1992; *Nowhere On.* London: Calder, 1992; *Dream of Fair to Middling Women.* Eoin O'Brien & Edith Fournier, eds. Dublin: Black Cat Press, [1992]; *Samuel Beckett's Company/Compagnie and A Piece of Monologue/Solo: A Bilingual Variorum Edition.* Charles Krance, ed. New York & London: Garland, 1993. In 1971, *The Collected Works of Samuel Beckett* was published by Grove in 19 volumes.   REFERENCES: Acheson, James, & Arthur, Kateryna, eds. *Beckett's Later Fiction and Drama.* [Basingstoke & London]: Macmillan, [1987]; Admussen, Richard L. *The Samuel Beckett Manuscripts: A Study.* Boston: G. K. Hall, 1979; Alvarez, A. *Beckett.* 2d ed. [London]: Fontana, [1992]; Amiran, Eyal. *Wandering and Home: Beckett's Metaphysical Narrative.* University Park: Pennsylvania State University Press, [1993]; Andonian, Cathleen Culotta. *Samuel Beckett: A Reference Guide.* Boston: G. K. Hall, 1989. (Bibliography of Criticism); Armstrong, Gordon. *Samuel Beckett, W. B. Yeats, and Jack Yeats: Images and Words.* Lewisburg, Pa.: Bucknell University Press, [1990]; *As No Other Dare Fail: For Samuel Beckett on His 80th Birthday by His Friends and Admirers.* London: John Calder/New York: Riverrun, [1986]; Astro, Alan. *Understanding Samuel Beckett.* [Columbia]: University of South Carolina Press, [1990]; Athanason, Arthur N. *Endgame: The Ashbin Play.* New York: Twayne, 1993; Bair, Deirdre. *Samuel Beckett.* New York: Harcourt Brace Jovanovich, 1978. (Biography); Beja, Morris; Gontarski, S. E., & Astier, Pierre, eds. *Samuel Beckett: Humanistic Perspectives.* Columbus: Ohio State University Press, 1983; Ben-Zvi, Linda. *Samuel Beckett.* Boston: Twayne, [1986]; Brater, Enoch, ed. *Beckett at 80/Beckett in Context.* New York & Oxford: Oxford University Press, 1986; Brater, Enoch. *Beyond Minimalism: Beckett's Later Style in the Theatre.* New York & Oxford: Oxford University Press, 1987; Brater, Enoch, ed. *Beckett in Dublin.* [Dublin]: Lilliput, [1992]; Brater, Enoch. *The Drama in the Text: Beckett's Later Fiction.* New York & Oxford: Oxford University Press, 1994; Brienza, Susan D. *Samuel Beckett's New Worlds: Style in Metafiction.* Norman & London: University of Oklahoma Press, [1987]; Bruzzo, Francois. *Samuel Beckett.* Paris: Veyrier, 1991; Bryden, Mary. *Women in Samuel Beckett's Prose and Drama.* [Basingstoke & London]: Macmillan/[Lanham, Md.]: Barnes & Noble, [1993]; Burkman, Katherine H., ed. *Myth and Ritual in the Plays of Samuel Beckett.* Rutherford, Madison & Teaneck, N.J.: Fairleigh Dickinson University Press, [1987]; Butler, Lance St John, ed. *Critical Thought Series: 4. Critical Essays on Samuel Beckett.* [Aldershot, Hants]: Scholar Press, [1993]; Buttner, Gottfried. *Samuel Beckett's Novel Watt.* Philadelphia: University of Pennsylvania Press, [1984]; Cohn, Ruby. *Samuel Beckett: The Comic Gamut.* New Brunswick, N.J.: Rutgers University Press, 1962; Cohn, Ruby, ed. *Samuel Beckett: A Collection of Criticism.* New York: McGraw-Hill, 1975; Cohn, Ruby. *Just Play: Beckett's Theatre.* Princeton, N.J.: Princeton University Press, [1980]; Connor, Steven. *Samuel Beckett: Repetition, Theory and Text.* [Oxford]: Basil Blackwell, [1988]; Cooke, Virginia. *Beckett on File.* London & New York: Methuen, 1985; Cormier, Ramona, & Pallister, James L. *Waiting for Death: The Philosophical Significance of Beckett's En Attendant Godot.* University: University of Alabama Press, [1979];

Cousineau, Thomas. *Waiting for Godot: Form in Movement.* New York: Twayne, 1990; Davis, Paul. *The Ideal Real: Beckett's Fiction and Imagination.* Rutherford, Madison & Teaneck, N.J.: Fairleigh Dickinson University Press, [1994]; Davis, Robin J. *Samuel Beckett: Checklist and Index of His Published Works 1967–1976.* Stirling: Library, University of Stirling, for the Author, 1979; Davis, Robin J., & Butler, Lance St. J. *"Make Sense Who May": Essays on Samuel Beckett's Later Works.* Gerrards Cross: Colin Smythe, 1988; Dearlove, J. E. *Accommodating the Chaos: Samuel Beckett's Nonrelational Art.* Durham, N.C.: Duke University Press, 1982; Di Pietro, John C. *Structures in Beckett's* Watt. York, S.C.: French Literature Publications, 1981; Doll, Mary A. *Beckett and Myth: An Archetypal Approach.* [Syracuse, N.Y.]: Syracuse University Press, [1988]; Ekbom, Torsten. *Samuel Beckett.* Stockholm: Natur och Kultur, 1991; Elovaara, Raili. *The Problem of Identity in Samuel Beckett's Prose.* Helsinki: Suomalainen Tiedeakatemia, 1976; Esslin, Martin, ed. *Samuel Beckett: A Collection of Critical Essays.* Englewood Cliffs, N.J.: Prentice-Hall, 1965; Esslin, Martin. *The Theatre of the Absurd.* Rev. ed. [Harmondsworth]: Penguin, [1968]; Federman, Raymond. *Journey to Chaos, Samuel Beckett's Early Fiction.* Berkeley & Los Angeles: University of California Press, 1965; Federman, Raymond, & Fletcher, John. *Samuel Beckett, His Works and His Critics.* Berkeley & Los Angeles: University of California Press, 1970. (Bibliography); Fitch, Brian T. *Beckett and Babel: An Investigation into the Status of the Bilingual Work.* Toronto, Buffalo & London: University of Toronto Press, [1988]; Fletcher, Beryl S., & Fletcher, John. *A Student's Guide to the Plays of Samuel Beckett.* 2d ed. London: Faber, 1985; Fletcher, John. *Samuel Beckett's Art.* London: Chatto & Windus, 1967; Fletcher, John, & Spurling, John. *Beckett the Playwright.* London: Methuen, [1985]. (3d, expanded edition of *Beckett: A Study of His Plays*); Foster, Paul. *Beckett and Zen: A Study of the Dilemma in the Novels of Samuel Beckett.* London: Wisdom, [1987]; Friedman, Alan Warren et al. *Beckett Translating/Translating Beckett.* University Park: Pennsylvania State University Press, [1987]; Friedman, Melvin J., ed. *Samuel Beckett Now.* Chicago: University of Chicago Press, 1970; Gidal, Peter. *Understanding Beckett: A Study of Monologue and Gesture in the Works of Samuel Beckett.* [Basingstoke & London]: Macmillan, [1986]; Gluck, Barbara Reich. *Beckett & Joyce: Friendship in Fiction.* Lewisburg, Pa.: Bucknell University Press, [1979]; Gontarski, S. E. *Beckett's "Happy Days": A Manuscript Study.* Columbus: Ohio State University Libraries, 1977; Gontarski, S. E. *The Intent of Undoing in Samuel Beckett's Dramatic Texts.* Bloomington: Indiana University Press, [1985]; Gontarski, S. E. *On Beckett: Essays and Criticism.* New York: Grove, [1986]; Gontarski, S. E., ed. *The Beckett Studies Reader.* Gainesville: University Press of Florida, [1993]; Graver, Lawrence, & Federman, Raymond, eds. *Samuel Beckett: The Critical Heritage.* London: Routledge, 1979; Hale, Jane Alison. *The Broken Window: Beckett's Dramatic Perspective.* West Lafayette, Ind.: Purdue University Press, [1987]; Harrington, John P. *The Irish Beckett.* [Syracuse, N.Y.:] Syracuse University Press, [1991]; Hauck, Gerhard. *Reductionism in Drama and the Theatre: The Case of Samuel Beckett.* Potomac, Md.: Scripta Humanistica, 1992; Hayman, Ronald. *Samuel Beckett.* 3d ed. London: Heinemann, [1980]; Henning, Sylvie Debevec. *Beckett's Critical Complicity: Carnival, Contestation, and Tradition.* [Lexington]: University Press of Kentucky, [1988]; Hill, Leslie. *Beckett's Fiction in Different Worlds.* Cambridge: Cambridge University Press, [1990]; Homan, Sidney. *Beckett's Theatres: Interpretations for Performance.* Lewisburg, Pa.: Bucknell University Press, [1984]; Homan, Sidney. *Filming Beckett's Television Plays: A Director's Experience.* Lewisburg, Pa.: Bucknell University Press, [1992]; Junker, Mary. *Beckett: The Irish Dimension.* Dublin: Wolfhound, 1995; Kalb, Jonathan. *Beckett in Performance.* Cambridge: Cambridge University Press, [1989]; Kennedy, Andrew K. *Samuel Beckett.* Cambridge: Cambridge University Press, [1989]; Kenner, Hugh. *Samuel Beckett: A Critical Study.* New York: Grove, 1961/London: J. Calder, 1962/revised, Berkeley & Los Angeles: University of California Press, 1969; Knowlson, James, & Pilling, John. *Frescoes of the Skull: The Later Prose and Drama of Samuel Beckett.* London: J. Calder, 1979/New York: Grove, 1980; Locatelli, Carla. *Unwording the World: Samuel Beckett's Prose Works after the Nobel Prize.* Philadelphia: University of Pennsylvania Press, [1990]; Levy, Eric P. *Beckett and the Voice of Species: A Study of the Prose Fiction.* [Dublin]: Gill & Macmillan/Totowa, N.J.: Barnes & Noble, [1980]; Levy, Shimon. *Samuel Beckett's Self-Referential Drama.* [Basingstoke & London]: Macmillan, [1990];

Lyons, Charles R. *Samuel Beckett.* New York: Grove, [1983]; McCarthy, Patrick A. *Critical Essays on Samuel Beckett.* Boston: G. K. Hall, 1986; McMillan, Dougald, & Fehsenfeld, Martha. *Beckett in the Theatre: The Author as Practical Playwright and Director.* Vol. I. *From* Waiting for Godot *to* Krapp's Last Tape. London: J. Calder/New York: Riverrun, [1988]; McMullen, Anna. *Theatre on Trial: Samuel Beckett's Later Drama.* New York & London: Routledge, [1993]; Mercier, Vivian. *Beckett/Beckett.* New York: Oxford University Press, 1977; Miller, Lawrence. *Samuel Beckett: The Expressive Dilemma.* [Basingstoke & London]: Macmillan/[New York]: St. Martin's, [1992]; Mitchell, Breon. "A Beckett Bibliography: New Works 1976–1982." *Modern Fiction Studies* 29 (Spring 1983): 131–151; Morot-Sir, Edouard; Harper, Howard, & McMillan, Dougald, eds. *Samuel Beckett: The Art of Rhetoric.* Chapel Hill: University of North Carolina Press, 1976; Murphy, P. J. *Reconstructing Beckett: Language for Being in Samuel Beckett's Fiction.* Toronto, Buffalo & London: University of Toronto Press, [1990]; O'Brien, Eoin. *The Beckett Country: Samuel Beckett's Ireland.* Dublin: Black Cat/London: Faber, 1986; Pilling, John, & Bryden, Mary, eds. *The Ideal Core of the Onion: Reading Beckett Archives.* Reading: Beckett International Foundation, 1992; Pountney, Rosemary. *Theatre of Shadows: Samuel Beckett's Drama 1956–76.* Gerrards Cross: Colin Smythe/Totowa, N.J.: Barnes & Noble, [1988]; Raghavan, Hema V. *Samuel Beckett: Rebels and Exiles in His Plays.* [Liverpool]: Lucas, [1988]; Ricks, Christopher. *Beckett's Dying Words: The Clarendon Lectures.* Oxford: Clarendon, 1990; Schulz, Hans-Joachim. *This Hell of Stories: A Hegelian Approach to the Novels of Samuel Beckett.* The Hague & Paris: Mouton, 1973; Smith, Joseph H., ed. *The World of Samuel Beckett.* Baltimore & London: Johns Hopkins University Press, [1991]; Solomon, Philip H. *The Life after Birth: Imagery in Samuel Beckett's Trilogy.* University, Miss.: Romance Monographs, 1975; Topsfield, Valerie. *The Humour of Samuel Beckett.* [Basingstoke & London]: Macmillan, [1988]; Webb, Eugene. *Samuel Beckett: A Study of His Novels.* London: Peter Owen, [1970]; Whitelaw, Billie. *Billie Whitelaw . . . Who He?* [London]: Hodder & Stoughton, [1995]; Worth, Katherine, ed. *Beckett the Shape Changer.* London & Boston: Routledge & Kegan Paul, [1975]. Since 1976, Florida State University, in Tallahassee, has published a *Journal of Beckett Studies.*

BEHAN, BRENDAN [FRANCIS] (1923–1964), playwright and novelist. Behan was born in Dublin on February 9, 1923, while the Irish Civil War was drawing to a close and his father was imprisoned for Republican activities. This conflict was to mold Behan's career: he spent many of his formative years in prison for political offenses, and there he found the raw material for his major works. Though his writings reflected a growing disenchantment with all kinds of violence, he clung to the ideal of a free Ireland, and when he died on March 20, 1964 he was given a military-style funeral by the illegal Irish Republican Army.

From the beginning, Behan's literary activities were a function of his dedication to the creation of an Irish republic. As a member of Fianna Éireann, the junior branch of the IRA, he contributed patriotic prose and verse to the magazine *Fianna: The Voice of Young Ireland* and to other radical organs. Brought up to revere the memory of those who had fought and suffered for Irish freedom, he longed to strike a blow himself. The campaign of bombing which the IRA launched in England in 1939 seemed an ideal opportunity: Behan was trained in the use of explosives but waited in vain for the call to active service. In November 1939, despite the appeals of family and friends, he traveled to Liverpool where he was spotted and soon picked up by detectives. On February 7, 1940, he was tried, convicted of possessing explosives, and sentenced to three years' detention at Borstal—the maximum sentence a frustrated judge could hand down to a juvenile.

Behan enjoyed most of his time in Borstal; he served only two years and was deported to Ireland in November 1941. Shortly afterwards he was in court again, this time for firing several shots at a detective during an IRA ceremony on April 5, 1942. He was considered fortunate to escape a death sentence. Instead, he got fourteen years, of which he served five before being released under a general amnesty at the end of 1946. These were relatively pleasant and fruitful years for him, and he remembered them as a period of higher education. Various classes were organized by Republican prisoners: there was a fairly high standard of instruction, which led to a wide range of debate, reading, and writing. Behan's convivial wit was well known, while his literary ability was noted by Sean O'Faolain,* who published *I Become a Borstal Boy* in *The Bell** in June 1942. With the assistance of Seán Ó Briain, a fellow prisoner who was a native speaker of Irish, Behan studied the language and literature of Gaelic Ireland. With the idea of writing in Irish, he glimpsed the possibility of integrating his literary and political aspirations. He translated his play *The Landlady* into Irish and submitted it to the Abbey Theatre* without success. He also offered the Abbey a play about hanging entitled *Casadh Súgáin Eile (The Twisting of Another Rope)*, on which he continued to work outside prison.

In December 1946, Behan's first poem in Irish, in honor of an IRA leader who had died on a hunger-strike, was published in *Comhar,* the Irish language magazine. Over the next six years, he wrote some dozen short poems in Irish, two of which were included in *Nuabhéarsaíocht,* an anthology of contemporary verse edited by Seán Ó Tuama in 1950. The quality of Behan's Gaelic verse is uneven. In the more sombre lyrics, he found a medium of self-scrutiny, which often escaped him when writing in English. Such efforts revealed a vulnerable personality, prone to anguish at the frustration of his dreams. More jovial pieces suggested a clash between his own hopes for a revival of Irish culture and his lack of sympathy with those of the revivalist establishment whom he found dull and puritanical. In *Guí an Rannaire (The Rimer's Prayer),* he seemed to imply that his poetic gift was insufficient to provide the desired revolution; shortly afterwards he abandoned Irish verse.

By the late 1940s, Behan was beginning to establish himself as a writer in English and as a Dublin "character." After short spells in prison and an effort to settle in Paris, he returned to Dublin in 1950 to make his living as a journalist while working on what would become *The Quare Fellow* and *Borstal Boy.* In the early 1950s, he published three short stories, "A Woman of No Standing" (*Envoy,* Dublin, 1950), "After the Wake" (*Points,* Paris, 1950), and "The Confirmation Suit" (*The Standard,* Dublin, 1953); two short plays for radio, *Moving Out* and *A Garden Party* (1952); and a very entertaining crime story which was serialized in *The Irish Times* in 1953 and published in book form as *The Scarperer* in 1964. The exceptions among these are "A Woman of No Standing" and "After the Wake," one a story of forbidden love, the other of homosexuality, both written in a quiet contemplative style. Almost all the other works depict Behan's particular demimonde of early-opening pubs and extravagant characters, which were realized in what may be termed *Behanese*, a highly cultivated comic language based on the working-class dialect of Dublin and liberally laced with ballads and historical allusions.

In 1954, the year of his marriage to Beatrice Salkeld, Behan's play about hanging, *The Quare Fellow,* was accepted by the Pike Theatre in Dublin. The full story of the production is told by Alan Simpson in *Beckett and Behan and a Theatre in Dublin* (London, 1962). Two years later, a splendid production of the play by the Theatre Workshop in London earned Behan critical esteem outside Ireland. He himself won another kind of fame by appearing drunk on television—then considered an outrage—and by generally presenting an image of himself as a roaring boy to the gratified media. *The Quare Fellow* was taken as a protest against capital punishment but was much more than that and never lapsed into propaganda: with gruesome humor it lacerated the idea of institutionalized violence and celebrated man's efforts to cope with oppression and death. Seen in the context of Behan's career, it was an attempt to exorcise the nightmare memory of his own narrow escapes from execution.

Behan was now in great demand. *The Big House,* commissioned by the BBC and broadcast in 1957, is an exhilarating romp on the fate of the Anglo-Irish after Irish independence, similar in tone and texture to the pieces Behan wrote in his *Irish Press* column. *An Giall (The Hostage)* was written for An Halla Damer, a small Irish-language theatre in Dublin. That Behan, on the crest of an international wave, provided a play for the Damer showed his deep commitment to the ideal of an Irish Ireland; the play itself marked his imaginative rejection of political violence and fanaticism and his sympathy for those caught up in ideological conflicts. The applause which greeted *An Giall* in 1958 was soon drowned in the outbursts of wild enthusiasm which greeted *The Hostage* and Behan in London, Paris, and New York. *The Hostage* was by no means a simple translation of *An Giall,* and Behan's part in the metamorphosis of a naturalistic tragedy into a music hall *mélange* of song, dance, and knockabout satire is a matter of dispute. The success of *The Hostage* showed that it was right for the time, and the script was continually changed to keep it so. It is doubtful if the play will retain its initial impact.

No such doubts arise in the case of *Borstal Boy,* which also appeared in 1958. This creative autobiography pretended to be a spontaneous account of Behan's detention in England from 1939 to 1941; in fact, it was a carefully wrought portrait of the artist as a young prisoner. The narrator was not so much a pioneer of the British as of his own inherited prejudices; these were severely tested when he came face to face with the old enemy and found much to love and admire in him. The young Brendan of *Borstal Boy* remains Behan's finest creation, while some of the episodes—The Stations of the Cross, for example— are among the best in comic literature.

Towards the end of *Borstal Boy,* there were signs of a slight loss of control.

By 1958, Behan was a prisoner of his own success, unable to climb off the international merry-go-round, discard the mask of the roaring boy, and return to the typewriter. He spoke into tape recorders the books he was unable to write; not surprisingly, there was a falling off in quality. *Confessions of an Irish Rebel* takes up the story of *Borstal Boy*, but that is all. Behan made little progress with a novel of Dublin life to be called *The Catacombs*. English and Irish versions of a new play, *Richard's Cork Leg*, were rejected as mere drafts. His efforts to begin again were thwarted by diabetes and alcoholism, and he had abandoned writing when he died in 1964. Many of the thousands who attended his funeral had probably read none of his books, but to working-class Dublin, Behan was much more than a writer: he was a favorite, charming, wayward son.

COLBERT KEARNEY

WORKS: *An Giall*. Dublin: An Chomhairle Naisunta Dramaoichta, n.d.; *Borstal Boy*. London: Hutchinson, 1958/New York: Knopf, 1959. (Prison autobiography); *Brendan Behan's Island*. London: Hutchinson/New York: Bernard Geis, 1962. (Includes "The Big House," "The Confirmation Suit," and "A Woman of No Standing"); *Hold Your Hour and Have Another*. London: Hutchinson, 1963/Boston: Little, Brown, 1964. (Sketches); *Brendan Behan's New York*. London: Hutchinson, 1964; *The Scarperer*. New York: Doubleday, 1964/London: Hutchinson, 1966. (Novel); *Confessions of an Irish Rebel*. London: Hutchinson, [1965]/New York: Bernard Geis, 1966; *The Complete Plays of Brendan Behan*. London: Eyre Methuen, 1978; *Brendan Behan: Poems and a Play in Irish*. Prionsias Ní Dhorchaí, ed. Dublin: Gallery, 1981. (Includes *An Giall*) *After the Wake*. Peter Fallon, ed. Dublin: O'Brien, [1981]. (Stories); *An Giall* [and] *The Hostage*. Washington, D.C.: Catholic University of America Press/Gerrards Cross: Colin Smythe, 1987. (*An Giall* translated into English by the editor Richard Wall and printed with Behan's English version); *Letters of Brendan Behan*. E. H. Mikhail, ed. Toronto: McGill-Queen's University Press, 1992.   REFERENCES: Arthur, Peter. *With Brendan Behan, A Personal Memoir*. New York: St. Martin's, 1981/London: Routledge, Kegan Paul, 1982; Behan, Beatrice, with Des Hickey & Gus Smith. *My Life with Brendan*. London: Leslie Frewin, 1973; Behan, Dominic. *My Brother Brendan*. London: Leslie Frewin, 1965; Boyle, Ted E. *Brendan Behan*. New York: Twayne, 1969; Cronin, Anthony. *Dead as Doornails*. Dublin: Dolmen, 1975. (Reminiscences of Behan and others); de Burca, Seamus. *Brendan Behan, a Memoir*. rev. 3d ed. Dublin: P. J. Bourke, 1993; Gerdes, Peter Rene. *The Major Works of Brendan Behan*. Berne: Herbert Lang/Frankfurt: Peter Lang, 1973; Goorney, Howard. *The Theatre Workshop Story*. London & New York: Eyre Methuen, 1981; Jeffs, Rae. *Brendan Behan, Man and Showman*. London: Hutchinson, 1966; Kearney, Colbert. *The Writings of Brendan Behan*. Dublin: Gill & Macmillan, 1977; McCann, Sean, ed. *The World of Brendan Behan*. London: New English Library, 1965/New York: Twayne, 1966; Mikhail, E. H., ed. *The Art of Brendan Behan*. London: Vision/New York: Barnes & Noble, 1979; Mikhail, E. H. *Brendan Behan: An Annotated Bibliography of Criticism*. London: Macmillan, 1982; Mikhail, E. H. *Brendan Behan: Interviews and Recollections*. 2 vols. London: Macmillan/Dublin: Gill & Macmillan, 1982/New York: Barnes & Noble, 1983; O'Connor, Ulick. *Brendan*. London: Hamish Hamilton, 1970/Englewood Cliffs, N.J.: Prentice-Hall, 1971. (Biography); Porter, Raymond J. *Brendan Behan*. New York & London: Columbia University Press, 1973. (Pamphlet); Simpson, Alan. *Beckett and Behan and a Theatre in Dublin*. London: Routledge & Kegan Paul, 1962/New York: Hilary House, 1966.

BEHAN, BRIAN (1927–199?), novelist and memoirist. Behan was born in Dublin, the third son of Kathleen and Stephen Behan and the brother of Brendan* and Dominic Behan.* An active trade unionist in his earlier years, he visited the Soviet Union, where he met Stalin, and China, where he met Chairman Mao. When about forty, he became a mature student at Sussex University and later taught at the London College of Printing.

His *Kathleen, A Dublin Saga* (1988) is a novel loosely based on the life of his mother and with a character closely resembling his brother Brendan dominating the concluding pages. Some historical characters, such as Pearse,* Connolly, and Larkin, are given their real names; but for some reason others, such as W. B. Yeats,* Maud Gonne, and Roger Casement, are given fictional names. For window dressing, Leopold Bloom and Bessie Burgess make appearances, although Mrs. Burgess little resembles Sean O'Casey's* character. Behan also takes certain liberties with facts, such as giving his heroine a lover resembling Synge* and another resembling O'Casey. For a Dublin man, he makes a few curious errors, such as situating the Queen's Theatre in Abbey Street. On the whole, the volume is a fairly readable amalgam of insight and spuriousness. A more authentic and better book is *Mother of All the Behans* (1984), his transcription of his mother's reminiscences.

WORKS: *With Breast Expanded.* London: MacGibbon & Kee, 1964. (Memoir); *Time to Go.* London: Martin Brian & O'Keeffe, [1979]. (Novel); *Mother of All the Behans: The Autobiography of Kathleen Behan as Told to Brian Behan.* [London]: Hutchinson, [1984]; *Kathleen, A Dublin Saga.* London: Century, [1988].

BEHAN, DOMINIC (1923–1989), novelist, playwright, biographer, and folksinger. Behan was the brother of Brendan* and Brian* and the son of Stephen Behan, a sign painter, and his wife Kathleen Furlong (born Kearney). Brought up in the same socialist-republican atmosphere as his brothers, Dominic in his unpublished play *Posterity Be Damned* (Gaiety Theatre, Dublin, February 28, 1960) voiced an early rejection of the old family cause. He became first known as a dramatist, but in this he was overshadowed by his elder brother Brendan. His own account of the family appeared as *Teems of Times and Happy Returns* (1961) and *My Brother Brendan* (1965). After a great deal of journalism and radio work and many years as a professional folksinger, he returned to writing with a 1988 biography of the Irish comedian Spike Milligan* and a novel, *The Public World of Parable Burns* (1989). Though lacking the feckless charm of Brendan, the harder life of Dominic (and Brian) made for tougher books, which were not negligible among the literary outpourings of a remarkable family. After his death in Scotland in the summer of 1989, his ashes were scattered on August 13, 1989, on the Royal Canal, behind the old family home at 14 Russell Street, north Dublin.

PETER COSTELLO

WORKS: *Teems of Times and Happy Returns.* London: Heinemann, 1961/as *Tell Dublin I Miss Her.* New York: G. P. Putnam's Sons, [1962]. (Autobiography); *My Brother Brendan.* London: Leslie Frewin, 1965; with George Tardios. *A Modern Tower Reading.* Newcastle upon Tyne: Modern Tower, 1976. (Poetry pamphlet); *A Tribute to Malachy McGurran.* London, 1979; *Milligan— The Life and Times of Spike Milligan.* London: Methuen, 1988; *The Public World of Parable Jones.* London: Collins, 1989. (Novel). REFERENCE: *Irish Times,* August 14, 1989.

BELL, THE (1940–1954), literary magazine. *The Bell,* together with Seumas O'Sullivan's* *The Dublin Magazine,** shares the honor of being the longest lived and most distinguished modern Irish literary magazine. It was founded by Sean O'Faolain* in October 1940, and its distinguished first number included stories, poems, essays, and reviews by O'Faolain, Frank O'Connor,* Elizabeth Bowen,* Patrick Kavanagh,* Brinsley MacNamara,* Flann O'Brien (Brian O'Nolan),* Peadar O'Donnell,* Lennox Robinson,* Maurice Walsh,* and Jack B. Yeats.* Succeeding numbers continued that high standard. The magazine published items by most of Ireland's established writers and fostered the early work of Bryan MacMahon,* John Montague,* Conor Cruise O'Brien* ("Donat O'Donnell"), James Plunkett,* Anthony Cronin,* and Val Mulkerns,* among others.

Under the wartime editorship of O'Faolain, *The Bell* emerged as a lonely liberal voice evaluating and criticizing establishment standards, such as the government censorship of books. This social orientation was even more emphasized when Peadar O'Donnell, the novelist, succeeded O'Faolain as editor in 1946. Rudi Holzapfel, the magazine's subsequent bibliographer, wrote that *The Bell* under O'Donnell "seemed to lose favour among the Irish people due to its aggressive, punchy left-wingism. However, to be fair, it is precisely this increased interest in Irish social welfare which makes the later issues of *The Bell* such a valuable document for historians of the day."

The magazine ceased publication in its fifteenth year with the December 1954 issue, its one-hundred and thirty-first number.

REFERENCES: Holzapfel, Rudi, comp., *The Bell: An Index of Contributors.* Blackrock: Carraig Books, 1970; McMahon, Sean, ed., *The Best from The Bell.* Dublin: O'Brien, 1978.

BELL, SAM HANNA (1909–1990), novelist, short story writer, and broadcaster. Bell was born in Glasgow on October 16, 1909, of Irish emigrant parents. His father worked as a journalist on the *Glasgow Herald,* but when he died, young Bell was sent to live with his mother's people at Raffrey, near Strangford Lough. A rather patchy rural education was followed by a brief period in Belfast Art School, and then Bell held a wide variety of jobs, including night watchman, laboratory attendant, salesman, and clerk with the Canadian Steamship and Railway Company. His first writing was for the BBC in Belfast, and he was greatly encouraged by Louis MacNeice.* Like other Northern writers of his generation who were without the fare to London, Bell turned also to Dublin for encouragement. He received it from Sean O'Faolain,* who was then editing *The Bell.** Sam Hanna Bell wrote some short stories for the magazine, which were collected in 1943 as *Summer Loanen and Other Stories.*

Bell's major work, the novel called *December Bride* (1951), grew out of a comic short story that O'Faolain stimulated Bell to write about his mother's family. Written in an old-fashioned prose style reminiscent of Hardy, the book marvelously evokes the harshness of rural life in the Ards Peninsula at the turn of the century. The plot centers around a servant girl, Sarah Gomartin, and her affair with two brothers. Her refusal to name the father of her child or to marry either of them leads to ostracism and other savage reprisals from the narrow rural community. Sarah, an interesting study of a strong-willed, manipulating woman who resents the strictures of her time, finally bows to public opinion and marries for the sake of her daughter. The attitudes of Presbyterians toward their Catholic neighbors are skillfully depicted, and there is also one especially funny episode in a Belfast pub when an old drunk, not realizing he is in a Catholic pub, requests an Orange song. The novel was banned in the 1950s in the South, although it is difficult now to see why. A film of it was released after Bell's death.

Bell wrote three other novels—*The Hollow Ball* (1961) about a footballer and unemployment, *A Man Flourishing* (1973) about the 1798 Rising, and *Across the Narrow Sea* (1987), an historical novel set in County Down in 1608. The latter book is rich in detail and depicts a church-ridden Ulster where no effort was made by the Scottish immigrants to integrate as the Normans and early English settlers had in the rest of Ireland. The main focus of the plot is a romantic love story that tends to slump in the middle but is, in some ways, an interesting illumination of the problems of Ulster today. Nevertheless, *December Bride* is justly considered Bell's best work. He also wrote a folklore volume entitled *Erin's Orange Lily* (1956) and a theatrical history entitled *The Theatre in Ulster* (1972). After retiring as a features producer for the BBC in Belfast in 1969, Bell continued to freelance and also to run the literary section of the *Ulster Tatler*. He died in Belfast on February 9, 1990.

MARY ROSE CALLAGHAN

WORKS: *Summer Loanen and Other Stories.* Newcastle, County Down: Mourne, 1943; *December Bride.* London: Dobson, [1951]/Belfast: Blackstaff, 1974. (Novel); ed., with Nesca A. Robb & John Hewitt, *The Arts in Ulster.* London: Harrap, [1951]; *Erin's Orange Lily.* London: Dobson, 1956. (Folklore); *The Hollow Ball.* London: Cassell, 1961. (Novel); *The Theatre in Ulster.* Dublin: Gill & Macmillan, 1972; *A Man Flourishing.* London: Gollancz, 1973. (Novel).

BENNETT, LOUIE (1870–1956), novelist, woman's activist, and trade union organizer. Bennett was born in Blackrock, County Dublin, and educated at Alexandra College, in England and in Bonn. She was principally notable for her social activism, particularly in the women's suffrage movement in the early years of the century, in proselytization against the First World War, and later in the Irish labor movement. She did write, however, two romantic novels of quite minor merit. She died in November 1956.

WORKS: *The Proving of Priscilla.* London & New York: Harper, 1902; *A Prisoner of His Word.* Dublin: Maunsel, 1908. REFERENCE: Fox, R. M. *Louie Bennett, Her Life and Times.* Dublin: Talbot, 1957.

BENNETT, RONAN (1950s–   ), novelist. Bennett was born in Belfast. In the 1970s, he was imprisoned in Long Kesh and in Brixton Prison for republican activities but defended himself successfully against conspiracy charges in a

three-month trial at the Old Bailey. After graduating in history, he completed a
Ph.D. in legal history at London University. He was involved in the campaign
to free the Guildford Four and in 1990 cowrote Paul Hill's book *Stolen Years:
Before and After Guildford.* His first novel, *The Second Prison* (1991), is a well-
characterized and well-plotted story about Augustine Kane, an Irish Republican
Army (IRA) member who has spent eleven years in prison and on his release
is bent on killing a childhood friend who betrayed him. However, the pattern
of betrayal is more complicated than Kane thinks, and finally even such an
embittered character as he has a change of heart. The scenes in prison and the
trial sequences are excellently done.

WORKS: *The Second Prison.* London: Hamish Hamilton, [1991]; *Overthrown by Strangers.* London: Hamish Hamilton, 1992.

BERKELEY, GEORGE (1685–1753), philosopher. Berkeley, bishop of
Cloyne, Ireland's most eminent philosopher, was born on March 12, 1685, in
County Kilkenny. He attended Kilkenny College and then entered Trinity College, Dublin, at the early age of fifteen. He received his B.A. in 1704 and his
M.A. in 1707, when he also received a fellowship. As an undergraduate, he
became acquainted with John Locke's *Essay Concerning Human Understanding,*
in reaction to which he wrote his major works—*Essay Towards a New Theory
of Vision* (1709), *The Principles of Human Knowledge* (1710), and *Three Dialogues between Hylas and Philonous* (1713). With these three volumes, Berkeley
defined his philosophical position; for the last forty years of his life, his interest
was in a variety of concerns other than philosophy.

In 1713, Berkeley went to London and made the acquaintance of the leading
literary men of the day: Swift,* Steele,* Addison, Pope, and Arbuthnot. Then
for several years he traveled in France and Italy, first as chaplain (on Swift's
recommendation) to Lord Peterborough and later as a tutor. He returned to
Ireland in 1723 when he received the deanery of Dromore and later the deanery
of Derry. In 1725, he received half of the estate of Hester Vanhomrigh, Swift's
Vanessa, although she had never or, at most, briefly met him.

Much of his energies in the 1720s were taken up with advancing a project to
found a college in the Bermudas, and for a time he seemed likely to receive
£20,000 from the government to inaugurate the college. He moved to America
and lived for nearly three years in Newport, Rhode Island, at the end of which
time he despaired of ever receiving aid for the college, and so returned in 1732
to London.

In 1734, Berkeley was consecrated bishop of Cloyne where he spent most of
the next eighteen years. In that time, he wrote pacificatory essays on the state
of Ireland, and he wrote on economics, somewhat anticipating the theories of
Adam Smith. However, he was interested chiefly in promoting a resinous fluid
called tarwater as an almost universal panacea. His last major work, *Siris* (1744),
was written largely as a result of his interest in tarwater, and its rambling erudition added nothing to his reputation.

He retired in bad health to England in 1752, and he died in Oxford on January 14, 1753.

Berkeley's philosophic position was developed as a refutation of John Locke whose espousal of a material universe seemed to Berkeley to have pernicious implications for religion. Locke accepted a Newtonian universe of real matter which presumably God had set in motion, but which now, like some vast machine, ticked on by its own self-sustaining and inexorable rules. To Berkeley, there was very little need or place for God in such a universe, and very little place either for soul or spirit. Consequently, to put God and soul back into the center of things, Berkeley posited that matter was, in fact, nonexistent. A weakness of Locke's position is that man perceives matter only by an idea of it in his mind, but, to Berkeleyan common sense, there is no way of ascertaining whether any perception is in fact true. Berkeley asserted that all one could be certain of was the idea in one's mind and that there need be no corresponding matter to the idea at all. In Berkeley's view, what exists is not material bodies in a material universe, but only in the mind of God who communicates the ideas of matter to the finite minds of man.

Berkeley systematically elaborated this view in *The Principles of Human Knowledge* and proselytized for it in the quite readable *Three Dialogues.* Despite his pious motivations and his reliance on common sense, Berkeley seemed nonsensical to most of his contemporaries. As one later writer remarked, "In assaulting matter he seemed to destroy reality." The view of the ordinary thinking man was well summed up by Dr. Johnson who kicked a stone and truculently remarked, "Thus I refute Berkeley." However, as G. J. Warnock wrote: "Locke gave the classic exposition of one of the traditional accounts of perception and the material world, Berkeley set out no less ably the classic response; and between them they established a pattern of argument on this subject which has remained central in philosophy right down to the present day." (Introduction to *The Principles of Human Knowledge and Other Writings.* London: Collins/Fontana, 1962.) By his *Principles of Human Knowledge* Berkeley became a central figure in modern philosophy; but in his *Three Dialogues* he wedded, as had Plato before him, philosophy to literature.

WORK: *The Works of George Berkeley, Bishop of Cloyne.* A. A. Luce & T. E. Jessop, eds. 9 vols. London: Nelson, 1948–1957.   REFERENCES: Bracken, H. M. *Berkeley.* London: Macmillan, 1974; Jessop, T. E. *A Bibliography of George Berkeley . . . with Inventory of Berkeley's Manuscript Remains* by A. A. Luce. 2d ed. The Hague: Martinus Nijhoff, 1973; Keynes, Geoffrey. *A Bibliography of Berkeley.* Oxford: Clarendon, 1976; Luce, A. A. *Berkeley's Immaterialism.* London: Nelson, 1945; Luce, A. A. The *Life of George Berkeley, Bishop of Cloyne.* London: Nelson, 1949; Pitcher, George. *Berkeley.* London: Routledge & Kegan Paul, 1977; Rossi, M. M. *Bishop Berkeley.* London: Faber, 1931; Walmsley, Peter. *The Rhetoric of Berkeley's Philosophy.* Cambridge: Cambridge University Press, 1990; Warnock, G. J. *Berkeley.* London: Pelican, 1953.

BERKELEY, SARA B. (1967–   ), poet and short story writer. Born in Ireland, Berkeley took a B.A. in English literature and German at Trinity College, Dublin, studied at the University of California at Berkeley, and received an M.Sc.

in technical writing from South Bank Polytechnic in London. Dermot Bolger* published her two volumes of poetry while she was still a student at Trinity, and the first one, *Penn* (1986), was short-listed for the Irish Book Awards and the *Sunday Tribune* Arts Award. She currently works for a computer company in San Francisco.

WORKS: *Penn.* Dublin: Raven Arts/Saskatchewan: Thistledown, [1986]. (Poetry); *Home-Movie Nights.* Dublin: Raven Arts/Saskatchewan: Thistledown, [1989]. (Poetry); *The Swimmer in the Deep Blue Dream.* Dublin: Raven Arts/Saskatchewan: Thistledown, [1991]. (Stories); *Facts about Water.* Newcastle upon Tyne: Bloodaxe/New Island Books/Saskatchewan: Thistledown, [1994]. (Poetry).

BERNEN, ROBERT (ca. 1930–   ), writer of tales and sketches. Robert Bernen was born in New York, taught Greek and Latin at Harvard when he was in his early twenties, and lived in a number of countries until 1970, when he and his wife bought an isolated farm nine miles north of Donegal town near the Blue Stacks mountains. ''Around these hills,'' he wrote, ''lives a small group of farmers whose lives continue to be rooted in eighteenth-century patterns, or earlier.'' Although the old ways are dying out, ''[c]rops of potatoes and corn are still sown and reaped entirely with spade and scythe; hay is mown by hand; fuel is won from the surrounding bog by laborious hand-cutting and sun-drying.'' The tales and sketches in Bernen's two books, *Tales from the Blue Stacks* (1978) and *The Hills: More Tales from the Blue Stacks* (1983), are about his own learning to cope with this life, and his teachers are the weather, animals, and neighbors steeped in old ways. It is more, however, than practical expertise he learns; it is also an appreciation of an old cast of mind and its values. Life in the hills was primitive and arduous, and he evokes it memorably in these precise and unromantic pieces. Although American, his years in Donegal have produced in his two short books an authentic sense of the old Ireland that does not pale even in comparison with the best of Peadar O'Donnell* and M. J. Molloy.* His Donegal neighbors, nevertheless, are said not to have liked the books. After a heart attack, Bernen returned to America.

WORKS: *Tales from the Blue Stacks.* London: Hamish Hamilton, 1978; *The Hills: More Tales from the Blue Stacks.* London: Hamish Hamilton, 1983.

BERRY, JAMES (1842–1914), folklorist. Berry was born in Louisburgh, County Mayo, educated in hedge schools, and died in Carna, County Galway. His anecdotes and descriptions of life and legends of the west of Ireland appeared originally in the *Mayo News* from 1910 to 1913. Like M. J. Molloy's* unpublished collection of tales and superstitions, they are a rich repository of rural memories.

WORK: *Tales of the West of Ireland.* Gertrude M. Horgan, ed. Dublin: Dolmen/Chester Springs, Pa.: Dufour, 1967.

BIBBY, THOMAS (1799–1863), poetic dramatist. Bibby was born in Kilkenny town and educated there and at Trinity College, Dublin. At the age of thirteen, he won a gold medal for science and became one of the best Greek students of his day. After he graduated in 1816, he led a studious and reclusive life in Kilkenny and grew eccentric enough to be thought insane. He produced, however, two connected dramatic poems, *Gerald of Kildare* (1854) and *Silken Thomas* (1859). He died in Kilkenny on January 7, 1863.

WORKS: *Gerald of Kildare*. Dublin: S. Lowen, 1854; *Silkin Thomas; or, Saint Mary's Abbey*. Dublin: S. Lowen, 1859.

BICKERSTAFFE (or BICKERSTAFF), ISAAC (ca. 1735–ca. 1812), dramatist. Swift* had used the name of Isaac Bickerstaff in his jape against Partridge the almanac maker in 1708, and Steele* later used it for *The Tatler*. The real Bickerstaffe was born in Dublin and, as a boy, became page to Lord Chesterfield, then lord lieutenant of Ireland, and Chesterfield subsequently obtained a commission for him in the marines. In London, Bickerstaffe became friendly with Dr. Johnson, Goldsmith,* and Garrick and wrote many popular comedies, farces, and ballad operas—among them, *Thomas and Sally; or, the Sailor's Return* (1760), *Love in a Village* (1762), and *The Maid of the Mill* (1765), based on Samuel Richardson's *Pamela*. His plays were popular for many years, and in his day he was considered the equal of John Gay. He was, however, expelled from the marines for some heinous offense and fled to the Continent, where he lived for some years in misery and poverty. His pieces have not held the stage.

MODERN REPRINTINGS: *Lionel and Clarissa*. London: Martin Secker, 1925; *Love in a Village*. London: Martin Secker, 1928. REFERENCE: Tasch, Peter A. *The Dramatic Cobbler. The Life and Works of Isaac Bickerstaff*. Lewisburg, Pa.: Bucknell University Press, [1971].

BINCHY, DAN (1940–   ), novelist. Binchy was born in County Limerick and educated by Christian Brothers and Benedictine monks. He still lives in County Limerick, with his wife and four children, where he has been a farmer. He knows his rural Ireland all too well, warts and all. In his novels, his wit is sharp-edged, and his plots and characters are hilariously real. His three novels all concern characters and events in Brulagh, a small coastal backwater of a town. In *The Neon Madonna* (1991), Father Gerry O'Sullivan comes home to die but takes on a new lease of life; Maggie Flannery and his housekeeper Julia May see the statue of the Virgin Mary move; and Mick Flannery, the local T.D., indulges in extramarital shenanigans with the wife of the bank manager. In *The Last Resort* (1992), some of Brulagh's citizens attempt various plays to put the town on the tourist map, and an American called Abe Linovitz has to escape from Brulagh by fishing boat. In *Fireballs* (1993), the enterprising Ways and Means Committee tries to organize a pop concert; Flannery schemes to turn the town into a coastal port, using coal brought in from America in a barge towed by an oceangoing tug; and, more successfully, as it is financed by an exiled African chief, Abe and Flannery establish a factory to produce peat pellets to fuel the local power-generating station. Mayhem and chaos reign in Binchy's little world of Brulagh, and he is a broadly comic writer not to be missed.

DOROTHY ROBBIE

WORKS: *The Neon Madonna.* London: Century, [1991]; *The Last Resort.* London: Century, [1992]; *Fireballs.* London: Century, Random House, 1993.

BINCHY, MAEVE (1940–   ), novelist, short story writer, and journalist. Binchy was born in Dublin on March 28, 1940, grew up in Dalkey, and attended the Holy Child Convent in Killiney, which was then considered a progressive school. She later took a history degree at University College, Dublin, and taught in various girls' schools, while writing her first travel articles in the summer holidays. There is a story that one of these, originally a letter home, led to her employment by the *Irish Times* in 1969. She soon became a popular columnist, writing twice-weekly articles distinguished by a quirky, self-deprecating humor. She was woman's editor during the first days of Irish feminism. She later moved to London, where she met and married Gordon Snell, a BBC presenter and later a writer of children's books.

My First Book is a collection of her newspaper articles. The Dublin section contains insightful case histories that prefigure her novelist's interest in character. The rest of the book is mainly humorous, and particularly droll is her account of a skiing holiday, "I Was a Winter Sport." Her next three books are collections of short stories. Two, *Central Line* (1977) and *Victoria Line* (1980), depict life in London, while *Dublin 4* (1982) is set in middle-class Dublin. These Irish stories could have been cut, but they are nonetheless enjoyable and perceptive. The best is about an alcoholic who works in Radio Telefis Éireann (RTÉ).

Light a Penny Candle (1982), her first novel, has all of the features that distinguish her fiction: a strong sense of place, a good story, and sympathetic characters. Here we meet the types that populate her later books: the capable wife, the good but blundering father, the kind doctor, the spoiled son, the village gossip, the nun, the priest, the feckless charmer. Also some favorite and recurrent themes are introduced: the parent–child relationship, the illusion of romance, the talented and capable character who, although underused, makes life purposeful. The novel juxtaposes two worlds, small-town Ireland and war-torn England, and tells the story of Aislinn and Elizabeth over a period of twenty years, during and after the Second World War. The two worlds meet and contemplate each other in the girls. In Ireland, status is endowed by money or a profession, but England is completely different. Although war-weary, it is a land of greater opportunity and less hypocrisy. In Aislinn, however, Binchy wonderfully captures Ireland of the frozen 1950s. It is an isolated world with an innocent charm, but it has its barbarities. Aislinn is married to a drunk, and her mother, a most moving and representative character, insists on her remaining married. Binchy has a great grasp of the rituals and minutia of small-town life; she describes, for instance, the clothes worn at a country wedding with a painter's skill.

The Lilac Bus (1984) is an enjoyable collection of linked short stories. In it,

Binchy enters the modern, changing Ireland of post-Vatican Two and gay lib. It is a world that has changed, but not that much. The ice is cracking, but there is still the need to keep up appearances. All of the characters are passengers on a bus that brings them from Dublin to the west for a weekend. Among them is the girl having an affair with an older man, the son involved with criminals, the gay son of Anglo-Irish parents. All are in flight from the lingering national oppressions; and, although they come to terms with their different problems, Binchy offers no tidy solutions.

In the novel *Echoes* (1985), Binchy again depicts, with a fine eye for sea and landscape, a small Irish town. It comes to life in the summer with gaiety and buckets and spades but is correspondingly bleak in winter. The novel focuses on Clare O'Brien, a shopkeeper's daughter who escapes to the big world of University College, Dublin. Other characters in the rigid social pecking order are not so lucky. Clare's childhood crush, Gerry Doyle, a photographer, remains to fester. As a character, he is more memorable than the doctor's handsome son, whom Clare marries. In Gerry, we recognize the youthful Romeo with whom everyone is in love but who never grows or amounts to anything in life. Other characters do, and changing Ireland is depicted in a priest who marries. Even Clare and her doctor's son learn some harsh lessons in their growth to maturity.

Firefly Summer (1987) is probably Binchy's least satisfying novel, for one of the main characters, a returned American in search of his roots, is a bit of a stereotype. However, the plot has sudden and unexpected twists that rivet the reader. Also, we see again Binchy's grasp of marriage and her uncanny knowledge of children, in the twins Dara and Michael, whose heartbreaks are beautifully caught. The parent–child relationship is also expertly depicted, particularly in Patrick and his selfish son Kerry.

Silver Wedding (1988) returns to the world of the London Irish and tells the story of a family through the eyes of its members and friends. The plot focuses on a party that a rather conventional couple is giving for their twenty-fifth wedding anniversary. They have had the usual ups and downs but cling to respectability. This need to keep up appearances involves one of their daughters in a sad episode that is at the heart of the novel. Helen is a dippy, superbly caught character who attempts to save her father's job by offering herself to his boss. She later enters a convent but is so forgetful that she is told to leave. In her, we see Binchy's comic ability, which unfortunately appears more in her journalism and early pieces than in her big novels.

Circle of Friends (1990) is probably Binchy's best novel. Its strength lies in the character of Benny, a large child who has to break away from comfortable but smothering small-town parents. Again the plot revolves around the friendship between two girls, Benny and Eve, the cast-off daughter of the Protestant Big House. Eve's dead mother was a Catholic, so Eve is brought up by nuns, who are kind and understanding and who present probably a truer and saner picture of religious life than the grotesqueries so frequent in recent Irish fiction.

Two worlds are again juxtaposed: professional upper-middle-class Dublin and a small country town. Benny herself loves and loses but learns that she can be a person in her own right. For anyone who was at University College, Dublin, in the 1950s or 1960s, the book will evoke heart-scalding memories of the Great Hall, the seedy Ladies Reading Room, the smell of dinner in the annex.

The Copper Beech (1992) is another collection of linked short stories that can be read as a novel. Although the book could have been fuller and shows some signs of having been written quickly, it contains some fine stories. "Dr. Jims," about a strained father–son relationship, is Chekhovian in its pain and insight.

Her novel *The Glass Lake* (1994) has been described by one critic as a "cosy read . . . like pulling up a chair in your favourite tea shop." This could not be further from the truth. Although we have the familiar Binchy world, the story is tragic. Here, fate is determined by character. A woman feels trapped in an unhappy marriage and runs away to England with an ex-boyfriend. There she changes her name and lives a lie, pretending she is dead. In one heartbreaking scene she meets her daughter and in the end loses everything, even her lover. She has remade herself, but at enormous cost. The book has serious things to say about marriage and woman's role in society, and there are skillful twists to the plot that keep the reader enthralled.

Binchy has also written plays. *End of Term* was performed in the Peacock Theatre in 1976, and *Deeply Regretted By* was a television play that won two Jacob's Awards and the Best Script Award at the Prague Film Festival. While continuing to write a weekly column in the *Irish Times,* Binchy is probably Ireland's currently most popular novelist. Some works have been televised, and *Circle of Friends* has been made into a Hollywood movie. To coincide with the film, a second million copies of that novel were printed. Her books have been translated into twelve languages, including Korean and Hebrew. To some academic critics, this popularity might seem suspect, but the novel has always been a popular art. In Victorian times, people read novels in vast numbers, and Binchy is in this tradition. She depicts humankind in society with the skill of a modern-day Trollope. If some of her books are alike, so are those of Jane Austen and Jennifer Johnston.* She holds a mirror up to our world, and one can only be in awe of her energy and talent.

MARY ROSE CALLAGHAN

WORKS: *My First Book.* Dublin: The Irish Times, 1976? (Essays); *Central Line.* Dublin: Ward River, 1977/London: Quartet, 1978. (Stories); *Maeve's Diary.* Dublin: The Irish Times, 1979. (Essays); *Victoria Line.* Dublin: Ward River/London: Quartet, 1980. (Stories); *Dublin 4.* Dublin: Ward River, 1982/London: Century, [1983]. (Stories); *Light a Penny Candle.* London: Century, 1982/New York: Viking, 1983. (Novel); *The Lilac Bus.* Dublin: Ward River, 1984/London: Century, 1986. (Stories); *Echoes.* London: Century, [1985]/New York: Viking, 1986. (Novel); *Firefly Summer.* London: Century Hutchinson, 1987/[New York]: Delacorte, [1988]. (Novel); *Silver Wedding.* London: Century Hutchinson, 1988/New York: Delacorte, 1989. (Novel); *Circle of Friends.* London: Random Century Group, 1990/[New York]: Delacorte, [1991]. (Novel); *The Copper Beech.* London:

Orion, 1992/[New York]: Delacorte, [1992]. (Novel); *The Glass Lake.* London: Orion, 1994. (Novel); *Dear Maeve.* Dublin: Poolbeg, 1995. (Newspaper columns).

BIRDSALL, BEN

WORK: *Blue Charm.* Belfast: Blackstaff, 1995. (Novel).

BIRMINGHAM, GEORGE A. (1865–1950), novelist, playwright, and humorist. George A. Birmingham was the pseudonym of Canon James Owen Hannay, who is rather unfairly remembered only as a prolific writer of humorous light fiction. Hannay was born in Belfast on July 16, 1865, the son of the Reverend Robert Hannay. He was educated at Haileybury and Trinity College, Dublin, from which he graduated in 1887. He was ordained a deacon of the Church of Ireland in 1888 and served as curate in Delgany, County Wicklow. He was ordained a priest in 1889 and appointed in 1892 to the parish at Westport, County Mayo, where he served until 1913.

Birmingham met and was much influenced by Standish O'Grady,* Horace Plunkett, the agricultural reformer (1854–1932), Arthur Griffith,* and particularly Douglas Hyde,* with whom he was involved in the Gaelic League. He began publishing a series of political novels in 1905 with *The Seething Pot,* but it was not until the great success of *Spanish Gold* in 1908 that he found a wide popular audience. His books appeared regularly at about yearly intervals. He also did some writing for the stage, including *Eleanor's Enterprise* performed by Count Markievicz's Independent Theatre in 1911, and *General John Regan* performed with much success by Charles Hawtrey in London in 1913. When a touring company presented *General John Regan* in Westport in 1914, it occasioned a night of rioting far more violent than the more celebrated frays over *The Playboy of the Western World* and *The Plough and the Stars.* As with *The Playboy,* the audience rioted over a presumed insult to Irish womanhood.

After an extended lecture tour to America before the war, Birmingham served as a chaplain in France in 1916 and 1917. From 1918 to 1920, he was rector of a small parish in County Kildare and chaplain to the lord lieutenant of Ireland. He resigned these posts in 1922 and went to Budapest for two years as chaplain of the British legation. In 1924, he accepted a living in Mells in Somerset. After his wife died, he moved to a small London parish in 1934. He was awarded a D. Litt. from Trinity College, Dublin, in 1946, and he died in London on February 2, 1950. He was a man of immense industry, publishing over eighty books, as well as uncounted fugitive pieces in newspapers and magazines. While he was active in many public capacities, he was even more active in the ministry and always put his priestly functions before his writing.

Despite the extreme popularity of his light fiction, the more patriotic Irish often suspected Birmingham of being Ascendancy and Protestant in his views. D. P. Moran, the editor of the patriotic journal *The Leader,* for instance, usually referred to him as "the bigot of Westport," and the citizens of Westport burned him in effigy during the *General John Regan* riot. Nothing could have been further from the truth than the charge of bigotry or bias, however, and even in his serious novels about the contemporary scene, Birmingham was scrupulously fair in seeing all sides. Indeed, his rather dull *Benedict Kavanagh* fails largely because much of the book is a plea not only for the Gaelic League, but also for mutual religious tolerance. The best of these early serious novels are *The Seething Pot* (1905), *Hyacinth* (1906), and *The Northern Iron* (1907). As R.B.D. French justly remarks of them, "The spirit of comedy in these novels and a new gift for satiric portraiture is revealed, but they are fundamentally serious works, even tragic in their implications, and they are the work of a Christian moralist."

Birmingham followed up the charming *Spanish Gold* of 1908 with several similar volumes, especially *The Search Party* (1909), *Lalage's Lovers* (1911), *The Inviolable Sanctuary* (1912), and *The Adventures of Dr. Whitty* (1913). In such books, he mined a vein of happy-go-lucky adventures involving amiable follies and engaging characters. Like the Irish R. M. stories of Somerville and Ross,* they are full of keen observation, deft phrasing, and, despite some droll comedy about the "mere Irish," utter tolerance. Birmingham's Reverend J. J. Meldon of *Spanish Gold* and some other books is one of the truly endearing comic creations of modern Irish literature. As a comic writer, Birmingham is not quite of the first rank, and his plots tend to fade in the memory. Nevertheless, one may return to the best of these books at intervals with unstinted delight.

The more political books which followed these comedies were increasingly permeated by good spirit and jovial satire, but they were not the kind of books to endear Birmingham to his Irish readers. For instance, the excellent *The Red Hand of Ulster* (1912) appeared in the midst of the Home Rule ferment, and the satiric *reductio ad absurdum* of its plot (in which Ulster is so opposed to Home Rule that it stages its own revolt and sets up its own independent government) was far too close to what might actually happen. *Up the Rebels!*, which appeared in the bad times of 1919, was full of gaiety, tolerance, and lightheartedness, but it could hardly have gone down well with the Irish patriots, for the charmingly foolish rebellion of the book was much too close in time to the ferocities of Easter Week.

Birmingham left Ireland for England in the early 1920s. His books continued to appear with their usual frequency, but there was a slow falling away from the excellence of his first twelve or fifteen years. Birmingham was rarely a hard satirist like Sean O'Casey* or Eimar O'Duffy,* but the times were out of joint for even mild satire. Still and all, he was a congenial, civilized, and humane writer, and, although thus far he rates merely a sentence in the literary histories, he is an immensely better writer than many with much more inflated reputations.

WORKS—as J. O. Hannay: *The Life of Frederick Richards Wynne.* London: Hodder & Stoughton, 1897; *The Spirit and Origin of Christian Monasticism.* London: Methuen, 1903; *The Wisdom of the Desert.* London: Methuen, 1904; *Is the Gaelic League Political?* Dublin: 1906. (Pamphlet); *Can I Be a Christian?* London: Hodder & Stoughton, 1923; *The Consecration of Churches.* London: Humphrey Milford, 1927; *Early Attempts at Christian Reunion.* London: 1929. (Pamphlet); *The*

Potter's Wheel. London: Longman's, 1940. as George A. Birmingham: *The Seething Pot.* London: Edward Arnold, 1905; *Hyacinth.* London: Edward Arnold, 1906; *Benedict Kavanagh.* London: Edward Arnold, 1907; *The Northern Iron.* Dublin: Maunsel, 1907; *The Bad Times.* London: Methuen, 1908; *Spanish Gold.* London: Methuen, 1908; *The Search Party.* London: Methuen, 1909; *Lalage's Lovers.* London: Methuen, 1911; *The Lighter Side of Irish Life.* London & Edinburgh: T. N. Foulis, 1911; *The Major's Niece.* London: Smith, Elder, 1911; *The Simpkins Plot.* London: Nelson, 1911; *The Inviolable Sanctuary.* London: Nelson, 1912; *The Red Hand of Ulster.* London: Smith, Elder, 1912; *The Adventures of Dr. Whitty.* London: Methuen, 1913; *Fidgets.* London: Hodder & Stoughton, 1913; *General John Regan.* London: Hodder & Stoughton, 1913. (Novel); *Irishmen All.* London & Edinburgh: T. N. Foulis, 1913; *The Lost Tribes.* London: Smith, Elder, 1914; *Gossamer.* London: Methuen, 1915; *Minnie's Bishop.* London: Hodder & Stoughton, 1915; *The Island Mystery.* London: Methuen, 1918; *A Padre in France.* London: Hodder & Stoughton, 1918; *An Irishman Looks at His World.* London: Hodder & Stoughton, 1919; *Our Casualty.* London: Skeffington, 1919; *Up, the Rebels!* London: Methuen, 1919; *Inisheeny.* London: Methuen, 1920; *Good Conduct.* London: John Murray, 1920; *Lady Bountiful.* London: Christophers, 1921; *The Lost Lawyer.* London: Methuen, 1921; *The Great-Grandmother.* London: Methuen, 1922; *A Public Scandal.* London: Hutchinson, 1922; *Fed Up.* London: Methuen, 1923; *Found Money.* London: Methuen, 1923; *King Tommy.* London: Hodder & Stoughton, 1923; *Send for Dr. O'Grady.* London: Hodder & Stoughton, 1923; *The Grand Duchess.* London: Hodder & Stoughton, 1924; *Bindon Parva.* London: Mills & Boon, 1925; *The Gun-Runners.* London: Hodder & Stoughton, 1925; *A Wayfarer in Hungary.* London: Methuen, 1925; *Goodly Pearls.* London: Hodder & Stoughton, 1926; *The Smuggler's Cave.* London: Hodder & Stoughton, 1926; *Spillikins.* London: Methuen, 1926. (Essays); *Now You Tell One.* Dundee & London: Valentine, 1927; *Ships and Sealing Wax.* London: Methuen, 1927. (Essays); *Elizabeth and the Archdeacon.* London: Gollancz, 1928; *The Runaways.* London: Methuen, 1928; *The Major's Candlesticks.* London: Methuen, 1929; *Murder Most Foul!* London: Chatto & Windus, 1929; *The Hymn Tune Mystery.* London: Methuen, 1930; *Wild Justice.* London: Methuen, 1930; *The Silver-Gilt Standard.* London: Methuen, 1932; *Angel's Adventure.* London: Methuen, 1933; *Connaught to Chicago.* London: Methuen, 1933; *General John Regan.* London: G. Allen & Unwin, 1933. (Play); *Pleasant Places.* London: Heinemann, 1934. (Autobiography); *Two Fools.* London: Methuen, 1934; *Love or Money.* London: Methuen, 1935; *Millicent's Corner.* London: Methuen, 1935; *Daphne's Fishing.* London: Methuen, 1937; *Isaiah.* London: Rich & Cowan, 1937; *Mrs. Miller's Aunt.* London: Methuen, 1937; *Magilligan Strand.* London: Methuen, 1938; *Appeasement.* London: Methuen, 1939; *God's Iron.* London: Skeffington, 1939; *Miss Maitland's Spy.* London: Methuen, 1940; *Over the Border.* London: Methuen, 1942; *Poor Sir Edward.* London: Methuen, 1943; *Lieutenant Commander.* London: Methuen, 1944; *Good Intentions.* London: Methuen, 1945; *The Piccadilly Lady.* London: Methuen, 1946; *Golden Apple.* London: Methuen, 1947; *A Sea Battle.* London: Methuen, 1948; *Laura's Bishop.* London: Methuen, 1949; *Two Scamps.* London: Methuen, 1950; *Golden Sayings from George A.* Birmingham. London: L. B. Hill, 1915.

BLACKBURNE, E. OWENS (1845–1894), novelist, poet, biographer, and feminist. Elizabeth Owens Blackburne Casey was born on May 10, 1845, in Slane, County Meath. At about eleven years of age, she lost her sight and remained blind until treatments by Sir William Wilde* restored her vision. After moving to London, in 1873 or 1874, her literary career was at first successful but then declined to the point of leaving her in poverty. In later life, she received assistance from the Royal County Fund. After returning to Dublin, she burned to death in an accident the month prior to her fifty-ninth birthday.

Casey was better known as a novelist than a poet. She was also the author of an early feminist encyclopedia, *Illustrious Irishwomen,* a two-volume set that was the first endeavor of its kind. In the preface, Casey explains that her original intent was to include living Irishwomen but that she was persuaded otherwise, probably due to legal concerns. The book covers the early and medieval periods of Irish myth and history, from Queen Macha to Elizabeth Hamilton (1641–1700), before switching format to classify the more contemporary women by occupation: famous actresses, literary women, and a miscellaneous category, where famous beauties like the Gunning sisters share space with the Ladies of Llangollen and Sarah Curran. Casey's dictionary is her most valuable work, both from the standpoint of generating further efforts in chronicling Irishwomen's lives and for her nineteenth-century view of eighteenth-century Irish women authors. Her description of the countess of Warwick's "Occasional Meditations upon Sundry Subjects" provides an excellent sample of her observations:

These meditations abound in fine metaphorical language, although the subjects of some of them seem almost too trivial to be so seriously treated. They are pervaded by a spirit of fervent Christianity; and exemplify the pure and exalted mind of the writer.

Casey's novels are typically set in Ireland, usually detailing aspects of peasant life. *A Woman Scorned* (1876) takes place in Casey's home territory near the Boyne. It follows the story of Katherine, the young stepsister pursued by the desirable Captain Fitzgerald, while the woman scorned, Katherine's elder stepsister, seeks to prevent their union. The couple triumphs while the sister dies an unhappy death. This plot, with variations, is the nucleus of Casey's novels. *A Bunch of Shamrocks* (1879) is a collection of short stories, tales, and sketches of Irish life. Stephen Brown said the volume illustrates "for the most part the gloomier side of the national character, viewed, apparently, from a Protestant standpoint" (*Ireland in Fiction*, p. 35).

ANNE COLMAN

WORKS: *A Woman Scorned.* 3 vols. London: Tinsley, 1876; *Illustrious Irishwomen.* 2 vols. London: Tinsley, 1877; *The Way Women Love.* 3 vols. London: Tinsley, 1877; *A Bunch of Shamrocks.* London: Newman, 1879. (Tales and sketches); *Molly Carew.* 3 vols. London: Tinsley, [1879]; *The Glen of Silver Birches.* 2 vols. London: Remington, 1880; *My Sweetheart When a Boy.* Moxon's Select Novelettes, No. 1. London, [1880]; *As the Crow Flies.* Moxon's Select Novelettes, No. 4. London, [1880]; *The Love That Loves Always.* 3 vols. London: F. V. White, 1881; *The Heart of Erin.* 2 vols. London: Sampson Low, 1882; *Con O'Donnell, and Other Legends and Poems for Recitation.* London, 1890; *Aunt Delia's Heir; In the Vale of Honey; Shadows in the Sunlight; A Modern Parrhasius; The Quest of the Heir; Philosopher Push; Dean Swift's Chest; A Chronicle of Barham.* REFERENCE: Sillard, P. A. "A Notable Irish Authoress." *New Ireland Review* 27 (August 1907): 369–372.

BLACKER, WILLIAM (1777–1855), poet. Blacker was born on September 1, 1777, at Carrickblacker, County Armmagh. He received a B.A. from Trinity College, Dublin, in 1799 and an M.A. in 1803. He had a military career, rising to the rank of lieutenant colonel, and wrote several tracts on economics, agriculture, and politics. As a poet, he wrote vigorous Orange ballads such as "The

Battle of the Boyne'' and "Oliver's Advice,'' with its rousing refrain. One
stanza may suffice:

> Then cheer, ye hearts of loyalty, nor sink in dark despair,
> Our banner shall again unfold its glories to the air.
> The storm that raves the wildest the soonest passes by;
> Then put your trust in God, my boys, and keep your powder dry.

The Oliver of the title was, of course, Cromwell. Blacker died on November
25, 1855.

LITERARY WORKS: *Ardmagh, a Chornicle.* . . . Armagh: J. Thompson, 1848; *Early Piety.* Por-
tadown: G. Wilson, 1853; *A Tale of Woe, for Children.* Portadown: G. Wilson, 1854; *Emmaus, a
Tale for Easter.* Portadown: Wilson, 1855. REFERENCES: "The Orange Minstrel." *Irish Book
Lover* 4 (1913): 163–165; "Our Portrait Gallery no. 18: Lieut-Col. Blacker," *Dublin University
Magazine* 17 (1841): 628–633.

BLACKWOOD, CAROLINE [MAUREEN] (1931–   ), novelist and short
story writer. Lady Caroline Hamilton-Temple-Blackwood was born in Northern
Ireland on July 16, 1931, the daughter of the fourth marquis of Dufferin and
Ava. On her mother's side she is a Guinness, and on her father's side she is a
direct descendant of Richard Brinsley Sheridan.* Her first husband was a grandson of Sigmund Freud, and her third husband was the American poet Robert
Lowell.

Her first book, *For All That I Found There* (1974), is a collection of short
stories, journalism, and memoirs of an Ulster childhood. Although funny, the
stories are also sad illustrations of human weakness and vulnerability. They
portray an unstable world where the props, such as the kind old priest of "How
You Love Our Lady" and the nanny of "Baby Nurse," are only temporary.
Among the journalistic articles is an hilarious account of a women's lib meeting, as well as a terrifying report of a visit to a hospital for burns. The memoirs
of childhood are perhaps the best parts of the book, especially "Piggy," the
account of a prep school bully, and "Never Breathe a Word," the writer's weird
experience with her pony's groom.

The Stepdaughter, her first novel, won the David Higham Prize for fiction in
1976. The book is a haunting indictment of the callous treatment of a young
girl by her father and his stepdaughter but is so skillfully done that the reader
feels as much for the awful adults as for the unhappy, rejected child.

Great Granny Webster, a best-selling novella published in 1977, traces the
influence of a grim, parsimonious old woman on three generations of her family.
The novella contains some marvelous characterization and a memorable depiction of life in an Anglo-Irish mansion reeking of damp and madness. Blackwood
contrives to treat madness with a witty detachment, and her depictions of the
pathetic life in a leaky mansion are both sad and funny. Nevertheless, although
characters like Lavinia and Granny Webster are memorably drawn, some of the
other characters are elusive. In addition, some questions are raised and never

answered. Why, for instance, is the narrator's father so unhappy? What happened to the narrator's mother? One gets the feeling that the book was, at one time, longer, and one wishes that it still were. There is so much suggestion of underdeveloped plot in the present book that one wishes the author had worked it out fully and given us more than brilliant sketches of several characters.

The title character of *The Fate of Mary Rose* (1981) is an undernourished, almost catatonic little girl with a mother whose obsessions lie in protecting her and in being fanatically tidy. When a neighborhood child is raped and murdered, the mother's protectiveness accelerates into madness, and her nominal and self-centered husband is finally driven to abduct Mary Rose to save her. As they are pursued by the police, the girl jumps out of the speeding car and is killed. The narrator-husband then surmises that his wife will plausibly give evidence against him and that he will certainly be convicted of the child's murder. Practically all of the characters in this fluently written and well-structured book are selfish, quarrelsome, or obsessed, and one reviewer called the book "[e]legant and unpleasant." It certainly shows Blackwood at her most morbid.

Good Night Sweet Ladies (1983) contains ten stories as well as three essays reprinted from her first book. "The Interview" is a dialogue between a journalist and the impossible old widow of a noted painter. It is more character sketch than story, but the character is memorable and has many telling and bitchy lines, such as, "He was always someone who made you feel that if you were to cut open his brain, you would find it all pitted and eaten up with some sort of dreadful dry-rot of morbid fears," or, "She looks rather insipid to me with her mousey-pale curls—a little too like some damp, slightly soiled, powder puff." Indeed, a wittily caught characterization is the notable quality of most of the stories: Miss Renny, the fat and awful title character of "The Baby Nurse"; Angeline, the frumpy hairdresser of "Who Needs It?"; Mrs. Ripstone, the rich and self-centered woman meeting her teenage illegitimate son for the first time and flirting with the social worker who accompanies him. The stories present a consistently bleak view but are accomplished work.

Corrigan (1984) is a leisurely novel about how a presumably crippled man, Corrigan, bilks a widow out of large contributions to a nonexistent nursing home and of how he actually moves into her house, which she remodels to accommodate his wheelchair. In the process, however, he becomes truly fond of her, they companionably drink champagne and read poetry together, and he actually awakens her from a torpor of mourning for her husband and gives purpose and meaning to her last months. This is a satisfying book, something of a slowly developing mystery, and has, in Mrs. Blunt, her Irish maid, and her daughter and son-in-law, Blackwood's usual deft characterization. Corrigan, for most of the book, is the most elusive character, but his falsely florid speech is excellently caught.

MARY ROSE CALLAGHAN

WORKS: *For All That I Found There*. [London]: Duckworth, [1973]/New York: George Braziller, 1974. (Stories and essays); *The Stepdaughter*. [London]: Duckworth, [1976]/New York: Scribner's,

[1977]. (Novelette); *Great Granny Webster.* [London]: Duckworth/New York: Scribner's, [1977]. (Novelette); with Anna Haycroft, *Darling, You Shouldn't Have Gone to So Much Trouble.* London: Jonathan Cape, 1980. (Cookbook); *The Fate of Mary Rose.* London: Jonathan Cape/New York: Summit, 1981. (Novel); *Goodnight Sweet Ladies.* London: Heinemann, 1983. (Short stories); *On the Perimeter.* London: Heinemann, 1984/New York: Penguin, 1985. (On the Greenham Common Nuclear protest); *Corrigan.* London: Heinemann, [1984]/New York: Viking, 1985. (Novel); *In the Pink: Caroline Blackwood on Hunting.* London: Bloomsbury, 1987; *The Last of the Duchess.* London: Macmillan, 1995. (On the latter days of the duchess of Windsor).

BLESSINGTON, LADY. *See* POWER, MARGUERITE.

BODKIN, M[ATTHIAS] M[cDONNELL] (1850–1933), novelist, journalist, and lawyer. Bodkin was born in Tuam, County Galway, son of a surgeon, Thomas Bodkin* ("the poor man's doctor"), and his wife, Maria, one of the MacDonnells of Cloona, Westport. He was educated by the Jesuits at St. Stanislaus College, Tullabeg, and at the Catholic University. Called to the bar in 1877, he took silk in 1894. In 1889, he married Arabella Norman, and their sons were Thomas Bodkin, the art critic, and Fr. Mathias Bodkin, a Jesuit. He was nationalist MP for North Roscommon from 1892 to 1895 and an anti-Parnellite. A strenuous journalist, he was chief leader writer for *United Ireland* and later for the *Freeman's Journal.* From 1907 to 1924, he was County Court judge for Clare. During the Troubles, he courageously criticized the activities of the government forces from the bench; and the Bodkin Report, which he read in open court in February 1921, listed 139 outrages. It was described by Asquith in the House of Commons as "one of the gravest indictments ever presented by a judicial officer against the Executive Government in a free country." Though his memoirs are of interest for the sidelights they cast on Irish life and politics, he is remembered today as a pioneer detective story writer, the creater of Paul Beck, Dora Myrle, and their son Paul Beck, Jr., who were, according to Julian Symons, "the best Plain Man detectives of their era." Bodkin told one of his sons in later years that he was disappointed that the detective story later developed into the murder story, as murderers in his experience were all too often stupid; con men made better material. He died on June 7, 1933.

PETER COSTELLO

WORKS: As Crom-a-boo: *Poteen Punch.* Dublin: M. H. Gill, 1890; *Pat O' Nine Tales.* Dublin: M. H. Gill, 1894. Under his own name: *Lord Edward Fitzgerald.* London: Chapman & Hall, 1896. (Historical romance); *White Magic.* London: Chapman & Hall, 1897; *Paul Beck, the Rule of Thumb Detective.* London: C. Arthur Pearson, 1898; *A Stolen Life.* London: Ward, Lock, [1898]; *The Rebels.* Dublin: Duffy/London: Ward, Lock, 1899; *Dora Myrl, the Lady Detective.* London: Chatto & Windus, 1900; *A Bear Squeeze.* London: Ward, Lock, 1901; *A Modern Miracle.* London: Ward, Lock, 1902; *Shillelagh and Shamrock.* London: Chatto & Windus, 1902; *In the Days of Goldsmith.* London: John Long, 1903; *A Modern Robyn Hood.* London: Ward, Lock, 1903; *Patsy the Omadhaun.* London: Chatto & Windus, 1904; *A Madcap Marriage.* London: John Long, 1906; *A Trip to the States and a Talk with the President.* Dublin: Duffy, 1907; *The Quest of Paul Beck.* London: T. Fisher Unwin, 1908; *The Capture of Paul Beck.* London: T. Fisher Unwin, 1909; *True Man and Traitor.* Dublin: Duffy/London: T. Fisher Unwin, 1910; *Young Beck, A Chip off the Old Block.* London: T. Fisher Unwin, 1911; *Grattan's Parliament, Before and After.* London: T. Fisher Unwin,

1912; *His Brother's Keeper.* London: Hurst & Blackett, 1913; *The Test.* London: Everett, [1914]; *Behind the Picture.* London: Ward, Lock, 1914; *Reflections of an Irish Judge.* London: Hurst & Blackett, 1914; *Pigeon Blood Rubies.* London: Eveleigh Nash, 1915; *Old Rowley.* London: Holden & Hardingham, [1917]; *Famous Irish Trials.* Dublin & London: Maunsel, 1918; *When Youth Meets Youth.* London: T. Fisher Unwin/Dublin: Talbot, 1920; *Kitty the Madcap.* Dublin & Cork: Talbot, [1927]; *Guilty or Not Guilty.* Dublin & Cork: Talbot, [1929]. REFERENCES: Denson, Alan. *Thomas Bodkin: A Bio-Bibliographical Survey with a Bibliographical Survey of His Family.* Dublin, 1966; Greene, Hugh, ed. *Further Rivals of Sherlock Holmes.* London: Bodley Head, 1971; Symons, Julian. *Bloody Murder.* London: Faber, 1971.

BODKIN, THOMAS PATRICK (1887–1961), art historian, biographer, poet, and radio and television performer. The elder son of Matthias McDonnell Bodkin* by his wife, Arabella Norman, Bodkin was born in Dublin on July 21, 1887. He was educated at Belvedere College, Clongowes Wood College, and the Royal University of Ireland (University College). He was called to the bar at King's Inn, Dublin, in 1911, and practiced as a barrister from 1911 to 1916. From 1916 to 1935, he was secretary to the Commissioners of Charitable Donations and Bequests in Ireland. His early personal friendship with Sir Hugh Lane sharpened Bodkin's good taste in the fine arts, and from July 1927 until February 28, 1935, he was director of the Irish National Gallery, an appointment formerly held by Lane. His power of decision coupled with good taste made his directorship memorable for significant purchases. The foundation trustees of the Barber Institute within Birmingham University offered him the directorship of their new gallery, undertaking to back his artistic judgment with trust money to ensure wise purchases. Bodkin ran the Barber Institute Collection from March 1, 1935, until September 30, 1952, remaining as sole adviser on purchases until failing physical health enforced his retirement on October 15, 1959. The Barber Collection is the finest formed in the U.K. in this century.

Bodkin had a mind both trenchant and witty. Fools he would not suffer gladly, making enemies easily as a consequence. More curiously, his considerable attainments as a poet have been almost entirely neglected despite the memorable skill he showed in translating from the French in *May It Please Your Lordships* (1917). Adroit and felicitously phrased, a new edition with Alan Denson's memoir is in preparation. Bodkin's original English poetry is of a high quality and characteristic of his precise thinking. Aside from a sheaf issued in 1939 as *Eight Poems,* he published a few in newspapers and journals. But the typed large collection formerly owned by his widow deserves publication.

Of all of Bodkin's scholarly books and articles, the one best-seller was his inimitable *The Approach to Painting* (1927), and its last paperback edition in 1954 was the best of all. Bodkin was, throughout his life, unusually honorable, and he built up a personal art collection only while he was not employed at the National Gallery and the Barber Institute.

He became very well known as a lucid conversationalist on BBC radio and television. A devout Catholic, he died in Birmingham on April 21, 1961, and was interred in his parents' grave in Dublin's Glasnevin Cemetery.

ALAN DENSON

WORKS: *May It Please Your Lordships. Reproductions of Modern French Poems.* Dublin & London: Maunsel, 1917; *Four Irish Landscape Painters.* Dublin: Talbot/London: T. Fisher Unwin, 1920; *A Guide to Caper.* London: Chatto & Windus, 1924; *The Approach to Painting.* London: George Bell, 1927/London: Collins, 1954; *Hugh Lane and His Pictures.* London: Pegasus Press for the Irish Free State, 1932; *The Importance of Art to Ireland.* Dublin: At the Sign of the Three Candles, 1935; *Eight Poems.* Birmingham: School of Painting, 1939; *Twelve Irish Artists.* Dublin: Victor Waddington, 1940; *The Paintings of Jan Vermeer.* London: Allen & Unwin, 1940; *My Uncle Frank.* London: Robert Hale, 1941; *Dismembered Masterpieces.* London: Collins, 1945; *Rembrandt Paintings.* London: Collins, 1948; *Report on the Arts in Ireland.* Dublin: Stationery Office, 1951. REFERENCE: Denson, Alan. *Thomas Bodkin. A Bio-Bibliographical Survey. With a Bibliographical Survey of His Family.* Dublin: Bodkin Trustees, 1966.

BOLAND, BRIDGET (1913–1988), memoirist, playwright, screenwriter, and novelist. Boland was born on March 13, 1913, in London, the daughter of John Pius Boland, Irish nationalist MP, who was later general secretary of the Catholic Irish Truth Society in England. She gives a fine evocation of her family and childhood, with its background of nationalist politics, in her very popular *At My Mother's Knee* (1978). She was educated at the fashionable Sacred Heart Convent, Roehampton, and at Oxford, where she received her B.A. in 1935. From 1937 onward, she was a screenwriter with many films to her credit, but the success of her 1953 play, *The Prisoner,* made her generally known. It was later filmed with Alec Guinness. She also wrote three novels, among them *The Wild Geese* (1938), a historical tale told through letters. In later years, she was known for her gardening books. She died on January 19, 1988.

PETER COSTELLO

WORKS: *The Wild Geese.* London: Heinemann, 1938. (Novel); *Portrait of a Lady in Love.* London & Toronto: Heinemann, 1942. (Novel); *The Return.* London: Samuel French, [1954]. (Play); *The Prisoner.* New York: Dramatists Play Service, [1956]. (Play); *Temple Folly.* London: Evans, 1958. (Play); *Caterina.* London: Souvenir, 1975. (Novel); with Maureen Boland. *Old Wives' Lore for Gardeners.* London: Bodley Head, 1976; *Gardener's Magic and Other Old Wives' Lore.* London: Bodley Head, 1977; *At My Mother's Knee.* London: Bodley Head, 1978. (Memoir); ed., after Muriel St. Clare Byrne. *The Lisle Letters: An Abridgement.* London: Secker & Warburg, 1982. Her films and plays include *Cockpit* (1948), *The Damascus Blade* (1950), *Terrible Folly* (1952), *The Rates* (1953), *The Prisoner* (staged 1953, filmed 1955), *Gordon* (1960), *The Zodiac in the Establishment* (1965), *Time Out of Mind* (1970), and others.

BOLAND, EAVAN (1944–), poet and critic. Boland, one of Ireland's leading contemporary poets, was born in Dublin on September 24, 1944, and was educated in Dublin, London, and New York. While the sense of displacement and exile that marked her childhood has been a theme in her poems, the sense of there being a world greater than the island of Ireland has enriched her work as a critic, and she has written with rigor and style of writers from many countries, among them Wallace Stevens, Anna Akhmatova, and Adrienne Rich.

Boland was the daughter of a diplomat, her father, Frederick, having been

Irish ambassador to the Court of Saint James and Ireland's permanent representative at the United Nations. Her mother's fondness for the visual arts has been translated into Boland's work with a strong sense of physical form, a variety of artistic references, and a feeling for color and for objects as still, potent lives.

In Dublin, Boland was educated at Trinity College, where her contemporaries included the poet Brendan Kennelly.* In 1986, writing in the *Irish Times,* he recalled her as being "brilliant and beautiful, with a mind fiercely her own . . . and an aggressive conviction that Dublin is the only *really* worthwhile spot on earth." She lives in Dublin now with her husband, the novelist Kevin Casey,* and their two daughters. She has worked as a freelance lecturer and has also been a pivotal figure for many writers who attended workshops that she has run from time to time.

From the very start, Boland's poems were distinguished by that sense of force and form that marks the arrival of an important and original voice. Her first book, *New Territory,* was published in 1967, when she was twenty-three, and many of its poems contained hints of themes that would strengthen and deepen in later books: Irish history, a feeling for the classical, an interest in paintings, the importance of journeys and migration, the place of the past. Its finest poems had an incredible assurance that never—as is too often the case with first books—seemed youthful arrogance but, instead, seemed earned, assured, and true.

The question of the role of women in poetry became central for Boland and became an object of intense questioning. Part of a generation that included President Mary Robinson, who quoted from Boland's work in her inauguration speech, Boland was acutely aware of the pressures under which women in Ireland had labored and of the role that convention forced women poets to inhabit. Her book *In Her Own Image* (1980) was a cutting loose, and it gave the impression of a writer who had been suddenly freed into a new expression of self. The lives and troubles of women became the subject of her poems, as the titles often indicate: "Anorexic," "Mastectomy," "Menses." While the book was thematically important, it worked less well as poetry, and its lean lines lack the packed power that marks her best work. The same is true of some poems in her book *Night Feed* (1982), though again there is an important declaration of themes.

While she developed themes of domesticity, motherhood, suburbia, and the lives of women, the relationship between Ireland and her work as a poet was also becoming an important issue. Many of her ideas on this theme can be found in the essay "Outside History" (originally published in the American *Poetry Review* [March/April 1960]). There she describes how the idea of the Irish nation was a construct from which she felt excluded, alienated by its "rhetoric of imagery," which merged the feminine and the national. It was a powerful literary tradition in which women were more often a type of ornament: "I was a poet lacking the precedent and example of previous Irish women poets. . . . A hundred years ago I might have been a motif in a poem. Now I could have a complex self within my own poem."

Her struggle with the question of her own role within this world has been a key moment for Irish poetry and has resulted in some of her strongest work. In a sense, it is akin to the kind of poetry that becomes not just the voice of a single poet but part of the very voice of a country at a given time. This is the case with Anna Akhmatova and Russia, for example; and some of Boland's poems, too, ofter that same confluence of country and self.

She is also a writer who has trusted in the strength and worth of ordinary experience. Her poem "The Journey" ranks with Mahon's* "A Disused Shed in County Wexford" and Heaney's* "The Harvest Bow" as one of those poems that "sanctify the common" and that seem among the finest of their time. It combines the ordinary and the mythic in a typical conjunction, and it also marks her once again as a poet who is most successful when using a classical mode and voice. The wondrous thing is that she has done this in a way that has remained true to everyday experience. Her strong lines, often capable of sustaining long sentences that carry the reader along with the force of a current, have the resonance of a world where voice and vision are merged. History, dolls, famine ships, the Liffey, visions, the streets of Dublin, love, graying hair, a parcel, a fan, a cameo, motherhood—all of these can take their place in her work. Her forms—and this is true of too few poets—are often a pleasure in themselves, as, say, "At the Glass Factory in Cavan Town" testifies. She sometimes also uses short sentences as part of a technique that gives her tone its individuality, as in "Love."

Her career is at a fascinating point. Her most important achievements include her assertion of the worth of the ordinary and the creation of a voice that does not show her as an object within a poem but, instead, as a fine and important maker of poems who has enriched and expanded her country's literary tradition.

SEÁN DUNNE

WORKS: *23 Poems.* Dublin: Gallagher, 1962. (Pamphlet); *Eavan Boland Poetry/Prose Joseph O'Malley.* Dublin: Gallagher, 1963. (Pamphlet); *Autumn Essay.* Dublin: Gallagher, 1963; *New Territory.* Dublin: Allen Figgis, 1967; with Micheál Mac Liammóir. *W. B. Yeats and His World.* London: Thames, 1971/New York: Viking, 1972; *The War Horse.* London: Gollancz, 1975/Dublin: Arlen House, 1980: *In Her Own Image.* Dublin: Arlen House, 1980; *Introducing Eavan Boland: Poems.* Princeton, N.J.: Ontario Review, 1981; *Night Feed.* Dublin: Arlen House/London & Boston: Marion Boyars, 1982/[Manchester]: Carcanet, [1994]; *The Journey and Other Poems.* Dublin: Arlen House, 1986/Manchester: Carcanet, 1987; *Selected Poems.* Dublin: Arlen House/Manchester: Carcanet, 1989; *Outside History: Poems 1980–1990.* [Manchester]: Carcanet, [1990]/New York: Norton, 1991; *A Kind of Scar: The Woman Poet in a National Tradition.* Dublin: Attic, 1990. (Essay); *In a Time of Violence.* [Manchester]: Carcanet, [1994]; *Selected Prose.* New York: Norton/Manchester: Carcanet, 1994; *Object Lessons: The Life of the Woman and the Poet in Our Time.* Manchester: Carcanet, 1995; *Collected Poems.* [Manchester]: Carcanet, [1995]. REFERENCES: Allen-Randolph, Jody. "Ecriture Feminine and the Authorship of Self in Eavan Boland's *In Her Own Image."* *Colby Quarterly Review* 27 (March 1991); Dawe, Gerald. *How's the Poetry Going? Literary Politics and Ireland Today.* Belfast: Lagan Press, 1991; Dawe, Gerald. "The Suburban Night: On Eavan Boland, Paul Durcan and Thomas McCarthy" in *Contemporary Irish Poetry: A Collection of Critical Essays.* Elmer Andrews, ed. London: Macmillan, 1992; Dawe, Gerald & Foster, John Wilson, eds. *Poet's Place: Ulster Literature and Society; Essays in Honour of John Hewitt, 1907–1987.* Belfast: Institute of Irish Studies, 1991; Ó Siadhail, Micheál. "Eavan Boland Talks to Micheál Ó Siadhail." *Poetry Ireland Review* 27 (Autumn 1989); Roche, Anthony, ed., with Jody Allen-Randolph. *Irish University Review* 23 (Spring–Summer 1993). Special Eavan Boland Issue. (Contains articles by Derek Mahon, Medbh McGuckian, Terence Brown, and others, an interview with Boland, and a checklist by Allen-Randolph); Tall, Deborah. "Q. & A. with Eavan Boland." *Irish Literary Supplement* (Fall 1988); Wright, Nancy Means & Hannam, Dennis J. "Q. & A. with Eavan Boland." *Irish Literary Supplement* (Spring 1991).

BOLAND, ROSITA (1965–   ), poet and travel writer. Boland was born in Ennis, County Clare, and received a B.A. in English and history from Trinity College, Dublin. She traveled for a year in Australia, worked for two years in publishing in London, and wrote a travel book, *Sea Legs,* about hitchhiking around the West of Ireland.

WORKS: *Muscle Creek.* [Dublin]: Raven Arts, [1991]. (Poetry); *Sea Legs.* Dublin: New Island Books, 1992. (Travel).

BOLGER, DERMOT (1959–   ), novelist, playwright, poet, and publisher. Bolger was born in Finglas, a suburb of north Dublin, on February 6, 1959. His mother (who died in 1969) was the daughter of a Monaghan farmer, and his father (now retired) was a sailor. Bolger attended St. Canice's Boys National School and later Beneavin College, both in Finglas. In 1977, after finishing school, he spent a year trying to establish a community arts group, Raven Arts, staging festivals. To finance the project, he found a job in 1978 as a factory hand in a factory producing welding rods, an experience on which his first novel, *Night Shift* (1985), was based. In 1979, he started work as a library assistant, mainly working on mobile libraries on the outskirts of Dublin, until 1984, when he became a full-time writer and publisher. In 1979, he had founded the Raven Arts Press, which published some of his own books of poetry, his first novel, work by then-unnoticed writers such as Paul Durcan,* and Matthew Sweeney,* as well as various anthologies that he edited: *After the War Is Over* (1984), Irish writers' protest at the visit of Ronald Reagan; *The Bright Wave/An Tonn Gheal* (1986), the first dual-language anthology of contemporary Irish-language poetry; *Letters from the New Island* (1987–1989), a polemical series of pamphlets on Irish politics and culture. He closed down the Raven Arts Press in 1992 and is now executive editor of New Island Books, which brought out his editions of *Selected Poems of Francis Ledwidge** (1992) and *Ireland in Exile* (1993), the first anthology of writing by Irish writers living outside Ireland.

When Bolger was fifteen, Anthony Cronin* recognized his talent and got him published in the *Irish Times* and *Profile,* an anthology of new Irish writers. Since then, he has brought out five collections of poetry: *The Habit of Flesh* (1979), *Finglas Lilies* (1980), *No Waiting America* (1981), *Internal Exiles* (1986), and *Leinster Street Ghosts* (1989). He has had five plays produced in Dublin and elsewhere: *The Lament for Arthur Cleary* of 1989, which won the Samuel Beckett* Award, the Stewart Parker* BBC Award, and Edinburgh Fringe First; *Blinded by the Light* of 1990, which won the O. Z. Whitehead Prize; *In High Germany* of 1990; *The Holy Ground* of 1990; and *One Last*

White Horse of 1991. He has also published five novels: *Night Shift* of 1985, which won the AE Memorial Prize; *The Woman's Daughter* of 1987, which won the Macaulay Fellowship, was short-listed for the Hughes Fiction Prize, and appeared in an extended version in 1991; *The Journey Home* of 1990, which was short-listed for the Hughes Fiction Prize and in 1992 for the *Irish Times*/ Aer Lingus Prize; *Emily's Shoes* of 1992; and *A Second Life* of 1994.

One of the themes that seem to fascinate Bolger is how the past impinges upon the present. Thus, in the poems of *Leinster Street Ghosts* he deals with the presences that people leave behind. All who have passed remain as imperceptible witnesses. They are the people who have been written out of history. Bolger's work is an attempt to preserve the memory of wasted lives so that they may not have been in vain. The poems in the other collections—for instance, in *Internal Exiles*—reflect Bolger's concern for life in Ireland today, yet again seen against the background of historical influences.

A Dublin Quartet (1992), a collection of four of his plays, paints a grim picture of modern urban life in an Ireland poised on the uneasy edge of the European Community. In *The Lament for Arthur Cleary,* which, like *The Holy Ground* and *One Last White Horse,* is indebted to surrealist stream-of-consciousness theater, Bolger offers a lament for a man who cannot understand that the Ireland he left to go and fight on the Continent has, upon his return, become a completely different and more dangerous place, one run by crooks, property agents, modern-type gombeen-men and drug pushers, where people feel uprooted, exploited, dispossessed, and homeless. *The Holy Ground* presents the ruminations of a middle-aged woman who has poisoned her husband because he stole her youth and left her barren. *One Last White Horse* treats of how a young married father, as a result of the poverty-stricken existence he is forced to lead, becomes a heroin victim.

In *The Journey Home,* Francis Hanrahan, Hano to his friend Shay, is on the run. Thugs are on his heels. With Hano is Katie, or Cait, a street waif Shay had befriended. Shay has apparently been killed. Hano and Cait are on their journey home. Home they have found in a dilapidated house in the country. The narrative develops three skeins, one describing the actual journey home, the second giving an account of Hano's life and friendship with Shay, and the third offering material to effect a poetical note. Shay introduces Hano to a gray Dublin underworld of nixers and the dole, social and political corruption. The only time Hano had seemed at home was with an old woman in a caravan when he was still quite young. The woman represents "a part of that barbarous race who had once controlled the land," a stalwart counterpoint to the industrialized, Europeanized, present-day Ireland. The old Ireland, rural, racy, and rustic, is gone beyond retrieval; home is lost; a Europeanized world is taking over.

There are three voices in *The Woman's Daughter.* The initial one seems to strive toward investing the story with some kind of mythohistorical significance: "This is the spot where the archers' horses paused first by the stream. . . . The King rode past with his lieutenants and stopped to examine the trees." The story of the woman's daughter is told by a second, omniscient-like voice that remarks about the woman's daily activities. The third voice is the woman's own, trying to explain about the past. The story concerns a woman who has hidden her illegitimate daughter, begot in an incestuous affair with her own brother, in her house for some sixteen years, until a plumber discovered her. *The Woman's Daughter* is about memory, about communal archetypes that, like the titular rivulet of Part II, "flow" from generation to generation, even if underground, encompassing the king, his lieutenants, and all subsequent people and their fates—the stories and lives passed into the care of the remembering consciousness. For the new edition of the novel, Bolger has sandwiched a lengthy middle section, entitled "Victoriana," between the original two parts. It features two stories, one set in the late nineteenth century and the other in the present, of obsessive sexual attraction, and the stories are held together by a number of thematic and motific parallels. The new part underscores the "message" so pregnant in "The Crystal Rivulet" section: history repeating itself in subsequent generations.

In *Emily's Shoes,* Michael McMahon has been haunted for years by the same dream, that he has killed someone, and he wonders whether there is "something in the past which [he is] hiding from [himself]." He may have been hiding the fact that he failed to bid farewell to the girl, Maggie, who meant so much to him in his youth, when she left Ireland for Canada. Or there may be the faceless figure of his seafaring father, whom he never got to know. Or there may be his mother's untimely death. Michael appears to be entangled in a web of guilt and haunted by a sense of loss and bereavement. He goes to live with his Aunt Emily in Birmingham, and there he develops an overriding penchant for women's shoes. He is imbued with "a longing, a hunger," of which he cannot trace the source. But when he touches Emily's shoes, "that yearning [seems] to stop." Part II relates his affair with Maggie, back from Canada, which once again ends in loss; and Part III, tied up with Part I through motific echoes, tells of his relationship with a woman, Clare, over whom a sinister priest holds sway. Finally, all ends not too badly when Michael and Clare, almost like Leopold and Marion, find each other on Howth Head. Perhaps the shoe fetishism and the complex guilt-loss, bereavement syndrome are not worked out convincingly enough, and the disruption of chronology and the experimental use of typography look grafted on.

In *A Second Life,* Dublin photographer Sean Blake is clinically dead for several seconds after a car crash. He experiences the powerful sensation of being drawn toward a blissful afterworld, only to find his progress blocked by the haunting face of a man he only partially recognizes. He is resuscitated and rather reluctantly adjusts to the gift of a second life: at the age of six weeks, he was taken from his mother when, as an adolescent girl in rural Ireland in the 1950s, she was forced by nuns to give up her baby for adoption. Sean embarks on a quest for his real mother, sifting through the madeleines of his memory and bits of dreams, recalling places in his past life stimulated by photographs, and conducting research in the dust-covered archives of the Botanical Gardens. It is also a quest for his own identity. In parallel manner, his mother, now at an advanced age and her wits overpowered by curious sensations concerning her son's accident, is in search of Sean, whom she herself had called Paudi. With the help of various people, including an aunt in England, who tells him that his mother died ten weeks prior to his arrival, Sean is able to identify the convent in which he was born. He severely reproaches the nuns for their despicable conduct at the time, and there would appear to be in the accusation some of Bolger's own anger at a deplorable period in Ireland's history. But as one nun rightly puts it, "Unless you rid yourself of this anger you'll pass it on." Whether Bolger intends to pass on any anger is debatable, as is the issue of whether—as the blurb claims—Sean Blake's story, in fact, succeeds in exposing a festering wound from Ireland's past to shed light on a changing modern country, exploring how we must not only retain the past but try to redeem it.

$RÜDIGER\ IMHOF$

WORKS: *Never a Dull Moment.* Dublin: Raven Arts, 1979. (Poems); *The Habit of Flesh.* Dublin: Raven Arts, 1979. (Poems); *Finglas Lilies.* Dublin: Raven Arts, 1980. (Poems); *No Waiting America.* Dublin: Raven Arts, 1981. (Poems); ed., *After the War Is Over.* Dublin: Raven Arts, 1984; *Night Shift.* [Dingle, Co. Kerry]: Brandon, [1985]/Harmondsworth, Middlesex: Penguin, 1993. (Novel); with M. O'Loughlin, *A New Primer for Irish Schools.* Dublin: Raven Arts, 1985; *Internal Exiles: Poems.* Mountrath, Co. Laois: Dolmen, 1986; ed., *The Bright Wave/An Tonn Gheal: Poetry in Irish Now.* Dublin: Raven Arts, 1986; *The Woman's Daughter.* Dublin: Raven Arts, 1987. (Novel); *Invisible Cities: The New Dubliners.* Dublin: Raven Arts, 1988/reprinted and extended as *Invisible Dublin. Letters from the New Island.* Dublin: Raven Arts, 1987–1989/collected edition, 1992. (Essays); *Leinster Street Ghosts.* Dublin: Raven Arts, 1989. (Poems); *The Journey Home.* London: Viking, 1990. (Novel); *Emily's Shoes.* London: Viking, 1992. (Novel); *A Dublin Quartet.* Harmondsworth, Middlesex: Penguin, 1992. (Plays); ed., *Selected Poems of Francis Ledwidge.* Dublin: New Island, 1992; ed., *Ireland in Exile.* Dublin: New Island, 1993; ed., *The Picador Book of Contemporary Irish Fiction.* London: Picador, 1993; *A Second Life.* London: Viking, 1994. (Novel); *A Dublin Bloom: An Original Free Adaptation of James Joyce's* Ulysses. Dublin: New Island/London: Nick Hern, [1995]. (Play). REFERENCE: Imhof, Rüdiger. "How It Is on the Fringes of Irish Fiction." *Irish University Review* 22 (Spring–Summer 1992): 151–167.

BORAN, PAT (1963–   ), poet, fiction writer, and playwright. Boran was born on September 4, 1963, in Portlaoise and has been based in Dublin since 1982. Not unlike Dermot Bolger,* Boran has successfully turned his hand to producing works of excellence in several literary genres, winning awards in all of them. He is the author of three volumes of poetry, *The Unwound Clock, History and Promise,* and *Familiar Things,* and of one collection of short stories, *Strange Bedfellows.* He has had a number of plays broadcast on radio to great acclaim. Recently, he completed his first novel, entitled *Hynes' Sight,* which is awaiting publication. Boran is currently editor of *Poetry Ireland Review.*

Boran's versatility is also evident in the diversity of his subject matter, setting, and tone. He seems to write with equal ease about common occurrences and visionary truths, urban and rural life, young and old people, male and female perspectives, decrepit and successful characters—sometimes adopting a playful, humorous attitude toward his theme and sometimes displaying brooding, almost sinister points of view. He neither moralizes nor seems to get emotionally involved in his subject matter. It would appear that he is not interested in affirming his readers' cosy familiarity with their surroundings. Instead, he likes to present things from an unexpected, occasionally disturbing, but almost always oblique, angle. That makes for exciting, eminently entertaining reading with plenty of surprises.

BARBARA FREITAG

WORKS: *The Unwound Clock.* [Dublin]: Dedalus, [1989]. (Poetry); *History and Promise.* Blackrock: Irish University Press, 1990. (Poetry pamphlet); *Familiar Things.* [Dublin]: Dedalus, [1990]. (Poetry); *Strange Bedfellows.* [Galway]: Salmon, [1991]. (Short stories).

BOUCICAULT, DION (1820 or 1822–1890), playwright and actor. Playwright, adapter of plays and novels, actor, director, manager, commentator, and entrepreneur, Boucicault was perhaps the most eminent man in the theatre of England, America, and Ireland in the mid-nineteenth century. His birth and his parentage, like much else in his personal life, are mysterious. He was born Dionysius Lardner Boursiquot in Dublin in 1820 or 1822; he always gave his birthdate as December 26, 1822, thus establishing the record of his precocity in writing the hit *London Assurance* in 1841. No parish records exist. He was named after Dionysius Lardner, who became well known in London as a lecturer and encyclopedist, whom Boucicault much resembled and whose protege he became. Although his formal schooling from age seven on was English, he retained his brogue both on and off stage throughout his life. In his teens, he left his training as an engineer to become a provincial actor and playwright under the name of Lee Moreton. Encouraged by Charles Mathews of Covent Garden to write a modern comedy, he wrote (with some help from John Brougham* [1814–1880]) the comedy *London Assurance,* which ran for sixty-nine nights. For the next fifty years, he was so heavily involved in personal and theatrical activities that they can barely be summarized in a short space.

In his twenties, Boucicault wrote and adapted many plays, lived in France for several years, learning the language fluently, and returned to England following the mysterious death of his first wife, Anne Guiot. As a reader for Charles Kean at the Princess, he met Kean's protegee, the actress Agnes Robertson, with whom he moved to America, in 1853. While they may not have been legally married, they lived and worked together as a married couple for many years. She achieved instantaneous success in Boston as a matinee idol, and Boucicault wrote five plays for her in the star role, touring widely throughout the United States. Partly as a result of Boucicault's efforts, Congress in 1856 changed the U.S. copyright laws to ensure playwrights a greater reward from their productions. Boucicault's *The Poor of New York* (1857, variously titled according to the city it was playing in) and *The Octoroon* (1859) revealed his enormous skill for seizing a currently popular or inflammatory issue, simplifying it into melodramatic terms, and providing a "sensational" theatrical climax, usually in Act

Three of a three-act play. The burning of a tenement, the explosion of the river boat, the climb up and leap from the high tower, the rescue of the heroine from drowning, the enactment on stage of the Oxford-Cambridge boat race, and the heroine tied to the railroad track (a scene which he actually stole from Augustin Daly's *Under the Gaslight*) became the trademark of Boucicault's melodrama.

The success of *The Colleen Bawn* ("the fair-haired girl") in New York and London in 1861 and in Dublin in 1862 led to another Boucicault innovation, the touring company, and another Boucicault advance, his Irish plays. While stars had been touring for decades, generally they used local talent from repertory companies. Boucicault put together the whole show. By acting with Agnes Robertson in his own play and touring with his own company, he earned money as a manager, playwright, and actor. Simultaneously, he benefited by sending out other companies on tour and through the newly increased royalties. With a succession of hit plays, Boucicault was to earn an estimated $5 million in his theatrical lifetime, while at the same time advancing the importance of the playwright in the whole process of theatrical production. He toured throughout the United States and for many years played regularly in Boston, New York, and Philadelphia. He returned to Dublin three times and to London at least three, all but one of these engagements being successful.

With his play *The Colleen Bawn* (1860), he had discovered what was perhaps his most moving theatrical genre, the Irish play. Highly aware of the Stage Irishman as a long-established English stereotype, he reversed the stereotype by taking the same character traits and showing them favorably. His country people were not slovenly and stupid but charming and beguiling, with a native wit and resourcefulness that belied upper-class condescension and occasionally twitted the English. In 1864–1865, he produced *Arrah-na-Pogue* ("Arrah of the Kiss") in Dublin and London, and in 1874 he opened *The Shaughraun* ("The Wanderer") in New York, both of them enormously successful. Their melodrama and their sentimentality account for only part of their appeal. It lies also in the charming dialogue and the creation of vivid characters like Danny Mann and the scampish Myles na Coppaleen. Not all of Boucicault's Irish plays were as good as these two. As in many other of his potboilers, he had a strong tendency towards stage emotion and dialogue rather than real emotion.

Boucicault had a knack as an adapter of plays, usually French, which he produced as his own, and as a dramatizer of fiction, like Dickens' "Cricket on the Hearth" and Scott's *The Heart of Midlothian*. His version of *Rip Van Winkle* in 1865 established Joseph Jefferson as a star and is still the acted version. Boucicault was not as skilled as a theatrical manager because he usually overspent money on elaborate refurbishing of his theatres and on extravagant productions. At times he managed theatres in New Orleans, Washington, New York, and London. However, he was enormously skilled as a set designer and technician, attentive to the smallest details. His productions were noted for their sets, their special effects, and the well-rehearsed ensemble nature of the acting. Late in his life, Boucicault published papers on acting and for a short while directed an acting school for the entrepreneur A. M. Palmer at Madison Square Garden. His emphasis was on movement and gesture rather than on the elocutionary manner of speech then popular.

Boucicault's personal and financial lives were puzzles to his contemporaries and remain so to the modern student. He made and lost three fortunes, some in gold mine stock, some in bad theatrical management, and some in personal extravagance. Following *London Assurance,* he dressed, dined, and entertained in the highest style. He was devoted to the six children Agnes Robertson bore him, several of whom followed him onto the stage. In the early 1880s, he and Agnes separated. His subsequent marriage to the very young actress Louise Thorndike, while on tour in Australia in 1885, and the public bickerings over the divorce from Agnes caused scandal in New York and London—partly because Boucicault now denied they had ever been married. After his death in New York City on September 18, 1890, there was extended fighting over his estate, which seemed to be almost nonexistent. He was always in the public eye, and he had a wide circle of nontheatrical as well as theatrical friends. Thousands of mourners attended his funeral at the Little Church Around the Corner, and obituaries appeared in the hundreds of cities in the United States and England where he had played on tour. It was an internationally reported event.

Boucicault's theatrical influence was pervasive rather than sharply focused. He could fill the great theatres in the cities and in the remote provinces. With his *London Assurance* and his *Old Heads and Young Hearts* (1844), he helped carry on the English tradition of drawing room comedy. Through numerous comedies and thrillers adapted from the French, he carried on the joint influence of English and French theatre. The organization of the touring company brought New York professional theatre to the provinces—and helped kill local repertory theatre. In the age of the great actor-managers, of which he was one, he led the audiences to expect exciting staging and ensemble acting, and he increased the importance of the playwright. He helped launch the careers of Henry Irving and Joseph Jefferson, and he encouraged the young Oscar Wilde* in the early part of his American tour. To the Irish stage he gave respectability and three notable plays. While Edmund Booth concentrated on Shakespeare and Gilbert and Sullivan on operetta, Boucicault influenced all areas of the theatre. By the time of his death in 1890, his taste was out of touch with the emerging theatre of Wilde, Shaw,* Synge,* Ibsen, and Chekhov, and by an irony of fate, his very great fame was soon forgotten. The Hollywood feature film rather than the theatre continued his tradition of spectacular effects and melodrama. Douglas Fairbanks, Jr., played his *Corsican Brothers* (derived from Dumas) in a film as late as 1941. But both Shaw and O'Casey* acknowledged his early influence, and Chekhov, who surely did not know him but did know his French and German equivalents, strenuously wrote his theatre of real life against the Boucicault traditions, using it in order to change it.

SVEN ERIC MOLIN

WORKS: *London Assurance.* London: Printed for the Author, 1841; *The Irish Heiress* (also called

West End). London: Andrews, 1842; *Alma Mater; or, A Cure for Coquettes.* London: Webster, [1842?]; *Curiosities of Literature.* London: Webster, [1842?]; *Don Caesar de Bazan; or Love and Honour.* London: Acting National Drama, [1844]; *The Fox and the Goose; or, The Widow's Husband.* London: Acting National Drama, [1844]; *Old Heads and Young Hearts.* New York: French's Standard Drama, No. 62, n.d.; *A Lover by Proxy.* London: Acting National Drama, [1845?]; *The Wonderful Water Cure.* London: Acting National Drama, [1846?]; *The School for Scheming* (later revised and retitled *Love and Money).* London: Acting National Drama, [1847?]; *A Romance in the Life of Sixtus the Fifth, entitled the Broken Vow* (later called *The Pope of Rome,* and often referred to as *Sixtus the Fifth).* London: Hailes Lacy, 1851; *Love in a Maze.* London: Hailes Lacy, 1851; *The Queen of Spades; or, The Gambler's Secret* (also called *The Dame of Spades).* London: Hailes Lacy, 1851; *The Corsican Brothers; or, The Vendetta.* London: Hailes Lacy, [1852]; *The Vampire.* London: French, [1852?]/later shortened and retitled *The Phantom,* New York: French's Standard Drama, 1856; *Faust and Marguerite.* London: French, [1854?]; *The Willow Copse.* Boston: William V. Spencer, [1856?]; *Wanted a Widow, with Immediate Possession.* New York: Samuel French, n.d.; *The Poor of New York* (also produced under many other titles). New York: Samuel French, [1857?]; *Jessie Brown; or, The Relief of Lucknow.* New York: Samuel French, 1858; Pauvrette (also called *The Snow Flower).* New York: Samuel French, [1858?]; *The Colleen Bawn; or, The Brides of Garryowen.* [New York]: Printed but not published, [1860?]/also in *Nineteenth Century Plays,* ed. by George Rowell. London: Oxford University Press, 1853, and in *The Dolmen Press Boucicault,* ed. David Krause. Dublin: Dolmen, 1964; *The Lily of Killarney.* Philadelphia, 1867. An operetta based on *The Colleen Bawn,* with words by Boucicault and John Oxenford, and music by Sir Jules Benedict; *How She Loves Him.* London: Chapman & Hall, [1868]; *The Knight of Arva.* New York: French's Standard Drama, [1868?]; with Charles Reade, *Foul Play.* London: Bradbury, Evans, 1868. (Novel); *Arrah-na-Pogue; or, The Wicklow Wedding.* London: French's Acting Edition, [1865], also in *The Dolmen Press Boucicault; The Long Strike.* New York: Samuel French, [1870?]; *Foul Play.* Chicago: Dramatic Publishing Co., n.d.; *After Dark: A Tale of London Life.* New York: De Witt's Acting Plays, n.d.; *The Rapparee; or, The Treaty of Limerick.* Chicago: Dramatic Publishing Co., n.d.; *Jezebel; or, The Dead Reckoning.* Chicago: Dramatic Publishing Co., n.d.; *Elfie; or, The Cherry Tree Inn.* Chicago: Dramatic Publishing Co., n.d.; *Night and Morning* (also called *Kerry; or, Night and Morning).* Chicago: Dramatic Publishing Co., n.d.; reprinted in *Irish University Review 3* (Spring 1973); *Led Astray.* New York & London: French, [1873?]; *The Shaughraun.* Published in acting editions by French, Dicks, Lacy's, and Webster, and currently available in *The Dolmen Press Boucicault; The Story of Ireland.* Boston: James R. Osgood, 1881. (Short history); *Andy Blake; or, The Irish Diamond* (later called *The Dublin Boy* and *The Irish Boy).* London: Dicks' Standard Plays, [1884]; *A Legend of the Devil's Dyke.* London: Dick's Standard Plays, [1898]; *The Old Guard* (a revision of his first play, *Napoleon's Old Guard).* London: Dick's Standard Plays, [1900?]; *The Jilt.* London & New York: French, [1904]; *Daddy O'Dowd; or, Turn About Is Fair Play* (later revised as *The O'Dowd; or, Life in Galway,* and still later revised as *Suil-a-mor; or, Life in Galway).* London & New York: French, [1909]; *Belle Lamar* (revised as *Fin Mac Cool of Skibbereen),* in *Plays for the College Theatre.* Garrett H. Leverton, ed. New York: French, 1932; *Forbidden Fruit and Other Plays.* Princeton, N.J.: Princeton University Press, 1940. (Also contains *Louis XI, Presumptive Evidence, Dot,* and *Robert Emmet); Flying Scud; or, A Four Legged Fortune,* in *Favorite American Plays of the Nineteenth Century.* Barrett H. Clark, ed. Princeton, N.J.: Princeton University Press, 1943; *The Octoroon; or, Life in Louisiana* and *Rip Van Winkle,* in *Representative American Plays, from 1767 to the Present Day.* Arthur Hobson Quinn, ed. 7th ed. New York: Appleton-Century-Crofts, 1953; *The Dolmen Press Boucicault.* David Krause, ed. Dublin: Dolmen, 1964. (Contains *The Colleen Bawn, Arrah na Pogue,* and *The Shaughraun); Lost at Sea; or, A London Story,* in *The Golden Age of Melodrama.* Michael Kilgarriff, ed. London: Wolfe, 1974. (Abridged version); *Plays by Dion Boucicault.* Peter Thomson, ed. Cambridge: Cambridge University Press, 1984. (Contains *Used Up, Old Heads and Young Hearts, Jessie Brown, The Octoroon,* and *The Shaughraun); Dion Boucicault, The Shaughraun. Part Three: Three Early Plays.* S. E. Molin & R. Goodefellowe, eds. Newark, Del.: Proscenium, 1985. (Contains *London Assurance, Used Up,* and

Old Heads and Young Hearts)/*Part Four: Three Early Potboilers.* Newark, Del.: Proscenium, 1989. (Contains *The Knight of Arva, The Corsican Brothers* and *The Phantom*); *Selected Plays of Dion Boucicault.* Andrew Parkin, ed. Gerrards Cross: Colin Smythe, 1987/1926. To these might be added: *The Art of Acting.* New York: Publications of the Dramatic Museum of Columbia University, 19246; *The Art of Acting: A Discussion by Constant Coquelin, Henry Irving, and Dion Boucicault.* New York: Publications of the Dramatic Museum of Columbia University, 1926.

The preceding list is a fairly complete compilation of Boucicault's major published works. However, because most of his plays were printed cheaply in ephemeral acting editions, some problems in his bibliography will probably never be solved. Many of his plays were not printed at all, but for a listing of their first productions, consult Fawkes or Hogan (in References). REFERENCES: Fawkes, Richard. *Dion Boucicault, A Biography.* London, Melbourne, New York: Quartet Books, 1979; Hogan, Robert. *Dion Boucicault.* New York: Twayne, 1969; Korf, Leonard Lee. "An Examination of Some Obscurities in the Life of Dion Boucicault." Diss., University of California–Los Angeles, 1975; Molin, S. E. & Goodefellowe, R. *Dion Boucicault, The Shaughraun. Part One: The Early Years.* Newark, Del.: Proscenium, 1979/*Part Two: Up and Down in Paris and London.* Newark, Del.: Proscenium, 1982/*Part Five: The American Debut.* Newark, Del.: Proscenium, 1991; Pine, Richard, ed. *Dion Boucicault and the Irish Melodrama Tradition,* a special edition of *Prompts* (Bulletin of the Irish Theatre Archive) 6 (September 1983); Tolson, Julius H. "Dion Boucicault." Diss., University of Pennsylvania, 1951; Walsh, Townsend. *The Career of Dion Boucicault.* New York: Dunlop Society, 1915.

BOURKE, EVA

WORK: *Litany for the Pig.* [Galway]: Salmon, [1989]. (Poetry).

BOURKE, P[ATRICK] J. (1883–1932), playwright and actor-manager. Born in Dublin in 1883, Bourke was orphaned by the age of twelve and early began to earn his living by driving a department store van. By the age of twenty he was producing and acting in patriotic melodramas, and he had his own company, which toured for years, specializing in his plays and those of Boucicault* and Whitbread.* In 1913, he wrote and partially directed *Ireland a Nation,* the first Irish feature film. When it was eventually released in Dublin in 1917, it was banned by the British military. For several years he managed the Queen's Theatre in Dublin, and he founded a theatrical costumier's, which closed only in 1994. He himself died on July 20, 1932. He is the father of Seamus de Burca,* the playwright.

Among his patriotic melodramas are *When Wexford Rose* (produced in the Father Matthew Hall in 1910 and in the Queen's in 1912), *The Northern Insurgents* (1912), *In Dark and Evil Days* (1914), and *For the Land She Loved* (1915). Although *When Wexford Rose* has a romantic subplot, where an Irish soldier prevents an English general from stealing his beloved Grace Bassett, political and military elements overshadow the romance. Set in 1798, the play demonstrates the valor of Irishwomen, complicating stereotypes of Ireland as passive and feminized. Kitty Cassidy fights in battle, and Mary Doyle, the heroine at Ross, was equal to "half a dozen men" in combat. When Donal O'Byrne, the hero, gives her a sword as a reward, she says, "With this sword I swear to stand for Ireland." Toward the end of the play, she protects Donal from British soldiers, sacrificing herself in the process. Even Biddy Dolan, the informer, repents, hoping her death "will be a warning to all who in the future may depend on the generosity of the English government."

As with *When Wexford Rose, For the Land She Loved* contains many elements of a romantic comedy. Rather than relying on Irish men to save them, here again women take the initiative. Sheila deLacy uses a pistol to rescue her mistress, Betsy Gray, from being raped by Colonel Johnston. Betsy Gray leads the rebels in assaults on the English and toward the end kills her nemesis, Lady Nugent, in a duel for the love of Robert Munro. She herself dies when she thrusts herself between the battling swords of Munro and the English colonel.

If Bourke's plays were hardly literary drama, they were all very lively and swashbuckling.

WILLIAM G. DOLDE

WORKS: *Kathleen Mavourneen, A Play with Songs.* Dublin: P. J. Bourke, 1959; *The Northern Insurgents. The Journal of Irish Literature* 13 (January–May 1984): 7–74; *When Wexford Rose* and *For the Land She Loved.* In *For the Land They Loved: Irish Political Melodramas 1890–1925.* Cheryl Herr, ed. [Syracuse, N.Y.]: Syracuse University Press, [1991]. REFERENCES: de Burca, Seamus. *The Queen's Royal Theatre Dublin, 1829–1969.* Dublin: Seamus de Burca, 1983; Herr, Cheryl, op. cit.

BOWEN, ELIZABETH [DOROTHEA COLE] (1899–1973), novelist and short story writer. A line from her best novel, *Death of the Heart,* reveals the central conviction of all of Elizabeth Bowen's fiction: "Illusions are art, for the feeling person, and it is by art that we live, if we do." The consolation of sensibility and the support it provides in dealing with the trials of life provides a central theme for all of her stories and novels.

Born in Dublin on June 7, 1899, Bowen spent most of her life in England. However, her affection for her birthplace and her pride in the estate that she inherited, Bowen's Court, appear in many of her works. Her childhood was unhappy, and the lonely children in many of her novels and stories seem to be based on her own experiences. In her adult life, she was part of the literary set that included Virginia Woolf, E. M. Forster, and the Bloomsbury group. She was a prolific but careful writer, the author of ten novels, over seventy short stories, a half dozen works of nonfiction, and over 600 reviews and essays.

Her first publications were short stories, the first collection of which was *Encounters* (1923). These and later stories, particularly "The Demon Lover," demonstrate Bowen's gift for using setting to reveal inner unrest and her fascination with the mysterious. The stories typically center on alienated characters who speak a kind of wisdom that disarms the reasonable but conventional attitudes of others. The understatement of her stories makes the extreme anxiety of her characters even more evocative, and strong evocations of terror or anxiety are achieved through a minimum of description or commentary.

Her stories remain popular anthology pieces, but her reputation rests on her novels. One of the earliest and best, *The Last September* (1929), is set in Ireland during the Troubles. Although its plot is simple, this novel shows the consequences of destroying a Great House and conveys the paralyzing confusions of the time.

In *The House in Paris* (1935), Bowen first treats the subject that was to become her central concern: the relations of children to adults. In this novel, a confused mother tries to deal with her perceptive but lonely child in a time of tension. In the end, the adult tendency toward conformity is overshadowed by the child's sensitivity.

Bowen's masterpiece, *The Death of the Heart* (1938), carries that subject further. Portia, an adolescent who has lived her life throughout Europe with her mother, is orphaned and is put in the care of an uncle and his wife in London. For all her suffering, Portia is spontaneous, natural, and, to them, threatening, for she questions the conformity and sterility of their lives. For a while she lives in a seaside resort, where she discovers the disorderly life of a young smart set; in their smug contentment and crassness they are no better than the older generation and just as eager to control her. The novel's title points to its main theme: the process of maturing threatens to destroy a native sensitivity. Portia succeeds in adjusting to life with others who are jaded and corrupted, but at some loss of innocence. The book's characters are varied, each established with a minimum of description, yet each representing a type of compromise of idealism. Like novels by Forster and Woolf, the plot is apparently simple, but subtle and finally complex, as Portia advances in her accommodation to life. The novel relies on symbolism, oblique expression, and a complicated juxtaposition of perceptions, yet its impact is, in the end, strong and challenging.

Worth special mention is Bowen's novel *The Heat of the Day* (1949) for the strength of its depiction of war-torn London. While the contrast to the sophistication of the earlier novels is first apparent, its central concerns are the same: the sacrifice of personal values in a menacing environment. Her final novel, *Eva Trout* (1969), evoked a varied critical response, because of its less realistic plot structure and its startling conclusion, yet its thematic concerns are consistent with all her earlier works. The title character, like so many of Bowen's main characters, is ill adapted to the conventional world. When she acquires a child— and we are not informed of whether or not this was through the adoption black market—she attempts to accommodate herself and the child to the rest of the world. The results are so unsuccessful that the account is often comic, but ultimately tragic.

Elizabeth Bowen puts heavy demands on her reader, as the novels rely on symbolism, irony, and subtle implication. However, the novels are more than novels of sensibility, for Bowen exhibits formidable intellectual skills and a deep knowledge of literary traditions. For all their verbal polish and restraint, her novels and her many stories deal with intense passions such as love, jealousy, hatred and, most frequently, loneliness.

Bowen's pride in her Irish heritage is revealed in her account of the estate she inherited, *Bowen's Court* (1942), and in *The Shelbourne* (1951), about that famous Dublin hotel; but in many stories and essays, Irish settings, both barren landscapes and lush ones, are skillfully employed. One of her novels, *The Last September,* deals with a specifically Irish subject, but even here her real interests are not with national identities but personal relations and internal life.

JAMES KILROY

WORKS: *Encounters.* London: Sidgwick & Jackson, 1923/New York: Boni & Liveright, 1925/ republished in *Early Stories,* New York: Alfred A. Knopf, 1950; *Ann Lee's and Other Stories.* London: Sidgwick & Jackson, 1926/New York: Boni & Liveright, 1926/republished in *Early Stories,* New York: Alfred A. Knopf, 1950; *The Hotel.* London: Constable, 1927/New York: Dial, 1928; *Joining Charles and Other Stories.* London: Constable/New York: Dial, 1929; *The Last September.* London: Constable/New York: Dial, 1929; *Friends and Relations.* London: Constable/New York: Dial, 1931; *To the North.* London: Gollancz, 1932/New York: Alfred A. Knopf, 1933; *The Cat Jumps and Other Stories.* London: Gollancz, 1934; *The House in Paris.* London: Gollancz, 1935/ New York: Alfred A. Knopf, 1936; *The Death of the Heart.* London: Gollancz, 1935/New York: Alfred A. Knopf, 1936; *Look at All Those Roses.* London: Gollancz/New York: Alfred A. Knopf, 1941; *Bowen's Court.* London: Longmans, Green/New York: Alfred A. Knopf, 1942/2d ed., with Afterword, London: Longmans, Green/New York: Alfred A. Knopf, 1964; *English Novelists.* London: W. Collins, 1942; *Seven Winters: Memories of a Dublin Childhood.* Dublin: Cuala, 1942/ republished as *Seven Winters: Memories of a Dublin Childhood and Afterthoughts: Pieces on Writing,* New York: Alfred A. Knopf, 1962; *The Demon Lover and Other Stories.* London: Jonathan Cape, 1945/published in America as *Ivy Gripped the Steps,* New York: Alfred A. Knopf, 1946; *Anthony Trollope: A New Judgment.* New York & London: Oxford University Press, 1946; *Why Do I Write? An Exchange of Views Between Elizabeth Bowen, Graham Greene, and V. S. Pritchett.* London: Percival Marshall, 1948; *The Heat of the Day.* London: Jonathan Cape/New York: Alfred A. Knopf, 1949; *Collected Impressions.* London: Longmans, Green/New York: Alfred A. Knopf, 1950; *The Shelbourne: A Center in Dublin Life for More Than a Century.* London: George G. Harrap, 1951/published in America as *The Shelbourne Hotel,* New York: Alfred A. Knopf, 1951; *A World of Love.* London: Jonathan Cape/New York: Alfred A. Knopf, 1955; *Stories by Elizabeth Bowen.* New York: Alfred A. Knopf, 1959; *A Time in Rome.* New York: Alfred A. Knopf/London: Longmans, Green, 1960; *Afterthought: Pieces About Writing.* London: Longmans, Green, 1962; *The Little Girls.* London: Jonathan Cape/New York: Alfred A. Knopf, 1964; *A Day in the Dark and Other Stories.* London: Jonathan Cape, 1965; *The Good Tiger.* New York: Knopf, 1968/London: Jonathan Cape, 1969; *Pictures and Conversations.* Foreword by S. C. Brown. London: Allen Lane, 1975; *Irish Stories.* Swords, Co. Dublin: Poolbeg, 1978; *The Collected Stories of Elizabeth Bowen.* Introduction by Angus Wilson. London: Jonathan Cape, 1980/New York: Knopf, 1981; *The Mulberry Tree: Writings of Elizabeth Bowen.* Selected & introduced by H. Lee. London: Virago, 1986. REFERENCES: Austin, Allen. *Elizabeth Bowen.* New York: Twayne, 1971; Blodgett, Harriet. *Patterns of Reality: Elizabeth Bowen's Novels.* The Hague: Mouton, 1975; Craig, P. *Elizabeth Bowen.* Harmondsworth: Penguin, 1986; Glendinning, Victoria. *Elizabeth Bowen: Portrait of a Writer.* London: Weidenfeld & Nicolson, 1977; Heath, William. *Elizabeth Bowen, an Introduction.* Madison: University of Wisconsin Press, 1961; Hoogland, Renee C. *Elizabeth Bowen: A Reputation in Writing.* New York: New York University Press, 1994; Jordan, Heather Bryant. *How the Heart Will Endure: Elizabeth Bowen in the Landscape War.* Ann Arbor: University of Michigan Press, 1993; Kenny, Edwin J., Jr. *Elizabeth Bowen.* Lewisburg, Pa.: Bucknell University Press, 1975; Kiberd, Declan. "Elizabeth Bowen—The Dandy in Revolt" in *Inventing Ireland.* London: Jonathan Cape, 1995, pp. 364–379; Lee, H. *Elizabeth Bowen: An Estimation.* London: Vision/Totowa, N.J.: Barnes & Noble, 1981.

BOWLER, MICHAEL (fl. 1990s), novelist. Bowler was born and reared in County Kerry, and his novel, *Destiny of Dreams* (1990), is a lyric account of childhood and early adolescence in Cahirciveen. There are exquisitely evocative details in the book, and the account of a Christmas is particularly memorable. The accuracy of detail and the frequent fineness of the writing do not, however, quite make up for the very ambling pace of the narrative. Should Bowler be able to harness his observation and his prose to an architectured plot, he might be a very considerable writer indeed.

WORK: *Destiny of Dreams.* [Swords, Co. Dublin]: Poolbeg, [1990].

BOYCE, JOHN (1810–1864), novelist. Boyce was born in County Donegal, educated at Maynooth, and ordained in 1837. In 1845, he went to America and wrote popular comic novels under the pseudonym of Paul Peppergrass. A friend of Dickens and Thackeray,* he died in America in 1864.

WORKS: *Shandy McGuire; or, Tricks upon Travellers: Being a Story of the North of Ireland.* New York: Dunigan, 1848; *The Spaewife; or, the Queen's Secret: A Story of the Reign of Elizabeth.* Baltimore: Murphy, 1852; *Mary Lee; or, The Yankee in Ireland.* Baltimore: Kelly, Hedian & Piet, 1860. REFERENCE: Boyce, Rev. Charles. *Biographical Sketch of the Rev. John Boyce, D.D. (1810–64).* Dublin: Juverna, 1941.

BOYD, ERNEST A[UGUSTUS] (1887–1946), literary critic and journalist. Boyd was born in Dublin on June 28, 1887, the son of James Robert Boyd and his wife, Rosa (formerly Kempson). As a boy, he modeled for the figure of Christ in the set of stations of the cross in the Dublin Pro-Cathedral. He was educated privately with a French tutor and also at schools in Germany and Switzerland. From his early training, he emerged with an exceptional grasp of the languages and literatures of Europe, especially France.

In 1910, he went to work on the *Irish Times,* where he remained until 1913, when he entered the British Consular Service. He was posted as vice-consul to Baltimore, Maryland, in 1913, to Barcelona in 1916, and to Copenhagen in 1918. His nationalist feelings were said to have been looked on with suspicion by his superiors (the service having already harbored Sir Roger Casement), and he was falsely suspected of being a supported of Sinn Féin. Boyd resigned in 1919 and settled in New York in 1920.

During his time in Baltimore, he had become friendly with H. L. Mencken, who encouraged his literary ambitions and about whom he later wrote a book. At first he worked as a journalist on the *New York Post* and then became the reader and literary adviser on foreign literature to Alfred A. and Blanche Knopf, who were establishing their important publishing firm in whose list European writers were a strong feature. He also contributed to *The Literary Review* and read plays for the Theatre Guild. He returned to journalism in 1925, becoming editor of *The Independent* until 1928, of *The New Freeman* from 1931 to 1932, and of *The American Spectator* from 1932 to 1937. Thereafter, he worked as a freelance literary journalist. He was elected an associate member of the Irish Academy of Letters* when it was created by Yeats* and Shaw* in 1933, but the last years of his life were largely uncreative.

He began his literary career in 1913, writing for the Jesuit-inspired journals

The Irish Review and *Irish Monthly,* on those perennial topics of the current mismanagement of the Abbey Theatre,* the dogmatism of the Gael, and feminism. He made his name with *The Irish Literary Renaissance,* published in Ireland in 1916 and in a revised edition in America in 1922. This key work defined for two generations the history and members of the literary movement inspired by Yeats. For a time, he was a member of the movement, writing under a pen name *The Sacred Egoism of Sinn Féin* (1918) and two satirical plays, *The Glittering Fake* (1918) and *The Worked-Out Ward* (1918). He also wrote ''The Ballade of George Moore,*'' contributed to Susan L. Mitchell's* collection of satires, *The Secret Springs of Dublin Song,* and wrote an introduction for the Talbot Press edition of Standish O'Grady's* *Selected Essays and Passages* (1918).

He was fiercely criticized for his synthetic satire and ''bad guy'' attitudes in his own dramatic work, though his taste and scholarship as critic and translator were rightly appreciated. His appreciations of Joyce* helped persuade Judge Woolsey to allow *Ulysses* into the United States. Dressed always in brown, he cultivated a reputation as a raconteur and a model of the cultivated, civilized Irish gentleman. He was thought by some to lack a sense of humor and to be glumly, rather than joyously, aware of the beauties he appreciated. However, his appreciations of the Irish writers of the literary revival are of the greatest historical importance, and his history of the movement will always be a special resource.

In 1913, he married Madeline Elsie Reynier, herself a translator of note, from whom he was later divorced. She made their life together the subject of her only novel, *Life Makes Advances* (Boston: Little, Brown, 1939). He died in New York on December 30, 1946.

PETER COSTELLO

WORKS: *Ireland's Literary Renaissance.* Dublin & London: Maunsel, 1916/New York: Knopf, 1922; *Contemporary Drama of Ireland.* Boston: Little, Brown, 1917; new ed., Dublin: Talbot, 1918; *Appreciations and Depreciations.* Dublin: Talbot, 1917/New York: John Lane, 1918; as Gnathai Gan Iarraidh. *The Sacred Egoism of Sinn Féin.* Dublin & London: Maunsel, 1918; *The Glittering Fake* with *The Worked-Out Ward.* Dublin: Talbot, 1918. (Plays); ed. & translator. *Collected Novels and Stories of Guy de Maupassant.* 18 vols. New York: Knopf, 1922; *Portraits Real and Imaginary.* New York: George H. Doran/London: Jonathan Cape, 1924; *Studies in Ten Literatures.* New York: Scribner's, 1925; *H. L. Mencken.* New York: R. M. MacBride, 1925; *Guy de Maupassant—A Biographical Study.* New York & London: Knopf/Boston: Little, Brown, 1928; *Literary Blasphemies.* New York: Harper's, 1927; translator. *88 Short Stories by Guy de Maupassant.* New York: Knopf, 1930. REFERENCE: O'Hegarty, P. S. ''Ernest Boyd.'' *Dublin Magazine* 22 (April–June 1947): 50–51.

BOYD, JOHN (1912–), dramatist. Boyd was born on July 19, 1912, in Belfast and was educated at the Royal Belfast Academical Institution, Queen's University Belfast, and Trinity College, Dublin. He married Elizabeth McCune in 1939 and has three children. Before joining the Belfast BBC as a producer in 1947, he taught at grammar schools in Newry, Lisburn, and Belfast. He is at present literary adviser to the Lyric Theatre and editor, since 1971, of its publication *Threshold.*

Boyd has been active in encouraging Ulster writing, notably through the periodical *Lagan* (1942–1946), of which he was editor. As a BBC producer, he was responsible for a great number of valuable documentaries, interviews, and programs of criticism and reminiscence by such writers as Sean O'Faolain,* Frank O'Connor,* Louis MacNeice,* and, more recently, Brian Friel.*

Boyd now devotes himself to writing and is known primarily as a dramatist, his continuing interest being the heritage of the North and the outcroppings of its violent disunities. He renders the local language common to the adherents of the disunited faiths. Each can understand the idiom, though not sharing the belief, of the other. Boyd's plays draw on this common idiom for his dramatic statement of the origins and the manifestations of factional hatreds.

The Assassin (Gaiety, Dublin, 1969) opens into the frightening landscapes of ostensibly religious paranoia. *The Flats* (Lyric, 1971) places domestic tragedy in the midst of collective violence and the conflict of slogans that brutalize any genuine political critique. These naturalistic plays, together with *The Farm* (Lyric, 1972), *Guests* (Lyric, 1974), *The Street* (Lyric, 1977), *Summer School* (Lyric, 1987), and *Round the Clock* (Lyric, 1992), a Belfast chronicle play, speak to the local immediacies of tribal dispossessions and to Boyd's sense of the gulf between experience and its factional interpretations.

D.E.S. MAXWELL

WORKS: *The Flats.* Belfast: Blackstaff, 1974; *The Collected Plays.* 2 vols. Belfast: Blackstaff, 1981, 1982. (Volume 1 contains *The Flats, The Farm,* and *Guests;* Volume 2 contains *The Street* and *Facing North*)*; Out of My Class.* Belfast & Dover, N.H.: Blackstaff, [1985]. (Autobiography); *The Middle of My Journey.* [Belfast]: Blackstaff, [1990]. (Autobiography).

BOYD, THOMAS (ca. 1867–1927), poet. Of Boyd, Padraic Colum* wrote:

While living in London in desperately straitened circumstances (he was employed by some automatic machine company to collect the pennies out of the machines) he wrote some fine poems for Arthur Griffith's journal [*The United Irishman*] in Dublin. The Irish Literary Society in London gave him a better-paid and more congenial job as secretary. Unfortunately his morale was broken by this time. Thomas Boyd was a man of great sensibility, considerable accomplishment and a great deal of learning.

Boyd was an old-fashioned poet rather than a modern one, but until recent years such attractive poems as "The King's Son," "Love on the Mountain," and "To the Leanan Sidhe" appeared in anthologies.

WORK: *Poems.* Dublin, 1906.

BOYLAN, CLARE (1948–   ), novelist, short story writer, journalist, and broadcaster. Boylan was born Clare Selby on April 24, 1948, in Dublin, where she was educated. She married Alan Wilkes, a journalist, in 1970. She has been a feature writer for an evening newspaper and an editor of women's magazines and in 1973 received Ireland's Journalist of the Year Award. Since 1983, she has written four novels and two collections of short stories.

Her first novel, *Holy Pictures* (1983), is a poignant portrait of a young adolescent's growing up, and her Nan Cantwell suffers all the indignities and humiliations of the unemancipated female. In the book, Boylan establishes character types who will recur in later fiction, including the disillusioned wife who grows disinterested in her children, the female servant whose low pay and despair lead her to behavior of questionable morality, and the virginal child who learns about sex through hazy innuendo and grotesque tales. Cecil Cantwell, Nan's father, manufactures corsets and would probably prefer all women to be morally corseted. He, however, is unable to contain his own frailties, financial disintegration, and an indiscreet marriage while in India. Although he has legally changed his name to Webster, his bigamy and business failure are brought to light. His suicide brings more hardship upon the family, and the novel ends where it began, with the Cantwell sisters, Nan and Mary, holding a private Christmas celebration and hoping to please their mother with some small offering.

Presenting gifts to uncaring recipients is a motif that also appears in Boylan's short story collection, *A Nail on the Head* (1983). In "Housekeeper's Cut," Susan's cooking is taken for granted. The tram conductor in "Appearances" shows off his sodality medals to a young girl and is disillusioned at her impassive reaction. Mirabel of the title story willingly prepares frugal yet elegant meals for her husband's guests, who invade and virtually destroy her home. Often, Boylan's characters are chagrined to discover unexpected tendencies in spouses, lovers, and acquaintances, such as homosexuality in "Black Ice," a psychopathic murder history in "Some Retired Ladies on a Tour," and geriatric sexual prowess in "Bad-Natured Dog." Strange proclivities sometimes surface in the main characters themselves: Ormond murders his wife in "The Complete Angler," and Dora slits a gigolo's throat in "For Your Own Bad." Interestingly, Boylan treats such grimness with irony and even humor.

Irony dominates her second novel, *Last Resorts* (1984), the recounting of an artistic divorcée's attempts to keep her three errant teenagers on track and her own mind intact through annual vacations on a primitive Greek island. She is disheartened, however, by a lover who flees, fearing that his wife will notice his tan; she is baffled to find her beloved twins shunning her; and she is dismayed to discover that her youngest girl has explored the sexual revolution. Eventually, the heroine seeks her own liberation from family obligations, only to have her ex-husband resurface and reclaim the entire brood. She herself escapes to the developed island of Psiros, confirming that impermanence gives meaning to life. The many rapid-fire changes in a short space of time that conclude the novel are not awfully effective.

Problems with time are handled more gracefully in *Black Baby* (1989), a novel that has bothered some critics because of a dream sequence that is explained near the end. The elderly Alice Boyle's dream, however, imparts a significance to her life that is actualized with the appearance of the dynamic black woman Cora/Dinah, whom Boyle confusedly thinks is the grown-up ''pagan baby'' she had adopted from darkest Africa on the day of her First Communion. The spinster, who suffers a stroke after a burglary assault, imagines a life she could never have had as the dutiful daughter of demanding parents or the pitied aunt of two ''solicitous'' nephews and their greedy wives. Boylan's description of the woman preparing a burned/raw cake for an imagined houseful of guests is comic, touching, and apt, for Alice, while aged on the outside, is still virginal and inexperienced, like the inside of her cake.

Virginity as a metaphor is explored in the collection of short stories, *Concerning Virgins* (1989). In ''A Little Girl, Never Out Before,'' Frankie has been exposed to incestuous advances, childbearing, and caring for babies, while an older servant girl disposes of unwanted twins with total amorality. Intellectual and judgmental virginity appears in ''The Little Madonna,'' in which a naive public entrusts an infant to a sixteen-year-old impoverished and unstable mother. The virginal naiveté of a young male emerges in ''L'Amour,'' in which Nicholas confronts the carnivorous French paramour of his widowed father. In ''The Miracle of Life,'' a girl befriends a savvy new neighbor, thinking herself mature in their mutual appreciation for movie magazines and television, but nevertheless is offered a child's dress for Christmas.

Boylan's concern with the physical and mental molestation of women appears again in her novel *Home Rule* or *Eleven Edward Street* (1992). Called a ''prequel'' to *Holy Pictures,* the book deals with incest and its impact on the daughters of the Devlin family of Dublin. Daisy Devlin's mother is indifferent to her daughters; the father dies and leaves the family bankrupt; and Daisy is sent to a convent in England. Her encounter with a soldier whom she marries affords no hope for change, for the difficulties of childhood repeat themselves in adulthood. Boylan's ironies and pessimism preclude idyllic endings, but her characters generally remain pragmatic and are either strengthened by their ordeals or exact revenge upon their mental torturers.

MARGUERITE QUINTELLI-NEARY

WORKS: *Holy Pictures.* London: Hamish Hamilton/New York: Simon & Schuster, 1983. (Novel); *A Nail on the Head.* London: Hamish Hamilton, 1983/New York: Penguin Viking, 1985. (Short stories); *Last Resorts.* London: Hamish Hamilton, 1984/New York: Simon & Schuster, 1986. (Novel); *Black Baby.* London: Hamish Hamilton, 1988/New York: Doubleday, 1989. (Novel); *Concerning Virgins.* London: Hamish Hamilton, 1989/New York: Doubleday, 1990. (Short stories); *Home Rule.* London: Hamish Hamilton, 1992/also published as *Eleven Edward Street,* New York: Doubleday, 1992. (Novel); ed., *A Literary Companion to Cats.* [London]: Sinclair-Stevenson, [1994]; *That Bad Woman.* [London]: Little, Brown, [1995]. (Short stories).

BOYLAN, MARTIN (1944–), playwright. Boylan was born in Belfast on June 7, 1944, and educated at St. Malachi's College and Queen's University, Belfast, where he received a degree in chemical engineering. For a time, he lived in Canada and wrote some short stories for the Canadian Broadcasting Company. His theatrical productions include *Mick and Ed,* later developed as an RTÉ comedy series, produced at the Peacock in 1978, and *Thompsons,* produced in 1981 at the Peacock. He is part of a group of playwrights once known as the "Peacock Playwrights"—a group that included Frank McGuinness,* Graham Reid,* Bernard Farrell,* and Neil Donnelly*—and whose writings were cultivated by the then-Abbey script editor Sean McCarthy and the artistic director Joe Dowling. Boylan's other stage productions include *The Making of Father Sullivan* (1992), performed in Tübingen by the Anglo-Irish Theatre Group. He has won the O. Z. Whitehead Award and has produced several scripts for the BBC and RTÉ.

Thompsons, Boylan's only published play, concerns members of a family and their relationships with each other. It is set in the late 1950s and plays like an amalgam of American plays and novels from that era and a generation before, but given an Irish setting. The family is made up of a widower father with symptoms of advanced tuberculosis, a severely retarded son, a younger brother and sister in college, and another brother frustrated with his working-class lifestyle. The retarded son functions as a rather obvious metaphor for the family's dichotomy between external respectability and internal corruption and dysfunction. The other characters are little more than stereotypes drawn from the works of Miller, Steinbeck, O'Neill, and Williams. Boylan does little to develop the rich potential of the intellectually and creatively frustrated sons, nor does he explore the character of the daughter, who appears hard and cruel for most of the play and seemingly consumed with the prospect of landing a husband. The plot is as thin as the characterization. Moments offering opportunity for conflict and resolution are not staged, and some that are involve dialogue between an onstage character and a disembodied voice. *Thompsons* plays like more of a sketch than a good play and, being rather short, would benefit from revision and expansion.

BERNARD McKENNA

WORK: *Thompsons.* [Dublin]: Co-op Books, [1981].

BOYLE, PATRICK (1905–1982), short story writer and novelist. Boyle was born in Ballymoney, County Antrim, in 1905, and educated at the Coleraine Academical Institution. He worked for forty-five years for the Ulster bank, spending twenty of those years in Donegal and retiring as manager of the bank's Wexford branch. He did not turn to writing until late in life. In 1965, he submitted the fourteen stories of his first collection pseudonymously to a short story contest held by *The Irish Times* and judged by Terence de Vere White,* Mary Lavin,* and Frank O'Connor.* White later wrote, "When I came to look at the entries I found an extraordinary thing. The first, second, fourth, fifth had all been written by the one man, Patrick Boyle."

Boyle produced three excellent volumes of stories and one strong, if flawed, novel. The general impression left by his work is that it depicts mainly the middle-aged, hard-drinking, and wenching bachelor in the provincial town. Indeed, the main character of Boyle's novel, *Like Any Other Man* (1966), is just such a person. There is much that is excellent about this readable book, particularly the evocation of the pub milieu and of the daily business of a provincial bank. However, the melodramatic climax seems a bit too much, with Boyle punishing his protagonist more than the poor slob's character would warrant.

Boyle's stories have a considerable range of subject and of tone, and are generally much less hardhearted than his novel. Particularly notable are "Interlude," about the snaring of a bachelor into marriage; "Dialogue," a finely comic sketch of an eccentric priest and his dog; "Sally," an appealing tale of adolescent attraction; "A Quiet Respectable Couple," with its effective peasant melodrama; and "Age, I Do Abhor Thee," which must rank with Frank O'Connor's finest stories about small boys and their fathers. Indeed, Boyle has so many successes in his three collections of stories that one deeply regrets he did not start writing them thirty years earlier. He died in Dublin in 1982.

WORKS: *Like Any Other Man.* London: MacGibbon & Kee, 1966. (Novel); *At Night All Cats Are Grey and Other Stories.* London: MacGibbon & Kee, 1966; *All Looks Yellow to the Jaundiced Eye.* London: MacGibbon & Kee, 1969. (Stories); *A View from Calvary.* London: Gollancz, 1976. (Stories).

BOYLE, WILLIAM (1853–1923), playwright. Boyle, born in Dromiskin, County Louth, on April 4, 1853, was employed as an excise officer until his retirement in 1914. He died in London on March 6, 1923. His writing includes a collection of short stories, *A Kish of Brogues* (1899), and three remarkably popular plays for the Abbey*: *The Building Fund* (1905), *The Eloquent Dempsy* (1906), and *The Mineral Workers* (1906). In protest against the *Playboy,* he severed connections with the Abbey but returned in 1912.

His plays may be divided into two categories. *The Mineral Workers* and *Nic* (1916) examine the impact of modern ideas on traditional Irish life. The others are humorous (in the Jonsonian sense) studies of "deadly" sins: avarice in *The Building Fund,* political duplicity in *Dempsy,* and indolence in *Family Failing* (1912).

Symmetrically structured and broadly characterized, Boyle's plays are entertainments. Only in *Nic* is there a tragic figure—a gentle old farmhand who, urged to improve his economic lot, robs his employer. *The Building Fund* approaches dark comedy in the maneuverings of relatives and church workers for the estate of a dying, avaricious old woman, and *Dempsy* might have been an effective satire on political extremism. Generally, however, Boyle, to paraphrase the other Johnson, pleased his age and did not aim to mend.

WILLIAM J. FEENEY

WORKS: *A Kish of Brogues.* London: Simpkin, Marshall, 1899. (Stories); *The Building Fund.* Dublin: Maunsel, 1905; *The Mineral Workers.* Dublin: M. H. Gill, 1910; *The Eloquent Dempsy.* Dublin: M. H. Gill, 1911; *Family Failing.* Dublin: Dublin: M. H. Gill, 1912.

BRADFORD, ROY (fl. 1960s), novelist.

WORKS: *Valerie Scorby and the Big Port.* New York: Lone Star, [1960]; *Excelsior!* London: Arthur Barker, [1961].

BRADY, ANNE M. (1926–   ), novelist. Brady was born Anne Cannon in Dublin and received a B.A. from University College in 1947. She lived for four years in Canada and worked at Carleton University library. Now married, with four children, she lives in Dalkey, County Dublin. An interest in the sixteenth century has led to the publication of two novels, *The Winds of God* in 1985 and *Honey Off Thorns* in 1988. Also in 1985, she published with Brian Cleeve* the useful *Biographical Dictionary of Irish Writers,* which offers brief lives of about 1,200 writers.

The Winds of God deals with the Spanish Armada and religious persecution on both Catholic and Protestant sides during the reigns of Henry VIII and Elizabeth I in England and Phillip II in Spain. The plot involves the adventures of Ralph Paulet, born a Catholic in England but raised a Protestant and Una O'Boyle, an Irish hostage raised in the same household. Their lives intertwine, although Ralph makes his way to Spain to fight for the Catholic faith, and Una is sent back to her native Ireland.

In Spain and Portugal, Ralph finds persecution again, this time from the Inquisition, with Catholics calling all who do not adhere to their faith ''infidels.'' Ralph is forced to participate in the great Armada that sails to attack England, but the ''Winds of God'' wreak havoc on the ships, and they are all but annihilated. Ralph's ship is wrecked off the coast of Ireland, and he makes his way to Una. Together they escape to Holland, where again they face persecution in the name of religion. Finally, they depart for an uncertain future together.

Honey Off Thorns is also set in sixteenth-century England, with the theme a treatment of the lives of women. Isobel, the central character, is a nun who has entered the convent because there is no place else for her to go. She becomes pregnant and is forced to return to her family home, branded a whore and unwelcomed by her family. She escapes to France, where her fortune is to meet again the young nobleman Robert FitzHugh, the father of her child. He is on a mission to return a priceless treasure to the abbey of Citreaux. The title refers to a thirteenth-century parable that describes love.

Both novels are essentially historical romances, and the plots strain credulity. Nevertheless, the historical accuracy of the backgrounds and the understanding of conditions of life in the sixteenth century make them both worthy of reading.

JEAN FRANKS

WORKS: *The Winds of God.* London: Century, 1985; with Brian Cleeve, *A Biographical Dictionary of Irish Writers.* Mullingar: Lilliput, 1985. (Reference); *Honey Off Thorns.* London & New York: Severn House, 1988.

BRADY, JOSEPH (1892–1979), novelist. Brady was the pseudonym of Monsignor Maurice Browne, the brother of Cardinal Browne and brother-in-law of Sean McEntee. He was parish priest at Ballymore Eustace, County Kildare. His popular novel, *The Big Sycamore* (1958), is, as Brady* and Cleeve* justly note, in the Canon Sheehan* tradition.

WORKS: *Prelude to Victory.* Dublin: James Duffy, 1950; *The Big Sycamore.* Dublin: M. H. Gill, 1958; *In Monavalla.* Dublin: M. H. Gill, 1963. (A sequel to *The Big Sycamore*); *From a Presbytery Window.* Dublin: Talbot, 1971.

BREEN, MURIEL (1899–1996), memoirist. Breen was born on December 31, 1899, in Bangor, County Down, and her first book, *Liquorice All-Sorts, A Girl Growing Up,* was published in 1993, a fact that makes her apparently the oldest Irish author of a first book. The book is a charming evocation of a middle-class Protestant family in the North in the early years of this century. Holidays in Fermanagh before 1916 are seen as an idyllic time when sectarianism hardly seemed to exist. However, the effect of the modern world, particularly of World War I, on a Northern town is well caught also. Breen died in Dublin on January 16, 1996.

MARY ROSE CALLAGHAN

WORK: *Liquorice All-Sorts, A Girl Growing Up.* Dublin: Moytura, [1993].

BRENNAN, ELIZABETH (1922–   ), novelist. Brennan was born in Clonmel, County Tipperary, and educated at Sion Hill College, at Blackrock outside Dublin. Her work is mainly in the vein of light romantic and mystery fiction, although early in her career she published some agreeable retellings in prose and verse from Irish legendary lore. Since she began publishing her romances, she has received no critical attention, but her *Girl on an Island* won the Irish Countrywomen's Association Award in 1984. She later settled in Sligo, at Kilmore, Lecarrow.

PETER COSTELLO

WORKS: *Out of the Darkness.* Dublin: Metropolitan, 1945. (Novel); *The Wind Fairies.* Dublin: Metropolitan, 1946. (Children's stories); *Am I My Brother's Keeper?* Dublin & London: Metropolitan, 1946. (Novel); *Whispering Walls.* Dublin: Metropolitan, 1948. (Novel); *The Wind Fairies Again.* Dublin & London: Metropolitan, 1948. (Children's stories); *The Mystery of the Hermit's Cave.* Dublin: Metropolitan, 1948; *Wind over the Bogs.* Dublin: Metropolitan, 1950. (Poetry); *The Children's Book of Irish Saints.* London: Harrap, 1963; *His Glamorous Cousin.* London: Hale/Toronto: Thomas Allen, 1963. (Novel); *Her Lucky Mistake.* London: Hale, 1966. (Novel); *Retreat from Love.* London: Hale, 1967. (Novel); *Love in the Glade.* London: Hale, 1968. (Novel); *Patrick's Women.* London: Hale, 1969. (Novel); *Mountain of Desire.* London: Hale, 1970. (Novel); *Innocent in Eden.* London: Hale, 1971. (Novel); *No Roses for Jo.* London: Hale, 1972. (Novel); *Love's Loom.* London: Hale, 1973. (Novel); *A Girl Called Debbie.* London: Hale, 1975. (Novel); *Sweet Love of Youth.* London: Hale, 1978. (Novel); *Girl on an Island.* London: Hale, 1984. (Novel).   REFERENCE: *Poetry Ireland,* No. 15 (October 1951): 21–22.

BRENNAN, JAMES (1944–   ), novelist. Brennan was born in Dublin on October 18, 1944. He has published one short novel, *Seaman* (1978), which is a study of six people in Dublin in the summer of 1969, most of whom are afflicted with a profound sense of the worthlessness of existence. Although the opening seems to promise little more than another aimless literary pub crawl around the city, the novel settles down to a workmanlike evocation of character. The sketch of a Liam O'Flaherty*-like novelist is particularly well done. Although the prose is much less well considered than Hemingway's, the novel is reminiscent of a more self-indulgent *The Sun Also Rises.*

WORK: *Seaman.* [Dublin: Irish Writers' Co-Operative, 1978].

BRENNAN, JAN HERBIE (1940–   ), novelist. James Herbert Brennan was born in County Down and has worked as a journalist, magazine editor, and advertising director. Jan Herbie was the pseudonym he used for his novels, Herbie Brennan the pseudonym for his short stories, and J. H. Brennan for several volumes of nonfiction, principally on the occult, and for some novels, such as *The Crypts of Terror* and *The Curse of Frankenstein,* which need not concern us here.

LITERARY WORKS: *The Greythorn Woman.* London: Collins/Fontana, 1980; *The Dark Moon.* London: Michael Joseph, 1980.

BRENNAN, M[ATTHEW] M[ICHAEL] (fl. 1920s), playwright. In 1922, Brennan wrote two popular one-act farces for the Abbey Theatre.* Both were set in the Dublin slums, a setting previously treated only by A. Patrick Wilson* and Oliver Gogarty* and treated the next year by Sean O'Casey.* *The Young Man from Rathmines* is culturally interesting as a farcical piece of racism. The daughter of the family has a blind date with the young man, and the family's hopes are pinned on a suitor from the then-fashionable suburb of Rathmines. At the curtain, the family's hopes are dashed when the young man turns out to be a socially unpresentable "darky." For a number of years, the play was very popular among amateur societies. *A Leprecaun in the Tenement* was a farcical whimsy, chiefly notable on opening night for one of the Abbey's unfortunate uses of an animal actor.

WORKS: *The Young Man from Rathmines.* Dublin: Talbot, 1923; *The Big Sweep.* Dublin & Cork: Talbot, [ca. 1933]; *Fitzgerald and the 'Quins.'* Dublin: J. Duffy, 1944; *Napoleon and the Triplets.* Dublin: Talbot, [1946?].

BRENNAN, ROBERT (1881–1964), diplomat and author. Brennan was born in Wexford and became a journalist. During the 1916 Rising, he occupied Wexford with 600 men. After the surrender, he was initially condemned to death. On his release, he became director of publicity for the revolutionary movement, and during the civil war he took the republican side. Later he became a director of the *Irish Press,* de Valera's newspaper, and he held many important diplomatic posts, including being minister to the United States from 1938 to 1947. In 1947 and 1948, he was director of broadcasting for Radio Éireann. He wrote two mystery novels, a play, and his autobiography, *Allegiance* (1950). He died in Dublin on November 12, 1964.

WORKS: *The Toledo Dagger.* London: John Hamilton, [1927]. (Novel); *Allegiance.* Dublin: Browne & Nolan, [1950]. (Autobiography); *The Man Who Walked like a Dancer.* London & New York: Rich & Cowan, 1951; *Good Night Mr. O'Donnell.* Dublin: James Duffy, 1951. (Play).

BRENNAN, RORY (fl. 1970s–1990s), poet. Brennan has worked in education, broadcasting, and arts administration and has been secretary of *Poetry Ireland*. His first collection, *The Sea on Fire* (1979), won the Patrick Kavanagh Award. His second, *The Walking Wounded* (1985), displays an interest in controlled form, particularly in a section of sonnets called "Ten Sketches from a Greek Terrace." The dramatic image and an often powerful use of simile and metaphor take up the slack even in less formal poems like "Programme Note" and "A Child Witnesses a Domestic Row." A pared-down poem like the five-stanza "Little Tom Thumbscrew" weds startling imagery to tight form in a truly Audenesque fashion.

WORKS: *The Sea on Fire*. Dublin: Dolmen, 1979; *The Walking Wounded*. [Dublin]: Dedalus, [1985].

BRETT, HEATHER (1956–   ), poet. Brett was born in Newfoundland and raised in County Antrim and trained as a fashion designer in York Street Art College, Belfast. Her first volume, *Abigail Brown*, won the Brendan Behan Memorial Prize in 1992, and in that year she also received an Arts Council Bursary. She lives in County Cavan.

WORKS: *Abigail Brown*. [Galway: Salmon, 1991]; *The Touch-Maker*. [Carrickaboy, Co. Cavan: Alternative/Toronto: Literary, 1994].

BREW, MARGARET W. (fl. 1880s), novelist. Nothing is known of Brew other than that she was a County Clare lady who wrote for *The Irish Monthly* and other periodicals and who published two novels of Irish life, *The Burtons of Dunroe* (1880) and *The Chronicles of Castle Cloyne* (1885). *The Burtons*, which is set in County Limerick in the early nineteenth century, is a tragic love story between a Protestant young man and a Catholic girl. Robert Lee Wolff finds it "steeped in Victorian conventionality" but thinks that it and also *The Chronicles of Castle Cloyne*, which depicts scenes from the Famine, are redeemed by the author's authentic details.

WORKS: *The Burtons of Dunroe*. 3 vols. London: Samuel Tinsley, 1880/New York & London: Garland, 1979; *The Chronicles of Castle Cloyne; or, Pictures of the Munster People*. 3 vols. London: Chapman & Hall, 1885/New York & London: Garland, 1979.   REFERENCE: Wolff, Robert Lee. Introduction to the Garland editions.

BRITTAINE, GEORGE (ca. 1790–1847), novelist. Brittaine was born in Dublin and became a Protestant minister in Kilcormack. He published his novels anonymously and, as Patrick Rafroidi remarks, "devoted his literary energies to painting the blackest picture of the Irish peasants and to hysterically denouncing Catholicism." He also contributed stories to the *Dublin University Magazine*. He died in Dublin in 1847.

WORKS: *A Sermon Preached in the Cathedral Church of Elphin. . . .* Dublin: R. M. Tims, 1819; *The Confessions of Honour Delany*. Dublin: R. M. Tims, 1829; *Recollections of Hyacinth O'Gara*. Dublin: R. M. Tims, 1829; *Irish Priests and English Landlords*. Dublin: R. M. Tims, 1830; *Irishmen and Irishwomen.* Dublin: R. M. Tims, 1831; *Johnny Derrivan's Travels.* Dublin: R. M. Tims, 1833. (Short story); *Mothers and Sons.* Dublin: R. M. Tims, 1833; *Nurse McVourneen's Story.* Dublin: R. M. Tims, 1833. (Short story); *The Election: A Tale of Irish Life.* Dublin: R. M. Tims, 1849. *The Orphans of Dunasker* appeared in the *Dublin University Magazine* from November 1837 to June 1838.

BRODERICK, JOHN (1927–1989), novelist. Broderick was born in Athlone on July 30, 1927, where his family owned a prosperous bakery business. He attended six different schools but never completed his formal education. He was, nevertheless, well read and a witty conversationalist. He was also a self-confessed alcoholic, and his homosexuality he put to good literary use in some later novels. His last years were spent in Bath, where he died on May 28, 1989.

From 1961 to 1977, Broderick published six novels that were highly critical of life in the Irish Midlands. As Michael Paul Gallagher remarked in 1976, "He has stayed with one dominant theme so far, the 'snobberies, hypocrisies and pretensions' of the 'little grocer's republic' that he finds in provincial Ireland.... He sees a 'great field for an Irish Balzac,' and in the last three of his books shows an increasing concern to expose the masks of the moneyed bourgeoisie." In perhaps the best of these earlier novels, the powerful *The Waking of Willie Ryan* (1965), Broderick was indeed something of an Irish Balzac, but in the others he seemed a sour, dour, and awkward satirist. Many of his characters were not so much psychologically believable, as forced into the molds of Jonsonian humors by the author's themes. His best creations were often not his main characters but his peripheral ones, such as his choral gossips, Mrs. Fallon and Mrs. Lagan in *The Fugitives* (1962) and Miss Price and Miss Fall in *An Apology for Roses* (1973). The main characters were often so manipulated by his condemnatory attitude that they became not merely humors but thoroughly repellent ones placed in a gallery of grotesques. Few figures in the earlier novels were written with love or even sympathy; hence, these books possess a coldness ultimately and even triviality. Two fine exceptions are the decrepit Anglo-Irish ladies Bessie and Violet in *The Pride of Summer* (1977). They were treated with a gentle comedy and yet given a kindness, an indomitability, and a dignity lacking in nearly all of Broderick's other early characters. Indeed, most of those other characters are so warped by the theme that they become two-dimensional monsters.

The prime importance of theme to Broderick even harmed the earlier books stylistically. Gallagher noticed the frequency of authorial intrusions, what he called "essayism," in the stories, especially in *The Waking of Willie Ryan* and *Don Juaneen* (1963). Certainly, there were constant turgid generalizations, such as "Every woman who has been scorched by the fires of sensuality will always choose death rather than the lack of love," or "For a man the passivity of passion is never enough; for a woman it is the essence of love" (both from *The Fugitives*). Gallagher also noted a prolixity of adjectives and adverbs; these, however, seemed not an unconscious stylistic habit but a deliberate choice dictated by the author's attitude. For instance, in *The Fugitives,* the evocative words of one typical paragraph are these:

rusty, ancient, rattling, soiled, crouched, resigned, grey, humid, oyster-coloured, livid, unearthly, muffled, opaque, glassy, narrow, grey-green, muffled, filmy, putty-coloured, drooping, acid-yellow, black-clothed, grey-capped, heavy, flat, big-tongued, apathetic, grey, langourous, grey, dead, buried, mortified.

The descriptive details in this long paragraph (the second of Chapter 20) are overwhelmingly and pejoratively slanted. If there is a choice of an epithet, Broderick inevitably opts for the more dismal one. One's heart would hardly be leaping with Broderick's "drooping, acid-yellow daffodils." Through thousands of consciously stylistic choices throughout the novel, he consistently stacks his deck to impel the reader toward his own bleakly condemnatory attitude. Fair enough, and any author does something of the same, but Broderick was so thoroughgoing that the final effect is that of forcing a partial truth and a myopic vision upon the reader. He was so thoroughgoing that his style ceased to be effectively subliminal and became obtrusive and unconvincing.

Broderick's views, of course, determined the developments of his plots but sometimes also deflected them from their true and inevitable course. This fact is especially obvious in the one-sentence final chapter of *The Pilgrimage,* which reduces the entire, meticulously built-up realism to a sardonic and implausible joke. It is also obvious in *The Pride of Summer,* which contains some of his very best early work side by side with some of his most unconvincing. The characters of the heroine, of the two Anglo-Irish ladies, and perhaps even of the heroine's brother-in-law are excellently drawn. If their stories had been worked out with the appropriate realism in which they had been so lovingly established, Broderick would have drawn a superb portrayal of provincial life. However, he insisted that his village be seen not implicitly, but overtly, as a paradigm of modern Ireland. This insistence makes the other portions of the novel satirically exaggerated and out of tone. Broderick even goes so far as to give some characters names closely resembling those of certain eminent contemporary Irishmen. In one scene, some gigolos are compared to such politicians as Conor Cruise O'Brien,* and the result is a lengthy and mirthless satire that nearly swamps the book.

The Pride of Summer may be taken as representative of Broderick's earlier work and its problems. The chief of those problems was a morality so grim that he sometimes appeared to take a masochistic enjoyment in depicting what he was nominally condemning. In the 1980s, after Broderick had moved to England, he seemed consciously attempting, twice with much success, to broaden his range. His *London Irish* (1979) moves away from the Irish Midlands and depicts an elderly and successful Irish businessman in London who decides to marry a young American girl. His niece and nephew, up till then his heirs, fly quickly to his and their rescue. The uncle, Andy Pollard, however, discovers that the girl has a Scandinavian homosexual boyfriend, then has a stroke, and is cared for by a respectable, middle-aged and middle-class woman, whom he marries. The nephew, for once unselfish, dies when traveling in France with the American girl. Much of the action is motivated by money, and Broderick remarked that few people "escape the enslavement of money, a corruption which is particularly malignant in a society, like the well-to-do middle class in Ireland during the years 1950 to 1980." All of the characters are plausibly drawn, but the flamboyant homosexual Hansen is quite the most vivid. All of the others, however, are treated with sympathy, and even Broderick's prose is much less slanted. This is still a somber book, but *The Trial of Father Dillingham* (1982) has none of the unrelenting early grimness and is one of Broderick's best. It depicts the fortunes of several friends who have flats in a Georgian house in Dublin's Fitzwilliam Square, and the characters are treated with real affection. Jim Dillingham has left the priesthood after having written some books critical of the church, but he is finally persuaded to accompany his old bishop to Central America, if not as a priest, at least as a social worker. An elderly former opera singer, called with gentle satire the La and probably based on the late Margaret Bourke Sheridan, concocts gourmet meals for the other tenants, dispenses sympathy and wisdom, and is a hopeless kleptomaniac. In Eddie and the dying Maurice, Broderick describes the love of two homosexuals, and the death of Maurice is so moving that Broderick probably should have ended the novel there.

A Prayer for Fair Weather (1984) is set in London and is described as a thriller. Save for the homosexual Brendan Tupper, who seems in his intelligence and dandyism to resemble the author, there is little Irish about the book. Except for the effective description of a gay bar, little in the book stays long in the memory. *The Rose Tree* (1985), however, is a memorable novel indeed. It has almost the form of an Ibsen tragedy: a gripping present plot in England, which is partly hooded in mystery and which rises to a strong climax; and a dark story in the past of Ireland, which is slowly revealed. As in tragedy, there is even a feeling that young May Carron is tainted and doomed by her past, the rape and murder of her mother and sister by the Irish Republican Army (IRA), and her own contamination. Also, as in Ibsen, the other well-drawn main characters have their true natures revealed bit by bit. The attractive George Duncan is sadistic; the gossipy homosexual antique dealer, Maxwell Burden, is kind; the father, Pat Carron, whom the villagers suspect of incest, is really trying to protect his daughter. This is a superbly structured novel, its characterization alternately tough and compassionate and its prose possessing an honest and unslanted clarity.

The Flood (1987), set in a small Irish country town, is an attempt at a broad comic novel. However, it is too broad in its characterization, as such names as Gummy Hayes, Fenny O'Barrell, and Mrs. Pig may suggest. Its dialogue is heavy with "does dose did dat dese and dose an' me fadder and me mudder an' thinkin' an' trut' for truth and fate for faith." The dialogue also is filled with many word manglings that are more tedious than funny, such as "all extensible owners a' lan' in de beootifool area dat yer innerisked in."

Broderick's later novels lack the consistency of approach and subject and tone that his earlier books had, and they are certainly a mixed bag. The two or three best of them, however, show an able writer who was growing considerably in stature.

WORKS: *The Pilgrimage.* London: Weidenfeld & Nicholson, 1961/reprinted as *The Chameleons.* London: Panther Books, 1965; *The Fugitives.* London: Weidenfeld & Nicholson, 1962; *Don Juaneen.* London: Weidenfeld & Nicholson, 1963; *The Waking of Willie Ryan.* London: Weidenfeld & Nicholson, 1965; *An Apology for Roses.* London: Calder & Boyars, 1973; *The Pride of Summer.* London: George G. Harrap, 1977; *London Irish.* London: Barrie & Jenkins, 1979; *The Trial of Father Dillingham.* London: Marion Boyars, 1982; *A Prayer for Fair Weather.* London & New York: Marion Boyars, 1984; *The Rose Tree.* London: Marion Boyars, [1985]; *The Flood.* London & New York: Marion Boyars, 1987; *The Irish Magdalen.* London & New York: Marion Boyars, [1991]. REFERENCES: Gallagher, Michael Paul. "The Novels of John Broderick." In *The Irish Novel in Our Time.* Patrick Rafroidi & Maurice Harmon, eds. [Lille, France]: Publications de l'Université de Lille, [1976]; Lubbers, Klaus. "John Broderick." In *Contemporary Irish Novelists.* Rüdiger Imhof, ed. Tübingen: Narr, 1990; Murphy, Michael. "At Bay in Bath." *Irish Times* (September 3, 1985): 10; Murray, Patrick. "Athlone's John Broderick." *Éire-Ireland* 27 (Winter 1992): 20–39.

BROGAN, PATRICIA BURKE

WORK: *Above the Waves' Calligraphy.* [Galway]: Salmon, [1994]. (Poetry).

BROOKE, HENRY (1703?–1783), novelist and dramatist. According to Burtchaell and Sadleir's *Alumni Dublinensis,* Brooke was born in County Cavan, educated by Dr. Jones of Dublin, and admitted to Trinity College as a pensioner on February 6, 1720/21, aged seventeen. He is said by Henry Wilson in *Brookiana* to have been a pupil of Dr. Sheridan* before entering Trinity, but there is no hard evidence for the supposition. In 1739, his *Gustavus Vasa* was proscribed from production at Drury Lane, probably by Walpole. However, it was very successful when issued by subscription and when produced in Dublin as *The Patriot.* His *Jack the Giant-Queller* was produced in Dublin and also proscribed by the government. His tragedy, *The Earl of Essex,* was produced in 1749 in Dublin and then in London. It contained the passage, "Who rule o'er freemen should themselves be free," which Dr. Johnson lampooned with the line, "Who drives fat oxen should himself be fat." Garrick, however, is said to have so admired the plays that he offered Brooke a shilling a pound for whatever he would write, an offer haughtily refused. Brooke also wrote a number of political and economic treatises on Ireland, and of his 1745 pamphlets, *The Farmer's Letters to the Protestants of Ireland,* the *Field Day Anthology* remarks, "The rhetorical flourishes in these pamphlets are important in the history of eighteenth-century writing, coming halfway between Swift's use of such full-blown rhetoric for satiric purposes in the 1720s and the florid verbal excesses of the later eighteenth-century Irish parliament and bar." Brooke is most remembered, however, for his long novel *The Fool of Quality* in five volumes, which began to appear in 1766. He returned to Cavan, where he was tended by his daughter Charlotte, the sole survivor of a family of twenty-one. He died in Dublin on October 10, 1783. Charlotte Brooke is most known for her significant collection *Reliques of Irish Poetry* (1789).

Brooke's most notable work, *The Fool of Quality,* proved most attractive to the religiously minded of the day and even now has some oases of interest. However, as John Butt and Geoffrey Carnall remark in *The Mid-Eighteenth Century* (Oxford: Clarendon, 1979):

The Fool of Quality has never quite established itself as even a minor classic. Its unwieldy shape seems to have no discernible artistic function, and the self-indulgent turbulence has not worn well. It forms a strong contrast in these respects with a work, also first published in 1766, which one is tempted to describe as the most assured minor classic ever written, *The Vicar of Wakefield.*

PRINCIPAL WORKS: *Gustavus Vasa, the Deliverer of his Country.* London: R. Dodsley, 1739. (Verse play); *The Farmer's Six Letters to the Protestants of Ireland.* Dublin: G. Faulkner, 1745; *The Case of the Roman-Catholics of Ireland.* Dublin: Pat. Lord, 1760; *The Earl of Essex.* London: T. Davis, J. Coote, 1761. (Verse play); *The Fool of Quality; or, The History of Henry Earl of Moreland.* 5 vols. London: W. Johnston, 1766–1770/New York & London: Garland, 1979, Ronald Paulson, ed. (Novel); *Juliet Grenville; or, The History of the Human Heart.* 3 vols. London: G. Robinson, 1774. (Novel); *A Collection of the Pieces Formerly Published by Henry Brooke, Esq. To Which Are Added Several Plays and Poems, Now First Printed.* London: Printed for the Author, 1778; *The Poetical Works of Henry Brooke.* Edited by Miss Brooke. 3d ed. 4 vols. Dublin: Printed for the Editor, 1792. REFERENCES: Scurr, Helen. Margaret. *Henry Brooke.* Minneapolis: University of Minnesota Press, 1927; Wilson, Henry. *Brookiana.* 2 vols. London: Richard Phillips, 1804.

BROPHY, CATHERINE (twentieth century), novelist. Born in Dublin, Brophy received a B.A. from University College and has worked in such diverse locales as Mexico, Turkey, Yugoslavia, Austria, and the United States.

Her first book, *The Liberation of Margaret McCabe* (1985), is an account of the developing identity of a twentieth-century Irish girl who must reconcile what she has been taught with the reality of the world she lives in. Reconciliation is painful, for she finds, after leaving her family home at the age of thirty-four to live with a lover, that she has exchanged one uncongenial situation for another. Finally, she moves into her own flat, where her loneliness is assuaged by the friendships she has made with kindred spirits. No longer does she harbor the fantasy that life will provide the ideal lover and husband or that the role of woman is to fulfill that fantasy. She realizes, instead, that she values honesty and courage in human relationships above simple performance of expected roles.

The novel, despite its serious theme, is written in a comic vein and details disheartening episodes in a madcap and even hilarious tone. The central character is the narrator, who maintains comedy by occasional resort to hyperbole. As a result, she becomes unbelievably timorous, particularly in her relationship with her lover, and the characterization suffers. One receives the impression that, if she had maintained the independence of spirit that had first attracted him, the relationship might have fared better.

While the first novel might be considered another Irish-girl-coming-of-age tale, the second novel, *Dark Paradise* (1991), indicates the author's power of imagination. It is a science fiction tale, astounding in the final resolution. The story involves a highly developed but eerie civilization in which privileged inhabitants occupy a domed crystal structure protecting them from the universal environment. The life of the intellect is the supreme focus, but with the aid of technological equipment existence is dictated by uncompromising rule. Life forms have evolved into oversize heads, supported by headrests. Lower extremities have been discarded, and beings navigate on "floaters" to protect the crystal corridors. Reproduction is handled through a "Life Pool," as physical union is replaced by "mind fusion." Inevitably, young creatures rebel, and the resolution of this rebellion forms the climax of the novel. The final pages raise a question as to whether the author intended the theme to be pro-life.

JEAN FRANKS

WORKS: *The Liberation of Margaret McCabe.* Dublin: Wolfhound, 1985/rpt. 1992; *Dark Paradise.* Dublin: Wolfound, 1991.

BROUGHAM, JOHN (1814–1880), playwright, story writer, and actor. Brougham, who was thought to be the original of Lever's* Harry Lorrequer, was born in Dublin on May 9, 1814, studied at Trinity College, and then abandoned the study of medicine for acting. He was excellent in comic character parts, particularly Irish ones such as Sir Lucius O'Trigger, Dennis Brulgruddery, and Boucicault's* O'Grady in *Arrah-na-Pogue.* He was also effective as Dazzle in Boucicault's *London Assurance* and was even rumored to have had a hand in that play's authorship. Allardyce Nicoll credits him with writing more than 30 plays, but the number has also been estimated at over 100. Among them were adaptations of Dickens, Bulwer-Lytton, and Charlotte Brontë's *Jane Eyre.* A few, such as *The Irish Emigrant* (1854), had an Irish background, but none has survived its day. Brougham also turned his hand to Irish tales, fairy stories, and verse, some of which retain a genial, stage-Irish charm. He was occasionally in theatrical management in both London and America, albeit none too successfully. He continued acting until nearly the end of his life, which occurred in New York on June 7, 1880. As H. C. Bunner remarked of him:

> The actor's dead, and memory alone
> Recalls the genial magic of his tone. . . .

PRINCIPAL WORKS: *A Basket of Chips.* New York: Bunce, 1855. (Verse and tales); *A Recollection of O'Flannigan and the Fairies.* London, [1856]. Lacy's Acting Edition of Plays, Vol. 26. (One-act comedy); *The Bunsby Papers, Irish Echoes. . . .* New York: Derby & Jackson, 1857; *The Irish Yankee; or, The Birth-day of Freedom.* New York: Samuel French, [1865?]; *The Irish Emigrant.* London, [1869]. Lacy's Acting Edition of Plays, Vol. 82/as *Temptation; or, The Irish Emigrant.* London, [1885]. Dick's Standard Plays, No. 621; *Life, Stories and Poems of John Brougham.* William Winter, ed. Boston: J. R. Osgood, 1881.

BROWN, CHRISTY (1932–1981), novelist and poet. Brown was an extraordinary writer and personality. His finest book, the eloquent autobiographical novel *Down All the Days* (1970), was not merely a literary triumph but also a human triumph, testifying to the indomitable courage of the author, his family, and his friends.

Brown was born in Dublin on June 5, 1932. His father was a bricklayer, and his mother bore twenty-one children besides Christy, thirteen of whom lived into adulthood. He himself was born almost completely paralyzed by cerebral palsy. He could not speak but only grunt, and the only part of his body over which he had any control was his left foot. Many doctors regarded him as imbecilic, but his mother staunchly refused to believe them. Her faith was rewarded when he was five. He was watching his sister write on a slate when his foot almost involuntarily reached out, his toes grasped the chalk, and he attempted to write on the slate. With his mother's patient teaching, he slowly and painfully mastered the alphabet and finally put letters together to make words. In his teens he came to the attention of the physician and playwright Robert Collis,* who worked with him and slowly improved his coordination and speech. Collis also encouraged and coached him to write his first book. That book, *My Left Foot* (1954), is a short, factual account of his life, and it was laboriously typed with the little toe of his left foot.

As a writer, Brown is unusually uneven, and the strongest symptom of his varying quality is probably most apparent in his prose style. *My Left Foot* is told in an unadorned, terse prose that does not interfere with the interest and power of the narrative. *Down All the Days,* which is an emotionally charged fictional re-creation of the same events, is told in an elaborate, sometimes florid prose that owes much to the American writer Thomas Wolfe. Occasional passages are simply too lush to be effective, but at its overall best the prose lifts the deeply felt events to an emotional eloquence of high intensity. Brown's second novel, *A Shadow on Summer* (1974), is a fictional re-creation of a trip to America; the prose is elaborated to a turgidity that is nearly unreadable. At the same time, the events and preoccupations of the novel—the author-hero's casual personal relations, his casual loves, and his feelings about writing—have little of the intensity that was so remarkable in *Down All the Days.* Brown's third novel, *Wild Grow the Lilies* (1976), is an attempt to get outside the frame of autobiographical fiction and depicts the stage Ireland of Brendan Behan,* full of drinking and sex and utter falseness. While the prose is less self-indulgently florid, it is still overwritten and needed a drastic cutting. The book has been charitably described as refreshingly bawdy and hilariously vulgar, but it is tedious, interminable, contrived, and untrue. A posthumous novel, *A Promising Career* (1982), depicts the marital problems of a pop singer in London, her pop composer husband, and their agent. It has none of the falsity of *Wild Grow the Lilies,* but the prose is constantly clogged with long paragraphs full of lines like "the turgid water, pungent with brine and wastrel city odours, shaking the lachrymose trees in dry spasms of commotion."

Brown also published some volumes of poems. They were more personal statements than works of art, but rich phrases abound, and one or two pieces are unpolished gems.

In 1972, he married Mary Carr from Killarney. They lived in a cottage in County Kerry and also in Somerset, where he died on September 7, 1981, of shock and asphyxiation from choking on food. The *London Times* wrote of him that "the first impression he made on people was of a particularly cheerful and gregarious man. Few can have met him without finding the experience life-enhancing." The impressive film made out of *My Left Foot* by Jim Sheridan* and Shane Connaughton* won Academy Awards.

WORKS: *My Left Foot.* London: Secker & Warburg, 1954/New York: Simon & Schuster, 1955/ republished as *The Story of Christy Brown,* New York: Pocket Books, 1971, and as *The Childhood Story of Christy Brown,* London: Pan, 1972; *Come Softly to My Wake.* London: Secker & Warburg, 1971/published as *The Poems of Christy Brown,* New York: Stein & Day, 1973; *Background Music: Poems.* London: Secker & Warburg/New York: Stein & Day, 1973; *A Shadow on Summer.* London: Book Club Associates, 1974; *Wild Grow the Lilies.* London: Secker & Warburg/New York: Stein & Day, 1976; *Of Snails and Skylarks.* London: Secker & Warburg, 1978. (Poems); *Collected Poems.* London: Secker & Warburg, 1982; *A Promising Career.* London: Secker & Warburg, 1982.

BROWNE, FRANCES (1816–1879), poet, novelist, and writer of children's stories. Browne, "the blind poetess of Donegal," was born in Stranolar, County Donegal, on January 16, 1816. Although blind from infancy, as a result of an attack of smallpox, she grew up with a good grasp of English literature and earned her living by writing. Her first poem was published in *The Irish Penny Journal,* and later she published in *Hood's Magazine, The Keepsake,* and *The Athenaeum;* the editor of the last named did much to publicize her work. She left Ireland in 1847 and made her home in either Edinburgh or London. She was granted a small pension from the civil list by Sir Robert Peel and died in London on August 25, 1879.

During her life she published an autobiography, novels, stories for children, and many poems. Her poetry was well thought of in its day and is still not to be dismissed, but she is best remembered for *Granny's Wonderful Chair and Its Tales of Fairy Times,* a collection of fairy stories for children. These delight-ful fantasies, written in lucid prose, illustrate Christian values without ever de-scending to smugness. The book was deservedly a worldwide best-seller but had an unusual publishing history. First published in 1857, it went through two editions, which quickly sold out. Then, in 1877, Frances Hodgsen Burnett wrote her version of the stories and called them *Stories from the Lost Fairy Book as Retold by the Child Who Read Them.* It was soon discovered that the lost book was Frances Browne's *Granny's Wonderful Chair,* and it was republished in 1880. This edition sold out quickly, as did many others until in 1891 an edition with colored pictures by Mrs. Seymour Lucas had an enormous success. In recent years, the book has again fallen into obscurity, but its merits are so perennially appealing that it well may be discovered again.

MARY ROSE CALLAGHAN

WORKS: *The Star of Atteghei; the Vision of Schwartz; and Other Poems.* London: Moxon, 1844; *Lyric and Miscellaneous Poems.* Edinburgh: Sutherland & Knox, 1848; *The Ericksons. The Clever Boy; or, Consider Another (Two Stories for my Young Friends).* Edinburgh: Paton & Ritchie, 1852; *Pictures and Songs of Home.* London: Nelson, [1856]; *Granny's Wonderful Chair, and Its Tales of Fairy Times.* London: Griffith & Farren, 1857. (Many later editions); *Our Uncle the Traveller's Stories.* London: W. Kent, 1859; *My Share of the World. An Autobiography.* London: Hurst & Blackett, 1861; *The Castleford Case.* 3 vols. London: Hurst & Blackett, 1862; *The Orphans of Elfholm.* London: Groombridge, [1862]; *The Young Foresters.* London: Groombridge, [1864]; *The Hidden Sin.* 3 vols. London: n.p., 1866. (Published anonymously); *The Exile's Trust, a Tale of the French Revolution, and Other Stories.* London: Leisure Hour, [1869]; *The Nearest Neighbours, and Other Stories.* London: R.T.S., [1875]; *The Dangerous Guest. A Story of 1745.* London: R.T.S., [1886]; *The Foundling of the Fens.* London: R.T.S., [1886]; *The First of the African Diamonds.* London: R.T.S., [1887].

BUCHANAN, GEORGE [HENRY PERROTT] (1904–1989), journalist and man of letters. Buchanan was born in Kilwaughter, Larne, County Antrim, in 1904. He attended Larne Grammar School with his friend Lyle Donaghy,* the poet, and later attended Campbell College in Belfast. In 1925, he went to London, worked on various newspapers, and contributed many poems to journals and many reviews to the *Times Literary Supplement.* During World War II, he served in the Royal Air Force (RAF). He has published novels, journals, volumes of autobiography, collections of poems, and some plays. The background of Europe in economic depression and at war is strongly present in his work, which has sometimes been described as journalistic fiction. Thus far, little recognition or discussion has been given to his considerable and individual body of work. The best introduction is the excellent George Buchanan number of *The Honest Ulsterman* (March–June 1978).

WORKS: *Passage through the Present.* London: Constable, 1932. (Journal); *A London Story.* London: Constable, 1935. (Novel); *Dance Night.* London: [French's Acting Edition, 1935]. (Play); *Words for To-night.* London: Constable, 1936. (Journal); *Rose Forbes,* Part 1. London: Constable, 1937. (Novel); *Entanglement.* London: Constable, 1938. (Novel); *Serious Pleasures, the Intelligent Person's Guide to London.* London: London Transport, 1938/revised, Westminster: London Transport, 1939; *The Soldier and the Girl.* London, Toronto: Heinemann, 1940. (Novel); *Rose Forbes,* Parts 1 & 2. London: Faber, 1950; *A Place to Live.* London: Faber, 1952. (Novel); *Bodily Responses.* London: Gaberbocchus, 1958. (Poetry); *Conversation with Strangers.* London: Gaberbocchus, 1959. (Poetry); *Green Seacoast.* London: Gaberbocchus, 1959. (Autobiography); *Morning Papers.* London: Gaberbocchus, 1965. (Autobiography); *Annotations.* Manchester: Carcanet, 1970. (Poems); *Naked Reason.* New York: Holt, Rinehart & Winston, 1971. (Novel); *Minute-book of a City—Oxford.* Manchester: Carcanet, 1972. (Poetry); *Inside Traffic.* Manchester: Carcanet, 1976. (Poetry); *The Politics of Culture.* London: Menard, 1977. (Essays); *Possible Being.* Manchester: Carcanet, 1980; *Adjacent Columns.* London: Menard, Carcanet, 1982. REFERENCES: Foster, John Wilson. *Forces and Themes in Ulster Fiction.* Dublin: Gill & Macmillan, 1974, pp. 223–228; Ormsby, Frank, ed. *The Honest Ulsterman* 59 (March–June 1978): 17–87. (The George Buchanan Supplement includes an article on Buchanan's poetry by James Simmons, an article on his fiction by Val Warner, an article on his journals, autobiography, and essays by Arthur McMahon, and an interview by Ormsby.)

BULFIN, WILLIAM (ca. 1862–1910), journalist and author. Born around 1862 at Derrinlough, near Birr, County Offaly, Bulfin was educated at the Classical

Academy and at the Presentation School in Birr and later attended the Royal Charter School in Banagher and the Galway Grammar School. In 1884, with his brother, he emigrated to the Argentine, then opening up as a settlement to which many Irish people were attracted. There he worked on an *estancia* owned by an Irish rancher. He began his career by writing for the *Southern Cross,* a periodical that vigorously served the interests of the Irish Catholic community. He eventually moved to Buenos Aires to become the assistant editor and soon after its editor and owner. While still in South America, he published *Tales from the Pampas* (1900). In 1902, he returned to Ireland and began his travels around the country by bicycle. His sketches of his adventures and encounters appeared in his own paper and later in *The United Irishman, Sinn Féin,* and the *New York Daily News.* In one memorable incident, he describes visiting the tower in Sandycove during its occupancy by James Joyce.* The articles were collected as *Rambles in Eirinn* (1907), a book that still retains a readership for its lively style and historical interest. He returned to South America in 1904. For his work on behalf of the Irish community in the Argentine, he was awarded a papal knighthood. He returned again to Ireland in 1909 and traveled to the United States with the O'Rahilly to gain Irish-American support for a Sinn Féin newspaper. He returned home on January 1, 1910, and died at Derrinlough on January 30. He left a son and a daughter, later Mrs. Sean MacBride.

PETER COSTELLO

WORKS: *Tales from the Pampas.* London: T. Fisher Unwin, 1900; *Rambles in Eirinn.* Dublin: M. H. Gill, 1907.   REFERENCE: Kiely, Benedict. "The Man from the Pampas," *Capuchin Annual* (1948): 428–436.

BULLOCK, SHAN F. (1865–1935), novelist. Bullock wrote over a score of books, more than a dozen of these being novels and the rest volumes of stories, books of verse, and biographies. His most notable work is *Thomas Andrews, Shipbuilder* (1912), the story of the man who built the *Titanic* and lost his life when it sank. The author was born on May 17, 1865, in Crom, south Fermanagh, where his father was a steward on the Earl of Erne's estate. Soon after leaving Farra School, County Westmeath, Bullock went to London where he spent his working life as a civil servant. He died on February 27, 1935, at Cheam, Surrey.

The two vastly different experiences of Bullock's life, Fermanagh and London, were the biographical impetus behind most of his fiction. Out of voluntary incarceration as a minor official came *Robert Thorne: The Story of a London Clerk* (1907), an interesting sortie into Edwardian realism replete with documentary details of the lives, at desk and hearth, of "pendrivers," emasculated drudges beset by poverty, duty, and routine. The novel also attempts to write "a page from the awful Day-book of London town," a city paying "the penalty of civilisation"—adulterated food, jerry-built housing, and shoddy clothes. Thorne's deliverance at novel's end is by emigration to New Zealand, but the real answer lies in the "manliness" of life he might have achieved in his native Devon. *By Thrasna River: The Story of a Townland* (1895), a loose-limbed narrative that is one of Bullock's best, shows that whereas manliness is more likely in the countryside, its enemies—in this case poverty, land-hunger, and an adverse climate—can be as fatally powerful as in London. The unassured urban naturalism of *Robert Thorne* succeeded the more mature rural naturalism of this novel, wherein romanticism (represented by the absurd Englishman Harry Thomson driven off by the narrow-minded tenants of an estate for courting one of their daughters) is at once given a larger say and a more definitive routing. Sectarianism is knowingly handled in the novel.

In *After Sixty Years* (1931), an autobiography confined to the Fermanagh years and most of the events that are in *By Thrasna River,* Bullock admitted that he found it easier to portray Catholics than Protestants because, though himself Protestant, he felt drawn towards them. He described himself as a "poor child of a world between two gate-houses" (England and Ireland, Protestant and Catholic). His first and un-Protestant name, Shan, was self-bestowed and is a further indication that of all Ulster writers Bullock perhaps comes closest to an intimate knowledge of both sects. Yet, Catholic characters also permitted him to exercise that democratic and paradoxically Protestant sympathy for the underdog that runs through his fiction. *After Sixty Years* is low-keyed but occasionally moving. It is of great documentary value in depicting, through his father's recollections, the semi-feudal Ireland of pre-Famine and pre-Land Act days, and, through Bullock's own recollections, the end of the Big House. Benedict Kiely has remarked in *The Irish Times* (December 29, 1972) that Bullock was the last Irish writer to see the Big House functioning efficiently, though the view was that of an outsider, albeit favored.

The odd combination of rural naturalism and mock-romantic melodrama can be found in such attempts at tragedy as *The Squireen* (1903), *Dan the Dollar* (1905), and *The Loughsiders* (1924) in which Bullock tries to capture the hubris of his unprepossessing heroes. These novels exhibit the virtues and failings of all Bullock's fiction. They are enjoyably readable, fair-minded (no petty virtue in Ulster fiction), and valuable as social history, but the author staidly lacks sympathy with his own, often unpleasant, characters, particularly the Protestant characters. This lack drains his fictional world of warmth and life, despite the quirky humor. Moreover, there is no stable point of view, no intelligible signals to the reader that Bullock is or is not employing irony. It is not merely that Bullock's attitude to his chief characters is usually enigmatic, but that motives (for example, those of John Farmer, the narrator of *By Thrasna River,* or of Richard Jebb in *The Loughsiders*) are often damagingly garbled or obscure. This intractability of Bullock's fiction could be taken as an ironic comment on the Ulster border country (as it was later to become) that bred him.

JOHN WILSON FOSTER

WORKS: *The Awkward Squads and Other Stories.* London: Cassell, 1893; *By Thrasna River.* London: Ward, Lock & Bowden, 1895; *Ring o' Rushes.* London: Ward, Lock & Bowden, 1896; *The Charmer.* London: Bowden, 1897; *The Barrys.* London: Harper, 1899; *Irish Pastorals.* London: Grant Richards/New York: McClure, Phillips, 1901; *The Squireen.* London: Methuen, 1903; *The*

Red Leaguers. London: Methuen, 1903; *Dan the Dollar.* Dublin: Maunsel, 1905; *The Cubs.* London: Laurie, 1906; *Robert Thorne.* London: Laurie, 1907; *A Laughing Matter.* London: Laurie, 1908; *Master John.* London: Laurie, 1909; *Hetty.* London: Laurie, 1911; *Thomas Andrews, Shipbuilder.* Dublin & London: Maunsel, 1912/published in the United States as *A "Titanic" Hero.* Baltimore: Norman, Remington, 1913; with Emily Lawless, *The Race of Castlebar.* London: John Murray, 1913; *Mr. Ruby Jumps the Traces.* London: Chapman & Hall, 1917; *Mors et Vita.* London: Laurie, 1923. (Poems); *The Loughsiders.* London: Harrap, 1924; *Gleanings.* Sutton, Surrey: William Pile, 1926. (Poems); *After Sixty Years.* London: Sampson Low, 1931. REFERENCES: Foster, John Wilson. *Forces and Themes in Ulster Fiction.* Dublin: Gill & Macmillan/Totowa, N.J.: Rowman & Littlefield, 1974; Foster, John Wilson. *Fictions of the Irish Literary Revival.* Dublin: Gill & Macmillan/Syracuse: Syracuse University Press, 1987; Kiely, Benedict. *Modern Irish Fiction—A Critique.* Dublin: Golden Eagle Books, 1950.

BUNBURY, SELINA (1802–1882), novelist and travel writer. Bunbury was born in County Louth, one of fifteen children of a Methodist minister. After her father's bankruptcy in 1819, her mother and the children moved to Dublin, where Bunbury taught in a primary school and began secretly writing. Her early Irish travel books offer useful views of pre-Famine Ireland. About 1830, the family moved to Liverpool, and Bunbury continued writing and also kept house for her twin brother. After his marriage in 1845, she traveled and wrote moral tales, some set in Ireland and with an anti-Catholic view and some going into several editions. They do not require perusal today.

PRINCIPAL LITERARY WORKS: *Cabin Conversations and Castle Scenes.* London: J. Nisbet, 1827; *My Foster Brother.* Dublin: J. R. Tims, 1827; *The Abbey of Innismoyle.* Dublin: W. Curry, Jun., 1828; *Retrospections.* Dublin: W. Curry, 1829; *Annot and Her Pupil.* 2d ed. Edinburgh: W. Oliphant, 1830; *Eleanor.* Dublin: Curry, 1830; *Tales of My Country.* Dublin: W. Curry, 1833; *Coombe Abbey.* Dublin: W. Curry, 1843; *Rides in the Pyranees.* 2 vols. London: T. C. Newby, 1844; *The Star of the Court.* London: Grant & Griffith, 1844; *The Triumph of Truth.* London: R.T.S., 1847; *Evelyn.* 2 vols. London: R. Bentley, 1849; *The Blind Clergyman, and His Little Guide.* London: Wertheim & MacIntosh, 1850; *Our Own Story.* 3 vols. London: Hurst & Blackett, 1856; *Sir Guy d'Esterre.* 2 vols. London: Routledge, 1858; *Madame Constance.* 2 vols. London: T. C. Newby, 1861; *Tales.* London: Rivington, 1862; *Florence Manvers.* London: Newby, 1865.

BURKE, EDMUND (1729–1797), political philosopher and aesthetician. Burke, the father of modern conservatism, as some have called him, was born in Dublin on January 12, 1729. His father, an Anglican, was a solicitor of good middle-class standing; his mother was a Catholic, a fact that would later haunt him as he began his political career in the 1760s, only a few years after his marriage (in 1756) to Jane Mary Nugent, also a Catholic. In their public and private attempts to discredit him, Burke's enemies rarely failed to mention his "low" origins and his questionable family connections: his Dublin birthplace and suspected Roman leanings; his inability to claim a distinguished lineage; the large crowd of Irish relatives, some of them quite disreputable, who always hung about him and whom he protected lovingly, passionately, sometimes perhaps unwisely. Occasionally, Burke's friends were chagrined for him, but never Burke himself—at least not seriously. His persistent refusal to find any reason for embarrassment in his background and station provides a clue to some of the abiding preoccupations of his life and career. Always an Anglican, he was nonetheless a staunch defender of Catholic rights in England and Ireland alike. His posture in this matter on behalf of fundamental human rights is consistent with the stance he assumed during two of the momentous episodes of his political career: his lonely and unsuccessful campaign for conciliation with the American colonies in the early 1770s, and the many years (from 1786 to 1795) of equally unsuccessful impeachment proceedings against Warren Hastings for his major part in the corruption of the colonial government in India. Burke's lifelong devotion to a troublesome family suggests that for him, as an Anglican moralist and practical man, the family, though capable of imperfections, was an important personal and social tradition, a force for stability and humanity in the day-to-day business of living. The essence of every civilized tradition, as the inevitably flawed but necessary product of generations of trial and error, needs desperately to be preserved by those who have the capacity for thought and learning and judgment, preserved against the erosions of indifference or ignorance and against the mad zeal of democratic reformers whose impractical, abstract philosophical notions of a perfect human society are the results of but a moment's hysterical folly and can only bring chaos—so Burke said with matchless brilliance and eloquence in his *Reflections on the Revolution in France* (1790).

Paradoxically, one of Burke's last significant pieces of work, the *Letter to a Noble Lord* (1795), castigated the duke of Bedford, one of the truly conspicuous symbols of the aristocratic tradition Burke had so vigorously defended and sought to join. Bedford, he charged, was a weighty baggage who enjoyed his privileges by birth only, and not by merit; while he, Edmund Burke, a man of humble beginnings, had risen to a certain eminence and earned the reward of a government pension by dint of his effort. It is almost the statement of a democratic reformer, dangerously close (as some, including Samuel Taylor Coleridge, have thought) to the ideals of the leveling Jacobins whom Burke despised and wrathfully reviled. And yet what is really meant seems abundantly clear. The rabble is to be distrusted and feared, and even a duke of Bedford must be protected from its menace. But socially unpretentious men of intelligence, learning, industry, honor, and some wisdom possess a kind of natural nobility and surely ought not be denied the benefits of privilege or, more important, the opportunity to participate in carrying out the responsibilities for wise government that tradition, as the cohering force in social and political order, requires.

Burke had no systematic philosophy of government, and he cannot be reduced to a single statement. Yet, it is clear that his every action in public life announced his commitment to those virtues which he so justly ascribed to himself, with becoming modesty and with crystalline clarity of understanding and expression, in the *Letter to a Noble Lord*. Above all things, Burke admired practical wisdom, and it was to the past he looked as its source, though not worshipfully or in mere nostalgia.

Despite the important consistencies in Burke's life and public career, Isaac Kramnick has characterized him astutely in *The Rage of Edmund Burke* (1977) as an ambivalent man, a man of paradoxes. Born and educated (at Trinity College, Dublin) an Irishman, he became an authentic genius of English political and parliamentary history. As a young man, however, he was unable to finish his studies at the Middle Temple in London, where his father had sent him in 1750—the law did not "open and liberalize the mind," he said. Always suspicious of theory, in his youth he wrote an ingenious satire called *A Vindication of Natural Society* (1756) in which he impersonated Bolingbroke, making a mockery of that noble lord's doctrine of natural theology by translating it into the practical realm of politics. In the very next year, however, he published a profoundly important treatise on aesthetics, his *Philosophical Enquiry into the Origin of Our Ideas of the Sublime and the Beautiful* (1757), which is a brilliant study of the emotional responses called forth by a variety of images and effects. Burke was a deeply skeptical man, but he nevertheless reserved for tradition— tradition as a practical consequence of man's successful living—the kind of reverence by which idealism usually bows before some noble vision of the good. Many have always considered his conservative reaction to the French Revolution as a turnabout from his earlier "liberal" stand on the taxation of the American colonies. He was a Whig turned Tory defender, the same man who, some twenty years earlier, had published his *Thoughts on the Cause of the Present Discontents* (1770), an attack on Toryism and on some of the evils of monarchy embodied in George III and his court circle. And there is, of course, the *Letter to a Noble Lord*, wherein Burke the apologist for inherited privilege almost becomes the prophet of the self-made man, the proponent of merit as the chief measure, whatever one's class, of worth and fitness for position. Though it may seem a contradiction to say it, Burke was consistent in his principles but (sometimes) inconsistent in his behavior and public utterances. In other words, he was human. Until very recently, Burke studies have revered him as the almost legendary apostle of straightforward political conservatism—or occasionally of political liberalism. Now scholars are coming round to a new understanding of the kind of depth and complexity of feeling and thought hinted at in the title of Kramnick's book and made rather plain by Burke himself in the *Letter* to Bedford.

Burke's public career was spectacular, but only in the sense that the amazing brilliance of his speeches and essays on the great subjects of his day attracted everyone's attention and have continued to do so. Though he must be called a grand statesman, he never reached the pinnacle of power. He first came to the attention of those in political circles as the editor and chief writer for Robert Dodsley's *Annual Register* of current politics, history, and literature. After beginning this work in 1758, he became known as a young man possessed with immense knowledge of public affairs, and in 1759, he was made private assistant to William Hamilton, secretary to the lord lieutenant of Ireland. Following a short official stay in his native island, Burke returned to London in 1764 and, along with his old friends Samuel Johnson and Joshua Reynolds, was an original member of "The Club." He joined the short administration of the marquis of

Rockingham as private secretary to the prime minister in 1765 and was elected (with Rockingham's help) a member of Parliament from the borough of Windover. He enjoyed instant success as an orator in the House of Commons. In 1767, he undertook a venture as grand as any of his speeches when he borrowed a huge sum of money to purchase Gregories, his magnificent country estate at Beaconsfield, which he loved but which remained a crushing financial burden for the rest of his years.

Burke's *Speech on American Taxation* (1774) and his address on *Conciliation with America* (1775) were models of rhetorical eloquence and practical wisdom. Conciliation may not be pleasant, Burke argued, but it is the only expedient. Everyone marveled, even the staunchest exponents of English prerogatives, but Burke's advice was, of course, not followed, though he was proven right by the outcome of the Revolutionary War. His unpopular stand on the American question and his advocacy of religious toleration and of fair trade practices with Ireland cost him the Bristol seat he had won in 1774. In 1780, he was elected member of Parliament from Malton, the seat he held until his retirement to Beaconsfield in 1794.

Burke's next great undertakings included a magnificent *Speech on the Economical Reformation,* which he delivered upon taking his new seat (his economics was hardly distinguishable from Adam Smith's); a campaign for parliamentary reforms begun in his *Speech on the Representation of the Commons in Parliament* (1782); and pursuit of policies of fair treatment for Ireland (*Letter to a Peer of Ireland,* 1782). Burke joined the second Rockingham administration in 1782 and was briefly paymaster-general under the Fox-North coalition in 1783. He began to fade when the younger Pitt and his fresh generation came to power in 1784. He was all but thrown out of the Whig party following a dramatic break with Fox in 1791. He wrote about this event with feeling and characteristic eloquence in *An Appeal from the New to the Old Whigs,* which expressed his reverence for the ideals of the Old Whigs whose origins lay in the Glorious Revolution of 1688.

The last decade of Burke's career was largely consumed by the Hastings affair and the French Revolution, but he continued his abiding interest in the problems of Ireland. In fact, besides the *Reflections* and the *Letter to a Noble Lord,* his most important works during those last years concerned the plight of the Irish. Burke was much distressed by the political and social injustices visited upon the Roman Catholic majority, and he yearned for reforms, as he explained in his powerful *Letter to Sir Hercules Langrishe on the Subject of the Roman Catholics of Ireland* (1792). He dispatched his son Richard there, since he could not go himself, and restated his concerns publicly in *A Letter to Richard Burke* (1793). The subject preoccupied him until his death; the last thing he wrote, before he died at Beaconsfield on July 9, 1797, was a *Letter on the Affairs of Ireland.*

Burke's attitudes towards Ireland were consistent with his political attitudes generally and were a natural outgrowth from them. He was, always, committed to "the principle of *common naturalization* which runs through this whole empire," as he said in a *Letter to Sir Charles Bingham, Bart., on the Irish Absentee Tax* (1773). He exercised this principle in his public statements on Ireland, America, and India, and it was the foundation of his arguments for fair taxation policies, free trade, and religious tolerance. He despised gratuitous injustice and harmful prejudice, and hearkened to what he called the "tolerating maxims of the Gospel." In his *Speech at Bristol Previous to the Election* (1780), he told his listeners that he wished to cultivate "the locality of patriotism," to make the empire "one family, one body, one heart and soul," to follow "the grand social principle, that unites all men, in all descriptions, under the shadow of equal and impartial justice." To achieve this end, it was not necessary to destroy the traditions upon which rested a system that fostered injustice or oppression. However, it *was* necessary for men and their governments to act humanely, wisely, with a sense of their past as guide to their present and their future. Burke repeated this idea over and over again, in many forms and from many forums—indeed, it is the essence of his genius and his greatness. The eloquence with which he always said it, the stunning beauty of his language so rich in images, metaphors, and analogies, gave it form as a strong and enduring idea. Burke may never have reached the highest seat of power, and he may have enjoyed only limited success at the business of parliamentary maneuvering. But this Irishman of modest beginnings, through the sheer force of his mind and his language and his principles, had an enormous impact on political thought in his own day and left a legacy of brilliance which has affected the course of Western political history ever since.

JERRY C. BEASLEY

WORKS: *The Works of Edmund Burke.* 8 vols. Bohn's Standard Library. London: George Bell, 1900; *Burke's Politics: Selected Writings and Speeches of Edmund Burke on Reform, Revolution, and War.* Ross J. S. Hoffman & Paul Levack, eds. New York: Alfred A. Knopf, 1949; *Letters, Speeches, and Tracts on Irish Affairs by Edmund Burke.* Matthew Arnold, ed. London: Macmillan, 1881; *A Note-book of Edmund Burke.* H. V. F. Somerset, ed. Cambridge: Cambridge University Press, 1957; *Selected Writings of Edmund Burke.* W. J. Bate, ed. Modern Library Edition. New York: Random House, 1960; *The Correspondence of Edmund Burke.* Thomas W. Copeland, general ed. 10 vols. Chicago: University of Chicago Press/Cambridge: Cambridge University Press, 1958–1978. *The Writings and Speeches of Edmund Burke.* Paul Langford, general ed. Oxford: Clarendon, 1981– . REFERENCES—Biographies: Ayling, Stanley. *Edmund Burke: His Life and Opinions.* London: John Murray, 1988; Bryant, Donald Cross. *Edmund Burke and His Literary Friends.* St. Louis, Mo.: Washington University Press, 1939; Cone, Carl B. *Burke and the Nature of Politics.* 2 vols. Lexington: University of Kentucky Press, 1957; Magnus, Philip. *Edmund Burke: A Life.* London: John Murray, 1939; Morley, John. *Burke.* English Men of Letters. London: Macmillan, 1874; O'Brien, Conor Cruise. *The Great Melody: A Thematic Biography and Commented Anthology of Edmund Burke.* London: Sinclair-Stevenson/Chicago: University of Chicago Press, 1992; O'Brien, William. *Edmund Burke as an Irishman.* 2d ed. Dublin: M. H. Gill, 1926; Wector, Dixon. *Edmund Burke and His Kinsmen.* Boulder: University of Colorado Press, 1939. Critical Studies: Blakemore, Steven. *Burke and the Fall of Language: The French Revolution as Linguistic Event.* Hanover, N.H.: University Press of New England, 1988; Blakemore, Steven, ed. *Burke and the French Revolution: Bicentennial Essays.* Athens: University of Georgia Press, 1992; Boulton, James T. *The Language of Politics in the Age of Wilkes and Burke.* London: Routledge & Kegan Paul, 1963;

Browne, Stephen H. *Edmund Burke and the Discourse of Virtue.* Tuscaloosa: University of Alabama Press, 1993; Cameron, David. *The Social Thought of Rousseau and Burke.* Toronto: University of Toronto Press, 1973; Canavan, Francis P. *The Political Reason of Edmund Burke.* Durham, N.C.: Duke University Press, 1960; Chapman, Gerald W. *Edmund Burke: The Practical Imagination.* Cambridge: Harvard University Press, 1967; Cobban, Alfred B. C. *Edmund Burke and the Revolt against the Eighteenth Century.* London: Allen & Unwin, 1929; Copeland, Thomas W. *Our Eminent Friend Edmund Burke.* New Haven, Conn.: Yale University Press, 1949; Fasel, George. *Edmund Burke.* Boston: Twayne, 1983; Furniss, Tom. *Edmund Burke's Aesthetic Ideology.* [Cambridge]: Cambridge University Press, [1993]; Fussell, Paul. *The Rhetorical World of Augustan Humanism: Ethics and Imagery from Swift to Burke.* London: Oxford University Press, 1965; Krammick, Isaac. *The Rage of Edmund Burke: Portrait of an Ambivalent Conservative.* New York: Basic Books, 1977; Krammick, Isaac, ed. *Edmund Burke.* Great Lives Observed. Englewood Cliffs, N.J.: Prentice-Hall, 1974; Mahony, Thomas H. D. *Edmund Burke and Ireland.* Cambridge: Harvard University Press, 1960; Pappin, Joseph L. *The Metaphysics of Edmund Burke.* New York: Fordham University Press, 1993; Parkins, Charles. *The Moral Basis of Burke's Political Thought.* Cambridge: Cambridge University Press, 1956; Ritchie, Daniel, ed. *Edmund Burke: Appraisals and Applications.* New Brunswick, N.J.: Transaction Books, 1990; Ritchie, Daniel E. *Further Reflections on the Revolution in France/Edmund Burke.* Indianapolis: Liberty Fund, 1992; Stanlis, Peter J. *Edmund Burke: The Enlightenment and Revolution.* New Brunswick, N.J.: Transaction Books, 1991; *Studies in Burke and His Times.* Published three times a year. 1959– .

BURKE, HELEN LUCY (ca. 1940–   ). Novelist, short story writer, and journalist. Born around 1940 in Dublin, Helen Lucy Burke won the Irish PEN award in 1970 for her short story "Trio." Her only fiction consists of one excellent novel and one slim volume of short stories. She is a witty, satirical writer with a keen eye for the tragicomic. Her novel, *Close Connections* (1979), tells brilliantly of an almost ludicrous love affair between a balding, married editor of a farmers' journal and a plain, clumsy, romantic farmer's daughter. Her book of short stories, *A Season for Mothers* (1980), shows the same fine, witty observation, but its range is wide and varied. She writes equally well of men and women, and she views both sexes with the same tolerant but clinical eye. In recent years, she has been a freelance journalist with Dublin newspapers and with various magazines and writes of food, restaurants and, with commendable sternness, hotels.

DOROTHY ROBBIE

WORKS: *Close Connections.* Dublin: Poolbeg, 1979. (Novel); *A Season for Mothers.* Dublin: Poolbeg, 1980. (Short stories).

BURKE-KENNEDY, DECLAN (1944–   ), novelist and playwright. Burke-Kennedy was born in Tullamore, Co. Offaly. He was a founder-director of Dublin's Focus Theatre, has had several plays produced, and is married to the director-playwright Mary Elizabeth Burke-Kennedy. Since 1980, he has worked for the *Irish Times* and is currently assistant foreign desk editor. He has published two novels, and the second, *Leonie* 1995), is a particularly effective coming-of-age story in the 1960s in Co. Kildare. The title character, Leonie, has a significant role in both major plot strands, but the focus is mainly on two young men, one of a well-to-do family and the other poor. The writing is terse and crisp with much ably handled dialogue, and the large cast of characters is excellently realized. Particularly notable are one boy's grandparents, who have been unable to marry. The old man has great kindness and dignity, and the old woman is an intriguing mixture of scattiness and perception. Perhaps reflecting the author's theatrical background are a number of well-dramatized scenes, an especially notable one being a remarkable tennis match in which one of the participants must be pushed in his wheelchair.

WORKS: *Robert's Alibi.* Dublin: O'Brien, 1988; *Leonie.* [Dublin]: Poolbeg, [1995].

BURNSIDE, SAM (1943–   ), poet and story writer. Born on November 3, 1943, Burnside was reared in the rural north of Ireland, taking degrees at the University of Ulster at Coleraine and at Magee University College, Derry. A passionate advocate of the collective imagination, he is founder and director of the Verbal Arts Centre in Derry, where he lives with his family. A long poem, *The Cathedral* (1989), received a Hennessy Award. In *Walking the Marches* (1990), Burnside writes vigorously about the Northern landscape, its savage beauties, its people, and the ubiquitous rumblings of its past. He is frequently described as "the truest heir" to John Hewitt,* and there is an immediacy to his verse that is planted firmly in a wider observance, as in "Foyle," where his description of trees along a riverbank indicts the failure of the land to sustain its people.

IVY BANNISTER

WORKS: *The Cathedral.* Belfast: Freehold, 1989; *Writer to Writer.* Belfast: Worker's Educational Association, 1991. (Nonfiction); *Walking the Marches.* [Galway: Salmon, 1990]; *Horses.* Malin: Ballagh Studios, 1993; ed., *The Glow upon the Fringe: Literary Journeys around Derry and the North.* Londonderry: Verbal Arts Centre, 1994.

BUSHE, PADDY (1948–   ), poet. Bushe was born in Dublin, lived for two years in Australia, and now lives in Waterville, County Kerry.

WORKS: *Poems with Amergin.* Dublin: Beaver Row, [1989]; *Digging towards the Light.* Dublin: [Dedalus, 1994].

BUTLER, HUBERT (1900–1991), essayist. Butler, who became a Protestant gentleman of letters in postindependent Ireland, was born on October 23, 1900, at Maidenhall, Bennetsbridge, County Kilkenny. At a very young age and in spite of some discouragement from his mother, he made up his mind to live out his life in Maidenhall, his family home. This resolve was to be tested many times. The wishes of his parents, professional and job opportunities, and the expectations of the social class to which he belonged all pointed him toward England.

While attending Charterhouse School, he was awarded a scholarship to St. John's College, Oxford. There he became friends with another Irishman, Tyrone (Tony) Guthrie, later the eminent play director, and he was introduced to Tony's sister, Susan (Peggy), who became his wife. Another encounter that was to have considerable influence on Butler was meeting AE* and Horace Plunkett.

Between 1922 and 1924, he worked for the Carnegie Libraries in Ireland, and when that experiment failed, he left Ireland and from 1924 to 1926 led a peripatetic existence. He taught, for a very short time, at Oakdene Preparatory School, visited Christopher Scaife, who was with the foreign office in Egypt, and traveled to Italy, Cyprus, Leningrad, Croatia and Serbia, and Greece. In 1926, he met the Zinovievs, who taught him Russian; translated Leonid Leonov's *The Thief;* holidayed with the Guthries in Sligo; and stayed for lengths of time at their home, Annaghmakerrig. There was a pilgrim or crusading element in his travels, and today's equivalent would likely be involved in aid or peace programs. A close reading of his European essays reveals his awareness that he was traveling and living in postcolonial Europe. Whether in an imperial or an emergent country, he was aware of the political background, and his particular focus of interest was the relationship between the state and the individual. Three years, from 1934 to 1937, were spent in Yugoslavia on a scholarship from the School of Slavonic Studies.

In 1938, the year before the Second World War, Butler, in his essay "The Kagran Gruppe," talks of "one of the happiest times of my life when I was working for the Austrian Jews in Vienna." In 1939, he visited Paris, and later that year his mother died. When his father died in 1941, he returned to live in Maidenhall for the rest of his life.

Two issues dominated Butler's life after coming home—one a private, ethical issue concerning the stance to take when a granddaughter was born severely brain-damaged. In his essay "Little K," Butler meditates on the morality of living a life without meaning, and he comes down on the side of euthanasia. The other was a public matter that has come to be known in his family circle as "the Nuncio Affair." What he sought to do was to show the collaboration of the Catholic Church in Croatia with fascism during the stewardship of Cardinal Stepinach. A great public outcry was followed by years of ostracism and isolation. Both issues, if one is a Protestant, insistently demand the exercise of private judgment.

In his last years, between 1985 and 1990, three volumes of his essays were collected and brought belated attention to him. In these essays, his enduring interests were Ireland, localism, archaeology, and issues of public and private morality. These last included the right of divorce, legalized abortion, and euthanasia, which for him were matters of private judgment. The essays are set in Ireland, in Eastern and Southern Europe, and in North America. But of his writing he said many times that "even when these essays appear to be about Russia or Greece or Spain they are really about Ireland."

He died in Kilkenny on January 5, 1991.

KATE BATEMAN

PRINCIPLE WORKS: tr., *The Thief* by Leonid Leonov. London: Martin Secker, 1931; tr., *The Cherry Orchard* by Anton Chekhov. London: W. H. Deane, 1934; *Ten Thousand Saints: A Study in Irish and European Origins.* Kilkenny: Wellbrook, 1972; *Escape from the Anthill.* Mullingar: Lilliput, 1985; *The Children of Drancy.* Dublin: Lilliput, 1988; *Grandmother and Wolfe Tone.* Dublin: Lilliput, 1990; *The Sub-Prefect Should Have Held His Tongue and Other Essays.* R. F. Foster, ed. London: Allen Lane, Penguin, in association with Lilliput, [1990]. (A selection from the three Lilliput volumes). REFERENCES: Foster, R. F. "Introduction" to *The Sub-Prefect Should Have Held His Tongue;* McCormack, W. J. "Far-Seeing Gifts: Hubert Butler, 1900–1991." *Éire-Ireland* 26 (Spring 1991): 95–100.

BUTLER, PIERCE (ca. 1950–   ), novelist. Born and raised in Waterford city, Butler attended University College, Cork, and taught there for three years in the Civil Engineering Department and also at Harvard. His *A Malady* (1982) is a novella in which little happens for pages except that characters lie in bed and stare at cracks in the ceiling or take walks around their hospital grounds and think. It is full of passages like this:

The illusion of stability was shattered; everything was caught up in a mindless gyre. She was an insignificant cell in the great cauldron, an amoeba winking with brief life, nudging its neighbour in the feverish stream of living. And within her, creatures smaller still, microscopic organisms were rampant in her blood, in the minute pores of her skin.

Despite its writing and its static quality, if the reader persists, it does come to a kind of resolution.

WORK: *A Malady.* [Dublin]: Co-op Books, [1982].

BUTT, ISAAC (1813–1879), barrister, founder-namer of the Home Rule movement, editor, translator, and fiction writer. Butt was born in Cloghan, County Donegal, on September 6, 1813. His father was a Church of Ireland clergyman who moved to nearby Stranorlar a year later. He was educated at the Royal School, Raphoe, and Trinity College, Dublin, where he had enrolled as an undergraduate at the age of fifteen, having taken first place in the entrance examination. His father died a year later, and for years he had to endure the miseries of poverty and the drudgery of grinding pupils. He was called to the bar in 1838, having published translations of Ovid's *Fasti* and Virgil's *Georgics* and helped found the *Dublin University Magazine,* which he edited from 1834 till 1838 and which included among its early contributors Carleton,* Lever,* Maxwell,* Sheridan Le Fanu,* Lover,* and Mangan.* He became professor of political economy at Trinity in 1836 but abandoned the academic life in 1841 for the richer pickings and greater excitement of the courts.

His ultra-Unionism led to public debates with Daniel O'Connell, but the great Famine of the mid-1840s and what he saw as England's inadequate response to the catastrophe changed his mind about the Union. His legal career afterward was dominated by defense of nationalists, notably, Smith O'Brien in 1848 and the Fénians two decades later. He founded the Home Government Association in 1870, which became the Home Rule League in 1873. His extreme constitutionalism and respectful attitude to England caused such supporters as Joseph Biggar to grow impatient, and with the coming of Parnell in 1879 he was effectively dismissed as leader of the Irish Party in Westminster. He died in Dundrum, County Dublin, on May 5, 1879, and was buried in Stranorlar. His wife, Elizabeth Swanzy, who was five years his senior, died in 1897.

Butt's personal life was rather rackety: though quite handsome, he was slovenly in appearance, was reputed to have extramarital affairs, and served an eighteen-month sentence for debt in Dublin in 1886 and 1887, the situation caused by the unprofitable Fenian trials. His conversion to nationalism was never complete, and his gradualism was too radical for his Protestant friends and too ineffective for Catholics. Yet his conscientious rejection of his early conservatism was admirable, and his Home Rule ideas surely paved the way for the successes that followed. He was a prodigious lecturer and speech maker, but his nonpolitical writings, apart from the classical translations, are sparse. *Irish Life in the Castle, the Courts and the Country* (1840) had as hero a barrister called Tarleton, who was friendly with a Nationalist leader. *The Gap of Barnesmore* (1848), a well-known beauty spot near Stranorlar, is a tale of the aftermath of the Siege of Derry and contains a plea for amity and tolerance much more applicable to the 1840s. *Chapters of College Romance* (1863), written as by Edward J. O'Brien, was a collection of mainly lugubrious tales about Trinity from the *Dublin University Magazine*. They included such titles as "The Murdered Fellow," based on an actual eighteenth-century incident in which a fellow was shot at his window, "The Sizar," "Reading for Honours," "The Billiard Table," "The Bribed Scholar," and "The Duel."

SEAN McMAHON

PRINCIPLE WORKS: tr., *Ovid's Fasti.* Dublin: Milliken, 1833; tr., *The Georgics of Virgil.* Dublin: Milliken, 1834; *Irish Life in the Castle, the Courts and the Country.* 3 vols. London: How & Parsons, 1840. (Novel); *A Voice for Ireland. The Famine in the Land.* Dublin: M'Glashan, 1847; *Zoology and Civilization.* Dublin: M'Glashan, 1847; *The Gap of Barnesmore.* London: Smith, Elder, 1848. (Novel); *The Transfer of Land.* Dublin: Smith, 1857; *History of Italy from the Abdication of Napoleon.* 12 vols. London: Chapman & Hall, 1860; *Chapters of College Romance.* London: Skeet, 1863. (Short stories); "Bishop Berkeley and his Writings" in *Afternoon Readings in the Museum, St. Stephen's Green, Dublin.* London: Bell & Daldy, 1865, pp. 185–224; *The Liberty of Teaching Vindicated.* Dublin: Kelly/London: Simpkin, Marshall, 1865; *Land Tenure in Ireland: A Plea for the Celtic Race.* Dublin: Falconer, 1866; *The Irish Querist.* Dublin: Falconer, 1867; *The Irish People and the Irish Land.* Dublin: Falconer/London: Ridgeway, 1867; *A Practical Treatise on the New Law of Compensation.* Dublin: Falconer/London: Butterworth, 1871; *Home Government for Ireland.* Dublin: Irish Home Rule League, 1874; *The Problem of Irish Education.* London: Longman, 1875. REFERENCES: McCormack, W. J. "Isaac Butt and the Inner Failure of Protestant Home Rule" in *Worsted in the Game: Losers in Irish History.* Ciaran Brady, ed. Dublin: Lilliput, 1989, pp. 121–131; Thornley, David. *Isaac Butt and Home Rule.* London: MacGibbon & Kee, 1964; White, Terence de Vere. *The Road of Excess.* Dublin: Browne & Nolan, 1946.

BYRNE, DONN (1889–1928), novelist and short story writer. Byrne was born in New York City on November 20, 1889, and was christened Brian Oswald Donn-Byrne. His parents were from South Armagh where they returned after a few months in America and where young Donn-Byrne was raised. As a youth, as Brian O'Beirne, he became an enthusiastic Irish speaker, fluent enough to win prizes and to receive the commendation of Douglas Hyde,* one of his teachers in University College, Dublin. He is said to have studied at the Sorbonne and at Leipzig where, according to his biographer, he refused his Ph.D. on the grounds that no Irish gentleman could possibly wear the prescribed evening clothes in the morning. In about 1911, he moved to New York and married Dorothea Cadogan, a girl from the South of Ireland, who, later, as Dolly Donn Byrne, had some success as a playwright, her plays being produced both by the Ulster Theatre and on Broadway.

Under the semi-pseudonym of Donn Byrne, Brian began writing prolifically, first poetry and then short stories, for various New York magazines such as *The Smart Set, Red Book,* and *Scribner's.* His first book, a collection entitled *Stories Without Women,* appeared in 1915, and his first novel, *The Stranger's Banquet,* in 1919. Ten more novels, two more volumes of stories, and a short book about Ireland appeared in the 1920s. Byrne gained great popularity and earning power during this period. He lived in Europe during much of the 1920s; he died in a car accident at Courtmacsherry Bay in West Cork on June 18, 1928.

Despite his years in America, many of Byrne's stories and novels are Irish in subject, and the best are compulsively readable and highly entertaining. However, his work has been described as ''ersatz,'' his popularity is long past, and academic critics generally ignore him today. Although his poorest work has merely the smooth canniness of the slick magazine entertainer, his best trembles on the verge of something better. If he has never quite achieved literary respectability, the reasons are that his romanticism is too rampant and his morality too simplistic. His ability to spin a yarn, however, is so fine that he frequently buries one's critical sensibilities, and it is only after the book is put down that one feels the whole business has been a bit spurious.

If one puts Byrne's pretensions to artistry aside and takes him on his own legitimate ground, Byrne still can evoke pleasure. His short stories are probably his tinniest work, but among the novels, *Messer Marco Polo, The Wind Bloweth, Hangman's House, Brother Saul,* and *The Power of the Dog* all have their persuasive devotees.

WORKS: *Stories without Women.* New York: Hearst's International Library, 1915; *The Stranger's Banquet.* New York & London: Harper, 1919. (Novel); *The Foolish Matrons.* New York: Harper, 1920/London: Sampson Low, 1923. (Novel); *Messer Marco Polo.* New York: Century, 1921/London: Sampson Low, 1922. (Novel); *The Wind Bloweth.* New York: Century/London: Sampson Low, 1922. (Novel); *Changeling, and Other Stories.* New York: Century, 1923/London: Sampson Low, 1924; *Blind Raftery.* New York: Century, 1924/London: Sampson Low, 1925. (Novel); *O'Malley of Shanganagh.* New York: Century, 1925/also published as *An Untitled Story.* London: Sampson Low, 1925. (Novel); *Hangman's House.* New York: Century/London: Sampson Low, 1925. (Novel); *Brother Saul.* New York: Century/London: Sampson Low, 1927. (Novel); *Crusade.* Boston: Little, Brown/London: Sampson Low, 1928. (Novel); *Destiny Bay.* Boston: Little, Brown/London: Sampson Low, 1928. (Stories); *Field of Honor.* New York: Century, 1929/also published as *The Power of the Dog.* London: Sampson Low, 1929. (Novel); *Ireland: The Rock Whence I Was Hewn.* Boston: Little, Brown/London: Sampson Low, 1929. (Travel); *The Golden Goat.* London: Sampson Low, Marston, 1930. (Novel); *A Party of Baccarat.* New York & London: Century, [1930]; *Rivers of Damascus, and Other Stories.* London: Sampson Low, Marston, 1931; *Sargasso Sea, and Other*

Stories. London: Sampson Low, Marston, [1932]; *The Island of Youth and Other Stories.* London: Sampson Low, Marston, [1932]; New York: Century, [1933]; *A Woman of the Shee and Other Stories.* New York & London, [1932]; *An Alley of Flashing Spears, and Other Stories.* London: Sampson Low, [1933]/New York: D. Appleton-Century, 1934; *A Daughter of the Medici, and Other Stories.* London: Sampson Low, [1933]/New York: D. Appleton-Century, 1935; *The Hound of Ireland, and Other Stories.* London: Sampson Low, Marston, [1934]/New York: D. Appleton-Century, 1935; *Poems.* London: Low, Marston, 1934. REFERENCES: Bannister, Henry S. *Donn Byrne: A Descriptive Bibliography 1912–1935.* New York: Garland, 1982; Macauley, Thurston. *Donn Byrne, Bard of Armagh.* New York & London: Century, [1929]; Wetherbee, Winthrop. *Donn Byrne. A Bibliography.* New York: New York Public Library, 1949.

BYRNE, GABRIEL (1950–   ), memoirist and actor. Born in Dublin and educated at University College, Dublin, Byrne became a leading actor in films in the 1980s and occasionally also a producer of films.

WORK: *Pictures in My Head.* [Dublin]: Wolfhound, [1994]. (Memoir).

BYRNE, JOHN KEYES. *See* LEONARD, HUGH.

BYRNE, LAURENCE PATRICK. *See* MALONE, ANDREW E.

BYRNE, SEAMUS (1904–1968), playwright. Byrne was born in Dublin on December 17, 1904, and died in Dublin on May 17, 1968. He received an LL.B. from University College, Dublin, in 1927 and practiced law for nine years in Leitrim. In 1940, he was jailed for his involvement with the Irish Republican Army (IRA), but he was released nine months later after a hunger strike of twenty-one days.

A proposed hunger strike among political prisoners in Mountjoy Jail is the subject of Byrne's finest play, *Design for a Headstone* (Abbey,* 1950). The conflict in the play is basically between the prisoners' political loyalties and their religious ones. On the sixth night of production, some outspoken criticisms of the Catholic Church within the play caused a disturbance in the theatre by a right-wing Catholic organization. Police were brought into the theatre on the following night, and the protest, which had no popular support, died away. The play has occasionally been compared to Brendan Behan's* later and better known prison drama, *The Quare Fellow,* but there is little point to the comparison. Behan is to Byrne rather like O'Casey* is to Denis Johnston*; Behan's theme is a simple emotional statement, but Byrne's is deeper and much more complex. On a merely theatrical level, Behan's play has a freewheeling broadness which Byrne's lacks, but Byrne's has effective comedy as well as more deeply drawn characters and its own quite stark intensity.

Little City (Theatre Festival, 1964) is a three-pronged condemnation of the quality of life in modern Dublin. The strongest prong of the attack is directed at the social hypocrisies surrounding abortion, and this topic effectively delayed the play's production for years. There is some lack of proportion between the play's various strands of plots, and recent events have made the play something of a period piece. Nevertheless, Byrne again demonstrates that he was the strong-est, if not almost the only, social commentator writing for the Irish stage in the 1950s. To the detriment of the Irish drama, he has had few followers.

WORKS: *Design for a Headstone*. Dublin: Progress House, 1956; *Little City*. Dixon, Calif.: Proscenium, 1970.

BYRON, CATHERINE (1947–   ), poet. Born on August 22, 1947, in London, Byron describes herself in *Out of Step* as "half-English and half-Galway by blood, Belfast by raising; but," she says, "Donegal is my country of the mind." In 1965, she left Belfast for Oxford, where she received an M.A. and an M.Phil. in medieval English studies. Most of her subsequent life has been spent in England: there she has raised her two daughters and has worked as a freelance reviewer, creative writing teacher, and farmer. She received an East Midlands Art bursary in 1984 and published her first two books (including the radio play *Samhain*) with Taxus Press in the mid-1980s. In 1992 and 1993, Loxwood Stoneleigh republished those first two volumes under one cover and issued two more major works. Byron lives in Leicester but often travels in Ireland.

Her initial volume, *Settlements* (1985), was reviewed as a treatment of the "dilemma of exile," but, all along, Byron's work has been remarkable for its rendering of in-between states: she has presented herself as floating between various emblems of the natural world, between past and present, between ma-triarchy and patriarchy, between England and Ireland. The first book's title se-quence comments on Irish unsettledness, from the time of the Celts coming to Ireland, to the present.

The wordings in *Settlements* sound very much like those of Seamus Heaney,* and the prose volume *Out of Step: Pursuing Seamus Heaney to Purgatory* (1992; illustrated by its author), is a powerful personal tribute to Heaney, whose early books provided Byron with "essential nourishment . . . all through the exhaust-ing years of caring for small children." It is also an extended quarrel with the way his work invokes but silences the feminine. The occasion of *Out of Step* is Byron's pilgrimage to Lough Derg, which was a quest for the "unassimilated feminine." That demanding journey was undertaken and rendered earlier by Patrick Kavanagh* and Denis Devlin,* as well as by Heaney, the twelve parts of whose "Station Island" provide, in order, the subjects for Byron's Chapters 3 through 13. Ultimately, Byron comes to "understand more about the disabling links between feminine and masculine in Catholic culture, in Heaney's work—and, a little, in myself." Though she claims to arrive at "no illumination" of her central problem, she produces moving autobiographical commentary on the breakup of her marriage, intense examination of Irish ritual from Marian pro-cessions to hunger strikes, and fine criticism of the work of William Carleton,* of Heaney's versions of Dante, and especially of "Station Island." The final two chapters end by presenting Byron's characteristic positions: first wishing she could remain "for ever in the waters of Saint George's Channel, and never have to make landing on the coast of either of my countries" and then gazing from off the Antrim coast on a clear night, able to see "both countries, one on the west horizon, one on the east, all the way across."

Gillian Cross, naming *Out of Step* one of the "Books of the Year" for 1993 in the *Times Educational Supplement,* called it "a heady and compelling cocktail of feminist criticism, Catholic reminiscence, and painful honesty." But for Nuala Ni Dhomhnaill, speaking on RTÉ, the true fruits of Byron's "dismaying" subsequence to Heaney could emerge only in Byron's own ensuing poetry: Ni Dhomhnaill called the book a "clearing out of the Augean stables." Indeed, the ambitious, independent poems in *The Fat-Hen Field Hospital* (1993), published soon after *Out of Step,* chart her own pilgrimage, as she visits Inisheer and other islands under the heading of the Irish word "Turas," which names the book's last section. Though some of the book's best poems extend an earlier debt to one of Heaney's influences, Ted Hughes, in their presentation of the violence of farm births and deaths, Byron's avowedly feminine perspective does envision another new middle ground, between animal and human, in which pain done to animals becomes a version of doing harm to one's self and, more, to the people in one's care. In the counterpoint between "The Favour," in which Byron intrudes on an intimate all-male act of neutering calves, and the splendid "Let-Down," in which she recalls the uncertainties and spontaneities of breast-feeding, she offers her own best answer to the anguished question of *Out of Step:* "Where can I turn to hear a real heterodoxy?"

VICTOR LUFTIG

WORKS: *Settlements.* Durham: Taxus, 1985; "Anguish of Denial," *Midland Review* 3 (Winter 1986). (Essay); *Samhain.* Leicester: Taxus, 1987; ed., with John Lyons. *Northern Poetry One.* Todmordern: Littlewood, 1989; *Out of Step: Pursuing Seamus Heaney to Purgatory.* Bristol: Loxwood Stoneleigh, 1992; *The Fat-Hen Field Hospital, Poems 1985–1992.* Bristol: Loxwood Stoneleigh, 1993; *Settlements & Samhain.* Bristol: Loxwood Stoneleigh, 1993.

C

CABALL, JOHN (1909–), novelist. Caball was born in Tralee, County Kerry, graduated from University College, Dublin, and became a schoolmaster in Tralee. His historical novel, *The Singing Swordsman* (1953), is about Pierce Ferriter.

WORK: *The Singing Swordsman.* Dublin: Michael F. Moynihan, 1953.

CADDELL, CECILIA MARY (1814–1877), novelist and short story writer. Caddell was born at Harbourstown, County Meath. She was the second daughter of Richard O'Ferrall Caddell, of Harbourstown. Her mother was the Hon. Pauline, sister of Viscount Southwell, of an old Gormanston Catholic family, "which," according to Matthew Russell, "while clinging to the old faith, has had the knack of clinging also to the old homestead and the old family estates." She was born into a family of acknowledged social position and, with an abundance of leisure, wrote to fulfill her intellectual needs. She was also noted as a benefactor of orphanages. Her health deteriorated, the result of devoted attendance to her parents during their final illnesses. Her father died on January 3, 1856, and her mother on May 5. Caddell never recovered her own health and was an invalid for twenty years until her death on September 11, 1877. She is buried in the Caddell family vault in Stanmullen. She was primarily a novelist and short story writer, although she occasionally wrote hymns. Her hymns were anthologized in the collections of Orby Shipley, particularly in the *Lyra Messianica* collection of 1864. She was a frequent contributor to the *Irish Monthly, Lamp, Month,* and *Catholic World.*

Caddell's writings are heavily religious. She wrote hagiography, preferring to highlight the lesser-known saints and Irish Catholic history. Her most popular work was *Blind Agnes; or, the Little Spouse of the Blessed Sacrament* (1856), which was regularly reprinted until the 1920s and translated into French and

Italian. *Blind Agnes* was probably based on the murder of Father Robert Netterville, a Jesuit priest beaten to death by Puritans. The story of Blind Agnes
focuses on the religious conversions of the partially Protestant Netterville family
back to the true religion, Catholicism. Her novels tend to have historical settings,
with moralistic guidelines and predictable plots.

ANNE COLMAN

WORKS: *Flowers and Fruit; or, The Use of Tears.* Dublin: Duffy, 1856; *A History of the
Missions in Japan and Paraguay.* 2 pts. London: Burns & Lambert, 1856; *Marie; or, The Work-
woman of Liege.* New York: Kennedy, 1856; *Blind Agnes; or, The Little Spouse of the Blessed
Sacrament.* Dublin: Duffy, 1856; *Home and the Homeless.* 3 vols. London: T. C. Newby, 1858;
The Martyr Maidens of Ostend. 1858; *Nellie Netterville.* London: Burns, Oates & Washbourne,
[1867]; *Hidden Saints: Life of Soeur Marie; the Workwoman of Liege.* London: T. Richardson,
1869; *Hidden Saints: Life of Marie Bonneau de Miramion.* London: T. Richardson/New York:
H. H. Richardson, 1870; *Never Forgotten; or, The Home of the Lost Child.* London: Burns, Oates,
1871; *Wild Times.* London: Burns, Oates, 1872; *Summer Talks about Lourdes.* London: Burns,
Oates, 1874; *The Cross in Japan.* London: Burns, Oates, 1904; *Lost Genevieve.* London: Burns,
Oates & Washbourne, n.d.; *The Miner's Daughter.* London: Burns, Oates & Washbourne, n.d.; *A
Pearl in Dark Waters.* London: Burns, Oates & Washbourne, n.d.; *Father de Lisle: A Story of
Tyborne.* London: Burns, Oates & Washbourne, n.d.; *Blanch Leslie.* London: Burns, Oates & Wash-
bourne, n.d.; *Minister's Daughter.* London: Sadlier, n.d.; *Little Snowdrop.* London: Burns, Oates &
Washbourne, n.d.; *Tales for the Young.* London: Burns, Oates & Washbourne, n.d.
REFERENCES: Brown, Stephen J. *Ireland in Fiction.* Dublin: Maunsel, 1919; "Cecilia Mary Cad-
dell: A Short Biographical Note." *Irish Monthly* 44 (March 1916): 202–203; Russell, Matthew.
"Cecilia Caddell." *Irish Monthly* 5 (December 1877): 772–774.

CALLAGHAN, MARY ROSE (1944–   ), novelist and biographer. Born in
Dublin on January 23, 1944, Callaghan was educated from the age of nine
mostly in convent boarding schools, leaving school in 1962. After a year working at various jobs and reading books, she enrolled as a medical student at
University College, Dublin, but quickly changed her focus to arts and took her
B.A. in 1968. She taught for a year at Killester Vocational School before moving
to England and teaching English and history in various secondary schools, ending finally at Rye St. Antony School, Oxford, for nearly three years. From 1973
to 1975, she was an assistant editor of *The Arts in Ireland,* writing her first
journalistic pieces there. Moving to America in 1975, she began her first novel,
Mothers, finished in 1978 but not published until 1982. Since then she has
written steadily, finishing her fifth novel in 1994. She also worked as contributing editor for *The Journal of Irish Literature* from 1975 to 1993, was associate
editor for the first edition of this dictionary, and taught occasional classes in
writing at the University of Delaware.

Callaghan's power as a writer depends, for the most part, on four techniques:
her control of point of view, her ability to characterize deftly and precisely, her
penchant for literary allusion, and her humor. Rich in comic detail, her characters are memorable, and her plots wild and quirky. *Mothers* (1982) is a powerful first novel chronicling the lives of three Irishwomen from three generations
in dramatic monologues that overlap and comment upon one another. This novel

about motherhood principally explores marriage, adoption, pregnancy out of wedlock, and female sisterhood. Her second novel, *Confessions of a Prodigal Daughter* (1985) is a portrait of an artist as a young girl. Modeled loosely on Dante's *Comedia,* the novel, populated by a large cast of Dickensian caricatures, is comic and highly allusive but not as successful aesthetically as *Mothers.* In *The Awkward Girl* (1990), however, Callaghan's experimentation with point of view and plot structure carries over from her first novel; here she deftly weaves together no less than thirty-six minor characters and apparently fragmented short "stories" into a novel about one major title character. She pulls out all the stops here, balancing biting comedy with sympathetic characterization and constantly shifting her readers' sense of aesthetic distance as she manipulates her characters around the life and death of her main focus, Sally Ann Fitzpatrick.

In addition to the major novels, Callaghan was commissioned to write *Kitty O'Shea: A Life of Katharine Parnell* (1989). From the start, Callaghan is clear about her purpose: to attempt to show Katharine Parnell's life as a noble and courageous one, not simply one linked by chance to her famous husband's. The biography is readable and well researched, a fine work showing her background in history.

In 1990, Callaghan published a novel for young adults, *Has Anyone Seen Heather?,* a murder mystery that is fast-paced and action-filled, with a strong, suspenseful plot and likable characters.

Overall, Mary Rose Callaghan is currently one of Ireland's significant writers. At work at present on her fourth major novel, she promises to get better and better.

Callaghan's *Emigrant Dreams* (1996) is set in America and depicts the emotional problems of an Irish writer teaching in an American college, as she attempts to untangle the dubious involvement of an Irish-American ancestor who was involved in the real-life Becker murder trial of 1912.

MARYANNE FELTER

WORKS: *Mothers.* Dublin: Arlen House, 1982. (Novel); *A House for Fools* in *Journal of Irish Literature* 12 (September 1983): 3–67. (Play); *Confessions of a Prodigal Daughter.* London & New York: Marion Boyars, 1985. (Novel); *Kitty O'Shea: A Life of Katharine Parnell.* London: Pandora, 1989. (Biography); *The Awkward Girl.* Dublin: Attic, 1990. (Novel); *Has Anyone Seen Heather?* Dublin: Attic, 1990. (Novel for young adults); *Emigrant Dreams.* [Dublin]: Poolbeg, [1996]. (Novel).

CALLANAN, J. J. (1795–1829), poet. J. J. (Jeremiah Joseph, James Joseph, or even Jeremiah John) Callanan was born in Cork in 1795. After attending Maynooth and then Trinity College, Dublin, without graduating, Callanan spent much time collecting Irish legends and ballads. Of his translations, Padraic Colum* remarks, "The poet brought, in one instance, anyway, a recognisable Gaelic cadence into translations from the Irish. That cadence is in 'The Outlaw of Loch Lene.' " Although Callanan's English equivalents of Irish poetry are not particularly accurate, his renderings are fluent, as in these verses from "The Lament of O'Gnive":

How dimmed is the glory that circled the Gael
And fall'n the high people of green Innisfail;
The sword of the Saxon is red with their gore;
And the mighty of nations is mighty no more! . . .

O'Neil of the Hostages; Con, whose high name
On a hundred red battles has floated to fame,
Let the long grass still sigh undisturbed o'er thy sleep;
Arise not to shame us, awake not to weep.

Sometimes Callanan rises to a strength that quite overcomes the conventions of nineteenth-century poetic diction, as in this stanza from "O Say. My Brown Drimin":

When the prince, now an exile, shall come for his own.
The isles of his father, his rights and his throne,
My people in battle the Saxons will meet,
And kick them before, like old shoes from their feet.

Or, as in this curse from "Dirge of O'Sullivan Bear":

Scully! may all kinds
    Of evil attend thee!
On thy dark road of life
    May no kind one befriend thee!
May fevers long burn thee,
    And agues long freeze thee!
May the strong hand of God
    In His red anger seize thee!

In 1829, Callanan went to Lisbon for his health, but, when his condition rapidly deteriorated, he determined to die in Ireland and boarded a vessel bound for Cork. His tuberculosis was so advanced, however, that he was returned to shore, and he died on September 19.

WORKS: *The Recluse of Inchidony and Other Poems.* London: Hurst, Chance, 1830; *The Poems of J. J. Callanan.* Cork: Bolster, 1847; *The Poems of J. J. Callanan.* Cork: Daniel Mulcahy, 1861; *Gems of the Cork Poets: Comprising the Complete Works of Callanan, Condon, Casey, Fitzgerald, and Cody.* Cork: Barter, 1883.   REFERENCE: MacCarthy, Bridget G. "Jeremiah J. Callanan. Part I: His Life. Part II: His Poetry." *Studies* 35 (1946): 215–229, 387–399.

CAMPBELL, JOSEPH (1879–1944), poet. Campbell was born in Belfast, on July 15, 1879. From his father, William Henry, a building contractor, he inherited his strong nationalistic tendencies; from his gentle, cultured mother he received an interest in literature, music, art, folklore, and a love of everything Gaelic.

Literary criticism has generally belittled Campbell, and literary history has undervalued his part in the creative upsurge of the early twentieth century. Apart from his being represented in anthologies by a few of his more popular poems, Campbell's individual contribution to Irish life and literature is ignored.

Poet, patriot, scholar, writer, and a man of vision, culture, and idealism, Campbell was one of the rarest and most Gaelic of minds of our time, as, indeed, Austin Clarke* remarked on Radio Éireann in 1938. Campbell's knowledge of Gaelic life and literature was profound. He was steeped in traditional lore, and he stimulated an interest in Ireland's cultural heritage everywhere he went. His poetry differs in some respects from that of other Irish poets who were writing at the opening of this century. He is essentially a lyric poet inspired directly by Irish folklore and folksong, a poet who expresses in clear, simple English the traditional spirit of Irish life. A little unpublished poem entitled "The Key" (written on June 19, 1939) expresses his own consciousness of his "Irishness":

> Who would unlock me
> Must file for himself a key of three words—
> Vision, Energy, Bleakness.

Campbell considered these three qualities characteristic of Irish poetry, and he strove to maintain them in his poetry. Vision he understood as imagery, energy as avoidance of the commonplace, and bleakness as austerity. The austerity of early Gaelic art and its concentrated brevity inspired him. His power of expressing a memorable simplicity is the result not only of inspiration, but also of subtle art:

> I am the mountainy singer—
> The voice of the peasant's dream,
> The cry of the wind on the wooded hill,
> The leap of the fish in the stream.

The first stirrings of the Irish Literary Revival reached Belfast in the early years of the century, and Campbell, with other young Ulstermen, was attracted to it. Introduced in 1902 by his friend Padraic Colum* to the Dublin literary leaders, Campbell published articles and poems in Arthur Griffith's* *The United Irishman* and Standish O'Grady's* *All Ireland Review.* In 1904, he collaborated with Herbert Hughes, the musician, in the publication of *Songs of Uladh,* a collection of folksongs. Campbell supplied the words for these beautiful, long-forgotten traditional airs which Hughes had collected in Donegal—"My Lagan Love," "The Ninepenny Fidil," and others. These genuine folksongs so capture the artlessness, freshness, and liquid ease of the ballad that they have passed into the anonymous folk tradition of Anglo-Irish ballads whose authorship is forgotten. Friendship with Francis Joseph Bigger, the Ulster politician, brought Campbell into contact with the Ulster Literary Theatre, and he became an actor, playwright, and an editor of *Uladh,* its quarterly journal. The reception given his play *The Little Cowherd of Slainge,* produced by the company in May 1905, convinced him that his talent lay elsewhere, but as an actor of fine voice and presence he showed distinct promise.

After a short stay in 1905 in Dublin where, as an Ulsterman, he felt he got scant recognition, Campbell went to London in 1906 in search of a more sympathetic audience. He was employed as a teacher of English in the London County Council Schools. He also acted as secretary of the Irish Literary Society, London, and as assistant to Eleanor Hull of the Irish Texts Society. While in London, he became acquainted with the poetic theories and movements of the twentieth century, especially the Imagist movement, and he developed an interest in contemporary Russian, French, American, and German literature. Having married a London girl, Nancy Maude, who shared his literary interests, he returned to Dublin in 1911 and set up home outside the city on the Dublin-Wicklow border, hoping to settle down seriously to a literary career.

Campbell's early volumes of verse—*The Garden of the Bees* (1905), *The Rushlight* (1906), *The Man-Child* (1907), *The Gilly of Christ* (1907), and *The Mountainy Singer* (1909)—have a certain freshness and a distinct vein of originality. He wrote of the simple things of Irish life in an utterly individual and spontaneous manner reminiscent of Gaelic poetry. The traditions of the Irish people, their religious outlook, and their strong faith permeate these poems. Campbell is very unequal, however. Many of these earlier poems lack ease of utterance and smoothness, and reflect the difficult wrestling of a poet with his material. Many poems have a looseness of style reminiscent of Whitman, and others show the too active influence of English poetry, particularly that of the Romantic school. The best of the early poems have been included by Austin Clarke* in *Poems of Joseph Campbell* (1963).

Mearing Stones (1911) revealed Campbell in a new light, that of prose writer and artist. Subtitled *Leaves from My Note-book on Tramp in Donegal* and illustrated with black and white pencil drawings, this unusual collection of prose sketches showed Campbell's capacity for impressionistic portraiture verbally as well as visually. The book is alive with mood and atmosphere. In the following year, 1912, Campbell published a play, *Judgment,* set in the same wild mountain area of Donegal. The play, produced at the Abbey* in April, is one of social realism and recalls Synge* in its grim tragedy and wild beauty, although it was scarcely as effective as Synge in the theatre. A second play, *The Turn Out,* was published in *The Irish Review* * in 1912 but was not produced. Campbell lacked a sense of dramatic structure and a sure command of technique.

The later volumes of verse, *Irishry* (1913) and *Earth of Cualann* (1917), marked Campbell's highest achievement as a poet. These show a development of style, a distinct improvement in technique, a tightening of the line, a more marked subtlety in diction, and a more confident use of difficult meters and even of free verse. Austin Clarke claimed that Campbell was the first Irish poet to use free verse effectively and that *Earth of Cualann* was his greatest achievement. This book, inspired by the matchless beauty of the Wicklow countryside of Cualann, is deeply charged with atmosphere. The terse symbolism, the epigrammatic conciseness, the allusions to Gaelic myths, the austerity, and the restraint which Campbell sought lessen its appeal for the average reader. His more popular *Irishry,* with its vivid and realistic character lyrics, forms an interesting study of the people of the Irish countryside. A comparison with Padraic

Colum's lyrics is obvious, but the austerity, realism, and absence of sentiment in Campbell's portraits form a vivid contrast with Colum's kindlier, gentler approach. Included in *Irishry* is Campbell's little masterpiece, "The Old Woman":

> As a white candle
> In a holy place,
> So is the beauty
> Of an aged face.
>
> As the spent radiance
> Of the winter sun,
> So is a woman
> With her travail done.
>
> Her brood gone from her,
> And her thoughts as still
> As the waters
> Under a ruined mill.

This sensitive, impressionistic lyric was inspired by his mother. Campbell playfully remarked on Radio Éireann on January 28, 1942, "Poets rarely make money, but I have made some on that. Indeed it has gotten into so many anthologies that I have been accused of living on 'The Old Woman'!"

In 1913, Campbell became involved in the struggle for national freedom. He was one of the promoters of the Irish Volunteers, did rescue work in Dublin during the Easter Rising, acted as chairman of the Wicklow County Council in 1920 and 1921, opposed the setting up of the Irish Free State in December 1921, was arrested early in the Civil War, and was interned in Mountjoy Jail and later in the Curragh internment camp until the general jail delivery of Christmas 1923. A "Jail Journal" which he wrote still remains unpublished. On his release, a broken and dispirited man, disillusioned with life and with Ireland's political leaders, and despairing of ever finding happiness or suitable employment in Ireland, he decided to emigrate to America.

Campbell's life in New York from 1925 to 1939 marked a new beginning. This man, fired with enthusiasm and love for Ireland's cultural inheritance, dreamed of establishing in America a permanent center of Irish culture. It seems incredible that one man, burdened with financial worries and dogged by misfortune, could attempt so much. He founded the School of Irish Studies in New York in 1925, the Irish Foundation in 1931, and *The Irish Review* in 1934; he pioneered cultural travel trips to Ireland in 1933; he lectured on Irish literature at Fordham from 1927 to 1938; and through lectures, plays, recitals, summer schools, and exhibitions of Irish arts and crafts, he sought to bring Ireland to America and America to Ireland.

Financial worries, poor health, and a desire to get down to the publication of his Collected Poems and to complete some unfinished work brought Campbell

220   CAMPBELL, MICHAEL [MUSSEN]

back to Ireland in 1939, to the security of his mountain farm in Wicklow where he lived an eremitic existence until his death in June 1944.

Campbell slipped away quietly, almost unknown to the general public. The literary world paid a passing tribute and soon forgot him. Not a single one of his books was in print, and so his name became just a name "with a hundred others / In a book in the library." Austin Clarke's* publication in 1963 of *The Poems of Joseph Campbell*, a Joseph Campbell number of *The Journal of Irish Literature** in 1979, and a critical biography, *Joseph Campbell, Poet & Nationalist 1879–1944*, published in 1988, suggested some reawakened interest in Campbell's work. However, he still remains a forgotten poet, one of the most neglected and undervalued of our time.

N. A. SAUNDERS

WORKS: *The Little Cowherd of Slainge*, in *Uladh* 1 (November 1904). (Play); *The Garden of the Bees and Other Poems*. [Belfast: W. Erskine Mayne; Dublin: Gill, 1905]; *The Rushlight*. Dublin: Maunsel, 1906; *The Gilly of Christ*. Dublin: Maunsel, 1907; *The Man Child*. [Dublin?]: Loch Press Series, 1907; *The Mountainy Singer*. Dublin: Maunsel, 1909/Boston: Four Seas Co., 1919; *Mearing Stones*. Dublin: Maunsel, 1911; *Judgment*. Dublin & London: Maunsel, 1912. (Play); *Irishry*. Dublin & London: Maunsel, 1913; *Earth of Cualann*. Dublin & London: Maunsel, 1917; *Orange Terror*, by "Ultach." Dublin: Reprinted from *The Capuchin Annual*, 1943; *The Poems of Joseph Campbell*, ed. & with an Introduction by Austin Clarke. Dublin: Allen Figgis, 1963; "A Joseph Campbell Number." Ed. by N. A. Saunders. *Journal of Irish Literature* 8 (September 1979). Contains Saunders's "Notes toward a Biography," as well as a selection of poems, some previously unpublished, his "Northern Autobiography," a radio talk, and a reprinting of the play *Judgment*. REFERENCES: O'Hegarty, P. S. *A Bibliography of Joseph Campbell—Seosamh Mac Cathmaoil*. Dublin: A. Thom, 1940; Saunders, Norah, & Kelly, A. A. *Joseph Campbell, Poet & Nationalist 1879–1944*. [Dublin]: Wolfhound, [1988].

CAMPBELL, MICHAEL [MUSSEN] (1924–1984), novelist. Campbell, the fourth baron Glenavy, was born in Dublin on October 25, 1924, the younger son of the second Lord Glenavy and his wife, the artist Beatrice Elvery. His older brother was Patrick Campbell,* the humorist and television personality. He was educated at St. Columba's College, Rathfarnham, and at Trinity College, Dublin. He was called to the Irish bar in 1947 but became a journalist, working for the *Irish Times* in London. He wrote six novels, which achieved some réclame, but his most lasting work will undoubtedly be *Lord Dismiss Us* (1967), a sensitive and evocative study of love between boys at a school that resembles St. Columba's down to the fine details and incidental characters. The arrival of a new headmaster restores the status quo. *Peter Perry* (1956) was withdrawn for fear of a libel action, the circumstances of which are related fictionally in *Nothing Doing*. After this final novel in 1970, he lapsed into silence, a rich talent wasting away (largely due to the effects of drink, which plays a leading role in his other books). His early novels, which were largely amusing satires drawn from well-known characters, were readable and amusing, but his distinction as a novelist will always rest on *Lord Dismiss Us*, an exceptional work. The author sets it in England, but such is the closed nature of the life described that it may be taken as an account of homosexual experiences in Ireland, an unusual enough theme at the time.

He succeeded his brother to the Glenavy title in 1980, but with his death the barony and baronetcy became extinct. Sober in his last years, he was unable to write and devoted himself to working in his companion Michael Horden's bookshop near Regents Park. He died in June 1984.

PETER COSTELLO

WORKS: *Peter Perry.* London: Heinemann, [1956]/New York: Orion, [1960]; *Oh, Mary, This London.* London: Heinemann, 1959/New York: Orion, [1962]; *Across the Water.* London: Heinemann/New York: Orion, 1961; *The Princess in England.* London: Heinemann/New York: Orion, 1964; *Lord Dismiss Us.* London: Heinemann, 1967/New York: Putnam, [1968]; *Nothing Doing.* London: Constable, 1970/New York: Putnam, [1971].

CAMPBELL, PATRICK [GORDON] (1913–1980), humorous essayist. Campbell, the third baron Glenavy, was born on June 6, 1913, the older brother of Michael Campbell.* He was educated at Pembroke College, Oxford, and from 1941 to 1944 served in the Irish Marine Service. From 1944 to 1947, he wrote the "Irishman's Diary" column for the *Irish Times* and later in England wrote columns for many years for the *Sunday Dispatch* and from 1961 for the *Sunday Times.* Despite, or perhaps because of, a notable stammer, he was a popular television performer from 1962 to 1979 on the program "Call My Bluff." He died in France on November 9, 1980.

He published many collections of humorous essays, and the best are so irresistibly droll that one has to laugh out loud. Describing his height and thinness, he wrote:

at the age of sixteen, I stood six feet four in my army boots—a distinction reduced in importance by my weight, which remained constant at eight stone. It is not true to say that you couldn't see me sideways, but it certainly was necessary to narrow the eyes a little.

Describing a fluent and garrulous Finn, he wrote:

During supper he skimmed up and down and round about the English language with such mastery that gradually everyone else fell silent. To join with him in a discussion would have been like accompanying Caruso on a jew's-harp.

The *Sunday Express* described him as "the Charlie Chaplin of writing." The "Jacques Tati" would perhaps have been more accurate. In any event, Campbell is the perfect bedside read and a superb antidote to melancholia.

WORKS: *Round Ireland with a Golf Bag.* Dublin: Irish Times, [1936]; *A Long Drink of Cold Water.* London: Falcon, 1949; *An Irishman's Diary.* London: Cassell, 1950; *A Short Trot with a Cultured Mind.* London: Falcon, 1951; *Life in Thin Slices.* London: Falcon, 1951; *Patrick Campbell's Omnibus.* [London]: Hulton, 1954; *Come Here Till I Tell You.* London: Hutchinson, 1960; *Constantly in Pursuit.* London: Hutchinson, 1962; *How to Become a Scratch Golfer.* London: Anthony Blond, 1963; *Brewing Up in the Basement.* London: Hutchinson, 1963; *Rough Husbandry.* London: Hutchinson, 1965; *The P-P-Penguin Patrick Campbell.* Selected by Kaye Webb. Harmondsworth: Penguin, 1965; *All Ways on Sundays.* London: Anthony Blond, 1966; *A Bunch of*

New Roses. London: Anthony Blond, 1967; *The Course of Events.* London: Anthony Blond, 1968; *Gullible's Travels.* London: Anthony Blond, 1969; *The High Speed Gasworks.* London: Anthony Blond, 1970; *Waving All Excuses.* London: Anthony Blond, 1971; *Patrick Campbell's Golfing Book.* London: Blond & Briggs, 1972; with Frank Muir. *Call My Bluff: Frank Muir versus Patrick Campbell.* London: Eyre Methuen, 1972; *Fat Tuesday Tails.* London: Blond & Briggs, 1973; *35 Years on the Job: The Best of Patrick Campbell, 1937–1973.* London: Blond & Briggs, 1973; *My Life and Easy Times.* London: Anthony Blond, 1976; *A Feast of True Fandangles.* London: W. H. Allen, 1979; *The Campbell Companion: The Best of Patrick Campbell.* Ulick O'Connor, ed. London: Pavilion, 1987.

CAMPION, JOHN T[HOMAS] (1814–189?), poet and novelist. Campion was born in Kilkenny in 1814, practiced medicine there for most of his life, and died sometime in the 1890s. Both as poet and novelist, he can be taken as typical of dozens of popular nineteenth-century Irish writers whose literary abilities were not commensurate with their patriotism. In subject matter, Campion's works were jingoistically patriotic, but in manner they were conventionally imitative of English modes. Campion differs from many popular writers, however, in that some few works have a vigor that captured the popular imagination, and a vitality that sometimes transcends craftsmanship. For instance, his widely known poem ''Emmet's Death,'' which was originally published in *The Nation** in 1844, is a fair example of the patriotic poetry that was technically proficient enough to be stirring and that also had an honest although quite unsubtle emotionalism. These qualities go far to compensate for its basic badness. Its last stanza reads:

''He dies to-day,'' thought a fair, sweet girl—
    She lacked the life to speak,
For sorrow had almost frozen her head,
    And white were her lip and cheek—
Despair had drank up her last wild tear,
    And her brow was damp and chill,
And they often felt at her heart with fear,
    For its ebb was all but still.

Campion's novels and his novelized history of Michael Dwyer are marred by the faults of his poetry, as well as by the conventional excesses of popular English fiction and theatrical melodrama. For, instance, from *Michael Dwyer:*

    ''Your doom is sealed, Williams!''
    ''My doom was sealed when my name was first entered on your
    list. It was at once death or dishonour: I choose death!''
    ''And die you shall!''
    ''Praise be to God!''
    ''You blaspheme, rebel.''
    ''I am an Irishman, and I die for Ireland!''
    ''Faugh! Summon the court-martial.''

In their descriptive and narrative sections, Campion's fictions have a literary pretentiousness of style. However, in Campion, as in much better writers like Fenimore Cooper in America or Carleton* in Ireland, the florid writing is not sufficient to deflect the vigorous forward thrust of the narrative. Campion's work is more interesting as evidence of Irish political sentiment than as literature, but the tradition he was working in has been used by a few modern writers to great effect, as in, for instance, Denis Johnston's* *The Old Lady Says "No!"* and portions of Sean O'Casey's* *The Drums of Father Ned.*

WORKS: "Ballads and Poems," *Traces of the Crusaders in Ireland.* Dublin: Hennessy, 1856; *Alice: A Historical Romance of the Crusaders in Ireland.* Kilkenny: Coyle, 1862. (Novel); *The Last Struggles of the Irish Sea Smugglers.* Glasgow: Cameron, Ferguson, 1869. (Novel); *Michael Dwyer; or, The Insurgent Captain of the Wicklow Mountains.* Glasgow: Cameron, Ferguson, [ca. 1869].

CANNING, MAURICE

WORK: *Where the Purple Heather Grows.* Rathcomac, Co. Cork: Sycamore, 1991. (Poetry).

CANNON, MOYA (1956–   ), poet. Cannon was born in Dunfanaghy, County Donegal. She read history and politics at University College, Dublin, and at Corpus Christi, Cambridge. Her first collection, *Oar* (1990), received the Brendan Behan* Memorial Prize. She has given readings widely in Ireland and abroad. Her work has been set to music by, among others, Irish composer Jane O'Leary. Her poems have been broadcast by BBC Radio 4 and by RTÉ, and she is currently editor of *Poetry Ireland Review.*

Cannon is one of the more exciting poets to emerge from a poetry "renaissance" in the west of Ireland. Her concerns are rooted in the cycles of nature, the everyday, the ordinary, which can transform itself into the miraculous and extraordinary. The topography of Galway and Clare combines with notions and aspects of history, old customs, and quasi-religious beliefs to produce a rich poetic tapestry, full of newly created phrases and individually cast language. At the same time, there are a unique quietness about Cannon's poetry and a sense of fulfillment in the appreciation of the ordinary.

FRED JOHNSTON

WORK: *Oar.* [Galway]: Salmon, [1990].

CARBERY, ETHNA (1866–1902), poet and short story writer. Carbery was the pen name of Anna Isabel Johnston, who was born in Ballymena on December 3, 1866. She lived most of her life in Belfast, where, from 1896 to 1899, she and Alice Milligan* edited the nationalistic literary magazine *The Shan Van Vocht.* She was a prolific contributor of verse and stories to similar Irish periodicals. In 1901, she married Seumas MacManus,* the Donegal story writer, but their marriage was short-lived, for she died on April 21, 1902. Of all the many patriotic women poets of her day, Ethna Carbery, possibly because of her early death, generated the most excitement in patriotic clubs and debating societies. Her poems, collected in the volume *The Four Winds of Eirinn,* were

widely read and frequently reprinted, and as late as 1922 Padraic Colum* found them charming. While they are facile, they contain only the conventional sentiments and the usual phrasing of a hundred poets before her. One ballad, ''Roddy McCorley,'' is still sung today.

WORKS: *The Four Winds of Eirinn.* Dublin: Gill, 1902/new edition, with additional poems and a memoir by Seumas MacManus. Dublin: Gill, 1918; *The Passionate Hearts.* London: Isbister, 1903; *In the Celtic Past.* Dublin: Gill, 1904. (Stories).

CARBERY, MARY

WORK: *Mary Carbery's West Cork Journals (1898–1901).* Jeremy Sandford, ed. Dublin: Lilliput, 1995.

CARLETON, WILLIAM (1794–1869), novelist and short story writer. A native of County Tyrone, educated in a hedge-school, Carleton is cited as the quintessential peasant artist, Ireland's equivalent to Robert Burns. It was an image he cultivated, and with great success. However, like Burns and the best of those who played on a naive persona, there is more skill than might be first evident in his narratives. He built upon the oral tradition of the *seanachai* but incorporated political convictions into his accounts, so that within his lifetime he became a spokesman for the country people of Ireland at a time of severe trials. His accounts of farm life and particularly his depictions of the Famine years are notable for their detail and candor.

Born on February 20, 1794, into a large and poor family, the young Carleton early exhibited intellectual ambition. He studied for the priesthood, but while in formal study, he abandoned such a vocation and his religious affiliation as well. Under the influence of Caesar Otway,* he began to write sketches of Irish country life for the *Christian Examiner,* a journal professing to expose the malign influence of the Roman Catholic Church. However, Carleton's descriptive gifts quickly exceeded such propagandistic purposes, and he turned toward literary art. His first collection of what seemed to be simple folktales, *Traits and Stories of the Irish Peasantry* (1830), was so popular that it was soon followed by similar collections. These stories are deceptive in their simplicity, for they contain an undercurrent of resentment against injustices and a set of clear convictions.

His novels, particularly *Fardorougha the Miser* (1839) and *Valentine Mc-Clutchy* (1845), are more direct in their social commentary and more forceful. His last and best novel, *The Black Prophet* (1847), is particularly impressive for its horrifying description of the Great Famine. His narratives are clever, but the characters tend to be stereotypes, although the lively dialogue and occasional humor relieve the heaviness of the subject matter.

Carleton's *Autobiography,* left unfinished at his death on January 30, 1869, is a work of considerable literary merit, particularly for the accuracy of its descriptions.

Critics, including Yeats,* have praised Carleton for the accuracy of his recording of Irish character and speech. But he is important for expanding readership as well. Stephen Gwynn,* in *Irish Literature and Drama in the English Language,* first articulated what has become the accepted assessment: ''The most notable thing about Carleton is that one feels him to be writing for Ireland, not for England.'' The Ireland he wrote about and for is far different from the Celtic dreamland described by Matthew Arnold and perpetuated in popular songs and literature. Nor is it the savage place dismissed by writers from Spenser* to the present, a place of hypocrites and buffoons. It is a real place of human aspirations and human sufferings, and his stories contain a realistic admixture of humor and heroism as well as the routines of simple life.

Carleton's specific literary achievement is his reproduction of native Irish speech. At the time, when Irish was being replaced by English as the dominant language, Carleton records the speech of country people in which English is spoken in the syntax of the native Irish. As Thomas Flanagan* notes in *The Irish Novelists 1800–1850,* ''Half a century before John Synge* put his ear to a Wicklow floor to catch the talk of servant girls, Carleton had caught every turn and nuance of Irish speech.'' Several generations later, when the writers of the Irish renaissance sought to reproduce peasant speech, they found a mentor in William Carleton.

JAMES KILROY

WORKS: *Father Butler; The Lough Derg Pilgrim.* Dublin: Wm. Curry, 1829; *Traits and Stories of the Irish Peasantry.* 2 vols. Dublin: Wm. Curry, 1830; *Traits and Stories of the Irish Peasantry, 2nd Series.* 3 vols. Dublin: W. F. Wakeman, 1833; *Tales of Ireland.* Dublin: Curry/London: Simpkin & Marshall, 1834; *Fardorougha the Miser; or, The Convicts of Lisnamona.* Dublin: Wm. Curry, 1839; *The Fawn of Springvale, The Clarionet and Other Tales.* Dublin: Wm. Curry, 1841; *Art Maguire; or, The Broken Pledge.* Dublin: J. Duffy, 1845; *Parra Sastha; or, The History of Paddy-Go-Easy and His Wife Nancy.* Dublin: J. Duffy, 1845; *Rody the Rover; or, The Ribbonman.* Dublin: J. Duffy, 1845; *Tales and Sketches.* Dublin: J. Duffy, 1845. Later called *Tales and Stories of the Irish Peasantry; Valentine McClutchy, the Irish Agent; or, Chronicles of the Castle Cumber Property.* 3 vols. Dublin: J. Duffy, 1845; *The Black Prophet, A Tale of Irish Famine.* Belfast: Simms & McIntyre, 1847; *The Emigrants of Ahadarra, A Tale of Irish Life.* London & Belfast: Simms & McIntyre, 1848; *The Tithe Procter, a Novel. Being a Tale of the Tithe Rebellion in Ireland.* London: Simms & McIntyre, 1848; *Red Hall; or, The Baronet's Daughter.* 3 vols. London: Saunders & Otley, 1852/revised as *The Black Baronet.* Dublin: J. Duffy, 1857; *The Squanders of Castle Squander.* 2 vols. London: Illustrated London Library, 1852; *Willy Reilly and His Dear Colleen Bawn.* 3 vols. London: Hope, 1855; *The Evil Eye; or, The Black Spectre.* Dublin: J. Duffy, 1860; *The Double Prophecy; or, Trials of the Heart.* Dublin: J. Duffy, 1862; *Redmond, Count O'Hanlon, The Irish Rapparee.* Dublin: J. Duffy, 1862; *The Silver Acre and Other Tales.* London: Ward & Lock, 1862; *The Fair of Emyvale, and the Master and Scholar.* London: Ward, Lock & Tyler, 1870; *The Red-Haired Man's Wife.* Dublin: Sealy, Bryers/London: Simpkin & Marshall, 1889; *The Autobiography of William Carleton.* London: MacGibbon & Kee, 1968. REFERENCES: Boué, André. *William Carleton 1794–1869, romancier irlandais.* Paris: Publications de la Sorbonne, Imprimerie Nationale, 1978; Chesnutt, Margaret. *Studies in the Short Stories of William Carleton.* Göteborg: Gothenburg Studies in English 34, 1976; Flanagan, Thomas. *The Irish Novelists 1800–1850.* New York: Columbia University Press, 1959, pp. 255–330; Hayley, Barbara. *Carleton's Traits and Stories and the Nineteenth-Century Anglo-Irish Tradition.* Gerrards Cross: Colin Smythe, 1983; Hayley, Barbara. *A Bibliography of the Writings of William Carleton.* Gerrards Cross: Colin Smythe, 1985; Kiely, Benedict. *Poor Scholar. A Study of the Works and Days of William Carleton.* London: Sheed &

Ward, 1947/New York: Sheed & Ward, 1948; O'Donoghue, David J. *The Life of William Carleton: Being His Autobiography and Letters; and an Account of His Life and Writings from the Point at Which the Autobiography Breaks Off.* 2 vols. London: Downey, 1896; Shaw, Rose. "Carleton in His Own Country." In *Carleton's Country.* Dublin & Cork: Talbot, 1930, pp. 83–111; Sullivan, Eileen A. *William Carleton.* Boston: Twayne, 1983; Wolff, Robert Lee. *William Carleton. Irish Peasant Novelist.* New York: Garland, 1981.

CARNDUFF, THOMAS (1886–1956), poet and playwright. Carnduff, socialist and Orangeman, was born in Belfast, the son of an invalided army corporal and Jane (formerly) Bollard. The endemic of working-class life in Belfast was deepened by his father's rapid decline into ill health, ending in mental dissolution. The boy became an apprentice printer and served in the First World War. On his return he worked in the Belfast shipyards and later found employment as a binman. Carnduff was prominent in the Independent Orange Order, acting as master of an independent lodge in the 1920s and 1930s. He was instrumental in establishing the Belfast Poetry Circle in 1926 and the Ulster Society in 1936. During the Second World War, he joined civil defense. Twice married, with four sons by his first wife, who died in 1939, he lived on Hanover Street and was employed as caretaker at Linen Hall Library in his later years.

Carnduff's writings consistently express working-class sympathies and an affinity with the republican politics of radical Presbyterianism in Ulster—a literary consistency that he represented in Sean O'Faolain's* "Ulster Issue" of *The Bell** in July 1941. He later contributed articles such as "Belfast as an Irish City" to *The Bell* under the editorship of Peadar O'Donnell.* In the collections *Poverty Street* (1921), *Songs from the Shipyards* (1924), and *Songs of an Out-of-Work* (1932), his verse mixes political realism ("Ballad of the Hammer," "Riots, 1921") with pride in Ulster industry ("The Ship") and sentimental Irish patriotism ("Dear Little Shamrock"), as well as rather stagey verses on the horrors of Ypres. The dominant manner of *ballade engagée* is akin to that of the working-class and soldier songs by Patrick McGill.*

His socialist play *Workers,* which appeared at the Abbey* in 1932, is now extant in an incomplete stage-copy only. Others were *Machinery* (1933), *Traitors* (1934), *Castlereagh* (1934), and *The Stars Foretell* (1938), each staged in Belfast and Dublin. In 1937, Carnduff collaborated with Denis Johnston* on *Birth of a Giant,* a radio documentary about shipbuilding. Selections from his writings were reprinted in 1994 with an introductory biography by the Linen Hall librarian John Gray, following on the appearance of a selection of his poetry the year before.

BRUCE STEWART

WORKS: *Songs from the Shipyards and Other Poems.* Belfast: E. H. Thornton, [1924]; *Songs of an Out-of-Work.* Belfast: Quota, 1932; *Poverty Street and Other Poems.* Belfast: Lapwing, 1993; *Thomas Carnduff: Life and Writings.* John Gray, ed. Belfast: Lagan, 1994.

CARNEY, FRANK (1902–?), playwright. Carney was born in County Galway and educated in Tuam and at the National University. He was a civil servant in the Old Age Pensions Department. The Abbey* produced three of his plays: *They Went by Bus* (1939), *Peeping Tom* (1940), and *The Righteous Are Bold* (1946). The Gate produced another, *The Doctor's Boy* (1942). *They Went by Bus* was mildly notable for having a scene set in the interior of a bus, but *The Righteous Are Bold* proved a considerable popular success. This is a play about a young and innocent Irish girl who goes to England and becomes possessed by the devil. As Peter Kavanagh remarked, ''The bedevilled girl breaks so many statues and crucifixes on the stage while the priest is attempting to exorcise the spirit, that a well-known wit in Dublin, asked why he did not go to see the play, replied that a friend of his had gone and had got a splinter in his eye.'' The play still gets the occasional amateur production even in the mid-1990s.

WORKS: *Bolt from the Blue.* Dublin: James Duffy, 1950. (Adaptation of Temple Lane's novel, *Friday's Well*); *The Righteous Are Bold.* Dublin: James Duffy, 1959.

CARR, HUGH (ca. 1940–   ), playwright and novelist. Carr was born in Dunkineely, County Donegal. He studied at the Royal Irish Academy of Music and from 1962 to 1988 was a civil servant. His short stories have been broadcast by Radio Éireann, and his play *The Life and Times of Benvenuto Cellini* was presented by the Abbey.* His one published play, *Encounter in the Wilderness* (1980), is a retelling of the Heloise and Abelard story. His novel *Voices from a Far Country* (1995) is an account of a boy growing up in a South Donegal village during the 1940s and of his family, friends, and neighbors. The narrative is made up of short, disconnected vignettes arranged in the order they chronologically happened. People talk, argue, gossip, drink, play, marry, die, even commit suicide; and a kind of conclusion is reached when the boy's family moves away. Alternately funny, sad, and nostalgic, the narrative is simply told and beautifully observed.

Carr is the father of the playwright Marina Carr.*

WORKS: *Encounter in the Wilderness.* Newark, Del.: Proscenium, [1980]. (Two-act play); *Voices from a Far Country.* Belfast: Blackstaff, 1995. (Novel).

CARR, MARINA (1964–   ), playwright. Carr was born on November 17, 1964, in Dublin and, one of seven children of Hugh Carr,* was raised in County Offaly in a town called Pallas Lake near Tullamore. She read English and philosophy at University College, Dublin. Subsequently, she moved to New York City and taught first grade at Saint Anselm's Catholic School in Brooklyn for a year. She lives now in Dublin. Her staged work includes *Low in the Dark* (1989), produced by the Crooked Sixpence Theatre Company in the Project; *Deers Surrender* (1990), produced by the Gaiety School for Acting in the Andrews Lane Theatre, Dublin; *This Love Thing* (1991), staged in Belfast and Dublin; *Ullaloo* (1991), staged at the Peacock; and *The Mai* (1994), which was staged at the Peacock for the Dublin Theatre Festival and which won the Best New Irish Play Award. She has also won a Hennessy Award for her story ''Grow Mermaid.''

Her published plays include *Low in the Dark* and *The Mai.* The style of the production of *Low in the Dark,* its characters, its staging techniques, sparse scenery, and dialogue are reminiscent of Samuel Beckett's* work. However, the play is quite original, using Beckett's work as a model for Carr's themes of gendering and gender relations. It is quite a funny play. The characters communicate their misguided impressions rather than listen to each other. The male characters seem particularly clueless. Even in their efforts to escape from their gendering tropes, they imprison themselves in their perceptions. The female characters, although on the surface as clueless as the male figures, managed to produce and rewrite mythologies almost half-consciously. They work from sources taken from modern and ancient models, including Beckett's plays, the Christ story, the Oisin legend, and the Athena myth.

BERNARD McKENNA

WORKS: *Low in the Dark* in *The Crack in the Emerald.* Selected & introduced by David Grant. London: Nick Hern Books, 1990; *The Mai.* [Oldcastle, Co. Meath]: Gallery, [1995].

CARROLL, PAUL VINCENT (1900–1968), playwright. Carroll was born on July 10, 1900, at Blackrock, near Dundalk in County Louth, migrated to Scotland at the age of twenty-one, and taught school in Glasgow for sixteen years until success as a playwright enabled him to devote full time to writing. Although *Things That Are Caesar's* (1932) won an Abbey Theatre* prize, his first outstanding play was *Shadow and Substance,* produced at the Abbey in 1937. In America, it won the New York Drama Critics Circle Award for the best foreign play of the 1937–1938 season. In 1939, *The White Steed* also won the New York Critics Circle Award. Although Carroll had been active in the Scottish theatre, he settled permanently in England in 1945 and wrote film and television scenarios, as well as plays. The most significant of his later works was the satirical extravaganza *The Devil Came from Dublin* (1951). Carroll died of a heart attack at his home in Bromley, Kent, on October 20, 1968.

Most of Carroll's dramas were strongly influenced by Ibsen, and his most successful work was in the genre of the ''well-made play.'' He evinced a strong didactic strain, attempting to stimulate thought and to reform people through the medium of the stage. *Things That Are Caesar's* sounds a recurring conflict in Carroll's works: the struggle between materialism and man's higher aspirations. Julia and Peter Hardy struggle against each other with their daughter Eilish as prize. Julia hypocritically schemes for a loveless marriage, compromise, and mediocrity, while the scholarly and sensitive Peter wants Eilish to be a free spirit, to obtain vision, to develop her individuality, and illuminate the way for others. Julia wins the battle, and although Carroll later revised the play and allowed Eilish to escape from an uninspiring materialistic life, the revised version lacks verisimilitude.

Shadow and Substance focuses on the conflict between Canon Skerritt and schoolmaster Dermot O'Flingsley. Both are idealistic and talented figures who are scarred by hubris. They are contrasted strikingly with the gentle, innocent, and saintly servant girl Brigid. Her warm humanity and spiritual humility bring the two antagonists to an awareness of their shortcomings, but only after Brigid is accidentally killed. Throughout the play, Carroll insists that goodness, faith, and unselfish love are the redeeming virtues of mankind. He contends that the world can improve only when individual hearts become innocent and pure and allow their love to overflow upon humanity.

In *The White Steed,* Father Shaughnessy violates Carroll's credo of love and generosity. Shaughnessy, a rabid puritan and vigilante, is finally overcome by a gentle and humane Canon Lavelle and by Nora Fintry, a spirited librarian who symbolizes Niam, the beloved of Ossian in the ancient Irish legend. Niam is the past spirit of Ireland that will not accept servitude. Her struggle, like Carroll's, is to attain beauty and joy, tolerance and goodness, as well as a reasonable use of freedom.

After *The White Steed,* Carroll went through a period when he permitted his didactic bent to overwhelm his writing. In plays such as *Kindred* (1939) and *The Old Foolishness* (1940), Carroll turns to murky allegory and symbolism which renders his work excessively sentimental and melodramatic. Carroll became bogged down in "philosophical dustbins" and foggy characterizations. Thus, Carroll was working counter to his strengths as a playwright: stinging, pungent, precise dialogue uttered by well-delineated characters who performed in a realistic milieu impregnated with wit, satire, and irony. Without these qualities his lesser work, although always containing some effective passages, becomes vague, and his call for love and generosity and his emphasis on the artistic spirit and the creative mind become simplistic, maudlin, and farfetched.

Near the end of his active career, Carroll wrote two carefree satiric comedies—*The Devil Came from Dublin* and *The Wayward Saint* (1955). Although *The Devil* is the stronger of the two plays, both are merry and perceptive romps full of rollicking satiric humor and delicious observations of the foibles and contradictions of human nature.

Carroll's reputation as a significant dramatist is assured by *Shadow and Substance* and *The White Steed.* In addition to having created several memorable characters, Carroll has drawn the most varied and convincing portraits of Irish clergymen and clerical life ever presented on the stage. Furthermore, at the top of his form, Carroll was one of the wittiest and talented masters of satiric and ironic dialogue and commentary which the Irish theatre has produced.

PAUL A. DOYLE

WORKS: *Things That Are Caesar's.* London: Rich & Cowan, 1934; *Shadow and Substance.* New York: Random House, 1937/London: Macmillan, 1938; *The White Steed and Coggerers.* New York: Random House, 1939; *Plays for My Children.* New York: Julian Messner, 1939. (Contains "The King Who Could Not Laugh," "His Excellency—the Governor," "St. Francis and the Wolf," "Beauty Is Fled," "Death Closes All," and "Maker of the Roads," each short play published separately by Samuel French in London in 1947); *The Old Foolishness.* London: Samuel French, 1944; *Three Plays: The White Steed, Things That Are Caesar's, The Strings, My Lord, Are False.* London: Macmillan, 1944; *Green Cars Go East.* London: Samuel French, 1947; *Interlude.* London: Samuel French, 1947; *Conspirators.* London: Samuel French, 1947/earlier titled *Coggerers; The*

Wise Have Not Spoken. London: Samuel French, 1947/New York: Dramatists Play Service, 1954; *Two Plays: The Wise Have Not Spoken—Shadow and Substance.* London: Macmillan, 1948; *The Wayward Saint.* New York: Dramatists Play Service, 1955; *Irish Stories and Plays.* New York: Devin-Adair, 1958. (Contains a full-length play *The Devil Came from Dublin,* the short plays *The Conspirators, Beauty Is Fled,* and *Interlude,* and eight stories); *Farewell to Greatness.* Dixon, Calif.: Proscenium, 1966; *Goodbye to the Summer.* Newark, Del.: Proscenium, 1970; *The Journal of Irish Literature* (January 1972). (A Paul Vincent Carroll number, containing *We Have Ceased to Live,* a full-length play, as well as some letters and an interview); *Shadow and Substance.* Acting ed. New York: Dramatists Play Service, 1990; *The Wise Have Not Spoken.* Acting ed. New York: Dramatists Play Service, 1990. REFERENCES: Conway, John D. "Paul Vincent Carroll's Major Dramatic Triumphs." *Connecticut Review* 6 (1973): 161–169; Doyle, Paul A. *Paul Vincent Carroll.* Lewisburg, Pa.: Bucknell University Press, 1971; Hogan, Robert. "Paul Vincent Carroll: The Rebel as Prodigal Son." In *After the Irish Renaissance.* Minneapolis: University of Minnesota Press, 1967/ London: Macmillan, 1968; Pallette, Drew. "Paul Vincent—Since *The White Steed.*" *Modern Drama* 7 (February 1965): 375–381.

CARSON, CIARAN (1948–), poet. Carson was born in Belfast, and his first language was Irish. He studied at Queen's University, Belfast, was a civil servant and teacher, and then became traditional arts officer with the Arts Council of Northern Ireland. In 1976, the year his *The New Estate* was published, he won a Gregory Award. Much of the language in that early book is unadorned to the point of being simply flat, almost monosyllabic prose. The occasional metaphors are much needed and stand out in bold relief. The language of his later volumes is richer, more individual, and usually written in extremely long lines. *The Irish for No* (1987) won the Alice Hunt Bartlett Award. *Belfast Confetti* (1989) was short-listed for the Irish Book Award for Literature, the Whitbread Poetry Award, and the Christopher Ewart-Biggs Literary Prize and won the *Irish Times*-Aer Lingus Irish Literature Prize for Poetry. His current reputation is probably well summed up by John Banville's* remark that he "is one of the most original poets now at work in this country."

Belfast Confetti, which A. S. Byatt called "a marvellous work of art . . . full of surprises, savage, and witty, human and extravagant," is probably Carson's work with the broadest popular appeal. It is, of course, about Belfast and particularly its modern troubles. The book contains several prose passages, most of which seem attempts to give a sense of the city's past and growth. They are not written in what used to be called prose poetry, that rather lush language with little poetic control, but simply in casual, modern, first-person prose. Hence, they may prove something of an oasis for the reader who does not read much poetry. If not poetry themselves, however, they are an integral part of the book.

The poems themselves are about life in the violent present, and their most obvious characteristic is the length of the lines, which may go to seventeen or nineteen syllables without any notable rhythmical pattern. The diction is often arresting but nevertheless retains the flavor of casual speech, of a distinct individual's voice. That quality and the subject matter make for a wider appeal than does *First Language* of 1993.

Some poems in the later book effectively use rhyme or at least similarity of sound at the end of their long lines, although Carson's obeisance to form is more a distant nod than a genuflection. The only connection, for instance, between the poems called ''Sonnets'' and the sonnet form is that they have fourteen lines. The various translations—although more so from Baudelaire and Rimbaud than from Ovid—are less translations than loose but breezily written variations on a theme. The strength of Carson's later work is probably that of a flip, quirky, quite modern, and often distinctive diction.

WORKS: *The Insular Celts.* Belfast: Ulsterman, 1973; *The New Estate.* Belfast: Blackstaff/Winston-Salem, N.C.: Wake Forest University Press, 1976/enlarged ed., 1988; *The Pocket Guide to Irish Traditional Music.* Belfast: Appletree, 1986. (Nonfiction); *The Irish for No.* Dublin: Gallery/Winston-Salem, N.C.: Wake Forest University Press, 1987; *Belfast Confetti.* Belfast: Blackstaff, 1989; *First Language: Poems.* [Oldcastle, Co. Meath]: Gallery[1993]/Winston-Salem, N.C.: Wake Forest University Press, 1994; *Letters from the Alphabet.* [Oldcastle, Co. Meath]: Gallery, 1995. REFERENCE: ''Ciaran Carson Interviewed by Rand Brandes.'' *Irish Review* 8 (1990): 77–90.

CARY, [ARTHUR] JOYCE [LUNEL] (1888–1957), novelist. Cary was born on December 7, 1888, in Londonderry. His family had come to Ireland during Elizabeth's reign, and for generations had been respected landlords on the Inishowen Peninsula in Donegal. By the time of Cary's youth, the family fortunes had disappeared, and he was raised mainly in England, ultimately becoming one of the most admired of modern English novelists. Although Cary's best known works, such as *The Horse's Mouth* and *Mr. Johnson,* are set in England or Africa, he spent much time in his youth in Donegal, and his experiences there are used in two of his minor works, *Castle Corner* (1938) and *A House of Children* (1941). While neither book is without interest, neither is among Cary's best work. *Castle Corner,* a sprawling chronicle novel intended as the first of a trilogy, depicts the fortunes of an Anglo-Irish landowning family in the years around the turn of this century. Part of the novel is set in Donegal, part in England, and part in Africa. Although the entire book lacks real form, the Donegal sections are done with considerable intensity. *A House of Children* is not so much a novel as a narrative depicting several years in the childhood and young adulthood of a number of characters connected with the landowning class in Donegal. The book reflects much of Cary's own youth and is often lovingly evocative, but it lacks strong characterization and much narrative thrust. Nevertheless, as a view of the landlord class in a time now irretrievably gone, Cary's two Irish books will always be of significance in the literature of Ireland. *A House of Children* won the James Tait Black Memorial Prize in 1941.

Cary died on March 29, 1957, in Oxford.

WORKS: The best edition of Cary's work is the Carfax edition, begun in 1950 by Michael Joseph in London. REFERENCES: Allen, Walter. *Joyce Cary.* London: Longmans, Green, 1953/revised 1954 & 1956. Writers and Their Work pamphlet, No. 41; Bishop, Alan. *Gentleman Rider, A Life of Joyce Cary.* London: Michael Joseph, [1988]; Bloom, Robert. *The Indeterminate World. A Study of the Novels of Joyce Cary.* Philadelphia: University of Pennsylvania Press, [1964]; Cook, Cornelia. *Joyce Cary: Liberal Principles.* London: Vision, 1981; Fisher, Barbara. *Joyce Cary: The Writer and His Theme.* Gerrards Cross: Colin Smythe, 1980; Fisher, Barbara, ed. *Joyce Cary Remembered: In Letters and Interviews by His Family and Others.* Gerrards Cross: Colin Smythe, [1988]; Foster, Malcolm. *Joyce Cary, a Biography.* Boston: Houghton Mifflin, 1968; Hall, Dennis. *Joyce Cary: A Reappraisal.* London: Macmillan, 1983; Hoffman, Charles G. *Joyce Cary: The Comedy of Freedom.* [Pittsburgh]: University of Pittsburgh Press, [1964]; Larson, Golden L. *The Dark Descent. Social Change and Moral Responsibility in the Novels of Joyce Cary.* London: Michael Joseph, 1965; Makinen, Merja. *Joyce Cary: A Descriptive Bibliography.* London: Mansell, 1989; Wright, Andrew H. *Joyce Cary: A Preface to His Novels.* London: Chatto & Windus, 1958.

CASEY, ELIZABETH OWENS BLACKBURNE. *See* BLACKBURNE, E. OWENS.

CASEY, JOHN KEEGAN (1846–1870), poet. It is indeed easy to say that John Keegan Casey, the young Fenian, was a perfectly dreadful poet. Nevertheless, anyone capable of such a stirring ballad as "The Rising of the Moon" is worth some scrutiny.

Casey was born, the son of a peasant farmer, at Mount Dalton near Mullingar, on April 22, 1846. Despite poverty and hardship, he applied himself to study, and his first poem appeared in *The Nation** under his pseudonym of "Leo" when he was only sixteen. He became a mercantile clerk, but published enough verse to issue his first collection when he was only twenty. In 1867, he was arrested for his connection with Fenianism and for a time imprisoned. It is said that his sufferings in prison weakened him; he was seized with a hemorrhage of the lungs and died on March 17, 1870. His funeral is said to have been attended by fifty thousand people. This great throng may be attributed not merely to political feeling, but also to the extraordinary popularity of Casey's verses.

He is a popular poet, and his themes are the appealing ones of heroic patriotism and romantic, often blighted love. He has hardly a poem which is not marred by the clichés of popular writing, and even "Mairé My Girl," which Padraic Colum* thought enough of to anthologize, has at least one stanza that lapses into clichéd thinness. Nevertheless, if one looks closely, one can discern lines and stanzas in Casey's work which presaged, with the growth of knowledge and taste, a real poet. One can discern not merely a graceful mellifluousness, as in "Song of the Golden-Headed Niamh," but occasionally an utter tightness, as in this stanza from "Mairé My Girl":

> Down upon Claris heath
>   Shines the soft berry,
> On the brown harvest tree
>   Droops the red cherry;
> Sweeter thy honey lips,
>   Softer the curl
> Straying adown thy cheeks,
>   Mairé my girl.

WORKS: *A Wreath of Shamrocks: Ballads, Songs and Legends.* Dublin: McGee, 1866; *The Rising of the Moon, and Other Ballads, Songs and Legends.* Glasgow: Cameron & Ferguson, 1869; *Rel-*

iques of John K. Casey ("Leo"), Eugene David, ed. Dublin: Pigott, 1878. Davis's biographical and critical introduction on pages 1–54 is the fullest account of Casey's life and work.

CASEY, JUANITA (1925–   ), novelist, short story writer, and poet. Casey was born on October 10, 1925, in England. Her mother, Annie Maloney, was an Irish traveler or tinker who died when her daughter was born. Her father was Jobey Smith, an English Romany who disappeared when she was a year old. Her early life was divided between private boarding schools and the circus; and her circus background explains her deep affection for animals, particularly horses. She became horse master for Robert Brothers Circus and even succeeded in training that most recalcitrant beast, a zebra. She has been married three times—to an English farmer, a Swedish sculptor, and an Irish journalist—and has had a child from each marriage.

Casey turned to writing late, first publishing and illustrating a book of rather amateurish but highly individual short stores called *Hath the Rain a Father?* in 1966. A slim volume of verse with two more drawings, *Horse by the River,* followed in 1968. Her short and highly acclaimed novel *The Horse of Selene* appeared in 1971 and was followed by her novel *The Circus* in 1974. *A Sampling,* a slim collection of stories and poems, appeared in 1981, and *Eternity Smith,* a second collection of poems, appeared in 1985. In recent years, she has lived in Devonshire.

The evocative prose of her novels is more lyrical than her poetry, which is usually casual, even conversational free verse. Nevertheless, she has a quite individual poetic voice, and some of her verse, such as "And Thrips to You Too" from *Eternity Smith,* is extremely funny, a rare quality among contemporary Irish poets.

Casey's two novels are written with a vibrant feeling for language and achieve extraordinary moments of lyrical beauty. The primacy of words in her fictional technique may be suggested by her remarks about *The Circus:*

You know when you were young—before words really sort of crystallized and formed—you used to listen to grownups talking and the words used to flow over you. You'd get a word like "ambulance." It's a beautiful word, and you can see it in colors. So I tried to write this book where words, really, are meaningless and meaningless and meaningful at the same time. It's very, very difficult. It's a step forward from the early work, the stories, as different as the later James Joyce is from the early Joyce. It's about a kid who wants to go to the circus and never gets there. When she finally does, I won't say what happens, but it's completely, utterly spoiled. Words are beginning to harden into their real meanings. . . . Words are so extraordinary! And yet you have the awful feeling that they're not meaning anything at all. They go on and on—words being bastardized. They come out of newspapers at you and out of loudspeakers, and you suddenly see a swallow overhead not saying a fucking thing.

If Casey's novels have a major fault, it is that their plots are rather tenuous and tend to be overwhelmed by the lushness of the prose.

Casey's real strength in language is not lyric, but comic, and it is probably at its best in her uncollected short stories, which have a quirkiness of view and a rich whimsicality that have hardly been seen in Irish writing since Flann O'Brien/Myles na Gopaleen. For instance, there is the beginning of her inimitable story "O Come, O Come, Emmanuel":

Death! cried Emmanuel McGuirk, gardener.
    He pronounced it debt!
    And two slugs, vertically locked in slimy bliss, were cut off from all further enjoyment of one of life's supreme moments, reduced to a liquified Romeo and Juliet by the scandalized heel of his boot.
    He had not seen God, Who Had Had a Thought.
    How Very Pleasant, Thought God, To See A Garden Again. Not Eden, Of Course, A Bad Business, That. O, A Sad Business. A Let-Down. (You will note that God thought in capitals.)

Casey never became a disciplined writer, but she is an amateur of most individual brilliance. She has published much too little, but she has had a good deal else on her mind. She once described her idea of bliss as composed of "crystals, minerals, rocks, and fossils," and she also noted that she was "extremely active in quarries, fields containing fauna, angels, tramps, and silence."

WORKS: *Hath the Rain a Father?* London: Phoenix House, 1966. (Stories); *Horse by the River, and Other Poems.* Dublin: Dolmen, 1968; *The Horse of Selene.* [Dublin]: Dolmen/London: Calder & Boyars, 1971/New York: Grossman, 1972. (Novel); A Juanita Casey Number, *The Journal of Irish Literature* 1 (September 1972): 41–71; *The Circus.* Dublin: Dolmen, 1974/Nantucket, Mass.: Longship, 1978. (Novel); *A Sampling.* [Newark, Del.]: Proscenium, [1981]. (Stories & poems); *Eternity Smith.* [Mountrath, Co. Laois]: Dolmen, [1985]. (Poems). REFERENCE: Henderson, Gordon. "An Interview with Juanita Casey" in *Journal of Irish Literature* 1 (September 1972): 41–54.

CASEY, KEVIN [FRANCIS] (1940–   ), novelist and playwright. Casey was born in Kells, County Meath, on December 5, 1940, and was educated at the Christian Brothers school in Kells and at Blackrock College, County Dublin. He is married to the poet Eavan Boland.* When the Abbey* presented his play *The Living and the Lost* in 1962, he became the youngest author to be produced by the theater. His *Not with a Bang* was produced at the Dublin Theatre Festival in 1965, but he is best known as an intelligent and craftsmanlike novelist.

As a novelist, Casey is probably more esteemed than enjoyed, for the attitudes behind his books range only from the greyly bleak to the blackly pessimistic. The blackest in tone is his first novel, *The Sinner's Bell* (1968), which is a study of a young marriage in a small town in Meath. The characters are well drawn, and the writing is crisp, lean, clear, and exact in detail. However, probably not one detail in the entire book is affirmatively described. If it is coffee, the taste is strange; if it is tea, it is lukewarm and the taste is rankly tannic; if it is bread, it is becoming stale and the edges are beginning to curl; if it is weather, it is inevitably raining or about to rain; and if it is people, they are faithless, crude, ugly, blotchy, pimply, and afflicted with boils, drunkenness in its last stages, hatred, guilt, apathy, inadequacy, or despair. Indeed, the one sympathetic character, the young wife, has become so indoctrinated by the author's view by the end of the novel that her last reflection about having a baby is that it "would be years before the baby could learn to hate her." That savage glumness, only slightly tempered by pity, is the impelling view of this well-crafted, card-stacked novel.

Casey's second novel, *A Sense of Survival* (1974), is very much in the sour tradition of what Graham Greene called "an Entertainment." Indeed, the novel is so reminiscent of Greene that it seems almost a pastiche. It is set in a remote and exotic place, Tangier; it has a background of sordid intrigue and violence; and its descriptive details are, once again, inevitably depressing. Flakes of plaster fall from walls, a bicycle rusts in the street, flowers decay, a cat is strangled. Perhaps the chief difference between this novel and a Greene entertainment is that Casey's plot is much more in the background and is almost submerged by the emphasis on the limply developed non-love story. Lacking real narrative tension, the book, then, seems more of an able exercise in illustrating a despairing attitude. One would not readily return to a contemplation of these well-caught, sad, seedy, baffled characters.

Dreams of Revenge (1977) is a much less academic exercise. Basically, the novel seems an exploration of guilt and of mixed motives in personal relations. That sound and perceptive insight comes across with considerable power, and the plot is in bolder relief than the plot of *A Sense of Survival* or the simple accumulating chronology of *The Sinner's Bell*. If the novel has notable faults, they might be these two: one incident, in which the hero is apprehended and beaten by Provos in Belfast, is rather farfetched; and some passages of the generally excellent dialogue between hero and heroine do seem a bit too clever and overly long. Nevertheless, the descriptive details are not so horrifically stacked in this novel, and the investigation of the very three-dimensional hero is a distinct achievement. It provides a more intelligent, if dour, insight into the way people act than one is accustomed to from novels.

Among the new fiction writers of the 1970s, Kevin Casey seems perhaps the most conscious of his craft. Although steeped in gloom, his books are careful and polished. He has published no more of them in recent years.

WORKS: *The Sinner's Bell*. London: Faber, 1968; ed., *Winter's Tales from Ireland 2*. Dublin: Gill & Macmillan/[Newark, Del.]: Proscenium, [1972]. (Anthology of stories); *A Sense of Survival*. London: Faber, 1974; *Dreams of Revenge*. London: Faber, 1977.

CASEY, MICHAEL G. (fl. 1990s), novelist. Casey was educated in New Ross, Co. Wexford, and later studied economics at University College, Dublin, and at Cambridge. He worked for EC committees in Brussels and for the International Monetary Fund in Washington, D.C. His novel, *Come Home, Robbie* (1990) concerns brainwashing by a religious sect.

WORKS: *Come Home, Robbie*. Dublin: O'Brien, [1990].

CASEY, PHILIP (1950–   ), poet, playwright, and novelist. Casey was born in London and grew up in Hollyfort, a village near Gorey, County Wexford. He lives in Dublin and is a member of Aosdána.* Casey's first published work, *The Planets and Stars Become Friends,* was brought out at the Funge Art Centre in 1974. This volume was one of a series of chapbooks published during the Gorey Arts Festival, which, under the direction of Paul Funge, ran from 1970 to 1982—a summer cultural event in which Casey frequently participated. Casey has traveled widely, principally to Spain and Germany. His play *The Cardinal* was premiered in Hamburg in 1990. Casey has worked as a book reviewer, most often for the *Sunday Press.* He is an introverted poet of quality. His tone is contemporary: mildly liberal, slightly rueful, evenly paced. However, the reader senses a background of ill health and fatigue. He is a European poet, especially open to Continental and Central post-World War II methodologies. When he does touch on local subjects, he appears to gain in effectiveness, as in the steered long poem "The Irish Wait." His "Looking through the Gates of Mount St. Benedict" comes off as a crafted poetic discourse, using folk history. The accomplished "Tom Moore's Romantic Dancehall" defines the operations of a local psyche. This outline poem, opening up again the silvery eloquence of the modern Irish voice, is reprinted, with thirteen other poems from *After Thunder,* in *The Year of the Knife.* The later poetry in this volume is hewn from rigorous material. The sentiment is edged forward by the energy of the content. There are vignettes here of brothers and rural places, quietly drawn and sunk in memory. "Feasting and Country Western Song" marks the kind of cultural time the reader finds in Casey's somewhat skeptical stance. The surreal option is open but sometimes appears more harmonic than spontaneous. "Answering Each Other," a poem reminiscent of 1930s speech in line breaks, is a clever account of a railway excursion that progresses beyond its original delineation. Casey's poetics is evocative without being unnecessarily contrite.

JAMES LIDDY

WORKS: *The Planets and Stars Become Friends.* Gorey, Co. Wexford: Funge Art Centre, 1974; *Those Distant Summers.* Dublin: Raven Arts, 1980; *After Thunder.* Dublin: Raven Arts/Gerrards Cross: Colin Smythe, 1985; *The Year of the Knife: Poems 1980–1990.* [Dublin]: Raven Arts, [1991]; *The Fabulists.* [Dublin]: Lilliput, [1994]. (Novel).

CASEY, W[ILLIAM] F[RANCIS] (1884–1957), journalist, novelist, and playwright. Casey was born in Capetown, on May 2, 1884, educated at Trinity College, Dublin, and called to the bar in 1909. In 1908, his plays *The Man Who Missed the Tide* and *The Suburban Groove* were performed at the Abbey Theatre* and remained popular pieces in the repertoire for about ten years. *The Man Who Missed the Tide,* a serious study of failure and drunkenness, introduced a brilliant young actor, Fred O'Donovan. *The Suburban Groove* was a comic and satiric dissection of middle-class society in the then-posh Dublin suburb of Rathmines; it was also one of the first Abbey plays of note to break away from the subject of the Irish peasant.

Casey went to London in about 1910, first as a free-lance journalist, and then during the war as a sporting correspondent for *The Times*. He later became a knowledgeable foreign correspondent for *The Times* in Washington, Paris, and elsewhere, and finally the editor of the paper. "No editor," writes A. P. Robbins, "was better loved." He retired in 1952 and died in London on April 20, 1957.

Neither of Casey's plays has been published, but, despite their popularity, they seem to have had more theatrical than literary merit. He published three novels which were rather promising, but the busy life of a professional journalist kept him away from literature.

WORKS: *Zoe*. London: Herbert & Daniel, 1911; *Haphazard*. London: Constable, 1917; *Private Life of a Successful Man*. London: Dent, 1935.

CAVANAGH, MAEVE (fl. 1912–1932), poet and playwright. Cavanagh wrote poetry in the early decades of this century. She also wrote one three-act play, which was published in 1925. Most of her published work is propagandist, extolling the nationalist cause, sometimes with sharp invective. In his preface to her collection, *Soul and Clay* (1917), F. R. Higgins* wrote: "This book is not intended for a work of Art: our poetess simply sings for the Irish democracy, expresses her personal feelings and holds communion with those of her friends who have kept their tryst with Death. . . . Miss Cavanagh inclines her ear to the soul of Infinitude."

Her work weaves between the concerns of the public persona of the militant nationalist imbued with the philosophy of heroic self-sacrifice and those of the private persona of the woman trapped in her societal role and struggling for more:

> I scorn their fettered safety
> I loathe the tasks of each dull day—
> I want the best and worst to see
> Before my sun shall wane away.
>
> The great adventurous road to tread,
> Where even through all the aeons passed,
> The wilds—where wander-lust had led,
> To live and feel life deep and vast.
>
> Instead I sweep and wash and sew
> And walk to chapel once a week—
> The life I want they do not know,
> To them I am but fool or freak.

The poems often descend into sentimentality and occasionally burst into real passion or have a wistful Hardyesque quality, particularly those set at Lough Cutra, County Galway, and those that deal with her overcircumscribed existence. However, when she is being flagrantly political and propagandist, her work is characterized by strong invective as, for example, when she attempts to shame the "hireling," Francis Ledwidge,* "clad in the livery of Ireland's foe."

Her play, *In Time of the Tans,* is dedicated to "the men and women in the ranks." Set in a middle-class conservative family home, it shows the younger members' involvement with the revolutionaries and the dangers to which this exposes the family. It reflects a variety of attitudes to rebellion and war. While, on one hand, Christ-like idealistic pursuit of a goal is applauded, we are also invited to ponder the recognition that "war will brutalize and harden the greatest nature" and to realize that when the foreigner has been defeated, "we'll have to start then and fight the sweaters and the gombeen men and the profiteers." Women are seen in the play as those who "learn to suffer and endure," who will be lonely for their dead heroes but who "don't count where the Republic is concerned."

MARY BALL

WORKS: *A Flame from the Whins.* Dublin: W. H. West, 1912; *Sheaves of Revolt.* Dublin: City Printing Works, 1914; *A Voice of Insurgency.* Dublin: W. H. West, 1916; *Soul and Clay.* Dublin: W. H. West, 1917; *Passion Flowers.* Dublin: For the Author, 1917; as Maeve Cavanagh McDowell. *In Time of the Tans.* Dublin & Cork: Talbot, 1925. (Play); *Irish Songs of the Months. For the Eucharistic Year.* Dublin: Talbot, 1932. Also three broadside poems: "Ireland to Germany," published by Shan-Van-Vocht sometime during the First World War; "A Ballad for Rebels," no date or publisher but possibly 1917; and "Thomas Ashe," no date or publisher but possibly 1920.

CELTIC TWILIGHT, THE. This term was used as the title of an early (1893) volume of reminiscence and folklore by W. B. Yeats,* and it became a not entirely appropriate tag to describe the ferment of Irish literary activity in the 1890s and for a few years afterwards. The description called up a vision of the mournful, the moody, and the mystical which was, and perhaps even still is, one romantic way of viewing Ireland. This view had probably been fixed in the public consciousness earlier by Matthew Arnold's essay "On the Study of Celtic Literature," delivered at Oxford in 1867. Certainly the description was apt enough for much of young Yeats' work in the 1890s. But in the early years of this century when Yeats gathered around him such co-workers as George Moore,* Lady Gregory,* and J. M. Synge,* much of the Twilight mist began rapidly to be blown away. Other than Yeats, the true Celtic Twilight poets were probably to be found in the ranks of the imitative minor writers, such as Nora Hopper Chesson* or Ella Young.* With the advent of a new generation of realistic writers, such as Joyce,* O'Casey,* O'Flaherty,* O'Connor,* and O'Faolain,* the Celtic Twilight seemed anachronistic indeed. In an amusing couplet, John Montague* repeats Yeats' famous line about romantic Ireland being dead and gone, and the reason was that it was laid in its grave by O'Connor and O'Faolain.

CENTLIVRE, SUSANNAH (ca. 1667–1723), playwright and actress. Centlivre was born of English parents, probably in Ireland around 1667. There are conflicting stories about her early life, but apparently her parents died when she was young. She began writing, publishing her early plays under the name of Mrs. Carroll. She also acted in strolling companies in the English provinces and, when appearing at Windsor, attracted the attention of Joseph Centlivre, the principal cook to Queen Anne and George I, whom she married. She became friendly with Rowe, Farquhar,* and Steele* and wrote about twenty plays, of which fifteen were produced. Many of these borrowed or partly borrowed from Jonson, Molière, and others, but several had considerable popularity on the stage and went through many editions, particularly *The Busy Body* (1709), *The Wonder! A Woman Keeps a Secret* (1714), and *A Bold Stroke for a Wife* (1718). Nevertheless, in *The Oxford History of English Literature,* Bonamy Dobrée justly dismisses her comedies of intrigue with the remark:

It is difficult to imagine anything sillier or emptier, and their popularity does more than anything to attest the extremely low level of taste in the new middle-class audiences. Mrs. Centlivre was one of those writers who have what is known as ''a sense of the theatre'' and little other sense at all.

She died in London on December 1, 1723.

WORKS: *The Perjur'd Husband: or, The Adventures of Venice.* London: B. Banbury, 1700. (Tragedy); *The Beau's Duel: Or, A Soldier for the Ladies.* London: D. Brown, 1702; *Love's Contrivance; or, Le Medécin Malgre Lui.* London: B. Lintott, 1703. (After Molière); *The Stolen Heiress; or, The Salamanca Doctor Outplotted.* London: W. Turner, [1703]; *The Gamester.* London: W. Turner, 1705; *The Basset-table.* London: W. Turner, 1706; *Love at a Venture.* London: John Chantry, 1706; *The Platonick Lady.* London: J. Knapton, 1707; *The Busy Body.* London: G. H. Davidson, [1709]/Los Angeles: William Andrews Clark Memorial Library, University of California, 1949; *A Bickerstaff's Burying; or, Work for the Upholders.* London: B. Lintott, [1710]; *The Man Bewitch'd; or, The Devil to Do about Her.* London: B. Lintott, [1710]; *Mar-plot; or, The Second Part of The Busie-body.* London: J. Tonson, 1711/as *Marplot in Lisbon.* Dublin: G. Faulkner, 1760; *The Perplex'd Lovers.* London: O. Lloyd, 1712; *The Wonder! A Woman Keeps a Secret.* London: Longmans, Hurst, Rees, Orme & Brown, [1714]; *The Gotham Election.* London: S. Keimar, 1715; *The Humours of Election. And a Cure for Cuckoldom: or The Wife Well Manag'd.* London: Roberts, 1715; *The Cruel Gift.* London: E. Curl . . . & A. Bettesworth, 1717. (Tragedy); possibly with John Mottley, *A Bold Stroke for a Wife.* London: G. H. Davidson, [1718]/Lincoln: University of Nebraska Press, 1968/London: Edward Arnold, 1969; *The Artifice.* London: T. Payne, 1723; *The Works of the Celebrated Mrs. Centlivre.* . . . 3 vols. London: J. Knapton, [1760–1761]; *The Ghost.* London: J. Williams, 1767.

CHAIGNEAU, WILLIAM (1709–1781), novelist. Chaigneau was born in Dublin of Huguenot extraction on January 24, 1709. Having served in the army in Flanders, he lived most of his life in Dublin. He was a friend of the actor Tate Wilkinson and adapted a farce from the French that was produced for Wilkinson's benefit in Edinburgh in 1765. In 1752, he published anonymously one of the first Irish novels, *The History of Jack Connor,* which Brady* and Cleeve* rather prudishly describe as bawdy and scandalous. Although only the beginning and end are set in Ireland, Ian Campbell Ross more justly describes this picaresque piece as ''a conscious attempt at writing a specifically Irish novel'' and ''noteworthy for its detailed examination of the question of national identity.'' Although no *Tom Jones* or *Roderick Random,* the book remains entertainingly readable. It went through three editions. Chaigneau died in Dublin on October 1, 1781.

WORK: *The History of Jack Connor.* 2 vols. London: W. Johnston/Dublin: Abraham Bradley, 1752; 2d ed., corrected. London: W. Johnston., 1753/ 3d ed., corrected. Dublin: Abraham Bradley, 1753. REFERENCES: Ross, Ian Campbell. "An Irish Picaresque Novel: William Chaigneau's *The History of Jack Connor.*" *Studies* 71 (Autumn 1982): 270–279; Wilkinson, Tate. *Memoirs of His Own Life.* 4 vols. York: Printed for the Author, 1790.

CHAPMAN, PATRICK (fl. 1990s), poet.

WORK: *Jazztown.* Dublin: Raven Arts, 1991.

CHARLTON, MAUREEN (fl. 1960s–1990s), playwright and poet. Charlton has been involved in various musical adaptations for the stage, most notably in *The Heart's a Wonder,* a version of Synge's* *Playboy.* She also edits and publishes *Martello,* an excellent occasional magazine about art and literature.

WORK: *Lyrics from Nora Barnacle and Other Poems.* Dublin: Martello, 1990.

CHEASTY, JAMES (1928–), playwright and novelist. Cheasty was born in County Waterford and educated locally. Possibly his best play is *The Lost Years* (1958), a strong study of the farming middle class. Other works, such as *A Stranger Came* (1956) and *Francey* (1962), seem only pale versions of *Juno and the Paycock.*

WORKS: *A Stranger Came.* Dublin: Progress House, 1956; *The Lost Years.* Dublin: Progress House, 1958; *Francey.* Dublin: Progress House, 1962; *The Captive.* Dublin: Progress House, 1965. (Novel); *All Set for Birmingham.* Portlaw, Co. Waterford: Volturna, 1970; *Prisoners of Silence.* Portlaw, Co. Waterford: Volturna, 1971.

CHEAVASA, MOIRIN (1883–1972), biographer, playwright, poet, and translator. Moirin Cheavasa was born Agnes Fox, in Pinner, Middlesex, on September 7, 1883. She was one of four children born to Arthur Fox, and his wife, the former Miss Knox, whose family was connected to the earl of Ranfually. Agnes Fox was educated at home by her mother and governesses. The governesses were French and German, so Fox was fluent in both languages. In boarding school, she began developing an interest in writing. She was also a gifted pianist but shied away from performing in public. Her Protestant family held strict religious views, against which she quietly rebelled.

In 1904, Fox had a nervous breakdown and decided to move to Ireland on a small pension from her father. Her interest in the Celtic revival led her to study Irish and to assume the Irish translation of her name, Moirín Ní Sionnaig. She married Claude de Ceabasa, and the couple settled at Ross House, the former home of Violet Martin ("Martin Ross" of Somerville and Ross*), near Moycullen, County Galway. They kept an Irish-speaking household, in which their only child, Aebhgréine, was raised. Moirin Cheavasa died on May 8, 1972, following a lengthy illness.

Liadain and Curithir (1916), her versified translation of the ninth-century text, shows Cheavasa's ready ability as a translator. She acknowledges Kuno Meyer as a source and an influence on her translations. Aebhgréine Cheavasa reports that her mother did not feel comfortable writing original poetry in the Irish language, but her translations from existing texts were well received.

Her biography of Terence MacSwiney* was compliled from her own acquaintance and through mutual friends. *The Fall of the Year* (1940) is a collection of her translations and plays: "Liadain and Curithir," "From the Book of Cait Ni Duibir," "Midher and Etain," "The Fire-Bringers" (which was particularly admired by W. J. Lawrence*), and "The One Unfaithfulness of Naoise." She published under three variations of her name: Moireen Fox, Moirin Cheavasa, and Moirin Chavasse.

ANNE COLMAN

WORKS: *Liadain and Curithir*. Oxford: Blackwell, 1916; *Midhir and Etain; a Poem*. Dublin & London: Talbot Press Booklets, 1920; *The Fire-Bringers; A Play in One Act*. Dublin: Talbot Press Booklets, 1920; *The One Unfaithfulness of Naoise; A Poem*. Dublin: Talbot, 1940; *The Fall of the Year*. Dublin: Gayfield, 1940; *Terence MacSwiney*. Dublin: Clonmore & Reynolds, 1961.

CHERRY, ANDREW (1762–1812), dramatist and song writer. Cherry was born in Limerick on January 11, 1762. He was a quite successful comic actor, first in Dublin and then in England. His contemporary reputation as a wit may, possibly, be borne out by this note which he wrote to a former manager:

> Sir:—I am not so great a fool as you take me for! I have been bitten once by you, and I will never give you an opportunity of making two bites of
>
> A. CHERRY

He composed about a dozen popular plays of the day, several of which included some of his engaging songs. He is remembered today for his song "The Dear Little Shamrock of Ireland," which sounds a trifle inane even when sung by John McCormack. One of its three stanzas should be sufficient:

> There's a dear little plant that grows in our isle,
> 'Twas Saint Patrick himself, sure, that set it;
> And the sun on his labor with pleasure did smile,
> And with dew from his eye often wet it.
> It thrives through the bog, through the brake, through the mireland;
> And he called it the dear little shamrock of Ireland,
> The sweet little shamrock, the dear little shamrock,
> The sweet little, green little, shamrock of Ireland.

His one-act operetta, *Spanish Dollars* (1806), is set on the coast of Ireland and contains his other well-known song, "The Bay of Biscay." Cherry died on February 7, 1812, at Montmouth.

WORKS: *The Soldier's Daughter*. London: Printed for Richard Phillips, 1804. (Play in 5 acts); *Spanish Dollars; or, The Priest of the Parish*. London: Barker & Son, 1806. (One-act operatic sketch with music by J. Davy); *The Travellers; or, Music's Fascination*. London: Printed for Richard Phillips, 1806. (An operatic drama in 5 acts with music by Mr. Corri); *Peter the Great; or, The Wooden Walls*. London: R. Phillips, 1807. (An operatic drama in 3 acts).

CHESSON, NORA HOPPER (1871–1906), poet, novelist, and writer of sketches. Chesson was a Celtic Twilight* poetess who lived all her life in England. Her father, Captain H. B. Hopper, was Irish, but her mother was Welsh, and she herself was born at Exeter on January 2, 1871. Her father died when she was an infant, and she lived thereafter with her mother in London. In 1894, she published her first volume, *Ballads in Prose,* which was admired by W. B. Yeats,* although he felt that she came very close to plagiarizing both Katharine Tynan* and himself. Also in 1894, she met her future husband, W. H. Chesson, whom she married on March 5, 1901. She wrote the libretto for *The Sea Swan,* an Irish legendary grand opera in three acts which was performed at the Theatre Royal, Dublin, on December 7, 1903. George Moore* helped her with the plot; nevertheless (or, perhaps, therefore), Edward Martyn* disliked the piece. She died on April 14, 1906, in London.

Chesson published prolifically in the popular press and achieved a considerable following. Her verses have many allusions to and verbal touches of Ireland, and are usually graceful and mellifluous, if generally somewhat vague and somewhat thin in content. However, Yeats wrote that her *Ballads in Prose* "haunted me as few books have ever haunted me, for it spoke in strange wayward stories and birdlike little verses of things and persons I remembered or had dreamed of." Yeats was perhaps flattered by Chesson's imitation of his own early manner, and gently remarked that her pastiches were only "plagiarisms of inexperienced enthusiasm. . . . She had taken[n] us as documents, just as if we had written hundreds of years ago." However, Yeats liked her second volume, *Under Quicken Boughs* (1896), less than her first, and finally came to feel that "our Irish fairyland came to spoil her work. . . ." In another gentle summation, Ford Madox Ford found both her and her works abstracted and pleasant, and "If she seldom called a spade a spade it was because that particular tool seldom came into her purview." Her world is of fairies, princes slain by elf-bolts, fog, roses, and gently mournful lovers. She was probably the quintessence of what the public regarded as a Celtic Twilight poet—quietly charming and not unpleasantly vapid.

WORKS: *Ballads in Prose.* London: John Lane, 1894; *Under Quicken Boughs.* London: John Lane, 1896; *Songs of the Morning.* London: Grant Richards, 1900; *Aquamarines.* London: Grant Richards, 1902; *Mildred and Her Mills, and Other Poems.* London: Raphael Tuck, 1903; *Old Fairy Legends in New Colours,* by T. E. Donnison, with verses by N. Chesson. London: Raphael Tuck, 1903; *With Louis Wain to Fairyland.* London: Raphael Tuck, 1904; *The Bell and the Arrow: An English Love Story.* London: T. Werner Laurie, 1905; *Dirge for Aoine and Other Poems.* London: Alston Rivers, 1906; *A Dead Girl to Her Lover and Other Poems.* London: Alston Rivers, 1906; *Jack O'Lanthorn and Other Poems.* London: Alston Rivers, 1906; *The Happy Maid and Other Poems.* London: Alston Rivers, 1906; *The Waiting Widow and Other Poems.* London: Alston Rivers, 1906; *Father Felix's Chronicles.* W. H. Chesson, ed. London: Unwin, 1907. (Novel). REFERENCE: Marcus, Phillip L. *Yeats and the Beginning of the Irish Renaissance.* Ithaca & London: Cornell University Press, [1970]. Pp. 147–157.

CHILDERS, [ROBERT] ERSKINE (1870–1922), politician and novelist. Childers belongs more to Irish history than to literature, but he wrote one perennially delightful thriller, *The Riddle of the Sands* (1903). He was born Robert Erskine Childers in London on June 25, 1870. He took his B.A. In 1893 from Trinity College, Cambridge, and most of the years from 1895 to 1910 he spent as a clerk in the British House of Commons. He served in the Boer War and wrote several war histories and books of military strategy. He also served as an intelligence officer in the Royal Navy in World War I, was several times mentioned in dispatches, and was awarded the Distinguished Service Cross.

Many of the patriotic Irish regarded Childers as an Englishman, even though much of his youth had been spent in Ireland. He grew increasingly sympathetic to Irish nationalism. It was he on his yacht, the *Asgard,* who brought the guns to Howth in the celebrated gun-running incident of 1914. After the war, he became an even more fervent nationalist. He went with Arthur Griffith* to Versailles to present the case of Ireland to the Peace Conference, and he was also the principal secretary of the Irish Treaty delegation to London in 1921. However, he was opposed to the signing of the treaty and joined the Republican side in the civil war. For the Republicans, he edited and published the paper *Poblacht na h-Éireann.* He was arrested at his home in November 1922, court-martialed, and executed by a Free State firing squad at Beggar's Bush on November 24. In 1973, however, his son—also named Erskine—became the fourth president of Ireland.

Shortly after his college years, Childers spent his vacations sailing on his yacht in the Channel, in the North Sea, and off the German, Danish, and Baltic coasts, an experience that served as background in what must be the first successful thriller written by an Irishman. *The Riddle of the Sands* was apparently written with the serious purpose of alerting people to the imminent German threat. Taken simply as a thriller, the book must rank as one of the classics in its field and can be mentioned with the best of Buchan and Ambler.

PRINCIPAL WORK: *The Riddle of the Sands.* London: Smith, Elder, 1903/many reprints, including London: Penguin, 1952.   REFERENCES: Boyle, Andrew. *The Riddle of Erskine Childers.* London: Hutchinson, 1977; O'Hegarty, P. S. *A Bibliography of Erskine Childers.* Dublin: Printed for the author, 1948/reprinted from *Dublin Magazine* 23, No. 2, n.s.; Wilkinson, Burke. *The Zeal of the Convert.* Washington, D.C.: Robert B. Luce, 1974. (Biography).

CHILDREN'S LITERATURE. Throughout the literary world, writing for children has traditionally held an inconsequential position. Of course, there have been stalwart supporters of children's writing over the years; the mammoth work of people such as Margaret Meek, John Rowe Townsend, and, more recently, Peter Hunt bears witness to this fact. At last, however, there seems to be an increasing awareness of the importance of children's literature. More attention is being paid to what adults give children to read and, more important, to what children themselves like to read. The growing number of conferences, seminars, summer schools, and periodicals specifically on the subject of writing for children is some indication of this fact.

In Ireland, writing for children has tended to germinate slowly through this century and to blossom in the last decade or so. For many centuries a bicultural nation, Ireland has had the benefit of drawing on two traditions, as well as two languages. On one hand, there was the old Gaelic oral folklore—a wealth of stories of myth and legend, of ancient warriors and battles, of fantasy and fables. At the same time, there coexisted a quite different tradition belonging to the measured, edifying type of books to be found in Britain, such as *Early Lessons* (1801) by Maria Edgeworth.* However, within the last fifteen years or so, writing for children in Ireland has diversified and taken its own directions, using the best elements of the old traditions and moving forward to break new ground. With Swift's* publication of *Gulliver's Travels* (1726), we begin to see the roots of children's literature in Ireland. Although not written specifically for children, the book was soon widely favored by young people all over Europe, and within a year of publication a new children's edition was issued. Perhaps the element of fantasy, the exotic nature of Gulliver's travels, and the earthy, humorous reactions of the narrator account for the book's popularity with children through the centuries.

Over 100 years later, we find a blind poetess from Donegal, Frances Browne,* writing *Granny's Wonderful Chair* (1856). A series of stories about human people and their adventures with fairy folk and magic is united by the device of the talking chair. Here we find that easy blend of reality and unreality, and the line between the two is ever blurred. Drawing on both ancient Celtic and modern moral traditions, Frances Browne successfully pleases and instructs at one and the same time. The lines, "King Winwealth . . . married a certain princess called Wantall. . . . People thought she must have gained the King's love by enchantment, for her whole dowry was a desert island, with a huge pit in it that could never be filled," are a good illustration of this blend of traditions.

The influence of the old *seanchai,* the storytellers, can be clearly seen in the work of Padraic Colum,* among whose many books for children, *The King of Ireland's Son* (1916) is most notable. Ordinary people mix with royalty, with talking animals, enchanters, and magic, and everyone is caught in a web of trials of virtue and honor. Colum's poetic ear for language adds much to his stories. Lines such as, "Gilly of the Goatskin, the bow in his hand, sprang across the cradle, over the threshold of the door, and out into the width and the height, the length and the breadth, the gloom and the gleam of the world," illustrate the strong poetic rhythm and vision that carries the reader from story to story. There are echoes here of the earlier work by James Stephens,* *The Crock of Gold* (1912), which Walter de la Mare once described as "a crazy patchwork . . . which is more than a little crammed full of life and beauty."

In the 1930s, the works of the prolific children's writer Patricia Lynch* came to the force. *The Turf-Cutter's Donkey* series is perhaps her best-known work, and again we find that easy transition from the earthy reality of rural cottage life to the realms of magic and mystery, where animals talk and leprechauns make mischief. Lynch's extensive exposure as a child to the Irish oral storytelling tradition explains a confident, lyrical, pregnant prose. Long Ears, the donkey, embodies that bewitching combination of earthiness and ethereality that the two children, Eileen and Seamus, half delight in and half fear. This subtle depiction of their emotional dilemma makes the books memorable. The fickleness of fortune plays a strong part also in *The Grey Goose of Kilnevin* (1939), but all the intricate loose ends are eventually tied up in the magically satisfying ending. The characterization of the protagonist Sheila is stronger than in the "Turf-Cutter" series, and Sheila's artlessness endears her to the reader from the start. Perhaps the most memorable scene is where Fat Maggie discovers the gray goose, and pandemonium ensues. "Let that creature come in again, if it dare," declares the formidable woman. The magic in this book is heightened by taking place in a recognizable domestic world, with realistic characters. Lynch's successful combination of the ordinary and the extraordinary makes for humorous stories, full of warmth and enchantment.

Eileen O'Faolain also sets her tales of fantasy in a familiar, everyday world. As in Lynch, the mortals in O'Faolain's stories hold the fairy-folk or *sluagh sidhe* in great awe, a fact that emphasizes the mystery and magical qualities of her stories. In *The Little Black Hen* (1940), the two children and the aged heroine Biddy try to save their three pets from the clutches of the *sluagh sidhe,* but, in fact, the bravery and ingenuity of the animals themselves earn them their freedom. O'Faolain's language is deliberately colorful and colloquial. The grammatical structure of the sentences, laced here and there with expressions such as "agrah," "aroo," "a stor," follows the inflections of the Irish language, and this adds a lyricism that sets the stories above the mundane.

By 1945, Mary Flynn was publishing her "Cornelius" books about a family of rabbits living in an idyllic little town called Tang. The everyday humdrum of the rabbits' lives is dotted with a variety of events, some dramatic, others less so, some humorous, and some edifying. Throughout, there is a strong sense of morality, the necessity of "good behaviour" from children, but this is softened by the humor and the characterization. The reader could hardly forget Tiny and his constant willingness to point out his "favouritest" things or forget Edward, the clumsy and bashful elephant, or forget the Rabbit family's hotel lunch where each chooses the most unlikely dishes from the menu—lamb, Irish stew, chicken!

Up to this point, most Irish children's books vacillated between everyday, familiar, usually rural life and the "otherworld" of the fairies, the *sluagh sidhe,* of magic and bewitching mystery. At the same time, there were animal stories such as Mary Flynn's and books that combined both the fairy and animal elements, such as O'Faolain's *Little Red Hen.* However, in the same year as Flynn's "Cornelius" books, Maura Laverty's* *Cottage in the Bog* (1945) was published. An adventure story right to the exciting end, this book departed from its predecessors by straying away from fantasy. Firmly rooted in their comfortable family life, the children, Essie, Con, and Mike, unravel a local mystery to discover the lost treasure of Fionn MacCumhaill. "So that's the stuff that men are willing to rob and kill and fight for? Well, well! I'd rather be looking for a field of ripe wheat any day in the week,'' says Granda, looking over the glittering treasure. This is very much an Irish adventure story; good sense and sound family values count for more than any amount of treasure.

The adventures of ''Specs McCann'' began in 1955, and Janet McNeill's* often hilarious stories about the redoubtable duo, Specs and Curly, have delighted generations of children in Ireland—so much so that a reissue of *My Friend Specs McCann* appeared in late 1995. Set in Ulster, these are stories of two schoolboys with an unfailingly dry sense of humor who fall into all manner of fantastic adventures. This is fantasy writing solidly rooted in the mundane life at boarding school. The language is comfortably Northern Irish, laced with expressions such as ''browned off'' and ''right enough, so I had,'' which help to localize the stories set in County Down. The humor is pervasive—from simple puns to the elaborate, farcelike denouement of Mr. Wutherspindle's lions in *Specs Fortissimo* (1958). McNeill's understated language is a perfect foil for the overstated farcical action.

Eilis Dillon* began writing for children in 1948. Spanning over four decades, her prolific work has always been well received by critics and children alike, and the versatility of her books is matched by her storytelling technique, like that of the old *seanchai* long ago. Each novel is filled with believable characters, and each set of children around whom the novels center grows up in maturity as the novels' actions unfold. *The Lost Island* (1952) is an adventure story with such diverse characters as the sensible hero Michael, the shady rogues Matt and Pat, and the brief, yet memorable appearance of the threatening Mikus. The suspense builds up to a well-crafted crescendo and a very satisfying ending. Similarly, *The Island of Ghosts* (1990) has its own set of widely differing characters, all brought together and forced to interact in a small, tight community. Here, however, Dillon's masterly portrayal of the learned man who imprisons the two intelligent boys on an island is what we remember of the adventure. We never totally dislike the man, and, along with his captive Dara, we come to admire the island way of life he has created and cherished.

Initially, Eilis Dillon's final book for children, *The Children of Bach* (1993), appears very different from her earlier work. It is the story of a family of Jewish children fleeing from the Nazi occupation of Hungary. From the first pages, the reader's interest is tightly gripped. One by one, the children return from school to an empty apartment that shows signs of having been hastily deserted. Gradually, it dawns on them that the Nazis have taken their parents, and how they escape in a custom-built furniture van to Italy makes for an exciting read. But the depiction of how the central characters relate to each other, intensified by the tight space in the van, makes the book stand out. Dillon's skill in unfolding a story with an intuitive sense of episodic timing and drama is perhaps shown here at its best. Uniformly, she tells powerful and interesting tales, with credible characters, and each book is filled with the musicality of human speech, whether from the West of Ireland or from Hungary.

While Dillon continued to write for children in the 1960s, two other notable authors were producing books of a very different nature. Walter Macken's* tale of two orphans' return to Ireland in search of love and family, *The Flight of the Doves* (1968), has been popularized in film as well as in book form for many years. Macken's ability to unravel a story swiftly, drawing out the drama and suspense in each situation, is laudable. Characters are boldly sketched, and the overall result is a good read. Sinead de Valera, on the other hand, was retelling the old stories of ancient warriors and heroes. Her gift as a writer lies in her use of natural idiomatic dialogue, and thus these old fairy tales of Ireland come to life with a refreshing and charming immediacy.

In terms of new Irish writers for children, the 1970s were not very prolific. This decade is dominated by the writer Joan Lingard,* and the great popularity of her "Kevin and Sadie" quintet can still be felt today. The stories begin in a working-class, religiously divided Belfast, where two young people from opposite divides find themselves increasingly attracted to one another. The unfolding of their story and the difficulties they experience in trying to shake off the religious prejudices of their parents are sensitively handled. Reflecting the natural growth of maturity, the series increases in complexity and seriousness as the young couple move through their teenage years to the responsibilities of young parenthood. Joan Lingard has written many other fine novels, but in an Irish context the "Kevin and Sadie" series is notable.

Peter Carter's *Under Goliath* (1977) is similar in that it relates the growth of friendship between two Belfast boys of opposite persuasions. Carter's ear for language is evident in the dialogue, especially in the portrayal of the band leader MacKracken. As the boys separate at the end, each understanding the other's world yet powerless to alter the deep divide between them, the book takes on great pathos. "A murderous rage at the waste and folly of it all but most of all I feel a rage at borders without meaning except that they divide the hearts of men." In many ways, this was a book ahead of its time, raising interests and painting pictures of war-torn Belfast that had hardly been recognized before in children's literature.

The publication of *The Lucky Bag* (1984), an anthology of classic Irish children's stories, was a significant landmark. For the first time ever, in one volume came together many well-loved and half-forgotten stories, from such writers as Swift and Micheál Mac Liammóir* and even the adult writers James Plunkett* and Brian Friel.* The editors, Pat Donlon, Eilis Dillon, Patricia Egan, and Peter Fallon,* were already well-respected Irish writers, and their choice of stories was clever and far-reaching. *The Lucky Bag* brought stories from lesser-known writers such as Kathleen Fitzpatrick and mixed them with the work of well-established writers such as the O'Faolains. It also brought stories from writers such as Janet McNeill, Maura Laverty, and Mary Lavin* to a new generation of Irish children. The irascible Jimeen, created by Padraig O'Siochfhrada and often hailed as the Irish "William," first appeared in the English language in *The Lucky Bag.*

Many of the stories belong to the oral tradition—the "once upon a time" fireside tales that grip the reader from start to finish. Interspersed between these are "the surprises" Eilis Dillon refers to in her introduction. Janet McNeill's "The Breadth of a Whisker" is a taut, thought-provoking story. Polly Devlin's* "The China Doll," extracted from *The Far Side of the Lough,* has a shock ending to an otherwise simple story. The inclusion of Frank O'Connor's* "First Confession" was inspired, for, although not written specifically for children, it captures the mentality of the little boy narrating the story. The aim of the collection was to provide a taste of classic Irish stories for children in order to spur the reader on to look for, as Dillon noted, "more work by the same authors. One book, or one story, should always lead to another."

For a number of years, the prolific work of Martin Waddell, sometimes under his pseudonym Catherine Sefton, has earned him a position of honor in children's literature. He has written books for practically every age and stage of childhood—from picture books for the very young, to the newly independent reader, to the football fanatic, to the more serious and searching adolescent. There are always humor, a set of believable characters, a tangible and realistic backdrop, and natural dialogue. The picture book probably most associated with Waddell is *Can't You Sleep, Little Bear?* (1988). With the charming illustrations of Barbara Firth, it is a delightful exploration of the I-can't-get-to-sleep routine most parents experience at some time with their children. The pervading gentleness of this book for young children is in total contrast to the action-packed stories of the football hero Napper McCann and also of the "Dingwell Street School" stories, aimed at solo readers. Waddell invariably has the intuitive power to hit the right note, to pitch at exactly the right level for each particular age. Slightly older readers will enjoy Catherine Sefton's *Along a Lonely Road* (1991), a suspense-filled story that, at the same time, quietly explores that point in childhood where one is neither child nor full-fledged teenager. During the course of this hostage story, Ruth comes to adopt a pragmatic approach to the family's situation, and this leads to a more mature understanding of her own and her mother's role in the whole affair. All in all, consistent quality is the hallmark of Waddell's many books for children.

The retelling of old tales has always been part of the Irish culture for both adults and children. Two writers of this tradition who figure largely in this last decade and a half are Morgan Llywelyn* and Michael Mullen. Both painstakingly strive for historical accuracy, yet taking care not to sacrifice the drama of the story. Llywelyn's two historical novels, *Brian Boru: Emperor of the Irish* (1990) and *Strongbow: The Story of Richard and Aoife* (1992), are packed with action, fights, treachery, and love, reflecting the turbulent times in which they are set. The details, such as Aoife's favorite food of mushrooms roasted with hazelnuts, and the strong protagonists humanize these distant events. For this reason, Llywelyn can justifiably call her works "biographical novels."

Michael Mullen's novels span a wide range of Irish history, from Viking Dublin to the Battle of the Boyne in 1690, and in each there is sorrow at the cruelty and harshness of war. He sensitively depicts the tragic results of battle when Irish people turn on their own, when people betray each other in order to survive, and when loved ones die. *The Long March* (1990) perhaps best displays Mullen's ability to re-create the excitement and fear of battle and the desolation and deprivation the people endure in their harrowing march across Ireland to escape their enemies. The address of O'Sullivan Beare to his flagging troops is reminiscent of the addresses of Anglo-Saxon heroic leaders, and there is a great sense of loss in this book as, repeatedly, characters tell each other "the old cause is dead." However, there is hope, and it lies in the young people. "Before them, lay the future" are the simple yet inspiring final words of *The Long March*.

No better proof of the popularity of historical fiction is to be found than in the work of Marita Conlon-McKenna. Set in the Irish Famine years, *Under the Hawthorn Tree* (1990) tells the vivid story of how one family of children survives the loss of their parents. Their perilous journey to find distant relatives ends in success, and the sequel, *Wildflower Girl* (1992), follows the younger sister's travels to America to seek her fortune. Conlon-McKenna's talent is to tell a story swiftly and simply with all the immediacy that a young solo reader expects. *The Blue Horse* (1992) departs from historical fiction and describes the fortunes of a girl in the traveling community in modern Ireland. Issues such as bullying and ostracism are touched on lightly, but Conlon-McKenna's preoccupation is always with the telling of a good tale.

Siobhan Parkinson's historical novel *Amelia* (1993) is set in the early twentieth century and similarly follows the central character through a dramatic change in family fortune, exploring the growth of Amelia's maturity in her now less-privileged life. Parkinson's sensitivity to personal relationships and the interaction of her characters gives depth to her novels, and Amelia's learning to shift her focus from outward appearances to an appreciation of inner strength is subtly portrayed. *No Peace for Amelia* (1994) takes up Amelia's story again years later, with the First World War and the 1916 Easter Rising in Dublin as a strong background.

The Second World War years are the setting for Joan O'Neill's* *Daisy Chain War* (1990), a marvelously vivid depiction of domestic life in Ireland during those deprived years. With the immediacy of a first-person narrative, we can appreciate the growth of Lizzie's maturity through the obvious widening of her vision and understanding

Michael Scott writes both historical and modern fiction. His great interest in the retelling of the old Celtic tales is evident in all of his historical work. *The Last Feast of the Fianna* (1987) is a re-creation of the Oisin story, with a memorable portrayal of the formidable Niamh Golden Hair. His "De Danann" fantasy series delights in the sorcery and mysticism of the Pre-Flood Age. Writing for teenagers as Mike Scott, he creates the disparate characters of the wealthy Judith and the traveler Spider in the "Judith and Spider" series (1992). There is a certain amount of clichéd romanticism about the heroes, but Scott handles the cliché cleverly. He tells an action-packed story but makes his characters real enough to escape sentimentality. The Dublin underground of crime is realistically portrayed, and the contrast between Spider's street-wiseness and Judith's naïveté often sparks humor.

The Northern writer Sam McBratney produced a memorable historical novel in *The Chieftain's Daughter* (1993). Set at the beginning of Christianity in Ireland, it tells the fascinating story of a young noble boy brought up by strangers and the growing friendship between him and the chieftain's daughter. The slightly archaic language is a clever reminder that we are reading of ancient Ireland and adds to the almost elegiac tone of the ending. McBratney's versatility can be clearly seen when we turn to his *Put a Saddle on the Pig* (1992), where contemporary Ireland provides the backdrop for a feud between a mother and teenage daughter. The humor and the sensitivity to teenage life distinguish this novel from others of its type. The picture book *Guess How Much I Love You* (1994) is successfully aimed at much younger readers. McBratney's work to date is both original and impressive.

Parnell's Ireland in 1890 is the setting for Elizabeth O'Hara's *The Hiring Fair* (1993), the story of a young girl who is forced to become a hired girl after her father's untimely death. O'Hara's strength is her ability to create a heroine with faults who is nonetheless likable. Sally's growth to maturity is gradual and surprises even herself. Perhaps this is the key to her attractiveness—her capacity to analyze and laugh at herself. *Blaeberry Sunday* (1994) continues the story of this interesting heroine from Donegal.

Tom McCaughren's latest book, *In Search of the Liberty Tree* (1994), follows the adventures of two boys in County Antrim during the 1798 Rising. The atmosphere and re-creation of the treachery of the times is excellent. The "Fox" trilogy is perhaps McCaughren's best-known work for children. Beginning with *Run with the Wind* (1983), we come to admire the noble character of the fugitive foxes and to regard Man's ignominious role with disgust. The landscapes can be friendly, but McCaughren does not forget the harsh, cruel side of nature.

The Summer of Lily and Esme (1991) by John Quinn is a fine piece of historical fiction, yet it is set in modern Ireland. The historical aspect is embodied in the two elderly sisters, Lily and Esme, living next door to Alan's new home in the country. The two confused sisters' memories are locked in the times of their girlhood during the First World War. The sensitivity and appreciation that Alan and his friend show these two old ladies is heartwarming. A deep sense of nostalgia pervades the books and lends it a lyrical quality befitting the connection with the poet Ledwidge.* Quinn's *Duck and Swan* (1993) is in stark contrast, in that it is definitely set in contemporary Galway. Great humor and banter derive from the relationship between the schoolgirl Emer and Duck, an orphan boy on the run. Quinn's ear for dialogue is accurate, and the character of Granny Flynn is remarkable in this fast-moving and funny book.

Fantasy has always held a strong place in Irish children's writing and is today as popular as ever. It ranges from animal stories such as McCaughren's "Fox" books to the mystical worlds of Orla Melling's novels and the "Giltspur" trilogy of Cormac MacRaois.

Born in Ireland, raised in Canada, and now back living and writing in Ireland, Orla Melling has produced some fine fantasy books over the last few years. As a scholar of Celtic studies, her books understandably glory in the ancient past of Ireland, celebrating its rich culture of music, sorcery, enchantment, treachery, and violent battles. Her use of the time-travel device allows subtle comparisons and contrasts between contemporary Ireland and its ancient past. For example, in *The Singing Stone* (1993), tapestry threads weave in and out through different ages, and Melling tantalizingly connects the present and the past. Strong characterization, combined with a lyrical appreciation of the natural elements, gives her work gnomic stature.

Time travel is also used by Yvonne MacGrory in "The Ruby Ring" series. Through coming to live in very different worlds from their own, the heroines grow in maturity and understanding. The historical detail is accurate, particularly in the second book, *Martha and the Ruby Ring,* which takes place during the 1798 Rebellion. MacGrory tells a gripping story, filled with believable characters, and her books are full of vivid, accurate period detail.

The three "Giltspur" novels (1988–1991) by Cormac MacRaois are fantasies set in contemporary Wicklow, with three children as central characters. Each book builds skillfully to a climax and to a final battle. MacRaois cleverly harnesses nature to reflect the menacing growth of evil in the unsuspecting world of the three children: rooks cast black shadows, flit across fields, and hide in hedges. MacRaois cleverly re-creates such childish, irrational fears and shockingly makes them materialize. Although evil does fight a strong battle, good always triumphs in these books, and the reader's focus is on the fun and good humor throughout.

Maeve Friel's *Distant Voices* (1994) is an unusual Viking time-travel fantasy book in which an ancient Viking warrior, disturbed by the injustice of his untimely death and a foreboding about his future, contacts Ellie, a young teenage girl living in modern Derry. How she helps set the Viking spirit to rest is a haunting tale full of pathos.

Fiction that raises social and moral issues has of late become popular in both adult and children's writing, and Irish writing is no exception. Many modern books for children, while not necessarily setting out to raise a specific issue, often do so.

The work of Margrit Cruickshank clearly falls into this category. Most notable is her "S.K.U.N.K" series, begun in 1990, in which a girl and several eccentric characters have various adventures trying to combat that dreaded organization involved in Skullduggery, Killing, Unscrupulousness, Nastiness, and Corruption. There is much humor in the books, and the irrepressible Aisling catches our attention from the start. Various issues appear, particularly of the environmental kind, but essentially our attention is focused on the twists of the plot. *Circling the Triangle* (1991) is a novel for teenagers and deftly encapsulates the feelings of isolation so often typical of this age. The generation gap and the attraction to the opposite sex are examined sensitively and with a dry sense of humor.

Tony Hickey has been writing for children for a decade and a half, and his work ranges from stories for younger children to stories for the older child who likes mystery and adventure. "The Matchless Mice" series is popular with young readers, for it is crammed with cartoonlike chases, escapes, and cheeky, streetwise characters. By contrast, Hickey's "Joe-in-the-middle" series combines intrigue and adventure with thought-provoking issues such as attitudes to the Travelling Community in Ireland. Characterization and dialogue are strong, and the reader is quickly involved in the plots.

The West of Ireland is the strong setting for Geraldine Mitchell's *Welcoming the French* (1992). It is a pleasant adventure story where a thirteen-year-old-girl gets caught up in a whirlwind of preparations to receive a group of traumatized French teenagers into a small, rural community. Great humor and sensitivity to changes of mood give Mitchell's writing distinction.

Coping with Mum when you are a teenage girl whose father is not long dead and you have just moved to Ireland is the subject of Bernadette Leach's lively *I'm a Vegetarian* (1992). Leach has a good understanding of the swings of teenage moods, and the stormy mother–daughter relationship is funny and sympathetic. The sequel, *Summer without Mum,* is equally full of vitality.

Rose Doyle's* *Goodbye, Summer, Goodbye* (1994) rises above the usual generation-gap strife to produce a book full of unique characters, and great sadness lies in the fact that few of them realize how dependent they are on each other. The subtlety of Doyle's writing is appealing, yet not precious. The central character of Martha ensures a solid, frank voice throughout.

Teenage romance is sensibly handled in Marilyn Taylor's *Could This Be Love? I Wondered* (1994). Expanding one's set of friends beyond the school-class circle, coping with jealousies, financial stress, parents' trust—all of these issues are raised, but, above all, the reader is engagingly interested in the ups and downs of the Jackie–Kev relationship.

The teenage novels of June Considine have proved popular in recent years. The "Beachwood" series conducts a large group of characters through a series of trying incidents; she shows the maturing process as funny, frivolous, and exciting and also painful and lonely. Considine is very strong on teenage moods, as her short novels move through friendships, bullying incidents, and, inevitably, romance. However, in *View from a Blind Bridge* (1992), her ability to control the emotions within a taut and tragic story comes to full light. This story of "loss and love," of having and not having, is gripping and far-reaching. The sequel, *The Glass Triangle* (1994), is equally sensitive.

When Stars Stop Spinning (1993) by Jane Mitchell is an unusual book, set in a rehabilitation center where the main character is recovering from severe head injuries after a joyriding incident. The close friendship he develops with another gifted but dying boy is poignant. This is a moving, serious book, but there are enough humor and "craic" to soften the tragic moments.

Until quite recently, Irish picture books have been very few. With the notable exception of Don Conroy's *The Owl Who Couldn't Give a Hoot* (1984) and *The Tiger Who Was a Roaring Success* (1985), Irish books have relied on simple black and white drawings. The appearance, however, of *The Sleeping Giant* (1991) by Marie-Louise Fitzpatrick was a welcome breath of fresh air. For many years, the work of Belfast-born P. J. Lynch has been greatly admired, although to date most of his work has been U.K.-published. His illustrations for the Oscar Wilde *Stories for Children* (1990) brought him great acclaim. Like the best illustrators, Lynch illuminates and extends the text, and his use of color reflects the various moods of these adultlike fairy tales. Lynch's work has obviously been influenced by the large screen; the angles from which he views his subjects and the often three-dimensional quality of his illustrations bear witness to this fact. The illustrations of the Steadfast Tin Soldier's fall from a high window ledge is reminiscent of scenes in children's cartoons. Lynch is an already well established name in children's writing, and one gets the feeling that he has only just started.

Since the 1980s, the output of children's literature in Ireland has significantly increased, and at the same time it has improved in variety and quality. Patricia Donlon, director of the National Irish Library, once wrote, ''Each child's reading matter should consist of as much variety as possible—something old and classic, something new and exciting, a little 'rubbish' now and again for light relief, lots of magic, fantasy, adventure, poetry and a smattering of factual books.'' Irish children's literature seems now at the stage where it can offer something for each category of book mentioned. As Donlon also remarked, ''The Children's Literature of each nation is a reflection in miniature of the world it portrays,'' and this thought seems sufficiently broad to describe what is happening in children's literature in Ireland today. Historical fiction, fantasy, and modern realistic fiction are all popular genres, both in adult and in children's writing. They are a reflection of a society deeply, emotionally rooted in its past, realistically recognizing its own limitations and problems, yet still capable of looking beyond to greater possibilities.

HELEN RYAN

NOTABLE WORKS: Browne, Frances. *Granny's Wonderful Chair*. London: Griffith & Farran, 1857; Carter, Peter. *Under Goliath*. Oxford: Oxford University Press, 1977; Colum, Padraic. *The King of Ireland's Son*. New York: Macmillan, 1916/London: Harrap, 1920; Conlon-McKenna, Marita. *Under the Hawthorn Tree*. Dublin: O'Brien, 1990, and *Wildflower Girl*. Dublin: O'Brien, 1992, and *The Blue Horse*. Dublin: O'Brien, 1992; Conroy, Don. *The Owl Who Couldn't Give a Hoot*. Wicklow: Rainbow, 1985, and *The Tiger Who Was a Roaring Success*. Wicklow: Rainbow, 1985; Considine, June. *View from a Blind Bridge*. Dublin: Poolbeg, 1992, and ''The Beechwood Series'' (*The Debs Ball*. Dublin: Poolbeg, 1993; *The Slumber Party*. Dublin: Poolbeg, 1993; *School Bully*. Dublin: Poolbeg, 1993; *The Glass Triangle*. Dublin: Poolbeg, 1994); Cruickshank, Margrit. ''S.K.U.N.K Series'' (*S.K.U.N.K. and the Ozone Conspiracy*. Dublin: Poolbeg, 1990; *S.K.U.N.K. and the Nuclear Waste*. Dublin: Poolbeg, 1992; *S.K.U.N.K. and the Freak Flood Fiasco*. Dublin: Poolbeg, 1994; *Circling the Triangle*. Dublin: Poolbeg, 1991); de Valera, Sinead. *Fairy Tales of Ireland*. Dublin: C. J. Fallon, 1967; Devlin, Polly. *The Far Side of the Lough*. London: Gollancz, 1993; Dillon, Eilis. *The Lost Island*. London: Faber, 1952/New York: Funk & Wagnall's, 1954, and

The Island of Ghosts. London: Faber, 1990, and *The Children of Bach*. London: Faber, 1993; Doyle, Rose. *Goodbye, Summer, Goodbye*. Dublin: Attic, 1994; Fitzpatrick, Kathleen. *They Lived in County Down*. London: Chatto & Windus, 1905; Fitzpatrick, Marie-Louise. *The Sleeping Giant*. [Dingle, Co. Kerry]: Brandon, [1991]; Flynn, Mary, *Cornelius Rabbit of Tang*. Dublin: Talbot, 1944, and *Cornelius on Holidays*. Dublin: Talbot, 1945, and *Cornelius in Charge*. Dublin: Talbot, 1946; Friel, Maeve. *Distant Voices*. Dublin: Poolbeg, 1994. Hickey, Tony. *The Matchless Mice*. Dublin: Geraldine, 1979, and *The Matchless Mice's Adventure*. Dublin: Children's, 1984, and *The Matchless Mice in Space*. Dublin: Children's, 1986, and *The Matchless Mice's Space Project*. Dublin: Children's, 1989, and *Joe in the Middle*. Dublin: Poolbeg, 1988, and *Where Is Joe?* Dublin: Poolbeg, 1989, and *Joe on Holiday*. Dublin: Poolbeg, 1991; Laverty, Maura. *The Cottage in the Bog*. Dublin: Browne & Nolan, 1945. Lavin, Mary. *A Likely Story*. New York: Macmillan/Dublin: Dolmen, 1957. Lingard, Joan. "Kevin and Sadie Quintet" (*The Twelfth Day of July*. London: Hamish Hamilton, 1970; *Across the Barricades*. London: Hamish Hamilton, 1972; *Into Exile*. London: Hamish Hamilton, 1973; *A Proper Place*. London: Hamish Hamilton, 1975; *Hostages to Fortune*. London: Hamish Hamilton, 1976); Leach, Bernadette. *I'm a Vegetarian*. Dublin: Attic, 1992, and *Summer without Mum*. Dublin: Attic, 1993; Llywelyn, Morgan. *Brian Boru, Emperor of the Irish*. Dublin: O'Brien, 1990, and *Strongbow: The Story of Richard and Aoife*. Dublin: O'Brien, 1992; *The Lucky Bag*. Eilis Dillon, Pat Donlon, Patricia Egan & Peter Fallon, eds. Dublin: O'Brien, 1984 (Anthology); Lynch, Patricia. "The Turf-Cutter Series" (*The Turf-Cutter's Donkey*. London & Toronto: Dent/New York: E. P. Dutton, 1935; *The Turf-Cutter's Donkey Goes Visiting*. London: Dent, 1935; *Long-Ears*. London: Dent, 1935; *The Turf-Cutter's Donkey Kicks Up His Heels*. Dublin: Browne & Nolan, 1946. *The Grey Goose of Kilnevin*. Dublin: Dent, 1939); Lynch, P. J. *Stories for Children* by Oscar Wilde. London: Simon & Schuster, 1990, and *The Steadfast Tin Soldier* by Hans Christian Anderson. London: Anderson, 1991/London: Red Fox, 1993; McBratney, Sam. *Put a Saddle on the Pig*. London: Methuen, 1992, and *The Chieftain's Daughter*. Dublin: O'Brien, 1993, and *Guess How Much I Love You*. London: Walker/Dublin: O'Brien, 1994; McCaughren, Tom. "The Fox Trilogy" (*Run with the Wind*. Dublin: Wolfhound, 1983; *Run to Earth*. Dublin: Wolfhound, 1984; *Run Swift, Run Free*. Dublin: Wolfhound, 1986. *In Search of the Liberty Tree*. Dublin: Anvil Books, 1994); McNeill, Janet. *My Friend Specs McCann*. London: Faber, 1955, and *Specs Fortissimo*. London: Faber, 1958; MacGrory, Yvonne. *Martha and the Ruby Ring*. Dublin: Children's, 1993; Macken, Walter. *Flight of the Doves*. London: Macmillan, 1968; MacRaois, Cormac. *The Battle below Giltspur*. Dublin: Wolfhound, 1988, and *Dance of the Midnight Fire*. Dublin: Wolfhound, 1989, and *Lightning over Giltspur*. Dublin: Wolfhound, 1991; Melling, Orla. *The Singing Stone*. Dublin: O'Brien, 1993; Mitchell, Geraldine. *Welcoming the French*. Dublin: Attic, 1992; Mitchell, Jane. *When Stars Stop Spinning*. Dublin: Poolbeg, 1993; Mullen, Michael. *The Long March*. Dublin: Poolbeg, 1990; O'Connor, Frank. "First Confession" in *Traveller's Samples*. London: Macmillan/ New York: Knopf, 1951; O'Faolain, Eileen. *The Little Black Hen*. Oxford: Oxford University Press, 1940; O'Hara, Elizabeth (Eilis Ní Dhuibhne). *The Hiring Fair*. Dublin: Poolbeg, 1983, and *Blaeberry Sunday*. Dublin: Poolbeg, 1994; O'Neill, Joan. *Daisy Chain War*. Dublin: Attic, 1990; O'Siochfhrada, Padraig. "Jimeen" in *The Lucky Bag*. Dublin: O'Brien, 1984/First published in Irish as *Jimeen Mhaire Thaidgh*. Dublin: Maunsel agus Roberts, 1921; Parkinson, Siobhan. *Amelia*. Dublin: O'Brien, 1993, and *No Peace for Amelia*. Dublin: O'Brien, 1994; Quinn, John. *The Summer of Lily of Esme*. Dublin: Poolbeg, 1991, and *Duck and Swan*. Dublin: Poolbeg, 1993; Scott, Michael, "De Dannan Series" (*Windlord*. Dublin: Wolfhound, 1991; *Earthlord*. Dublin: Wolfhound, 1992; *Firelord*. Dublin: Wolfhound, 1994; *The Last of the Fianna*. Dublin: O'Brien, 1992); Scott, Mike. *Judith and the Traveller*. Dublin: Wolfhound, 1991, and *Judith and the Spider*. Dublin: Wolfhound, 1992; Sefton, Catherine (Martin Waddell). *Along a Lonely Road*. London: Hamish Hamilton, 1991; Stephens, James. *The Crock of Gold*. London: Macmillan, 1912; Swift, Jonathan. *Gulliver's Travels*. First published, 1726/Swift's revised edition, Dublin: Faulkner, 1735; Taylor, Marilyn. *Could This Be Love, I Wondered?* Dublin: O'Brien, 1994; Waddell, Martin, *Can't You Sleep, Little Bear?* London: Walker, 1988, and "Napper McCann Series" (*Napper Goes for Goal—Striking Again*). London: Penguin, 1981. 2 vols.; *Napper's Golden Goals*. London: Penguin, 1984; *Napper, Super-*

Sub. London: Penguin, 1993; *Napper's Big Match.* London: Penguin, 1993), and "Dingwell Street School Series" (*Fishface Feud.* Dublin: O'Brien, 1993; *Rubberneck's Revenge.* Dublin: O'Brien, 1993).

CLARKE, AUSTIN [AUGUSTINE JOSEPH] (1896–1974), poet, playwright, and novelist. Clarke was born on May 9, 1896, in Dublin. He was educated at Belvedere College and University College, Dublin, from which he received a B.A. in 1916 and an M.A. in 1917, and was then appointed assistant lecturer in English to replace Thomas MacDonagh.* His *The Vengeance of Fionn,* sponsored by AE,* was published in 1917 and widely noticed and admired. In 1927, he wrote his first verse play, *The Son of Learning.* From 1929 to 1937, he worked in England, reviewing and writing poems, plays, and his novels *The Bright Temptation* and *The Singing Men at Cashel,* both of which were banned by the Free State government. In 1940, he and Robert Farren* founded the Dublin Verse-Speaking Society which performed on radio and in the Abbey Theatre.* In 1944, he founded with Farren the Lyric Theatre Company which performed at the Abbey until the 1951 fire. He continued to write prolifically, and his old age became his most accomplished period. In 1962 his first autobiography, *Twice Round the Black Church,* appeared, followed in 1963 by *Collected Plays* and *Flight to Africa,* and in 1968 by another autobiography, *A Penny in the Clouds.* At his death, he was generally considered the finest Irish poet of the generation after Yeats.* Clarke died on March 19, 1974, at the age of seventy-seven. His first book, a narrative poem called *The Vengeance of Fionn* was published in 1917. His last work, a narrative poem called *The Wooing of Becfola,* appeared in the year of his death. In his long working career, while earning his living mainly by literary journalism in Ireland and England, he published verse, plays, novels, two books of memoirs, and numerous books of poetry, many in fugitive form. The *Collected Poems,* a book of almost six hundred pages, appeared shortly after his death as a memorial volume, making it possible for the first time to see his poetry as a whole. It is an important document in modern poetry. And yet, outside of Ireland, Clarke's poetry is scarcely heard of.

There are reasons. To begin with, his work is uneven. He was capable, at any stage of his career, of writing poorly. Even whole books can, on the whole, disappoint, as with *Old-Fashioned Pilgrimage,* published in 1967; though the book that preceded it and the book that followed contain some of his best work. Given this unevenness, the reading of his poetry is a constant test of discrimination and patience. At the same time the range of Clarke's interests is narrow. His poems, with few exceptions, reflect only the immediate milieu. In his narrowness of reference much of his work raises the question of legitimate obscurity. There are poems of such economical means, like "Usufruct" in *Too Great a Vine* (1952) that the essential facts, on whose basis the poem communicates, need to be extracted with Holmesian care. But the facts are there. And a reading of "Miss Marnell," two pages after "Usufruct," acts as a confirming footnote. The poems accumulate, particularly the later ones, and illuminate one another.

A number of times during his career the attention of Clarke's poetry turned completely inward; in psychic experiment on a small scale, sometimes in whole gnomic poems, sometimes in the detail of longer poems or in the prolonged presentation of special situations. *Mnemosyne Lay in Dust* (1966) is a dramatic poem about a patient confined in an asylum. It is a demanding and successful poem of twenty-five pages, set entirely inside the patient's disturbed state of mind, in phases of upset, confusion, or terror. The settings of place are specific and important, but their significance is often private, sometimes even dramatically forgotten.

There is also a problem of verbal idiosyncrasy. With one of his strongest books *Night and Morning,* published in 1938, Clarke abandoned the derivative richness of his earlier work for a compacted and constricted diction in which the elements of grammar and syntax transfer and contort. The mature style of his later work absorbs these complexities, but it does not simplify them. The diction of his last poems is a vivid, particular voice, rich and supple; nothing is unsayable. But it is no "natural" voice.

The effect is compounded by Clarke's early interest in Gaelic prosody. He was not the only Irish writer who wanted to write intricately in the Gaelic manner, but he was the only one to make this element a part of his poetic nature. It became an essential vehicle of expression for him, and though it resulted in a number of poems which are little more than exercises, it also helped him to many fine statements, even on urgent contemporary matters. It works strongly in *Mnemosyne Lay in Dust,* his most intensely personal poetry.

Kindred idiosyncrasies have not prevented the appreciation of say, Ezra Pound. Mere idiosyncrasy is not the difficulty. But, taken with the narrowness of reference or the private focus, and the absence of ordinary communication, it sets a problem for the casual reader. It is the energetic reader, meeting the poetry's demands in the way of modern art, who finds that it meets his. And who finds by way of consolation poems of total lucidity and naturalness scattered here and there in early books and late.

It was Yeats who aroused Clarke's interest in poetry. The first excitement was centered on the Abbey Theatre: "All the dear mummocks out of Tara / That turned my head at seventeen." The Abbey and verse drama remained lifelong enthusiasms. Yeats himself was a lifelong fixation, an object of inspiration and emulation, and a cross; directing Clarke, by his example, toward Irish history, legend and literature; hypnotizing him even from the grave.

Clarke's early narrative poems appear to have been planned as a new retelling of the old sagas in verse, and the poems in *Pilgrimage and Other Poems,* published in 1929, are exhibits from Irish history, apparently in continuation or modification of the plan. In *Night and Morning,* published in 1938, these historical exercises are virtually abandoned. Another and profounder theme is introduced: a Joycean* struggle with issues of conscience and authority, Faith and the Church. Over the book hangs the tortured darkness of apostasy, with the poet in "Tenebrae" an agonized Luther:

> I hammer on that common door,
> Too frantic in my superstition,
> Transfix with nails that I have broken,
> The angry notice of the mind.

Then, for almost twenty years, Clarke wrote no further narrative or lyric poetry. During those years he was involved in practical theatrical affairs and wrote a series of verse plays. But the interruption may also have had something to do with difficulties encountered in the development of his late manner.

Whatever the cause of the interruption, Clarke emerged from his silence in 1955 with *Ancient Lights,* the first of three pamphlets of "poems and satires," making use still of the half-rhymes and internal assonance of his early Gaelic manner, but equipped with new emotional fire and a new epigrammatic power:

> What Larkin bawled to hungry crowds
> Is murmured now in dining-hall
> And study. Faith bestires itself
> Lest infidels in their impatience
> Leave it behind. Who could have guessed
> Batons were blessings in disguise,
> When every ambulance was filled
> With half-killed men and Sunday trampled
> Upon unrest? Such fear can harden
> Or soften heart, knowing too clearly
> His name endures on our holiest page.
> Scrawled in a rage by Dublin's poor.
>   ("Inscription for a Headstone")

In 1961 the three recent pamphlets and the contents of *Night and Morning,* long out of print, were published by the Dolmen Press* as *Later Poems,* giving Clarke a wider audience for his later poetry. The important changes were sensed by a few reviewers, and Clarke had suddenly a discerning, if tiny public. In continuation of the release begun in 1955, he produced an enormous quantity of poems, very uneven, in a very short time; these were published in *Flight to Africa* in 1963. It is probably his most important single book. Longer than all the *Later Poems,* and more varied in content and manner, it contains a number of major poems, including poems of Dublin detail and character, like the long poem "Martha Blake at Fifty-One," which (with related poems in other books) combine into a presentation of the human situation in his mid-twentieth century Dublin setting.

After finishing *Mnemosyne Lay in Dust* in 1966, Clarke entered a mood of cheerful good temper which made possible some of the finest poetry of his last phase: a series of wickedly glittering narratives culminating in *Tiresias;* poetry as pure entertainment, serious and successful.

THOMAS KINSELLA

WORKS: *The Vengeance of Fionn.* Dublin & London: Maunsel, 1918; *The Fires of Baal.* Dublin & London: Maunsel & Roberts, 1921; *The Sword of the West.* London: Maunsel & Roberts, 1921;

The Cattledrive in Connaught. London: Allen & Unwin, 1925; *The Son of Learning.* London: Allen & Unwin, 1927; *Pilgrimage and Other Poems.* London: Allen & Unwin, 1929; *The Flame.* London: Allen & Unwin, 1930; *The Bright Temptation.* London: Allen & Unwin, 1932; *Collected Poems.* London: Allen & Unwin, 1936; *The Singing Men at Cashel.* London: Allen & Unwin, 1936; *Night and Morning.* Dublin: Orwell, 1938; *Sister Eucharia.* Dublin: Orwell/London: Williams & Norgate, 1939; *Black Fast.* Dublin: Orwell, 1941; *The Straying Student.* Dublin: Gayfield, 1942; *As the Crow Flies.* Dublin: Bridge, 1943; *The Viscount of Blarney and Other Plays.* Dublin: Bridge/London: Williams & Norgate, 1944; *First Visit to England and Other Memories.* Dublin: Bridge, 1945; *The Second Kiss.* Dublin: Bridge/London: Williams & Norgate, 1946; *The Plot Succeeds.* Dublin: Bridge, 1950; *The Sun Dances at Easter.* London: Andrew Melrose, 1952; *The Moment Next to Nothing.* Dublin: Bridge, 1953; *Ancient Lights.* Dublin: Bridge, 1955; *Too Great a Vine: Poems and Satires.* Dublin: Dolmen, 1957; *The Horse-Eaters.* Dublin: Bridge, 1960; *Later Poems.* Dublin: Dolmen, 1961; *Forget-Me-Not.* Dublin: Dolmen, 1962; *Poetry in Modern Ireland.* Cork: Mercier (for the Cultural Relations Committee of Ireland), 1962; *Twice Round the Black Church.* London: Routledge & Kegan Paul, 1962; *Collected Plays.* Dublin: Dolmen, 1963; *Flight to Africa.* Dublin: Dolmen, 1963; *Mnemosyne Lay in Dust.* Dublin: Dolmen, 1966; *Old-Fashioned Pilgrimage and Other Poems.* Dublin: Dolmen, 1967; *A Penny in the Clouds.* London: Routledge, 1968; *A Sermon on Swift and Other Poems.* Dublin: Bridge, 1968; *The Echo at Coole and Other Poems.* Dublin: Dolmen, 1968; *Two Interludes Adapted from Cervantes.* Dublin: Dolmen, 1968; *The Celtic Twilight and the Nineties.* Dublin: Dolmen, 1969; *Orphide.* Dublin: Bridge, 1970; *Tiresias.* Dublin: Bridge, 1971; *The Impuritans.* Dublin: Dolmen, 1973. (Play); *Collected Poems.* Dublin: Dolmen/London & New York: Oxford University Press, 1974; *The Third Kiss.* Dublin: Dolmen, 1976. (Play); *Liberty Lane.* [Mountrath, Portlaoise]: Dolmen, [1978]. (Play); *Reviews and Essays of Austin Clarke.* Gregory A. Schirmer, ed. Gerrards Cross: Colin Smythe, 1995. REFERENCES: Clarke, Dardis. "Austin Clarke at Templeogue." *Poetry Ireland Review* 21 (1988): 167–175; Halpern, Susan. *Austin Clarke, His Life and Works.* Dublin: Dolmen, 1974; Harmon, Maurice. *Austin Clarke: A Critical Introduction.* Dublin: Wolfhound/Totowa, N.J.: Barnes & Noble, 1989; *Irish University Review.* Maurice Harmon, ed. 4 (Spring 1974). (A Clarke number containing detailed biographical notes by Harmon, critical essays on various aspects of Clarke's work, and Gerard Lyne's bibliography. Clarke himself contributed a play, *The Visitation.*); Ricigliano, Lorraine. *Austin Clarke: A Reference Guide.* New York: G. K. Hall, [1993]; Schirmer, Gregory A. *The Poetry of Austin Clarke.* Mountrath, Portlaoise: Dolmen/Notre Dame, Ind.: Notre Dame University Press, 1983; Tapping, Craig G. *Austin Clarke: A Study of His Writings.* Dublin: Academy, 1981.

CLARKIN, SEAN (1941–), poet. Clarkin was born in New Ross, County Wexford, in 1941. He was educated at the Gregorian University in Rome, at University College, Cork, and at Trinity College, Dublin. In 1971, he won the first Patrick Kavanagh Poetry Award, and he has published one pamphlet of verse. His work is in short lines of free verse, and his rhythms and sentences are abrupt and often fragmentary. He is capable of sharp images and, occasionally, witty comparisons, as when he describes a man being as un-Italian "as tinned spaghetti."

WORK: *Without Frenzy.* Dublin: Gallery, 1974.

CLEARY, BRENDAN (1958–), poet. Cleary was born in County Antrim and has edited *The Echo Room,* a poetry magazine in Newcastle upon Tyne.

WORK: *The Irish Card.* Newcastle upon Tyne: Bloodaxe, 1993.

CLEEVE, BRIAN [TALBOT] (1921–   ), novelist. Cleeve was born in Essex to an Irish father and an English mother. At the age of seventeen, he ran away to sea, and during the Second World War he worked in the Merchant Navy and in military intelligence. After the war, he traveled in Europe and was a journalist in South Africa, from where he was expelled for writing against apartheid. He is a graduate of the University of South Africa. Returning to Ireland in 1954, he received a Ph.D. from the National University, was twice épée fencing champion of Ireland, and for ten years was a scriptwriter and broadcaster for RTÉ.

Despite this active life, he has written prolifically. Most of his output has been craftsmanlike popular fiction and ranges from Regency romances à la Georgette Heyer to thrillers that are forgettable but effective. *Death of a Painted Lady,* for instance, paints a glumly evocative picture of certain aspects of Dublin in the early 1960s. His more serious work would include a volume of short stories, *The Horse Thieves of Ballysaggert* (1966), which is uneven but contains at least two admirable tales. More ambitious works are two long novels, *Cry of Morning* (1971) and *Tread Softly on This Place* (1972). The first deals with the modern Dublin of building developers and television antennas, and the second is a study of the clash between the modern world and provincial Ireland. Both books seem consciously intended for the mass best-seller market. The writing is fluent, and the reader is easily carried along by a large number of well-differentiated, if not deeply drawn, characters, in rather complex plots. Both novels provide pleasant enough reading, but both fade quickly in the memory, as does the work, say, of a Leon Uris or an Arthur Hailey. They are serious but slick, and similar Irish writers who come to mind are David Hanly* or, to a lesser extent, W. J. White.* Cleeve's best-drawn character is probably Margaret Sullivan, the heroine of the more recent novel, *A Woman of Fortune* (1993), a fine study of an uneducated Dublin woman amassing a fortune by her own innate acumen and then nearly losing it in old age by being duped, because of loneliness, by the attentions of a younger man.

Cleeve is also the author of a *Dictionary of Irish Writers* (1967–1971), later revised and expanded with Anne M. Brady* under the title of *A Biographical Dictionary of Irish Writers* (1985), which offers capsule biographies and often short evaluations of about 1,200 writers in English and Irish. To both editions, this volume is indebted.

PRINCIPAL WORKS: *The Far Hills.* London: Jarrolds, 1953; *Portrait of My City.* London: Jarrolds, 1953; *Birth of a Dark Soul.* London: Jarrold's, 1953/published in America as *The Night Winds,* Boston: Houghton Mifflin, 1954; *Assignment to Vengeance.* London: Hammond, Hammond, [1961]; *Death of a Painted Lady.* London: Hammond, Hammond, [1962]; *Death of a Wicked Servant.* London: Hammond, Hammond, [1963]; *Vote X for Treason.* London: Collins, 1964; *Dark Blood, Dark Terror.* London: Hammond, Hammond, [1966]; *The Horse Thieves of Ballysaggert.* Cork: Mercier, 1966. (Stories); *Violent Death of a Bitter Englishman.* New York: Random House, 1967; *Dictionary of Irish Writers.* 3 vols. Cork: Mercier, [1967–1971]/revised and expanded with Anne M. Brady as *A Biographical Dictionary of Irish Writers.* [Mullingar, Co. Westmeath]: Lilliput, 1985; *Cry of Morning.* London: Michael Joseph, 1971; *Tread Softly in This Place.* London: Cassell, 1972; *The Dark Side of the Sun.* London: Cassell, 1973; *Sara.* London: Cassell, 1976; *Kate.* London:

Cassell, 1977; *Judith.* London: Cassell, 1978; *Hester.* London: Cassell, 1979/New York: Coward, McCann & Geoghegan, 1980; *The House on the Rock.* London: Watkins, [1980]. (Metaphysical speculation); *The Seven Mansions.* London: Watkins, ca. 1980; *1938: A World Vanishing.* London: Buchan & Enright, 1982; *A View of the Irish.* London: Buchan & Enright, 1983; *A Woman of Fortune.* [Dingle, Co. Kerry:] Brandon, [1993].

CLERKE, ELLEN MARY (1840–1906), poet. Clerke was the daughter of John William Clerke and his wife, the former Miss Deasy, sister of Lord Justice Deasy. She was born on September 26, 1840, in Skibbereen, County Cork. The Clerke family moved to Dublin in 1861, then relocated to Queenstown in 1863. They traveled during the winters: Rome in 1867 and 1868, Naples in 1871 and 1872, and Florence during the winters from 1873 to 1876. It is not, then, surprising that Clerke and her sister Agnes Mary (1842–1907) were fluent in Italian and Latin. Ellen was a noted translator and wrote a number of "versified translations" of Italian poetry for the *History of Italian Literature* by R. Garnett. She also wrote articles in German and Arabic for various periodicals. Her literary reputation was based on her devotional poetry, and her *The Flying Dutchman, and Other Poems* (1881) was an immediate success. In her memoir of the Clerke sisters, Lady Huggins states that Ellen was "a devoted and exemplary Catholic." She also wrote articles on geology, astronomy, the Arabic language, and mathematics. She was a talented musician and a gifted guitarist. She and her sister were inseparable, living together throughout their lives. Ellen Clerke died in London on March 2, 1906.

Agnes Clerke was famous among the nineteenth-century astronomers of Europe. *A Popular History of Astronomy During the Nineteenth Century* was a standard textbook, and portions of it were actually written when the author was but fifteen years of age.

ANNE COLMAN

PRINCIPAL WORKS: *The Flying Dutchman, and Other Poems.* London: Satchell, 1881; *Jupiter and His System.* London: Edward Stanford, 1892; translations contributed to *History of Italian Literature* by R. Garrett. 1898; *Fable and Song in Italy.* London: Grant Richards, 1899; *Flowers of Fire.* London: Hutchinson, 1902. REFERENCE: Huggins, Lady. *Agnes Mary Clerke and Ellen Mary Clerke; an Appreciation.* Printed for private circulation, 1907.

CLERY, ARTHUR E. (1879–1932), controversialist, lawyer, and academic. Clery was born in Dublin, the son of barrister Arthur Clery, K. C. He was educated at University School, Dublin, at Clongowes Wood College, and at University College, Dublin. He was called to the bar in 1902 and in 1910 became professor of law of property and contracts at University College, Dublin. From college days on, he wrote under the pen name of "Chanel," after the martyred French missionary. As "Chanel," he wrote *The Idea of a Nation* (1907), and as "Arthur Synon" he wrote a short novel, *The Coming of the King* (1909), a light historical fantasy of an invasion of Ireland by James II. It is aided by Swift* but fails to seize Dublin Castle through sectarian divisions. In 1918, he wrote appreciations of the poets of the Easter Rising, Pearse,* Plunkett,* and MacDonagh.* He was a member of the Dail Éireann Supreme Court from 1920 to 1922. Anti-Treaty in sentiment, he stood as Independent Republican T. D. for University College in 1927. He never married and was described by a friend as "a devout and militant Catholic." A portrait painting hangs in Newman House. He died on November 20, 1932.

PETER COSTELLO

PRINCIPAL WORKS: *The Idea of a Nation.* Dublin: Duffy, 1907; *The Coming of the King.* Dublin: Catholic Truth Society, 1909/St. Louis: Herder, 1914; "Pearse, MacDonagh and Plunkett: An Appreciation" in *Poets of the Insurrection.* Dublin & London: Maunsel, 1918; *Dublin Essays.* Dublin: Maunsel/New York: Brentano's, 1919. He wrote also some legal works and much journalism in *Studies* and elsewhere.

CLIFFORD, SIGERSON (1913–1985), ballad writer and man of letters. Edward Bernard Clifford was born in 11 Dean Street, Cork, in 1913 to Mary Anne Sigerson and Michael Clifford. Both of his parents were from Kerry, and the family moved to Cahirciveen in the South Kerry peninsula when Edward was two years old. Educated at the Christian Brothers Primary and Secondary schools, he began to write poems in his early teens. At this time he used the Irish form of his name, Eamonn Ó Clubhain, but he soon adopted the name Sigerson as his Christian name. It was a significant development, marking the beginning of his writing career and showing his respect for the traditions of his grandfather, Ned Sigerson, a stonemason, general handyman, and noted storyteller.

The natural beauty of Cahirciveen, its many fine sportsmen, and the older characters of the town held a fascination for him from an early age and became dominant features of his work. The Rocky Road, the Fair Field, the Old Road, and Barr na Sraide became his canvas. Though physically parted from them for much of his adult life, the man and the place were inseparable.

Clifford joined the Irish civil service at the age of nineteen and worked in employment exchanges throughout the country, including Dungloe, Tralee, Cahirciveen, and Cork. In 1943, he was transferred to the Department of Social Welfare in Dublin, and he remained there until he retired in 1973.

In 1945, he married Marie Eady from Cork. They had seven children, two girls and five boys. He died in Glenageary, County Dublin, on January 1, 1985, and was buried, in compliance with his wishes, in Cahirciveen, with some lines from his song, "The Boys of Barr na Sraide," as his epitaph:

> I'll take my sleep in those green fields, the place my life began,
> Where the Boys of Barr na Sraide went hunting for the wran.

Today he is remembered mainly as the man who wrote "The Boys of Barr na Sraide," a song that became hugely popular through the singing of Sean Ó Siochain on Radio Éireann's "The Ballad-Maker's Saturday Night" in the 1940s and 1950s. It is not unusual, however, to meet people who have memorized "The Ballad of the Tinker's Son," "The Boy Remembers His Father," and "I Am Kerry," which were first published in the still-popular *Ballads of a Bogman* (1955).

Most of his poems were written in early manhood, and from the age of thirty-one his creative energy was devoted almost entirely to drama. *The Great Pacificator,* a play based on the life of Daniel O'Connell, was produced by the Abbey Theatre* in 1947, while *Nano, The Glassy Man,* and *The Devil's Dust* received much acclaim. Indeed, all of his eleven plays met with much success on the amateur drama circuit.

Although he wrote many stories and articles for the Irish press, including the stories in *The Red-Haired Woman* (1989), Clifford was basically a ballad poet. His verses show a keen sense of place and a celebration of a town—its scenery, its people, and their everyday activities. He exalted the humble and therefore unknowingly struck a chord that still resonates.

TIM DENNEHY

WORKS: *Travelling Tinkers.* Dublin: Dolmen, 1951; *Lascar Rock.* Dublin: Dolmen, 1953; *Ballads of a Bogman.* London: Macmillan/New York: St. Martin's, 1955; *An Banbh Beag.* Dublin: An Gum, 1969. (Children's story, translated into Irish by Peadar Ó Muircheataigh); with T. Crofton Croker. *Legends of Kerry.* Tralee: Geraldine, 1972. (Folklore); with W. MacLysaght. *The Tragic Story of the Colleen Bawn.* Tralee: Anvil Books, 1966. (Consists of MacLysaght's reconstruction of the murder and of Clifford's adaptation of Griffin's *The Collegians*); *The Red-Haired Woman and Other Stories.* Cork: Mercier, 1989.

CLIFTON, HARRY (1952–   ), poet. Clifton was born in Dublin and educated at University College, Dublin. He lives in Italy and is the author of six books of poetry as well as some short stories and essays. Since "New Irish Writing" in the *Irish Press* first published Clifton's poems in 1970 and a story in 1978, his work has appeared in many newspapers, magazines, and anthologies. He was the 1982 winner of the Patrick Kavanagh* Award and has had bursaries from the Irish Arts Council. He has been a guest writer at the Tyrone Guthrie Centre at Annaghmakerrig, the Iowa International Writers' Program, and the Robert Frost Place in New Hampshire.

Clifton's poetry reflects not only his roots in Dublin but also his varied experiences in Europe, Africa, Asia, and America. Many poems in his first volume, *The Walls of Carthage* (1977), show the dense, difficult meditations of a scholastic Catholic mind encountering the realities of Irish life. The epiphanies may suggest a latter-day Stephen Dedalus, but the highly wrought style may recall Wallace Stevens, the subject of Clifton's 1975 M.A. thesis at University College, Dublin. For the young poet, words alone are certainly good in trying to make sense of experience, but he is also aware of bookish limitations, as he remarks in "The Cang."

Office of the Salt Merchant (1979) begins in Ireland but soon moves to West Africa. Clifton's two years of teaching English in Nigeria from 1976 to 1978 and his related travels provided him with two dozen poems alive with vivid perceptions and wry reflections on cultures very different from his Dublin background. Estranged both at home and abroad, the Irish poet in Africa feels a detachment, as when the persona of the poems notices and ponders the "health inspectors" hovering like vultures over the carcasses during Rhamadan in "Catarrh" or when he notices the many typing errors in the draft constitution in "Government Quarters."

The appropriately entitled collection *Comparative Lives* (1982) also begins and ends in Ireland, but most of the poems move through, and capture the spirit of, many places. Many poems in the book revolve around his two years, 1980 to 1982, in Bangkok, Thailand, administering United Nations/Concern refugee aid programs. Particularly interesting are two five-part sets, "Sketches from Berlin" and "Indian Sequence," in which a sure sense of place soon expands to a sad sense of history. The five sonnets of "Indian Sequence" maintain a composure as they move through "a disconnected wilderness, dharma without destination." ("Disconnected" is a recurrent word in his work.) As in his poems set in other countries, there is a general sense of "power failure."

"Monsoon Girl" is electric with erotic and political tension, with its hints of miscarriage of justice. The woman as sexual object, sometimes a Third World prostitute, is a common figure. "Death of Thomas Merton" is perhaps Clifton's best long poem. It is both sensitive to, and critical of, Merton, a "holy fool." "Field Hospital, Thailand, 1982" and "The Holding Centre" reflect upon Clifton's two years, from 1980 to 1982, administering aid programs for Indo-Chinese refugees. These two poems, like much of his work, show a compassion for the victims of history whose pervasive misery history does not always record. They also articulate the dilemma of the poet surrounded by mass suffering and his desire to clear a space in which his imagination can be free from certain responsibilities. Clifton would claim that all his poems are merely efforts to capture experiences and would deny that they have any political purpose, but the human situations he so beautifully records are vibrant with political implications.

In Clifton's 1988 collection, *The Liberal Cage,* poems recollect his African and Asian experiences, brood upon present conditions in Ireland, explore aspects of American culture, and delight in his married life with novelist Deirdre Madden* in Perugia. Many poems remain deeply introspective. In *Night Train through the Brenner* (1994), the disengaged poet continues his "travels in search of a Rubicon." But now he has someone else inside his solitary world to look out on the different cities, whether they are crossing borders or hibernating in temporary homes. Two examples of his finest love poems in one of his richest collections are the dedicatory prologue to Deirdre Madden, "In our own city, we are exiles—" and "Where We Live."

Clifton's short stories range from the lives of night watchmen on the Dublin docks to an Irish whiskey priest in northern Nigeria ("Where the Track Fades") to an attempted coup in Bangkok. Clifton's short fiction has been published in Irish newspapers since 1978. An early Joycean example is "Alexandria Sheds," which explores the dark underbelly of student life in the 1970s, showing "the squalor and inertia we thought was free living." Postgraduate night watchmen on the Dublin docks were "like night animals in an underworld . . . each of us looking for his favourite hole to lurk in, solitary, nightbound and, in some ways, at peace." This extended story allows Clifton to deal less cryptically with many concerns that recur in his poems, whether they be about solitary figures in Dublin, western Africa, or Southern Asia.

CHRISTOPHER GRIFFIN

WORKS: *The Walls of Carthage.* [Dublin]: Gallery, [1977]; *Office of the Salt Merchant.* [Dublin]: Gallery, [1979]; "Alexandria Sheds." *Irish Press,* January 17, 1979. (Short story); *Comparative Lives.* [Dublin]: Gallery, [1982]; "Where the Track Fades." *Irish Times,* August 12, 1987. (Short story); *The Liberal Cage.* [Dublin]: Gallery, [1988]; *Desert Route: Selected Poems, 1973–1988.* [Oldcastle, Co. Meath]: Gallery, [1992]; *Night Train through the Brenner.* [Oldcastle, Co. Meath]: Gallery, [1994]

COADY, MICHAEL (1939–   ), poet. Coady was born in Carrick-on-Suir, County Tipperary, and he still lives in his native town. He was educated there and in University Colleges Galway and Cork. He works in Carrick-on-Suir as a teacher and has also been a prominent local musician—a talent he inherits from his mother and one that has served him well both in the making of his poems and in their content. He has written a column for a local newspaper, the *Clonmel Nationalist,* and his weekly reflections on aspects of local life and wider themes have, at their best, displayed fastidious care and a love of locale that sets them among the best columns in contemporary Irish journalism. He has published two books of poems and has encouraged many younger writers.

His poems exhibit a number of themes, but many of them are connected by their concern for the details of everyday local life. The streets, characters, history, and customs of Carrick-on-Suir figure in his work, as in the poem "Two for a Woman, Three for a Man." In an age where the planetary can take precedence over the parochial, and where the personal often gives way to the faceless, Michael Coady is one of those writers—Patrick Kavanagh* and the essayist Hubert Butler* were others—for whom the local is richly supreme. His work illustrates what many writers have realized: that to tap into the local is to tap into an expression that is ultimately universal. His work is witty and shows many elements of a balladic, songwriting tradition. His awareness of local fidelities is combined with an empathy with history, as in his poems inspired by the dedications on old headstones. Like other Irish poets, he has written about the Irish experience in America. His awareness of hurt is balanced by an awareness of a healing element; or, as he says in one of his poems, although there are torturers, "[t]here are also musicians" in the world.

SEÁN DUNNE

WORKS: *Two for a Woman, Three for a Man.* [Dublin]: Gallery, [1980; *Oven Lane.* [Dublin]: Gallery, [1987].

COCHRANE, IAN (1942–   ), novelist. Cochrane was born in Northern Ireland. His first novel, *A Streak of Madness* (1973), details the life of a poor Ulster family. The book examines feckless and incapable parents, a stereotypically "good" schoolteacher, and the requisite young artist. Cochrane's next novel, *Gone in the Head* (1974), is narrated by a fourteen-year-old-boy named Frank Broodie and written in a prose reminiscent of the simple, although sometimes self-conscious, thoughts and memories of early teenage years. Despite its often clichéd plot and predictable characterization—a drunken father, a desperately religious mother, and a wise simpleton whose candor is not always timely and appreciated—the novel is eminently readable, funny, and, on occasion, quite moving. Its narrative voice conveys familiar elements with the freshness of youthful perspective and innocence. *Jesus on a Stick* (1975) examines random sexuality, unemployment, boredom, and a sensitive narrator trapped in a cruel world. However, the prose style and the use of the present tense save the work from cliché and monotony. *Ladybird in a Loony-Bin* (1978) also addresses familiar topics for the modern novelists, such as the deformity and confusion of industrialized society, and also is redeemed by its colorful prose. Unlike Anne Devlin* and Christina Reid,* whose recent works search for ritual and meaning in a time of war and violence, Cochrane's work finds meaning in the Northern violence only through the individual human voice. Clearly, he chooses common themes to demonstrate their universality and the hopelessness of individuals' lives, but unlike many contemporary novelists, he does not seem deadened by such themes. Despite misery, cruelty, and purposelessness, his characters exist and suffer daily through issues that have become clichés. *F for Ferg* (1980) continues and expands this effort. Although reviewers have criticized the plot and characterization as melodramatic and "stage Irishy," this seems to be Cochrane's point. People do act cruelly and without concern for self or others, but some people are sensitive enough to discern these traits and too sensitive to dismiss them. Cochrane's most recent novel, *The Slipstream* (1983), is set in London and explores the lives of unemployed young people coming to terms with the meaninglessness and desperation of their lives. Once again, these familiar themes are saved from cliché by Cochrane's innocent narrative voice. The totality of Cochrane's work portrays thoughtful, intelligent, and sensitive individuals perceiving and conveying the horror of the ordinary, the cliché. Although his work sometimes becomes too monotonous and predictable, his style is unique and moving. Further, his work warrants a wider audience, and Irish literature has suffered from the author's recent silence.

BERNARD McKENNA

WORKS: *A Streak of Madness*. London: Allen Lane, 1973; *Gone in the Head*. London: Routledge & Kegan Paul, 1974; *Jesus on a Stick*. London: Routledge & Kegan Paul, 1975; *Ladybird in a Looney-Bin*. London: Weidenfeld & Nicolson, 1978; *F for Ferg*. London: Gollancz, 1980; *The Slipstream*. London: Gollancz, 1983.

COFFEY, BRIAN (1905–1995), poet. The son of Denis J. Coffey, first president of University College, Dublin (UCD), Brian Coffey was born near Dublin on June 8, 1905. (He should not be confused with an American fiction writer who sometimes uses "Brian Coffey" as a pseudonym.) After attending Clongowes Wood College, he received a bachelor's degree from Institution St. Vincent in 1924 and then studied for two more bachelor's and a master's of science at UCD until 1930. In that year, he met Denis Devlin,* and the two together issued a volume of poems. By 1934, Samuel Beckett's* essay on "Recent Irish Poetry" would call Coffey and Devlin "the most interesting of the youngest generation of Irish poets." Coffey's *Three Poems* appeared in 1933 and was followed by *Third Person* in 1938, the year of his marriage. But a long hiatus then followed before he published, in the 1960s, a series of works, including "Missouri Sequence" (1962), the poem for which he is best known, as well as translations of Mallarmé and others. At least half of the works included in his *Poems and Versions 1929–1990* (1991) appeared first in the 1975 *Irish University Review* special issue on Coffey, or later. After Devlin's death, Coffey edited two volumes of his longtime friend's work.

That Coffey may be known mainly through excerpts from "Missouri Sequence" (the only sampling of his work included in, for instance, *The Field Day Anthology* and *The Faber Book of Irish Verse*) means that readers may be greatly misled: that somber poem's absorbing but accessible consideration of the familiar theme of emigration is formally and idiomatically unique in Coffey's oeuvre. Like Thomas Murphy's* *A Crucial Week in the Life of a Grocer's Assistant*, "Missouri Sequence" suggests that what is at stake in Irish emigration is not a socially or economically constructed choice between leaving and staying, but rather a moral self-evaluation occasioned by a personal crisis:

> How the will shifts from goal to goal
> for who does not freely choose.
> Some choose, some are chosen
> to go their separate paths.
> I would choose, I suppose, yet would be chosen
> in some equation between God's will and mine,
> rejecting prudence to make of conflict
> a monument to celtic self-importance.
>
> The truth is, where the cross is not
> The Christian does not go.

Coffey insists: *"none chooses who were not first chosen / to greet fairly their cross."* Elsewhere in the poem he arraigns himself for "having failed to choose / with loving wise choice." These moments anticipate Eavan Boland's* "An Irish Childhood in England: 1951," with its suspended question, "Did I choose to—?" No twentieth-century Irish poem offers a more urgent examination of the moral and epistemological meanings of "choice" than does "Missouri Sequence."

But exile, Coffey's characteristic theme, figures in his work "not so much a social condition as an ontological given, the necessary ground of existence," as Stan Smith has observed. What "Missouri Sequence" gives voice to, according to Smith, "is a natural and inevitable vagrancy." The early "Quay" is another poem of departure, as is the late "Window in the Sky." But in much of Coffey's work, deeply immersed in religious meditation and strongly influenced by French surrealism, the themes and tones are much more difficult to identify. J.C.C. Mays, introducing the *Poems and Versions,* recalls having "heard someone complain you need a degree in Thomas Aquinas to get anything out of [Coffey's poetry], and another that you have to be well-read in French poetry." Mays' insistence that Coffey's "method assumes," on the contrary, that "book-learning will not help in the last ditch" may not reassure puzzled readers. But Mays rightly gives priority to the way Coffey's poems sound. Their syntax and rhythms are often reminiscent of Pound—especially in the translations—and Eliot.

Still, some of the illustrated works of the 1960s, such as *Monster, A Concrete Poem* (1966), share more elements with the Beatles' *Yellow Submarine* than with modernist inheritors like Thomas Kinsella* or James Merrill. John Ashberry may ultimately be the best analogue; though it seems unsurprising that John Montague,* also influenced by the French, is the anthologist who has been most ready to include Coffey's work—in both *Bitter Harvest* and the *Faber Book.* Even *Abcedarian* (1974), which looks like a children's alphabetical bestiary, seems to posit a rather sophisticated readership with

> I'm a Newt.
> A Yank I met
> in a think-tank
> Said, "You're Kute."

and

> I'm a Viper.
> Sunning
> on a stone I lie:
> "Horseman, pass by."

The bitter, obscure joke in *The Big Laugh* (1976) depends on presenting Beckettian characters in sometimes Wakean language; Coffey relates laughter and apocalypse in the way of Ted Hughes's *Crow,* but without the poetic energy. Coffey's stylistic "vagrancy" often makes his work seem listless, even static. In "Xenia" (1978), his characteristic repetition of words in individual verse lines gives the sonnet the feeling of a villanelle. Coffey is apt to turn to Joyce's* themes and cadences, but without offering Joyce's sense of profusion: "All wanting fruit of other's will / is wanting sadly wanting," he says in "The Time the Place." But in that poem, as in the longer *Advent* (1986) and *The Death of Hektor* (1979), Coffey may also achieve moments of sad beauty, such as in the concluding

> Prone I stared at the night sky
> quite recognizably starred

knew as little as he or she
how another mewards fared

Coffey died on April 14, 1995, in Southampton.

VICTOR LUFTIG

WORKS: With Denis Devlin. *Poems.* Dublin: A. Thom, 1930; *Three Poems.* Paris: Librarie Jeanette Monnier, 1933; *Third Person.* London: George Reavy, 1938; ed., *Collected Poems* by Denis Devlin. Dublin: Dolmen, 1964; *Dice Thrown Will Never Annul Chance.* Dublin: Dolmen, 1965. (Translation of Mallarme); *Monster, A Concrete Poem.* London: Advent, 1966; ed., *The Heavenly Foreigner* by Denis Devlin. Dublin: Dolmen, 1967; *Selected Poems.* Dublin: New Writers, 1971/ Dublin: Raven Arts, 1983; *Abcedarian.* London: Advent, 1974; *The Irish University Review* 5 (Autumn 1975). (A Brian Coffey Special Issue); *The Big Laugh.* Dublin: SugarLoaf, 1976; *The Death of Hektor.* Guildford: Circle, 1979; *Topos and Other Poems.* Bath: Mammon, 1981; *Chanterelles: Short Poems, 1971–1983.* Wilton: Melmoth, 1985; *Slight Song.* London: Menard, 1985. (After Mallarmé); *Advent.* London: Menard, 1986. (After Mallarmé); *Salut.* Dublin: Hardpressed, 1988. (After Mallarmé); *Poems of Mallarmé.* London: Menard, 1990; *Poems and Versions 1929–1990.* Dublin: Dedalus, [1991]. REFERENCE: Morgan, Jack. " 'Missouri Sequence': Brian Coffey's St. Louis Years, 1947–1952.'' *Éire-Ireland* 28 (Winter 1993): 100–114.

COFFEY, THOMAS (1925–   ), playwright. Coffey, an extremely popular and promising playwright in the early 1960s, was born on September 3, 1925, in Ennis, County Clare. After graduating from St. Flannan's College in Ennis, he worked at a variety of jobs before qualifying as a teacher of English, Gaelic, and mathematics. In the mid-1950s, he won prizes for short plays in Irish and had several short plays in English broadcast on Irish radio. His first full-length stage play, *Stranger Beware* (Abbey,* 1958), is set in West Kerry; it is more interesting for its realistic observation than for its melodramatic plot. Other plays include *Anyone Could Rob a Bank* (Abbey, 1959), a broad farce and his most popular piece; *The Long Sorrow* (Abbey, 1960), a one-act plea for tolerance between the North and the South; and *Them* (Eblana, 1962), a superb study of how a family copes with an imbecile son. *Gone Tomorrow* (Gate,* 1965), a technically accomplished study of sensitive youth, won the Irish Life Drama Award. *The Call* (Abbey, 1966), a study of religious fanaticism in a small town, is written with little distinction. In the mid-1960s, Coffey gave up teaching, moved to Limerick, and went into business. Since then, he has apparently written little.

WORKS: *The Call.* Dublin: James Duffy, 1967; *Anyone Could Rob a Bank.* Dublin: James Duffy, 1974. REFERENCE: Hogan, Robert. *After the Irish Renaissance.* Minneapolis: University of Minnesota Press, 1967. Pp. 82–85.

COGHILL, RHODA [SINCLAIR] (1903–   ), poet. Born in Dublin, Coghill was educated at Alexandra College, Read Pianoforte School, and Trinity College. She was a concert pianist, taught piano, and in 1939 became accompanist for Radio Éireann. She turned to poetry after an illness and published two slim and interesting collections. *The Bright Hillside* (1948) has considerable range of subject, from rather conventional descriptions in the early pages to pieces suggestive of Emily Dickinson or H. D. in the later ones. The technique is equally varied. She fluently handles conventional iambics and, of course, free verse, and she gets considerable effect with spondees. Indeed, when she adds alliteration in such lines, she sounds almost like Hopkins. She often uses rhyme, indeed sometimes a too-complicated Dylan Thomas rhyme scheme, as in the ABCDE EDCBA of "Revolt." However, in a piece like "Poem," she substitutes assonance for rhyme with the assurance of an Austin Clarke.* *Time Is a Squirrel* (1956) is only a twenty-page pamphlet, but it contains two charming children's poems, "The Bird's Garden" and "In the Train," as well as the strong depiction of a woman avoiding an old lover in "Flight." If Coghill's slim collections are too eclectic in their references to allow for an individual voice, their various voices are often polished and arresting.

WORKS: *The Bright Hillside.* Dublin: Hodges, Figgis, 1948; *Time Is a Squirrel.* [Dublin]: Published for the author at Dolmen, 1956.

COLIN SMYTHE, LTD., publishing house. This publishing house was founded in 1966, the initial finance coming from the sale of the publisher's collection of first editions of W. B. Yeats* and Dun Emer/Cuala Press* publications to the Dublin City Library. The company moved to Gerrards Cross, Buckinghamshire, in 1967, and its extensive Irish list was conceived in 1968 after Lester Connor at the Yeats Summer School wondered why the company was not publishing Lady Gregory's* books. The result was the *Coole Edition* of Lady Gregory's works (general editors, T. R. Henn and Colin Smythe, 1970–   ). The list developed with editions of individual works and of the *Collected Edition* of AE's* writings, some George Moore titles (including the three volumes-in-one edition of *Hail and Farewell!,* edited by Richard Allen Cave), the three-volume *Dramatic Works of Denis Johnston,** and the *Irish Literary Studies,* containing about fifty volumes, which has covered most aspects of Irish literature in the twentieth century and also includes critical studies of some nineteenth-century authors. Other series published by the company are *Irish Drama Selections* (general editors, Joseph Ronsley and Ann Saddlemyer), *The Princess Grace Irish Literary Series* and *The Princess Grace Irish Library Lectures* (the general editor of both being C. George Sandulescu), and *Ulster Editions and Monographs* (general editor, Robert Welch).

On the demise of the Dolmen Press* in 1987 after the death of its founder, Liam Miller, who had designed and printed some of Colin Smythe's publications, including *A Book of Devotions* by Queen Elizabeth I, all Dolmen's stock was bought from the liquidators by Colin Smythe, and so the firm now has one of the largest Irish-interest lists of any publisher.

COLIN SMYTHE

COLLINS, MICHAEL (1964–   ), novelist and short story writer. Collins was born in Limerick and educated in Ireland and the United States. He now lives in Chicago and teaches at the University of Notre Dame. One quote on the dust jacket of his volume of short stories, *The Meat Eaters* (1992), compares him to Joyce* and Beckett,* and the comparison, particularly to Beckett, is not entirely inexact. The eccentric, maimed, and insane characters of many of his stories sit around interminably, not doing much of anything, and their milieu is ultra-Beckettian:

[H]e sidestepped the slick entrails of fish guts and shining fish heads. There were old crates strewn everywhere. Blanched heads of cabbages and cauliflowers withered in the cold puddles of water. Blackened potatoes decayed in spongy mush.

Or:

He felt a slight tinge of horror as his thick nostrils inhaled the pervasive fetid alchemy of stale vomit and urine. He groped at the cold slimy walls and the clinging moss that suffocated the walls issuing forth pungent black water. . . . A profound surging impotency rose in his body.

The most powerful story borrows its title, "The Dead," from Joyce, but it is a meticulously detailed account of an extended Irish Republican Army (IRA) torturing. Its details finally become so ferocious that it becomes a kind of pornography of violence and is probably one of the most inhumane and repellent pieces in recent Irish fiction. It makes another book blurb quote from the *Times* seem plausible, if not attractive: "Reading Collins' stories . . . is like being mugged in a savage land."

His novel, *The Life & Times of a Teaboy* (1994), is not a violent but a pervasively glum account of the life of Ambrose Feeney, who grows up in Limerick, hates his mother, becomes a civil servant in the Department of Agriculture and Fisheries, has a breakdown, is diagnosed as a schizophrenic, and winds up probably not too unhappily in a lunatic asylum. Not much dramatic happens, but most of the characters are physically as well observed as any writer has done since the early Brian Moore.* Also, many passages, such as a long bus journey in the company of a fat drunk, are rendered with a convincing precision. The reader, nevertheless, frequently wonders just why they are there. Beckett makes an appearance toward the end in Ambrose's mind; and, like *Finnegans Wake,* the book's last sentence is also its first. That may, possibly, encourage some masochistic readers to read it again.

WORKS: *The Meat Eaters.* London: Jonathan Cape, [1992]. (Short stories); *The Man Who Dreamed of Lobsters.* New York: Random House, 1993; *The Life & Times of a Teaboy.* London: Phoenix House, [1994]. (Novel); *The Feminists Go Swimming.* London: Phoenix House, [1995]. (Short stories).

COLLIS, JOHN STEWART (1900–1984), farmer, ecologist, and philosopher. Collis was born at Kilmore, Killiney, County Dublin, on February 16, 1900, the son on W. S. Collis and his wife, Edith Barton, and the brother of Maurice* and twin brother of Robert Collis.* He was educated at Rugby and at Balliol

College, Oxford; and he married Eilene Joy, with whom he had two daughters. He served as lieutenant in the Irish Guards during World War I, was a land worker from 1940 to 1945, and was a fellow of the Royal Society of Literature. In 1974, he married Lady Beddington-Behrens. He was the author of a remarkable series of books about man and his true relationship with the soil, which, having lapsed into obscurity, were revived and acclaimed in his old age, from 1971 onward. His friend Richard Ingrams provides in his memoir a vivid glimpse of Collis's philosophic old age. The most remarkable and influential of a remarkable and influential family, he died at Abinger Common, near Dorking, Surrey, on March 2, 1984.

PETER COSTELLO

WORKS: *Shaw.* London: Cape, 1925; *Forward to Nature.* London: Cape, 1927; *Farewell to Argument.* London: Cassell, 1935; *The Sounding Cataract.* London: Cassell, 1936; *An Irishman's England.* London: Cassell, 1937; *While Following the Plough.* London: Cape, 1946; *Down to Earth.* London: Cape, 1947; *The Triumph of the Tree.* London: Cape, 1950; *The Moving Waters.* London: Rupert Hart-Davis, 1955; *Paths of Light.* London: Cassell, 1959; *The Artist of Life: Havelock Ellis.* London: Cassell, 1959; *Marriage and Genius.* London: Cassell, 1963; *Tolstoy: A Pictorial Biography.* London: Burns & Oates, 1969; *Bound upon a Course.* London: Sidgwick & Jackson, 1971; *The Carlyles.* London: Sidgwick & Jackson, 1972; *The Vision of Glory.* London: Charles Knight, 1972; *The Worm Forgives the Plough.* London: Charles Knight, 1973; *Christopher Columbus.* London: Macdonald, 1976; *Living with a Stranger.* London: Macdonald, 1978. REFERENCE: Ingrams, Richard. *John Stewart Collis, A Memoir.* London: Chatto & Windus, 1986.

COLLIS, MAURICE (1889–1973), Indian civil servant, man of letters, and critic. Born in Dublin on January 10, 1889, the brother of John Stewart* and Robert Collis,* Collis was educated at Rugby School and at Corpus Christi College, Oxford. He joined the Indian civil service in 1911 and was posted to Burma. By 1928, he was a district magistrate in Rangoon. In November 1934, he retired and at once commenced a second career as an author, luckily helped by a childhood friendship with his publisher Geoffrey Faber. His first book, *Siamese White* (1936), about the massacre at Mergui in 1784, was an immediate success. In all, he published some twenty-nine books, mostly on Oriental themes, though he also wrote on art, notably about his friends Lowry, Mervyn Peake, and Stanley Spencer. Painting was an interest he took up only at the age of sixty-eight, but he had two one-man shows with some success and liked to be photographed with his brushes. He was art critic for *Time and Tide,* for which he also reviewed books on the East and travel. Having lived for many years at Maidenhead, he died on January 12, 1973, in London.

PETER COSTELLO

PRINCIPAL WORKS: *Danse Macabre.* London: Selwyn & Blount, 1922. (Poetry); *Siamese White.* London: Faber, 1936; *Lords of the Sunset.* London: Faber, 1938; *Trials in Burma.* London: Faber, 1938; *Sanda Mala.* London: Faber, 1939. (Novel); *The Dark Door.* London: Faber, 1940. (Novel); *British Merchant Adventurers.* London: Collins, 1942. (Pamphlet); *The Burmese Scene.* Bognor Regis & London: John Crowther, 1943; *The Land of the Great Image.* London: Faber, 1943; *The Motherly and Auspicious.* London: Faber, 1943. (Play); *White of Mergen.* London: Faber, 1945. (Play); *Foreign Mud.* London: Faber, 1946; *Quest for Sita.* London: Faber, 1946; *Lord of the Three*

Worlds. London: Faber, 1947. (Play); *The Descent of God.* London: Faber, 1948; *The Grand Per-egrination.* London: Faber, 1949; *Marco Polo.* London: Faber, 1950; *The Mystery of Dead Lovers.* London: Faber, 1951; *The Discovery of L. S. Lowry.* London: A. Reid & Lefevre, 1951. (Pamphlet); The Journey Outward. London: Faber, 1952. (Memoirs); *Last and First in Burma, 1941–1948.* London: Faber, 1956; *The Hurling Times.* London: Faber, 1958. (History of England, 1346–1381); *Nancy Astor.* London: Faber, 1960. (Biography); *Stanley Spencer.* London: Harvill, 1962. (Biography); *Wayfoong.* London: Faber, 1965. (History of the Hongkong & Shanghai Bank); *Raffles.* London: Faber, 1966. (Biography); *Somerville and Ross.* London: Faber, 1968. (Biography); *The Journey Up: Reminiscences, 1934–1968.* London: Faber, 1970; *The Three Gods.* Gerrards Cross: Colin Smythe, 1970; *Diaries, 1949–1969.* Introduction by Louise Collis. London: Heinemann, 1976.

COLLIS, [WILLIAM] ROBERT [FITZGERALD] (1900–1975), playwright, author, and pediatrician. Sons of a wealthy lawyer, Robert Collis and his twin brother, John Stewart* (author of *The Vision of Glory, The Worm Forgives the Plough,* and others), were born in 1900 at Kilmore, a beautiful house over-looking Dublin's Killiney Bay. There were also an elder brother, Maurice* (au-thor of *Trial in Burma, Siamese White,* and others), and two sisters. Educated at Aravon School in Bray, Rugby School, Cambridge, and King's College Hos-pital, London, Collis graduated in medicine in 1925. He was Sir Frederick Still's resident at the Hospital for Sick Children, Great Ormond Street, and decided to become a pediatrician. His research dealt with rheumatic fever.

His *The Silver Fleece* (1936) is an autobiographical idyll enriched by the happiness of youth, its events placed against the beauty of Irish landscapes, London's Twickenham (where he played rugby for Ireland), the russet woods of New England, Johns Hopkins Hospital, and the rolling Maryland countryside. It concludes with his return to Ireland and a horseback ride into the Wicklow hills.

Settling in Dublin with appointments at the Meath, National Children's, and Rotunda Hospitals, he became aware of a direct relationship between poverty and disease and joined the Citizens' Housing Council. At the suggestion of Frank O'Connor,* he wrote a play, *Marrowbone Lane,* which was staged suc-cessfully at the Gate* in 1939 and revived at the larger Gaiety Theatre. His royalties went to the Marrowbone Lane Fund set up to combat tuberculosis. *The Barrel Organ,* Collis's second play, opened at the Gaiety in 1941.

To Be a Pilgrim (1975), a second autobiography, presents more somber sit-uations: Belsen, which Collis entered with a Red Cross team in 1945; Ibadan, where kwashiorkor was a common cause of death in children; apartheid in South Africa. Christy Brown,* who owed much to Collis, contributed a foreword.

Collis's move from Dublin to a larger stage was occasioned by domestic problems, ennui, professional jealousy, and the conviction that broader measures must have fuller rewards. That phase of his career devoted to education in Africa was the greater. With his second wife, Han Hogerzeil, he retired to County Wicklow, where in May 1975, he died, thrown by a young horse.

J. B. LYONS

PRINCIPAL LITERARY WORKS: *The Silver Fleece. An Autobiography.* London: Nelson, 1936; *Marrowbone Lane.* Monkstown, Dublin: Runa, 1943. (Play); with Han Hogerzeil. *Straight On.*

London: Methuen, 1947. (On Red Cross work in German concentration camps after the surrender); The *Ultimate Value.* London: Methuen, 1951. (On refugee children); *A Doctor's Nigeria.* London: Secker & Warburg, 1960; *Nigeria in Conflict.* London: 1970; *To Be a Pilgrim.* London: Secker & Warburg, 1975.   REFERENCE: Coakley, Davis. *Irish Masters of Medicine.* Dublin: Town House, 1992, pp. 320–331.

COLUM, MARY [CATHERINE GUNNING MAGUIRE] (1887–1957), critic and autobiographer. Colum was born June 13, 1887 and was educated in convents and at University College, Dublin. She taught at St. Ita's, Padraic Pearse's schools for girls, and in 1912 married Padraic Colum,* the poet. Her *Life and the Dream* (1947) gives a romantic view of the Irish Revival as seen by an impressionable student. Her gift for anecdote is also apparent in passages about Joyce* collected after her death in *Our Friend James Joyce* (1958). Her other book, *From These Roots,* explores the origins of modernism. From 1914 she and her husband resided in the United States and were very active in New York literary circles. Colum became a well-known literary critic, serving as literary editor of the *Forum,* critic for *The New York Times* and *Tribune,* and a frequent contributor to the major literary periodicals in the United States and Ireland. Colum died on October 22, 1957.

RICHARD M. KAIN

WORKS: *From These Roots: The Ideas That Have Made Modern Literature.* New York: Scribner's, 1937; *Life and the Dream.* Garden City, N.Y.: Doubleday/London: Macmillan, 1947; with Padraic Colum, *Our Friend James Joyce.* Garden City, N.Y.: Doubleday, 1958.

COLUM, PADRAIC (1881–1972), poet, playwright, biographer, novelist, short story writer, essayist, folklorist, and writer of children's stories. Colum was a practitioner of so many of the literary arts that he is difficult to label. He wrote sixty-one books and hundreds of essays, articles, and introductions and separately published poetry as well as a number of plays. His career spans nearly a century, beginning with the early days of the Irish renaissance and extending into the seventh decade of the twentieth century. An intimate friend of the giants of modern literature in America and France, as well as in England and Ireland, Colum had a major part in shaping the direction of the Irish theater and in bringing classical literature to children in comprehensible, appealing form.

Padraic was born to Patrick and Susan Colum on December 8, 1881, in the workhouse at Longford where Patrick was the master. His early years were spent in Longford and Cavan before the family moved to Sandycove, where the elder Colum got a job as railway station master. Colum attended the Glasthule National School in Sandycove and worked for his father delivering packages until he graduated. When he was seventeen, he obtained a position as clerk in the Irish Railway Clearing House; he worked there for five years until he was given a five-year scholarship by a wealthy American to pay for a period of study, development, and writing.

Around 1902, his poems began to appear in Arthur Griffith's* *United Irishman,* and he won a contest of the *Cumann na nGaedeal* with his early play *The*

Saxon Shillin'. Colum became a member of the National Theatre Society, was an original Abbey* charter signer, and wrote three of the Abbey's earliest plays, *The Fiddler's House* (1907), *The Land* (1905), and *Thomas Muskerry* (1910). By this time, his poetry was extremely popular, and he was an intimate of George Russell,* W. B. Yeats,* Lady Gregory,* and James Stephens.*

Colum met Mary Catherine Gunning Maguire while she was a student at University College, Dublin, and married her in 1912. Padraic and Mary both taught at St. Ita's and St. Enda's and began *The Irish Review** with two of their colleagues, David Houston and Thomas MacDonagh.*

The Colums migrated to America in 1914, where Colum began a new career in children's literature by writing a series of stories for the children's column of the *New York Sunday Tribune*. Publication in 1916 of a volume of his poetry, *Wild Earth,* and his first volume of children's stories, *The King of Ireland's Son,* quickly established his reputation in the United States. Colum supported himself throughout his life principally with his popular children's books and his translations of the classics and mythology. Under a commission from the Hawaiian legislature, he recorded in three volumes the lore of the islands for children in Hawaiian schools.

The Colums lived in Paris and Nice from 1930 to 1933. They finally returned to the United States, first settling in New Canaan, Connecticut, and later in New York City, where they both taught part-time at Columbia University. After Mary died in 1957, Colum divided his time among New York, Woods Hole, Massachusetts, and Ireland. He never stopped writing poetry; a new poem written in his ninetieth year in a nursing home in Connecticut was subsequently published in the *New York Times,* and *Carricknabauna,* a musical based on his poems and songs, was produced in New York in 1967. He was completing a series of Noh plays at the time of his death on January 11, 1972. He was interred in Ireland.

Colum's poetry, as all his work, is characterized by simplicity and craftsmanship. His character studies in verse, such as "An Old Woman of the Roads," "The Toy-Maker," "The Poor Scholar," and "The Ballad Singer," embody the essence of a nearly forgotten rural picture-book Ireland. His poetry, generally regular in meter and rhyme, captures the rustic peasant speech of the Midlands. Colum had the ability to re-create the past authentically, and for many American Irish as well as modern-day citizens of Ireland, his work is an echo of the idyllic Ireland they had only heard about at their parents' knees.

Colum's early plays appealed to a large popular audience in Ireland and England, and he was hailed as one of the greatest young writers of the Irish theater. Unfortunately, that early promise as a dramatist never completely materialized. Although he continued to write plays throughout his life and thought of himself as a dramatist, his later works never were as successful as his earliest productions.

Colum's close ties with the great Irishmen of his times led him to write two widely read biographies—one of Arthur Griffith,* *Ourselves Alone* (1959), and the other, *Our Friend James Joyce* (1958). The first was principally a scholarly history of the Sinn Féin party, and the second a collection of personal reminiscences, written in collaboration with Mary Colum. The tone of the two books is so different that it is difficult to think they came from the same pen. *Ourselves Alone* is written in stark, matter-of-fact language and is well researched, full of dates, and heavily annotated. *Our Friend James Joyce* is a conversational, largely anecdotal series of personal reminiscences.

Colum's two novels are also widely contrasting. The first, *Castle Conquer* (1923), is an apprentice work, full of nationalistic propaganda, but the second, *The Flying Swans,* written thirty-four years later, is a classic in its own right, though largely ignored by the critics. It captures in realistic but picturesque prose the verisimilitude of life in late nineteenth-century Ireland.

Colum's many volumes of Irish essays and children's stories are written in the same style. Never condescending to children, he writes with the same simplicity in both children's works and in his Irish travel stories for adults. His character studies are largely one-dimensional and easy to understand—often vignettes—but they have a unique archetypal quality. Colum's work often contains the expected, but it is said with such simple eloquence that the experience remains a pleasant memory long after the bizarre and unusual are forgotten. Colum falls easily into the role of storyteller, much like the itinerant poets and raconteurs he knew in his youth. Tales are told for their wonder, humor, and familiarity, their ultimate aim being the delight and enjoyment of the audience.

ZACK BOWEN

WORKS: *The Land.* Dublin: Abbey Theatre, 1905. (Play); *The Fiddler's House.* Dublin: Maunsel, 1907. (Play); *Heather Ale.* 1907. (Poetry pamphlet); *Studies.* Dublin: Maunsel, 1907. (Sketches and a short play); *Wild Earth.* Dublin: Maunsel, 1907. (Poetry); *Thomas Muskerry.* Dublin: Maunsel, 1910. (Play); *The Desert.* Dublin: Devereux, 1912. (Play); *My Irish Year.* London: Mills & Boon, 1912; *A Boy in Eirinn.* New York: E. P. Dutton, 1913/London: Dent, 1915; *The King of Ireland's Son.* New York: Macmillan, 1916/London: Harrap, 1920; *Wild Earth, and Other Poems.* New York: Holt/Dublin: Maunsel, 1916. (A new edition with additional poems); *Mogu the Wanderer.* Boston: Little, Brown, 1917. (New version of *The Desert*); *Three Plays.* Dublin & London: Maunsel, 1917/ revised, New York: Macmillan, 1925. (Contains *The Fiddler's House, The Land,* and *Thomas Muskerry*); *The Boy Who Knew What the Birds Said.* New York: Macmillan, 1918; *The Adventures of Odysseus.* New York: Macmillan, 1918/London: Harrap, 1920; *The Girl Who Sat by the Ashes.* New York: Macmillan, 1919; *The Boy Apprenticed to an Enchanter.* New York: Macmillan, 1920; *The Children of Odin.* New York: Macmillan, 1920/London: Harrap, 1922; *The Golden Fleece and the Heroes Who Lived Before Achilles.* New York: Macmillan, 1921; *The Children Who Followed the Piper.* New York: Macmillan, 1922; *Dramatic Legends and Other Poems.* New York: Macmillan, 1922; *Castle Conquer.* New York: Macmillan, 1923. (Novel); *At the Gateways of the Day.* New Haven, Conn.: Yale University Press, 1924; *The Island of the Mighty.* New York: Macmillan, 1924; *The Peep-Show Man.* New York: Macmillan, 1924; *Six Who Were Left in a Shoe.* London: Brentano, 1924; *The Bright Islands.* New Haven, Conn.: Yale University Press, 1925; *The Forge in the Forest.* New York: Macmillan, 1925; *The Voyagers.* New York: Macmillan, 1925; *The Road Round Ireland.* New York: Macmillan, 1926; *Creatures.* New York: Macmillan, 1927. (Poems); *The Fountain of Youth.* New York: Macmillan, 1927; *Balloon.* New York: Macmillan, 1929. (Play); *Cross-Roads in Ireland.* New York & London: Macmillan, 1930; *Old Pastures.* New York: Macmillan, 1930. (Poems); *Orpheus. Myths of the World.* New York & London: Macmillan, 1930; *Three Men.* London: Elkin Mathews & Marrot, 1930. (A story); *A Half-Day's Ride.* New York: Macmillan, 1932. (Essays); *Poems.* New York & London: Macmillan, 1932; *The Big Tree of Bun-*

lahy. New York: Macmillan, 1933/London: Macmillan, 1934 (Stories); *The White Sparrow.* New York: Macmillan, 1933; *The Legend of Saint Columba.* New York: Macmillan, 1935/London: Sheed & Ward, 1936; *Legends of Hawaii.* New Haven, Conn.: Yale University Press, 1937; *The Story of Lowry Maen.* New York & London: Macmillan, 1937; *Flower Pieces: New Poems.* Dublin: Orwell, 1938; *The Jackdaw.* Dublin: Gayfield, 1939 (Pamphlet poem); *Where the Winds Never Blew and the Cocks Never Crew.* New York: Macmillan, 1940; *The Frenzied Prince, Being Heroic Stories of Ancient Ireland.* Philadelphia: McKay, 1943; *The Collected Poems of Padraic Colum.* New York: Devin-Adair, 1953; *A Treasury of Irish Folklore.* New York: Crown, 1954; *The Vegetable Kingdom.* Bloomington, Ind.: Indiana University Press, 1954. (Poems); *The Flying Swans.* New York: Crown, 1957. (Novel); *Ten Poems.* Dublin: Dolmen, 1957; *Garland Sunday.* Dublin: Dolmen, 1958. (A poem); *Irish Elegies.* Dublin: Dolmen, 1958/augmented, 1961 & 1966. (Poems); with Mary Colum, *Our Friend James Joyce.* Garden City, N.Y.: Doubleday, 1958; *Ourselves Alone.* New York: Crown, 1959/European edition entitled *Arthur Griffith (1872–1922),* Dublin: Browne & Nolan, 1959. (Biography of Griffith); *The Poet's Circuits. Collected Poems of Ireland.* London: Oxford University Press, 1960; *Story Telling, New and Old.* New York: Macmillan, 1961; *Moytura: A Play for Dancers.* Dublin: Dolmen, 1963; *The Stone of Victory and Other Tales of Padraic Colum.* New York: McGraw-Hill, 1966; *Images of Departure.* Dublin: Dolmen, 1969/Chester Springs, Pa.: Dufour, 1970; *The Journal of Irish Literature* 2 (January 1973), a Padraic Colum number. Zack Bowen & Gordon Henderson, eds.; *Selected Short Stories of Padraic Colum.* Sanford Sternlicht, ed. Syracuse, N.Y.: Syracuse University Press, 1985; *Selected Plays of Padraic Colum.* Sanford Sternlicht, ed. Syracuse, N.Y.: Syracuse University Press, 1987; *Selected Poems of Padraic Colum.* Sanford Sternlicht, ed. Syracuse, N.Y.: Syracuse University Press, 1989.   REFERENCES: Barton, Yancy. "Padraic Colum's *The Children's Homer:* The Myth Reborn." In *Touchstones: Reflections on the Best in Children's Literature.* Perry Nodelman, ed. West Lafayette, Ind.: Children's Literature Association, 1987; Bowen, Zack. *Padraic Colum: A Biographical-Critical Introduction.* Carbondale: Southern Illinois University Press, 1970; Denson, Alan. "Padraic Colum: An Appreciation with a Checklist of His Publications." *Dublin Magazine* 6 (Spring 1967): 50–67; Greene, Ellin. "Literary Uses of Traditional Themes: From "Cinderella" to *The Girl Who Sat by the Ashes* and *The Glass Slipper.*" *Children's Literature Association Quarterly* 11 (Fall 1986): 128–132; Huse, Nancy. "Padraic Colum's *The Golden Fleece:* The Lost Goddesses." In *Touchstones: Reflections on the Best in Children's Literature.* Perry Nodelman, ed. West Lafayette, Ind.: Children's Literature Association, 1987; Murphy, Ann. "Appreciation: Padraic Colum (1881–1972), National Poet." *Éire-Ireland* 17 (Winter 1982): 128–147; Sternlicht, Sanford. *Padraic Colum.* Boston: Twayne, 1985; Sternlicht, Sanford. "Padraic Colum: Poet of the 1960s." *Colby Library Quarterly* 25 (December 1989): 253–257.

CONCANEN, MATTHEW (1701–1749), poet and editor. His comedy, *Wexford Wells,* was produced at the Smock Alley Theatre, Dublin, in 1720, when he was only nineteen. In the next year, he published *A Match at Foot-ball,* an entertaining mock-heroic poem in three cantos, which features a game between Lusk and Swords in north County Dublin. In 1722, his *Poems upon Several Occasions* appeared. Moving to London, Concanen became involved in party politics and wrote on behalf of the government. His editorship of *Miscellaneous Poems* (1724) earns him a place in literary history: the volume, which contains work by Swift,* Delany,* the elder Thomas Sheridan,* and others, is the first anthology of Irish verse. Concanen figures as a minor dunce in Pope's *The Dunciad* and was ridiculed by Swift in "Poetry, A Rhapsody." In 1732, Concanen was appointed attorney general of Jamaica. He returned to England, a wealthy man, in 1743; and he died in London of consumption in January 1749.

AILEEN DOUGLAS

occasional verse, and carefully revised his writings for a three-volume collected *Works* (1710).

Congreve's plays were the main object of attack in Jeremy Collier's *Short View of the Immorality and Profaneness of the English Stage,* published in 1698, to which Congreve (and several others) replied later in the year with his *Amendments of Mr. Collier's False and Imperfect Citations.* In the sense that Collier's *Short View* spoke for the rising taste for reform of the stage in the direction of exemplary sentimental comedy, it and his *Defence of the Short View* (also 1698) were the victors. At times, Collier seems to attack all theatre, or at least all comic theatre. In the sense that Congreve's *Amendments* presented the classic defense of comedy from its beginnings to the present day, he was the victor: the morality of comedy consists not of preaching and of poetic justice, but of holding folly and vice up to ridicule. Nonetheless, Congreve was hurt by the attack, and he left the stage partly because he was aware that his own and his audience's tastes were at odds.

For ten years Congreve was friendly with the famous actress Mrs. Bracegirdle, for whom he wrote the celebrated part of Millamant, and in his later years with Henrietta, second duchess of Marlborough, who erected his monument in Westminster Abbey. He lived his last years as a retired gentleman, suffering from ill health and supported by government sinecures. In a famous meeting, the young Voltaire scorned Congreve's pose as a gentleman rather than a writer. Through the turmoil surrounding the death of Queen Anne and the Hanoverian succession, Congreve stayed aloof from politics. He managed to remain in the Whig Kit-Cat Club and to keep the friendship and respect of his fellow Irishmen Swift and Steele* as well as of Addison and Pope. He was widely mourned at his death in 1729, for what seemed the passing of the earlier generation of wit.

SVEN ERIC MOLIN

WORKS: *The Complete Works of William Congreve.* Montague Summers, ed. London: Nonsuch, 1923; *The Works of Congreve,* F. W. Bateson, ed. London: Peter Davies, 1930; *The Comedies of William Congreve.* Anthony G. Henderson, ed.   REFERENCES: Avery, Emmett Langdon. *Congreve's Plays on the Eighteenth-Century Stage.* New York: Modern Language Association of America, 1951; Bartlett, Laurence. *William Congreve: A Reference Guide.* Boston: G. K. Hall, [ca. 1979]; Dobree, Bonamy. *William Congreve.* London: Longmans, Green, 1963. (Pamphlet); Gosse, Edmund. *Life of Congreve.* New York: Scribner's, 1924; Hodges, John C. *William Congreve, the Man.* New York: Modern Language Association of America, 1941; Hodges, John C., ed. *William Congreve: Letters and Documents.* New York: Harcourt, Brace & World/London: Macmillan, 1964; Holland, Norman N. *The First Modern Comedies: The Significance of Etherege, Wycherley and Congreve.* Cambridge: Harvard University Press, 1959; Jantz, Ursula. *Targets of Satire in the Comedies of Etherege, Wycherley and Congreve.* Salzburg: Institut für Englische Sprache und Literatur, Universität Salzburg, 1978; Lindsay, Alexander & Erskine-Hill, Howard, eds. *William Congreve: The Critical Heritage.* London: Routledge, 1989; Love, Harold. *Congreve.* Totowa, N.J.: Rowman & Littlefield, 1975; Lynch, Kathleen Martha. *A Congreve Gallery.* Cambridge: Harvard University Press, 1951; Novak, Maximillian E. *William Congreve.* New York: Twayne, 1971; Van Voris, W. H. *The Cultivated Stance. The Designs of Congreve's Plays.* [Chester Springs, Pa.]: Dufour, [1967]; Williams, Aubrey L. *An Approach to Congreve.* New Haven, Conn.: London: Yale University Press, 1979.

CONLON, EVELYN (1952–   ), fiction writer. Evelyn Conlon was born in Rockcorry, County Monaghan. She published her first short story when she was eighteen in David Marcus's* "New Irish Writing" in *The Irish Press.* After traveling in Australia, Asia, and Russia, she took a B.A. at St. Patrick's College, Maynooth, and taught English for two years. She has published two collections of short stories and a novel and in 1988 received an Arts Council Bursary. She was a founder member of the Rape Crisis Centre. She lives in Dublin with her two children.

She writes with fluency and sensuality and primarily for women. Her short stories are well crafted, often with a bittersweet sting at the end. The stories are rather more readable than the novel because of her penchant for overanalysis. Every sensation, every feeling has to be minutely scrutinized. The result, particularly in the case of the novel, *Stars in the Daytime,* is to bury the narrative in a welter of detail.

DOROTHY ROBBIE

WORKS: *My Head Is Opening.* Dublin: Attic, [1987]. (Short stories); *Stars in the Daytime.* Dublin: Attic, [1989]. (Novel); *Taking Scarlet as a Real Colour.* Belfast: Blackstaff, [1993]. (Short stories).

CONNAUGHTON, SHANE (late 1946–   ), fiction writer, playwright, and screenwriter. Connaughton was born in Kingscourt, County Cavan, and lived in Redhills, County Cavan, until 1957. He was educated at Saint Bridgid's National School, Redhills, and at Saint Tiarnach's, Clones. In the mid-1960s, he trained as an actor with the Bristol Old Vic Theatre School. His awards include the Royal Court, Sloane Square Most Promising Playwright Award, and the Hennessy Award for New Irish Writing. His plays have included works for the National Theatre (London), the Half Moon Street Theatre, Bubble Theatre, the Dublin Theatre Festival, the Victoria Theatre, and television for the BBC. His film credits include *My Left Foot, The Playboys,* and *The Run of the Country.*

Of his published works, *My Left Foot* is the dramatization of the film's screenplay, cowritten with Jim Sheridan,* and details in an unsentimental manner the life of Irish writer and painter Christy Brown.* *A Border Station* (1989) is a collection of seven short stories written in the literary tradition of Joyce's* *Dubliners* or Sherwood Anderson's *Winesburg Ohio,* in that it is not, strictly speaking, a novel but rather a collection of interrelated stories. They center around a boy's experience living in a village on the border between the six counties and the republic. Each story marks a stage in the growth and development of the young boy and traces his relationship with his father, a Garda sergeant, and with his mother, his religion, and his peers. Reviewers have compared the boy to Stephen Dedalus in the sense that the feelings and experience of Connaughton's boy are marked by an artistic sensitivity. In addition to the development of the main character, Connaughton's descriptions of landscapes and supporting characters are written in simple, elegant prose that is remarkable for its clarity and power. Connaughton's second major published work is *The*

Run of the Country (1991). More traditionally a novel, the book shares much with the earlier collection of stories. Both are set on the border between Cavan and Northern Ireland. Both involve a young boy and the experiences that mark his development—his relationship with his father, his experience with love and romance, his adolescent adventures dodging border patrols, playing tricks on farmers, gambling. Each of the last experiences highlights the development of the young boy's friendship with his young companion, Prunty. Prunty is a classic comic type in the tradition of Huck Finn and serves as effective foil to the protagonist. Curiously, Connaughton never discloses the name of his main character, but this technique produces an intimacy with the protagonist, a casual familiarity in which names become unnecessary. Both *The Run of the Country* and *A Border Station* posit an elaborate metaphor between the border dividing North and South and the division between the possibilities of youth and the reality of maturity with its attendant random violence and ultimate frustrations. Connaughton's writings reveal not only the author's ability to create convincing characters, draw intensely dramatic situations juxtaposed with wonderfully comic scenes, and write effective and often stunningly beautiful prose but also to reveal an understanding of the complexities of a divided nationhood and the effect of intermittent war on the sensibilities of those growing and living in its context.

BERNARD McKENNA

WORKS: With Jim Sheridan: *My Left Foot.* London: Faber, 1989. (Screenplay); *A Border Station.* London: Hamish Hamilton/New York: St. Martin's, 1989. (Short stories); *The Run of the Country.* London: Hamish Hamilton/New York: St. Martin's, 1991. (Novel); *A Border Diary.* London: Faber, 1995. (Autobiographical).

CONNELL, VIVIAN (1905–1981), novelist and playwright. Connell was born in Cork in 1905 and lived there until he was thirty, after which he traveled on the Continent and lived in Sussex, Sicily, and the south of France. His last years were spent in Bray, County Wicklow, where he died in 1981. His first story was published by AE* in *The Irish Statesman,** after which he had nothing more published for over a decade. He wrote a number of plays, the most successful being *The Nineteenth Hole of Europe* (1943), but his great success was the novel *The Chinese Room* (1942), which sold over 3 million copies. On the dust jacket of one of his books, he is quoted as saying:

I was taught to read and write by my father. I gathered the rest of my education in the Irish pubs, the hurling fields, and on the athletic track. I have carried a horn with several packs of hounds. And I once ran the half-mile and mile. I consider the habit of physical endurance thus gathered, through long days of riding or running across the Irish country, an explanation of my ability to drive on a play or book to the end without flagging.

Connell gives such a background and such tenacious literary ability to the obviously autobiographical novelist hero of *The Golden Sleep* (1948), who finishes his novels in two months flat. Cleeve* calls Connell a distinguished man of letters, but he belongs more in the company of the Donn Byrnes* and Constantine Fitzgibbons* than of the Shaws* and Joyces.* His novels have a portentousness and yet a spuriousness. They have a sleek craft that makes them easy to read, while they also have heavy pretensions to deep meaning. The popularity of *The Chinese Room* in the 1940s arose partly from its theme, which is an attack on sexual inhibition and a celebration of sexual openness. The book owes a heavy debt to the later, and at that time banned, D. H. Lawrence, but it is a Lawrence euphemized for the coffee tables of the day. At the same time, the book has a running mystery story plot (in which the villain turns out to be the most mechanically sexual character), and finally there is an embroidery of Sax Rohmer hocus-pocus.

Ultimately, this book and its less popular successors ring tinny. First, the characters, especially the women, are the stereotypes of racy and romantic fiction; and second, the writing at the intense and crucial moments sinks into the most hackneyed banality. In fact, there can be no greater condemnation of Vivian Connell than to quote him. The following is from *The Golden Sleep:*

He stopped and bent down and kissed her and she had the odor of the figs in Spain in her mouth and her lips clung in the plasm of desire. . . .

"I . . . I think I've come asunder. . . . I . . . Let me alone for a minute."

He walked onto the quay and knew that everything he had felt in his life was only an illusion compared to this surging and genetic love that left his body now quivering like a seismograph and his soul riding out on midnight air.

WORKS: *The Peacock Is a Gentleman.* New York: Dial, 1941. (Novel); *The Squire of Shaftesbury Avenue.* London: Constable, [1941]. (Play); *Throng o' Scarlet.* London: Constable, [1941]. (Play); *The Chinese Room.* New York: B. C. Hoffman, Dial, 1942. (Novel); *The Nineteenth Hole of Europe.* London: Secker & Warburg, 1943. (Play); *The Golden Sleep.* New York: Dial, 1948. (Novel); *A Man of Parts.* New York: Fawcett, 1950. (Novel); *The Hounds of Cloneen.* New York: Dial, 1951. (Novel); *September in Quinze.* London: Hutchinson/New York: Dial, 1952. (Novel).

CONNER, [PATRICK] REARDEN (1907–1991), novelist. Conner was born on February 19, 1907, in Dublin. His father was a head constable in the Royal Irish Constabulary, and he was educated at Presentation College, Cork. He went to England when he was in his teens and worked at a variety of jobs, principally that of gardener. His first published novel, *Shake Hands with the Devil* (1933), has been his most successful; it was a book club choice in America and some twenty-five years later was made into a film. The book still stands up as one of the better novels of Irish political violence and can be ranked with the well-known works of Liam O'Flaherty* and F. L. Green.* Conner's novel depicts the period of the Black and Tan War which he observed as a boy, and he is about equally critical of both sides. The book is not as crudely written as is O'Flaherty's *The Informer,* nor as floridly as is Green's *Odd Man Out.* Unlike those other two volumes, it also contains a good deal of specific detail and realistic observation, but it would finally have to be called powerful rather than deeply realized. Perhaps Conner's other important book is the autobiographical

A Plain Tale from the Bogs (1937) which describes his life in Ireland from Easter Week through the Black and Tan War, but which is more interesting in its depiction of the life of a manual laborer in London during the depression. Conner died in August 1991. An unimpressive posthumous novel, *Epitaph,* was published in 1994.

WORKS: *Shake Hands with the Devil.* London: J. M. Dent, 1933; *Rude Earth.* London: J. M. Dent, 1934/published in America as *Salute to Aphrodite,* New York: Bobbs-Merrill, 1935; *I Am Death.* London: Chapman & Hall, 1936; *Men Must Live.* London: Cassell, 1937; *A Plain Tale from the Bogs.* London: John Miles, 1937. (Autobiography); *The Sword of Love.* London: Cassell, 1938; *Wife of Colum.* London: Michael Joseph, 1939; *The Devil Among the Tailors.* London: MacDonald, 1947; *My Love to the Gallows.* London: MacDonald, 1948; *Hunger of the Heart.* London: Mac-Donald, 1950; *The Singing Stone.* London: MacDonald, 1951; *The House of Cain.* London: Mac-Donald, 1952. (as Peter Malin): *To Kill Is My Vocation.* London: Cassell, 1939; *River, Sing Me a Song.* London: Cassell, 1939; *Kobo the Brave.* London: Warne, 1950; *Epitaph.* London: Janus, [1994].

CONNOLLY, JAMES (1868–1916), labor leader, socialist theoretician, and nationalist. Connolly was born on June 5, 1868, in Edinburgh and was executed on May 12, 1916, for his prominent part in the Easter Rising. Much of Connolly's life was spent in Scotland and America, but the most significant part was undoubtedly the years from 1910 when, after Jim Larkin had gone to America, he emerged as the major spokesman for organized labor in Ireland and as a fiery proponent of armed rebellion. Connolly's major works are *Labour in Irish History, The Reconquest of Ireland,* and the long essay *Labour, Nationality and Religion.* He has been called "one of the first great working class intellectuals" and "the only Irish philosopher of consequence since the days of Bishop Berkeley*." Such strong claims for Connolly as a deep or original economic thinker seem extravagant, however, and are based on a general regard for the man's character and accomplishment. Connolly was primarily a political activist, and his prolific writing practically always had an immediate propagandistic function. For Ireland, his significant positions were his Marxian reading of Irish history, his attempt to reconcile Catholicism and socialism, and his assumption that Irish nationalism and Irish socialism were inextricably intertwined. Much of his writing has a fiery, if traditional, vigor, and all of it is permeated by an utter dedication and a burning sincerity. His occasional poems and apparently his two unpublished plays were also motivated more by propaganda than by art. Connolly is important as a social force and a humane conscience more than as an original journalist or artist or economic thinker. However, in modern Ireland his influence has remained more latent and superficial than active and profound.

WORKS: *Labour, Nationality and Religion.* Dublin: Harp Library, 1910; *Labour in Ireland* (containing *Labour in Irish History* and *The Reconquest of Ireland*). Dublin: Maunsel, 1917; *Socialism and Nationalism: A Selection from the Writings of James Connolly.* D. Ryan, ed. Dublin: Sign of the Three Candles, 1948; *The Workers' Republic: A Selection from the Writings of James Connolly.* Dublin: Sign of the Three Candles, 1951; *The Best of Connolly.* Proinsias Mac Aonghusa & Liam Ó Reagain, eds. Cork: Mercier, 1967; *James Connolly: Selected Writings.* P. Berresford Ellis, ed. Harmondsworth, Middlesex: Penguin/New York: New Monthly, 1973; *James Connolly: Selected*

Political Writings. Owen Dudley Edwards & B. Ransom, eds. London: Jonathan Cape, 1973; *James Connolly: Selected Writings.* London: Pluto, 1990.   REFERENCES: Allen, K. *The Politics of James Connolly.* London: Pluto, 1990; Edwards, Owen Dudley. *The Mind of an Activist—James Connolly.* Dublin: Gill & Macmillan, 1971; Edwards, Ruth Dudley. *James Connolly.* Dublin: Gill & Macmillan, 1981; Freitag, Barbara. "Literature Rewrites History: James Connolly and James Larkin Larger than Life." *Journal of Irish Literature* 22 (May 1993): 25–38; Greaves, C. Desmond. *The Life and Times of James Connolly.* London: Lawrence & Wishart, 1961; Levenson, Samuel. *James Connolly.* London: Martin Brian & O'Keeffe, 1973; Morgan, A. *James Connolly: A Political Biography.* Manchester: Manchester University Press, 1988; Nevin, D. *Connolly Bibliography.* Dublin: Irish Congress of Trade Unions, 1968; Ransom, B. *Connolly's Marxism.* London: Pluto, 1980; Ryan, Desmond. *James Connolly: His Work and Writings.* Dublin: Talbot, 1924.

CONNOLLY, SUSAN (1956–   ), poet. Connolly was born in Drogheda, Co. Louth and studied Italian and music at University College, Dublin.

WORK: *For the Stranger.* [Dublin]: Dedalus, [1993].

CONNOR, ELIZABETH. *See* WALSH, UNA TROY.

CONYERS, [MINNIE] DOROTHEA [SPAIGHT SMYTH] (1871–1949), novelist. Conyers was born at Limerick, the daughter of Colonel J. Blood Smyth. Her first marriage was to Lieutenant Charles Conyers, who died in 1915. Two years later she married Captain Joseph White, but she continued to publish under the name Dorothea Conyers. She died in 1949, in Limerick.

Her many romance novels usually center on horses and hunting. She frequently includes in her works the problems involved in buying, selling, and maintaining horses. Conyers specialized in Anglo-Irish settings for her popular romances. Typical in this regard is *Some Happenings of Glendalyne* (1911), where the heroine, Eve O'Neill, is reunited with her wealthy Anglo-Irish family, including a mad uncle, horses, and hunts. *Irish Stew* (1920) is a collection of short stories, peopled with Irish characters frequently speaking in dialect. Dorothea Conyers and Nannie Lambert O'Donoghue were perhaps the most horse-conscious of the nineteenth century, Anglo-Irish women authors.

ANNE COLMAN

WORKS: *The Thorn Bit.* London: Hutchinson, 1900; *Bloom or Blight.* London: Hurst & Blackett, 1901; *The Boy, Some Horses, and a Girl: A Tale of an Irish Trip.* London: Edward Arnold, 1903; *Peter's Pedigree.* London: Edward Arnold, 1904; *Cloth versus Silk.* London: Hutchinson, 1905; *The Strayings of Sandy.* London: Hutchinson, 1906; *Aunt Jane and Uncle James.* London: Hutchinson, 1908; *Three Girls and a Hermit.* London: Hutchinson, 1908; *The Conversion of Con Cregan, and Other Stories.* London: Hutchinson, 1909; *Lady Elverton's Emeralds.* London: Hutchinson, 1909; *Two Imposters and Tinker.* London: Hutchinson, 1910; *For Henri and Navarre.* London: Hutchinson, 1911; *Some Happenings of Glendalyne.* London: Hutchinson, 1911; *The Arrival of Antony.* London: Hutchinson, 1912; *Sally.* London: Methuen, 1912; *Sandy Married.* London: Methuen, 1913; *Old Andy.* London: Methuen, 1914; *Meave.* London: Hutchinson, 1915; *A Mixed Pack.* London: Methuen, 1915; *The Financing of Fiona.* London: Unwin, 1916; *The Scratch Pack.* London: Hutchinson, 1916; *The Experiments of Ganymede Bunn.* London: Hutchinson, 1917; *The Blighting of Bartram.* London: Methuen, 1918; *B. E. N.* London: Methuen, 1919; *Tiranogue.* London: Methuen, 1919; *Irish Stew.* London: Skeffington & Son, 1920; *Sporting Reminiscences.* London: Methuen, 1920; *Uncle Pierce's Legacy.* London: Methuen, 1920; *The Mating of Moya.* London: Hutchinson,

1921; *The Toll of the Black Gate.* London: Hutchinson, 1922; *Rooted Out.* London: Hutchinson, 1923; *The Adventures of Gerry.* London: Hutchinson, 1924; *The Two Maureens.* London: Hutchinson, 1924; *Sandy and Others.* London: Mills & Boon, 1925; *Treasury Notes.* London: Hutchinson, 1926; *Grey Brother, and Others.* London: Mills & Boon, 1927; *Hounds of the Sea.* London: Hutchinson, 1927; *Bobbie.* London: Hutchinson, 1928; *Follow Elizabeth.* London: Hutchinson, 1929; *Denton's Derby.* London: Hutchinson, 1930; *Hunting and Hunted.* London: Hutchinson, 1930; *Managing Ariadne.* London: Hutchinson, 1931; *Whoopee.* London: Hutchinson, 1932; *A Meave Must Marry.* London: Hutchinson, 1933; *A Good Purpose.* London: Hutchinson, 1934; *The Fortunes of Evadne.* London: Hutchinson, 1935; *The Elf.* London: Hutchinson, 1936; *Phil's Castle.* London: Hutchinson, 1937; *A Lady of Discretion.* London: Hutchinson, 1938; *Gulls at Rossnacorey.* London: Hutchinson, 1939; *The Best People.* London: Hutchinson, 1941; *Rosalie.* London: Hutchinson, 1945; *Dark.* London: Hutchinson, 1946; *Kicking Foxes.* London: Hutchinson, 1947; *A Kiss for a Whip.* London: Hutchinson, 1948; *The Witch's Samples.* London: Hutchinson, 1950.

COOGAN, BEATRICE (1906–), novelist. Coogan was raised in Dublin and in the 1920s acted at the Abbey Theatre.* She turned to writing seriously in the 1950s, and her only novel to date, *The Big Wind* (1969), won her the Author of the Year Award at the Frankfurt Bookfair. *The Big Wind* is a a huge, sprawling novel that races through the events of Irish—and, fleetingly, American—history from 1839 to 1867, as they affect the life and loves of her spirited and beautiful heroine, Sherrin. The book is best described as an Irish answer to *Gone with the Wind.* We even find the heroine, at one point when the family fortunes are at their lowest, reminding us of Scarlett by wearing a bodice of green velvet made over from her dead father's breeches.

The book is overlong but readable. The author has well researched her period, but there is too much crammed in to make the reader care unduly. The characters remain shadowy, and Thomas, the hero, is particularly unlikely. Also the horrors of the potato failure, the subsequent Famine, and the terrible evictions are not so much evoked as cited. Yet, throughout the book, there are indications that Coogan might have written less of a best-seller and more of a literary success.

One of her children is the journalist and historian Tim Pat Coogan.

DOROTHY ROBBIE

WORK: *The Big Wind.* London: Michael Joseph, 1969.

COOGAN, PATRICK (1950–), novelist. Coogan was born in Belfast and, after attending school in the Falls Road, won the Director of Studies Award at the Royal Military Academy, Sandhurst. In 14 years, he rose from private to major in the British army. He is now retired and lives in Essex. His well-received thriller *The General* was published in 1993.

WORK: *The General.* [London]: Sinclair-Stevenson, [1993].

COOKE, EMMA (1934–), fiction writer. Emma Cooke was born in 1934 in Portalington. She was educated at Alexandra College in Dublin and at the Mary Immaculate Training College in Limerick. She worked as a secretary in Dublin and London but since her marriage in 1959 has lived in Limerick, where she has a large family and organizes the Killaloe Writers' Group. She began writing in 1970 and has published a collection of short stories, *Female Forms* (1980), as well as two novels, *A Single Sensation* (1981) and *Eve's Apple* (1985). She writes with sensitivity and in fine detail of women and their relationships. The relationships between women and men are rarely happy ones, however, and her heroines often end up in hopeless situations. The reader is presented with a dark view of Irish suburban attitudes, and, as Cooke writes well and with bleak perception, her books leave one with a sense of despair.

DOROTHY ROBBIE

WORKS: *Female Forms.* [Dublin]: Poolbeg, [1980]. (Stories); *A Single Sensation.* [Dublin]: Poolbeg, [1981]. (Novel); *Eve's Apple.* [Dublin]: Poolbeg, [1985]. (Novel); *Wedlocked* [Dublin]: Poolbeg. [1994].

CORK DRAMATIC SOCIETY (1908–1914), amateur dramatic group. The Cork Dramatic Society was formed by Daniel Corkery* and others in Cork city in 1908. Originally, the group intended to produce new plays by its members as well as translations by its members from various foreign languages. No translations were ever produced, but for a few years the group produced new Cork plays in a Gaelic League hall in Queen Street, and on one occasion even played for several days in the Cork Opera House. The Society brought forth no masterpieces, but it did produce seventeen new plays by new Cork writers—among them Corkery himself, Terence J. MacSwiney,* T. C. Murray,* Lennox Robinson,* Con O'Leary,* and J. Bernard MacCarthy.* A handful of the Cork plays were later produced by the Abbey Theatre,* and about half of them have been published.

WORKS: Hogan, Robert, and Burnham, Richard, eds. *Lost Plays of the Irish Renaissance. Vol. II, The Cork Dramatic Society.* Newark, Del.: Proscenium, 1979.

CORK REALISTS. This term, apparently coined by W. B. Yeats,* was used as a blanket description of several playwrights who were first performed by the Abbey Theatre* in the years immediately following the death of J. M. Synge.* Principally, Yeats was referring to Lennox Robinson,* T. C. Murray,* and R. J. Ray,* and had in mind such plays as Robinson's *The Cross Roads* (1909), Ray's *The White Feather* (1909), and Murray's *Birthright* (1910). Robinson and Murray both had early one-acts performed by the Cork Dramatic Society,* but there was really no school of realistic drama growing up in Cork, and these three men at the time hardly knew each other. They were simply writing "strong" dramas in a language which mirrored life around them, rather than heightened reality as did Synge's dialogue. Yeats' descriptive term was a journalistic label of no more relevance than "The Beat Generation" or "The Angry Young Men." Playwrights such as Padraic Colum,* St. John Ervine,* and W. F. Casey* were writing realistically about other sections of the country at the same time.

CORKERY, DANIEL (1878–1964), man of letters. Corkery, whose life centered in Cork, was born in that city on February 14, 1878, to William and Mary Corkery, and was paternally a descendant of generations of carpenter-craftsmen. Crippled in one leg, supposedly by poliomyelitis, he matured into a puritanical, deeply religious man, very lucky in friends. Unmarried, he was cared for by his sister Mary until the two were persuaded to join a niece (Maureen) in her home on the Lee in County Cork. There he died on December 31, 1964, to be buried in St. Joseph's Cemetery, Cork.

Corkery's life was relatively quiet and his education, very sparse: a period (followed by a monitorship) at the Presentation Brothers Elementary School, Cork; a year at St. Patrick's College, Dublin, 1906–1907; and night study at the Crawford Municipal School of Art, Cork, which eventually led to his sensitive water colors of the Lee Valley. Meanwhile, his violent fanaticism for the Irish language had begun in 1901, though presumably he never became fluent in writing it. In 1908, he helped organize the Cork Dramatic Society and thus got into playwriting. Miscellaneous teaching preceded his M.A. for independent research on Synge* from the National University (1929) and his professorship in English at University College, Cork (1931–1947), which gave him an honorary D.Litt. after retirement. He served in the Seanad Éireaan from 1951 to 1954 and on the Arts Council from 1952 to 1956. For the rest, he wrote, reviewed, and painted, sometimes exhibiting.

Corkery's efforts at scholarship—*The Hidden Island* (1925), *Synge and Anglo-Irish Literature* (1931), and *The Fortunes of the Irish Language* (1954)— have stirred much controversial, sometimes acidulous, opinion, and it seems that there is a good basis for the negative assessment. Certainly Corkery's linguistic fanaticism, with extravagant claims of literary significance; inadequate knowledge; chauvinism; religious zealotry; and propagandistic inclination are hardly impressive guarantees of scholarship. One must turn to the creative work, and much of that is unexciting: e.g., the mild verse (cf. *I Brhreasil/A Book of Lyrics,* 1921), the sentimental novel (*The Threshold of Quiet,* 1917), most of the MS plays, and two that got printed (the mawkish "Resurrection": *Theatre Arts Monthly,* April 1924; and the tractarian *The Labour Leader,* 1920). But the best of the creative work is very fine indeed. *The Yellow Bittern and Other Plays* (1920) concentrates in three one-acters the finest of Corkery's dramatic work; they are spiritual, moving, poetic, and compassionate, and its title piece is in the "miracle" tradition, as Frank O'Connor* recognized. The romantic, though imperfect play, *Fohnam the Sculptor* (1973) could be associated with it. The grey-toned short stories (except for *The Hounds of Banba,* 1920, a pathetic and sentimental memorialization of Irish guerrilla activities) are Corkery's prime claim to distinction, established by *A Munster Twilight* (1916). *The Stormy Hills* (1929) and portions of *Earth Out of Earth* (1939) helped to consolidate that claim; the tension of suppressed wildness often underlies these tales.

Corkery's realistic, but never vulgar, handling of Cork and Kerry life; his handling of colloquial speech; his poetic response to the malign and uncontrollable in nature; and his sheer originality in such tales as "The Ploughing of Leaca-na-Naomh," "The Stones," and "Refuge" place him in the forefront of the short story writers of his day.

GEORGE BRANDON SAUL

WORKS: *A Munster Twilight.* Dublin & Cork: Talbot, 1916/New York: Stokes, 1917; *The Threshold of Quiet.* Dublin & Cork: Talbot/London: Unwin, 1917; *The Hounds of Banba.* Dublin & Cork: Talbot, 1920/New York: Huebsch, 1922; *The Labour Leader.* Dublin: Talbot/London: Unwin, 1920; *The Yellow Bittern and Other Plays.* Dublin: Talbot/London: Unwin, 1920; *I Bhreasail/A Book of Lyrics.* Dublin: Talbot/London: Mathews & Marot, 1921; *Rebel Songs* by "Reithin Siubhalach." [Cork]: Provinces Publishing Co., [1922]; *The Hidden Ireland/A Study of Gaelic Munster in the Eighteenth Century.* Dublin: Gill, 1925; *The Stormy Hills.* Dublin: Talbot/London: Jonathan Cape, 1929; *Synge and Anglo-Irish Literature.* Cork: Cork University Press/London: Longmans, Green, 1931; *Earth Out of Earth.* Dublin & Cork: Talbot, 1939; *Resurrection.* Dublin & Cork: Talbot, n.d.; *What's This About the Gaelic League?* Ath Cliath: Connradh na Gaedhilge, n.d.; *The Philosophy of the Gaelic League.* Dublin, 1948; *The Wager and Other Stories.* New York: Devin-Adair, 1950; *An Doras Dunta.* Baile Atha Cliath, 1953; *The Fortunes of the Irish Language.* Dublin: Fallon, 1954; Fohnam the Sculptor. Newark, Del.: Proscenium, 1973; "Three Stories." *Journal of Irish Literature* 22 (September 1993): 3–17. REFERENCES: Hutchins, Patricia. "Daniel Corkery, Poet of Weather and Place." *Irish Writing* 25 (December 1953): 42–49; Maume, Patrick. *'Life That Is Exile': Daniel Corkery and the Search for Irish Ireland.* Belfast: Institute of Irish Studies, Queen's University, Belfast, 1993; O'Faolain, Sean. "Daniel Corkery." *Dublin Magazine* 11 (April–June 1936): 49–61; Saul, George Brandon. *Daniel Corkery.* Lewisburg, Pa.: Bucknell University Press, 1973.

COSTELLO, MARY (1955–   ), memoirist. Born in Belfast.

WORK: *Titanic Town: Memoirs of a Belfast Girlhood.* London: Methuen, 1992.

COSTELLO, PETER (1946–   ), biographer, cultural historian, and critic. Costello was born in Dublin on April 3, 1946, the youngest son of James C. Costello, professor emeritus of architecture, University of Michigan, and his wife, Margaret (née Walsh). He was educated in Dublin by the Jesuits at Gonzaga College and graduated from the University of Michigan in 1969. He has written, edited, or contributed to some twenty-four books; and his interests have been extraordinarily wide-ranging—from Irish cultural and business histories, to books on animal mythology, to research on the Piltdown man hoax of 1912, and to books on Jules Verne and Sherlock Holmes. For Irish literature, his important volumes are two: *The Heart Grown Brutal* (1977), which was a learned but very readable study of writers who flourished from the death of Parnell to the death of Yeats* and which called attention to several significant figures outside the academic pantheon; and *James Joyce—The Years of Growth, 1882–1915* (1992), which provided new information and perspectives on a subject often thought to be exhausted. Two other works must also be cited: his appreciative and knowledgeable *Flann O'Brien* (1987), written with Peter van de Kamp; and his charming novel, *Leopold Bloom* (1981), which has a circumstantiality that Joyce himself could not but have admired. There is something of a tradition in Irish literature of the independent scholar, perhaps maintained in modern times by D. J. O'Donoghue* and W. J. Lawrence,* who has an erudition embarrassing to the professional academic; Costello is a contemporary embodiment of it.

PRINCIPAL IRISH WORKS: *The Heart Grown Brutal: The Irish Revolution in Literature from Parnell to the Death of Yeats.* Dublin: Gill & Macmillan/Totowa, N.J.: Rowman & Littlefield, 1977; *The Life of Leopold Bloom.* [Schull, West Cork]: Roberts Rinehart, 1981. (Novel); with Peter van de Kamp. *Flann O'Brien: An Illustrated Biography.* London: Bloomsbury, 1987; *James Joyce— The Years of Growth, 1882–1915.* [London]: Kyle Cathie, [1992].

COTTER, PATRICK (1963–   ), poet. Cotter was born in Cork and studied German and English at University College, Cork.

WORK: *The Misogynist's Blue Nightmare.* Dublin: Raven Arts, [1990]. (Poetry pamphlet).

COULTER, JOHN (1888–1980), playwright. Coulter, born in Belfast on February 12, 1888, divided his life span almost evenly between Ireland and Canada. While living in Ireland, he witnessed the rise of the Abbey* and the Ulster Literary Theatre*; moving to Toronto in 1936, he became an important figure in the development of Canadian drama. He and his wife, née Olive Clare Primrose, had two daughters. Coulter died in Toronto on December 1, 1980.

Coulter's plays of Ulster life include *The House in the Quiet Glen* (1925), a matchmaking comedy, and *Family Portrait* (1935), a satire on a materialistic Belfast family. *The Drums Are Out,* a drama of divided loyalties, set in Belfast during the Troubles, enjoyed a long run at the Abbey beginning on the anniversary of the Battle of the Boyne, appropriately, on July 12, 1948. A two-part tragedy, *God's Ulsterman* (1974), traces the legacy of sectarian hatred bequeathed to Ireland by Cromwell from the civil war of the 1640s to the era of Ian Paisley. These plays take no dogmatic stance and offer no solution to the torment of the North. If any hope is intimated, it lies in the possibility that the young will ultimately reject the ancient hostilities.

In addition to his plays, Coulter wrote a short novel entitled *Turf Smoke* (1945), adapted from his play *Holy Manhattan* (1941); this is the wistful tale of an elderly emigrant who tries to maintain a rural Ulster life-style in the canyons of New York. Coulter also wrote the libretto for Healey Willan's opera *Deirdre of the Sorrows* (1944).

Coulter's principal contribution to Canadian drama is the *Riel* trilogy (1950, first major production 1975). In 1869 and 1885, Louis Riel, a man of French and Metis Indian parentage, led uprisings in what is now Manitoba to protest wrongs done to the Metis people. There are some similarities between Riel and some Irish revolutionary leaders, between the situation in nineteenth-century Manitoba and in contemporary Quebec and Belfast. While the Ulster plays of John Coulter are a sensitive distillation of first-hand knowledge, *Riel* may be considered his masterwork because of its originality of subject and treatment.

WILLIAM J. FEENEY

WORKS: "The Catholics Walk." *Living Age,* 323 (November 22, 1924): 433–435. (Fiction); *The House in the Quiet Glen* and *Family Portrait.* Toronto: Macmillan, 1937; *Deirdre of the Sorrows:* An Ancient and Noble Tale Retold by John Coulter for Music by Healey Willan. Toronto: Macmillan, 1944. 2d ed., 1965; *Churchill.* Toronto: Ryerson, 1944. (Biography); *Turf Smoke.* Toronto: Ryerson, 1945; *The Blossoming Thorn.* Toronto: Ryerson, 1946. (Poetry); *The Trial of Louis Riel.* Ottawa: Oberon, 1968; *The Drums Are Out.* Irish Drama Series, Vol. 6. Chicago: De Paul University, 1971; *Riel.* Hamilton: Cromlech, 1972. Coulter's plays, stories, articles, radio and television scripts, and other documents are stored in the Coulter Archives, Mills Memorial Library, MacMaster University, Hamilton, Ontario, Canada. REFERENCES: Anthony, Geraldine. *John Coulter.* Twayne's World Author Series. Boston: G. K. Hall, 1976; Anthony, Geraldine. "Coulter's *Riel:* A Reappraisal." *Canadian Drama* 11 (1985): 321–328; Dempsey, Marion. "Profile: John Coulter." *Performing Arts* 8 (Spring 1971): 20–21; Garay, Kathleen. "John Coulter's *Riel:* The Shaping of a Myth for Canada." *Canadian Drama* 11 (1985): 293–309.

COUPER, LOUISE (fl. 1990s), novelist. Couper was born in Dublin and graduated from University College, Dublin. With her husband and two sons, she lives on an organic farm in Co. Westmeath.

WORK: *Philippa's Farm.* [Dublin]: Poolbeg, [1995].

COUSINS, JAMES H[ENRY SPROULL] (1873–1956), poet and playwright. Cousins was born in Belfast on July 22, 1873. He was educated at a national school in Belfast and then became an office boy, a clerk, and the private secretary to the lord mayor. In 1897, he moved to Dublin where he was first a clerk in a coal and shipping firm, and where he met AE,* Yeats,* Martyn,* Hyde,* and other writers of the Literary Revival. In 1901, he met Frank and Willie Fay and, learning of their desire to produce Irish plays, introduced them to AE who had written the first act of his *Deirdre.* Cousins acted in small parts for the newly formed Irish National Theatre Society, and he also wrote a number of plays, among them *The Sleep of the King* (1902), *The Racing Lug* (1902), and *The Sword of Dermot* (1903). Some of his short pieces were poetic versions of Irish stories and, except in quality, were not unlike some of the early plays of Yeats. Yeats, however, deplored "too much Cousins," succeeded in squashing a production of Cousins' comedy *Sold,* and firmly detached Cousins from the theatre movement.

In 1905, Cousins became an assistant master of English at the High School in Harcourt Street. In 1908, he joined the Theosophical Society. He was also a prolific poet. It was probably his volume *The Bell-Branch* (1908) which Joyce* had in mind in "Gas from a Burner" when he referred to a "tablebook of Cousins" which would "give you a heartburn in your arse." Cousins also edited a suffragette journal and rode many other hobbyhorses, among them vegetarianism.

In 1913, he and his wife left Dublin for Liverpool and then for India. On this occasion, the Theatre of Ireland gave him a special benefit evening, and Yeats made some amends by contributing £5 and writing a letter mentioning how much he valued Cousins. Cousins spent most of the rest of his life in India as a much admired individual and a highly valued teacher. He continued to write prolifically, and he died in India on February 20, 1956.

As a playwright, Cousins' most successful piece was the short tragedy *The Racing Lug* which predates John Synge's* somewhat similar *Riders to the Sea*. His bibliographer Alan Denson thinks, rather too enthusiastically, that "There are perhaps fifty poems of James Cousins which will endure." However, Denson goes on to note that "Much of his verse is in one key, and palls if read often."

Cousins is more interesting as a personality than as a writer. Although he was a catalyst in the early days of the theatre movement, he is most memorable as an engaging and enthusiastic eccentric. Perhaps the best judgment on him is again Denson's:

The unflattering (and offensive) gibes levelled at him in the W. B. Yeats and James Joyce canon deserve to be weighed against one important fact. Neither Yeats nor Joyce appears to have had any knowledge of Cousins' books written after 1915. Whilst they lived out their lives in service to their own self-centered ideals James Cousins devoted his best energies and his subtlest intellectual powers to the education of the young and the welfare of the poor and oppressed.

WORKS: *Ben Madighan and Other Poems*. Belfast: Marcus Ward, [1894]; *The Voice of One*. London: T. Fisher Unwin, 1900. (Poems); *The Quest*. Dublin: Maunsel, 1906. (Poems). *The Awakening and Other Sonnets*. Dublin: Maunsel, [1907]; *The Bell-Branch*. Dublin: Maunsel, 1908. (Poems); *Etain the Beloved and Other Poems*. Dublin: Maunsel, 1912; *The Wisdom of the West*. London: Theosophical Publishing Society, 1912. (Mythological studies); *The Bases of Theosophy*. Madras, Benares & Chicago: Theosophical Publishing House, 1913; *Straight and Crooked*. London: Grant Richards, 1915. (Poems); *The Garland of Life*. Madras: Ganesh, 1917. (Poems); *New Ways in English Literature*. Madras: Ganesh, [1917] revised, 1919; *The Renaissance in India*. Madras: Ganesh, [1918]; *Footsteps of Freedom*. Madras: Ganesh, 1919. (Essays); *The King's Wife*. Madras: Ganesh, 1919. (Play); *Moulted Feathers*. Madras: Ganesh, 1919. (Poetry); *Sea-Change*. Madras: Ganesh, 1920. (Poetry); *Modern English Poetry*. Madras: Ganesh, 1921; *The Cultural Unity of Asia*. Adyar, Madras: Theosophical Publishing House, 1922; *Surya-Gita*. Madras: Ganesh, 1922. (Poetry); *Work and Worship*. Madras: Ganesh, 1922. (Essays); *The New Japan, Impressions and Reflections*. Madras. Ganesh, 1923; *Forest Meditation and Other Poems*. Adyar, Madras: Theosophical Publishing House, 1925; *Heathen Essays*. Madras: Ganesh, 1923; *The Philosophy of Beauty*. Adyar, Madras: Theosophical Publishing House, 1925; *Samadarsana . . . A Study in Indian Psychology*. Madras, Ganesh, 1925; *Above the Rainbow and Other Poems*. Madras: Ganesh, 1926; *The Sword of Dermot*. Madras: Shama's Publishing House, 1927. (Play); *The Girdle*. Madras: Puck/Ganesh, 1929. (Poems); *The Wandering Harp, Selected Poems*. New York: Roerich Museum Press, 1932; *A Bardic Pilgrimage, Second Selection of the Poetry of James H. Cousins*. New York: Roerich Museum Press, 1934; *A Study in Synthesis*. Madras: Ganesh, 1934; *The Oracle and Other Poems*. Madras: Ganesh, 1938; *Collected Poems, 1894–1940*. Adyar, Madras: Kalakshetra, 1940; *The Faith of the Artist*. Adyar, Madras: Kalakshetra, 1941. (Essays); *The Hound of Uladh, Two Plays in Verse*. Adyar, Madras: Kalakshetra, 1942; *The Aesthetical Necessity in Life*. Kitadistan, Allahabad: University of Madras, 1944; *Reflections Before Sunset*. Adyar, Madras: Kalakshetra, 1946. (Poems); *Twenty-four Sonnets*. Adyar, Madras: Kalakshetra, [1949]; *We Two Together*, with Margaret E. Cousins. Madras: Ganesh, [1950]. (Autobiography).   REFERENCE: Denson, Alan. *James H. Cousins and Margaret E. Cousins, a Bio-Bibliographical Survey*. Kendal: Alan Denson, 1967. (An authoritative listing of many minor works not included above.)

COWMAN, ROZ (1942–   ), poet. Cowman was born in Cork and received a B.A. from University College, Cork. She has taught French in Ireland and Ni-

geria and now lives in Cork with her family. In 1985 she won the Patrick
Kavanagh Award, and her volume of poetry, *The Goose Herd* (1989), is a short
book of short, free-verse poems. Its notable quality is its arresting word choice,
which runs from the breezily colloquial ("Well, you can shove it, / Love. . . .")
to words like "flenses," "monofilament, "gastropod," "brumous," "rauwolf,"
and "glissades" as a verb. Sometimes the images startle, as in "bluebottles,
stewed, / bristling, juicy—." Sometimes they are more puzzling than startling,
as in "my father's crotch / moved like simmering stew." Sometimes they are
tersely effective:

> . . . Aghast
> at the explosion of sound,
> our little group falls silent,
>
> like birds after thunder.

WORK: *The Goose Herd.* [Galway: Salmon, 1989].

COX, WALTER ["WATTY"] (ca. 1770–1837), journalist and dramatist. Described by John [Purcell] O'Donovan* as "one of the many disgraces to the
craft of journalism produced by Ireland," Cox was the son of a Westmeath
blacksmith who came to Dublin, worked as a gunsmith, and edited scurrilous
journals designed to be the mouthpiece of the United Irishmen, although he
himself was suspected of having been an informer in 1798. Despite fines and
imprisonments for libelous attacks against figures as divergent as Major Sirr and
Daniel O'Connell, the government awarded him a pension on condition that he
leave the country. He spent some years in America but eventually returned to
Dublin, where he died on January 17, 1837. His principal attack on O'Connell,
The Cuckoo Calendar (1833), contains notable examples of his vitriolic worst.
His only extant play, *The Widow Dempsey's Funeral,* in an abridged version by
J. Crawford Neil, was revived in December 1911 by the Theatre of Ireland. It
was dismissed by W. J. Lawrence* as "merely a social satire arranged somewhat
amorphously in dialogue" and as possessing "no dramatic quality."

PRINCIPAL LITERARY WORKS: As Julius Publicola: *The Tears of Erin, A Poem Founded
upon Facts.* Dublin: Cox, 1810. As Cox: *The Widow Dempsey's Funeral.* Dublin: Printed for the
Author, 1822. (Three-act play); *The Cuckoo Calendar, Anecdotes of the Liberator, Containing some
Humorous Sketches of the Religious and Politcal Cleverness of the Great Mendicant.* Dublin: Printed
by J. Bryan, 1833. REFERENCES: Madden, Richard R. *The United Irishmen, Their Life and
Times.* London: Madden, 1842, Vol. 2, pp. 55–81; Ó Casaide, Séamus. "Watty Cox and His
Publications." *Bibliographical Society of Ireland Publications* 5 (1935): 17–38.

COX, WILLIAM TREVOR. *See* TREVOR, WILLIAM.

COYLE, KATHLEEN (1886–1952), novelist. Coyle was born and brought up
in the west of Ireland, with an Irish father and an American mother. She was
educated by governesses and by her father's library. For many years, she lived

in Paris; in 1942 she moved to New York, and in 1951 to Philadelphia, where, her husband having predeceased her, she died on March 25, 1952. She long suffered poor health and remarked, "Writing . . . was my only outlet. I was good for nothing else. Of my novels only one, *A Flock of Birds,* is of any value. The others are, and were meant to be, means of earning a livelihood. *The French Husband* was written in eleven days." *A Flock of Birds* (1930) is a finely realized and painful but very slowly moving book. Told through the consciousness of a woman whose son has been convicted of a political murder, it covers the few days from the end of the trial to the execution.

WORKS: *Piccadilly.* London: Jonathan Cape/New York: E. P. Dutton, 1923; *The Widow's House.* London: Jonathan Cape/New York: E. P. Dutton, 1924; *Shule Agra.* New York: E. P. Dutton, [1927]/ as *Youth in the Saddle.* London: Jonathan Cape, 1927; *It Is Better to Tell.* London: Jonathan Cape/ New York: E. P. Dutton, [1927]; *Liv.* London: Jonathan Cape, 1928/New York: E. P. Dutton, [ca. 1929]; *A Flock of Birds.* London: Jonathan Cape/New York: E. P. Dutton, [1930]; *There Is a Door.* Paris: Edward W. Titus, 1931; *The French Husband.* London: Pharos Editions/New York: E. P. Dutton, 1932; *The Skeleton.* New York: E. P. Dutton, 1933/London: Ivor Nicholson & Watson, 1934; *Morning Comes Early.* New York: E. P. Dutton, 1934; *Undue Fulfillment.* New York: William Morrow/London: Ivor Nicholson & Watson, 1934; *Immortal Ease.* New York: E. P. Dutton, 1939/ London: Gollancz, 1941; *Who Dwell with Wonder.* New York: E. P. Dutton, [ca. 1940]; *Brittany Summer.* New York & London: Harper, [ca. 1940]; *Josephine.* New York & London: Harper, [1942]; *To Hold against Famine.* New York: E. P. Dutton, 1942; *Major and the Others.* New York: E. P. Dutton, 1942. (Short stories); *The Magical Realm.* New York: E. P. Dutton, 1943. (Autobiography); "My Last Visit with James Joyce." *Tomorrow* 2 (October 1950): 15–17.

COYLE, ROBERT C. (1936–   ), novelist.

WORK: *The Grainne Journals.* Dublin: Basement, 1[995]. REFERENCE: Kelly, Shirley. "Michael Collins: The Novel." *Books Ireland,* No. 185 (April 1995): 77–78.

COYNE, JOSEPH STIRLING (1803–1868), playwright and humorist. Born in Birr, County Offaly, Coyne wrote farces for the Theatre Royal in Dublin and then, armed with an introduction from Carleton* to Crofton Croker,* removed to London, where he wrote for *Bentley's Miscellany* and was involved in the foundation of *Punch.* He was most noted as a playwright, and Nicoll attributes over 60 farces, comedies, melodramas, and dramas to him. The number has also been estimated at over 100. Coyne's pieces proved quite ephemeral, and the only one to be published in our day is a one-act farce from the French called *How to Settle Accounts with Your Laundress.* There is nothing of literary merit to it, and, if performed today, it could succeed only with consummate farcical acting and pacing. Coyne's uncollected sketches of Irish life are of a broadly popular nature, as this dialogue from "Tim Hogan's Ghost" may suggest:

"And now, boys and girls," said he, elevating his voice, "as surveyor and directhor of this fantastic and jocular meeting, I direct the demonsthrations to begin. You all know the rules. The best couple of dancers win the cake. So take to your partners, and commence your flagitious recrayations."

Coyne died in London on July 18, 1868.

WORK RECENTLY IN PRINT: "How to Settle Accounts with Your Laundress" in *The Magistrate and Other Nineteenth-Century Plays.* Michael R. Booth, ed. London: Oxford University Press, 1974.

CRAIG, MAURICE [JAMES] (1919–   ), social historian, essayist, and poet. Craig was born on October 25, 1919, in Belfast, and was educated at Magdalene College, Cambridge, and at Trinity College, Dublin, from which he received his Ph.D. In the 1940s, he published some superb poetry. His understanding of traditional form is finely apparent in, for instance, "Ballad to a Traditional Refrain," where he suffuses the simple public form of the popular ballad with a pervasive irony and uses a Yeatsian refrain with devastating cumulative effect. Craig gave up the writing of poetry, however, and his best-known work is *Dublin, 1660–1860,* a companionable social and architectural history of immense information and consummate taste. His more recent books usually deal with Irish architecture, but in 1990 he published *The Elephant and the Polish Question,* a book of discursive essays on language and other subjects.

PRINCIPAL WORKS: *A Poem: Black Swans.* Dublin: Gayfield, 1941; *Twelve Poems.* Dublin: Privately printed, 1942; *Some Way for Reason.* Toronto: Heinemann, 1948; *The Volunteer Earl, Being the Life and Times of James Caulfield, First Earl of Charlemont.* London: Cresset, 1948; *Dublin, 1660–1860.* London: Cresset, 1952/Dublin: Figgis, 1969; *Irish Bookbinding, 1660–1800.* London: Cassell, 1954; *The Personality of Leinster.* Dublin: Colm Ó Lochlainn for the Cultural Relations Committee of Ireland, 1961; *Classic Irish Houses of the Middle Size.* London: Architectural Press, 1976; *Architecture in Ireland.* Dublin: Department of Foreign Affairs, 1978; with the Knight of Glin, *Ireland Observed: A Handbook to the Buildings and Antiquities of Ireland.* Dublin: Mercier, 1980; *The Architecture of Ireland from Earliest Times to 1880.* London: Batsford, 1982; *The Elephant and the Polish Question.* Dublin: Lilliput, [1990].   REFERENCE: Bernelle, Agnes, ed. *Decantations: A Tribute to Maurice Craig.* [Dublin]: Lilliput, [1992].

CRANE BAG, THE (1977–1985), magazine. Edited by Mark Patrick Hederman and Richard Kearney,* *The Crane Bag* printed articles on art, literature, philosophy, and cultural and political issues. Its contributors included many leading Irish intellectuals of the day, such as Conor Cruise O'Brien,* Seamus Deane,* Vivian Mercier,* Declan Kiberd,* Thomas Kilroy,* W. J. McCormack,* and many others. Its focus was not narrowly Irish, and it contained, among other matter, interviews with Herbert Marcuse and Noam Chomsky. Although many of its articles tended to be rather too short for profundity, it was one of the few forums for intellectual debate in the country.

REFERENCES: *The Crane Bag Book of Irish Studies (1977–1981).* Dublin: Blackwater, [1982]. (A reprinting of the first five volumes); *The Crane Bag Book of Irish Studies 1982–1985.* Dublin: Wolfhound/St. Paul, Minn.: Irish Books & Media, 1987. (A reprinting of the last four volumes).

CREGAN, CONOR

WORKS: *Chrissie.* [Swords, Co. Dublin]: Poolbeg, [1992]. (Novel); *The Poison Stream.* [Swords, Co. Dublin]: Poolbeg, [1993]. (Novel).

CROFTS, FREEMAN WILLS (1879–1957), writer of mystery fiction. Crofts was born in Dublin in June 1879 to an army medical officer and became a pupil in civil engineering to the chief engineer of the Belfast and Northern Counties Railway. He worked on northern railways from 1900 to 1929, when his health gave way, and he turned to writing full-time. His first and most famous novel, *The Cask,* was begun in 1919 and translated into nine languages; and he was probably the most prolific and popular Irish writer of detective fiction. A practitioner of the "classic" detective story, he was eminently fair in planting clues for his readers, but his dogged amassing of detail can seem more than a bit phlegmatic. He died in Worthing, Sussex, on April 11, 1957.

WORKS: *The Cask.* London: W. Collins, [1920]; *The Ponson Case.* London: W. Collins, 1921; *The Pit-Prop Syndicate.* London: W. Collins, [1922]; *The Groote Park Murder.* London: W. Collins, [1924]; *Inspector French's Greatest Case.* London: W. Collins, [1925]; *Inspector French and the Cheyne Mystery.* London: W. Collins, [1926]; *Inspector French and the Starvel Tragedy.* London: W. Collins, [1927]; *The Sea Mystery.* London: W. Collins, [1928]; *Inspector French's Case Book.* London: W. Collins, [1928]; *The Box Office Murder.* London: W. Collins, [1929]; *Sir John Magill's Last Journey.* London: W. Collins, [1930]; *Mystery in the Channel.* London: W. Collins, [1931]; *Sudden Death.* London: W. Collins, [1932]; *Death on the Way.* London: W. Collins, [1932]; *The Freeman Wills Crofts Omnibus.* London: W. Collins, [1932]; *The Hog's Back Mystery.* London: Hodder & Stoughton, 1933; *Mystery on Southampton Water.* London: Hodder & Stoughton, 1934; *The 12.30 from Croydon.* London: Hodder & Stoughton, 1934; *Crime at Guildford.* London: W. Collins, [1935]; *The Loss of the "Jane Vosper."* London: W. Collins, [1936]; *Man Overboard!* London: W. Collins, [1936]; *The Mystery of the Sleeping Car Express and Other Stories.* London: Hodder & Stoughton, 1936; *Found Floating.* London: Hodder & Stoughton, 1937; *The End of Andrew Harrison.* London: Hodder & Stoughton, 1938; *Antidote to Venom.* London: Hodder & Stoughton, 1938; *Fatal Venture.* London: Hodder & Stoughton, 1939; *Golden Ashes.* London: Hodder & Stoughton, 1940; *James Tarrant, Adventurer.* London: Hodder & Stoughton, 1941; *The Losing Game.* London: Hodder & Stoughton, 1941; *Fear Comes to Chalfont.* London: Hodder & Stoughton, 1942; *The Affair at Little Wokeham.* London: Hodder & Stoughton, 1943; *The Hunt Ball Murder.* London: Todd, [1943]; *Mr. Sefton, Murderer.* London: Vallancy, 1944; *Enemy Unseen.* London: Hodder & Stoughton, 1945; *Death of a Train.* London: Hodder & Stoughton, 1946; *Murderers Make Mistakes.* London: Hodder & Stoughton, 1947; *Young Robin Brand, Detective.* London: University of London Press, 1947; *Silence for the Murderer.* London: Hodder & Stoughton, 1949; *French Strikes Oil.* London: Hodder & Stoughton, 1952; *Many a Slip.* London: Hodder & Stoughton, 1955; *Anything to Declare?* London: Hodder & Stoughton, 1957.

CROKER, MRS. B. M. (ca. 1850–1920), novelist and short story writer. Croker was the only daughter of Reverend William Sheppard, rector of Kilgefin, County Roscommon. She was educated at Rockferry, then at Cheshire and Tours. After her marriage to Lieutenant-Colonel Croker of the Royal Munster Fusiliers, she spent fourteen years in India and Burma, and most of her extremely popular books are set there. Only eight of her nearly forty volumes are set in Ireland or populated with Irish characters: *Beyond the Pale, A Bird of Passage, Bridget, Johanna, In the Kingdom of Kerry, Lismoyle, A Nine Days' Wonder,* and *Terence.* Several of these novels were set in Kerry, and the author shows a familiarity with the Waterville area. Following her return from the East, she lived in London and Folkestone until her death in 1920. Her works were frequently translated into German and French.

Croker's novels were generally popular romances, and the majority provide glimpses of British military life in colonized areas. The relationships between the British mistresses and their native servants are especially well drawn, as is the social hierarchy of the officers' wives. One particularly fine novel is *Angel,* where the protagonist is a young girl who views her world with the eye of a practiced spectator. Two of her Irish novels are worth reading for their insights into the life of the Protestant upper class. *Terence* (1899) is set in Waterville among holidaying Protestant anglers, and the plot involves a romance complicated by jealousy. *A Nine Days' Wonder* (1905) displays the social chaos caused when Mary Foley, who has been raised in an Irish cabin during her formative years, suddenly finds herself pronounced to be the missing Lady Joseline Deane, daughter of English nobility. Mary's lack of social graces, blunt tongue, and forthright manner assure the heroine of a comical and chaotic introduction into British society. Croker's novels were eminently suitable for the young ladies of her day, and as such they stress the elements of patience, charity, and womanly virtues.

ANNE COLMAN

WORKS: *Pretty Miss Neville.* 3 vols. London: Tinsley, 1883; *Proper Pride.* London: Ward & Downey, 1885; *Some One Else.* 3 vols. London: Sampson Low, Marston, Searle & Rivington, 1885; *A Bird of Passage* 3 vols. London: Chatto & Windus, 1886; *Diana Barrington: A Romance of Central India.* 3 vols. London: Ward & Downey, 1888; *Two Masters.* 3 vols. London: F. V. White, 1890; *Interference.* 3 vols. London: F. V. White, 1891; *A Family Likeness: A Sketch in the Himalayas.* 3 vols. London: Chatto & Windus, 1892; *A Third Person.* 2 vols. London: F. V. White, 1893; *"To Let,"* etc. London: Chatto & Windus, 1893; *Mr. Jervis.* 3 vols. London: Chatto & Windus, 1894; *Married or Single?* 3 vols. London: Chatto & Windus, 1895; *Village Tales and Jungle Tragedies.* London: Chatto & Windus, 1895; *In the Kingdom of Kerry, and Other Stories.* London: Chatto & Windus, 1896; *The Real Lady Hilda.* London: Chatto & Windus, 1896; *Mrs. Balmaine's Past.* London: Chatto & Windus, 1898; *Peggy of the Bartons.* London: Methuen, 1898; *Beyond the Pale.* London: Chatto & Windus, 1899; *Infatuation.* London: Chatto & Windus, 1899; *Jason and Other Stories.* London: Chatto & Windus, 1899; *Terence.* London: Chatto & Windus, 1899; *Angel: A Sketch in Indian Ink.* London: Methuen, 1901; *A State Secret, and Other Stories.* London: Methuen, 1901; *The Cat's Paw.* London: Chatto & Windus, 1902; *Her Own People.* London: Hurst & Blackett, 1903; *Johanna.* London: Methuen, 1903; *The Happy Valley.* London: Methuen, 1904; *A Nine Days' Wonder.* London: Methuen, 1905; *The Old Cantonment, and Other Stories of India and Elsewhere.* London: Methuen, 1905; *The Youngest Miss Mowbray.* London: Hurst & Blackett, 1906; *The Company's Servant: A Romance of Southern India.* London: Hurst & Blackett, 1907; *The Spanish Necklace.* London: Chatto & Windus, 1907; *Katherine the Arrogant.* London: Methuen, 1909; *Babes in the Wood: A Romance of the Jungles.* London: Methuen, 1910; *Fame.* London: Mills & Boon, 1910; *A Rolling Stone.* London: F. V. White, 1911; *The Serpent's Tooth.* London: Hutchinson, 1912; *In Old Madras.* London: Hutchinson, 1913; *Lismoyle: An Experiment in Ireland.* London: Hutchinson, 1914; *Quicksands.* London: Cassell, 1915; *Given in Marriage.* London: Hutchinson, 1916; *A Rash Experiment.* London: Hutchinson, [1917]; *The Road to Mandalay: A Tale of Burma.* London: Cassell, 1917; *Bridget.* London: Hutchinson, 1918; *Blue China.* London: Hutchinson, [1919]; *Jungle Tales.* London: Holden & Hardingham, 1919; *Odds and Ends.* London: Hutchinson, [1919]; *The Pagoda Tree.* London: Cassell, [1919]; *The Chaperon.* London: Cassell, [1920]; *The House of Rest.* London: Cassell, 1921.

CROKER, JOHN WILSON (1780–1857), politician and man of letters. Croker was born in Galway on December 20, 1780, educated at Trinity College, Dublin, and at Lincoln's Inn, and admitted to the Irish bar in 1802. He wrote a few early satires and historical essays about Ireland which are little read today. His real career was in England as a member of Parliament, as secretary to the Admiralty, and as one of the founders (in 1809) of the influential *Quarterly Review* for which he wrote over 250 articles. His literary criticism for the *Review* was not always very perceptive (see his damning notice of Keats' "Endymion" in September 1818); and his edition of Boswell's *Life of Johnson* was savagely attacked by his frequent sparring partner, Thomas Babington Macaulay, in *The Edinburgh Review*. His own ferocious assault on Macaulay's *History of England* was defined by Sydney Smith as an attempt at murder that ended in suicide. He also quarreled with Lady Morgan,* and he was unfairly pilloried as the despicable Rigby in Disraeli's *Coningsby*. He died at Hampton, Middlesex, on August 10, 1857.

PRINCIPAL WORKS: [*The Opinion of an Impartial Observer Concerning the Late Transactions in Ireland.* Dublin: J. Parry, 1803.]; *An Intercepted Letter, from J—T—, Esq., Writer at Canton, to His Friend in Dublin, Ireland.* Dublin: M. N. Mahon, 1804; *Familiar Epistles to Frederick J.—S, Esq. on the Present State of the Irish Stage.* Dublin: John Barlow, 1804; *The Amazoniad; or, Figure and Fashion.* Dublin: John King, 1806; *A Sketch of the State of Ireland Past and Present.* Dublin: M. N. Mahon, 1808; *The Battles of Talavera.* Dublin: Mahon, 1809; ed., *Life of Samuel Johnson, by James Boswell.* London: John Murray, 1831; *Essays on the Early Period of the French Revolution.* London: John Murray, 1857; *The Croker Papers.* Louis J. Jennings, ed. 3 vols. London: John Murray, 1884; *The Croker Papers 1808–1857.* Bernard Pool, ed. London: Batsford, 1967. REFERENCE: Brightfield, M. F. *John Wilson Croker.* Berkeley: University of California Press, 1940.

CROKER, T[HOMAS] CROFTON (1798–1854), folklorist. Croker, the pioneering collector of Irish folklore, was born in Buckingham Square, Cork, on January 15, 1798. At the age of fifteen, he was placed as an apprentice in a mercantile firm in Cork, but his main interest was already in old legends and stories. He made several excursions throughout the South of Ireland to sketch and to study the traditions of the countryside. In 1818, after the death of his father, he moved to London. John Wilson Croker,* who was no relation, secured him a clerkship at the Admiralty, where he served until his retirement in 1850.

In 1830, Croker married Marianne Nicholson who published two novels, *The Adventures of Barney Mahoney* and *My Village Versus Our Village* (both 1832), under her husband's name.

Croker's own first book, *Researches in the South of Ireland* (1824), was admired but not greatly successful. However, his *Fairy Legends and Traditions of the South of Ireland* (1825) was an immediate popular success, and also brought the author enthusiastic praise from Wilhelm Grimm, Maria Edgeworth,* and Sir Walter Scott. (On his first meeting with Croker, Scott described him as "little as a dwarf, keen-eyed as a hawk, and of easy, prepossessing manners, something like Tom Moore.") *Fairy Legends* is a collection of tales about such strange and wondrous beings as Banshees, Merrows, Phookas, and Cluricaunes. The stories are perhaps not as faithfully rendered as modern folklorists would desire, but they are delightful stories. Croker did not merely take them down verbatim, but arranged them into effective narrative structures. "The Haunted Celler" is an obvious example of how successfully Croker rearranged his incidents to lead to an effective climax. However, it was not only the charm of his subjects and the craft of his organization, but also the terse yet rich prose that captivated his readers. As W. B. Yeats* remarked, Croker "caught the very choice of the people, the very pulse of life—giving what was most noticed in his day. Croker, full of the ideas of harum-scarum Irish gentility, saw everything humorized. His work is touched everywhere with beauty—a gentle Arcadian beauty."

Croker's last years were busy ones, and his important publications include *Legends of the Lakes; or Sayings and Doings at Killarney* (1829), *A Memoir of Joseph Holt* (1838), and *Popular Songs of Ireland* (1839). He died on August 8, 1854, at Brompton, leaving behind at least one volume, *Fairy Legends,* which is as fresh and captivating today as it was 150 years ago.

WORKS: *Researches in the South of Ireland,* London: J. Murray, 1824/reprint. Dublin: Irish University Press, 1968, with an introduction by Kevin Danaher; *Fairy Legends and Traditions of the South of Ireland.* London: J. Murray, 1825 & 1828; *Daniel O'Rourke; or, Rhymes of a Pantomime.* London: Ainsworth, 1828; *Legends of the Lakes; or, Sayings and Doings at Killarney.* London: Ebers, 1829; *Landscape Illustrations of Moore's "Irish Melodies".* London: Power, 1835; *The Tour of the French Traveller M. de la Boullaye le Gouz in Ireland. A. D. 1644.* London: T. & W. Boone, 1837; *Memoirs of Joseph Holt, General of the Irish Rebels in 1798.* London: H. Colburn, 1838; *The Popular Songs of Ireland.* London: H. Colburn, 1839; *The Historical Songs of Ireland.* London: Printed for the Percy Society by G. Richards, 1841; *Narratives Illustrative of the Contests in Ireland in 1641 and 1690.* London: Printed for the Camden Society by J. Bowyer Nichols, 1841; *A Kerry Pastoral.* London: Reprinted for the Percy Society by T. Richards, 1843; *The Keen of the South of Ireland.* London: Printed for the Percy Society by T. Richards, 1844; *Popular Songs, Illustrative of the French Invasions of Ireland.* London: Percy Society, 1845–1847; *A Walk from London to Fulham.* London: W. Tegg, 1860. REFERENCE: MacCarthy, Bridget G. "Thomas Crofton Croker 1798–1854." *Studies* 32 (1943): 539–556.

CROLY, GEORGE (1780–1860), poet, fiction writer, playwright, and essayist. If Croly is remembered today, it is because of Byron's remark in Canto XI of *Don Juan:*

> The Muses upon Sion's hill must ramble
>   With poets almost clergymen, or wholly;
> And Pegasus has a psalmodic amble
>   Beneath the very Reverend Rowley Powley,
> Who shoes the glorious animal with stilts,
> A modern Ancient Pistol—by the hilts!

Byron was not entirely fair. It is true that Croly is capable of beginning a poem like "Approach of Evening" with "Night's wing is on the east" and then have the clouds reposing

> Like weary armies of the firmament,
> Encamped beneath their vanes of pearl and rose. . . .

and then have "the wind's sudden trumpet" shaking "their pavilions" and conclude with a remark about "the dew distilled / From Evening's airy urns." However, in the same poem, Croly can write with effective simplicity:

> This is the loveliest hour of all that Day
> Calls upwards through its kingdom of the air.
> The sights and sounds of earth have died away;
> Above, the clouds are rolled against the glare
> Of the red west. . . .

Also much—not all—of his play, *Catiline* (1822), has an unadorned and terse dramatic speech rare enough among the fustian tragedies of the nineteenth century.

Croly was born in Dublin, educated at Trinity College, and ordained in 1804. In 1810, he moved to London and began to publish verse, tales, and essays, including ones on Burke* and Curran.* In 1835, he was made rector of St. Stephen's, Walbrook, London. In 1847 he was appointed afternoon preacher at the Foundling Hospital and made a considerable reputation as a preacher. He died on November 24, 1860.

PRINCIPAL WORKS: *Paris in 1815.* 1st part. London: Murray, 1817. (Poem)/2d part. London: J. Warren, 1821. (With other poems); *The Angel of the World; An Arabian Tale—Sebastian; A Spanish Tale.* London: J. Warren, 1820. (Poetry); *Gems Principally from the Antique. . . .* London: Hurst, Robinson, 1822. (Poetry to illustrate etchings by Richard Dagley); *Catiline.* London: Hurst, Robinson, 1822. (Verse tragedy); *Salathiel.* 3 vols. London: H. Colburn, 1829. (Novel); *The Poetical Works of the Rev. G. Croly.* 2 vols. London: H. Colburn & R. Bentley, 1830; *Historical Sketches, Speeches and Characters.* London: Seely & Burnside, 1842. (Essays); *The Modern Orlando.* London: H. Colburn, 1846. (Poetry); *Marston; or, The Soldier and Statesman. . . .* 3 vols. London: H. Colburn, 1846. (Novel).   REFERENCE: Kerring, R. *A Few Personal Recollections of the Late Rev. G. Croly.* London: Longman, 1861.

CROMMELIN, MAY DE LA CHEROIS (ca. 1850–1930), novelist, travel writer, and poet. Crommelin was the daughter of S. de la Cherois Crommelin, himself a descendant of Louis Crommelin, of Huguenot descent, who was a founder of the Ulster linen industry. She was born at Carrowdore Castle in County Down. Educated at home, she spent her childhood in Ireland before moving to London. She traveled widely—to South America, the West Indies, Syria, Palestine, and elsewhere—and she included her own adventures in her travel books. Crommelin also wrote novels and poetry, generally under the names of Mary Henrietta de la Cherois or May Crommelin. She died on August 10, 1930.

Crommelin wrote romance novels, in a variety of geographic settings. Only four of her novels were set in Ireland: *Orange Lily* (1879), *Black Abbey* (1880), *Divil-May-Care* (1899), and *The Golden Bow* (1912). In these Northern Ireland novels, she tends to write of County Down or the Antrim areas. Her use of the Northern peasant dialect is refreshingly deft, and her peasant characters are well drawn. Her Irish novels reveal the Northern Orange society, and she rarely slips into religious or political stereotypes, although Stephen J. Brown finds "a tinge of stage Irishman" in *Divil-May-Care*. She may have written another dozen novels, which cannot be properly substantiated.

ANNE COLMAN

WORKS: *Queenie*. 3 vols. London, 1874; *My Love, She's But a Lassie*. 3 vols. London, 1875; *A Jewel of a Girl*. 3 vols. London, 1877; *A Jewel of a Girl*. New York: Harper, 1878; *Orange Lily and Other Tales*. 2 vols. Dublin: Hurst & Blackett/New York: Harper, 1879; *Black Abbey*. 3 vols. London: Sampson Low, Marston, Searle & Rivington, 1880; *Miss Daisy Dimity*. 3 vols. London: Hurst & Blackett, 1881; *Brown Eyes*. London: Arrowsmith's Christmas Annual, 1882; *In the West Countrie*. 3 vols. London: Hurst & Blackett, 1883/New York: Harper, [1884]; *My Book of Friends: Pen and Ink Portraits by Themselves*. London & New York: George Routledge, 1883; *Joy; or, The Light of Cold-Home Ford*. 3 vols. London: Hurst & Blackett/New York: Harper, 1884; *Goblin Gold*. London: Frederick Warne/New York: Harper, 1885; *Love, the Pilgrim*. 3 vols. London: Hurst & Blackett, 1886; *Poets in the Garden*. London: Fisher Unwin, 1886/New York: A. C. Armstrong, 1887. (Poetry); *Dead Men's Dollars*. Bristol: J. W. Arrosmith, [1887]; *The Freaks of Lady Fortune*. 2 vols. London: Hurst & Blackett/New York: J. W. Lovell, 1889; *Violet Vyvian, M. F. H.* London: Hurst & Blackett, 1889/New York: J. W. Lovell, [1890]; *Cross-Roads*. 3 vols. London: Hurst & Blackett, 1890/as *Love Knots; or, Cross Roads*. London & Sydney: Eden, Remington, 1892; *Midge*. London: Trischler, 1890; *For the Sake of the Family*. New York: J. W. Lovell, [1891]/London & Sydney: Eden, Remington, 1892; *Mr. and Mrs. Herries*. London: Hutchinson, 1892; *Dust before the Wind*. 2 vols. London: Bliss, Sands & Foster, 1894; *Over the Andes; from the Argentine to Chili and Peru*. London: Bentley/New York: Macmillan, 1896. (Travel); *Half round the World for a Husband*. London: T. Fisher Unwin, 1896/as *Half around the World to Find a Husband*. Chicago & New York: Globe Library, 1898; *Divil-May-Care*. 8 vols. London: F. V. White, 1899; *Kinsah, a Daughter of Tangier*. London: John Long, 1899; *Bay Ronald*. 3 vols. London: Hurst & Blackett, 1899/rev. ed., London: Jarrold, 1899; *Bettina*. London: John Long, 1900; *The Luck of a Lowland Laddie*. London: John Long/New York: F. M. Buckles, 1900; *The Vereker Family*. London: Digby, Long, 1900; *A Woman—Derelict*. London: John Long, [1901]; *A Daughter of Old England*. London: John Long, [1902]; *Her Faithful Knight*. New York: A. L. Burt, [1902]; *Partner's Three*. London: John Long, 1903; *Some Arts and Crafts*. London: Chapman & Hall, 1903; *Crimson Lilies*. London: John Long, 1903; *One Pretty Maid, and Others*. London: John Long, 1904; *The White Lady*. London: John Long, 1905; *Phoebe of the White Farm*. London: John Long, 1906; *The House of Howe*. London: John Long, 1907; *"I Little Knew—!"* London: John Milne, [1908]; *Lovers on the Green*. London: Hutchinson, 1910; *The Isle of the Dead*. London: Hutchinson, 1911. (With A. Williams); *Madame Mystery: A Romance in Touraine*. London: Hutchinson, 1910/Boston: D. Estes, 1912; *The Golden Bow*. London: Holden & Hardingham, 1912; *Pink Lotus: A Comedy in Kashmir*. London: Hurst & Blackett, 1914; *Little Soldiers*. London: Hutchinson, [1916]; *Sunshine on the Nile*. London: Jarrolds, [1920]; *Aunt Angel*. London: Odhams, [1921]; *Halfpenny House*. London: Hurst & Blackett, [1924].

CRONE, ANNE (1915–1972), novelist. Although she was born in Dublin on September 16, 1915, Crone's father was from Belfast, and her mother from County Fermanagh. She was educated at Methodist College, Belfast, and at Somerville College, Oxford. She received a Double First in modern languages in 1936 and a B. Litt. in 1940. She taught modern languages in Belfast and became head of the Department of Modern Languages in Princess Gardens School, Belfast. She published three novels, and she died on October 15, 1972, of asthma, from which she had suffered since childhood.

Crone's novels focus on rural Ulster families whose histories are narrated by young women. Land and love are her main themes. For example, the orphaned Catholic heroine of *Bridie Steen* (1948) roams the shores of Lough Erne free of any ties until she falls in love with her cousin, who reunites her with her termagant Protestant grandmother. A painful love affair matures her, but when her grandmother, an embittered Protestant, presses her to renounce her religion to inherit family land, the conflict drives her to her death. The novel has other charming characters in addition to Bridie, and it is a passionate, nonpartisan plea for religious tolerance in Ulster.

This Pleasant Lea (1951) is also set on the windy shores of Lough Erne. Faith, the young heroine, falls in love, suffers the pain of rejection and the dissipation of her family's land by a feckless brother, but finally finds happiness in marriage to a wealthy farmer. Like Bridie, she is an intense, romantic young woman whose fortunes command our interest and sympathy. Not so Grace Maguire, the heroine of *My Heart and I* (1955), whose self-effacing virtue is tedious in the extreme. No doubt hers is a realistic portrait of Irish womanhood, but it is without humor. The novel is thematically sound, however: Grace is finally cared for by her lost love, whose life has been ruined by his ties to the land.

Crone's writing, though sensitive and lyrical, is mannered and dated. Nonetheless, she does understand human emotions and does know the foibles of her characters. Her characterization of young women is excellent. *Bridie Steen* may not warrant Lord Dunsany's* description as "one of the great novels of our time," but it has something of Emily Brontë's depth of feeling and Jane Austen's charm and common sense. *This Pleasant Lea* is almost as good as *Bridie Steen,* but *My Heart and I* is much inferior.

MARY ROSE CALLAGHAN

WORKS: *Bridie Steen.* New York: Scribner's, 1948/London: Heinemann, 1949; *This Pleasant Lea.* New York: Scribner's, 1951/London: Heinemann, 1952; *My Heart and I.* London: Heinemann, 1955.

CRONIN, ANTHONY (1928–   ), biographer, broadcaster, columnist, critic, editor, novelist, and poet. Born in Wexford and educated at University College, Dublin, Cronin has had a very varied, interesting career on the Dublin literary scene. During the early 1950s, he worked with Peadar O'Donnell* on *The Bell,* formally becoming associate editor with the January 1954 issue. From 1956 to 1958, he served as literary editor of *Time and Tide.* From 1966 to 1968, he was visiting lecturer in English at the University of Montana, and from 1966 to 1968 he was poet in residence at Drake University. From 1980 to 1983 and from 1987 to 1992, he was cultural adviser and artistic adviser to the prime minister, Charles J. Haughey, and in that capacity an instigator of Aosdána.* In 1983, he received the Marten Toonder Award for his contribution to Irish literature. He has produced four books of poetry, two novels, four collections of criticism, a biography of Flann O'Brien, numerous newspaper columns particularly for the *Irish Times,* and a variety of edited journals and other publications. During these years, though principally in the 1960s, he has also lived in England, Spain, and the United States. Friend or acquaintance of Brendan Behan,* Patrick Kavanagh,* Flann O'Brien, and others, he more than many literary figures—even in Ireland—has been prolific in contributing to almost all of the genres, and he has made his mark as an influential figure on the public scene.

As a novelist, he has been called (by James Cahalan in *The Irish Novel*) a conventional realist. *The Life of Riley* (1964) and *Identity Papers* (1979) both depend heavily on close observation of the Dublin pub scene, an outcast world of "gurrierdom," where "unsuccess was looked upon with favor." Cronin's heroes, if they can be called that, meander through some great drinking scenes and awkward situations, sometimes painstakingly described; he is perhaps too fond of interjection, qualification, the appositive, of the "as it were" variety, to maintain a plausible fictional line. Setting is all-important, plot generally less so; characters are comic, silly, exasperating, sometimes leaving the feeling that one has read all this somewhere else, perhaps in *The Ginger Man* or in Behan. As Dublin reminiscence, the novels seem, literally, second-rate, but there are moments of comedy, passion, and insight. The plot of *Identity Papers* approaches the intriguing with a teasing touch whereby the main character labors under the delusion that he is the grandson of Richard Pigott, the nineteenth-century forger.

Cronin's poetry is better than his fiction. Generally careful, taut, and crafted and frequently clever, witty, and original, he fronts a number of issues, themes, emotions, states of being—despair, fear, failure, loneliness, frustration, pride. Settings are frequently bleak: "the grimy primrose / That is the western sky of winter London" or, frequently, "rain-swept" cities in autumn gloom. He probes what "steers us to destruction" in "R. M. S. Titanic," one of his longer poems (331 lines), though, invariably, "[w]e live by living, survive by mere surviving. / Stubborn beyond our stubbornness or strength / Our virtues, like our weaknesses, prevail." A more ambitious effort, "The End of the Modern World" (161 mostly sonnet-length pieces), purports to be "a poetic view of the psychic history of western civilisation [since the Middle Ages] and the stage at which it has arrived today." But because Cronin is always the analyst, the dissector, the player of contrasts, it is difficult to find much synthesis or unified effect in this long and discursive work; the final poem ends with history having reached a culmination in Manhattan, "seen at sunset from the harbour, / Meaningless, astonishing and simple." "Letter to an Englishman" (1985) has, in 608 lines, the avowed purpose of explaining "the Irish Question" to an English friend. It contains much historical reference and a great deal of social criticism of Ireland since 1916; he is particularly concerned with what might be called Paudeenism in "the second generation," that is, among the sons who inherited wealth and influence as a result of a parent's role in the War of Independence. He suggests that the nub of the Northern Irish problem is the English ruling class, "those who've run your show since sixty-six, / I mean ten, not nineteen"; that is, specifically, the desire of militarists in that ruling class to protect England's back door—Ireland—on the Atlantic seaways. If this seems a simplified explanation of England's continued interest in Ireland, so does Cronin's final eloquent plea:

> Go north, come south, the primary fixation
> Is still the hypothesis of the Irish Nation,
> Where else but here could controversy, hate
> Attend the concept of the nation state?

One wonders—Cyprus? Lebanon? Yugoslavia?

A number of Cronin's poems deal with the poet and his craft, with struggling away in the small hours over "the poem I'm able / Instead of the one I will never be able to write." However, he is certainly able to write some very good poems. "A Form of Elegy for the Poet Brian Higgins (1930–1965)" is simple, clever, and intensely moving. He shows particular insight about the peculiar problems of being an Irish author, for example, "The Man Who Went Absent from the Native Literature." "Responsibilities" is deservedly the most frequently anthologized of his poems.

Cronin's criticism, arguably his strongest genre, began with articles in *The Bell* that lamented "a country which is politically and socially in a slough . . . unlikely to provide the atmosphere of intellectual excitement which sustains the good monthly or weekly magazine." ("This Time, This Place," July 1954). His memoir, *Dead as Doornails* (1975), is an excellent picture of the Dublin literary scene in the 1950s and 1960s. *Heritage Now* (1982) collects essays "extensively added to and rewritten" from various newspapers and broadcasts in an interesting attempt to discuss the long-standing controversy of what is and is not Anglo-Irish literature and whether it speaks for the nation of Ireland: "To put it briefly, confronted with the phenomenon of *Ulysses,* with the poems of Yeats's full maturity, with Kavanagh's poems or *Finnegans Wake* or *At Swim-Two-Birds* or *Black List, Section H* or the Beckett trilogy, there is not much point in talking about Anglo-Irish literature. Whatever else these works are, they are not Anglo-Irish anything. . . . And the truth is that Ireland now has quite a considerable literature of its own in the English language to which the term Anglo-Irish, though still used in universities, is entirely inapplicable." He is similarly negative and outspoken about academically accepted terms like "the Celtic Twilight" or "the Irish literary revival." Despite its pungency, *Heritage Now* is a lucid, very readable treatment of writers from Maria Edgeworth* to Flann O'Brien, the latter, of course, the subject of a full-length biography by Cronin, which is gentle, sympathetic, but also balanced in its coverage of a man whom he knew and admired.

In sum, Cronin has been a prolific writer, one who speaks, according to Seamus Deane,* with Kavanagh, Behan, and O'Brien, with a spirit that counters "the very real grimmness of the general situation with a comic verve that is often generated by the camaraderie of an outcast group."

JOHANN A. NORSTEDT

WORKS: *Poems*. London: Cresset, 1957; ed., with Jon Silken, *New Poems*. London: Hutchinson, 1960; ed., *The Courtship of Phelim O'Toole*. London: New English Library, 1962. (Stories by William Carleton); *The Life of Riley*. London: Secker & Warburg, 1964. (Novel); *A Question of Modernity*. London: Secker & Warburg, 1966. (Criticism); *Collected Poems, 1950–1973*. Dublin: New Writers', 1973; *Dead as Doornails*. Dublin: Dolmen, 1975. (Memoir); *Identity Papers*. Dublin: Co-op Books, [1979]. (Novel); *Reductionist Poem*. Dublin: Raven Arts, 1980; *R. M. S. Titanic*. Dublin: Raven Arts, 1981. (Long poem); *New and Selected Poems*. Manchester: Carcanet New/ Dublin: Raven Arts, [1982]; *Heritage Now: Irish Literature in the English Language*. [Dingle, Co. Kerry]: Brandon, [1982]/New York: St. Martin's, 1983. (Criticism); *An Irish Eye: Viewpoints*. [Dingle, Co. Kerry]: Brandon, [1985]. (Essays); *Letter to an Englishman*. Dublin: Raven Arts, 1985. (Poem); *The End of the Modern World*. Dublin: Raven Arts, 1989. (Poetry sequence); *No Laughing Matter: The Life and Times of Flann O'Brien*. London: Grafton, 1989. (Biography); *Edward McGuire, RHA*, ed. by Brian Fallon. Blackrock, Co. Dublin: Irish Academic, 1991. (Memoirs by Cronin and others); *Relationships*. Dublin: New Island Books, 1992. (Poetry). REFERENCE: Scully, Maurice. "A Chat with Anthony Cronin." *Icarus* (May 1976).

CROSS, ERIC (ca. 1905–1980), writer of sketches and stories. Cross, born in Newry, County Down, was a scientist, inventor, chemist, and general philosopher, as well as a writer. He lived in the west of Ireland for many years and is the author of the minor Irish classic *The Tailor and Anstey* (1942), an ever-fresh and ripely witty collection of sketches commemorating the talk of his friend, the Tailor of Gougane Barra. In 1943, Cross's book was banned by the Irish Censorship Board, one of the more ludicrous instances of holy narrowness in those insular de Valera years. The Tailor's friend, Frank O'Connor,* remarked of the four-day debate in the Irish Senate about the banning, "Reading it is like a long, slow swim through a sewage bed."

In 1978, after a long silence, Cross collected his fugitive pieces under the title *Silence Is Golden*. The book is an uneven but engaging collection of the whimsical, the fey, and the supernatural. Its best pieces are the rural japes and exaggerations, such as "The Power of Levity," which recall the brilliance of his collaboration with the Tailor. He died in County Mayo in 1980.

WORKS: *The Tailor and Anstey*. London: Chapman & Hall, 1942/Cork: Mercier, 1970; *Silence Is Golden and Other Stories*. Dublin: Poolbeg, 1978.

CROWE, EYRE EVANS (1799–1868), fiction writer, historian, and journalist. Crowe was born at Redbridge, Southhampton, on March 20, 1799, of Irish parents. His mother died soon after, and the boy was educated in Carlow and began studies at Trinity College, Dublin, but left before taking his degree and become a journalist. He spent two years in Italy, contributing articles to *Blackwood's Magazine* on Italian affairs and was Paris correspondent of the *London Morning Chronicle* from 1830 to 1844. He joined the staff of the new *Daily News*, the liberal paper that briefly had Dickens as its first editor in 1846, and was editor himself from 1850 to 1851.

Apart from journalism, Crowe's main work was historical: *History of Louis XVIII and Charles X* (1854) and *History of France* in five volumes (1858–1868). His contribution to Irish literature consists of two books, *Today in Ireland* (1825) and *Yesterday in Ireland* (1829), both published anonymously, in standard three-volume format. The books consist of long stories of novella length, the first dealing with aspects of Irish life viewed from the perspective of Catholic Emancipation, the second set in the century before Crowe's birth. His sympathies are firmly on the side of the oppressed Catholic peasantry and town poor, but his view of Ireland ranges from the clear-eyed to the acid. The first volume contains the notably contrasting tales "The Carders," "Connemara," "Old and New Light," and "The Toole's Warning." The first and much the longest is set on the Shannon near Athlone ("the strongest garrison of a numerously garrisoned kingdom") and deals with the eponymous "carders," a nationalist secret society like the Whiteboys whose chief weapon was the savage comb used for carding flax. The unselective nature of the "outrages," the presence of the informer, that essential element of any Irish conspiracy, the papist-hunting Orange curate, all give "The Carders" a rare authenticity that is only weakened by an unlikely and overdrawn Jesuit, straight from Protestant propaganda. The other pieces are shorter and less significant. "Connemara" is funny and might be thought stage-Irish except that the more extreme characters are drawn from life. The medieval independence of some western lands was a fact that the authorities in Dublin had to admit. "Old and New Light" is a genial account of the impact of the new evangelism on the easygoing Church of Ireland, while "The Toole's Warning" is a retelling of a tale from the store of oral folklore.

Yesterday in Ireland has two stories. The first, "Corramahon," set in a post-Stuart Ireland bereft of the Wild Geese and crushed under penal laws, contains one of the best fictional portraits of a "rapparee" in Ulick O'More. Most impressive of all Crowe's work is the final story, "The Northerners of 1798." Its proposition is that the Catholics of Ulster were the sufferers, victims of a kind of moral entrapment, caught between the naive revolutionary temper of the United Irishmen, largely Presbyterian, and the "yeomen," the mainly Orange defenders of a smug and insensitive establishment, blessed by the very established Church of Ireland. "Protestants were the instigators. . . . Catholics were universally the sufferers and dupes." Crowe's portraits of a certain type of unyielding Ulster loyalist are still relevant.

Crowe was essentially a benevolent Tory, a prototype of those who would later hope to "kill Home Rule with kindness," but his knowledge of actual conditions was sound and his account of them unblinking. According to the *Dictionary of National Biography,* he died "after a painful operation" on February 25, 1868, and was buried in Kensal Green cemetery in London.

SEAN McMAHON

IRISH WORKS: *Today in Ireland.* London: Charles Knight, 1825; *Yesterday in Ireland.* London: Henry Colburn, 1829. REFERENCE: Wolff, Robert Lee. Introduction to reprint edition. New York: Garland, 1979.

CROWLEY, ELAINE (ca. 1930–   ), novelist and short story writer.

WORKS: *Dreams of Other Days.* London: Penguin, 1984. (Novel); *A Man Made to Measure.* London: Penguin, 1986. (Novel); *Waves upon the Shore.* London: Penguin, 1989. (Novel); *The Petunia-Coloured Coat.* London: Penguin, 1991. (Stories).

CROWLEY, VICKI (1940–   ), poet and painter. Crowley was born in Malta and was educated there, in Ethiopia, Libya, and England and since 1970 has lived in Galway.

WORK: *Oasis in a Sea of Dust.* [Galway: Salmon, 1992].

CUALA PRESS (formerly the Dun Emer Press), publishing house. The Dun Emer Industries were established at Dundrum, County Dublin, in 1902 by Evelyn Gleeson "to find work for Irish hands in the making of beautiful things." All the workers were Irish girls, and the industries originally comprised embroidery on Irish linen, the weaving of tapestry and carpets, and the printing of books by hand. A bookbinding workshop was added later.

Elizabeth Corbet Yeats and her sister Lily returned to Ireland from London to assist Gleeson in establishing the Industries. Lily Yeats organized the embroidery workshop, and Elizabeth founded the Dun Emer Press as part of the scheme. Their brother W. B. Yeats* acted as editorial adviser to the Press, and Emery Walker, who had worked as adviser to the Kelmscott Press, the Doves Press, and several other notable private presses in England, advised on typography and book production.

The typeface chosen for the Press was Caslon, and all text composition was done in the fourteen point size of that face. The printing was done on an Albion hand press which was built in 1853, and a special paper was made in County Dublin for all the regular books printed at the Press. The format of the books was a small quarto, with a page size of 8¼ × 5¾ inches. The books, with the exception of the first, were issued in colored boards with an Irish linen spine.

Printing of the first book was completed on July 16, 1903. This was *In the Seven Woods,* a collection of new poetry by W. B. Yeats, together with his play *On Baile's Strand.* The edition consisted of 325 copies, priced at 10s 6d. This was the first of many books by living Irish writers to appear from the Press over the next forty-three years, almost thirty of them by Yeats.

Although few of the books were illustrated, most of them had one or more decorative devices, usually on the title page. The first such symbol appeared in the second book, *The Nuts of Knowledge* by AE.* A pressmark, engraved on wood by Elinor Monsell and depicting the Lady Emer, was first used in 1926. Other devices were designed by AE, Robert Gregory, T. Sturge Moore, Edmund Dulac, and E. C. Yeats.

The first series of *A Broadside* was issued from 1908 to 1915. Each number contained ballad poetry, new and traditional, with three drawings by Jack B. Yeats.* Many of the drawings were colored by hand, and the series ran to eighty-four numbers. Two later series were published, in 1935 and 1937, each of twelve parts, and these had illustrations by several other artists as well as the music of the airs for the songs.

In addition to the books and *A Broadside,* the Press also published many hand-colored prints and greeting cards, and undertook commissions to print private editions of some thirty books and booklets. Bookplates were also designed and printed at the Press, including those for John Quinn, Lennox Robinson,* and members of the Yeats family. In 1908, after eleven books had been published and the first series of *A Broadside* commenced, the Yeats sisters left the Dun Emer Industries and, as Cuala Industries, continued the embroidery and hand printing. The first book from the Cuala Press, *Poetry and Ireland* by W. B. Yeats and Lionel Johnson,* was finished in October 1908. Sixty-six Cuala Press books were published before publication of books was suspended in 1946. During this period, the Press was first at Churchtown in County Dublin and later at Merrion Square, at Baggot Street, and at Palmerstown Road in Dublin.

In addition to books by W. B. Yeats, his father, and his brother, the Press published books by, among others, AE, Douglas Hyde,* Lady Gregory,* J. M. Synge,* Lord Dunsany,* Rabindranath Tagore, John Masefield, Ezra Pound, Oliver St. John Gogarty,* Frank O'Connor,* F. R. Higgins,* Louis MacNeice,* Donagh MacDonagh,* Elizabeth Bowen,* and Patrick Kavanagh.*

Elizabeth Corbet Yeats died in 1940, and a memorial tribute by her sister Lily was printed at the Press. The work was continued under the management of Mrs. W. B. Yeats. Fifteen additional books were published between 1940 and 1946, when publication was suspended with the seventy-seventh book, *Stranger in Aran,* written and illustrated by Elizabeth Rivers. The Press continued to produce hand-colored prints and greeting cards until the death of Mrs. Yeats in August 1968.

The Cuala Press was reorganized in 1969 to continue the tradition established in 1903 by its founder, Elizabeth Corbet Yeats. Since then, the Press has printed seven other books in the regular series, as well as some booklets. Prints from designs by Jack B. Yeats and illuminated poems by W. B. Yeats are also being printed. The aim of the Press is to include the best new work being written in Ireland, and to print it with the same craftsmanship and care that has distinguished its work since 1903.

Cuala Press prints and greeting cards are still available in shops, but otherwise the press has been inactive in recent years.

LIAM MILLER

REFERENCES: Lewis, Gifford. *The Yeats Sisters and the Cuala.* Dublin: Irish Academic, 1994; Miller, Liam. *The Dun Emer Press, Later the Cuala Press.* Dublin: Cuala, 1973; also issued in 1973 by Dolmen as No. 7 of the *New Yeats Papers.*

CULLEN, LEO (1948–   ), short story writer. Cullen was born in County Tipperary and now lives in Monkstown, County Dublin. His *Clocking Ninety on the Road to Cloughjordan* (1994) is a collection of connected stories set in rural Ireland in the 1950s. It describes about a dozen years in the young life of Lally Connaughton: his relations with his mother, who dies, with his father, who is variously hotelier, undertaker, horse trainer, and farmer, and with his friends, with whom he stages a fiasco of a raid on an apple orchard. It describes his first misadventures with a shotgun and with drink and a family trip to Sunday mass on a snowy road. A solid accomplishment, it is excellently characterized, contains a wealth of well-evoked details, and is a funny and often sad depiction of normality, a quality frequently undervalued in contemporary Irish fiction.

WORK: *Clocking Ninety on the Road to Cloughjordan and Other Stories.* Belfast: Blackstaff, [1994].

CULLEN, LINDA (1963–), novelist. Cullen was born in Dublin and educated at the Sacred Heart Convent in Monkstown and at the Dominican Convent, Sion Hill. She is a television and video director. *The Kiss* (1990) deals with the question of relationships and sexuality in the manner of a bildungsroman. The heroine grows up against the background of the floundering marriage of her parents and the painful experience of relationships at school. As a young adult, her friendship through school days with Helen develops into a love affair that is unsatisfactory since Helen cannot decide to leave her male lover. The novel circles around various issues relevant to the girls' relationship—the positive effect it has on Joanna's self-acceptance, the awkwardness she feels in society, and the threats to which it is exposed. Cullen's style is direct and carefully managed and accords with the voice of her narrator and principal character, Joanna. It also, perhaps, reflects her own work with scriptwriting for television and radio in its visual and dramatic qualities.

MARY BALL

WORK: *The Kiss.* Dublin: Attic, 1990.

CULLY, KEVIN (1950–), novelist. Cully was born in Dublin and educated at Blackrock College and University College, Dublin. He worked as a teacher in inner London and as a reviewer and television critic. He lives in Cornwall. His novel, *A Ring of Rocks* (1992), tells of the misadventures of a family living near Blackrock in an old house overlooking Dublin Bay. Much of the difficulty is caused by the father, Jack Culhane, a civil servant who romantically stops working to write a novel based on old Irish legends. He has no ability whatsoever as a writer. The problems of the Culhanes are, however, nothing compared to those of their even more romantic and feckless neighbors, the Sheehans, whose roof collapses, whose boiler explodes, and whose house becomes utterly uninhabitable. At the end of a family vacation to the country in a borrowed car, Culhane visits his old home, which is now itself a shambles. He leaves, locks the door, gives the key to a friend, and returns to Dublin to take up his job. The period is 1959 and 1960, when the Lemass government was attempting to attract foreign investment into the country and turning its back on de Valera's vision of an isolated and innocent country; and Cully's book seems to suggest that Irishmen now must turn their backs on the romantic past and the irresponsible present and cope with the practical necessities. The story is episodic, but the details of the time are lovingly observed.

WORK: *Ring of Rocks.* London: Hutchinson, [1992].

CUMMINS, G[ERALDINE] D[OROTHY] (1890–1969), woman of letters and psychic. Cummins was born in Cork in 1890. She was active in the woman's suffrage movement with her friend Suzanne R. Day,* with whom she wrote two comic plays produced by the Abbey Theatre*—*Broken Faith* (1913) and *Fox and Geese* (1917). *Fox and Geese* is a genial matchmaking comedy set among the Cork peasantry. If not brilliant, it was written in short, supple lines and was eminently playable. Cummins also wrote two novels, *The Land They Loved* (1919) and *Fires of Beltane* (1936), as well as a volume of short stories entitled *Variety Show* (1959). Her stories are a mixed bag in subject, tone, and quality: some are tragic vignettes of the peasantry, some are comic glimpses of the middle class, and one is a sophisticated account of a dissolving marriage in the upper middle class. Cummins is at her best in "The Tragedy of Eight Pence," with its two misers, who are almost Jonsonian humors. Among her other writings are a biography of Edith Somerville* and quite a number of volumes of psychical research. Many of the psychical volumes were dictated to her by an unseen intelligence when she was in a light trance. During World War II, she received in this fashion a message for President Roosevelt and duly forwarded it via the American ambassador. She died in Cork in 1969.

PRINCIPAL LITERARY WORKS: *Fox and Geese,* with Suzanne R. Day. Dublin & London: Maunsel, 1917. (Play); *The Land They Loved.* London: Macmillan, 1919. (Novel); *Fires of Beltane.* London: Michael Joseph, [1936]. (Novel); *Unseen Adventures.* London: Rider, 1951. (Autobiography); *Dr. E. OE. Somerville.* London: Dakers, [1952]. (Biography); *Variety Show.* London: Barrie & Rockliff, 1959. (Short stories).

CUNNINGHAM, PETER (1947–   ), novelist. Cunningham was born and raised in Waterford. He graduated from University College, Dublin, in 1967, and in 1971 he became a chartered accountant. He has worked in New York, London, and Dublin as a trader of commodities and now lives in Kildare. In 1989, he became a full-time writer and after several thrillers produced the well-received *Tapes of the River Delta* (1995). This is a long, intricately plotted novel that deals with the lives of three generations and that effectively flits back and forth in time to chart the lives of a large cast of characters. There is a mystery about the hero, Theo Shortcross, who does not really know whose son he is; and this uncertainty perhaps parallels a moral uncertainty. He becomes an important official in Customs and Excise and is torn between the positions of two childhood friends, the venal pragmatism of Bain Cross, who has become prime minister, and the moral rectitude of Pax Sheehy, who has become a superintendent of police. Much of the plot slides over into the melodramatic, but the theme of the complicated action seems to be that love usually involves betrayal. Some of the characters, even important ones such as the hero's grandfather and his nominal mother, remain curiously shadowy. Some of the incidents are almost the perfervid stuff of Jacobean Blood Tragedy. Some of the frequent sex scenes are notably lurid in style, and other scenes are rather exaggeratedly lyrical. Like a Blood Tragedy, the novel presents something of a gloss on life, a heightened reality, but it has an undeniable power.

WORKS: *All Risks Mortality.* London: Michael Joseph, 1987; *The Snow Bees.* London: Sphere, 1989; *The Bear's Requiem.* London: Sphere, 1990; *Who Trespass against Us.* London: Century, [1993]; *Tapes of the River Delta.* London: Century, [1995].

CURRAN, JOHN PHILPOT (1750–1817), orator and poet. Curran was born on July 24, 1750, in Newmarket, County Cork. He was a poor youth, physically unprepossessing, and afflicted with a stutter. Nevertheless, he became the most eloquent orator in Grattan's Parliament. He was educated at Trinity College, Dublin, and the Middle Temple in Dublin. He was called to the bar in 1775 and entered the Irish Parliament in 1783. He defended several of the United Irishmen, including Hamilton Rowan, William Drennan, Wolfe Tone,* the Reverend William Jackson, and the Sheares brothers. He advocated Catholic emancipation and attacked government patronage. In despair about its corruption, he finally resigned from Parliament in 1797. After the Rising of 1803, Curran discovered that his daughter Sarah was secretly engaged to Robert Emmet,* and his anger drove her from his house. In 1806, he was appointed master of the rolls and given a seat in the Privy Council. In 1814, he retired and moved to London, where he enjoyed the company of other congenial, witty spirits such as Lord Byron, Richard Brinsley Sheridan,* and Thomas Moore.* He died at Brompton, Middlesex, on October 14, 1817, and he is buried in Glasnevin Cemetery.

In a great age of oratory, Curran is eminent. His control of sentence structure is masterly, and his use of balance, parallelism, and antithesis markedly effective. He utilizes allusion and classical quotation and even succeeds with an occasional extended metaphor. Nevertheless, there are a tightness, a frequent terseness, and an urgency to his speeches that one would not expect from language that uses all of Johnson's rhetorical devices. To compare Curran's speeches with Sheridan's famous speeches against Warren Hastings is to discover the difference between true eloquence and melodramatic fustian.

Curran's occasional poems have not been collected but are very adroit and often witty. His "The Deserter's Meditation," which Padraic Colum* thought "the first attempt—very likely unconscious—to give Gaelic structure to a poem in English," is a good example:

> If sadly thinking, with spirits sinking,
> Could, more than drinking, my cares compose
> A cure for sorrow from sighs I'd borrow,
> And hope to-morrow would end my woes.
> But as in wailing there's nought availing,
> And Death unfailing will strike the blow,

Then for that reason, and for a season,
Let us be merry before we go.

To joy a stranger, a wayworn ranger,
In every danger my course I've run;
Now hope all ending, and death befriending,
His last aid lending, my cares are done.
No more a rover, or hapless lover,
My griefs are over—my glass runs low;
Then for that reason, and for a season,
Let us be merry before we go.

Curran was also renowned as a wit, and the stories about him are legion. Two may suffice. When riding with the hanging judge Lord Norbury, they passed a gallows, and Norbury said, "Where would you be, Curran, if that scaffold had its due?"

"Riding alone, my lord."

During his final illness, his doctor remarked one morning that he was coughing with more difficulty.

"That is surprising," he said, "as I have been practising all night."

WORKS: *The Speeches of the Right Hon. John Philpot Curran. Complete and Correct Edition. Ed., with Memoir and Historical Notes, Thomas Davis.* Dublin: James Duffy, 1845; *Letters of Curran to the Rev. H. Weston, Written in the Years 1773 and 1774.* London: T. Hookham, 1819. REFERENCES: Curran, W. H. *The Life of the Rt. Hon. John Philpot Curran.* 2 vols. London: Longman/Edinburgh: Constable, 1819/with additions and notes by R. Shelton Mackenzie. New York: Redfield, 1855; Davis, Thomas. *The Life of the Right Hon. John Philpot Curran.* Dublin: James Duffy/London: Simpkin, 1846; Hale, Leslie. *John Philpot Curran (1750–1817), His Life and Times.* London: Jonathan Cape, 1958; O'Regan, William. *Memoirs of the Legal, Literary and Political Life of the Late Right Hon. John Philpot Curran . . . Comprising Copious Anecdotes of His Wit and Humour; and a Selection of His Poetry. . . .* London: Harper/Dublin: Milliken, 1817; Phillips, C. *Recollections of Curran and Some of His Contemporaries.* London: Hookham & Baldwin/Dublin: Milliken, 1818.

CURTIS, EDMUND (1881–1943), historian. Curtis was born of a Donegal father and a Belfast mother on March 25, 1881, at Bury, Lancashire. By good luck and his own considerable ability, he succeeded in entering Oxford in 1900, and he graduated with a First in modern history four years later. By 1914, he was appointed professor of modern history at Trinity College, Dublin. He is known for his *History of Medieval Ireland* (1923) and his *History of Ireland* (1936). T. W. Moody has written of his "bold and original scholarship" and has remarked that "he had the merits of a pioneer." His obituary in *The Irish Times* remarks that he brought Irish history to the fore at Trinity College at a time when little provision was made for it. His writing is ever in a terse, fluent style that has as its best a dramatic immediacy about it. He died in Dublin on March 25, 1943.

At one time he was married to Margaret Barrington.*

WORKS: *A History of Mediaeval Ireland.* Dublin: Maunsel & Roberts, 1923; *A History of Ireland.* London: Methuen, 1936/revised 1937, 1943.

CURTIS, TONY (fl. 1990s), poet. Curtis lives in Balbriggan, Co. Dublin.

WORK: *This Far North.* Dublin: Dedalus, [1994].

CUSACK, MARGARET (1829–1899), poet, mystery writer, hagiographer, historian, translator, theological writer, and composer. Margaret Cusack was born on May 6, 1829, in Dublin and rose to fame as "the Nun of Kenmare." She was noted for her multiple religious conversions, from Protestant to Catholic to Protestant, and for religious changes among the Catholic orders. Her parents were Samuel and Sarah Cusack, a substantial Episcopalian couple from York Street, Dublin. Samuel was a medical doctor whose speciality was obstetrics. Margaret's upbringing was somewhat unconventional, as she had an excellent education and much personal freedom, both physical and intellectual. She also had the personal funds to allow her independence. Her parents separated during her childhood, and her mother took the two children to live with wealthy relatives in Exeter.

Cusack joined the Anglican sisterhood established by Edward Pusey in the early 1850s. This convent community was never acceptable to either the High Church or the Protestant community. The sisterhood's hierarchy and internal politics caused the disillusioned Cusack to depart after a few years. She converted to Catholicism on July 2, 1858, and added the name Anna. She then entered the Christian Sisters of Penance, in Staffordshire. Finding the order too restrictive, Cusack then traveled to Ireland and became Sister Mary Francis Clare, entering the Poor Clare Convent in Newry, on July 2, 1859. When the mother abbess and six nuns left to establish a Poor Clare convent at Kenmare, County Kerry, Sister Mary Frances was among that group. In Kenmare, she wrote a considerable number of texts on Irish history and established Kenmare Publications, which she personally controlled while a cloistered nun. She was allowed a separate and private bank account for the company and organized the printing and distribution of the books. Kenmare Publications was responsible for printing and distributing possibly as many as 200,000 volumes in ten years. Two full-time secretaries were kept busy within the cloister, attending to the business.

Sister Mary Frances Clare was also the first to establish a Famine relief fund when the Kerry farmers began to experience difficulties in the 1870s. Her external commitments, however, created internal problems for the Kenmare community and for Cusack, and so she decided to open a convent and vocational school for women at Knock. In 1882, permission was granted, and the Convent of St. Joseph of the Ave Maria opened. The new order in Knock created hostility within the Church in Ireland, and Cusack found herself again caught in ecclesiastical politics. Her venture in Knock ended, and she was invited to open a new community in Nottingham. Pope Leo XIII granted permission for the new

St. Joseph's Sisters of Peace in 1884, at a personal meeting with Mother Clare in Rome. Again, church politics intervened, and she emigrated to America. In Jersey City, New Jersey, she established the American branch of St. Joseph's Sisters of Peace in 1885. The persistent church problems followed her, and she ultimately resigned from the Catholic Church. Thereafter, she lived with relatives in Leamington, England, writing and lecturing about the evils of the Catholic Church. It is rumored that she may have returned to Catholicism on her deathbed, but it is impossible to substantiate this claim. She died on June 5, 1899, in Leamington.

Cusack began writing at the instigation of Cardinal Manning, who was distressed by the lack of educational texts stressing the Catholic history of Ireland. Her early efforts were historical texts, hagiography, and biographies. Her lone mystery novel was *Ned Rusheen* (1871). She usually published under the name of M. F. Cusack. Her two-volume *The Liberator (Daniel O'Connell)* (1872) was extremely popular, as was *The Life of St. Patrick* (1871). Controversy followed the publication of *A History of the Kingdom of Kerry* (1871), in which she expressed her opposition to absentee landlords, particularly to the Lansdowne family and their estate managers. These attitudes came to full fruition in *The Present Case of Ireland Plainly Stated* (1881).

Cusack was an early feminist, concerned with the issues of education and vocational training for girls. She advocated a core curriculum of Latin, science, politics, and economics, coupled with vocational education. Cusack equated economic independence with the freedom of personal choice for nineteenth-century women. Her later work, after she left the Catholic Church, was concerned with exposing the inequities of Catholicism. *The Nun of Kenmare: The True Facts,* written by Sister Philomena McCarthy of the Kenmare Poor Clares convent, presents the community's response to Cusack's autobiographies and suggests mental illness as the cause of her decision to foresake Catholicism. Biographies of her tend generally to be polarized, categorizing her either as a saint or as a sinner.

ANNE COLMAN

PRINCIPAL WORKS: *The Patriot's History of Ireland.* Kenmare, 1869; *The Student's Manual of Irish History.* London: Longmans, Green, 1870; *Ned Rusheen.* London: Burns, Oates/Dublin: Elwood/Boston: Patrick Donohoe/Melbourne: George Robertson, 1871. (Mystery novel); *The Life of Saint Patrick, Apostle of Ireland.* London: Longmans, Green, 1871; *A History of the Kingdom of Kerry.* London: Longmans, Green, 1871; *The Liberator (Daniel O'Connell): His Life and Times, Political, Social and Religious.* London: Longmans, Green, 1872; *The Life of St. Aloysius Gonzaga, of the Society of Jesus.* 1872; *Advice to Irish Girls in America.* New York, 1872; *The Book of the Blessed Ones.* London: Burns, Oates, 1874; *The Life of Father Matthew, the People's Soggarth Aroon.* Dublin, 1874; *Women's Work in Modern Society.* Kenmare, 1874; *Devotions for Public and Private Use at the Way of the Cross.* London: R. Washbourne, 1875; *A History of the City and County of Cork.* Cork: Francis Guy/Dublin: McGlashan & Gill, 1875; *The Speeches and Public Letters of the Liberator, with Preface and Historical Notes.* 2 vols. Kenmare, 1875; *In Memoriam Mary O'Hagan, Abbess and Foundress of the Convent of the Poor Clares, Kenmare.* London: Burns, 1876; *The Lives of St. Columba and St. Brigit.* Dublin: Kenmare Series of the Lives of Irish Saints, 1877; *Tim O'Halloran's Choice; or, From Killarney to New York.* London: Burns, 1877; *The Trias*

Thaumaturge; or, Three Wonder-Working Saints of Ireland. London: J. G. Murdoch, [1877]; *A Nun's Advice to Her Girls.* 3d ed. Kenmare: Kenmare Publication Agency, 1877; *Good Reading for Girls.* London: Burns, Oates/Dublin: Gill, 1877; *The Life and Times of Pope Pius IX.* Kenmare, 1878; *The Life of the Most Rev. Joseph Dixon DD, Primate of All Ireland.* Dublin, 1878; *The Apparition at Knock....* London: Burns & Oates/Dublin: M. H. Gill, [1880]; *Cloister Songs.* London: Burns/Dublin: Gill, 1881; *The Present Case of Ireland Plainly Stated: A Plea for My People and My Race.* New York: P. J. Kenedy, 1881; *Three Visits to Knock.* Dublin: Gill & Son/London: R. Washbourne, 1882; *A Patriot's History of Ireland.* Dublin, 1885; *The Question of To-day.* Chicago & New York: Belford, Clarke, [1887]; *The Nun of Kenmare: An Autobiography.* London: Jonah Child, [1888]; *Life inside the Church of Rome.* London: Hodder & Stoughton, 1889; *The Story of My Life.* London: Hodder & Stoughton, 1891; *What Rome Teaches.* London: Marshall Bros., 1892; *The Black Pope: A History of the Jesuits.* London: Marshall, Russell/Brighton: D. B. Friend, [1896]; *Revolution and War: The Secret Conspiracy of the Jesuits in Great Britain.* London: Swan Sonnenschein, 1910. REFERENCES: Eagar, Irene Ffrench. *The Nun of Kenmare.* Cork: Mercier, 1970; McCarthy, Philomena. *The Nun of Kenmare: The True Facts.* Killarney: Killarney Printing Works, 1989; O'Neill, Margaret Rose. *The Life of Mother Clare.* Seattle: Sisters of St. Joseph of Peace, 1990.

D

DALACOURT (or DELACOUR), JAMES (1709?–1781?), poet. Dalacourt was born in Bantry, County Cork, possibly in March 1709. He was educated at Trinity College, Dublin, and while a student published his long poem *Abelard to Eloisa, in Answer to Mr. Pope's Fine Piece of Eloisa to Abelard.* He also became involved in the literary war between his friend Charles Carthy, whose verses the formidable William Dunkin* and others satirized. Dalacourt took Holy Orders in 1737 and from 1744 to 1755 was curate at Ballinaboy, County Cork. Patrick Fagan remarks: "It was a vocation for which he was quite unfitted. Rhyming and congenial company . . . were more to his taste. With the advance of age his brain became affected. He fancied himself a prophet and became known as 'the mad parson.' " He died in either 1781 or 1785. As a poet, he was extremely smooth and often witty, even when his topic was glum, as in "An Epitaph on Mr. Edward Stockdale, an Eminent Tallow-chandler":

Here lies Ned Stockdale, honest fellow,
who died by fat, and lived by tallow;
his light before men always shone,
his mould is underneath this stone.
Then, taking things by the right handle,
is not this life a farthing candle,
the longest age but a watch taper,
a torch blown out by every vapour,
today will burn, tomorrow blink,
and end, as mortals, in a stink.
If this be true, then worthy Ned
is a wax-light among the dead;
his fluted form still sheds perfume
and scatters lustre round his tomb.
Then what is mortal life?—why, tush,
this mortal life's not worth a rush.

WORKS: *Abelard to Eloisa, in Answer to Mr. Pope's Fine Piece of Eloisa to Abelard.* Dublin, 1730; *The Progress of Beauty. A Poem.* Dublin, 1732; *A Prospect of Poetry: Address'd to the Right Honourable John, Earl of Orrery. To Which Is Added a Poem to Mr. Thomson on His Seasons.* Dublin: William Heatley, 1734/London: J. Roberts, 1734; *Poems.* Cork: Thomas White, 1778/as *A Prospect of Poetry. With Other Poems.* Cork: John Harris, 1807. REFERENCES: Coleborne, Bryan. "Jonathan Swift and the Dunces of Dublin." Ph.D. diss., National University of Ireland, 1982; Fagan, Patrick. *A Georgian Celebration.* Dublin: Branar, [1989]; von Dietrich, Andrea. "Satirische Techniken in den persönlicken Schmähschriften der Dubliner "University Wits," James Delacourt, Charles Carthy, William Dunkin und Ambrose Philips." Staatsexamen thesis, Technical University of Berlin, 1985.

D'ALTON, JOHN (1792–1867), poet, historian, and antiquarian. D'Alton was born at Bessville, County Westmeath, on June 20, 1792. He was educated at Trinity College, Dublin, and was called to the bar in 1813. In 1814, he published a now-forgotten romance in twelve cantos called *Dermid, or Erin in the Days of Boroimhe.* He made a good many translations from the Irish for Hardiman's *Irish Minstrelsy* (1831), and, although his translations are seldom reprinted, his "Why, Liquor of Life!" after Carolan and his own "Carroll O'Daly and Echo" are both deft and droll. Indeed, even his conventionally patriotic "Oh! Erin!" has a couple of admirable lines. He died in Dublin on January 20, 1867.

WORKS: *Dermid; or, Erin in the Days of Boroimhe.* London: Longman/Dublin; J. Cumming, 1814; *Essay on the History, Religion, Learning, Arts and Government of Ireland.* Dublin: R. Graisberry, 1830. Vol. 16 of *Transactions of the Royal Irish Academy; The History of Ireland.* 2 vols. Dublin: Published by the author, 1845; (Also some translations in Hardiman's *Irish Minstrelsy.* 2 vols. London: Joseph Robins, 1831).

D'ALTON, LOUIS [LYNCH] (1900–1951), playwright and novelist. D'Alton, son of actor-producer Frank Dalton, was born in Dublin in 1900. After working as a civil servant and a cartoonist, he joined Victor O'Donovan Power's* traveling drama company, acted briefly at the Queen's, Dublin, and then formed his own touring company. Two novels, *Death Is So Fair* (1936) and *Rags and Sticks* (1938), preceded most of his dramatic work. *The Man in the Cloak,* staged in 1937, marked the beginning of his association with the Abbey* as playwright, actor, and producer. He died in London on June 15, 1951.

The Man in the Cloak, based on the life of poet James Clarence Mangan* (1803–1848), effectively combines an impressionistic study of Mangan's chaotic personality and an almost documentary treatment of Dublin slums during a cholera epidemic. Published with the Mangan play is *The Mousetrap,* a pallid offspring of O'Casey's* *Juno* in theme—unwedded pregnancy—and dialogue. *To-morrow Never Comes* (1939) charts the psychological breakdown of a weakminded, frightened murderer. *The Spanish Soldier* (1940) deals with the troubled return to civilian life of an Irish volunteer in Franco's army.

The Money Doesn't Matter (1941) is the first of a series of thematically related plays. Rags to riches businessman Michael Mannion spends freely to buy or coerce the affection of his children. In every case, through their failure or his,

Mannion is disappointed. At the close, a creature of habit, he continues to claw for the money that doesn't matter.

Lovers Meeting (1941) might be called a matchmaking tragedy. Mrs. Jane Sheridan, overcoming the scruples of her husband Tom, matches their daughter Mary to a grizzled boor. Mary's lover, Joe Hession, thinking Mrs. Sheridan has written him off as a poor provider, kills his uncle so that he can inherit land and money. But the money doesn't matter. The buried truth emerges: Joe is Mrs. Sheridan's illegitimate son. The ending resembles Greek tragedy, with the elder Sheridans separated, Joe hanged, and Mary a suicide.

Garrulous, improvident Bartley Murnaghan, in *They Got What They Wanted* (1947), represents another aspect of the money doesn't matter theme. He has none, but by manipulating the nebulous possibility of an inheritance and the greed and gullibility of his neighbors, he becomes a small town financier. It is not the best of D'Alton's plays, but it was made into a movie, *Smiling Irish Eyes,* by an English producer.

Money enters peripherally into *The Devil a Saint Would Be* (1951). Seventy-year-old Stacy, advised by a saint visible only to herself, gives her money to a doubtfully deserving lot of poor folk as a means of attaining sanctity. Everybody but the parish priest considers her "certifiable": he rightly fears that the saint is an evil spirit. The real saint, whom the evil spirit counterfeited, defines saintliness: "There is no virtue without humility, and the temptation of the saints is to think of themselves as saints." Part of the delightful third act is a colloquium at the gate of Heaven between Stacy, a sorely tried Peter, and the saint embarrassed by Stacy's loquacity.

This Other Eden (1953) is the land across the Irish Sea, depending on the direction in which one is facing. An Irish girl escapes from religiosity and parochialism to find freedom—in Birmingham; an Englishman fed up with the welfare state and, ironically, with an influx of "foreigners" buys an estate in Ireland. A woefully confused commemorative service for a clay-footed IRA hero provides the framework for what is basically a discussion drama, in the manner of Bernard Shaw,* of life in Ireland.

Cafflin' Johnny (1958) slightly resembles the comic reprobate sketches of George Shiels.* Johnny Fortune's Excelsior banner is inscribed Do Nothing, and to the end he holds it aloft with eloquence and wistful pride.

D'Alton's novels are overshadowed by his reputation as playwright. *Death Is So Fair* examines differing responses to the Easter Week Rising. Its terrible beauty inspires Manus Considine to become an idealistic revolutionary. Andrew Gilfoyle, seeing it as a fiasco of poets playing soldier, becomes an efficient killer. *Rags and Sticks* relates the decline and fall of the Superlative Dramatic Company, a tattered, anachronistic survival of vagabond tradition. Both novels are masterful in characterization and description, but D'Alton sometimes indulges in speechmaking and intrusive commentary.

As playwright, D'Alton in his mature work updates traditional themes such as made marriages and money-grubbing, bestowing on them a cerebral quality which makes most of the earlier specimens seem gauche by comparison. His finest play, *This Other Eden,* skillfully blends crackling dialogue with a thoughtfully posed question, "how's dear old Ireland and how does she stand three decades after the Treaty?"

WILLIAM J. FEENEY

WORKS: *Death Is So Fair.* London: Heinemann, 1936; *Rags and Sticks.* London: Heinemann, 1938; *Two Irish Plays (The Man in the Cloak* and *The Mousetrap).* London: Macmillan, 1938; *Tomorrow Never Comes: A Play in Three Acts.* Dublin: Duffy, 1945/new edition, Dublin: Bourke, 1968; *The Devil a Saint Would Be: A Morality in Three Acts.* Dublin: Bourke, 1952; *They Got What They Wanted: A Comedy in Three Acts.* Dundalk: Dundalgan, 1953; *This Other Eden: A Play in Three Acts.* Dublin: Bourke, 1954; *The Money Doesn't Matter: A Play in Three Acts.* Dublin: Duffy, 1957; *Lovers Meeting: A Tragedy in Three Acts.* Dublin: Bourke, 1964; *Cafflin' Johnny.* Dublin: Bourker, [1966]. REFERENCES: Hogan, Robert. *After the Irish Renaissance.* Minneapolis: University of Minnesota, 1967; Hogan, Thomas. "Theatre." *Envoy* 2 (May 1950): 80–84. (Review of *They Got What They Wanted*); *The Irish Sunday Independent,* June 17, 1951, 1:3–5. (Obituary).

DALY, ITA (1944?–), novelist and short story writer. Daly was born in County Leitrim in 1944 or 1945 and moved with her family to Dublin when she was thirteen. She was educated at University College, Dublin, majoring in English and Spanish, and receiving a B.A. and an M.A. She taught for eleven years, married the novelist and literary editor David Marcus,* and has one child. Her short stories, which were collected in *The Lady with the Red Shoes* (1980), won two Hennessey Literary Awards and the *Irish Times* Short Story Competition. Since then she has published four novels.

The Lady with the Red Shoes contains ten stories of about a dozen pages each. All are about women, and all but one are narrated by women. In them, Daly's strengths are her characterization and her effective control of the reader's reactions. In "Hey Nonny No" and "Compassion," for instance, the reader is adroitly led to view the narrator very differently from the way that the narrator herself does. Most of the stories are about dreary lives, disaffection, and failure. All, however, are written in a terse, controlled prose, and all contain terse and precise detail.

About three-fifths of Daly's first novel, *Ellen* (1986), is a cosy tale about an awkward young woman who begins to blossom after finding, for the first time, a girlfriend and moving away from home to share a room. Sprucing the place up, giving a disastrous comic dinner party, entertaining the girlfriend's beau, and even attracting an unprepossessing beau herself all seem the details of a nice, comfortable read for teenage girls. Then, however, Ellen discovers the girlfriend entertaining her own beau. Although she does not particularly fancy the young man, she abruptly and startlingly stabs her girlfriend with a kitchen knife. The remainder of the story tells how Ellen blossoms or, more aptly, withers into a typical Daly heroine. Solely in order to attain a comfortable security, she contrives to become engaged to her dead girlfriend's young man, whom also she does not particularly fancy. A resumé makes the heroine sound like a villainess from melodrama, but actually the book is a flatly stated character sketch of a self-contained young woman who does not want or need love. Despite the abrupt shift in the book's tone, *Ellen* is a singular study of an emotionally stunted ego. If somewhat repellent, it is a perfect antidote to innumerable volumes of romantic fiction.

A Singular Attraction (1987) is rather a companion volume, but the woman who leaves home after her mother's death and takes a place of her own is a thirty-eight-year-old virgin named Pauline. She is even more self-contained than Ellen, and the sparse, spartan furnishings of her own place really mirror her own spare, virginal life. Nevertheless, when a nice and attractive Dane moves in across the hall, she finds that she does want to discover what she has been missing, sex and even love. When finally they do go to bed, she is embarrassed by being a middle-aged virgin and explains the blood on the sheets by saying that she is recovering from venereal disease. He immediately leaves for Denmark; and she, deciding that sex and love are overrated, continues with her assured, serene, and arid life.

Martina of *Dangerous Fictions* (1989) is another of Daly's emotionally deficient women, whose lacks break up her marriage, estrange her daughter, and drive her to defecate on her mother-in-law's grave. At novel's end, she has an undemanding job in Spain and a basically solitary life. Then, after a visit from her daughter, she comes to realize that there is something "more monstrous by far than indifference or ingratitude or love outgrown. Or the desecration of someone's grave." Her realization is of her own mortality; however, for the present she is still alive, and "[t]omorrow she would laugh at the gods of creation, inviting them to do their damnedest." That assertion about the value of life, even as narrow and solitary a life as hers, is something of a triumph for a Daly heroine.

All Fall Down (1992) is a new departure that, until the conclusion, takes a much less bleak view of human relations. It is, for most of its length, a comic novel about some of the hypocrisies and absurdities of contemporary Ireland. Several of the characters—particularly the overwhelming millionaire businessman, the foolish, frightened rabbit who is minister for the arts, and a retired country and western singer from Cavan—are drawn with a sympathetic warmth not evident in Daly's earlier books and are rather more than satiric caricatures. The novel's chief fault is probably its plotting. After a leisurely introduction of her characters, Daly launches into an engaging plot about a sex scandal involving the arts minister and the singer. She winds up this plot and then introduces another about a political pageant, which itself concludes abruptly and disconcertingly with the accidental death of the millionaire's daughter. The glumness of the ending is quite out of tone with all that went before, but consistent enough with Daly's previous themes.

WORKS: *The Lady with the Red Shoes.* Swords, Co. Dublin: Poolbeg, 1980. (Short stories); *Ellen.* London: Jonathan Cape, 1986. (Novel); *A Singular Attraction.* London: Jonathan Cape, 1987. (Novel); *Dangerous Fictions.* London: Bloomsbury, 1989. (Novel); *Candy on the Dart.* Swords. Co. Dublin: Poolbeg, 1989. (Children's book); *All Fall Down.* London: Bloomsbury, 1992. (Novel).

DALY, LEO (1920–   ), novelist and critic. Daly was brought up in Mullingar, Country Westmeath, and worked as a psychiatric nurse before turning to broadcasting and journalism. His most notable work is the 1984 novel about the Aran Islands entitled *The Rock Garden*. In it, a nurse from the mainland marries Michael James Flaherty, the son of a prominent islander, and finds herself enmeshed in a web of spite, sex, and madness that has been festering over years. The book is far from a romanticization of island life; and, although its conclusion is a revelation about the past rather than a dramatic culmination in the present, it has a somber power.

WORKS: *James Joyce and the Mullingar Connection.* [Dublin]: Dolmen, 1975; *Oileáin Árann.* Swinford: A. Kennedy, 1975. (Guidebook); ed., with others. *The Midlands.* Dublin: Albertine Kennedy, 1979. (Guidebook); *Titles.* Mullingar, Co. Westmeath: Lilliput, 1981. (Essays); *The Rock Garden* [Mullingar: Co. Westmeath]: Lilliput, [1984].

DALY, PADRAIG J[OHN] (1943–   ), poet. Daly was born on June 25, 1943, in Dungarvan, County Waterford. In 1960 he joined the Augustinian Order and has worked as a priest in John's Lane and Ballyboden, Dublin. He also spent time in Italy, where he studied theology at the Gregorian University in Rome.

Daly has published six collections of poetry, and his reviewers have commented on the scope of his preoccupations and the effectiveness of his delicate technique. John Jordan* wrote in *The Irish Independent:* "Father Daly sees Christ in all things: he does not go about stridently invoking Him, but 'sees' Him in all manner of things and people, 'the treetops reaching invisibly to sky / Or the circle of lamplight on the shrubs / Falling tenderly on the woman as she sings.' Elsewhere Father Daly excels in quiet audacity." Brendan Kennelly,* in *The Sunday Independent,* observed: "In one of his poems, Padraig J. Daly says that he, as a priest, belongs 'out by the side of things.' This is why, I think, his experience and portrayal of loneliness is counterbalanced by a sustained projection of sympathy, the heart lucidly manifesting its subtle acts of understanding in a way the mind, by itself, never quite can." Writing in the *Poetry Ireland Review,* Roz Cowman* stated: "His vision is loving and tender, but there is no sentimentality, rather an appalled awareness of cruelty and suffering." In *Ambit* Herbert Lomas commented: "These poems aim to state the nuances of feeling as humbly and clearly as possible. . . . This is the best kind of religious poetry: the presence of God is felt in the confession of humanity."

JACK HARTE

WORKS: *Nowhere But in Praise.* [Clondalkin, Co. Dublin]: Profile, [1978]; *Augustine: Letter to God.* [Dublin]: St. Bueno's, [1978]. (Poetry pamphlet); *This Day's Importance.* Dublin: Raven Arts, 1981; *Dall' Orlo Marino del Mondo.* Rome: Libreria Editrice Vaticana, 1982. (Poems in English with Italian translations by Margherita Guidacci); *A Celibate Affair.* [Drogheda]: Aquila, 1984; *Poems Selected and New.* Dublin: Dedalus, 1988; *Out of Silence.* [Dublin]: Dedalus, [1993].

DANA. *See* EGLINTON, JOHN.

D'ARCY, MARGARETTA (1934–), playwright. D'Arcy was born into a Dublin working-class family. Her father was a veteran of the Irish Republican Army during the War of Independence and fought on the antitreaty side in the civil war. Her mother was of Russian-Jewish heritage. D'Arcy went to school in Dublin, including time in a Domenican convent, but left at age fifteen to pursue a career in the theater. She first worked on the Dublin stage and then, at age twenty, moved to the London stage. While in London, she met her husband, John Arden.

Arden is British. He was born in Barnsley, Yorkshire, on October 26, 1930, educated at Sedberg School in Yorkshire, at King's College, Cambridge, and at the Edinburgh School of Art. He married Margaretta D'Arcy in 1957, and they have five sons. With such plays as *Sergeant Musgrave's Dance,* he became one of the most notable of postwar British playwrights.

In 1958, D'Arcy decided to break away from the established theater because of its, as she saw it, patriarchal influences. She then studied nontraditional theater in England, Scotland, Ireland, and the United States, including spending time with the San Francisco Mime Troupe. In 1968, she decided to return to Ireland to participate more actively in the civil rights movement and the republican movement. After her return, she joined and was subsequently expelled from the "official" Sinn Féin. She organized artist and theatrical protests against the British government's policy regarding the six counties. She formed the Galway Theatre Workshop as a showcase for "anti-repression" and "anti-imperialist" plays. She served time in prison as a result of her political activities. For most of the past decade, D'Arcy has worked almost exclusively with small groups of women over long periods of time in the Galway area initiating, as part of her work, informal improvisations that function as art therapy, helping the women come to terms with, and grow away from, abuse and oppression. The work intends to give women a voice to articulate the specific nature of their oppression and then to free themselves from the oppressive masculinist-dominated discourse that so consumes their lives. As part of this work, she has formed Galway Women's Entertainment (1982) and Women's Scaeal Radio (1986). Her work, in large measure, developed directly from her prison term in Armagh Gaol, participating in the "no-wash" protest with women such as Mairead Farrell, who was later shot by the British troops in Gibraltar. D'Arcy's politics are unapologetically republican and feminist. Indeed, most, if not all, of her work speaks to a very clear political agenda. However, it is far from propaganda, functioning as more an expression about political oppression rather than as political statement. Indeed, her published work includes *Tell Them Everything,* an account of her time in Armagh. The work is a moving, vivid account of the experiences of D'Arcy's terms in prison. It speaks of the absurdities of her arrests, the brutalities of her imprisonments, and the community of the women in the prison.

D'Arcy's collaborations with her husband are, with the exception of some essays on the theater, plays. They include *The Happy Haven,* produced by the

Drama Studio in Bristol; *The Business of Good Government: A Christmas Play,*
produced in 1960 in Saint Michael's Church in Brent Knoll in Somerset and
revised and staged in 1978 in London; *Ars Longa, Vita Brevis,* a children's play
put on in London in 1964 by the Royal Shakespeare Company; *Friday's Hiding,*
produced by the Royal Lyceum theater in Edinburgh in 1966; *The Royal Pardon,*
produced by the Bedford Arts Centre in Devon in 1966; *The Hero Rises Up,*
produced in 1968 at the Roundhouse in London; *Harold Muggins Is a Martyr,*
produced in 1968 by the Unity Theatre in London; *Two Hundred Years of
Labour History,* produced in London in 1971; *Granny Welfare and the Wolf,*
also produced in London in 1971; *My Old Man's a Tory,* produced in London
in 1971; *Rudi Dutschke Must Stay,* produced in London in 1971; *The Ballygombeen Bequest,* produced in 1972 at St. Mary's College in Belfast and later revised and produced as *The Little Grey Home in the West* by the Drama
Department of Birmingham University; *The Island of the Mighty,* produced by
the Aldwych Theatre in London in 1972; *The Devil and the Parish Pump,*
produced in Galway in 1974; *The Crown Strike Play,* produced in Galway in
1975; *The Non-Stop Connolly Show,* produced in Dublin in 1975 at Liberty
Hall; *Sean O'Scruda,* produced in Galway in 1976; *The Mongrel Fox,* produced
in Galway in 1976; *No Room at the Inn,* produced in Galway in 1976; *Silence,*
produced in Galway in 1977; *Blow-in Chorus for Liam Cosgrave,* produced in
Galway in 1977; *Vandaleur's Folly,* produced by the Nuffield Studio Theatre
at the University of Lancaster in 1978; *The Mother,* produced in London in
1984; *The Making of Maxwell Hill,* also produced in London in 1984; and *The
Pinprick of History.* Arden and D'Arcy have also written plays for television
and radio. In 1973, they put together a documentary titled *Sean O'Casey: Portrait of a Rebel.* For radio they have written *Keep Those People Moving* (1972),
The Manchester Enthusiasts (1984), and *Whose Is the Kingdom?* (1988). D'Arcy
has also written numerous community film and education projects in County
Galway, most notably with the community of Corrandulla.

Her work for the theater includes many published plays. However, it must be
remembered that many of these works, especially the ones that came from the
Galway Theatre Workshop, were almost constantly revised. Consequently, their
published form represents only one aspect or snapshot of their staged form. Of
these published works, four have received the most critical attention. *The Non-
Stop Connolly Show* is a play in six parts that runs for approximately twenty-
six hours. It considers the life of Irish trade unionist James Connolly.* D'Arcy
called it "the first ever mammoth left-wing statement on the Irish stage." In
this context, the play considers such issues as the relationship between republicanism and Marxism, the role of women, and the meaning of revolution. *The
Little Grey Home in the West,* a revised version of *The Ballygombeen Bequest,*
studies issues of land and ownership. The play, in its original form, staged and
clearly took sides in an actual land dispute. The revision stages a broader historical dispute and speaks to the inheritance of revolution by the present-day
Irish government. *Vandaleur's Folly* considers an agricultural cooperative so-

ciety that actually existed in Ralahine in 1831. *Whose Is the Kingdom?*, commissioned by BBC Radio, is a historical drama about Constantine the Great and
early Christianity. The play considers the interrelationship between religion and
power, between individual desire for expression and community demands on
the individual for conformity, and the role of women in the early church. Critics
praise the collaborative work of Arden and D'Arcy and the ability of their
sometimes radical expressions to maintain their dramatic integrity and to avoid
the somewhat dubious distinction as mere propaganda.

BERNARD McKENNA

WORKS: *Tell Them Everything: A Sojourn in the Prison of Her Majesty Queen Elizabeth II at
Ard Macha (Armagh).* London: Pluto, 1981. With John Arden: *Business of Good Government: A
Christmas Play.* London: Methuen, 1963/New York: Grove, 1967; *The Happy Haven* in *New English
Dramatists 4.* London: Penguin, 1964/in *Three Plays.* London: Penguin, 1964/New York: Grove,
1966; *Ars Longa, Vita Brevis* in *Eight Plays for School I.* Malcolm Staurt Fellows, ed. London:
Cassell, 1965; *Friday's Hiding* in *"Soldier, Soldier" and Other Plays.* London: Methuen, 1967;
The Royal Pardon: or, The Soldier Who Became an Actor. London: Methuen, 1967; *The Hero Rises
Up: A Romantic Melodrama.* London: Methuen, 1969; *The Impromptu of Muswell Hill* in *Two
Autobiographical Plays.* London: Methuen, 1971; *The Ballygombeen Bequest. Scripts* 1 (September
1972): 4–50; *The Island of the Mighty: A Play on a Traditional British Theme.* London: Eyre
Methuen, 1974; *To Present the Pretence.* London: Eye Methuen, 1977. (Collection of essays by
Arden but containing two cowritten with D'Arcy); *Vandaleur's Folly.* London: Eyre Methuen, 1981;
The Little Grey Home in the West. London: Pluto, 1982. (Revised version of *Ballygombeen Bequest*);
The Non-Stop Connolly Show. London: Methuen, 1986. (Originally published in five books
containing the six parts of the play by London's Pluto Press in 1978); *Awkward Corners: Essays,
Papers, Fragments.* London: Methuen, 1988; *Whose Is the Kingdom?* London: Methuen, 1988;
*Plays I: The Business of Good Government, The Royal Pardon, The Little Grey Home in the West,
Ars Longa Vita Brevis, Friday's Hiding, Vandaleur's Folly, Immediate Rough Theatre, Sean
O'Scrudu, The Hunting of the Mongrel Fox, No Room at the Inn,* and *A Pinprick of History.* London:
Methuen, 1991. (Some of the preceding titles are published as by Arden and D'Arcy, and others
as by D'Arcy and Arden). REFERENCES: Bleike, Werner. *Prods, Taigs and Brits: Die Ulster-
Krise als Thema im nordirischen und britischen Gegenwartsdrama.* Frankfurt am Main: Verlag
Peter Lang, 1990; Broich, Ulrick. "Wandlungen des Melodramas: Boucicault's *Arrah-na-Pogue,*
Shaw's *The Devil's Disciple,* and Arden/Darcy's *Vandaleur's Folly*" in *Gatlungsprobleme in der
anglo-amerikanischen Literatur.* Raimund Borgmeier, ed. Tübingen: Niemeyer, 1986, pp. 108–124;
Cohen, Michael. "A Defence of D'Arcy and Arden's *Non-Stop Connolly Show.*" *Theatre Research
International* 15 (Spring 1980): 78–88; Goring, Michael. *Melodrama heute: die Adaption melod-
ramatischer Elemente und Strukturen im Werk von John Arden und Arden/D'Arcy.* Amsterdam: B.
R. Gruner, 1986; Hammerschmidt, Hildegard. "John Arden und Margaretta D'Arcy: *The Island of
the Mighty*" in *Das Englische Drama der Gegenwart Interpretationem.* Horst Oppel, ed. Berlin:
Schmidt, 1976; Hohne, Horst. "The Struggle of Working Class Ireland in the Plays of John Arden
and Margaretta D'Arcy" in *Irland: Gesellschaft und Kultur.* Dorothea Siegmund-Schultze, ed.
Halle, 1976, pp. 148–165; Hozier, Anthony. "From Galway to Managua." *Red Letters: A Journal
of Cultural Politics* 17 (March 1985): 11–26; *John Arden and Margaretta D'Arcy: A Casebook.*
New York: Garland, 1985; Klotz, Gunther. "Ein irisches Vermachtnis: *The Ballygombeen Bequest*
von John Arden und Margaretta D'Arcy." *Zeitschrift für Anglistik und Amerikanistik* 22 (1974):
419–424; Krahe, Peter. "John Arden und Margaretta D'Arcy's *The Hero Rises Up:* Ein zeitkritsches
Melodrama" in *Von Shakespeare bis Chomsky.* Elfi Bettinger, ed. Frankfurt: Peter Lang, 1987;
Lumsden, Andrew. "D'Arcy Protest Swings On." *New Statesman* 111 (June 13, 1986): 5(1); Lumsden, Andrew. "Margaretta D'Arcy Takes on the Irish Theatre Establishment." *New Statesman* 111
(May 9, 1986): 5(1); Malick, Shah Jaweedul. *The Dramaturgy of John Arden: Dialectical Vision
and Popular Tradition.* DAI, Ann Arbor, Mich., 46 (May 1986); Marsh, Paddy. "Easter at Liberty

Hall: The Ardens' *Non-Stop Connolly Show.*" *Theatre Quarterly* 5, (1975): 133–141; Morsiani, Giovanni. "Margaretta d'Arcy a il problema della co-autrice" in *Il teatro e le donne: Forme drammatiche e tradizione al femminile nel teatro inglese.* Raffaella Baccolini, Vita Fortunati & Romana Zacchi, eds. Urbino: Quattroventi, 1991, pp. 169–182; Winkler, Elizabeth. "Modern Melodrama: The Living Heritage in the Theatre of John Arden and Margaretta D'Arcy" in *Melodrama.* James Redmond, ed. Cambridge: Cambridge University Press, 1992, pp. 255–267.

DARLEY, GEORGE (1795–1846), poet, mathematician, and art and drama critic. Darley was born in Dublin in 1795. He studied classics and mathematics at Trinity College and received his B.A. in 1820. He went to London and began to write art and drama criticism, often of considerable asperity, for the *London Magazine* and the *Athenaeum.* He also published several treatises on geometry, algebra, and trigonometry, which were much respected. His poetry, however— although admired by Coleridge, Lamb, Carlyle, and Tennyson—was never popular. In 1950, A. J. Leventhal tried to revive interest in Darley, noting that he was ahead of his time and that some of his poetry seems particularly modern. The truth seems to be that Darley was distinctly out of his time. His poetic diction is both archaic and very literary, and his most famous lyric, "It is not beautie I demande," was printed as a genuine anonymous Caroline lyric in the 1861 edition of Palgrave's *Golden Treasury.* Also, despite being a London drama critic, Darley's plays were so entirely for the closet that there was never any thought of their being staged. In his public work, there is little of Irish inspiration, although his letters reveal some preoccupation with, and nostalgia for Ireland.

His younger brother Charles (1800–1861) was a clergyman and professor of modern history and English literature at Queen's College, Cork; and Charles's play, *Plighted Troth,* was produced with great lack of success by Macready at Drury Lane in 1842. At about the same time, Darley himself was publishing his own virtually ignored closet dramas on English history. This dual failure may have been galling to the Darley brothers particularly because their scapegrace young nephew, Dion Boucicault,* had made the hit of the 1841 season with his comedy *London Assurance.* The brothers never, in any document so far discovered, mentioned their precocious and raffish nephew, but Boucicault said in later life that they both regarded him as a schoolboy who ought to be whipped back to his lessons.

Darley may have been out of his time partly because of an appalling stutter, which was a considerable social embarrassment. In any event, his reclusive life and elegant but formal verses largely succeeded in minimizing his quite real personal wit and warmth. He died on November 23, 1846.

PRINCIPAL WORKS: *The Errors of Ecstasie: A Dramatic Poem. With Other Pieces.* London: G. & B. Whittaker, 1822; *The Labours of Idleness, or, Seven Nights' Entertainments,* under the pseudonym of Guy Penseval. London: John Taylor, 1826; *Sylvia; or, The May Queen. A Lyrical Drama.* London: John Taylor, 1827; *The New Sketch Book,* under the pseudonym of Geoffrey Crayon, Jr. 2 vols. London: Printed for the Author, 1829; *Nepenthe.* London: ?, 1835/London: E. Matthews, 1897; *Thomas A. Beckett. A Dramatic Chronicle.* London: Edward Moxon, 1840; *Ethelstan; or, the Battle of Brunanburgh. A Dramatic Chronicle.* London: Edward Moxon, 1841; *Se-*

lections from the Poems of George Darley, with an Introduction and Notes by R. A. Streatfield. London: Methuen, 1904; *The Complete Poetical Works of George Darley.* Ramsay Colles, ed. London: G. Routledge/New York: E. P. Dutton, 1908; *Selected Poems of George Darley.* Anne Ridler, ed. London: Merrion, 1979. REFERENCES: Abbot, Claude C. *The Life and Letters of George Darley, Poet and Critic.* Oxford: University Press/London: Humphrey Milford, 1928; Heath-Stubbs, J. *The Darkling Plain: A Study of the Later Fortunes of Romanticism in English Poetry from George Darley to W. B. Yeats.* London: Eyre & Spottiswoode, 1950; Leventhal, A. J. *George Darley (1795–1846).* [Dublin]: Dublin University Press, 1950.

DAUNT, WILLIAM JOSEPH O'NEILL (1807–1894), historical writer and novelist. Daunt was born at Tullamore, King's County, on April 28, 1807. A convert to Catholicism, he acted as secretary to Daniel O'Connell, whom he admired inordinately and of whom he wrote his *Personal Recollections* (1848). His *Eighty-five Years of Irish History* (1886) and his posthumous *A Life Spent for Ireland* (1896) are fluently written with much humorous observation, a point applicable also to his neglected novels. He died on June 29, 1894.

LITERARY WORKS: *The Wife Hunter & Flora Douglas, Tales by the Majority Family.* London: Bentley/Philadelphia & Hart, 1838. (Published under the pseudonym of Denis Ignatius Moriarty); *The Husband Hunter.* Philadelphia: Lea & Blanchard, 1839. (Published under the pseudonym of Denis Ignatius Moriarty); *Innisfoyle Abbey: A Tale of Modern Times.* 3 vols. London: C. Dolman, 1840/Dublin: James Duffy, 1844. (Published under the pseudonym of Denis Ignatius Moriarty); *Hugh Talbot: A Tale of the Irish Confiscations of the Seventeenth Century.* Dublin: James Duffy, 1846; *The Gentleman in Debt.* London: Newby, 1851.

DAVIS, FRANCIS (1810–1885), poet. Davis was born in Cork but became a muslin weaver in Belfast, where he died. He was sometimes called "the Belfast Man" and, with more enthusiasm than justice, "the Burns of Ireland."

WORKS: *Miscellaneous Poems and Songs.* Belfast: J. Henderson, 1847; *Lispings of the Lagan.* Belfast: J. Henderson, 1849; *Belfast the City and the Man, A Poem.* Belfast, 1855; *The Tablet of Shadows: A Phantasy and Other Poems.* London: Hamilton & Adams/Dublin: McGlashan/Edinburgh: Nimms/Belfast: Phillips, Henderson, 1861; *Leaves from Our Cypress and Our Oak.* London: Macmillan, 1863; *Earlier and Later Leaves; or, An Autumn Gathering.* Belfast: Mallon, 1878. (His collected works with an introduction by Columban O'Grady).

DAVIS, THOMAS (1814–1845), poet, patriot, and journalist. Davis was born in Mallow on October 14, 1814, the posthumous child of a surgeon in the Royal Artillery, John Thomas Davis. His mother was Mary Atkins, a lady who included the O'Sullivan Beare family among her ancestors. The family removed to Dublin when Thomas was four years old, and he was educated there (showing no particular promise) at the school of a Mr. Mongan and at Trinity College. At Trinity he came under the influence of a group of young Protestant intellectuals who were developing a national consciousness in the wake of the eclipse of the Irish Ascendancy ruling class by the transfer of the center of power to London under the Act of Union 1800. Davis graduated in 1836, kept his law terms in London, and was called to the bar in 1837. Reared as a high Tory Episcopalian, he was at this time a utilitarian. In 1840, he was auditor of the

College Historical Society, and his inaugural address included the famous phrase "Gentleman, you have a country."

The dominant figure in the Irish politics of this epoch was, of course, Daniel O'Connell, and in 1841 Davis joined O'Connell's Repeal Association (agitating for repeal of the Act of Union) and was put on the general committee and several subcommittees. In 1842, with Charles Gavan Duffy* and John Blake Dillon, he founded *The Nation** newspaper, a weekly of advanced national views and considerable journalistic merit. *The Nation* reached a circulation of eleven thousand, although newspaper prices were still remarkably high and the paper sold at sixpence.

In 1843, Davis became disenchanted with O'Connell, following O'Connell's cancellation of the proclaimed mass meeting at Clontarf, and adopted a federalist position, which O'Connell regarded as less than the Repeal movement demanded. A final rift with O'Connell came when Davis and his immediate colleagues, known as the Young Ireland group, favored acceptance of a government proposal for the establishment of nondenominational third-level education, while O'Connell and the conservatively minded clergy claimed to regard it as state-sponsored godlessness. The confrontation, at which O'Connell proclaimed his allegiance to Old Ireland, took place at a meeting at which Davis took the chair and was reduced to tears.

Davis died on September 16, 1845 of scarletina, after a brief illness. In his last years, he had a charming relationship with Annie Hutton, to whom he was engaged at the time of his death.

Davis' principal achievements were his enthusiasm in the national cause, which won over many of his associates, and his articulation of a nationalist apparatus of thought in his essays in *The Nation*. He had broad cultural as well as political interests and wrote on Irish music and the Irish language, for example, with intense feeling. His style was that of polished journalism, with rhetorical flourishes typical of his age. His verse is false and bombastic to the modern ear and reveals a racialist preoccupation kept in restraint in the more controlled prose.

Through Fenianism, Sinn Féin, the Rising of 1916, and up to modern times, Davis has been a main inspiration of the nationalist movement. He was canonized, so to speak, when Pearse* included him in his list of the four evangelists of separatism in the pamphlets Pearse published in the last months of preparation for the Easter Rising.

Davis' manner and personality exercised a great influence on his contemporaries, and by their accounts he was a person of immense personal charm. The principal source is Sir Charles Gavan Duffy's *Thomas Davis, the Memoirs of an Irish Patriot* (London, 1890), in which Duffy, an intimate friend and colleague, quotes a large number of letters and other writings by Davis. There is a considerable volume of later scholarship on the politics of the period, though it is to be noted that many later anthologists have failed to give integral texts of what purport to be reprints of Davis' works.

ALF MacLOCHLAINN

WORKS: *The Poems of Thomas Davis.* Dublin: Duffy, 1846; *Literary and Historical Essays.* Dublin: Duffy, 1846; *Letters of a Protestant, on Repeal.* Thomas Meagher, ed. Dublin: Irish Confederation, 1847; *Prose Writings of Thomas Davis.* T. W. Rolleston, ed. London: W. Scott, [1890]; *Essays Literary and Historical,* with notes by D. J. O'Donoghue and an essay by John Mitchel. Dundalk: W. Tempest, 1914; *Thomas Davis, the Thinker and Teacher.* Arthur Griffith, ed. Dublin: Gill, 1914; *Essays and Poems.* Dublin: Gill, 1945.   REFERENCES: Ahern, J. L. *Thomas Davis and His Circle.* Waterford: Carthage, 1945; Duffy, Charles Gavan. *Thomas Davis: The Memoirs of an Irish Patriot, 1840–6.* London: Kegan Paul, Trench & Co., 1892; Hone, J. M. *Thomas Davis.* London: G. Duckworth/Dublin: Talbot, 1934; MacLochlainn, A. ''The Racism of Thomas Davis.'' *Journal of Irish Literature* 5 (May 1976): 112–122; MacManus, M. J., ed. *Thomas Davis and Young Ireland.* Dublin: Stationery Office, 1945; Moody, T. W. *Thomas Davis, 1814–45.* Dublin: University of Dublin Historical Society, 1945; Quigley, Michael, ed. *Pictoral Record: Centenary of Thomas Davis and Young Ireland.* Dublin: Public Sales Office, 1945; Sullivan, Eileen. *Thomas Davis.* Lewisburg, Pa.: Bucknell University Press, 1978; Yeats, W. B. *Tribute to Thomas Davis.* Cork: Cork University Press, 1947; Yeats, W. B., & Kinsella, Thomas. *Davis, Mangan, Ferguson?* Dublin: Dolmen, 1971.

DAVISON, PHILIP (1957–   ), novelist and film writer. Davison was born in Dublin. *Twist and Shout* (1983) is a novella about a successful saxophone player who returns to Dublin for the wedding of an old girlfriend. The mildly eccentric characters are well drawn, and the writing is often clever:

We would arrive in the morning and find the chairs carelessly stacked upside-down on the tables—it was a lion-tamer's paradise.

. . . words were as useful to me as a wet cardboard box.

What it all means, however, is problematic. *The Illustrator* (1988) is a short novel about an Irish illustrator living in London whose wife leaves him, and it traces his frantic and unsuccessful attempts to find her. It is clearly written with much dialogue and good comic detail, and the character's hysteria is well caught.

WORKS: *The Book-Thief's Heartbeat.* Dublin: Co-op Books, 1981; *Twist and Shout.* [Dingle]: Brandon, [1983]; *The Private Citizen.* [Dingle]: Brandon, [1985]; *The Illustrator.* [Dublin]: Wolfhound, [1988].

DAVYS, MARY (1674–1732), woman of letters. Born in Dublin, Davys was married to the headmaster of the school attached to St. Patrick's Cathedral in Swift's* day. Swift's editor, Harold Williams, accurately describes her novels and plays as ''minor.''

WORK: *The Works of Mrs. Mary Davys: Consisting of Plays, Novels, Poems, and Familiar Letters.* 2 vols. London: H. Woodfall, 1725.

DAWE, GERALD (1952–   ), poet and critic. Dawe was born in Belfast and educated at the New University of Ulster in Coleraine and at University College,

Galway. He taught at UCG for some years before moving to Dublin, where he works as a lecturer in the School of English at Trinity College. He is the founder-editor of *Krino,* one of Ireland's leading literary journals, and he is also an anthologist.

At once a poet and an intellectual with a keen sense of history, Dawe has also written essays, many of them critiques of contemporary Irish culture and society. More than most Irish critics—most of whom are, in truth, reviewers rather than critics—he has a sharp awareness of the connections that exist between literature and the society out of which it comes. In this way, his prose is at once a reading of a literature and of a place. Many of his essays display an autobiographical base that serves to root them in experience and also to make Dawe's own life a starting point for eventual judgments. Considering his past—a Belfast Protestant working in the south—this has made for a sharp and important perspective at a critical and troubled state of contemporary Irish history.

Of his work, he once wrote: "Poetry for me is a way of getting things clear: of sorting things out. I like the statement of Jacques Villon, the French painter, when he said: 'I seek to avoid confusion.' " His poems can range in theme from simple, everyday experiences to a more complex meshing of the personal and the political. He uses words in a plain manner, and in both his prose and poems there is an avoidance of the rhetorical and the pompous. He can create both clear images and clear statement, and while his words can have a stripped feel, they are modestly at ease rather than stark.

His poems are firmly set in the real world of children's cries, the west of Ireland, domestic relationships, gardens, local pubs, a Belfast childhood, the Troubles, a radio that "blinks alive with Morning Ireland." Yet history is there, too, as in his second collection, *The Lundys Letter* (1985), where Edward Carson, Carlyle, and Lieutenant Colonel Lundy (the military governor during the Siege of Derry) are among the shadows cast by and over the poems. Again, history does not exist in the formalin of the past but is forcefully present in everyday events.

The subjects of Dawe's essays and reviews include Patrick Kavanagh,* the Protestant imagination in modern Ireland (also the subject of a book he edited with Edna Longley*), literary politics, his own experience of life in the North and in the republic. At their best, they typify an engagement with both literature and society, and they are also distinguished by an absolute refusal to accept any of the superficial and journalistic clichés with which literary life in Ireland is too often imbued.

SEÁN DUNNE

WORKS: *Sheltering Places.* Belfast: Blackstaff, 1978; ed., *The Younger Irish Poets.* Belfast: Blackstaff, 1982; *The Lundys Letter.* [Dublin]: Gallery, [1985]; ed., with Edna Longley. *Across a Roaring Hill: The Protestant Imagination in Modern Ireland.* Belfast: Blackstaff, 1985; *The Water Table.* [Belfast]: Honest Ulsterman, [1990]. (Poetry pamphlet); *Sunday School* [Oldcastle, Co. Meath]: Gallery, [1991]; *How's the Poetry Going? Literary Politics and Ireland Today.* Belfast: Lagan, 1991. (Criticism); *Water Table.* Belfast: Honest Ulsterman, 1991. (Poetry pamphlet); *A Real Life Elsewhere.* [Belfast]: Lagan, [1993]. (Criticism); *Poems.* Biddulph Moor: Rudyard, 1993; ed.,

Yeats: The Poems. Dublin: Anna Livia, 1993; *False Faces: Poetry, Politics & Places.* [Belfast]: Lagan, [1994]. (Essays); *Heart of Hearts.* [Oldcastle, Co. Meath]: Gallery, [1995]. (Poetry).

DAY, S[USANNE] R[OUVIER] (1890–1964), novelist and playwright. Day was born in Cork and died in London and is said to have been a Quaker, a suffragette, a keen ornithologist, a nurse in France during World War I, and an employee throughout World War II of the London Fire Service. In 1913, the Abbey Theatre* produced the unpublished *Broken Faith,* a two-act play by her and Geraldine D. Cummins,* about a heroic woman, but even the suffragette paper thought it "a sordid tragedy." In 1917, the Abbey produced *Fox and Geese,* a three-act comedy by Day and Cummins. The play translates into an Irish "folk" setting the conventional comic situation of a number of young men and women scheming to overcome obstacles to their love and finding themselves caught by their schemes. The language is lively, with the kind of metaphor and imagery that Synge's characters might have used. While the plot is thin, there are sufficient twists and reversals to engage interest and generate humor. It is interesting to note that the initiative lies with the female characters. W. B. Yeats,* who disliked the play, called it "a bad example of the Miss Barlow,* Miss Lawless* peasant literature."

In 1916, Day published *The Amazing Philanthropists. Being Extracts from the Letters of Lester Martin.* In the preface, she explained that the contents were a "record of personal experience. . . . The characters are not those of individuals but are types, composite creations intended to portray the qualities—human passions, emotions, ambitions—which may sway the minds and influence the judgments of any elected Board or Council in Ireland." Lester Martin is a young woman from the Ascendancy, fired by a keen desire to play an active part in relieving the conditions of the poor. She gets herself elected as a poor law guardian and brings to the hitherto all-male board a practical wisdom that achieves results: "What angers me most is the WASTE, the pitiful tragic, terrible waste of human life and energy and thought and action." The novel takes the form of a series of letters to her friend, Jill, now living in England, to whom she recounts her experiences from the initial canvassing for election to the approving of a badly needed extension to the local hospital. Her accounts are humorous, compassionate, often ironical, and sometimes critical. She is acute in her observation of human nature and perceptive in her analysis of the cause of abuse. The social ills with which the fiction deals are at the forefront of the material but never allowed to efface the comic vision of life: "Well in Ireland, thank God, one is never far from the comedy of life, no matter how insistent the tragedy."

Round about Bar-le-Duc (1918) is a series of reflections and descriptions of life as a relief agent in Bar-le-Duc in 1917 in the months leading up to, and following, the Battle of Verdun. It records the sufferings, heroism and idiosyncrasies that survive in spite of the appalling human degradation caused by war. The strength of her writing again lies in her ability to portray the comic situation that can exist side by side with the deepest tragedy—though here the mood is quite somber, and her compassion extends only to the French.

Where the Mistral Blows (1933) bears little resemblance to the previous works either in style or in content, being much more like a travelogue, more intent on the history and description of the various towns and sites of Provence. It includes the occasional anecdote but is an altogether more objective book of information.

MARY BALL

WORKS: With G. D. Cummins. *Fox and Geese.* Dublin & London: Maunsel, 1913. (Play); *The Amazing Philanthropists. Being Extracts from the Letters of Lester Martin.* London: Sidgwick & Jackson, 1916. (Novel); *Round about Bar-le-Duc.* London: Skeffington & Sons, 1918. (Nonfiction); *Where the Mistral Blows.* London: Methuen, 1933. (Travel).

DAY-LEWIS, C[ECIL] (1904–1972), poet. Although born in County Laois on April 27, 1904, and distantly related to Goldsmith,* Day-Lewis was taken to England when eighteen months old and is basically an English poet. Nevertheless, he valued his Irish connection, and, when he wrote about Ireland, he wrote knowledgeably and well. The best of such poems are "The House Where I Was Born," "Fishguard to Rosslare," "My Mother's Sisters," and "Remembering Con Markievicz." *The Private Wound,* one of the detective novels that he wrote under the pseudonym of Nicholas Blake, is laid in the west of Ireland. His name is frequently connected with W. H. Auden and Stephen Spender as a prominent example of the English social poets of the 1930s. In 1968, he succeeded John Masefield as poet laureate of England. Yeats* once proposed him for the Irish Academy of Letters, but he was blackballed for his left-wing views. In 1968, however, Trinity College awarded him an honorary degree. He died on May 22, 1972, in London at the home of his friend Kingsley Amis.

PRINCIPAL WORKS: *The Buried Day.* London: Chatto & Windus, 1960. (Autobiography); *The Complete Poems.* [London]: Sinclair-Stevenson, [1992]; as Nicholas Blake. *The Private Wound.* London: Collins, 1958.   REFERENCES: Day-Lewis, Sean. *C. Day-Lewis, An English Literary Life.* London: Weidenfeld & Nicholson, [1980]; Handley-Taylor, Geoffrey, & d'Arch Smith, Timothy. *C. Day-Lewis, The Poet Laureate, A Bibliography.* Chicago & London: St. James, 1968; Riddell, Joseph N. *C. Day Lewis.* New York: Twayne, 1971. Neither Handley-Taylor nor Riddell contains an adequate bibliography of the Nicholas Blake books.

DEALE, KENNETH [EDWIN LEE] (1907–1974), barrister, judge, and playwright. Deale was born in Dublin on January 17, 1907, admitted to the Irish bar in 1935, took silk in 1950, and became a judge of the Circuit Court in 1955 and of the High Court in 1974. From 1941, he wrote about 150 scripts for Radio Éireann; in the late 1950s and 1960s, he wrote several unpublished plays dealing with crime for the BBC; and in 1966 he wrote an Abbey* play, *The Conspiracy.* In addition to several legal works, he published two volumes of general interest about notable Irish trials.

WORKS OF LITERARY INTEREST: *Memorable Irish Trials.* London: Constable, 1960; *Beyond Any Reasonable Doubt? A Book of Murder Trials.* Dublin: Gill & Macmillan, 1971.

DEANE, JOHN F. (1943–   ), poet, fiction writer, and publisher. Deane was born on December 8, 1943, on Achill Island. He was educated at Mungret

College, Limerick, and at University College, Dublin, from which he received
an M.A. in modern English and American literature. He taught at St. Aidan's
Secondary School in Whitehall, Dublin, until 1979. He then resigned to write
full-time and to develop the national poetry society, Poetry Ireland, which he
founded in 1978. He is the director of the Heinrich Böll Cottage on Achill
Island, and he is the founder and editor of the Dedalus Press.*

He has published five principal volumes of poetry and has given poetry read-
ings in Ireland, England, Yugoslavia, Denmark, France, Italy, and the United
States. His poems have been translated into Italian, French, Danish, Serbo-
Croatian, and Swedish. He has published translations of the Romanian poet Marin
Sorescu, the Swedish poet Tomas Transtromer, and the Danish poet Uffe Harder.

A review in *The Poetry Ireland Review* speaks of his "sensibility of impressive calibre. . . . his style is capable of conveying a wide range of perceptions
and concerns . . . a capacity to communicate, at one and the same time, both a
sense of control over the most potentially overwhelming emotions, even distance
from them, and the most sensitive openness to them, even rawness." In the
Connacht Tribune, Mary O'Donnell* wrote of *The Stylized City* (1991), "Deane
commits, over and over, the gross sin of writing beautifully, of approaching
language and handling it with tenderness, respect and sensitivity. . . . [It] is a
beautiful, meditative and colourful depiction of life for a man who finds himself
too frequently at a crossroads but paradoxically who moves on, finding wonder,
glimpses of hell and profane visions of God on the way. These poems will
endure long after current belle epoch Big Bang poetry has whimpered into silence." The *Times Literary Supplement* spoke of *Far Country* (1992) as a "taut,
fluent sequence . . . a beautifully wrought poem."

Deane recently began to write fiction, and his stories have been short-listed
twice for the Francis MacManus Award and once for the Hennessy Award. In
April 1994, Wolfhound published his first collection, *Free Range,* and in September 1994 Poolbeg published his first novel, *One Man's Place.* Of *Free
Range,* the *Irish Independent* wrote, "With all 13 stories carefully-chosen images cause a deep impact on the reader in the briefest of space"; and the *Irish
Times* spoke of "a sureness of style, and confident humour and evidence of a
keen ear."

Deane's *Free Range* is a collection of a dozen brief stories and a novella.
The stories are straightforwardly told, generally glum in outlook, and often violent in their conclusions. The most impressive piece is *The Juniper Files,* a
telling novella about clericalism and sexual frustration. His novel, *One Man's
Place,* covers much the same thematic ground as the novella but adds the theme
of nationalism. The bulk of the book traces the life of a man from his boyhood,
shows his father's involvement with the republicans during the Troubles, his
own becoming a Christian brother and teacher, his frustrations about sex, his
eventual (and very skimpily treated) marriage, and a rather far-fetched final
section in which he is forced into an assassination attempt on de Valera. This
he refuses to do at the last moment and attacks his Irish Republican Army (IRA)

handler. The book is told in alternate sections, the present moments through the mind of the man's son as he watches his father dying. Little is added in these sections except a reiteration of grief, and little is added by the author's free-verse poems that appear throughout the text. Much of the father's episodic story, however, is well dramatized and engrossing.

JACK HARTE

WORKS: *Stalking after Time.* [Clondalkin, Co. Dublin]: Profile, [1977]; *Island.* [Dublin]: St. Bueno's, [1978]. (Poetry pamphlet); *Sea-Songs.* [Portmarnock, Co. Dublin]: St. Bueno's, [1979]. (Poetry pamphlet); *High Sacrifice.* [Portlaoise, Co. Laois]: Dolmen, [1981]; *Voices.* Drogheda: Aquila, 1983. (Poetry pamphlet); tr. *The Truth Barrier,* by Tomas Transtromer. Drogheda: Johnston Green, 1984. (In *Tracks 4); Winter in Meath.* [Dublin]: Dedalus, [1985]; tr. *The Wild Marketplace,* by Tomas Transtromer. Dublin: Dedalus, 1985; *Road with Cypress and Star.* Dublin: Dedalus, 1988; ed., *Irish Poetry of Faith and Doubt: The Cold Heaven.* Dublin: Wolfhound, 1990); *The Stylized City: New and Selected Poems.* [Dublin]: Dedalus, [1991]; *Far Country.* Dublin: Dedalus, 1992; *Free Range.* [Dublin]: Wolfhound, [1994]. (Short stories); *One Man's Place.* [Dublin]: Poolbeg, [1994]. (Novel); *Walking on Water.* Dublin: Dedalus, 1994. REFERENCE: O'Brien, Catherine. "La nudita tragica delle cose nella poesia di John Deane." *Citta de Vita* 46 (May–June 1991): 247–255.

DEANE, RAYMOND (1953–   ), composer and novelist. Deane was born on Achill in 1953 and as a classical composer is a member of Aosdána.* His only novel, *Death of a Medium* (1991), is a peculiar but arresting book, a latter-day Gothic novel set in nineteenth-century Ireland and France, with a villain who has affinities both to Dracula and to the Wandering Jew. In its lurid subject matter and perfervid style, it seems a pastiche of Maturin,* Poe, Sheridan LeFanu,* and Bram Stoker* combined. Its remarkable and charmingly archaic prose is full of words like "wyverns," "vrykolakases," "tragelaphs," "somniloquism," and, of course, Poe's "tintinnabulation." Not to mention phrases like "a fetid pool of steaming ichor" and sentences like, "And so I resolved to repugn this pernicious fate and, even if successful—nay, *particularly,* if successful—not to live out the residuum of my dreary days in obscure and eremitic reparation."

WORK: *Death of a Medium.* [Vale, Guernsey, Channel Islands]: Odell & Adair, [1991].

DEANE, SEAMUS (1940–   ), poet and critic. Deane was born in Derry on February 9, 1940, and educated at St. Columb's College. He received his B.A. in 1961 and M.A. in 1963 from Queen's University, Belfast, and his Ph.D. from Cambridge University in 1966. He has taught extensively on both sides of the Atlantic, at Reed College in Oregon (1966–1967), at the University of California at Berkeley (1967–1968, 1978), at the University of Washington in Seattle (1987), and at Carleton College in Minnesota (1988). From 1980 until 1993, he was professor of modern English and American literature at University College, Dublin, and since August 1993 has been Keough Professor of Irish Studies at the University of Notre Dame in Indiana. He is a member of the Royal Irish Academy, a director of Field Day Theatre and Publishing Company, and a member of Aosdána.* He received the AE Memorial Prize for Poetry in 1973 and the American-Irish Fund Award for Literature in 1989.

Deane published three major collections prior to his *Selected Poems* in 1988: *Gradual Wars* (1972), *Rumours* (1977), and *History Lessons* (1983). A novel, *Reading in the Dark,* is forthcoming, as also are his Clarendon lectures entitled *Strange Country: Ireland, Nation and State.* He has published extensive scholarship and criticism on many Irish writers (Banville,* Beckett,* Clarke,* Edgeworth,* Friel,* Goldsmith,* Joyce,* Lavin,* O'Casey,* Swift,* Synge,* and Yeats*) as well as English writers (Conrad, Ford, Hardy, and Godwin). His eclectic and cosmopolitan scholarly interests include work on politics and political philosophy; he has written about Edmund Burke,* Charles Steward Parnell, Montesquieu, and Voltaire and about Irish historical themes, the writer and the Troubles, Irish poetry and nationalism, the revival, nineteenth-century fiction and poetics, the Irish national character, and nationalism and imperialism. Perhaps his most notable work is his general editorship of the three-volume *Field Day Anthology of Irish Writing* (1991).

Deane's poetry reveals a concern with causes and effects of violence and with "the compensating power of culture to restore some sense of the human community." Like Brian Friel and Eavan Boland,* Deane focuses much of his attention on the human memory with its attendant power to distort and restore, much like historical scholarship. Deane shares with James Joyce a sense of history, with W. B. Yeats his coming to terms with the self in the larger cultural context. In "Strange Country," he uses almost Yeatsian rhythms and haunting images of a troubled Ireland. His recent work demonstrates his sense of European history and indicates a "desire to locate Irish experience as part of that wider pattern."

Deane makes clear the connection between present and past history in "Reading *Paradise Lost* in Protestant Ulster 1984" from *Selected Poems,* in which the speaker finds a parallel between Milton's devils and present-day "zombie soldiers and their spies." Nor can the next generation escape; the sins of the parents are visited upon the children throughout history.

Similarly, in "History Lessons," the title poem of Deane's third volume, the speaker compares the burning of Moscow by Napoleon and Hitler to the burning of houses in his own country. He compresses European, Irish, and personal history in order to demonstrate that "history lessons" are not new but are always being learned and that truth is made manifest through living.

"A World without a Name," also from *History Lessons,* describes the manner in which we carry the past with us whether we want to or not. In "Great Times Once," from *Gradual Wars,* the speaker confronts his own personal history in Wordsworthian fashion when he sees "[t]he child looking out of my face." The first poem in the volume titled *Rumours,* "Migration," investigates the process of coming to understand the self by identifying what one is and then leaving it ("migrating").

Deane's work, while finding the connection between personal feeling and public consciousness, is neither confessional nor especially personal. Although he writes about relationships between fathers and children, the reader learns less about the poet but gains an awareness of common heritage. Private feelings and experience parallel public events just as Ireland's history parallels Europe's. The "rumors" of Deane's second volume of poetry are hints of the past that we all carry within us, public events that are foreshadowed by private feelings and that lead us to the lessons of history. Although the private life is hidden, the description of streets, back lanes, and fields reveal our connection to a history that we all share.

DEBORAH FLEMING

WORKS: *While Jewels Rot.* Belfast: Festival, Queen's University of Belfast, [1967]. (Poetry pamphlet); *Gradual Wars.* Dublin: Irish University Press, 1972. (Poetry); *Rumours.* Dublin: Dolmen, 1977. (Poetry); *History Lessons.* Dublin: Gallery, 1983. (Poetry); *Civilians and Barbarians.* Derry: Field Day, 1983. (Essay); *Heroic Styles: The Tradition of an Idea.* Derry: Field Day, 1984. (Essay); *Celtic Revivals: Essays in Modern Irish Literature, 1880–1980.* London: Faber, 1985/Salem, N.C.: Wake Forest University Press, 1987; *A Short History of Irish Literature.* London: Hutchinson, 1986/ Notre Dame, Ind.: University of Notre Dame Press, 1987; *The French Revolution and Enlightenment in England, 1789–1832.* Cambridge & London: Harvard University Press, 1988; *Selected Poems.* [Oldcastle, Co. Meath]: Gallery, [1988]; general editor, *The Field Day Anthology of Irish Writing.* 3 vols. Derry: Field Day, [1991]; ed., *Penguin Twentieth Century Classics: James Joyce.* 6 vols. London: Penguin, 1992; ed., *Field Day Essays: Critical Conditions.* Cork: Cork University Press/ Notre Dame, Ind.: Notre Dame University Press, 1995; *Reading in the Dark.* London: Granta/New York: Knopf, 1995. (Novel).

DE BLACAM, AODH (1890–1951), novelist, critic, and journalist. De Blacam was born Hugh Blacam in London of an Ulster family. He learned his Irish there from Robert Lynd* and began using an Irish form of his name, although some of his works appeared under the English form in America. He came to Ireland in 1915 as a journalist, using the pen name "Roddy the Rover." In Ireland he became a Roman Catholic. His novel *Holy Romans* (1920) charts a similar course for Shane Lambert from childhood to his marriage just after the 1916 Rising. De Blacam's involvement with Sinn Féin and the republican movement of the day got him interned during the Troubles. He contributed to a wide range of magazines and journals and for many years to the *Irish Press.* His enthusiasms make him a very typical figure of the period, but little that he wrote survives rereading except for his important study, *Gaelic Literature Surveyed* (1929), which has become a standard work. He died in Dublin on January 31, 1951.

PETER COSTELLO

WORKS: *Dornan Dan.* Dublin: Talbot, 1917. (Poetry); *Towards the Republic: A Study of New Ireland's Social and Political Aims.* Dublin: T. Kiersey, 1918/rev. ed., 1919; *The Ship That Sailed Too Soon, and Other Stories.* Dublin & London: Maunsel, 1919; *The Druid's Cave: A Tale of Mystery and Adventure for Young People of Seven to Seventy.* Dublin: Whelan, 1920; *Holy Romans.* Dublin & London: Maunsel, 1920. (Novel); *Songs and Satires.* Dublin: Talbot/London: T. Fisher Unwin, 1920. (Pamphlet in English and Irish); *What Sinn Fein Stands For.* Dublin: Mellifont/ London: Chapman & Dodds, 1921; *From a Gaelic Outpost.* Dublin: Catholic Truth Society of Ireland, 1921; *Tales of the Gaels.* Dublin: Mellifont, 1921. (Children's book); *Patsy Kehoe, Co-*

dologist. Dublin & London: Mellifont, [1923]. (Humorous tales); *Gaelic Literature Surveyed.* Dublin & Cork: Talbot, 1929/rev. ed., 1933/reissued, with additional chapter by Eoghan O hAnluain, 1973; *The Lady of the Cromlech.* London: John Murray, 1930/as *The Flying Cromlech* by Hugh de Blacam. New York: Century, 1930. (Novel); *A First Book of Irish Literature.* Dublin: Talbot, [1934]/ Port Washington, N.Y.: Kennikat, 1970; *The Life Story of Wolfe Tone.* Dublin: Talbot/London: Rich & Cowan, 1935; *The Story of St. Columcille.* Dublin: Browne & Nolan, 1935; *Roddy the Rover and His Aunt Louisa, MCMXXXIII.* Dublin: Browne & Nolan, [1935]; *For God and Spain. The Truth about the Spanish War.* Dublin: Irish Messenger Office, 1936. (Political pamphlet); *Golden Priest.* Dublin: M. H. Gill, [1937]. (One-act play about Oliver Plunkett); *The Black North.* Dublin: M. H. Gill, 1938. (On the six counties); *St. Patrick, Apostle of Ireland.* Milwaukee: Bruce, 1941; *O'Kelly's Kingdom.* Dublin: M. H. Gill, 1943. (Novel); *Ambassador of Christ.* Dublin: M. H. Gill, 1945. (Three-act play about St. Patrick); *St. John of God 1495–1550.* Dublin: Irish Messenger Office, 1950. (Pamphlet).

DE BURCA, SEAMUS (1912–   ), playwright. De Burca was born James Bourke in Dublin on March 16, 1912. His father was P. J. Bourke,* the actor, costumier, and author of several neo-Boucicaultian patriotic melodramas; his uncle was Peadar Kearney,* the author of the Irish national anthem "The Soldier's Song"; and his cousin was Brendan Behan.* De Burca's early theatre experience was at the Queen's which his father managed in the 1920s, and the best of his own plays, such as *Limpid River* (1962), reflect the influence of the popular theatre of the past. De Burca is steeped in Dublin's past. That knowledge is shown in his droll and savage *The Howards,* which was given a semi-professional production at the Gate* in 1959, and also in his broadly comic and rambling imitation of Brendan Behan, *The End of Mrs. Oblong* (1968). This preoccupation with the past also seems apparent in two excellent theatrical adaptations—*Knocknagow* (1945) after Charles Kickham,* which has been produced on several occasions by the Dublin comedian Jack Cruise, and *Handy Andy* after Samuel Lover* which remains unproduced. De Burca has also written a biography of Peadar Kearney and a short memoir of Brendan Behan. On paper, much of de Burca's work seems slovenly, long-winded, and even amateurish, but on stage, in a sympathetic production, it can be splendidly theatrical.

WORKS: *Find the Island.* Dublin: P. J. Bourke, [1940?]. (Play); *Two Plays: Michael Dwyer Keeps His Word* [and] *They Met Again.* Dublin: P. J. Bourke, [1944?]; *Knocknagow, or The Homes of Tipperary.* Dublin: P. J. Bourke, 1945. (Play after Kickham); *Family Album.* Dublin: P. J. Bourke, 1952. (Play); *Phil Lahy the Tailor.* Dublin: P. J. Bourke, [1953]. (One-act version of *Knocknagow*); *The Soldier's Song: The Story of Peadar O Cearnigh.* Dublin: P. J. Bourke, 1957 (Biography); *The Howards.* Dublin: P. J. Bourke, [1960]. (Play); *The Boys and Girls Are Gone.* Dublin: P. J. Bourke, 1961. (Play); *Thomas Davis.* Dublin: P. J. Bourke, 1962. (Play); *Limpid River.* Dublin: P. J. Bourke, 1962. (Novel); *The End of Mrs. Oblong.* Dixon, Calif.: Proscenium, 1968. (Play); *Brendan Behan, a Memoir.* Newark, Del.: Proscenium, 1971/3d ed. revised, Dublin: P. J. Bourke, 1993; *Down to the Sea in a Tanker.* Dublin: P. J. Bourke, 1972. (Pamphlet); *The Queen's Royal Theatre Dublin 1829–1969.* Dublin: Seamus de Burca, 1983. (History); *Handy Andy* in *Journal of Irish Literature* 13 (January–May 1984): 87–140. (Play after Lover); *Nostalgia.* Dublin: P. J. Bourke, 1985. (Play); *Limpid River: "Mrs. Josephine Jordan."* Dublin: P. J. Bourke, 1985. (Play).   REFERENCE: Jacobsen, Kurt. "An Interview with Seamus de Burca." *Journal of Irish Literature* 13 (January–May 1984): 75–85.

DEDALUS PRESS, THE (1985–   ), publishing house. On April 7, 1985, two books were launched at a reading in Buswell's Hotel, Dublin. The books were *A Bright Mask,* new and selected poems by Robert Greacen,* and *Age of Exploration,* a new collection of poems by Conleth Ellis.* These were the first books to be published by the Dedalus Press, whose founder and editor was John F. Deane.* By the end of 1995, over 100 titles had been published, and in those years the press established itself as one of the leading poetry publishers in Ireland.

At the time of the first launch, Dolmen Press* was extinct, and its demise left a great gap in poetry publishing in Ireland. Other poetry presses had marked out lines of form, matter, and commitment that were not suitable to the Greacen and Ellis books, while several other poets were translating poetry from other languages, and there was no outlet for such work in Ireland.

The Dedalus Press has quite deliberately avoided any attempt at fixing demarcation lines, in terms of subject matter, style, or form. New young poets have been consistently encouraged. What has been stressed has been the publication of the best poetry available, original and in translation.

Several of the younger Dedalus poets are accomplished translators, and Dedalus has published the work of such poets as Agnes Nemes Nagy (Hungary), Mario Luzi (Italy), Tomas Transtromer (Sweden), Lorand Gaspar (France), and Ivan V. Lalic (Yugoslavia). The press also tries to introduce poets from other English-speaking countries by publishing a series of introductory booklets. James Merrill, just before his untimely death, published a thirty-two-page booklet with Dedalus; and there have been booklets by William Scammell and others.

The great influences on Irish poetry have been Yeats,* Clarke,* and Kavanagh,* but there has been the more curious influence of Joyce* and a group of poets associated with him. These include Denis Devlin* and Brian Coffey,* and Dedalus has published large volumes of the work of both. Also the press has continued to develop the interim publications of Thomas Kinsella* in his Peppercanister series.

Dedalus has also attempted to forge a religious poetry in Ireland. The work of Patrick O'Brien,* Paul Murray,* and Padraig J. Daly* has contributed much to this emphasis, and the activist American priest Daniel Berrigan has published a selection of poems with Dedalus.

Gradually, the press has been creating new spaces for Irish poetry and poets. It is to be hoped that the careers of certain fine poets—among them, John Ennis,* Macdara Woods,* Pat Boran,* Gerry Murphy,* and Susan Connolly*— will grow and develop through the work of the press. It is also to be hoped that the horizons will never be so fixed as to make the publications of the press predictable and uniform.

JOHN F. DEANE

DEELEY, PATRICK (1953–   ), poet. Deeley was born in County Galway and teaches in Ballyfermot, Dublin.

WORKS: *Intimate Strangers*. Dublin: Dedalus, 1986; *Names for Love*. [Dublin]: Dedalus, [1990]; *Turane: The Hidden Village*. Dublin: Dedalus, [1995].

DEEVY, TERESA (1894–1963), playwright. Deevy was born in Waterford on January 21, 1894, the last of thirteen children. A clever pupil, she was educated at the Ursuline Convent in Waterford and then attended University College, Dublin. While there, she suffered the early stages of Ménière's disease, which in her case resulted in total deafness and quashed her hopes of becoming a teacher. She then transferred to University College, Cork, graduating with an arts degree. She went to London to study lip reading, and her later plays showed an extraordinary sensitivity to the nuances of speech. She also became an avid playgoer and, on her return to Ireland in 1919, began avidly to write plays.

Her first Abbey* play, *The Reapers* (March 18, 1930), was followed by the one-act comedy *A Disciple* (August 24, 1931). In 1931, she and Paul Vincent Carroll* were the joint winners of an Abbey play competition, and her prize-winning play *Temporal Powers* was produced on August 24. Her best-known one-act play, *The King of Spain's Daughter,* was done on April 29, 1935, and was followed by her memorable *Katie Roche* on March 16, 1936. The Abbey produced her *The Wild Goose* on November 9, 1936, and her one-act *Light Falling* was presented in its Experimental Theatre on October 25, 1948. Her *Wife to James Whelan* was done at Madame Bannard Cogley's Studio Theatre club on October 4, 1956. Many of her later plays, including the excellent *Beyond Alma's Glory* (1951), were written for radio.

Deevy is remembered most for her brilliant portraits of high-strung, romantic young women caught in rural Ireland. Through remarkable poetic dialogue, she catches them almost in flight at a moment in life when they put aside their youthful illusions and accept a grayer but more plausible adult reality. Her best character in this mold is Annie Kinsella, the heroine of *The King of Spain's Daughter,* a mad, wild young girl who lives completely in her dreams. She is roughly brought down to earth by her brute of a father, who forces her to marry Jim Harris, "a sensible boy." She has to agree, but she is determined to make her world what she wants it to be. Her man will be heroic, and that is that. Browsing through his notebook, she discovers that he has methodically entered an account of his weekly savings, and suddenly she exults. "He put by two shillings every week for two hundred weeks. I think he is a man that—supposin' he was jealous—might cut your throat."

The heroine of *Katie Roche* is a more developed version of Annie Kinsella. Katie marries a dull older man, Stanislaus Gregg, but after the marriage she continues to flirt with a local young man. Her husband, exhausted by what he has taken on, disappears to Dublin. When Katie discovers that she is the illegitimate daughter of the local Big House, it seems to her a most fitting origin. Reuben, a wandering mystic and her father in disguise, realizes that Katie's wild temperament needs a strong man. He talks to Stanislaus, who finally brings Katie firmly off to Dublin, where she will be out of temptation. Like Annie, Katie decides there is glamour in facing the future bravely, but her character is more complex than Annie's. Katie's motives in marrying Stanislaus and then in flirting as she does are never clearly understood. For this reason and because of a looseness in plot, the play is not as successful as *The King of Spain's Daughter.* Here Deevy has tried to do more than the simple art of the drama will allow, but if she has failed, she has done so brilliantly.

In Search of Valour and *The King of Spain's Daughter* were performed with considerable success by the BBC in the pioneering days of prewar television. The heroine of *In Search of Valour,* Ellie Irwin, precedes Annie and Katie, but she shares their characteristics. She works as a maid and wants a man like Coriolanus, who "done things proper." She is fascinated by the local bandit, Jack the Scalp, and sees a comparison between him and Mr. Glitterton, the local squire who has just divorced his wife. Both are like the heroes of old, unafraid to act. When Ellie actually meets Mr. Glitterton, however, she cannot believe that the little old man hobbling about on a stick is her hero. "—An' I thinkin' of him! Dreamin' of him!—"

The plays ends on a comic but dismal note. Ellie is trapped in a house with her hero Jack the Scalp. She offers herself to him defiantly, but he refuses her, afraid of losing his soul. When he runs from her arms to the police, she shouts after him, "I hopes they'll get you! I hopes you'll be hanged!" Then she laments to herself, "Them were best off that were born long ago. Wirra—why weren't I born in a brave time?!"

Another romantic character is Martin Shea, the hero of *The Wild Goose,* a play set in rural Ireland at the end of the seventeenth century. Usually, a dramatic hero has the dilemma of two simple alternatives, but here Teresa Deevy poses a more complex problem. Martin vacillates among the church, the army, and marriage, and while this psychological portrait is recognizable, it is doubtful whether it is successful for the stage. Moreover, Martin is always seen through the eyes of the other characters, and so he never gets an opportunity to explain himself as Katie Roche and Annie Kinsella do. Hence, he is an intangible character, indecisive and never progressing to maturity; correspondingly, the plot seems to wander and appears weak and ill made.

Two small pieces that are generally considered outside Deevy's range are *Strange Birth* and *Going beyond Alma's Glory. Strange Birth* is a tightly woven one-act set in a guest house. Sara Meade is a servant girl of about thirty who serves as a link to all the other characters in the play. She is unmarried and the only person in the house who does not feel the stab of love. All the others do and suffer accordingly, and Sara has to prop them all up by being constantly cheerful. The postman enters and declares his love and desire to marry Sara. At first she refuses, but realizing what she is missing by not loving anyone, she accepts. *Going beyond Alma's Glory* is a radio play, but with its simple set it could easily be staged. It concerns the attempts of two middle-aged people to retrieve a lost past. There are two excellent characterizations, Martin Spillane and his wife, Mona Pewitt. Here we get an opportunity to see not the usual young Deevy romantics, but older and faded members of the same family, for whom romance has failed.

In world terms, Deevy's talent might have been small, but in any terms it was definite. Her dialogue is often close to brilliant, and one cannot but regret that she was restricted by the Catholic Ireland of the 1930s and 1940s. In her later years, she remarked to the Waterford playwright James Cheasty* that a number of poor productions had diminished her popularity. If she had found a more accommodating stage than the Abbey Theatre of those years, her talent might have flowered. Her last production in the Abbey was *Light Falling* of 1948. For twelve years previous to that she had no Abbey productions. For a dramatist of her stature, the first essential is a stage; plays for religious orders or scripts for radio, both of which occupied many of her later years, are poor substitutes. *Katie Roche,* however, was revived by the Abbey in the 1970s and again in 1994. She herself died in Waterford on January 19, 1963.

MARY ROSE CALLAGHAN

PRINCIPAL WORKS: "The Enthusiast." *One Act Play Magazine,* 1 (1938); *Three Plays.* London: Macmillan, 1939. (Contains *Katie Roche, The King of Spain's Daughter,* and *The Wild Goose*); *The King of Spain's Daughter and Other One-Act Plays.* Dublin: New Frontiers, 1947. (Also contains *In Search of Valour* and *Strange Birth*); "Going beyond Alma's Glory." *Irish Writing,* 17 (December 1951): 21–32; "Temporal Powers." *Journal of Irish Literature* 14 (May 1985): 18–75. (Three-act play). "Wife to James Whelan." *Irish University Review* 25 (Spring/Summer 1995): 29–87. (Three-act play). REFERENCES: Dunne, Sean. "Teresa Deevy, an Introduction" and "The Plays of Teresa Deevy, a Checklist." *Journal of Irish Literature,* 14 (May 1985): 3–17; Kearney, Eileen. "Teresa Deevy: Ireland's Forgotten Second Lady of the Abbey Theatre." *Theatre Annual* 40 (1985); Murray, Christopher, ed. *Irish University Review* 25 (Spring/Summer 1995). ("A Teresa Deevy and Irish Women Playwrights" number, which prints "Wife to James Whelan," several essays about Deevy, and Martina Ann O'Doherty's Bibliography); Riley, J. D. "On Teresa Deevy's Plays." *Irish Writing* 32 (Autumn 1955).

DELANEY, EAMON (1956–   ), novelist. Delaney works as a third secretary in the Department of Foreign Affairs.

WORK: *The Casting of Mr. O'Shaughnessy.* London: Bloomsbury, 1995.

DELANEY, FRANK (1942–   ), novelist and nonfiction writer. He was born on October 24, 1942, in County Tipperary and educated at Ross College, Dublin. After an early career in banking, Delaney worked as newsreader with RTÉ, as freelance journalist, and then as current affairs reporter for the BBC in Belfast. Moving to London, he helped to inaugurate the program "Bookshelf" for the BBC and, for Radio Four, the language series "Word of Mouth."

Delaney's popular novels make good "train journey" reads. He is not afraid of big, rambling plots, and there is more than a hint of the journalist in his crisp, fluent style. A chief weakness is his characterization. He almost succeeds in Ellen, the mother in *A Stranger in Their Midst* (1995), and to a lesser extent in her husband Thomas. His books are basically well written, well researched, well paced blockbusters, which are not so much bodice-rippers as fly-openers. His nonfictional books are more rewarding.

DOROTHY ROBBIE

WORK: *James Joyce's Odyssey: A Guide to the Dublin of* Ulysses. London: Hodder & Stoughton, 1981; *A Walk in the Dark Ages.* London: William Collins, 1988; *Legends of the Celts.* London: Hodder & Stoughton, 1990; ed., *The Hutchinson Book of Essays.* London: Hutchinson, 1990; *The Sins of the Mothers.* London: HarperCollins, 1992. (Novel); *Telling the Pictures.* London: HarperCollins, 1993. (Novel); *A Walk to the Western Isles after Boswell and Johnson.* London: HarperCollins, 1993. (Travel); *A Stranger in Their Midst.* [London]: HarperCollins, [1995]. (Novel).

DELANEY, MARY

WORK: *The Correspondence of Mary Delaney.* Belfast: Friar's Bush, 1991.

DELANTY, GREG (1958–   ), poet. Born in Cork, Delanty was educated at University College, Cork, and now teaches in St. Michael's College, Vermont. In 1983, he won the Patrick Kavanagh Memorial Award and in 1986 the Alan Dowling Poetry Fellowship in the United States.

The one unconventional, formal element in Delanty's clear and direct writing is his use of the ampersand. Now and then, however, he will use both it and "and" in the same poem. In "Thrust & Parry," which appears in both of his collections and in *The Field Day Anthology,* he does it twice. This is a trivial matter, but perhaps a symptomatic one because one futilely wonders why. Indeed, many of Delanty's practices make one wonder why. "The Bridegroom's Tale," for instance, is composed of five groups of six lines each. Each second line is slightly indented, each third line is slightly more indented, and so on. The poetic convention of indentation is traditionally to indicate the rhyme pattern. There is some rhyming in the poem, but there is no pattern. In prose, the indentation of the paragraph is connected to the meaning, but here that does not seem to be the case. So, again, why? Is it merely that the appearance of the lines is attractive on the page? There seems little consistent rhythm in most of Delanty's work, but some poems utilize rhyme or slant rhyme. They do so, however, in such an on-again, off-again, patternless manner that one wonders why. It is merely that here a rhyme occurred to the poet, and there it did not?

Delanty can frequently write the arresting line. "Corc's Gold Vessel," for instance, opens with, "The putrefied slug-slithering Lee." The final stanza of "Setting the Type" offers a fine contrast of the unpoetically prosaic with the lyrical last line:

> impressed by the common raised type on the 3rd floor
> of Eagle Printing Company, 15 Oliver Plunket [*sic*] Street,
> in the summer-still, ticking heart of Cork City.

The earlier poems in *Southward* (1992) are about memories of youth—going fishing, sitting in a classroom, hanging around a printing shop, watching a Tom and Jerry cartoon and a James Bond film—and they have a distinct nostalgic charm.

WORKS: *Cast in the Fire*. Dublin: Dolmen, 1986; *Southward*. Dublin: Dedalus, [1992]: *American Wake*. Belfast: Blackstaff, 1995.

DELANY, PATRICK (ca. 1685–1768), poet, religious writer, clergyman, and teacher. Born at Rathkrea, Queen's County, the son of a small farmer, Delany was admitted to Trinity College on September 13, 1701, aged seventeen. He received a B.A. in 1706, became a Fellow in 1709, received an M.A. in 1709, and a B.D. and D.D. in 1722. An extremely popular tutor and lecturer, he was appointed Archbishop King's Lecturer in 1722 and professor of oratory and history in 1724. An early friend of Thomas Sheridan the elder* and highly valued by Swift,* he was also an able poet. Indeed, in 1718, Swift suggested that the frivolous and combative Sheridan should take Delany as his poetic model. Also an anonymous broadside of 1726, "An Epistle in Behalf of Our Irish Poets to the Right Hon. Lady C------t," remarks:

> But if Sw--t or D-l--y should go off to London,
> Poor Dublin, alas! would be perfectly undone.
> Then take whom you will of the musical herd,
> But Patrick and Jonathan cannot be spared.

Despite wit and fluency, however, Delany's poems were the occasional and casual work of his left hand, and there has not thus far been a collected edition. Some of the best, such as "News from Parnassus," "Sent by Dr. Delany to Dr. S---t, in order to be admitted to speak to him," and "Verses on the Deanery Window," have, however, stayed in print in various editions of Swift's verse. Delany is a more circumspect poet than Swift and Sheridan, and their occasional divagations into the vulgar or scabrous he deplored. In his excellent defense of Swift, *Observations upon Lord Orrery's Remarks,* he attacks the brilliant fourth book of *Gulliver's Travels* as "a piece more deform, erroneous, and (of consequence) less instructive, and agreeable, than any of his productions." He even remarks, "who would not wish rather to be the author of one ARCADIA, than fifty LAPUTA'S[,] LILLIPUTS, and HOUYHNHNMS"; and even goes so far as to call Swift's "latter works, among the follies of his life." Nevertheless, he was too clever a man not to be amused by some of the poetic trifles and verse warfares in Swift's set; and he defended even such playful works as riddles and wrote a few himself. What he considered his important work is of little interest today: volumes of sermons and treatises on transubstantiation and polygamy and a fluently written, multivolume history of King David.

Upon the house and grounds of his small estate, Delville, in Glasnevin, he spent much attention and money and thus came in for some poetic ridicule from Sheridan and others. In 1744, he was appointed Dean of Down, but his later years were harried by a lawsuit arising out of his disposal of the property of his first wife, and he died in Bath on May 6, 1768.

His second wife, Mary Pendarves (1700–1788), was a notable needleworker and a friend of the royal family and of various literary ladies such as Mrs. Montague and Fanny Burney. Her autobiography and correspondence are of interest.

PRINCIPAL LITERARY WORKS: *Observations upon Lord Orrery's Remarks.* . . . Dublin: Robert Main, 1754. (Short biography of Swift). Individual poems may be found in Harold Williams's edition of *The Poems of Jonathan Swift* (Oxford: Clarendon, 1958) and in Robert Hogan's edition of *The Poems of Thomas Sheridan* (Newark: University of Delaware Press, 1994). REFERENCE: Ehrenpreis, Irvin. *Swift, the Man, His Works, and the Age.* Vol. 3. London: Methuen, 1983.

DENHAM, SIR JOHN (1615–1669), poet and playwright. Denham was born in Dublin and educated at Trinity College, Oxford, and at Lincoln's Inn. He loved gambling and, after he inherited the family mansion at Egham, Surrey, squandered several thousand pounds by gambling. During the civil war, he supported the royalists, and upon the Restoration he was knighted and given the office of surveyor of the royal works. He was also one of the architects of Burlington House and Greenwich Hospital. Pepys and others suspected him of murdering his second wife. After his death in the middle of March 1668/69, he was buried in Westminster Abbey.

His most famous work was the eclogue *Cooper's Hill,* which combined description of the scenery around Egham with an appeal to national sentiment. Dryden thought that it established "the exact standard of good writing," and Pope used it as something of a model for *Windsor Forest.* Bonamy Dobrée remarked in *English Literature in the Early Eighteenth Century:*

To read Denham side by side with Pope offers an amusing exercise in comparative criticism, though little is to be gained from a comparison of the versification, since the differences are obvious. Denham had made great steps in the use of the closed couplet, but Pope's is already brilliant, masterly, and modulated.

WORKS: *Poems and Translations, with the Sophy.* 2 pts. London: H. Herringman, 1668/4th ed. *To Which Is Added, Cato-Major of Old Age.* 3 pts. London: H. Herringman, 1703; *The Poetical Works of Sir John Denham. With the Life of the Author.* Edinburgh: Apollo, 1779. (The Life is by Samuel Johnson); *The Poetical Works of Sir John Denham.* Edited with Notes, an Introduction and a Bibliography by Theodore Howard Banks. New Haven, Conn.: Yale University Press/London: Oxford University Press, 1928. REFERENCES: O'Hehir, Brendan P. *Harmony from Discords. A Life of Sir John Denham.* Berkeley & Los Angeles: University of California Press, 1968. (Contains "A revised canon of the works of John Denham"); O'Hehir, Brendan P., ed. *Expans'd Hieroglyphicks.* Berkeley & Los Angeles: University of California Press, 1969. (A critical edition of *Cooper's Hill*).

DENMAN, PETER (1948–   ), poet and critic. Denman was born in Guernsey, grew up in Cork, and was educated at University College, Cork, and at the University of Keele. He now lectures in St. Patrick's College and lives in Maynooth. He has been editor of *Poetry Ireland Review.*

WORKS: *Sour Grapes.* Belfast: Ulsterman, 1980. (Poetry); *Samuel Ferguson: The Literary Achievement.* Gerrards Cross: Colin Smythe/Atlantic Highlands, N.J.: Barnes & Noble, 1990; *The Poet's Manual.* [Maynooth, Co. Kildare]: Sotto Voce, 1991. (Poetry).

DERMODY, THOMAS (1775–1802), poet. Dermody was an astonishing child prodigy whose precocious abilities as a classical scholar and poet were rivaled only by his equally precocious proclivities as a toper. He was born on January 15, 1775, in Ennis, County Clare, the son of a schoolmaster. At the age of four, his father set him to learning Latin and Greek, and by the age of nine he was teaching these subjects in his father's school. When a younger brother died of smallpox in 1785, Thomas produced a commemorative poem entitled ''Corydon,'' which reads in part:

> ''Yet cease to weep, ye swains; for if no cloud
>   Of thwarting influence mar my keener sight,
>   I mark'd stranger-star serenely bright,
> Burst from the dim inclosure of a shrowd.
> 'Twas Corydon! a radiant circlet bound
> His brow of meekness; and the silver sound
> Shook from his lyre, of gratulations loud,
>   Smooth'd the unruffled raven-plum of Night.''—
> Thus chanted the rude youth his past'ral strain,
>   While the cold earth his playmate's bosom press'd.
> And now the sun, slow westing to the main,
>   Panted to give his wearied coursers rest;
> The azure curtains took a crimson stain,
>   And Thetis shone, in golden garments drest.
> The shepherd-minstrel bent his homeward way,
> And brush'd the dew-drops from the glitt'ring spray.

Although filled with echoes of Milton and of his classical reading, young Dermody's poem was an extraordinary production for a boy of ten. The influence of his father may undoubtedly be seen in Dermody's early training as may a more baneful paternal influence, his father's habitual drunkenness. By the age of ten, young Dermody was already an experienced drinker and, chafing at the constraints of home life, ran away to Dublin where he arrived penniless. He was shortly discovered reading Anacreon at bookstore stalls and received the protection of various charitable and learned people who were dazzled by his broadness of reading, his ability to translate almost instantly the classics into English poetry, and the facility of his own poetic invention. Dermody was always lucky in his patrons, and some of the early ones were Robert Owenson, Lady Morgan's* father, the dowager countess of Moira, Lord Chief Justice Kilwarden, and Henry Grattan.* Inevitably, however, he disillusioned and rebuffed them all, and refused every opportunity to advance himself, including the opportunity of attending Trinity College. In personality, he seemed to shift from the proud and autocratic to the humble and engaging, but he was always devious, untrustworthy and willing to waste all of his income on conviviality and drink. At one time he is said to have characterized himself by the remark, ''I am vicious because I like it.''

In his early teens, Lady Moira brought him to the village of Killeigh to continue his studies under the local clergyman, but he found the life of the village tavern more congenial and celebrated it in a number of rollicking songs reminiscent of Burns. Particularly fluent is "Lory's of the Lane" which begins:

> There never was sa rare a fight
> Described since Kirst-kirk squabble,
> As that which hap'd on Tuesday night
> At Lory's near the stable:
> For all the lads were drunken quite,
> To stand or sit unable;
> Some lay in hole till morning light,
> Some underneath the table,
>   Fu black that night.

"My Own Epitaph" with its deft heroic couplets is also quite remarkable; as is "An Ode to Myself," which begins:

> Thrice hail, thou prince of jovial fellows,
> Turning so blithe thy lyric bellows,
> Of no one's brighter genius jealous;
>   Whose little span
> Is spent 'twixt poetry and alehouse,
>   'Twixt quill and can!

Back in Dublin, Dermody went from bad to worse, often pawning his clothes or appearing in filthily unpresentable fashion. On one occasion he walked into Wicklow from Dublin, borrowed £5 from Grattan, but had drunk and dispersed all of it by the time he got back to the city. He then walked three miles out to Ranelagh and attempted to arouse his future biographer, James Grant Raymond, by heaving stones through the windows. By the time Raymond was aroused, so was the entire neighborhood, and the drunken and disheveled poet had been collared by the watch.

After being saved from having been pressed into the army on two occasions, Dermody finally enlisted as a private, and, with only occasional drunken lapses, served with such distinction in France that he was raised to the rank of second lieutenant. Twice wounded and mustered out on halfpay, he spent the rest of his life in London, writing, alienating his friends and becoming a hopeless alcoholic. He died in utter poverty on July 15, 1802, at Sydenham in Kent. He was only twenty-seven years old.

Dermody wrote a few perceptive critical essays, but his serious work was poetry. His more formal pieces tended to be conventional and imitative, and were permeated with echoes of his voluminous reading. All his works, however, reflect his consummate ease of expression, and often an individual note brilliantly breaks through. That individuality is most apparent in his pieces of invective, satire, or whimsy. His "Battle of the Bards," for instance, is one of the very few productions of its time to beg comparison with Pope's "Rape of the Lock.'' His ''Farewell to Ireland'' commences with the marvelously energetic lines

Rank nurse of nonsense; on whose thankless coast
The base weed thrives, the nobler bloom is lost:
Parent of pride and poverty, where dwell
Dullness and brogue and calumny:—farewel!

Such lines make him a superb antidote to the multitude of patriotic poets discussed elsewhere in this volume, but it might be noted that Dermody's poem also contains the lines

For spite of anger, spite of satire's thrill
Nature boils o'er; thou art my country still.

Dermody the man is difficult to sum up, for, as his dozens of begging letters show, he was an accomplished self-dramatizer. In one vein, he may truculently assert:

'Fore heav'n! you'll find no saint in me,
    From passion's furnace glowing hot;
And as for prim hypocrisy,
    Hypocrisy! I know her not.

But in a more self-pitying manner, he will advise Ireland to:

Thy artists cherish; bid the mighty soul
Of wisdom range beyond cold want's control;
And haply when some native gem you see
Unknown, unfriended, lost—oh, think on Me!

Nevertheless, the reader's final judgment might best be based on his lines from his ''The Fate of Genius,'' which are engraved on his tombstone:

And though fell passion sway'd his soul,
By Prudence seldom ever won,
Beyond the bounds of her control,
He was dear Fancy's favour'd son.

Now a cold tenant does he lie
Of this dark cell, all hush'd his song:
While Friendship bends with streaming eye,
As by his grave she wends along;

On his cold clay lets fall a holy tear,
And cries, ''Though mute, there is a poet here.''

WORKS: *Poems.* Gilbert Austin, ed. Dublin: Chambers, 1789. *Poems, Consisting of Essays, Lyrics, Elegiac, & c., Written between the 13th and 16th Year of His Age.* Dublin: J. Jones, 1792; *The Rights of Justice; or, Rational Liberty.* Dublin: J. Mehain, 1793. (Essay); *Poems, Moral, and*

Descriptive. London: Vernor & Hood/Lackington, Allen, 1800; *The Histrionade,* by Marmaduke Myrtle (pseud). London: R. S. Kirby, 1802; *Poems on Various Subjects.* London: J. Hatcherd, 1802; *The Harp of Erin.* James G. Raymond, ed. 2 vols. London: Richard Phillips, 1807. REFERENCE: Raymond, James Grant. *The Life of Thomas Dermody: Interspersed with Pieces of Original Poetry . . . and Containing a Series of Correspondence . . .* 2 vols. London: Miller, 1806.

DERRICK, SAMUEL (1724–1769), poet and playwright. Derrick was born in Dublin, was apprenticed to a linendraper, and then went unsuccessfully upon the stage. In London, he became acquainted with Dr. Johnson and Goldsmith* and published his *A Collection of Original Poems* (1755). However, when Johnson was asked whether Derrick or Smart were the greater poet, he delivered himself of the opinion that there was "no setting the point of precedency between a louse and a flea." Nevertheless, Derrick had more success as a playwright than did Johnson, and his criticisms of plays are not without interest. After the death of Beau Nash in 1760, Derrick was appointed master of ceremonies at Bath, and he kept that and a similar position at Tunbridge Wells until his death at Tunbridge Wells on March 28, 1769.

WORKS: *Remarks upon the Tragedy of Venice Preserved. . . .* London: Richard Manby & H. S. Cox, 1752; tr., *Sylla.* London: P. Vaillant, 1753. (A version of a play by Frederick II of Prussia); *A Collection of Original Poems.* London: For the Author, 1755; *Letters Written from Leverpoole, Chester, Cork, the Lake of Killarney, Dublin, Tunbridge-Wells, Bath.* London: L. Davis & C. Reymers/Dublin: G. Faulkner, 1767; *Derrick's Jests; Or, the Wits Chronicle. . . .* London: I. Fell, 1769.

DEVAS, NICOLETTE (1912–1987), novelist and memoirist. The daughter of the notorious Francis MacNamara, a landed heir of Doolin House in County Clare, Nicolette MacNamara was the sister of Caitlin Thomas, wife of the poet Dylan Thomas. Their mother brought them up in England after separating from their father, and they were reared near the family of Augustus John at Fordingbridge. She studied at the Slade art school, and in 1931 she married the painter Anthony Devas (1911–1958), by whom she had two sons and a daughter. She began to write during the night watches of the war, publishing three novels, one of which grew out of her interest in birds. In *Two Flamboyant Fathers* (1966), her most successful book, she gives an account of the circumstances of her early life and upbringing. *Susannah's Nightingales* (1978) is about her French ancestry and family background. In 1965, she married the artist Rupert Shephard, also a contemporary at the Slade, who illustrated her last novel, *Pegeen Crybaby,* privately published in 1986. Her death in London was announced in May 1987.

PETER COSTELLO

WORKS: *Bonfire.* London: Chatto & Windus, 1958. (Novel); *Nightwatch.* London: Chatto & Windus, 1961. (Novel); *Two Flamboyant Fathers: Reminiscences of Francis MacNamara and Augustus John.* London: Collins, 1966; *Black Eggs.* London: Collins, 1970; *Susannah's Nightingales: A Companion to Two Flamboyant Fathers.* London: Collins & Harvill, 1978; *Pegeen Crybaby.* London: Gronow, 1986. REFERENCE: Obituary, *Times* (London) (May 20, 1987).

DE VERE, SIR AUBREY (1788–1846), poet and dramatist. De Vere was born Vere Hunt at Curragh Chase, County Limerick, on August 28, 1788, and was educated at Harrow with Byron and Peel. He was an enlightened and responsible landlord and wrote little until he was thirty. His most ambitious works were a number of verse dramas, of which the best is probably the posthumously published *Mary Tudor* (1847). This drama is written in a much more muscular style than some of the more famous closet dramas of the nineteenth century.

Some of de Vere's poems were about Ireland, and the best were in the form of the sonnet which he came to practice and to admire. As a sonneteer, he was a disciple, and also a good friend, of Wordsworth who called de Vere's sonnets "the most perfect of our age." Wordsworth's judgment was much too kind, but it was not ridiculous. De Vere's Irish sonnets are typical of his style. However, they were less successful than his more general work because the English manner, the Wordsworthian romantic diction, just did not graft well onto the Irish subject matter. De Vere is also extremely uneven from line to line in the same poem. He is capable of a line of authentic Wordsworthian simplicity, or even grandeur, as in "Lismore" where he writes of Raleigh:

> . . . now soon his star
> Should set, dishonoured, in a bloody sea!

But in the same poem he has a good deal of soporific and vague romantic imagery such as:

> . . . umbrageous glade;
> Dark, dimpling eddies, 'neath bird-haunted shade. . . .

In "The Sea-Cliffs of Kilkee," he can dust off a line from the lumber-room of poetry, like:

> Ere the poised Osprey stoop in wrath from high.

And in the same poem he is capable of an incredibly flat line like:

> Awfully beautiful art thou, O sea!

Or he can even palm off such a flat line and then redeem it by one which is utterly tight:

> Where all is simply great that meets the eye—
> The precipice, the ocean, and the sky.

Contemporary taste would probably deem no one de Vere poem thoroughly admirable. Yet, he is worth reading, for among the sunbeams and the rills, the bastioned islets and the desecrated fanes, one will constantly meet lines like these from the first poem in "Glengarriff":

> Gazing from each low bulwark of this bridge,
> How wonderful the contrast! Dark as night,

> Here, amid cliffs and woods, with headlong might,
> The black stream whirls, through ferns and drooping sedge. . . .

De Vere's second son, Sir Stephen, was a translator of Horace; his third son was Aubrey Thomas de Vere,* a neglected but quite considerable Irish poet. De Vere died at Curragh Chase on July 5, 1846.

WORKS: *Ode to the Duchess of Angoulême.* London: Longman, 1815; *Julian, the Apostate; a Dramatic Poem.* London: Warren, 1822; *The Duke of Mercia; an Historical Drama. The Lamentation of Ireland and Other Poems.* London: Hurst, Robinson, 1823; *A Song of Faith, Devout Exercises and Sonnets.* London: Pickering, 1842; *Inaugural Address . . . At the House of the Limerick Philosophical and Literary Society.* Dublin: Grant & Bolton, 1842; *Mary Tudor, an Historical Drama, The Lamentation of Ireland and Other Poems.* London: Pickering, 1847; *Dramatic Works.* London: Pickering, 1858. REFERENCES: De Vere, Aubrey Thomas. *Recollection of Aubrey De Vere.* New York: Arnold, 1897. (This is an autobiography, but it contains many recollections of the author's father); Dixon, William Macneile. "The Poetry of the De Veres." *In the Republic of Letters.* London: Nutt, 1898, pp. 64–118.

DE VERE, AUBREY THOMAS (1814–1902), poet. De Vere, the third son of Sir Aubrey de Vere,* was born at the family estate, Curragh Chase, County Limerick, on January 10, 1814. He was educated at Trinity College, Dublin. He then traveled a good deal in Europe and was frequently in England where he became friends with many of the eminent men of the day, including Wordsworth, Tennyson, Carlyle, Sir Henry Taylor, and Cardinal Newman. He was a deeply pious man who never married. After long consideration, he left the Anglican faith in 1851 and was received into the Roman Catholic by his friend, the future Cardinal Manning.

De Vere was much concerned with the problems of Ireland, and he and his family worked diligently to alleviate the sufferings in their neighbourhood during the Famine. In 1848, he published a book on the Irish situation called *English Misrule and Irish Misdeeds.* This was not precisely the work of an Irish patriot, but of an enlightened Christian gentleman of his class. Concerning the book, modern sentiment would probably agree with John Stuart Mill who wrote to de Vere, ". . . I look much more than you do to reclamation of waste lands and alteration of landed tenures, and less to emigration as a remedy." However, one of his biographers, Mary Paraclita O'Reilly, notes that, "Throughout his life he worked diligently in behalf of his countrymen, promoting religious equality, lending his support to the Irish Land Act of 1881, to the earlier establishment of the Irish Church, and to the cause of popular education."

De Vere was a cultivated man of leisure who devoted much of his life to writing. He produced four volumes of essays, two of travel, one of *Recollections,* six of poetry and two poetic dramas, in addition to much fugitive work. He is little read today. One critic in a recent literary history devotes only two sentences to him, misspelling his name once and remarking that he "produced some superficially 'Irish' poetry, but rarely gives the impression that he is more than a conventional Victorian who occasionally successfully exploited material from his Irish homeland" (Richard Fallis, *The Irish Renaissance,* 1978). Patrick Rafroidi's view that de Vere is, with Sir Samuel Ferguson* and Standish O'Grady,* a major link between the Romanticism of the early nineteenth century and the Celtic Renaissance at the end is a much sounder position (*L'Irlande et le Romantisme*, 1972).

Perhaps only a third or a fourth of de Vere's poetic production can strictly be labeled Irish, but much of that is extremely interesting. His retelling of the *Tain* under the title of *The Foray of Queen Maeve* is certainly spotted with some nineteenth-century poetic diction and some poetic inversions, but mainly it impresses by a terse (sometimes almost too terse) masculine style that hurtles the story fluently along. Of nearly equal interest are his retellings of "the Sons of Usnach" and "The Children of Lir." His best Irish work may be in two shorter pieces, "Oiseen and Saint Patrick" and "The Bard Ethell." These works reflect his deeply felt Christianity and yet do not dissipate the un-Christian heroism of an earlier day. In the metrically jaunty first part of his Oiseen and Patrick colloquy, the pagan hero loses none of his intractability by his confrontation with the Christian saint:

> "Old man, thou hearest our Christian hymns;
> Such strains thou hadst never heard—"
> "Thou liest, thou priest! for in Letter Lee wood
> I have listened its famed blackbird!
>
> "I have heard the music of meeting swords,
> And the grating of barks on the strand,
> And the shout from the breasts of the men of help
> That leap from the decks to land!"

The character of the thirteenth-century poet in "The Bard Ethell" is a beautifully drawn sketch of pagan surliness not yet entirely dimmed by conversion to Christianity. Ethell can still say:

> Man's deeds! Man's deeds! they are shades that fleet,
> Or ripples like those that break at my feet;
> The deeds of my chief and the deeds of my King
> Grow hazy, far seen, like the hills in spring.
> Nothing is great save the death on the Cross!
>   But Pilate and Herod I hate, and know,
>   Had Fionn lived then, he had laid them low. . . .

According to Robert Welch,* the best recent commentator on de Vere, his most accomplished poem is *Inisfail* (1861). In any event, de Vere is not a modern poet, but his handling of Irish themes is no more superficial than that of Yeats,* who had a good word or two to say for him. Further, he is not an inconsiderable poet, for he can handle strong narrative, draw a memorable character, and fashion fluent verse. He died on January 21, 1902.

WORKS: *The Waldenses, or The Fall of Rora: A Lyrical Sketch. With Other Poems.* Oxford: John Henry Parker/London: Rivingtons, 1842. *English Misrule and Irish Misdeeds.* London: Murray,

1848; *Picturesque Sketches of Greece and Turkey.* London: Bentley, 1850; *The Sisters and Inisfail.* London: Longmans, 1867. (Poems); *Ireland's Church Question.* London: Longmans, 1868; *(Irish Odes and Other Poems.* New York: Catholic Publication Society, 1869); *May Carols.* London: Richardson, 1870; London: Burns & Oates, 1881. (Poetry); *Alexander the Great.* London: King, 1874. (Poetic drama); *Saint Thomas of Canterbury.* London: King, 1876. (Poetic drama); *Antar and Zara: An Eastern Romance.* London: King, 1877; *Legends of the Saxon Saints.* London: Kegan, Paul, 1879; *Constitutional and Unconstitutional Political Action.* Limerick: McKern, 1881; *The Foray of Queen Maeve.* London: Kegan, Paul, Trench, 1882; *The Search after Proserpine and Other Poems.* London: Kegan, Paul, 1884; *Legends and Records of the Church and Empire.* (Poetry); *Essays, Chiefly on Poetry.* London: Macmillan, 1887; *Legends of St. Patrick.* London: Cassell, 1889; London: Macmillan, 1892. (Poetry); *Mediaeval Records and Sonnets.* London: Macmillan, 1893; *Religious Problems of the Nineteenth Century.* London: St. Anselm's Society, 1893; *Selections from the Poems of Aubrey de Vere,* ed. George Edward Woodberry. New York: Macmillan, 1894; *Recollections.* New York: Arnold, 1897; *Poems from the Works of Aubrey de Vere,* ed. Lady Margaret Domvile. London: Catholic Truth Society, 1904; *The Poetical Works of Aubrey de Vere.* Vols. 1–3. London: Kegan Paul, 1898; Vols. 4–6. London: Macmillan, 1898.   REFERENCES: Gunning, John P. *Aubrey de Vere: A Memoir.* Limerick: Guy/London: Simpkin & Marshall, 1902; Reilly, Mary Paraclita. *Aubrey de Vere, Victorian Observer.* Lincoln: University of Nebraska Press, 1953; Ward, Wilfrid. *Aubrey de Vere: A Memoir.* London: Longmans, Green, 1904; Welch, Robert. "Aubrey de Vere: An Attempt at Catholic Humanity." In *Irish Poetry from Moore to Yeats.* Gerrards Cross: Colin Smythe/Totowa, N.J.: Barnes & Noble, 1980, pp. 156–177; Winckler, Paul A. & Stone, William V. "Aubrey Thomas de Vere 1814–1902: A Bibliography." *Victorian Newsletter,* No. 10, Supplement (1956): 1–4.

DEVLIN, ANNE (1951–   ), playwright and short story writer. Anne Devlin was born in Belfast, educated in Ireland, and now lives in Birmingham and has held a post as visiting lecturer and playwright in residence at the University of Birmingham. She has written plays for the Liverpool Playhouse Studio, the Royal Court Theatre (London), BBC television, the Royal Shakespeare Company, and the Birmingham Repertory Theatre. In addition, she adapted D. H. Lawrence's *The Rainbow* for BBC television and *Wuthering Heights* for Paramount Pictures. She has received numerous awards and wide-ranging recognition for her work, including a Hennessy Literary Award in 1982 for her short story "Passages," which was later adapted for television under the title *A Woman Calling.* She has also received the Samuel Beckett Award; the Susan Smith Blackburn Prize; the Eight International Celtic Film Festival Prize for *Naming the Names,* a television adaptation of her short story; and the San Francisco Film and Television Best Drama Award for her play *The Venus de Milo Instead.* In the early 1980s, she began to publish stories in a variety of periodicals including *Threshold, Woman's Journal, Argo, The Ulster Tatler, Bananas, Irish Press, Cosmopolitan, Good Housekeeping, Literary Review,* and *The Female Line.*

The range and diversity of these journals speak to the broad appeal of her writing. Her stories, collected under the title of *The Way Paver* (1986), share common themes of relationships and love and detachment. The women in her stories—and almost all the major characters are women—find themselves unable to connect fully with a male other—a husband, brother, father, friend, lover.

The sense of disconnectedness comes from the inadequacy of memory, the gender tropes endemic to society, and the sense that any genuine affection will not be able to sustain itself. Further, her characters seem separated from the events they experience. They assume an emotional distance from the Northern war, sexual violation, and the witness of sadomasochistic death.

Her first collection of plays, *Ourselves Alone* (1986), contains *A Woman Calling, The Long March,* and *Ourselves Alone.* This last play, first produced by the Liverpool Playhouse Studio on October 24, 1985, details the lives of working-class women in Belfast during the Troubles. The women are active participants in the violent struggle for Catholic nationalism. They attempt fulfillment in the acts of delivering explosives, hiding fugitives, and basically ''supporting'' the male-dominated movement. *A Woman Calling* effectively stages Devlin's short story, set in County Down in the early 1980s. The play centers around a woman's adult recollection of a childhood memory involving strangulation and sexuality. On one level, the play and story are psychological thriller, a murder mystery. On another level, the play addresses the issues of male dominance and the vocation of the artist and her call to be witness of her experience, even if that witness involves recalling painful memory. *The Long March,* first performed on BBC television on November 20, 1984, is set in West Belfast and Stranmillis. The play's action covers an eighteen-month period from early spring of 1979 to early winter of 1980. The protagonist returns to Belfast from Leeds after her marriage breaks up and becomes involved with a member of the Irish National Liberation Army (INLA), at a time when the INLA takes responsibility for killing Airey Neave. The events also cover the hunger strike and the death of Bobby Sands.* As is the case in much of her writing, Devlin's female protagonists seem controlled and manipulated by the forces around them—the forces of history, of male dominance, of political violence, of love and affection.

Of her remaining works, *After Easter,* first performed by the Royal Shakespeare Company on May 18, 1994, carries forward Devlin's familiar themes of exile and return, male–female relations, and the backdrop of political violence in Northern Ireland. Like her other plays and stories, *After Easter* contains Devlin's characteristic dark humor and a sensitive female protagonist. However, *After Easter* not only carries forward the themes and motifs of her earlier works but also attempts an integration between the protagonist and all that drove her to exile and a sense of powerlessness—religion, violence, and family relations. *Heartlanders,* a play written with Stephen Bill and David Edgar to commemorate Birmingham's centenary, was first performed at the Birmingham Repertory Theatre on October 19, 1989. The play, set in Birmingham, carries forward Devlin's themes of women trying to live their lives and find fulfillment in a world that offers only seeming opposition to their quest.

BERNARD McKENNA

WORKS: *The Way Paver.* London: Faber, 1986. (Short stories); *Ourselves Alone with A Woman Calling and The Long March.* London: Faber, 1986. (Plays); *After Easter.* London: Faber, 1994. (Play). In addition, Devlin's stories and plays have appeared in a variety of journals, anthologies, and periodicals. Notably, "Five Notes after a Visit" in *State of the Art: Short Stories by New Irish Writers.* David Marcus, ed. London: Sceptre, 1992. Also, *Ourselves Alone* appeared in *Contemporary Plays by Women.* Emilie Kilgore, ed. New York: Prentice-Hall, 1991. REFERENCES: Bankowicz, Ryszard. "Towarzyska kochanka." *Dialog: Miesiecznik Poswiecony Dramatugii Wspolczsnej: Teatralnej, Filmowej, Telewizyj* 34 (November–December 1989): 146–153; Bort, Eberhard. "Female Voices in Northern Irish Drama" in *Standing in Their Shifts Itself... Irish Drama from Farquhar to Friel.* E. Bort, ed. Vol. 1. Bremen: European Society for Irish Studies, 1993, pp. 263–280; Lojek, Helen. "Difference without Indifference: The Drama of Frank McGuinness and Anne Devlin." *Éire-Ireland* 25 (Summer 1990): 56–68; McClone, Martin. "Cinema Irish Style." *Studies: An Irish Quarterly Review* 74 (Summer 1985): 220–224.

DEVLIN, DENIS (1908–1959), poet, translator, and diplomat. Devlin was born in Greenock, Scotland, on April 15, 1908, the son of a prosperous Irish businessman. In 1918, when Devlin was ten, the family returned to Ireland. Devlin was the eldest of nine children, and the interests of his large, hospitable family were lively. There was a formidable library and much stimulating discussion of current affairs, the household being frequented by such political notables as Michael Collins and Éamon de Valera with whom Devlin retained acquaintance throughout his life.

Devlin received his primary education from the Christian Brothers and his secondary education from the Jesuits at Belvedere College, Dublin, the school attended by James Joyce.* He spent one year in seminary at Holy Cross College, Clonliffe, before deciding, despite his religious fervor, not to enter the priesthood. He entered University College, Dublin, and gave himself over with characteristic vitality to pursuits artistic as well as intellectual. He acted in dramatic productions, among them *Twelfth Night,* and was one of the founders of the Dramatic Society. He also began his career as a poet with the publication of a few poems in *The National Student.* In 1930, he and his friend and fellow poet Brian Coffey* had a slim volume of their combined efforts privately printed at their own expense. The collection contained four poems by Devlin and five by Coffey and, as Coffey says, was intended to "show that the pre-treaty tradition of writing from U.C.D. was not dead" (*University Review* 2, No. 10). In *Advent VI,* a publication devoted to Devlin, Mervyn Wall,* the novelist and lifelong friend who had met Devlin at Belvedere, remembers him as "the perfect friend, very well-read, humorous, and always radiating a quiet charm... who introduced me to Eliot and Pound." Wall gives this portrait:

While standing and listening to what others had to say, Denis often adopted a slightly comic stance, his arms and hands hanging loosely by his sides. A College cartoonist once drew him as a penguin with a cherrywood pipe in its mouth, and those who saw the drawing immediately recognized whom the cartoon represented.

After taking a degree in languages at University College, Dublin, Devlin made a brief visit to the Blaskets to improve his knowledge of Gaelic, and then went on scholarship to study at Munich University (1930–1931) and at the Sorbonne (1931–1933). During these years, he and his friend Niall Montgomery took on the unorthodox challenge of translating nineteenth-century French poetry into

Gaelic; their manuscript remains unpublished. There was also a short trip to Spain with American journalist Sam Pope Brewer. Devlin was to capture his reactions to that country in the poem "Meditations at Avila." For a short time, he was assistant lecturer in English Literature at University College, Dublin. The salary, however, was quite small, and Mervyn Wall recalls the poet's struggle in deciding to leave teaching for a more lucrative position with the Irish diplomatic service: " 'I know the academic life is the superior,' he said, 'but I admit that the diplomatic life attracts me' " (*Advent VI*).

Devlin left the university in 1935 and entered the Department of External Affairs as a cadet. He was to remain in the Irish diplomatic service until his death in 1959, becoming progressively more proficient in the execution of his duties. But his dedication to poetry remained constant, and the successful pursuit of this avocation runs parallel to his successful pursuit of his vocation. Indeed, poetry was as much his vocation as was diplomacy. All that he encountered in his travels provided his poetry with a world vision that is perhaps unequaled in modern poetry, with the exception of Ezra Pound, with whom he shares many affinities.

Intercessions, a collection of fifteen poems, appeared in 1937. The technical control, rich and complex imagery, broad vocabulary, and themes of love, justice, family, and mystical union that mark the later work abound in these early poems of passionately religious fervor. They reflect his thorough acquaintance with and respect for European literature, and the influence of those French poets he held in highest regard: Gide, Villon, and most particularly Eluard. Coffey tells us that "Devlin used a copy of *Longer Poems of the English Language* until it fell apart" and that he always kept Eluard beside him (*University Review* 2, No. 10). In certain of the poems, the mimicry of the French *symbolistes* is awkward and inhibiting, and echoes of Baudelaire are destructive. In "Est Prodest" and "Argument with Justice," however, Devlin's own unique voice emerges. His poetic development, as Frank Kersnowski says, his "progression . . . from a surrealistic portrayal of disgust to a mythic celebration of love" (*Sewanee Review,* Winter 1973), has only just begun and is only just perceptible. Several of the poems in *Intercessions* reappear in *Selected Poems* (1963) and one, "The Statue and the Perturbed Burghers," has been anthologized.

In 1938, Devlin went to Rome as first secretary to the Legation to Italy and made a first visit to Greece. In 1939, he left for the United States where he spent one year as consul in New York and six years (1940–1947) as first secretary to the Irish Legation in Washington. It was there, at the home of Katherine Anne Porter, that he met Robert Penn Warren, who two years earlier had read and admired his "Lough Derg" and published it in *The Southern Review.* Many of Devlin's poems appeared in American journals and magazines during this time. One may find them in *Accent, Briarcliff Quarterly, New Republic, Sewanee Review, Poetry,* and *Maryland Quarterly,* among others. America gave Devlin a wife as well as an audience: in 1946, he married Marie Caren Radon, an American of French descent.

A great deal of Devlin's poetic virtuosity may be attributed to his translations, particularly those of French poets. A series of his translations of Saint John Perse were published immediately following the war, culminating in the publication of the bilingual edition *Exile and Other Poems* in New York in 1949.

A collection of his own verse, *Lough Derg and Other Poems,* was published in New York in 1946. Included in the collection were many of the best poems previously published in *Intercessions* and in various periodicals. The volume was quite favorably received, despite one critic's reaction that "Devlin is a learned rather than an accomplished craftsman" (Babette Deutsch, *Weekly Book Review,* July 28, 1946). Although there are poems in the book that would create that impression, the title poem is not one of them. "Lough Derg" is of primary importance among Devlin's work. The story centers around an Irish abbey famous for centuries as a place of religious pilgrimage, and the reference to Dante, who centuries before had celebrated the spot, is more than incidental. In "Lough Derg," the poet-pilgrim reaches a celebration of life derived from a Blakean awareness of mystical union and reunion, which may serve as an analogue for Devlin's search for poetic vision in general. Inez Boulton accurately remarks that "the poet gives us a glimpse of that philosophy which recognizes the unity of all consciousness. . . . This thought stream runs through all the poems. Sometimes it is bright with humor, sometimes dim in the tarnishment of life's tragic background, but always an essential part of the pattern" (*Poetry,* December 1946). More than one critic has commented that "Lough Derg" will stand beside Stevens' "Sunday Morning" and Eliot's "Gerontion" as an answer to the modern dilemma. As Mary Salmon puts it, Devlin approaches the theme of modern man's "loss of God and the seeming bankruptcy of efforts at replacement . . . from the standpoints of humanism ancient and modern, the theocratic symbolism of European Christianity and the emotional piety which he found in the Ireland of his time" (*Studies,* Spring 1973).

Returning to Europe in 1947, Devlin was assigned the post of counsellor attached to the Office of the High Commission, London. He returned to headquarters in Dublin in 1949. In 1950, he went to Italy, and most of the ensuing years were spent there, first as minister plenipotentiary and later (1958) as Ireland's first ambassador to Italy. A brief post as minister plenipotentiary to Turkey in 1951 is reflected in the poem "Memoirs of a Turkish Diplomat," first published in *Botteghe Oscure* and later in both *Selected Poems* and *Collected Poems.* This poem is not one of Devlin's best, but it displays the complex patterning of irony that runs through most of his work. Its counterpointing of philosophical argument and evocative imagery, standing out as it does, prepares the reader for that more subtle rhetoric and obscure metaphor that moves the better poems. Not the least of the merits of "Memoirs" is its exploitation of the culturally alien situation for the purpose of contrast which highlights the universal human condition. As always, Devlin's keen sensibilities penetrate the variety of experience and synthesize it to poetic advantage.

Devlin died on August 21, 1959, in Dublin. He was survived by his wife,

Caren, and his son, Stephen. During the years following his return from America, a few new poems were published in literary journals, but no books appeared. It is known that he was busy translating, among others, the work of Goethe, Appolinaire, and Quasimodo, and that he was working on an autobiography, unfinished and unpublished.

In 1963, *Selected Poems by Denis Devlin*, edited and prefaced by Robert Penn Warren and Allen Tate, appeared, as well as *Collected Poems*, edited and introduced by Brian Coffey. There are forty-two poems in *Selected Poems*, representing approximately half of those finished by the poet. Among the most notable not heretofore published in book form are the long poems "The Tomb of Michael Collins," "The Passion of Christ" (dedicated to Allen Tate), and "The Colours of Love" (dedicated to Caren). These are beautifully crafted poems, wherein Devlin's celebration of man's divinity, in several ways, is carried off in lyrical and grand style. In these poems, the vision of a fragmented world is unified by a resounding metaphysical awareness of oneness, and in retrospect much of the irony and paradox of the earlier poems is illuminated. Maurice Harmon says of "The Passion of Christ": ". . . the grandeur of theme is matched with suitable elevation of language . . . Devlin seems to have found a mode entirely suitable to his needs as man and poet: the great theme of Christ, son of man and son of God, the act of atonement and the act of redemption, the absolute certainty of the journey towards transfiguration" (*Advent VI*). By *Selected Poems*, the poet has found his vision and his voice. Tate and Warren, whose affectionate preface is primarily biographical, consider "The Passion of Christ," "From Government Buildings," and "Lough Derg" to be Devlin's best poems. They find his work neither Irish nor English (there is little there, they say, of Yeats*), but rather European in the manner of Valery and St. John Perse. However, when they refer to what they consider Devlin's "eccentricity" in punctuation and his deviation from iambic pentameter in parts of "Lough Derg," they evoke a response from Brian Coffey, whose *Collected Poems* appeared almost simultaneously with their edition. In *Poetry Ireland* (Spring 1973), Coffey "vindicates" Devlin's technique—to use a term which Coffey tells us Devlin applied to the responsibility of the poet to his talent (*University Review* 2, No. 10).

In *Collected Poems* (Dublin, 1963 and 1964), Coffey has gathered all of the poems published during the poet's lifetime (with the exception of the translations), all of the poems published posthumously, and some few others not before published. Coffey was named executor of Devlin's manuscripts upon his death. The introduction to *Collected Poems* is valuable for a variety of reasons, particularly for the information drawn from unpublished notes and poems and the autobiography. Coffey has also provided a critical edition of "The Heavenly Foreigner," Devlin's most difficult poem, at least in terms of its obscurity, and perhaps his best work in terms of complexity and completeness of vision. *The Heavenly Foreigner* (Dolmen Press, 1967) is the first edition of the revised edition of the poem; it was completed before the poet's death and contains his worksheets. "The Heavenly Foreigner" was originally published in *Poetry Ireland* in 1950, and Coffey includes in his text Niall Sheridan's* introduction to that version. What Sheridan says of the poem holds true for all of Denis Devlin's verse: that it makes "what may seem unusual demands on the reader," but that "on careful reading, superficial obscurities vanish, new imaginative horizons open," as "complexities of thought and feeling fuse into a glowing lyricism. . . ." In handling the themes of "Time and human destiny" and "the anguished alliance of flesh and spirit," Devlin "shows a rare power of stating abstract ideas and philosophical concepts in terms of poetry."

Devlin brought much to his poetry: excellent education, broad cultural experience, religious training and genuine conviction, native intelligence, and a gift for language and its cadence. In reading his work, one is reminded as much of Blake and his fellows as of Yeats and the moderns of French and English verse, especially of Pound. His bent is surely romantic, and his technique is strikingly modern. An effort must be made to avoid confusing his sophistication with artifice. Critics place him with Austin Clarke* and Patrick Kavanagh*; he ranks with Yeats. It is only exposure that is lacking; wider circulation will surely yield greater critical acclaim.

NORA F. LINDSTROM

WORKS: with Brian Coffey, *Poems*. Dublin, 1930; *Intercessions*. London: Europa, 1937; *Lough Derg and Other Poems*. New York: Reynal & Hitchcock, 1946; trans., *Exile and Other Poems*, by Saint John Perse. New York: Pantheon Books, 1949; *Selected Poems*. Robert Penn Warren & Allen Tate, eds. New York: Holt, Rinehart & Winston, 1963; *Collected Poems*. Brian Coffey, ed. Dublin: Dolmen, 1964. (Previously published as a special number of *University Review,* University College, Dublin, 1963); *The Heavenly Foreigner*. Brian Coffey, ed. Dublin: Dolmen, 1967; *Collected Poems of Denis Devlin*. J.C.C. Mays, ed. Dublin: Dedalus, 1989/Winston-Salem, N.C.: Wake Forest University Press, 1990; *Translations into English from French, German and Italian Poetry*. Roger Little, ed. Dublin: Dedalus, 1992.   REFERENCES: *Advent VI*. Denis Devlin Special Issue. Southhampton: Advent Books, 1976; Coffey, Brian. "Of Denis Devlin: Vestiges, Sentences, Presages." *University Review* 2 (1965): 3–18; Dowhey, William G., Jr. "Thinking of Denis Devlin." *Éire-Ireland* 14 (Spring 1979): 102–114; Kersnowski, Frank L. "The Fabulous Reality of Denis Devlin." *Sewanee Review* (Winter 1973): 113–122; Salmon, Mary. "Modern Pilgrimage: Denis Devlin's 'Lough Derg.' " *Studies: An Irish Quarterly Review* (Spring 1973): 75–83.

DEVLIN, POLLY (1944–   ), woman of letters. Devlin was born in Ardboe, County Tyrone. In 1964, she won a talent competition sponsored by *Vogue* and worked for that magazine, doing interviews with Bob Dylan, Barbra Streisand, her brother-in-law Seamus Heaney,* and others. As a journalist she has traveled widely and written much for magazines and newspapers, including the *Sunday Times*. In 1992, she was awarded an OBE for her writing. She has three children and divides her time among Somerset, London, and Ireland.

Her *All of Us There* (1983) is less a memoir of her early life with five sisters and a brother than it is a celebration of how life was lived near Lough Neagh in Tyrone in the 1950s. It is more essayistic than interested in narrative or characterization, but it is a memorable evocation of place, with a telling eye for detail. For instance:

The nuns in the order that ran the day-school had a narrowness of outlook and apparent evaporation of earthly expectation, emotion, or fulfilment that gave all their faces a pinched, curdled look. . . . before you saw them or, even earlier, heard their rustling, rattling approach, you felt a precursory cold ooze.

Also Devlin's ear for local language is excellent. When the girls come in dirty and bedraggled, Ellen, the well-realized servant girl, says, "In clabber to your lugs . . . and worsen pigs, for they *have* to be in it, and there's no having on you, only wanting to puddle in muck and glaur."

Her novel, *Dora* (1990), is a long, leisurely study of a woman's relationships with a couple of violent and savage lovers and with a patient and loving husband. The occasional dramatized scenes are like oases, for most of the book is composed of Dora's interminable reflections about this and that, and many of these lengthy paragraphs could have been profitably pruned. Also, the heroine's character seems very different at different stages. The longest section, in which she is trying to choose between family and lover, shows her as petulant, quarrelsome, selfish, and probably more unsympathetic than the author intended. The book has a hasty resolution, if hardly a climax, and the ending is a tacked-on, perhaps peaceful coda, mainly about characters who have not appeared before. Despite considerable felicity in the writing, this is, for the most part, a tedious tale.

WORKS: *The Vogue History of Photography*. London: Thames & Hudson/New York: Simon & Schuster, 1979; *All of Us There*. London: Weidenfeld & Nicholson, [1983]. (Memoir); *The Far Side of the Lough*. London: Gollancz, 1983. (Children's stories); *Dora, or the Shifts of the Heart*. London: Chatto & Windus, [1990]. (Novel).

DILLON, EILIS (1920–1994), novelist, playwright, editor, translator, and non-fiction writer. Born in Galway on March 7, 1920, Dillon at first studied music with the goal of being a professional cellist. But having composed her first story at the age of seven and "never remember[ing] a time when [she] did not want to write," Dillon turned to writing; her first novel, *An Choill bheo* was published in 1948. Since that time, she has published over forty books, spanning genres and aiming at different age groups. As a professional writer, she lectured on creative writing at Trinity College, Dublin, in 1971 and 1972 and at University College, Dublin, in 1988, as well as in various American colleges. She has won a number of awards, including the Irish Children's Book of the Year Award in 1991 for *Island of Ghosts* and the American Library Association Award and the Lewis Carroll Shelf Award in 1970 for *A Herd of Deer*. She was a fellow of the Royal Society of Literature and a member of Aosdána.* In 1991, she was awarded a D. Litt. (honoris causa) from the National University of Ireland. She is the mother of Eilean Ni Chuilleanain,* and her second husband was Vivian Mercier.* She died in July 1994.

Dillon's adolescent books are quite fresh and exciting, even though some were written almost thirty years ago. The many well-read, thumbed-through library copies attest to the popularity of her writing for this age group. Some are adventure stories in the Robert Louis Stevenson vein, full of daring feats and improbable plots where young adolescents take center stage in heroic adventures. The stories are action-packed, the life-and-death plots centering around romantic, fantastical situations: there are the voyage to Spain and the potential shipwreck in *The Cruise of the Santa Maria* (1967), the cattle stampedes of *The Singing Cave* (1959), and a fort full of old Spanish doubloons in *The Fort of Gold* (1961), to name a few. The settings, mostly on the west coast of Ireland and its islands, are vividly captured and powerfully drawn; Dillon evokes the mystery and the folklore and local legends handed down by generations of local inhabitants as well as domestic scenes of thatched cottages and Irish-speaking peasants with potatoes on the fire. Many of the stories focus on a male narrator and often a friend, who goes off on adventures defying all odds and adult prohibitions. Dillon maintains suspense and an aura of mystery as the young heroes face adventure after adventure. Her power as a storyteller is impressive, and these stories capture the young reader's attention. More than this, they focus on the concerns of their audience: they show children as heroes and problem solvers—children who weigh and make decisions about families and about community ethics, children who have strength of character and great fortitude but who face and overcome their natural fears.

Dillon's historical fiction for young readers, when it is set outside Ireland, is not quite as powerful as the tales she sets in the places she knows best. *The Shadow of Vesuvius* (1978) and *Living in Imperial Rome* (1974) are somewhat flat and perhaps a bit schoolbookish with cardboard characters. Even in *Children of Bach* (1992), although the story line is full of suspense, the characters and the settings lack the power and grip of her Irish books. Given the subject, Jewish children escaping from the Nazis in World War II Austria, Dillon hardly realizes the potential power of her prose and seems to minimize the dangers and terrors inherent in the situation. Compared with other children's books on the same subject, this one seems to use the Holocaust as a mere backdrop for a family story. In all, Dillon has written thirty-five books for children. Especially given her output, the quality of these books is impressive.

Dillon's adult fiction is not as impressive as her fiction for young adults and children. Her mystery *Death at Crane's Court* (1953) lacks the typical suspense and horror of the genre, although *Sent to His Account* (1954) and *Death in the Quadrangle* (1956) are somewhat better. *The Bitter Glass* (1959) is the first in a series of historical novels that merge traditional, romantic love stories with Irish political events. Here the engagement between an Irish Catholic and member of the gentry is set against the struggles between nationalists and the Black and Tans. The characterization is weak, and though the plot is tighter than that of *Blood Relations,* still it lacks power. *Blood Relations* (1977) is a rambling, episodic historical romance set against the background of the Easter rebellion. Dillon loses focus here, dismissing the most interesting of her characters, the heroine's father, Henry, by shipping him off to America and letting her heroine, and insipid and silly woman, Molly, take center stage with the heroes of 1916.

Her earlier novel *Across the Bitter Sea* (1973) was much more successful at merging the love story and the historical novel and was quite a blockbuster when first published. Alice, daughter of the tallywoman of a local, wealthy, Protestant landlord, marries the son of that landlord. But she is constantly torn between her affection for her husband, who is so good to her, and her romantic passion for Morgan, a patriot during the rebellion. The story is tightly constructed, and the political events are well integrated; however, the plot seems too pat when Alice's husband conveniently dies, leaving her free for her soul mate, Morgan.

Besides her fiction, Dillon has written plays and nonfiction. She edited *Modern Irish Literature* (1994), a book by her husband, Vivan Mercier, admirably organizing his extensive drafts and notes, though Mercier died with the project far from complete. Especially noteworthy is her book *Inside Ireland* (1982). Instead of the expected tour guide of the various countries, Dillon starts with her family history as representative of Irish history in general. She goes back to her Dillon and Plunkett ancestors and shows, through their lives, the major movement of Irish history from the end of the last century to the present. The book is informative, enjoyable, and eminently readable.

MARYANNE FELTER

WORKS: Children's books—*Midsummer Magic*. London: Macmillan, 1949; *The Lost Island*. London: Faber, 1952/New York: Funk & Wagnalls, 1954; *The San Sebastian*. London: Faber, [1953]/New York: Funk & Wagnalls, 1954; *The House on the Shore*. London: Faber, [1955]/New York: Funk & Wagnalls, 1956; *The Little Wild House*. London: Faber, 1955/New York: Criterion, [1957]; *The Island of Horses*. London: Faber/New York: Funk & Wagnalls, 1956; *Plover Hill*. London: Hamish Hamilton, 1957; *Aunt Bedelia's Cats*. London: Hamish Hamilton, 1957; *The Singing Cave*. London: Faber/New York: Funk & Wagnalls, 1959; *The Fort of Gold*. London: Faber, 1961/New York: Funk & Wagnalls, 1962; *King Big-Ears*. London: Faber, [1961]; *Pony and a Trap*. London: Hamish Hamilton, 1962; *The Cat's Opera*. London: Faber, [1962]/Indianapolis: Bobbs-Merrill, [1963]; *The Coriander*. London: Faber, 1963/New York: Funk & Wagnalls, [1964]; *A Family of Foxes*. London: Faber, 1963/New York: Funk & Wagnalls, [1964]; *The Sea Wall*. London: Faber/New York: Farrar, Straus & Giroux, [1965]; *The Lion Club*. London: Hamish Hamilton, 1966/New York: Duell, Sloan & Pearce, [1967]; *The Road to Dunmore*. London: Faber, 1966; *The Key*. London: Faber, 1967/"The Road to Dunmore" and "The Key" also published as *Two Stories*. New York: Meredith, [1968]; *The Cruise of the Santa Maria*. New York: Funk & Wagnalls, [1967]; *The Seals*. London: Faber/New York: Funk & Wagnalls, 1968; *Under the Orange Grove*. London: Faber/New York: Meredith, 1968; *A Herd of Deer*. London: Faber/New York: Funk & Wagnalls, 1969; *The Wise Man on the Mountain*. London: Hamish Hamilton, 1969/New York: Atheneum, [1970]; *The Voyage of Mael Duin*. London: Faber, [1969]; *The King's Room*. London: Hamish Hamilton, 1970; *The Five Hundred*. London: Hamish Hamilton, 1972; *Living in Imperial Rome*. London: Faber, 1974/Nashville: Thomas Nelson, 1976; *The Shadow of Vesuvius*. London: Faber/New York: Thomas Nelson, 1978; *Down in the World*. London: Hodder & Stoughton, 1983; *The Horse-Fancier*. Basingstoke: Macmillan, 1985; *The Seekers*. Basingstoke: Macmillan/New York: Scribner's, 1986; *The Island of Ghosts*. Basingstoke: Macmillan/New York: Scribner's, 1989; *Children of Bach*. Basingstoke: Macmillan, 1992. Adult Fiction—*Death at Crane's Court*. London: Faber, [1953]/New York: Walker, [1963]; *Sent to His Account*. London: Faber, [1954]/New York: Walker, 1966; *Death in the Quadrangle*. London: Faber, 1956/New York: Walker, 1965; *The Bitter Glass*. London: Faber, [1958]/New York: Appleton-Century-Crofts, 1959; *The Head of the Family*. London: Faber, [1960]; *Bold John Henebry*. London: Faber, [1965]; *Across the Bitter Sea*. London: Hodder & Stoughton/New York: Simon & Schuster, 1973; *Blood Relations*. New York: Simon &

Schuster, 1977/London: Hodder & Stoughton, 1978; *Wild Geese.* London: Hodder & Stoughton/ New York: Simon & Schuster, 1981; *Citizen Burke.* London: Hodder & Stoughton, 1984; *The Interloper.* London: Hodder & Stoughton, 1987. Plays—*Manna,* Radio Eireann, 1962; *A Page of History,* Abbey, 1966; *The Cat's Opera,* Abbey, 1981. Works in Irish—*An Choill bheo* (The Living Forest), Oifig an tSolathair, 1948; *Oscar agus an Coiste se nEasog* (Oscar and the Six-Weasle Coach), Oifig an tSolathair, 1952; *Ceol na Coille* (Song of the Forest), Oifig an tSolathair, 1955. Other—*The Hamish Hamilton Book of Wise Animals.* London: Hamish Hamilton, 1973; *Inside Ireland.* London: Hodder & Stoughton, 1982; ed., *Modern Irish Literature* by Vivian Mercier. Oxford: Clarendon, 1994.

DODDS, E[RIC] R[OBERTSON] (1893–1979), classicist, translator, and autobiographer. Born on July 25, 1893, at Bambridge, County Down, Dodds was the oldest son of Robert Dodds, headmaster of Banbridge Academy. Educated at Campbell College, Belfast, and University College, Oxford, Dodds became lecturer in classics at University College, Reading, from 1919 to 1924, being recommended by Gilbert Murray. From 1924 to 1936, he was regius professor of Greek at the University of Birmingham, and from 1936 to 1960 he was regius professor of Greek at Oxford. His family's Protestant and Unionist stance, he rejected. As a teacher, he influenced several generations at Birmingham and Oxford. Childhood reading of Walter Scott's novels stimulated his imagination, and this expansion of his childish awareness that history matters was somewhat spoiled by the plethora of "romantic nonsense, especially about women, which lingered uncriticized and was to be the ultimate source of many misjudgments in later life."

Dodds's *Missing Persons. An Autobiography* (1977) included revealing portraits of W. H. Auden and Louis MacNeice,* in addition to affecting insights into his own younger and matured self. His *Thirty-two Poems* (1929) included the memorable "When the Ecstatic Body Grips," although Dodds's analysis of the book is disparaging.

Dodds's most enduring work was as a classicist, translator, and analytical propagandist for the human values expressed by "pure learning." His *Select Passages Illustrative of Neo-Platonism* (2 vols., 1923, 1924) and *Proclus: Elements of Theology* (1933) are still dependable texts. As an editor of English writers, his reputation remains equally secure on the basis of his *Journals and Letters of Stephen MacKenna* (1936) and as literary executor of MacNeice. Dodds enabled MacKenna* to complete his English version of *Plotinus' Enneads* by introducing his pupil B. S. Page to MacKenna, the final volume being their joint translation. His *Plato: Gorgias. A Revised Text with Introduction and Commentary* (1959) is scrupulous, illuminating, and "a good read." Dodds was also much interested in psychic research. He died on April 8, 1979.

ALAN DENSON

PRINCIPAL WORKS: *Select Passages Illustrative of Neo-Platonism.* 2 vols. London: S.P.C.K./ New York: Macmillan, 1923 & 1924; *Thirty-two Poems.* London: Constable, [1929]; *Proclus: Elements of Theology.* Oxford: Clarendon, 1933; ed., *Journals and Letters of Stephen MacKenna.* London: Constable, 1936. (With a lengthy memoir); *The Greeks and the Irrational.* Berkeley: University of California, 1951; tr., *Plato: Gorgias. A Revised Text with Introduction and Commen-*

tary. Oxford: Clarendon, 1959; *Pagan and Christian in an Age of Anxiety.* Cambridge: Cambridge University Press, 1965; ed., *The Collected Poems of Louis MacNeice.* London: Faber, [1966]/New York: Oxford University Press, 1967; *The Ancient Concept of Progress and Other Essays on Greek Literature and Belief.* Oxford: Clarendon, 1973; *Missing Persons. An Autobiography.* Oxford: Clarendon, 1977. REFERENCES: An account of Dodds by D. A. Russell was published in *Proc. of the British Academy* 65 (1979), and by H. Lloyd Jones in *Gnomon,* iii (1980). Jones also has an article in *DNB 1971–1980,* pp. 245–247.

DOLMEN PRESS For the first edition of this dictionary, Liam Miller wrote the following entry for the Dolmen Press:

The Dolmen Press was founded by Liam and Josephine Miller in Dublin in 1951 as a small handpress to publish the works of Irish writers as well as works of Irish interest by writers from other countries. Since then, over 250 books have appeared under the Dolmen imprint, and the list, which has an emphasis on poetry, includes most of the foremost Irish writers of the present day. The scope of the list has broadened over the years so that the current titles include fiction, drama, poetry, biography, and bibliography.

Several Dolmen poetry titles have been choices or recommendations of the Poetry Book Society in London. Other awards to authors have included the AE Memorial Award, the Irish Arts Council Poetry Award, the Marten Toonder Award, the Kavanagh Award, the W. H. Smith Award, the Irish-American Cultural Foundation Award, and bursaries from the Arts Council of Great Britain and of Northern Ireland.

The Dolmen Press undertakes almost all of its own printing and, in addition, offers clients the services of its printing house. Although the press is small in size, it carries a distinguished range of typefaces and prints many kinds of letterpress work, especially bookwork, for publishers in Europe and America.

Illustration is often a feature of the Dolmen Press books. Such distinguished graphic artists as Tate Adams, Leonard Baskin, Jack Coughlin, S. W. Hayter, Louis le Brocquy, Elizabeth Rivers, and Anne Yeats are represented by cover design and illustrations. Several of the books have received design awards in Ireland. A comprehensive bibliography appeared in 1976 to mark the first twenty-five years of the press.

While most of the early editions from the press were limited, publications now include paperbacks, general books in hardcover, and limited editions. Several continuing series are published; among them are "Dolmen Editions," which are limited editions of the best Irish writings, often with illustrations, and "The Tower Series of Anglo-Irish Studies," which consists of essays published in conjunction with the Anglo-Irish Department in University College Dublin. An Irish Theatre series is devoted to the Irish theater and includes critical works and a documentary history of modern Irish drama. New Yeats Papers, studies of the poet's life, work, and influences, have been appearing since 1971.

Liam Miller died in Dublin in May 1987 at the age of sixty-three. He was a native of Mountrath, County Laois, and trained as an architect. He was also a director of the Lantern Theatre and a notable set designer. He was an authority on Yeats* and on Irish philately, on both of which subjects he published excellent books. He was probably most eminent, however, as a book designer, and his greatest achievements were probably the Roman Missal in 1974 and Thomas Kinsella's* translation of *The Tain* in 1969, with its striking illustrations by le Brocquy. In its last years, the press was in some financial difficulty, and it was dissolved with the death of its founder, its stock eventually being acquired by Colin Smythe, Ltd.* However, with the Cuala Press* and with Maunsel and Company,* it brought great distinction to Irish publishing.

REFERENCE: Miller, Liam, comp. *Dolmen XXV: An Illustrated Bibliography of the Dolmen Press 1951.* Dublin: Dolmen, 1976.

DONAGHY, JOHN LYLE (1902–1949), poet. Donaghy was born near Larne, County Antrim, on July 28, 1902. He was educated at Larne Grammar School, where he was a childhood friend of George Buchanan,* and at Trinity College, Dublin. He once acted with the Abbey* as "the Christ" in Lady Gregory's* *The Story Brought by Brigit,* and later he played Marlowe's Doctor Faustus in his own production at the Abbey. After his marriage, he completed his B.A. at Trinity and taught for several years in Ireland and England. He had two children, separated from his wife, and, as Dardis Clarke remarks, "had a nervous breakdown and for the rest of his life he was to have occasional visits to mental hospitals. . . . He returned to Ireland in the 1930s and lived in various small holdings in Wicklow, wrote poetry and contributed articles to various magazines. His meagre income from this pursuit was supplemented by his mother." He died on May 4, 1949, in Dublin.

He published, both as John Lyle Donaghy and as Lyle Donaghy, much fugitive verse and several slim volumes. Some critics believe that he could have developed into a significant talent; however, he was never able to harness an apparently terrific poetic ambition to an effective form. His *Primordia Caeca* (1927) is mystical in content, elevated in manner, and written in florid prose poetry. Its most ambitious poem, "The Pit," is a conversation on elemental questions between the author and Virgil, Dante, and Milton. The poems in *The Flute over the Valley* (1931) are much simpler, but they are also slack and metrically muddled with many flabby lines that exist merely to fill out a stanza scheme or to make up a rhyme. The poems in *The Blackbird* (1933) are mainly romantic descriptions of nature and apostrophes to love and God. The diction is hardly individual, but the rhyming verses are more controlled, and there is the occasional tight line in such poems as "The Heron," "The Falcon," or "Dreadnought." Nevertheless, even his *Selected Poems* (1939) contains many examples of the poet's inability to control his form. His longest and last book, *Wilderness Sings* (1942), abandons form almost entirely and is a nearly unreadable volume of ecstatic free verse and prose poetry, in which the syntax often disappears. Yet, if he wound up with this final, formless shout, he was occasionally capable of writing, as in "A Thought of Suicide," some very mordant lines indeed.

WORKS: *At Dawn above Aherlow: Poems.* Dublin: Cuala, 1926; *Primordia Caeca: Poems.* Dublin: Eason, 1927; *Ad Perennis Vitae Fontem.* Dublin: Minorca, 1928; *The Flute over the Valley: Antrim Song.* Larne: Inver, 1931; *The Blackbird, Songs of Inisfail.* Larne: Inver, 1933; *Into the Light, and Other Poems.* Dublin: Cuala, 1934; *Selected Poems.* Dublin: Orwell, 1939 (Tower Press Booklets, ser. 3, no. 6); *Wilderness Sings.* Dublin: Printed for the Author by Wood Printing Works,

1942. REFERENCES: Buchanan, George. "Lyle Donaghy: A Personal Note." *The Honest Ulsterman,* No. 63 (July/October 1979): 17–23; Clarke, Dardis. "A Neglected Poet." *Irish Times* (June 8, 1883): 8; "John Lyle Donaghy, 1902–1949, Memorial Number." *Rann,* No. 6 (Autumn 1949).

DONLEAVY, J[AMES] P[ATRICK] (1926–   ), novelist. Donleavy was born in Brooklyn, New York, on April 23, 1926. After World War II, he attended Trinity College, Dublin, and was one of the Bohemian group that gathered in the Georgian cellar known as the Catacombs. Other notable habitués were Brendan Behan,* Anthony Cronin,* and a rather legendary American named Gainor Christ, who was attending Trinity on the GI Bill and who became the model for the protagonist of Donleavy's first and most famous novel, *The Ginger Man* (1955). The book's hero, Sebastian Dangerfield, has much in common, in both eloquence and fecklessness, with John Osborne's angry young man Jimmy Porter in *Look Back in Anger.* Nevertheless, his story makes one of the most rowdy, raucous, vulgar, funny, and thrillingly written books about Dublin in the last forty years. *The Ginger Man* established its author's international reputation, but a lively stage version was withdrawn in Dublin in 1959 as a result of clerical pressure.

Donleavy's later novels are either moderately conventional or distinctly odd. Of the moderately conventional, *The Beastly Beatitudes of Balthazar B* (1968) is largely laid in Ireland, and the Darcy Dancer trilogy is almost wholly laid there. These books may be taken as representative of the best of Donleavy's later work. They are picaresque *Tom Jones*-like novels, but their exuberance, broad satire, and often effectively exaggerated comic scenes stamp them as inimitably Donleavy's. Another noticeable characteristic of his work is an overwhelming preoccupation with sex, which is often described in a tongue-in-cheek, apparent parody of the literary pornography of the Victorian age. *Leila* (1983), for instance, the second of his ambitious Darcy Dancer trilogy, is a fair example of the best of the later Donleavy. The writing retains its breezy cleverness. The comic details about the hero's moldering Big House are heaped up extravagantly but stay within distinct hailing distance of reality: the roof leaks, there are holes in the floor, and the whole place is overwhelmed with dry rot, rising damp, and unpaid bills. The lazy, slovenly, incompetent, dishonest, and—in the Irish sense—"cute" servants have a long tradition in Irish writing, which Donleavy's versions do not transcend but do not disgrace. Here, for instance, is the breakfast served by Darcy Dancer's kitchen maid:

My fingertips pressing into a thick smear of butter on the bottom of my tray as I reached to lift it. The cream sour that I poured on my porridge. Yolks fried solid on my eggs. And although congealed in their fat, at least my sausages weren't wrapped in hairs. But on lifting the cover to the pot, a dead summer mummified fly was on top of my raspberry jam.

This all approaches the stage-Irish, but it is still funny. On the debit side, the book is overlong and has less a plot than a narrative. Also, it is not about much, except possibly the hero's problems about sex, which seem expressed on a pretty adolescent level: "I shall burst my fly open with the present obelisk one sports." This and the descriptions of desirable women owe more to a Frank Harris*-like silliness than to literature.

One of the more eccentric of Donleavy's later fictions is *De Alfonce Tennis: The Superlative Game of Eccentric Champions, Its History, Accoutrements, Rules, Conduct and Regimen* (1984). About half of this quirky book is a facetious description of the rules and conduct of Donleavy's made-up game; the rest is a narrative with some lively writing and little characterization and is basically on the level of undergraduate humor.

That charge of puerility would seem applicable also to his occasional nonfictional books. For instance, *The Unexpurgated Code: A Complete Manual of Survival & Manners* (1975) is a collection of reflections ranging from half a line to three or four pages, upon such solid topics as Being Old, Religions, and Euthanasia. However, it is far from the excellence of Flaubert's *Dictionary of Received Ideas,* and his more usual topics are such peculiar preoccupations as Farting, Bodily Stench, Bad Breath and Toothpicks, Pimples and Black Head Squeezing, and Solitary Masturbation. Even a breezy style cannot raise this adolescent vulgarity to wit.

Donleavy has written two nonfictional books about Ireland. The more recent, *A Singular Country* (1989), presents a very limited view of the country, largely from such a position as on the back of a horse while fox hunting. The style is an intermittently amusing parody of colloquial speech, in which many paragraphs begin with "Ah," and even a couple of "bedads" and "begorrahs" are resorted to. His 1994 memoir *A History of the Ginger Man* discusses his own early days in Dublin, hobnobbing with Gainor Christ and Brendan Behan. In it, Donleavy comes across as a sort of Wild Irish Boy or Hibernian Hemingway, and there is a plethora of monumental drinking bouts and fistfights. Certainly, Donleavy has never lost the initial comic brilliance or the glittering prose style of *The Ginger Man,* but as a writer he has neither grown nor grown up.

He became an Irish citizen in 1967. He lives on the shores of Lough Owel near Mullingar, County Westmeath.

WORKS: *The Ginger Man.* Paris: Olympia, [1955]/London: Spearman, [1956]/revised, New York: McDowell, Obolensky, 1958/complete & unexpurgated edition, London: Corgi, 1963/New York: Delacorte, [1965]; *Fairy Tales of New York.* New York: Random House/Harmondsworth, Middlesex: Penguin, [1961]. (Play); *What They Did in Dublin with* The Ginger Man, *A Play.* New York: Random House/[London]: MacGibbon & Kee, [1961]; *A Singular Man.* Boston: Little, Brown, [1963]/London: Bodley Head, 1964. (Novel); *Meet My Maker the Mad Molecule.* Boston: Little, Brown, [1964]/London: Bodley Head, 1965. (Stories); *A Singular Man, A Play.* London: Bodley Head, 1965; *The Saddest Summer of Samuel S.* New York: Delacorte, [1966]/London: Eyre & Spottiswoode, 1967. (Novel); *The Beastly Beatitudes of Balthazar B.* New York: Delacorte, [1968]. (Novel); *The Onion Eaters.* New York: Delacorte/London: Eyre & Spottiswoode, 1971. (Novel); *The Plays of J. P. Donleavy.* [New York]: Delacorte, [1972]; *A Fairy Tale of New York.* London: Eyre Methuen/[New York: Delacorte/S. Laurence, [1973]. (Novel); *The Saddest Summer of Samuel S.* New York: Delacorte, 1972/London: Penguin, 1974. (Play); *The Unexpurgated Code: A Complete Manual of Survival & Manners.* New York: Delacorte/London: Wildwood House, 1975; *The Des-*

tinies of Darcy Dancer, Gentleman. New York: Delacorte, [1977]/London: Allen Lane, 1978. (Novel); *Schultz.* New York: Delacorte/London: Allen Lane, 1980. (Novel); *Leila: Further in the Destinies of Darcy Dancer, Gentleman.* New York: Delacorte/London: Allen Lane, 1983. (Novel); *De Alfonce Tennis: The Superlative Game of Eccentric Champions, Its History, Accoutrements, Rules, Conduct, and Regimen.* London: Weidenfeld & Nicolson, 1984/New York: Dutton, 1985; *Ireland: In All Her Sins and in Some of Her Graces.* London: Joseph/New York: Viking, 1986; *Are You Listening Rabbi Low.* London: Viking, 1987/New York: Atlantic Monthly, 1988. (Novel); *A Singular Country.* Peterborough: Ryan, 1989/New York: Norton, 1990. (Nonfiction); *That Darcy, That Dancer, That Gentleman.* London: Viking, 1990/New York: Atlantic Monthly, 1991. (Novel); *A History of the Ginger Man.* London: Viking, 1994. (Memoir).   REFERENCES: Lawrence, Seymour. "Adventures of J. P. Donleavy: or, How I Lost My Job & Made My Way to Greater Glory." *Paris Review* 116 (Fall 1990): 187–201; Masinton, Charles G. *J. P. Donleavy: The Style of His Sadness and Humor.* Bowling Green, Ohio: Popular, 1975; Sharma, R. K. *Isolation and Protest: A Case Study of J. P. Donleavy's Fiction.* New Delhi: Ajanta, 1983.

DONNELLY, CHARLES [PATRICK] (1914–1937), poet and political activist. Donnelly was born on July 10, 1914, near Dungannon in County Tyrone. In 1917, his parents moved to Dundalk, where his father opened a greengrocer's shop, bought land, and prospered and where Donnelly received his early education from the Christian Brothers. After the death of his mother in 1927, the family moved to Dublin, and in 1931 Donnelly entered University College, Dublin, as an arts student. He became a friend of Donagh MacDonagh* and Niall Sheridan,* read widely, and wrote poems. He failed, however, to pass his first-year examinations, for he had become a Marxist, an idealistic political activist, a member of the republican Congress, and a contributor to its newspaper. Arrested in January 1935 for picketing, he was jailed for a month in Mountjoy and on his release left for London. There, he prolifically wrote stories, poems, reviews, and articles on history, economics, and politics for various left-wing magazines and papers. An opponent of fascism, he fought in the Irish section of the International Brigade in the Spanish civil war. Shortly before he was killed in battle on February 27, 1937, a fellow soldier observed him:

We ran for cover. Charlie Donnelly, Commander of the Irish company is crouched behind an olive tree. He has picked up a bunch of olives from the ground and is squeezing them. I hear him say something quietly between a lull in machine-gun fire: "Even the olives are bleeding."

This ability to find the striking phrase is the best quality in Donnelly's small body of verse. The fourteen poems printed in his biography by Joseph O'Connor* are in free verse, and about half of them are about death. They were promising work.

REFERENCE: Joseph O'Connor. *Even the Olives Are Bleeding: The Life and Times of Charles Donnelly.* Dublin: New Island Books, [1992]. (Contains also a selection of Donnelly's poems and a bibliography of fugitive material, letters, and unpublished manuscripts).

DONNELLY, NEIL (1946–   ), playwright. Donnelly was born in Tullamore, County Offaly, on June 21, 1946. He studied with the Christian Brothers in

Tullamore and took a degree in education from Saint Mary's College in London. He has worked as a teacher in London on both the primary and secondary levels. As a playwright, he has written scripts for the stage and radio (*Rotunda Blue, Upstarts, Flying Home,* and *The Loop*), and he has also written several screenplays (*No Prisoners, Brown Lord of the Mountain,* and *The Big Buck*). His first dramatic work, *Dust,* was produced in New York and Farnhaun in 1972, but he made his reputation as a playwright writing for the Abbey Theatre* and the Peacock Theatre. In fact, he is part of a group of playwrights known as the "Peacock Playwrights"—a group that includes Frank McGuinness,* Graham Reid,* Bernard Farrell,* and Martin Boylan*—whose work is particularly suited to the smaller, intimate stage of the Peacock and whose writings were cultivated by the then-Abbey script editor Sean McCarthy and the then-Abbey artistic director Joe Dowling. In 1993, he was writer in residence with the Mayo County Council. In 1994, he began a tenure as "Ansbacher Writer-in-Association" with the Abbey Theatre. He was also cofounder in 1973 of the Wheeles Theatre-in-Education (TIE) Company. Based in Hertfordshire, Wheeles was one of the first TIE companies in Great Britain. He served on the board of Shane Connaughton's* the Irish Company, a group dedicated to performing Irish plays in England. Between 1984 and 1991, Donnelly served as director of the Playwrights and Actors Company, which developed the "One-Act Play Lunchtime Series" at the Gaiety Theatre in 1985 and at the Peacock in 1988. He has directed two productions, *Goodbye Carraroe* in the Peacock in 1989 and *Can't Stand Up, for Falling Down* at the Bank of Ireland Arts Centre in 1993. He received bursaries from the Arts Council in 1981 and 1986.

Donnelly's numerous productions for the National Theatre include *The Duty Master* (Peacock, 1995), *Goodbye Carraroe* (Peacock, 1989), *The Reel McCoy* (Peacock, 1989), *The Silver Dollar Boys* (Peacock, 1981; Abbey, 1986), *Chalk Farm Blues* (Peacock, 1984), *Flying Home* (Peacock, 1983), and *Upstarts* (Peacock, 1980). Outside the National Theatre, Donnelly's work has appeared at the Olympia during the Dublin Theatre Festival, in Belfast, in New York, in Scotland, and in Australia. The TEAM Theatre Company performed *Blindfold,* a play commemorating the twenty-fifth anniversary of Amnesty International. *Blindfold* explores issues of human rights and personal and societal responsibility for the rights of others.

Of his published work, *The Silver Dollar Boys* won the Harvey Award for best play of 1981–1982. It considers the school life and family influences on a young boy at a Christian Brothers school in the Irish Midlands and how those influences led to his fate as a terrorist bank robber. Originally expressionistic in style, the play was revised to its advantage into a largely naturalistic piece for the Peacock. The revised work more fully develops the supporting characters and consequently lends depth to the protagonist. *Upstarts,* Donnelly's most widely staged piece, is also set in the Midlands and explores life in a Gardai Station. It traces the activities of three garda. One is a new recruit earnestly pursuing his duties with a diligence not always appropriate and not always welcome by his fellow officers. Another is a middle-aged officer who in his youth served as part of President Kennedy's Honor Guard and as an undercover operative on the border. Being abducted and almost shot by the Irish Republican Army (IRA) have left him damaged in a way that lends his activities a flavor of harsh and unexpected violence, mixed with a sharp wit and a desperate faith. The sergeant, having seen the Ireland in which he grew up disappear, prepares to emigrate with his family to Australia and a job as a custodian. He tries desperately to avoid controversy and trouble before his departure.

In addition, Donnelly takes a particular pride in his educational videos. These works include *Lifestyles,* a series of six dramas commissioned by the Health Education Bureau in 1983; *Just a Little Virus,* dealing with the AIDS dilemma; and *The Man in New York,* filmed in 1994 as part of a Health Education Project.

BERNARD McKENNA

WORKS: *The Plays of Neil Donnelly.* [Dublin: Co-op Books, 1982]. (Contains *The Silver Dollar Boys* and *Station Master*); *Upstarts.* Dublin: Co-op Books, 1982.   REFERENCE: O'Toole, Fintan. "Today: Contemporary Irish Theatre—The Illusion of Tradition." *Ireland and the Arts.* Tim Pat Coogan, ed. London: Namara, 1983, pp. 132–137.

DONOGHUE, DENIS (1928–   ), literary critic. Donoghue was born at Tullow, County Carlow, on December 1, 1928, the son of a sergeant of police. He grew up in Warrenpoint, County Down, and was educated at University College, Dublin, where he eventually became professor of modern English and American literature. In 1980, he became Henry James Professor at New York University, and in 1989 he received an honorary degree from UCD. He was undoubtedly the first modern Irish literary critic of international stature, and his thoughtful and often lengthy essays frequently appear in such publications as *The New York Review of Books,* the *New York Times Book Review,* the *London Review of Books,* and the *Times Literary Supplement.* A typical collection of such essays would be *We Irish: Essays on Irish Literature and Society* (1986). Although he has little to say about O'Casey's* and Synge's* letters other than that O'Casey was combative and Synge was glum, more complicated topics such as Yeats* and Joyce* and Austin Clarke* show him at his superb best, raising new ideas and drawing on an immense reading. His writing probably appeals more to the academic than to the generally cultured mind: for instance, his prose can produce a delightful remark like, "Reading AE's poems is like being inside a feather mattress"; however, his prose can also grow pedantic and spoil the previous simile by adding its unnecessary explanation of "embarrassed by texture absurdly in excess of structure and ossature." Even his memoir of growing up, *Warrenpoint* (1990), shows this ivory-tower quality, for Donoghue is less a raconteur remembering a place, incidents, and people than he is an essayist reflecting on Irish history, Wittgenstein, Wordsworth, Leibniz, Eliot, Emmanuel Levinas, and a host of other topics from his well-stocked mind. As a critic of books and society, he is probably more an F. R. Leavis than an Edmund Wilson, but he has become for Irish literature something of an intellectual conscience.

He is the father of Emma Donoghue,* the novelist.

PRINCIPAL WORKS: *The Third Voice: Modern British and American Verse Drama.* Princeton, N.J.: Princeton University Press, 1959; ed., *The Integrity of Yeats.* Cork: Mercier, 1964/Philadelphia: R. West, 1976; ed., with J. R. Mulryne, *An Honoured Guest: New Essays on W. B. Yeats.* London: Edward Arnold, 1965; *Connoisseurs of Chaos: Ideas of Order in Modern American Poetry.* London: Faber, 1966/New York: Columbia University Press, 1984; *The Ordinary Universe: Soundings in Modern Literature.* London: Faber, 1968; ed., *Swift Revisited.* Cork: Mercier, 1968; *Emily Dickinson.* Minneapolis: University of Minnesota Press, 1969. (Monograph); *Jonathan Swift: A Critical Introduction.* London: Cambridge University Press, 1969; ed., *Jonathan Swift, a Critical Anthology.* Harmondsworth, Middlesex: Penguin, 1971; *Yeats.* London: Fontana, 1971; ed., *W. B. Yeats Memoirs: Autobiography and First Draft Journal.* London: Macmillan, 1972; *Thieves of Fire.* London: Faber, 1973/New York: Oxford University Press, 1974; *Imagination, the Twenty-Fifth W. P. Ker Memorial Lecture.* Glasgow: University of Glasgow Press, 1975; ed., *Seven American Poets from MacLeish to Nemerov.* Minneapolis: University of Minnesota Press, 1975; *The Sovereign Ghost: Studies in Imagination.* Berkeley: University of California Press, 1976/London: Faber, 1978; ed., *Poems of R. P. Blackmur.* Princeton, N.J.: Princeton University Press, 1977; *Ferocious Alphabets.* London: Faber, 1981/New York: Columbia University Press, 1984; *The Arts without Mystery: Reith Lectures.* London: BBC, 1983; *We Irish: Essays on Irish Literature and Society.* Brighton: Harvester, 1986/New York: Knopf, 1986; *Reading America: Essays on American Literature.* New York: Knopf, 1987; *England, Their England: Commentaries on English Language & Literature.* New York: Knopf, 1988; *Warrenpoint.* New York: Braziller, 1990/London: Jonathan Cape, 1991.

DONOGHUE, EMMA (1969–   ), novelist and playwright. Donoghue was born in Dublin, the eighth and youngest child of the critic Denis Donoghue* and his wife, Frances. Emma Donoghue studied arts at University College, Dublin, obtaining a double first in her B.A. and winning a scholarship to Cambridge. Her history, *Passions between Women: British Lesbian Culture, 1668–1801,* appeared in 1993; and her play, *I Know My Own Heart,* based on the Regency diaries of Anne Lister, was produced in both Cambridge and Dublin.

Stir Fry (1994), her first novel, tells the story of Maria, a country girl, who comes to UCD and shares a flat with two older students, whom she gradually realizes are lovers. Each of the flatmates falls for Maria, and she, after having flirted with boys, falls in love with one of them. The book is a touching read, and Maria has an appealing wit, especially in the use of cooking imagery. The other characters are well realized: Maria's country parents, other students and friends, and nosy Aunt Thelma—although the reader expected more of her unexpected visit to the flat. There is a good sense of place, and the Belfield campus particularly comes to life. The sex is all the better for being underplayed, and the reader is so in sympathy with Maria's youthful emotional confusion that the book works polemically as well.

Her 1995 novel, *Hood,* is disappointing. Pen, a primary school teacher, has lost her lover, Cara, in a car crash. Although both girls are well realized, almost the whole novel looks backward to this passionate but one-sided affair. Pen's numb grief is totally believable; she thinks constantly of her lost lover, trying to come to terms with loss and semiunrequited love. The trouble is that the reader is made into a voyeur by endless sexual reenactments. If grief is a private thing, so is sex. Also, some of the details are tasteless, such as smelling soiled underwear and the lovers drinking each other's menstrual blood. Further, the main action is in the past, and so the present plot is weak. The reader, not being involved in an action, merely feels manipulated. The author seems bashing us over the head with her message that lesbian life is not a cosy knitting club but much more physically sexual than the tame heterosexual world. If so, there must be a more unpolemical way of expressing it.

There are good things about the novel: the drab primary school world is utterly believable, and the insight into lesbian society enlightening. There is a lovely scene at the end when Pen brings Cara's clothes to a memorial service, and people take what they want to remember her by. Mr. Wall, Cara's father, is a touching character who finally totally accepts Pen as his daughter's lover, while Pen just cannot tell her own mother. On this final page, the novel finally makes a moving plea for sexual tolerance and compassion. Emma Donoghue is a considerable talent, which she probably now needs to stretch by writing a greater book about a wider society.

MARY ROSE CALLAGHAN

WORKS: *Stir Fry.* London: Hamish Hamilton, [1994]; *Passion between Women: British Lesbian Culture 1668–1801.* London: Scarlet, 1994; *Hood.* London: Hamish Hamilton, [1995].

DONOHOE, M. J. (1932–), short story writer.

WORK: *So So Stories.* New York: Vantage, 1989.

DONOVAN, GERARD (fl. 1990s), poet.

WORKS: *Columbus Rides Again.* Galway: Salmon, 1992; *Kings and Bicycles.* Dublin: Salmon, 1995.

DONOVAN, KATIE (1962–), poet. Katie Donovan spent her early youth on a farm in County Wexford. She studied at University College, Dublin, and at the University of California, Berkeley, and she now works as a journalist for the *Irish Times.* The pieces in her collection, *Watermelon Man* (1993), should perhaps be called lyrical prose rather than poetry. They are straightforward, with a clarity enhanced by an often striking use of metaphor. The lines are very short, generally from two to no more than eight syllables, and they are arranged in stanzas of varying lengths even in the same poem. For instance, "Night Music" has a stanza of five lines, then one of eight, another of five, one of seven, and one of ten. Apparently, the stanza lengths are determined not by formal pattern but by content. The punctuation is individual rather than conventional but does not interfere with the sense. There does not appear any even amorphous rhythmical pattern. The content ranges from descriptions of places, to sex, to a pious micturation on Queen Medbh's cairn.

Her 1994 anthology, *Ireland's Women,* edited with A. Norman Jeffares* and Brendan Kennelly,* was looked forward to as an antidote to the small representation of women in *The Field Day Anthology.* However, the briefness of the many snippets made the volume more advertisement than literature.

WORKS: *Irish Women Writers: Marginalised by Whom?* Dublin: Raven Arts, 1988. (Essay); ed., with Brendan Kennelly. *Dublines.* [Newcastle upon Tyne]: Bloodaxe, 1993; ed., with A. Norman Jeffares & Brendan Kennelly. *Ireland's Women: Writings Past and Present.* [London]: Kyle Cathie, [1994].

DORCEY, MARY (1950–   ), short story writer and poet. Dorcey was born in Dublin and has lived in France, England, America, and Japan and now lives in County Kerry. An activist in the Irish feminist movement for many years, she is a landmark figure in modern Irish literary history, in being one of the first writers to acknowledge being lesbian and to write candidly about the lesbian experience. Since the 1980s, when her work first appeared, several other women have followed suit, but she must be accredited with taking the initial, courageous step.

Her collection of short stories, *A Noise from the Woodshed* (1989), which won the Rooney Prize for a first work of fiction, consists of story about female experiences and especially about female lesbian experience. The most successful story, however, is "The Husband," which recounts the coming out of a woman from the point of view of the man who is still in love with her. It is a compassionate and beautifully written story. Its main strength is that, by using the persona of the husband as the main voice of the tale, Dorcey establishes an artistic distance between herself and her subject.

Several of the stories are too loosely constructed to achieve narrative integrity. They have, however, many other excellent qualities. The vocabulary is well chosen, rich, and sensuous, particularly when the natural world is described. Sexual love is portrayed with extraordinary precision and joyful exuberance. The raw material and themes of the stories are important in their revolutionary novelty, and for that reason this book will always have a place in any history of modern Irish literature. In a way, the very strength of the work is also its weakness: many of the stories indulge in polemic on behalf of feminism and lesbianism. While this is understandable and perhaps necessary from an ideological point of view, it can be artistically destructive.

Dorcey's poetry shares the virtues of her short stories. Her themes are lesbian love, nature, women's lives, and sexual politics. She is at her best in the nature and love lyrics. As with the stories, the author's ardent feminist allegiances occasionally express themselves too bluntly and prosaically, to the detriment of poems like "Coming Home" from *Kindling* (1982). A poem such as "Colonised Minds," from the same volume, indicates, however, that Dorcey is well aware of the complexity of feminism and human nature and can express this poetically and subtly.

In both short stories and poetry, Dorcey exhibits an acute sensitivity to language and a fundamental literary sensibility. Above all, she has something new and important to say.

                                                        EILÍS NÍ DHUIBHNE

WORKS: *Kindling.* London: Onlywomen, 1982. (Poetry); *A Noise from the Woodshed: Short Stories.* London: Onlywomen, 1989. *Moving into the Space Cleared by Our Mothers.* Galway:

Salmon, 1991. (Poetry); *The River That Carries Me.* [Galway]: Salmon, [1995]. (Poetry). REFERENCE: Quinn, Antoinette. "Speaking of the Unspoken: The Poetry of Mary Dorcey." *Colby Quarterly* 28 (December 1992): 227–238.

DORGAN, THEO (1953–   ), poet. Dorgan was born in Cork and received a B.A. in English and philosophy and an M.A. in English from University College, Cork, where he later tutored and lectured. He has been the literature officer with the Triskel Arts Centre in Cork and the director of the Cork Film Festival from 1986 to 1989. At present, he is director of Poetry Ireland, the national poetry organization, and the presenter of *Inprint,* a books program on RTÉ radio. He frequently broadcasts on BBC radio and contributes to Irish-language television for RTÉ. He was editor of the 1993 Thomas Davis lecture series on contemporary Irish poetry on RTÉ radio, which was published as *Irish Poetry after Kavanagh.* He has published two poetry pamphlets, *Slow Air* (1975) and *A Moscow Quartet* (1989), and two collections of poems, *The Ordinary House of Love* (1991) and, *Rosa Mundi* (1995).

The poems in *The Ordinary House of Love* are intimate, thoughtful, and low-key, yet not without a confident, rhythmic energy. Dorgan is one of the least showy poets on the contemporary scene in Ireland. He avoids gimmickry and rhetorical stridency, but his quiet and confident voice impressively plumbs the depths of friendship and love, which are among his favorite themes. Eileen Battersby in the *Irish Times* praised his "instinctive sharpness of phrase"; James Liddy* in *Éire-Ireland* praised his "acuteness of eye"; and Hugh McFadden in *Salmon* noted his clarity of vision. The poet's control of the speaking voice was admired, and Eamon Grennan* in *Poetry Ireland Review* thought that the "chanting inevitability, the repetition of sounds" produced "a species of spoken ritual." It has also been suggested that Dorgan's poetry demonstrates a wide range of influence, including Auden, Graves, and Valentin Iremonger,* although at his best his voice is very much his own.

JONATHAN ALLISON

WORKS: *The Ordinary House of Love.* [Galway]: Salmon, [1991]; *Rosa Mundi.* [Galway]: Salmon, [1995]. REFERENCE: Donovan, Katie. "Wheeling, dealing, dreaming in poetry," *Irish Times* (November 23, 1995).

DOUGLAS, JAMES (1929–   ), playwright and fiction writer. Douglas was born in Bray, County Wicklow, on July 4, 1929, and after school became an electrician. His first produced play, *North City Traffic Straight Ahead,* was directed by Alan Simpson for the 1961 Theatre Festival. In the 1963 Theatre Festival, the musical *Carrie* was based on one of his stories. In the 1964 Festival, his *The Ice Goddess* was produced at the Gate,* and in 1970 his *The Savages* was produced at the Eblana and, later, off-off Broadway. His *Time Out of School* won the O. Z. Whitehead Award for one-act plays; and his *What Is the Stars?,* written in collaboration with Robert Hogan, won the final Irish Life Award. That last play was a study of a playwright resembling Sean O'Casey,* and its award was rescinded when O'Casey's widow threatened a lawsuit. He has written frequently for television and devised and spent twenty-six painful weeks writing the serial "The Riordans," which remained for about twenty years the most popular drama on Irish television and radio. Some of his other television plays include *The Bomb, The Hollow Field, How Long Is Kissing Time?,* and *Babbi Joe,* which appeared off-off Broadway in an expanded stage adaptation in 1978. His short stories have appeared in many Irish literary periodicals but have not been collected.

Douglas' first two plays, *North City Traffic* and *The Ice Goddess,* have a tersely distinctive style that seems mannered upon the page but can be most effective upon the stage. Beginning with *The Savages,* this stylized simplicity begins to change to a fuller, more realistic dialogue, and in his recent work he has allowed his rhetorical range to expand enormously. His first long stage plays are about defeat, disillusionment, weltschmerz, and anguish. Only their solid theatrical sense keeps them from being depressingly bleak. His recent work contains, however, much comedy and even farce. Similarly, his early short stories were generally glumly contemporary and powerfully brackish, but in 1993 he published in collaboration a comic historical novel entitled *Murder at the Abbey Theatre.* This is a semifictional re-creation of the events surrounding the riots over J. M. Synge's* *The Playboy of the Western World* in 1907. Among its principal characters are versions of Synge, W. B. Yeats,* Lady Gregory,* Oliver Gogarty,* and Joseph Holloway.* Douglas's portions of the narrative are very effective. Most of his other recent work has been in radio drama.

WORKS: *The Bomb.* Dixon, Calif.: Proscenium, 1966. (One-act play); *The Ice Goddess,* in *Seven Irish Plays, 1946–1964,* R. Hogan, ed. Minneapolis: University of Minnesota Press, 1967; *North City Traffic Straight Ahead.* Dixon, Calif.: Proscenium, 1968; *The Savages.* Newark, Del.: Proscenium, 1979; as Robert James, *The Writers' Trilogy,* comprising *There Are Joys, What Is the Stars?,* and *Cast a Cold Eye,* in *Journal of Irish Literature* 10 (January, May, and September 1981); "Catalogue" in *4 Irish Plays.* Newark, Del.: Proscenium, 1983. (One-act play); "The Old Markers Don't Work Anymore." *George Spelvin's Theatre Book* 5 (Fall 1983). (Radio play); as Robert James, *The Wild Turkey* and *The Balloon Factory,* in *George Spelvin's Theatre Book* 6 (Fall 1984); "James Douglas & Radio Drama," comprising his essay "Radio Drama" and his radio play "Cross Words." *Journal of Irish Literature* 19 (January 1990); "Indigo Days," radio play. *Journal of Irish Literature* 20 (January 1991); *Murder at the Abbey Theatre,* novel with Robert Hogan. Dublin: Moytura, [1993].

DOWLING, RICHARD (1846–1898), journalist, humorist, and novelist. Dowling was born in Clonmel on June 3, 1846. He wrote for *The Nation,* edited the comic periodical *Zozimus,* and wrote for *Ireland's Eye,* before going to London and writing for *The Illustrated Sporting and Dramatic News* and editing his own comic paper, *Yorick.* He deserves some contemporary attention, for he had a good comic talent and wrote with fluency. His chief work of fiction is *The Mystery of Killard,* which is in a mordant vein. He died in 1898.

WORKS: *The Mystery of Killard,* 3 vols. London, 1879/London: Tinsley, 1884; *The Sport of Fate.* 3 vols. London: Tinsley, 1880; *Under St. Paul's.* 3 vols. London: Tinsley, 1880; *The Weird*

Sisters, 3 vols. London: Tinsley, 1880; *The Duke's Sweetheart.* 3 vols. London: Tinsley, 1881; *The Husband's Secret.* 3 vols. London: Tinsley, 1881; *A Sapphire Ring, and Other Stories.* 3 vols. London: Tinsley, 1882; *Sweet Inisfail.* 3 vols. London: Tinsley, 1882; *The Last Call.* 3 vols. London: Tinsley, 1884; *On the Embankment.* London: Tinsley, 1884; *The Hidden Flame.* 3 vols. London: Tinsley, 1885; *Fatal Bonds.* 3 vols. London: Ward & Downey, 1886; *The Skeleton Key.* London: Ward & Downey, 1886; *Tempest-Driven.* 3 vols. London: Tinsley, 1886; *With the Unhanged.* London: Swan Sonnenschein, 1887; *Miracle Gold.* 3 vols. London: Ward & Downey, 1888; *Ignorant Essays.* New York: Appleton, 1888; *Indolent Essays.* London: Ward & Downey, 1889; *An Isle of Surrey.* 3 vols. London: Ward & Downey, 1889; *The Crimson Chair, and Other Stories.* London: Ward & Downey, 1891; *Catmur's Caves; or, the Quality of Mercy.* London: A. & C. Black, 1892; *While London Sleeps.* London: Ward & Downey, 1895; *Old Corcoran's Money.* London: Chatto & Windus, 1897; *A Baffling Quest.* 3 vols. London: Ward & Downey, n.d.; *Below Bridge.* London: Ward & Downey, n.d.; "Letters to a Young Writer." *Cornhill Magazine, NS* 15 (1903): 80–86; *Zozimus Papers.* New York: Kennedy, 1909. (as Marcus Fell): *London Town: Sketches of London Life and Character.* 3 vols. London: Tinsley, 1880. (as Emmanuel Kirk): *On Babies and Ladders. Essays on Things in General.* London: Hotten, [1873]; *School Board Essays.* London: Ward & Downey, 1888.

DOWNEY, EDMUND (1856–1937), fiction writer and publisher. Downey was born in Waterford on July 24, 1856, the son of a shipowner and broker. He was educated locally and went to London in 1878 and worked in the offices of Tinsley, the publisher. He became a partner in the publishing firm of Ward and Downey but retired from it in 1890. In 1894, he formed his own firm of Downey and Company, which published many of his own sea stories and Irish tales, which he often wrote under the pseudonym of F. L. Allen. In 1906, he became editor of the *Waterford News,* and he died in Waterford on February 11, 1937. Downey's Irish stories are broadly brogued and whimsical, for instance, this typical passage from "From Portlaw to Paradise," a story about how an Irishman squeezes into Heaven:

He reeled off his sins, mortial an' vanyial, to the priest by the yard, an' begor he felt mighty sorrowful intirely whin he thought what a bad boy he'd been, an' what a hape of quare things he'd done in his time—though, as I've said before, he was a dacent little man in his way, only, you see, bein' so close to the other side of Jordan, he tuk an onaisy view of all his sayin's and doin's.

Nevertheless, Sean O'Faolain* called Downey's *Clashmore* (1903) "a pleasant book . . . so authentic that despite the passage of time . . . it sounds as fresh today as when it was written." *The Merchant of Killogue* (1894) is a more serious effort and suggests that Downey, if he had not succumbed to entertaining, might have been a substantial novelist.

WORKS: *Anchor-Watch Yarns.* 2 vols. London: Tinsley, 1883; *The Land Smeller, and Other Yarns.* London: Ward, Downey, 1893; *The Merchant of Killogue: A Munster Tale.* London: Heinemann, 1894; *Charles Lever. His Life in His Letters.* 2 vols. Edinburgh & London: William Blackwood, 1903; *Clashmore.* London: Simpkin, Marshall, 1903; *The Brass Ring.* London: Simpkin, Marshall, 1904; *Dorothy Tuke: A Story of the Sea.* London: Hurst & Blackett, 1905; *Twenty Years Ago: A Book of Anecdote Illustrating Literary Life in London. . . .* London: Hurst & Blackett, 1905; *Dunleary. Humours of a Munster Town.* London: Sampson Low, [1911]; *The Story of Waterford.* Waterford: Waterford News Printing Works, 1914. (Nonfiction); *Waterford: An Illustrated Guide.*

Waterford: Waterford News, 1915; *Waterford's Bridges.* Waterford: Waterford News, [ca. 1923]; *Morrissey.* London: John Lane, 1924. As F. L. Allen: *Through Green Glasses.* London: Ward & Downey, 1887; *The Voyage of the Ark.* London: Ward & Downey, 1888; *From the Green Bog.* London: Ward & Downey, 1889; *Captain Lanagan's Log.* London: Ward & Downey, 1891; *The Round Tower of Babel.* London: Downey, 1891; *Green as Grass.* London: Chatto & Windus, 1892; *Ballybeg Junction.* London: Downey, 1895; *The Little Green Man.* [London]: Downey, [1895]. (Fairy tale); *Pinches of Salt.* London: Downey, 1896; *London's Past.* London: Downey, [1900]; *Glimpses of English History.* London: Downey, 1901.

DOWNING, ELLEN MARY (1828–1869), poet. Downing was the daughter of the resident medical officer at Cork Fever Hospital and was born on March 19, 1828. Her parents, especially her mother, gifted their child with a love of literature. She was an especially delicate child, plagued by shyness and an intensely nervous temperament. She began to compose poetry orally as a young child. In her midteens, she became an avid reader of *The Nation,** with a particular fondness for the ballads and lyrics it contained. Thomas Davis* and Denis Florence MacCarthy* were among her favorite writers. Her first poem appeared on May 10, 1845, in *The Nation*'s "Answers to Correspondents" section, under the pseudonym of Kate. She subsequently used a variety of pseudonyms: Kate, Mary, Ellen, or her initials, E.M.P.D. As a result of her poetic success in *The Nation,* she was involved to an undetermined extent with one of the Young Ireland writers, probably Joseph Brennan. Their relationship apparently ended prior to his transportation for political activities.

Downing decided to stop writing for *The Nation* around 1847, and her final contribution appeared in the New Year's Day 1848 edition. Thereafter, her poetry appeared chiefly in the *United Irishman.* In the spring of 1849, her health failed, and she visited a relative at the North Presentation Convent, Cork, while recuperating. By July 1849, she had expressed her desire for a nun's life and chose Mary Alphonsus as her convent name. Her poetry made a corresponding shift from the nationalistic to the devotional at this time. She became a novice on October 14, 1849, but was deemed unfit within a year, due to a mysterious illness characterized by periods of total physical paralysis lasting for weeks. Then a sudden recovery would occur, and she would return to full mobility. Her precarious health caused her to leave the convent in the spring of 1851, but she continued to use her religious name as she became a member of the Third Order of St. Dominic, living as a Dominican Tertiary.

By December 1868, she entered Mercy Hospital when her paralysis became permanent, with light and sound now unbearable to her. An untitled poem, beginning "Deep in the shadow of my room," records her physical and mental state shortly before her death, which occurred on January 27, 1869:

> What a fierce torment she can be
> Imagination proves to me,
> Who but her hideous nightmares see.

Words, thoughts, and deeds that once seemed good,
Have now become a monster brood
Of ills, too clearly understood.

Sharp, fiery pains like arrows fly,
And as they strike in passing by,
I hear my own affrighted cry!

Yet, Lord! through all how faith can see
That every blow is struck by Thee,
And struck in changeless love to me.

Downing was considered one of the finest women poets of *The Nation*. Passionate in her political beliefs and frequently building her poems on Irish folklore, she was a formidable voice for nationalism. Her political poems were published as single submissions to periodicals. Her later devotional poetry, written with children and converts in mind, was collected in volume form.

                                                                ANNE COLMAN

WORKS: *Voices of the Heart.* Most Rev. J. P. Leahy, Bishop of Dromore, ed. Dublin, 1868/ revised and enlarged. Dublin: Gill, 1881; *Novenas and Meditations.* Dr. Leahy, ed. Dublin, 1879; *Poems for Children.* Dublin, 1881. REFERENCES: Anton, Brigitte. "Women of the *Nation.*" *History Ireland* 1 (Autumn 1993): 34–37; Cumming, G. F. "Mary of the *Nation.*" *Irish Rosary* 28 (1924): 649–655; Ghall, Sean (pseudonym). "An Irish Woman-Poet." *United Irishman* (March 15, 1902): 7/(March 22, 1902): 6–7/(March 29, 1902): 7/(April 5, 1902): 6–7/(April 12, 1902): 6–7; Markham, Thomas. *Ellen Mary Downing: "Mary of* The Nation." Dublin: Catholic Truth Society, 1913; O'Delany, M. Barry. "The Centenary of 'Mary of *The Nation.*' " *Irish Rosary* 32 (1928): / 001014/182; Russell, Matthew. "Ellen Downing: 'Mary' of *The Nation.*" *Irish Monthly* 6 (August– October 1878): 459–465, 506–512, 573–580, 621–630, 661–667; Russell, Matthew. "More about 'Mary' of *The Nation.*" *Irish Monthly* 36 (February 1908): 69–82; Russell, Matthew. "Unpublished Relics of Ellen Downing." *Irish Monthly* 12 (1884): 315–320, 425–432, 534–540.

DOWSLEY, WILLIAM GEORGE (1871–1947), novelist. Dowsley was born in Clonmel, County Tipperary. After being ordained, he went to South Africa and was chaplain and master of St. Andrew's College in Grahamstown. He died in Capetown. Other than works on farming, he wrote some plays and two novels with an Irish background.

PRINCIPAL WORKS: *Travelling Men.* Dublin: Talbot/London: Simpkin, Marshall, 1925; *Long Horns. (The O'Brien of the Glen's Story).* London: John Heritage, 1937.

DOYLE, LYNN (1873–1961), humorist. Lynn Doyle was the pseudonym of Leslie Alexander Montgomery, who was born at Downpatrick, County Down, on October 5, 1873. Educated in Dundalk, he entered the Northern Banking Company when he was sixteen and remained until his retirement. He is remembered chiefly for several volumes of broadly comic stories in dialect about the fictional Northern village of Ballygullion. His best stories are as fresh today as when they first began to appear in 1908. Lynn Doyle also wrote a number of plays, mainly for the Ulster Literary Theatre*; one of them, *Love and Land*, was produced successfully in London under the title of *Persevering Pat.* Montgomery's pseudonym was originally Lynn C. Doyle, which was suggested by a bottle of linseed oil he saw in a grocer's shop. He was briefly a member of the Irish Censorship Board in 1936 and 1937. He died on August 13, 1961, leaving behind a long series of entertainments that must certainly rank just below those of Somerville and Ross* and of George A. Birmingham.*

WORKS: *Ballygullion.* Dublin: Maunsel, 1908. (Stories); *An Ulster Childhood.* Dublin & London: Maunsel & Roberts, 1921; *Mr. Wildridge of the Bank.* London: Duckworth, [1916]; *Lobster Salad.* London: Duckworth, [1922]. (Stories); *Dear Ducks and Other "Ballygullion" Stories.* London: Duckworth, 1925; *The Lilac Ribbon.* Dublin: Talbot, [1927]. (One-act play); *Love and Land (Persevering Pat).* Dublin: Talbot, [1927]. (Four-act play); *Turncoats.* Dublin & Cork: Talbot, [1928]. (One-act play); *Me and Mr. Murphy.* London: Duckworth, 1930. (Stories); *Rosabelle and Other Stories.* London: Duckworth, 1933; *Ballygullion Ballads and Other Verses.* London: Duckworth, 1936; *Fiddling Farmer.* London: Duckworth, 1937; *The Shake of the Bag.* London: Duckworth, 1939. (Stories); *Lilts and Lyrics.* Dublin: Talbot, 1941. (Verse); *Yesterday Morning.* London: Duckworth, 1943; *Babel Babble,* an extravaganza. Transliterated and translated from the original Assyrian Brickfield by Gil McGamish. Dublin: Talbot, 1945. (Poem); *A Bowl of Broth.* London: Duckworth, 1945. (Stories); *Not Too Serious.* London: Duckworth, 1946. (Essays); *Green Oranges.* London: Duckworth, 1947. (Stories); *Love and Roberta.* Belfast: Carter, 1951; *Back to Ballygullion.* London: Duckworth, 1953. (Stories).

DOYLE, RODDY (1958–   ), novelist, playwright, and screenwriter. Doyle grew up in the Kilbarrack area of Dublin, the inspiration for his "Barrytown" settings. He earned a degree from University College, Dublin, and later a diploma in education. From 1979 until 1993, he taught English at the Greendale Community School. Doyle's greatest gift as a writer is transliterating Dublin speech; his skill with dialogue is unparalleled in contemporary Irish fiction because of the way he captures the urban voice, often ugly, always accurate. His attention to detail, particularly the use of the "f-word" by young Dubliners, has earned him a substantial amount of condemnation, to which he once replied: "I've been criticized for the bad language in my books—that I've given a bad image of the country. There's always a subtle pressure to present a good image, and it's always somebody else's definition of what is good" (*Maclean's* magazine, August 30, 1993, p. 50).

Doyle's literary career began in 1987, when he and a friend formed a small press, King Farouk, to publish *The Commitments,* which was later picked up by a British publisher. In 1991, the novel was turned into a successful film by director Alan Parker, with Doyle writing the screenplay. Doyle's second novel, *The Snapper* (1990), was also turned into a film, directed by Stephen Frears, and it also won critical acclaim. The third work of "the Barrytown Trilogy," *The Van* (1991), was short-listed for the Booker Prize and also filmed. In 1993, Doyle became the first Irish writer to win the prestigious Booker Prize for *Paddy Charke Ha, Ha, Ha.*

Doyle's *The Commitments* was an impressive debut that earned him praise for his microscopic picture of contemporary Dublin. The novel centers around the dream of Jimmy Rabbitte Jr., a young Dubliner who wants to put together and manage an Irish soul band. Though the prospective bandmates are skeptical at first, Jimmy convinces them that the music of James Brown, Otis Redding, and black America is also the music of working-class Ireland. A great strength of the work is the vitality, which makes each character believable and entertaining, from the forty-something trumpeter, Joey "The Lips" Fagan, to the hard-drinking and hard-headed lead singer, Decco, to Jimmy's Elvis-worshiping father, Jimmy Sr. The key question in the novel is whether The Commitments will stay together as a band to get a record contract. The book is a striking achievement for two main reasons: the candid dialogue and the author's ability to make the music lively even when all the reader has to rely on are the printed lyrics.

Doyle followed *The Commitments* with his first play, *Brownbread,* which was first staged in September 1987, at the SFX Centre, Dublin. The action centers on three nineteen-year-old Dubliners who kidnap an Irish bishop because "there was nothin' on the telly; yeh know; snooker or cricket." With a Barrytown setting, *Brownbread,* which is slang for being "dead," shares many of *The Commitment*'s qualities: quick-witted dialogue, coarse but entertaining humor, and a keen ability to poke fun at modern Dublin sensibilities. In 1990, Doyle's second play, *War,* was presented at the SFX Centre. In *War,* the setting is a pub, and the action centers around a quiz contest. While not as engaging as *Brownbread,* the play again contains Doyle's witty dialogue, outrageous humor, and astute eye for the human condition.

Also appearing in 1990 was the second installment of the Rabbitte trilogy, *The Snapper.* Like its predecessor, the book comprises mostly dialogue. This time, however, the focus is solely on the Rabbitte family, though not Jimmy Jr. Rather, twenty-year-old Sharon is the center of the story, and Doyle presents a more fleshed-out picture of the peculiar Rabbitte household. The action in *The Snapper* centers around Sharon's pregnancy and the subsequent birth of baby Gina (in Irish slang, "the snapper"). The conflict in the story is that unmarried Sharon will not say who the father is, when, in fact, she was raped by a middle-aged family friend. Despite that dreary plotline, *The Snapper* is strikingly humorous as the Doyle family adjusts to the arrival of a new baby. The most endearing character is Jimmy Sr. His lack of experience with things "feminine" is the source for much waggery, yet his effort to understand Sharon and Gina illustrates the "black affection" that holds the Rabbitte family together.

Fortunately for Doyle's readers, Jimmy Sr. returns in the last of the Barrytown trilogy, *The Van.* That 1991 book represents a change in writing style that shows that Doyle is more than a fine composer of dialogue. While *The Van* has the witty and sometimes biting repartee of the earlier books, it tells the story more fully, with a good deal of description. The protagonist is Jimmy Sr., who has "become redundant" at work; that is, he was fired. For Jimmy Sr., the major drawback with being fired is that he can go to the pub only a few nights a week because of the Rabbitte family's pressing financial situation. Eventually, he and a fellow unemployed friend, Bimbo, decide to invest in a "Chipper van" called

"Bimbo's Burgers," with the slogan "Today's Chips Today." The time is the summer of 1990, and all of Ireland is fanatical about the Italia '90 World Cup, which the Republic of Ireland team has qualified for, for the first time. Amid the drunken chants of "Olé, Olé, Olé" and "Ooh, Aah, Paul McGrath," Jimmy Sr. and Bimbo see a chance to make a lot of money when the hungry soccer fans exit from the pubs at closing time. In the end, though, the business is doomed to fail. The partners have little business sense, but most of the problems rise because Bimbo owns the van, and his wife wants to control the business. Eventually, a health inspector closes down "Bimbo's Burgers," and after a fistfight with Jimmy Sr., whom he blames for the shutdown, Bimbo drives the van into the Irish Sea. Despite all of the bickering, the fighting, and the lost money, Jimmy Sr. and Bimbo remain best friends at the end of the story.

In many respects, *The Van* is the most complete work in the Barrytown trilogy. Doyle's development of Jimmy Sr. is multidimensional and memorable. He is no longer merely the Elvis-crazed man who appeared in *The Commitments,* but funny, scared, lonely, emotional, and sometimes confused. The novel also portrays a darker side of middle-class Dublin—being on the dole, sorting out family problems, and the struggle to feel needed. Like the earlier novels, *The Van* has plenty of laughs, yet Doyle does not patronize the characters. Jimmy Sr., Bimbo, and the others seem more like neighbors than fictional characters.

Paddy Clarke Ha, Ha, Ha signaled a new direction for Doyle. Although the setting is still Barrytown, the time is 1968, and the Rabbitte family is nowhere to be found. Instead, we have Paddy Clarke, a ten-year-old boy who is the son of a printer and a homemaker. Paddy lives in a new middle-class housing development: the city of Dublin is on one side, the soon-to-be-developed open fields of suburbia on the other. Paddy is like most ten-year-olds of his time— he worships George Best of Manchester United, he likes to pop hot tar bubbles with a stick to trap bees, and he has to deal with being picked on by older boys, and, in return, he picks on his younger brother, Sinbad. Doyle's attention to the details of a young boy's life is impressive. Without relying on nostalgia or sentimentality, he re-creates the honest thoughts of a ten-year-old boy. While Paddy may be more sensitive and aware than most children of his age, Doyle does not spoil the narrative with "witty adult observations." Indeed, one of the most attractive aspects of the work is the development of the tension between Paddy's father and mother and their eventual separation. The poignant portrayal of Paddy's struggle to find normality in his family gives the novel much of its excellence. With this work, Doyle has cemented his reputation as one of Ireland's best novelists. He does continue to work in other media, however, and his four-part television series of 1994, "Family," occasioned much public comment for its strong depiction of brutalized lives, wife battering, and drugs.

SHAWN O'HARE

WORKS: *The Commitments.* Dublin: King Farouk, 1987/London: Heinemann, 1988/New York: Vintage, 1989/Great Britain: Mandarin Paperbacks, 1990/London: Minerva, 1991; *War.* Dublin: Passion Machine, 1989. (Play); *The Snapper.* London: Secker & Warburg, 1990/London: Minerva,

1991/New York: Penguin, 1992; *The Van.* London: Secker & Warburg, 1991/New York: Viking, 1992/Great Britain: Mandarin, 1992; *The Barrytown Trilogy: The Commitments, The Snapper, The Van.* London: Secker & Warburg, 1992/London: Minerva, 1992; *Brownbread and War.* London: Secker & Warburg, 1992/London: Minerva, 1992. (Plays); *Paddy Clarke Ha, Ha, Ha.* London: Secker & Warburg/New York: Viking, 1993.

DOYLE, ROSE (fl. 1990s), novelist. Doyle completed her education in the 1930s, worked for the *Irish Press,* and lives in Dublin with her husband and two sons. Her two adult novels provide a well-crafted "easy read." The story lines race along, the events come fast and furious, and there is evidence that some research was done: on the art scene, on alcoholism, on drugs in *Images* (1993) and on horses and horse people in *Kimbay* (1994). Doyle is an extremely competent writer who deliberately uses her talent to sell her books to the widest possible woman's audience. Her books are full of golden people who are instantly forgettable.

DOROTHY ROBBIE

WORKS: *Tarantula.* Dublin: Poolbeg, 1992. (Children's book); *Images.* Dublin: Poolbeg, 1993; *Kimbay.* Dublin: Town & Country in association with Macmillan, 1994; *The Invisible Monk.* Dublin: Poolbeg, 1994. (Children's book).

DRENNAN, WILLIAM (1754–1820), nationalist and poet. Drennan was born in Belfast on May 23, 1754; he received an M.A. in 1771, and a doctorate in medicine from Edinburgh in 1778. A founder of the nationalist organization the United Irishmen, he was tried for sedition with Hamilton Rowan for issuing the Address of the United Irishmen to the Volunteers of Ireland. Although he had written the address, he was acquitted, while Rowan was fined and imprisoned. His most notable poems include "The Wake of William Orr" and "When Erin First Rose"; in the latter he coined the phrase "the Emerald Isle." Even in these, the best of his poems, he verges from conventional phrasing to extreme tightness and strength. His sons, William Drennan, Jr. (1802–1873) and John Swanwick Drennan (1809–1895), both contributed work to his best volume, *Glendalloch and Other Poems.* He died in Belfast on February 5, 1820.

WORKS: *Fugitive Pieces in Verse and Prose.* Belfast: Printed by F. D. Finlay, & sold by R. Rees, 1815; *The Electra of Sophocles.* Belfast: Printed by F. D. Finlay, 1817; *Glendalloch and Other Poems,* 2d ed., with additional verses by his sons. Dublin: W. Robertson/London: Simpkin/Edinburgh & Belfast, 1859; *The Drennan Letters.* D. A. Chart, ed. Belfast: His Majesty's Stationary Office, 1931. REFERENCES: Curley, P. G. "William Drennan and the Young Samuel Ferguson: Liberty, Patriotism and Senses of Protestantism in Ulster Poetry between 1775 and 1848." Diss., Belfast: Queen's University, 1987, Larkin, John, ed. *The Trial of William Drennan.* Blackrock: Irish Academic, 1991.

DRUID THEATRE, THE (1975–   ), Galway. Beginning as a venue for the entertainment of summer visitors, the Druid was launched as an independent year-round theater by three members of the student drama society at University College, Galway, and An Taibhdeharc: Garry Hynes, Marie Mullen, and Mick Lally. Against the odds and with small Bord Failte and Arts Council grants, they survived. Their perseverance paid off in the spring of 1977 with a fine production of Paul Foster's *Tom Paine,* which made their critical reputations and played to full houses. This success enabled them in 1978 to convert a disused warehouse near the Spanish Arch into the Druid Lane Theatre.

Under Garry Hynes' dynamic leadership, they quickly gained a reputation for original, vigorous interpretations of Irish and Continental works: Ibsen, Beckett, Dario Fo, Brecht, Boucicault,* Sheridan,* and Wilde.* Their specialization was in West of Ireland playwrights, particularly J. M. Synge,* M. J. Molloy,* and Tom Murphy,* whose work got unsentimental, detailed, colorful treatment. In 1980, they won major awards at the Edinburgh Fringe Festival, and in 1982 they made "the definitive production" of Synge's *Playboy of the Western World.* Similarly successful was the 1983 production of Molloy's *The Wood of the Whispering.* The triumphant 1985 London production of the *Playboy* was filmed by Channel Four, and it was taken to New York in 1986. Thomas Murphy's *Bailegangaire* received its first production on December 5, 1985.

Although drawing its strength from its roots in the Galway community, the Druid is no longer a regional theater. Through its passionate engagement with rural life, it has brought new styles of performance to the Irish stage. Its impact has been disproportionate to its size, age, and location. The departure of its founders for international careers leaves open the question whether the inevitable tensions between success and local loyalty can be turned to creative ends.

CÓILÍN OWENS

REFERENCE: Burke, David. *Druid: The First Ten Years.* Galway: Druid Performing Arts, 1985.

DRUMMOND, WILLIAM HAMILTON (1778–1865), poet. Drummond was born in August 1778 at Larne, County Antrim, and was educated at Glasgow University. In 1800, he became pastor of a congregation in Belfast and in 1815, pastor of a congregation in Dublin. Some of his poems are on Irish subjects— *Hibernia, The Giant's Causeway, Clontarf, Bruce's Invasion of Ireland.* In his *Ancient Irish Minstrelsy,* he made some translations from the saga stories of Finn and his companions. Occasionally, he manages a strong eighteenth-century line, as in these couplets from *The Giant's Causeway:*

> The victor here and vanquished side by side
> Sleep ghastly pale, sad wrecks of human pride. . . .

> And cursed Ambition, drunk with folly, plan
> The guilt, the crimes, and miseries of man!

But more often he simply has the eighteenth-century mannerisms, as in his references to "Ye feathered tribes" and "Ye finny nations" in "Benevolence of the Good Man to the Inferior Animals." His versions of the Irish stories, despite an archaic fluency, are finally incongruous in their smooth English meters and diction. Drummond died on October 16, 1865.

WORKS: *Hibernia.* Belfast, 1797; *The Man of Age.* Belfast, 1797; *The Battle of Trafalgar.* Belfast: Archer & Ward, 1806; *The Giant's Causeway.* Belfast: Longman, 1811; *An Elegiac Ballad on the Funeral of Princess Charlotte.* Dublin: Graisberry & Campbell, 1817; *Who Are the Happy?* Dublin: Graisberry & Campbell, 1818; *Clontarf.* Dublin: Archer, Hodges & McArthur, 1822; *Bruce's Invasion of Ireland.* Dublin: Hodges & McArthur, 1826; *The Pleasures of Benevolence.* London: Hunter/Dublin: Wakeman, Hodges & Smith, 1835; *Life of Michael Servetus.* London: Chapman, 1848; *Ancient Irish Minstrelsy.* Dublin: Hodges & Smith, 1852; (Also some translations in Hardiman's *Irish Minstrelsy.* 2 vols. London: Joseph Robins, 1831).

DRUMMOND, WILLIAM HENRY (1854–1907), poet. Born at Mohill, County Leitrim, and reared at Tawley, County Donegal, W. H. Drumm[ond] was the eldest of the four sons of an Irish constabulary officer, George Drumm, and his wife, Elizabeth Morris Soden. Falling on hard times, the family emigrated to Canada and settled in Montreal, where, within a few years, George Drumm died.

In order to assist his mother in the maintenance of the family, young William worked as a telegrapher in the lumber camps. Fascinated by the speech of the *voyageurs* and *habitants* whom he came to know, he used their dialect for the verses he wrote for recital by the campfire.

Returning eventually to the city, he completed his education and graduated in medicine. Urged by a self-styled cousin, the family changed their name officially to Drummond, under which the doctor published the first of his verse collections, *The Habitant and Other French-Canadian Poems* (1897), an immediate best-seller. Other popular books followed, and Drummond's ties with the medical profession loosened. He died suddenly from a cerebral hemorrhage in 1907.

J. B. LYONS

WORKS: *The Habitant and Other French-Canadian Poems.* New York & London: Putnam's Sons, 1897; *Phil-o-Rum's Canoe and Madelaine Vercheres.* New York: Putnam's Sons, 1898; *Johnnie Courteau and Other Poems.* New York: Putnam's Sons, 1901; *The Voyageur and Other Poems.* New York: Putnam's Sons, 1905; *The Great Fight: Poems and Sketches.* Edited, with a biographical sketch by May Harvey Drummond. London & New York: Putnam's Sons, 1908; *Poetical Works of William Henry Drummond, MD.* New York: Putnam's Sons, 1912. *Dr. W. H. Drummond's Complete Poems.* With an Appreciation by Neil Munro. Toronto: McClelland & Stewart, [1926]. REFERENCES: Bianquis, Geneviève. "Un Poète Canadien." *La Revue* [Paris]. Serie 7, Tome 113 (1915): 642–654; Lyons, J. B. *William Henry Drummond: Poet in Patois.* Markham, Ontario: Fitzhenry & Whiteside, 1994.

DUBLIN MAGAZINE, THE (1923–1958), literary magazine. *The Dublin Magazine,* founded by the poet and bibliophile Seumas O'Sullivan* (the pen name of James Sullivan Starkey), has been called "the major Irish literary periodical of its day" and "Ireland's greatest literary periodical." In modern times, it was the longest lived literary magazine, and over six hundred writers appeared in its pages. It was founded as a monthly in August 1923, and it ran in that format until the August 1925 issue. Its original cover was a stylish Beardsley-like drawing by Harry Clarke, and its original number contained stories, poems, and articles by, among others, James Stephens,* Brinsley MacNamara,* Donn Byrne,* John Masefield, Ella Young,* and O'Sullivan himself.

After the first two years of publication, as a result of lack of money, insufficient original material, and editorial overwork, the magazine had to appear less frequently. In its new format as a quarterly, the magazine reappeared in January 1926, and it continued until its editor's death, the final issue being that for April–June 1958.

In its long life, the magazine was sometimes uneven, but it published a very large amount of excellent and even extraordinary work. Most of the major figures of the time contributed, and the magazine was particularly strong in its poets; among the most frequently represented were Padraic Colum,* Austin Clarke,* F. R. Higgins,* Patrick Kavanagh,* John Lyle Donaghy,* and Padraic Fallon.* However, among the short story writers were O'Flaherty* and O'Connor,* and also the young Mary Lavin* who received particular encouragement. Rather unusually, the magazine printed quite a few plays, among them those of Rutherford Mayne,* John MacDonagh,* Lennox Robinson,* Seumas O'Kelly,* Padraic Colum, Paul Vincent Carroll,* Austin Clarke, Gerald MacNamara,* and Padraic Fallon. Of special interest was the first printing of the *Diarmuid and Grania* of W. B. Yeats* and George Moore,* as well as (to O'Sullivan's great credit) the printing of no less than eight plays by George Fitzmaurice.*

As an enthusiastic bookman, O'Sullivan included a generous selection of short but interesting reviews, as well as commentaries on book catalogues and highly useful bibliographies by P. S. O'Hegarty and M. J. MacManus. Criticism, and even scholarship, were well represented by many contributors, including W. J. Lawrence* and La Tourette Stockwell. Nor was the magazine provincial in its outlook: it gave much space to translation and to consideration of foreign works.

As O'Sullivan was married to the artist Estella Solomons, the magazine was often and beautifully illustrated by artists such as Nora McGuinness, Harry Kernoff, Sean Keating, Sarah Purser, Jack B. Yeats,* Augustus John, and Solomons herself.

The thirty-five year achievement of *The Dublin Magazine* can hardly be underrated, and Irish letters owes an immense debt to O'Sullivan's brave tenacity. When his magazine ceased publication, it left a gap that has never been filled.

REFERENCES: Burnham, R. "The Development of Seumas O'Sullivan and *The Dublin Magazine*. Dublin: National University of Ireland, Ph.D. dissertation, 1977; Holzapfel, Rudi. *An Index of Contributions to The Dublin Magazine*. Dublin: Museum Bookshop, 1966; Holzapfel, Rudi. "A Note on *The Dublin Magazine*," *The Dublin Magazine*† 4 (Spring 1965): 18–27; Pressley, Stuart, "The Archives of *The Dublin Magazine, 1923–58*." *The Long Room*, No. 7 (Spring 1973).

DUFFAUD, BRIEGE (ca. 1950s–), novelist and short story writer. Duffaud, née Finnegan, was born near Crossmaglen in County Armagh, Northern Ireland. She has lived in England and Holland and now lives in Brittany, France. She has worked as a freelance journalist.

†A later literary magazine of the 1960s and 1970s, which grew out of *The Dubliner*.

Her 1993 novel, *A Wreath upon the Dead,* takes its title from a poem by Patrick Kavanagh* and is an impressive debut; by focusing on two families, the novel attempts to explore the history of Claghan in one corner of Northern Ireland. The story is told through several voices, both native and settler. Maureen Murphy, a romantic novelist living in France, researches the story of Cormac O'Flaherty with a view to writing a novel about him. He is a jockey who, before the Famine of the 1840s, eloped with his landlord's daughter, Marianne Mc-Leod. It was considered an unforgivable act by her family, and the couple came to a tragic end. One of their direct descendants, Kathleen O'Flaherty, is Maureen's best friend, while another McLeod descendant, Eric, fathers Kathleen's illegitimate child. It is a tangled web, and at first the plot is difficult to unravel, but finally it is well worth the effort. The book comes to life with Marianne's mid-nineteenth-century journal, which portrays her Scottish family, who bought a run-down estate in Ulster. Another sympathetic and memorable character is Lizzie, a maid for Cormac O'Flaherty's descendants who eventually becomes Kathleen's mother and the solace of Kathleen's alienated, republican daughter. The book interweaves myth and historical truth and shows the often unrealized connections between the different traditions in the North. It charts the civil rights movement and ends in the Troubles of today. It is never didactic, and the reader feels that the author is unbiased. Some of the most sympathetic characters are Protestants, and the Catholics are not depicted as saints and martyrs, but as human beings caught in a class, as much as a religious, conflict.

Nothing like Beirut (1994), a collection of short stories, is not as good. Some of the characters reappear in different stories, and in most the main character is a woman who moves from Ireland to England or France and finds that life abroad is not perfect either. On the whole, there is too much narration, and the stories tend toward gloom. However, in some, characters do jump to life. Flanagan in "Things Fall Apart" evokes pity as he labors in an appalling but recognizable English school. In "Escape," there are an unforgettable three-year-old-girl and an equally unforgettable French mother. "Swan Song," a story about an ugly duckling, is a modern fable reminiscent of Orwell. Duffaud's stories are, nevertheless, something of a letdown after her novel, which must be one of the best recently written books on Northern Ireland.

MARY ROSE CALLAGHAN

WORKS: *A Wreath upon the Dead.* [Swords, Co. Dublin]: Poolbeg, [1993]; *Nothing like Beirut.* [Dublin]: Poolbeg, [1994]. (Short stories).

DUFFERIN, LADY (1807–1867), poet, novelist, and playwright. Helen Selina Sheridan Blackwood, Lady Dufferin, was the granddaughter of Richard Brinsley Sheridan* and the elder sister of Caroline Norton.* She was born in England in 1807. Early in her childhood, she accompanied her parents to South Africa, returning to England on her father's death, when her mother was given lodgings at Hampton Court. In 1825, at the age of eighteen, she married Captain Price Blackwood, heir to the marquess of Dufferin. To escape his family's disapproval, the couple lived at first in Italy, and in 1826 a son was born, later the distinguished British diplomat Lord Dufferin* and Ava. In 1841 her husband died, and she remained a widow for twenty-one years, until 1862, when she married the dying earl of Gifford. She was widowed again after a few months, and she died on June 13, 1867. Caroline Blackwood* is her direct descendant.

Unlike her sister, Caroline Norton, Lady Dufferin never regarded herself as a serious writer. She is remembered today for sentimental ballads, such as "Terence's Farewell" and particularly "The Lament of the Irish Emigrant," where she partially succeeds in lifting sentiment to a higher level. Such poems were widely anthologized, and some were set to music. Her real successes, however, were light verses, such as "The Charming Woman," "The Fine Young Englishman," and the deft and delightful "Donna Inez's Confession." Her one stage play, *Finesse,* was brought out anonymously at the Haymarket in 1863 and is a bit too skimpily developed to be a memorable comedy. The comedy, however, of her short satire of travel memoirs, *Lispings from Low Latitudes; or, Extracts from the Journal of the Hon. Impulsia Gushington,* is excellently droll. The title is a joke at the expense of her son's much-read Icelandic journal, *Letters from High Latitudes,* and the tale relates how a romantic and credulous English spinster comes to various embarrassing griefs as she travels alone in Egypt. A second extract from Impulsia's ebullient pen was promised but did not appear; however, the fragment we have of her misadventures is too charming to gather dust on library shelves. Before her death, her son had erected on his estate, Clandeboye, near Bangor, a four-story tower dedicated to her. On the walls of the top story are tablets engraved with poems to her, including ones by Tennyson and Browning.

MARY ROSE CALLAGHAN

WORKS: *Lispings from Low Latitudes; or, Extracts from the Journal of the Hon. Impulsia Gushington.* London: J. Murray, 1863; *Songs, Poems, and Verses by Helen, Lady Dufferin (Countess of Gifford).* Edited with a Memoir and Some Account of the Sheridan Family by her Son the Marquess of Dufferin and Ava. London: J. Murray, 1884; *A Selection of the Songs of Lady Dufferin (Countess Gifford).* Marquess of Dufferin and Ava, ed. London: J. Murray, 1895.

DUFFERIN, LORD (1826–1902), diplomat and author. Frederick Temple Hamilton Temple Blackwood, who was to be the fifth Baron Dufferin and the first marquis of Dufferin and Ava, was born at Florence, Tuscany, on June 21, 1826, and educated at Oxford. He was a descendant of Richard Brinsley Sheridan* through the playwright's granddaughter Helena Selina Sheridan, his mother, who married Price Blackwood, the fourth Baron Dufferin. In 1860 he was appointed commissioner in Syria, advancing to undersecretary of state for India, and for war (1864–1866), until he abandoned politics in 1871. He was governor general of Canada from 1872 to 1878 and ambassador, in turn, at St. Petersburg from 1879 to 1881, at Constantinople from 1881 to 1882, at Rome in 1888, and at Paris from 1892 to 1896. But his central role was as viceroy of India from 1884 to 1888. He was made an earl in 1871 for his work in settling relations between Turkey and Egypt (allowing, naturally, a major British role in Egypt); and, after his conquest of Upper Burma and the overthrow of King Thebaw in January 1886, he was given his other title of Ava upon leaving India in 1888. His last years were clouded, and his death hastened by his taking moral responsibility for the Globe Finance Corporation, a company that failed and of which he carelessly accepted the chairmanship, although it gave him no control.

His writings are largely political except for *Letters from High Latitudes* (1857), a witty masterpiece of travel writing recounting a voyage to Iceland and retaining its freshness to this day. The house he built at Clandeboye outside Bangor is among the most remarkable in Ireland, both for its appearance and for the relics of the former empire that it contains. His nephew Harold Nicolson has given a warm account of both the man and the house. He died in his beloved house on February 12, 1902.

PETER COSTELLO

WORKS: *Letters from High Latitudes.* London: John Murray, 1857; *Contributions to an Inquiry into the State of Ireland.* London: John Murray, 1866; *Irish Emigration and the Tenure of Land.* London: John Murray, 1867; *Speeches and Addresses.* London: John Murray, 1882; *Speeches in India.* London: John Murray, 1890. REFERENCES: Lyall, Sir Alfred. *The Life of the Marquis of Dufferin and Ava.* 2 vols. London: John Murray, 1905; Nicolson, Harold. *Helen's Tower.* London: Constable, 1937.

DUFFY, BERNARD (1882–1952), playwright and novelist. The plays of Duffy prove that modern knockabout comedy is not vastly different from Tudor-era interludes. He relies on such time-hallowed devices as the cheater cheated in *The Coiner* and *The Plot;* farcical matchmaking with surprise endings in *The Counter Charm* and *Cupboard Love;* blundering burglars who solve domestic problems in a home they invade in *Special Pleading;* the triumph of the clever little fellow, seasoned with political jokes, in *Fraternity;* the smile and the tear in *The Old Lady,* wherein a sweet Irish mother rescues her son from a predatory chorus girl.

Of his Abbey* plays—*Fraternity, The Coiner,* and *The Counter* Charm (all in 1916) and *The Piper of Tavran* (1921)—only the last, adapted from a Douglas Hyde* tale, rises above situation comedy. An old piper who has converted a wicked woman to the good life comes to exorcise a devil from an abbey. While the man dreams of a beautiful tune the sainted woman is teaching him, the devil is blasted by lightning. The poor piper wakes, cannot remember the tune, and leaves the abbey unrewarded.

Duffy also wrote two novels. *Oriel* (1918) is another "coming-of-age in Ireland" story. *The Rocky Road* (1929) has an old flute player and a young girl singer earning their way along country paths and in Dublin slums. His stories, like his plays, are pleasantly subliterary. He died on March 31, 1952.

WILLIAM J. FEENEY

WORKS: *Four Comedies (The Counter Charm, The Coiner, Special Pleading, The Old Lady).* Dublin: Talbot, 1916; *Oriel.* Dublin: Talbot, 1918. (Novel); *The Rocky Road.* Dublin: Talbot, 1929. (Novel); *Cupboard Love.* Dublin: Duffy, 1930. (Play); *The Plot.* Dublin: Duffy, 1941. (Play).

DUFFY, SIR CHARLES GAVAN (1816–1903), journalist, politician and poet. Duffy was born in Monaghan on April 12, 1816, and became a journalist in Dublin and Belfast. In 1842, with Thomas Davis* and John Blake Dillon (1816–1866), he founded *The Nation,** the famous nationalist paper which published the fiery young patriots of the Young Ireland group. After the collapse of that group and his own trial for sedition, Duffy entered Parliament in 1852. Then, losing all hope for parliamentary agitation, he emigrated to Australia, where he became prime minister in 1871. In 1873, he was knighted, and in 1880, he retired to Nice where he died on February 8, 1903. He edited *The Ballad Poetry of Ireland,* an anthology which contained pieces by John Banim,* J. J. Callanan,* William Carleton,* Thomas Davis, William Drennan,* Samuel Lover,* James Mangan,* Thomas Moore,* and many others, and which went through more than fifty editions. His own few poems are spirited and fluent, if conventional.

WORKS: ed., *The Ballad Poetry of Ireland.* Dublin: Duffy, 1845; *Young Ireland: A Fragment of Irish History, 1840–1850.* London & New York: Cassell, Petter, Galpin, 1880–1883; *Four Years of Irish History, 1845–1849.* London & New York: Cassell, Petter, Galpin, 1883. *The League of North and South: An Episode in Irish History, 1850–1854.* London: Chapman & Hall, 1886; *Thomas Davis.* London: Kegan Paul, Trench, 1890; *Conversations with Carlyle.* London: Sampson, Low, 1892; *What Irishmen May Do for Irish Literature.* London, 1892; *The Prospects of Irish Literature for the People.* London: Printed for private circulation, 1893; *The Revival of Irish Literature.* Addresses by Sir Charles Gavan Duffy, Dr. George Sigerson, & Dr. Douglas Hyde. London: Fisher Unwin, 1894; *My Life in Two Hemispheres.* 2 vols. London: Fisher Unwin, 1898. REFERENCES: O Broin, Leon. *Charles Gavan Duffy: Patriot and Statesman.* Dublin: Duffy, 1967; Pearl, Cyril. *The Three Lives of Gavan Duffy.* Dublin: O'Brien, 1979.

DUFFY, JAMES (ca. 1809–1871), publisher. Duffy, the founder of the publishing house that bore his name, was born in County Monaghan in about 1809 and educated at a hedge-school. He became a small Dublin bookseller, establishing himself by buying up Protestant Bibles, which the Bible Society would give to Catholics and which the Catholics would pawn. He then took the Bibles to Liverpool and traded them for more salable volumes. Originally in an obscure shop in Anglesea Street, Duffy had been publishing popular thrillers that sold at a mere twopence each, when he was approached by the editors of *The Nation** to print books for them. *The Spirit of the Nation* and the "Library of Ireland" volumes sold hugely, and Duffy was able to move to larger premises on Wellington Quay, where, at one time, he is said to have employed 120 people, whom he never allowed a holiday. After 1848, his business was in occasional difficulties, but he continued to run it, his patriotic Young Ireland books being the staple of his list. He died on July 4, 1871.

During most of the twentieth century, James Duffy and Company was located in Westmoreland Street and published many plays by new Irish writers, although the Duffy list in no measure rivaled that of Maunsel and Company* in excellence. During the great flourishing of the amateur drama that lasted at least until the advent of television in the early 1960s, there was a good market for inexpensive acting copies. That market has much diminished, but the firm lingered on, publishing a few volumes each year from obscure premises on Shaw Street, until it finally expired in the early 1980s.

DUGDALE, NORMAN (1931–1995), poet. Dugdale was born in Burnley, Lancashire, and educated at Burnley Grammar School and Manchester University. He moved to Belfast in 1948, to join the Northern Ireland Civil Service. In 1970 he became permanent secretary at the Department of Health and Social Services, and held that position until his retirement in 1984. He died in Belfast on October 27, 1995.

Dugdale has a distinct poetic voice. His poems contain frequent classical allusions and scraps of Greek. His diction is peppered with recondite words. For instance, from the volume *Running Repairs* (1983): "discarnate," "lithomantic," "knurl," "carious," "mephitic," "smegna," "prepuce." Yet he does not seem pedantic, for he is capable of the conversational line such as "The same old sorry human mess, I'd say," or of the effective juxtaposition of conventional description with the strongly contrasting word, as in:

> This pitching night flecked by the spume
> And slobber of the maniacal sea.

In one poem, he seems almost to deride "stiff metre, rigid form" as "conventional" and "boring." Yet he is quite capable of it, particularly in occasional epigrammatic quatrains or couplets. His recent work often deals dourly with aging.

WORKS: *The Disposition of the Weather*. Belfast: Festival, Queen's University of Belfast, [1967]. (Poetry pamphlet); *A Prospect of the West: Poems*. London: Barrie & Jenkins, [1970]; *Corncrake in October*. Belfast: Blackstaff, 1978; *Running Repairs*. Belfast: Blackstaff, 1983; *Limbo*. Belfast: Blackstaff, [1991].

DUN EMER PRESS. *See* CUALA PRESS.

DUNKIN, WILLIAM (ca. 1709–1765), poet. In a letter of January 17, 1737/38, Swift* described William Dunkin as "a gentleman of much wit and the best English as well as Latin poet in this kingdom." A modern scholar, Bryan Coleborne, describes him in *The Field Day Anthology* as "probably the most underrated poet of eighteenth century Ireland." Although Swift's other cronies, Thomas Sheridan the elder* and Patrick Delany,* are strong candidates for being considered the second Irish poet of the age, the poetic credentials of Dunkin are indeed persuasive.

He was born in Dublin, probably between 1706 and 1709, and was educated at Trinity College. He received a B.A. in 1729 and a D.D. in 1744. The *Dictionary of National Biography* notes, "His ordination by the Archbishop of Cashel in 1735 and the increase of the annuity which he received from Trinity College from 70£ to 100£ in 1736 were both due to Swift's intercession, which caused his marriage and other imprudent acts to be overlooked.'' While probably still a student, he translated Swift's Latin poem "Carberiae Rupes.'' In 1734, he, abetted by Sheridan and probably by Swift, engaged in a witty verse warfare (on their side) against Charles Carthy for a poor translation of Horace. After having worked in Dublin for several years as a schoolmaster, he was appointed master of Portora Royal School in Enniskillen by Chesterfield in 1746, and he held that post until his death in Dublin on November 24, 1765.

His fluency in Latin and Greek may be seen in a number of his poems, particularly in "Origo Faulkneriana,'' which appears in his *Select Poetical Works* not only in Latin with an English translation but also in Greek with a different English translation. His great ability as a comic poet is apparent in long pieces such as "The Art of Gate-Passing: or, The Murphaeid'' (which also has a Latin version), about Trinity students attempting to sneak through the gates after hours, and also in "The Parson's Revels,'' which makes effective use of a broad brogue:

> At this O Murphy, like a nag
> Spurr'd to his mettle, would not lag:
> Quoth he, "I am na ribil rag-
> A-muffin,

> But ov dhe reight Hibarnian seed,
> Aldough mey fadhir cud nat reed,
> Nat lek yur black fanaatic breed,
> You puffin'.

Like Swift and Sheridan, he can effectively descend to the scabrous, as in these satirical lines from "Receipt for Making a Doctor'':

> A wise physician still consults
> his patient's eyes, his tongue and pulse,
> and thinks it also not amiss
> to view the colour of his piss,
> mark this, and what on this may border,
> nay, condescend to taste the ordure.

His control of form is probably more pronounced than that of the sometimes careless Sheridan, and the tight iambic tetrameters of his moving "Epistle to Robert Nugent Esq. with a picture of Dr. Swift'' are effortless in their wedding of sense to form. His wit, unlike Sheridan's, hardly ever gets out of hand, even when joined to a serious subject, as in the epigram "On the Earl of Warwick's two Daughters, who were drowned together'':

> What to the faithless ocean now is due?
> She gave one Venus, and has taken two.

However, he can be just as effective in an entirely sober vein, as in his "Epitaph Designed for the Author's Father'':

Here lies (if truth was ever yet averr'd)
The best of husbands, fathers, friends, interr'd,
Fill'd with the Muses, who he ne'er profess'd,
Just to her fortunes, which he ne'er possess'd:
Much injur'd, and opprest, afflicted, brave,
Like Job he brought his virtue to the grave.
O! be it lawful for his offspring here
To wet his ashes with a pious tear;
And yet an other, and an other yet—
Alas, my life will never pay the debt.

There has lamentably been no modern edition of his works.

WORKS: *Select Poetical Works of the Late William Dunkin, D.D.* Vol. 1. Dublin: W. G. Jones, 1769/Vol. 2. Dublin: S. Powell, 1790. REFERENCES: Day, Joseph C. "William Dunkin: "Best Poet" in the Kingdom? A New Look at His Augustan Burlesque." M.A. thesis, National University of Ireland, 1978; von Dietrich, Andrea. "Satirische Techniken in den persönlicken Schmähschriften der Dubliner 'University Wits,' James Delacourt, Charles Carthy, William Dunkin und Ambrose Philips." Staatsexamin thesis, Technical University of Berlin, 1985.

DUNLOP, ANNE (1968–   ), novelist. Dunlop was born in Castledawson, County Derry, Northern Ireland. She studied agricultural science at University College, Dublin, graduating in 1991. She then returned to Northern Ireland to do postgraduate work. Her trilogy, comprising *The Pineapple Tart, The Soft Touch,* and *The Dolly Holiday* and published in 1992 and 1993, records the burlesque adventures of the Gordon sisters who come to Dublin to "shift" men by the dozen and who subsequently return manless to their Northern parents' farm, Derryrose. The series starts out very promisingly in *The Pineapple Tart,* which, like the others, is narrated by Helen Gordon. Her lovely, outrageous humor, which sends up feminism and modern political correctness, is so amusing that the lack of plot is forgiven—the narrative that focuses on the story of her family carries the book. One can open the book anywhere and come across an acerbic gem: "Laura left for America at the end of June and we all cried for precisely ten minutes, then promptly forgot about her. It's out of sight, out of mind at Derryrose." Also Dunlop's characters are gorgeously comic—eccentric Aunt Maisie, the menopausal mother, the Orange Lodge father who will not refer to his grandson by name because he is called Shaun, after *The Quiet Man.* Indeed, Helen grew up thinking Northern Ireland was an island. In Ireland today, this is a very healthy and refreshing comic voice. It is sustained in the next two books, both published in 1993, *The Soft Touch* and *The Dolly Holiday,* but by this time the reader is crying out for a story. Anne Dunlop's characters are wonderful, but they are characters in search of a plot. It is not enough to pile on the comic details, for the reader wants a story. It is the reason one reads a novel. Here one gets an impression of indecent haste. However, Anne Dunlop has published at a very young age, so perhaps the fault will be corrected in the future. Because of her rare comic flair, one hopes so.

MARY ROSE CALLAGHAN

WORKS: *The Pineapple Tart.* [Swords, Co. Dublin: Poolbeg, 1992; *The Dolly Holiday.* [Swords, Co. Dublin]: Poolbeg, [1993]; *A Soft Touch.* [Swords, Co. Dublin]: Poolbeg, [1993].

DUNNE, JOHN

WORK: *Purtock.* Dublin: Anna Livia, 1992.

DUNNE, [CHRISTOPHER] LEE (1934–   ), novelist and scriptwriter. Dunne was born in Dublin on December 21, 1934, and grew up in a group of Corporation flats in Ranelagh called the Hill. He has followed many professions—sailor, singer, actor, taxidriver in London, and scriptwriter for an interminable serial, *Harbour Hotel,* on Radio Éireann. His first and very promising novel, *Goodbye to the Hill* (1965), contains an evocative re-creation of working-class Dublin. Even his poorer second novel, *A Bed in the Sticks* (1968), contains interesting details about an actor's life in the fit-ups, or provincial touring companies that played in the smallest towns. In these novels, his style is colloquial and simple, and in the first person. It seems modeled on the neo-American style of "tough" writing for popular magazines. A typical paragraph reads:

On the way down we went into the convent at Milltown. Ma held me with one hand. In the other she carried a half-gallon can. An old nun filled the can with soup and bits of meat and potatoes and my mother thanked her, and there was a lot of talk about the good God in his almighty glory, blessing you and yours. I hated the sight of the nun in her long robe or whatever it's called, but I gave her a smile that warmed her feet. I liked the look of the soup.

This pared-to-the-bone prose, a legacy from Hemingway and his many imitators, can be effective and can also quickly pall. Dunne's subsequent novels have been simple and lurid entertainments for the mass paperback market. A recent example, *Requiem for Reagan* (1990), is a spy thriller adeptly imitating Ian Fleming, Jack Higgins, Tom Clancy, even John le Carré, and even what used to be called pornography. A cold war fiction about an attempted assassination of Ronald Reagan on his Irish visit of 1984, it was meant to be a time-passer but is really a time-waster. Dunne's stage version of *Goodbye to the Hill* was produced at the Oscar Theatre in Dublin in the fall of 1978, revived at the Olympia in 1985, ran for three years and thirteen weeks at the Regency Hotel in north Dublin, and was revived at the Tivoli in 1994. The play, like the originating novel, was almost good, and the pity is that Dunne's real talent has been squandered on so much hack writing.

WORKS: *Goodbye to the Hill.* London: Hutchinson, 1965; *A Bed in the Sticks.* London: Hutchinson, 1968; *Does Your Mother.* London: Arrow, 1970; *Paddy Maguire Is Dead.* London: Arrow, 1972; *Midnight Cabbie.* London: Coronet, 1974; *The Cabbie Who Came in from the Cold.* London: Coronet, 1975; *The Cabfather.* London: Coronet, 1975; *The Day of the Cabbie.* London: Futura, 1975; *Big Al.* London: Futura, 1975; *Maggie's Story.* London: Futura, 1975; *The Virgin Cabbies.* London: Futura, 1976; *Harbour Hotel.* [Wicklow: Pal Paperbacks, 1977]; *Ringmaster.* Dublin: Wolfhound, 1986; *Requiem for Reagan.* [Dublin]: Kildanore, [1990].

DUNNE, SEAMUS

WORK: *The Gardener.* Dublin: Wolfhound, 1993. (Novel).

DUNNE, SEÁN (1956–1995), poet. Dunne was born in Waterford and received a B.A. from University College, Cork. He became a journalist and was the editor of the *Cork Examiner*'s weekend supplement. His *In My Father's House* (1991) was a lyrical memoir about growing up in Waterford in the 1960s. His two volumes of verse have a fine clarity of detail and some arresting achievements of sound. He edited two useful anthologies of poetry, an edition of the *Cork Review* devoted to Sean O'Faolain* and an issue of *The Journal of Irish Literature** devoted to Teresa Deevy,* as well as writing many fugitive essays and reviews and *The Road to Silence* (1994), a kind of spiritual reflection. He died most prematurely and unexpectedly in his sleep of a coronary on August 3, 1995, in Cork.

WORKS: ed., *Poets of Munster.* [London]: Anvil Press Poetry/[Dingle, Co. Kerry]: Brandon, 1985; *In My Father's House.* Dublin: Anna Livia, 1991. (Memoir); *The Sheltered Nest.* [Oldcastle, Co. Meath]: Gallery, [1992]; *The Road to Silence: An Irish Spiritual Odyssey.* Dublin: New Island, [1994]; ed., *Something Understood: A Spiritual Anthology.* Dublin: Marino, 1995.

DUNSANY, LORD (1878–1957), fantasist, playwright, and short story writer. The ancestral home of Edward John Morton Drax Plunkett, the eighteenth Baron Dunsany, is near Tara in County Meath, but the future Lord Dunsany was born on July 24, 1878, at 15 Park Square in the Regents Park Section of London. Dunsany was the chess champion of Ireland, a great sportsman, a brave soldier, a dedicated family man, and an adventurer, as well as a man of letters. Unlike other writers of the Irish Renaissance, such as Yeats,* Synge,* Colum,* and even James Joyce,* Dunsany was not of old Celtic stock, Irish Catholic peasantry, or Protestant ascendancy-turned-Irish-nationalist. He was a loyal British subject who fought for the Crown in Africa, France, and Dublin, and his associations were with the British aristocracy more than with the Irish serfdom with whom many of his contemporaries sought so painstakingly to identify themselves. One of the principal aims of the Irish Literary Revival, the glorification of Ireland, had no place in the Dunsany canon, although he knew all of the main figures in the movement and his first play, *The Glittering Gate* (1909), was written in response to a request from Yeats for a production for the Abbey.*

The Dunsany family was founded by a Norman, John Plunkett, after the Norman conquest of Ireland in the twelfth century. Dunsany's remarkable life encompassed eighty years and represented the nearly idyllic combination of activities requisite of one of the oldest peerages in the British Empire. His first formal training came from a local school in Kent. He then attended his father's school, Cheam, where he learned the Greek language and the mythology which he emulated in so many of his works. He also became acquainted with Grimm's and Anderson's fairy tales, the works of Edgar Allan Poe, and the strategies of tournament chess.

From Cheam he went to Eton, and then to a crammer in Dublin, later qualifying for Sandhurst, from which he graduated with a military education. He
next joined the Coldstream Guards and was soon transferred to Gibraltar. There
he developed his fascination for the Near East in the settings that he was to use
in his tales *The Fall of Babbulkund* and *A Fortress Unvanquishable Save for
Sacnath.* With the beginning of the Boer War, Dunsany transferred to South
Africa, where he saw extensive combat and met Rudyard Kipling, who became
a lifelong friend.

After the war, he returned to Meath and the duties of his estate. In 1904, he
married Lady Beatrice Villiers, who became his most devoted reader, his sometime secretary, and his honest critic. His first book, *The Gods of Pegana,* was
published at his own expense in 1905 by Elkin Mathews. The book was successful and was followed quickly by two others, *Time and the Gods* and *The
Sword of Welleran.* He began to dictate to Lady Dunsany and wrote with exceptional speed and great productivity. Dictation accounts in part for the enormous quantity of his writing, but even in Lady Dunsany's absence he turned
out whole plays in an afternoon with quill and ink. Although the Dunsanys
traveled a great deal in Europe, America, North and Central Africa, and India,
all the time he was producing short stories, plays, and novels at an exceptionally
rapid pace.

During World War I, Dunsany joined the Royal Inniskilling Fusiliers. While
at home on a weekend pass for the Easter holiday of 1916, he came to Dublin
to see how he might help quell the rebellion. He was shot through the head and
taken to a hospital which was under siege for nearly a week. He recovered
slowly and then was sent to France, where he again saw front-line combat. Later
during the war, he was transferred to British Intelligence, where he wrote propaganda items, articles, stories, and books for the government. The least of his
literary accomplishments, *Tales of War* (1918), was a product of his military
service. Between the two world wars, Dunsany became an international chess
player, a big game hunter, and a celebrated lecturer in the United States and
Great Britain. During those years, his literary acquaintanceships included H. G.
Wells, Oliver St. John Gogarty,* and Mary Lavin.*

Throughout his career, Dunsany felt the lack of critical scholarly recognition
of his work on the one hand and a good deal of popular success, especially with
his dramas and fantasies, on the other. He sensed a sort of reverse snobbery in
the critical barbs he received, feeling that critics considered him a sort of dil-
ettante, taking bread out of the mouths of honest professional writers. He was
often regarded as being in a sort of literary limbo. Perhaps much of this attitude
stemmed from the fact that Dunsany did not write for any identifiable literary
movement or faction. Although he produced a few plays for Yeats and the
Abbey Theatre over the course of years, and though these were popular successes in America as well as in England and Ireland, Dunsany could hardly have
received great national accolades in a country in which he was so preeminently
for the British Crown and so apolitical in his creative work. His reputation as

a playwright equals his fame as a fiction writer. He specialized in one act plays, though his full-length plays were among his best.

His prose works are primarily stories of the fantastic and beautiful. His prose is much like poetry, often nearly metrical and highly stylized, occasionally even Biblical. His stories dealing with the remote and exotic are heavily romantic in character. A forerunner of such writers as Tolkien, Dunsany created his own mythology with people, planets, and lands removed from ours in time and temperament, but redeemed by a pervasive humor which was part of Dunsany's own character both in and out of his literary works. He was unpretentious throughout his life and possessed a sense of the incongruous which was reflected in his stories by a puckish sense of the ludicrous.

Dunsany collaborated with the well-known illustrator S. H. Sime on a large number of his works. Sime's illustrations, uncharitably called by a critic a combination of Blake and Beardsley but without the messages of either, were as fanciful and elaborate as Dunsany's tales. They are neither deep nor difficult to grasp but are filled with the exotic wonder of fantasy and fairy tales. Dunsany eschews the difficult and erudite, claiming such heavy intellectual endeavors are out of place as the matter of serious literature, which he regarded as principally escapist and pleasure producing.

Most of Dunsany's characters, lacking individuality, depth, and verisimilitude, are principally the instruments of plot. His narratives inspire readers with leaps of fantastic imagination, but make little attempt to probe psychological complexities or establish intricacies of theme or symbol. Later Dunsany critics often saw his work as heavily symbolic, but such symbolism was certainly not part of the author's initial intent.

Dunsany, did, however, develop one of the drollest contemporary literary characters in a barfly named Joseph Jorkens, whose fabulations, chiefly in return for drinks at the mythical Billiards Club, encompassed five volumes. Jorkens' character is archetypal, lovable, and often Dickensian. While Jorkens expected to be believed, his tales defy credulity. In a sense, Jorkens and Dunsany are much alike in their narration of the fantastic, in their search for artistic approbation, and in their abundant good humor. Dunsany's prolific career is evidenced by more than fifty-five published volumes and hundreds of plays, articles, and introductions. He died in Dublin on October 25, 1957.

ZACK BOWEN

WORKS: *The Gods of Pegana*. London: Elkin Mathews, 1905; *Time and the Gods*. London: Heinemann, 1906; *The Sword of Welleran*. London: George Allen, 1908; *A Dreamer's Tales*. London: George Allen, 1910; *The Book of Wonder*. London: Heinemann, 1912; *Five Plays*. London: Grant Richards, 1914; *51 Tales*. London: Elkin Mathews, 1915; *Tales of Wonder*. London: Elkin Mathews, 1916; *Plays of Gods and Men*. Dublin: Talbot, 1917; *Tales of War*. London & New York: Putnam, 1918; *Tales of Three Hemispheres*. Boston: Luce, 1919; *Unhappy Far-off Things*. London: Elkin Mathews, 1919; *If*. London & New York: Putnam, 1921; *The Chronicles of Rodrigues*. London & New York: Putnam, 1922; *Plays of Far and Near*. London & New York: Putnam, 1922; *The King of Elfland's Daughter*. London & New York: Putnam, 1924; *Alexander*. London & New York: Putnam, 1925; *The Charwoman's Shadow*. London & New York: Putnam, 1926; *The Blessings of*

Pan. London & New York: Putnam, 1927; *Seven Modern Comedies.* London & New York: Putnam, 1928; *50 Poems.* London & New York: Putnam, 1929; *The Old Folk of the Centuries.* London: Elkin Mathews, 1930; *The Travel Tales of Mr. Joseph Jorkens.* London & New York: Putnam, 1931; *Lord Adrian.* Cranberry, N.J.: Golden Cockerel Press, 1933; *If I Were Dictator.* London: Methuen, 1934; *Jorkens Remembers Africa.* London: Heinemann, 1934; *The Curse of the Wise Woman.* London: Heinemann, 1935; *Mr. Faithful.* New York: Samuel French, 1935; *Up in the Hills.* London: Heinemann, 1935; *My Talks with Dean Spanley.* London: Heinemann, 1936; *Rory and Bran.* London: Heinemann, 1936; *My Ireland.* New York: Jarrolds, 1937; *Plays for Earth and Air.* London: Heinemann, 1937; *Mirage Water.* London & New York: Putnam, 1938; *Patches of Sunlight.* London: Heinemann, 1938; *The Story of Mona Sheehy.* London: Heinemann, 1939; *Jorkens Has a Large Whiskey.* London & New York: Putnam, 1940; *War Poems.* London: Hutchinson, 1940; *Wandering Songs.* London: Hutchinson, 1943; *Guerilla.* London: Heinemann, 1944; *The Journey.* London. Macdonald, 1944; *While the Sirens Slept.* London: Hutchinson, 1944; *The Donellan Lecture 1943.* London: Heinemann, 1945; *The Sirens Wake.* London & New York: Jarrolds, 1945; *A Glimpse from a Watchtower.* London & New York: Jarrolds, 1946; *The Year.* London & New York: Jarrolds, 1946; *The Man Who Ate the Phoenix.* London & New York: Jarrolds, 1947; *The Odes of Horace,* translated into English Verse. London: Heinemann, 1947; *The Fourth Book of Jorkens.* London & New York: Jarrolds, 1948; *To Awaken Pegasus.* Oxford: G. Ronald, 1949; *The Strange Journeys of Colonel Polders.* London & New York: Jarrolds, 1950; *His Fellow Men.* London & New York: Jarrolds, 1951; *The Last Revolution.* London & New York: Jarrolds, 1951; *The Little Tales of Smethers.* London & New York: Jarrolds, 1952; *Jorkens Borrows Another Whiskey.* London: Michael Joseph, 1954. POSTHUMOUS EDITIONS: *At the Edge of the World.* New York: Ballantine, 1970; *Beyond the Fields We Know.* New York: Ballantine, 1972; *Gods, Men, and Ghosts: The Best Supernatural Fiction of Lord Dunsany.* New York: Dover, 1972; *Over the Hills and Far Away.* New York: Ballantine, 1974; *The Ghosts of the Heaviside Layer and Other Phantasms.* Philadelphia: Owlswick, 1980; *Verses Dedicatory: 18 Previously Unpublished Poems.* Montclair, N.J.: Charnel House, 1985. REFERENCES: Amory, Mark. *A Biography of Lord Dunsany.* London: Collins, 1972; Anderson, Angelee Sailer. "Lord Dunsany, The Potency of Words and The Wonder of Things." *Mythlore* 55 (Autumn 1988): 10–12; Bassnett, Susan. "From Gods to Giants— Theatrical Parallels between Edward Dunsany and Luigi Pirandello." *The Yearbook of the British Pirandello Society* 6 (1986): 40–49; Bierstadt, Edward Hale. *Dunsany the Dramatist.* Boston: Little, Brown, 1917; Boyd, Ernest A. *Appreciations and Depreciations.* Dublin: Talbot, 1917/New York: John Lane, 1918; Burleson, Donald R. "On Dunsany's 'Probable Adventure of the Three Literary Men.' " *Studies in Weird Fiction* 10 (Fall 1991): 23–26; Cantrell, Brent. "British Fairy Tradition in *The King of Elfland's Daughter. The Romantist* 4–5 (1980–1981): 51–53; Duperray, Max. "Lord Dunsany: Sa Place dans une Eventuelle Litterature Fantastique Irlandaise." *Études Irlandaises* 9 (December 1984): 81–88; Gayford, Norm. "The Influence of Two Dunsany Plays." *Lovecraft Studies* 19–20 (Fall 1989): 49–55, 62; Joshi, S. T. & Schweitzer, Darrell. *Lord Dunsany: A Bibliography.* Metuchen, N.J.: Scarecrow, 1993; Littlefield, Hazel. *Lord Dunsany: King of Dreams: A Personal Portrait.* New York: Exposition, 1959; Saul, George Brandon Saul. "Strange Gods in Far Places: The Short Stories of Lord Dunsany." *Arizona Quarterly* 19 (Autumn 1963): 197–210; Schweitzer, Darrell. "How Much of Dunsany Is Worth Reading?" *Studies in Weird Fiction* 10 (Fall 1991): 19–23; Schweitzer, Darrell. "Lord Dunsany: Visions of Wonder." *Studies in Weird Fiction* 5 (Spring 1989): 20–26; Schweitzer, Darrell. "The Novels of Lord Dunsany." *Mythlore* 7 (Autumn 1980): 39–42; Schweitzer, Darrell. *Pathways to Elfland: The Writings of Lord Dunsany.* Philadelphia: Owlswick, 1989; Walker, Warren S. " 'Tales That One Never Wants to Hear'—A Sample from Dunsany." *Studies in Short Fiction* 22 (Fall 1985): 449–454.

DUNTON, JOHN (1659–1733), publisher, bookseller, and pamphleteer. Dunton was born on May 4, 1659, in England, the son of a clergyman and fellow of Trinity College, Cambridge. He was apprenticed to a bookseller in London at the age of fourteen and became a bookseller and publisher who brought out, according to his own account, over 600 works. He was, however, frequently in debt, a fact that occasioned visits to New England, Holland, Germany, and Dublin, where he conducted book auctions. A quarrel with a Dublin bookseller resulted in *The Dublin Scuffle* (1699), a still readable if somewhat suspect account of Dublin at the end of the century. His later writings showed his eccentricity degenerating into madness, and he died in obscurity in 1733.

PRINCIPAL WORKS: *The Athenian Gazette.* London, 1690–1696; *The Dublin Scuffle.* London: For the Author, 1699; *The Case of John Dunton, with Respect to Madam Jane Nicholas of St. Albans, His Mother-in-Law.* London, 1700; *The Life and Errors of John Dunton Esquire.* London, 1705; *Dunton's Whipping-Post; or, a Satire upon Everybody. . . .* London, 1706; *Athenianism; or, the New Projects of Mr. John Dunton. . . .* London, 1710; *Neck or Nothing.* London, 1716; *Mordecai's Memorial; or, There Is Nothing Done for Him; a Just Representation of Unrewarded Services.* London, 1716; *An Appeal to His Majesty.* London, 1723; *A Cat May Look at a Queen; or, a Satire upon Her Present Majesty.* London, n. d.   REFERENCES: Hill, Peter Murray. *Two Augustan Booksellers: John Dunton and Edmund Curll.* Lawrence: University of Kansas Libraries, 1958; Parks, Stephen. *John Dunton and the English Book Trade: A Study of His Career with a Checklist of His Publications.* New York: Garland, 1976.

DURCAN, PAUL (1944–   ), poet. Durcan was born in Dublin on October 16, 1944. He received a B.A. from University College, Cork, and won the prestigious Whitbread Prize for Poetry in 1990 for *Daddy, Daddy.* He is generally regarded as a social critic and satirist, his main targets Irish social and religious institutions, but this hardly honors the complexity of his often surreal, idiosyncratic, iconoclastic, relentlessly contemporary outrage against the antilife forces that he sees about him. For a variety of conflicting reasons, he has been compared with Patrick Kavanagh* (for his attacks on Irish society), D. H. Lawrence (for his tendency to write the "poetry of the present moment"), Yeats* (for measuring contemporary Ireland against a legendary backdrop), and Walt Whitman (for his evangelism).

Seamus Heaney* detects a "tension between the lyrical and the anti-lyrical, between intensity and irony, between innocence and fear" in Durcan's work, and this is certainly true not only in his apparent political nonpartisanship (e.g., he opposes both the British and the Irish Republican Army) but also in a style that is often characterized as uneven. Typically, a Durcan poem will begin with an engagingly patterned lyricism that, as one gets further into the poem, seems to gravitate (deteriorate?) into, as David Profumo says, "corrugated vernacular prose." This may, to some, seem an evocative "montage of the banal and exotic," as Gerald Dawe* puts it, but to more traditional others it seems a calamitous disregard of craft.

Durcan's titles deserve mention simply because of their succinct wit. Often the title itself is a précis of the poem proper: "Three Hundred Men Made Redundant," "The Bishop of Cork Murders His Wife," "The Perfect Nazi Family Is Alive and Well and Prospering in Modern Ireland," or "The Vasectomy Bureau in Lisdoonvarna." A distinct, jokey roguishness to Durcan's art wins him such sobriquets as the "Playboy of Western Surrealism" or "Stevie Smith imitating Damon Runyon." This might cause some to wonder if his admittedly powerful urgent energy is not bought at the expense of salutary restraint.

Durcan has been publishing his poetry since the late 1960s but only gained serious critical notice with *The Selected Paul Durcan* in 1982. This collection contains poems from four previous volumes: *O Westport in the Light of Asia Minor* (1975), *Teresa's Bar* (1976), *Sam's Cross* (1978), and *Jesus, Break His Fall* (1980). *Jumping the Train Tracks with Angela* (1983) is an unevenly eccentric collection of the ridiculous and the sublime, full of jokes (both good and bad) with a touch of dark humor directed at the repressive social and religious practices in Ireland. *The Berlin Wall Cafe* (1985) has a sharper focus but still raises the question, For all its inventiveness and wit, does one want to read any of the poems again? *Daddy, Daddy* (1990), as the title suggests, concerns the death of Durcan's father but also touches on the poet's characteristic political, social, and religious concerns.

He is a member of Aosdána.*

THOMAS F. MERRILL

WORKS: *Endsville*, with Brian Lynch. Dublin: New Writers, 1967; *O Westport in the Light of Asia Minor*. [Dun Laoire]: Anna Livia, [1975]; *Teresa's Bar*. Dublin: Gallery, 1976; *Sam's Cross: Poems*. Portmarnock, Co. Dublin: Profile, 1978; *Jesus, Break His Fall*. Dublin: Raven Arts, 1980; *Ark of the North*. Dublin: Raven Arts, 1982; *The Selected Paul Durcan*. Belfast: Blackstaff, 1982; *Jumping the Train Tracks with Angela*. Dublin: Raven Arts/Manchester: Carcanet New, 1983; *The Berlin Wall Cafe*. Belfast: Blackstaff, 1985; *Going Home to Russia*. Belfast: Blackstaff, 1987; *In the Land of the Punt*. Dublin: Clashganna Mills, 1988; *Jesus and Angela: Poems*. Belfast: Blackstaff/ Philadelphia: Dufour, 1988; *Daddy, Daddy*. Belfast: Blackstaff, 1990; *Crazy about Women*. Dublin: National Gallery, 1991; *A Snail in My Prime*. Belfast: Blackstaff, 1993; *Give Me Your Hand*. London: Macmillan, published in association with National Gallery, [1994].

E

EDGEWORTH, MARIA (1767–1849), novelist. In charting the development of the novel, Edgeworth was proclaimed by no less than Sir Walter Scott to be the first regional novelist. Although that may seem a slender claim to a place in literary history, the immense popularity of that genre in the nineteenth century and the admitted influence on subsequent writers make Maria Edgeworth a truly important figure.

She was born on January 1, 1767, the third child of Richard Lovell Edgeworth, a figure of considerable interest on his own, as a radical theorist on education. As soon as she was mature enough, Maria was enlisted by her father to help in the task of educating her numerous stepbrothers and stepsisters, Richard's children by his four wives. From 1782, when the family settled in Edgeworthstown, County Longford, Maria helped him formulate a system of education that was described in *Practical Education* (1798). Like John Stuart Mill's father, whom he resembled in many ways, Richard Edgeworth was a powerful influence on his children, expecting of them mature analysis and emphasizing principles of utility and equity in all that he taught.

Her early contributions to his collections of essays on education led quickly to her first attempts at serious literature: *The Parent's Assistant; or Stories for Children* (1796). Despite the unrelieved moralizing, these tales have a simple charm and reveal nascent narrative skills.

Her masterpiece, *Castle Rackrent,* appeared as early as 1800 and thus conveniently marks the beginning of the century and the first production that can be termed a work of Anglo-Irish literature. The novel records the decline of the Rackrent family over several generations, as told by the family steward, Thady Quirk. Although the novel is short, and the plot uncomplicated, Edgeworth's skill at characterization is impressive. Each of the characters is established with telling gestures and qualities, and while each is easily distinguishable from the others, he or she reveals a common family strain that leads to the dissolution of the line. The moral implicit in such an account is clear and strong, but the tendency toward judgment is counterbalanced by the narrator's treatment of the family and by the irony of his account. The narrator, Thady, is a memorable character; while he claims to be objective, he is clearly an unreliable reporter, for he was involved in much that went on. In the end Thady inherits the estate, an ironic twist that makes the final impact both amusing and enlightening at the same time. Although Thady's dialect is stylized, his speech patterns suggest the same mixture of the serious with the ironic. In terms of literary history, Edgeworth's use of such an involved and unreliable narrator advanced the novel in important ways, and it extended the audience for such fiction at the same time. The novel was so popular that it prompted a taste for fiction about Ireland in the salons of London. The publication of this novel in the very year of the Act of Union was particularly auspicious, for it was seen as extending the realm of subject matter of British art to include Ireland. None of her subsequent novels were as popular in her lifetime.

In her later fiction, Edgeworth continued to favor Irish subjects and even to take up the causes of the most enlightened Irish gentry. In *Ennui* (1809) and *The Absentee* (1812), she continued the attack on the irresponsibility of landlords begun in her 1800 novel. But these and many of her novels seem heavy because of the more elaborate plotting and tendency toward digression. One novel, *Ormond* (1817), deserves special mention for its resemblances to Fielding's *Tom Jones*. The comparison is not incidental, because the main character is lively and appealing, and the plot is fast-paced and humorous. It is a novel of education, like most of Edgeworth's tales, but even here the English are reminded of how little they ever bothered to learn about Ireland.

After her father's death in 1817, Edgeworth slowed down somewhat in her production of fiction, although her output was still remarkable. Her collected works came to eighteen volumes. She continued to publish children's stories as well as novels, often in the later years centering on confident and articulate young women who became models of behavior. Her own life was, in many respects, exemplary; her neighbors record her tireless work in aiding tenant farmers during the Great Famine. She died shortly after that time of trial, on May 22, 1849.

Often cited as a literary influence on Sir Walter Scott, William Makepeace Thackeray, and even Ivan Turgenev, Edgeworth earned fame in her lifetime. She was a deft critic of English pretensions and insensitivities, particularly as they misunderstood and neglected their Irish tenants, yet she was gentle and usually humorous in such deflations. Often her observations are so intellectually clever as to merit comparison with Jane Austen. She was an original theorist on education, both in her essays and in her remarkable correspondence with friends. Throughout her work, her sense of humor lightens the seriousness of her subject matter. Her depiction of, and sympathy for, children are rare for the period; in fact, she is one of the earliest to treat them as other than miniature adults. If, in her novels, she did not present the Irish peasants with the same authority and precision as did successors, particularly Carleton,* she did portray them with sympathy and manifest concern. She spoke for the landed class in Ireland, undoubtedly, and some of their narrow prejudices are evident in her; but she cited the responsibility of her own class for the improvement of the lives of the Irish lower classes. She is consistently humane and sympathetic, if limited in her exposure to the realities of the life of the poor.

Most enduring of the effects of her works are their redeeming humor and irony. Like Jane Austen, she is clearly aware of the pretenses of her characters, and she seems to revel in hinting at the irony of their self-serving maneuvers. Characteristic of the period, the novels have explicit morals, but they are rarely ponderous, lightened as they are with humor. She comments with skill on the place of women in her society, exposing the chauvinism of the males. In short, the novels balance substantial intellectual content, such as theories on education, social action, and individual responsibility, with a delight in humankind. Enjoyable as are her fictional works, the breadth and depth of her concerns are best revealed in her correspondence, where many of her observations seem uncanny in their contemporary relevance.

JAMES KILROY

WORKS: *Letters for Literary Ladies.* London: J. Johnson, 1795; *The Parent's Assistant; or Stories for Children.* 2 vols. London: J. Johnson, 1796. (An expanded edition in 6 vols. appeared in 1800); *Practical Education.* 2 vols. London: J. Johnson, 1798; *A Rational Primer.* London: J. Johnson, 1799; *Castle Rackrent.* London: J. Johnson, 1800; *Early Lessons.* London: J. Johnson, 1801; *Belinda.* 3 vols. London: J. Johnson, 1801; *Moral Tales for Young People.* 5 vols. London: J. Johnson, 1801; *Essay on Irish Bulls,* with Richard Lovell Edgeworth. London: J. Johnson, 1802; *Popular Tales.* London: J. Johnson, 1805; *Leonora.* 2 vols. London: J. Johnson, 1806. *Essays on Professional Education.* London: J. Johnson, 1809. (This volume was published solely under her father's name, but Maria collaborated on it); *Tales of Fashionable Life.* 3 vols. London: J. Johnson, 1809; *Tales of Fashionable Life.* 3 vols. London: J. Johnson, 1812; *Continuation of Early Lessons.* 2 vols. London: J. Johnson, 1814; *Patronage.* 4 vols. London: J. Johnson, 1814; *Readings on Poetry,* with Richard Lovell Edgeworth. London: R. Hunter, 1816; *Harrington, a Tale; and Ormond, a Tale.* 3 vols. London: R. Hunter, Baldwin, Cradock & Joy, 1817; *Comic Dramas in 3 Acts.* London: R. Hunter, etc., 1817. (Contains *Love and Law, The Two Guardians,* and *The Rose, Thistle and Shamrock*); *Memoirs of Richard Lovell Edgeworth, Esq.,* begun by himself and concluded by Maria. 2 vols. London: R. Hunter, etc., 1820; *Rosamund.* 2 vols. London: R. Hunter, etc., 1821; *Frank.* 3 vols. London: R. Hunter, etc., 1822; *Harry and Lucy.* 4 vols. London: R. Hunter, etc., 1825; *Tales and Miscellaneous Pieces.* 14 vols. London: R. Hunter, etc., 1825; *Little Plays for Children.* London: R. Hunter, etc., 1827; *Garry Owen; or, The Snow-Woman: and Poor Bob, the Chimney-Sweeper.* London: J. Murray, 1832; *Tales and Novels.* 18 vols. London: Baldwin, etc., 1832–1833; *Helen.* 3 vols. London: R. Bentley, 1834. *Orlandino.* Edinburgh: W. & R. Chambers, 1848; *The Novels of M. Edgeworth.* 12 vols. London: J. M. Dent/New York: Dodd, Mead, 1893. REFERENCES: Butler, H. J. & Butler, H. E. *The Black Book of Edgeworthstown and Other Memories.* London: Faber & Gwyer, 1927; Butler, Marilyn. *Maria Edgeworth: A Literary Biography.* Oxford: Clarendon, 1972; Clarke, Isabel C. *Maria Edgeworth, Her Family and Friends.* London: Hutchinson, 1949; Colvin, Christina, ed. *Maria Edgeworth: Letters from England 1813–1814.* Oxford: Clarendon, 1971; Colvin, Christina, ed. *Maria Edgeworth in France and Switzerland.* Oxford: Oxford University Press, 1979; Dunne, Tom. *Maria Edgeworth and the Colonial Mind.* Cork: Cork University Press, 1984; Edgeworth, Mrs. F. A. *A Memoir of M. Edgeworth with Selections from Her Letters.* 3 vols. London: Privately printed, 1867; Flanagan, Thomas. *The Irish Novelists 1800–1850.* New York: Columbia University Press, 1959, pp. 53–106; Harden, O. Elizabeth McWhorter. *Maria Ed-

geworth's Art of Prose Fiction. The Hague: Mouton, 1971; Harden, O. Elizabeth McWhorter. *Maria Edgeworth.* Boston: Twayne, 1984; Hare, Augustus. *The Life and Letters of Maria Edgeworth* 2 vols. London: Arnold, 1894; Hausermann, H. W. *The Genevese Background.* London: Routledge & Kegan Paul, 1952; Hawthorne, Mark D. *Doubt and Dogma in Maria Edgeworth.* Gainesville: University of Florida Press, 1967; Hill, Constance. *Maria Edgeworth and Her Circle in the Days of Buonaparte and Bourbon.* London & New York: John Lane, 1910; Hurst, Michael. *Maria Edgeworth and the Public Scene.* London: Macmillan, 1969; Inglis-Jones, Elisabeth. *The Great Maria.* London: Faber, 1959/Westport, Conn.: Greenwood, 1979; Kowaleski-Wallace, Elizabeth. *Their Father's Daughters.* New York: Oxford University Press, 1991; Lawless, Emily. *Maria Edgeworth.* London: Macmillan, 1904; McCormack, W. J. *Ascendancy and Tradition in Anglo-Irish Literary History from 1789 to 1939.* Oxford: Clarendon, 1985; MacDonald, Edgar E., ed. *The Education of the Heart: The Correspondence of Rachel Mordecai Lazarus and Maria Edgeworth.* Chapel Hill: University of North Carolina Press, 1977; Newby, Percy H. *Maria Edgeworth.* London: A. Barker, 1950; Newcomer, James. *Maria Edgeworth the Novelist, 1768–1849.* Fort Worth: Texas Christian University Press, 1967; Owens, Coilin. *Family Chronicles. Maria Edgeworth's "Castle Rackrent."* Dublin: Wolfhound, 1987; Zimmern, Helen. *Maria Edgeworth.* London: Allen, 1883.

EDWARDS, RUTH DUDLEY (1944–   ), historian and novelist. Edwards was born in Dublin into a family of academicians who also specialize in histories. She was educated at Catholic schools in Ireland and received her undergraduate and postgraduate degrees in history from University College, Dublin. She worked for the post office and served in the Department of Industry before pursuing a writing career. She lives in London.

Edwards' first two histories are distinguished by their conciseness and thoroughness. *An Atlas of Irish History* (1973) provides an overview of all things Irish; no doubt, teachers have flouted copyright laws to distribute photocopies of her chapters and W. H. Bromage's accompanying maps in introductory Irish history and literature courses. Her *Patrick Pearse: The Triumph of Failure* won the National University of Ireland Prize for Historical Research in 1978 and has been lauded as "definitive" and "indispensable."

Critics have complained that Edwards' biographies of Harold Macmillan (1983) and publisher Victor Gollancz (1987), as well as her history of *The Economist* (1993), cling so tightly to primary sources that they lack the perspective that secondary sources would have afforded. There was also grousing about the biographies being painfully complete: *Gollancz,* which won the James Tait Black Prize for Biography, is almost 800 pages, and *Pursuit of Reason* is over 1,000. Nevertheless, the same critics have praised Edwards' ability to remain objective under circumstances that would unnerve less fearless historians: writing for a publisher who commissioned the book in honor of a family member, a founder, or itself.

Edwards' four mysteries feature the bloody adventures of solid Scotland Yard detective James Milton; urbane, chronically unemployed civil servant Robert Amiss; and two sidekick-policemen who are given dialogue on an as-needed basis. Amiss's banter is more entertaining than the mysteries are challenging, primarily because Edwards relies on expositions over cocktails. Still, she tells a good story. Perhaps most interesting is seeing Edwards recycle elements of her own life—for example, her civil service background and her brother's (Owen Dudley Edwards) interest in Sherlock Holmes—into the mysteries. Even a copy of *The Economist* becomes a deadly weapon.

Edwards easily reconciles her interests in histories and murder mysteries by noting that "both my serious books and my crime novels are mainly about people and their motivation."

PRISCILLA GOLDSMITH

WORKS: *An Atlas of Irish History*. London: Methuen, 1973/2d ed., 1981; *Patrick Pearse: The Triumph of Failure*. London: Victor Gollancz/New York: Taplinger, 1977/London: Faber, 1979/ Dublin: Poolbeg, 1990; *James Connolly*. Dublin: Gill & Macmillan, 1981. (Short biography); *Corridors of Death*. London: Quartet, 1981/New York: St. Martin's, 1982. (Mystery); *Harold Macmillan: A Life in Pictures*. London: Macmillan, 1983; *The Saint Valentine's Day Murders*. London: Quartet, 1984/New York: St. Martin's, 1985. (Mystery); *Victor Gollancz: A Biography*. London: Gollancz, 1987; *The School of English Murder*. London: Gollancz, 1990/as *The English School of Murder*, New York: St. Martin's, 1990. (Mystery); *Clubbed to Death*. London: Gollancz/ New York: St. Martin's, 1992. (Mystery); *The Pursuit of Reason:* The Economist *1843–1993*. London: Hamish Hamilton/New York: Penguin, 1993; *The Best of Bagehot*. London: Hamish Hamilton, 1993. (An edition of pieces by Walter Begehot, third editor of *The Economist*); *True Brits: Inside the Foreign Office*. London: BBC Books, 1994. (Companion book to a BBC series).

EGAN, DESMOND (1936–   ), poet. Born on July 15, 1936, in Athlone, Desmond Egan gained international acclaim with the publication of his *Collected Poems* in 1983, which won the National Poetry Foundation of America Award that year. Up to that time his primary vocation was teaching English and classical Greek at Newbridge College, although he published a number of volumes of poetry through his own Goldsmith Press in Kildare, beginning with *Midland* (1972) and including *Leaves* (1974), *Siege!* (1976), *Woodcutter* (1978), *Athlone?* (1980), *Snapdragon* and *Seeing Double* (1983), volumes from which the *Collected Poems* drew. Since then the University of Maine in association with the Goldsmith Press has published *Poems for Peace* (1986) and *Song for My Father* (1989).

Egan's style has been justly characterized as experimental, eccentric, American, Poundian. His aim is to "catch a moment of living, a pervasive mood." He explains, "When the times no longer rhyme, then neither will poetry." He adds that "to write in the traditional way in the later Twentieth Century—even in Ireland—is pure insensitivity." Accordingly, he strives for "a syntax which might reflect the flux and confusions of our present . . . but not from a theoretical stance. . . . Each attempt at making a poem must uncover its own new shape; each line discover its own peculiar rhythm." He captures the flux and confusion of our present in many of his poems by forgoing punctuation; in others by a contrapuntal device, most obvious in *Seeing Double,* where he confronts us with a page bearing a single title under which appear two columns of words, each column a separate poem. In this way an interaction between the two apparently autonomous texts is forced, often with surprising interpretive "accidents."

In the early *Midland,* which characteristically includes drawings, Egan celebrates place in brief, taut, imagistic poems that blend the landscapes of the Irish Midlands with images of Crete. *Leaves* is a more personal collection. Intense and introspective, it contains a number of passionate love lyrics. In *Siege!*, however, there is a turn from lyricism to contemporary politics—the kidnapping of a Dutch industrialist by the Irish Republican Army. In Egan's own words, it is about "changing Irish society and the gradual betrayal of the ideals of the 1916 Rebellion."

Woodcutter contains illustrations by Alberto Giacometti and is seen by Egan as "a different book" with "all sorts of contradictions in it." He describes it as "a kind of summary of what had gone before. But there's also that in it which is experimental and pointing towards the future." Its last poem, "Late But? One for Ezra," suggests the impact that Pound would have on that future. "Reading the *Cantos* of Pound," says Egan, "I saw that he tried to involve everything he knew, remembered, was interested in, was even casually interested in, the people he knew—to heave the whole lot into poetry. And I wanted to do that in a poem, to get the whole range of human response, not just the romantic little things, to get memory, to get cross-references, to get intellect, to get one's response to the thing itself."

Athlone? strives "to get memory" into its poems, mapping Egan's childhood in the town in which he grew up. "I'm from the Midlands, from Athlone, County Westmeath," said Egan. "Bred, born and raised there—something I have gradually come to value greatly." *Snapdragon* is a book of love poems, but love poems grounded in simple ordinary experience, what Egan calls in one poem "the small change of your everydays."

Seeing Double is a tribute to the richness of the passing moment—so rich that it requires a double vision to take it all in. The double vision is realized in Egan's technique of placing complementary poems side by side under a single title. "I want to make people aware of what is going-on on the right-hand side while they are looking at the left."

The increasing political nature of Egan's work is exemplified in *Poems for Peace,* which rails against the pervasive injustice of the world, a theme that reappears in more covert form in the two-sectioned *A Song for My Father.* Section one is reminiscent of *Midland* in the way it juxtaposes the local and the international: poems about Midlanders mingle with figures such as Benjamin Moloise, the South African freedom fighter.

Egan's most recent works include a collection of essays called The *Death of Metaphor* (1990), a translation of Euripides' *Medea* (1991), and *Poems for Eimear* (1993), a sequence of ten elegiac poems on the death of a six-and-a-half-year-old girl, Eimear Cullen.

THOMAS F. MERRILL

WORKS: *Midland.* Newbridge, Co. Kildare: Goldsmith, 1972; *Leaves.* Newbridge: Goldsmith, 1974; *Siege!* Newbridge: Goldsmith, 1976; *Woodcutter.* Newbridge: Goldsmith, 1978; *Athlone?* Newbridge: Goldsmith, 1980; *Snapdragon.* Little Rock, Ark.: Milestone, 1983; *Seeing Double.* [Newbridge: Goldsmith, 1983]; *Collected Poems.* Orono, Maine: National Poetry Foundation, 1983/

2d ed., Newbridge: Goldsmith, 1984; *Poems for Peace*. Dublin: [Afri], 1986; *A Song for My Father*. Newbridge: Kavanagh/Calstock: Peterloo Poets, 1989; *The Death of Metaphor*. Gerrards Cross: Colin Smythe/Newbridge: Kavanagh, 1990. (Essays); *Euripides' Medea*. Newbridge: Kavanagh, 1991. (Translation); *Peninsula: Poems of the Dingle Peninsula*. Newbridge: Kavanagh, 1992; *Selected Poems*. Hugh Kenner, ed. Newbridge: Goldsmith/Omaha: Creighton University Press, 1992; *Poems for Eimear*. Little Rock, Ark.: Milestone, 1993; *In the Holocaust of Autumn*. [Newbridge, Co. Kildare]: Goldsmith, 1994.   REFERENCES: Arkins, Brian. *Desmond Egan: A Critical Study*. Newbridge: Goldsmith, 1992/Little Rock, Ark.: Milestone, 1993; Johnston, Conor. "The Passionate Transitory in the Collected Poems of Desmond Egan." *Massachussetts Review* 29 (Spring 1988): / 001014/168; Kenner, Hugh, ed. *The Poet and His Work: Desmond Egan*. Orono, Maine: Northern Lights, 1993; Roche, Anthony. "Q. & A. with Desmond Egan." *Irish Literary Supplement* 8 (Fall 1989): 22–23; van de Kamp, Peter. "Desmond Egan: Universal Provincialist" in *The Crows Behind the Plough: History and Violence in Anglo-Irish Poetry and Drama*. Geert Lernout, ed. Amsterdam: Rodopi, 1991, pp. 143–158.

EGAN, PIERCE (1772–1849), sports journalist and humorist. Egan was born of Irish parents in either London or Dublin. He made a reputation for his descriptions of pugilism, collected as *Boxiana* (1812–1821), and especially for his racy sketches about London low life, *Life in London* (1822).

WORK OF IRISH INTEREST: *Real Life in Ireland; or, The Day and Night Scenes, Rovings, Rambles and Sprees, Bulls, Blunders, Bodderation and Blarney of Brian BORU, Esq. and His Elegant Friend Sir Shawn O'Dogherty*. London: Jones & J. L. Marks, 1821.   REFERENCE: Reid, J. C. *Bucks and Bruisers: Pierce Egan and Regency England*. London: Routledge & Kegan Paul, 1971.

EGERTON, GEORGE (1859–1945), novelist, short story writer, and playwright. George Egerton was the pseudonym of Mary Chavelita Dunne, who was born in Melbourne, Australia, on December 14, 1859, the eldest daughter of a cashiered Irish officer. His rambles with his large family took her to New Zealand, Chile, and eventually back to Ireland. Her father had much charm but no settled occupation: twice he was the governor of prisons—in Nenagh and Castlebar—but lost these posts when he fell into debt. He did, however, find time to write *How and Where to Fish in Ireland,* which is considered a classic. The accounts of the suffering of his children in George Egerton's published correspondence are graphic. When she was fourteen, and her mother died, bailiffs were in the house. She was sent by relatives to Germany for two years' study. Next she tried her hand at nursing in London, then went to New York, where she took low-paying jobs as a journalist and lived in a boardinghouse, experiences described in her novel *Wheel of God*. Through all of these misadventures, she somehow remained close to her father, whom she loved, despite his fecklessness, because he treated her as an equal and taught her such male sports as fly-fishing.

   She returned to Ireland to help care for her impoverished family, then in 1887 became the traveling companion of her father's friend, Henry Higginson, and of Higginson's wife, the widow of the author Whyte Melville. Higginson, who was already a bigamist, "eloped" with her to Norway, where they set up as a wealthy English couple. He turned out to be drunken and violent (she writes about this in her story "Under Northern Sky"), but, luckily for her, he, died in two years. Meanwhile, she had learned Norwegian, become interested in the Scandinavian realists, and sought out Knut Hamsun (she describes their relationship—conducted primarily through correspondence—in "Now Spring Has Come"). In 1890, she was in London again, working on a translation of *Hunger*.

In 1891, she met George Egerton Clairmonte, an attractive but ineffectual Newfoundlander; they married and moved to County Cork to live cheaply. Soon they were impoverished, and she tried her hand at fiction based primarily on her experiences in Norway. She submitted a book of six stories, which eventually became *Keynotes* (1893), to Heinemann, using her husband's name for a nom de plume. It was rejected but accepted by John Lane, and immediately its attractive, daring, and somewhat argumentative author became a literary sensation and darling of the fin-de-siècle movement. Another book of longish short stories, *Discords* (1894), was greeted with more applause. In the mid-1890s in London, George Egerton was at the height of her fame, counting among her acquaintances Yeats* and Havelock Ellis.

In 1895, a son was born, but her marriage was failing. Her husband, who resembled her father in his general ineptitude, in effect deserted her, going first to South Africa and then to the United States. She divorced him and in 1899 met Reginald Golding Bright, a drama critic turned theatrical agent who was fifteen years her junior. Her career as a writer of fiction seemingly stalled, she began, possibly at Bright's urging, to write drama. She had an affair with a young Norwegian who, she stated, was the only man she was ever physically attracted to (a version of her letters to him was published in *Rosa Amorosa*), but in 1901 she married Bright. Thereafter she devoted herself primarily to the writing of drama. Shaw,* among others, tried to offer assistance, and three of her plays were staged, but all were failures. Golding Bright's success and status grew, and her fame diminished. The death of her son in World War I greatly saddened her, and as the years passed, she wrote less and less, then not at all. Although she maintained a genuine interest in Ireland, she rarely visited there during the last half century of her life and died at Crawley, Sussex, on August 12, 1945, at the age of eighty-five, largely forgotten except by historians of literature.

Egerton recognized that her real genius was for the long short story, but publishers told her there was a declining market for this genre, and she abandoned it. She was not a true novelist; short stories, based on experience, came naturally to her, but to write novels she was forced to contrive and pad. Her plays were laughed off the stage. Shaw believed that she had talent but that her loquaciousness—a trait she bequeathed to her stage characters—drove people away. Her best work was based on personal experience, but once she had utilized the fund of her youthful adventures, she had little to say. Her earlier work, however, which celebrates the Ibsenite woman, was revolutionary in its treatment of the subtle nuances of personal relationships, the politics of power within the sexual union, and the attitude of women toward marriage and children. She championed greater frankness and honesty, particularly in sexual matters, insisting that a woman must be true to her nature, rather than to the role in which society had traditionally cast her. She celebrates the "wildness" that she felt was the essence of women's nature, and her best writing has a naturalness and directness that is tonic. Despite her admiration for masterful, dominant, "manlike" (her word) women in her fiction, in her personal and professional life, her relationships were not so confident or magisterial. When the fin-de-siècle sensibility ceased to be fashionable, her fame waned, but contemporary critics, feminists especially, have, to a degree, resuscitated her. There was a reprinting of *Discords* by Garland Press of New York in 1977 and of *Keynotes* and *Discords* in one volume by Virago Press of London in 1983. Her correspondence and diary have been edited by Terence de Vere White,* who was a close friend.

WILLIAM J. LINN

WORKS: *Keynotes*. London: Elkin Mathews & John Lane/Boston: Roberts Bros., 1893/rpt. London: Virago, 1983. (Stories); *Discords*. London: John Lane/Boston: Roberts Bros., 1894/rpt. New York: Garland, 1977/London: Virago, 1983. (Stories); *Young Ofeg's Ditties*. London: John Lane, 1895. (Translated from the Swedish of Ola Hansson); *Symphonies*. London & New York: John Lane, 1897. (Stories); *Fantasias*. London & New York: John Lane, 1898. (Stories); *The Wheel of God*. London: Grant Richards/New York: E. P. Dutton, 1898. (Novel); *Hunger*. London: L. Smithers, 1899/New York: Knopf, 1920/London: Duckworth, 1921. (Translated from the Norwegian of Knut Hamsun); *Rosa Amorosa: The Love-Letters of a Woman*. London: Grant Richards/New York: Brentano's 1901. (Novel); *Flies in Amber*. London: Hutchinson, 1905. (Novel); *A Leaf from the Yellow Book*. Terence de Vere White, ed. London: Richards Press, 1958. (Correspondence). REFERENCES: Foerster, Ernst. *Die Frauenfrage in den Romanen englischer Schriftstellerinnen der Gegenwart (George Egerton, Mona Caird, Sara Grand)*. Marburg, 1907; Gawsworth, John. *Ten Contemporaries. Notes toward Their Definitive Bibliography*. London: Ernest Benn, 1932.

EGLINTON, JOHN (1868–1961), essayist. John Eglinton was the pseudonym of William Kirkpatrick Magee, who was born in Dublin in 1868, the second son of a Presbyterian clergyman. Magee and W. B. Yeats* were classmates at the High School. Magee then went on to be a classical honorsman at Trinity College and four times won the Vice-Chancellor's Prize for the best composition in English, Greek, or Latin verse, the examiners being the redoubtable trio of Mahaffy,* Tyrrell, and Dowden. After his graduation, he went to work at the National Library, much against his will, and remained there from 1895 to 1921. He appears in the Scylla and Charybdis chapter of Joyce's* *Ulysses,* which is set in the library, and is treated with more respect than Joyce usually accorded his real-life subjects. Magee was an early member of the theosophical movement in Dublin, and his many friends included AE,* Stephen MacKenna,* and George Moore* who describes him in *Hail and Farewell* as "a sort of lonely thorn tree." Magee, who for a time acted more or less as Moore's secretary, said that Moore was "almost intolerably tedious about literary trifles."

Although somewhat austere and aloof, Magee's John Eglinton essays were highly regarded. His two early volumes, *Two Essays on the Remnant* and *Pebbles from a Brook,* are full of transcendental generalization. He later wrote of them, "There was a young man in the nineties into whom the very breath of Emerson and Thoreau had entered, with those tongue he spoke (or at least in their tone of voice). Now there is a battered and somewhat incredulous person who blushes when he runs across some quotation from either book." Nevertheless, W. B. Yeats, who crossed swords with Magee in the press, called him "our one Irish critic," but one who was "in permanent friendly opposition to our national literary movement." "Opposition" was too strong a word, for Magee and Fred Ryan* did launch one of the important, if too shortlived, magazines of the literary movement. This was *Dana,* which appeared twelve times from May 1904 through April 1905. Among the contributors were AE, Colum,* Gogarty,* Joyce (whose *Portrait of the Artist* was rejected as a serial), George Moore, Seumas O'Sullivan,* and W. B. Yeats. In 1920, Magee married M. L. O'Leary who worked with him at the National Library. After the formation of the Free State, Magee found himself out of sympathy with the new Ireland and moved to England where he died in Bournemouth on May 9, 1961. His important later books were his *Irish Literary Portraits* (1935) and *Memoir of A.E.* (1937).

WORKS: *Two Essays on the Remnant.* Dublin: Whaley, 1894; *Literary Ideals in Ireland,* with W. B. Yeats, A. E. & W. Larminie. London: T. Fisher Unwin/Dublin: Daily Express Office, 1899; rpt., New York: Lemma, 1973; *Pebbles from a Brook.* Kilkenny & Dublin: Standish O'Grady, 1901; *Some Essays and Passages by John Eglinton,* selected by W. B. Yeats. Dundrum: Dun Emer, 1905; *Bards and Saints.* Dublin: Tower Press Booklets, Maunsel, 1906; *Anglo-Irish Essays.* Dublin: Talbot/London: T. Fisher Unwin, 1917; ed. and trans., G. Moore, *Letters to Edouard Dujardin.* New York: Crosby Gaige, 1929; *Irish Literary Portraits.* London: Macmillan, 1935; rpt., Freeport, N.Y.: Books for Libraries, 1967; *A Memoir of A.E.* London: Macmillan, 1937; ed., *Letters of George Moore, with an Introduction by John Eglinton, to Whom They Were Written.* Bournemouth: Sydenham, [1942]; *Confidential; or, Take It or Leave It.* London: Fortune, 1951. (Poems). REFERENCES: Boyd, Ernest. *Ireland's Literary Renaissance.* Dublin: Maunsel/New York: John Lane, 1916; Boyd, Ernest. "An Irish Essayist: John Eglinton" in *Appreciations and Depreciations: Irish Literary Studies.* Dublin: Talbot/London: T. Fisher Unwin, 1917; Lenoski, Daniel S. "Yeats, Eglinton, and Aestheticism." *Eire–Ireland* 14 (Winter 1979): 91–108.

ELLIS, CONLETH (1937–1988), poet. Ellis was born in Carlow and taught in Belfast and Athlone. His substantial 1971 collection *Under the Stone* is a book that improves and becomes more impressive with each page. The first section, which apparently contains earlier poems, includes a conventional and not very memorable sonnet called "After Love" and a poem called "Belfast, 1960," with its notable grammatical error and a far-fetched image like "The bell of the abbey wrapped / Sparrows' singing in folds of serge." Several other pieces, however, like "Encounter with the Poet Sweeney" and "Under the Stone," show a quite deft handling of conventional form. In still others, like "Walls" or "Ash," the poet commences the tinkering with rhythm and rhyme discernible in the most interesting poems of the rest of the book.

The second section remains eclectic in form, from the ABAB iambic pentameter of "Young Poet," to the effective free verse of "Passion" and the even more interesting use of spondees and alliteration in the imagistic poem "Good-

bye''—for instance, in a line like ''Rain round street lamps lighted like lace.''
This last technique is most apparent in the final half-dozen poems of the book's
last section—in such pieces as ''Islands,'' ''Sequences,'' or ''Sunday Morning,'' in which last piece Ellis sounds almost Hopkins-like. Rhythmically, Ellis
can veer fascinatingly from a swinging looseness to the effectively clotted: from
''The kestrel drops by the black / Elms where the horses turn for home'' of
''Ploughman and Kestrel,'' to ''The pock-marked stone falls when winds
heave'' from ''West of Here.'' The poems of *Under the Stone* are those of a
writer still experimenting with sound and rhythm, but in at least a dozen pieces
experimenting successfully and excitingly.

Ellis's posthumous volume *Darkness Blossoming* (1989) is a collection about
Africa, which the author visited before his death in 1988. The book is a distinct
disappointment and seems almost written by another man. The poems are direct,
disarmingly simple, often even rather flat. Sometimes, as in ''Gloss,'' the simplicity of a number of metaphors and conceits about fireflies in the woods works.
At other times, as in the line ''a red snake suddenly grated like iron / on iron
into the leaves of the fallen years,'' the poet seems less effective than affected.
In almost no place does the volume fulfill the formal promise of *Under the
Stone*.

WORKS. *Under the Stone*. Dublin: Gill & Macmillan, [1971]; *After Doomsday*. Dublin: Raven
Arts, 1982; *The Age of Exploration*. Dublin: Dedalus, 1985; *Aoibhinn An Galor*. Dublin: Coisceim,
1985; *Seabhac Ag Guirdeal*. Dublin: Coisceim, 1985; *Darkness Blossoming*. Dublin: Dedalus,
1989.   REFERENCE: Kelly, Rita E. ''Suaimhneas Ort: Conleth Ellis 1937–1988.'' *Innti* 12 (1989):
85–91.

ELLMANN, RICHARD (1918–1987), American biographer and critic. Although American, Richard Ellmann made a major contribution to Irish letters
by his superbly thorough biography of James Joyce.* He also edited a two-
volume addition to Stuart Gilbert's collection of Joyce's letters and wrote some
subtle academic criticism of W. B. Yeats.* Shortly before his death, he completed an admirable biography of Oscar Wilde,* although it is not quite on a
par with his Joyce. He was born on March 15, 1918, in Highland Park, Michigan, and was educated at Yale and at Trinity College, Dublin. He taught at
Harvard, Northwestern, Indiana, Chicago, and Oxford; and he died in Oxford
on May 13, 1987.

WORKS: *Yeats, the Man and the Masks*. New York: Macmillan, 1948/London: Macmillan, 1949;
The Identity of Yeats. London: Macmillan/New York: Oxford University Press, 1954; rev. ed.,
London: Faber/New York: Oxford University Press, 1964; *James Joyce*. New York: Oxford
University Press, 1959; rev. ed., London and New York: Oxford University Press, 1982; ed., *Letters
of James Joyce*. Vols. 2 & 3. New York: Viking, 1966; *Eminent Domain: Yeats among Wilde,
Joyce, Pound, Eliot, and Auden*. New York: Oxford University Press, 1967; *Ulysses on the Liffey*.
New York: Oxford University Press, 1972; *Codgers*. New York: Oxford University Press, 1973;
ed., *Selected Letters of James Joyce*. New York: Viking, 1975 (Contains some significant and
elsewhere unpublished letters from Joyce to his wife); *Oscar Wilde*. New York: Knopf/London:
Hamish Hamilton, 1987.   REFERENCE: Dick, Susan, Kiberd, Declan, McMillan, Dougald, & Ronsley, Joseph, eds. *Omnium Gatherum. Essays for Richard Ellmann*. Gerrards Cross: Colin Smythe/

Montreal: McGill University Press, 1989. (Contains several essays about Ellmann and a full bibliography.)

EMMET, ROBERT (1778–1803), nationalist. Emmet was born in Cork on March 4, 1778, and was executed in Dublin on September 20, 1803. The abortive rising that he led had enormous impractical influence on Irish history. His speech from the dock and his appealing love affair with Sarah Curran have captured the imagination of succeeding generations. The tale of Bold Robert Emmet, the Darlin' of Erin, has been celebrated by many writers, among them his friend Thomas Moore,* and by the playwrights Lennox Robinson,* Denis Johnston,* Paul Vincent Carroll,* John O'Donovan,* and Conor Farrington.* There are several versions of his stirring speech, probably none of them completely authentic. One particularly eloquent version concludes:

I have but one request to make at my departure from this world, it is—the charity of its silence. Let no man write my epitaph; for as no man, who knows my motives, dare now vindicate them, let not prejudice or ignorance asperse them. Let them rest in obscurity and peace! Let my memory be left in oblivion, and my tomb remain uninscribed, until other times and other men can do justice to my character. When my country takes her place among the nations of the earth, *then,* and *not till then,* let my epitaph be written. I have done.

By his speech, Emmet made a small eloquent addition to Irish literature; by his death, he had an incalculable emotional effect on Irish history.

REFERENCES: Landreth, Helen. *The Pursuit of Robert Emmet.* New York: McGraw-Hill, 1948/ 2d ed., Dublin: Browne & Nolan, 1949; Madden, Richard R. *The Life and Times of Robert Emmet, Esq.* Dublin: Dublin: Duffy, 1847; O Broin, Leon. *Emmet.* Baile Átha Cliath: Sairseal agus Dill, 1954; Vance, N. C. "Text and Tradition: Robert Emmet's Speech from the Dock." *Studies* (Summer 1982): 185–191.

ENNIS, JOHN (1944–   ), poet. Ennis, born in Westmeath in 1944, was educated at University College, Cork, and at University College, Dublin. He lives in Butlerstown, County Waterford, and is head of humanities in the Waterford Regional Technical College. He won the Patrick Kavanagh Award in 1975; published his first volume, *Night on Hibernia,* in 1976; and won the Open Poetry Competition at Listowel Writers' Week in 1976 and 1977. His "Orpheus," which won at Listowel in 1977, forms the bulk of his book published later in that year, *Dolmen Hill.*

Night on Hibernia is rather foppishly full of unusual words, such as lixiviate, helices, guillemot, filbert, haulms, glaubed, grume, waifed, berried, undine, lactic, staggy, glaur, condescent, britchen, cutis, smalt, prepuce, amnion, nard, pelagic. It is also full of many faintly awkward coined words, such as hiss-lipped, haw-warm, grassovered, dew-greasy, thunder-tiered, starling-crowned, defunct-winged, truthhoods. And many of the sentences are rather scrunched up, as if written by an enormously literate Tarzan. For instance, "Son, father wake, exit greyly once-trodden familiar haunts/Kitchen, sheds, fields.'' Nevertheless, the volume reeks with talent.

Dolmen Hill is even more interesting. In this work, Ennis writes in extremely long lines; therefore, his occasional rhyming is usually ineffective. Still, as symptoms of growth, it might be noted that the erratic punctuation of the first volume is less in evidence, and the language is fascinating. Many tersely jammed-up short sentences still occur without that usual grease of discourse, the article ''the''; and so the poet still sometimes sounds like a lobotomized German in a basic English-language course. But his ''Orpheus,'' for all of its cluttering obfuscation and giddy eclecticism of diction, must still be considered possibly the most astonishing long poem any Irish poet has written since Kavanagh's* *The Great Hunger.*

For several years, Ennis seemed to develop along the lines laid down in his first books. For instance, his long poem *Arboretum,* which won a prize at Listowel Writers' Week in 1990, appears to be about a family outing in the John F. Kennedy Park in Wexford and may reflect the father's concern about his young son's growing up. It is difficult to say, for Ennis's passion for obscure words increasingly tends to obscure rather than clarify his statement. Words like ''phloem,'' ''streal,'' ''panicles,'' ''nymphaea,'' ''ordovician,'' ''alnus,'' ''shinato,'' ''robus,'' ''cratageous,'' ''pinnate,'' ''paliuris,'' ''chamaecyparis,'' and ''phyllodoce'' are scattered throughout, as are obscure place-names and the Latin names for trees—''Tamarix ramosissima,'' ''Taxodum ascendens mutans,'' ''beluta pubsescens,'' and the like. In this book, Ennis's language has grown so obtrusive that he is in danger of talking mainly to himself.

In a 1979 article in *The Crane Bag,* Sean Golden remarked that Ennis, like Paul Muldoon* and Eilean Ni Chuilleanain,* wrote ''naturally'' and ''unselfconsciously.'' A more inappropriate statement would be hard to imagine—at least until Ennis's 1994 collection, *Down in the Deeper Helicon.* This is quite different from his previous work, having really none of his erudite diction. The directness of the simple language of ''Father Hopkins in Old Age'' or ''The Knife'' or, indeed, many other poems in the collection is a notable contrast to his earlier work. What he loses in richness, however, he gains in power. Most of the poems are a kind of variation of the sonnet form. They have fourteen lines and a rhyme scheme, and the lines are sometimes in iambic pentameter. Very often, however, the lines have six or eight or even more stresses, with considerable variety in the number and placement of unstressed syllables. Despite the loose freedom Ennis allows himself and also despite the usual awkwardness of the long line in English verse, he consistently succeeds, both rhythmically and rhetorically, as in the concluding couplet of ''Joyce Cycling to Oughterard and Vico'':

> Till I'm young enough again the face the spittle and the blows,
> Who may not last, like that boy will, beyond the winter snows.

The poetic voice in this large collection is as distinctive as Ennis's earlier one and more effectively public.

WORKS: *Night on Hibernia.* [Dublin]: Gallery, [1976]; *Dolmen Hill.* [Dublin]: Gallery, [1977]; *A Drink of Spring.* [Dublin]: Gallery, [1979]; *The Burren Days.* [Dublin]: Gallery, [1985]; *Arboretum.* [Dublin]: Dedalus, [1990]; *In a Green Shade.* [Dublin]: Dedalus, [1991]; *Down in the Deeper Helicon.* Dublin: Dedalus, [1994]; *Telling the Bees.* Dublin: Dedalus, [1995].

ENRIGHT, ANNE (1962–   ), short story writer. Born in Dublin in 1962, Anne Enright attended school there, including Trinity College, Dublin, and lives there still. She has also lived in Vancouver, Canada, and attended the University of East Anglia. She has worked as an actress and writer and is currently a producer/ director for RTÉ.

Enright's collection of short stories, *The Portable Virgin* (1991), won the Rooney Prize and shows brilliant technical skill, impressive handling of images, and great promise. The power of Enright's language carries both plot and character. Enright's characters often want revenge; they are out of touch, often out of control. Mrs. Hanratty in "Luck for a Lady" numbers everything; she is incapable of not seeing life as arithmetically perfect. Cathy in "(She Owns) Everything" sells handbags and keeps her life and the lives of her customers orderly until one day a customer challenges her judgment. Cathy falls in love, loses control, abuses her handbag, and starts to sleep around. The characters are all "grotesques," Enright exaggerating particular elements of their personalities and showing how those elements play out.

The prose is intelligently and dryly witty. Although the subjects of the stories are often painful, harsh, and violent, Enright maintains throughout an underlying humor, albeit fairly sharp. The prose relies on series of images that are often surrealistic and disjointed. Also, the stories seem to get more difficult and fragmented as they go along, all of them having a somewhat cold, spiteful, violent underpinning. The last story, "Mr. Snip Snip Snip," provides the focus for the entire collection: the flashing images of the cinema, fragmentary as if large parts have been edited or "snipped" out, mirror Enright's process of composition. Most of the stories have a very cinematic quality, focusing on the flat image that suggests but does not delineate.

The collection is, in fact, full of self-reflexive commentary. "The House of the Architect's Love Story," for example, provides the "architectural plan" for the reading of the book:

In the house of an architect's love story the light is always moving, the air is thick with light. From outside, the house of the architect's love story is a Neo-Palladian villa, but inside, there are corners, cellars, attics, toilets, a room full of books with an empty socket in the lamp. . . . cubbyholes that smell of wet afternoons. . . . vaults, a sacristy, an office with windows set in the floor. . . . a sky-blue nursery where the rockinghorse is shaped like a bat and swings from a rail. And in the centre of it all is a bay window where the sun pours in.

The image conjures up the very way her prose affects the reader. The technique, the crafting, the polish of the surface belie what is behind the door of the facade. At first, dazzled by the brilliance of the prose, the reader explores the inner recesses, finding ever more to look at, ever more to ponder, ever more to puzzle over.

Enright's first novel, *The Wig My Father Wore* (1995) carries on many of the stylistic techniques of the story collection. She uses the surrealistic, dreamlike technique of fragmented images colliding. The strength of the images is, again, in their very concreteness used to capture the ineffable. It is a book about love— the love between parent and child and between lovers and the glitzy, superficial love portrayed by the media, here represented by the television show where the main character works, the "LoveQuiz." Each different kind is problematic: the "LoveQuiz" represents the falsity, the fakery, the shallowness of our percep- tions about love. The relationship between the narrator and her father carries that theme into another level: the wig her father wears suggests the falsity of his character; and her father, who is lapsing into senility throughout the book, is not a character Grace can actually talk about or grasp. Still, she looks at the love that existed between her parents, as well as the feelings she still has for her father, and the reader gets the sense that love, somehow, sustains, in spite of falsity. Finally, Grace's lover Stephen is, literally, an angel, a noncorporeal substance who is, in his own way, as glitzy and unreal as the television show but who suggests a powerful level of idealized love. The book ends with a dream image of spilled milk, unanswerable questions of childhood, the love of the angel Stephen, and Grace's realization that making love has not changed anything. Although the style and content are more difficult to sustain than in the short stories, still the novel shows Enright's powerful language and ability to capture daily human experience.

MARYANNE FELTER

WORKS: *The Portable Virgin*. London: Martin & Secker, 1991; (Short stories); *The Wig My Father Wore*. London: Jonathan Cape, 1995. (Novel).

ENVOY (1949–1951), literary magazine. *Envoy* was the lively but short-lived literary magazine whose editor was John Ryan* and whose poetry editor was Valentin Iremonger.* The magazine first appeared in December 1949, and in all, it published twenty monthly numbers. It is important chiefly for the forum it gave to Patrick Kavanagh,* but Brendan Behan,* Brian O'Nolan,* Sean O'Faolain,* Francis Stuart,* and many other important writers also appeared in its pages.

ERVINE, ST. JOHN GREER (1883–1971), playwright. John Greer Ervine (the "St." was added when he began to write) was born in Ballymacarrett, in suburban Belfast, on December 28, 1883. Moving to London at the age of seventeen, he became acquainted with Bernard Shaw* and the Fabian Society, and developed an interest in repertory theatre. Between 1911 and 1915, Ervine contributed to the Abbey* four plays of Ulster life: *Mixed Marriage, The Magnanimous Lover, The Orangeman,* and *John Ferguson.*

Ervine was appointed manager of the Abbey in the autumn of 1915. Rejecting all that was distinctive in the theatre, he sought to convert it into a typical repertory theatre. By the end of the season, all of the actors had resigned or were dismissed by the contentious, outspoken manager. The Abbey directors had to replace Ervine and rebuild a company. He then went into military service and in 1918 suffered a wound which necessitated the amputation of one leg.

In the 1920s, Ervine wrote drawing room comedies for London theatres. His only work for the Abbey was the sarcastically titled *The Isle of Saints.* In 1924, the Gaiety, Dublin, staged Ervine's *The Ship,* a father-son conflict spoiled by an operatic ending. In 1936, he returned to the Abbey stage and an Ulster locale with *Boyd's Shop,* followed by *William John Mawhinney* (1940) and *Friends and Relations* (1941). The Ulster Drama Group in Belfast performed three of his less important plays—*My Brother Tom, Ballyfarland's Festival,* and *Martha*—in the 1950s.

His formidable productivity included several novels, abrasive commentary on the theatre of his time (the Abbey did not appear to advantage), and biographies of such personalities as Shaw, Parnell, and Wilde,* which, like Johnson's *Lives,* were more notable for the opinions than for the scholarship. A collection of stories, *Eight O'Clock and Other Studies,* was published in 1913. Typical is "The Burial," in which two men of the North discuss as matters of equal significance the death of a young woman and the market price of cattle. The novel *Changing Winds* (1917) follows its quasi-autobiographical hero, Henry Quinn, an Ulsterman with Southern connections, to Dublin during Easter Week and eventually to the Western Front.

As drama critic for the *New York World* in 1928 and 1929, he predictably was at odds with other critics. Ervine married Leonora May Davis in 1911; they had no children. He died in London on January 24, 1971.

Like Lennox Robinson,* Ervine began with localized realism, turned to Londonized sophistication, and then came back to Erin. But whereas Robinson's earliest dramas were apprentice work, Ervine's first creations were successful.

In Ervine's 1911–1915 Ulster dramas, the dominant figure is the fundamentalist patriarch, dogmatic in all things religious and political. Into the seemingly rigid format implied by such characterization Ervine introduced variety. For John McClurg, in *The Orangeman* (1914), July 12 is a chamber of horrors; rheumatism keeps him out of The Parade, and a rebellious son breaks John's drum. John Rainey, in *Mixed Marriage* (1911), is an extremely unwilling party to two "mixed marriages," one between his son and a Catholic girl, and another between Catholic and Protestant workers on strike. Bigotry, in the latter instance, cannily augmented by management, shatters both alliances. At the catastrophic close, with religious warfare churning in the streets and his sons estranged from him, Rainey mutters his apologia, "A wus right." The strength of otherwise melodramatic *John Ferguson* (1915) is molded in the title character, whose Old

Testament concepts of right and wrong are shaken when his daughter is raped and his son carries out violent reprisal.

Ulster phariseeism is the topic of *The Magnanimous Lover* (1912). Henry Hinde, "born again" years after fathering an illegitimate child, offers marriage to the mother, whom he admittedly does not love. She turns him down. Replying to journalists who found the subject matter offensive, Ervine wrote *The Critics* (1913), in which reviewers sit in the vestibule of the Abbey and condemn an anti-Irish play by one of the Cork realists, entitled *Hamlet*.

Ervine's work for British theatres has not aged well. The best of the lot, *Mary Mary Quite Contrary* (1923), lightheartedly examines show business personalities. *Anthony and Anna* (1926) is the old formula of the brash, penniless man and the spoiled rich girl. *The First Mrs. Fraser* (1929), a box office triumph, tells of a middle-aged man who wants to end his marriage to a trashy young thing and remarry his first wife. *The Christies* (Glasgow, 1947; Belfast, 1948) is a semi-serious treatment of the rehabilitation of an unrepentant financier who was imprisoned for fraud.

In *Boyd's Shop* (Liverpool, 1936; Abbey, 1936) one sees a changed Ulster, or a changed Ervine. It is no longer the greybeards but the young who are dogmatic and intolerant. The peaceful realm of Andrew Boyd, a grocer descended from grocers, and a superannuated Presbyterian minister, the Reverend Arthur Patterson, is invaded by John Haslett, a rival grocer with modern ideas, and the Reverend Ernest Dunwoody, an ordained social climber. Boyd, too, can say in effect at the close, "A wus right," but his rightness comes from a shrewd, yet kindly, understanding of his fellow men. *Friends and Relations* is set in suburban Belfast, but only the servants are stock Ulster types. Crusty old Sir Samuel Lepper wills his estate to his second cousin, Adam Bothwell, an unread novelist who does not want the money but whose friends and relations do.

Ervine's main contribution to Irish literature is a realism diverging from that of the Cork writers. They see men coarsened by bleak environment; the hardness of Ervine's Ulstermen is a projection of their stony creed. The mothers in Lennox Robinson's and T. C. Murray's* early plays are aggressive and manipulative. The mothers in Ervine's Ulster plays, Martha Martin in his novel *Mrs. Martin's Man* (1914), and the heroine of his play *Jane Clegg* (Manchester, 1913) all have an infinite capacity for endurance and self-denial.

Life in the North is judiciously examined in Ervine's writing. One finds characters narrow in bigotry and supple in hypocrisy, along with those who possess the traits Ervine commends—integrity, patience, and industry. Throughout his biography of Bernard Shaw, he praises the upright workingman and worries about the erosion of character which a welfare state might cause. Ervine also brought the agonies of divided Belfast onto the stage several years before Sean O'Casey* did as much for Dublin.

Compared to the coarse texture of his serious work, Ervine's comedies may have a satiny feel, but ideas sometimes lurk behind the sheen. *Anthony and*

Anna, Friends and Relations, The Christies, and, to some extent, *Boyd's Shop*
bear the common theme of what Alexander Pope called the Use of Riches.

Whatever his truculent personality, whatever temporary harm he wrought as
manager of the Abbey, St. John Ervine was a conscientious craftsman, artistically at home in a ''smart set'' drawing room or in an Ulster cottage.

WILLIAM J. FEENEY

PRINCIPAL WORKS: *Eight O'Clock and Other Studies.* Dublin & London: Maunsel, 1913.
(Short stories); *Four Irish Plays (Mixed Marriage, The Magnanimous Lover, The Critics, The Or-
angeman).* London & Dublin: Maunsel/New York: Macmillan, 1914; *Jane Clegg.* London: Sidgwick
& Jackson/New York: Henry Holt, 1914. (Play); *Mrs. Martin's Man.* London & Dublin: Maunsel,
1914. (Novel); *Alice and a Family.* London & Dublin: Maunsel/New York: Macmillan, 1915.
(Novel); *John Ferguson.* Dublin: Maunsel/New York: Macmillan, 1915. (Play); *Sir Edward Carson
and the Ulster Movement.* Dublin & London: Maunsel/New York: Dodd, Mead, 1915; *Changing
Winds.* Dublin & London: Maunsel/New York: Macmillan, 1917. (Novel); *The Foolish Lovers.*
London: Collins/New York: Macmillan, 1920. (Novel); *Some Impressions of My Elders.* New York:
Macmillan, 1922/London: Allen & Unwin, 1923. (Essays); *The Ship.* London: Allen & Unwin/New
York: Macmillan, 1922. (Play); *Mary, Mary, Quite Contrary.* London: Allen & Unwin/New York:
Macmillan, 1923. (Play); *The Lady of Belmont.* London: Allen & Unwin/New York: Macmillan,
1923. (Play); *The Organized Theatre: A Plea in Civics.* London: Allen & Unwin/New York: Mac-
millan, 1924; *Anthony and Anna.* London: Allen & Unwin/New York: Macmillan, 1925/revised ed.,
1936. (Play); *Parnell.* London: Ernest Benn/London: Queensway/Boston: Little, Brown, 1925. (Bi-
ography); *The Wayward Man.* London: Collins/New York: Macmillan, 1927. (Novel); *How to Write
a Play.* London: Allen & Unwin/New York: Macmillan, 1928; *The Mountains and Other Stories.*
London: Allen & Unwin, 1928; *Four One-Act Plays (The Magnanimous Lover, Progress, Ole
George Comes to Tea, She Was No Lady).* London: Allen & Unwin/New York: Macmillan, 1928;
The First Mrs. Fraser. London: Chatto & Windus, 1929/New York: Macmillan, 1930. (Play); *The
First Mrs. Fraser.* London: Collins/New York: Macmillan, 1931. (Novel); *The St. John Ervine
Omnibus.* London: Collins, 1933. (Includes the novels *The Foolish Lovers, The Wayward Man, &
The First Mrs. Fraser*); *The Theatre in My Time.* London: Rich & Cowan, 1933/New York: Loring
& Mussey, 1934/Toronto: Ryerson, 1936; *God's Soldier: General William Booth.* London & To-
ronto: Heinemann, 1934/New York: Macmillan, 1935. (Biography); *Boyd's Shop.* London: Allen &
Unwin/New York: Macmillan, 1936. (Play); *People of Our Class.* London: Allen & Unwin, 1936.
(Play); *Robert's Wife.* London: Allen & Unwin/New York: Macmillan, 1938. (Play); *Sophia.* Lon-
don: Macmillan, 1941. (Novel); *Friends and Relations.* London: Allen & Unwin, 1947. (Play);
Private Enterprise. London: Allen & Unwin, 1948. (Play); *The Christies.* London: Allen & Unwin,
1949. (Play); *Craigavon, Ulsterman.* London: Allen & Unwin, 1949. (Biography); *Oscar Wilde: A
Present Time Appraisal.* London: Allen & Unwin, 1951/New York: Macmillan, 1952/New York:
William Morrow, 1952. (Biography); *My Brother Tom.* London: Allen & Unwin, 1952. (Play);
Bernard Shaw: His Life, Work and Friends. London: Constable/New York: William Morrow, 1956.
(Biography); ''St. John Ervine's Broadway, Part 1.'' Peter Drewniany & Robert Hogan, eds. *George
Spelvin's Theatre Book* III (Spring 1980): 1–97. (Theatrical criticism from *The New York World* for
1928–1929 season); ''St. John Ervine's Broadway, Part 2.'' *George Spelvin's Theatre Book* 3 (Sum-
mer 1980): 1–94; *Selected Plays of St. John Ervine.* John Cronin, ed. Gerrards Cross: Colin Smythe/
Washington, D.C.: Catholic University of America Press, 1988.   REFERENCES: Bell, Sam Hanna.
Theatre in Ulster. London & Dublin: Gill & Macmillan, 1972; Boyd, John. ''St. John Ervine, a
Biographical Note.'' *Threshold* 25 (Summer 1974): 101–115; Ireland, Denis. ''Red Brick City and
Its Dramatist: A Note on St. John Ervine.'' *Envoy* 1 (March 1950): 59–67; Vance, Norman. *Irish
Literature: A Social History.* London: Basil Blackwell, 1990.

ESLER, ERMINDA (1860?–1924), novelist and short story writer. Esler was
from County Donegal, the daughter of the Reverend Alexander Rentoul, of

Manorcunnigham, who was also a medical doctor. She was educated privately and then abroad at schools in Nimes and Berlin. In 1879, she graduated from Queen's University with a first honors certificate. She married a physician, Robert Esler, of London and Marlow House, Ballymena, in 1883, and thereafter lived in London, where she bore two sons.

Esler wrote much of her fiction for English magazines, her stories appearing in *Cornhill*, *Chambers'*, *Quiver*, and *Sunday at Home*. Most of her work is set in rural England, but her most popular work has Irish settings. *The Way They Loved at Grimpat* (1894) is a collection of brief love stories touched with satire. *A Maid of the Manse* (1895) is a novel about Presbyterian clerical life in mid-nineteenth-century Donegal. Reviewers described its tone as "essentially Scotch." *The Wardlaws* (1896), set in rural Ireland and in the tradition of *Castle Rackrent*, describes an Irish family's decay over a half century; it was her most popular work. *The Trackless Way* (1904) is set in Garvaghy, County Innismore, Ulster. The hero is a Presbyterian minister, Gideon Horville, who is dismissed for teaching "erroneous" doctrine. He then helps a friend, Lord Tomnitoul, with socialistic plans. The clergyman's inner struggle and the narrow-minded mean-spiritedness of his social circle are described so realistically that readers concluded the work was based upon firsthand knowledge.

Scotch-Irish, Presbyterian values pervaded both Esler's work and her personal life. In *Who's Who*, she listed her recreations as "walking, reading [and] conversation with people of individual mind." She belonged to the Lyceum Club and spent her final years in Bexley, Kent.

WILLIAM J. LINN

WORKS: *Almost a Pauper*. London: Christian Knowledge Society, [1888]. (Novella); *The Way of Transgressors*. 3 vols. London: Sampson Low, 1890. (Novel); *The Way They Loved at Grimpat*. London: Sampson Low, 1894. (Short stories); *Village Idylls*. London: Sampson Low, Marston/Lepizig: Tauchnitz, 1894; *A Maid of the Manse*. London: Sampson Low, 1895. (Novel); *'Mid Green Pastures*. London: Sampson Low/New York: J. Pott, 1895. (Short stories); *The Wardlaws*. London: Smith, Elder, 1896; *Youth at the Prow*. London: J. Long, 1898. (Novel); *The Awakening of Helena Thorpe*. London: S. W. Patridge, [1902]. (Novel); *The Trackless Way*. London: Brimley Johnson, 1904.

ETTINGSALL, THOMAS (ca. 1800–ca. 1850), humorist. Ettingsall kept a fishing-tackle establishment on Wood Quay about 1824, and his books are about fishing. A contributor also to various magazines, his droll story "Darby Doyle's Voyage to Quebec," which originally appeared in *The Dublin Penny Journal* on December 15, 1832, has sometimes been attributed to Lover.* He died, apparently in poor circumstances, about 1850.

WORKS: With H. B. Code. *The Angling Excursions of Gregory Greendrake, Esq.* 2 pts. Dublin: Archer, 1824, 1826. (Sketches); *The Green Bank, or An Hour's Amusement for the Young Angler*. Dublin: Gunn & Cameron, 1843. (Poetry); *The Angling Philosopher. Dedicated to All Fishers*. Dublin: Charles, ca. 1850.

EVA OF THE *NATION*. *See* KELLY, MARY EVA.

EVANS, EMYR ESTYN (1905–1989), geographer and humanist. Evans was born on May 29, 1905, the fourth son of the Reverend G. O. and Elizabeth Evans. He was educated at Welshpool County School and at the University of Wales, Aberysthwayth, where he received a B.A. in geography and anthropology in 1925, an M.A. in 1931, and a D.Sc. in 1939. The major influence on his intellectual life was H. J. Fleure, who introduced a new concept of human geography to him. In 1931, he married Gwyneth Lyon Jones, the daughter of Professor Jones of Aberysthwayth. From 1924 to 1970, he taught at Queen's University, Belfast: he became reader in geography in 1944, professor in 1945, and first director of the Institute of Irish Studies in 1968. Through a remarkable series of books, he mingled the insights of both geography and anthropology to create a totally new notion of man and landscape in Ireland and a whole new approach to the past and the present that proved highly influential. Dismissing the myths of nationalism and Unionism, he said, "I've always felt Irish history to be one-sided because we haven't looked enough at the land itself." He died in Belfast on August 12, 1989.

KELLY MARY EVA

WORKS: *France, A Geographical Introduction.* London: Christophers, 1937; with David A. Chart & others, *A Preliminary Survey of the Ancient Monuments of Northern Ireland.* Belfast, 1940; *Irish Heritage.* Dundalk: W. Tempest, 1942; *Northern Ireland.* London: W. Collins, 1951; *Mourne Country.* Dundalk: Dundalgan, 1951; *Lyles Hill: A Late Neolithic Site in County Antrim.* Belfast: [Archaeological Research], 1953; *Irish Folk Ways.* London: Routledge & Kegan Paul, 1957; *Prehistoric and Early Christian Ireland.* London: B. T. Batsford, 1966; ed., *Facts from Gweedore,* by Lord George Augustus Hall. Belfast: Queen's University of Belfast, Institute of Irish Studies, 1971; *The Personality of Ireland: Habitat, Heritage and History.* London: Cambridge University Press/ enlarged ed. Belfast: Blackstaff, 1981; *The Personality of Wales.* 1973; ed., *Harvest Home, the Last Sheaf: A Selection from the Writings of T.G.F. Patterson Relating to County Armagh.* Armagh: Armagh County Museum, 1975; *Ireland's Eye: The Photographs of Robert J. Welch.* Belfast: Blackstaff for the Ulster Museum & the Arts Council of Northern Ireland, 1977; *Ulster, the Common Ground.* [Gigginstown, Co. Meath]: Lilliput, 1984; *The Irishness of the Irish.* Belfast, 1986. (Essays). REFERENCE: Obituary. *Irish Times* (August 16, 1989).

EVANS, MARTINA (1961–   ), poet. Evans was born in Cork.

WORK: *The Iniscarra Bar and Cycle Rest.* Ware, Herts: Rockingham, 1995.

EVERETT, KATHERINE (1872–?), memoirist. Everett was born Kathleen Olive Herbert in 1872, at the family home, Cahirnane, near the Lakes of Killarney. Although not affluent herself, many of her connections were. A greatuncle had owned Muckross House and entertained Queen Victoria. Her cousin was Lady Ardilaun. Her books, *Bricks and Flowers* (1949) and *Walk with Me* (1951), tell much of life in Ireland from the view of a humane and highly competent Anglo-Irish woman. *Bricks and Flowers* also tells of her considerable abilities as a gardener and a builder of new houses and renovator of old ones. It recounts her travels, including a miserable three-month voyage to Australia on a decrepit sailing ship, and is often superb in its evocation of character, particularly of her feckless and dotty Aunt Aurelia. There are interesting glimpses of Wilde* and Yeats,* and the book is beautifully written. Its first paragraph, for instance, concludes:

No money was spent on amusements: books were not bought, holidays were not taken, and our clothes were made at home of harsh Kerry frieze, woven of the wool shorn off our own sheep into a material which we hated, for it tickled, and looked like dirty porridge.

Everett deplored the 1916 Rising, had some good words for the Black and Tans, and was deeply distrustful of democracy, but her books are entertaining and companionable.

WORKS: *Bricks and Flowers*. London: Constable, 1949; *Walk with Me*. London: Constable, 1951. (Short stories).

F

FAGAN, J[AMES] B[ERNARD] (1873–1933), playwright and producer. Fagan was born in Belfast and began as an actor, playing with Benson and Tree. He gave some notable productions of Shakespeare during his management of the Court Theatre; from 1923 to 1925, such actors as Flora Robson, John Gielgud, Tyrone Guthrie, and Raymond Massey played under him in Oxford; in 1929, he became director of the Festival Theatre, Cambridge. He managed many productions for Arthur Sinclair's Irish Players, and he was O'Casey's* first London producer. Of his own plays, the most successful were a rousing adaptation of *Treasure Island* (1922) and *And So To Bed* (1926) about Samuel Pepys. His short Irish farce, *Doctor O'Toole,* became an effective vehicle for Sinclair.

WORKS: *The Prayer of the Sword: A Play in Five Acts.* London: R. B. Johnston, 1904; *The Earth: A Modern Play in Four Acts.* London: T. Fisher Unwin, [1910]; *The Wheel: A Play in Two Acts.* London: Duckworth, 1922; *And So To Bed.* London: Putnam, 1926; *The Improper Duchess: A Modern Comedy in Three Acts.* London: Gollancz, 1931; *Treasure Island.* London: Cassell, 1936; *Doctor O'Toole: A Farcical Comedy.* London: Samuel French, 1938.

FALCONER, EDMUND (1814–1879), playwright, actor, and manager. Falconer was a sentimental melodramatist in the manner of Boucicault.* His real name was Edmund O'Rourke, and he was born in Dublin and went on the stage at an early age, playing utility roles in the country. He was introduced as a writer to London with the successful production of *The Cagot; or, Heart for Heart* at the Lyceum on December 6, 1856. In August 1858, he went into management with Ben Webster at the Lyceum and staged a number of his own pieces. This was a busy time, for he played Danny Mann in the first London production of Boucicault's *The Colleen Bawn,* which opened at the Adelphi on July 18, 1860, and ran for 231 nights. His own *Peep o' Day* opened at the Adelphi on November 9, 1861, and ran for more than a year. It was based on John Banim's* novels *John Doe* and *The Nowlans.* Having made £13,000 at the Lyceum, he became in 1862 joint lessee of Drury Lane, for which, among other things, he produced *Galway Go Bragh,* his dramatization of Lever's* *Charles O'Malley,* in which he played the role of Mickey Free. Producing Shakespeare at Drury Lane, however, lost him all of his money; consequently, he retired from the management in September 1866. He went to America for about three years, both acting and writing. Returning to London, he had several successful productions before he died at his house in Russell Square on September 29, 1879. He also wrote opera librettos for Balfe and published a couple of volumes of poems.

Falconer's Irish works manifest a shift in attitude toward Anglo-Irish relations. Although both *Peep o' Day* and *Eileen Oge* (1871) are romantic comedies ending with festive marriage ceremonies, *Peep o' Day*'s reconciliation differs from *Eileen Oge*'s. The former reconciles the English and Irish. Harry Kavanaugh, leader of the rebels, receives not only pardon but the hand of Mary Grace because he nobly lays down his arms to the British officers. In *Eileen Oge,* however, Henry Loftus, an English landlord who has schemed to win Eileen from his tenant Patrick O'Donnell, does not share in the final festivities. Indeed, he goes to prison for having framed O'Donnell five years previously and having him transported. Loftus misjudges both O'Donnell's endurance and the loyalty of his Scot and Irish helpers, Maclean and Tim the Penman; Tim is an Irish peasant who forges an incriminating letter but repents and rebukes his employer five years later. There may be still some sparks of vitality left in Falconer's best Irish plays, but, unlike Boucicault's, they have not been revived.

WILLIAM G. DOLDE

WORKS: *The Cagot; or, Heart for Heart.* London: J. Mitchell, [1856?]; The *Husband of an Hour.* New York: Samuel French, 1857/Boston: W. V. Spencer, [1857?]/London: T. H. Lacy, n.d.; *The Rose of Castille.* London: Cramer, [1857?]/Philadelphia: Ledger Job Printing Office, 1867. (Opera composed by Balfe, with libretto by Falconer & Augustus Harris); *Satanella; or, The Power of Love.* London: Published and sold in the theater, [1858?]. (Opera composed by Balfe, with libretto by Falconer & Augustus Harris); *Extremes; or, Men of the Day.* London: T. H. Lacy, n.d./New York: Samuel French, [1858?]; *Victorine.* London: Published and sold in the theater, [1859]. (Opera in three acts composed by Alfred Mellon); *Chrystabelle; or, The Rose without a Thorn.* London: T. H. Lacy, [1860?]; *The Family Secret.* London: T. H. Lacy, [ca. 1860]; *Next of Kin.* London: T. H. Lacy, [1860?]; *Ruy Blas.* London: T. H. Lacy, [1860?]. (After Victor Hugo); *Too Much for Good Nature.* London: T. H. Lacy/New York: Samuel French, [ca. 1860]; *Peep o' Day; or, Savourneen Deelish.* Chicago: Dramatic, [1861?]/New York: Samuel French, [ca. 1867]; *Memories, the Bequest of My Boyhood.* London: Tinsley, 1863. (Poems); *Murmurings in the May and Summer of Manhood. . . .* London, 1865. (Poems); *Does He Love Me?* London: T. H. Lacy, n.d./London: Samuel French, n.d.; *Eileen Oge; or, Dark's the Hour before the Dawn.* London: T. H. Lacy, n.d./ London & New York: Samuel French. [197?]/Chicago: Dramatic, 1876. Many of Falconer's plays remain unpublished; however, a list of first productions occurs in Volume 5 of Allardyce Nicoll's *A History of English Drama 1660–1900.* 2d ed. (Cambridge: Cambridge University Press, 1959). The Lacy or French acting editions are hard to come by, but various plays are available on microform or microfiche.

FALLER, KEVIN (1920–1983), poet. Faller was born in Galway city and worked from 1945 until his death as a journalist in Dublin. He generally wrote brief poems with short lines and was capable, as in his poems "Landscape" and "First Light," of beautifully controlling his constricted form.

WORKS: *Genesis.* London & New York: T. V. Boardman, 1953. (Novel); *Island Lyrics.* Dublin: Colm O Lochlainn, [1963]; *Lament for the Bull Island, and Other Poems.* [Dublin]: Goldsmith, [ca. 1973]; *The Lilac Tree and Other Poems.* [Portmarnock, Co. Dublin]: St. Bueno's, [1979]. (Poetry pamphlet); *Memoirs.* Mornington, Co. Meath.: Tracks, 1983.

FALLON, ANNE C. (fl. 1990s), mystery novelist. Fallon is a Bostonian who lived in Ireland for twelve years and who received her M. Litt. from Trinity College, Dublin. She is now an assistant professor in New York. She has published several novels about James Fleming, a Dublin solicitor who solves crimes.

WORKS: *Blood Is Thicker.* Dublin: Town House, 1994; *Where Death Lies.* Dublin: Town House, 1994.

FALLON, PADRAIC (1905–1974), poet and playwright. Fallon is one of the most accomplished and, until recently, most neglected of modern Irish writers. He was born in Athenry, County Galway, on January 3, 1905, and he worked as a customs official for forty years, mainly in Wexford. His first work was published by AE* in the *Irish Statesman,* and he continued to publish prolifically—poems, stories, and reviews—in many periodicals. No collection of his work appeared, however, until shortly before his death. That fact certainly contributed to his being much less well known than Austin Clarke* and Patrick Kavanagh,* with whom he can be ranked. He died on October 8, 1974, in Aylesford, Kent, and he is buried in Kinsale.

His *Poems* (1974) collected some of the most controlled and craftsmanlike poems to appear in many years. In his poem "Fin de Siecle," Fallon wrote "Who makes the rhyme / Will have the resonance." However, his own poems do not resonate merely with rhyme, but also with unexpected patterns of rhyme and, more usually, off-rhyme which is used most subtly and satisfyingly. No particular manner or tone of voice or subject is discernible from poem to poem, for the poet plays eclectically with line and stanza length, and his subjects are most various. Those subjects range from local descriptions, dialogues of the blind nineteenth-century Irish poet Anthony Raftery, love poems with a Yeatsian bite, and indeed some of the best poems about Yeats,* as well as some religious poems which are probably his weakest, and some poems of personal reminiscence, such as "Poem for My Mother," "Painting of My Father," and "March Twentysix," which are among his strongest. If any qualities are constant in Fallon's poetry, they would be the richness of his imagery and the power of his rhetoric. His diction ranges from the casual to the eloquently formal, and he is such a phrasemaker that one cannot begin to quote with fairness. His sentences can be a terse five words or lengthy in the Faulknerian mode. *Poems and Versions,* edited by his son, appeared in 1983 and added many previously uncollected poems as well as translations from the Greek, Latin, and French. A

Collected Poems finally appeared in 1990. Obviously, he is a major poetic voice, demanding study and assimilation, quite as much as Clarke or Kavanagh.

Fallon also wrote two plays for the stage, *The Seventh Step* (1954) and *Sweet Love Till Morn* (Abbey, 1971), as well as several plays which were broadcast over Radio Éireann. His radio plays included his finest dramatic work, his *Diarmuid and Grainne* (Radio Éireann, 1950) and his masterly *The Vision of Mac Conglinne* (Radio Éireann, 1953). Michaeál Ó hAodha, who produced his radio plays, has written that "In many respects, these two plays are the most successful modernizations of old Irish Literature" (*Theatre in Ireland,* 1974). That seems a highly extravagant statement when one considers that Yeats, Synge,* Stephens,* and so many other remarkable writers have turned their hands to modern versions of classic Irish material. Nevertheless, to anyone who has read the unpublished pieces, the wit, the gusto, and the riot of rhetorical exuberance seem rarely paralleled and hardly excelled in modern Irish dramatic writing.

PRINCIPAL WORKS: *Lighting-up Time.* Dublin: Orwell, 1938. (Story); *Poems.* [Dublin]: Dolmen, [1974]; *Poems and Versions.* Brian Fallon, ed. Manchester: Carcanet/Dublin: Raven Arts, 1983; *Collected Poems.* [Oldcastle, Co. Meath]: Gallery/Manchester: Carcanet, [1990]; "The Vision of Mac Conglinne" in *Irish Drama, 1900–1980.* Coilin D. Owens & Joan Radner, eds. Washington, D.C.: Catholic University of America Press, 1990, pp. 456–538.   REFERENCES: Davie, Donald. "Austin Clarke and Padraic Fallon" in *Two Decades of Irish Writing.* Douglas Dunn, ed. Cheadle: Carcanet/Chester Springs, Pa.: Dufour, 1975, pp. 37–58; Fallon, Brian. "Afterword" in *Poems and Versions,* pp. 101–112; Garrett, R. F. *Modern Irish Poetry: Tradition and Continuity from Yeats to Heaney.* Berkeley, Los Angeles & London: University of California Press, 1986, pp. 70–77; Grennan, Eamon. "Affectionate Truth: Critical Intelligence in the Poetry of Padraic Fallon." *Irish University Review* 121 (Autumn 1982): 173–188; Harmon, Maurice. "The Poetry of Padraic Fallon." *Studies* (Autumn 1975): 269–281; Heaney, Seamus. Introduction to *Collected Poems;* O'Driscoll, Dennis. "Padraic Fallon Rediscovered." *Poetry Ireland Review* 19 (1990): 34–46.

FALLON, PETER (1951–   ), poet and publisher. Fallon was born in Germany of Irish parents on February 26, 1951; a few years later his family moved to County Meath. Fallon's poems appeared first in 1967 and have subsequently been printed in various anthologies he has coedited as well as in six volumes from Gallery Press,* the publishing house he founded in 1970, when he was an undergraduate at Trinity. In the ensuing decades, under Fallon's directorship, Gallery has become Ireland's foremost poetry house, both introducing and reissuing works by many of Ireland's most celebrated contemporary poets while also publishing an important series of Irish plays. Fallon's own verse has, since the mid-1970s, consisted primarily of quiet lyrics evoking life on and near the Meath sheep farm where he has lived with his wife and children.

By the time Fallon was twenty-three, he had published his third book, the jacket of which could announce, "I earn my living from the readings I give, often visiting schools around the country." Many of his early poems are love lyrics that rely on a symbolic weightiness absent in later work. Fallon's first book uses long verse lines; the second uses shorter, more clipped ones that are characteristic of all his subsequent poetry. The turning point in his poetic career comes with the second half of the third book, *The First Affair* (1974), which addresses the realities of winter and rough weather—his constant themes thereafter. Many of these latter poems from *The First Affair* reappeared, four years later, in *The Speaking Stones* (1978), often significantly and meticulously refined: for instance, the last line in "Nettle" that had an italicized *"you"* loses, in republication, its artificial emphasis.

The lighter touch has been maintained through the subsequent volumes. Maurice Harmon, reviewing *Winter Work* (1983), described Fallon's poetry as "both formal and relaxed, measured in movement and unhurried"; George McWhirter said of the same book that Fallon's "words can hug the home ground, fit tight to spare and familiar things." But Harry Clifton's* later survey of Fallon's career noted that Fallon's "innocent . . . visions . . . have a borrowed air about them" (with his "visions borrowed from Kavanagh, . . . his style from Frost, Heaney,* and Paul Muldoon*") and called Fallon's poetic mind "cold, exploitative."

Eye to Eye (1992), dedicated to the "memory of John Fallon, born 7 December, died 8 December 1990," received attention for its treatment of the death of a child; even forums not usually attentive to poetry, such as an afternoon talk show on a Midlands radio station, discussed the book. *Eye to Eye* casts an eerie light on the poems in preceding volumes that had dealt, continually, with the difficulties and tragedies of farm births: "Lennoxbrook," in *The Speaking Stones;* "Stillborn," which appeared in the second part of the "Gravities" sequence in *Winter Work* but was omitted from the abbreviated version that appeared in the *Selected Poems;* "Fostering," called by McWhirter the "centre" of *Winter Work;* and "Caesarean" in *The News and Weather* (1987). But perhaps Fallon's soft-spoken reflections on such subject matter previously handled by Heaney* and by Ted Hughes may best distinguish him from those poets. In *Eye to Eye,* "Grace," mostly about lambs that "thrive" but also about those that are "mismothered," gives way to the series of poems on the dead infant son.

Fallon's vision is summed up in the last of the four lines that make up his slight "The Herd," about every lamb being a lamb of God. His poems argue for the value of "talk in small communities" ("The Heartland") and for the adequacy and importance of familiar phrases—like the one that gives *Eye to Eye* its title and that recurs throughout that book—or phrases slightly turned. Several of his poems on farm life end with references to "shit," thus reaching for a toughness that they do not achieve otherwise. Others, such as "El Dorado" and "Country Music," claim the authenticity of somewhat humorous pub talk.

Founded in Dublin, Gallery moved in the late 1980s to Fallon's home at Oldcastle, County Meath, from which it produced editions of such important works as Nuala Ni Dhomhnaill's *Pharaoh's Daughter* and Heaney's *The Midnight Verdict.* By this stage, Gallery could surely be described as an established press, both for its having forged its own prominent reputation and for its tendency to produce the work of already well respected writers. It had long been liable to criticism for a certain narrowness of representation, especially for its having published a small proportion of women writers and, after a certain point, first books; still, it had been responsible for such publications as the Kavanagh Award-winning initial volume by Nuala Archer.* Fallon could rightly claim a central role in guiding contemporary Irish poetry to the position of prominence it occupied as the end of the century approached. Perhaps the best fusion of his roles as writer and publisher is in "The Hares" from *Winter Work,* which may be read as a vision of the way poets may outrun the care of one who has done much to foster them.

VICTOR LUFTIG

WORKS: *Among the Walls.* Dublin: Tara Telephone, 1971. (Poetry pamphlet); *Coincidence of Flesh.* Dublin: Gallery, 1972; *The First Affair.* Dublin: Gallery, 1974; ed., with Dennis O'Driscoll. *The First Ten Years, Dublin Arts Festival Poems.* Dublin: Dublin Arts Festival, 1974; *A Gentler Birth.* Deerfield, Mass.: Deerfield, 1976; *Victims.* Deerfield, Mass.: Deerfield, 1977; *Finding the Dead.* Deerfield, Mass.: Deerfield, 1978; *The Speaking Stones.* Dublin: Gallery, 1978; ed., with Sean Golden. *Soft Day: A Miscellany of Contemporary Irish Writing.* Dublin: Wolfhound/South Bend, Ind.: Notre Dame University Press, 1979; ed., with Andrew Carpenter. *The Writers: A Sense of Ireland.* Dublin: O'Brien/New York: George Braziller, 1981; *Winter Work.* [Dublin]; Gallery, [1983]; *The News and Weather.* [Oldcastle, Co. Meath]; Gallery, [1987]; ed., with Derek Mahon. *The Penguin Book of Contemporary Irish Poetry.* London: Penguin, 1990; *News of the World: Selected Poems.* Wake Forest University Press, 1993; *Eye to Eye.* [Oldcastle, Co. Meath]: Gallery, [1992]. REFERENCE: Lincecum, Jerry B. "Peter Fallon: Contemporary Irish Poet, Editor, and Publisher." *Notes on Modern Irish Literature* 3 (1991): 52–58.

FANNING, GERARD (fl. 1990s), poet. Fanning's first collection, *Easter Snow* (1992), won the Brendan Behan Memorial Prize and the Rooney Prize for Irish Literature.

WORK: *Easter Snow.* Dublin: Dedalus, [1992].

FARQUHAR, GEORGE (1677–1707), playwright. Biographical information on dramatist George Farquhar is sketchy. The son of an Anglican clergyman, he was born in 1677 in Londonderry, lived through the siege of that city, and may have been with the Williamite army at the Boyne in 1690. After mediocre performances as a student at Trinity and as an actor in Dublin's Smock Alley Theatre, he went to London in 1697 with the script of a comedy, *Love and a Bottle,* which was staged in 1698. His second play, *The Constant Couple* (1699), was a major triumph, but his next three works, *Sir Harry Wildair* (1701), *The Inconstant* (1702), and *The Twin-Rivals* (1702), were failures. Farquhar was chronically impecunious during his short life, and marriage in 1703 brought him a meager dowry. His last two plays are his masterpieces. *The Recruiting Officer* (1706) was based on Farquhar's experience as a recruiter in Shrewsbury in 1704. *The Beaux Stratagem,* written during a fatal illness, was brought on stage shortly before the author's death on about May 23, 1707.

Of the Irish characters in his plays, the most important is Roebuck, "an Irish gentleman of a wild, roving temper, newly come to London," in *Love and a*

Bottle. He is a gauche precursor to the urbane rakes of the later comedies. Teague, the loyal comic servant in *The Twin-Rivals,* and Macahone, the booby squire from Tipperary in *The Stage Coach* (1704), differ only in name. Foigard, chaplain to French prisoners-of-war in *The Beaux Stratagem,* in spite of his atrocious pidgin-Irish dialect, pretends to be a native of Brussels. His Jesuitical role in the attempted seduction of an English lady makes Foigard a more complex and less likable figure than Farquhar's other "Teagues" who are cut from the regular Stage Irish pattern. Anti-Catholicism, probably heightened by the religious warfare in Ireland, surfaces often, as in the character of Foigard and in *The Constant Couple,* which ridicules the pomp and commercialism of papal authority.

When Farquhar arrived in London, Restoration drama was coming under attack by moralists, and sentimental comedy was in its formative state. He worked in both genres. His early and middle period plays, in the Restoration mode, were inferior to the verbal rocketry of Congreve* and the tormented intensity of Wycherley. In *The Recruiting Officer* and *The Beaux Stratagem,* he grafts leering Restoration dialogue and the sexual poaching plot onto a quasi-sentimental attitude from which the wits and scintillating ladies of good King Charles' golden days would have recoiled in horror: there is life, pleasant life, in the outer space beyond London; small-town girls have their own sweet style—they are neither apple-checked hoydens nor easy conquests for smugly confident city rakes; and elderly persons are capable of wisdom and simple dignity.

Full-blown sentimental comedy, with its thick-ankled altruism and weepy distresses, as in Richard Steele's* *The Conscious Lovers,* seems to a modern reader as unintentionally campy as *Ten Nights in a Bar-room.* Farquhar's variations, as their long stage history will attest, have passed through the wild vicissitudes of taste and have kept most of their bounce.

WILLIAM J. FEENEY

WORK: *The Works of George Farquhar.* 2 vols. Oxford: Clarendon/New York: Oxford University Press, 1988. REFERENCES: Connely, Willard. *Young George Farquhar: The Restoration Drama at Twilight.* London: Cassel, 1949; Farmer, Albert. *George Farquhar.* London: Longman's, 1966; James, Eugene E. *George Farquhar: A Reference Guide.* Boston: G. K. Hall, 1986; Jordan, Robert J. "George Farquhar's Military Career." *Huntington Library Quarterly* 37 (1973–1974): 251–264; Roper, Alan. "The Beaux Stratagem, Image and Action" in *Seventeenth Century Imagery: Essays on Uses of Figurative Language from Donne to Farquhar.* Earl Miner, ed. Berkeley: University of California Press, 1971; Rothenstein, Eric. *George Farquhar.* New York: Twayne, 1967.

FARRELL, BERNARD (ca. 1939–   ), playwright. Farrell was born in Sandycove, County Dublin, and educated at Monkstown Park. After having worked in British Rail and the Sealink Shipping Company for twenty years, he arrived on the theatrical scene to great acclaim with *I Do Not Like Thee, Doctor Fell* in 1979. He is often linked with Hugh Leonard* in that both are highly popular writers of (mainly) satiric comedy, commercially viable, and great favorites on the amateur dramatic circuit. Like Leonard's Farrell's work is accessible, favoring traditional forms, careful construction, and vivid characterization—in other words, a good story and a good night out.

"I have been asked," Farrell says, "when I was going to write a serious play. I think all my plays are serious plays—I think they use comedy to make serious points." His work is entertaining, but it is not frivolous; problems as diverse as middle-aged redundancy, labor relations, homosexuality, and the oppression of women and the old are introduced.

His favorite satiric target is the young middle-class couple with social ambitions, and there is an antithesis in many of his plays between the values of these people and the values of an older and less pretentious generation. This conflict is represented emblematically in *Forty-Four Sycamore Street,* where the elderly Mr. Prentice is beaten up on stage by a pair of yuppies whose claim to social sophistication is based on the extent of their electronic gadgetry.

The typical Farrell work deals with a middle-class family or grouping (office workers, holidaymakers, an encounter group, a school reunion) whose foibles and eccentricities are recognized and enjoyed by the audience but whose pretensions are mercilessly unmasked. The stripping away of pretension—particularly social pretension—is Farrell's major concern, and most of his plays are movements toward a final scene of revelation and exposure. (It is no coincidence that he has adapted a play of Molière's.) A dissenting character in *Dr. Fell* comments that what group therapy participants really need is "a good boot in the arse." In his plays, Farrell creates situations where this action is called for, as he creates characters who are on hand to deliver it.

There is, however, a tendency (especially in his middle plays) to slip too easily into farce and thus undermine serious social commentary. He is at his best where the comedy and the social issues are well balanced, as in *Dr. Fell, Canaries,* and *Forty-Four Sycamore.*

His most recent work, *The Last Apache Reunion* (1993), which examines retrospectively school rituals and allegiances and bullying, marks a new departure. It corresponds to the Farrell formula in that there is a stripping away of layers of evasion and deceit, until in the final sequence the truth is laid bare. But in this play the emphasis is not so much on a general social issue as on the hidden hurts of private lives, and it reveals a new intensity and a wider range of feeling. Though there is comedy in abundance, it is there to express the underlying desperation of characters whose lives have made a wrong turning or—worse—no turning at all. That Farrell himself, although successful in his writing, is not afraid to take new turns indicates the vitality of his talent.

His produced plays include *I Do Not Like Thee, Doctor Fell* (Abbey,* 1979), *Legs Eleven* (Moving Theatre, 1979), *Canaries* (Abbey, 1980), *All in Favour Said No!* (Abbey, 1981), *Petty Sessions* (after Boucicault's *Forbidden Fruit,* Abbey, 1983), *Don Juan* (from Molière, Peacock, 1984), *Then Moses Met Marconi* (Team Theatre, 1984), *All the Way Back* (Abbey, 1985), *Because Just Because* (Team Theatre, 1986), *Say Cheese!* (Abbey, 1987), *Forty-Four Sycamore* (Red Kettle, 1992), *The Last Apache Reunion* (Abbey, 1993). His television plays include *Lotty Coyle Loves Buddy Holly* (RTÉ, 1984). Among his radio plays is *The Year of Jimmy Somers,* which was the RTÉ entry for the 1987 Prix Italia.

He was awarded the Rooney Prize for Irish Literature in 1980 and was elected to Aosdána* in 1989.

JOHN BARRETT

WORKS: *I Do Not Like Thee, Doctor Fell.* [Dublin]: Co-op Books, [1979]/Dublin: Brophy, 1988; *Canaries.* [Dublin]: Co-op Books, [1980]/Galway: Campus, 1992; *The Plays of Bernard Farrell.* [Dublin]: Co-op Books, [1982]. (Contains *I Do Not Like Thee, Doctor Fell, All in Favour Said No!* and *Lotty Coyle Loves Buddy Holly*); *All the Way Back.* Dublin: Brophy, 1988; *When Moses Met Marconi.* In *Three Team Plays.* Dublin: Wolfhound, 1988; *Say Cheese!* [Galway]: Campus, [1994]; *Forty-Four Sycamore.* Cork: Mercier, 1994; *The Last Apache Reunion.* Cork: Mercier, 1994.

FARRELL, J[AMES] G[ORDAN] (1935–1979), English novelist. Farrell was born on January 23, 1935, in Lancashire. Only one of his six completed novels, *Troubles* (1970), is about Ireland. That book is set in 1919 in a decaying Big House now converted into an unsuccessful hotel inhabited by old ladies and cats. Farrell spent much of his childhood in Ireland, and his re-creation of the strife-torn times after World War I seems as utterly authentic as his loving portrayal of down-at-the-heels Anglo-Irish. The volume is one of the most re-alized and satisfying novels written about Ireland by anyone since World War II, and it won the Faber Memorial Prize in 1971. His novel about India, *The Siege of Krishnapur* (1973), won the Booker Prize. A few months before the end of his life, Farrell moved to an old farmhouse in West Cork, and on August 12, 1979, he was swept into the sea while fishing.

IRISH WORK: *Troubles.* London: Cape, 1970/New York: Knopf, 1971. REFERENCES: Allen, Brigid. "Feline Friend: Memories of J. G. Farrell (1935–1979)." *London Magazine* 32 (May 1992): 64–75; Binns, Ronald. *J. G. Farrell.* London & New York: Methuen, [1986]. See also the essays by John Spurling, Margaret Drabble, and Malcolm Dean in Farrell's posthumous *The Hill Station.* London: Weidenfeld and Nicolson, 1981.

FARRELL, MICHAEL (1899–1962), novelist. Farrell was born in 1899 in Carlow, where his parents were prominent in business. He was educated at Knockbeg College and Blackrock College and studied medicine at the National University. During the Troubles, with which he was only peripherally involved, he was imprisoned in Mountjoy Jail for six months. On his release, he went on a walking tour of France before taking a job as marine superintendent in the Belgian Congo. He returned in 1927 to Ireland, and in 1930 he married Frances Cahill, who ran the Crock of Gold, a handweaving business in Dublin. He resumed his medical studies at Trinity College, Dublin, but made little headway and so finally stopped. For the next seven or eight years, he worked on a draft of his novel *Thy Tears Might Cease,* before plunging full-time into journalism. He was compere, scriptwriter, and producer for Radio Éireann, and for several years he ran the program "Radio Digest." During the war he wrote under the pseudonym of "Gulliver" for Sean O'Faolain's* *Bell.** He finally abandoned journalism altogether and took over the management of his wife's handweaving business. He died on June 24, 1962. Mervyn Wall* has a vivid, if unflattering portrait of him in the play *Lady in the Twilight.*

Farrell's life work, the novel *Thy Tears Might Cease,* has an unusual publishing history. It originally ran to five unwieldy volumes, and in 1937 Sean O'Faolain brought these to London in a suitcase. The publisher agreed to accept them when complete, but, O'Faolain writes, "the author viewed this encouraging news with the sort of haughty smile proper to an aristocrat who has just heard he is for the guillotine in the morning. It was his constant attitude toward his MS.: avid to see it printed, terrified to let it go." The book was finally published posthumously in 1963 through the efforts of Monk Gibbon,* who cut it by 100,000 words. In that form, it became something of a best-seller.

In the novel, orphan Martin Matthew Reilly grows to manhood during ten vital years of Ireland's history. The halcyon days of Redmond's Home Rule Party are reflected in his early life. He moves from his prosperous Catholic merchant uncle's home to a pleasant boarding school, from which he spends holidays with his dead mother's landed Protestant friends. In this way, Catholic Martin sees the Irish question from both sides. In spite of bereavements, he is happy. He makes idyllic childhood friendships, and there are cosy nursery tea, order, harmony. With the coming of World War I, this peace begins to crack. Martin's painful adolescence is not helped by the death of his guardians. He changes school, loses his religion, and falls in love. The 1916 Rising, which changed Ireland, effects a similar drastic change in him. Once unsympathetic to the Irish cause, he now throws himself into Ireland's fight for freedom.

The novel gives a clear feeling of what life before World War I must have been like, both in the prosperous country towns and in the homes of the landed gentry. There are many memorable minor characters and much exciting action, but the book is marred by passages of lush writing and hazy romanticism. Up to the Rising, it reads almost like a boy's book, and after that the change in Martin seems too drastic. Even though it is marvelously readable and accurate social history, the book owes nothing to modern fiction and could almost have been published not in 1963, but in 1863 by a second cousin of the Brontës.

MARY ROSE CALLAGHAN

WORK: *Thy Tears Might Cease.* London: Jonathan Cape, 1963/New York: Knopf, 1964.   REFERENCE: Costello, Peter. *The Heart Grown Brutal.* Dublin: Gill & Macmillan/Totowa, N.J.: Rowman & Littlefield, 1977.

FARREN, ROBERT. *See* Ó FARACHÁIN, ROIBÉARD.

FARRINGTON, CONOR [ANTHONY] (1928–   ), playwright and actor. Farrington was born on June 17, 1928. After graduating from Trinity College, he acted with an English touring company in Malta and India, and from 1955 to 1993 he was a member of the repertory company of Radio Éireann. He has written many radio and stage plays, the most successful of which have been *The-*

Last P. M., or Stella and the Big Bang and *Aaron Thy Brother. The Last P. M.,* which was performed by the Gate Theatre* for the 1964 Dublin Theatre Festival, is a satirical fantasy that was highly regarded by Frank O'Connor* and Micheál Mac Liammóir.* *Aaron Thy Brother,* performed by the Abbey* in the Peacock in 1969, is a historical play about John Philpot Curran but has a modern chorus of Irish soldiers serving with the United Nations in the Congo. In 1987, his *Ground Work Limited* shared the O. Z. Whitehead Prize. His unproduced *The Lifted Staff,* set in the twelfth century in the time of Strongbow, was published in 1990. His stage plays are usually in loose free verse, and he is one of the few modern Irish dramatists who consistently write in verse.

WORKS: "Playwrights and the Stationary Carrot." *Theatre Arts* 46 (February 1962): 21–22; "The Ghostly Garden." In *Prizewinning Plays of 1964.* Dublin: Progress House, 1965. (One-act play); *Aaron Thy Brother.* Newark, Del.: Proscenium, [1975]; *The Lifted Staff.* Dublin: Saor-Ollscoil, [1990].

FAULKNER, GEORGE (1699–1775). Printer, publisher, and bookseller. Called by Swift* "the Prince of Dublin printers," Faulkner published Swift's works in 1735, and by 1769 there were twenty volumes of them. He also published *The Dublin Journal,* in the pages of which are various items by Swift and Dr. Sheridan.*

REFERENCE: Ward, Robert E. *Prince of Dublin Printers, The Letters of George Faulkner.* Lexington: University Press of Kentucky, 1972.

FEE, DEREK (1947–   ), novelist. Fee was born in Dublin and works in Brussells for the European Union.

WORK: *Cartel.* Dublin: Townhouse, 1994. (Thriller).

FEENEY, JOHN (1948–1984), journalist, fiction writer, and publisher. Feeney was born in Dublin and graduated from University College, Dublin. He was an able journalist, writing originally on religious matters and editing *The Standard.* He published a gentle monograph on Archbishop McQuaid, a somewhat crude and awkward novel about television journalism, and a volume of short stories entitled *Mao Dies* (1977). One story in that collection, "The Exorcism," is gratuitously horrendous but, nevertheless, memorable and his best work. He was involved in two publishing ventures, the Irish Writers' Cooperative and his own Egotist Press, which published interesting work by Brian Power,* Fred Johnston,* and Lucile Redmond,* as well as some of Hugh Leonard's* lively journalism. In later years, Feeney was a popular and readable journalist for the *Evening Herald,* and with several other journalists he died in a plane crash in England in 1984. In a short life crammed with activity, he did not reach his full potential as a writer.

WORKS: *John Charles McQuaid.* Dublin: Mercier, 1974; *Worm Friday.* Dun Laoghaire: Anna Livia, 1974. (Novel); *Mao Dies and Other Stories.* Dublin: Egotist, 1977.

FERGUSON, KATHLEEN (1958–   ), novelist. Ferguson was born in Tam-naherin, County Derry, and took a doctorate in English literature at the University of Ulster, where she later taught. She now writes full-time. Her *The Maid's Tale* was short-listed for the 1994 Whitbread First Novel Award and won the *Irish Times* Literature Prize for Fiction in 1995. The book tells the story of Brigid Keen, a young woman who was reared in a Derry orphanage and later became a priest's housekeeper. It is written in Brigid's own words:

The Catholic church was father, mother and family to me for over fifty years. You can imagine what I felt, then, when the bishop dropped me like that—like yesterday's newspaper he'd throw at his backside whenever he'd done with it. After I'd given Father Mann what many a wife never gave her husband.

What she gave him was her life. Yet, despite this strong opening, Brigid becomes bitter and disillusioned only at the end of her years of service. Although her mother had died violently, Brigid's childhood was not desperately unhappy. However, there were few opportunities for her. She finds limited happiness with Father Mann, who comes across as very human, if a bit chauvinistic. The strength of Ferguson's book is that she avoids the usual stereotyping of the clergy one finds in many Irish novels. There are no monsters here, but warmly comic scenes—one priest is an alcoholic, and one gets cold feet about his ordination. Only the bishop is coldly inhuman. He chucks Brigid out, as easily as he gets rid of demented Father Mann. The book is about the abuse of power, but it also asks questions about priestly celibacy. While there is no hint of anything improper between Brigid and her employer, the relationship is deeply touching. In the end, she is the only one who cares for him. The reader cannot help but be moved by his plight and wonder about all the other lonely clerics who are deprived of the support of families because of church rule.

MARY ROSE CALLAGHAN

WORK: *The Maid's Tale*. [Dublin]: Poolbeg, [1994].

FERGUSON, SIR SAMUEL (1810–1886), poet. In the efforts to reconstruct native Irish culture during the nineteenth century, Ferguson's contributions in research, verse translations, and popular writings were indispensable.

Born in Belfast on March 10, 1810, Ferguson advanced in his literary career at an early age. "The Forging of the Anchor," a poem in praise of industrial progress, was published when he was only twenty-one, but it was cited by Christopher North as superior to works contained in Tennyson's 1830 volume of poetry. From the start his special interest was Ireland, although his sympathies were clearly antinationalist. His most virulent attack on the excesses of Irish nationalism is contained in "An Irish Garland," which was published in *Blackwoods* in 1833.

Despite Ferguson's abhorrence of the nationalist cause, his best work resulted from his extensive investigations of native Irish folklore and, particularly, the Gaelic sagas and legends. His verse renderings of those were both more accurate than previous translations and better verse as well; in fact, they were so popular that he devoted his subsequent career to composing poems based on the Irish heroic legends, versions of the bardic verses, and translations on a wide variety of Irish originals. He neglected in his study the most insistently patriotic verse of previous centuries, unlike his contemporary, James Clarence Mangan,* who emphasized precisely those poems in his efforts at translation.

Ferguson's work was widely read and respected in his lifetime, so that he was named president of the Royal Irish Academy. He died on August 9, 1886, in Howth, near Dublin.

W. B. Yeats* was generous in his praise of Ferguson. In an 1886 essay in *The Dublin University Review,* Yeats claimed that while almost all poetry of his time was academic and bookish, Ferguson's was "truly bardic, appealing to all natures alike, to the great concourse of the people." But to twentieth-century readers his long heroic tales seem tendentious and flaccid. Even *Congal: A Poem in Five Books* (1872), his best long work, seems overly decorated and contrived. The descriptions are so long as to become distracting, and prosody is almost comically contrived. His version of the most famous love tale in Celtic mythology, *Deirdre* (1880), is also flawed by its pretty diction and rhetorical excesses. He reduces the most sensual and violent tales in Irish legend to mere sentimental parlor tales, making them sentimental and mildly amusing. While such domestication of folklore was common enough in Victorian times, one cannot help but contrast his decorated verse with the vigorous and challenging poems of Mangan,* his contemporary.

Nevertheless, in his steady work at reviving Irish legend and mythology, Ferguson made a valuable contribution. Like Yeats, he aspired to write the Irish epic; and if he did not succeed in producing a work of genuine conviction, he did expand the audience for Irish writing, at a critical time. Furthermore, he treated the supernatural elements of Irish folklore—ghosts, fairies, and magic— seriously, an effort that appealed particularly to Yeats. Finally, he was a real scholar, whose efforts elevated the study of Irish mythology to a level of real seriousness.

JAMES KILROY

WORKS: *Cromlech on Howth.* . . . London: Day, 1841. (Poetry); *On the Expediency of Taking Stock: A Letter to James Pim, Jun., Esq.* Dublin: McGlashan, 1847; *Dublin, a Satire.* Dublin, 1849. (Poetry); *Inheritor and Economist.* Dublin: McGlashan, 1849. (Poetry); *Father Tom and the Pope; or, a Night at the Vatican.* . . . Baltimore: Robinson, 1858. (Prose); *Lays of the Western Gael, and Other Poems.* London: Bell & Daldy, 1865; *Congal; a Poem in Five Books.* Dublin: E. Ponsonby/ London: Bell & Daldy, 1872; *Deirdre: A One-Act Drama of Old Irish Story.* Dublin: Roe, 1880; *Poems.* Dublin: W. McGee/London: G. Bell, 1880; *The Forging of the Anchor.* London, Paris, New York: Cassell, 1883. (Poetry); *Hibernian Nights' Entertainments.* Dublin: Sealy, Bryers & Walker/ London: G. Bell, 1887. (Prose); *Ogham Inscriptions in Ireland, Wales, and Scotland.* Edinburgh: Douglas, 1887; *The Remains of St. Patrick.* . . . Dublin: Sealy, Bryers & Walker/London: G. Bell, 1888. (Translation from Latin into English blank verse); *Lays of the Red Branch,* with an introduction by Lady Ferguson. London: T. Fisher Unwin/Dublin: Sealy, Bryers & Walker, 1897; *Poems of Sir Samuel Ferguson,* with an Introduction by Alfred Perceval Graves. Dublin: Talbot/London: T. Fisher Unwin, [1918]; *Poems.* Padraic Colum, ed. Dublin: A. Figgis, 1963. REFERENCES:

Brown, Malcolm. *Sir Samuel Ferguson.* Lewisburg, Pa.: Bucknell University Press, 1973; Brown, Terence & Hayley, Barbara, eds. *Samuel Ferguson, a Centenary Tribute.* Dublin: Royal Irish Academy, 1987; Denman, Peter. *Samuel Ferguson: The Literary Achievement.* Gerrards Cross: Colin Smythe/Savage, Md.: Barnes & Noble, 1990; Ferguson, Lady Mary C. *Sir Samuel Ferguson in the Ireland of His Day.* 2 vols. London: W. Blackwood, 1896; O'Driscoll, Robert. *An Ascendancy of the Heart: Ferguson and the Beginnings of Modern Irish Literature in English.* Dublin: Dolmen, 1976; Yeats, W. B. "The Poetry of Sir Samuel Ferguson." In *Uncollected Prose by W. B. Yeats.* Vol. 1. John P. Frayne, ed. [London]: Macmillan, [1970], pp. 81–104.

FIACC, PADRAIC (1924–   ), poet. Padraic Fiacc is the pseudonym of Patrick Joseph O'Connor, who was born in the Lower Falls Road, Belfast, in 1924. He spent his childhood in the "Markets" area and then emigrated with his family to New York City where he was educated at Commerce and Haaren High Schools and then at St. Joseph's Seminary in Calicoon. He returned to Belfast in 1946.

Fiacc is perhaps the most considerable poet emerging from the Ulster disturbances and is more committed to enduring the terror and the blood letting than any other Northern Irish writer. Fiacc's early poems are pleasantly low-keyed and sometimes suggest translation from early Irish nature poetry. This bright visual quality is present in his later work, but lyric absorption reaches for social absorption. As Terence Brown has written, Fiacc's Gaelic vision of purity is "tested against brutally explicit images of sectarian warfare and guerilla activity."

With the publication of *Odour of Blood* (1973) and *Nights in the Bad Place* (1977), Fiacc becomes the first of a European species to appear in Irish writing: a Holocaust child, whose mental cast is formed by a milieu of violence. In "Son of a Gun," the poet is more involved than Yeats* was in "Easter 1916." He feels guilt because he is unable to fulfill his parents' role; he cannot carry a gun. The surface of the poem is dismembered like a dream. Fiacc's lyricism reads like a Rimbaudian enactment of Hell. His poems jerk, grimace, and end quickly to convey the idea that there is no way out of the pain. In "The British Connection," he senses racial calamity for the minority: a British-unionist nexus that is itself hopelessly involved. In another fine poem, "Glass Grass," he walks through scorched and burnt Catholic Belfast to give a reading in Ballymurphy. "The Black" is in him, the poison born of violence. The poem attacks all those who can take it less easily than himself. Belfast is quiet, "a beaten sexless dog," waiting for the next outrage. In his controversy with James Simmons in *The Honest Ulsterman* (November 1974–February 1975), Fiacc defends his seminal anthology *The Wearing of the Black:* "The bad odour surrounding *The Wearing of the Black* is the bad odour of blood and it stinks of a society that has hopelessly degraded itself and consequently degraded those of us who have to exist in it."

A tragedy in Fiacc's life was the murder of a young poet, Gerry McLaughlin, whom he commemorates in a lovely elegy in *Nights in the Bad Place.*

A major figure in Fiacc is Padraic Pearse*; the landscape of young men caught up, dying in terrible actions, reflects Pearse's ideals and poetry. The sensual theme connects Fiacc and Pearse to Whitman. Fiacc typically is not Anglo-Irish in his verse methods. He organizes a free verse technique, and he is influenced by William Carlos Williams and the Black Mountain School of poets in America.

He won the AE* Memorial Award in 1957 and received an Arts Council of Northern Ireland bursary in 1976, an Arts Council of Northern Ireland major award in 1980, and a *Poetry Ireland* award in 1981. He is a member of Aosdána.*

JAMES LIDDY

WORKS: *By the Black Stream.* Dublin: Dolmen, 1969; *Odour of Blood.* Newbridge, Co. Kildare: Goldsmith, 1973; ed., *The Wearing of the Black.* Belfast: Blackstaff, 1974. (Poetry anthology); *Nights in the Bad Place.* Belfast: Blackstaff, 1977; *The Selected Padraic Fiacc,* Introduction by Terence Brown. Belfast: Blackstaff, 1979; *Missa Terribilis.* Belfast: Blackstaff, 1986; *Ruined Pages: Selected Poems of Padraic Fiacc.* Gerald Dawe & Aodhán Mac Phóilín, eds. Belfast: Blackstaff, [1994]; *Woe to the Boy.* Belfast: Lapwing, 1994. REFERENCES: Brown, Terence. *Northern Voices: Poets from Ulster.* Dublin: Gill & Macmillan, 1975; Liddy, James. "Ulster Poets and the Catholic Muse." *Éire-Ireland* 18 (Winter 1978).

FIELD DAY THEATRE COMPANY (1980–   ), a politicocultural enterprise, was founded by Brian Friel* and Stephen Rea in 1980 in Derry City. It soon included Seamus Heaney,* Tom Paulin,* David Hammond, and Seamus Deane* among its directors. Impelled by the continuing political crisis in the North of Ireland, they undertook a reappraisal of Ireland's political and cultural situation. Their aim was to help resolve the crisis by producing analyses of established opinions, myths, and stereotypes that they considered both symptoms and causes of the impasse.

Thus, they undertook a threefold program: theatrical production, the publication of a series of pamphlets, and the editing of the *Field Day Anthology of Irish Writing.* Beginning with the assumption that national identity is a created, and not a natural, phenomenon, Field Day's analyses of popular, political and literary Irish culture center on the premise that its underlying mythology is politically grounded and expresses itself in the rhetoric of separation or antagonism between two cultures. The ensuing debate about demythologizing, it was hoped, would liberate public consciousness from a fated view of history, alleviate the more lethal expressions of opposition, and allow room for constructive options.

Beginning with Friel's *Translations* in September 1980, the central feature of the project has been an annual dramatic production originating in Derry City, and from there touring Ireland. Among these have been Friel's *Three Sisters* (1981) and *The Communication Cord* (1982), Athol Fugard's *Boseman and Lena* (1983), Tom Paulin's *The Riot Act* (a version of *Antigone,* 1984), Thomas Kilory's* *Double Cross* (1986), and Friel's *Making History* (1988). These plays examine political or cultural crises and the conflicting loyalties they produce: to language, place, community, and inherited values.

The Field Day pamphlets appeared in five three-item series between 1983 and 1988. Each series offered complementary essays on the political-cultural problem facing the North of Ireland, dealing, respectively, with language, literature, religious history, law, and colonialism. Their common purpose was to embarrass even the most innocent-looking literary discourse by exposing its covert burden of stereotyping, prejudice, and evasion.

The *Field Day Anthology,* a massive compilation of some 4,000 finely printed pages, has several purposes: to enlarge the embrace of the term "Irish"; to show that the tradition has expressed itself in several languages; to expand the range of documents beyond the traditional genres to include popular, philosophical, and polemical texts; and to situate the selections against a colonial-imperial historical paradigm. By reprinting substantial selections from such writers as Spenser,* Berkeley,* Swift,* and Wilde,* the anthology challenges the English canonical hegemony in many gratifying and, in the event, controversial ways. By similarly contextualizing Yeats* and Joyce,* it implicitly reclaims them from international modernism and problematizes once again the terms "Irish," "Gaelic," and "Anglo-Irish." Despite some inconsistencies and omissions, the anthology is a sterling achievement for its intelligence and breadth, the theoretical sophistication of its introductions, its enlightening annotations, and useful bibliographies. It demonstrates the complex hospitality of Irish written expression over the past millennium and a half.

CÓILÍN OWENS

WORKS: Heaney, Seamus. *Sweeney Astray: A Version from the Irish.* Derry: Field Day, 1983/ New York: Farrar, Straus, Giroux, 1984; Paulin, Tom. *A New Look at the Language Question.* Field Day Pamphlet #1, Derry: Field Day Theatre Company, 1983; Heaney, Seamus. *An Open Letter.* Pamphlet #2, 1983; Deane, Seamus. *Civilians and Barbarians.* Pamphlet #3, 1983; Deane, Seamus. *Heroic Styles: The Tradition of an Idea.* Pamphlet #4, 1984; Kearney, Richard. *Myth and Motherland.* Pamphlet #5, 1984; Kiberd, Declan. *Anglo-Irish Attitudes.* Pamphlet #6, 1984; Brown, Terence. *The Whole Protestant Community: The Making of an Historical Myth.* Pamphlet #7, 1985; Elliott, Marianne. *Watchmen in Sion: The Protestant Idea of Liberty.* Pamphlet #8, 1985; McCartney. R. L. *Liberty and Authority in Ireland.* Pamphlet #9, 1985; Mulloy, Eanna. *Emergency Legislation: Dynasties of Coercion.* Pamphlet #10, 1986; Farrell, Michael. *Emergency Legislation: The Apparatus of Repression.* Pamphlet #11, 1986; McGrory, Patrick J. *Emergency Legislation: Law and Constitution: Present Discontents.* Pamphlet #12, 1986; Eagleton, Terry. *Nationalism: Irony and Commitment.* Pamphlet #13, 1988; Jameson, Frederic. *Modernism and Imperialism.* Pamphlet #14, 1988; Said, Edward W. *Yeats and Decolonization.* Pamphlet #15, 1988; Deane, Seamus, Carpenter, Andrew, Williams, Jonathan, et al., eds. *The Field Day Anthology of Irish Literature.* 3 vols. Derry: Field Day/New York: Norton, 1991.   REFERENCE: Richtarik, Marilyn. *Acting between the Lines: The Field Day Theatre Company and Irish Cultural Politics 1980–1984.* Oxford: Clarendon, 1995.

FIELDEN, OLGA (1903–?), novelist and playwright. Born in County Antrim.

WORKS: *Island Story.* London: Jonathan Cape, 1933. (Novel); *Stress.* London: Jonathan Cape, 1936. (Novel); *Three to Go.* Belfast: H. R. Carter, 1950. (Play).

FIGGIS, DARRELL [EDMUND] (1882–1925), politician and man of letters. Figgis was born in Rathmines, a suburb of Dublin, in 1882 of an Anglo-Irish family. As a child he lived in India, and as a young man he worked in London for a firm of tea merchants. He then turned to journalism and to more ambitious writing, and also became deeply involved in the Irish nationalist movement. It was he, for instance, who negotiated the purchase of arms that were landed in Howth in the famous gun-running incident of 1914. Immediately after the Rising, in which he did not take part, he was interned in England for several months as a prominent member of the Volunteers. He was again interned for a longer period in 1919. He drew up the Constitution for the Irish Free State, and he was a member of Dail Éireann for County Dublin. His wife shot herself in 1923, and in 1925 Figgis himself committed suicide.

Both his life and his writing were active and so curiously various that he really seems several different individuals. When his best known novel, *The Return of the Hero,* was published under the pseudonym of Michael Ireland in 1923, it was generally thought to be the work of James Stephens,* because of its subject, its style, and its whimsical tone. Indeed, the book so little resembles anything else by Figgis that James Stephens remarked in his introduction to the American edition: ''. . . if Darrell Figgis wrote *The Return of the Hero,* then literary criticism stands baffled, and we must admit that occasions can arise in which the impossible becomes possible, and the unbelievable is to be credited.''

As a writer, Figgis' work falls into the broad categories of historical and political journalism, of poetry and of verse drama, of literary criticism, and of the novel. As an historian and political journalist, his work was mainly for the moment and need not concern us here, although his two short ''Jail Chronicles'' do possess an eloquent simplicity. As a poet, Figgis seems a talentless AE* (to whom, indeed, he dedicated his volume *The Mount of Transfiguration*). His subjects are cosmic emotions and vaguely perceived nature. His higgledypiggledy rhyming only faintly suggests some sort of form and does not disguise a surprisingly faulty control of meter. This lack of control is noticeable also in the frequent and awkward syntactical inversions. He is much given to poetic spelling and archaic words, such as, for instance, the verb ''to high-trape.'' His favorite adjective seems to be ''dewy,'' and a typical line is, ''Visions of light that fill the air with brightness like a floating mist.'' G. K. Chesterton thought him, with Francis Thompson, one of a poetic breed of new Elizabethans, an opinion which must rank in the vanguard of G.K.C.'s most misguided. Figgis' play, *Queen Tara* (1913), was produced by F. R. Benson. Despite its title, it is not Irish in subject matter but takes place in a Maeterlinckean Ruritania. Although the piece received long and respectful reviews on its Dublin appearance, it is distinctly closet drama. As a literary critic, Figgis is more various. Most of his essays are simply long pieces culled from his journalism, but he is interesting on the subject of J. M. Synge* and well worth attention on the subject of his friend AE, about whom he wrote a short book. Figgis' best and most extended piece of criticism is his *Shakespeare, a Study* (1911). This volume is neither modern nor scholarly criticism, but on a continuum of Shakespearean criticism ranging from the lively unprofessionalism of a Frank Harris to the magisterial analyses of an A. C. Bradley, Figgis would be fairly close to the middle. He is extremely knowledgeable and full of plausible ideas always delivered gracefully, if sometimes upon insufficient evidence. He makes some provocative comparisons to the practices of playwrights in other eras, particularly to Ibsen, and he is extremely interesting on Shakespeare's plot structure. This remains a book worthy of some attention.

Nevertheless, Figgis is most important for his five unread and out-of-print novels, of which the most significant are the last three: *Children of Earth* (1918), *The House of Success* (1921), and *The Return of the Hero* (1923). These books are so different in both subject and style that their author seems a literary chameleon. *Children of Earth* is probably his finest novel, and it is an extraordinary one—visually evocative, structurally powerful, and rhetorically eloquent. It takes place on an island, like Achill where Figgis lived for several years, off the West Coast, and it is a study of the elemental life and peasant character formed there. Much of the book seems an emulation of Thomas Hardy with the Wessex dialect replaced by the dialect of the Synge of *In the Shadow of the Glen* or *The Well of the Saints*. However, Figgis' attempt in the last fifty pages to portray a state of mind in a sort of mystical communion with the earth is eerily reminiscent of a book written at almost the same time by Thomas Hardy's most distinctive pupil—that is, *The Rainbow* by D. H. Lawrence. There are some lengthy descriptive passages in Figgis' novel, particularly at the beginning of sections, that do not work because he is waxing too poetic. That flaw apart, this novel grows in beauty and power. It has been long out of print and is unmentioned by critics or historians, who have called lesser books masterly.

If *Children of Earth* is redolent of Hardy, *The House of Success* is permeated by the spirit of Henry James. There is a quintessentially Jamesian narrator, and there is the prudish avoidance of the specific that lifts the whole story out of the real world into the ambiguities of Jamesian psychology. The book is mainly a leisurely contrast between a successful, self-made entrepreneur of a father and a son eventually hardened by patriotic idealism. The major events lead up to the 1916 Rising and its aftermath, but are related mainly in terms of the emotional struggle between father and son, which takes place within the confines of their own sitting room. The novel is basically about two views of what is good for Ireland; although in the novel the palm is given to the son, the father's personal qualities are more dynamic and perhaps more admired. Figgis' diagnosis was, of course, correct, for the somewhat unscrupulous gombeen (or business) man and the sometimes fanatical patriot have been the major figures in Irish political life until today. The book is not entirely a success because of its technique and its style, but it does have two strongly developed characters and some intense moments.

The subject of *The Return of the Hero* is the famous Oisin-St. Patrick colloquy after the hero has returned from the Land of Youth. This clash between the Irish legendary past and the beginnings of modern Irish Christianity is developed with a simple charm and a mild humor. Nevertheless, it implies a genial criticism

of contemporary established religion and its inability, even at its best inten-
tioned, to deal with the unfamiliar. Although the book is little read today, it is
not in the least dated and deserves the small but irreducible stature of a minor
classic. That small but irreducible stature is also the least that Darrell Figgis
himself deserves.

WORKS: *A Vision of Life,* Introduction by G. K. Chesterton. London & New York: J. Lane,
1909. (Poems); *Broken Arcs.* London: Dent, 1911/New York & London: M. Kennerley, 1912.
(Novel); *The Crucibles of Time and Other Poems,* London: Dent, 1911; *Shakespeare, a Study.*
London: Dent, 1911/New York & London: M. Kennerley, 1912; *Studies and Appreciations.* London:
Dent, 1912. (Essays); *Queen Tara.* London: Dent, 1913. (Play); *Jacob Elthorne.* London & Toronto:
Dent, 1914. (Novel); *The Mount of Transfiguration.* Dublin: Maunsel, 1915. (Poems); *AE (George
W. Russell), a Study of a Man and a Nation.* Dublin & London: Maunsel, 1916; *A Chronicle of
Jails.* Dublin: Talbot, 1917; *The Gaelic State in the Past and Future.* Dublin & London: Maunsel,
1917; *Bye-Ways of Study.* Dublin: Talbot/London: Urwin, 1918. (Essays); *Children of Earth.* Dublin:
Maunsel, 1918. (Novel); *A Second Chronicle of Jails.* Dublin: Talbot, 1919; *The Economic Case
for Irish Independence.* Dublin & London: Maunsel, 1920; *The Historic Case for Irish Indepen-
dence.* Dublin & London: Maunsel, 1920; *The House of Success.* Dublin: Gael Co-operative Society,
1921. (Novel); *The Irish Constitution.* Dublin: Mellifont, [1922]; *The Return of the Hero.* London
& Sydney: Chapman & Dodd, 1923, published under the pseudonym of Michael Ireland/New York:
C. Boni, 1930, published under his own name, with an Introduction by James Stephens and a second
unsigned Introduction probably by Padraic Colum; *The Paintings of William Blake.* London: E.
Benn/New York: Scribner's, 1925; *Recollections of the Irish War.* London: E. Benn, 1927.   REF-
ERENCES: Costello, Peter. *The Heart Grown Brutal.* Dublin: Gill & Macmillan/Totowa, N.J.:
Rowman & Littlefield, 1977; Dunn, John J. "Darrell Figgis, A Man Nearly Anonymous." *Journal
of Irish Literature* 15 (January 1986): 33–42; Wessel-Felter, Maryanne. "Darrell Figgis: An Over-
view of His Work." *Journal of Irish Literature* 22 (May 1993): 3–24; Gonzalez, Alexander G.
Darrell Figgis: A Study of His Novels. Butler, Pa.: Kopper, 1992. (Monograph).

FINLAY, LILIAN ROBERTS (1915–   ), novelist and short story writer. Finlay, although born in Malta on February 21, 1915, was reared in Dublin. Her
Welsh father died of Spanish flu as he made his way home after the war. Her
mother worked hard to ensure Finlay's education at Mount Sackville, although
she did not live to see her complete it; she died when her daughter was thirteen.
After finishing school, Finlay studied acting at the Abbey Theatre* between
1936 and 1939, when she married. She reared a large family, augmenting her
income by publishing short stories and articles in *The Holly Bough, Peg's Paper,
Home Notes, The Lady, The Strand,* and *Argosy.*

Her first novel, *Always in My Mind,* was published in 1988. The background
for this and *Forever in the Past* (1993), its sequel, is based on Finlay's memories
of the Dublin of her childhood and young adulthood; and *Stella* was inspired
by Finlay's time in Philadelphia after her husband's death. The strongest elements in the first two books are Finlay's evocation of Dublin between the wars
and her ability to capture both the intensity and the strangely random nature of
women's lives in that social setting. *Stella* is less successful, giving the impression that Finlay had inadequate time to explore the unfamiliar environment in
which she found herself, though she does convey the nightmare quality of Stella's time as a nanny with a spectacularly disfunctional American family. In their

compression, the short stories in *A Bona Fide Husband* show Finlay at her best. They are informed by a view of human nature that is always compassionate and often uncompromisingly ironic and by her wide experience and clear-sighted observation of the relationships between women and men.

SHEILA BARRETT

WORKS: *Always in My Mind*. London: Collins/New York: St. Martin's, 1988. (Novel); *A Bona Fide Husband*. [Swords, Co. Dublin]: Poolbeg, [1991]. (Short stories); *Stella*. [Swords, Co. Dublin]: Poolbeg, [1992]. (Novel); *Forever in the Past*. [Swords, Co. Dublin]: Poolbeg, [1993]. (Novel).

FINNEGAN, SEAMUS (fl. 1980s–1990s), playwright.

WORKS: *North: Four Plays*. London: Marion Boyars, 1987. (Contains "North," "Soldiers," "Act of Union," and "Mary's Men"); *Cemetery of Europe*. London: Marion Boyars, 1991; *James Joyce and the Israelites and Dialogues in Exile*. Switzerland: Harwood Academic, 1994. (Contemporary Theatre Studies, Vol. 7); *It's All Blarney: Four Plays*. Switzerland: Harwood Academic, 1994. (Contemporary Theatre Studies, Vol. 8).

FINNEY, PATRICIA (1958–) novelist.

Nearly the most precocious writer included in this dictionary is Patricia Finney, who was born on May 12, 1958, in London and who published two impressive novels on Irish themes before she was twenty. The first novel, *A Shadow of Gulls* (1977), won the David Higham Award for Best First Novel of the Year. Although she is English by birth and upbringing and of Hungarian extraction on her mother's side, her father's people came from Cork, and her great-uncle was Frank Gallagher,* the short story writer and journalist. Her second novel, *The Crow Goddess,* was written and published while she was studying modern history at Wadham College, Oxford. She has worked as a journalist and is now married with two children. In 1988, her radio play, *A Room Full of Mirrors,* won the Radio Times Drama Award.

A Shadow of Gulls and *The Crow Goddess* actually form one long narrative. The story takes place early in the second century A.D. and is set in Ireland and Britain. It is the story of an Irish harper named Lugh Mac Romain, whose life is closely bound up with the events recounted in the Ulster Cycle of hero tales. The chief events of the Ulster Cycle—the stories of Deirdre of the Sorrows, the Cattle Raid of Cooley, and the life and death of Cuchulain—are all woven into the story of Lugh, as are various historical personages such as the Roman emperor Hadrian. The author cites Lady Gregory's* *Cuchulain of Muirthemne* as her main source of Irish legend, but she seems as much indebted to Sir James Frazer and Robert Graves for her treatment of myth and ancient religion. Her story has considerable narrative skill and emotional power. Even more remarkable is her convincing re-creation of a far-distant time and realistic humanizing of the legend, thereby making it both plausible and modern.

Her most recent novel, *Firedrake's Eye* (1992), is similarly rich in its evocation of the past, but the past is the late sixteenth century, and the setting is London.

WORKS: *A Shadow of Gulls.* London: Collins, 1977; *The Crow Goddess.* London: Collins, 1978; *Firedrake's Eye.* London: Sinclair-Stevenson/New York: St. Martin's, 1992.

FITZGERALD, BARBARA (1911–1982), novelist. The younger daughter of Archbishop Gregg of Armagh, Fitzgerald was born in Cork on December 16, 1911, raised in Dublin and Kilkenny, schooled in England, and graduated from Trinity College, Dublin. On August 21, 1935, she married Michael Fitzgerald Somerville, a nephew of Edith Somerville* and a son of Admiral Boyle Somerville, who was murdered on March 14, 1936, by the Irish Republican Army. (This act was at the behest of General Tom Barry, who objected to the admiral's signing papers of recommendation for local boys who wished to join the British merchant marine.) Fitzgerald and her husband were abroad at this time, as he was an oil executive with Texaco, and they spent much time in West Africa. They had two children, a daughter and a son. She returned to England during the war and worked in intelligence. While living in Armagh after 1944 with her children, she wrote her first novel about the Anglo-Irish situation, *We Are Besieged* (1946), which indirectly drew on her family background but is, in fact, a generalized book about the Protestant position in the new Free State. It was commended by Sean O'Faolain*: "What makes the novel so interesting is that it lights an old story from a fresh angle. . . . it is a genuine novel of Ireland's passions refreshingly told from a new angle and as such ought to be read by every Irishman." A second, more psychological novel, *Footprints upon Water,* was completed in 1955 but failed to find a publisher and appeared only after her death. She and her husband retired to Ireland in 1968, but her last years were clouded by the advent of early senility, and she died in County Dublin on May 21, 1982.

PETER COSTELLO

WORKS: *We Are Besieged.* London: Peter Davies, 1946; *Footprints upon Water.* Belfast: Blackstaff, 1983.   REFERENCE: O'Faolain, Sean. *The Bell* 12 (May 1946): 172–173.

FITZGERALD, PERCY HETHERINGTON (1834–1925), man of letters. Fitzgerald was born in the Fane Valley, County Louth, and educated at Stonyhurst and Trinity College, Dublin. He became crown prosecutor on the northeast circuit but forsook law and country to become a writer in London. He was one of Dickens's protégés, a contributor to *Household Words,* and, though twenty-two years younger, a personal friend of Dickens. In fact, Dickens encouraged him to court his daughter Mamie. This intimacy lends a rare authority to his book, *The Life of Charles Dickens—As Revealed in His Writings* (1905). Other similar work includes *The Life, Letters and Writings of Charles Lamb* (1876) and a lengthy biography of the Sheridan family. He was a prolific author of fiction, biography, histories, and plays, many written from a formally Catholic point of view. His work is almost entirely unavailable, but he is credited with authorship of more than 200 books. More lasting memorials are his sculptures

of Johnson in the Strand, of Dickens in Bath, and of Boswell in Lichfield. He
died in London.

SEAN McMAHON

NOTABLE WORKS: *Lives of the Sheridans*. London: Bentley, 1886; *Life of Charles Dickens*.
London: Chatto & Windus, 1905; *The Life, Letters, and Writings of Charles Lamb*. 6 vols. London:
E. Moxon, 1876/London: Gibbings, 1895/London: Constable, 1924.

FITZGIBBON, [ROBERT LOUIS] CONSTANTINE [LEE-DILLON]

(1919–1983), novelist, journalist, and translator. Fitzgibbon was born on June
8, 1919, in Lenox, Massachussetts, of an American mother and a Northern Irish
father. He was educated at Munich University, the Sorbonne, and Exeter College, Oxford. During World War II, he served first in the British army and then
in the American army. Then, after a short period of schoolmastering in Bermuda,
he turned full-time to writing. He lived for about ten years in England before
moving to Ireland. He became an Irish citizen and was elected to the Irish
Academy of Letters. His first wife was Theodora Fitzgibbon,* the cookery
writer, and his second wife was Margorie Fitzgibbon, the sculptress. He died
on March 23, 1983.

Fitzgibbon was a prolific translator of war memoirs from the French and
German. He himself wrote about thirty volumes of fiction and nonfiction, including the life of Dylan Thomas and an effective thriller-fantasy in the *1984*
vein called *When the Kissing Had to Stop*. His Irish writing consists of a biography of de Valera, some short popular histories, and a novel about Michael
Collins entitled *High Heroic*. That novel has a professional fluency and craft
but treats its subject with little more than a plausible superficiality.

PRINCIPAL IRISH WORKS: *Miss Finnigan's Fault*. London: Cassell, 1953. (Travel in Ireland);
High Heroic. London: Dent, 1969. (Novel); *Out of the Lion's Paw*. London: Macdonald, 1969.
(History); *Red Hand: The Ulster Colony*. London: Joseph, 1971. (History); *The Life and Times of
Eamon de Valera*. Dublin: Gill & Macmillan, 1973. REFERENCE: ''Constantine Fitzgibbon: A
Portrait.'' *New Criterion* 8 (February 6, 1990): 34–39.

FITZGIBBON, THEODORA (1916–1991), cookery writer and woman of let-

ters. Fitzgibbon was born in London of Irish parents, educated in England,
Belgium, and France, and lived in India, America, France, Italy, and Ireland.
She was married to Constantine Fitzgibbon* and later to George Morrison, the
Irish filmmaker and photographic archivist. She was best known for her cookery
books, particularly *A Taste of Ireland* (1968). However, she also wrote a short
novel, *Flight of the Kingfisher* (1967), which was made into a play for television.
Her two volumes of autobiography, *With Love* (1982) and *Love Lies a Loss*
(1985), are racy and easy to read but neither reveals much of the author or the
people she lived or rubbed shoulders with. The war years are well described,
and there are attractive descriptions of houses and places. The name-dropping,
however, is obtrusive, and little of real interest is told the reader of the famous
people the author met. It is all too bland, and even Caitlin and Dylan Thomas

remain washed-out figures. There are times in the books when one is sadly reminded of a harmless and superficial gossip column.

DOROTHY ROBBIE

PRINCIPAL WORKS: *Flight of the Kingfisher.* London: Dent, 1967. (Novel); *A Taste of Ireland.* New York: Avenal Books, 1968. (Cookbook); *With Love: An Autobiography, 1938–46.* London: Century, 1982. (Autobiography); *Love Lies a Loss: An Autobiography, 1946–1959.* London: Century, 1985. In addition, Fitzgibbon published about two dozen cookbooks.

FITZMAURICE, GABRIEL (1952–   ), poet. Fitzmaurice was born on December 7, 1952, in Moyvane, County Kerry, where he now teaches in the National School. He is also director of Listowel Writers Week. He has written both in English and Irish, as well as producing translations from the Irish and children's verse. His poems are straightforward and simple, and the speaker's voice is clear, colloquial, conversational. The early work is generally free verse that is very free; the later work tends to be tighter, with a loose but basically iambic meter and, if not always rhyme, some similarity of sound at the end of the second and fourth lines of a quatrain.

WORKS: *Rainsong.* Dublin: Beaver Row, 1984; *Road to the Horizon.* Dublin: Beaver Row, 1987; *Nocht.* Dublin: Coisceim, 1989. (Irish poems); *The Moving Stair.* Tralee: Kerryman, 1989/Dublin: Poolbeg, 1993. (Children's poems); tr., *The Purge.* Dublin: Beaver Row, 1989; *Dancing Through.* Dublin: Beaver Row, 1990; ed., with Declan Kiberd. *The Flowering Tree/An Crann Faoi Bhláth.* Dublin: Wolfhound, 1991; ed., *Between the Hills and the Sea: Songs and Ballads of Kerry.* Ballyheigue: Oidhreacht, 1991; ed., *Con Greany: Traditional Singer.* Ballyheigue; Oidhreacht, 1991; *The Father's Part.* [Brownsville, Oreg.]: Story Line, 1992; *Kerry through Its Writers.* Dublin: New Island Books, 1993; *The Space Between: New and Selected Poems 1984–1992.* Indreabhán, Conamara: Cló Iar-Chonnacta, [1993]; ed., *The Listowel Literary Phenomenon.* Indreabhán, Conamara: Cló Iar-Chonnachta, [1994].

FITZMAURICE, GEORGE (1877–1963), playwright. Fitzmaurice was first a writer of broad, conventional peasant comedy in his short stories and in his most popular play, *The Country Dressmaker.* Then, partly impressed by Synge* and partly motivated by his own eccentric individuality, he wrote a number of short, grotesque tragicomedies, such as *The Pie-dish* and *The Magic Glasses.* Withdrawing ever more into his own rich imagination and from the theatre—and, indeed, from the ordinary concourse of life—he followed his fantastic fairy tale *The Dandy Dolls* with increasingly fanciful and sardonic plays. In posthumously produced works such as *The Enchanted Land* and *The King of the Barna Men,* he has created an Irish never-never land rivaled only by that of James Stephens.*

Fitzmaurice was born on January 28, 1877, in Bedford House, near Listowel, County Kerry. His father was a Church of Ireland minister and his mother a Catholic, and he was the tenth of twelve children. After working briefly in a bank in Cork, he moved to Dublin where he was a clerk in the civil service for most of the rest of his life. He was out of Dublin only for a period of service in the British Army in World War I and for occasional visits back to Kerry.

Although Yeats* had predicted that Fitzmaurice's first produced play, *The*

Country Dressmaker, would be even more inflammatory than Synge's *The Playboy of the Western World,* the *Dressmaker,* after its initial production in October 1907, became one of the most popular of all Abbey* plays. In 1908, the Abbey produced *The Pie-dish* and in 1913 *The Magic Glasses,* but these rich one-act tragicomedies were before their time, and Abbey audiences did not quite know how to react to them. Yeats himself did not rank Fitzmaurice highly. A number of other Fitzmaurice plays were rejected, among them his strong peasant tragedy *The Moonlighter* and a peasant comedy which Fitzmaurice wrote with John Guinan.*

After the war, Fitzmaurice returned to Dublin to work with the Land Commission, and in 1919 he wrote *'Twixt the Giltinans and the Carmodys.* This rather conventional peasant farce was staged at the Abbey in March 1923, about a month before the first production of O'Casey's* *The Shadow of a Gunman.* This was the last Fitzmaurice play to be staged by the Abbey in his lifetime. Acutely sensitive to criticism, Fitzmaurice withdrew his plays from the Abbey. He lived for forty years more, and he continued to write new work and to revise old work, but during that time he received only the slimmest handful of productions. His name was kept before the public only by his friend Seumas O'Sullivan,* who occasionally persuaded him to allow a play to appear in *The Dublin Magazine.**

There is the tendency to see Fitzmaurice simply as the product of a rich folk culture, but, because his father was an Anglo-Irish minister, Fitzmaurice had only one foot in the door of the whitewashed cabin. Even his early popular stories, informed as they are, tend to see the peasant from the outside. Fitzmaurice was no rural realist like T. C. Murray*; he was more like Lady Gregory,* presenting and exaggerating the foibles of the peasant for the purpose of often quite broad comedy. And so Fitzmaurice's best folk plays present a galaxy of the quaint, the eccentric, and the mad. We are presented with Jaymoney Shanahan who hides in his loft seeing visions in his magic glasses; with Morgan Quille the quack doctor; with Leum Donoghue the fanatical creator of the pie dish, and with Lena Hanrahan the beauty who wears false teeth, a wig, and a wooden leg.

From the exaggerations of the comic vision, it is not far to the exaggerations of satire and fantasy. As Fitzmaurice grew older and further removed from a past that he was not even originally firmly rooted in, satire and fantasy began to take over. We see this particularly in *The Waves of the Sea, The Linnaun Shee,* and *The Green Stone,* and triumphantly in *The Enchanted Land* and *The Ointment Blue.* Fitzmaurice did make a couple of attempts to write about the city. One, *The Coming of Ewn Andzale,* is his only really tedious play, but the other, *One Evening Gleam,* is a little *tour de force.* However, Fitzmaurice was such a recluse that he was never really of the city, and his most characteristic and finest work came out of memory and a most extraordinary imagination.

If this isolation gave Fitzmaurice his strength as a writer, it also gave him two weaknesses. His language is generally as Synge would have wanted it: as

ripe as a berry. It is rare, rich, hypnotically fluent, and as playfully inventive as
the Synge of *The Playboy* or the O'Casey of *Purple Dust.* In the hands of a
memorable Kerry actor, such as Eamon Kelly or Eamon Keane, Fitzmaurice's
long fancies are often a memorable joy. But the long speeches are also a problem
in many of the later plays. Despite engaging experiments with sound, repetition,
malapropisms, and different levels of language, many of these speeches are more
literary than dramatic. If the speeches are read as portions of a novel in dialogue,
they are delightful. If they are read with a theatrical ear, as scripts to be spoken
in plays to be staged, they are a bit of a problem. Engaging, charming, even
marvelous, but a bit of a problem.

A second symptom of Fitzmaurice's isolation is the frequent laziness of his
plot construction. A prime example is the published version of his brilliant *The
Enchanted Land.* The first and second acts are loaded down with exposition
which could profitably and excellently have been dramatized. Indeed, they cry
out to be dramatized. The result is that much of the chat in Act One simply
tells us what should have been the dramatized story of Act One. Fitzmaurice
has attacked his story at the wrong place and has caused his director a quite
unnecessary problem of dullness.

Nevertheless, in these brilliant fantasies, Fitzmaurice has truly created his own
worlds, just as did Lewis Carroll or James Stephens or Kenneth Grahame. The
use of fantasy was the making of Fitzmaurice as an artist. Fantasy allowed him
free play for gaiety and wit, and was a liberating influence. Poorer writers have
usually but one tone, one emotional slant, one angle of vision on the world.
Fitzmaurice seems to have had three: the grotesque in such early work as *The
Magic Glasses* and *The Pie-dish;* the bleakly glum, in which so many of his
plays are concluded with a stoical acceptance of failure or, at best, second-best;
and the fantastic which allowed him to palliate the grotesquerie and to alleviate
the glumness.

Fitzmaurice died on May 12, 1963, in his room at 3 Harcourt Street in Dublin.
After his death, all of his available printed plays and manuscripts were collected
and published in three volumes. Several of them have been either revived or
produced for the first time at the Abbey Theatre. Among the early Abbey playwrights, his reputation today is probably second only to that of Synge. He probably would have found some dour solace in that.

WORKS: *Five Plays.* London & Dublin: Maunsel, 1914/Boston: Little, Brown, 1917. (Includes
The Country Dressmaker, The Moonlighter, The Pie-Dish, The Magic Glasses, and *The Dandy
Dolls*); *The Plays of George Fitzmaurice.* Vol. 1, *Dramatic Fantasies,* with an Introduction by
Austin Clarke. Dublin: Dolmen, 1967. (Includes *The Magic Glasses, The Dandy Dolls, The Linnaun
Shee, The Green Stone, The Enchanted Land,* and *Waves of the Sea*); *The Plays of George Fitz-
maurice.* Vol. 2, *Folk Plays,* with an Introduction by Howard K. Slaughter. Dublin: Dolmen, 1970.
(Includes *The Ointment Blue or The King of the Barna Men, The Pie-Dish, The Terrible Baisht,
There Are Tragedies and Tragedies,* and *The Moonlighter*); *The Plays of George Fitzmaurice.* Vol.
3, *Realistic Plays,* with an Introduction by Howard K. Slaughter. Dublin: Dolmen, 1970. (Includes
The Toothache, The Country Dressmaker, One Evening Gleam, 'Twixt the Giltinans and the Car-

modys, The Simple Hanrahans, and *The Coming of Ewn Andzale*); *The Crows of Mephistopheles,* ed., with an Introduction by Robert Hogan. Dublin: Dolmen, 1970. (Stories); ''Chasing a Ghoul.'' *The Irish Emerald* (June 24, 1905/reprint, *Journal of Irish Literature* 6 (September 1977): 57–63. (Story); with Guinan, John. *The Wonderful Wedding. Journal of Irish Literature* 6 (September 1978): 3–36. REFERENCES: Gelderman, Carol W. *George Fitzmaurice.* Boston: Twayne, [1979]; McGuinness, Arthur E. *George Fitzmaurice.* Lewisburg, Pa.: Bucknell University Press, [1975]; Slaughter, Howard K. *George Fitzmaurice and His Enchanted Land.* Dublin: Dolmen, 1972.

FITZPATRICK, NINA (fl. 1990s), novelist. Fitzpatrick's first novel, *Fables of the Irish Intelligentsia,* briefly won the prestigious *Irish Times*/Aer Lingus Literature Prize for Fiction in 1991. However, the prize was withdrawn after it was charged that she was not an Irish citizen. Then, as her publisher remarks on the book blurb of her second novel, ''her name, her nationality, her sex, her number and her very reality became a matter for fierce debate.'' In any event, *Fables* is a clever, witty, often bawdy, and thoroughly knowledgeable collection of tales in which the author takes a barbed but often amused and very amusing look at aspects of modern Irish intellectual life. Her characters are varied, eccentric, and extremely articulate. Sometimes, as in the opening sentence of ''The Missionary,'' the author seems striving mainly for the startling effect: '' 'Father Boniface, you're a real shit,' said the Abbot of Petra Fertilis.'' But generally the writing is legitimately fresh and arresting, as in the opening paragraph of ''Easter Journey'':

> The buses are brazen today. They trundle past without the slightest intention of stopping. Sly-boots, pretending not to see me. Buttery eyes, greasy arses, wobbly torsos. Heaving and spewing water all over the place. They hate me.

The plots quickly become rather vague in the memory, as do the characters, but the style is as individual as any Irish writer's since Tom MacIntyre's* early pieces—and a good deal less cutesy.

Fitzpatrick's second novel, *The Loves of Faustyna* (1994), is set in last decade of communist Poland but nevertheless contains many Irish jokes and allusions. Again Fitzpatrick writes with an inimitably witty and sharply pointed pen, and her tragicomic characters are painted with truth, bite, and economy of words. Ireland nowadays has too few comic writers to afford a cultural disfranchisement of Nina Fitzpatrick.

DOROTHY ROBBIE

WORKS: *Fables of the Irish Intelligentsia.* London: Fourth Estate, [1991]; *The Loves of Faustyna.* London: Fourth Estate, [1994].

FITZPATRICK, WILLIAM J[OHN] (1830–1895), historian. Fitzpatrick was born in Dublin in 1830 and died there in 1895. He was a prosperous tallow merchant who spent part of his profits on acquiring Secret Service records and other useful historical documents from government archives. Such materials were supposed to be in safe keeping at Dublin Castle, but unaccountably kept turning up in the private market. With these sources of inside information, supplemented by *viva voce* inquiries throughout a city whose remarkable acoustics were so admired by George Moore,* Fitzpatrick uncovered many deplorable governmental activities and practices. He then published his findings in a series of books which caused virtuous indignation or hilarity among readers according to their temperament. The best of these books are *The Life, Times and Contemporaries of Lord Cloncurry* (1855), *Ireland Before the Union* (1867), and *"The Sham Squire"* (1866).

ANDREW MARSH

WORKS: *The Life, Times and Contemporaries of Lord Cloncurry.* Dublin: James Duffy, 1855; *Who Wrote the Waverly Novels?* London: Effingham Wilson, 1856; *A Note to the Cornwallis Papers.* Dublin: W. B. Kelly, 1859; *Lady Morgan.* London: C. J. Skeet, 1860; *The Life, Times, and Correspondence of Dr. Doyle, Bishop of Kildare and Leighlin.* Dublin: James Duffy, 1861/new ed., greatly enlarged, 1880; *Memoirs of R. Whatley, Archbishop of Dublin.* London: R. Bentley, 1864; *"The Sham Squire" and the Informers of 1798.* London: W. B. Kelly/London: Simpkin, Marshall/ New York: J. W. Bouton, 1866; *Curious Family History; or, Ireland before the Union.* . . . Dublin & London: James Duffy, 1867; *Irish Wits and Worthies; Including Dr. Lanigan.* . . . Dublin: James Duffy, 1873; *The Life of Charles Lever.* London: Chapman & Hall, 1879/new ed., revised, London: Ward, Lock [1884]; *The Life of . . . Thomas N. Burke.* London: Kegan Paul, 1885/new ed., revised, 1894; *Secret Service under Pitt.* London & New York: Longmans, 1892/2d ed., enlarged, 1892; *Memoirs of Father Healy of Little Bray.* London: Richard Bentley, 1896; *History of the Dublin Catholic Cemeteries,* continued & edited by Gerald P. Fitzpatrick. Dublin: [Catholic Cemeteries Offices], 1900.

FITZSIMON, ELLEN O'CONNELL (1805–1883), poet. Fitzsimon, the eldest daughter of Daniel O'Connell, was born in Dublin on November 12, 1805. She is remembered for her poem "The Song of the Irish Emigrant in America," which is not only the prototypical nostalgic song, but also contains the immortal line "my ears are full of tears." She died in 1883.

WORK: *Darrynane in Eighteen Hundred and Thirty-two, and Other Poems.* Dublin: W. B. Kelly, 1863.

FLANAGAN, THOMAS [JAMES BONNER] (1923–   ), critic, historian, and novelist. Flanagan was born in Greenwich, Connecticut, on November 5, 1923, the son of Owen Flanagan, an oral surgeon, and his wife, Mary Helen Bonner, all Flanagan's grandparents having emigrated from County Fermanagh. He has stated, in the *San Francisco Chronicle* of May 22, 1994, that he feels no Ulster creative resonance, but Fermanagh may be too close as well as too remote for him to summon up. Three of his finest critical studies are concerned with figures not far from the Fermanagh frontier: William Carleton,* Maria Edgeworth,* John Mitchel.*

Flanagan served in the U.S. Navy in the Pacific in World War II. He received a B.A. from Amherst and an M.A. in 1948 and a Ph.D. in 1958 from Columbia University, where he was an assistant professor from 1948 to 1960.

Flanagan's dissertation, published as *The Irish Novelists 1800–1850* (1959), showed a delicate psychological perception utterly free from jargon. He grounded his work firmly in history from the beginning:

The Ireland of the nineteenth century was a fragmented culture, a dismaying and complicated tangle of classes, creeds, loyalties, and aspirations.

The Year of the French would express this thesis for 1798, but in 1959 Flanagan's future fictions were visible only in his discussion of novelists for whom he revealed a certain austere kinship. Above all, he gave them a function, where Irish historians cleansing their art from propaganda found themselves ill at ease among storytellers. Or the more urban did. Those aware of their rural roots, such as Maureen Wall, would join Flanagan in acclaiming Carleton as unsurpassable if unreliable evidence. As Flanagan anatomized:

In its characteristic form, the Irish novel is an attempt to define the nature of Irish society and to relate its present graces and disorders to the island's tragic past. The myths, justifications, and visions, which such novels embody, are attempts to reconcile in symbolic terms the conflicting elements of a culture at war with itself.

He was choosing five novelists—Edgeworth, Lady Morgan,* John Banim,* Gerald Griffin,* Carleton—and said the book could "be called a study of five islands, for each writer had his own intense understanding of the country which he had taken as his subject."

Flanagan sought to instill a cool suspense of passions while using literature to win back the mind of the past from which modern scholarship was divorcing itself. He trained his readers to keep their feet on Irish ground without being swallowed by it. The oscillation in reputation of his five novelists gave its own warnings but also its own insurance:

In Ireland their books had been greeted with that mixture of lavish praise, and hoarse indignation, with which all public events, great or small, were celebrated. And abroad they had been accepted, each in turn and despite all contradictions, as the delineations of the "real" Ireland.

The Irish revival and its successors had largely condemned the five novelists as false in moral and political terms. Flanagan now reclaimed them as historical evidence no less than as forgotten literature.

Flanagan moved to the University of California at Berkeley as associate professor and remained there for eighteen years until he took his last academic post at the State University of New York at Stony Brook. In 1960, he also visited Ireland as a Guggenheim fellow, establishing a pattern of nearly annual visits. He was now at work on a sequel to *The Irish Novelists.* Although this has not been completed, its design dominated his creative life and dramatically affected his vision as a novelist. He intended to single out certain writers, often for one specific work. Some were obvious, such as Joyce's* *Ulysses;* others were surprising preferences. His essay "The Big House of Ross-Drishane" implies that the major Somerville and Ross* work under discussion would be *The Big House of Inver,* "one of the most remarkable books ever written in Ireland. Its worth begins with its abrupt dismissal of all apology, all pleading, all recrimination." But the big surprise would have been *When We Were Boys* by Parnell's fervent apostle and reluctant apostate William O'Brien.* Swept away and forgotten with the glories of the old Home Rule Party, Flanagan was almost alone in rediscovering it. As a social witness to late nineteenth-century Catholic Ireland before Joyce, it is indeed unrivaled in its wit, perception, and humanity. Flanagan owes it a new edition with an appreciative critical introduction, for O'Brien was to inspire the closest approximation to a hero in *The Tenants of Time*.

Flanagan would ensure a modern edition of one major Irish classic, not nominally a work of fiction: John Mitchel's *Jail Journal*. Its philosophy of war and hatred, its refusal to concede fair hearing to any opponent, and its phenomenal wit, charm, imagery, grandeur, and bite were handled by Flanagan in statesmanlike terms. Up to now, Mitchel was idolized by undiscriminating followers such as Arthur Griffith* or Patrick Pearse* or else disdainfully ignored by critics. Flanagan used his own appreciation for the stylistic genius of the work to show Mitchel essentially as self-destructive.

Flanagan came to know Ireland in the 1960s partly through travel, partly through research, partly through friends such as Seamus Heaney,* Benedict Kiely,* and Conor Cruise O'Brien,* but the friendship that probably taught him most about being an Irish writer of the past was that with Frank O'Connor.* O'Connor taught him, by argument, much of the mind of Irish nationalist rebellion, but he also gave Flanagan, in flesh and blood, the Cork past, whence presumably Cork's major place in *The Tenants of Time* and, to a lesser extent, *The End of the Hunt*. There is this difference: the unmistakable Cork you see in Flanagan and you hear in O'Connor.

Flanagan began writing *The Year of the French* one day at Berkeley when his wife telephoned to say she would be a couple of hours late in picking him up.

On impulse, I picked up a pad of blue interoffice paper and began writing. It was a description of a man walking along a strand on the west coast of Ireland. He was wearing a frock coat, a very torn frock coat, so I knew it was in the past. But I didn't know why I was writing it.

That survived to become the opening of *The Year of the French*. The man proved to be Owen MacCarthy, the emblem of the Gaelic Ireland that had so little to do with the warring factions in 1798 and yet was doomed with it and is hanged at the end. The novel as a whole is extraordinary in its interweaving of disparate cultural voices as historical sources, making a far more credible history than any finished narrative. No Irish historical novelist has shown so Homeric a fairness.

The Year of the French, which received the American National Book Critics Circle Award in 1979, dealt with the impact of the belated Revolutionary French troops' landing at Killala in 1798 after the main insurrections were over in Wexford and Antrim-Down. As the French-Irish television production stressed, Flanagan gave fine French cameos as well as a multitude of Irish and English narratives. *The Tenants of Time* (1988) was subtler in title, symbolizing the land war but also linking past with present to show that Man may live within a long lease whence Time may suddenly evict him. Many of the protagonists meet that fate: Parnell himself, living in his "Marriage" with Katharine O'Shea, which suddenly turns from his haven into his doom; Bob Delaney, inspired by William O'Brien but meeting a Parnellesque fate in a rural Irish Catholic context; the survivors of an abortive Fenian rising discovering catastrophically twenty-five years later what had really happened to them. Meanwhile, the rise of the Irish Catholic bourgeoisie unfolds inexorably behind the tapestry of Fenianism, Parnellism, land war, village, cottage, and Big House. Sardonically, in the third novel, allusions are made to a later generation of Catholic capitalists rising on the rapacity of their grandfathers and the self-destruction of their fathers.

The End of the Hunt (1994) covers the Irish rebellion and civil war, 1919–1923, but with a quicker pace: it is a twentieth century of train and motorcar with a corresponding speed in change of locale. No longer do the characters await history to engulf them: they devour it before it eats them. Possibly Flanagan's greatest achievement is to have captured the zeitgeist of 1798, 1867–1892, and 1919–1921. Flanagan, teacher to the last, seems to say that neither will the raw sources of 1919–1923 reach the stature of 1798, nor its memoirs approach the quality of William O'Brien's or of his contemporaries'. We are allowed to see the major figures more directly, above all, the implacable yet deeply sympathetic republican Frank Lacy, whose impossibilism is as obviously anathema to Flanagan as its integrity is unanswerable. The subtlety of more civilized strategists, capable of even more sinister means, is caught among British and Irish visionaries.

Mary Renaúlt, possibly the greatest historical novelist of her time, saluted Thomas Flanagan, probably the greatest Irish historical novelist of his, as one whose work "should not be missed by anyone prepared to learn from history." Even less should it be missed by anyone prepared to learn history. Flanagan has vindicated the historical novel as a form of science, no less than as a form of art.

OWEN DUDLEY EDWARDS

WORKS: *The Irish Novelists 1800–1850.* New York: Columbia University Press, 1959; "The Big House of Ross-Drishane." *Kenyon Review* 28 (January 1966): 54–78; "Frank O'Connor, 1903–1966." *Kenyon Review* 28 (September 1966): 439–455; *The Year of the French.* New York: Holt Rinehart/London: Macmillan, 1979; "Critical Introduction" to *Jail Journal* by John Mitchel. N.p.: University Press of Ireland, 1982, pp. vii–xxxv; *The Tenants of Time.* New York: Dutton/London: Bantam, 1988; "Literature in English, 1801–91." In *A New History of Ireland,* Vol. 5, Ireland under the Union I. 1801–70, W. E. Vaughan, ed. Oxford: Oxford University Press, 1919, pp. 482–522; *The End of the Hunt.* New York: Dutton, 1994/London: Sinclair-Stevenson, 1995.   REFERENCE: Donoghue, Denis. "*The Year of the French.*" In *We Irish.* Berkeley, Los Angeles & London: University of California Press, pp. 258–266.

FLECKNOE, RICHARD (?–1678?), man of letters. Flecknoe is chiefly remembered because of Dryden's withering remarks about him in "Mac Flecknoe":

> All human things are subject to decay,
> And when Fate summons, monarchs must obey.
> This Flecknoe found, who, like Augustus, young
> Was call'd to empire, and had govern'd long:
> In prose and verse, was own'd without dispute,
> Thro' all the realms of *Nonsense,* absolute.

Although very well known in the London of his day, little is known about Flecknoe now. He is said to have been an Irish priest and to have traveled widely: to the Low Countries in the early 1640s, to Rome in 1645, to Constantinople around 1647, to Portugal and Brazil in 1648. Returned to London, he was described by Marvell as being extremely lean and with an appetite for reciting his own verse. His play, *Love's Kingdom,* was performed but generally judged insipid. His *Ariadne* was possibly the first English opera, although his music to it has been lost. Despite Dryden's strictures, Flecknoe has had a few defenders and mild admirers, among them Southey and Lamb and, in modern times, Alfred Noyes and Shane Leslie,* who saw fit to include two poems in Catholic anthologies of verse. In *The Oxford History of English Literature,* James Sutherland remarks that ''a few of his poems are considerably better than one would expect.'' Incidentally, this is how Flecknoe praised Dryden in an epigram:

> . . . the Muse's darling and delight,
> Than whom none ever flew so high a flight.

PRINCIPAL WORKS: *Miscellania: or, Poems of All Sorts, with Divers Other Pieces.* London: Printed by T. R., 1653; *Ariadne Deserted by Theseus, and Found and Courted by Bacchus. A Dramatick Piece Adapted for Recitative Musick.* London, 1654; *Love's Kingdom, A Pastoral Tragecomedy . . . With a Short Treatise of the English Stage.* London: Printed by R. Wood for the Author, [1664]. (Apparently a revision of the earlier *Love's Dominion*); *Rich. Flecknoe's Aenigmatical Characters. Being Rather a New Work, Than New Impressions of the Old.* London: Printed by R. Wood, for the Author, 1665; *Epigrams of All Sorts, Made at Several Times, on Several Occasions.* 2 pts. London: Printed for the Author, 1671.

FLITTON, SHEILA (1935–   ), playwright, novelist, and actress. Born and raised in Cork, Flitton lived briefly in England before returning to Ireland to raise her four children and to pursue her acting career. Her 1979 play, *Harbour Nights,* received excellent reviews, and from that time on she combined her acting career with her writing. Her first full-length play, *For Better or For Worse,* won the 1982 Listowel Writers' Week Award; an exploration of wife-battering, it has been produced in Ireland and America. Other plays include *Heavenly Visitation,* a one-act comedy, and *Beezie (A Ghost's Story),* a one-woman show, cowritten with her son David, about a Sligo wisewoman. Flitton has recently achieved commercial success with three novels: *Notions* (1991), *Whispers* (1992), and *More Notions* (1993). A fourth, *Waiting in the Wings,* will be published in 1996. Flitton's work is notable for its humor, even when depicting serious issues, and for the incredible joie de vivre of her characters.

KATHLEEN A. QUINN

WORKS: *Notions*. Cork: Glencree, 1991; *Whispers*. Cork: Glencree, 1992; *More Notions*. Cork: Emperor, 1993.

FLOOD-LADD, DORIS (fl. 1980s), novelist.

WORK: *The Irish*. London: Star, 1982/New York: Banbury, 1983.

FLOWER, ROBIN [ERNEST WILLIAM] (1881–1946), Celtic scholar, translator, and poet. Flower, one of the most erudite of Celtic scholars and graceful of translators, was born in England on October 16, 1881. He was educated at Leeds Grammar School and Pembroke College, Oxford; from 1929 to 1944, he was deputy keeper of manuscripts at the British Museum. Flower did not live to complete a history of Irish literature which he had been preparing for years, but his many translations and scholarly works (particularly *The Irish Tradition*), are an admirable body of work. His reminiscences of life on the Great Blasket Island, *The Western Island*, is a loving recreation of a vanished way of life, written with an appreciative poet's eye. He died in Southgate, London, on January 16, 1946.

WORKS: *Eire, and Other Poems*. London: Locke Ellis, 1910; *Hymenaea, and Other Poems*. London: Selwyn & Blount, 1918; *The Leelong Flower*. [London]: 1923. (Poems); with Ida M. Flower, *The Great Blasket*. London, 1924. (Poems); *Love's Bitter-Sweet: Translations from the Irish Poets of the Sixteenth and Seventeenth Centuries*. Dublin: Cuala, 1925; *Monkey Music*. London, 1925. (Poems); *Trirech inna n-én, From the Irish*. London: Donald Macbeth, 1926. (Poems); *The Pilgrim's Way*. London, 1927. (Poems); *Fuit Ilium*. London, 1928. (Translations of Irish poems); *Ireland and Medieval Europe*. London, [1928]. (Lecture); *Poems and Translations*. London: Constable, 1931; *The Islandman*, by Tomas Ó Criomhthain. Dublin: Talbot/London: Chatto & Windus, 1934. (Translation of Irish memoir); *The Western Island; or, the Great Blasket*. Oxford: Clarendon, 1944; *The Irish Tradition*. Oxford: Clarendon, 1947.   REFERENCE: Bell, Sir Harold Idris. *Robin Ernest William Flower, 1881–1946*. London: Geoffrey Cumberlege, [1948]. (Pamphlet).

FLYNN, [GERARD] MANNIX (1957–   ), novelist and actor. Flynn was born in Dublin and, according to a brief biography in his novel *Nothing to Say,* was educated ''at Whitefriar Street National School, St. Joseph's Industrial School, St. Patrick's Institution, and Mountjoy Prison.'' He has acted in the Project, and an unpublished play, *He Who Laughs Wins,* was performed at a fringe theater in London. His novel appeared in 1983 to considerable acclaim and depicts the young life of Gerard O'Neill, growing up in a large family in inner-city Dublin. His family life is turbulent, his father is seldom around, his mother drinks, and his various siblings form a background chorus of chaos. Gerard mitches from school, steals from shops, and is finally apprehended riding a stolen bicycle. For this, he is sent to a reform school in the West of Ireland, run by some often brutal and sadistic Christian Brothers. Flynn's young boy is no childish monster like Patrick McCabe's* Butcher Boy, but a very vulnerable and appealing creation. His story is told from his point of view but a few years later, when he is leaving Ireland, and the language is more lean and straightforward than McCabe's. Nevertheless, it catches the language of the street accurately and forcefully: "This was my new abode," reminisces the older Gerard, "and if Charles Dickens could have seen the place, he would have dropped fucking dead." It has its own horrific imaginative details: "My skin felt as if it was trying to get away from the pyjamas. It was like eating with a spoon with maggots on it, and it getting closer and you not being able to close your mouth." Flynn's impoverished inner city is not described with the romanticized eloquence of a previous generation's Sean O'Casey,* but with an effective and memorable realism.

Unfortunately, there have been no further books from Flynn, but, despite some obstreperous collisions with the Garda Siochána, he has frequently been effectively seen on the Dublin stage and in the occasional film.

WORK: *Nothing to Say.* [Swords, Co. Dublin]: Ward River, [1983].

FOLEY, MICHAEL (1947–   ), poet and novelist. Foley was born in Derry and educated at St. Columb's College, Derry, and at Queen's University, Belfast. He lives in London, where he lectures in information technology at the University of Westminster.

In *The Go Situation* (1982), he uses a colloquial hip diction that is often a refreshing contrast to the solemnity of much modern Irish verse. He includes such words as "uh," "hee-hee," "oh-ho!" and "yukky," as well as more than a smattering of the usual four-letter ones. Some readers would doubtless find him invigoratingly tasteless in such poems as "Howdy!" which is a refutation of his critics and concludes, "Love you all madly, you dumb assholes!" Nevertheless, Foley is an often funny poet, as in:

> The men doze in chairs
> while the women sort out their affairs—
> an extreme case of aunts-in-the-pants.

The flipness of Foley's style often belies the seriousness of his content, and with more tightening up, the flipness could sometimes be raised to wit.

In *Insomnia in the Afternoon* (1994), Foley has developed along predictable lines. Its very first poem is entitled "Chickenshit" but contains the superb line "It's all hot air, a *succes de steam.*" Some poems, such as "Heaven," are probably more breezy than funny; and to many people breeziness would hardly atone. In that poem, God is described as "The old cunt," and remarks, "Son, I wouldn't know peace of mind if it / Stuck its hand into my shorts and *jerked me off.*" However, if not a reverential, Foley is a referential poet who can incorporate lines from Byron or Whitman or references to old Glenn Ford or Burt Lancaster or even Rhonda Fleming movies, as well as superbly embody the more culturally—and not always morally—vulgar argot of the modern world. There is little care for form in Foley's slapdash work, but there is much in his diction that is vital and individual—and also abrasive and callow.

WORKS: *True Life Love Stories: Poems.* Belfast: Blackstaff, 1976; *The Irish Frog: Adaptations from Rimbaud, Corbiere, Laforgue.* Belfast: Ulsterman, 1978; *The Go Situation.* [Dundonald,

N. I.]: Blackstaff, [1982]. (Poetry); *The Life of Jamesie Coyle.* Belfast: Fortnight, 1984. (Novel); *Insomnia in the Afternoon.* Belfast: Blackstaff, 1994.

FOLKLORE, IRISH. The oral tales, beliefs, and traditions of the Irish peasantry attracted little attention or admiration prior to the nineteenth century. Collectors of Irish folklore were inspired by the enormous popularity of Jacob and Wilhelm Grimm's early nineteenth-century folklore collections and of Sir Walter Scott's *Minstrelsy of the Scottish Border* (1803) and Waverley novels, which Scott claimed in the Postscript to *Waverley* had been inspired by Maria Edgeworth's* portraits of the Irish peasant. The anthologies of Thomas Crofton Croker* (1798–1854) encouraged the collection of Irish folklore both by demonstrating the continued existence of what many had believed to be forgotten superstitions and by proving how much the beliefs and legends of the Irish countryside appealed to the curiosity of the reading public. Croker's most well-known collection, *Fairy Legends and Traditions of the South of Ireland* (1825), became so popular that a second series dedicated to Walter Scott and a third series dedicated to Wilhelm Grimm were published in 1828; the entire work was reissued throughout the century. Croker patronizingly presented his materials as antiquarian curiosities and transformed them into fiction. Croker's collections reflected a dichotomy between folklore and fiction reminiscent of Scott: while the tales themselves were highly fictionalized narratives, Croker's "Notes" after each story offered a wealth of unadorned information about local legends, customs, and beliefs. Croker attempted to expand the significance of Irish folklore with numerous references to English literary parallels and international analogues.

The popularity of Croker's collections encouraged Irish novelists to write about the peasantry. William Carleton,* John and Michael Banim,* Samuel Lover,* and Gerald Griffin* recorded many of the tales, beliefs, and customs of rural Ireland in their novels. William Carleton (1794–1869), whose mother and father were both Gaelic-speaking peasants noted for their knowledge of traditional songs and stories, presented the most complete and authentic picture of pre-Famine peasant life in nineteenth-century Irish fiction, especially in the two series of *Traits and Stories of the Irish Peasantry* (1830, 1833) and in *Tales and Sketches Illustrating the Character of the Irish Peasantry* (1845). John and Michael Banim's *Tales of the O'Hara Family* (1825, 1827), Samuel Lover's *Legends and Stories of Ireland* (1831, 1834), and Gerald Griffin's *Holland-Tide* (1827), *Tales of the Munster Festivals* (1827), *The Collegians* (1829), and *Talis Qualis; or Tales of the Jury Room* (1842) also include a great deal of Irish folklore. However, the folklore depicted in these works, as in Carleton's, inevitably was colored by the propaganda, sentimentality, and comic caricature which pervade much of nineteenth-century Irish fiction. The popularity and literary possibilities of materials from Irish folklore were also demonstrated by Thomas Moore's* *Irish Melodies.*

Literary periodicals like the *Dublin University Magazine* and the *Dublin and*

London Magazine were the major publishers of Irish folklore during the forty years after Croker's collections of the 1820s. Their anonymous contributors made no effort to preserve the oral tales and traditions of the country peoplein their original form. Usually what was presented as folklore in such periodicals kept to the tradition of "literary folklore" begun by Croker. Supposedly authentic peasant legends were rewritten to conform to nineteenth-century standards of fiction. The introductions to such "legends" contained other, unelaborated examples of the beliefs and tales of the peasantry plus skeptical, patronizing comments by the "enlightened" narrator. However, the folklore in such articles was generally less adulterated than in Croker's collections and in Irish novels. The least adulterated Irish folklore was contained in some of the many county histories published throughout the century.

Patrick Kennedy (1801–1873), who had contributed folklore to the *Dublin University Magazine,* published several important collections of the tales and traditions of his native County Wexford. Kennedy's *Legends of Mount Leinster* (1855), *The Banks of the Boro* (1876), and *Evenings in the Duffrey* (1869) present Irish folklore against a fictional background. Kennedy had read Croker, Carleton, and Griffin, but his work represents significant advances in the collection of Irish folklore. His collections contain relatively few literary mannerisms and are much closer to the original idiom and structure of oral traditions. Kennedy was motivated by an antiquarian zeal similar to Croker's, but whereas Croker had presented only legends, Kennedy's collections of tales, *Legendary Fictions of the Irish Celts* (1866), *The Fireside Stories of Ireland* (1870), and *The Bardic Stories of Ireland* (1871), included the entire spectrum of oral prose traditions in Ireland. The Ossianic tales which Kennedy recorded in *Legendary Fictions* demonstrated that the native heroic and mythological cycles found in medieval manuscripts in Dublin libraries also existed in oral form among the peasantry. Later in the century the noted Celtic folklorist, Alfred Nutt (1856–1912), would claim that the medieval Irish manuscripts themselves were derived from a worthy and poetic oral folk tradition still current among the nineteenth-century Irish peasantry. The great popularity of Kennedy's collections and the revelation that the peasantry of predominantly English-speaking County Wexford had preserved an exclusively Gaelic tradition for over one thousand years encouraged further collecting, especially in the Irish-speaking districts in the west of Ireland, by literary nationalists in the last quarter of the century.

Ancient Irish myths and hero tales were given a new scholarly significance by nineteenth-century developments in philology, anthropology, and comparative mythology. Ireland's ancient literature underwent the same process of popularization and literary transformation in the last quarter of the century that the more contemporary tales, beliefs, and traditions of the peasantry underwent throughout the century. Standish J. O'Grady* freely rewrote ancient Irish myths and legends in the guise of a nineteenth-century novel in his immensely popular and influential *History of Ireland: Heroic Period* (1878) and its sequel, *Cuchulain and His Contemporaries* (1880). As with the Irish folklore published throughout the century, the intrinsic quality and importance of O'Grady's materials transcended the limitations of his style and inspired Irish literature and politics for years to come.

The nationalism implicit in earlier anthologies of Irish folklore and mythology became obvious propaganda in Lady Wilde's* collections *Ancient Legends, Mystic Charms, and Superstitions of Ireland* (1887) and *Ancient Cures, Charms, and Usages of Ireland* (1890). Lady Wilde (1826–1896), who had contributed to *The Nation** under the pseudonym "Speranza," filled her anthologies with materials which her husband, Sir William Wilde* (1815–1876), an eye surgeon, occultist, and antiquarian, had collected after he published *Irish Popular Superstitions* (1853). The folklore in Lady Wilde's collections is colored by her political and ethnological nationalism and her occult theories rather than by literary elaboration.

In the last quarter of the century, the study of Irish folklore fostered some of the worst and some of the best literature ever written in Ireland. Literary popularizations of Irish folklore such as David Rice McAnally's *Irish Wonders, The Ghosts, Giants, Pookas, Demons, Leprechawns, Banshees, Fairies, Witches, Widows, Old Maids and Other Marvels of the Emerald Isle* (1888) reduced the Irish peasantry to humorous, sentimental buffoons who spoke a ridiculous dialect. On the other hand, the early energies of the Irish Renaissance were generated in large part by the study of Ireland's ancient and contemporary traditional literature. William Butler Yeats,* John M. Synge,* and Lady Gregory* all collected Irish folklore and transformed it into great literature. As Yeats remarked in *The Celtic Twilight,* "Folk art is . . . the soil where all great art is rooted."

William Butler Yeats (1865–1939) devoted much time and effort in the 1880s and 1890s to collecting Irish folklore from printed and oral sources while preparing his three anthologies of Irish folklore. In *Fairy and Folk Tales of the Irish Peasantry* (1888) and *Irish Fairy Tales* (1892), Yeats surveyed, organized, and, in some cases, freely rewrote the available corpus of Irish folklore. Yeats' appreciation of Irish folklore as a serious subject matter and the quality of his introductions and notes in these anthologies represent important advances in the study of Irish folklore. In 1893, Yeats published the folklore he had collected from oral sources in *The Celtic Twilight, Men and Women, Dhouls and Faeries,* which he revised and enlarged in 1902. The fairy beliefs and visionary traditions of Irish folklore provided Yeats with a perfect link between his literary nationalism and his occult interests. He also selected materials from novels about the Irish peasantry for his two anthologies of nineteenth-century Irish fiction, *Stories from Carleton* (1889) and *Representative Irish Tales* (1891). Irish folklore offered Yeats a link with Ireland's heroic past, a living mythological tradition, a folk speech which invigorated his poetic vocabulary, and a subject matter and symbolism at once ancient and novel for his poetry and plays.

The writings of John Millington Synge (1871–1909) are even more markedly focused on subjects from Irish peasant life and traditions. The plots and the dialect of all his plays are derived from Irish folklore and folklife. Synge recorded his first-hand observations of the Irish peasantry and their lore in *The Aran Islands* (1906) and *In Wicklow, West Kerry, and Connemara* (1912). Like Yeats, Synge found in Irish folklore a joyous energy and a simplicity of life and language next to which modern life and literature seemed pallid and sterile indeed.

Lady Gregory (1859–1932) shared Yeats' view that Irish folklore was a living link with Ireland's heroic past and that a great literature could be re-created for modern Ireland from contemporary folklore and ancient legends. With Yeats' encouragement, she retold the two major legend cycles of ancient Ireland in *Cuchulain of Muirthemne: The Story of the Men of the Red Branch of Ulster* (1902) and *Gods and Fighting Men: The Story of the Tuatha de Danaan and of the Fianna of Ireland* (1904). During the 1890s, she had taught herself Irish and, inspired by Yeats' *The Celtic Twilight* and Douglas Hyde's* *The Love Songs of Connacht*, avidly collected folklore in her native County Galway. She published several rich collections of this folklore: *Poets and Dreamers* (1903), *The Kiltartan History Book* (1909), *The Kiltartan Wonder Book* (1910), *The Kiltartan Poetry Book* (1918), and *Visions and Beliefs in the West of Ireland* (1920). Her collections represented a significant development in the study of Irish folklore because she presented literal, objective accounts of her materials without the literary elaboration, sentimentality, comedy, nationalistic propaganda, or patronizing commentary which had marred so many of the earlier collections. Nor did she use folklore as a vehicle for personal reverie as Yeats and Synge had done in *The Celtic Twilight* and *The Aran Islands*. Her collections were a scholarly achievement, just as her folk-history plays and her comedies of peasant life were an artistic achievement.

The nationalistic, literary, and scholarly significance of Irish folklore culminated in the work of Douglas Hyde (1860–1949), a preeminent folklorist who was also a nationalist, poet, and scholar. Hyde, the founder of the Gaelic League, devoted his life to the preservation of the Irish language and culture. Hyde's literary genius is apparent in his prose and verse translations from the Irish in *Beside the Fire: A Collection of Irish Gaelic Folk Stories* (1890) and in *The Love Songs of Connacht* (1893) which capture the beauty and vigor of the Irish originals and demonstrate the poetic richness of the English spoken by the Irish peasantry. A scholar as well as a poet and nationalist, Hyde accurately recorded and carefully annotated the folklore he collected and published. Hyde's collections inspired Yeats. Synge, and Lady Gregory in their collection and literary adaptation of Irish folklore. Hyde himself wrote many poems and plays based on Irish folklore. In addition, his scholarship elevated Irish folklore into a respected field of knowledge. Under his influence, William Larminie* and Jeremiah Curtin (1835–1906) published important collections during the 1890s. Like Hyde, Larminie and Curtin collected their materials in Irish, published literal translations and some annotation, and valued the scholarly as well as the imaginative significance of Irish folklore. Hyde's preeminence as a nationalist poet and playwright, as the first president of the Republic of Ireland, and as an outstanding collector and scholar of Irish folklore exemplifies the closely related literary, political, and scholarly dimensions of Irish folklore.

Hyde's accomplishments were largely responsible for the founding in 1926 of the Folklore of Ireland Society, the first organized effort to collect and to study the entire spectrum of Irish oral tradition. In 1935, the Irish government created the Irish Folklore Commission for the purpose of collecting, cataloguing, and publishing Irish folklore. A rich tradition remained to be explored—in 1935, the parish of Carna in West Galway had more unrecorded folktales than the whole of Europe. By 1964, manuscript collections in the commission's archives totaled more than 1.5 million pages. Today the Irish Folklore Commission (now the Department of Folklore at University College, Dublin) is renowned for the abundance and quality of its folklore research. Sean O'Sullivan's *A Handbook of Irish Folklore* (1942) is the foremost such guide in the world. With Reidar Christiansen, O'Sullivan published *The Types of the Irish Folktale* (1963), an index to the forty-three thousand versions of popular tales collected during the commission's first twenty-one years. Kevin Danaher's massive bibliography of Irish folklore studies, published in 1978, attests to the magnitude of Irish folklore research. Once the hobby of amateur collectors in search of antiquarian curiosities, Irish folklore was a crucial influence in the literary and political history of late nineteenth-century and early twentieth-century Ireland and today is in the forefront of international folklore studies.

In recent decades, Irish folklore scholarship has expanded beyond its earlier emphasis on the Irish and nationalistic dimensions of its subject to explore English-language as well as Irish-language materials, urban as well as rural traditions, and the living present as well as the ancient past. Henry Glassie's declaration in his Introduction to *Irish Folk Tales* (1985) that the significance of Irish folklore transcends its antiquity, academic typologies, and issues of language and national identity and his interest in English-language materials from Northern Ireland typify this expansion of Irish folklore studies. Clodagh Brennan Harvey's study of the English-language tradition and of the impact of folklore collecting itself on traditional storytelling in *Contemporary Irish Traditional Narrative* (1992) is a more recent example of how both primary and secondary materials in Irish folklore represent an important and ever-evolving tradition that illuminates the study of Irish culture, history, and literature in the past and in the present.

MARY HELEN THUENTE

REFERENCES: The following works provide a good introductory survey of the materials and the historical developments involved in the study of Irish folklore: Evans, E. Estyn. *Irish Folk Ways.* London: Routledge & Kegan Paul, 1957; Glassie, Henry, ed. *Irish Folk Tales.* New York: Pantheon, 1985; O'Sullivan, Sean. *Folktales of Ireland.* Chicago: University of Chicago Press, 1966; O'Sullivan, Sean. *A Handbook of Irish Folklore.* Detroit: Singing Tree, 1970; Yeats, W. B., ed. *Fairy and Folk Tales of Ireland.* 2d ed. Gerrards Cross: Colin Smythe, 1977.

FORRISTAL, DESMOND [TIMOTHY] (1930–   ), playwright. Forristal was born in Dublin on September 25, 1930. He was educated at the O'Connell

School, at Belvedere College, and at University College, Dublin, where he received a Ph.D. in philosophy in 1956. He was ordained a Roman Catholic priest in 1955 and has worked for many years in the field of communications. He has written books on communications and on religious subjects, but is best known as a playwright. His plays include *The True Story of the Horrid Popish Plot* (Gate,* 1972), *Black Man's Country* (Gate, 1974), *The Seventh Sin* (Gate, 1976), *Captive Audience* (Gate, 1979), and *Kolbe* (Abbey, 1982). *Black Man's Country*, the more moving of his two published pieces, is about Catholic missionaries in Nigeria. The often breezy fluency of the dialogue sets a tone that is impressively counterpointed by the somber political action and the moving personal one. Like his other works, the play views a complex problem with a wry clarity. If Forristal has a particular lack as a playwright, it would seem to be the quality of his writing in the serious scenes. There, the prose is straightforward and adequate enough, but hardly of the excellence of the lighter moments. In any event, he was one of the most intelligent of Irish playwrights of the 1970s, and his work has a solid merit. Since 1985, he has been parish priest of Dalkey, County Dublin.

PRINCIPAL LITERARY WORKS: *Black Man's Country.* Newark, Del.: Proscenium, 1975; *The True Story of the Horrid Popish Plot.* Dublin: Veritas, 1976.

FOSTER, AISLING (1949–), novelist. Foster was born in Dublin on September 6, 1949, and educated at the National College of Art and at University College, Dublin. She is married to the historian Roy Foster,* and they have two sons. She commenced her career in journalism and broadcasting and has written plays for Radio 4 and a novel for young adults, *The First Time* (1988), which could be read happily by any age. The narrator, Rosa O'Grady, is the daughter of a feisty Irish single mum who has just found a new man and expects Rosa to do the same. However, Rosa is in her last year at school and keen to do well in art. Her world revolves around her friends and her art master, who encourages her work. The characters are beautifully caught, as is the world of a seedy London comprehensive school in post-Thatcher Britain.

Her adult novel, *Safe in the Kitchen* (1993), tells the story of Rita Fitzgerald, a young lady who came "out" in the Dublin season of 1916. Revolution was in the air at home, while abroad the young men who should have been dancing with her were dying in the trenches. Rita defies her upper-middle-class family by marrying Frank Fee, a follower of de Valera, whom she has met at the Gaelic League. She travels with him to America to raise funds for Ireland. They encounter some eccentric Russians, and Rita has a serious but hilarious lesbian affair with one of them. In an early form of money laundering, the Russians pawn the Crown jewels in exchange for Irish fund money. These jewels become the focus of the plot. Frank, who has Irished his name to O'Fiaich and has also changed into a dour and reclusive Irish husband, is given charge of them; and his wife's only outlet is secretly trying them on.

Safe in the Kitchen can be classified as a feminist, revisionist, comic-historical novel. It is rich in period detail and has wonderful touches, particularly the appearance of real people. As well as portraying a sad marriage, it shows up Dublin middle-class society, from the 1920s to the 1970s, as a place with little fresh air and few rights for women. Rita's only outlet is meeting a school friend in Brown Thomas's Social and Personal Café. Despite this, the book is an able and very enjoyable debut.

MARY ROSE CALLAGHAN

WORKS: *The First Time*. London: Walker Books, [1988]. (Young adult novel); *Safe in the Kitchen*. London: Hamish Hamilton, 1993.

FOSTER, R[OBERT] F[ITZROY] (1949–   ), historian and biographer. The son of a schoolmaster, Roy Foster was born in Waterford on January 16, 1949, and educated at the Newtown School in Waterford and at St. Andrew's School, Middletown, Delaware. In 1968, he entered Trinity College, Dublin, where he became a foundation scholar in 1969. In 1975, Foster completed his Ph.D. dissertation, "Charles Stewart Parnell: The Man and His Family," under the influential supervision of T. W. Moody. He then took up a lectureship in the History Department at Birkbeck College, in the University of London. Here he was to work alongside some of the most celebrated English historians of modern Europe, notably, E. J. Hobsbawm, Richard Evans, and David Blackbourn; and there seems little doubt that his membership of what was to become a world-class history department helped to give Foster's work an extra edge and intellectual ambition. Foster may at times have missed Trinity College, but London was to provide vastly greater stimulus. At this time, he was also very sensitive to some of the new trends in British political history, in particular, the "high politics" approach embodied in A. B. Cooke and J. R. Vincent's *The Governing Passion* of 1974.

Not long after his appointment at Birkbeck, Foster became review editor of *History* and rapidly established himself as a regular reviewer for the *Times Literary Supplement*. His reviews—which were never lazy but always elegantly constructed—exploited, in part, his subtle skills of literary appreciation as well as historical knowledge. In 1976, his doctoral study of Parnell was published by Harvester and deservedly received outstanding reviews.

In 1982, he brought out his brilliant *Lord Randolph Churchill: A Political Life*, a work that owed something to John Vincent in particular. Foster's reputation, however, rests on his magnificent, wide-ranging survey *Modern Ireland 1600–1972* (1988). It was widely perceived to be, and in part was, a synthesis of a generation's work of revisionist scholarship in Irish history. Somehow this notion does not convey the full range and quality of this stunning work. Written in a flawless style—save perhaps for an addiction to the word "bizarre"—it engaged the sympathies of intelligent readers in both Ireland and England in a way that no other Irish scholar of this generation could even think of doing.

Because Foster was the supreme stylist of his generation, readers sometimes failed to register the sheer meticulous professionalism of his approach as an historian. How many Foster interpretations have ever been successfully challenged? In short, he had a penchant for accuracy as well as wit that often left his critics floundering. It was noticeable how often critiques, especially from literary critics, degenerated into the personal. It was almost as if Foster's crime was a generalized failure to emote in the approved manner, and even where he had done so, as in his discussion of the Famine as a "holocaust" or of Ulster Unionism as "ludicrously extreme," "antirevisionist" opponents appeared not to notice. This is not to say that there were no difficulties with Foster's work. He was a true child of the Republic of Ireland, as he always insisted, and nowhere is this more obvious than in his relative lack of interest in Northern Ireland. The dreary steeples of Fermanagh and Tyrone—even the shenanigans of what he once, in a memorable phrase, called "the lumpen bourgeoisie" of Belfast—left him cold. Duty at times forced him to comment, but it is always clear that, quite understandably, the heart lay elsewhere.

In 1991, Foster left his chair at the University of London to take up the Carroll Chair of Irish History at the University of Oxford. In Oxford, he established a vigorous Irish studies seminar and, more generally, gave Irish history a presence at the heart of British life that it had never previously enjoyed. He continued also to publish—a provocative collection of essays, *Paddy and Mr. Punch* (1993), and his stimulating inaugural lecture, *The Story of Ireland* (1994). Most of his energy, however, in those years went into his full-scale biography of W. B. Yeats,* a project he had inherited from the late F.S.L. Lyons and one that seemed perfectly designed to exploit his unusual skills as a political historian and literary critic. Foster's nationalistic critics claimed that he was all too easily co-opted into the British establishment; in fact, only the most insensitive readers and observers could fail to detect a passionate commitment to the serious study of Irish history.

He is married to Aisling Foster,* the novelist.

PAUL BEW

WORKS: *Charles Stewart Parnell: The Man and His Family.* Hassocks, Sussex: Harvester, 1976/ Atlantic Highlands, N.J.: Humanities, 1979; *Political Novels and Nineteenth Century History.* Winchester: King Alfred's College, 1981; *Lord Randolph Churchill: A Political Life.* Oxford & New York: Oxford University Press, 1982; *F.S.L. Lyons 1923–1983.* London: British Academy/ Wolfeboro, N.H.: Longwood, 1986; *Modern Ireland 1600–1972.* [London], Allen Lane/ New York: Viking Penguin, 1988; ed., *Oxford Illustrated History of Ireland.* Oxford & New York: Oxford University Press, 1989; ed., *The Sub-Prefect Should Have Held His Tongue.* [London]: Allen Lane, Penguin, in association with Lilliput, [1990]. (Essays by Hubert Butler); *Paddy and Mr. Punch: Connections in Irish and English History.* [London]: Allen Lane, Penguin, [1993]; *The Story of Ireland.* Oxford: Clarendon, 1994.

FRANCIS, M. E. (1859?–1930), novelist and short story writer. M. E. Francis is the pseudonym of Mrs. Francis Blundell, née Mary Sweetman, who was born in Killiney Park, near Dublin, of Catholic parents. She was educated in Queen's County, her mother's home, and then in Belgium. Her Catholicism was an important factor in her writing. She first published at the age of fourteen in the

Irish Monthly, edited by Father Matt Russell. In 1879 she married Francis Blundell, and they settled in the village of Crosby, near Liverpool in Lancashire; this village became the setting of many of her works. Widowed in 1884, she resumed her literary career, partly for financial reasons, partly to ward off depression, with a serial, *Molly's Fortunes,* which appeared in the *Irish Monthly.* She was very productive, writing over thirty books, some collections of "tales," others novels, all set in Ireland, Lancashire, Dorset, or Wales.

In a North Country Village (1893) describes life in her Lancashire village of Great Crosby; *The Story of Dan* (1894) is a tale of a peasant infatuated with a worthless girl. *A Daughter of the Soil* (1895) is a romantic story set in rural Lancashire. *Frieze and Fustian* (1896) is in two parts, one treating the Irish peasant, the other his English counterpart; much of the book is in dialect. *Maime o' the Corner* (1897) concerns the altruistic poor of Liverpool and Lancashire. *Miss Erin* (1898), included in Benzinger's (New York) Series of Standard Catholic Novels, tells the story of a poor girl who becomes a landowner and dramatically describes an eviction. *Yeoman Fleetwood* (1900), set in Lancashire, describes the love of a yeoman for a girl of the upper class. *Pastorals of Dorset* (1901) is a collection of short stories; *Fiander's Widow* (1901) centers around the machinations of a Dorset widow to secure a husband to work her farm. *North, South, and over the Sea* (1902) is a collection of fifteen stories, five of which describe poverty-stricken Irish; the brogue is especially well rendered, and the author strives for psychological realism. *Lychgate Hall* (1904), subtitled "a Romance," is set in Great Crosby; the "hall" is haunted. *Wild Wheat* (1905) is about the poor of Dorset; *Dorset Dear* (1905) is more of the same, containing mostly short stories reprinted from various periodicals. *Simple Annals* (1906) describes the everyday lives and dreams of Lancashire working women. *Margery o' the Mill* and *Stepping Westward* were both published by Methuen in 1907; the subject—again the good-hearted, rural poor—continued to find readers, as it also did with the Dorset tale *Hardy-on-the-Hill* (1908). *Children of Light and Other Stories* (1907) contains "touching" sketches, the heroes of some of them being Catholic clergy. According to S. J. Brown, the theme illustrated that "only through sorrow do the 'Children of the Light' learn life's lessons." *Galatea of the Wheatfield* (1909) shows the author returning to an old theme—love between people of different classes, in this case a Dorset peasant girl and a gentleman. In 1919, Mrs. Blundell changed publishers, and Smith, Elder brought out *The Wild Heart,* whose main character was a love-smitten poacher. In *Gentleman Roger* (1911) the title figure must perform the déclassé work of a common laborer in order to win the heart of a farmer's daughter.

The Story of Mary Dunne (1913) is a tragedy about a girl from Glen Malure who is forced into prostitution; this is a melodramatic, moral tale probably intended to warn the naive. *Dark Rosaleen* (1915) is a tragic story of a marriage between a Catholic girl from Connemara and a Protestant engineer from Belfast; the difference in faith turns out to be insurmountable. Some excellent descriptions of Galway are included. In 1917, Mrs. Blundell published *A Maid o'*

Dorset but in 1922 switched her venue to Wales for *Many Haters. Young Dave's Wife* (1924) describes the lives of the poor who lived in the mountains of Wales, and *Wood Sanctuary* (1930), softer in tone, portrays life in a Welsh village.

Mrs. Blundell's only son, Francis, was MP for Ormskirk from 1922 to 1929. She died at Mold on March 9, 1930. She had written of her Irish upbringing in *The Things of a Child* (1918), and in 1935 a posthumous autobiography, *An Irish Novelist's Own Story,* appeared. She was one of the seemingly numberless prolific female novelists of the late nineteenth and early twentieth centuries. During her day, her work was admired for its "pleasant" atmosphere and realistic depiction of the character of rural people and the everyday details of their lives. Nationalist Irish critics praised her sympathetic portrayal of the Catholic peasantry.

WILLIAM J. LINN

WORKS: *Whither?* 3 vols. London: Griffith Farran, 1892; *In a North Country Village.* London: Osgood, 1893; *The Story of Dan.* London: Osgood, M'Ilvaine, 1894; *A Daughter of the Soil.* London: Osgood, M'Ilvaine/New York, Harper, 1895; *Frieze and Fustian.* London: Osgood, 1896; *Maime o' the Corner.* London: Harper, 1897; *Miss Erin.* London: Methuen, 1898; *The Duenna of a Genius.* London: Harper/Boston: Little, Brown, 1898; *Yeoman Fleetwood.* London: Longmans, 1900; *Pastorals of Dorset.* London: Longmans, 1901; *Fiander's Widow.* London: Longmans, 1901; *The Manor Farm: A Novel.* London: Longmans, 1902; *North, South, and over the Sea.* London: George Newnes, 1902; *Christian Thal.* New York & London: Longmans, Green, 1903; *Lychgate Hall: A Romance.* London: Longmans, 1904; *Wild Wheat: A Dorset Romance.* London: Longmans, 1905; *Dorset Dear: Idylls of Country Life.* London: Longmans, 1905; *Simple Annals.* London: Longmans, 1906; *Margery o' the Mill.* London: Methuen, 1907; *Stepping Westward.* London: Methuen, 1907; *Children of Light and Other Stories.* London: Catholic Society, 1907; *Hardy-on-the-Hill.* London: Methuen, 1908; *Galatea of the Wheatfield.* London: Methuen, 1909; *The Wild Heart.* London: Smith, Elder, 1910; *Gentleman Roger.* Edinburgh: Sands/New York: Benziger, 1911; *Honesty.* London: Hodder & Stoughton, [1912]; *The Story of Mary Dunne.* London: John Murray, 1913; *Molly's Fortunes.* London: Sands, [1913]; *Our Alty.* London: John Long, [1914]; *Dark Rosaleen.* London: Cassell, [1915]/New York: P. J. Kennedy, 1917; *Penton's Captain.* 1916; *A Maid o' Dorset.* London: Cassell, 1917; *The Things of a Child.* London: W. Collins, 1918; *Beck of Beckford.* London: G. Allen & Unwin, 1920; *Rosanna Dew.* London: Odhams, [1920]; *Renewal.* London: 1921; *Many Haters.* London: Hutchinson, 1922; *The Runaway.* London: Hutchinson, [1923]; *Young Dave's Wife.* London: Hutchinson, 1924; with Margaret Blundell, *Lady Jane and the Small Holders.* London: Hutchinson, [1924]; with Agnes Blundell, *Golden Sally.* 1925; *Cousin Christopher.* London: T. Fisher Unwin, [1925]; *Napoleon of the Looms.* London: Hutchinson, [1925]; *Tyrer's Lass.* London: Sands, 1926; *Idylls of Old Hungary.* London: Sheed & Ward, 1926; *Mossoo.* London: Hutchinson, [1927]; *The Evolution of Oenone.* London: Hutchinson [1928]; *Wood Sanctuary.* London: Allen & Unwin, 1930; *An Irish Novelist's Own Story.* 1935.

FRAZER, JOHN D[E JEAN] (ca. 1810–ca. 1850), poet. Frazer (or Fraser) was a cabinet maker by trade and hence sometimes known as the "Poet of the Workshop." He was born in Birr, King's County (now County Offaly). The date of his birth is variously given as 1804, 1809, and 1813, and the date of his death as 1849 and 1852. He contributed much verse about the beauties of nature and the ills of Ireland to *The Nation** and *The Irish Felon.* Despite his fluency, he lacks judgment, and both his meter and his diction sometimes become amusingly incongruous. For instance, his "Lament for Thomas Davis" bears some resemblance metrically to W. S. Gilbert's "The Flowers that Bloom in the Spring," with the "tra-la" being replaced by such lines as "Woe, woe" or "Gloom, gloom." Similarly, despite some sincerity and real feeling that manages to break through his conventional poetic diction, the effect is often silly. For example, in his description of "The Holy Wells," he writes:

How sweet of old the bubbling gush—no less to antlered race
Than to the hunter and the hound that smote them in the chase.

In his patriotic moments, he is extremely jingoistic. In "The Holy Wells" again, Ireland is "The Emerald garden, set apart for Irishmen by God." At the same time, his martial poetry is full of tyrants and cowards, gauntlets and swords. Probably his most anthologized piece is "Song for July 12th, 1843," four lines of which O'Casey* quotes for comic effect in *The Drums of Father Ned.*

WORKS: *Eva O'Connor, a Poem in Three Cantos by an Author Yet Unknown.* Dublin: Milliken, 1826; *Poems for the People.* By J. De Jean. Dublin: J. Browne, 1845; *Poems.* By J. De Jean. Dublin: J. McGlashan, 1851; *Poems.* By J. De Jean. With a Memoir by James Burke. Dublin: Mullany, 1853.

FRENCH, [WILLIAM] PERCY (1854–1920), humorist and entertainer. French was born in Cloonyquin, County Roscommon, on May 1, 1854. He was educated at Trinity College, Dublin, and became a civil engineer, but his great talent was as a humorist in prose and in verse. Many of his pieces appeared in his comic paper *The Jarvey.* Their delightful quality may be suggested by the beginning of his sketch "The First Lord Liftinant":

"Essex," said Queen Elizabeth, as the two of them sat at break-whisht in the back parlor of Buckingham Palace, "Essex, me haro, I've got a job that I think would suit you. Do you know where Ireland is?"
"I'm no great fist at jografy," says his lordship, "but I know the place you name. Population, three millions; exports, emigrants."

French was best known as a public entertainer, playing the banjo, making lightning sketches, and singing his own songs. Many of those songs—such as "Come Back, Paddy Reilly," "The Mountains of Mourne," "Phil the Fluter's Ball," and "Are Ye Right There, Michael?"—have never lost their popularity. Indeed, a popular musical of the 1950s, *The Golden Years,* was based on French's life and songs. He died at Formby, Lancashire, on January 24, 1920.

WORKS: *The First Lord Liftinant and Other Tales.* Dublin: Mecredy & Kyle, 1890; *The Irish Girl, Comedy Opera.* Book & lyrics by Percy French, assisted by Brendan Stewart. London: Boosey, 1918; *Chronicles and Poems of Percy French.* Mrs. de Burgh Daly, ed. Dublin: Talbot, 1922; *Our House-Warming.* London & New York: Samuel French, 1925. (Eight-page monologue); *Prose, Poems and Parodies.* Mrs. de Burgh Daly, ed. Dublin: Talbot/London: Simpkin, Marshall, 1925. REFERENCE: Healy, James N. *Percy French and his Songs.* Cork: Mercier/London: Herbert Jenkins, 1966; O'Dowda, B. *The World of Percy French.* Belfast: Blackstaff, 1981.

FRIEL, BRIAN (1929–   ), playwright and short story writer. Friel was born in Omagh, County Tyrone, on January 9, 1929. He was educated in Derry at Long Tower School, where his father taught; at St. Columba's College; and at Maynooth College, County Kildare. He left Maynooth in 1948, after two years, for St. Joseph's Teacher Training College, Belfast.

Teaching in Derry from 1950 to 1960, Friel began writing short stories, mainly for *The New Yorker,* and radio plays (which he prefers to forget) for the BBC. The territory of the short stories stretches from County Tyrone to County Donegal. Their characters are mostly from the rural poor. For all of their inventive humor and satire of Irish cant, the stories essentially celebrate the small gains of loss endured, the solace of illusions that do not wholly deceive: what "Among the Ruins" calls "continuance, life repeating itself and surviving."

Friel's drama inhabits the same regions. Its first major success was *Philadelphia, Here I Come!* at the 1964 Dublin Theatre Festival. It established designs ramified in his early plays. The complementary public and private voices of Gar O'Donnell, about to emigrate to America, scrutinize his present with his taciturn father in Friel's fictional Donegal town, Ballybeg, both prudishly restrictive and "not a bad aul' bugger of a place."

In the search for selfhood, the exchanges between Gar and his alter ego rehearse figments of an enchantingly Arcadian past—his dead mother from "beyond the mountains," an idyllic childhood fishing trip—personal and hearsay. It is a common enough situation in Irish drama. Here it is preserved from sentimentality by the intervention of a ribald comic spirit and by the status of Gar's evocations of the past as perhaps mere solacing contrivances of fond memory, uncorroborated and finally unresolved.

Through the malleable circuits of memory, Friel's characters reconstruct dispiriting circumstances. In *The Loves of Cass McGuire,* Cass, returned to her family after squalid years in America, romanticizes her exile into the illusions that comfort her existence in an old people's home. Fox, of *Crystal and Fox,* in a series of callous rejections, destroys his ramshackle traveling show to regain a past that, if it ever existed, is irrecoverable. This kind of beguiling fiction is the target of *The Gentle Island.* It brutally revokes urban myths of serene pastoral on an island off Donegal and inaugurates new directions in Friel's next plays, notably, *The Freedom of the City, Volunteers, Aristocrats,* and *Faith Healer.*

In *The Freedom of the City,* set in the Derry of Bloody Sunday, the three victims, having spent lives of dispossession, are dispossessed of life. Their most articulate speech is Skinner's nihilistic chat, partly a form of escape but, in the final tableau, of the three standing, arms raised, in some way reassessing an imaginative defiance, however doomed, of Auden's "lie of authority." *Volunteers* is set in a Viking dig manned by five political prisoners, flouting their organization's edict of noncooperation. Among the relics is Leif's skeleton, witness to ancient sacrifices. Skinner's equivalent is Keeney, his subservient patter distancing but unable to prevent their eventual execution by their comrades. In these places, political forces dominate individual fates. They echo on the margins of *Aristocrats,* where Casimir's ludicrous fables of his family's Catholic Big House counterpoint its decline.

Faith Healer consolidates the themes of these plays. Its risky form—four monologues splendidly modulating tragic and comic energies—delivers a riddling account of Frank Harvey's capricious healing powers and suicidal death, thereby subtly exploring analogous acts of the creative imagination. In one aspect, it questions whether art leaves any imprint on a world where the debased rhetoric of politics, of authority, of the group or community declares its strident claims. *Translations* canvasses another loss, the dissolution of the old Gaelic culture, reinforced by the Anglicizing of its place-names. Essentially a lament, it accommodates mordant, skeptical undertones enlarged in the mockery of *The Communication Cord*'s "restored" Donegal cottage.

Dancing at Lughnasa articulates afresh the questions ambient throughout the plays. In a small house outside Ballybeg, five sisters contrive to subsist. The Old Adam/Eve, an unsublimated paganism that Catholic sanctimony can neither repress nor absorb, finally fragments it. Yet the household's remembered dances and songs of the 1930s temper, without blinking, the tragic outcome. In *Wonderful Tennessee,* a picnic party's all-night vigil of reminiscence, storytelling, and song partly exorcises the characters' masking fictions of their relationships.

Though Friel deploys music and dance, words remain his necessary medium. His drama's conflict is between the autocratic vocabulary of power—whether vested in regime, family, or religion—and the antic, imagining self, the victim, the outsider, the dispossessed. Their voices seek a dignity, some integration with their place, through stories, lies, fictions. Success is, at best, partial. Within the tragedy and farce that Friel's wide-ranging dramatic language encompasses, the characters' shifts and stratagems are more ends in themselves than a reforming force, solace hard won, not solution.

D.E.S. MAXWELL

WORKS: *The Saucer of Larks.* London: Gollancz, 1962. (Stories); *Philadelphia, Here I Come!* London: Faber, 1965; *The Gold in the Sea.* London: Gollancz, 1966. (Stories); *The Loves of Cass McGuire.* London: Faber, 1967; *Lovers.* New York: Farrar, Straus & Giroux, 1968/London: Faber, 1969; *Crystal and Fox.* London: Faber, 1970; *Two Plays.* New York: Farrar, Straus & Giroux, 1970. (Contains *Crystal and Fox* and *The Mundy Scheme*); *The Gentle Island.* [London]: Davis-Poynter, [1973]; *The Freedom of the City.* London: Faber, 1974; *The Enemy Within.* Newark, Del.: Proscenium, 1975/Dublin: Gallery, 1979; *Living Quarters.* London: Faber, 1978; *Volunteers.* London & Boston: Faber, 1979; *Faith Healer.* London & Boston: Faber, 1980; *Aristocrats.* Dublin: Gallery, 1980/London: Faber, 1984; *Translations.* London & Boston: Faber, 1981; *The Three Sisters* (after Chekhov). Dublin: Gallery, 1981; *The Communication Cord.* London & Boston: Faber, 1983; *Selected Plays.* Seamus Deane, ed. London: Faber, 1984/Washington, D.C.: Catholic University Press of America, 1985; *Fathers and Sons* (after Turgenev). London: Faber, 1987; *Making History.* London: Faber, 1989; *Dancing at Lughnasa.* London: Faber, 1990; *The London Vertigo* (one-act version of Macklin's *True-Born Irishman*). Dublin: Gallery, 1990; *Wonderful Tennessee.* Dublin: Gallery, 1993; *Molly Sweeney.* [Oldcastle, Co. Meath]: Gallery, [1994]. REFERENCES: Andrews, Elmer. *The Art of Brian Friel.* London: Macmillan, 1995; Dantanus, Ulf. *Brian Friel: The Growth of an Irish Dramatist.* Atlantic Highlands, N.J.: Humanities, 1986; Etherton, Michael. *Contemporary Irish Dramatists.* London: Macmillan, 1989, pp. 147–208; Maxwell, D. E. S. *Brian Friel.* Lewisburg,

Pa.: Bucknell University Press, 1973; O'Brien, George. *Brian Friel.* Dublin: Gill & Macmillan, 1989; Peacock, Alan, ed. *The Achievement of Brian Friel.* Gerrards Cross: Colin Smythe, 1993; Pine, Richard. *Brian Friel and Ireland's Drama.* London: Routledge & Kegan Paul, 1990; Richtarik, Marilyn. *Acting between the Lines: The Field Day Theatre Company and Irish Cultural Politics 1980–1984.* Oxford: Clarendon, 1995.

FULLER, JAMES FRANKLIN (1835–1924), architect and novelist. Fuller was born in Denniquinn, County Kerry, and became an extremely successful architect, designing many churches and several country mansions. In addition to some short works on genealogy, he wrote three admired novels of the day and, in his eighties, a still interesting autobiography. He died in Dublin on December 8, 1924.

LITERARY WORKS: *Culmshire Folk. By Ignotus.* London: Macmillan, 1872; *John Orlebar, Clk.* London: Smith, Elder, 1878; *Chronicles of Westerley, a Provincial Sketch.* Edinburgh: W. Blackwood, 1872; *Omniana: The Autobiography of an Irish Octogenarian.* London: Smith, Elder/ New York: E. P. Dutton, 1916.

FURLONG, ALICE (ca. 1875–1946), poet. Furlong was born in Tallaght, County Dublin, in about 1875. Her older sister Mary (ca. 1868–September 22, 1898) was a frequent contributor of romantic verse to the popular press; her ability may be judged by the first stanza from "An Irish Love Song":

> I love you, and I love you, and I love you, O my honey!
> It isn't for your goodly lands, it isn't for your money;
> It isn't for your father's cows, your mother's yellow butter.
> The love that's in my heart for you no words of mine may utter!

Apparently inspired by both the quality and content of her sister's verse, Furlong became a prolific writer of poems for the nationalist press and of stories for the popular press. Her subjects are Ireland—its romance, its whimsy, its weather, and its landscape. She is a better poet than Mary and has had a few successes, as in "The Warning" and "The Betrayal."

WORKS: *Roses and Rue.* London: E. Mathews, 1899; *Tales of Fairy Folks, Queens and Heroes.* Dublin: Browne & Nolan, [1907].

FURLONG, THOMAS (1794–1827), poet. Furlong, although a poet of great skill, is unfortunately neglected today. At his best, as in his long poem "The Doom of Derenzie," he tells a powerful, Wordsworthian story movingly, and his handling of the blank verse is exceptionally fluent. He was born at Scara-walsh, County Wexford, in 1794, the son of a small farmer. With little education, he was apprenticed to a Dublin grocer. An elegy which he wrote on the death of his master came to the notice of Jameson the whiskey distiller, who encouraged him in his writing efforts. His poem "The Misanthrope" gained him the friendship of Thomas Moore* and Lady Morgan.* He became a regular contributor to Dublin journals and helped found *The New Irish Magazine* in 1821. His political satire "The Plagues of Ireland" appeared in 1824, and he became a friend and confidant of O'Connell. He produced a graceful translation of "The Remains of Carolan" and other poems from the Irish, about which he also wrote:

> Fling, fling the forms of art aside—
>> Dull is the ear that these forms enthrall;
> Let the simple songs of our sires be tried—
>> They go to the heart, and the heart is all.

Nevertheless, his own supple translations did not fling the forms of art aside. Furlong died of consumption on July 25, 1827, and is buried in Drumcondra.

WORKS: *The Misanthrope, and Other Poems.* London: H. Colburn, 1819/Dublin: Underwood, 1821; *The Plagues of Ireland.* Dublin: Printed for the Author, 1824; *The Doom of Derenzie.* London: J. Robins, 1829. (Furlong also has some translations from the Irish in Hardiman's *Irish Ministrelsy.*) 2 vols. London: Robins, 1831. Indeed, Brian McKenna attributes nearly all the translations in Vol. I to Furlong. REFERENCES: De Blacam, Aodh. "Two Poets Who Discovered Their Country." *Irish Monthly* 74 (1946): 357–365; Hardiman, James. "Memoir of Thomas Furlong." *In Irish Ministrelsy* (London: Robins, 1831. Vol. I, pp. lxix-lxxx; Russell, Matthew. "Our Poets, No. 17: Thomas Furlong." *Irish Monthly* 18 (1888): 421–426.

G

GALLAGHER, BRIAN

WORK: *Invincible Town*. Dublin: Town House, 1993. (Novel).

GALLAGHER, FRANK (1893–1962), journalist, historian, and short story writer.

Gallagher was born in Cork in 1893. He became a member of the Irish Volunteers and later worked closely with Erskine Childers* on the publicity staff of the Republican government and as editor of the clandestine *The Irish Bulletin*. He was several times in prison and was once involved in a long hunger strike which he described in one of his short stories and in *Four Glorious Years*. He was editor of the *Cork Free Press* and of *The Irish Press* from 1931; deputy director of Radio Éireann; head of the Government Information Bureau; and from 1954, a member of the National Library.

As an historian, Gallagher was diligent and as accurate as partisanship would allow. His best book is a collection of journalistic pieces, *Four Glorious Years* (1953). This is a totally slanted, occasionally overwritten, often tedious, and yet intermittently fascinating personal reminiscence of the years leading up to the signing of the Anglo-Irish Treaty. His *The Indivisible Island* (1957) is a well-researched, book-length tract against partition. *The Anglo-Irish Treaty*, posthumously published in 1965, was part of an uncompleted biography of de Valera. Its separate publication was scarcely warranted, for the fragment adds little or nothing to Frank Pakenham's previously published study of the Treaty negotiations, *Peace by Ordeal*. Under one of his pseudonyms, David Hogan, Gallagher published some short stories dealing with the Troubles. These stories are leanly written and technically craftsmanlike, but with their patriotic simplicity, melodrama, and romance, they cannot be considered seriously as literature. Gallagher died in Dublin in July 1962.

WORKS: As Frank Gallagher: *Days of Fear*. London: John Murray, 1928; *The Indivisible Island* London: Gollancz, 1957; *The Anglo-Irish Treaty*, ed. With an Introduction by Thomas P. O'Neill.

London: Hutchinson, 1965. As David Hogan: The Challenge of the Sentry, and Other Stories of the Irish War. Dublin & Cork: Talbot, 1928; Dark Mountain, and Other Stories. Dublin & Cork: Talbot/London: Harold Shaylor, 1931; The Four Glorious Years. Dublin: Irish, 1953.

GALLAGHER, MIRIAM (1940–   ), playwright. Born in County Waterford.

WORKS: Let's Help Our Children Talk. Dublin: O'Brien, 1977. (Prose); Fancy Footwork: Selected Plays. Dublin: Society of Irish Playwrights, 1991.

GALLAGHER, PATRICK (PADDY THE COPE) (1870?–1964), autobiographer. Gallagher was born in Cleendra, just outside Dungloe, County Donegal, possibly on Christmas Day in 1870, although his exact date of birth cannot really be determined. His birth certificate lists May 23, 1871. Early editions of his autobiography list Christmas Day, 1873, and later editions list Christmas 1871. As it seems unlikely that his birth certificate was recorded before he was born, as parents occasionally misreported winter births when the weather and time proved an inconvenience, and as the law required that they report a birth within ninety days, it seems likely that the May date is also in error. His education was scarcely more formalized. He studied at school for only three to five years. At ten he was sent to the hiring fair at Strabane, where his services for six months were purchased for three pounds, and this labor continued until he was sixteen. Then he worked in England for several years as a manual laborer. He gained, nevertheless, a remarkable reputation as a storyteller and entrepreneur. In fact, his reputation and autobiography base themselves on his life and career as organizer and founder of the Templecrone Co-operative Agricultural Society, which gave its nickname, the ''Cope,'' to its founder. Thus, American editions of his book are titled Paddy the Cope. His accomplishments with the cooperative should not be underestimated, for they demanded tenacity, discipline, and ingenuity. The organization began with the intention of allowing people to become involved with their economic well-being without the inherent disadvantage and endemic corruption of the local shopkeeper. However, what began as a local retail shop in Dungloe soon expanded into other town lands and eventually led to businesses associated with manufacturing, shipping, fishing, milling, and utilities. Gallagher began his autobiography with the encouragement of his wife, Sally, and of George Russell (AE*), then editor of The Irish Homestead. Most critics have limited their examinations of Gallagher to short passing commentaries on his thoughts and life, including brief mentions by Benedict Kiely* and Terence Brown. However, a recent book by Lawrence Scanlon places Gallagher's autobiography in the context of literary and public autobiographies and explores Gallagher's moving and simple tale as something more than simply an account of a farming cooperative. Scanlon correctly observes that the cooperative system and even the facts of Paddy the Cope's life highlight the themes of cooperation and communities that can empower themselves through working together.

BERNARD McKENNA

WORK: *My Story*. London: Jonathan Cape, 1939. (Also published by the Templecrone Co-operative Society and by Devin-Adair in New York under the title of *Paddy the Cope*, with introductions by E. P. McDermott, Dorothy Canfield Fisher, and Peadar O'Donnell). REFERENCE: Scanlon, Lawrence. *The Story He Left Behind Him: Paddy the Cope*. Lanham, Md.: University Press of America, 1994.

GALLAHER, LEE (ca. 1935–   ), playwright. Gallaher was born in Bray, County Wicklow, in the mid-1930s, and after 1969 his plays began to be produced at Trinity College and at the Focus, Lantern, and Project Theatres. He was awarded the Abbey Theatre* Playwright's Bursary for 1973 and 1974. His most talked-about play has probably been *The Velvet Abbatoir* (Project, 1976), which was a mixed media show that also featured his collages. He has published two one-acts, *Kiss Me, Mr. Bogart* (Lantern, 1970) and *All the Candles in Your Head* (Lantern, 1974). The more effective of the two, the *Mister Bogart* play, is a Pinter-like exercise in what used to be called the Theater of Menace. In 1983 and 1984, he cowrote the RTÉ television serial "Glenroe." In recent years, his radio plays have often been heard on RTÉ and the BBC.

WORK: *Two Plays*. Dublin: Lantern Writers Workshop, 1974.

GALLERY PRESS (1970–   ), publishing house. Gallery Press was founded by Peter Fallon* when he was an eighteen-year-old student at Trinity College. In the twenty-five years or so since then, the press, first from Dublin and then from County Meath, has published over 300 volumes. Primarily a publisher of poetry, the Gallery list reads rather like a who's who of contemporary Irish verse—among many, Eileán Ní Chuilleanáin,* Pearse Hutchinson,* Desmond O'Grady,* Derek Mahon,* Michael Hartnett,* Medbh McGuckian,* and Fallon himself. In 1979, the press also began to publish plays, and the present ratio of poetry to plays is about three to one. Among the Gallery playwrights are some of the country's most distinguished—Brian Friel,* Tom Kilroy,* Tom Murphy,* Eugene McCabe.* That the press has existed for so long while publishing work so usually unprofitable as poems and plays is a considerable achievement. Although inexpensive, the Gallery books are consistently distinctive and handsome.

REFERENCE: Battersby, Eileen. "The View from Gallery—25 Years On." *Irish Times* (February 7, 1995): 10, Johnston, Dillon. " 'My Feet on the Ground': An Interview with Peter Fallon," *Irish Literary Supplement* 14 (Fall 1995): 4–5.

GALLIVAN, G[ERALD] P. (1920–   ), playwright. Gallivan was born on July 29, 1920, in Limerick. Upon graduating from Crescent College at eighteen, he wrote a book, which he could not get published. In 1940, he emigrated to England, where he worked until 1946, when he returned to Ireland and found a job in business. His first six plays were produced in Limerick by the College Players when he was working for Trans-World Airlines at Shannon. His first Dublin production was *Decision at Easter* (Globe, 1959) about the 1916 Rising.

This play was followed by *Mourn the Ivy Leaf* (Globe, 1960) about Parnell and by *The Stepping Stone,* which was produced in Cork, Belfast, and Dublin in 1963 and was about Michael Collins. *Campobasso* (Theatre Festival, 1965) and *A Beginning of Truth* (Lantern, 1968) were about modern politics. *Campobasso* is set in some unspecified European country but has distinct parallels to the career of de Valera. *A Beginning of Truth* is set in present-day Ireland and is probably his best play. *The Dail Debate* (Peacock, 1971) was a docudrama, but proved little more than an undramatic stringing together of excerpts from the discussions about whether to accept the Anglo-Irish Treaty of December 1921. *Dev* (Project, 1977) was an overt consideration of de Valera but did not probe very deeply into his complex character. In 1980, a commercial ''musical'' based on the life and songs of John McCormack was something of a crowd-pleaser because of a popular tenor in the lead, but McCormack's life obdurately resisted drama. In 1981, *Watershed* was published and proved to be a rambling, lengthy, three-handed lament about the life of a middle-aged couple. In 1983, *And a Singing Bird* was published and was a return to Gallivan's forte of historical drama. Its main character was a plausible Maud Gonne, but its W. B. Yeats* was done with no more panache than Gallivan's Bernard Shaw* in a 1994 Radio Éireann play. Throughout his career, Gallivan has written much journeyman work for Irish television and radio, but his serious preoccupation has been with political and historical drama for the stage. The modern Irish theater has certainly a crying need for such topics. Nevertheless, despite his early promise, his seriousness, and his application, Gallivan's plays are generally not as interesting as their subjects.

WORKS: *Decision at Easter.* Dublin: Progress House, [1960]; *Mourn the Ivy Leaf.* Dublin: Progress, [1965]; *Dev.* [Dublin]: Co-op Books, [1978]; *Watershed.* Newark, Del.: Proscenium, [1981]; *And a Yellow Singing Bird.* Dublin: Elo, 1983

GALVIN, PATRICK (1927?–   ), poet, playwright, autobiographer, and ballad singer. Galvin was born in Cork, although the exact day and even the exact year are a matter of some doubt, as his birth records were corrupted in his youth. He has been a bookseller, film critic, folksinger, and editor of the Tone Press. Additionally, he has served as writer in residence for the West Midlands Arts Association. His publications total seventeen volumes, containing extracts from songs, stories, plays, and folktales. Galvin's first plays, *Cry the Believers* and *And Him Stretched,* were staged at the Dublin Theatre Festival, and two of his plays have been staged at the national theater: *We Do It for Love* (Abbey,* 1976) and *Last Burning* (Peacock, 1989). These two plays and *Nightfall to Belfast* were written under the Leverhulme Fellowship for Belfast's Lyric Players Theatre* and represent, by far, Galvin's most accomplished and influential work as a writer.

Nightfall to Belfast was first staged in July 1973 in Belfast and ran through the beginning of September. The play, directed by Mary O'Malley, considers the life of the Catholic working class. It is not a naturalistic play, and, consequently, more traditional critics have expressed reservations about a lack of characterization and plot development. However, the piece does stage well as a metaphor for the Troubles. Societal and government institutions plague an individual family whose members try to live out their lives in the context of the Northern violence. Although it played to small audiences, the play's controversial subject apparently made an impression on one group; the day after the play closed, three men were arrested outside the theater attempting to detonate a bomb, and during the play's runs actors confessed to fears and threats of violence.

We Do It for Love opened in May 1975 and played to huge audiences. Public demand extended its run numerous times, and over 20,000 saw the play. It incorporated songs and characters and instances readily recognizable to Belfast audiences into a montage of tragic and comic scenes. The songs, in fact, were gathered by Galvin from the Catholic communities of West Belfast. In sequences reminiscent of Gay's *The Beggar's Opera,* new words replaced the familiar ones, and the songs directly addressed the violence in the North. Like *Nightfall to Belfast,* the play is not naturalistic. The central and unifying image is that of a merry-go-round upon whose horse's bodies are placed the heads of various players in the Troubles—politicians, paramilitary leaders, religious figures, ordinary people, and their children. The play has been justifiably criticized for its lack of ''literary'' significance. It tends to be, especially in the second act, overly romantic and sentimental. Further, because many of the songs are taken directly from the Belfast of the early 1970s, its broad appeal and potential for revival are limited. However, its immediate significance for the community cannot be underestimated. Most notably, the production inspired a generation of Northern dramatists, including Martin Lynch.* Galvin has also written *The Last Burning* (1974) and *My Silver Bird* (1981) for the Lyric.

Galvin's numerous volumes of poetry owe much to his background in music. In fact, they much resemble the collections of folk ballads he published early in his career. What his poems lack in literary merit, they make up for in enthusiasm and stylish bravado. Galvin has also published two volumes of reminiscences about his childhood in Cork, *Song for a Poor Boy* (1990) and *Song for a Raggy Boy* (1991). Both are moving and humorous accounts of a childhood between the wars. The stories address the serious issues of the Catholic Church's support of the fascists in the Spanish civil war and latent Irish anti-Semitism. Galvin also explores the difficult issues of Irish neutrality and shame. However, he tells, too, of a love affair with the movies and his imagined romances with film stars. In all, these memoirs represent the best of Galvin's nontheatrical work, combining his ability to tell a compelling story with his natural dramatic flair.

In addition to his many volumes of poetry and stories, he contributed regularly to *Threshold* and *Fortnight* magazines. However, he will be most remembered for his work with the Lyric in the mid-1970s.

He is a member of Aosdána.*

BERNARD McKENNA

WORKS: *Irish Songs of Resistance*. London: Worker's Music Association, 1955; *Heart of Grace*. London: Linden, 1957. (Poetry); *Christ in London*. London: Linden, 1960. (Poetry); *Letter to the Minister*. Brighton, Sussex: Tone, 1970; *Five Irish Poets: Anthony Blinco, Patrick Galvin, Seán Lucy, Donal Murphy, Seán Ó Críadáin*. Seán Lucy, ed. Cork: Mercier, [1970]; *Beg to Report the Following: "Good News from Ireland" as Expressed in a Letter by Engism Jones*. Brighton, Sussex: Tone, 1971; *By Nature Different: A Poem*. Brighton, Sussex: Tone, 1971; *On the Murder of David Gleason, Bailiff and Citizen of this Parish*. Brighton, Sussex: Tone, 1971; *Letter to a British Soldier on Irish Soil*. Highland Park, Mich.: Red Hanrahan, 1972; *The Wood-Burners*. Dublin: New Writers', 1973. (Poetry); *Three Plays*. Belfast: Threshold, Lyric Players' Theatre, 1976; *Man on the Porch*. London: Martin Brian & O'Keeffe, 1980. (Poetry); *Folk Tales for a General*. Dublin: Raven Arts, 1989. (Poetry); *Song for a Poor Boy: A Cork Childhood*. Dublin: Raven Arts, [1990]; *Song for a Raggy Boy: A Cork Boyhood*. Dublin: Raven Arts, [1991]. (Memoir); *Madwoman of Cork*. Cork: Three Spires, 1991. (Poetry); *Miss Elderberry Swim*. Cork: Three Spires, 1994. (Poetry pamphlet). REFERENCES: Kiely, Niall. "The Saturday Interview." *Irish Times* (July 24, 1976); O'Malley, Conor. *A Poets' Theatre*. [Dublin: Elo, 1988]; O'Malley, Mary. *Never Shake Hands with the Devil*. Dublin: [Elo], 1990; O'Malley, Mary, & John Boyd, eds. *A Needle's Eye*. Belfast: Lyric Player's Theatre, 1979.

GAMBLE, JOHN (ca. 1770–1831), travel writer and novelist. Gamble was born in Strabane, County Tyrone, and received an M.D. from Edinburgh. After serving as an army surgeon in the Low Countries, he traveled often on foot around Ireland gathering material for his perceptive travel writings and his novels.

WORKS: *Sketches of History, Politics, and Manners, in Dublin, and the North of Ireland, in 1810*. London: C. Cradock & W. Joy, 1811/new ed., London: Baldwin, Cradock & Joy, 1826; *A View of Society and Manners, in the North of Ireland, in the Summer and Autumn of 1812*. London: C. Cradock & W. Joy, 1813; *Sarsfield; or Wanderings of Youth, An Irish Tale*. London: Craddock & Joy, 1814; *Howard*. 2 vols. London: Baldwin, Cradock & Joy, 1815; *Northern Irish Tales*. London: Longman, Hurst, 1818; *Views of Society and Manners in the North of Ireland, in a Series of Letters Written in the Year 1818*. London: Longman, Hurst, Rees, Orme & Brown, 1819; *Charlton; or, Scenes in the North of Ireland. A Tale*. 3 vols. London: Baldwin, Cradock & Joy, 1823.

GANLY, ANDREW (1908–1982), playwright and novelist. Ganly was born in Dublin, educated at Trinity College, and became a dentist. His classmate at Trinity, Samuel Beckett,* was one of his patients, and Ganly had to extract a great many of his rotten teeth. Frank O'Connor,* who had been appointed to the Abbey* Board of Directors in 1935, persuaded Ganly to try his hand at playwriting, and one result was "The Dear Queen" (Abbey, 1938). This one-act is a touching, bittersweet study of three old Anglo-Irish ladies, remembering their youth in the days of Queen Victoria. A less successful "prequel" titled "The Dance in Nineteen Hundred and Ten" was not produced by the Abbey, but the Gate* had produced the unpublished, full-length *Murder like Charity* in 1937, and the Abbey produced the unpublished, full-length *The Cursing Fields* in 1942. Ganly's most notable published work, however, was his novel, *The Desolate Sky* (1967), which has some of the warmth and humor of his short plays, but this study of the breakup of a Big House has its harder, sullen, and even ferocious passages also. Unlike many more recent novels, the book is not an ambling narrative but has an effective, well-wrought plot with telling and thoroughly dramatized scenes. Also, unlike more recent novels, it does not depend on one developed character, usually the narrator, while all of the other characters remain wraithlike and wispy. Ganly has perhaps a dozen realized and even memorable characters, particularly the narrator, once the scion of a Big House, now a seedy alcoholic who can be quite ruthless in getting money for drink. *The Desolate Sky* has been rather overlooked in the strident puffing for much less well crafted work that came later. Indeed, Ganly himself has been rather overlooked. He did rate a mention in passing in *The Field Day Anthology,* but his last name was misspelled.

WORKS: *The Desolate Sky.* London: W. H. Allen, 1967. (Novel); "The Dear Queen." *Journal of Irish Literature* 5 (May 1976): 93–111. (One-act play); "The Dance in Nineteen Hundred and Ten." *Journal of Irish Literature* 6 (September 1977): 89–102. (One-act play).

GANNON, NICHOLAS JOHN (1829–1875), novelist, poet, and critic. Gannon was born probably in County Kildare. He was educated at Clongowes Wood College and became a barrister. He died at Kingstown (now Dun Laoghaire) on January 22, 1875.

WORKS: *An Essay on the Characteristic Errors of Our Most Distinguished Poets.* Dublin, 1853; *The O'Donoghue of the Lakes, and Other Poems.* London: Bosworth & Harrison, 1858; *Above and Below.* 2 vols. London, 1864. (Novel); *Mary Desmond, and Other Poems.* London: S. Tinsley, 1873.

GATE THEATRE, THE (1928–   ) The Gate Theatre has been a complement to rather than a rival of the Abbey Theatre.* At times in their histories, especially when the Gate productions have been particularly scintillating and the Abbey productions dully pedestrian, the Gate has seemed the more important theatre. Any such comparison of relative importance is irrelevant, however, for the aims of the two organizations have always been different. The Abbey has been engaged primarily in producing new Irish plays, and even at the dreariest periods in its long history, it has never wavered from that intention. In contrast, the younger Gate, from its founding in 1928, has concentrated on producing an eclectic selection from world drama in nearly every period. While the Gate has sporadically produced new Irish plays, some of which have been extremely distinguished, its founders have never viewed their primary function as the encouragement of native Irish drama.

The Gate was founded by a young English actor, Hilton Edwards, and a young, nominally Irish actor and painter, Micheál Mac Liammóir.* They were inaugurating nothing new in the Irish theatre but were continuing an impulse that had been present from the beginning. In the early years of the dramatic movement, three strands of future development may be distinguished: the poetic drama of W. B. Yeats,* the realistic native drama of Padraic Colum,* and the interest in the continental drama of Ibsen and Strindberg. This interest in continental drama was most evident in the plays of Edward Martyn.* Although Martyn's own dramatic talent was small, he continued to be involved in and even to launch small theatres, such as the Irish Theatre in Hardwicke Street, that produced some of the more interesting and depressing contemporary European plays. However, two of Martyn's key people, Thomas MacDonagh* and Joseph Mary Plunkett,* were executed after the 1916 Rising. Hence, the Dublin Drama League was initiated in 1918 by Yeats,* Robinson,* James Stephens,* and others, to continue the production of foreign masterpieces that would not otherwise be seen in Dublin. The League existed for ten years, staging intermittent productions of one or two performances and using actors recruited from the Abbey and from the amateur movement. In 1928, Edwards and Mac Liammóir, who had met while touring in Anew McMaster's company, joined forces to produce a season of plays at the Abbey's little experimental theatre, the Peacock. The season began with a noteworthy performance of *Peer Gynt* and continued with two plays by O'Neill and others by Wilde,* Evreinov, Mac Liammóir, and Elmer Greensfelder. Its second season, also in the Peacock, saw works by Tolstoy, Rice, Capek, Galsworthy, Evreinov, and Paul Raynal, as well as three new Irish plays, the finest being Denis Johnston's* now-famous *The Old Lady Says "No!"* With these exciting productions, the new theatre was obviously the heir of Edward Martyn's tradition.

After this second season, Edwards and Mac Liammóir moved their operations to the Rotunda where a second-storey ballroom was converted into a theatre. There the Gate has maintained its permanent home ever since. From that third season in 1930, the Gate has produced well over three hundred plays from world drama, ranging from the high tragedy of Aeschylus, Sophocles, and Shakespeare, to the high comedy of Shaw,* Wilde, and Sheridan,* to broad farce, airy romance, poetic drama, expressionism, and the Broadway and West End success. The company is not associated with any individual style. Rather, the productions have been noted for an eclecticism of approach, as well as consummate taste in staging and a meticulous professionalism. In the thirty years after 1930 until the advent of television, there was no more potent force than the Gate in educating Ireland in the drama.

The interest of the Gate for literature lies in the new Irish plays and playwrights that it has fostered. The most significant new Irish plays produced by the Gate were those by Denis Johnston, Lord Longford,* Lady Longford,* and Mary Manning,* but it also presented plays by such interesting dramatists as Padraic Colum,* T. C. Murray,* Lennox Robinson, Austin Clarke,* St. John Ervine,* Andrew Ganly,* Maura Laverty,* Donagh MacDonagh,* and others. In the 1960s, the theatre attained international success with plays by the Northern writer Brian Friel* and attracted considerable local admiration with the plays of Desmond Forristal.*

Of these writers, the most eminent theatrically is Johnston, whose reputation finally, in its different way, is beginning to rival that of O'Casey.* Some of Johnston's plays were produced by the Abbey, but his most experimental were done by the Gate, including *The Old Lady* and *A Bride for the Unicorn*. In the 1930s, the Gate had an aura of clever sophistication that did not at all attach to the Abbey, which at that time was largely producing "kitchen comedies" (and indeed one wit compared the differences between the Gate and the Abbey as the differences between Sodom and Begorrah). If there was a kind of Gate play, it was a clever, witty satire or satirical comedy. The most brilliant writers of this genre were Mary Manning, Lady Longford, and Mac Liammóir himself. In such pieces as *Youth's the Season—?*, *Mr. Jiggins of Jigginstown,* and *Ill Met by Moonlight,* the Gate managed enormously stylish productions.

In 1936, Lord Longford, who had been a major financial supporter of the theatre, formed his own company, Longford Productions. For many years, Longford shared the building on a half-yearly basis with the original company. In the 1970s, after more than forty years of financial struggle, the Gate received a subsidy from the Irish government. However, Mac Liammóir died in 1978, and Edwards died in 1982. Since December 1983, Michael Colgan has been the director of the Gate and has basically followed the theater's traditional policy of a mixture of modern and classic plays with an occasional new Irish play. Some, if not all, of the last decade's productions have received admirably rich stagings. The Joe Dowling production of O'Casey's *Juno and the Paycock,* with Donal McCann and John Kavanagh, is likely to be the definitive production for this generation. The theater has also staged short Beckett* and Harold Pinter seasons. In 1991, a new stage and seating were installed, the auditorium refurbished, and the foyer extended.

If the Gate is not as prominent as the Abbey in either literary or theatrical history, the reason may be that its main interest was never the production of new Irish plays. However, much of what the theater has produced—including well over fifty new Irish plays—it has done brilliantly.

REFERENCES: Hobson, Bulmer, ed. *The Gate Theatre, Dublin.* Dublin: Gate Theatre, 1934. (Contains articles, list of productions, sketches, and many photographs); Edwards, Hilton. *The Mantle of Harlequin.* Dublin: Progress House, 1958; Mac Liammóir, Micheál. *All for Hecuba.* Dublin: Progress House, 1961; Mac Liammóir, Micheál. *Each Actor on His Ass.* London: Routledge & Kegan Paul, 1961; Mac Liammóir, Micheál. *Theatre in Ireland.* 2d ed. Dublin: Cultural Relations Committee of Ireland, 1964; Luke, Peter, ed. *Enter Certain Players, Edwards-Mac Liammóir and the Gate.* [Dublin]: Dolmen, [1978]; O hAodha, Micheál. *The Importance of Being Michael: A Portrait of MacLiammóir.* [Dingle, Co. Kerry]: Brandon, [1990]; Fitz-Simon, Christopher. *The Boys.* London: Nick Hern, [1994].

GÉBLER, CARLO (1954–   ), novelist. Gébler is the son of Ernest Gébler* and Edna O'Brien.* His first excellently realized novel, *The Eleventh Summer* (1985), is about an eleven-year-old boy who does not like his father and whose mother is dead and who spends a summer in the west of Ireland with his grandparents. The action is less a plot than a gathering of disparate but arresting incidents, such as a horse race, the boy's first experiments with sex, the burning down of the house, and his grandfather's death. At the end the boy is unwillingly taken away by his father. It is less the action than the plausible characterization of the boy and the precise and accurate details that give the novel its considerable merit. On any page, however, the details are given a pejorative slant. To take some random examples:

Behind his bare knees he could feel the always damp, always sticky wooden pew.

The legs of the sheep were like spindles, their faces were sooty black and their coats matted and dirty.

The smell of his tobacco was honeyed and slightly sickly.

The invariably slanted details are probably justified, for this is not exactly an idyllic summer.

Work and Play (1987) is, in its details, even bleaker:

A nurse showed him into a room which smelled of fart and cabbage.

The chips were dried twigs; the beans had a scum around the edges; and the sausages were like slivers of dry turf.

The mental malaise of the protagonist, Fergus Maguire, is heightened by his father's death after a swimming accident and by having been left out of his father's will. He flees Dublin, and most of the action is set in London in the 1980s. Fergus gets a dull job answering letters for a television company, but spends his free time aimlessly sleeping with various girls and taking drugs. In one typical scene, Laura takes off all of her clothes in a restaurant and empties a glass of Perrier water over another girl's head. When a policeman comes, Fergus "pushed a wedge of Camembert cheese onto the envelope of cocaine and swallowed the lot." The ending of the novel, however, is, surprisingly, upbeat. After failing to rescue an Indian family from a fire, Fergus "was heavy with the sense of how he had wasted his time" and that in the future "[h]e had to take responsibility himself."

Malachi and His Family (1990) is the story of an American boy who, discovering his real father was an illegal Irish immigrant, traces his father to a London suburb. The father has married a Hungarian refugee, and the boy becomes involved with the family—his stepmother, her mother, his half-brother and sister. The ultimate suicide of the half-sister seems to arise out of the trauma of their Hungarian background, which is traced in flashbacks from the end of the First World War. The book has Gébler's usual characteristics—an ambling narrative, well-developed characters, precise details, and a gloomy view.

WORKS: The *Eleventh Summer*. London: Hamish Hamilton/ New York: Dutton, [1985]; *August in July*. London: Hamish Hamilton, 1986; *Work and Play*. London: Hamish Hamilton, [1987]/New York: St. Martin's, 1988; *Driving through Cuba: An East-West Journey*. London: Hamish Hamilton, 1988. (Reportage); *Malachi and His Family*. London: Hamish Hamilton, [1990]; *The Cure*. London: Hamish Hamilton, 1991; *Life of a Drum*. London: Hamish Hamilton, [1991]; *The Glass Curtain: Inside an Ulster Community*. London: Hamish Hamilton, 1991. (Nonfiction).

GÉBLER, ERNEST (1915–   ), novelist. Gébler was born in Dublin and lived some years in England and America before returning to Ireland. He was married to Edna O'Brien* and at one time claimed to have much to do with the writing of her early work. He is the father of Carlo Gébler.* His first novel, *He Had My Heart Scalded* (1946), concerns growing up in Dublin, but his later work is set elsewhere. His most successful book, *The Plymouth Adventure* (1950), was a best-seller in America and was filmed.

WORKS: *He Had My Heart Scalded* (London: Sampson Low, Marston, [1946]; *The Plymouth Adventure: A Chronicle Novel on the Voyage of the Mayflower.* Garden City, N.Y.: Doubleday, 1950/London: Cassell, 1952; *A Week in the Country.* London: Hutchinson, 1958; *The Love Investigator.* London: Pan, 1963; *The Old Man and the Girl.* Garden City, N.Y.: Doubleday, 1968; *Shall I Eat You Now?* London: Macmillan, 1969/published also as *Hoffman.* Garden City, N.Y.: Doubleday, 1969.

GENTLEMAN, FRANCIS (1728–1784), playwright and theatrical critic. Gentleman was born in York Street, Dublin, on October 13, 1728, the son of an army officer. He himself was in the army but left to appear under Thomas Sheridan the younger's* management at Smock Alley, where he successfully appeared in Southerne's* *Oroonoko* and other plays. In England, he played in the provinces and under Foote at the Haymarket. Many of his plays were produced, among them adaptations of Ben Jonson and Southerne. The *Dictionary of National Biography* calls *The Modish Wife* "his masterpiece, if such a term may be used." Probably his most important work was *The Dramatic Censor* (1770), two volumes of criticism of plays of the day. He also edited Bell's acting edition of Shakespeare, which has been called the worst that ever appeared of any English author. His later years were spent trying not too successfully to make ends meet, and he spent the last seven in Dublin, where he died on December 21, 1784.

PRINCIPAL WORKS: *A Trip to the Moon.* London: Crowder, 1765. (Fantasy); *Royal Fables.* London: T. Beckett & P. A. De Hondt, 1766; *The Stratford Jubilee.* London: T. Lowndes, 1769. (Two-act comedy); *The Sultan; or, Love and Fame.* London: J. Bell, 1770. (Tragedy); *The Dramatic Censor; or, Critical Companion. . . .* 2 vols. London: J. Bell, 1770; *The Tobacconist.* London: J. Bell, 1771. (Two-act farce, after Jonson's *The Alchemist*); *The Pantheonite. A Dramatic Entertainment.* London: J. Bell, 1773; *The Modish Wife.* London: T. Evans & J. Bell, [1774].

GEOGHEGAN, ARTHUR GERALD (ca. 1810–1889), poet. Geoghegan was born in 1809 or 1810, worked in the civil service, and was a collector of Irish antiquities. His long narrative poem, *The Monks of Kilcrea,* appeared anonymously but went into two editions and was translated into French. He wrote for *The Dublin Penny Journal, The Dublin University Magazine, The Nation,* * and many other magazines. His work is consistently euphonious, and his deft little "After Aughrim" is sometimes reprinted. He died in London in November 1889.

WORKS: *The Monks of Kilcrea, a Ballad Poem.* Dublin: J. McGlashan, 1853; *The Monks of Kilcrea, and Other Ballads and Poems.* London: Bell & Doldy, 1861.

GIBBON, [WILLIAM] MONK (1896–1987), poet and man of letters. Gibbon was born in Dublin on December 15, 1896, and was educated at St. Columba's College, Rathfarnham, and at Keble College, Oxford. He served in World War I from 1914 until he was invalided out in 1918. While home on leave during the 1916 Rising, he witnessed the execution of Francis Sheehy-Skeffington.* After the war he taught at Oldfield School, Swanage, Wales, for twelve years and continued to teach until he was almost eighty. He was a member of the Irish Academy of Letters and a Fellow of the Royal Society of Literature. He succeeded in reducing the huge, inchoate mass of Michael Farrell's* novel *Thy Tears Might Cease* into publishable form. On the occasion of his ninetieth birthday, the Irish Tourist Board paid him the uncommon compliment, for a living author, of placing a plaque on his house. He died in Killiney on October 29, 1987.

As a poet, Gibbon is conventional and even old-fashioned. He is capable of poetic spellings such as "o'er," of poetic inversions such as "chestnuts young" or "they turned from him away," of personifications of Love and Truth and "blind grief," "deaf pride," and "purse-proud Time," and his work is full of poetic diction such as "O," "Ah," "Aye," "Nay," "oft," "spake," "alas," "thou," and "thy," "art," "wilt," "lest," "twixt," "pelf," and so on. All of these archaic qualities notwithstanding, Gibbon is, at his best, graceful, terse, immediate, and strong. What, for instance, could be tighter or defter than his excellent poem "Microcosm"? He handles conventional quatrains and couplets and sonnets with ease and fluency and can even manage effective pastiches of Gerard Manley Hopkins, who is far from his own style. He is not a highly individual poet, but he has had so many successes that a Selected Poems would well be in order.

Gibbon did a good deal of miscellaneous writing, including prose poems, travel books, some criticism, a novel, a biography, a refractory critical memoir of Yeats* (who found him argumentative), and some autobiographical volumes, of which the best are *The Seals* (1935) and *Mount Ida* (1948). *The Seals* is a reflective narrative of a seal hunt in Donegal and is curiously reminiscent of (and far superior to) Hemingway's *Green Hills of Africa*. *Mount Ida* has the same beautifully lucid prose but is a self-indulgent, lengthy account of three romances at various times in the author's life and in various places—Wales, Italy, and Austria. Although much too long for the strength of emotion involved or the amount of action, the book has charm; at half its length it could have been a minor classic.

WORKS: *The Tremulous String.* Fair Oak: A. W. Mathews, 1926. (Prose poems); *The Branch of Hawthorn Tree.* London: Grayhound, 1927. (Poems); *For Daws to Peck at.* London: Gollancz/ New York: Dodd, Mead, 1929. (Poems); *A Ballad.* Winchester: Grayhound, 1930; *Seventeen Sonnets.* London: Joiner & Steele, 1932; *The Seals.* London: Jonathan Cape, 1935; ed and with an introductory essay, *The Living Torch* by AE. London: Macmillan, 1937; *Mount Ida.* London: Jonathan Cape, 1948; *The Red Shoes Ballet.* [London]: Saturn, [1948]. (Criticism); *Swiss Enchantment.* London: Evans, 1950. (Travel); *This Insubstantial Pageant.* London: Phoenix House, 1951. (Prose poems); *The Tales of Hoffmann: A Study of the Film.* London: Saturn, 1951; *An Intruder at the*

Ballet. London: Phoenix House, 1952. (Criticism); *Austria.* London: Batsford, 1953. (Travel); *In Search of Winter Sport.* London: Evans, 1953. (Travel); *Western Germany.* London: Batsford, 1955; *The Rhine and its Castles.* London: Putnam, 1957. (Travel); *The Masterpiece and the Man: Yeats as I knew Him.* London: Hart-Davis, 1959; *Netta.* London: Routledge & Kegan Paul, 1960. (Biography); *The Climate of Love.* London: Gollancz, 1961. (Novel); ed. with an Introduction, *Poems from the Irish* by Douglas Hyde. Dublin: Figgis, 1963; ed. with an Introduction, *The Poems of Katharine Tynan.* Dublin: Figgis, 1963; *The Brahms Waltz.* London: Hutchinson, 1970. (Autobiographical); *The Velvet Bow and Other Poems.* London: Hutchinson, 1972; *The Pupil: A Memory of Love.* Dublin: Wolfhound, [ca. 1981].   REFERENCE: Inverarity, Geoffrey. "Q & A: Monk Gibbon." *Irish Literary Supplement* 6 (Fall 1987): 29–30.

GIBBONS, MARGARET (1884–1969), novelist, poet, and religious historian. Margaret Gibbons was born in July 1884, the daughter of a member of the Royal Irish Constabulary. One of four children, Margaret's brother, Edward, became a priest in the diocese of Meath. Her sister Maria became Mother Columba of the Loreto Convent in Navan and wrote the ballad "Who Fears to Speak of Easter Week?" Her sister Kitty became Mrs. O'Doherty and was occasionally a secret messenger for de Valera. Margaret was an avid reader, completing Dickens's works by age nine and Shakespeare's by age eleven. She wrote her first poem at ten. The pseudonyms under which she occasionally published were Eithne and Meda. She was educated at the Fore National School at Collinstown, County Westmeath, and at St. Mary's College, Belfast, where she qualified as a teacher. She taught in the Scottish islands and at Cannistown, near Navan. One of her later efforts was a book of hymns intended to unify the pilgrims' singing at Lough Derg. At the age of seventy-two, she journeyed to India to research the life of Mar Ivanios, who had converted to Catholicism at the Eucharistic Congress of 1932 and was later made archbishop of Trivandrum. She died in Dublin in January 1969 and is buried at Fore in Westmeath.

Gibbons's early works were novels, eight of which were published by D. C. Thomson and Company as part of their Red Letter Novels series. She was quite successful as a popular novelist but began to focus on religious history in the 1930s. Her work in this area was warmly received, beginning with *Glimpses of Catholic Ireland in the Eighteenth Century* (1932). The title is somewhat misleading, as the volume is really a history of the Irish Brigidine Sisterhood. Gibbons's novels are fairly pedestrian, but her later religious works were deservedly popular. Her attempts to recapture the Catholic history of Ireland, particularly during the period of suppression, are remarkably balanced for one so devout. Her Lough Derg volumes were among the first to chronicle the island's history.

ANNE COLMAN

WORKS: *The Good-Night Stories.* London: Year Book, 1912; *The Rose of Glenconnel.* London: Herbert Jenkins, 1917/London: D. C. Thomson, [1921]; *An Anzac's Bride.* London: Herbert Jenkins, 1918; *Whom Love Hath Chosen.* London: Herbert Jenkins, 1920; *Hidden Fires.* London: Herbert Jenkins, 1921; *Each Hour a Peril.* London: D. C. Thomson, [1921]; *The Highest Bidder.* London: D. C. Thomson, [1921]; *The Bartered Bride.* London: Herbert Jenkins, 1921; *The Flame of Life.* London: Herbert Jenkins, 1922; *Shifting Sands.* London: Herbert Jenkins, 1922; *His Dupe.* London:

D. C. Thomson, 1922; *Molly of the Lone Pine.* London: D. C. Thomson, [1922]; *A Lover on Loan.* London: D. C. Thomson, [1923]; *Her Undying Past.* London: Herbert Jenkins, 1924; *Lone—and Carol.* London: Herbert Jenkins, 1925; *Love's Defiance.* London: D. C. Thomson, 1926; *Her Dancing Partner.* London: Herbert Jenkins, 1926; *My Pretty Maid: Talks with Girls by Eithne . . .* London: Sands, 1927; *The Ukelele Girl.* London: Herbert Jenkins, 1927/London: D. C. Thomson, 1927; *The Life of Margaret Aylward: Foundress of the Sisters of the Holy Faith.* London: Sands, 1928; *Nellie of Holy God.* London: Sands, [1929]; *Dancers in the Dark.* London: Herbert Jenkins, 1929; *Painted Butterflies.* London: Herbert Jenkins, 1931; *Glimpses of Catholic Ireland in the Eighteenth Century: Restoration of the Daughters of St. Brigid by Most Rev. Dr. Delany.* Dublin: Browne & Nolan, 1932; *Guide to St. Patrick's Purgatory, Lough Derg.* Dublin: Talbot, 1932; *Hollywood Madness.* London: Herbert Jenkins, 1936; *Loreto, Navan: One Hundred Years of Catholic Progress, 1833–1933.* Navan: Meath Chronicle, 1937; *The Ownership of Station Island, Lough Derg.* Dublin: Duffy, 1937; *Station Island, Lough Derg: With Historic Sketch of the Pilgrimage and Chronology* Dublin, 1950; *Mar Ivanios, 1882–1953: Archbishop of Trivandrum.* Dublin: Clonmore & Reynolds, 1962.

GIBSON, MAGGIE (1948–   ), novelist. Margaret Ann Gibson, the second of five children, was born in Yorkshire of Irish parents on May 8, 1948. The family kept close links with Ireland, summering in her mother's home, Westport, County Mayo. In the early 1970s, they returned to Ireland to live. Gibson herself moved to Westport after her divorce in 1985. She lives in a shop built in 1905 by her great-great-great-great-grandfather, and she runs her hairdressing business from the premises.

After buying a personal computer for her business, Gibson began to write, using the spell-checker as a corrective for her dyslexia. Freed by the spell-checker, she "bought a 'How To' book and started to bash away." She chose to write crime fiction because that is what she enjoys reading.

Grace, the Hooker, the Hard Man and the Kid (1995) is the first of a trilogy of mystery stories featuring Grace de Rossa. De Rossa becomes embroiled in a case that includes child abuse, murder, and corruption within the police. The story moves at a pace that precludes the development of any of the characters, including the heroine, although her discontent and need to change her lot form the spine of the story. Despite stock characters and some awkward writing, it is an energetic debut, a welcome foray into the "humorous mystery" by an Irish writer. The second novel in the trilogy, *The Longest Fraud,* is scheduled for publication in 1996.

SHEILA BARRETT

WORK: *Grace, the Hooker, the Hard Man and the Kid.* Dublin: Poolbeg, 1995.

GILBERT, LADY (1841–1921), novelist, short story writer, and poet. Lady Gilbert was born Rosa Mulholland in Belfast in 1841. She married John T. Gilbert,* the historian, in 1891, and she became a prolific writer for the popular press. Her fiction is informed by some real knowledge of the peasantry of the West but is overly romantic and heavily religious. Like the hero of one of her books, Lady Gilbert wrote for "the nobler and purer-minded section of the reading public." The intellectual level of that public may perhaps be demonstrated by the conclusion of her novel, *The Wild Birds of Killeevy* (1883):

We will now take leave of our hero and heroine on a summer evening after sunset as they sit in their own little territory—a garden of roses extending down to the cliffs, with the crimsoned ocean at their feet and all the hundred isles they know so well burning on it like so many jewels, set with amethyst and amber and gold.

Kevin has just finished reading his new poem to Fanchea. Her hand is in his; her eyes are full of tears. She is not thinking of the applause of the world which may follow this work, but of the higher audience that have been present at the reading, the choirs of angels that have witnessed this new utterance of a strong man's soul. "Let them be the judges," is the thought of her heart; and she smiles, feeling conscious of their approval.

A cloud of sea-birds rises from their favorite island; they circle and wheel, and fly off in a trail towards the glory of the sun.

So wing all white souls to a happy eternity.

After penning hundreds of such sweet and innocuous fictions, she died in Dublin in 1921.

WORKS: *Hester's History,* published anonymously. 2 vols. London, 1869; *The Wicked Woods of Tobereevil.* London, 1872/London: Burns & Oates, [1897]; *The Little Flower Seekers.* London, [1873]; *Eldergowan . . . and Other Tales.* London, 1874; *Five Little Farmers.* London, 1876; *Four Little Mischiefs.* London: Blackie, 1883; *The Wild Birds of Killeevy.* London: Burns & Oates, [1883]; ed., *Gems for the Young from Favourite Poets.* Dublin: Gill, 1884; *Hetty Gray, or Nobody's Bairn.* London: Blackie, 1884; *The Walking Trees, and Other Tales.* Dublin: Gill, 1885; *The Late Mrs. Hollingford.* London: Blackie, [1886]; *Marcella Grace, an Irish Novel.* London: Kegan Paul, 1886; *Vagrant Verses.* London: Kegan Paul, 1886/London: E. Mathews, [1889]; *A Fair Emigrant.* London: Kegan Paul, 1888; *Gianetta.* London: Blackie, 1889; *The Mystery of Hall-in-the-Wood.* London: Sunday School Union, [1893]; *Marigold and Other Stories.* Dublin: Eason, 1894; *Banshee Castle.* London: Blackie, 1895; *Our Own Story and Other Tales.* London: Catholic Truth Society, [1896]; *Nanno.* London: Grant Richards, 1899; *Onora.* London: Grant Richards, 1900/later published as *Norah of Waterford,* London & Edinburgh: Sands, 1915; *Terry; or, She Ought to Have Been a Boy.* London: Blackie, [1900]; *Cynthia's Bonnet Shop.* London: Blackie, 1901; *The Squire's Grand-Daughters.* London: Burns & Oates/New York: Benziger, 1903; *The Tragedy of Chris.* London, Edinburgh: Sands, 1903; *A Girl's Ideal.* London: Blackie, 1905; *Life of Sir John T. Gilbert.* London: Longman's, 1905; *Our Boycotting.* Dublin: Gill, 1907. (Play); *Our Sister Maisie.* London: Blackie, 1907; *The Story of Ellen.* London: Burns & Oates/New York: Benziger, 1907; *The Return of Mary O'Murrough.* Edinburgh & London: Sands, 1908; *Spirit and Dust.* London: Elkin Mathews, 1908; *Cousin Sara.* London: Blackie, 1909; *Father Tim.* London & Edinburgh: Sands, 1910; *The O'Shaughnessy Girls.* London: Blackie, 1911; *Fair Noreen.* London: Blackie, 1912; *Twin Sisters, an Irish Tale.* London: Blackie, 1913; *Old School Friends.* London: Blackie, 1914; *The Daughter in Possession.* London: Blackie, 1915; *Dreams and Realities.* London & Edinburgh: Sands, 1916. (Poems); *Narcissa's Ring.* London: Blackie, 1916; *O'Loughlin of Clare.* London & Edinburgh: Sands, 1916; *The Cranberry Claimants.* London: Sands, [1932].

GILBERT, SIR JOHN T[HOMAS] (1829–1898), historian and antiquary. Gilbert was born on January 23, 1829, in Dublin. He wrote the first real history of that city, a book that is still most readable and full of valuable fact and excellent anecdote. Boylan remarks, "His criticisms of the official treatment of Irish historical documents led to the founding of the Public Record Office by the government in 1867," and he was appointed its secretary. He was also librarian of the Royal Irish Academy for thirty-four years, published a *History of the Viceroys of Ireland,* and retrieved and published many valuable historical documents.

He married Rosa Mulholland in 1891, was knighted in 1897, and died on May 23, 1898. His invaluable collection of books, broadsides, and manuscripts, cataloged by D. J. O'Donoghue* and Douglas Hyde,* is housed in the Pearse Street Library, Dublin.

PRINCIPAL WORK: *A History of the City of Dublin.* 3 vols. Dublin: James McGlashan, 1854–1859/Dublin: James Duffy, 1861. Gilbert wrote a good deal of other scholarly historical work, but probably nothing else of great literary interest. REFERENCE: Gilbert, Lady. *Life of Sir John T. Gilbert.* London: Longmans, 1905.

GILBERT, STEPHEN (1912–   ), novelist. Gilbert, born in July 1912, at Newcastle, County Down, was the elder son of William Gilbert, a wholesale seed and tea merchant of Belfast. He was a reporter on the *Northern Whig* from 1931 until 1933, when he joined his father at Samuel McCausland, Limited. On the death of his father, he was appointed a director. At the outbreak of World War II, Gilbert joined the 3rd Ulster Searchlight Regiment as a gunner. He was awarded the Military Medal in 1940, and later in that year he was commissioned. In 1941, he was released from service to return to business. He was actively associated with the Campaign for Nuclear Disarmament in Northern Ireland, acting as secretary for two years.

Gilbert's latest novel, *Ratman's Notebooks,* was published in 1968 and was made into the very successful film *Willard.* The book was subsequently reissued in paperback with the latter title and has also been translated into Italian, German, Portuguese, Dutch, and Japanese. His previous publications are *The Landslide* (1943), *Bombadier* (1944), *Monkeyface* (1948), and *The Burnaby Experiments* (1952).

Gilbert stands apart from other Irish writers both in subject matter and style. Although his fantasies are influenced by the work of his friend Forrest Reid,* Gilbert broke free of that influence with the publication of *Bombadier,* one of the best written novels of World War II. His highly imaginative prose is marked by its extreme lucidity and simplicity. Though *Ratman's Notebooks* is his most popular novel, *The Landslide* is perhaps his outstanding achievement, formally and stylistically.

Gilbert is married and has four children. He is director or chairman of a number of companies operating in Ireland, Scotland, and England. He lives about twelve miles from Belfast in County Antrim, where his wife farms seventy-five acres of land and breeds Shetland ponies.

JOHN BOYD

WORKS: *The Landslide.* London: Faber, 1943; *Bombadier.* London: Faber, 1944; *Monkeyface.* London: Faber, 1948; *The Burnaby Experiments.* London: Faber, 1952; *Ratman's Notebooks.* London: Michael Joseph, 1968.

GILL & MACMILLAN (1968–   ), publishing house. Gill & Macmillan is the largest trade publisher in Ireland, publishing over eighty titles per annum. The list is primarily a general-interest, nonfiction one, focusing principally on history, reference, biography, psychology, religion, and tourist guidebooks. There is also an academic and recently published professional list. In addition, Gill & Macmillan is a major educational publisher of textbooks for use in Irish schools and overseas: about half of the company's business lies in this area.

The company was formed in 1968 from the association of two long-established publishing houses: M. H. Gill & Son, Ltd., in Dublin (founded 1856) and Macmillan & Company of London (founded 1843). Both companies have been in family control since their foundation. Macmillan remains the largest privately owned book publisher in Britain while Gill family interests hold majority ownership of Gill & Macmillan. In early 1985, Verlagsgruppe Georg von Holtzbrinck, a privately owned German company, acquited a majority shareholding in Macmillan.

Among Gill & Macmillan's earliest ventures was the eleven-volume paperback Gill History of Ireland (1972–1975), which was a standard textbook series for many years. It has recently been replaced by the six-volume New Gill History, now nearing completion. Individual history titles have ranged from J. H. Whyte's seminal *Church and State in Modern Ireland* to more recent volumes such as Christine Kinealy's major reexamination of the Famine, *This Great Calamity.*

Biography and autobiography have ranged across a list of subjects as diverse as Eamon de Valera, Garret FitzGerald, Noel Browne, and Gay Byrne. In addition, the sixteen-volume Gill's Irish Lives (1980–1983) repeated the small paperback formula originally employed in the Gill History of Ireland.

The reference list embraces dictionaries of biography, history, literature, and religion. This latter category reflects a long-standing commitment. The original reputation of M. H. Gill & Son as religious publishers has been developed and enhanced with the publication of books by internationally established theologians such as Werner Jeanrond, Enda McDonagh, Donal Dorr, and Avery Dulles. Gill & Macmillan is also the English-language publisher of Michel Quoist, one of the most popular devotional writers of the last twenty years.

A general-interest list based in a thinly populated country will necessarily be eclectic. Gill & Macmillan's tourist publishing is hardly literary—it is not intended to be—but it reflects the growing professionalism of Irish publishing generally. Even then, a title like Peter Harbison's *Guide to the National and Historic Monuments of Ireland,* never out of print since it was first published in 1970 and at present in its fourth edition, combines outstanding scholarship with accessibility. Similarly, the astonishingly successful Darina Allen, whose cookbooks have sold over half a million copies in less than ten years, has raised this kind of publishing to a new level in Ireland. In addition, the Gill & Macmillan list has addressed major areas of political and social concern in modern Irish life, not least in Frank McDonald's *The Destruction of Dublin* (1985), a no-holds-barred account of the ravages of property speculators on the capital's architectural fabric from the 1960s on.

The company has selling arrangements internationally through other companies in the Macmillan Group and specialized independent agents. It provides sales representation in Ireland, the U.K., and Europe for publishers based in Britain, Canada, and Australia. It also provides distribution services for twelve other publishers based both in Ireland and Northern Ireland.

GILTINAN, DONAL (1908–   ), playwright, novelist, and radio and television scriptwriter. Giltinan was born in Cork on March 1, 1908. He worked as a customs and excise official in Dublin before turning to full-time writing. More than 600 of his radio programs were broadcast, as well as a number of television plays for the BBC and ITV in England. He was also a prolific writer for the stage, and the Abbey* produced four of his pieces: *Goldfish in the Sun* (1950), *The Gentle Maiden* (1952), *The Flying Wheel* (1957), and his Robert Emmet* play *A Light in the Sky* (1962). A novel, *Prince of Darkness,* was published in 1955.

GLAVIN, ANTHONY (1945–   ), poet. Glavin was born in Dublin and became a teacher at the Royal Irish Academy of Music. In 1987 he received the Patrick Kavanagh Award. He is not to be confused with the short story writer of the same name.

WORK: *The Wrong Side of the Alps.* [Oldcastle, Co. Meath]: Gallery, [1989].

GLAVIN, ANTHONY (1946–   ), short story writer. Glavin was born in Boston in 1946 and, like Robert Bernen,* went to live in the Blue Stacks mountains of Donegal. His collection of stories about his experiences, *One for Sorrow* (1980), describes the old customs and ways, but the author seems a bit like Lady Gregory searching out the quaint. Another problem is that the stories are not about very much; one, perhaps symptomatically, is called "Killing Time." A second problem is that the author seems less interested in Donegal than in himself; one story, "Of Saints and Scholars," is about an American writer in Donegal who is trying to write a story about Donegal. The texture of Glavin's work is professional enough, but the substance is often arbitrary or thin.

WORK: *One for Sorrow.* [Swords, Co. Dublin]: Poolbeg, [1980].

GOGARTY, OLIVER ST. JOHN (1878–1957), poet. Gogarty was born in 5, Rutland (now Parnell) Square, Dublin on August 17, 1878. He attended the local Christian Brothers school and, after his father's early and unexpected death from appendicitis, was a boarder at Mungret, Stonyhurst, and Clongowes. Following a period at the Royal University, he entered the medical school of Trinity College.

Gogarty's amusing personality and athletic prowess ensured his popularity with fellow students. For a time he and James Joyce* were close friends, a relationship discussed in J. B. Lyons, *James Joyce and Medicine* (1973). The dons, too, were impressed by his knowledge of literature and his flair for parody. He formed lasting friendships with the Trinity College classical scholar, Robert Yelverton Tyrrell (1844–1914) and John Pentland Mahaffy,* and won the Vice-Chancellor's Prize for English Verse in 1902, 1903, and 1905. Hoping for similar success with the Newdigate Prize, he spent a term at Worcester College, Oxford, in 1904 but placed second to G.K.C. Bell, a future bishop of Chichester. His letters to Bell (*Many Lines to Thee,* 1971) display a sensitivity concealed in his correspondence with Joyce where a cynical bawdiness predominates.

While at Oxford, he became friendly with R. S. Chenevix Trench who stayed with him in a Martello Tower in Sandycove which he rented in the autumn of 1904. James Joyce was the third member of the party. The young men are featured in *Ulysses* as Buck Mulligan, Haines, and Stephen Dedalus, respectively.

Gogarty's multifarious interests (he was a strong swimmer and a champion cyclist) conflicted with professional studies and delayed graduation until 1907. Meanwhile, he had married Martha Duane of Moyard, Connemara. (They were to have three children.) A period of postgraduate study in Vienna equipped him to practice ear-nose-and-throat surgery. He purchased a house in Ely Place, Dublin, where his neighbors included George Moore* and Sir Thornley Stoker whose brother Bram Stoker* was the author of *Dracula.*

As an undergraduate, Gogarty published signed and unsigned poems and articles in *Dana* and other periodicals, but the conservative traditions of the medical profession obliged him to delay a public appearance as a poet. He used a pseudonym when his plays *Blight* (1917), *A Serious Thing* (1919), and *The Enchanted Trousers* (1919) were staged in the Abbey Theatre.* His personality was too strong, however, to be fettered, and through politics he became a national figure when appointed to the Irish Free State Senate in 1922. Unfortunate consequences in those troubled times were an attempt on Senator Gogarty's life and the burning of his country property, Renvyle House, where his guests had included W. B. Yeats* and Augustus John.

The Senate provided Gogarty a forum for advising on how the building of the new state should proceed and for castigating political opponents. On the whole, his advice was sound, and peppered with wit. His castigations, though not undeserved, were almost indecently vehement, his special target being Eamon de Valera. The remark that "Dev" looked like "a cross between a corpse and a cormorant" was made in private, but in the Senate he referred to "our Celtic Calvin" and on another occasion said, "Instead of seizing the opportunity of Plenty, like a fanatical edition of St. Francis he is to wed his Lady Poverty . . ." Giving tit for tat, Sean MacEntee said that Gogarty reminded him "of a surgeon operating with a pickaxe."

When Gogarty's patients in the Meath Hospital overflowed into the beds of his colleague Sir Lambert Ormsby, a general surgeon, Ormsby's assistant remonstrated, saying that Ormsby needed the beds. "Beds!" exclaimed Gogarty, "he needs slabs." The remark is characteristic of his mordant wit. The publication of *As I Was Going Down Sackville Street* (1937) led to a libel suit which Gogarty lost. This is his best known book, an interesting memoir of his times, but inferior in comic individuality to *Tumbling in the Hay* (1939). The latter work, incidentally, describes an evening in Holles Street Hospital that may have been Joyce's inspiration for the Oxen of the Sun episode of *Ulysses*. The third major prose work is *I Follow Saint Patrick* (1938).

Gogarty left Ireland in 1939 and, apart from occasional visits home, spent the remainder of his life in America, a period considered by J. B. Lyons in *Oliver St. John Gogarty: The Man of Many Talents* (1980). He died in New York City on September 22, 1957. During his years abroad, the novels *Going Native* (1940), *Mad Grandeur* (1941), and *Mr. Petunia* (1945) were published, as well as an autobiography *It Isn't that Time of Year at All* (1954) and books of essays and reminiscence. Some of these, deriving from repetitive homeward glances, lack freshness, but in any case Gogarty's principal claim on our attention is through his poetry. He had emerged from the cloak of anonymity with *An Offering of Swans* (1923), *Wild Apples* (1928), and a larger volume, *Selected Poems* (1933). His *Collected Poems* was published in 1950.

Envious contemporaries thought W. B. Yeats* overvalued Gogarty in the Preface to the *Oxford Book of Modern Verse* (1936) when he called him "one of the great lyric poets of our age." Today, Gogarty is under-valued except by eclectics who are still receptive to themes, moods, and measures influenced by antiquity and the Elizabethans and owing nothing to Pound and Eliot. The future will surely bring redress, with adequate appreciation of Gogarty's exquisite lyrics and of epigrams worthy of the *Greek Anthology*.

A. N. Jeffares remarks in "Oliver St. John Gogarty, Irishman" (*The Circus Animals,* 1970) that the volume *Collected Poems* contains what "would be considered a dangerous spread of subject by some of our contemporary critics who confuse solemnity with seriousness." Vivian Mercier has written perceptively of Gogarty in *Poetry* (1958, 93, 35); he regards "Leda and the Swan" as a masterpiece of great originality. David R. Clark contributes an analysis of "The Crab Tree" in *Lyric Resonance* (1972); he selects "Ringsend" as deserving of Yeats' high praise and disagrees with both Mercier's and Jeffares's assessment of this poem. A fuller critical evaluation is offered by James F. Carens in *Surpassing Wit* (1979).

The infinite range of personal tastes helps to explain the irreconcilable judgments on Gogarty. One should perhaps turn to a nonacademic opinion. The late William Doolin, an erudite medical editor, made the enthusiastic affirmation (*The Lancet,* October 5, 1957) that Gogarty's lyrics will be remembered "so long as there are men to quote them."

J. B. LYONS

WORKS: *Hyperthuleana.* Dublin: Printed by F. J. Walker, at the Gaelic Press, 1916. (Poems); *Blight, the Tragedy of Dublin,* with Joseph O'Connor, under the pseudonyms of Alpha and Omega. Dublin: Talbot, 1917; *The Ship and Other Poems.* Dublin: Talbot, 1918; *An Offering of Swans.* Dublin: Cuala, 1923; London: Eyre & Spottiswoode, [1934?]. (Poems); *To My Mother . . . 1924.*

GOLDEN, FRANK

Prize ode, written by Gogarty, with music by Louis O'Brien. Dublin: Pigott, [1924]; *Wild Apples.* Dublin: Cuala, 1928, 1930; New York: J. Cape & H. Smith, [ca. 1929]. (Poems); *Selected Poems.* New York: Macmillan, 1933, published in U.K. as *Others to Adorn.* London: Rich & Cowan, 1938; *As I Was Going Down Sackville Street.* London: Rich & Cowan; New York: Reynal & Hitchcock, 1937. (Reminiscences); *I Follow Saint Patrick.* London: Rich & Cowan; New York: Reynal & Hitchcock, 1938; London: Constable, 1950; *Elbow Room.* Dublin: Cuala, 1929; New York: Duell, Sloan & Pearce, 1940. (Poems); *Tumbling in the Hay.* London: Constable; New York: Reynal & Hitchcock, 1939. (Novel); *Going Native.* New York: Duell, Sloan & Pearce, 1940; London: Constable, 1941. (Novel); *Mad Grandeur.* Philadelphia & New York: J. B. Lippincott, [1941]; London: Constable, 1943. (Novel); *Mr. Petunia.* New York: Creative Age, [1945]; London: Constable, 1946. (Novel); *Perennial.* London: Constable, 1946. (Poetry); *Mourning Becomes Mrs. Spendlove, and Other Portraits Grave and Gay.* New York: Creative Age, [1948]. (Stories and essays); *Rolling Down the Lea.* London: Constable, 1950; *Intimations.* New York: Abelard, [1950]. (Essays); *The Collected Poems of Oliver St. John Gogarty.* London: Constable, 1951; New York: Devin-Adair, [1954]; *It Isn't This Time of Year at All!* London: MacGibbon & Kee; Garden City, N.Y.: Doubleday, 1954. (Autobiographical); *Unselected Poems.* Baltimore: Contemporary, 1954; *Start from Somewhere Else; An Exposition of Wit and Humour, Polite and Perilous.* Garden City, N.Y.: Doubleday, 1955; *The Plays of Oliver St. John Gogarty,* James F. Carens, ed. Newark, Del.: Proscenium, 1971; *Many Lines to Thee,* James F. Carens, ed. Dublin: Dolmen, 1971. (Letters). REFERENCES: Carens, James F. "Four Revival Figures: Lady Gregory, A.E. (George W. Russell), Oliver St. John Gogarty, and James Stephens." In *Anglo-Irish Literature, a Review of Research,* Richard J. Finneran, ed. New York: Modern Language Association of America, 1976; Carens, James F. *Surpassing Wit: Oliver St. John Gogarty, His Poetry and His Prose.* Dublin: Gill & Macmillan, 1979; Lyons, J. B. *Oliver St. John Gogarty.* Lewisburg, Pa.: Bucknell University Press, 1976; Lyons, J. B. *Oliver St. John Gogarty: The Man of Many Talents: A Biography.* Dublin: Blackwater, [1980]; O'Connor, Ulick. *Oliver St. John Gogarty: A Poet and His Time.* London: Jonathan Cape, 1964.

GOLDEN, FRANK (1957–   ), poet. Born in Dublin.

WORKS: *In Partial Settlement.* [New York]: Wiffle, [1987]. (Poetry pamphlet); *On Route to Leameneh.* Dublin: Raven Arts, [1990]; *The Two Women of Aganatz.* Dublin: Wolfhound, 1994.

GOLDSMITH, OLIVER (1728–1774), man of letters. Goldsmith is one of Ireland's greatest contributions to English literature. He was the second son and fifth child of a clergyman, and was born at Pallas, near Ballymahon, County Longford, on November 10, 1728. He entered Trinity College, Dublin, on June 11, 1744, and was a contemporary though probably not an acquaintance of Edmund Burke* at that time. (Statues of the two eminent alumni now stand flanking the entrance gates to Trinity in College Green.) After a rackety and impoverished college career, Goldsmith received his B.A. on February 27, 1749. He then began his travels, studied medicine at Edinburgh, and wandered around the Continent, picking up a living as best he could. In 1756, he reached London and embarked upon a literary career which involved him in much hack writing as well as in the production of several minor but enduring masterpieces in several genres. His poems "The Traveller" and "The Deserted Village," his essays in *The Bee* and *The Citizen of the World,* his novel *The Vicar of Wakefield,* and his comedy *She Stoops to Conquer* were among the happiest productions of their day and have continued to charm and delight readers and audiences ever since.

The clearest picture of Goldsmith is probably in Boswell's *Life of Johnson*. Boswell can hardly be exempted from the charge of painting Goldsmith's foibles in bold strokes, but undoubtedly Goldsmith was one of the most feckless, if lovable, of men.

The Irish influence in Goldsmith is small, although it has been justly pointed out that the description of Sweet Auburn in "The Deserted Village" owes much to Goldsmith's memories of his native Lissoy.

He died in London on April 4, 1774, much mourned by his friends. As a counter to Boswell's picture of Goldsmith as the consummate booby, it might be noted that his intimate friends included the most eminent men of the day— Burke, Reynolds, and Dr. Johnson.

WORKS: *New Essays by Oliver Goldsmith*. R. S. Crane, ed. Chicago: University of Chicago Press, 1927; *The Collected Letters of Oliver Goldsmith*. Katherine Balderston, ed. Cambridge: Cambridge University Press, 1928; *Collected Works of Oliver Goldsmith*. Arthur Friedman, ed. 5 vols. Oxford: Clarendon, 1966. REFERENCES: Bloom, Harold, ed. *Oliver Goldsmith*. New York: Chelsea, 1987; Boswell, James. *The Life of Samuel Johnson*. G. B. Hill, ed. Revised, L. C. Powell. 6 vols. Oxford: Oxford University Press, 1939–1950; Ginger, John. *The Notable Man: The Life and Times of Oliver Goldsmith*. London: Hamish Hamilton, 1977; Hopkins, Robert. *The True Genius of Oliver Goldsmith*. Baltimore: Johns Hopkins University Press, 1969; Kirk, Clara M. *Oliver Goldsmith*. New York: Twayne, 1967; Lyons, J. B. *The Mystery of Oliver Goldsmith's Medical Degree*. Blackrock: Carraig Books, 1978; Lucy, Sean, ed. *Goldsmith: The Gentle Master*. Cork: Cork University Press, 1984; Mikhail, E. H., ed. *Goldsmith: Interviews and Recollections*. New York: St. Martin's, 1993; Quintana, Ricardo. *Goldsmith: A Georgian Study*. New York: Macmillan, 1967/ London: Weidenfeld & Nicolson, 1969; Rousseau, George Sebastian, ed. *Goldsmith, the Critical Heritage*. London & Boston: Routledge & Kegan Paul, 1974; Scott, Temple (pseud. of J. H. Isaac). *Oliver Goldsmith Bibliographically and Biographically Considered*. New York: Bowling Green, 1928; Sells, A. Lytton. *Oliver Goldsmith, His Life and Works*. London: Allen & Unwin/New York: Barnes & Noble, 1974; Swarbrick, Andrew, ed. *The Art of Oliver Goldsmith*. London: Vision/ Totowa, N.J.: Barnes & Noble, 1984; Taylor, Richard C. *Goldsmith as Journalist*. Rutherford, N.J.: Fairleigh Dickinson University Press, 1993; Wardle, Ralph M. *Oliver Goldsmith*. Lawrence: University of Kansas Press/London: Constable, 1957; Woods, Samuel H., Jr. *Oliver Goldsmith: A Reference Guide*. Boston: Hall, 1982; Worth, Katherine. *Sheridan and Goldsmith*. New York: St. Martin's, 1992; Zack, Wolfgang. "Oliver Goldsmith on Ireland and the Irish: Personal Views, Shifting Attitudes, Literary Stereotypes" in *Studies in Anglo-Irish Literature*. Heinz Kosok, ed. Bonn: Bouvier, 1982.

GORE-BOOTH, EVA [SELENA] (1870–1926), poet and verse dramatist. Gore-Booth was born at Lissadell, County Sligo, on May 22, 1870, the third child of a prominent Anglo-Irish landlord and the younger sister of Countess Constance Markievicz (1868–1927), the nationalist. Of the sisters, W. B. Yeats* wrote one of his finest poems, "In Memory of Eva Gore-Booth and Con Markievicz" (1927).

While her older sister Constance was most dramatically engaged in the major Irish social and political questions of the day, Eva spent her life much less flamboyantly as a social worker in Manchester. In her quiet but useful and busy life, she found time to write enough poems and verse dramas to fill nearly 650 pages when they were posthumously collected. She was not actively engaged in the Irish Literary Revival, but she was certainly much influenced by it. One of her verse dramas, *Unseen Kings,* about Cuchullain, was considered for production by the Irish National Theatre Society but was finally rejected because it was technically impossible to manage certain of the play's requirements, such as birds flying across the stage. Gore-Booth's poetic plays were really closet dramas, but both they and many of her poems were impelled by a strong feeling for her country. Unfortunately, she was influenced most by the Celtic Twilight* school of Irish writing. Hence, although she is always graceful, she is usually conventional. Like that other mystic AE,* her poems seem dully similar, but also like AE, she can occasionally startle with a tersely controlled passage. For instance, from "The Body to the Soul":

> You were the moonlight, I lived in the sun;
> Could there ever be peace between us twain?
> I sought the Many, you seek the One,
> You are the slayer, I am the slain.

Or the last stanza of "Three Ways of Love":

> Love that is Life and Light,
> Radiance, reflected far
> From the million mirrors of night—
> The Love of the Sun for a Star.

She died in Hampstead on June 30, 1926.

WORKS: *Poems of Eva Gore-Booth,* with a biographical introduction by Esther Roper. London: Longmans, Green, 1929. (Collected works); *The Buried Life of Deirdre.* London: Longmans, 1930; *The Plays.* F. S. Lapisardi, ed. San Francisco: E. M. Text, 1991. REFERENCE: Lewis, Gifford. *Eva Gore-Booth and Esther Roper.* London, Sydney & Wellington: Pandora, 1988.

GORMAN, MICHAEL

WORK: *Up She Flew.* Salmon: Galway, 1991. (Poetry).

GRATTAN, HENRY (1746–1820), orator, politician, and lawyer. Grattan was born in Dublin on July 3, 1746. He was the moving spirit of the Irish Parliament from 1782 until it dissolved itself by the Act of Union in 1800. He was also one of the most eloquent orators of his day. Lecky* the historian has probably given the last word on Grattan's language:

The eloquence of Grattan in his best days was in some respects perhaps the finest that has been heard in either country since the time of Chatham. Considered simply as a debater he was certainly inferior to Fox and Pitt, and perhaps to Sheridan; but he combined two of the very highest qualities of a great orator to a degree that was almost unexampled. No British orator except Chatham had an equal power of firing an educated audience with an intense enthusiasm, or of animating and inspiring a nation. No British orator except Burke had an equal power of sowing his speeches with profound aphorisms, and associating transient questions with eternal truths. His thoughts naturally crystallized into epigrams; his arguments were condensed with such admirable force and clearness that they assumed almost the appearance of axioms; and they were often interspersed with sentences of concentrated poetic beauty, which flashed upon the audience with all the force of sudden inspiration, and which were long remembered and repeated.

Grattan died in London on June 4, 1820, and was buried against his wishes in Westminster Abbey. His flamboyant statue, however, stands in College Green opposite the old House of Parliament.

WORKS: *The Speeches of the Rt. Hon. Henry Grattan.* D. O. Madden, ed. Dublin: James Duffy, 1853. REFERENCE: McHugh, Roger. *Henry Grattan.* Dublin: Talbot/London: Duckworth, 1936.

GRAVES, ALFRED PERCEVAL (1846–1931), poet. Graves, the son of the Protestant bishop of Limerick, was born in Dublin on July 22, 1846. He was educated in England and at Trinity College, Dublin, but he lived most of his life in London and was an official of the Board of Education. He was a frequent and fluent author of sentimental and humorous verse, much of it set to Irish airs. His most famous piece is the rollicking "Father O'Flynn." Graves also wrote the libretto of a one-act opera, *The Postbag,* which was subtitled "A Lesson in Irish." The music was composed and arranged from old Irish airs by Michele Esposito, and was presented at the Gaiety Theatre, Dublin, in March 1902. Although received with little enthusiasm, the piece was one of the earliest of the very few attempts at an Irish opera.

Graves was a member of a talented writing family, the most notable of which is his son, the English poet and novelist Robert Graves. (Incidentally, Robert Graves once remarked, "Yeats'* father once confided to my father: 'Willie has found a very profitable little by-path in poetry'. . . .") Alfred Perceval Graves died in Harlech, North Wales, on December 27, 1931.

WORKS: *Songs of Killarney.* London, 1873; *Irish Songs and Ballads.* Manchester: A. Ireland, 1880; ed., *Songs of Irish Wit and Humour.* London: Chatto & Windus, 1884; *Father O'Flynn and Other Irish Lyrics.* London: Swan Sonnenschein, 1889; ed., *The Irish Song Book.* London: Unwin, 1894; *The Postbag: A Lesson in Irish.* Libretto by Graves, music by M. Esposito. London: Boosey, [1902]; *The Irish Poems of Alfred Perceval Graves.* Dublin: Maunsel/London: Unwin, 1908; with W. W. Keene, *Lyrics from "The Absentee,"* an Irish Play in Two Acts. London: Women's Printing Society, [1908]; *An Irish Fairy Book.* London: Unwin, [1909]/London: A. & C. Black, 1938; *Poems for Infants and Juniors.* London: Sir Isaac Pitman, [1910]; ed., *The Poetry Readers.* London: Horace Marshall, [1911]; ed., *The Golden Dawn Reader.* London: James Nisbet, [1911–1917]; *Irish Literary and Musical Studies.* London: Elkin Mathews, 1913; ed., *The Book of Irish Poetry.* London: Unwin, [1914]; with Guy Pertwee, *The Reciter's Treasury of Irish Verse and Prose.* London: Routledge, [1915]; *A Celtic Psaltery.* London: S. P. C. K., 1917. (Translations from the Irish and Welsh; *Songs of the Gael.* Dublin: Talbot, [1925]; *Irish Doric in Song and Story.* London: Unwin, 1926; ed., *The Celtic Song Book.* London: E. Benn, 1928. (Folk songs); *To Return to All That.* London, Toronto: Jonathan Cape, 1930. (Autobiography); *Lives of the British and Irish Saints.* London & Glasgow: Collins' Clear-Type Press, [1934].

GRAVES, ARNOLD FELIX (1847–1930), poet. Graves was born in Dublin on November 17, 1847, into one of the most distinguished families of nine-teenth-century Anglo-Irish society. His father was Charles Graves, bishop of Limerick. Arnold was the third son. Both of his older brothers were knighted, and the second brother was Sir Alfred Perceval Graves,* the author and father of Robert Graves. His sister, Ida, married Admiral Sir Richard Poore and wrote her memoirs under the title *Recollections of an Admiral's Wife.* Arnold was educated at Windemere College and Trinity College, Dublin. He began his studies at Trinity when he was only sixteen on July 1, 1864, the same day as his more famous elder brother Alfred. At Trinity, Arnold outshone Alfred in both academics and athletics, taking a first-class honours degree in mathematics, serving as captain of the university's football team, and playing cricket for Ireland from 1865 to 1868. After taking his degree in 1868, he intended to serve in the colonial administration of Britain's Indian colonies. He passed the first exam for the "Indian Civil" with one of the highest scores on record but failed the law section of the second exam because of an attack of opthalmia. After this "failure," Graves devoted himself to charities and educational ventures in Ireland, serving as founder, organizer, and benefactor for the City of Dublin Technical Schools, the Pembroke Technical Schools, the Technical Education Association, the Irish Artisan's Association, the Irish Industries Association, the Royal Society for the Training and Employment of Women, and the City of Dublin Libraries Committee. He married Constance Weatherley, and they had four sons and one daughter. Three of his children died in the First World War.

His reputation as a writer suffers from comparison with his more famous relatives, and in truth only *Clytaemnestra* (1903) warrants any sustained critical attention. It is an adaptation of the Greek story based largely on the *Choephori* and *Electra,* written in verse that is readable and unaffected. Graves changes the original story to comment on early twentieth-century British society, having Orestes witness as a young man, rather than as a child, his father's murder and having him accidentally kill his mother. Significantly, Graves also attributes his characters' motives and actions to human rather than divine sources. He died on May 24, 1930.

WORKS: *Prince Patrick: A Fairy Tale.* London: Downey, 1898; *Clytaemnestra.* London: Longmans, 1903. (Verse tragedy); *The Long Retreat, and Other Doggerel.* London: John Murray, 1915; *The Turn of the Tide.* London: John Murray, 1916. (Poetry); *Healthy, Wealthy and Wise.* London: Methuen, 1925. (Nonfiction).

GRAY, TONY (1922–), novelist, journalist, and nonfiction writer. Gray was born in Dublin and worked for twenty years for the *Irish Times,* succeeding Brian Inglis and Patrick Campbell* in writing the popular "Irishman's Diary" column. In 1959, he moved to London, worked for the *Daily Mirror,* wrote television scripts, several novels, and several useful nonfictional books, including *The Irish Answer* (1966), *The Orange Order* (1972), and *Ireland This Century* (1994).

PRINCIPAL WORKS: *Starting for Tomorrow.* London: Heinemann, 1965. (Novel); *The Irish Answer: An Anatomy of Modern Ireland.* London: Heinemann, 1966; *The Real Professionals.* London: Heinemann, [1966]. (Novel); *Gone the Time.* London: Heinemann, 1967. (Novel); *The Last Laugh.* London: Heinemann, 1972. (Novel); *The Orange Order.* London: Bodley Head, 1972; *Psalms and Slaughter: A Study in Bigotry.* London: Heinemann, 1972; *Fleet Street Remembered.*

London: Heinemann, 1990; *"Mr. Smyllie, Sir."* Dublin: Gill & Macmillan, 1991; *Europeople.* London: Macdonald, 1992; *Ireland This Century.* London: Little, Brown, 1994.

GREACEN, ROBERT (1920–   ), poet. Greacen was born in Derry on October 24, 1920, and was educated at the Methodist College, Belfast, and at Trinity College, Dublin. He married the critic Patricia Hutchins and worked in England as a teacher. In the mid-1980s, he returned to Ireland and settled in Dublin. In 1990, he remarked, "Before I was 21 I had poems in *The Bell** and *Horizon.* . . . I was in the poetry business. . . . In my mid-thirties I ditched poetry. Or did poetry ditch me? The reasons are too complex to go into here. Unexpectedly at fifty plus I felt the urge again and created the character Captain Fox. For nearly twenty years I've been writing poems again."

In the 1940s, he published two volumes of poetry, but no further volumes appeared until 1975. His 1940 poems are extremely various in style, ranging from the tightly formal to the loosely casual. Such poems as "Written on the Sense of Isolation in War-time Ireland" are almost Yeatsian; others, such as "Chorus of Irresponsibles," "The Kingdom Shall Come," and "On My Arm Your Drowsy Head," are quite reminiscent of Auden. These tightly controlled pieces strike one as much better than the freer "The Poet Answers" or "Lament for France." At his best, Greacen writes in sharply etched images and strong phrasing that make many of his short pieces, such as "Through the Red Canyon" or "The Hopeless Man," cling in the memory. His 1975 volume, *A Garland for Captain Fox,* is a sequence of poems that characterize a shady but civilized wheeler-dealer. The book is even more notable than the early books for its colloquial ease and freshness of diction. His *Collected Poems 1944–1994* won the *Irish Times* Literature Prize for Poetry in 1995.

WORKS: Ed., *Poems from Ulster.* (Belfast: [Erskine Mayne], 1942; ed., with Alex Comfort, *Lyra: An Anthology of New Lyrics.* Billerclay: Gray Walls, 1944); ed., *Northern Harvest.* Belfast: Derrick MacCord, [1944]. (Anthology of Ulster writing); *One Recent Evening.* London: Favil, 1944. (Poetry); ed., *Irish Harvest.* Dublin: New Frontiers, 1946; *The Undying Day.* [London]: Falcon, [1948]. (Poetry); ed., with Valentin Iremonger, *Contemporary Irish Poetry.* London: Faber, [1949]; *The World of C. P. Snow.* London: Scorpion, 1952; *The Art of Noel Coward.* Aldington, Kent: Hand & Flower, [1953]; *Even without Irene.* Dublin: Dolmen, 1969/rev. & enlarged, Belfast: Lagan, 1995. (Autobiographical); *A Garland for Captain Fox.* Dublin: Gallery, 1975. (Poetry); *I, Brother Stephen.* Dublin: St. Bueno's hand-printed Limited Editions, [1978]. (Poetry pamphlet); *Young Mr. Gibbon.* Dublin: Profile, 1979. (Poetry); *A Bright Mask: New and Selected Poems.* Dublin: Dedalus, 1985; *Carnival at the River.* Dublin: Dedlaus, 1990; *Brief Encounters: Literary Dublin and Belfast in the 1940s.* [Dublin]: Cathair Books, 1991. (Short memoir); *The Only Emperor.* Belfast; Lapwing, 1994. (Poetry pamphlet); *Collected Poems 1944–1994.* Belfast: Lagan, 1995. REFERENCES: Brown, Terence. "Robert Greacen and Roy McFadden: Apocalypse and Survival." In *Northern Voices: Poets from Ulster.* Dublin: Gill & Macmillan, 1975, pp. 128–140; Brennan, Rory, ed. *Robert Greacen: A Tribute at the Age of Seventy.* Dublin: Poetry Ireland, 1990. (Pamphlet).

GREEN, ALICE STOPFORD (1847–1929), historian. Alice Sophia Amelia Stopford was one of nine children born in Kells to Edward Adderley Stopford, archdeacon of Meath, and Anne Duke Stopford, a native of County Sligo. Alice was educated in the strongly evangelical household by a series of governesses. She developed a serious eye problem about 1860 and spent a year in a darkened room and a further seven years without reading. Her eyes continued to be troublesome throughout her life. In 1873, her family moved to Dublin, and she persuaded the College of Science to allow her to attend lectures in physics, provided she was accompanied by another woman. In 1877, she married John Richard Green, the English historian. He was the perfect tutor for her, and she the perfect nurse and research assistant for him. He died in 1882, leaving her, however, financially secure. For the next thirty-five years, she lived in London, became deeply interested in Africa, and was a member of the Africa Society.

Green moved to Dublin in 1918, remaining there until her death. She helped to found the School of Irish Studies and concentrated her attention on Ireland's political developments and the cultural revival. She strongly believed that the Irish people before the Norman conquest were lawmakers and law-abiding, which placed her in opposition to the British historians of her day. She further believed that the binding element of Irish society was spiritual, not economic. Thus, she was extremely concerned with the cultural aspects of Irish nationalism. Her volume *The Making of Ireland and Its Undoing* (1908) was criticized for her use of early Irish literature as historical sources. She was, however, one of the first to take a revisionist stance toward the history of Ireland as disseminated by British historians. She was completely unable to understand the Ulster Unionists' views. Her pamphlet *Ourselves Alone in Ulster* (1918) charges the Unionists with creating their own version of Sinn Féin to ensure their economic interests were protected during the political upheavals. Her home was raided several times due to her political stance, and she was reported to have been greatly amused when two bags of shot were confiscated. She had used them for paperweights. She died on May 28, 1929, in Dublin, after a short illness.

Her 1913 volume, *A Woman's Place in the World of Letters,* is a study of the nature of women writers and scholars. She cites Catherine Macauley as the first woman historian and states that the history of women as writers is cloaked in reluctance and pseudonyms, "a very complicated story, this story of precaution and disguise." Women, she believed, were creatures of strong curiosity and natural anarchy who must learn the history and philosophy of men in order to be successful interpreters of their own experiences. The modern woman was reluctant to enter the fields of history, theology, or philosophy, because "for her the world has practically no past—it begins here and now where she stands."

ANNE COLMAN

PRINCIPAL WORKS: *The Making of Ireland and Its Undoing.* London: Macmillan, 1908; *Irish Nationality.* London: Williams & Norgate, 1911; *The Old Irish World.* Dublin: Gill/London: Macmillan, 1912; *Woman's Place in the World of Letters.* London: Macmillan, 1913; *Loyalty and Disloyalty: What It Means to Ireland.* 1918; *Ourselves Alone in Ulster.* Dublin & London: Maunsel, 1918; *The Irish National Tradition.* Dublin: Maunsel, 1921; *The Government of Ireland.* London: Labour Publishing 1921; *The Irish and the Armada.* 1921; *A History of the Irish State to 1014.* London: Macmillan, 1925; *Irish History Studies.* Six parts. Dublin: Browne & Nolan, 1926. (School texts). REFERENCE: McDowell, R. B. *Alice Stopford Green; A Passionate Historian.* Dublin: Allen Figgis, 1967.

GREEN, F[REDERICK] L[AWRENCE] (1902–1953), English novelist. Green was born in Portsmouth in 1902 and died in Bristol on April 14, 1953. In 1932, he settled in Belfast and spent much of the rest of his life there. His most valuable contribution to Irish literature is his 1945 novel *Odd Man Out,* which is something of a Graham Greene-like entertainment or thriller with distinctly serious overtones. The story tells of the aftermath of an IRA raid, in which the leader is gravely wounded and wanders, dying, around the city as both the police and his friends attempt to find him. Green's primary interest is not the recreation of an historical situation but rather a probing into more elemental questions of how men should regard each other. Although the narrative interest of the book is considerable and the characterization is at least adequate, *Odd Man Out* is not up to the standards of a Graham Greene, for it is consistently flawed by florid and pretentious writing, such as: "Whereas it was an immortal soul in its raiment of flesh and bone. This was a curious phenomenon which has emerged from aeons of life on the world. The body was sustained by certain known processes. But the forces which supported the soul were secret and unfathomable." The quite faithful film of the book, for which Green and R. C. Sheriff wrote the script, is considered one of the finest cinematic treatments of an Irish subject, and probably ranks with the films *Man of Aran* and *The Informer.* It contains some excellent performances by Irish actors, among whom are W. G. Fay, Maureen Delany, Denis O'Dea, Cyril Cusack, and a rare and superb film appearance by F. J. McCormick.

WORKS: *Julius Penton.* London: John Murray, 1934; *On the Night of the Fire.* London: Michael Joseph, 1939; *The Sound of Winter.* London: Michael Joseph, 1940; *Give Us the World.* London: Michael Joseph, 1941; *Music in the Park.* London: Michael Joseph, 1942; *A Song for the Angels.* London: Michael Joseph, 1943; *On the Edge of the Sea.* London: Michael Joseph, 1944; *Odd Man Out.* London: Michael Joseph, 1945; *A Flask for the Journey.* London: Michael Joseph, 1946; *A Fragment of Glass.* London: Michael Joseph, 1947; *Mist on the Waters.* London: Michael Joseph, 1948; *Clouds in the Wind.* London: Michael Joseph, 1950; with R. C. Sheriff, *Odd Man Out* in *Three British Screenplays.* Roger Manvell, ed. London: Methuen in association with the British Film Academy, 1950, pp. 83–202; *The Magician.* London: Michael Joseph, 1951; *Ambush for the Hunter.* London: Michael Joseph, 1952.

GREENE, ANGELA (fl. 1990s), poet. Greene was born in Dublin and now lives in Drogheda, County Louth. She won the Patrick Kavanagh Award in 1988 and in 1989 was short-listed for the *Sunday Tribune*/Hennessy Literary Award. Her collection *Silence and the Blue Night* (1993) can slide from trite imagery to lush: from "their burning kisses" to a description of a woman's thighs as "bruised poppies," both from "Destiny," the book's first poem. Usually, however, her writing is exact and appropriate for her subject matter, which is mainly the stuff of daily life—raising children, cooking, gardening, looking at pictures, sitting on the seashore. Occasionally she rises to the really striking phrase or idea, such as easing her bones into the universe from "Letting Go." It is basically the phrasing by which Greene's work can be judged or admired, for it is the most formless of free verse, with little even dimly consistent rhythm from line to line. Indeed, one poem, "Recipe," is simply a transcription from a 1935 cookbook, with Greene stopping the lines at major or minor syntactical breaks or, possibly, where it just feels good. Like many of Greene's original pieces, "Recipe" is well written; whether it or her own original work be poetry is another matter.

WORK: *Silence and the Blue Night.* [Swords, Co. Dublin]: Salmon, [1993].

GREGORY, DAME ISABELLA AUGUSTA (1852–1932), playwright and folklorist. Lady Gregory was hailed by Bernard Shaw* as "the greatest living Irishwoman." She was born Isabella Augusta Persse at Roxborough, County Galway, on March 15, 1852. As a playwright, essayist, poet, translator, and editor, she could not have differed more from her proselytizing, unionist, non-literary, gentleman-farming family. Even in childhood she showed her sympathy for the rebel stories and folktales told by her Irish-speaking nurse by collecting Fenian pamphlets and ballad poetry. Later, she established a solid grounding in agrarian economy, forcing the local shopkeepers to cut their prices by setting up in competition on her brother's estate. With her marriage to Sir William Gregory of neighboring Coole on March 4, 1880, she gained access to the political, artistic and social life of Europe. Sir William, thirty-five years her senior, had recently retired as governor of Ceylon but continued to maintain his trusteeship of the National Gallery, his keen interest in the tenant rights for which he had campaigned as member of Parliament for Galway City, and the knowledge of classical literature and antiquities which he shared with his close friend Sir Henry Layard. Married life alternated between London for the season, Coole for the shooting, and travel to India, Ceylon, Egypt, Spain, and Italy. Their only son, William Robert, was born in London in May 1881; Sir William died in March 1892.

By this time, Lady Gregory had already begun her literary career, drawing on her experiences both at home and abroad. Encouraged by Sir William and the poet W. S. Blunt who became a lifelong friend, in 1882 she published a pamphlet defending the Egyptian officer Arabi Bey's revolt against Turkish rule. During the following decades, she campaigned in similar manner for funds for a parish in south London (*Over the River,* 1888 and 1893), support of cottage industries in the west of Ireland (*Gort Industries,* 1896), Irish tax rebates (*A Short Catechism on the Financial Claims of Ireland,* 1898), and against Gladstone's Home Rule bill (*A Phantom's Pilgrimage,* 1893). Although she was constant in her concern that Ireland be sufficiently prepared for the responsibilities of independence, her political beliefs altered radically during the 1890s. In editing her husband's autobiography (1894) and selections from the correspondence of Sir William's grandfather during his years as undersecretary of state for Ireland (*Mr. Gregory's Letter Box 1813–1830*), she laid the foundation both for her own easy, graceful prose style and her determination to rescue Ireland from the English "overgovernment." By 1898, she had become a sufficiently strong nationalist to be involved in the celebrating of the centenary of the 1798 Fenian uprising; three years later, she edited a collection of essays debating literary nationalism (*Ideals in Ireland,* 1901). A combination of social tact and disinterested service enabled her to retain the friendship and active support of such unionist and conservative friends of her late husband as the historian W.E.H. Lecky* and the English diplomat Sir Henry and his wife Enid Layard.

By the 1890s, too, she had begun the collection of folktales and legends of Galway which was to absorb her for the rest of her life, leading to the publication of five volumes of folktales and folk history (*A Book of Saints and Wonders,* 1906; *The Kiltartan History Book,* 1909; *The Kiltartan Wonder Book,* 1910; and the two-volume *Visions and Beliefs in the West of Ireland,* 1920). Although the original impetus for these collections came from her jealousy of W. B. Yeats'* collection of tales for Sligo, *The Celtic Twilight* (1893), it was not until 1896 that she met the poet, who was visiting her neighbor Edward Martyn.* An invitation to Coole led to the lifelong relationship of which Yeats was later to write in his *Memoirs* (1972): "She has been to me mother, friend, sister and brother. I cannot realize the world without her—she brought to my wavering thoughts steadfast nobility." Shortly after her meeting with Yeats, she assisted Douglas Hyde* in founding a Kiltartan branch of the Gaelic League, revived her own earlier desire to learn Irish, and embarked on the ambitious task of translating the epics *Cuchulain of Muirthemne* (1902) and *Gods and Fighting Men* (1904), followed by *The Kiltartan Poetry Book, Translations from the Irish* (1919).

Meanwhile, collaboration with Yeats, Hyde, and Martyn led to the work which was to become Lady Gregory's chief concern: the establishment of an Irish literary theatre. At first considered primarily a fundraiser, she was soon suggesting scenarios for little plays in Irish to Hyde and, while taking dictation, recommending phrases to Yeats. She discovered to her great surprise that the years of listening to good talk, directing affairs in London, Roxborough, and Coole, and researching historical manuscripts in the Royal Irish Academy and the British Museum had sharpened her ear for dialogue, developed clarity of argument, and provided keen insight into character and action. So, at the age of fifty she saw produced the first of her forty plays, most of them written in the Kiltartan dialect which, along with the language of Hyde's *Love Songs of Connacht* (1893), was to offer John Millington Synge* the key he, too, was seeking. From now on her interests—restoring the language and literature of Ireland to its rightful esteem, preparing the country for political independence, and freeing art from the bondage of patriotism and propaganda—merged and led to the foundation, first with Yeats, Martyn, and George Moore,* and later with Yeats, Synge, and the Fay brothers, of the Abbey Theatre* movement.

From the beginning, Lady Gregory had hoped for a touring company which would carry plays based on Irish history and legend to all parts of the country. Her two volumes of folk-history plays, even her later children's wonder plays, were written with that goal in mind. But the plays most frequently associated with her name, the one-act comedies, provided what she was later to refer to in *Our Irish Theatre* (1913) as "the base of realism" balancing the apex of her colleagues' poetic dramas. In these plays, she developed a genius for comedy which is almost eighteenth century in the balanced precision and deliberate avoidance of sentiment. Set in the mythical township of Cloon, yet readily identifiable as the west of Ireland, her characters thrive and act upon "the talk." *Spreading the News,* the title of one of her most delightful comedies, is also an apt description of the life force pervading the "Gregorian universe." Like Don Quixote, one of her favorite literary models (and the subject of her last play, *Sancho's Master,* 1927), her characters assert, believe, and thereupon act, frequently leading to a conundrum of argument and activity which involves the entire community. When still more comedy was required, not surprisingly she turned to Molière. Her adaptation into Kiltartan of *The Doctor in Spite of Himself* (1906), *The Rogueries of Scapin* (1908), *The Miser* (1909), and *The Would-Be Gentleman* (1926) were spirited successes on the Abbey stage.

To one intensely devoted to preserving the history and folklore of her country, the temptation to mythologize which she observed in her countrymen did not always lead to lighthearted comedy. One of her earliest plays, *The Rising of the Moon* (1904), combined the surprised self-commentary of her comic characterizations with the revolutionary spirit of the folk ballad. Her own favorite three-act play, *The Image* (1909), celebrates the leader who follows his heart-secret to tribulation and certain defeat. *The Deliverer* (1911) looks back not only to Moses, but also to the defeat and rejection of Charles Stewart Parnell; *The Story Brought by Brigit* (1924) is a sombre reinterpretation of the passion play as seen through the eyes of one of Ireland's saintly "traveling women." Her strangely powerful but unsuccessful mystery play *Dave* (1927) explores the dark side of the dreamer without the sentiment clinging to *The Travelling Man* (begun with Yeats as early as 1902). Yet, although many of her folk-history plays are aptly labeled "tragic comedies," she wrote few tragedies, the most successful being the one-act threnody *The Gaol Gate* (1906), rising simply, like the keen, to a passionate outburst of heroic grief. Of *Dervorgilla* (1907) Frank O'Connor* wrote in *The Saturday Review* (December 10, 1966): "Her last great speech is as noble as anything in Irish literature." Yeats commented in his journal of her first, much revised history play, *Kincora* (1909): "This play gives me the greatest joy—colour, speech, all has music, and the scenes with the servants make one feel curiously intimate and friendly with those great people who otherwise would be far off—mere figures of speech." More frequently, the mixture of mythmaking and mischief is introduced under the guise of laughter. Her fondness for the cracked idealist and personal idiosyncrasy led to the harmless worlds of *The Jester* (1923, a graceful tribute to her good friend Bernard Shaw), *Hyacinth Halvey* (1906, her version of the paradox of Synge's *Playboy*), and

The Full Moon (1910, drawing on the character Yeats would later mythologize as Crazy Jane).

In her seventy-fifth year, Lady Gregory decided to stop writing plays, but she remained a staunch help to the Abbey Theatre as director, administrator, fundraiser, teacher, and critic. She was chiefly responsible for the discovery of Sean O'Casey* and defender of the rights, both at home and on tours to Britain and America, of many another playwright whose work she may have personally disliked. But more and more of her energy, especially after the death of her son during World War I, was taken up with unsuccessfully persuading the British government to honor the unwitnessed codicil to his will prepared by her nephew Hugh Lane, leaving his collection of Impressionist paintings to Ireland. One of her last stage pieces was the monlogue "The Old Woman Remembers," recited on the Abbey stage on December 31, 1923, by her favorite performer Sara Allgood. Her final publication during her lifetime, in 1931, was a return to her starting place, a spare and powerful evocation of the house, library, and lands of Coole. A selection from her journals edited by Lennox Robinson* was published in 1946. Forty years after her death, the typescript of *Seventy Years,* the autobiography she worked on with the help of Yeats, was discovered and subsequently published by Colin Smythe in his Coole series of her collected works.

The complexity of Lady Gregory's activities and interests over an energetic lifetime makes it difficult to define her clearly. Having begun her writing career as a strong unionist, she then courageously defended Synge's *Playboy of the Western World* against overzealous patriots and Shaw's *Shewing-up of Blanco Posnet* against the Castle. Later, she published outspoken articles on the Black and Tan atrocities. A romantic idealist who delighted in her countrymen's "incorrigible genius for myth-making," she continually fought against any trace of sentimentality in her life and her work. She never allowed delicacy of feeling to dull truth in her history plays, yet she did not hesitate to refine and simplify the ancient sagas for drawing room and cabin. An unflinching realist with a keen sense of the practical, she nevertheless wrote what Shaw called one of the best ghost plays he had ever seen (*Shanwalla,* 1915) and with Yeats consulted mediums in an effort to make contact with the spirit of Hugh Lane. Although she was a natural moralist and believed in rigid standards of behavior, she wrote comedies in which a strain of daftness is revealed through horseplay, harmless magic, and innocent shape-changing, as well as near-tragedies based on the themes of conflicting loyalties and the need to follow one's dream despite the consequences. The most flexible and experimental of the early Abbey dramatists, she possessed a strong sense of what was possible on stage and in dialogue, reveling in clarity of action, motive, setting, and characterization. At the same time, she pushed her creations—and frequently her audiences—through the door of wonder into a world ruled by beggar, ballad-maker, and weird messenger. Unless one attempts to reconcile these apparent contradictions, it is dangerously easy to over-simplify both her character and her contribution.

Perhaps the most damaging misconception of all has to do with what George

Moore described in *Hail and Farewell* as "the interdependence of these two minds," Lady Gregory's and Yeats'. Beginning with *Cathleen ni Houlihan* (1902) and *The Stories of Red Hanrahan* (1904) until as late as *King Oedipus* (1928), she helped Yeats with dialogue and sometimes plot. At times the debt is obvious, as in *The Plot of Broth* (1902) and *The Unicorn from the Stars* (1907), but at other times the collaboration extended over so many revisions and such a length of time that identification of contribution becomes impossible. Throughout his lifetime, Yeats never hesitated to acknowledge gracefully the great debt he owed his closest friend and helper. A scribbled note of thanks written on her deathbed movingly records her own tribute to that unique and unbroken partnership. As image-maker herself and helper of countless other workers for Ireland, like her hero Patrick Sarsfield of *The White Cockade* (1905), her name too should be "set in clean letters in the book of the people." She died at Coole Park on May 22, 1932.

ANN SADDLEMYER

WORKS: *Arabi and His Household.* London: Privately printed, 1882; *Over the River.* London: Privately published, 1888/revised 1893; *A Phantom's Pilgrimage; or, Home Ruin,* published anonymously. London: Ridgway, 1893; ed., *The Autobiography of Sir William Gregory.* London: John Murray, 1894; "Ireland, Real and Ideal," *The Nineteenth Century* (November 1898): 770–774; ed., *Mr. Gregory's Letter Box, 1813–1830.* London: Smith, Elder, 1898; ed., *Ideals in Ireland.* London: Unicorn, 1901; *Cuchulain of Muirthemne.* London: John Murray, 1902; *Gods and Fighting Men.* London: John Murray, 1904; *A Book of Saints and Wonders.* Dundrum: Dun Emer, 1906; *The Kiltartan History Book.* Dublin: Maunsel, 1909; *Seven Short Plays.* Dublin: Maunsel, 1909. (Contains *The Rising of the Moon, Spreading the News, Hyacinth Halvey, The Gaol Gate, The Jackdaw, The Travelling Man,* and *The Workhouse Ward*); *The Kiltartan Molière.* Dublin: Maunsel, 1910. (Contains *The Doctor in Spite of Himself, The Rogueries of Scapin,* and *The Miser*); *The Kiltartan Wonder Book.* Dublin: Maunsel, 1910; *Irish Folk History Plays, First Series.* London: Putnam, 1912. (Contains *Kincora, Dervorgilla,* and *Grania*); *Irish Folk History Plays, Second Series.* London: Putnam, 1912. (Contains *The White Cockade, The Canavans,* and *The Deliverer); New Comedies.* New York & London: Putnam, 1913. (Contains *The Full Moon, McDonagh's Wife, The Bogie Men, Damer's Gold,* and *Coats*); *Our Irish Theatre.* London: Putnam, 1913; *The Golden Apple.* London: John Murray, 1916; *The Kiltartan Poetry Book: Translations from the Irish.* London: Putnam, 1919; *Visions and Beliefs in the West of Ireland.* With two essays and notes by W. B. Yeats. 2 vols. London: Putnam, 1920; "A Week in Ireland," *The Nation* (October 16, October 23, November 13, December 4, December 18, 1920); *Hugh Lane's Life and Achievement.* London: John Murray, 1921; *The Image and Other Plays.* London: Putnam, 1922. (Contains also *The Wrens, Shanwalla,* and *Hanrahan's Oath*); *Three Wonder Plays.* London: Putnam, 1923. (Contains *The Dragon, The Jester,* and *Aristotle's Bellows*); *Mirandolina.* London: Putnam, 1924, (After Goldoni); "The Old Woman Remembers," *The Irish Statesman* (March 22, 1924): 40–41; *The Story Brought by Brigit.* London: Putnam, 1924; *A Case for the Return of Sir Hugh Lane's Pictures to Dublin.* Dublin: Talbot, 1926; *On the Racecourse.* London: Putnam, 1926; *Three Last Plays.* London: Putnam, 1928. (Contains *The Would-Be Gentleman, Sancho's Master* and *Dave*); *My First Play: Colman and Guaire.* London: Elkin Mathews & Marot, 1930; *Coole.* Dublin: Cuala, 1931; *Lady Gregory's Journals, 1916–1930.* Lennox Robinson, ed. London: Putnam, 1946; "The Lady Gregory Letters to Sean O'Casey." A. C. Edwards, ed. *Modern Drama* 8 (May 1965): 95–111; "Lady Gregory's Letters to G. B. Shaw." Daniel Murphy, ed. *Modern Drama* 10 (February 1968): 331–345; *Theatre Business: The Correspondence of the Abbey Theatre Directors.* Ann Saddlemyer, ed. Gerrards Cross: Colin Smythe, 1982; *Lady Gregory's Diaries, 1892–1902.* Pethica, James, ed. Gerrards Cross: Colin Smythe, 1995. The complete writings of Lady Gregory, including much formerly unpublished material, can be found in *The Coole Edition of Lady Gregory's Writings.* Colin Smythe & T. R. Henn, general eds. Gerrards Cross: Colin Smythe/New York: Oxford University Press, 1970– . Of particular interest among the volumes published thus far is Lady Gregory's autobiography, *Seventy Years* (1974) and *Lady Gregory's Journals,* Parts 1 & 2 (1978, 1987). REFERENCES: Adams, Hazard. *Lady Gregory.* Lewisburg, Pa.: Bucknell University Press, 1973; Coxhead, Elizabeth. *Lady Gregory: A Literary Portrait.* Revised ed., Gerrards Cross: Colin Smythe, 1966; Gregory, Anne. *Me and Nu: Childhood at Coole.* Gerrards Cross: 1966; Kohfeldt, Mary Lou. *Lady Gregory: The Woman behind the Irish Renaissance.* New York: Atheneum, 1985; Kopper, Edward A. *Lady Gregory: A Review of the Criticism.* Butler, Pa.: Kopper, 1991; Mikhail, E. H., ed. *Lady Gregory: Interviews and Recollections.* Totowa, N.J.: Rowman & Littlefield, 1977; Saddlemyer, Ann. "Augusta Gregory, Irish Nationalist." In *Myth and Reality in Irish Literature.* Joseph Ronsley, ed. Waterloo, Ontario: Wilfrid Laurier University Press, 1977, pp. 29–40; Saddlemyer, Ann. *In Defence of Lady Gregory, Playwright.* Dublin: Dolmen, 1966; Saddlemyer, Ann & Smythe, Colin, eds. *Lady Gregory Fifty Years After.* Gerrards Cross: Colin Smythe, 1987; Smythe, Colin, ed. *Robert Gregory, 1881–1918.* Gerrards Cross: Colin Smythe, 1981; Yeats, William Butler. *Memoirs.* Denis Donoghue, ed. London: Macmillan, 1972.

GREGORY, PADRAIC (1886–1962), poet. Born in Belfast, Gregory became a prolific maker of old-fashioned ballads, often in dialect. His work was simple and unsubtle and often told a story. Fluently conventional in rhythm and rhyme, it had considerable popular appeal.

WORKS: *The Ulster Folk.* London: David Nutt, 1912; *Old World Ballads.* London: David Nutt, 1913; *Love Sonnets.* Belfast: G. M. Harvey, 1914; *Ireland: a Song of Hope and Other Poems.* Dublin: Talbot, 1917; *Ulster Songs and Ballads.* Dublin: Talbot, 1920; *Coming of the Magi: Sacred Drama of the Epiphany.* Dublin: Talbot, 1932; *Complete Collected Ballads of Padraic Gregory (1912–1932).* London: Burns Oates & Washbourne, [1935]; *Complete Collected Ulster Songs and Ballads.* Belfast: W. Mullan, 1959.

GRENNAN, EAMON (1941–   ), poet. Grennan, born on November 13, 1941, in Dublin, attended the Cistercian College in Roscrea and then went to University College, Dublin, where he earned a B.A. in 1963 and an M.A. in 1964. He completed a Ph.D. in English at Harvard in 1973, taught at City University of New York and then at Vassar, where he is now professor of English. He received a Guggenheim Fellowship in 1995.

His three major volumes—*Wildly for Days* (1983), *What Light There Is* (1987), and *As If It Matters* (1991)—have been published in the United States and Ireland. His translations of Leopardi appeared in 1995. He has published criticism on Shakespeare, Spenser, and Chaucer and written extensively on Irish poetry, particularly on Yeats,* Kavanagh,* MacNeice,* and Kinsella.*

One reviewer describes Grennan's work as not experimental; he offers no technical surprises but draws on, and delights in, the traditional sources of language. He takes a "painterly" approach to poetry, using adjectives of color and images of light effects. Grennan admires James Wright's "pure, clear word" but not his austerity. As Seamus Deane* said of Patrick Kavanagh, his work displays "fidelity to the miracle of the actual." Grennan, in fact, cites Kavanagh as the poet who made contemporary Irish poetry possible.

Grennan's frequent choice of relationship and domesticity as themes leads him to be compared with Eavan Boland* and Seamus Heaney.* Throughout his three chief volumes and in many uncollected poems, we see an illusory security, a human figure in a darkening landscape, and we feel the inevitability of extinction. In "Breaking Points," the poet discovers that we "make and break" the world for ourselves, "flail our way to freedom of a sort" to find ourselves alone, bewildered, in the ruins of a life that looks as if it were the result of will.

Grennan's poems about separation are concerned not with nationality but mostly with children growing up. When he turns to Irish politics, as in "Sea Dog," his choice of metaphor reveals his focus on the ordinary. Surrounded by children playing on a beach, Grennan discovers the carcass of a dog noosed and drowned by its owner and describes with devastating precision the betrayal of trust: "Such a neat knot: someone knelt safely down to do it, pushing those ears back / with familiar fingers." The final vision suggests another betrayal: over the scene of innocent play, "a sudden flowering shaft of sunlight / picks out four pale haycocks / saddled in sackcloth," reminiscent of the Four Horsemen of the Apocalypse as well as the four fields of Ireland, still entangled in betrayal and murder.

The organizing principle of *As If It Matters* is not politics but family relationships. Poems about journeys with his son and daughter begin and end the book; in its center we find an elegy to his father. Indeed, Grennan's newest volume contains many elegies and elegy-like poems connected with the death of his mother. It would be misleading, however, to suggest that he provides no optimistic note. The poem that follows the elegy to his father is a meditation on the purpose of art. "The Cave Painters," in the poem of that name, "came to terms / with the given world" and left "something / upright and bright behind them in the dark." In "At Home in Winter," from *What Light There Is,* although the house is threatened with snow and the speaker with worry, he finds solace and inspiration in a sudden moment of understanding. In "Conjunctions," which closes that volume, after enduring the ordeal of separating from his children, he finds not loss or fear but the image of endurance embodied in a fox. The natural world provides hope in a darkening landscape.

A sense of community unifies the poems in Grennan's three volumes. The words "common gound" echo like a refrain in poems such as "Men Roofing," "Four Deer," and "Cows." A sense of common space, spiritual as well as physical, which we share with each other and with the creatures of the natural world, allows us to transcend the visible and temporal and the inevitability of extinction. Grennan's poetry leads us to discover our commonality of experience and feeling.

DEBORAH FLEMING

WORKS: *Wildly for Days.* [Dublin]: Gallery, [1983]; *What Light There Is.* [Dublin]: Gallery, [1987]; *Twelve Poems.* Woodside, Calif.: Occasional Works, 1988. (Poetry pamphlet); *What Light There Is & Other Poems.* San Francisco: North Point, 1989; *As If It Matters.* [Oldcastle, Co. Meath]: Gallery, [1991]/St. Paul: Graywolf, 1992; tr. *Leopardi: Selected Poems.* Dublin: Dedalus, [1995]. REFERENCES: Fleming, Deborah. "The 'Common Ground' of Eamon Grennan."

Éire-Ireland 28 (Winter 1993): 133–149; Tillinghast, Richard. ''Eamon Grennan: To Leave Something Bright and Upright Behind.'' *New England Review* 15 (Spring 1993): 189–195.

GRIERSON, CONSTANTIA (ca. 1705–1732), poet. Grierson was born to the Crawley family, of Graiguenamanagh, County Kilkenny. Her parents were uneducated but had advanced ideas for their era and provided Constantia with the best education allowed by their limited funds. The local minister tutored her briefly, and she taught herself Hebrew, Greek, Latin, and French, before she journeyed to Dublin about 1721, as an apprentice midwife to Dr. Van Lewen. She became friends with Van Lewen's daughter Laetitia, who later became Laetitia Pilkington,* herself a poet. Mary Barber* reportedly tutored Constantia, to some degree, in history, theology, and philosophy. Also, Constantia met George Grierson, a Dublin printer who possessed a substantial library to which he gave her access. Grierson had a virtual monopoly on Bible printing in Ireland, and Constantia became his second wife in 1726.

Constantia wrote poetry in Latin, Greek, and English, but before her death, she burned much of her work, as she felt the pieces were substandard. The poems she wrote for her friends, particularly those to Mrs. Barber, were preserved. She corrected George Grierson's editions of *Terence* (1727) and *Tacitus* (1730), and her work on these editions was widely praised. George Grierson received the patent of King's Printer in Ireland, at the instigation of Lord Carteret, then lord lieutenant of Ireland. Constantia was a member of Swift's* literary circle and was complimented by Swift in a letter to Alexander Pope. She had four children, three of whom died in infancy. Her second son, George, succeeded his father as King's Printer in Dublin but died at the age of twenty-seven, in 1755. Constantia had also died at the age of twenty-seven, on December 2, 1732, following a long and painful illness that probably was tuberculosis.

Her poetry appeared in Mary Barber's *Poems* (1734), in Volume 1 of Laetitia Pilkington's *Memoirs* (1748), and in *Poems by Eminent Ladies* (1755). Her frequently cited poem ''To Miss Laetitia Van Lewen'' celebrates the friendship between the two women poets. A. C. Elias has recently discovered a manuscript notebook containing her published and unpublished writings.

ANNE COLMAN

WORKS: Contained in Mary Barber's *Poems on Several Occasions* (London: C. Rivington, 1734), in Laetitia Pilkington's *Memoirs,* Vol. 1 (Dublin, 1748), and in *Poems by Eminent Ladies* (1755). REFERENCES: Blackburne, E. Owens. *Illustrious Irishwomen.* Vol. 2 (London: Tinsley, 1877); Elias, A. C. ''A Manuscript Book of Constantia Grierson's.'' *Swift Studies* 2 (1987): 33–56; Lonsdale, Roger. *Eighteenth-Century Women Poets.* Oxford: Oxford University Press, 1989; Tucker, Bernard. ''Swift's 'Female Senate.' '' *Irish Studies Review* 7 (Summer 1994): 7–10.

GRIFFIN, GERALD (1803–1840), novelist and man of letters. Griffin, born on December 12, 1803, at Limerick, was the ninth child (and seventh son) of an Irish family with the ancestral name O'Griobhth. The family moved to Fairy Lawn (1810) on the Shannon; then the parents emigrated to Pennsylvania

(1820), and the remaining children moved to Adare and then to Pallas Kenry, which remained Griffin's home in Ireland.

In autumn 1823, Griffin went to London where John Banim* encouraged his writing. He lived in extreme poverty while working as anonymous hack, translator, book reviewer, and parliamentary reporter until 1827 when he became famous for *Holland Tide*. An attack of rheumatism in 1825 left him with recurrent illness the rest of his life.

The year 1829 marked three events: the publication of *The Collegians;* his term as London law student as an alternative to the "fickleness of public literary taste"; and a meeting in Limerick with a Quaker, Mrs. Lydia Fisher, who became "the secret patron of his minstrelsy." Around 1830, his religious habits gained ascendancy over his literary aspirations, and at Pallas Kenry he even began catechizing neighborhood children.

In 1836, he spent some time at Taunton and in Paris. In 1835, Griffin went to Scotland, and on his return he burned his manuscripts preparatory to joining, in September, the Christian Brothers at Dublin. From there he moved to the monastery in Cork, where he died of typhus on June 12, 1840.

Griffin was a romanticist who drew on history for examples of devoted and virtuous women and for heroes who strove for loyalty and honor in the face of conflicting values. His subjects ranged from lycanthropy and self-combustion, to magical folklore and supernatural tales, including a vampire story.

His best remembered works are the song "Aileen Aroon" and the novel *The Collegians* (1829), based on a true account of an Irish colleen who was drowned by her husband so that he might marry a woman of wealth. Now judged by some as the best nineteenth-century Irish novel, it became the play *Colleen Bawn* by Dion Boucicault* and the opera *Lily of Killarney* by Jules Benedict. Its plot reappears in Theodore Dreiser's *American Tragedy.*

Much folklore may be found in *Tales of the Munster Festivals,* which appeared in three volumes under the titles *Holland-Tide* (1827); *Card Drawing, The Half-Sir,* and *Suil Dhuv the Coiner* (1829); and *The Rivals* and *Tracy's Ambition* (1830). He also wrote *The Christian Physiologist* (1830), *Tales of My Neighbourhood* (1835) in three volumes, and *Tales of the Jury Room* (1842). His historical novels are *The Invasion* (1832), set in the eighth century, and *The Duke of Monmouth* (1836), set in 1685. His tragedy *Gisippus* was performed at Drury Lane in 1842. Griffin's *Life and Letters* (1843) was written by his brother Daniel. His known letters and manuscripts are held by the Christian Brothers— "Commonplace Book A" in Dublin and letters in the archives in Rome.

Throughout his fifteen years of writing poems, plays, operas, essays, juvenile tales, stories, and novels, Griffin was caught between the restrictions of religion and the expanse of knowledge that he admitted contradicted many of his tales, while he lamented the failure of literature as adequate moral instruction. Amid many reversals in his attitudes and subjects, he compromised his excellent folklore with apologies and explanations.

Many of the virtues and sentiments Griffin extolled have passed out of style.

William Butler Yeats* praised Griffin's work as an authentic source for Irish folklore; this fact, plus his rich dramatic qualities and scenes of stark realism, constitute his strongest attractions.

GRACE ECKLEY

WORKS: *Holland-Tide; or, Munster Popular Tales.* London: W. Simpkin & R. Marshall, 1827; *Tales of the Munster Festivals.* 3 vols. London: Saunders & Otley, 1826–1827; *The Collegians.* 3 vols. London: Saunders & Otley, 1829; *The Christian Physiologist.* London: E. Bull, 1830. (Stories); *The Invasion.* 4 vols. London: Saunders & Otley, 1832; *Tales of My Neighbourhood.* 3 vols. London: Saunders & Otley, 1835; *The Duke of Monmouth.* 3 vols. London: Bentley, 1836; *Gisippus.* London: Maxwell, 1842. (Play in 5 acts); *Talis Qualis; or, Tales of the Jury Room.* 3 vols. London: Maxwell, 1842; *The Works of G. Griffin.* 8 vols. London: Various publishers, 1842–1843; *The Works of Gerald Griffin.* 10 vols. New York: D. & J. Sadlier, 1857; *The Poetical and Dramatic Works.* Dublin: J. Duffy, 1877.   REFERENCES: Cahalan, James M. *Great Hatred, Little Room: The Irish Historical Novel.* Syracuse, N.Y.: Syracuse University Press/Dublin: Gill & Macmillan, 1984; Cronin, John. *Gerald Griffin 1803–1840: A Critical Biography.* Cambridge: Cambridge University Press, 1978; Flanagan, Thomas. *The Irish Novelists, 1800–1850.* New York: Columbia University Press, 1958; Gill, W. S. *Gerald Griffin, Poet, Novelist, Christian Brother.* Dublin: M. H. Gill, 1940; Griffin, Daniel. *Life of Gerald Griffin, Esq.* London: Simpkin & Marshall, 1843/rev. ed. Dublin: J. Duffy, 1857; Kiely, Benedict. "The Two Masks of Gerald Griffin." *Studies* 61 (Autumn 1972): 241–251; MacLysaght, William. *Death Sails the Shannon: The Tragic Story of the Colleen Bawn.* Tralee: Anvil Books, 1953; Mannin, Ethel. *Two Studies in Integrity.* New York: G. P. Putnam's/London: Jarrolds, 1954; Sloan, Barry. *The Pioneers of Anglo-Irish Fiction 1800–1850.* Gerrards Cross: Colin Smythe/Totowa, N.J.: Barnes & Noble, 1986.

GRIFFITH, ARTHUR (1872–1922), journalist and politician. Griffith is important to Irish literature for his brilliant editing of *The United Irishman* (1889–1906) and *Sinn Féin* (1906–1914). He was born in Dublin on March 31, 1872, the son of a printer. From 1896 to 1899, Griffith was in the Transvaal, editing a small paper. When he returned to Dublin, his new paper, *The United Irishman,* quickly became the most important organ of the Irish national movement. In 1904, he published his influential pamphlet, *The Resurrection of Hungary, a Parallel for Ireland.* He was the initiator of the Sinn Féin movement, and, although he did not take part in the 1916 Rising, he was interned after it. With Michael Collins, he headed the Treaty delegation to London in 1921 and was the head of government in the new Free State after the de Valera split. He died of overwork on August 12, 1922, in Dublin.

Although the purpose of Griffith's journals was primarily political, they were cordially receptive to new Irish writing and encouraged such major new talents as Padraic Colum* and James Stephens.* However, Yeats,* Martyn,* Gogarty,* Alice Milligan,* Seumas O'Sullivan,* James Cousins,* and many others (including the awful poet Lizzie Twigg, who is mentioned in Joyce's *Ulysses*) often appeared in their pages. As James Stephens wrote, "the best poetry and literary criticism in the English language was written weekly by us in The United Irishman." The intimate connection between politics and the literary movement received an early partial rupture, however, over the plays of John Synge.* Griffith is remembered by literary historians for his vehement criticism of Synge and

GRIFFITH, RICHARD

his growing antipathy to Yeats and to the Abbey Theatre.* Nevertheless, that fact does not obscure the immense early service of Griffith to Irish letters.

Of Griffith's own writing, Stephens remarked:

His was one of the easiest pens that ever took naturally to ink, and at its best his prose was actually masterly. He was, in my opinion, the greatest journalist working in the English tongue, with an astonishing lucidity of expression, and with a command of all the modes of tender, or sarcastic or epigrammatic expression, and always that ample, untroubled simplicity of utterance which ranks him among the modern masters of the English language.

PRINCIPAL WORK: *The Resurrection of Hungary: A Parallel for Ireland.* Dublin: James Duffy, 1904. REFERENCES: Colum, Padraic. *Ourselves Alone: The Story of Arthur Griffith and the Origin of the Irish Free State.* New York: Crown, 1959/published as *Arthur Griffith.* London & Dublin: Browne & Nolan, 1959; Davis, Richard P. *Arthur Griffith and Non-Violent Sinn Fein.* Dublin: Anvil Books, 1974; Davis, Richard P. *Arthur Griffith.* Dundalk: Dundalgan, for the Irish Historical Association, 1976; Glandon, V. E. *Arthur Griffith and the Advanced Nationalist Press: Ireland, 1900–1922.* New York: Lang, 1985; Lyons, G. A. *Some Recollections of Griffith and His Times.* Dublin: Talbot, 1923; Ó Luing, Sean. *Art Ó Griofa.* Dublin: Sairseal agus Dill, 1953; Stephens, James. *Arthur Griffith, Journalist and Statesman.* Dublin: Wilson, Hartnell, [1922]; Younger, Carlton. *A State of Disunion.* London: Fontana, 1972; Younger, Carlton. *Arthur Griffith.* Dublin: Gill & Macmillan, 1981.

GRIFFITH, RICHARD (1704?–1788), novelist and playwright. Griffith's family settled in Ireland during the reign of James I. If he be the Richard Griffith who received a B.A. from Trinity College, Dublin, in 1721 and an M.A. in 1724, he may have been born about 1704. He attempted farming in County Kilkenny, and about 1752 he married Elizabeth Griffith (1720?–1793), an actress, fairly successful playwright, and novelist. In 1757, they published their love letters under the title of *A Series of Genuine Letters between Henry and Frances.* In 1769, they published a similar volume, *Two Novels, in Letters.* By himself, Griffith published *The Triumvirate* (1764) and *The Posthumous Works of a Late Celebrated Genius* (1770), both notable for the strong and lively influence of Sterne.* His play, *Variety,* was produced at Drury Lane on February 25, 1782, and has been called "uniformly dull." He died at his son's residence in Naas, County Kildare, on February 11, 1788.

WORKS: With Elizabeth Griffith: *A Series of Genuine Letters between Henry and Francis.* London: W. Johnston, 1757; *Two Novels, in Letters.* 4 vols. London: T. Becket, 1769. (Contains *The Delicate Distress* and *The Gordian Knot*). By himself: *The Triumvirate; or, The Authentic Memoirs of A, B, and C. . . .* London: W. Johnston, 1764/Dublin: J. Hoey, 1765; *The Posthumous Works of a Late Celebrated Genius, Deceased.* London: W. & J. Richardson, 1770. (Also called *The Koran; or, The Life, Character and Sentiments of Tria Juncta in Una, M. N. A., or Master of No Arts*).

GRIMSHAW, BEATRICE ETHEL (1870–1953), journalist, novelist, short story writer, travel writer. The majority of Grimshaw's forty books reflect her intimate knowledge of the South Seas. Born at Cloona House, County Antrim, one of the six children of a declining mercantile family, whose money had come from Ulster's textile industry, Grimshaw was educated at Victoria College, Belfast, at Bedford College, London, at Queen's College, Belfast, and at Caen. By the 1890s, she was living in Dublin, a Catholic convert embarked on a lively career as a journalist and editor. Athletic and industrious, she soon became holder of the women's world twenty-four-hour cycling record and published a novel, *Broken Away* (1897). Moving to London, she dreamed of the Southern Hemisphere, so she wangled free passage by promising publicity to the shipping agents and exotic copy to the newspapers. Bewitched by what she found "between the magic lines of Cancer and Capricorn," she wrote, "[t]he South Sea world is infinite; to know it, you must make your home in it—forget your own people and your father's house"; and by 1906, she had.

In the Strange South Seas (1907) and *From Fiji to the Cannibal Islands* (1907) offer real insight into a then-remote world. As travel books, they weave a vividly detailed tapestry of description, adventure, and practical economic advice to prospective settlers. Grimshaw's humor delights, as does her considerable facility with language. Faced with a smoking, 800-foot volcanic cone, she writes, "[t]he crater expands like a bursting red flower, while I, deprived of my lawful inches and comfortable self-importance, stand like a wretched little insect, a speck that does not count, on the verge of utter immensity." However, a novel, *Vaiti of the Islands* (1907), made money and established Grimshaw's name. The heroine, Vaiti, an irresistible *picara* who seems to reflect Grimshaw's own powerful personality, propels the vivid narrative stew of incest, violence, and cannibalism. But to dismiss Grimshaw's fiction as romantic adventure is to undervalue her understanding of the native mind, her frequently lyrical expression of the mysteries of her chosen world, and her facility with either the male or female perspective. Dozens of stories and some twenty novels followed, among them Grimshaw's favorite, *When the Red Gods Call* (1911), and the sequel, *Queen Vaiti* (1921).

She continued to explore, living for months at a time in isolated houses of her own design, spectacularly located, as on a precipice overlooking the Rona Waterfall. She was not shy of employing cannibals, controlling them with "a meaningless but effective language of intimidation using words from geometry with considerable effect." In her fifties, she became the first white woman to journey up the Sepik and Fly Rivers, notorious for their headhunters, with whom she rubs shoulders, describing the preservation of their trophies in graphic detail in *Isles of Adventure* (1930). This latter volume, referred to as autobiography, is mostly travel writing, offering little concrete personal information and no glimpse of Grimshaw's private persona. The last fourteen years of her long life were spent in quiet retirement in Australia, where she died in some obscurity.

IVY BANNISTER

WORKS: *Broken Away*. London & New York: Lane, 1897; *Vaiti of the Islands*. London: Eveleigh Nash, 1907. (Novel); *In the Strange South Seas*. London: Hutchinson, 1907; *From Fiji to the Cannibal Islands*. London: Eveleigh Nash, 1907; *The New New Guinea*. London: Hutchinson, 1910; *When the Red Gods Call*. London: Mills & Boon, 1910/New York: Moffat & Yard, 1911. (Novel);

Guinea Gold. London: Mills & Boon, 1912; *The Sorcerer's Stone.* London: Hodder & Stoughton, 1914. (Novel); *Red Bob of the Bismarcks.* London: Hurst & Blackett, 1915. (Novel); *Adventures in Papua with the Catholic Mission.* Melbourne: Australian Catholic Truth Society, 1915; *Nobody's Island.* London: Hurst & Blackett, 1917; *Kris-girl.* London: Mills & Boon, 1917. (Novel); *The Terrible Island.* New York: Ridgway, 1919/London: Hurst & Blackett, 1920. (Novel); *White Savage Simon.* London, 1919/London: Newnes, 1929; *The Coral Queen.* London, 1919/London: Newnes, 1925; *Queen Vaiti.* London: Newnes, 1921; *My South Sea Sweetheart.* New York: Macmillan, 1921. (Novel); *The Little Red Speck and Other South Seas Stories.* London: Hurst & Blackett, 1921; *Conn of the Coral Seas.* New York: Macmillan, 1922. (Novel); *The Long Beach and Other South Sea Stories.* London: Hurst & Blackett, 1923; *The Valley of Never-Come-Back, and Other Stories.* London: Hurst & Blackett, 1923; *Helen of Man O' War Island.* London: Hurst & Blackett, 1924. (Novel); *The Sands of Oro.* London: Hurst & Blackett, 1924. (Novel); *The Candles of Katara.* London: Hurst & Blackett, 1925; *The Wreck of the Redwing.* New York: Henry Holt, 1926/London: Hurst & Blackett, 1927. (Novel); *Black Sheep's Gold.* London: Hurst & Blackett, 1927; *Eyes in the Corner and Other Stories.* London: Hurst & Blackett, 1927; *The Paradise Poachers.* London: Hurst & Blackett, 1928; *My Lady Far-Away.* London: Cassell, 1929; *Isles of Adventure.* London: Jenkins, 1930; *The Star in the Dust.* London: Cassell, 1930; *The Beach of Terror, and Other Stories.* London: Cassell, 1931; *The Mystery of Tumbling Reef.* Boston & New York: Houghton Mifflin/London: Cassell, 1932; *The Long Beaches, and Other South Sea Stories.* London: Cassell, 1933; *Victorian Family Robinson.* London: Cassell, 1934; *Pieces of Gold, and Other South Sea Stories.* London: Cassell, 1935; *Rita Regina.* London: Herbert Jenkins, 1939; *South Sea Sarah and Murder in Paradise. Two Complete Novels.* Sydney: New Century, 1940; *Lost Child.* London: Herbert Jenkins, 1940.   REFERENCES: Gardner, Susan Jane. *"For Love and Money: Beatrice Grimshaw's Passage to Papua."* Diss., Rhodes University, 1985; Kelly, A. A. *Wandering Women.* Dublin: Wolfhound, 1995, pp. 149–169.

GROARKE, VONA (1964–   ), poet. According to her poem "Patronage," Groarke was born in the ballroom of Maria Edgeworth's* house in Edgeworthstown, County Longford. She grew up on a farm near Athlone and took degrees from Trinity College, Dublin, and from University College, Cork. She has worked in England, the United States, and Norway. In 1992, she received a bursary from the Arts Council. In 1994, she was joint winner of the Listowel Writers' Week Sonnet Competition, and she has also won the Hennessy Award for Poetry and the *Sunday Tribune* New Irish Writer of the Year Award. She lives in Dublin and is curator of Newman House. Her collection, *Shale* (1994), tends to be loose in form but intense in statement, less wrought than overwrought. See, however, her adroit use of sound in "For the Unkept House" and "Reflections."

WORK: *Shale.* [Oldcastle, Co. Meath]: Gallery, [1994].

GROVES, EDWARD (ca. 1775–ca. 1850), playwright. Groves was educated at Trinity College, Dublin, and ordained around 1800. He was a Protestant patriot and a friend of O'Connell. His play, *The Warden of Galway,* ran for a remarkable forty-five nights in Dublin in 1831. He was also interested in promoting a universal language.

PRINCIPAL WORKS: *Pasilogia, An Essay towards the Formation of a System of Universal Language.* . . . Dublin: J. McGlashan, 1846; *The Warden of Galway.* Dublin: A. Thom, 1876.

GUBBINS, CHARLOTTE (1827–1889), poet. Charlotte Gibson was born in 1827, and a footnote to her poem "The Beacon" states that it was written when she was twelve. She married Blakeney Gough Gubbins, an inspector of the Sligo Revenue Police, and the family lived in Sligo from the 1840s until the early 1870s. Charlotte contributed poems to *Chamber's Journal* in the 1840s, as well as to the Sligo newspaper. In 1871, a piece in the Sligo paper gave Rathmines as her address, but by 1880 the family was back in Sligo, where she died on April 25, 1889.

Charlotte Gubbins's poetry is unique, particularly for a woman poet, as much of her verse pertains to her husband's work with the Revenue Police and thus with raids on poteen stills. The first five poems of her single volume combine to make a single day's entry into the Revenue inspector's journal. They tell the story of a Lieutenant Herbert of the Revenue Police and his love for Isoline, the only daughter of wealthy parents. Another couple, of less moneyed and social prominence, also features in the same five poems: Lilla, Isoline's maid, and Bryan, Lilla's unemployed suitor. Gubbins is in full sympathy with the brave Lieutenant Herbert, as evidenced in "In Quarters," where she describes the inspector's job:

> These to detect, pursue, arrest,
> It was his duty: and at night
> The smuggler's haunt approaching best,
> Unseen, and guided by the light
> Which sometimes from the "still-house" gleams;
> Thus oft he took his weary way,
> (While others happy in their dreams,
> In slumber's sweet oblivion lay),
> With twelve brave men at his command. . . .
> It was a life he could not love;
> But light of heart, of courage high,
> He met with fate contentedly. . . .

"The Still-House" provides a description of poteen making, and Herbert's raid on the cabin creates the following response among the poteen makers:

> The still they seemed to contemplate,
> Which, in its long accustomed nook,
> Unconscious of impending fate,
> Reposed in dignity sedate.
>   Then, starting wildly to their feet,
>   Each differing impulses obeyed;
> A feeble movement of retreat
> By one without success was made;
> The others all their efforts gave
> Their scanty property to save.

Gubbins has a deft poetic style, except for her tendency to italicize poteen-related words she uses as puns. She was a firm Unionist, and "Britannia's Wreath" celebrates the union of Ireland, Scotland, and England.

ANNE COLMAN

WORK: *One Day's Journal: A Story of the Revenue Police, and Other Poems.* Sligo: Printed at the *Independent* and General Printing Office, by Alexander Gillmore, 1862. REFERENCES: Co. Sligo Library, local authors' collection.

GUINAN, JOHN (1874–1945), playwright. Guinan was born in Ballindown, Birr, Offaly, in 1874. A civil servant, he spent much of his working life in the offices of the Congested Districts Board and of the Land Commission. He was a frequent writer of short stories for the popular press and had four plays produced at the Abbey Theatre*: *The Cuckoo's Nest* (1913), *The Plough Lifters* (1916), *Black Oliver* (1927), and *The Rune of Healing* (1931). His plays tend to be rather overelaborated in dialogue and overconvoluted in plot. He collaborated on a play, probably called *The Wonderful Wedding,* with George Fitzmaurice* with whom he worked in the Land Commission. A conventional matchmaking comedy, the piece was hardly the best work of either Fitzmaurice or Guinan; it was rejected by the Abbey but was finally published in 1978. Guinan died in Sutton on March 7, 1945.

WORKS: *Black Oliver* in *One-Act Plays for Stage and Study: Fifth Series.* New York: 1929; *The Cuckoo's Nest.* Dublin: Gill, [1933]; with George Fitzmaurice, "The Wonderful Wedding" in *The Journal of Irish Literature* 7 (September 1978): 3–36.

GUINAN, JOSEPH (1863–1932), novelist. Canon Guinan served in Liverpool and then as parish priest in County Longford. His novels, often about the clerical life, were serious moral entertainments, and *The Soggarth Aroon* (1906) was widely read, even until fairly recently.

WORKS: *Scenes and Sketches in an Irish Parish; or, Priest and People in Doon.* 4th ed. Dublin: M. H. Gill, 1906; *The Soggarth Aroon.* New York: Benziger, 1906/Dublin & Cork: Talbot, [1944]; *The Moors of Glynn.* New York: Benziger, 1907; *The Island Parish.* Dublin & Waterford: M. H. Gill, 1908; *The Curate of Kilcloon.* Dublin & Waterford: M. H. Gill, 1912; *Months and Days: Their Silent Lessons.* Dublin: Catholic Truth Society of Ireland, [1920]/2d ed., rev. & enlarged, [1925]. (Nonfiction); *Annamore; or, The Tenant at Will.* London: Burns & Oates, 1924; *The Patriots.* New York: Benziger, 1928. REFERENCE: Candy, Catherine. *Priestly Fictions: Popular Irish Novelists of the Early 20th Century.* Dublin: Wolfhound, 1995.

GUINNESS, BRYAN [WALTER] (1905–1992), man of letters. Guinness, the second Baron Moyne, was born on October 27, 1905. A member of the famous brewing family, he was educated at Eton and at Christ Church, Oxford, where he received a B.A. in 1928 and an M.A. in 1931. He was called to the English bar in 1930. In Ireland, he was a noted patron of the arts, supporting the Guinness Poetry Awards and the Wexford Opera Festival; and he received honorary degrees from Trinity College and the National University. He was also a member of the Irish Academy of Letters and governor of the National Gallery of Ireland. He died on July 6, 1992.

Guinness was a prolific and varied writer, and his writing included poetry, novels, short stories, plays, children's stories, and autobiography. Most of his work has an English background and is informed by charm, delicacy, and a mild wit. A good introduction to his prose, showing both his excellences and limitations, would be the volume of stories entitled *The Girl with the Flower* (1966). A good introduction to his poetry would be the selection of old and new work that he made for the posthumously published *On a Ledge* (1992). His subjects are usually descriptions of nature or reflections on love. He is an imitative amateur as a poet, basically wedded to form and to meter, but not always in control of them. In "Parties," for instance, there are awkward inversions of syntax. In "Paris," the diction is old-fashioned and even trite: "the bitter sky," "solemn steps," "Lo," "smiling fields," "Apollo's car," "vibrant life." He has, nevertheless, his successes, such as this stanza from "Winter Landscape":

> The crows devour the liver
>   Of carrion on the hill;
> The lingering hare must shiver;
>   The lurking fox must kill.

Indeed, there are six or eight tightly effective pieces that would not disgrace any anthology, among them "Harmonics," "Thrift," "The Rose in the Tree," "Love in a Crowd," "Love's Isolation," and "The Pretty Girl Milking the Cows."

WORKS: *Twenty-three Poems*. London: Duckworth, 1931; *Singing Out of Tune*. London: Putnam, 1933. (Novel); *Landscape with Figures*. London: Putnam, 1934. (Novel); *Under the Eyelid*. London: Heinemann, [1935]. (Poems); *The Story of Johnny and Jemima*. London: Heinemann, 1936. (Children's story); *A Week by the Sea*. London: Putnam, 1936. (Novel); *Lady Crushwell's Companion*. London: Putnam, 1938. (Novel); *The Children in the Desert*. London: Heinemann, 1947. (Children's story); *Reflexions*. London: Heinemann, 1947. (Poems); *The Animals' Breakfast*. London: Heinemann, 1950. (Children's story); with Desmond MacCarthy. *The Story of a Nutcracker*. London: Heinemann, 1953. (Free version of a tale by E.T.W. Hoffmann); *Collected Poems, 1927–1955*. London: Heinemann, 1956; *A Fugue of Cinderellas*. London: Heinemann, 1956. (Novel); with Ronald Pym, *The Story of Catriona and the Grasshopper*. London: Heinemann, 1958. (Children's story); with Ronald Pym, *The Story of Priscilla and the Prawn*. London: Heinemann, 1960. (Children's story); *Leo and Rosabelle*. London: Heinemann, 1961. (Novel); *The Giant's Eye*. London: Heinemann, [1964]. (Novel); *The Rose in the Tree*. London: Heinemann, 1964. (Poems); *The Girl with the Flower and Other Stories*. London: Heinemann, [1966]; *Diary Not Kept: Essays in Recollection*. Salisbury, Wilts: Compton, 1975; *The Clock: Poems and a Play*. [Dublin]: Dolmen/New York: Humanities, 1973; *The Engagement*. Cambridge: Rampart Lion, n. d. (Novel); *Hellenic Flirtation*. Salisbury: Compton, 1977. (Novelette); *Personal Patchwork 1939–1945*. London: Cygnet, [ca. 1986]. (Memoirs); *On a Ledge: New and Selected Poems*. [Dublin]: Lilliput, 1992.

GWYNN, STEPHEN [LUCIUS] (1864–1950), politician and man of letters. Gwynn was born on February 13, 1864, at St. Columba's College near Dublin. His father, John Gwynn, was the warden of the college and became Regius professor of divinity at Trinity College. His mother was the daughter of William

Smith O'Brien, the patriot, while one of his brothers became provost of Trinity and another brother vice-provost.

Gwynn attended Brasenose College, Oxford, graduated with distinction in 1896, and then turned to journalism in London. He returned to Ireland to live in 1904, and from 1906 to 1918 he was a nationalist member of Parliament for Galway City. Despite his age, he entered World War I as a private. He was promoted to captain, served in France until 1917, and was made a chevalier of the Legion of Honor. In late life, he was honored by the Irish Academy of Letters and awarded a D. Litt. both from the National University and Trinity. He died in Dublin on June 11, 1950.

Gwynn led an intensely active public life, and yet his literary output was immense. He attempted with distinction practically every literary form except the drama. He wrote poems, novels, sketches, stories, essays, books on fishing, guidebooks to Ireland, works on politics, biographies of Thomas Moore,* Scott, Swift,* Goldsmith,* Robert Louis Stevenson, and others, and he was a prolific editor and a particular authority on the eighteenth century.

The extraordinary fact about Gwynn's work is that, despite its great bulk, it is unvaryingly competent. He has no lost masterpieces, but he is a supple and vigorous writer of prose and the best of genial companions. While he sometimes repeats his best stories in different works, he always has ideas, his literary taste is excellent, and his political remarks are full of humane good sense. For instance, there could be few more succinct and more telling characterizations of the nineteenth-century Irish novel than his seventeen-page essay in *Irish Books and Irish People* (except perhaps the next essay in the book on Irish humor which covers the same ground). One may dip into Gwynn almost at random— say, in his autobiography, *Experiences of a Literary Man,* or in his discursive books on fishing, or in a loving recreation of Dublin and its characters like his *Dublin Old and New*—and find interest, information, and charm.

Oliver Gogarty* thought Gwynn "a considerable poet," and he has indeed a fine command of technique. He is at his best as a poet in the old-fashioned, but stirring, "A Lay of Ossian and Patrick." Gogarty also summed him up well:

Gwynn's long life witnessed many changes both slow and abrupt: three major wars, a rebellion, and a civil war. None of these affected his imperturbability. He was stationary but not a recluse. Unobtrusively he lived and died, but for patriotism, scholarship, and integrity he was the greatest figure in the Ireland of his time.

WORKS: *Memorials of an Eighteenth Century Painter: James Northcote.* London: Unwin, 1898; *The Repentance of a Private Secretary.* London: John Lane, 1898. (Novel); *The Decay of Sensibility.* London: J. Lane, 1899. (Sketches, essays); *Highways and Byways in Donegal and Antrim.* London: Macmillan, 1899; *The Old Knowledge.* London: Macmillan, 1901. (Novel); *The Queen's Chronicler.* London & New York: J. Lane, 1901. (Poems); *John Maxwell's Marriage.* London: Macmillan, 1903. (Novel); *To-day and To-morrow in Ireland.* Dublin: Hodges, Figgis, 1903. (Essays); *A Lay of Ossian and Patrick.* Dublin: Hodges, Figgis/London: Macmillan, 1904. (Poems); *Fishing Holidays.* London: Macmillan, 1904; *The Masters of English Literature.* London: Macmillan, 1904; rev. ed., 1925; 2d ed., 1938; *Thomas Moore.* London: Macmillan, 1905; *The Fair Hills of Ireland.* Dublin: Maunsel/London: Macmillan, 1906. (Guidebook); *The Glade in the Forest.* Dublin: Maunsel, 1907. (Stories); *A Holiday in Connemara.* London: Methuen, 1909; *Robert Emmet.* London: Macmillan 1909. (Novel); *Beautiful Ireland.* London: Blackie, 1911. (Guidebook); *The Case for Home Rule.* Dublin: Maunsel, [1911]; *The Famous Cities of Ireland.* Dublin & London: Maunsel/ New York: Macmillan, 1915; *For Second Reading.* Dublin & London: Maunsel, 1918. (Essays); *John Redmond's Last Years.* London: Edward Arnold/New York: Longmans, Green, 1919. (Biography); *Irish Books and Irish People.* Dublin: Talbot/London: Unwin, 1920; *Garden Wisdom.* Dublin: Talbot/London: Unwin, 1921. *The Irish Situation.* London: Jonathan Cape, 1921; *Collected Poems.* Edinburgh & London: Blackwood, 1923; *The History of Ireland.* London: Macmillan/Dublin: Talbot, 1923; *Duffer's Luck.* Edinburgh & London: Blackwood, 1924. (Fishing); *Ireland.* London: E. Benn, 1924/New York: C. Scribner's, 1925; The *Student's History of Ireland.* London: Longman's, 1925; *Experiences of a Literary Man.* London: Thornton Butterworth, 1926. (Autobiography); *In Praise of France.* London: Nisbet, 1927; *Captain Scott.* London: J. Lane, 1929. (Biography); *Saints and Scholars.* London: Thornton Butterworth, 1929; *Burgundy.* London: Harrap, 1930; *The Life of Horace Walpole.* London: Thornton Butterworth, 1932; *The Life of Mary Kingsley.* London: Macmillan, 1932; 2d ed., 1933; *The Life of Sir Walter Scott.* London: Thornton Butterworth, 1932; *The Life and Friendships of Dean Swift.* London: Thornton Butterworth, 1933; *Claude Monet and His Garden.* London: Country Life, 1934; *Mungo Park and the Quest of the Niger.* London: J. Lane, 1934. *Ireland in Ten Days.* London: Harrap, 1935; *Oliver Goldsmith.* London: Thornton Butterworth, 1935; *Irish Literature and Drama in the English Language.* London: Nelson, 1936; *The Happy Fisherman.* London: Country Life, 1936; *River to River.* London: Country Life, 1937; *Dublin, Old and New.* Dublin: Browne & Nolan/London: Harrap, [1938]; *Fond Opinions.* London: Frederick Muller, 1938. (Essays); *Munster.* London & Glasgow: Blackie, [1938]; *Two in a Valley.* London: Rich & Cowan, [1938]. (Travel); *Henry Grattan and His Times.* Dublin: Browne & Nolan, 1939; *Robert Louis Stevenson.* London: Macmillan, 1939; *Salute to Valour.* London: Constable, 1941. (Poems); *Aftermath.* Dundalk: W. Tempest, 1946. (Poems); *Memories of Enjoyment.* Tralee: Kerryman, [1946]. (Selections from his writing).

HACKETT, FRANCIS (1883–1962), novelist, historian, and critic. "A myopic, astygmatic, fatty, apprehensive bundle of human expectancy," Hackett was born on January 21, 1883, in Kilkenny. After completing his only formal education at Clongowes Wood College, he emigrated to the United States at eighteen. An editorial writer for the *Chicago Evening Post,* he graduated to editor of its weekly review, from which he moved to the position of editor of the just-established *New Republic* in 1914. By 1922, he had married Danish-born Signe Toksvig and published his two books on Ireland: *Ireland: A Study in Nationalism* (1918) and *The Story of the Irish Nation* (1922). There were also two early collections of essays and reviews: *Horizons* (1918) and *The Invisible Censor* (1921).

In 1922, Hackett left the *New Republic* in order to pursue a more creative literary career and moved to southern France where he wrote a first novel, *That Nice Young Couple* (1925). Free-lance writing for various American papers and literary magazines preceded his first historical biography, *Henry the Eighth,* written and published after Hackett and his wife had settled in Ireland in 1926, first in Clonsharragh Lodge, Duncannon, County Wexford, and from May 1929 in Killadreenan House in County Wicklow. The American publication of *Henry the Eighth* in 1929 and its immediate choice as a Book-of-the-Month Club "first" was a personal and financial triumph after seven years of penury. Another five years brought *Francis the First, Gentleman of France* (1934), followed by the autobiographical novel *The Green Lion* (1936). When the Irish Censorship Board simultaneously banned this novel and his wife's second novel, *Eve's Doctor* (1937), the Hacketts left Ireland on the anniversary of Parnell's death for Signe Toksvig's native Denmark. They settled in Copenhagen.

In December 1939, the novel *Queen Anne Boleyn,* considered for dramatic adaptation, brought the Hacketts to New York. The German Occupation of Denmark prevented their return to Denmark, and the adaptation was canceled. They then rented a house on Martha's Vineyard where Hackett wrote a biweekly literary review for *The New York Times* and completed his semi-autobiographical *. . . I Chose Denmark,* for which he was later awarded the King Christian Liberty Medal. This work was followed by his Washington novel *The Senator's Last Night* (1943).

After the war, Hackett returned to Copenhagen, edited a collection of reviews, *On Judging Books* (1947), and pursued an independent and chosen life. He died on April 25, 1962, at the age of seventy-nine.

Politics, history and literary criticism were Hackett's keenest interests. Consequently, with the singular exception of *Queen Anne Boleyn,* which is a novel only in the fact that Hackett invents dialogue for his historical characters, his novels, spaced between other works requiring a greater exactitude, are often simply entertainments. *The Green Lion* and *The Senator's Last Night,* however, reveal his egalitarian political principles. *The Green Lion,* banned because its Irish hero is the bastard child of a passionate mountain girl and a neophyte in the Church, is the story of a young boy's hero-worship of Parnell and of a half-understood but wholly felt love of liberty. The political liberalism of *The Green Lion* found more mature expression in *The Senator's Last Night,* in which the senior senator from Nebraska suffers a living death on the night he is later to die. The senator represents all that is reprehensible to Hackett: an isolationist in time of war; a power-mogul whose rise from penury to wealth and power makes him a secret admirer of Hitler; a husband whose sexual loyalties lie elsewhere; a father without a shred of paternal feeling. Hackett's obvious delight in doing him in is a fine example of his assurance that in politics as in all things, there is progress.

Somewhat dampened political optimism emanates from his expository works on Ireland. *Ireland, A Study in Nationalism* (a separately published "Preface," *The Irish Republic,* accompanied the printing of the third edition in 1920) fully blames British insensitivity for the Easter Rising but conservatively pleads for Dominion Home Rule to save Ulster from the exclusion of Republicanism. Hackett recants in the "Preface" of 1920 in which he argues complete separatism. *The Story of the Irish Nation,* written in response to Herbert Bayard Swope's challenge that Hackett could write a history of Ireland in three days, took three months, with the obvious result that Ireland from the Firbolgs to the Treaty of 1921 skims glibly along the surfaces of time.

Hackett's excellence lies in his focused histories (with which must be included the novel *Queen Anne Boleyn*) and in part, too, in his detailed and dramatic evocation, and in his finding of an "objective correlative" he did not have when writing about Ireland directly. The two histories, *Henry the Eighth* and *Francis the First,* discuss the birth and tenure of nationalism. Henry VIII's harsh and uncompromising consolidation of England under Crown authority (an authority which was nearly undermined by the commoner's daughter, Anne Boleyn, whose gift it was to foment power struggles which a country just emerging from feudalism was only too ready to engage in) is contrasted to the rule of Francis

I. Youthful and extravagant, militarist and gangster, friend of Rabelais and patron of Cellini, a king who made mistakes, Francis I ushered his country into the glories of the Renaissance. These two men together form Hackett's symbol of leadership: authority for the child in man; pride, for his self-respect; a common humanity, in which he hopes to see himself; a paternalism to which he clings; and a flamboyance, for his aspirations, his entertainment, and just for the fun of it. If everyman sees enough of himself in his nation's leader, enough of himself will become his country.

Perhaps it was such thinking which led Hackett to "choose" Denmark, a country which having achieved nationhood, allowed its symbols of nationality to recede. Denmark's symbolic monarchy and social progressiveness was a twentieth-century ideal of authority and democracy functioning in accord. In . . . *I Chose Denmark,* Hackett (indirectly saying a great many things about his native Ireland) praises a nation not only for its cleanliness, honesty, and independence, but also for the fact that its premier rides a streetcar, its farming cooperatives work, and only ten taxpayers earn more than $100,000 in a single year. Its citizens, freed from social, political and economic harassment, express themselves without fear. In *On Judging Books,* Hackett wrote: "The might of judgment adheres in a free man. . . . Religious have wiped out books. States have burned them. The right of private judgment is obviously the passkey out of prison. Without it men are dependents, whether happy or unhappy, and dependents end as slaves." To this ideal Francis Hackett adhered and towards its realization he wrote.

M. KELLY LYNCH

WORKS: *Ireland, a Study in Nationalism.* New York: B. W. Huebsch, 1918; *Horizons.* New York: B. W. Huebsch, 1918. (Literary criticism); ed., *On American Books.* New York: B. W. Huebsch, 1920; *The Invisible Censor.* New York: B. W. Huebsch, 1921. (Sketches and reviews); *The Story of the Irish Nation.* New York: Appleton-Century, 1922; *That Nice Young Couple.* London: Jonathan Cape, 1925. (Novel); *Henry the Eighth.* London: Jonathan Cape, 1929. (History); *Francis the First, Gentleman of France.* London: Heinemann, 1934. (History); *The Green Lion.* London: I. Nicholson & Watson, 1936. (Novel); *Queen Anne Boleyn.* New York: Doubleday, Doran, 1939. (Novel); . . . *I Chose Denmark.* New York: Doubleday, Doran, 1940. (Autobiography and political and social commentary); *The Senator's Last Night.* New York: Doubleday, Doran, 1943. (Novel); *On Judging Books in General and in Particular.* New York: J. Day, 1947. (Essays and reviews); *American Rainbow.* New York: Liveright, 1971. Signe Toksvig, ed. (Reminiscences). REFERENCE: Pihl, Lis, ed. *Signe Toksvig's Irish Diaries 1926–1937.* Dublin: Lilliput, 1994.

HAIRE, WILSON JOHN (1932–   ), playwright. Haire was born in Belfast on April 6, 1932, to a Protestant father and a Catholic mother. His early life was spent on the Shankill Road, but, while still young, his family moved to Carryduff in County Down. His literary career began with a series of short stories published in the *Irish Democrat.* The first was written under the pseudonym "Fenian," which he adopted as a symbol of resistance. His formal association with the theater began as an actor with London's Unity Theatre. He subsequently codirected London's Camden Group Theatre. His first play, a one-act entitled "The Cockin' Hen," was produced in 1968 in London and explores a demonstration in Catholic West Belfast by an Ian Paisley-like figure and the consequent resistance and trial of a Catholic and a Protestant demonstrator. Set in 1966, the play accurately represents the atmosphere that would lead to a later outbreak of violence. Later productions include *The Diamond, Bone and Hammer and Along the Sloughs of Ulster* (London, 1969), *Within Two Shadows* (London, 1972; New York, 1974), *Bloom of a Diamond Stone* (Abbey,* 1972), *Echoes from a Concrete Canyon* (London, 1975), *Lost Worlds: Newsflash, Wedding Breakfast* and *Roost* (London, 1978), and *Worlds Apart* (Glasglow, 1981). Haire has also written two television plays—*Letter from a Soldier* (1975) and *The Dandelion Clock* (1975). He has received the George Devine Award, the Thames Television Award, and the *Evening Standard* Award. He has served as playwright in residence at the Royal Court Theatre in London and at the Lyric Players Theatre* in Belfast. The Lyric Players staged his *Within Two Shadows* to open their 1972–1973 season.

Haire's career coincided with the beginnings of the Troubles, and his later work explored the Northern issue directly. When *Within Two Shadows* opened at the Royal Court on April 12, 1972, there had been no major staged treatment of the Northern violence on the London stage. A careful examination of the text reveals moving sequences in which humor and tragedy mix, the rhythm of the language betrays a character's inner torment, and other characters raise the level of their dialogue to near poetic discourse. Critics have commended Haire's sensitive and accurate ability to display both the Protestant and Catholic experience. In fact, the two shadows of the play's title are the darkness cast by the experiences of living in a mixed household strained to breaking in the face of sectarian violence. In *Bloom of the Diamond Stone* a young man and woman, one Catholic and the other Protestant, fall in love and find that the violence of the streets translates into the dynamics of the relationships that dominate their lives—friends, family, work contacts. The television play *Letter from a Soldier* explores the efforts of a British soldier to describe his term of service to his family, and *The Dandelion Clock* examines the life of a girl growing up in the midst of violence.

Haire's career has been punctuated by exceptionally well crafted plays mixed with less successful work. *Echoes from a Concrete Canyon,* although it explores a meaningful theme of the failed marriage and the wife's subsequent life with her daughter, lacks precisely what made Haire's other work more successful— humor mixed with pathos, precise and moving language. Haire produced two plays for the Lyric Players under the Leverhulme Fellowship, but Mary O'Malley felt that his insistence on remaining in London contributed to the plays' lack of suitability. However, Haire's enduring value rests with works that explore the genesis and early manifestations of the Troubles' effect on lives overwhelmed, irrevocably altered, and destroyed by violence.

BERNARD McKENNA

WORKS: *Bloom of the Diamond Stone.* London: Pluto, 1973; *Lost Worlds.* London: Heinemann,

516

HALDANE, SEAN

1978. (Contains *Newsflash, Wedding Breakfast,* and *Roost*); *Within Two Shadows.* London: Davis-Poynter, 1979.   REFERENCES: Buchloh, Paul, G. & Rix, Walter T. "Wilson John Haire: *Within Two Shadows* und *The Bloom of the Diamond Stone*" in *Englische Literatur der Gegenwart, 1971–1975.* Rainer Lengler, ed. Düsseldorf: Bagel, 1977, pp. 117–132; Deutsch, Richard. "*Within Two Shadows:* The Troubles in Northern Ireland." In *The Irish Novel in Our Time.* Patrick Rafroidi & Maurice Harmon, eds. Lille: Publications de l'Université de Lille, 1977, pp. 133–134; O'Malley, Conor. *A Poet's Theatre.* Dublin: Elo, 1988; O'Malley, Mary. *Never Shake Hands with the Devil.* Dublin: Elo, 1990.

HALDANE, SEAN

WORK: *Dance in Belfast.* Belfast: Blackstaff, 1992. (Novel).

HALL, PAULINE (1930s?–   ), novelist. Hall was born in Dublin, probably in the middle or late 1930s. She took degrees at University College, Dublin (UCD) and Yale and taught part-time at UCD in the English and French departments. She lives in Dublin with her husband and four children. The episodic story of her novel *Grounds* (1983) depicts moments in the life of Margaret Hogan, from childhood during World War II to a visit twenty years later to Arus an Uachtarain to present an award to the aged de Valera. Along the way we see her studying in France, at UCD, and in America. Few of the episodes are greatly dramatic, but the excellence of the book is the author's ability to catch character and to focus on the telling detail. She is particularly fine in conjuring up an authentic feel of the Dublin of the 1950s and 1960s. Her book, as Anthony Cronin* remarked, "is as authentic as Pembroke Road."

WORK: *Grounds.* [Dingle, Co. Kerry]: Brandon, [1983].

HALL, MRS. S. C. (1800–1881), novelist and short story writer. Mrs. Hall was born Anna Maria Fielding in Dublin on January 6, 1800, but she lived most of her first fifteen years at Bannow in County Wexford. She was taken to London where she met and, in 1824, married Samuel Carter Hall. Her husband was born on May 9, 1800, near Waterford where his father, an army officer, was stationed. After a few years in Cork, Hall moved to London and founded a number of journals, such as *The Amulet* and *The Art Journal,* in which much of his wife's work appeared. She was vastly productive of sketches, stories, and novels of Irish peasant life, and it has been estimated that she published over five hundred books, some of which she wrote in collaboration with her husband. Like Maria Edgeworth,* Somerville and Ross,* and Lady Gregory,* Mrs. Hall was observing the peasant from the outside. Unfortunately, she had little of the comic genius of these writers, and, while some of her work is pleasant enough, little of it is memorable. Her rather awesome energies were also utilized in a good deal of philanthropic work, as well as in anti-alcoholic campaigns, proselytization for women's rights, and spiritualism. She died in East Mousley on January 30, 1881. Her husband died in Kensington on March 16, 1889.

WORKS: *Sketches of Irish Character.* London: F. Westley & A. H. Davis, 1829; *Sketches of Irish Character, Second Series.* London: F. Westley & A. H. Davis, 1831; *The Buccaneer.* London:

R. Bentley, 1832; *The Outlaw*. London: R. Bentley, 1835; *Tales of Woman's Trials*. London: Houlston, 1835; *Uncle Horace*. London: H. Colburn, 1837; *The Groves of Blarney*. London: Chapman & Hall, ca. 1838. (Three-act play); *Lights and Shadows of Irish Life*. London: H. Colburn, 1838; *Marian*. London: H. Colburn, 1840; with S. C. Hall, *Ireland*. London: How & Parsons, 1841; with S. C. Hall, *A Week at Killarney*. London: J. How, 1843; *The Whiteboy*. London: Chapman & Hall, 1845; *A Midsummer Eve*. London: Longman, 1848; *Stories of the Irish Peasantry*. Edinburgh: W. & R. Chambers, 1850; *The Fight of Faith*. London: Chapman & Hall, 1869.   REFERENCES: Anon. "The Didactic Irish Novelists: Carleton, Mrs. Hall." *Dublin University Magazine* 26 (1845): 737–752; Hall, S. C. *Retrospect of a Long Life*. New York: Appleton, 1883; Mayo, Isabella Fyvie. "A Recollection of Two Old Friends: Mr. and Mrs. S. C. Hall." *Leisure Hour,* 38 (1889): 303–307.

HALPINE, CHARLES GRAHAM (1829–1868), journalist and popular writer. Halpine was born in Oldcastle, County Meath, on November 20, 1829. His father, Nicholas John Halpine, after a brilliant career at Trinity College, was editor for many years of *The Dublin Evening Mail*. Halpine himself graduated from Trinity and then turned to journalism, first in Dublin and then in London. In 1851, he emigrated to America where he became for a while the private secretary to P. T. Barnum. His journalistic career flourished, and he distinguished himself in the American Civil War and retired a brigadier general. He was a prominent member of the Democratic party of his day and an outspoken critic of municipal corruption. He died on August 3, 1868, from an accidental overdose of chloroform.

Halpine's verses, written under the pseudonym of Private Miles O'Reilly, are comic, patriotic, and sentimental. The worst of them are rather dreadful, but a few, such as "Irish Astronomy," are somewhat clever. In that poem we learn how St. Patrick placed O'Ryan [*sic*] in the firmament as thanks for the following occasion:

> St. Patrick wanst was passin' by
>   O'Ryan's little houldin',
> And, as the saint felt wake and dhry,
>   He thought he'd enther bould in.
> "O'Ryan," says the saint, "avick!
>   To praich at Thurles I'm goin',
> So let me have a rasher quick,
>   And a dhrop of Innishowen."
>
> "No rasher will I cook for you
>   While betther is to spare, sir,
> But here's a jug of mountain dew,
>   And there's a rattlin' hare, sir." . . .

Halpine also wrote two Irish historical novels which are justifiably neglected.

WORKS: *Lyrics by the Letter H* (published anonymously). New York: J. C. Derby/Cincinnati: H. W. Derby, 1854; *The Poetical Works of Charles Graham Halpine (Miles O'Reilly)*, R. B. Roosevelt, ed. New York: Harper, 1869; *The Patriot Brothers; or, the Willows of the Golden Vale*. Dublin: A. M. Sullivan, [1869]; *Mountcashel's Brigade; or, the Rescue of Cremona: an Historical Romance*. 5th ed. Dublin: T. D. Sullivan, 1882. As Miles O'Reilly: *Baked Meats of the Funeral. A*

Collection of Essays, Poems, Speeches, Histories and Banquets. New York: Carleton, 1886; *The Life and Adventures, Songs, Services . . . of Private Miles O'Reilly.* New York: Carleton, 1864/ Tarrytown, N.Y.: W. Abbatt, 1926.

HAMILTON, ELIZABETH (1758–1816), novelist and writer on education. Elizabeth was born on July 25, 1758, the daughter of Charles and Katherine Mackay Hamilton of Belfast. Her father died in 1759, and her mother in 1767. There were two other children in the family, Katherine and Charles, and the three children were separated after their parents died. Elizabeth was sent to live with her paternal aunt, Mrs. Marshall, on a Stirlingshire farm. She was educated at a local Stirling school and received tutoring in womanly tasks. A meeting with her brother in 1772 led to a lengthy correspondence and what she called her "second education." The Marshalls later moved to Ingram's Cook in Scotland, and Elizabeth settled into a tranquil life. Charles, her brother, sailed for India at about the time she moved to Scotland, and his return in 1786 afforded her the opportunity to study Indian literature while assisting him with his translations. Charles and Elizabeth were later reunited with their sister, Katherine, and the trio moved to London where they lived until Charles died in 1792. The influence of Charles' accounts for the Indian themes of *Hindoo Rajah* (1796), Elizabeth's first book. She used the pseudonym of Almeria.

Elizabeth's health deteriorated, and she moved to Bath, where she wrote her memoirs. She was concerned with educational philosophies and policies, advocating the education of the poor. She was an opponent of Godwin, Rousseau, and their followers, as evidenced by *Memoirs of Modern Philosophers* (1800). Her most popular work was the novel *The Cottagers of Glenburnie* (1808), which regularly occasioned new editions until 1885. Her later work is heavily moralistic, with piety, cleanliness, and a work ethic as ideals. She lived in Edinburgh, where she helped found a House of Industry, before returning to Bath in 1812. She died on July 23, 1816, at Harrogate.

ANNE COLMAN

WORKS: *Translations of the Letters of a Hindoo Rajah.* 2 vols. London: G. G. & J. Robinson, 1796; *Memoirs of Modern Philosophers.* 2d ed. 3 vols. Bath: Printed by R. Cruttwell/London: G. G. & J. Robinson, 1800. (Novel); *Letters on the Elementary Principles of Education.* Dublin: H. Colbert, 1801; *Memoires of the Life of Agrippina, the Wife of Germanicus.* 3 vols. Bath, 1804; *Letters Addressed to the Daughter of a Nobleman on the Formation of Religious and Moral Principle.* 2 vols. London, 1806; *The Cottagers of Glenburnie.* Edinburgh: Manners and Miller, 1808; *Exercises in Religious Knowledge.* Edinburgh, 1809; *A Series of Popular Essays Illustrative of Principles Connected with the Improvement of the Understanding, the Imagination and the Heart.* Edinburgh, 1813; *Hints Directed to Patrons and Directors of Schools. . . .* London & Edinburgh, 1815. REFERENCES: Benger, E. O. *Memoirs of the late Mrs. Elizabeth Hamilton. With a Selection from Her Correspondence, and Other Unpublished Writings.* 2 vols. London: Longman, 1818; Fowler, Kathleen L. "Elizabeth Hamilton." In *An Encyclopaedia of British Women Writers.* Paul Schleuter & June Schleuter, eds. Chicago & London: St. James, [1988], pp. 216–217.

HAMILTON, HUGO (1953–   ), novelist. Hamilton was born in Dun Laoghaire to an Irish father and a German mother. He spent several years in

Berlin working for a publishing company, and his three novels are set in Germany. His second novel, *Last Shot,* won the Rooney Prize in 1991. His prose style has been much praised, but *Books Ireland* was able to spot this sentence from *Surrogate City* (1991): "On the evening of the party the guests began to arrive at six in the evening."

WORKS: *Surrogate City.* London: Faber, 1991; *Last Shot.* London: Faber/New York: Farrar Straus, 1991; *The Love Test.* London: Faber, 1995.   REFERENCE: "Breaking the Bounds of Nationality." *Books Ireland* 184 (March 1995): 45–46.

HAMILTON, M. (ca. 1860–?), novelist. M. Hamilton was the pseudonym of Mrs. Churchill-Luck, formerly Miss Spottiswood-Ashe, who was born around 1860 in County Derry. She was a resident of County Derry for most of her life, although she was living in London by 1919.

She produced three novels specifically set in Ulster: *Across an Ulster Bog* (1896), *Beyond the Boundary* (1902), and *On an Ulster Farm* (1904). Of these, *Across an Ulster Bog* was her most popular and her best work. Stephen J. Brown called it "an ugly, but very powerful, tale of seduction." The novel centers around the seduction of a Protestant peasant girl, Ellen Linsay, by the local reverend, the son of a successful farming family from Southern Ireland. The relationship between Reverend Duffin and Ellen culminates in an unacknowledged child and an unsuccessful suicide attempt by Ellen. Hamilton explores all aspects of social relationships in the small Ulster village of Ballyturbet: between landed gentry and clergy, relationships among Protestant denominations, Catholic and Protestant relationships, the social hierarchy of the peasants. The central focus, however, remains Reverend Duffin, a man completely unsuited to fulfill his lifelong ambition of becoming a gentleman and attaining the social equality he technically is supposed to have with the local gentry. Ellen's brother, Willy, merits special attention as the drunken Orangeman and good churchman who never attends church services but hates all the proper denominations. This is an unusual novel, as it concentrates on the relationships between Protestant people and interdenominational Protestant strife rather than the usual Protestant–Catholic conflict.

Hamilton's other two Ulster-based novels also explore social class structures. *Beyond the Boundary* is set among the Ulster peasantry and focuses on a cowardly peasant who is mistakenly decorated for heroics in war. He marries an impoverished girl of good breeding, the sister of the true war hero. Her growing dissatisfaction with the marriage parallels the rising threat to her husband's secret cowardice. Hamilton has a light, convincing touch with this story and with the subsequent *On an Ulster Farm.* For the latter novel, she studies the workhouse system through the eyes of a child sent to service with a rigid Ulster family of Scottish decent. The novel is interesting for its character development. Relationships between individuals, between social classes, and between social groups are the dominant element of M. Hamilton's novels.

ANNE COLMAN

IRISH WORKS: *Across an Ulster Bog.* London: Heinemann, 1896; *Beyond the Boundary.* London: Hurst & Blackett, 1902; *On an Ulster Farm.* London: Everett, 1904.

HAMILTON, SIR WILLIAM ROWAN (1805–1865), mathematician, astronomer, and poet. This extraordinary nineteenth-century mathematician was born in Dublin at midnight between August 3 and 4, 1805, and died there on September 2, 1865. He is remembered for his *A Theory of Systems of Rays* (1828), his *Lectures on Quaternions* (1853), and his posthumous *The Elements of Quaternions* (1866). He was also deeply interested in poetry and a friend of Wordsworth and Southey. His fugitive pieces were not collected in his lifetime, but many are gathered in R. P. Graves's *Life* (1882). Hamilton uses the poetic diction, the syntactical inversion, and the lyric apostrophes of his times, but many of his poems retain a straightforward clarity, strength, and dignity.

WORKS AND REFERENCE: Graves, R. P. *Life of Sir W. Rowan Hamilton.* . . . 3 vols. Dublin: Hodges Figgis/London: Longmans, 1882.

HANLY, DAVID (1944–   ), novelist, broadcaster, and journalist. Hanly was born on April 25, 1944, in Limerick, where he was educated by the Sexton Street Christian Brothers. After school, he briefly entered the civil service but in 1964 joined RTÉ, where he wrote the popular radio serial "The Kennedys of Castleross" and the popular television serial "The Riordans." In 1970, he joined the Irish Tourist Board, and his six years there provided the background for his novel *In Guilt and in Glory,* a story of how Tourist Board representatives accompany an American television crew around Ireland. Set in the late 1970s, it is that rarity in Irish fiction, a novel of ideas. It discusses with occasional simplicity, but frequent trenchancy and pervasive glumness, the changes taking place in Ireland as it joins the modern world. Some of the most telling examples are beyond satire and simply taken directly from life, such as the exhibition as a work of art of some squiggles that a German artist had made on a blackboard during a lecture. In reality, the squiggles were made by the artist Joseph Beuys, called in the novel Joseph Goils. The book's weaknesses are that much of the plot is impelled by the thematically irrelevant question of who sleeps with whom and impaired by the two-dimensional characterization. Although some characters are limp, satirical versions of prominent people such as Conor Cruise O'Brien* or Edna O'Brien,* the two-dimensionality is especially evident in the sketch of a loutish best-selling American novelist who has settled in Ireland to take advantage of the tax exemption for writers. His bald vulgarity is underlined when another character reads a description of sex from one of his novels. The description, although tellingly appalling, is not greatly different from two of Hanly's own descriptions, and that fact seems symptomatic of the faults of this ambitious and readable, but finally flawed and forgettable, book.

In recent years, Hanly has been a news reporter for Irish radio, a literary interviewer for Irish television, and a columnist for the *Sunday Tribune.*

WORK: *In Guilt and in Glory*. London: Hutchinson, [1979]. REFERENCE: Battersby, Eileen. "Morning Becomes David." *Irish Times* (April 21, 1994): 13.

HANNA, DAVOREN (1975–1994), poet. Hanna was born in Dublin in 1975, and his slim volume of strong free-verse poems, *Not Common Speech,* appeared when he was only fifteen. His poetry received the Christy Brown* Award and the British Spastics Society Award and won the Welsh Academy Young Writers' Competition and *The Observer* National Children's Poetry Competition. These honors were well deserved, for his voice is a highly individual one. Like the work of Christy Brown and Christopher Nolan,* the work is itself extraordinary, but perhaps even more extraordinary is that it was produced with more physical difficulty than even theirs. As he remarked in his preface:

Limbs as sclerotic as mine have little or no voluntary movement. When you think of Christy Brown you think of feet. My feet are ice-fettered inside boots of lead. When you think of Christopher Nolan you see head-cupped unicorns tumbling among meadows of mellifluous words. But I can't even hold up my head or point with my eyes, so limp is my body at times.

He died in Dublin on July 18, 1994.

WORK: *Not Common Speech: The Voice of Davoren Hanna.* Dublin: Raven Arts, [1990].

HANNAY, CANON JAMES OWEN. *See* BIRMINGHAM, GEORGE A.

HARBINSON, ROBERT (1928–), short story writer, autobiographer, and travel writer. Harbinson was born Robin Bryans, a name he still used for many travel books, in Ballymacarrett, Belfast, on April 24, 1928. He was educated in Belfast and in Enniskillen. In 1944, he left to study theology at South Wales Bible College. He subsequently taught in England, Canada, and Venezuela, and he has been a diamond prospector in Canada and South America. He now lives in London.

His account of his childhood and youth in prewar Belfast, as an evacuee in Fermanagh, as a youthful Christian, and as an evangelical preacher is recorded in a memorable four-volume autobiography beginning with *No Surrender* (1960), possibly the finest (and funniest) account of the making of an Ulster working-class Protestant. Admirable as entertainment, the books are invaluable as social documents, essential for the understanding of the current (and perennial) problems in Northern Ireland. In 1974, while making a film based on his autobiographical tetralogy, he wrote *Songs Out of Oriel,* a free-verse sequence in twenty-four cantos that covers with greater compression and lyrical intensity and the same ornithological and botanical expertise (but without the demotic humor) the material of the earlier prose works.

Tattoo Lily, and Other Ulster Stories (1961) is a collection of gentle stories set mainly in Fermanagh in the years of Harbinson's own youth. "Benedicite" describes the anticlimax of a returned missionary who finds her cottage in

County Antrim morally and physically confining but who discovers fresh missionary field in the London of the 1960s. The title story, the longest in the collection, is the weakest; Harbinson's forte of kindly, uncritical humor does not suit the farce attempted here. He is best with children and the old. "Cage," about a child's acceptance of school life, and "Shanty," about a teacher's acceptance of imperfection in the young, show his talents better.

SEAN McMAHON

WORKS: *No Surrender: An Ulster Childhood.* London: Faber, 1960. (Autobiography); *Song of Erne.* London: Faber, 1960. (Autobiography); *Up Spake the Cabin Boy.* London: Faber, 1961. (Autobiography); *Tattoo Lily, and Other Ulster Stories.* London: Faber, 1961; *The Far World, and Other Ulster Stories.* London: Faber, 1962; *The Protege.* London: Faber, 1963. (Autobiography); *Lucio: A Novel.* London: Faber, 1964; *Songs Out of Oriel.* London: G. H. & R. Hart: B.G.M. Productions, 1974. (Poetry). As Robert Harbinson-Bryans: *Ulster: A Journey through the Six Counties.* London: Faber, 1964. Also travel books on Iceland, Morocco, Pakistan, Brazil, Denmark, and so on.

HARDING, MICHAEL (1953–   ), novelist and playwright. Harding was born in County Cavan and has worked as a teacher and social worker and was ordained a priest in 1981. Indeed, much of his work betrays a fascination for ritual and ritualized expression. His productions for the National Theatre include *Misogynist,* staged at the Abbey* in 1990, and three productions for the Peacock—*Strawboys* (1987), *Una Pooka* (1989), and *Hubert Murray's Widow* (1993). He has frequently been produced elsewhere—*The Kiss* at the Project Arts Centre, *Where the Heart Is* by Passion Machine and by the Lyric Players' Theatre* in Belfast, and *Backsides in the Wind* at the Theatre Royal in Waterford. He has also published two novels—*Priest* (1986) and *The Trouble with Sarah Gullion* (1988). His short stories have appeared in the *Irish Press* and *Drumlin,* and he has received a Stewart Parker Theatre Bursary.

Priest is a series of related episodes that examine the life and desperation of the clergy. Harding details the separateness of a life of celibacy, a separateness that engenders suicide and self-maiming. One of his priests hangs himself, and another gouges out his own eyes. It is a beautifully written work that demonstrates a reverence for language and a prose style that fluently carries forward themes and characterizations. *The Trouble with Sarah Gullion* is a short novel about a young woman who moves from her home in the South of Ireland to her husband's village in the Six Counties. Metaphorically, Sarah also moves from an almost numbing calm to a violent awareness of the limitations of her married life, including a lack of intellectual stimulation and a physically and emotionally abusive relationship. She takes desperate measures to relieve her growing isolation, and again the novel's prose reflects a rare sensitivity to language.

Harding's Abbey play *Misogynist* also shares a reverence for language and an appreciation for ritual. Like Brian Friel's* *Dancing at Lughnasa,* Vincent Woods's* *At the Black Pig's Dyke,* and Anne Devlin's* *After Easter,* Harding's play attempts to demonstrate through ritual the emptiness of a life without ceremonial rites as well as the regenerative force of Christian and non-Christian liturgies. An attentive reader will notice subtle references to Greek ceremonial drama and not-so-subtle references to the Catholic mass. Significantly, Harding reverses the traditional roles and portrays women raising the chalice and holy men in drag. Critics and reviewers, although praising aspects of the play's imagery and composition, criticized the lack of theatrical technique not only in *Misogynist* but in his other dramatic works.

BERNARD McKENNA

WORKS: *Priest.* Belfast: Blackstaff, 1986. (Novel); *The Trouble with Sarah Gullion.* Belfast: Blackstaff, 1988. (Novel); *The Misogynist* in *A Crack in the Emerald: New Irish Plays.* Introduction by David Grant. London: Nick Hern, 1990; *Una Pooka* in *First Run 2: New Plays by New Writers.* Introduction by Kate Harwood. London: Nick Hern, 1990.

HARRIS, EOGHAN (1943–   ), playwright and journalist. Harris was born in Cork and educated at University College, Cork, studying under the revisionist historian John A. Murphy. He has been a journalist, columnist, editor, and producer for a variety of television broadcasts, including "The Greening of America" (Jacobs Award) and "Darkness Visible" (Silver Bear Award). He has been associated with the Workers Party, formerly the Official Sinn Féin, contributing to the composition of several of their pamphlets, including *Irish Oil and Gas Robbery* (1973), *Irish Industrial Revolution* (1976), *The Land for the People* (1978), and *Television and Terrorism* (1987). He has written three plays, including *The Ballad of Jim Larkin* (the Gaiety, 1972) and *The Pope's Gig* (Damer, Dublin, 1984). However, his literary reputation is based on *Souper Sullivan,* produced at the Abbey* in 1985.

Souper Sullivan, subtitled *A Play for Protestants,* stages the struggles of the "spaleens," unskilled laborers, of Tooremoore with the local merchants and shopkeepers. Only a local rector and an English engineer show any sympathy for their plight. Set in the Great Famine, the laborers convert to the Protestant church for soup. Harris seeks to represent the plight of the Protestant poor far from the Anglo-Irish Big House. His own boyhood in Cork included no association with his Protestant neighbors because of the memories of the Famine and the still lingering anger and hostility of the local population. In interviews before the production, Harris told the story of Ronald Reagan's visit to Cork when graffiti proclaimed the Protestant president a "Souper" because of his conversion from Catholicism.

For all his literary achievement, Harris considers his first love politics, and he worked for Mary Robinson's successful presidential campaign as adviser and campaign strategist, much to the dismay of the more powerful members of the party. He has developed a reputation among critics and supporters alike of being brilliant and energetic but also abrasive and arrogant. In addition, in 1995, the *Sunday Independent* named him one of the twelve sexiest men in Ireland.

BERNARD McKENNA

REFERENCES: Barry, Kevin. "Feasts, Festivals, and Famines in the Irish Theatre: The Souper Sullivan Controversy." *Irish Literary Supplement* 5 (Spring 1986): 11; Bell, J. Bowyer. *The Irish*

Troubles: A Generation of Violence, 1967–1992. Dublin: Gill & Macmillan, 1993; O'Sullivan, Michael. *Mary Robinson—The Life and Times of an Irish Liberal.* Dublin: Blackwater, 1993.

HARRIS, FRANK (1856–1931), editor and author. Harris was born an ugly baby in the city of Galway of Welsh parents and baptized James Thomas Harris. He had two brothers and two sisters. The father, a naval lieutenant, commanded a revenue cutter and was harsh and strict. Mrs. Harris, frail and ladylike, cherished Frank but died of tuberculosis when he was four.

Then the doughty lieutenant dragged his family on a succession of postings to dreary Irish ports. During his absences at sea, Frank was left in the care of the other children, who bullied him. Once ashore, the sailor was virtually manic in his desire to instill his offspring with virtue and learning. Punishments were meted out for any shortcomings. The sensitive Frank became imbued with a great fear of his father and blustered to conceal it. There was neither softness nor sympathy in his life, and he early began to seek solace in feminine company.

At the age of twelve, he was sent to a boarding school in England. Life there proved little different from home: he was abused by his teachers and bullied by his fellows. After three years, he won a school prize of ten pounds and ran away, using the money to buy a ticket from Liverpool to New York. On the passage, he succeeded in his first real attempt at seduction.

In New York, he worked first as a shoeblack, then as a sandhog under the East River, during the building of Brooklyn Bridge. He moved to Chicago to become a night clerk in the Fremont House Hotel. Cunning by then, physically brave, and bursting with self-confidence, he had learned how to take care of himself. After Chicago, in search of money and adventure, he teamed up with a gang of cattle thieves. He had also begun to write short sketches of the life he saw around him, and these were published in small local papers.

Finally, he arrived at Lawrence, Kansas, looking like some strange, strutting bird. Five feet five inches tall, his biceps were huge, and his barrel chest strained the buttons of a gaudy waistcoat. His black hair, parted in the middle, was plastered down about two gigantic ears; alert brown eyes flashed from beneath a simian brow; a great, beaklike nose twitched aggressively above a magnificent moustache; and his booming voice sounded much too large for so short a body.

Harris remained in Lawrence for a year, attending university under Professor Byron Smith as a special student of the humanities. He impressed with the power of his presence, the quickness of his mind, and the scope of his knowledge. Arrogant and opinionated and aged about twenty, he was admitted to the bar of Lawrence.

At the year's end, he returned to England, was reconciled with his father, and became briefly an assistant schoolmaster at Brighton. The next few years were spent in France and then in Germany, where he attended the universities of Heidelberg and Göttingen. He studied Greek and Latin and perfected his German. His twin pleasures were Shakespeare and seduction.

After a stint as correspondent reporting the Russo-Turkish War, he returned to England and broke into journalism by writing book reviews for *The Spectator*. A couple of years later, aged twenty-eight, he bluffed his way into the editorship of the ailing *Evening News*. Totally without scruples, full of brash energy, he gave his readers a sensational diet of sex, sport, and politics, the like of which was never before experienced in a British paper. Circulation increased from 7,000 to 70,000.

Sorely aware that he was catering to the masses, he really wanted to be taken seriously by the upper middle class, which, however, regarded the *Evening News* as vulgar and its editor a cad. He ran the paper for eight years, but, finally becoming bored and negligent, he was sacked.

He next determined to resuscitate the sober *Fortnightly Review,* then suffering a slow death from respectability. He bullied until he became its editor. Then he boomed and bellowed to dislodge many venerable contributors. The magazine did improve during the eight years of his editorship, for he had no wish to disconcert the Establishment and close the doors of power and prestige. Radicals did not appear in his pages. Wilde's* *The Portrait of Mr. W. H.,* for instance, was rejected. Harris had his sights on the House of Commons.

While continuing to have many liaisons, he met and married Edith Mary Clayton, a circumspect but wealthy Yorkshire widow. She entertained lavishly, and royalty were not infrequent guests at her house in Park Lane. With Lord Randolph Churchill as his chief backer, Harris was selected as Conservative Party candidate for Hackney.

Oscar Wilde said of him, "Frank Harris has been to all the great houses of England—once!" Determined to make a success of his marriage and his social and political careers, Harris set out to please his straitlaced wife. He curbed his sexual appetite, moderated his drinking, and refrained in crowded drawing rooms from such bellowed remarks as, "Rape? Why, any sensible woman would just lie back and enjoy it!"

The accumulated weight of all that dignity and decorum proved too much of a constriction. Harris clawed himself out of the aspic of respectability, got gloriously drunk, insulted his sedate wife and her friends, delivered a speech in defense of Kitty O'Shea, and declared that he regarded sexual restraint as an interference with nature. Inevitably, he was scrubbed as candidate for Hackney, sacked from *The Fortnightly,* and separated from Mrs. Harris.

Next, with a down payment of 10% and promises that some powerful friends soon enabled him to fulfill, he bought the old *Saturday Review*. He made this journal his very own, being free from every constraint and publishing exactly whom and what he wished. He had a sharp eye for writing talent, both established and budding. Among the tried and the tyros that he engaged were Bernard Shaw* to write on theater, John Runciman on music, H. G. Wells on books, D. S. McColl on art, Chalmers Mitchell on science, and Cunningham Graham on travel. He turned *The Saturday Review* into a vital, stimulating, and exceedingly profitable journal.

At the height of his editorial fame, he became obsessed with a beautiful Dublin girl, Helen O'Hara, twenty years his junior. In 1898, he persuaded her to elope with him. Harris, his way of life, and his many mistresses vulgarized Nellie; but she remained with him, tough and supportive, until his death thirty years later. In the misery of old age, he would often remark, "Nellie's still with me, anyway; that's something."

In 1898 also, Harris sold *The Saturday Review* and used the considerable sum realized to finance a couple of hotels in the South of France and an art gallery in London. His businesses and other investments failed, and he supported himself and Nellie on the proceeds of swindles, blackmail, and plagiarism. He also edited a number of magazines, great and small, in Britain and America, including *Vanity Fair, Hearth and Home, Pearson's,* and *Modern Society.* He grew increasingly unscrupulous in his shady moneymaking schemes, but he also published three volumes of short stories, the first in 1894. There were some novels and five collections of *Contemporary Portraits.* When some of those depicted in the latter complained of not recognizing themselves, Harris replied that he was an artist, not a reporter.

He wrote a play, *Mr. and Mrs. Daventry,* based on a scenario by Wilde, who claimed that Harris had stolen and spoiled his work. While the dialogue does not have Wilde's fizz, and the plot creaks, the play was first produced with Mrs. Patrick Campbell in the lead. Some money was made, and Wilde and Harris fought over the royalties.

He wrote biographies of Shakespeare, Wilde, and Shaw. Each caused conflict and controversy and revealed more of Harris than of his subjects.

If Harris is remembered today, it is as the brilliant editor of *The Saturday Review* and as the notorious author of *My Life and Loves,* a pornographic exaggeration in four volumes, which shortage of money persuaded him to write in his old age. The first volume of this "black harvest" appeared in 1925.

Harris died in a villa at Nice in 1931, aged seventy-five. The tough but faithful Nellie was by his side. Shaw, who remained his friend till the end, once wrote to him, "Like everyone else I took you to be much more of a man of the world," but, in fact, Harris, "the buccaneer of Monte Carlo, was a romantic boy and even a sensitive child without the ghost of a notion of the sort of society he was living in and the people he was up against."

JAMES DOUGLAS

WORKS: *Elder Conklin and Other Stories.* London: Heinemann, 1895; *A Daughter of Eve.* Paris: Privately printed, 1898. (Story); *The Bomb.* London: John Long, [1908]/New York: M. Kennerley, 1909. (Novel); *Montes the Matedor, and Other Stories.* London: Grant Richards, 1909/New York: M. Kennerley, 1910; *The Man Shakespeare and His Tragic Life Story.* London: Frank Palmer/New York: M. Kennerley, 1909; *Shakespeare and His Love.* London: Frank Palmer, [1910]. (Play); *The Women of Shakespeare.* London: Methuen/New York: M. Kennerley, 1911; *Unpath'd Waters.* London: John Lane, 1913; *Great Days.* London: John Lane/Toronto: Bell & Cockburn/New York: M. Kennerley, 1914. (Novel); *The Yellow Ticket and Other Stories.* London: Grant Richards, 1914; *England or Germany?* New York: Wilmarth, 1915. (Nonfiction); *Contemporary Portraits.* 4 vols. London: Methuen, 1915–1924; *Love in Youth.* New York: Doran, 1916; *Oscar Wilde: His Life and*

Confessions. New York: Author, 1916; *Oscar Wilde: His Life and Confessions, with "Memories of Oscar Wilde" by G. B. Shaw.* New York: Author, 1918/London: Constable, 1938; *Undream'd of Shores.* London: Grant Richards/New York: Brentano's, 1924. (Short stories); *My Life and Loves.* 4 vols. Various private publishers, 1925–1929/Paris: Obelisk, 1945. (Pornography); *Joan La Romee.* Nica: Nicaise/London: Fortune/New York: Frank Harris, 1926. (Play); *Latest Contemporary Portraits.* New York: Macaulay, 1928; *On the Trail. My Reminiscences as a Cowboy.* London: John Lane, 1930/as *My Reminiscences as a Cowboy.* New York: C. Boni, 1930; *Confessional . . . A Volume of Intimate Portraits, Sketches and Studies.* New York: Panurge, [1930]; *Pantopia.* New York: Panurge, 1930. (Pornography); *Bernard Shaw, An Unauthorized Biography . . . with a Postscript by Mr. Shaw.* Garden City, N.Y.: Garden City/London: Gollancz, 1931; *Mr. and Mrs. Daventry.* London: Richards, 1956. (Play based on a scenario by Oscar Wilde). REFERENCES: Bain, Linda Morgan. *Evergreen Adventurer. The Real Frank Harris.* London: Research, 1975; Brome, Vincent. *Frank Harris.* London: Cassell, 1959; Kingsmill, Hugh. *Frank Harris.* London: Jonathan Cape, 1932; Pearsall, Robert B. *Frank Harris.* New York: Twayne, [1970]; Puller, Philippa. *Frank Harris.* London: Hamilton, 1975; Root, Edward M. *Frank Harris.* New York: Odyssey, 1947; Sherard, Robert. *Bernard Shaw, Frank Harris & Oscar Wilde.* London: T. Werner Laurie, 1937; Tobin, A. I. & Gertz, Elmer. *Frank Harris.* Chicago: Madelaine Mendelsohn, 1931.

HARRISON, SHANE

WORK: *Blues before Dawn.* Dublin: Poolbeg, 1992. (Novel).

HART, JOSEPHINE

WORKS: *Damage.* London: Chatto & Windus; *Sin.* London: Chatto & Windus/New York: Knopf, 1992. (Novel).

HARTE, JACK (1944–), fiction writer. Harte was born on September 1, 1944, near Easkey in County Sligo and is the principal of Lucan Community College in County Dublin. He was involved in Profile Press in the mid-1970s and was the founder of the Irish Writers' Union and the Irish Writers' Centre in the 1980s. He is married to Celia de Freine. His *Murphy in the Underworld* (1986) is an imaginative collection of stories, tales, and fables that range in setting from Hades, to small Irish towns, to the moon. Not all are totally successful, but the title story, as well as "The Land of Dwarfs" and "Three for Oblivion," is impelled by a fancy that is a welcome respite from the realism of much modern Irish writing. Indeed, the well-conceived narrator of one particularly relevant story is actually a bee. His rather less successful novella *Homage* (1992) depicts a contest in Sligo in which a poet, a sculptor, and a traditional musician write, sculpt, and compose for the affections of a young woman. However, neither the poem nor the sculpture is very good, and the song is not original. The point seems to be, as the musician remarks, "I'm not going to spend my life brooding about love. If I don't find satisfaction in one woman's arms, then by Christ I'll find it in another's." Despite this healthily unromantic conclusion, the characters are not vividly realized, and in the eighty-six pages of text there are twenty-three very short chapters, many of only a page or two.

WORKS: *Murphy in the Underworld.* [Dun Laoghaire]: Glendale, [1986]. (Short stories); *Homage.* [Dublin]: Dedalus, [1992]. (Novella).

HARTIGAN, ANNE LE MARQUAND (1937–), poet, playwright, and painter. Born in England of an Irish mother and a Jersey father, Hartigan grew up and was educated in Reading, studying fine art (painting) at university. In 1962, she moved to Ireland, where she lived near Drogheda and raised six children. She now lives in Dublin. Although her short stories frequently appear in anthologies, Hartigan is better known for her poetry and its lush imagery— unquestionably a reflection of her artistic training. In addition, Hartigan has written several excellent plays: *Strings,* a one-act, appeared in a workshop production in the 1981 Galway Arts Festival; her experimental full-length play, *Beds,* was in the 1982 Dublin Theatre Festival; *I Do Like to Be beside the Seaside* was first produced as a rehearsed staged reading in 1984 at the Abbey Theatre*; *La Corbiere,* the first of the Jersey Lilies trilogy, was in the 1989 Dublin Theatre Festival; the second of the trilogy, *Le Crapaud,* was first performed in 1994; and her epic poem, *Now Is a Moveable Feast,* has been frequently performed on stage and on the radio. Her most recent play, *A Secret Game,* won the Mobil (Ireland) competition in 1995.

KATHLEEN A. QUINN

WORKS: *Long Tongue.* Dublin: Beaver Row, 1982. (Poetry); *Return Single.* Dublin: Beaver Row, 1986. (Poetry); *The Mute Voice, the Deaf Ear: Women Writing.* Dublin: University College, Dublin: Women's Studies Forum, 1987. (Pamphlet); *Now Is a Moveable Feast.* Galway: Salmon, 1991. (Poetry); *Clearing the Space: The Why of Writing.* Dublin: Salmon, 1992. (Essay); *Immortal Sins.* [Dublin]: Salmon, [1994]. (Poetry).

HARTLEY, MARY ("MAY") LAFFAN (1850?–1916), novelist and short story writer. Little is known of this writer's life other than that she was born in Dublin and that in 1882 she married Walter Noel Hartley, distinguished chemist and fellow of the Royal Society, lecturing at King's College, London, where the Hartleys lived. Between 1876 and 1887, Mrs. Hartley published anonymously five volumes. They include some very poignant analysis of the conditions of the lives of the poor in Dublin during the 1870s, as well as a more satirical treatment of the social posturing and maneuvering of the up-and-coming Catholic middle classes.

In "Flitters, Tatters, and the Counsellor," a long short story in her 1881 volume of that name, she tells a story of three Dublin "street Arabs" who are forced to live by their wits. She shows their courage and heroic loyalty to one another. While the final outcome may border on the sentimental, the situations are not overstated, and the story unfolds with just the right amount of detail. The sordid lives of the slum dwellers are described against the backdrop of a city with great natural beauty and a society able to enjoy the advantages of a prosperous (for some!) capital. The children in her stories are treated with compassion, while the adults are shown to be almost brutalized by their poverty, but at the same time supportive of one another through an innate generosity: "What do you care so long as you have a bit to eat? And if you haven't it, won't anyone give it to you?" remarks one of the characters with typical confidence.

In "The Game Hen," she tells a tragic tale of a young mother ostracized and ultimately destroyed by jealousy and the narrow prejudice of two women living along her street. When they finally recognize what they have done, they set about sharing what little they have to save the children the mother has been driven to neglect.

The novels deal with Irish politics, social climbing, intermarriage between Catholics and Protestants, and the Catholic education system. The opening scenes of *Hogan, M.P.* (1876) are reminiscent of George Moore's* *Drama in Muslim,* and her characters have been compared with similar figures in Zola, Twain, and Trollope. Ruskin was particularly moved by the story of "Flitters, Tatters, and the Counsellor," which was described by Stephen J. Brown in 1915 as "quite the most perfect thing that has been written about Dublin life." Certainly, Mrs. Laffan was a mordant and powerful social critic, and few Irish writers of the nineteenth century have been so shamefully neglected.

MARY BALL

WORKS: *Hogan, M.P.* 3 vols. London: Henry S. King, 1876/London: Macmillan, 1881/New York & London: Garland, 1979; *The Hon. Miss Ferrard.* 3 vols. London: Guildford, 1877/New York: H. Holt, 1878; *Christy Carew.* New York: Holt, 1878/3 vols. London: R. Bentley, 1880; *Flitters, Tatters, and the Counsellor, and Other Sketches.* New York: G. Munro, 1879/Philadelphia: Lippincott, 1879/3d ed. London, Dublin, [1879]/London: Macmillan, 1881/New York & London: Garland, 1979; *Baubie Clark.* Edinburgh & London: W. Blackwood, 1880. (Short story); *The Game Hen.* Dublin: Gill, 1880. (Short story); tr., *No Relations.* New York: G. Munro, 1880. (Translation of a French novel by Hector Malot); *A Singer's Story.* London: Chapman & Hall, 1885/New York: G. Munro, [1886]; *Ismay's Children.* 3 vols. London: Macmillan, 1887.

HARTNETT, MICHAEL (1941–   ), poet. Hartnett was born in 1941 in Newcastle West, County Limerick. He came to school late and did not receive his leaving certificate until he was twenty. Nevertheless, he is fluent in Irish and has a reading competence in several other languages. After working for many years in the Department of Posts and Telegraphs, he became a lecturer in creative writing at Thomand College in Limerick. He received the Irish-American Cultural Institute Award in 1980, the Irish Arts Council Award for the best book in Irish in 1986, the Irish American Cultural Institute Award in 1988, and the American-Ireland Fund Literary Award in 1990. He is a member of Aosdána* and lives in Dublin.

His first small collection of verse, *Anatomy of a Cliché* (1968) is a talented, if overwrought collection of love poems, in which the writer eschews capital letters, consistent punctuation, conventional syntax, and discernible rhythm, although he rhymes when convenient. The diction ranges from the flat to the florid, that is, from "love is . . . wonderful!" to "delicate footsteps of spring." There is some pretentious phrasing such as "conceptual orgasms" and one bizarre personification of Ireland as a multibreasted female who invites her children to suckle her many breasts, after which she promises to make them love her by devouring them and then vomiting them up.

In *Selected Poems* (1970), Hartnett is more concerned with form, but in such pieces as "I Have Exhausted the Delighted Range," "I Have Managed," "Fairview Park: 6 A.M.," "The Lord Taketh Away," and "For My Grandmother, Bridget Halpin," the form is uncontrolled and disintegrates before the close of the poem. "The Poet as Black Sheep" and "The Poet as Woman of Ireland" are somewhat better, despite a couple of metrical breakdowns. *A Farewell to English* (1975) was a definite advance, and there are some strong images in "The Oat Woman" and "Death by the Santry River." The longish title poem, however, veers between limp eloquence and lame satire, with detours into rather frantic imagery. There is, for instance, one extraordinary and extended image about deformed dwarfs riding other deformed dwarfs around a racetrack while jabbing them with electric prods and while being covered with mucous and excrement. The purpose of this activity is to win an anus made of glass and concrete.

Despite such silliness, the sentiment of the title poem received considerable publicity at the time. Hartnett's farewell to English was not total, for his next two volumes were written in English; however, for ten years he did concentrate on writing in Irish. In recent years, he has continued to publish frequently, both original work in English and translations, especially from the Irish. His reputation has grown greatly, and Seamus Heaney* has written that he is "one of the truest, most tested and beloved voices in Irish poetry in our time."

At this writing, the best introduction to his work is the Gallery Press* *Selected and New Poems* (1994), which contains work spanning his career from *Anatomy of a Cliché* to the present. In this selection, there is much less of the overlush diction of his earlier work, and a phrase like "purple thunder" from the late poem "He'll to the Moors" is a rarity. Occasionally, a line really requires an explanatory note. For instance, in his very effective "That Actor Kiss" about his dying father, he lists the numbers '29, '41, and '84. In a radio reading of the poem, Hartnett explained that these were significant dates in his father's life and what the significance was. Without such information, this line and others remain meaningless.

Nevertheless, Hartnett is not basically an obscure poet. Also, he can command meter well enough to diverge from it effectively by intruding two or three stressed syllables together. He is not interested in imitating conventional form, and when, for instance, he writes a sonnet, he will often give it a most unconventional rhyme scheme. One might not quite agree with Brendan Kennelly's* assessment that Hartnett's work has "here and there a hint of that brave, rounded humanity which earns the right to be called divine." Nevertheless, one must certainly agree that Hartnett's talent and technique has matured over the years.

WORKS: *Anatomy of a Cliché*. Dublin: Dolmen, 1968; *The Hag of Beare, a Rendition of the Old Irish*. Dublin: New Writers', 1969; *Selected Poems*. Dublin: New Writers', 1970; *Tao: A Version of a Chinese Classic of the Sixth Century, B.C.* Dublin: New Writers', 1971; *Gipsy Ballads: A Version of the Romancero Gitano (1924–27) of Federico Lorca*. Dublin: Goldsmith, 1973; ed., with Desmond Egan. *Choice*. Dublin: Goldsmith, 1973. (Poetry anthology); *A Farewell to English*. Dublin: Gallery, 1975/enlarged ed., 1978; *The Retreat of Ita Cagney/Culu Ide*. Dublin: Goldsmith, 1975; *Poems in English*. Dublin: Dolmen, 1977; *Adharca Broic*. Dublin: Gallery, 1978; *An Phurgoid*.

Dublin: Coiscéim, 1983; *Do Nuala: Foighne Crainn.* Dublin: Coiscéim, 1984; *Collected Poems in English.* 2 vols. Dublin: Raven Arts, 1984–1985; *Inchicore Haiku.* Dublin: Raven Arts, 1985; *Ó Bruadair: Selected Poems of Daithi Ó Bruadair Translated and Introduced by Michael Hartnett.* Dublin: Gallery, 1985; *A Necklace of Wrens: Selected Poems in Irish with English Translations by the Author.* Dublin: Gallery, 1987; *Poems for Younger Women.* [Oldcastle, Co. Meath]: Gallery, [1988]; *Farewell to English.* Rev. ed. [Dublin]: Gallery, [1991]; *A Killing Dreams.* [Oldcastle, Co. Meath]: Gallery, [1992]; *Haicead.* [Oldcastle, Co. Meath]: Gallery, [1993]. (Translations from the seventeenth-century Irish Dominican Padraigin Haicead); *Selected and New Poems.* [Oldcastle, Co. Meath]: Gallery/Winston-Salem, N.C.: Wake Forest University Press, 1994. REFERENCE: White, Victoria. "Heartbreak in Two Languages." *Irish Times* (December 15, 1994): 14. (Interview).

HARVEY, FRANCIS (1925–   ), poet and playwright. Harvey was born in Enniskillen and has lived in County Donegal. He has written plays for Radio Éireann, and one of his plays won the O. Z. Whitehead Award.

WORKS: *In the Light of the Stones.* [Dublin]: Gallery, [1978]; *The Rainmaker.* [Dublin]: Gallery, [1988].

HAYES, DAVID (1919–1994), playwright. Hayes was born in Dublin on June 7, 1919, and graduated from University College, Dublin. He worked in industry for many years, before turning to writing full-time. Most of his work was done for radio and television. For radio, he created the popular soap opera, "The Foley Family," and his *Gift of Tears* won the play competition that marked the twenty-first anniversary of the Radio Éireann repertory company. His stage play, *Sorry! No Hard Feelings?,* is a rather sadistic black comedy about government's inhumanity to man. His long one-act, "Legend," is a garrulous but strong satiric fantasy set in a prison. He died unexpectedly at his home in County Louth on January 16, 1994.

WORK: *Sorry! No Hard Feelings?* Newark, Del.: Proscenium, 1978; "Legend" in *4 Irish Plays* (called in Ireland *4 One-Act Plays*). [Newark, Del.]: Proscenium, [1982].

HAYES, KATY (1965–   ), short story writer and playwright. Hayes lives in Dublin with her husband, the academic writer Anthony Roche. She has worked in the theater, staging plays by women for the now defunct Glasshouse Productions. Her one-act *Playgirl* was commissioned by the Abbey* and staged at the Peacock in October 1995. Her collection of short stories, *Forecourt* (1995), is enjoyable and promising. The stories focus on young women, children in suburban housing estates, women coming to terms with themselves and their sexuality, unemployed actors, and successful stage directors. The title story about a young woman petrol pump attendant who masturbates is particularly funny and won the Francis MacManus Award and the Mercier Press Jubilee Prize. "Stepford" has a beautifully bizarre touch that makes one laugh aloud when the roller-skating heroine chats to her food processor and calls her children after washing products. This comic quality is seen again in a dinner party conversation in "Something Formal." "Getting Rid of Him" and "Dead Wood" are excellent studies of obsession. On the whole, the book has a hopeful quality that makes it cheerful, unsentimental reading.

MARY ROSE CALLAGHAN

WORK: *Forecourt.* [Dublin]: Poolbeg, [1995].

HAYWARD, H. RICHARD (1892–1964), travel writer. Hayward was born in Larne in 1892 and died in an auto crash on October 13, 1964, in Belfast. His career was enormously busy and varied. He published a novel and many travel books about Ireland. He wrote two curtain-raisers for the Ulster Players; he was a prominent actor with the group and managed it for some years. He was later the founder of the Belfast Repertory Theatre and, with Tyrone Guthrie, of the Belfast Radio Players. As a ballad singer, he cut over a hundred records, and he directed the first sound motion picture made in Ireland. His travel books are informal and minutely knowledgeable, but finally a bit irksome to read because of his obtrusive stage-Ulster jocularity. More dated but charming companions for travelers are Colum's* *The Road Round Ireland,* Harold Speakman's *Here's Ireland,* or even Thackeray's *Irish Sketch Book.*

WORKS: *The Jew's Fiddle,* with Abram Rish. Dublin: Talbot/London: Unwin, 1921. (One-act play); *Sugarhouse Entry.* London: Barker, 1936. (Novel); *In Praise of Ulster.* London: Barker, 1938/ revised, Belfast: William Mullan, 1946; *Where the River Shannon Flows.* London: Harrap, 1940; *The Corrib Country.* Dundalk: W. Tempest, 1943; *In the Kingdom of Kerry.* Dundalk: W. Tempest, 1946; *This Is Ireland. Leinster and the City of Dublin.* London: Barker, 1949; *This Is Ireland. Ulster and the City of Belfast.* London: Barker, 1950; *Belfast through the Ages.* Dundalk: Dundalgan, 1952; *This Is Ireland. Connacht and the City of Galway.* London: Barker, 1952; *The Story of the Irish Harp.* Dublin: Arthur Guinness, 1954. (Pamphlet); *This Is Ireland. Mayo, Sligo, Leitrim and Roscommon.* London: Barker, 1955; *Border Foray.* London: Barker, 1957; *Munster and the City of Cork.* London: Phoenix House, 1964.

HEAD, RICHARD (1637?–1686?), bookseller, novelist, playwright, and poet. Head was born in Ireland, his father a nobleman's chaplain who was killed by Irish rebels in 1641. Head and his mother escaped to Belfast and then to England, where he attended grammar school at Bridport, Dorsetshire, and then was admitted to Oxford. He soon left to become apprentice to a London bookseller and eventually opened his own bookshop. Gambling, however, ruined him, and he retired to Dublin, where he wrote *Hic et Ubique; or, the Humours of Dublin,* which was privately performed with some success. Returning to London in 1663, he printed the play and again attempted bookselling and again was ruined by gambling and reduced to scribbling for booksellers himself. His *The English Rogue* (1665) pretended to be the autobiography of a thief and was racy, indecent, and extremely popular. Several sequels, which he denied having a hand in, repeated its success. In the same vein were *Nugae Venales, or Complaisant Companion* (1675) and *The Life and Death of Mother Shipton* (1677). He was not lacking in wit, as may be seen by his *Proteus Redivivus: or, The Art of Wheedling* (1675). He led a rackety and dissipated life and drowned, possibly in 1686, crossing to the Isle of Wight.

PRINCIPAL WORKS: *Hic et Ubique; or, The Humours of Dublin.* London: For the Author, 1663; *The English Rogue, Described in the Life of Meriton Latroon.* . . . London: F. Kirkman, 1665; *The Canting Academy; or, The Devil's Cabinet Opened.* . . . London: M. Drew, 1673; *The Floating Island: or, A New Discovery.* . . . London, 1673; *Jackson's Recantation; or, The Life & Death of the Notorious High-way-man.* . . . London: T. B., 1674; *The Miss Display'd, with All Her Wheedling Arts and Circumventions.* London, 1675; *Nugae Venales, or Complaisant Companion.* London: W. D., 1675; *O-Brazile; or the Inchanted Island.* . . . London: W. Crook, 1675; *Proteus Redivivus: or, The Art of Wheedling.* . . . London: W. D., 1675; *The Life and Death of Mother Shipton.* London: B. Harris, 1677.

HEALY, DERMOT (1947–   ), novelist, short story writer, and poet. Healy was born in Finea, County Westmeath, and has lived in Cavan, Dublin, and London. His short stories won Hennessy Awards in 1974 and 1976, and his first collection, *Banished Misfortune,* won the Tom Gallon Award in 1983. The twelve stories in the collection are of various lengths and two manners. "Reprieve" and "Betrayal" are less than two pages long; the remainder range from about five to fifteen pages. "Reprieve" and particularly "The Tenant" are told in a conventional manner; the remainder, which really set the tone for the book, are written with a denser obliquity than that of his near contemporaries, Desmond Hogan* and Neil Jordan,* and may owe something to writers like Aidan Higgins* and Tom MacIntyre,* who have admired his later work. Healy does not, however, depend on unusual or foreign words or startling images, but rather on an eccentric punctuation linking or, more usually, separating sentences, clauses, and fragments of sentences. A typical passage is this from "First Snow of the Year":

It stopped snowing, the brittle stars came out. Would the dead forgive him if his hand wandered over Helen's face in darkness of the mourning house, touching and parting flesh here, and folding his body around her against death. The canoe to the sea. He walked across a new planet, journeying inwards, without thought of his fellows. There were so many clear stars that he found the gravel track on the far side of the bog as in a dream, all beaten up and restored, like the others of his tribe.

Not a totally baffling paragraph but, if regarded closely, in part a puzzling one. The attractions of such a style are its freedom, its individuality, and its suggestion of a sensitive, mysterious, and wildly inexplicable persona. However, the dangers are obvious: certain phrases lose their syntactical anchor so that their position gets puzzling, and their meaning murky; the public presentation of a narrative gets camouflaged, and indeed the narrative becomes less prominent than the narrating.

Healy's first novel, *Fighting with Shadows* (1984), was published to considerable acclaim. Higgins, for instance, called it "the best novel to come out of Ireland since *Malone Dies*," and MacIntyre remarked, "Not since [Francis] Stuart's* *Black-List* have I read an Irish novel that kept my hand so tight to the page." Nevertheless, the problems of Healy's short story collection seem, if anything, more pronounced in his novel, and the problems are as much of diction as of syntax. He is capable of the arresting simile like "The line of trees . . .

blew down the crest of the hill to the lake like a horse's mane,'' but it will be immediately followed by something more ''poetic'' like ''At the water's edge the hills drank.'' The overwriting finally overwhelms the good lines, and the book is full of florid writing like ''the deep-throated sound of the night,'' ''And the earth lulled by inactivity grew desperate for growth and space and life from another world,'' ''Frank went down the tortured path of longing,'' and ''his eyes took a swallowdive through the thick lines on his temple.'' Again, the prose overwhelms the narrative and characterization and makes the reader wonder with some impatience, When is he going to get on with it?

Healy's collection of poems, *The Ballyconnell Colours* (1992), gets its effects not from form but from a strong, terse clarity. Mainly, it is flat statement and sometimes entirely too flat, as in the ten-line, three-line piece ''Two Moons.''

In 1995, his novel *Goat's Song* won the Encore Award for the best second novel to be published in Britain. He is a member of Aosdána.*

WORKS: *Banished Misfortune and Other Stories.* London & New York: Allison & Busby/[Dingle, Co. Kerry]: Brandon, [1982]; *Fighting with Shadows; or Sciamachy.* London: Allison & Busby/[Dingle, Co. Kerry]: Brandon, [1984]. (Novel); *A Goat's Song.* London: Collins Harvill, 1990. (Novel); *The Ballyconnell Colours.* [Oldcastle, Co. Meath]: Gallery, [1992].

HEALY, GERARD (1918–1963), playwright and actor. Healy was born in Dublin in 1918, and was educated at the Synge Street Christian Brothers School. After working in a Dublin drapery store, he joined the Gate Theatre* as assistant stage manager and toured with the company to the Balkans and to Egypt. He married one of the company's actresses, Eithne Dunne, and played himself in a number of Gate productions. In 1939, he and his wife moved to the Abbey* and played there for five years. In 1943, the Abbey produced his first play, *Thy Dear Father.* In 1945, he helped to form the short-lived Players' Theatre, which staged in that year his second play *The Black Stranger.* Illness forced him temporarily from the stage, and he wrote radio notes for *The Irish Times* before joining the Radio Éireann Repertory Company. He wrote many scripts and documentaries for radio, and also became a member of Austin Clarke's* verse-speaking team on Radio Éireann. When asked why he did not write more plays, he replied, ''I cannot satisfy myself. . . . Playwriting is an art. I'm afraid my work is purely ephemeral.''

While *Thy Dear Father* would probably not bear revival, as a study of fanatic religiosity it was an outspoken piece for the 1940s. A stronger work is *The Black Stranger,* which is set during the Potato Famines of the 1840s and sees this overwhelming national trauma through the microcosm of two families. The play is a leanly written, understated, tightly structured piece of realism that remains persuasive, powerful, and moving.

Healy wrote his two plays in his middle twenties. Although he lived about twenty years longer, he regrettably wrote no more for the stage. He died in London on March 9, 1963, while playing the role of the Jesuit in Hugh Leonard's* *Stephen D.*

WORKS: *The Black Stranger.* Dublin: James Duffy, 1950; *Thy Dear Father.* Dublin: P. J. Bourke, 1957.

HEALY, SHAY (1943–   ), novelist and entertainer. Healy was born in Dublin in 1943, the son of Seamus Healy the actor. He has been a singer, a songwriter, and a popular entertainer on Irish television. His novel *The Stunt* authentically depicts the Dublin Rock scene and adds liberal saltings of sex, violence, and profanity. Its unadorned, utilitarian prose makes it an easy read; its characters are simple but well defined; and it has a structured plot from which emerges a theme of human values triumphing over greed. It is a serious entertainment, as is his second novel, *Green Card Blues* (1994), which is set in New York City.

WORK: *The Stunt.* Dublin: O'Brien, 1992; *Green Card Blues.* Dublin: O'Brien, 1994.

HEANEY, SEAMUS (1939–   ), poet. One of the two or three most important poets writing in English today, Seamus Heaney was born on April 13, 1939, in County Derry. After secondary education at St. Columb's College, he attended Queen's University, where he took first class honours in English language and literature in 1961. Subsequently, he has held a number of academic appointments, including lectureships at St. Joseph's College and Queen's and department head of English at Carysfort College. He was a guest lecturer at the University of California, Berkeley, and a visiting professor at Harvard. Since 1984, he has been the Boylston Professor of Rhetoric and Oratory at Harvard and in 1989 was made professor of poetry at Oxford. In addition, Heaney has contributed to the BBC and Radio Éireann and is a founding editor of Field Day* Publishing. Besides eight major volumes of poetry, Heaney has published *Sweeney Astray* (1984), a translation of the medieval Irish poem *Buile Suibhne,* and a play, *The Cure at Troy* (1990), a version of Sophocles' *Philoctetes.* He has also published three collections of critical essays. His numerous prizes and awards include the E. C. Gregory Award, the Somerset Maugham Award, the Geoffrey Faber Prize, the Denis Devlin* Award, the Duff Cooper Memorial Prize, the Whitbread Prize, and in 1995, the Nobel Prize for literature.

In an early essay, Heaney quotes approvingly from Shakespeare's *Timon of Athens,* "our poesy is a gum / Which oozes whence 'tis nourished." Beginning with his first two collections, *Death of a Naturalist* (1966) and *Door into the Dark* (1969), the sensuous particularity of his own poetry does indeed ooze with the bogs, potato drills, and farmyards of rural Ulster. While it is a poetry that led to almost universal admiration for Heaney's concrete physicality, some early critics saw Heaney merely as a competent regional poet. Such reactions, however, oversimplify a sensibility in Heaney that has been fundamental to his work throughout his career. It is a sensibility that is informed by the textures of his surroundings but that sees beneath the superficial "visual pleasure" they provide. Heaney talks about the possibility of seeing "the features of the landscape [as] . . . a mode of communion with a something other than themselves, a something to which we ourselves still feel we might belong."

If a sense of belonging to place was evident in Heaney's first two books, with *Wintering Out* (1972), his third volume, critics noted a change in the poetic weather where there were "many poems . . . about the estrangement and isolation the poet feels." This sense of isolation might well have been the result of increasing pressure on Heaney at the time to "be more Irish, to be more political, to 'try to touch the people,' to do Yeats's* job again instead of his own." With its publication coinciding with increasing sectarian violence in Northern Ireland and with Heaney's removal from Ulster to the republic, the book does appear to be "everywhere bruised by northern politics, even though rarely confronting them directly." Rather, in keeping with his established technique, Heaney looks to the land itself as a way to find terms "adequate to [Ulster's] predicament." By "[l]ovingly dwelling on place, name, and place-name he . . . opens up much wider perspectives of history." One poem in particular, "The Tollund Man," signals an important new direction for Heaney's poetry. One of the Iron Age victims of a sacrificial killing exhumed from the bogs of Jutland, the Tollund Man becomes for Heaney a symbol for

> The scattered, ambushed
> Flesh of labourers,
> Stockinged corpses
> Laid out in the farmyards.

In an interview, Heaney has explained how "potent" he found "the sacrificial element, the territorial religious element, the whole mythological field surrounding" such exhumed corpses.

This concern with the territorial, archetypal nature of the conflict in Northern Ireland dominates Heaney's fourth book, *North* (1976), where such poems as "Funeral Rites," "Kinship," "Punishment," "Bone Dreams," "Bog Queen," and "The Grauballe Man" further explore the related impulses behind Iron Age and present-day Ireland. In the second half of *North,* Heaney also deals with the political more directly in poems like "The Ministry of Fear," "A Constable Calls," and "Orange Drums, Tyrone, 1966." But perhaps the final poem, "Exposure," speaks best of Heaney's complicated relationship with his battered homeland:

> . . . I sit weighing and weighing
> My responsible *tristia.* . . .
>
> I am neither internee nor informer;
> An inner émigré, grown long-haired
> And thoughtful; a wood-kerne
>
> Escaped from the massacre,
> Taking protective colouring
> From bole and bark, feeling
> Every wind that blows. . . .

Here is a sensibility that, while alienated from, is also, paradoxically, deeply imbued with, place.

The pressures and intransigencies of the Northern Ireland situation surface in *Field Work* (1979) but without the archetypal weight of the drowned bog victim. Elegies to victims of the sectarian violence like "Casualty" and the "Stand at Lough Beg" emphasize the personal over the tribal and focus on the individual victims and their relationships to personal places. Heaney explains that after *North* he had begun to feel "a danger in that responsible adjudicating stance towards communal experience." More important, the lyric poems in *Field Work*, especially in the central sonnet sequence "The Glanmore Sonnets," with its keen awareness of the interpenetration between poet and place, demonstrate Heaney's assertion that the

lyric stance is not an evasion of the actual conditions. . . . The purely poetic force of the words is a guarantee of a commitment which need not apologise for not taking up cudgels since it is raising a baton to attune discords which the cudgels are creating.

While Heaney's early poetry showed the influence of Kavanagh,* Wordsworth, Frost, Hopkins, and Hughes, the last poem in *Field Work*, "Ugolino," acknowledges Dante as a new, fruitful influence. The title sequence of Heaney's sixth book, *Station Island* (1985), details a Dantesque pilgrimage to Lough Derg, the site of Catholic pilgrimages in Ireland since the Middle Ages. Along the way, Heaney meets the ghosts of friends, victims of political violence, and other writers (William Carleton,* Kavanagh, and Joyce*). The sequence ends with the shade of Joyce urging Heaney to "Keep at a tangent" and to "swim / out on your own and fill the element / with signatures on your own frequency." In addition to this central title sequence, *Station Island* contains two other sections. Part One is a collection of lyrics on people, places, and things that one critic sees as having a "harsher, more astringent quality than the richly sensuous music of *Field Work*." Part Three, "Sweeney Redivivus," is, as Heaney's note explains, "voiced for Sweeney, the seventh-century Ulster king who was transformed into a bird-man" and whom Heaney calls in his introduction to *Sweeney Astray* (1984) "a figure of the artist, displaced, guilty, assuaging himself by his utterance."

Assuaging himself by utterance and keeping at a tangent continue in Heaney's seventh collection, *The Haw Lantern* (1987). The book contains a number of parable poems and allegories that are unlike anything in his earlier work. Poems like "From the Republic of Conscience," "From the Land of the Unspoken," and "The Mud Vision" are at once familiar yet disorienting and have the wary guardedness to them that seems influenced by Eastern European poets like Zbigniew Herbert and Miroslav Holub. However, *The Haw Lantern* also contains a more typically Heaneyesque sonnet sequence, "Clearances," written in memory of the poet's mother. Like "The Glanmore Sonnets," these poems are deeply rooted in particular places. Yet there is a powerful tension between the clarity

of Heaney's recollection and his recognition that the places and people are no
more:

> I thought of walking round and round a space
> Utterly empty, utterly a source
> Where the decked chestnut tree had lost its place
> In our front hedge above the wallflowers. . . .
> Deep planted and long gone, my coeval
> Chestnut from a jam jar in a hole,
> Its heft and hush become a bright nowhere.

This tension between the absolute necessity of the concrete and the ineluc-
tability of its absence is one of the features of Heaney's most recent volume,
Seeing Things (1991), where in one poem he juxtaposes "Ultimate / Fathom-
ableness, [and] ultimate / Stony up-againstness." He then asks, "could you
reconcile / What was diaphanous there with what was massive?" The
interesting variation that Heaney plays here on his usual concern with the pal-
pability of place led one critic to note that these poems are "aimed squarely at
transcendence." Many of the poems exhibit what Heaney has seen in the poetry
of Elizabeth Bishop: "poems with a dream truth as well as a daylight truth
about them, they are as hallucinatory as they are accurate." Elsewhere in the
volume, Heaney acknowledges that perhaps he has been suffering from "Heaviness of being. And poetry / Sluggish in the doldrums of what happens." He
recognizes a need "To credit marvels." Thus, in "Skylight" from the sonnet
sequence "Glanmore Revisited," which documents Heaney's return to his "lo-
cus amoenus" of *Field Work,* Heaney details his resistance to putting a skylight
in the "claustrophobic, nest-up-in-the-roof" room and the subsequently miraculous way "Sky entered and held surprise wide open." Or in the poem "Mark-
ings" he describes with great particularity boys marking out a football field at
twilight and then playing until "a limit had been passed," and "There was
fleetness, furtherance, untiredness / In time that was extra, unforeseen and
free."

These are apt images for Heaney's work at midcareer, a work confidently
grounded in place but able, at the same time, to use that place as a jumping-off
point. Or, as another poem from *Seeing Things,* a poem about skating on ice,
describes it, Heaney's work now is capable of a

> Running and readying and letting go
> Into a sheerness that . . . [is] its own reward:
> A farewell to surefootedness, a pitch
> Beyond our usual hold upon ourselves.

CHRISTOPHER PENNA

WORKS: *Death of a Naturalist.* London: Faber/New York: Oxford University Press, 1966; *Door
into the Dark.* London: Faber/New York: Oxford University Press, 1969; *Wintering Out.* London:
Faber/New York: Oxford University Press, 1972; *North.* London: Faber, 1975/New York: Oxford
University Press, 1976; *Field Work.* London: Faber/New York: Farrar, Straus & Giroux, 1979;
Selected Poems 1965–1975. London: Faber, 1980; *Poems 1965–1975.* New York: Farrar, Straus &
Giroux, 1980; *Preoccupations: Selected Prose 1968–1978.* London: Faber/New York: Farrar, Straus

& Giroux, 1980; *The Rattle Bag: An Anthology of Poetry.* Selected by Heaney & Ted Hughes. London: Faber, 1982; *Sweeney Astray.* Derry: Field Day, 1983/London: Faber, 1984/New York: Farrar, Straus & Giroux, 1985; *Station Island.* London: Faber, 1984/New York: Farrar, Straus & Giroux, 1985; *The Haw Lantern.* London: Faber/New York: Farrar, Straus & Giroux, 1987; *The Government of the Tongue: The 1986 T. S. Eliot Memorial Lectures and Other Critical Writings.* London: Faber, 1988; *The Place of Writing.* Atlanta, Ga.: Scholars Press, 1989; *New Selected Poems 1966–1987.* London: Faber, 1990; *The Cure at Troy: A Version of Sophocles' Philoctetes.* Derry: Field Day, 1990; *Seeing Things.* London: Faber, 1991. *The Midnight Verdict.* [Oldcastle, Co. Meath]: Gallery, [1994]. *The Redress of Poetry.* London: Faber, 1995. (Lectures); *Laments* by Jan Kochanowski. Translated by Heaney and Stanislaw Baranczak. London: Faber, 1995. REFERENCES: Andrews, E. *Seamus Heaney: The Realms of Whisper.* London: Macmillan, 1989; Bloom, Harold, ed. *Seamus Heaney.* New Haven, Conn., New York, Philadelphia: Chelsea House, 1986; Buttel, R. *Seamus Heaney.* Lewisburg, Pa.: Bucknell University Press/London: Associated University Presses, 1975; Corcoran, Neil. *Seamus Heaney.* London: Faber, 1986; Foster, John Wilson. *The Achievement of Seamus Heaney.* [Dublin]: Lilliput, 1995; Foster, Thomas C. *Seamus Heaney.* Dublin: O'Brien/ Boston: Twayne, 1989; Hart, Henry. *Seamus Heaney, Poet of Contrary Progressives.* [Syracuse, N.Y.:] Syracuse University Press, [1992]; Hofmann, Michael. "Dazzling Philosophy." *London Review of Books* (August 15, 1991): 14–15; King, P. R. *Nine Contemporary Poets.* London: Methuen, 1979; Longley, Edna. *"North:* 'Inner Emigre' or 'Artful Voyeur'?" In *The Art of Seamus Heaney.* Tony Curtis, ed. Bridgend: Poetry Wales, 1982/Chester Springs, Pa.: Dufour, 1985, pp. 63–95/[Dublin]: Wolfhound, [1994]; Molino, Michael R. *Questioning Tradition, Language, and Myth: The Poetry of Seamus Heaney.* Baltimore: Catholic University of America Press, 1994; Morrison, Blake. *Seamus Heaney.* London: Methuen, 1982; O'Donoghue, Bernard. *Seamus Heaney and the Language of Poetry.* Hemel Hampstead: Harvester Wheatsheaf, 1994; Parker, Michael. *Seamus Heaney: The Making of the Poet.* Iowa City: University of Iowa Press/[Basingstoke]: Macmillan, 1993; Randall, James. "An Interview with Seamus Heaney." *Ploughshares* 53 (1979): 7–22.

HEARN, LAFCADIO (1850–1904), travel writer, storyteller, critic, journalist, translator, and chronicler of Japan. Hearn was born on the Greek island of Lefkos, from which he was named, on June 27, 1850. He was the son of Charles Bush Hearn, an Anglo-Irish surgeon who worked with the British army, and of Rosa Cassimati Hearn, who was Greek. After his father went to the West Indies, Lafcadio and his mother went to Dublin to live with his grandaunt, Sarah Brenane, a woman whose influence upon the boy was profound. His mother never settled in Dublin but returned to Greece, where, later, she went insane. Her son never met her again. His father transferred to India, and, on his last meeting with his son, they walked along the beach in Tramore, County Waterford. Lafcadio spent his holidays in Tramore, and many years later, as he listened to old fishermen in Japan tell ghost stories, he recalled hearing such folktales in County Waterford and also in Mayo.

Hearn was educated at Ushaw in England, at Saint Cuthbert's College. His memories of that school were hurtful; decades later, when he heard a student in Japan singing hymns, he asked the young man to desist as the sound reminded him of his unpleasant school days.

Hearn's features were marred by a boyhood accident. In most photographs, he is seen only in profile as, like Patrick Pearse,* he hid his bad eye.

When he was nineteen, Hearn went to America and worked as a journalist in

Cincinnati, where newspaper readers came to know him as Paddy Hearn. He was a superb chronicler of the grotesque, and the thread of horror that runs with a frisson through his best journalism also runs through his other work. He sensed aspects of the ghastly in many situations and loved supernatural tales. Like Poe, he had a Gothic imagination, which some of those who met him interpreted as morbidity. One senses a kind of demented, delighted energy behind his description of a corpse or of begrimed scavengers. He worked hard and, at his most productive, managed 150 pages a month. He moved to New Orleans and, together with journalism, produced literary translations, among them works by Flaubert and Gautier, and a Creole cookbook. Again, he collected folktales and legends. After a two-year visit to Martinique, he wrote in 1890 an account of life in the French West Indies.

Hearn visited Japan in 1890, initially working on an assignment for *Harper's New Monthly* magazine. He became obsessed with the country and its ways, and in the following years he became the foremost interpreter of Japan for the West. His best writing on Japan displays not merely an understanding of Japanese culture but also a deep empathy with the land and its spirit. In a sense, Japan became his birthplace. He idealized it. He chronicled Japanese legends and habits, and many of these legends are collected in *Kwaidan* (1904), a wonderful book that is still in print. His other works on Japan include *In Ghostly Japan* (1899) and *Gleanings in Buddha Fields* (1971). He married a Japanese and in time taught English literature in the Imperial University of Tokyo. In Japan, he was known as Koizumi Yakumo.

Hearn admired the works of other Irish writers, among them W. B. Yeats* and Sheridan Le Fanu.* Yeats admired Hearn's statement that "there is something ghostly in all great art." While his work can be seen as part of the Gothic strain in Irish literature, Hearn is of importance in another way: he was one of those writers who opened the way to the East. Others—Fenellosa and Pound, for example—would take this much further later on, but their interest was more purely literary. Whether writing of insects, the Japanese smile (which, like Irish eloquence, sometimes serves to hide rather than to explicate) or of religion or folklore, Hearn helped the West to understand Japan. He also helped Japan to understand itself. He died on September 26, 1904, at Okubo.

Yone Noguchi's praise of Hearn, written in 1910, sums it up: "We Japanese have been regenerated by his sudden magic, and baptised afresh under his transcendent rapture; in fact, the old romances which we had forgotten ages ago were brought again to quiver in the air. . . . He made us shake the old robe of bias which we wore without knowing it, and gave us a sharp sensation of revival."

SEÁN DUNNE

PRINCIPAL WORKS: *Two Years in the French West Indies.* New York & London: Harper, 1890; *Glimpses of Unfamiliar Japan.* 2 vols. Boston: Houghton, 1894/London: Osgood & McIlvaine, 1894/London: Kegan Paul, 1903; *Out of the East.* Boston: Houghton Mifflin, 1897; *In Ghostly Japan.* Boston: Little, Brown/London: Sampson Low, 1899; *Japan: An Attempt at Inter-*

pretation. New York: Macmillan, 1904; *Kwaidan: Stories and Studies of Strange Things.* Boston: Houghton Mifflin, 1904; Bisland, Elizabeth, ed. *The Japanese Letters of Lafcadio Hearn.* London: Constable/Boston & New York: Houghton Mifflin, 1910; King, Francis, ed. *Lafcadio Hearn: Writings from Japan.* London: Penguin, 1984. Many of Hearn's books were reprinted in the 1970s by the Charles E. Tuttle Company, of Rutland, Vermont, and Tokyo.   REFERENCES: Kunst, Arthur E. *Lafcadio Hearn.* New York: Twayne, [1969]; Murray, Paul. *The Life and Literature of Lafcadio Hearn.* Folkstone, Kent: Japan Library, 1993; Ronan, Sean G. & Koizumi, Toki. *Lafcadio Hearn (Koizumi Yakumo), His Life, Work, and Irish Background.* Dublin: Ireland Japan Association, 1991.

HECTOR, ANNIE FRENCH (1825–1902), fiction writer. Hector was born in Dublin on June 23, 1825, the daughter of Robert French and Anne Malone. She was educated in Dublin and in France, and in 1858 she married Alexander Hector, hence her usual pseudonym of Mrs. Alexander. She was a very popular and extremely prolific writer, pouring out over forty novels and many short stories. These works were mainly page-turning romantic entertainments, but they had a certain professionalism to them that looked forward to modern writing. There were certain things that Mrs. Alexander would not do, as may be seen in her 1897 criticism of Caroline Norton's* *Stuart of Dunleath* when she complained of lengthy preambles with an "account of the hero and heroine's families, even to the third and fourth generation." Looking back to the novels of the mid-nineteenth century, she also complained that the "people are terribly consistent in good or evil":

The dignity, the high-mindedness, the angelic purity of the heroine is unsupportable, and the stainless honour, the stern resistance to temptation, the defiance of tyrannical wrong-doers, makes the hero quite as bad.

She died in London in July 10, 1902.

PRINCIPAL WORKS: *Kate Vernon.* 3 vols. London: Thomas Cautley Newby, 1854; *Agnes Waring.* 3 vols. London: Thomas Cautley Newby, 1856; *Which Shall It Be?* 3 vols. London: R. Bentley, 1856/New York: H. Holt, 1874; *Look Before You Leap!* 2 vols. London: R. Bentley, 1865/ rev. ed., London: R. Bentley/New York: H. Holt, 1882; *The Wooing O't.* 3 vols. London: R. Bentley/ New York: H. Holt, 1873; *Ralph Wilton's Weird.* 2 vols. London, 1875; *Her Dearest Foe.* 3 vols. London: R. Bentley/New York: H. Holt, 1876; *The Heritage of Langdale.* 3 vols. London: R. Bentley/New York: H. Holt, 1877; *Maid, Wife or Widow?* London: Chatto & Windus/New York: H. Holt, 1879; *The Admiral's Ward.* London: R. Bentley/New York: H. Holt, 1883; *At Bay.* 3d ed. London: F. Warne, [1882]/New York: H. Holt, 1885; *The Freres.* 3 vols. London: R. Bentley/New York: H. Holt, 1882; *The Executor.* 3 vols. London: R. Bentley/New York: H. Holt, 1883; *A Second Life.* 2 vols. London: R. Bentley/New York: H. Holt, 1885; *By Woman's Wit.* 2 vols. London: F. V. White, 1886; *Beaton's Bargain.* New York: H. Holt, 1886/London: F. Warne, 1887; *Mona's Choice.* 3 vols. London: F. V. White/New York: J. W. Lovell, 1887; *Forging the Fetters.* New York: J. W. Lovell, [1887]/London: Spencer Blackett, 1890; *A Life Interest.* 2 vols. London: R. Bentley/New York: H. Holt, 1888; *A Crooked Path.* 3 vols. London: Hurst & Blackett/New York: H. Holt, 1889; *A False Scent.* London: F. V. White/New York: G. Munro, 1889; *Blind Fate.* London: F. V. White/New York: H. Holt, 1890; *Well Won.* London: F. V. White/New York: J. A. Taylor, 1891; *A Woman's Heart.* 3 vols. London: F. V. White, 1891; *Mammon.* New York: J. W. Lovell, [ca. 1891]/London: Heinemann, 1892; *For Her Sake.* 3 vols. London: F. V. White/Philadelphia: J. B. Lippincott, 1892; *The Snare of the Fowler.* 3 vols. London & New York: Cassell, 1892; *Found Wanting* 3 vols. London: F. V. White/Philadelphia: J. B. Lippincott, 1893; *A Choice of Evils.* 3

vols. London: F. V. White, 1894; *Broken Links.* New York: Cassell, [ca. 1894]; *A Ward in Chancery.* 2 vols. London: Osgood, McIlvaine/New York: D. Appleton, 1894; *What Gold Cannot Buy.* London: F. V. White, 1895; *A Fight with Fate.* London: F. V. White/Philadelphia: J. B. Lippincott, 1896; *A Warning Hazard.* London: T. Fisher Unwin/New York: D. Appleton, 1896; *A Golden Autumn.* London: F. V. White, 1896/Philadelphia: J. B. Lippincott, 1897; *Mrs. Crichton's Creditor.* London: F. V. White/Philadelphia: J. B. Lippincott, 1897; *Barbara, Lady's Maid and Peeress.* London: F. V. White, 1897/Philadelphia: J. B. Lippincott, 1898; *The Cost of Her Pride.* London: F. V. White, 1898/Philadelphia: J. B. Lippincott, 1899; *Brown, V. C.* London: T. Fisher Unwin/New York: R. F. Fenno, 1899; *The Step-Mother.* London: F. V. White, 1899/Philadelphia: J. B. Lippincott, 1900; *Through Fire to Fortune.* London: T. Fisher Unwin/New York: R. F. Fenno, 1900; *A Missing Hero.* London: Chatto & Windus/New York: Fenno, 1901; *The Yellow Fiend.* London: T. Fisher Unwin/New York: Dodd Mead, 1901; *Stronger than Love.* London: T. Fisher Unwin: New York: Brentano's, 1902; *Kitty Costello.* London: T. Fisher Unwin, 1904; *The Crumpled Leaf: A Vatican Mystery.* London: H. J. Drane, [1911].

HENRY, JAMES (1798–1876), classical scholar. Henry, sometime vice president of the King and Queen's College of Physicians of Ireland, reflected not only an acquaintance with "the Two Cultures" but in the liberal arts was a profound scholar of both English literature and ancient classics. His eccentricity must have made him endearing as well as infuriating, and his decision to avoid commercial booksellers (his privately published books were presented to friends and scholars) may explain his present neglect. His pamphlets, verse collections, and exegetical works (details of which are given in J. B. Lyons's *Scholar and Sceptic,* 1985) are now collectors' items. His major contribution was to Virgilian studies. His own creative efforts are uneven, descending at times to doggerel. He was an instinctive satirist, however, and many passages in his longer poems show a remarkable ability to interweave his lines with detailed botanical knowledge.

Born in Dublin in 1798, the son of Robert Henry, a woolen draper, and his wife, Katharine Olivia Elder, he took a degree in classics in Trinity College before studying medicine. He practiced his profession in York Street and Fitzwilliam Square and to the irritation of his colleagues declared the usual guinea fee excessive. He charged five shillings, to be paid in silver. He married Anne Patton of County Donegal; of their three daughters, only the youngest, named Katharine Olivia after her grandmother, survived to adult life.

During his years in practice, James Henry wrote a number of pamphlets, of which *A Dialogue Between a Bilious Patient and a Physician* (1838) and *An Account of the Drunken Sea* (1840) deal with constipation and alcoholism, respectively. Ireland's domination by her neighbor is the theme of *Little Island and Big Island* (1841), and *An Account of the Police in the City of Canton* (1840) tilts at the newly established Dublin Metropolitan Police.

A legacy Henry received in the mid-1840s enabled him to devote himself wholly to classical study. He spent almost the remainder of his life traveling on foot from one great European library to another collating Virgilian manuscripts. This labour resulted in *Notes of a Twelve Years Voyage of Discovery in the First Six Books of the Eneis* (1853) and the five-volume *Aeneidea,* most of which was published posthumously. Robert Yelverton Tyrrell in *Latin Poetry* (1894) described this monumental work as "perhaps the most valuable body of original comment and subtle analysis which has even been brought together for the illustration of a Latin poet." R. D. Williams, in an appraisal in *Hermathena* (1973, pp. 27–43), states that more than a thousand authors are cited. Indeed, it is remarkable with what ease Henry, in order to emphasize a point, can supply an apt quotation from, say, Milton or Scott.

In *Poematia* (1866), he admitted that "To bid me write's to bid the drunkard drink / The miser hoard, the dice player play on." The verses included in *My Book* (1853), *A Half-Year's Poems* (1854), and *Poems Chiefly Philosophical* (1856) are for the greater part the art of the rhymer, but he has a flair for epigrams: "All the whole world loves twaddle—'How do you know?' / All the whole world reads Harriet Beecher Stowe."

One suspects that when versifying, Henry was filling in time as another might have occupied himself with crossword puzzles, but he is a master of rhetorical prose with a taste for polemics. No respector of persons, he dismisses Dryden's translation of the *Aeneid* contemptuously: "—that translation which, up to the present day, is the only recognised representative at the court of English literature, of the sweet, modest, elegant, and generally correct muse of Virgil. Blush, England! For shame, English criticism! English poets, what or where are ye?" Wordsworth fares worse. Having quoted a passage from the Second Book of the *Aeneid,* Henry remarks: "It is one of the finest passages which ever issued from the hand of man which is thus—shall I say travestied? or shall I say degraded?"

Librarians overzealous in the guardianship of their treasures, especially those of the Vatican and the British Museum, he regarded as his natural enemies. *The Dictionary of National Biography* credits him with a combination of kindness and rudeness, of softness and severity: "His long white locks and somewhat fantastic dress were combined with great beauty and vivacity of countenance . . ."

Henry's wife died in 1849 in Arco, but Katharine Olivia remained his companion in travels during which they crossed the Alps at least seventeen times. One such journey from Dresden to Venice is described in *Thalia Petasata Iterum* (1877). Here, Henry displays a detailed knowledge of natural history, indulges his agnosticism and anticlericalism, and composes a palinode inspired by the vines, before reaching their destination and the lodgings on the Ripa dei Schiaveni which had once been Petrarch's.

Eventually, "the wandering Irish Gleeman and his daughter" returned to Ireland and lived for some years in Dalkey Lodge, Dalkey, County Dublin, where she died on December 11, 1872. Henry himself died on July 14, 1876. The neglected genius is paid a fitting tribute by W. B. Stanford, who in *Ireland and the Classical Tradition* (1976) ranks him with other scholar-physicians—Linacre, Campion, and Sir Thomas Browne.

J. B. LYONS

WORKS: *My Book.* Dresden, 1853; *Notes of a Twelve Years Voyage of Discovery in the First Six Books of the Eneis.* Dresden, 1853; *A Half-Year's Poems.* Dresden: Meinhold, 1854; *Poematia.* Dresden: Meinhold; 1866; *Aeneidea: or, Critical, Exegetical, and Aesthetical Remarks on the Aeneis.* Vol. 1, London, 1872; Vol. 2, London, 1878; Vol. 3, Dublin, 1881; Vol. 4, Dublin, 1889; *Thalia Petasata Iterum.* Leipsig: Gieseche & Devrient, 1877.   REFERENCES: Lyons, J. B. "Doctors and Literature." *Conjoint Annual General and Scientific Meeting Proceedings, 1976.* Dublin: Irish Medical Association, 1976, pp. 164–173; Richmond, John. *James Henry of Dublin.* Dublin: Published by the Author, 1976.

HEWITT, JOHN (1907–1987), poet. Hewitt was born of nonconformist parents in Belfast on October 28, 1907. He was educated at Queen's University in Belfast, receiving a B.A. in English in 1930. From 1930 to 1957, he was on the staff of the Belfast Museum and Art Gallery. From 1957 to 1972, he was director of the Herbert Art Gallery and Museum, Coventry. In 1972, he returned to Ireland to spend his retirement in his native city. His chief volumes of poetry include *Conacre* (1943), *Compass* (1944), *Those Swans Remember* (1956), *Collected Poems 1932–1967* (1968), *Out of My Time: Poems 1967–1974* (1974) *Time Enough: Poems New and Revised* (1976), *The Rain Dance: Poems New and Revised* (1978), *Mosaic* (1981), *Loose Ends* (1983), *Freehold and Other Poems* (1986), and a posthumous and definitive *Collected Poems,* edited by Frank Ormsby* (1991).

The recurrent poetic concerns in Hewitt's measured cumulative output have been an involvement in modes owing something to eighteenth-century English landscape poetry and something to Wordsworth. He has drawn the Ulster countryside and attempted to define the nature of Ulster Protestant identity and the relation of the planter stock in the province with the Irish past and present. Poems like "A Country Walk in March" are notable for topographical accuracy; "First Snow in the Glens," "Colour," and "The Ram's Horn" for a Wordsworthian joy in the landscape; while "Once Alien Here," "Ireland," and "The Colony" are analyses of the planter in the Irish context which do not hesitate to confront political and social issues. (Hewitt has always declared himself to be a member of the left.)

During the 1840s, Hewitt was involved in an Ulster regionalist movement in the arts and a revival of poetry in Belfast. At that time, he hoped a cultivation of local traditions and pieties might help solve the political and national conflicts experienced in his province. His M.A. thesis was on the forgotten minor poets of early nineteenth-century Ulster, and his *Rhyming Weavers and Other Country Poets of Antrim and Down* was published in 1974. He was associate editor of *Lagan* (1945–1946), the Belfast literary periodical edited with regionalist intentions, and of the volume *The Arts in Ulster* (1951). From 1957 to 1962, he was poetry editor of the literary periodical associated with Belfast's Lyric Theatre,* *Threshold.* He also edited the poems of the nineteenth-century Donegal poet, William Allingham* (with whose poetry his own has affinities); in 1967 and 1975, his monograph on the Ulster painter, Colin Middleton, appeared. In the 1960s, Hewitt's work influenced the young poets writing in Belfast at that time.

Since his return to Belfast in 1972, he has given generously of his time and energy in furthering the arts under the most difficult of circumstances.

Hewitt's poetry has a strength and integrity of purpose that can occasionally suggest limitations of range and depth but that remind us of human continuities and moral courage in the midst of historical flux and the permanencies of nature. His lifelong attachment to the local has been a strongminded celebration of man the maker in his society, family, and tribe. The scrupulous care of his art is a reflection of his faith in human making, while its moments of calm lyricism are his testimony to the fundamentally benign realities of man's life.

In 1983, Hewitt was awarded the degree of doctor of literature (*honoris causa*) by Queen's University, Belfast, and in 1984 he was awarded the Gregory Medal by the Irish Academy of Letters.* In May 1986, his verse play *The Bloody Brae* was performed in Belfast by the Lyric Players Theatre.* He died in Belfast on June 17, 1987.

TERENCE BROWN

WORKS: *Conacre.* Belfast: Privately published, 1943; *Compass: Two Poems.* Belfast: Privately published, 1944; *No Rebel Word.* London: Frederick Muller, 1948; ed., with Sam Hanna Bell & Nesca Robb. *The Arts in Ulster.* London: Harrap, 1951; *Those Swans Remember: A Poem.* Belfast: Privately published, 1956; *Tesserae.* Belfast: Festival, Queen's University Belfast, 1967. (Poetry pamphlet); *Collected Poems 1932–1967.* London: MacGibbon & Kee, 1968; *The Day of the Concrake: Poems of the Nine Glens.* N.p.: Glens of Antrim Historical Society, 1969/rev., 1984; *The Planter and the Gael: Poems by John Hewitt and John Montague.* Belfast: Arts Council of Northern Ireland, 1970; *An Ulster Reckoning.* Coventry: Author, 1971. (Poetry pamphlet); *Out of My Time. Poems 1967–1974.* Belfast: Blackstaff, 1974; *Scissors for a One-Armed Tailor: Marginal Verses 1929–1954.* Belfast: Privately published, 1974; *The Chinese Fluteplayer.* Lisburn: Privately published, 1974; ed., *Rhyming Weavers, and Other Country Poets of Antrim and Down.* Belfast: Blackstaff, 1974; *Time Enough: Poems New and Revised.* Belfast: Blackstaff, 1976; with Theo Snoddy. *Art in Ulster: Paintings, Drawings, Prints and Sculpture for the Last 400 Hundred [sic] Years.* Belfast: Blackstaff, 1977; *The Rain Dance: Poems New and Revised.* Belfast: Blackstaff, 1978; ed., *John Luke 1906–1975.* Belfast & Dublin: Arts Councils of Ireland, 1978; *Kites in Spring: A Belfast Boyhood.* Belfast: Blackstaff, 1980; *The Selected John Hewitt.* Alan Warner, ed. Belfast: Blackstaff, 1981; *Mosaic.* Dundonald: Blackstaff, 1981. (Poetry pamphlet); *Loose Ends.* Dundonald: Blackstaff, 1983; *Freehold and Other Poems.* Belfast: Blackstaff, 1986; *Ancestral Voices: The Selected Prose of John Hewitt.* Tom Clyde, ed. Belfast: Blackstaff, 1987; *The Collected Poems of John Hewitt.* Frank Ormsby, ed. Belfast: Blackstaff, [1991]. (Contains a Chronology of Hewitt's life, and an Introduction, copious notes, and a Bibliography that includes fugitive articles and reviews). REFERENCES: Brown, Terence. *Northern Voices: Poets from Ulster.* Dublin: Gill & Macmillan, 1975, pp. 86–97; Brown, Terence. "The Spark of a Slim-Volume Man." *Irish Literary Supplement* 11 (2) (Fall 1992): 21; Foster, John William. "The Landscape of Planter and Gael in the Poetry of John Hewitt and John Montague." *Canadian Journal of Irish Studies* 1 (November 1973); Heaney, Seamus. "The Poetry of John Hewitt." *Threshold* 22 (Summer 1969): 73–77/ reprinted in Heaney's *Preoccupations.* London & Boston: Faber, 1980, pp. 107–110; Montague, John. "Regionalism into Reconciliation." *Poetry Ireland* 3 (Spring 1964): 113–118; Sealy, Douglas. "An Individual Flavour: *The Collected Poems of John Hewitt.*" *Dublin Magazine* 8 (Spring–Summer 1969): 19–24.

HICKEY, CHRISTINE DWYER (1958–   ), novelist and short story writer. Hickey was born in Dublin and twice won the Listowel Writers' Week Short Story Competition and also an *Observer* short story award.

WORK: *The Dancer.* [Dublin]: Marino, [1995].

HICKEY, EMILY HENRIETTA (1845–1924), poet, religious writer, essayist, and editor. Emily Hickey was born on April 12, 1845, at Macmine Castle, near Enniscorthy, County Wexford, the daughter of Reverend J. S. Hickey of Goresbridge, County Carlow, and the former Miss Stewart of Stewart Lodge in County Carlow. Emily's mother was a descendant of the Stuart royal family, and her paternal grandfather, Reverend William Hickey, wrote "agricultural novels" under the pseudonym of Martin Doyle. Emily's father was rector of Goresbridge, where she was raised, but she was born in the maternal family's ancestral castle because her mother planned a visit to coincide with her birth. Both mother and daughter were proud of the nobility of the maternal family. However, Enid Dinnis's biography makes the point that, while Emily may have overemphasized her noble heritage, she also lived a noble life. The Hickeys were Loyalist and Protestant.

Hickey began writing poetry shortly after she was sent to boarding school at the age of thirteen. Her early poetic influences were Scott, Tennyson, and Elizabeth Barrett Browning. Her father refused to allow her to read any Shakespeare, as he believed the writing was "marred by Elizabethan coarseness." Hickey and Dr. Furnivall founded the Browning Society in 1881. She had earned first-class honours at Cambridge by 1912 and became a lecturer in English literature at the London Collegiate School and Cambridge correspondence classes. She received the Cross Pro Ecclesia Et Pontifice from Pius X in 1912.

Hickey lived most of her life in England. She was received into the Catholic Church on July 22, 1901, and Catholicism became the dominating element of her later poetry. Following her conversion, she retracted her first three collections of poetry. *A Sculptor* (1881), *Verse-Translations* (1891), and *Michael Villiers, Idealist* (1891) had expressed ideas at odds with Hickey's adopted Catholic beliefs. Katharine Tynan* felt that Hickey's later works, with their strong focus on Catholicism, were "a great advance on those earlier pieces, which were full of the religion of humanity." The critical reception of her later work generally disagrees with Tynan's assessment, discounting the postconversion poetry for its emphasis on piety at the cost of style. The earlier works had utilized Irish legends and history in a manner typical of the Celtic revival movement. "The Ballad of Lady Ellen" utilizes the same myth as W. B. Yeats's* play *The Countess Cathleen,* although Hickey adds a note to indicate that the original legend was not Irish but French. She also stresses the considerable "alterations and additions" between her version and Yeats's. An excerpt from "Two Women and a Poet" illustrates her early style:

> We poets are forerunners of the time
> When all shall run in rhythmic harmony:
> We, the great poets, like the Weimar sage,
> Who keeps us calm amid the tempest's roar.
> The lesser poets are beaten, driven about,
> Are passion's slaves. Well, well, they have their place;
> They take the big world's anguish on their heart,

And so their songs, half-stifled, only rise
To sink; a poet shoud be no mere man. . . .

Hickey's later religious verses tend to be instructional, introspective, and moralistic, sacrificing craft for content. Katharine Tynan's own religious poetry shows a more delicate hand, while expressing an equally devout heart. Hickey died on September 19, 1924.

ANNE COLMAN

WORKS: *A Sculptor, and Other Poems*. London: Kegan Paul, 1881; *Browning's Strafford, Edited and Annotated*. London: G. Bell, 1884; *Verse-Tales, Lyrics and Translations*. Liverpool: W. & J. Arnold, 1889; *Verse-Translations, and Other Poems*. London, 1891; *Michael Villiers, Idealist, and Other Poems*. London: Smith, Elder, 1891; *Poems*. London: E. Mathews, 1896; *Ancilla Domini, Thoughts in Verse on the Life of the Blessed Virgin Mary*. London: Printed by the author, [1898]; *St. Patrick's Breastplate: A Metrical Translation*. London: Catholic Truth Society, [1902]. (Prose translation by Whitley Stokes and metrical renderings by Cecil F. Humphreys and Hickey); *Our Lady of May*. London: Catholic Truth Society, 1902; *Havelock the Dane*. London: Catholic Truth Society, 1902; *Thoughts for Creedless Women*. London: Catholic Truth Society, [1906]; *A Parable of a Pilgrim, etc.: Selections from Walter Hylton*. 1907; *Lois*. London: Burns, Oates & Washbourne, 1908; *Our Catholic Heritage in English Literature*. London: Sands, 1910; *Later Poems*. London: Grant Richards, 1913; *The Bishop and the Three Poor Men*. London: Catholic Truth Society, 1922; *Devotional Poems*. London: Elliot Stock, 1922; *Jesukin, and Other Christmastide Poems*. London: Burns, Oates, 1924. REFERENCES: Dinnis, Enid. *Emily Hickey: Poet, Essayist, Pilgrim—A Memoir*. London: Harding & More, 1927; Furlong, Alice. "Emily Hickey." *Irish Monthly* 53 (January 1925): 16–20

HIGGINS, AIDAN (1927–   ), novelist and short story and travel writer. Higgins was born on March 3, 1927, in Celbridge, County Kildare, in a Georgian house on a seventy-two-acre farm. He had a happy childhood and was educated at Clongowes Wood College. There he had a few "disciplinary problems" and rejected the "republican bigotry" of his Jesuit Irish teacher. As their fortunes declined, his family moved to Greystones, Dalkey, and Dun Laoghaire. After leaving Clongowes, Higgins wandered through the country and from job to job in England, reading Joyce,* spending time in the company of Patrick Collins the painter, and in Clonskea Fever Hospital recovering from scarlet fever brought on by malnourishment. He met his wife, Jill Damaris Anders, in London, and with her and John Wright's Marionette Company, toured much of Europe, the then-Rhodesia, and South Africa. He lived in South Africa for two years and subsequently in Spain, Germany, London, Connemara, and County Cork. His fiction has won him numerous prizes and distinctions, including the James Tait Black Memorial Award, an Irish Academy of Letters Award, the Daad Scholarship of Berlin, and an American Irish Foundation Literary Award. His works have been translated into a dozen languages.

His first work, *Felo de Se* (1960), consists of six stories (one a novella) of the characters' drift toward self-destruction. Set in Ireland, England, Germany, and South Africa, they are told in a rich, dark, grotesque, painterly prose that ushers their blundering characters to their various dooms. These virtuoso stories are full of comic savagery, melancholia, and violence.

Langrishe, Go Down (1966), a development of one of its stories, "Killachter Meadow," handsomely fulfills the promise of *Felo de Se*. This account of a love affair between Imogen Langrishe, the last flower of a decaying Anglo-Irish family, and Otto Beck, an aging (thirty-five-year-old) German student of phenomenology with Bohemian tastes, is set in north Kildare in the 1930s. In a densely evocative style and with unflagging attention to detail, Higgins manages an acute, poignant rendition of the period, the daily life of the village, and the thwarted sensitivities of his characters. In many ways a return to the late Victorian novel, it contrasts the ambience of a leisured, feckless Big House gentility with the intellectualism, brutality, and self-centeredness of the new rulers of Europe. Higgins sets his account of the seduction and abandonment of Imogen into a mosaic of images from the landscape, its birds and animals, local history, the nooks and shadows of Springfield House, fragments of philosophical German, and glimpses of contemporary newspaper headlines on the approaching war. The method sets Higgins apart from the more parochial realists writing in Ireland in the 1960s, but the theme is a rather belated subscription to the Yeatsian version of Irish history. Despite some structural flaws and occasional shreds of self-consciousness, this study of entropy is a stylistic performance of a high order, which rightly gained its author several prizes and accolades. Harold Pinter wrote a screenplay from the novel and produced it on BBC television in 1978. It was also well received.

In 1971, *Images of Africa: Diary (1956–60)* appeared. It is a vivid account of its author's voyage to Rhodesia, his life in Johannesburg, and his return to England. It contains a minutely observed account of South Africa before the Sharpville massacre and exemplifies Higgins's search for the telling image.

His second novel, *Balcony of Europe* (1972), is set in Nerja, Andalusia, in 1962–1963 and centers on the clandestine love affair between a middle-aged Irish painter and a complacent young Jewish-American wife. The background to this encounter is richly textured with exotica, recherché allusions, and semantic jokes. It seems larger in ambition than in feeling: the main characters lack sufficient weight to counterbalance all of these devices, so that the effect is portentous.

Higgins' return home in his next work, *Scenes from a Receding Past* (1977), promised a more passionate concern. But this attempt to rediscover an Irish childhood and adolescence as dispassionate impressions and the extension of that into adult life as an ironic self-examination is another misjudged effort. A brave experiment in style and form, it falsifies the consciousness of the child and betrays the effects of earnest literary labor.

Bornholm Night-Ferry (1983) is an epistolary novel that revisits a familiar Higgins scenario. Elin, a Danish poet, and Finn, an Irish writer, are lovers. The records of their passionate love bear five years of postmarks, recording their mutual passion, silence, and tensions with their respective families. Despite the liveliness of much of the writing, it does not move the reader to care for the characters.

The year 1989 saw the publication of two retrospective collections: *Helsingør Station & Other Departures* (shorter fiction) and *Ronda Gorge & Other Precipices* (travel). These pieces confirm a growing impression of the meretriciousness of Higgins' work. His gifts are primarily linguistic and stylistic: at his best, he writes fine prose poems. But he seems to be the victim of his own gifts: a collector of polyglot locutions, rather than the possessor of any sustaining vision. If fragmentation appeared to be the subject of *Langrishe, Go Down,* it is the condition of the later work.

Lions of the Grunewald (1993) is, in many ways, a summative Higgins novel. Thematically similar to *Bornholm Night-Ferry* and expressly cannibalizing *Ronda Gorge,* it is a farcical reduction of the method and material of *Balcony of Europe.* This time it is Dallan Weaver, an Irish writer on a temporary academic appointment to West Berlin, who abandons his wife and son for the passionate Lore Schroder. Many scenes are vintage Higgins: crackling with observation, energy, and humor. But the whole is less than the parts. Lacking the energy of Donleavy's* Ginger Man, Weaver's obsessive priapism is repellent. A typical Higgins phrasemonger, he moves among a throng of imaginary and historical characters (including Sir Kenneth Clark and Samuel Beckett*) with heartless brio. But such endorsements do not rescue this connoisseur of lusts from the readers' indifference. Again, the verve and control of *Langrishe, Go Down* have yielded to a mannered narcissism. He has not done better than *Langrishe, Go Down.* Few have.

CÓILÍN OWENS

WORKS: *Felo de Se.* London: John Calder, 1960/reissued as *Killachter Meadow.* New York: Grove, 1961/republished as *Asylum and Other Stories.* London: John Calder/Dallas: Riverrun, [1978]; *Langrishe, Go Down.* London: Calder & Boyars, 1966/New York: Grove, 1967/London: Minerva, 1993; *Images of Africa: Diary (1956–60).* London: Calder & Boyars, 1971; *Balcony of Europe.* London: Calder & Boyars, 1972/New York: Delacorte, 1973; *Scenes from a Receding Past.* London: John Calder/Dallas: Riverrun, 1977; *Bornholm Night-Ferry.* London: Allison & Busby, 1983; *Ronda Gorge and Other Precipices: Travel Writing 1956–1989.* London: Secker & Warburg, 1989; *Helsingør Station and Other Departures: Fictions and Autobiographies 1956–1989.* London: Secker & Warburg, 1989; *Lions of the Grunewald.* London: Secker & Warburg, 1993; *Donkey's Years.* London: Secker & Warburg, 1995.   REFERENCES: Beja, Morris. "Felons of Our Selves: The Fiction of Aidan Higgins." *Irish University Review* 3 (Autumn 1973): 163–178; Garfitt, Roger. "Constants in Contemporary Irish Fiction." In *Two Decades of Irish Writing.* Douglas Dunn, ed. [Cheadle, Cheshire]: Carcanet/Chester Springs, Pa.: Dufour, [1975]; Skelton, Robin. "Aidan Higgins and the Total Book." *Mosaic* 10 (Fall 1976): 27–37; Special Aidan Higgins Issue, *Review of Contemporary Fiction* 3 (Spring 1983): 106 ff.; *Dictionary of Literary Biography.* Vol. 14, pp. 389–394.

HIGGINS, F[REDERICK] R[OBERT] (1896–1941), poet. Born in Foxford, County Mayo, on April 24, 1896, in the Catholic and Gaelic-speaking West, Higgins grew up in the English Pale. His father, a County Meath engineer, was a strict Unionist of the Protestant Ascendancy tradition. Fred Higgins was, among other things, a pioneer of the labor movement. He founded a Clerical Workers Union, started a paper called the *Irish Clerk,* edited several trade journals with titles such as *Oil and Colour Paint Review* and *The Furniture Man's Gazetter,* and established an early woman's magazine in Ireland. This magazine ran for two issues; the first issue was called *Welfare,* and the second *Farewell.* Higgins was also a contributing editor to several short-lived literary papers such as *The Klaxon* (1923–1924) and *To-Morrow* (1924). However, it is a poet passionately interested in Irish folk tradition that Higgins will be remembered.

In 1923, the Irish Bookshop published six of his poems in an eight-page pamphlet called *The Salt Air.* The edition was limited to five hundred copies and, although the poems in it were melodic and delicately wrought, they suffered because they were too wistful and overembroidered. Higgins' second book of poetry, *Island Blood* (1925), established a distinctly Irish note. Its poems were full of phrases that breathed Connemara. However, it was in his third book of poetry, *The Dark Breed* (1927), that Higgins began to publish appealing and sophisticated folk poems like "The Island Dead of Inchagoill." In this poem, he lamented the death of an island through the use of contrasting sounds, both past and present. Higgins' poem, like much of Austin Clarke's* historical and mythic poetry, reflected a richness of life and the intensity of a dark people. It evoked the spirit of a particular time and place, and restated Higgins' belief that Irish poets "must work more and more out of that realistic beauty found only in the folk, fusing nature with a personal emotion that incidentally revealed the all important quality of a racial memory."

In 1933, Higgins published his fourth volume of poetry, *Arable Holdings.* One of the best poems in this volume was "The Woman of the Red-Haired Man," which discussed the plight of one man in love with another man's wife. In this poem, Higgins appeared to be concerned more with imagery, melody, and the texture of language than with theme. He believed that poetry should aspire to the condition of music and produce an effect so absolutely aesthetic that understanding would be held in abeyance. He frequently tried to make sounds and associations do all the work so that meaning would almost not matter. Echoes of sweet harmony and the assonance found in many a Connacht song were present in the first two stanzas of "The Woman of the Red-Haired Man."

After the publication of *Arable Holdings,* Higgins' approach to the writing of poetry changed. He discarded the image of himself as a folk poet, and the lyricism which had been present in so much of his early verse vanished. The first stanza of the poem "The Past Generation," first published in the October 1936 *Dublin Magazine,** indicated this change. Once Higgins lost his lyrical touch, symbolism became too overt, and in his search for passion and quick emotional effects he created clichés.

By 1935, Higgins had become an intimate friend of W. B. Yeats* and a director of the Abbey Theatre* for which he wrote a remarkably unsuccessful Dublin verse play, *The Deuce of Jacks.* Higgins' late writing, like Yeats', coarsened. Although Higgins claimed that Yeats never tried to shape and form his writing, no young writer as susceptible to the heroic as Higgins could live long in the company of the master of Byzantium and remain indifferent. Higgins only published one more book of poetry, *The Gap of Brightness,* before his death on January 8, 1941.

ℛ𝐼𝒞ℋ𝒜ℛ𝒟 ℬ𝒰ℛ𝒩ℋ𝒜ℳ

WORKS: *Island Blood.* London: John Lane, 1925; *The Dark Breed.* London: Macmillan, 1927; *Arable Holdings.* Dublin: Cuala, 1933; *The Gap of Brightness.* London: Macmillan, 1940. REFERENCES: Farren, Robert. *The Course of Irish Verse.* London: Sheed & Ward, 1948, pp. 128–150; Kavanagh, Patrick. "The Gallivanting Poet." *Irish Writing* 3 (November 1947): 63–70; MacManus, M. J. "A Bibliography of F. R. Higgins." *Dublin Magazine,* new series, 12 (1937): 61–67.

HIGGINS, MICHAEL D. (1941–   ),

poet and politician. Higgins was born in Limerick on April 18, 1941, and raised on a small farm in County Clare. He was educated at University College, Galway, where he later taught sociology and political science, and at Indiana University and Manchester University. He has been a Labor deputy in Dail Éireann and twice lord mayor of Galway and in the coalition government of 1993 was appointed minister of culture, arts and the Gaeltacht. His poems are clear, sincere, conversational, and sometimes, as in "The Student Who Wanted to Do an M.A. on God" or "Bank Manager Faints at the Mayor's Wall," funny. The only reason for calling his work poetry, however, is that the quite arbitrary line lengths make it look like poetry on the page.

WORKS: *The Betrayal.* [Galway: Salmon, 1990]; *The Season of Fire.* [Dingle]: Brandon, [1993].

HIGGINS, PADRAIG J.

WORKS: *Ballybawn.* [Dingle, Co. Kerry]: Brandon, [1991]. (Novel).

HIGGINS, RITA ANN (1955–   ),

poet and playwright. Higgins was born on May 26, 1955, in Galway. Her formal education ceased when she was a teenager. She began her literary self-education much later, while recovering from tuberculosis; and she began writing in 1982, her early efforts encouraged by fellow members in a local workshop. Higgins is the most prominent of a group of Galway poets whose work has been published by Jessie Lendennie's Salmon Publishing*; others include Eva Bourke,* Moya Cannon,* and Anne Kennedy.* Higgins' first two volumes of poetry, *Goddess on the Mervue Bus* (1986) and *Witch in the Bushes* (1988), were reprinted first in one volume entitled *Goddess & Witch* and then again separately, in 1993, at about the same time as her 1992 *Philomena's Revenge.* Large-print runs of these later editions, issued under Salmon's new agreement with the Dublin publisher Poolbeg,* attest to the widespread popularity of Higgins' work. In the early 1990s, two of her plays, *Face Licker Come Home* and *God-of-the-Hatch Man* (the latter an expansion of a poem in her first volume), were produced by Galway's Punchbag Theatre. She has received bursaries from the Arts Council and, in 1989, the Peadar O'Donnell Award.

Eva Bourke, introducing *Goddess & Witch,* notes that Higgins "deals with subjects usually considered unfit for poetry." Indeed, though the narrator of the first poem in her first volume cradles "an anthology of the Ulster poets," her attention to Heaney,* Mahon,* and Ormsby* is interrupted or punctuated by the coughing of a nearby consumptive. In "Poetry Doesn't Pay," the narrator explains to the rent man that people keep telling her,

> "Your poems, you know,
> you've really got something there,
> I mean really."

To which he responds,

> "If you don't come across
> with fourteen pounds and ten pence soon
> you'll have something at the side of the road,
> made colourful by a little snow."

Its dedication page announces that the book is "for" Higgins' husband, her two daughters, "and the rent man." Still, many of the poems suggest that a kind of magic may lurk even in the most economically troubled circumstances, such as that of the butcher who wants to shout, "Lapis Lazuli, Lapis Lazuli" (but instead says, "You wouldn't put a dog out in it"), and that of the elderly unemployed man whom Higgins portrays as "The Lotus Eater from Bohermore."

That latter poem's fine, stable rhythm and clever use of rhyme are unmatched in Higgins' subsequent work. *Witch in the Bushes* most often stakes its claims on explicit, sardonic social commentary, in poems like "All Because We're Working Class," "Anything Is Better Than Emptying Bins," "Woman's Inhumanity to Woman (Galway Labour Exchange)," and "Blanket Man." Perhaps the most memorable of these is "Some People," a list of the indignities that "some people" know ("to be called a cunt in front of their children / to be short for the rent / to be short for the light/ . . . to be half strangled by your varicose veins, but you're 198th on the list") and that "other people don't." The book also includes two relatively controversial poems. "The KKK of Kastle Park," a bitter comment on an antitravelers meeting in Higgins's own neighborhood, elicited a good deal of local hostility and attention from the national newspapers. "Daughters of the Falls Road," with its dedication to Mairéad Farrell, one of the three Irish Republican Army members killed by British forces in Gibraltar in 1988, was judged by Patrick Crotty in the *Irish Times* to be "slipshod and morally myopic," though it is, in fact, a rather subtle commentary on public reation to the event: "it got into / the minds of the people. / And it was bigger than them / and they feared it / they feared the bullet / and the bomb, / but mostly their own thoughts." The most memorable poems in *Philomena's Revenge,* such as "I'll Have to Stop Thinking about Sex" and "I Want to Make Love to Kim Basinger," aim for laughter, but the book also includes "The H-Block Shuttle," with its depiction of bus riders who are able to "see nothing" on their way to visit political prisoners "(and no one really knows / what side they are on)."

Her first play, *Face-Licker Come Home,* marks a new departure for Higgins. Its method is sometimes reminiscent of the poetry of Mebdh McGuckian,* both because of its playful, antisyntactical language (according to which "experience" metamorphosizes into "expire," and "saint" and "genius" become verbs connoting violent action) and because that linguistic flexibility is a response to constraining circumstances. The lone character, Ellen, must spend the whole play in her bathroom because of her "hair-trigger colon," but language allows her to find there enormous imaginative freedom and range. Still, she spends much of the play mourning lost marital hopes; her wayward husband, the "face licker" (an alibi for one who provides cunnilingus), comes and goes outside. *God-of-the-Hatch Man* was misunderstood by some reviewers as anti-working class, but it continues the sometimes bitter, often humorous response to the troubled circumstances of the Irish 1980s and 1990s that has characterized Higgins' poetry. Her work incorporates the elements of consumer culture that provide substance in those difficult circumstances—signs of what McGuckian, reviewing Higgins' first book, called "the second-rate, Housing Executive environment of leatherette belts and brown acrylic pullovers, the Quinnsworth, Dunne's and bingo paradise"—and makes of them scavenged emblems of strength.

VICTOR LUFTIG

WORKS: *Goddess on the Mervue Bus.* Galway: Salmon, 1986. (Poetry); *Witch in the Bushes.* Galway: Salmon, 1988. (Poetry); *Goddess & Witch.* Galway: Salmon, 1990. (Poetry); *Face-Licker Come Home.* Galway: Salmon, 1991. (Play); *Philomena's Revenge.* Galway: Salmon, 1992. (Poetry).

HILL, GEOFF

WORK: *Smith.* Belfast: Blackstaff, 1993. (Novel).

HILL, NIKI (fl. 1990s), novelist. Hill was born and educated in Northern Ireland and is the editor of *Women's News* in Belfast.

WORK: *Death Grows on You.* London: Paladin, 1992. (Novel).

HINKSON, H[ENRY] A[LBERT] (1865–1919), novelist. Hinkson was born in Dublin on April 18, 1865. He was educated at Dublin's High School, at Trinity College, Dublin, in Germany, and received an M.A. in classical honours at the Royal University of Ireland in 1890. He was for a time senior classical tutor at Clongowes Wood but became a barrister and after 1914 was the resident magistrate for South Mayo. He married Katharine Tynan* in 1893 and was the father of Pamela Hinkson.* His novels, now generally neglected, are certainly full of arresting incident. For instance, in *The King's Deputy* (1899), the heroine, disguised as a man, successfully fights a duel. Nevertheless, his scenes often seem flatly narrated rather than starkly dramatized. His *O'Grady of Trinity*

(1896) is interesting for its depiction of university life. He died on January 11, 1919.

WORKS: *Golden Lads and Lasses.* London: Downey, 1895; ed., *Dublin Verses. By Members of Trinity College.* London: Elkin Mathews, 1895; *O'Grady of Trinity, A Story of Irish University Life.* London: Lawrence & Bullen, 1896; *Up for the Green: A Romance of the Irish Rebellion of 1798.* London: Lawrence & Bullen, 1898; *When Love Is Kind.* London: J. Long, 1898; *The King's Deputy.* London: Lawrence & Bullen, 1899; *The Point of Honour.* London: Lawrence & Bullen, 1901; *Fan Fitzgerald.* London: Chatto & Windus, 1902; *Silk and Steel.* London: Chatto & Windus, 1902; *Copyright Law.* London: A. H. Bullen, 1903; *The Wine of Love.* London: Eveleigh Nash, 1904; *The Splendid Knight.* Dublin: Sealy, Bryers/London: F. V. White, 1905; *Sir Phelim's Treasure.* London: Christian Knowledge Society, [1907]; *Golden Morn.* London: Cassell, 1907; *The Castaways of Hope Island.* London & Edinburgh: T. C. & E. C. Jack, 1907; *Father Alphonsus.* London: T. Fisher Unwin, 1908; *The King's Liege.* London: Blackie, 1910; *The Considine Luck.* London: Stephen Swift, 1912; *Glory of War.* London: Christian Knowledge Society, [1912]; *Gentleman Jack.* London: Christian Knowledge Society, [1913].

HINKSON, PAMELA [MARY TYNAN] (1900–1982), novelist, travel writer, writer of children's stories, and journalist. Hinkson was born in London, the daughter of Katharine Tynan* and H. A. Hinkson.* She was educated privately in Ireland, Germany, and France. She traveled in India and lectured on that country in the United States. During World War II, she worked for the Ministry of Information and after the war lectured to British troops abroad. Her *Irish Gold* (1939) is a readable collection of sketches, and her most popular novel, *The Ladies' Road* (1932), sold 100,000 copies in its Penguin edition. She died on May 26, 1982.

WORKS: *The End of All Dreams.* London: First Novel Library, 1923. (Novel); *The Girls of Redlands.* London: S. W. Partridge, [1923]. (School story); *Patsy at School.* London: T. Nelson, [1925]. (School story); *St. Mary's.* London: Longmans, 1927. (School story); *Wind from the West.* London: Macmillan, 1930. (Novel); *Schooldays at Meadowfield.* London & Glasgow: Collins, [1930]. (School story); *The Ladies' Road.* London: Gollancz, 1932. (Novel); *Victory Plays the Game.* London & Glasgow: Collins, [1933]. (School story); *The Deeply Rooted.* London: Gollancz, 1935. (Novel); *The Light on Ireland.* London: Frederick Miller, 1935. (Novel); *Victory's Last Term.* London & Glasgow: Collins, [1936]. (School story); with Elizabeth Plunkett, countess of Fingall. *Seventy Years Young. Memories of Elizabeth, Countess of Fingall.* London: Collins, 1937; *Irish Gold.* London: Collins, [1939]. (Sketches); *Indian Harvest.* London: Collins, 1941. (Travel); *Golden Rose.* London: Collins, 1944. (Novel); *The Lonely Bride.* London: Collins, 1951.

HOBHOUSE, VIOLET (1864–1902), novelist. Hobhouse was the eldest daughter of Edmund McNeill of Craigdunn, County Antrim, and she married Reverend Walter Hobhouse, the second son of Bishop Hobhouse. She was a firm Unionist and in 1887 and 1888 was a frequent public speaker against Home Rule. She also spoke Irish, however, and was deeply interested in Irish culture, traditions, and myths.

Hobhouse's first volume, *An Unknown Quantity* (1898), is a love story set primarily in London. Although the heroine and Maria, the nurse, are Irish, there is little else concerning Ireland in the novel. However, her second book, *Warp and Weft* (1899), takes place in a Northern Ireland linen-weaving district among the Presbyterian people with whom she felt at home. The heroine, Esther MacVeagh, is a strong woman who rises above the unscrupulous behavior of her husband and sets such a noble example that she eventually reforms him. Hobhouse is wonderfully adept in portraying Esther's character and in developing the psychological aspects of Esther's vows and decisions. The Northern Presbyterian psyche is well presented, and the author handles the sectarian elements with grace and neutrality. Hobhouse's only volume of poems, *Speculum Animae,* was a slim collection of devout verses, posthumously printed for private circulation among her close friends.

ANNE COLMAN

WORKS: *An Unknown Quantity.* London: Downey, 1898; *Warp and Weft: A Story of the North of Ireland.* London: Skeffington & Son, 1899; *Speculum Animae.* N.p.: Privately printed, 1902.

HOEY, MRS. CASHEL (1830–1908), novelist and journalist. Hoey was born Frances Sarah Johnston at Bushy Park, County Dublin, on February 14, 1830, and was largely self-educated. She was married at sixteen and widowed at twenty-five. In 1853, she had begun contributing to *The Freeman's Journal* and to *The Nation,** and after her husband's death she went to London with a letter of introduction from Carleton* to Thackeray. There she married John Cashel Hoey, who had been editor of the revived *Nation.* She became a Roman Catholic like her second husband and launched into a prolific career as journalist, translator from the French, and novelist. Although admired by such an astute critic as Mary Manning,* Mrs. Hoey's usual quality may be seen in this typical extract from one of her romantic and melodramatic productions about fashionable life:

She drew a little nearer; a wild light came into her eyes, her white cheeks were streaked with crimson. Her hands fluttered like leaves, and her gown stirred with the trembling of her knees.

"I will repent, I will repent, if the chances are for you; and, if you will give me a chance then, Dominick, my darling, my lover—I love you—how shall it be, since you have beaten me, and I cannot die for you, if the chances are for you?"

She clasped her hands, and stretched them towards him. A terrible yearning, half madness, half memory, all anguish, was in her beautiful, dreadful face. He recoiled still farther, and answered her thus:

"Woman, if the chances were for me, I would rather be hanged twice over than see your face again."

Elizabeth Lee in *The Dictionary of National Biography* says that Mrs. Hoey collaborated on the following novels which appeared under the name of Edmund Yates: *Land at Last* (1866), *Black Sheep* (1867), *Forlorn Hope,* and *Rock Ahead* (1868). Lee also states that *A Righted Wrong* (1870), published under Yates' name, was entirely written by Mrs. Hoey. In 1892, she was awarded a Civil Pension List of £50, and she died on July 8, 1908, at Beccles, Suffolk.

WORKS: *A House of Cards.* 3 vols. London: Tinsley, 1868; *Falsely True.* 3 vols. London: Tinsley, 1870/revised, London: Ward & Downey, 1890; *A Golden Sorrow.* 3 vols. London: Hurst & Blackett/New York: Harper, 1872; *Nazareth.* London: Burns & Oates, 1873. (Nonfiction); *Out of Court.* 3 vols. London, 1874; *The Blossoming of an Aloe, and the Queen's Token.* 3 vols. London: 1875/New York: Harper, 1875; *Griffith's Double.* 3 vols. London, 1876; *Kate Cronin's Dowry.* New York: Harper, 1877; *Ralph Craven's Silver Whistle.* London, 1877; *All or Nothing.* 3 vols. London, 1879; *The Question of Cain.* 3 vols. New York: Harper, 1881/London: Hurst & Blackett, 1882/ revised, London: Ward & Downey, 1890; *The Lover's Creed.* 3 vols. London: Chatto & Windus/ New York: G. Munro, 1884; *A Stern Chase.* 3 vols. London: Sampson Low/New York: Harper, 1886; *The Queen's Token.* London, 1888.

HOGAN, DAVID. *See* GALLAGHER, FRANK.

HOGAN, DESMOND (1950–   ), novelist and short story writer. Hogan was born in Ballinasloe, County Galway, on December 10, 1950, educated at Garbally College in Ballinaslow from 1964 to 1969, and at University College Dublin from 1969 to 1973. He received a B.A. in English and philosophy in 1972 and an M.A. in 1973. In recent years he has lived in England. Since the age of seventeen, he has published fairly prolifically, and his work thus far includes four collections of short stories, four novels, a travel book, and some early plays produced in Dublin and on the BBC. In 1971 he won the Hennessy Award, and in 1977 the Rooney Prize, and in 1980 his stories *The Diamonds at the Bottom of the Sea* won the John Llewellyn Rhys Memorial Prize. Generally, he has received considerable critical acclaim. For instance, a writer in the *Times* wrote "No one will ever push Joyce* or MacNeice* off my raft, but Mr. Hogan joins them," while in the *Irish Times* Augustine Martin remarked, "His imaginary world will probably haunt me to my dying day."

The themes of Hogan's early work were the traumas of early adolescence and a somewhat ambiguous preoccupation with homosexuality. Both themes are prominent in his short novel, *The Ikon Maker,* published in 1976 by the Irish Writers Co-operative, which he helped to found. The main characters of the book, a mother and her son, appear more manipulated than real. The son is misty, romantic, Byronic; the mother suffers, suffers, suffers. Indeed, there is a good deal of crying in the rambling plot. To take a random sample of consecutive pages, we find that the girlfriend cries on page 114, the mother cries on page 115 and again on pages 116 and 117 and on page 119 ("She stood weeping. Tears flowed. Her whole being became like a tidal wave"), a baby cries on page 122, the mother cries on page 123, and so on. Much of the novel is written in sentence fragments and in one-line paragraphs, but the style is clear and, in places, vivid.

Hogan's subject matter has somewhat broadened as he and his heroes have aged. From writing obliquely about the suppressed homosexuality of twelve-year-old boys, he turned to vague Grafton Street Byrons, who sat in Stephen's Green in the aftermath of the late 1960s, sipped coffee in Bewley's, smoked pot in seedy bedsits, and had unsatisfying and glancing relations with wraithlike characters who were doing the same things. Most recently, the heroes have approached middle age, achieved success of some sort, and transferred their broodings and their now overt homosexuality to Shepherd's Bush or San Francisco or New York.

As a short story writer, Hogan's constant and obtrusive faults are basic ones. He does usually narrate a tale rather than slap down a sketch, but the tale meanders shapelessly, without architecture, without proportion. His characters, save for the protagonist, are thin; and the protagonist is usually a journalist, an artist, or someone called Desmond. The other characters are so sieved through the psyche of the protagonist that they remain tersely described, undeveloped, and lifeless. For instance, in the story "Southern Birds," Hogan uses his favorite triangle of two young men and a woman. Here, the woman embodies some of the most recognizable characteristics of Juanita Casey,* who is probably about the most personally individual Irish writer since Brendan Behan.* But even here, Hogan flattens the character, reduces it to a wispy ectoplasm; and, considering his model, this is quite a dreary accomplishment. In another triangle story, "A Poet and an Englishman," the female character is as unbelievable and as manipulated as D. H. Lawrence's wish fulfillment of a heroine in "The Woman Who Rode Away." Hogan's story ends:

She'd never know how Peader had picked up a young boy from Cahirciveen who's been drunkenly urinating and made love to him in the tent, kissed his white naked pimples as Michael Gillespie had kissed his years before.

She'd never know but when she woke in the morning between Peader and a young boy she knew more about life's passion than she'd ever known before. She rose and put on a long skirt and looked at the morning, fresh, blue-laden, as she'd never seen it before.

The novels are like the short stories in that the characters are not strongly realized, and the narrative is related rather than dramatized. The most notable characteristic of the late novels is undoubtedly their prose style. In *The Ikon Maker* and the early stories, the prose was often in sentence fragments or one-sentence paragraphs containing lyric, quirky, and often arresting comparisons. In the later novels, the style is much less telegraphic in sentence structure, and the diction has grown florid, sometimes puzzling, and often tasteless. One critic, however, notes about *A Curious Street* (1984) that "there isn't a page without a strong flight of prose poetry" and that "Hogan's stylistic felicities are abundant." His stylistic infelicities are even more abundant. For instance, from *A New Shirt* (1986):

His eyes were snails in mustard lassitudes of lines.

In the orchestra, a chopped-hay headed boy with hare front teeth and a face that dropped into his teeth, salivated over his banjo.

His head corroding the pillow

Nessan was aware of the tribulation in his blood vessels on trains taking him home.

Clothes dripped from her.

Tufts of cotton clouds got entangled with the nonchalant mountains.

boys in white shorts with legs the amber of dollops of fried banana shuffling on the tennis court.

Nessan . . . blubbered quietly, silent jets of red and blue tears eventually on stoic exhibition.

His brows took on a blanch and became thick and surprised railway tracks.

His stylistic infelicities are even more abundant in his frequent descriptions of buttocks, penises, and testicles. We have, for instance, "his rodent skimpy buttocks . . . his antelope buttocks . . . his rock hard Unionist buttocks . . . two taciturn buttocks . . . the saucers of those buttocks. The fierce and multifarious buttocks of middle-aged ladies," and so on. We have, even more lyrically:

mangy looking priests in black soutanes suspiciously eyed the ermine of boys' penises curling upon themselves in the showers

I sailed around New York, my genital area blown apart by lightness. Parachutes dropped through the lightness.

The aura around his genitalia had changed, flecks of dust fighting around it like warring aeroplanes.

His bottom, the protruding defiance of it, steered a defiant course for her rippling breasts.

Hogan's late novels have really little to offer but their appalling prose style; and stylistically he has, despite an originally promising talent, developed into a kinky Amanda M'Kittrick Ros.* Ros, at least, was unintentionally very funny; Hogan in his late novels is unintentionally silly and almost unreadable.

   A Farewell to Prague (1995) is also almost unreadable, but not because of his style, which is less quirky and more effective. The book is nearly 250 pages of generally short and self-contained paragraphs that seem to have been taken verbatim from the writer's notebooks and that are descriptive jottings about people in places ranging from San Francisco, to the American Deep South, to Dublin and London and various Continental cities. Individual details are often nicely noted, but the paragraphs are but brief snapshots that neither create character nor cohere into a narrative. Hogan's subject has always been much more himself than the world. Here, the narrator is again named Des, and the book is finally about Des's sensibility as a casual observer. It is really too narrow a base for what is nominally a novel.

   WORKS: *The Ikon Maker.* Dublin: Co-op Books, 1976. (Novel); *A Short Walk to the Sea,* published with *The Swine and the Potwalloper* by Paschal Finnan. Dublin: Co-op Books, 1979. (One-act play); *The Diamonds at the Bottom of the Sea.* London: Hamish Hamilton, 1979. (Stories); *The Leaves on Grey.* London: Hamish Hamilton, 1980. (Novel); *Children of Lir.* London: Hamish Hamilton, 1981. (Stories); *A Curious Street.* London: Hamish Hamilton, 1984. (Novel); *A New Shirt.* London: Hamish Hamilton, 1986. (Novel); *The Mourning Thief.* London: Faber, 1987. (Stories); *Lebanon Lodge.* London: Faber, 1988. (Stories); *The Edge of the City.* Dublin: Lilliput, 1993. (Travel); *A Farewell to Prague.* London: Faber, [1995].

HOGAN, MICHAEL (1832–1899), poet. Hogan, "the Bard of Thomond," was born at Thomond Gate, County Limerick, in 1832 and published much abominable verse in *The Nation** and lesser known periodicals of the day. His patriotic, satiric, and humorous squibs are indeed fluent but could have been written by dozens of other public poets of the day. A few commentators, including Críostóir Ó Flynn,* have claimed that Hogan was a genius. Ó Flynn, for instance, makes the extraordinary claim that *Drunken Thady and the Bishop's Lady* is a masterpiece, "much more masterly," in fact, than Burns' "Tam o Shanter." The Bard Hogan, a nominal employee of the Limerick Corporation, died in 1899. He produced many poetry pamphlets in small editions, and most of them are quite rare. The following list of his works, then, is undoubtedly incomplete.

WORKS: *The Light of Munster.* Limerick: Goggin, 1852; *Anthems to Mary; For the Month of May.* Dublin: Mullany/London: Catholic Publishing & Bookselling Co., 1859; *Songs and Legends of Thomond.* Dublin: Mullany/London: Catholic Publishing & Bookselling Co., 1860; *Lays and Legends of Thomond.* Limerick: Munster News Office, 1865–1869; Dublin: Gill, 1880; *The Story of Shawn-a-Scoop, Mayor of Limerick* . . . , Nos. 1–4. Dublin: Author, 1868–1870; Nos. 5–8, Limerick: Author, 1871–1876; *The Limerick Election 1880.* . . . Limerick, 1880; *The Pictorial Gallery of the Limerick Election.* . . . Limerick: Author, 1880; *Newest Romance of Love.* Limerick, 1883; *Drunken Thady and the Bishop's Lady.* C. Ó Flynn, ed. [Dun Laoghaire?: Ó Flynn?, ca. 1976]. REFERENCE: Herbert, Robert. "A Bibliography of Michael Hogan, 'Bard of Thomond.'" *Irish Book Lover* 27 (1941): 276–279; Correction by Seamus Ó Casaide, *Irish Book Lover* 28 (1941): 36.

HOLLAND, DENIS (1826–1872), novelist and journalist.

WORKS: *The Landlord in Donegal: Pictures from the Wilds.* Belfast: *Ulsterman* Office, ca. 1859; *Ulic O'Donnell: An Irish Peasant's Progress.* London: Catholic Publishing & Bookselling, 1860; *Donal Dun O'Byrne: A Tale of the Rising in Wexford in 1798.* Glasgow: Cameron & Ferguson, 1869.

HOLLOWAY, JOSEPH (1861–1944), diarist. Holloway, one of the notable Dublin characters of his day, was an unacademic student of the Irish stage, an unsystematic collector of theatrical memorabilia, and the author of a unique theatrical diary. He was born on March 21, 1861, in Dublin, attended the School of Art in Kildare Street, then studied architecture, and finally set up as a practicing architect in 1896. Architecture, however, did not deeply or long engage his attention. Possessed of a small private income, he was able to devote most of his life to his great love, the theatre. Over the course of about sixty years he attended practically every first night in the Dublin theatre. He was an enthusiastic supporter of the Irish Literary Theatre* and attended so many rehearsals of its successor, the Irish National Theatre Society, that he was considered something of an unofficial adviser or mascot. When A.E.F. Horniman was planning a permanent home for the Society, she hired Holloway to renovate the old Mechanics' Theatre which became, of course, the Abbey.*

Deeply religious and thoroughly conservative, Holloway early fell out of total sympathy with the Abbey Theatre. He incurred the suspicion and dislike of Yeats* and Lady Gregory* for his violent objections to Synge's* *The Playboy* *of the Western World* and later, to some extent, to Sean O'Casey's* *The Plough and the Stars.* Nevertheless, his theatrical knowledge was so extensive and his theatrical taste so generally sound that many playwrights and actors continued to value his opinions and to seek out his advice. Mary Walker, one of the early actresses, remarked that Holloway was the finger which the players kept upon the public pulse.

Every day of his adult life, Holloway wrote about two thousand words in his diary, describing what he had seen and whom he had talked to that day. The basic diary, housed in the National Library of Ireland, consists of 221 manuscript volumes and totals approximately 25 million words. Written in a semi-legible scrawl and with scant attention to style, spelling, or punctuation, the diary is an immense desert of aridity which is dotted with innumerable oases of fascination. It has long served as a mine of information and gossip for scholars, and four volumes of selections have been quarried from it. In addition to his diary, which he called *Impressions of a Dublin Playgoer,* Holloway edited a shortlived Irish theatrical journal, *The Irish Playgoer,* in the 1890s; he published a slovenly but still unsuperseded bibliography of the Irish drama in Stephen J. Brown's *A Guide to Books on Ireland* (1912); and he wrote innumerable, if mainly inconsequential, pieces on the theatre for the Dublin press.

As a person, he was both crusty and kind; as a scholar, he was amateurish but encyclopedic; as a critic, he was often predictably narrow but basically surprisingly broad. He died in Dublin on March 13, 1944.

WORKS: *Joseph Holloway's Abbey Theatre.* Robert Hogan & M. J. O'Neill, eds. Carbondale & Edwardsville: Southern Illinois University Press, 1967; *Joseph Holloway's Irish Theatre, Vol. One—1926–1931.* Robert Hogan & M. J. O'Neill, eds. Dixon, Calif.: Proscenium, 1968; *Joseph Holloway's Irish Theatre, Vol. Two—1932–1937.* Robert Hogan & M. J. O'Neill, eds. Dixon, Calif.: Proscenium, 1969; *Joseph Holloway's Irish Theatre, Vol. Three—1938–1944.* Robert Hogan & M. J. O'Neill, eds. Dixon, Calif.: Proscenium, 1970.

HOLMES, MÁIRE C. (1952–), poet, playwright, and short story writer. Holmes was born in Dublin and now lives in Spiddal, County Galway. A writer in both English and Irish, her only work in book form thus far is a volume of poems in Irish. Her short story in English, however, "Smile for Mammy," won a Hennessy Award in 1988; and her play, *The Butterfly Who Couldn't Dance,* was staged at the Peacock in 1989

WORK: *Dúrún.* Baile Atha Cliath: Coiscéim, 1988. (Poetry).

HOLMQUIST, KATHRYN (1957–), autobiographer, playwright, and journalist. Holmquist was born on January 2, 1957, in Vermont. She grew up in Baltimore and Chatham, Massachussetts, taking her primary degree at Oberlin College, Ohio. In the 1980s, she emigrated to Dublin, where, after studying at Trinity College, she became a staff journalist with the *Irish Times* in 1986. *A Good Daughter* (1991) interweaves an account of her own turbulent coming-of-age with the tragic history of her mother's death from cancer. More than au-

tobiography, this is a poignant, poetically written probing of the mother–
daughter relationship. Holmquist is married to Ferdia MacAnna.*

IVY BANNISTER

WORK: *A Good Daughter*. Dublin: Raven Arts, 1991.

HONE, JOSEPH (1937–   ), novelist and travel writer. Born in London, Hone
is a grandson of Joseph Maunsel Hone.* He was educated at Kilkenny College
and St. Columba's in Dublin. He has been a freelance writer and broadcaster
since 1968.

WORKS: *The Private Sector*. London: Hamish Hamilton, 1971. (Novel); *The Sixth Directorate*.
London: Secker & Warburg, 1975. (Novel); *The Dancing Waters: Collected Travels*. London: Ham-
ish Hamilton, 1975; *The Paris Trap*. London: Secker & Warburg, 1977. (Novel); ed., *Irish Ghost
Stories*. London: Hamish Hamilton, 1977; *The Flowers of the Forest*. London: Secker & Warburg,
1980. (Novel); *Gone Tomorrow: Some More Collected Travels*. London: Secker & Warburg, 1981;
The Valley of the Fox. London: Secker & Warburg, 1982. (Novel); *Children of the Country: Coast
to Coast across Africa*. London: Hamish Hamilton, 1986; *Duck Soup in the Black Sea: Further
Collected Travels*. London: Hamish Hamilton, 1988; *Summer Hill*. London: Pan, 1990. (Novel);
Return to Summer Hill. London: Pan, 1992. (Novel).

HONE, JOSEPH [MAUNSEL] (1882–1959), biographer. Hone was probably
the foremost Irish literary biographer. He was born on February 8, 1882 in
Killiney, County Dublin, and was educated at Cheam School, Wellington College, and Jesus College, Cambridge. He was one of the founders of the distinguished publishing house of Maunsel and Company.* His own most notable
works were well researched and quite readable lives of Berkeley,* George
Moore,* and W. B. Yeats.* In 1957, he was elected president of the Irish Academy of Letters. He died on March 26, 1959.

WORKS: *Bishop Berkeley*. London: Faber, 1931. (Introduction by W. B. Yeats); *Ireland Since
1922*. London: Faber, 1932. (Pamphlet); *Thomas Davis*. London: G. Duckworth, 1934; with M. M.
Rossi, *Swift; or, the Egoist*. London: Gollancz, 1934; *The Life of George Moore*. London: Gollancz,
1936; *The Life of Henry Tonks*. London, Toronto: Heinemann, 1939; *The Moores of Moore Hall*.
London: Jonathan Cape, 1939; *W. B. Yeats, 1865–1939*. London: Macmillan, 1942. ed., *J. B. Yeats,
Letters to His Son W. B. Yeats and Others, 1869–1922*. London: Faber, 1944. (as Nathaniel Marlowe): with Warre Bradley Wells, *History of the Irish Rebellion of 1916*. Dublin & London: Maunsel, 1916; with Warre Bradley Wells, *The Irish Convention and Sinn Féin*. Dublin & London:
Maunsel, 1918. Hone also did many translations, including Halévy's life of Nietzsche, Montegut's
life of Mitchell, and Rossi's *Viaggio in Irlanda*.

HOPKIN, ALANNAH (1949–   ), novelist, journalist, and travel writer. Hopkin was born on September 6, 1949, in Singapore but spent her early childhood
in Cork. The family moved to England when she was four, and she was educated
at More House in London. She went on to Queen Mary College, University of
London, graduating with a B.A. (Hons) in English in 1974; and she obtained
her M.A. in sociology of literature in 1976 at the University of Essex.

All of Hopkin's work is informed by her acute awareness of place. The psychological effects of place determine the direction taken by the lives of her

protagonists in *A Joke Goes a Long Way in the Country* (1982) and *The Out-Haul* (1985). In the first novel, Alex Buckley settles into Castletownbere and finds that the "petty worries of the last few weeks and longer-established doubts, the detritus of years of misjudged decisions and impulsive experiments" have fallen away. "She knew she was all right. She had arrived." In *The Out-Haul,* Celia finds "beauty, and a continuity of life that made the rest seem petty and transitory."

In their retreat from restless, urban lives in London to the small-town quietness of Castletownbere or "Bally C" in West Cork, Hopkin's heroines reflect the author's belief in the spiritual resonances of specific places, which finds expression also in *The Living Legend of Saint Patrick.* This well-documented history of the folk practices based on the veneration of Patrick in Ireland and abroad makes deceptively easy reading. In it Hopkin first teases out the various strands that form both life and legend of the St. Patrick of the Confessions ("Patricius"), giving the reader a sound basis for understanding the observances that have sprung up over the years. Part of the charm of this book and its usefulness for the enthusiast comes from Hopkin's personal exploration of, and reaction to, the patrician sites she visits. The "great sense of peace and regeneration" and "new perception of yourself in relation to the material world and your own life" that she describes at the end of her chapter on Lough Derg could equally apply to the feelings of the heroines of her novels after they have been regenerated by the life and surroundings of West Cork.

Inside Cork: An Independent Guide to Cork City; West Cork; East Cork; South Cork; North Cork is extraordinarily informative. Entries reflect Hopkin's skills at research, her inquiring eye, and inexhaustible willingness to explore the terrain.

All of these virtues inform the novels, making them pleasingly readable, though not, perhaps, as emotionally arresting as they might be. Both heroines arrive at their earthly salvation almost by chance. In *A Joke Goes a Long Way in the Country,* Alex is set on her own course of action (in her case, deliberate nonaction) by a sudden death and a legacy, followed by the equally unexpected end of her flat-sharing arrangement. When Celia, in *The Out-Haul,* "thought about the random chain of events that took her back to Bally C she almost became mystic." In both novels, the real protagonist is the place, which exerts its influence on these young women when they seem most passive. Because of this, *A Joke* loses the chafing, insistent, potentially explosive causality generated by character, and the reader can sympathize with those friends of Alex who "found her bland confidence that something would turn up rather irritating."

Partly because of this, structure seems to be arbitrarily imposed on *A Joke* from outside. Hopkin interrupts the sequence of the narrative, shifting it from present to past and back again, giving each section a title: "Prologue," "Exposition," and so on, and interleaving the sections with quotations taken from other writings about the area. In *The Out-Haul,* a chapter is devoted to each month in the heroine's life from August to March. During this orderly progress of the seasons, Celia develops wisdom and, with it, an abiding relationship with Jimmy, her lover. Here Hopkin achieves the difficult aim of showing how, through being passive, a character is enabled to learn, to change, and finally to act.

SHEILA BARRETT

WORKS: *A Joke Goes a Long Way in the Country.* London: Hamish Hamilton, 1982/New York: Atheneum, 1983/London: Sphere, 1983; *The Out-Haul.* London: Hamish Hamilton, 1985/London: Sphere, 1986; *The Living Legend of St. Patrick.* London: Grafton, 1989/New York: St. Martin's, 1990; *Inside Cork.* Cork: Collins, 1991. REFERENCES: Delaney, Frank. "Ireland's Icon." *Sunday Times* (March 12, 1989); Keane, Molly. "Caught in the Nets." *Irish Times* (February 9, 1985); Updike, John. *"A Joke Goes a Long Way in the Country." The New Yorker* (May 2, 1983).

HOULT, [ELEANOR] NORAH (1898–1984), novelist and short story writer. Hoult was born in Dublin on September 10, 1898, of Anglo-Irish parents who died in her early childhood. She was educated in various boarding schools in England but returned to Ireland to collect material for her writing from 1931 to 1937. Just prior to World War II, she spent two years in America. She spent her last years in Greystones, County Wicklow, where she died on April 6, 1984.

Her first book, *Poor Women!,* appeared in 1928. This collection of short stories was a critical success and has been reprinted several times, both individually and in selected editions. The stories explore the consciousness of women in different walks of life; the best of them is "Bridget Kiernan," a study of a young domestic servant in prewar Britain. The other stories, especially "Violet Ryder," are interesting psychological studies, but Hoult tends to overburden them with dull realistic details and thus to impede the action. This unselectivity was to become a marked feature of her later style.

Since 1928, Hoult has published a formidable list of titles, but only two books, *Holy Ireland* (1935) and its sequel *Coming from the Fair,* (1937), are concerned with Irish life. They depict Irish family life from the end of the nineteenth century up to 1916 and particularly explore religious prejudice. In *Time Gentlemen! Time!* (1930), we see the horror of marriage to an alcoholic waster and the grimness of middle-class poverty. Here the drab realism is probably accurate enough but grows depressingly soporific in its accumulation. *Only Fools and Horses Work,* a later novel, is a more cheerful study of widowhood.

MARY ROSE CALLAGHAN

WORKS: *Poor Women!* London: Scholartis, 1928. (Stories); *Time Gentlemen! Time!* London: Heinemann, 1930; *Violet Ryder.* London: E. Mathews & Marot, 1930. (Novelette); *Apartment to Let.* London: Heinemann, 1931; *Ethel.* London: Peppercorn, 1931. (Story, first published in *Poor Women!*); *Youth Can't Be Served.* London: Heinemann, 1933; *Holy Ireland.* London: Heinemann, 1935; *Coming from the Fair.* London: Heinemann, 1937; *Nine Years Is a Long Time.* London: Heinemann, 1938. (Stories); *Four Women Grow Up.* London: Heinemann, 1940; *Smilin' on the Vine.* London: Heinemann, 1941; *Augusta Steps Out.* London: Heinemann, 1942; *Scene for Death.* London: Heinemann, 1943; *There Were No Windows.* London: Heinemann, 1944; *House Under Mars.* London: Heinemann, 1946; *Selected Stories.* London, Dublin: Maurice Fridberg, 1946; *Farewell Happy Fields.* London: Heinemann, 1948; *Cocktail Bar.* London: Heinemann, 1950. (Stories); *Frozen Ground.* London: Heinemann: 1952; *Sister Mavis.* London: Heinemann, 1953; *A Death*

Occurred. London: Hutchinson, 1954; *Journey into Print*. London: Hutchinson, 1954; *Father Hone and the Television Set*. London: Hutchinson, 1956; *Father and Daughter*. London: Hutchinson, 1957; *Husband and Wife*. London: Hutchinson, 1959; *The Last Days of Miss Jenkinson*. London: Hutchinson, 1962; *A Poet's Pilgrimage*. London: Hutchinson, 1966; *Not for our Sins Alone*. London: Hutchinson, 1972; *Two Girls in the Big Smoke*. London: Hale, 1977.

HOWARD, GORGES EDMOND (1715–1786), playwright and poet. Howard was born to a captain of dragoons in Coleraine on August 18, 1715. He was educated at Dr. Thomas Sheridan's* school in Dublin and actually published a volume of apothegms and maxims, as Sheridan himself had proposed to do in the 1730s. He became a prosperous solicitor and land agent and for his services to Dublin received the freedom of the city in 1766. He advocated a relaxation of the penal laws, and he died well-off in Dublin in June 1786.

As the *Dictionary of National Biography* amusingly remarks, ''His laborious efforts . . . to achieve reputation as a poet, dramatist, and literary moralist failed signally. The pertinacity with which he wrote and printed contemptible tragedies, none of which were acted, led to the publication of facetious satires, written mainly by Robert Jephson* in 1771.'' These satires took the form of fictitious letters written between Howard and George Faulkner,* the publisher, in ''the confused and jumbled styles'' of both, and copiously and amusingly annotated.

LITERARY WORKS: *A Collection of Apothegms and Maxims for the Good Conduct of Life*. . . . Dublin S. Cotter, 1767; *Almeyda: or, The Rival Kings*. Dublin: E. Lynch, 1769/3d ed., with alterations. London: Robinson & Roberts, 1769; *A Candid Appeal to the Public, on the Subject of a Late Epistle*. Dublin, 1771. (Pamphlet about the Jephson pamphlets); *The Life of Man. An Allegorical Vision*. 2d ed. Dublin: S. Powel, 1772. (Poetry); *The Miscellaneous Works, in Verse and Prose, of Gorges Edmond Howard*. 3 vols. Dublin: S. Price, W. Watson, 1782.

HUGHES, DECLAN (1963–   ), playwright. Hughes was born in Dublin and writes for the theater company Rough Magic. He was joint winner of the 1990 Stewart Parker* Playwright Bursary and the BBC (Northern Ireland) TV Drama Award. His *Digging for Fire* was first produced at the Project Arts Centre in Dublin on October 16, 1991, and later opened at the Bush Theatre, London, on March 20, 1992. Although another play in which a handful of people sit around for two hours and discuss their noneventful past, it is done with vigor and does in its last acts develop considerable conflict. A reunion of seven college friends ten years on, its first acts contain an effective indictment of contemporary Irish society. As one character says:

[T]he chaos *is* here—wannabees and weirdoes on the airwaves, brains fried from TV and video and information overload—so acknowledge it, don't pretend that there's some unique sense of community, that Ireland's some special little enclave—things are breaking down as fast here as anywhere else.

His second published play, *New Morning*, was first performed by Rough Magic at the Bush Theatre on April 2, 1993, and at the Project Arts Centre on April 28. It is a similar but lesser work in which two sisters argue about their past for three acts. It is somewhat arbitrarily enlivened by a wrestling match and a sinister dream figure with some resemblance to Elvis Presley. Hughes' dialogue is consistently strong and racy, and his characters well drawn. Thus far, these are his strong points, rather than his plotting.

WORKS: *Digging for Fire* and *New Morning*. [London]: Methuen, [1994].

HUGHES, JOHN (1962–), poet. Hughes was born in Belfast, grew up in Downpatrick, County Down, and took a B.A. in English and scholastic philosophy from Queen's University, Belfast, in 1984. He worked in New York City from 1988 to 1991 and now lives in Belfast. He has said that the writers he most admires are Borges, Vasko Popa, Robert Louis Stevenson, and Emily Dickinson. His poems have appeared in many journals, and he has published two collections, *The Something in Particular* (1986) and *Negotiations with the Chill Wind* (1991).

Hughes' second book resembles his first in its fascination with outrageous possible worlds and with potential and realized violence and in its tough, unemotional narrative style. In these new poems, systems of order, like the astronomical patterns of the night sky or the ritual patterns of a dance or the scholarly apparatus of a historical text, are backdrops for a vicious quotidian life, in which a violent randomness prevails. Lovers jilt each other, bystanders are killed by bombs, and a vampire is destroyed by fire. But despite the high level of punitive violence, justice is rarely seen to be done. Hughes' characters are more sinned against than sinning; indeed, Hughes' imaginative world is populated by victims, women victims in particular. Due to the rather detached and unemotive voice of the speaker in the poems, the reader is sometimes left wondering what to make of it all. These are brutal parables of suffering, fables of a feral world, produced by an imagination whose violence, in Wallace Stevens' phrase, is equal to the violence pushing against it from within. Surely with this in mind, Gerald Dawe* wrote of the poems in the *Irish Times* (January 4, 1992): "[T]here is a kind of belligerence about them: no fawning to the audience, no heart on the sleeve, no saying the acceptable, soulful things."

In "Relativity Avenue," a car bomb explodes and kills a number of people deep in conversation about the origin of the universe. This melodramatic contrast between the stylishly theoretical and the brutally violent is typical of the tone of the poems. Hughes refers in this poem to "the world we make up as we go along," a phrase that points to his major theme, for the makeup of his poetry is a fantastic environment of alchemists, astronomers, foreign kings, emperors and empresses, dictators, angels, wolves, and horsemen, where the possibilities of fable continually resist the probabilities of fact. The poems are disturbing and powerful, all the more so since the real world of political violence in Northern Ireland is sensed beyond the thin curtain of these impure fictions.

Gerald Dawe and Nicholas Murray both detect the considerable influence of Paul Muldoon* on Hughes. Murray in the *Times Literary Supplement* (August

14, 1992) writes: "[I]n the careful insouciance and laconic eloquence, the trans-atlantic orientation, the name dropping, the recondite vocabulary . . . and occasional downright impenetrability of these poems we can see the affinity with [Muldoon]." On the other hand, Dawe concludes that Hughes' poetry "is one of the most definite artistic accomplishments to have come out of the North in recent years."

JONATHAN ALLISON

WORKS: *The Something in Particular.* Dublin: Gallery, 1986; *Negotiations with the Chill Wind.* Dublin: Gallery, 1991/Newcastle upon Tyne: Bloodaxe, 1992.

HUGHES, MATTHEW FRANCIS (1834–1895), poet.

WORK: *Lyrics and Sonnets of Ireland, by Conaciensis.* Dublin: Fowler, 1871.   REFERENCE: McCall, John. "Matthew Francis Hughes: Memoir of Another Forgotten Irish Writer, with Selections from His Poems." *Irish Emerald* 7 (1898): 87–88, 103–104, 119–120, 135–136, 151–152, 191–192, 208, 224, 239–240, 256.

HUGHES, SEAN

WORK: *Sean's Book.* London: Pavilion, 1993. (Novel).

HULL, ELEANOR [HENRIETTA] (1860–1935), translator, historian. Hull was born in Manchester, the daughter of Professor Edward Hull, whose family claimed permanent residence in County Down from the early seventeenth century. Her father served as Director of the Geological Survey of Ireland from 1870 to 1890, and her grandfather was Reverend J. D. Hull, a minor poet. The Hulls returned from England to Dublin while Eleanor was a young girl. She was educated at Alexandra College and lived in Dublin until she was about twenty.

Hull was a student of Irish studies under Kuno Meyer and Standish O'Grady.* "A Personal Reminiscence" and an analytical article on O'Grady's work for the journal *Studies,* show his influence on her life and work. She helped found the Irish Texts Society in 1899 and served as secretary for almost thirty years. She edited the *Irish Home Reading Magazine* with Lionel Johnson,* in 1894. She was the recipient of a D.Litt. degree, and she died on the eve of her seventy-fifth birthday, in 1935. She made substantial contributions as an Irish historian in the late nineteenth and early twentieth centuries. Her two studies of the Cuchulainn myth were very popular, and both went into second editions.

ANNE COLMAN

WORKS: ed. *The Cuchullin Saga.* London: D. Nutt, 1898; *Pagan Ireland.* London: D. Nutt/Dublin: Gill, 1904; *Early Christian Ireland.* London: D. Nutt/Dublin: Gill, 1905; *A Text Book of Irish Literature.* 2 vols. Dublin: M. H. Gill/London: David Nutt, 1906–1908; *Cuchulainn, the Hound of Ulster.* London: G. G. Harrap, 1909; tr. *The Poem Book of the Gael.* London: Chatto & Windus, 1912/Chicago: Browne & Howell, 1913; *The Northmen in Britain.* London: G. G. Harrap/New York: Thomas Y. Crowell, 1913; *A History of Ireland and Her People to the Close of the Tudor Period.* 2 vols. London: G. G. Harrap, [1926–1931] *Folklore of the British Isles.* London: Methuen,

[1928]. REFERENCES: Biographical Sketch, in "Queries." *Irish Book Lover* 2 (July 1911): 194; Obituary. *Irish Book Lover* 23 (July–August 1935): 82.

HUNGERFORD, MARGARET WOLFE (1855–1897), fiction writer. Born in Rosscarberry, County Cork, Hungerford was the daughter of Rev. Fitzjohn Stannus Hamilton, rector of Ross and canon of Ross Cathedral. She was educated at Portarlington College, and in 1872 she married Edward Argles, a Dublin solicitor, and had three daughters. After his death, she married Henry Hungerford of Bandon, County Cork, in 1892 and had two sons and a daughter. She was an enormously popular and prolific writer of light romantic fiction, and her books went through innumerable editions in the English-speaking world. She turned out short stories, novellas, and three-volume novels, often under the pseudonym of "the Duchess" or as "By the Author of *Phyllis*" or "of *Molly Bawn*," possibly her best known works. She generally wrote of romantic love and courtship among the landed gentry, never among the peasantry. Of her work, Phyllis J. Scherle aptly remarked, "Although largely superficial, sentimental, and clearly lacking in serious intent, H[ungerford]'s works are still readable, even somewhat entertaining." It might be added that her best work is distinctly a cut above the Mills & Boon romances of the present and just as distinctly a cut or two below those of, say, Georgette Heyer. She died in Bandon on January 24, 1897, of typhoid fever.

PRINCIPAL WORKS: *Phyllis.* 3 vols. London, 1877/Philadelphia: Lippincott, 1877; *Molly Bawn.* 3 vols. London: Smith, Elder/Philadelphia: Lippincott, 1878; *"Airy, Fairy Lilian."* 3 vols. London: Smith, Elder, 1879/New York: G. Munro's Sons, n.d.; *Beauty's Daughter.* 3 vols. London: Smith, Elder, 1880/Chicago: W. B. Conkey, n.d.; *The Honorable Mrs. Vereker.* New York: J. W. Lovell, [1880]/London, 1888; *Faith and Unfaith.* 3 vols. London: Smith, Elder, 1881/New York: J. W. Lovell, [1881?]; *Mrs. Geoffrey.* 3 vols. London, 1881/New York: Universal, [1881?]; *Portia; or "By Passions Rocked."* 3 vols. London, 1883; *Rossmoyne.* 3 vols. London, 1883/New York: J. W. Lovell, [1883]; *Loÿs, Lord Berresford, and Other Tales.* 3 vols. London, 1883/New York: J. W. Lovell, 1883; *Twitching Horn and Other Stories.* New York: G. Munro, [1884]; *Doris.* 3 vols. London: Smith, Elder, 1884/New York: J. W. Lovell, [1884]; *A Week in Killarney.* New York: J. W. Lovell, [1884]/reissued as *Her Week's Amusement.* London, 1886/New York: J. W. Lovell, [1888]; *In Durance Vile, and Other Stories.* 3 vols. New York: J. W. Lovell, [1885]/London: Ward & Downey, 1889; *A Maiden All Forlorn, and Other Stories.* 3 vols. London: Ward & Downey/New York: J. W. Lovell, 1885; *A Mental Struggle.* 3 vols. New York: G. Munro, [1885]/London, 1886; *Dick's Sweetheart.* New York: J. W. Lovell, [1885]; *Mildred Trevanion.* New York: G. Munro, [1885]; *Lady Branksmere.* 3 vols. London: Smith, Elder/New York: J. W. Lovell, 1886; *Dolores; or Green Pleasures and Grey Grief.* 3 vols. London: Smith, Elder, [1886]; *The Haunted Chamber.* New York: J. W. Lovell, [1886]; *Lady Valworth's Diamonds.* New York: J. W. Lovell, [1886]; *A Life's Remorse.* 3 vols. Philadelphia: Crawford, 1887/London: F. V. White, 1890; *The Duchess.* New York: J. W. Lovell, [1887]/London: Hurst & Blackett, 1888; *A Modern Circe.* 3 vols. London: Ward & Downey/New York: J. W. Lovell, 1887; *Marvel.* 3 vols. London: Ward & Downey/New York: J. W. Lovell, 1888; *Under-currents.* 3 vols. London: Smith, Elder/New York: G. Munro, 1888; *A Troublesome Girl.* New York: J. W. Lovell, [1889]/London, 1889; *Her Last Throw.* London: F. V. White/New York: J. W. Lovell, 1990; *A Born Coquette.* 3 vols. London: Spencer Blackett/New York: J. W. Lovell, 1890; *April's Lady.* 3 vols. New York: J. W. Lovell, [1890]/London: F. V. White, 1891; *A Little Rebel.* New York: J. W. Lovell, 1890/London: F. V. White, 1891; *A Little Irish Girl, and Other Stories.* London: Henry/Philadelphia: Lippincott, 1891;

Nor Wife Nor Maid. 3 vols. New York: Hovendon, [1891]/London: Heinemann, 1892; *Nora Creina.* 3 vols. New York: Hovendon, [1892]/London: F. V. White, 1893; *The O'Connors of Ballinahinch.* New York: Hovendon, [1892]/London: Heinemann, 1893; *A Conquering Heroine.* London: F. V. White, 1892/New York: Tait, [ca. 1892]; *Lady Patty.* London: F. V. White/Philadelphia: Lippincott, 1892; *Lady Verner's Flight.* 2 vols. London: Chatto & Windus/New York: J. A. Taylor, 1893; *A Mad Prank.* London: F. V. White/New York: J. A. Taylor, 1893; *The Hoydon.* 3 vols. Philadelphia: Lippincott, 1893/London: Heinemann, 1894; *The Red-House Mystery.* 2 vols. London: Chatto & Windus, 1893/as *The Red House.* Chicago & New York: Rand, McNally, 1894; *Peter's Wife.* 3 vols. London: F. V. White/Philadelphia: Lippincott, 1894; *An Unsatisfactory Lover.* London: F. V. White, 1894; *The Professor's Experiment.* 3 vols. London: Chatto & Windus, 1895/New York: R. F. Fenno, [ca. 1895]; *The Three Graces.* 2 vols. London: Chatto & Windus/Philadelphia: Lippincott, 1895; *A Tug of War.* London: F. V. White, 1895; *Molly Darling and Other Stories.* London: T. Fisher Unwin/Philadelphia: Lippincott, 1895; *A Point of Conscience.* 3 vols. London: Chatto & Windus/Philadelphia: Lippincott, 1896; *A Lonely Maid.* Philadelphia: Lippincott, 1896/as *A Lonely Girl.* London: Downey, 1896; *Lovice.* London: Chatto & Windus/Philadelphia: Lippincott, 1897; *The Coming of Chloe.* London: F. V. White/Philadelphia: Lippincott, 1897; *An Anxious Moment.* London: Chatto & Windus, 1897. (Stories).

HUTCHINSON, [WILLIAM PATRICK HENRY] PEARSE (1927–   ),

poet. Hutchinson was born in Glasgow on February 16, 1927, of Irish parents. He was the last pupil to be enrolled in St. Enda's school and was also educated at the Christian Brothers school in Synge Street and at University College, Dublin. From 1951 to 1953, he worked as a translator for the International Labor Organization in Geneva. From 1957 to 1961, he was a drama critic for Radio Éireann. He has worked as a journalist in Dublin and lived for long periods in Spain and elsewhere in Europe. From 1971 to 1973, he was Gregory fellow in poetry at the University of Leeds. He was awarded the Butler Prize in 1969 and an Arts Council bursary in 1978. He was one of the founding editors of the magazine *Cyphers,* and he is a member of Aosdána.*

Hutchinson's work is sparing of simile and metaphor and even, relatively, of imagery. His earlier poems tended toward some formality, but his recent work has become much looser, conversational, even colloquial. However, even when the early work resorts to meter, the meter does not merely loosen before the poem concludes; it disintegrates. Hutchinson is seen at his best in such early pieces as "Petition to Release" and "Málaga," and at his worst in such late pieces as "All the Old Gems." His early work is superior to his later because the earlier poems usually preserved a certain authorial detachment, and many of the later ones are directly, even baldly personal. Moreover, his later work, no matter into what line lengths it is arbitrarily chopped, has diverged more and more into prose. Nevertheless, in both early and late work, Hutchinson is always capable of the utterly arresting line, for instance, "Love takes a long and garrulous time to die."

WORKS: Tr., *Poems* by Josep Carner. Oxford: Dolphin, 1962. (From the Catalan poet); *Tongue without Hands.* Dublin: [Dolmen], 1963; *Faoistin bhacach.* Baile Atha Cliath: An Clochomar, 1968; *Expansions.* Dublin: Dolmen, 1969; tr. *Josep Carner: 30 Poems.* 1970; tr., *Friend Songs: Medieval Galaico-Portuguese Love Poems.* Dublin: New Writers', 1970; *Watching the Morning Grow.* Dublin: Gallery, [1973]; *The Frost Is over All.* Dublin: Gallery, 1975; *Selected Poems.* [Dublin]: Gallery,

[1982]; *Climbing the Light.* [Dublin]: Gallery, [1985]; *The Soul That Kissed the Body.* [Oldcastle, Co. Meath]: Gallery, 1990; *Barnsley Main Seam.* [Oldcastle, Co. Meath]: Gallery, [1995].

HUTCHINSON, RON (1946–   ), playwright and radio and television writer. Hutchinson was born in Lisburn, County Antrim, on November 29, 1946. He was raised in Belfast and Port Muck, County Antrim, and in Coventry, Warwickshire. Before he was able to make a career as a playwright, he earned his living at a variety of jobs, including fish-gutter, salesman, bookseller, fraud investigator for the department of Social Security, social worker, and clerk at the Ministry of Defence and the Ministry of Labour in Coventry. While a clerk, he began to write for radio and television. His radio productions include *Roaring Boys* (1977), *Murphy Unchained* (1978), *There Must Be a Door* (1979), *Motorcade* (1980), *Risky City* (1981), *Troopers* (1988), and *Larkin* (1988). *Roaring Boys,* written for BBC Radio, was the first radio play to address issues associated with the Northern Troubles. He also wrote the first television play about the Troubles. His *Last Window Cleaner* (1979) studies, in a humorous way, Irish Republican Army compensation for injuries received from the violence in the North. His other television productions include *Twelve Off the Belt* (1977), *Deasy Desperate* (1979), *The Out of Town Boys* (1979), *Deasy* (1979), *The Winkler* (1979), *Bull Week* (1980), the *Bird of Prey* series (1982 and 1984), the *Connie* series (1985), *The Marksman* (1987), *Murderers among Us: The Simon Wiesenthal Story* (1988), *Dead Man Out* (1988), *Red King, White Knight* (1990), *The Josephine Baker Story* (1990), *Prisoners of Honor* (1991), *Blue Ice* (1992), *The Burning Season* (1994), *Against the Wall* (1994), and *Fatherland* (1994). His stage career includes being writer in residence at the Royal Shakespeare Company, and his productions include *Says I, Says He* (1977), *Eejits* (1978), *Jews/Arabs* (1978), *Anchorman* (1979), *Christmas of a Nobody* (1979), *The Irish Play* (1980), *Into Europe* (1981), *Risky City* (1981), *The Dillon* (1983), *Rat in the Skull* (1984), *Mary, After the Queen* (1985), *Curse of the Baskervilles* (1987), *Babbit: A Marriage* (1987), and *Pygmies in the Ruins* (1991). His numerous awards include a George Devine Award, the John Whiting Award, an Ace Award, and an Emmy Award. In 1986, he moved to California and began to write for film and television.

Of his published works, *Connie* (1985) is the novelization of the television series. *Says I, Says He* details the lives of two men who leave Northern Ireland for London and hoped-for success, which they achieve, in part, by using the threat of the violent Irish. The men are eventually killed just as they plan to return to England. The themes of attempting to escape Northern Ireland and its associated problems in exile and the inability to leave the violence and chaos of the Troubles are common to Hutchinson. In form, the play contains several musical numbers, some of which are obscene and all of which are funny. In addition, the play is a series of comic sketches that reveal the characters of his protagonists. *Rat in the Skull,* first produced at the Royal Court Theatre in 1984, again treats the violence of the Troubles and focuses on an interrogation scene in Paddington Green in which an Irish prisoner is brutalized. The dialogue is again quite funny, and its substance serves as sharp contrast to the tragic situation. Further, the absurdity of some of the characters, the deliberate play on racial attitudes and stereotypes, and the seeming inevitability of violence—a very human, rather than an institutionalized, violence—summon both the audience's outrage and sympathy and heighten the impact of the drama. These published works, like many of his television and radio plays and other stage productions, focus on individuals and their efforts to overcome the seemingly uncontrollable forces in their worlds—the forces of racism, of violence, of tyrannical government. At their best, his protagonists maintain their humanity, their humor, in the face of these uncontrollable powers. In his Irish plays, Hutchinson concentrates largely on the experience of the Irish outside Ireland and their efforts to come to terms in exile with their country's history, their country's violent present, and their country's persistent hold on the imagination and lives of its inhabitants, even those inhabitants in exile.

BERNARD McKENNA

WORKS: *Says I, Says He.* Newark, Del.: Proscenium, 1980. Part I published in *Plays and Players.* London (March & April, 1978); *Rat in the Skull.* London: Methuen, 1984; *Connie.* London: Severn House, 1985. (Novelization of television series).   REFERENCE: Etherton, Michael. *Contemporary Irish Dramatists.* London: Macmillan, 1989.

HYDE, DOUGLAS (1860–1949), scholar, poet, translator, founder of the Gaelic League, and first president of the Republic. Hyde was born on January 17, 1860. He was the third son of the Reverend Arthur Hyde, Protestant rector of Tibohine, Frenchpark, County Roscommon, and his wife Elizabeth, daughter of the Reverend John Oldfield, Protestant rector at Castlerea, County Roscommon. In 1873, Hyde was sent to a boarding school in Dublin, but after a few weeks he returned home to convalesce from the measles and did not return to school. He received a good education at home, especially in languages, but, more importantly, he developed an avid interest in Irish during these years which proved to be the determining force in his life. In 1874, Hyde began a series of diaries, composed in both Irish and English (and now at the National Library of Ireland), which record how eagerly he began learning Irish and collecting the oral songs and tales of the local country people. Hyde took the entrance examination for Trinity College, Dublin, in June 1880 and placed seventh out of a hundred candidates. His personal library at the time included over one hundred books written in Irish, twenty-four books mainly in English but on Irish subjects, and eighteen Irish manuscripts—an extraordinary collection for a young man of twenty who had never had a formal lesson in Irish languages or literature and who was about to enter a university which was a bastion of prejudice against Irish language and culture. Hyde perfunctorily fulfilled his formal studies at Trinity, first in divinity and then in law. He reserved his real enthusiasm for his ongoing efforts to teach himself Irish and to learn as much as possible about Irish culture. His early booklists indicate that by 1888 he had read almost all

Gaelic poetry in print and a considerable amount in manuscript. Hyde received an LL.D. in 1888, but the prizes he won while at Trinity—the Vice-Chancellor's Prize for English Verse in 1885, for prose in 1886, and both prizes in 1887— demonstrate that his genius and enthusiasm were for language and literature rather than for law.

Hyde had begun writing poetry in Irish and English in 1877. Between 1879 and 1883, he published original poems in Irish in *The Irishman* and *The Shamrock* under the pseudonym ''An Craoibhin Aoibhinn'' (the Pleasant Little Branch). The Fenianism he had absorbed in Roscommon and expressed in his early poetry and diaries was transformed into a cultural nationalism in Dublin during the 1880s. He was an active member of the Contemporary Club which Charles Oldham had founded in 1885. Its weekly meetings were a lively forum of debate about politics and literature among John O'Leary,* W. B. Yeats,* George Sigerson,* T. W. Rolleston,* and others who became the leaders of the Literary Revival. John O'Leary inspired Yeats to devote himself to producing a distinctively Irish literature written in English. But Hyde's devotion to the preservation of Irish language and culture made it inevitable that his nationalism would be modeled on that of George Sigerson who had succeeded James Clarence Mangan* as translator of the Irish poems in John O'Daly's *Poets and Poetry of Munster* (Second Series, 1860). Hyde devoted his life and his considerable talents as a poet, folklorist, and scholar to the restoration of Irish which he considered to be above and more important than divisive revolutionary nationalism. Nevertheless, his collection and translation of Irish oral traditions had a profound effect on Yeats and his literary movement, and Hyde's avowedly unpolitical propagandizing on behalf of Irish inevitably influenced Irish political events.

Hyde proclaimed his linguistic nationalism in an essay entitled ''A plea for the Irish Language'' in Charles Oldham's *Dublin University Review* in August 1885. Hyde's own immense knowledge of Irish oral tradition is apparent in the notes and three stories translated from the Irish which he contributed to W. B. Yeats' *Fairy and Folk Tales of the Irish Peasantry* (1888). In the same year, Hyde contributed six poems in English to the anthology of the emerging literary revival, *Poems and Ballads of Young Ireland.* His main interest, however, continued to be Irish, and his first book, *Leabhar Sgéulaigheachta* (1889), a collection of folk stories, rhymes, and riddles, was the first of its kind ever to be published in Irish. In *Beside the Fire: A Collection of Irish Gaelic Folk Stories* (1890), Hyde presented English translations of about half the stories in his first book, together with six other traditional tales in the original Irish with English translations. *Beside the Fire* is a landmark both in Irish folklore studies and in Irish literary history. Numerous collections of Irish folktales in English had been published throughout the nineteenth century, but Hyde was the first to present the exact language, names, and various localities of his informants. The ''Index of Incidents'' which he included at the end anticipated the use of motifs by twentieth-century folklorists. Hyde's forty-page preface reviewed the entire tradition of Irish folklore, presenting a scholarly evaluation of its significance and evaluating earlier collectors who had tampered with the substance and idiom of their originals. Hyde's own translations represented the first attempt to render Irish folklore in a true Anglo-Irish idiom. Hyde's prose bore little resemblance to the imaginary and ludicrous English of the Stage Irishman or the artificial literary style of his predecessors in the publication of Irish folklore. The poetic possibilities of this Anglo-Irish idiom were even more apparent in Hyde's translations of folk poetry, the "Songs of Connacht," which began to appear in serial form in *The Nation** in 1890. The fourth chapter of these songs, published in *The Weekly Freeman* in 1892 and early 1893 and in book form as the *Love Songs of Connacht* (1893), was a poetic and scholarly achievement and had immense literary significance. Hyde published the originals with translations to preserve them from oblivion and to aid students of Irish. He translated most of the poems twice. The first version, a free translation, reproduced the rhythm of the Irish verse; the second version, given as a footnote, was a literal translation. W. B. Yeats wrote that "the prose parts of that book were to me, as they were to many others, the coming of a new power into literature." Ironically, Hyde's achievement as a translator and a poet in the *Love Songs of Connacht* frustrated his own goal, for it furnished Yeats, Synge,* and Lady Gregory* with Irish themes in a beautiful idiom which made an Irish literature in English seem all the more possible.

The year 1893 also marked what Hyde considered to be the most important event in his life—his marriage to Lucy Kurtz, the daughter of a German research chemist who had left Russia to settle in England. The Hydes had two daughters, Nuala, who died of consumption in 1916, and Una, who married James Sealy, a Dublin judge.

On his return from a one-year interim professorship at the University of New Brunswick in 1891, Hyde had assumed the presidency of the new National Literary Society. His inaugural address, "The Necessity for De-Anglicising Ireland," given in November 1892, is his most famous and influential lecture. This lecture marked the beginning of an organized effort not only to preserve but to revive Irish language and culture. In 1893, largely as a result of Hyde's energetic propaganda on behalf of the language, the Gaelic League was founded with Hyde as its president. The two aims of the Gaelic League, which was founded as a cultural rather than as a political organization, were to revive Irish as the national language and to create a modern Irish literature. The Gaelic League was an immensely popular movement which attracted and inspired many literary as well as revolutionary nationalists. Hyde managed to keep the League from becoming politicized until 1915 when its constitution was amended to declare that its aim would be the realization of "a free, Gaelic-speaking Ireland." Hyde resigned immediately from the presidency and from the Gaelic League. In *The Young Douglas Hyde* (1974), Dominic Daly summed up the political implications of Hyde's movement as "immense and profound":

Although the actual course of events was not what he would have chosen, his ideology was the mainspring that set these events in motion. It was he who created the ground-swell on which the Volunteer movement was launched; his students and disciples were the officers and men of the insurrection. With the zeal of a convert he opened the eyes of Irish men and women to the source of their identity as a nation.

Hyde continued his work as a poet, folklorist, and scholar of Irish literature during and after the twenty-two years he was a very active president of the Gaelic League. He wrote *The Story of Early Gaelic Literature* (1895) as an answer to those who still repeated the popular fallacy that there was no literature in Irish. His *A Literary History of Ireland* (1899) surveyed the diversity and importance of Irish literature written in Irish. Hyde's achievements as a scholar were recognized when he was appointed to the chair of modern Irish at University College, Dublin, in 1905. His genius as a poet-translator produced three more chapters of the "Songs of Connacht": *Songs Ascribed to Raftery* (1903), which saved the oral poems of the blind poet Anthony Raftery (ca. 1784–ca. 1835) from oblivion, and two volumes of *Religious Songs of Connacht* (1906), which had been serialized in the *New Ireland Review* from June 1895 to June 1905.

Hyde was also a playwright and an amateur actor. He is credited with writing the first play in Irish produced at a professional theater. *Casadh an tSugáin* was performed by members of the Gaelic League Amateur Dramatic Society at the Gaiety Theatre, Dublin, on October 21, 1901, and translated by Lady Gregory as "The Twisting of the Rope." The play, with Hyde playing the principal part, was an immense success and both Synge and Padraic Colum* wrote of the audience's emotional and enthusiastic response at its first performance. From 1902 until 1904 Hyde wrote several more plays in Irish, often from scenarios by Yeats and Lady Gregory, to help the language movement: *The Tinker and the Fairy, The Marriage, The Nativity, The Lost Saint, The Bursting of the Bubble, King James, The Schoolmaster,* and *The Poorhouse. The Poorhouse* was rewritten by Lady Gregory as "The Workhouse Ward." Hyde's literary publications also include two additional collections of Irish folklore: *Legends of Saints and Sinners* (1916) and *Mayo Stories Told by Thomas Casey* (1939).

Hyde retired from University College in 1932 and went to live near French-park at Ratra, the house purchased and given to him by the Gaelic League. When the new Irish Constitution was adopted in 1938, Douglas Hyde was elected unopposed as the first president of the Republic of Ireland, an office he held until 1944. In 1940, he suffered a stroke which left him a semi-invalid. He died in Dublin on July 13, 1949, and is buried in the graveyard of the Protestant Church, Portahard, near Frenchpark.

Hyde's significance to the preservation of Irish and to the establishment of a free Ireland has been generally acknowledged, but his literary genius as a poet and translator and his influential pioneer work with the Anglo-Irish idiom have, until recently been unjustly overshadowed by the literary accomplishments of his more well-known contemporaries. Yet, Yeats, Synge, and Lady Gregory all acknowledged their immense debt to Douglas Hyde. Susan Mitchell's tribute to Hyde, written thirty-three years before his death in her book on George Moore,* was even more appropriate when Hyde died in 1949 because it recognized that Douglas Hyde's legacy to Ireland encompassed much more than language, poetry, folklore, and scholarship: "We who remember those days know what Ireland owes to Hyde's fiery spirit, his immense courage, his scholarship, his genius for organization, his sincerity, his eloquence, and the kindness of his heart."

MARY HELEN THUENTE

WORKS: *Beside the Fire: A Collection of Irish Gaelic Folk Stories.* London: David Nutt, 1890/ facsimile edition, New York: Lemma, 1973; *Love Songs of Connacht.* Dublin: Gill, 1893/facsimile edition, Shannon: Irish University Press, 1969; *A Literary History of Ireland from the Earliest Times to the Present Day.* London: Unwin, 1899/revised & edited by Brian Ó Cuív, London: Ernest Benn/ New York: Barnes & Noble, 1967; "The Necessity for De-Anglicising Ireland." In *The Revival of Irish Literature.* London: Unwin, 1901; *The Religious Songs of Connacht.* Dublin: Gill, 1906/facsimile edition, Shannon: Irish University Press, 1972. REFERENCES: Coffey, Diarmid. *Douglas Hyde: President of Ireland.* Dublin: Talbot, 1938; Conner, Lester. "The Importance of Douglas Hyde to the Irish Literary Renaissance." *Modern Irish Literature.* R. J. Porter and J. D. Brophy, eds. New York: Twayne, 1972, vol 1, pp. 95–114; Daly, Dominic. *The Young Douglas Hyde: The Dawn of the Irish Revolution and Renaissance 1874–1893.* Totowa, N.J.: Rowman & Littlefield, 1974; Dunleavy, Janet Egleson & Dunleavy, Gareth W. *Douglas Hyde: A Maker of Modern Ireland.* Berkeley & Los Angeles: University of California Press, 1991.

INGMAN, HEATHER (fl. 1980s–1990s), novelist. Heather Ingman has also published as Heather von Prondzynski, which seems an unlikely name for an Irish writer. In fact, she was born in Stockton-on-Tees in the north of England and studied at London University. Having completed a doctorate in French literature, she spent ten years teaching at Trinity College, Dublin. She also lived in Ecuador, which forms part of the setting of her novel *Sara*. She currently resides in Hull with her husband and two children and teaches at York University.

Her novel *The Quest* (1992) is set in Trinity, where, amid the politics and bureaucracy of academic life, Maggie James confronts the issues of personal and national identity. *The Quest* is an examination of struggle. It is a struggle not for independence, but rather of how one creates and perceives the self once that independence has been gained.

Maggie is seen as being "different" from other women because she has sacrificed having a family for her career. She fights against this image of herself and accepts the voices in her head as a manifestation of this struggle: "I believe women will always have such voices, until they become more certain of their identity." Only when Maggie learns to discard these voices can she come to terms with the life of an independent woman leading an unconventional life in a male-organized society.

Throughout the novel, parallels are drawn between the search for a woman's identity and the definition of a new Irish society. Patrick Brophy is the elderly writer who leads Maggie to the end of her quest. He questions why an Irish people fought for independence from England and then created the new Ireland in England's image.

If this novel seems contrived at times, it is also charming. The reader enters into Maggie James's dilemmas and joys and is carried along by the lively narrative and the quirky situations.

Ingman's recent novels, *Sara* (1994) and *Anna* (1995), are set, respectively, in the Irish Midlands and in Hull. Both detail the problems of able but insecure women. Sara is unable to conceive but desperately wants a child. Anna, a harried young widow attempting to raise two small boys, discovers that her husband had a daughter ten years earlier by an old girlfriend. Both characters are on the verge of hysteria, and both weep a lot, but both are convincing. The plots have a wealth of incident, the minor characters are excellently established, and the writing is clear and economical. Ingman is a very solid writer realistically addressing women's issues.

RACHEL DOUGLAS

WORKS: *The Dance of the Muses. A Novel on the Life of Pierre Ronsard.* London: Owen, 1987; *Machiavelli in Sixteenth-Century French Fiction.* New York: P. Lang, 1988; *The Quest.* Dublin: Attic, 1992; *Sara.* Dublin: Poolbeg, 1994; *Anna.* Dublin: Poolbeg, 1995.

INGOLDSBY, PAT (1942–   ), poet and children's writer. Ingoldsby has published and peddled most of his own books of verse himself, with some success. Most of his pieces are too formless to be called verse, and some are self-pityingly sentimental. Written in very short lines, all are tight and clear, and the best have an arrestingly fey idea to them. Fairly typical would be "I Hope So," which suggests that car tires have treads so they will not crush the insects. At best, Ingoldsby's work seems a mixture of e. e. cummings and Spike Milligan,* and one should not be too dismissive of that.

WORKS: *You've Just Finished Reading This Title.* [Blackrock, Co. Dublin: Author, 1977]; *Welcome to My Head.* Bray, Co. Wicklow: Rainbow, 1986; *Scandal Sisters.* [Dun Laoghaire, Co. Dublin]: Anna Livia, [1990]; *How Was It for You Doctor?* Dublin: Willow, [1994]; *Salty Water.* Dublin: O'Brien, 1994; *Poems So Fresh & So New . . . Yahoo!* Dublin: Willow, [1995].

INGRAM, JOHN KELLS (1823–1907), scholar and poet. Ingram was born at the rectory at Temple Crane, County Donegal, on July 7, 1823. He was educated at Trinity College, Dublin, received a B.A. in 1843, was elected a fellow in 1846, and continued his connection with the university for fifty-three years. In 1852, he was made Erasmus Smith professor of oratory and was thus the first to give formal instruction in English literature at the university; in 1866, he became Regius professor of Greek, in 1879 librarian, in 1884 senior fellow, in 1887 senior lecturer, in 1891 was awarded a D. Litt., and in 1898 became vice provost. He was also on the Board of the National Library and was involved in the founding of Alexandra College for Women in 1866. He wrote much on the history of religion and on political economy, and he translated Comte. As a literary man, he is remembered only for his poem "The Memory of the Dead" which he published anonymously as a young man. The first famous stanza reads:

Who fears to speak of Ninety-Eight?
  Who blushes at the name?
When cowards mock the patriot's fate,
  Who hangs his head for shame?

> He's all a knave or half a slave
>   Who slights his country thus:
> But a true man like you, man,
>   Will fill your glass with us.

Ingram did not formally acknowledge his authorship of the poem until 1900, and, in fact, became somewhat embarrassed by its fiery sentiments. He died in Dublin on May 1, 1907.

WORKS: *Sonnets, and Other Poems.* London: A. & C. Black, 1900. REFERENCES: Falkiner, C. L. *Memoir of John Kells Ingram.* . . . Dublin: Sealy, Bryers & Walker, 1907. (Pamphlet); Lyster, T. W. "Bibliography of the Writings of John Kells Ingram 1823–1907 with a Brief Chronology." *Leabharlann* 3 (1909): 3–46.

IRELAND, DENIS (1894–1974), autobiographer and writer on politics. Ireland was born in Belfast into a well-off linen manufacturing family, for which he commenced working as an agent in Britain, the United States, and Canada. He was educated at the Belfast Academical Institute and at Queen's University. During the World War I, he saw action with the Royal Irish Fusiliers in France and Macedonia, and was wounded "on the road to Byzantium." He developed the strongly-held nationalist opinions that remained with him for life through a chance encounter with a copy of P. W. Joyce's* *Irish Names and Places* which he found "hidden away on a shelf" when he was convalescing at Eccles Hotel in Glengarriff, County Cork—a conversion similar to Standish O'Grady's.* Besides much occasional literary journalism and broadcasting, he went on to write a short "biography" of Wolfe Tone*—actually a connected series of extracts from the diary—and issued a series of anti-Unionist polemics such as *An Irish Protestant Looks at His World* (1930) and *Six Counties in Search of a Nation* (1947). In 1948, he became the first Northern member of the Irish Senate and served as a member of the Irish delegation to the Council of Europe. He always retained the use of his wartime rank of captain. He died in Belfast on September 23, 1974.

Ireland regarded modern Unionism as a tragic aberration from the radical independence of more radical forefathers, and considered that the greatest Anglo-Irishmen loved their native country better than either Rome or England. Of his own case, he wrote, "It is easier for a camel to pass through the eye of a needle, than for a son of an Ulster Protestant industrialist to orientate himself in relation to his country's history." The break-up of the British Empire, which he regarded with satisfaction, argued that the dependence of Ulster would not for long be economically advantageous, and he endorsed the view (which he associated with Patrick Kavanagh*) that Catholic Ireland was always more influenced by continental Europe than by Britain. He was critical of the rural-peasant bias of the Irish literary revival, remarking, with others such as St. John Ervine,* that for W. B. Yeats* Northern Ireland was beyond the romantic pale: "factory chimneys and fairies were assumed to cancel one another out; if you had one, you couldn't have the other, and we had the factory chimneys." At the same time, he disparaged "the usual Anglo-Irish half truths about Ireland" which he discerned in the plays of Denis Johnston* and wrote admiringly of John Mitchel,* Daniel Corkery,* and Dan Breen. He contributed reviews and essays both to *The Bell** and its successor *Envoy,** and also to Robert Greacen's* anthology *Northern Harvest* (1944). The autobiographical chapters in *From the Irish Shore* (1936) are supplemented by the more occasional writings of *Statues Round the City Hall* (1939). A final collection, *From the Jungle of Belfast* (1973), reprinted earlier pieces with some newly-gathered material. His occasional writings and journals are often touched with high spirits, and he was not above parodying James Joyce's* *Ulysses.*

BRUCE STEWART

WORKS: *An Ulster Protestant Looks at His World: A Critical Commentary on Contemporary Irish Politics.* Belfast: Dorman, [1931]; *Ulster To-day and To-morrow.* London: L. & V. Woolf, 1931. (Pamphlet); *Portraits and Sketches.* Belfast: Vortex, [1935]; *From the Irish Shore: Notes on My Life and Times.* London: Rich & Cowan, 1936; *Patriot Adventurer.* London: Rich & Cowan, 1936. (Extracts from the writings of Wolfe Tone with Ireland's connecting narrative); *Statues Round the City Hall.* London: Cresset, 1939. (Stories and sketches); *Eamon de Valera Doesn't See It Through: A Study of Irish Politics in the Machine Age.* Cork: Forum, 1941. (Pamphlet); *The Age of Unreason: A Short History of Democracy in Our Times.* Dublin: Corrigan & Wilson, 1944. (Pamphlet); *Six Counties in Search of a Nation: Essays and Letters on Partition 1942–1946.* Belfast: Irish News, 1947; *From the Jungle of Belfast: Footnotes to History 1904–1972.* Belfast: Blackstaff, [1973].

IREMONGER, VALENTIN (1918–1991), poet and diplomat. Iremonger was born in Dublin on February 14, 1918, and was educated at the Synge Street Christian Brothers school and at Colaiste Mhuire. In 1945, he won the AE Memorial Prize for a manuscript collection of poems, some of which were printed in his first volume, *Reservations* (1950). In November 1947, supported by Roger McHugh,* he protested from the audience of the Abbey Theatre* that an inadequate production of O'Casey's* *The Plough and the Stars* was a debasement of the theatre's ideals. From 1949 to 1951, he was poetry editor of *Envoy,** which published his *Reservations.* He has spent most of his life in Ireland's foreign service—in London as first secretary and then counsellor, as ambassador to Sweden, Norway, and Finland, and as ambassador to India. He has made translations from the Irish of two modern prose narratives. His collected poems appeared in 1972 under the title *Horan's Field,* and some later pieces appeared in 1988 under the title *Sandymount, Dublin.*

Iremonger is a thoroughly glum poet, full of nostalgia, regret, remorse, and the consciousness of growing old. He speaks constantly of "the debris of the years." Winter is always coming, but in actuality spring and winter are pretty much the same. His work is in free verse at best and prose at worst, although sometimes the prose is decorated with rhyme. His sentence structure is generally straightforward, and his diction restrained, except for some awkwardly used colloquialisms. When he attempts to set up a rhyme scheme, as in "By the Dodder in Flood at Herbert Bridge" or in "Time, the Faithless," he cannot hold to it and either abandons it or settles for vague similarities of sound. Fairly often, however, he does manage a strong image or metaphor, even an extended one. One of his most effective pieces is the concluding poem in *Horan's Field,* a translation from Catullus in which the language is both modern and racy.

He died in Dublin on May 22, 1991.

WORKS: Ed. with Robert Greacen. *Contemporary Irish Poetry.* London: Faber, 1949; *Reservations.* Dublin: Envoy, 1950; ed., *Irish Short Stories.* London: Faber, 1960; trans., *The Hard Road to Klondike,* by Michael MacGowan. London: Routledge & Kegan Paul, 1962; trans., *An Irish Navvy, the Diary of an Exile,* by Donall MacAmhlaigh. London: Routledge & Kegan Paul, 1964; *Horan's Field and Other Reservations.* Dublin: Dolmen, 1972. (Contains his poems since 1950, with those poems from his first book that he wished to retain); *Sandymount, Dublin.* Dublin: Dedalus, 1988.

IRISH ACADEMY OF LETTERS. The academy was pretty much the brainchild of W. B. Yeats,* and one of his chief reasons was to found a prestigious organization that could effectively oppose the banning of books by the Irish Free State. The academy was inaugurated at a meeting at the Peacock Theatre on September 18, 1932, with Bernard Shaw* as president and Yeats as vice president. The initial members were AE,* Edith Somerville,* James Stephens,* Padraic Colum,* Lennox Robinson,* Seumas O'Sullivan,* T. C. Murray,* St. John Ervine,* Forrest Reid,* Brinsley MacNamara,* Austin Clarke,* F. R. Higgins,* Liam O'Flaherty,* Oliver St. John Gogarty,* Frank O'Connor,* Peadar O'Donnell,* Francis Stuart,* and Sean O'Faolain.* Associate membership, which was generally understood to mean not quite as Irish as ordinary membership, was given to Eugene O'Neill, Helen Waddell,* Walter Starkie,* J. M. Hone,* Stephen Gwynn,* T. E. Lawrence, L.A.G. Strong,* and John Eglinton.* Among those who were offered but refused membership were James Joyce,* George Moore,* Douglas Hyde,* Daniel Corkery,* Lord Dunsany,* Stephen MacKenna,* and Sean O'Casey.* The initial view—if there was one—of the man on the street toward the academy might be summarized by Joseph Holloway,* who wrote, "Its sole aim seemingly is to do away with the Censors and give all a free hand to flood the Free State with filth. I call the new venture the Irish Academy of Litters." Although the academy had singularly little success in stemming the notorious state censorship of books, it did, over the years, manage to give various awards and prizes of money to writers. In recent years, the academy gently dwindled away; and, although it has never been formally dissolved, it really does not exist anymore. However, its effective functions, the awarding of prestige and money, were taken over by the foundation of Aosdána* in 1981.

IRISH LITERARY THEATRE, THE. *See* ABBEY THEATRE.

IRISH REVIEW, THE (1911–1915), literary magazine. *The Irish Review* was founded by three young people who worked at Padraic Pearse's* St. Enda's

School, by a friend who lived down the road from the school, and by James
Stephens.* The three young people were Thomas MacDonagh,* Padraic
Colum,* and his future wife, Mary Maguire;* the friend was David Houston, a
North of Ireland man who worked at the College of Science and published a
magazine called *Irish Gardening.* As Padraic Colum wrote:

David Houston was an outgoing, enthusiastic, hospitable man, with a tinge of Orangism
that was provocative. Now his house open on Sunday afternoons was crammed with Irish
Revivalists. Thomas MacDonagh from the school down the road appeared amongst them.
So did James Stephens, who was now a cherished guest at every reception in Dublin. I
would come with M.C.M. [Mary Maguire], who was a favourite in the Houston household.

  One evening the sanguine householder announced to the four of us that he had the
establishment of an Irish monthly in mind. It is a measure of the faith that obtained in
those days that this disclosure was discussed, not merely seriously, but eagerly. Houston,
MacDonagh, Stephens and myself were to conduct it. We named the future publication—
at my suggestion, I think—*The Irish Review.* M.C.M. was to have the office of critic-
in-chief. And the Review, mind you, was not to be quarterly, but monthly, with the same
number of pages as a quarterly of today, and to be sold for sixpence. [*The Dublin
Magazine 5* (Spring 1966): 42–43.]

From 1911 to 1912, the main editor was Houston; from 1912 to 1913, Colum,
and from 1913 to 1914, Joseph Mary Plunkett.* Like most fine literary magazines, *The Irish Review* finally expired not because of lack of interest, but because of lack of funds. Nevertheless, in its short life, it published poems, stories,
plays, criticism, and reviews by and about the best writers of the day—among
them Yeats,* Pearse,* AE,* Corkery,* Dunsany,* Birmingham,* Gogarty,* Forrest Reid,* Eimar O'Duffy,* Douglas Hyde,* and Seumas O'Sullivan.*

IRISH STATESMAN, THE (1923–1930), magazine of contemporary comment.
The Irish Statesman was edited by AE* (George W. Russell) and is indispensable for the study of modern Irish letters. It grew out of *The Irish Homestead,*
the journal founded in 1895 by Sir Horace Plunkett (1854–1932) as the organ
for his Irish Agricultural Organisation Society, and edited from 1905 by AE.
The *Homestead* was interested mainly in agricultural matters, but did, especially
in its Celtic Christmas numbers, publish works of literary interest. James Joyce*
referred to it scathingly as "the pigs' paper," but that "bullock-befriending
bard" was willing to publish some early stories from *Dubliners* in it.
  The Irish Statesman, also supported by Plunkett, was much broader in its
interests than the *Homestead;* it gave a lively and intelligent survey of Irish,
and of foreign politics and art. Because of limited funds, AE had to write much
of the journal himself, but most of the important Irish writers of the day appeared
in it. Of AE's abilities as its editor, Monk Gibbon* wrote:

The most gentle and good-natured of editors, his good-nature never betrayed him into
publishing work which was shoddy. If there are any who doubt this they need only

consult the files. Apart from his more illustrious contributors like Yeats,* Bernard Shaw* and others, he discovered and encouraged a great deal of new talent. And though his own note might tend sometimes to echo itself he took care to introduce variety into what he accepted from others. He had no prejudices. His journal was open to contributors of any nationality, of any point of view, from any school, provided only their work was good. Nor were any allowed to dominate the paper or monopolise it to the point of wearying the reader. No hobby-horses were allowed to be ridden too long—unless perhaps those wonderful courses, the winged hobby-horses of A.E. himself.

REFERENCES: A. E. *The Living Torch.* Monk Gibbon, ed. New York: Macmillan, 1938. (A collection of AE's writings from *The Irish Statesman,* with a long introduction by Gibbon); Smith, Edward Doyle. "A Survey and Index of *The Irish Statesman.*" Ph.D. dissertation, University of Washington, 1966.

IRISH THEATRE, THE (1914–1920). Founded in 1914 by Edward Martyn,* Thomas MacDonagh,* and Joseph Plunkett,* the Irish Theatre was conceived as an alternative to the commercial playhouses in Dublin and to the "peasant drama" of the Abbey.* The directors announced that they would offer Irish language plays, contemporary continental masterpieces, and works by Irish writers who dealt with urban and upper middle-class life. Only a few Irish language plays were staged because few were being written; otherwise, the actual programming conformed to the original intent.

The theatre was located in an eighteenth century building in Hardwicke Street, in a North Dublin neighborhood sliding into shabby gentility. It had served as a convent for Poor Clare nuns, a Jesuit chapel and day school, and a Methodist normal school. In 1910, the derelict structure was purchased by the Plunkett family as a workshop for the Dun Emer Guild of female artisans who worked with textiles and precious metals, and as a place in which the family could put on private dramatic entertainments. From 1911 to 1912, the small auditorium was used by the Theatre of Ireland. It seated, with minimal comfort, about 120 patrons. While it was being renovated, the first Irish Theatre production, Edward Martyn's *The Dream Physician,* a satire aimed at Yeats,* Joyce,* and George Moore,* was presented in the Little Theatre, 40 Upper O'Connell Street, on November 2–7, 1914. Thereafter, all the plays were staged in the Hardwicke Street hall.

Most of the actors were professional persons for whom theatre was an avocation: J. B. Magennis, for instance, was a doctor, Norman Reddin a lawyer, and Katherine MacCormack a textile designer. Occasionally, an Abbey player, welcoming an opportunity to move outside his customary repertoire, moonlighted in Hardwicke Street, contributing his services because no salaries were paid. A few amateurs with professional aspirations had a chance to display their acting ability. Among those who appeared on the little stage were Frank Fay, Una O'Connor, Maire nic Shiubhlaigh (Mary Walker), F. J. McCormick, Paul Farrell, Noel Purcell, Patrick Hayden, Jimmy O'Dea (as old Firs in *The Cherry Orchard,* a part far removed from his later stage work), Nell Byrne (Blanaid

Salkeld),* and, diffidently under the stage name "Richard Sheridan," Thomas MacDonagh.* Young Mícheál Mac Liammóir* created the mountaintop set for the final act of Martyn's *Regina Eyre,* a spectacular set by Irish Theatre standards. It had a more favorable reception than the play.

Between 1914 and 1920, the Irish Theatre developed an able corps of actors, brought to Ireland for the first time a number of major continental dramas (no work by English playwrights was offered), and introduced some original Irish plays. It also sponsored the appearance of the young men of St. Enda's School in plays by Padraic Pearse* and a lecture by Pearse on May 20–22, 1915. John MacDonagh,* sometimes working with materials furnished by the ladies of Dun Emer Guild, achieved striking stage effects. On the negative side, the theatre was physically inadequate, dismal in atmosphere, and inconveniently located. If a play ran late, patrons had to scurry through dark streets to catch the last tram leaving Nelson's Pillar. Too, the subtleties of Maeterlinck, Strindberg, and Chekhov generally proved unpalatable to audiences habituated to Queen's Theatre melodrama or the sledgehammer comedy sometimes dispensed by the Abbey.

The Easter Week Rising crippled the Irish Theatre. Thomas MacDonagh, Joseph Plunkett, and William Pearse, Padraic's brother and an able actor, were shot. John MacDonagh, who doubled as actor and stage manager, and several other actors were interned. But by November 1916, Martyn, the only remaining director, John MacDonagh, and a sufficient number of players were able to regroup.

Martyn had hoped to develop a school of dramatists who, while writing of Irish life, would be open to the best continental influences. Only a few playwrights came forward. Eimar O'Duffy* contributed two thoughtful comedies, *The Phoenix on the Roof* and *The Walls of Athens* in 1915. Henry B. O'Hanlon,* like Martyn a dedicated Ibsenite, created *To-morrow* (1916), *Speculations* (1917), and *The All-Alone* (1918). John MacDonagh* wrote incisive topical comedies, *Author! Author!* (1915) and *Just Like Shaw* (1916), and a serious Chekovian play, *Weeds* (1919). It was one of the few Irish Theatre presentations from which patrons had to be turned away for lack of room; not uncommonly, there would be only a score of persons in the house. *Weeds* dramatized the transition, delayed by mutual hostility and suspicion, from the old Clanricardian concept of landownership (the tenants were weeds to be rooted out) to a more enlightened system. Martyn primed the pump with his own original plays and revivals: *The Dream Physician* (1914, 1915), *The Privilege of Place* (1915), *The Heather Field* (1916, 1918), *Romulus and Remus* (1916), *Grangecolman* (1917), and *Regina Eyre* (1919). But on the whole the response to his appeal for non-peasant drama was disappointing.

While it lasted, the theatre steadfastly refused to lower its standards and remained deaf to the taunts of Dubliners that it was a zoo populated by highbrows and freakish aesthetes. Late in 1919 began a series of unfortunate circumstances. Martyn's health and financial condition both took a sharp turn for the worse. John MacDonagh left to work in the developing Irish motion picture industry.

Martyn chose Robert Herdman Pender to replace him. During World War I, Pender, a British civilian, had been interned in a camp near Ruhleben, Germany. There he took part in literary and dramatic activities. The Irish Theatre company, many of them ardent nationalists, greeted him with open hostility. He produced only one play, Chekhov's *The Cherry Orchard,* which closed on January 31, 1920. Soon afterward the Plunkett family canceled the theater's lease to the Hardwicke Street building. It was a coup de grâce.

A few years later, another attempt was made to establish a sophisticated, unparochial playhouse in Dublin. This time, with a better company, somewhat better facilities, and certainly better fortune, the Gate Theatre* accomplished what the men and women of the Irish Theatre valiantly but unsuccessfully tried to bring about.

WILLIAM J. FEENEY

WORKS: Boyd, Ernest. "The Work of the Irish Theatre." *Irish Monthly* 47 (February 1919): 71–76; Feeney, William J. *Drama in Hardwicke Street: A History of the Irish Theatre Company.* Rutherford, Madison, Teaneck, N.J.: Fairleigh Dickinson University Press/London & Toronto: Associated University Presses, [1984]; Feeney, William J., ed. *Edward Martyn's Irish Theatre. Lost Plays of the Irish Renaissance,* Vol. 2. Newark, Del.: Proscenium, 1980. (Contains O'Duffy's *The Phoenix on the Roof* and *The Walls of Athens,* Thomas MacDonagh's *Pagans,* Martyn's *Romulus and Remus,* and O'Hanlon's *To-morrow*); MacDonagh, John. "Acting in Dublin." *Commonweal* 10 (June 19, 1929): 185–186; Martyn, Edward. "Astorea Redux." *Banba* 1 (May 1921): 57–59. (On why the Irish Theatre failed); Reddin, Gerard Norman. "A National Theatre." *Motley* 1 (March 1932): 6–8. (Capsule history of the Irish Theatre).

IRISH WRITERS' CENTRE. Founded in 1987 by Jack Harte,* the Irish Writers' Centre is based in 19 Parnell Square, Dublin, next door to, and linked into, the Dublin Writers' Museum at No. 18 Parnell Square. Established with the help of a grant from the first allocations of the National Lottery, the center accommodates various writers' organizations and projects, including the Irish Writers' Union,* the Society of Irish Playwrights, the Irish Translators' Association, and the Irish Children's Book Trust. The central aim of the center is to help writers pursue their work and their careers more effectively. It also promotes and organizes cultural exchange of a literary nature between Ireland and other countries. Within the center a program of literary activities, including seminars, readings, lectures, and workshops, is organized. Accommodation is provided for literary events such as book launchings. The center, therefore, seeks to cultivate an interest, both at home and abroad, in the work of contemporary Irish writers. It is supported financially by both Arts Councils in Ireland.

JACK HARTE

IRISH WRITERS' UNION. Founded by Jack Harte* in 1986, the Irish Writers' Union set out to put the relationship between writer and publisher on a professional footing. It rapidly forced the universal use of written contracts, which, up to then, had been rare. Payment of royalties in a regular and businesslike manner was a twin objective. The response of publishers in the early years to such demands was very positive. Many long-standing disputes between individual writers and their publishers were resolved by negotiation. On a wider front, the union has represented writers on such issues as censorship, playing an active role in the Salman Rushdie and the Alex Comfort *Joy of Sex* affairs. Copyright was another preoccupation, and the union was instrumental, with CLÉ, the Irish Publishers' Association, in establishing a copyright agency. Progress is also being made on the collecting of fees for photocopying and for public lending rights in libraries. The union is based in the Irish Writers' Centre* in Parnell Square, Dublin, and caters to all categories of writers, including fiction writers, poets, and nonfiction authors. Anyone who has had a book or similar body of work published may apply for membership.

JACK HARTE

IRISH WRITING (1946–1957), literary magazine. *Irish Writing* was a quarterly edited from 1946 to 1954 by David Marcus* and Terence Smith, and from December 1954 to its demise in 1957 by Sean J. White. Thirty-seven issues in all appeared, and its list of contributors was extraordinarily distinguished. Its first issue alone contained work by O'Flaherty,* O'Connor,* O'Faolain,* James Stephens,* Louis MacNeice,* Lord Dunsany,* Teresa Deevy,* Patrick Kavanagh,* Somerville and Ross,* L.A.G. Strong,* and Myles na gCopaleen.* Its second issue contained O'Casey,* Colum,* Mary Lavin,* Jim Phelan,* Ewart Milne,* Oliver Gogarty,* Seamus Byrne,* and others.

REFERENCE: *Irish Writing.* Nos. 1–28. Nendeln/Liechtenstein: Kraus Reprint, 1970.

IRVINE, ALEXANDER [FITZGERALD] (1862–1941), fiction writer, evangelist, and orator. Irvine was born on January 19, 1862, at Pogue's Entry, Antrim town, the son of a Protestant shoemaker, soon to be reduced to poverty by the spread of cheap manufactures, and of Annie (*née*) Gilmore, a Catholic and the "lady" of his classic Ulster reminiscence, *My Lady of the Chimney Corner* (1913). He went to work young as a stable boy in the local Big House, then briefly in a Scottish coal mine before enlisting in the Royal Marines, where he became a boxing champion and acquired the robust ideal of physical and spiritual health that remained with him for life. In the same period, he began reading widely. On leaving the service, he settled in New York and became involved in evangelical missions in the Bowery. With the help of benevolent patronage, he studied extramurally at Yale and was ordained a minister in 1903, briefly holding a pulpit in New York's Fifth Avenue Church. His increasingly socialist doctrines alienated his patrons, and he embarked on a career as a migrant preacher associated with the American labor movement and gained a national reputation as a reformer. His protest against chain gangs was anthologized by Upton Sinclair.

Irvine began writing after an encounter with Jack London, whom he greatly admired. As an author, he retained a high regard both for standard English and the usage of his childhood, writing in *My Cathedral* (1935), "When recounting the experiences of my youth I gave them in the Irish dialect. When I carried them along with me into a larger world, I used the best English at my command.'' He served as chaplain to American and British troops in the First World War and was called one of the six greatest living orators by Lloyd George. He revisited Ulster in 1934 and 1938 but was ill received by the members of the Presbyterian Church because of his socialism. John Hewitt,* on the other hand, was deeply impressed by him and counted him ''among the greatest men I have ever known.'' Shortly after Irvine's death in Los Angeles on March 15, 1941, his birthplace in Antrim town was turned into a museum.

His famous book was followed by *The Souls of Poor Folk* (1921) and *Anna's Wishing Chair* (1937), both in the same vein. *From the Bottom Up* of 1910, an autobiographical account of his life, was reissued in 1914. The later memoir, *A Fighting Parson* (1930), resulted from a request by the American ambassador Walter H. Page at a time when his services were sought to mediate in the General Strike in Britain. *The Man from World's End* (1926) was a collection of stories from which ''The Laying on of Hands'' was reprinted posthumously in Sean O'Faolain's* ''Ulster issue'' of *The Bell** in the sole gesture of recognition of his standing as an Irish writer outside Ulster.

BRUCE STEWART

WORKS: *The Master and the Chisel.* [New Haven, Conn.]: The People's Church, 1904; *Jack London at Yale.* Westwood, Mass.: Ariel, [1906?]. (Pamphlet); *From the Bottom Up.* London: Heinemann/New York: Doubleday, Page, 1910/London: Eveleigh Nash, 1914; *The Magyar; A Story of the Social Revolution.* Girard, Kans.: Socialist, [1911]; *Revolution in Los Angeles (1911).* Los Angeles, [1912?]; *My Lady of the Chimney Corner.* New York: Century/London: Eveleigh Nash, 1913/ Belfast: Appletree, 1980; *God and Tommy Atkins.* London: Hutchinson, 1918. (Addresses); *The Souls of Poor Folk.* London: Collins, [1921]; *The Carpenter and Some Educated Gentlemen.* London: Evans Brothers, [1921]; *The Carpenter and His Kingdom.* London: W. Collins/New York: Scribner's, 1922; *A Yankee with the Soldiers of the King.* New York: E. P. Dutton, [ca. 1923]; *The Life of Christ.* London: W. Collins, [ca. 1924]; *The Man from World's End, and Other Stories.* London: T. Fisher Unwin, 1926; *A Fighting Parson, The Autobiography of Alexander Irvine.* Boston: Little, Brown/London: Williams & Norgate, 1930; *My Cathedral, A Vision of Friendship.* Belfast: Quota, [1935]; *Anna's Wishing Chair and Three Other Chimney Corner Stories.* Belfast: Quota, [1937]. REFERENCES: Hewitt, John. ''Alec of the Chimney Corner.'' *Threshold* 35 (Winter 1984–1985): 34–39; MacKelvey, Robert Samuel James Houston. *''The Chimney Corner'': A Short Description of the Author Dr. Alexander Irvine's Childhood Home, His Life and His Writings.* Belfast: Antrim County Council, [1967]. (Pamphlet); Smythe, Alastair. ''Introduction.'' *My Lady of the Chimney Corner.* Belfast: Appletree, 1980.

IRVINE, JOHN (1903–1964), poet. Irvine was born in Belfast and issued several collections of Irish lyrics from small presses in Belfast and Dublin, among them *A Voice in the Dark* (1932), *Wind from the South* (1936), *The Quiet Stream* (1944), and *Lost Sanctuary* (1954), the last-named reflecting the impact of modern American poetry. *Willow Leaves* (1941) contains poems in the manner of early Chinese poets, and *The Fountain of Hellas* (1943) is a volume of translations from the Greek Anthology. *By Winding Roads* (1950) is a humorous celebration of Irish townships, North and South. Irvine contributed to such journals as *Capuchin Annual* and *Cross*. His *Treasury of Irish Saints* (1964), a slim collection of pious verses in pleasant quatrains, was issued by the Dolmen Press with woodcuts by Ruth Brandt and the imprimatur of the Catholic Bishop of Down and Connor. Irvine also edited *The Flowering Branch* (1945), an anthology of Irish poetry through the ages.

BRUCE STEWART

WORKS: *A Voice in the Dark.* Belfast: Quota, 1932; *Wind from the South.* Belfast: Mullan, 1936; *Willow Leaves, Lyrics in the Manner of the Early Chinese Poets.* Dublin: Belfast: Mullan/Dublin: Talbot, 1941; *Nocturne: Poems.* Dublin: Orwell, 1941; *Two Poems.* Dublin: Gayfield, 1942; *The Fountain of Hellas, Poems from the Greek Anthology Attempted in English Verse.* Belfast: Derrick MacCord, [1943]; *Sic Transit Gloria Mundi.* [Dublin: Sign of the Three Candles, 1943?]; *The Quiet Stream.* Belfast: MacCord, 1944; ed., *The Flowering Branch, an Anthology of Irish Poetry Past and Present.* Belfast: MacCord, 1945; *With No Changed Voice.* Belfast: Mullan/Dublin: Talbot, 1946; *Selected Poems.* [Belfast]: Arden, 1948; *By Winding Roads.* Belfast: H. R. Carter, 1950; *Green Altars.* [Belfast]: Owenvarra, 1951; *Lost Sanctuary and Other Poems.* Belfast: Quota, 1954; *A Treasury of Irish Saints.* Dublin: Dolmen, 1964.

IRWIN, THOMAS CAULFIELD (1823–1892), poet and fiction writer. Irwin was born on May 4, 1823, at Warrenpoint, County Down. His family was wealthy, and he was privately educated; however, the wealth had disappeared by 1848. Irwin then became a prolific writer for *The Nation,** *The Dublin University Magazine,* and other Irish journals. His fiction and verse are now little remembered, but he was highly skilled in both. Only one collection has been made of his stories and sketches, *Winter and Summer Stories* (1879), but they bear rereading especially for their gentle humor, and it might be a profitable task for a scholar to glean the best of his fugitive prose. Lorna Reynolds, in a perceptive couple of pages on Irwin's poetry, makes two sound points about it: that it is overly generalized and not sufficiently tied down to a specific place; and that it seems strongly influenced by the major nineteenth-century English poets. Certainly, one can see the influence of Keats and Shelley in ''Hymn to Eurydice,'' of Keats in ''An Urn,'' and of Tennyson in ''England.'' If Irwin never attained the individual voice of his masters, he did, at any rate, have an uncommon fluency and control of his medium. If he spoke in no inimitable voice, he did have many minor successes. His short poem ''A Character'' is much more specific than is his wont and is perfectly charming. His ''Hearth Song'' is excellently musical, and his ''L'Angelo'' has some effectively understated lines.

In old age, Irwin became increasingly eccentric, ''a weird and uncouth but venerable figure.'' John O'Donovan,* the great Celtic scholar, wrote of him to Sir Samuel Ferguson*:

I understand that the mad poet who is my next-door neighbor claims acquaintance with you. He says I am his enemy, and watch him through the thickness of the wall which divides our house. He threatens in consequence to shoot me. One of us must leave. I have a houseful of books and children; he has an umbrella and a revolver. If, under the circumstances, you could influence and persuade *him* to remove to other quarters, you would convey a great favour on yours sincerely.

Irwin died in Rathmines on February 20, 1892.

WORKS: *Versicles.* Dublin: W. M. Hennessy, 1856; *Poems.* Dublin: McGlashan & Gill, 1866; *Irish Poems and Legends.* Glasgow: Cameron & Ferguson, [1869]; *Songs and Romances.* Dublin: Gill, 1878; *Winter and Summer Stories, and Slides of Fancy's Lantern.* Dublin: Gill, 1879; *Pictures and Songs.* Dublin: Gill, 1880; *Sonnets on the Poetry and Problems of Life.* Dublin: Gill, 1881; *Poems, Sketches, and Songs.* Dublin: Gill, 1889. REFERENCES: Rooney, William. "Thomas Caulfield Irwin." *New Ireland Review* 7 (1897): 86–100; Taylor, Geoffrey. "A Neglected Irish Poet." *The Bell* 3 (1942): 308–312; Victory, Louis H. "Thomas Caulfield Irwin." *The United Irishman* (November 30, 1901): 6.

J

JACKMAN, ISAAC (1732?–?), dramatist and journalist. Jackman practiced law in Dublin, became editor of the *Morning Post* in London, and wrote farces, burlettas, and comic operas, which were popular enough to be often reprinted.

PRINCIPAL WORKS: *All the World's a Stage*. London: J. Dicks, n.d./Dublin: J. Byrn, 1777. (Two-act farce); *The Milesian*. London: J. Wilkie, 1777. (Comic opera in two acts); *The Divorce*. London: G. Kearsly, 1781; *Hero and Leander*. London: T. Hughes & J. Bysh, [1787?]. (Butletta in two acts); *The Man of Parts; or, A Trip to London*. Dublin: George Folingsby, 1795. (Two-act farce).

JACKSON, ROBERT WYSE (1908–1976), clergyman and man of letters. Jackson was born on July 12, 1908, and educated at Trinity College, Dublin, the Middle Temple, and the University of Manchester. His degrees included a B.A., LL.B., M.A., LL.D., Litt.D., and, in 1961, a D.D. He served as dean of Cashel from 1946 to 1960 and as bishop of Limerick, Ardfert, and Aghadoe from 1961 to 1970. In addition to religious works, he wrote on Swift* and Goldsmith,* as well as producing two novels and two plays. He died on October 21, 1976.

PRINCIPAL WORKS: *Jonathan Swift, Dean and Pastor*. London: S.P.C.R., 1939; *Brian Taafe's Money*. Dublin: James Duffy, 1944. (One-act comedy after a short story by Gerald Griffin); *Swift and His Circle*. Dublin: Talbot, 1945; *The Bible and Ireland*. Dublin: Hibernian Bible Society, 1950. (Pamphlet); *Oliver Goldsmith: Essays towards an Interpretation*. Dublin: A.P.C.K., 1951. (Monograph); *A Memorial Sermon Preached at Drumcliffe on the Occasion of the Centenary of the Birth of William Butler Yeats*. Dublin: Dolmen in association with J. M. Keohane, Sligo, 1965; *Archbishop Magrath: The Scoundrel of Cashel*. Dublin: Mercier, 1974.

JACOB, ROSAMUND (1888–1960), novelist. Jacob was born in Waterford to a Quaker family. From 1920, she lived in Dublin, becoming a suffragette and a member of Sinn Féin.

WORKS: *The Rise of the United Irishmen, 1791–94*. London: G. G. Harrap, [1937]. (History); *The Troubled House*. London: G. G. Harrap, 1938; *The Rebel's Wife*. Tralee: Kerryman, 1957; *The Raven's Glen*. Dublin: Allen Figgis, 1960.

JEFFARES, A[LEXANDER] NORMAN (1920–   ), critic, scholar, and poet. Jeffares was born in Dublin on August 11, 1920, and received his early education at the High School. He then received a Ph.D. from Trinity College, Dublin, and a D. Phil. from Oriel College, Oxford. He has taught at Trinity College, the University of Gronigen in Holland, and the University of Adelaide in Australia. In 1957, he became professor of English literature at Leeds, and in 1974 professor of English studies at Stirling. He received an honorary doctorate from the University of Lille, and he was the founding chairman of IASAIL, the International Association for the Study of Anglo-Irish Literature. He has been a prolific critic and editor with very wide-ranging interests, but probably his most valuable work has been on W. B. Yeats,* especially in *A Commentary on the Collected Poems of W. B. Yeats* (1968) and *A New Commentary on the Poems of W. B. Yeats* (1984). He has also, as Derry Jeffares, published two volumes of commendable verse.

PRINCIPAL WORKS: *W. B. Yeats: Man and Poet*. London: Routledge & Kegan Paul/New Haven, Conn.: Yale University Press, 1949/2d ed. London: Routledge & Kegan Paul/New York: Barnes & Noble, 1966; *A Commentary on the Collected Poems of W. B. Yeats*. London: Macmillan/ Stanford, Calif.: Stanford University Press, 1968; *The Circus Animals. Essays: Mainly Anglo-Irish*. London: Macmillan/Stanford, Calif.: Stanford University Press, 1970; with A. S. Knowland. *A Commentary on the Collected Plays of W. B. Yeats*. London: Macmillan/Stanford, Calif.: Stanford University Press, 1975; *A History of Anglo-Irish Literature*. London: Macmillan, 1982; *A New Commentary on the Poems of W. B. Yeats*. London: Macmillan/Stanford, Calif.: Stanford University Press, 1984; ed., *Poems of W. B. Yeats, A New Selection*. 2d ed. London & Basingstoke: Macmillan, 1987; *Brought Up in Dublin*. Gerrards Cross: Colin Smythe, 1987. (Poems); *Brought Up to Leave*. Gerrards Cross: Colin Smythe, 1987. (Poems): *Images of Invention: Essays on Irish Writing*. Gerrards Cross: Colin Smythe, 1995.   REFERENCES: Welch, Robert & Bushrui, Suheil Badi, eds. *Literature and the Art of Creation: Essays and Poems in Honour of A. Norman Jeffares*. Gerrards Cross: Colin Smythe/Totowa, N.J.: Barnes & Noble, 1988. (Contains a checklist of Jeffares's writings by Colin Smythe).

JENNETT, SEAN (1921–   ), poet, typographer, and travel writer. Jennett originally made his name with two small books of poems published under the aegis of T. S. Eliot, but the poetic streak in him died. He was the author of *The Making of Books* (1951), which became a standard work, passing through several editions and influencing the new typography of the 1950s. For a time from 1947, he was editor of the Crown Classics with the innovative but ill-fated Grey Walls Press. Most of his work was in travel writings, and for a time after 1964 he edited "The Travellers' Guides," a series for the Catholic publishers Darton, Longman, and Todd. An engaging writer, but not among the great talents of his field, his work on typography is likely to remain of interest.

                                                                        PETER COSTELLO

WORKS: *Always Adan*. [London]: Faber, [1943]. (Poetry); *The Cloth of Flesh*. [London]: Faber, [1945]. (Poetry); ed., Crown Classics. London: Grey Walls 1947–   ; *The Making of Books*. [London]: Faber, [1951]/5th ed., 1973; *Pioneers in Printing*. London: Routledge & Kegan Paul, 1958; *The Sun and Old Stones. A Tour through the Midi*. London: Faber, 1961; tr., *Beloved Son Felix. The Journal of Felix Platter, a Medical Student in Montpellier in the Sixteenth Century*. London: Frederick Muller, 1961; *The Young Photographer's Companion*. London: Souvenir, 1962; *Deserts of England*. London: Heinemann, 1964; *Munster*. London: Faber, 1967; *Connacht: The Counties Galway, Mayo, Sligo, Leitrim and Roscommon in Ireland*. London: Faber, 1970; with Sam Mac Gredy. *A Family of Roses*. London: Cassell, 1971; *The Pilgrim Way. Poems*. London: Batsford, 1973; *The Loire*. London & Sidney: Batsford/New York: Hastings House, 1975; *Paris*. London: Batsford, 1975; *The Ridgeway Path*. London: H.M.S.O., 1976; *South Downs Way*. London: H.M.S.O., 1977; *Cork and Kerry*. London: Batsford, 1977; *Official Guide to the Royal Parks of London*. London: H.M.S.O., 1979. (Pamphlet); *The West of Ireland*. London: Batsford, 1980.   REFERENCE: Cave, Roderick. "The Grey Walls Press Crown Classics." *Private Library*, 4th ser. 2, 3 (Autumn 1989): 100–117.

JEPHSON, ROBERT (1736–1803), playwright, poet, and satirist. Jephson is read no more and is accorded very little attention even by scholars. Nevertheless, he was a successful playwright in his day, an able poet, and a prose satirist of some ability. He was born in Ireland and educated in Dublin, one of his schoolmates being Edmond Malone.* He entered the army, became a captain, and after he retired on half-pay removed to England. A jocular and convivial man, he became friendly with Johnson, Burke,* Garrick, Goldsmith,* Burney, and others. After obtaining the post of master of the horse to Viscount Townshend, the lord lieutenant of Ireland, he returned to Dublin. Eventually, he received a permanent pension of £300, which was later doubled, and he also obtained a seat in Parliament. He died from paralysis in Blackrock on May 31, 1803.

In his earlier days in Dublin, he published several amusing pieces, among them *An Epistle to Gorges Edmond Howard, Esq.* (1771). This mock encomium is a poem "with Notes Explanatory, Critical, and Historical" purporting to have been written by George Faulkner,* Swift's* pompous and self-important printer. Howard has been described as "a dull legal compiler and unsuccessful dramatist." On any page, two lines of verse may be followed by four-fifths of a page of facetious, whimsical, macabre, mock-pedantic, and witty annotation. On Howard, for instance:

He hath amassed a considerable fortune by various means, and lived in tolerable repute, as a practicing attorney, till he quarrelled with the author hereof; who has since exposed him in sundry witty paragraphs, pointed epigrams, stinging repartees, facetious verses, biting epistles, humorous acrostics, sharp railleries, keen retorts, brilliant quibbles, and anonymous stanzas.

Several of his tragedies were brought out in London: *Braganza* at Drury Lane in 1775; *The Law of Lombardy* at Drury Lane in 1779; *The Count of Narbonne*, after Walpole's *The Castle of Otranto*, at Covent Garden in 1781; and *Julia, or the Italian Lover* at Drury Lane in 1787. A comic opera, *Campaign, or Love in the East Indies*, appeared at Covent Garden in 1785; and a farce, *Two Strings to Your Bow*, appeared at Covent Garden in 1791. In addition, his farce *The*

Hotel, or the Servant with Two Masters was produced in Smock Alley, Dublin, in 1784, with Mrs. Inchbald. Jephson's tragedies predictably contain some of the conventional tragic phrasing of the time, such as "Destruction! all's revealed!" or "Yes, in your gloomiest dungeon plunge me down, / Welcome, congenial darkness—Horrors, hail!" Nevertheless, his language never descends to the fustian that was to overwhelm the tragedies of the nineteenth century. Indeed, he generally writes a spare and vigorous blank verse that plunges into the plot and, even in its thinner moments, gives actors something to work with, for instance, in *Julia,* the heroine's death speech, which concludes the play:

> Bury these papers with me: lay that picture
> Close to my heart, and let my coffin rest
> In the same tomb that holds my murder'd Claudio.
> One love, one death, and the same sepulchre.
> I thank your tender tears. Fountain of mercy!
> Calm peace, and heav'nly light will dawn on my sense.
> My pains grow less; this load will soon fall off.
> I shall be happy—weep not—mercy!—Oh!—

A Mrs. Siddons could bring down the house with such a curtain speech, as she did. Jephson's tragedies were set in Italy or Spain, had nothing Irish about them, and are not lost masterpieces crying for revival. His comedy, however, is another matter. *The Hotel* follows the stock conventions, including the girl disguised as a young man. However, the succession of deftly managed situations, including the averted duel, would raise as many laughs now as in 1784; and his dialogue is as tight, flip, and sprightly as Boucicault's* would be. As a comic writer, he deserves a modern reappraisal.

Jephson's last notable work was *Roman Portraits, A Poem in Heroick Verse* (1794). In effect, it is a number of short poems on various classical Romans, such as Pompey, Cicero, and Julius Caesar. His copious notes often take up more space on the page than the text proper, but the text is in clear, strong, often tersely uncuttable heroic couplets.

WORKS: *An Epistle to Gorges Edmond Howard, Esq. . . . The Fifth Edition, with considerable Additions.* Dublin: Pat. Wogan, 1771; with John Courtenay. *Essays from the Batchelor, in Prose and Verse. . . .* 2 vols. London: T. Beckett, 1773; *Braganza.* London: T. Evans/Dublin: R. Moncrieffe, 1775; *The Law of Lombardy.* Dublin: Printed by R. Marchbank for the Company of Booksellers, 1779; *The Hotel: or, the Servant with Two Masters.* Dublin: W. Wilson, 1784; *Julia; or, The Italian Lover.* Dublin: W. Wilson, 1786/London: C. Dilly, 1787; *The Count of Narbonne.* 2d ed. Dublin: Printed by H. Chamberlaine, for the Company of Booksellers, 1788; *Roman Portraits, A Poem in Heroick Verse.* London: G. G. & J. Robinson, 1794. REFERENCE: Peterson, Martin Severin. *Robert Jephson, 1738–1803. A Study of his Life and Works.* Lincoln: University of Nebraska Press, 1930. (Monograph).

JESSOP, GEORGE H. (?–1915), novelist, short story writer, and playwright. Jessop was educated at Trinity College, Dublin, and emigrated to the United States in 1873. There, he contributed to humorous papers, edited the magazine *Judge* in 1884, and wrote some plays and novels, sometimes in collaboration with Brander Matthews. He also wrote the libretto for Charles Villiers Stanford's comic opera *Shamus O'Brien* (1896). He published a volume of short stories and two novels with an Irish background. He died in Hampstead.

WORKS: With Brander Matthews. *Check and Counter-Check: A Tale of Twenty-four Hours* in *Lippincott's Monthly Magazine* 41 (1888)/as *A Tale of Twenty-five Hours.* New York: D. Appleton, 1892. (Novella); *Judge Lynch.* Chicago, New York & San Francisco: Belford, Clarke, [1889]/London: Longmans, Green, 1989. (Novel); *George French's Friends.* New York: Longmans, Green, 1889/as *Gerald French's Friends.* London: Longmans, 1899. (Short stories); *Shamus O'Brien. A Romantic Comic Opera in Two Acts, Founded on the Poem by Joseph Sheridan Le Fanu....* London: Boosey, 1896. (Music by Charles Villiers Stanford, Libretto by Jessop); *My Lady Molly; a Comedy Opera in Two Acts.* London: Keith Prowse, 1902. (Book and lyrics by Jessop); with Brander Matthews. *A Gold Mine.* New York & London: S. French, [ca. 1908]. (Three-act play); *Where the Shamrock Grows.* London: Murray & Evender/New York: Baker & Taylor, 1911; *Desmond O'Connor.* London: Long, 1914; *Sam'l of Posen* in *Davy Crockett & Other Plays.* Isaac Goldberg, ed. Princeton, N.J.: Princeton University Press, 1940.

JOHNSON, LIONEL [PIGOT] (1867–1902), poet. Johnson was born at Broadstairs, Kent, on March 15, 1867. He was of Welsh descent, the third son of Captain William Victor Johnson of the 90th Regiment of Light Infantry, the grandson of Sir Henry Allen Johnson, 2nd baronet, and great-grandson of the first baronet, General Sir Henry Johnson. He was educated at Durdham Down, then at Clifton, and then in 1880 he won a six-year scholarship to Winchester College. There, he won the English Literary Prize in 1883, the English Essay Prize in 1885, and the Medal for English Verse in 1885 and 1886, the subjects being "Sir Walter Raleigh in the Tower" and "Julian at Eleusis." In December 1885, he won the Winchester Scholarship to New College, Oxford, where in 1890 he gained a second-class degree in classical moderations and a first in literae humaniores. At Oxford, Johnson modeled his prose style on Samuel Johnson, and aesthetically he was a disciple of Walter Pater. His family's Protestantism aroused his skepticism; and, finding Catholic mysticism to his taste, he was received into the Roman Catholic Church on June 22, 1891.

The Art of Thomas Hardy was published in 1894 and *Poems* in 1895. Johnson contributed to the *First* and *Second Book of the Rhymers' Club* in 1892 and 1894. His first visit to Ireland in September 1893 was often repeated. But, as the *Dictionary of National Biography* remarked, "[H]is own alleged Irish origin was a literary pose," and the sentimental Celtic influences in his life came from the head, not the loins or the genes.

Johnson contributed *The Gordon Riots* in 1893 as No. 12 of *Historical Papers* edited by John Morris, S.J.; and with Richard le Gallienne wrote *Bits of Old Chelsea* (1894). A reviewer for *Academy, Anti-Jacobin,* the *National Review, Daily Chronicle,* and *Pall Mall Gazette,* his earliest critical essay was "Fools of Shakespeare," published in *Noctes Shakesperianae* (1887). *Ireland, with Other Poems* was published in 1897. His essay on Pater, first printed in the *Fortnightly Review* in September 1894, was collected in *Post-Liminium. Essays and Critical Papers,* edited with an Introduction by Thomas Whittemore in 1911.

Apart from his fellows in the Rhymers' Club, the clearest summaries of Johnson's personality appear in George Santayana's evocative autobiography *Persons and Places,* Volume 2, *The Middle Span.* Johnson's other inimitable
remembrancer was John Francis Stanley, second Earl Russell, Bertrand Russell's
elder brother and the undeclared editor of *Lionel Johnson's Winchester Letters*
(1919).

Johnson was small and frail, his poetry "genuine but limited in inspiration"
(Dictionary of National Biography). His Fenianism was a fantasy, a Bacchic
intoxication, subjective and unreal. Santayana was fond of him seeing in him
"a child of premature genius and perpetual immaturity." Personal dissipation
wrecked Johnson by 1897. He died in St. Bartholomew's Hospital, London, on
October 4, 1902, and was buried at Kensal Green. His best poems are "The
Dark Angel" and "By the Statue of King Charles at Charing Cross."

ALAN DENSON

WORKS: *Sir Walter Raleigh in the Tower.* Chester: Philipson & Golden, [1885]; *The Gordon
Riots.* 1893; *The Art of Thomas Hardy.* London: Elkin Mathews & John Lane, 1894; *Poems.* London:
Elkin Mathews, 1895; *Ireland, with Other Poems.* London: Elkin Mathews, 1897; *Selections from
the Poems of Lionel Johnson . . . Including Some Collected for the First Time.* London: Vigo Cabinet
Series, No. 34, 1900; *Twenty-one Poems.* Dundrum: Dun Emer, 1904. (Selected by W. B. Yeats);
Post-Liminium. Essays and Critical Papers. Thomas Whittemore, ed. London: Elkin Mathews, 1911;
Some Poems of Lionel Johnson. London: Elkin Mathews, 1912. (Selected, with an Introduction by
Louise Imogen Guiney); *Poetical Works.* London: Elkin Mathews, 1915. (Selected by Ezra Pound);
The Religious Poems of Lionel Johnson. London: Burns Oates & Elkin Mathews, 1916; *Some
Winchester Letters.* London: Allen & Unwin/New York: Macmillan, 1919; *Lionel Johnson. Selected
Poems.* London: Elkin Mathews & Marrot, 1927. (Compiled by H. V. M[arrot]; *Selected Poems of
Lionel Johnson.* London: Burns Oates, 1934; *The Complete Poems of Lionel Johnson.* Iain Fletcher,
ed. London: Unicorn, 1953.   REFERENCE: Santayana, George. *Persons and Places.* W. G. Holz-
berger & H. J. Saatkamp, Jr., eds. Cambridge & London: MIT Press, 1986.

JOHNSTON, ANNA. *See* CARBERY, ETHNA.

JOHNSTON, [WILLIAM] DENIS (1901–1984), playwright. Johnston was
primarily a playwright, and a very distinguished one, but he was a multitude of
other things: lawyer, actor, play director, movie maker, war correspondent,
teacher, scholar, literary critic, and mystical philosopher. He was born in Dublin
on June 18, 1901, and was educated at St. Andrew's in Stephen's Green, at
Merchiston in Edinburgh, at Cambridge, and at Harvard Law School. While still
in his twenties, he wrote the brilliant *The Old Lady Says "No!"* and directed
King Lear for the Abbey.* In 1931, he became a director of the Gate,* which
produced some of his plays, as did Longford Productions, and he did some
directing and acting for both groups. In the late 1930s, he was a writer and
director for the BBC, first in radio and then in the prewar days for television.
During the war, he was a broadcaster in the Middle East, Africa, Italy, and
Germany; later, he wrote *Nine Rivers from Jordan,* a disconcerting, not entirely
realistic book about his experiences. After the war, he was for a year director
of programmes for the BBC. He then worked for NBC television in New York

but, disliking the job, began teaching in American colleges, first at Amherst, then at Mount Holyoke, and then at Smith. In 1955, on a Guggenheim Fellowship, he wrote a book called *In Search of Swift,* which has proved more disconcerting to scholars than his plays have to drama critics. After his retirement from Smith, he was a visiting professor at several American universities and published *The Brazen Horn,* an extraordinary mélange of personal mysticism and philosophy. He died on August 8, 1984, and was buried in the close of St. Patrick's Cathedral, near the grave of Lennox Robinson.* His daughter, Jennifer Johnston,* is one of the notable novelists to emerge in the 1970s.

Only in the 1970s did Johnston himself begin to emerge as an Irish playwright to be reckoned with on the same level as Synge,* Yeats,* and O'Casey.* The reason for his belated recognition is probably that his plays are so eclectic in technique and so complex in theme that they have resisted pigeonholing. His first produced play, *The Old Lady Says "No!",* produced by the Gate in 1928, was avant-garde both in its allusions to, and borrowings from, popular Irish literature. Indeed, he was using allusion in the drama rather as T. S. Eliot had in poetry and Joyce* had in fiction. In its dream technique, the play owed something to expressionism and more to the fluidity of the cinema. However, the broadness of its jokes and the trenchancy of its satire about the new Free State assured its local popularity for years. In Dublin, it was something of a highbrow play for the man in the street. Only in 1977, in a bland Abbey revival, did the play show signs of thinness and datedness.

Johnston's second play, *The Moon in the Yellow River,* is set in the aftermath of the Civil War, and it is too accomplished to seem either thin or dated. A conscious attempt to write an Abbey play, it was much too Chekhovian in technique and complex in theme to be a successful Abbey one. As Johnston remarked, "It was gently sabotaged by most of its original Abbey cast who until 1938 played it with that subtle air of distaste with which experienced actors can dissociate themselves from the sentiments expressed in their parts." The parts, however, are very rich; and the questions posed about human sympathy and public loyalty are ever relevant. The very theatrical comedy of the piece, juxtaposed against the melodramatics and even sentimentality of the plot, should not have bothered actors used to O'Casey. But the interweaving of broad theatrical techniques with a more complicated content than O'Casey's well might have. That fact also makes the play rather more than a Shavian sugarcoated pill.

A Bride for the Unicorn, staged by the Gate in 1933, is Johnston's most thematically opaque play and a bolder advance into theatrical allegory than his *Old Lady.* Never adequately staged and seldom revived, the piece remains to be theatrically tested, but it was Johnston's favorite play. *Storm Song,* produced by the Gate in 1934, was his least favorite, for it was written as a conscious attempt to achieve a hit. The play is about the shooting of a film very like *Man of Erin* but poses some noncommercial thoughts about art and commercialism. *Blind Man's Buff* (Abbey, 1936) and *"Strange Occurrence on Ireland's Eye"* (Abbey, 1956) are variations on a theme. Indeed, the second is sometimes a close paraphrase of the dialogue of the first, which was itself a broad adaptation of a German play by Ernst Toller. Perhaps both may be seen as attempts, by use of the evergreen stock situation of a murder trial, to capture a popular audience. Nevertheless, neither is merely a "whodunnit," but a thoughtful meditation on the nature of justice. *The Dreaming Dust* (Gate, 1940) is a technically adroit attempt to make sense of the enigmatic Jonathan Swift* and is intriguing in its complex presentation of his character. *The Golden Cuckoo* (Gate, 1939) attempts to wed thin farce to thick content and is reminiscent of the late Shaw.*

The Scythe and the Sunset (Abbey, 1958) must rank with Johnston's best work. A study of the Easter Rising, it is, as its title suggests, a companion piece—if not, indeed, something of an antidote—to O'Casey's *The Plough and the Stars*. However, where O'Casey's play is a straightforward emotional indictment of war, Johnston's play is an intellectual assessment of the personal and public issues. *The Scythe* is a less moving play, more sardonic in its humor, more complex in its motivation, but it is not the least less untheatrical in its technique.

Johnston's other dramatic work was chiefly for radio and television and is of less interest. However, he was the most intelligent and, with Samuel Beckett,* the most daring Irish playwright of his time. In criticizing Shaw, Johnston once remarked that it was impossible to teach an audience something that it did not already believe. Like Shaw, however, Johnston's best work may be seen as an attempt to do just that, and to do it by a Shavian mastery of all of the tricks of the trade. Unlike O'Casey, his work has rarely fallen much below a high level of excellence, and his finest plays are among the best the modern Irish theater has to offer.

WORKS: *Nine Rivers from Jordan.* London: Derek Verschoyle, 1953. (War memoir); *In Search of Swift.* Dublin: Allen Figgis, 1959. (Literary history); *John Millington Synge.* New York & London: Columbia University Press, 1965. (Literary criticism); *The Brazen Horn.* Dublin: Dolmen, 1977. (Philosophy); *The Dramatic Works, Vol. I.* Gerrards Cross: Colin Smythe, 1977; *The Dramatic Works, Vol. II.* Gerrards Cross: Colin Smythe, 1979; *The Dramatic Works, Vol. III, The Radio and Television Plays.* Joseph Ronsley, ed. Gerrards Cross: Colin Smythe, 1992; *Selected Plays.* Joseph Ronsley, ed. Gerrards Cross: Colin Smythe/Washington, D.C.: Catholic University of America Press, [1983]. (Contains a checklist of fugitive pieces); *The Old Lady Says "No!"* Christine St. Peter, ed. Washington, D.C.: Catholic University of America Press/Gerrards Cross: Colin Smythe, [1992]. (Valuably annotated edition); *Orders and Desecrations.* Rory Johnston, ed. [Dublin]: Lilliput, [1992]. (Autobiographical essays).   REFERENCES: Barnett, Gene A. *Denis Johnston.* New York: Twayne, 1978; Ferrar, Harold. *Denis Johnston's Irish Theatre.* Dublin; Dolmen, 1973; Ronsley, Joseph, ed. *Denis Johnston, A Retrospective.* Gerrards Cross: Colin Smith/Totowa, N.J.: Barnes & Noble, 1981.

JOHNSTON, FRED (1951–   ), poet and fiction writer. Johnston was born in Belfast and educated there and in Toronto. He has lived in Algeria and Spain and, since 1977, in Galway. In 1972, he received a Hennessy Award; in 1981 and 1982 the *Sunday Independent* Story and Poem of the Month Awards; and in 1988 an Arts Council bursary. One of the founders of the Irish Writers' Co-operative in the mid-1970s, in 1986, he cofounded CÚIRT, Galway's now annual poetry festival. His poems and stories have appeared in many periodicals and have been broadcast, and he has published a novel and four collections of poetry. He frequently and trenchantly reviews new poetry and fiction. His novel, *Picture of a Girl in a Spanish Hat* (1979), is ambling apprentice work about a sensitive young man and, although no poorer than Desmond Hogan's* early work—indeed, Hogan is referred to in it as "the sensitive poet"—is best forgotten. His poems, which he has described as concentrating "for the most part on alienation of the urban individual when confronted by the rural or natural," are often romantic in content and free in form and technique. His use or lack of use of punctuation is inconsistent but does not really muddle the basically clear meaning. In some later poems, he plays with sound at the end of lines, but his rhythms seem determined by content or dramatic effect, rather than having much connection from line to line. His diction is sometimes excellently striking, as in "you bled in aphorisms" from "Sinners."

WORKS: *Picture of a Girl in a Spanish Hat.* [Enniskerry, Co. Wicklow]: Egoist, [1979]. (Novel); *Life and Death in the Midlands.* Dublin: Tansey, 1979; *A Scarce Light.* Dublin: Beaver Row, 1985. (Poetry); *Song at the Edge of the World.* [Galway: Salmon, 1988]. (Poetry); *Measuring Angles.* Indreabhan, Conamara: Cló Iar-Chonnachta, [1993]. (Poetry); *Browne.* Belfast: Lapwing Pamphlets, 1993. (Long poem).

JOHNSTON, JENNIFER [PRUDENCE] (1930–   ), novelist. Johnston was born in Dublin on January 12, 1930, the first child of Denis Johnston* the playwright and of Shelagh Richards the actress and producer. She was educated at Park House School and Trinity College, Dublin. In 1951, she married Ian Smyth, and they have four children. She is now remarried to Denis Gilliland and lives in Northern Ireland.

Now considered one of Ireland's leading writers, Johnston has been publishing compact and highly praised novels regularly since 1972. These novels have won prizes, have been reprinted many times, and have been translated into many languages. They have also been adapted for television. Her main themes are change and the lack of communication that is the result of this change—between the Irish and the Anglo-Irish, individuals and mindless authority, or parents and children. Some of the novels end violently, but, in all, her protagonists make a choice by which they are redeemed.

Her first four novels center on an individual who loves someone of a different age or class, and this love is usually betrayed. In *The Gates* (1973), her first-written but second published novel, Minnie McMahon returns from England to live with her Uncle Prionnsias in their decaying Irish ancestral home. Her uncle mutters about renovating the house, but does nothing except rub his chilblains and drink in the boot room. He represents the declining Anglo-Irish tradition, while Minnie, the orphaned daughter of his republican brother and a shopgirl, bridges the two classes, the Irish and the Anglo-Irish. Minnie falls in love with Kevin, a local boy, and they decide to restore the vegetable garden. To raise money, they secretly sell the demesne gates to rich Americans. But Kevin, desperate to escape his unhappy background, pockets the money and leaves Minnie to face her uncle. That confrontation, however, unites the girl and her uncle, and the novel ends on a hopeful note. This is a skilled first novel with well-realized characters and some delightful comic touches.

The Captains and the Kings (1972), Johnston's first published novel, is a brilliant portrait of old age. Charles Prendergast, a scion of the Big House and the last of his family, awaits death as dispassionately as he has lived. His experiences in the trenches, where his gifted elder brother was killed, and his rejection by his mother have left him with a despair which no other relationship could eradicate. His isolation is disturbed by a local boy whose trust gradually transmutes the old man's exasperation into affection. Their relationship is most touching, but to the boy's loutish Irish Catholic parents it is homosexual and to be snuffed out. Although betrayed, the old man's love for the boy somehow redeems his life, and he dies happy.

In *How Many Miles to Babylon?* (1974), two young men do manage to defy class barriers and the even more rigid barriers of army rank to maintain a friendship, but in doing so they both die. The novel is the testimony of one of them, Alexander Moore, who is awaiting death for the mercy killing of the other, Gerry. Alexander is the only child of wealthy and estranged parents, and his friendship with a working-class boy, captured in delightfully comic flashbacks, has been his happiest experience. Parallels with *The Captains and the Kings* are obvious, and it is probably no accident that the author calls her hero Alexander, the name of Charles Prendergast's dead brother. This novel, however, catches the Big House in its heyday, before the final collapse brought about by the Great War and the 1916 Rising.

Johnston's fourth novel, *Shadows on Our Skin* (1977), departs from the great rooms of the Anglo-Irish to the mean streets of present-day Derry. Joe Logan, who lives with his parents in a Catholic working-class district, is a teenage boy who falls in love with a young woman teacher. When jealousy of his older brother, an IRA member, makes him reveal that the teacher is engaged to a British soldier, the retaliation is swift and the relationship is destroyed. The author is at her best in portraying adolescence. Joe is a beautifully realized character, and the intensity of his emotion is psychologically apt. The young woman's feelings and actions are not so easily understood, and Johnston descends, for the first time, into woolly romanticism. However, Joe's relationship with his mother who, like the women in O'Casey,* works to keep the home together, is touchingly rendered. The dialogue, although not quite working class, does not usually grate.

For a reader seeking an introduction to Johnston, her fifth novel, *The Old Jest,* is a delight. It won the Whitbread Award for the best novel of 1979 and is set during the Irish War of Independence. Nancy, the protagonist, is a wonderfully caught character who swings between bravado and vulnerability. She is an eighteen-year-old orphan about to enter Trinity and in love with a young man, Harry, who is a veteran of the trenches. She lives with her Aunt Mary, another well-realized character, in an old and gracious house, probably in Grey-stones, County Wicklow. The atmosphere of Dublin at the time and of its res-idential seaside suburb is brilliantly caught. However, this safe world cannot last. With the political change, a nouveau riche class is emerging. This class is represented by Maeve, whom Harry, much to Nancy's chagrin, is to marry. Like Johnston's previous heroine, Minnie, Nancy is fatherless and fantasizes that a republican fugitive she meets on the railway line is her father. The scenes in-volving them are deeply touching and provide the climax for the plot.

The Christmas Tree (1981) is about dying. Although sad, it is also uplifting, because Constance, the narrator, faces her death from cancer so bravely. It is set in the present, in the comfortable but stifling world of the south Dublin middle class. Constance has rebelled against this world by having a child out of wedlock and now waits for its father to come and claim it. However, she has not done the one other thing she wanted in life—write a book. The narration of the novel becomes this book, which is found by Bridie, her young servant. Like other Bridies in Johnston's fictional world, she provides comfort and con-trasts with the colder, more upper-class characters, represented here by the ghosts of Constance's parents.

The Railway Station Man (1984) moves to a remote Donegal fishing village. Here strong, opposing characters again try to communicate. This time the con-flict is between Helen, a grumpy, middle-aged woman and struggling artist, and her son, Jack, a bungling revolutionary. Helen, who has been widowed by the provisional Irish Republican Army (IRA), falls in love with an eccentric English railway enthusiast who is renovating the old station. Her son visits with a ghastly friend called Manus, and this visit provides the climax of the plot. Although the present Irish Troubles intrude, the novel is really a love story. As usual, the relationships are well caught and unsentimental, especially that of the mother and son.

In *Fool's Sanctuary* (1987), Johnston returns to the Big House and the Trou-bles of the early 1920s. Miranda Martin is the child of an innovating and ide-alistic landlord who befriends a young native Irishman called Charlie. Into this world come two British soldiers, the son of the house and his friend, both veterans of the Great War. The brother is a dour alcoholic, but the friend is a funny stammerer and provides humor. Charlie tips off the young men that they are to be executed by the IRA. However, he amazingly does nothing to save himself. He just waits for the gunmen. More than any of the others, this novel reads like a play. Indeed, Miranda, who has been frozen by the tragedy, assem-bles the cast to tell the story in her old age. The book is a gripping read, although afterward one wonders about Miranda. Did she do nothing for the rest of her life? Can one tragedy in youth completely freeze a character? In her next novel, *The Invisible Worm* (1991), Johnston addresses this very problem. Again a woman is blighted by the past—this time because of violent sexual abuse by her father. However, through the help of an ex-priest, she releases herself sym-bolically by burning the summerhouse where the rape took place.

Johnston's most notable characteristic as a writer is her distinctive prose style with its extraordinary terseness and civilized accuracy of diction. Sometimes, especially in the later novels, the terseness goes a bit too far. One longs for more meat on the bone. However, she remains very strong on character. Her people hop so clearly from the page that her considerable talent seems to be crying out for a stage. Indeed, she has published three one-act plays in *The Nightingale and Not the Lark* (1988), but the plots are too static to be memorable. Nevertheless, her first love was for the stage, and she wrote in her introduction: "I was a clumsy, uncoordinated child, with a sight problem but I had the notion in my head that on the stage I became transformed into whatever character it was that I was living at that moment." In her novels, at least, she has often worked such a magical transformation.

MARY ROSE CALLAGHAN

WORKS: *The Captains and the Kings*. London: Hamish Hamilton, [1972]; *The Gates*. London: Hamish Hamilton, [1973]; *How Many Miles to Babylon?* London: Hamish Hamilton, [1974]; *Shadows on Our Skin*. London: Hamish Hamilton, [1977]/Garden City, N.Y.: Doubleday, 1978; *The Old Jest*. London: Hamish Hamilton, [1979]; *The Christmas Tree*. London: Hamish Hamilton, [1981]; *The Railway Station Man*. London: Hamish Hamilton, [1984]; *Fool's Sanctuary*. London: Hamish Hamilton, [1987]/[New York]: Viking, [1988]; *The Nightingale and Not the Lark*. [Dublin]: Raven Arts, [1988]. (One-act plays); *The Invisible Worm*. London: Sinclair-Stevenson, 1991/New York: Carroll & Graf, 1993. (Novel); *Three Monologues*. Belfast: Lagan, 1995; *The Illusionist*. London: Sinclair-Stevenson, 1995. (Novel).   REFERENCES: Kamm, Jurgen. "Jennifer Johnston" in *Contemporary Irish Novelists*. Rüdiger Imhof, ed. Tübingen: Narr, 1990, pp. 125–144; Weekes, Ann Owens. "Jennifer Johnston: The Imaginative Crucible." In *Irish Women Writers: An Uncharted Tradition*. [Lexington]: University Press of Kentucky, [1990], pp. 191–211; Woodworth, Paddy. "Invisible Characters of the Heart: Jennifer Johnston Talks to Paddy Woodworth." *Irish Times* (February 23, 1991): Weekend, p. 5.

JOHNSTON, MYRTLE (1909–   ), novelist and short story writer.

WORKS: *Hanging Johnny*. London: Murray, 1927; *Relentless* London: Murray, 1930; *The Maiden*. London: Murray, 1932; *Laleen and Other Stories*. London: Murray, 1937; *The Rising*. London: Murray, 1939; *A Robin Redbreast in a Cage*. London: Heinemann, 1950.

JOHNSTONE (or JOHNSTON), CHARLES (1719?–ca. 1800), novelist. Johnston was born in County Limerick and studied at Trinity College, Dublin. He was called to the bar but because of deafness was engaged only as a chamber counsel. The most popular of his satirical novels was *Chrysal; or the Adventures of a Guinea* (1760), which went through many editions, partly because it was supposed to reveal political secrets and to expose the peccadilloes of the famous. However, it is also an engaging narrative that followed the adventures of a guinea from pocket to pocket. Told in the first person by the coin, the book sardonically flays human nature in all ranks of society and is so excellently adroit both in characterization and in dialogue that it could well be reprinted. Of his other volumes, the Irish interest is greatest in *The Adventures of Anthony Varnish* (1786). Earlier, in May 1782, Johnstone sailed for India, where he wrote for Bengal newspapers, became joint proprietor of one, and died well-off in Calcutta.

WORKS: *Chrysal; or the Adventures of a Guinea.* 2 vols. London: T. Beckett, 1760/4th ed., "greatly inlarged and corrected." 4 vols. London: T. Beckett, 1764; *The Reverie; or, A Flight to the Paradise of Fools.* Dublin: D. Chamberlaine, 1762/London: T. Beckett & P. A. DaHondt, 1763; *The History of Arsaces, Prince of Betlis.* 2 vols. London: T. Beckett, 1774/Dublin: United Company of Booksellers, 1774; *The Pilgrim; or, a Picture of Life.* Dublin: J. Potts, 1775/London: T. Cadell, [1775]; *The History of John Juniper, Esq. Alias Juniper Jack.* Dublin: S. Price/London: R. Baldwin, 1781; *The Adventures of Anthony Varnish; or, A Peep at the Manners of Society.* 3 vols. London: William Lane, 1786. REFERENCE: Scott, Sir Walter. "Charles Johnstone." In *Lives of the Novelists.* Paris: A. & W. Galignani, 1825/London & New York: F. Warne, 2887/London: J. M. Dent, 1910.

JOHNSTONE, ROBERT (1951–), poet. Born in Belfast.

WORKS: *Breakfast in a Bright Room.* Belfast: Blackstaff, 1983; *Eden to Edenderry.* Belfast: Blackstaff, 1989.

JONES, HENRY (1721–1770), poet and playwright. Jones was born near Drogheda, County Louth. He was a bricklayer, but he gained the approbation of Lord Chesterfield by a poem celebrating Chesterfield's arrival in Ireland as lord lieutenant. Chesterfield encouraged Jones to follow him to London in 1748, and with Chesterfield's help he published his *Poems on Several Occasions* in 1749. Chesterfield also recommended Jones's play, *The Earl of Essex,* to Colley Cibber, and, revised by Cibber and Chesterfield, it appeared at Covent Garden on February 21, 1753. With Spranger Barry in the title role, it ran for a very successful seventeen nights and brought Jones £500. Its success, however, owed more to Barry's artistic abilities than to Jones's.

Success quite undid Jones. As the *Dictionary of National Biography* censoriously remarks, "His drunken habits, indolence, coarse manners and arrogant temper soon disgusted most of his patrons, though by a carefully regulated system of hypocrisy he continued to keep on terms with Chesterfield for some years longer." However, he ran through his money and became quite an adroit sponger. He was run over in St. Martin's Lane in 1770 and died in the parish workhouse in April.

As a poet, Jones was generally no more than fluently, blandly conventional. On occasion, however, as in the concluding curse of "On the Death of a Favourite Nightingale," he could rise to something a bit better.

> May braying asses, bitterns from the mire,
> and croaking ravens haunt thee all thy life!
> may baleful cats and cackling hens conspire
> and, what's more dreadful still, a scolding wife.

PRINCIPAL WORKS: *The Bricklayer's Poem. Presented to His Excellency the Lord Lieutenant. On His Arrival in This Kingdom.* Dublin, 1745; *Poems on Several Occasions.* London: R. Dodsley, 1749/ Dublin: S. Powell, 1749; *An Epistle to the Right Honourable the Earl of Orrery Occasion'd by Reading His Lordship's Translation of Pliny's Epistles.* London: W. Owen, 1751; *The Earl of*

Essex. A Tragedy. London: R. Dodsley, 1753; *Merit. A Poem: Inscribed to the Right Honourable Philip Earl of Chesterfield.* London: R. & J. Dodsley, 1753; *The Relief; or, Day Thoughts.* London: J. Robinson, 1754; *Vectis. The Isle of Wight: A Poem. In Three Cantos.* London: W. Flexney, 1766/ as *The Isle of Wight.* Isle of Wight, 1782; *Clifton: a Poem, in Two Cantos, Including Bristol and All Its Environs.* Bristol, [1767]/3d ed. . . . *To Which Is Added, an Ode to Shakespear in Honour of the Jubilee.* . . . Bristol: T. Cocking, 1779; *Key Garden. A Poem in Two Cantos.* London: J. Dodsley, 1767; *The Arcana: or Mystic Gem. A Poem in Two Cantos.* . . . Wolverhampton: For the Author, 1769; *Shrewsbury Quarry.* Shrewsbury: J. Eddowes, 1769; *The Heroine of the Cave. A Tragedy.* London: T. Evans/Dublin: United Company of Booksellers, 1755. (Jones's three-act *The Cave of Idra* expanded to five acts by Paul Hiffernan).

JONES, MARIE (1951–   ), playwright. Jones was born in East Belfast on August 29, 1951. Her career in the theater began when she was sixteen as an actor in James Young's comedy show, which involved good-natured humor about sectarian issues. She has since played with amateur and professional companies and on television. In the early 1980s, she was one of the founders of the Charabanc Theatre Company, which was born largely of frustration at the lack of women's roles in the repertory. Charabanc produced a series of original plays involving collaborative composition. Jones also wrote scripts for the Replay Theatre Company, including their first production, *Under Napoleon's Nose* (1988), and four subsequent plays. In 1991, she was a founder of the Doublejoint Theatre Company, for which she wrote three scripts. She has been involved in the formation of various community theater companies and has written television plays for the BBC and Channel 4, including *Tribes* (1990), *Fighting the Shadows* (1992), *Wingnut and the Sprog* (1994), and an adaptation of her stage play *The Hamster Wheel* (1991). She played Sarah Conlon in the Jim Sheridan* film *In the Name of the Father.* She has received the John Hewitt Award for an outstanding contribution to culture, tradition, and arts in Northern Ireland. Married to the actor Ian McElhinney, she lives in Belfast.

Her published work, *The Hamster Wheel,* details the story of a married couple whose lives are substantially altered by the husband's stroke. The wife leaves her career and devotes herself to care for her husband, abandoning much that formerly gave her happiness. She passes through five stages characteristic of grief—anger, resentment, frustration, guilt, and understanding and acceptance. The play has been admired by critics for its sensitivity, power, and accuracy. It is, in fact, the result of extensive work with volunteer and professional care organizations in the community. As is the case with much of Jones's writings, *The Hamster Wheel* explores the feelings and responses of ordinary people, especially women, to the circumstances of daily life in Northern Ireland.

BERNARD McKENNA

WORKS: *The Hamster Wheel* in *The Crack in the Emerald.* David Grant, ed. London: Nick Hern Books, 1990; *A Night in November.* Dublin: New Island Books/London: Nick Hern Books, [1995]. REFERENCES: Bort, Eberhard. "Female Voices in Northern Irish Drama: Anne Devlin, Christina Reid, and the Charabanc Theatre Company." In *"Standing in Their Shifts Itself . . .": Irish Drama from Farquhar to Friel.* Bremen: European Society for Irish Studies, 1993; DiCenzo, Maria. "Charabanc Theatre Company: Placing Women Center-Stage in Northern Ireland." *Theatre*

Journal 45 (May 1993): 175–184; Grant, David. *Playing the Wild Card.* Belfast: Community Relations Council, 1993; Martin, Carl. "Charabanc Theatre Company: 'Quare' Women 'Sleggin' and 'Geggin' the Standards of Northern Ireland by 'Tappin' the People." *Drama Review* 31 (Summer 1987): 88–99; Wilmer, Steven. "Women's Theatre in Ireland." *New Theatre Quarterly* 7 (November 1991): 353–360.

JONES, T[HOMAS] MASON (fl. 1850–1870), novelist. Robert Lee Wolff in his introduction to the modern reprinting of Jones's *Old Trinity,* notes that he "ran the *Tribune* in Dublin in the fifties and was afterwards well-known in England as a lecturer of the Reform League." From a description in a Richard Bentley catalog, Wolff adds that Jones "was a reformer of the 'advanced school,' gave a series of 'orations' at Willis's Rooms in London in the 1850's on the British poets, and lectured in the United States in favor of the North during the Civil War. He ran unsuccessfully for Parliament." Jones's knowledge of Trinity College, Dublin, would make it likely that he was a student there, but Burtchaell and Sadleir's *Alumni Dublinensis* lists no plausible Thomas Jones.

Old Trinity is not really a unified book. Less than half is concerned with student life at Trinity College, and the rest takes place in Laois and Limerick and relates the hero's love affair and his accidental killing of his villainous rival. It culminates in an effective trial scene in which the defense attorney is modeled on Isaac Butt.*

Although intended as entertainment, the book has its serious preoccupations. As the hero remarks, "[t]he true artist finds his materials lying around him. . . . The writer need not resort to sensations or horrors." Thus, the depiction of student revelries is balanced by some serious critical discussion of what profession is worth pursuing; and the plot in the West, despite melodramatic moments, gives a fair portrayal of landlordism. Despite some romantically florid passages, the book is basically an engaging read.

WORK: *Old Trinity.* 3 vols. London: Richard Bentley, 1867; rpt., New York & London: Garland, 1979.

JONES, WALTER (ca. 1693–1756), poet? Jones was probably born in Headfort, County Leitrim. He was the eldest son of Theophilus Jones, MP for Sligo and later for Leitrim in the Irish Parliament. He graduated from Trinity College, Dublin, in 1715, and he died in May 1756. D. J. O'Donoghue* asserts that Jones was almost certainly the real author of the long, very popular jocular poem *Hesperi-neso-graphia: Or, a Description of the Western Isle* (1716), which eventually came to be known as *The Irish Hudibras.* The author usually cited for the piece is William Moffet.*

WORK: *Hesperi-neso-graphia: Or, a Description of the Western Isle. In Eight Cantos.* London: J. Baker, 1716/Dublin, 1724. Also published in some of its many editions as *The History of Ireland in Verse* and *The Irish Hudibras.*

JORDAN, JOHN (1930–1988), literary critic, short story writer, and poet. Jordan was born in Dublin on April 8, 1930, and was educated by the Christian

Brothers of Synge Street. Information on his childhood can be found in his letters to the critic James Agate in the latter's *Ego 8* and *Ego 9:* "There is nothing as boring as a conventional childhood for one who knows that there is such a thing as an unconventional childhood. People in my circle don't read anything worthwhile, don't say anything witty, and for a young prig like me that's unbearable." He obtained a first-class honours B.A. in English and French at University College, Dublin, an M.A. in 1954, and a B.Litt. from Oxford, where he worked on the verse letters of John Donne. In 1959, he became assistant lecturer to a professor of English at University College and college lecturer in 1965 and resigned in 1969. He was a member of Aosdána.* He died on June 6, 1988, in Wales.

Jordan involved himself in the theater, working with Micheál Mac Liammóir* and Hilton Edwards and with Edward and Christine Longford* at the Gate.* In the 1950s, he started to gain a reputation as a critic in many departments of letters. His most innovative criticism was the championship of the later O'Casey,* as in his essay, "Illusion and Actuality," in *Sean O'Casey,* edited by Ronald Ayling (1969). He also did pioneer work on other dramatists, such as Teresa Deevy* (*University Review,* Spring 1956). His stage knowledge and extensive memory of Dublin theater productions were something of a living archive.

A friend of writers such as Patrick Kavanagh* and Kate O'Brien,* Jordan has lavished the intelligent heart well on both of them. He has written the most seminal post-Yeatsian criticism of Irish poetry. He wore the novel reviewer's laurels with grace for the *Irish Times;* his main form as a commentator on cultural affairs remains his column in *Hibernia.* Jordan's mind was Alexandrian and nostalgic, with acerbic moods. As a writer of poetry and fiction, Jordan developed slowly, well behind his criticism. He published fugitive pieces in both genres under the name Stephen Renehen, in magazines such as *Irish Writing* and *Arena.* His collection of stories, *Yarns,* appeared only in 1977. The book at its best captures the seedy student Dublin of the late 1940s and 1950s; in this work, he exhibits a fine ear for the sentiments of fading, middle-aged ladies and unfading (as yet) young men. Where the stories are weak, as in "Miss Scott" and "Misadventure," either the character or the scene is miscast. The *Collected Short Stories* were published in 1991.

The later prose in *Blood and Stations* (1976) is private and hermetic. It may be his best. His poetry seems charming and febrile. In *A Raft from Flotsam* (1975), minimal elegance mocks itself, and confession rises from repression. The volume contains too much juvenilia, but the expanded and revised "Patrician Stations" in *Blood and Stations* reads better. Thematically and linguistically a meditation on Austin Clarke* under the eye of eternity, it combines tenderness and vituperation, particularly the latter in a splendid polemic against Robert Graves. Jordan's mannered life becomes cathartic as he explores his chlorotic Catholic humanism. Self-heroism expiates absolutely.

Now that John Jordan is dead, it should be pointed out that his life, like that of Mac Liammóir's before him, gave dignity to homosexuality in Ireland.

The posthumous *Collected Poems,* introduced by MacDara Woods,* is an arresting volume. It collects previously published work and adds later poems and some new early pieces. The impression is of sometimes brilliant occasional poetry. The early work combines pathos and charm, strong romanticism allied to a weak voice. Jordan's translations shimmer; his versions from the Irish of Mac Liammóir keep the secret flavor of the original. In the last section, comedy, Spain, and devotion to alcohol become a trinity. Literary and cultural ideas are put forward in a less than pious way. The sustained cursing of Robert Graves still reads well, and one must acknowledge an elegant twist in "During the Illness of Dolores Ibarruri": "And I think of Kathleen Daly Clarke / Whom we exported to English welfare, / And her spouse the tobacconist." Jordan had a tough sense of nostalgia.

JAMES LIDDY

WORKS: "Off the Barricades: Notes on Three Poets." In *The Dolmen Miscellany of Irish Writing* (Dublin: Dolmen, 1962), pp. 107–116; "Writer at Work." *St. Stephen's* (Michaelmas Term, 1962): 17–20; *Patrician Stations.* Dublin: New Writers', 1971; *A Raft from Flotsam.* Dublin: Gallery, 1975; *Blood and Stations.* Dublin: Gallery, 1976; *Yarns.* Dublin: Poolbeg, 1977; *With Whom Did I Share the Crystal?* Dublin: Limited Edition Handprinted by John F. Deane, 1977; ed., *The Pleasures of Gaelic Literature.* Dublin & Cork: Mercier & RTE, 1977; *Collected Poems.* Hugh McFadden, ed. Dublin: Dedalus, 1991; *The Collected Short Stories of John Jordan.* Introduction by Benedict Kiely. Dublin: Poolbeg, 1991. REFERENCE: Kilroy, Thomas & Liddy, James. "In Memoriam: John Jordan." *Irish Review* 6 (1989).

JORDAN, NEIL (1950?–   ), novelist, short story writer, and screenwriter. Jordan was born in Sligo in 1950 or 1951. He attended University College, Dublin, worked as a laborer, wrote plays, and with several other young writers established in 1974 the Irish Writers' Co-operative to publish new Irish fiction. His collection of stories, *Night in Tunisia,* was published by that group in 1976 and was generally regarded, even by Sean O'Faolain,* as a brilliant debut. In 1979, the book was joint winner of the Guardian Fiction Prize and a Somerset Maugham Award. Since then he has published a novel, *The Past* (1980), and a novella, *The Mark of the Beast* (1983). His principal activity in recent years, however, has been directing and writing films. Several of these, particularly *Company of Wolves, Mona Lisa,* and *The Crying Game,* have received much international acclaim, and in 1993 Jordan's script for *The Crying Game* won an Academy Award. He is regarded as one of contemporary Ireland's significant artists.

His fiction has, however, many problems. Most of the stories and sketches in the talented and slovenly *Night in Tunisia* are about adolescents who are blighted by love, and there is a good deal of frantic, inchoate emotion, such as:

he couldn't see my tears or see my smile.

She was crying, great breathful sobs.

He was crying, and his face looked more beautiful than ever through the tears.

I stopped my hate and felt baffled, sad, older than I could bear.

Generally, Jordan's early style is an understated lyricism, albeit much less florid than his contemporary Desmond Hogan's* and with fewer sentence fragments. However, there is little feeling for the architecture or even the basic syntax of a sentence. In fact, the basic conventions of writing are either ignored or simply misunderstood. The grammar is careless, the spelling a little too faulty, the punctuation confusing and inconsistent. Any page offers several examples:

He knew as he approached the baths to wash off the dust of a weeks labour, that this hour would be the week's high-point.

The tinker was on the burrows now, pulling the donkey by the hair of it's neck.

He felt that somewhere he knew as much as she. . . . And the boy saw the naked figure, smaller than him.

a ladies drink.

his father would stop and let him play on, listening. And he [who?] would occasionally look and catch that look on his [whose?] listening eyes, wry, sad and loving his [whose?] pleasure at how his son played only marred by the knowledge of how little it meant to him [whom?]. And he [who?]

She thought of all the times they had talked it out, every conceivable mutation in their relationship, able and disable, every possible emotional variant, despision [?] to fear, since it's only by talking of such things that they are rendered harmless.

All small flaws, but there are six or a dozen on every page and hundreds in the book.

Jordan's novel *The Past* (1980) is an immense advance. With the benefit of professional editing, the innumerable flaws of form have been eliminated, and the remaining errors are ones of fact—Thomas MacDonagh's* name is misspelled, as is Sara Allgood's and that of O'Casey's* hero Donal Davoren; Denis Johnston's* memorable play is called *The Moon on the Yellow River,* Great Brunswick Street is called Rutland Street, Greystones can be seen from the north slope of Bray Head, W. B. Yeats* sits in a private box in the Abbey Theatre,* in probably the 1920s the Abbey has a set built "on a circular rostrum, like a merry-go-round," and so forth.

The narrative has a small, mainly fictional cast of Irish actors, artists, and politicians and covers the years from 1912 to 1934. Most of these characters are well defined, but the book's real advance is in its prose, which, despite some quirkiness, is often exact and evocative. For instance:

You look at the yellow irises, flapping in their jam jars on the sill of the window, behind which the beech tree can be seen studded with green now as if the month of May has hastily flecked it with a stiff green paint brush. You can hardly isolate any one spot of green from the tentative mass but you still try, with your young girl's eyes, their imperfection of focus, their totality of concentration. The points which are in fact small buds and which in autumn will become broader leaves with the texture of beech nuts and bark resist all your attempts to isolate them, merge and separate and finally through the tiredness of your eyes become what seems to be a pulsating mist, forming a halo, the limits of which you can't define around that unlikely trunk, much like your own hair, which you also must be able to see reflected in the window-glass, and the image of your own blonde halo becomes merged with the first green pulsating of the month of May.

Such prose, of course, is also the book's chief problem, for it is descriptive rather than dramatic. It provides little forward thrust to the narrative, and one often gets bogged down in minor details and neo-Jamesian descriptions of sensibility.

The Dream of a Beast, Jordan's novella of 1983, has an arresting science-fictional premise of Dublin's being overwhelmed by a rampaging Nature and by some of its people, including the hero, being physically transformed into grotesque beasts. The 100-page work is divided into thirty-three chapters, some less than a page long, but the effect is less dramatic than lyric. Like *The Past,* the strength of the idea is largely dissipated by the story's being reflectively related and hardly ever dramatized. As a fiction writer, Jordan thus far evinced talent, individuality, a penchant for experimentation and little consideration for craftsmanship. He seemed trying to fly without ever having learned to walk.

Jordan's film scripts are necessarily much more dramatized than his fiction and generally are about the confrontation of innocence or naïveté with violence and a somewhat bizarre sexuality. Nevertheless, the need for a story and for dramatized scenes may have had a salutary effect on Jordan's next novel, *Sunrise with Sea Monster,* which appeared in 1994, more than a decade after *The Dream of the Beast.* This novel is easily his most accomplished, for it has a developed and even tense plot, three well-drawn central characters, and a moving conclusion. Set in Bray, as was his film *The Miracle,* it has a similar central situation—a father, a somewhat alienated son, and a woman they both love. The father, a member of the Free State government, is a widower and proposes to his son's piano teacher. The son, who has slept with the piano teacher, goes off to fight against Franco. Interned and in danger of being shot, he is eventually released. Returning to wartime Ireland, he makes a living as a fisherman, and he and the woman take care of the father, who has had a stroke and can barely communicate. Tension is added by the son's having to cooperate with the government by betraying a liaison between the Irish Republican Army and Germany. This would seem to parallel the personal betrayal of the father by the son, and the strength of the book is the son's growing love for the father and a final rather mystical reunion after the father's death. There is some quirky handling of dialogue early on, in which various unpunctuated speeches by different characters are huddled up in the same paragraph, but this technique in the latter pages is usefully semiabandoned. The book is quite Jordan's most realized fiction.

WORKS: *Night in Tunisia and Other Stories.* Dublin: Co-op Books, 1976/London: Hogarth, 1979; *The Past.* London: Jonathan Cape, 1980; *The Dream of a Beast.* London: Chatto & Windus, 1983/ London: Hogarth, 1989; *Mona Lisa,* with David Leland. London: Faber, 1986. (Film script); *Angel.*

London: Faber, 1989. (Film script); *High Spirits*. London: Faber, 1989. (Film script); *The Crying Game*. London: Faber, 1993. (Film script); *A Neil Jordan Reader*. New York: Vintage, [1993]. (Comprising *Night in Tunisia, The Dream of the Beast*, and *The Crying Game*); *Sunrise with Sea Monster*. London: Chatto & Windus, [1994]. (Novel).

JOURNAL OF IRISH LITERATURE, THE (1972–1993), literary magazine. Founded by Robert Hogan and edited later with Gordon Henderson and Kathleen Danaher, this magazine appeared thrice yearly and published plays, poems, short and long fiction, criticism, and book reviews. Of particular interest were the issues devoted to one single writer—such as Colum,* Stephens,* O'Riordan,* O'Duffy,* Kavanagh,* Frank O'Connor,* Flann O'Brien/Brian O'Nolan* Mervyn Wall,* and others—which usually published new material by those writers. The lively book reviews were probably too jokey for academic acceptance.

JOYCE, JAMES [AUGUSTINE] (1882–1941), novelist and short story writer. Joyce was born in Dublin on February 2, 1882, the oldest of ten children born to John Stanislaus and Mary Jane Murray Joyce. His father, an extroverted, witty man never able to live within his means, is accurately described in the autobiographical *A Portrait of the Artist as a Young Man:*

A medical student, an oarsman, a tenor, an amateur actor, a shouting politician, a small landlord, a small investor, a drinker, a good fellow, a storyteller, somebody's secretary, something in a distillery, a taxgatherer, a bankrupt and at present a praiser of his own past.

Having inherited some property in Cork, the elder Joyce did not see himself as poor, but rather as a man who suffered reverses. His days as a tax collector ended when he was forty-two, and he was pensioned off at a modest sum during a reorganization of the Rates Office. This small pension, his principal source of income, was not enough to sustain both his family and his intemperate habits. During James' childhood and youth, the monetary restraints caused the family to move constantly from one rented house to another. Such moves were accomplished by obtaining recommendations from landlords who wanted to get the family out of the house. The Cork properties eventually were sold along with all their furnishings.

John Joyce also was an ardent nationalist and had a great deal to say about the fall from power of Charles Stewart Parnell. Nine-year-old James, caught up in his father's fervor, wrote a poem entitled "*Et Tu,* Healy," which his father had published. Indeed, the Parnell episode sparked a deep distrust of the Roman Catholic Church in the elder Joyce, which left its mark on James as well. Joyce's mother, on the other hand, was as devout as John was anticlerical. Thus, their family life, particularly as James grew into puberty, was difficult in both religious and monetary matters.

James began his schooling at Clongowes Wood College in 1888 and went quickly to the head of his class. He was unable to return in 1891, however, and was forced to spend some time in a Christian Brothers school before enrolling in Belvedere, a Jesuit secondary school in Dublin, in 1893. This placement was made possible because Father John Conmee, formerly rector at Clongowes, had assumed the position of prefect of studies at Belvedere and, remembering James, arranged for him to study at Belvedere without fees. In Belvedere, James experienced violent changes in attitude and a new sense of isolation from parents, teachers, and religion. He began to write a series of prose sketches and a volume of verse.

Throughout his pubescence and early manhood, as the eldest child, Joyce was increasingly expected to assume the responsibility for his brothers and sisters. His decision to follow his art instead of being the family provider is outlined in *Portrait*.

Turning down an offer to study for the Holy Orders, Joyce was admitted to University College, Dublin, in 1898. By the time he graduated four years later, he already had a substantial local reputation as an eccentric intellectual and writer. Earlier he had become devoted to the works of Henrik Ibsen and was a staunch advocate of the playwright in a period in which Ibsen was condemned for immorality by many of Joyce's contemporaries and teachers. Joyce's essay "Ibsen's New Drama," published when he was just eighteen years old in no less prestigious a journal than *The Fortnightly Review,* drew considerable notice from his colleagues, especially when it was learned that Joyce had received payment of twelve guineas for his contribution. When Ibsen wrote a note of thanks, young Joyce was overwhelmed. After receiving it, he began the systematic study of foreign languages and literature, seeking to become European rather than merely Irish. "The Day of the Rabblement," an attack on what he saw to be the parochialism of the Irish theatre, was published at his own expense after it had been rejected by the school magazine, *St. Stephen's.* By now, Joyce's circle of literary acquaintances had expanded to include George Russell,* W. B. Yeats,* and Lady Gregory.*

On his graduation from University College, Joyce emigrated in December 1902 to Paris, where he was to undertake the study of medicine while supporting himself with some reviewing that Yeats and Lady Gregory had arranged. However, the nearly starved Joyce spent his days in arguments with John Synge* and in the literary section of the library, rather than the medical section, until his mother's failing health prompted his return to Ireland.

Once back in Dublin, he lived in the now famous Martello Tower in Sandycove with Oliver St. John Gogarty,* whose urbanity and wit grace the character of Buck Mulligan in *Ulysses.* Joyce took a job as teacher at the Clifton School in Dalkey, and on June 16, 1904, the date on which *Ulysses* occurs, he had his first date with Nora Barnacle, a Dublin boardinghouse employee. In October the couple left Ireland permanently, first traveling to Paris and then to Zurich and Trieste.

Joyce lived all his life with Nora, and though it was 1931 before they were formally married, it was a remarkably monogamous relationship—despite doubts about Nora's fidelity and occasional indiscretions of his own. The Joyces had two children, Giorgio and Lucia. Giorgio died in 1976, and Lucia spent most of her adult life in sanitariums until her death in 1982.

Joyce was befriended by Ezra Pound, who was then the most influential literary figure in Europe. Pound first published serially Joyce's *Dubliners* and *Portrait* in the *Egoist,* which he edited. He also introduced Joyce to Harriet Shaw Weaver, who took over the editorship of the *Egoist* and who supported Joyce for the rest of his life. Although Joyce had a great deal of difficulty with the publication of his stories and the *Portrait,* he had many friends and devoted followers who always regarded him as the genius the world was later to accept. Joyce knew all the major figures of the literary renaissance that occurred between the wars. He was a frequenter of the Shakespeare Bookshop in Paris, and it was under the auspices of Shakespeare and Company that *Ulysses* was first published in its entirety in 1922.

Joyce's life in Paris was interrupted by World War II; he fled the city ahead of the Germans to settle finally in Zurich (where he died on January 13, 1941). Always in need of money and continually fighting with editors and critics, Joyce nevertheless was surrounded by a host of friends and was supported by his family, especially his brother, Stanislaus, who criticized, edited, provided funds, and devotedly carped his way through decades of attempts to improve his brother's intemperate drinking and fiscal habits.

Joyce's eyes were never good, and they deteriorated over the years until he approached total blindness. He had a number of amanuenses, particularly as his last work progressed. The most famous of these was Samuel Beckett,* whose refusal of Lucia's affections may have been a major cause of her mental problems. Never a great family man, Joyce was a full-time artist, formal and reserved, distant from his children, living for his work, never doubting his own genius.

The fifteen years spent in the composition of his longest work, known for the major portion of its time in composition as ''Work in Progress,'' were spent in the company of great modern writers, and readings of the work were often given. Even before *Finnegans Wake* was formally published as a book, a number of essays on it were published and a full-length book of essays, *Our Exagmination Round His Factification for Incamination of Work in Progress,* was published in 1929, with studies by twelve outstanding men of letters of their day: Samuel Beckett, Marcel Brion, Frank Budgen, Stuart Gilbert, Eugene Jolas, Victor Llona, Robert McAlmon, Thomas MacGreevy,* Elliot Paul, John Rodker, Robert Sage, and William Carlos Williams.

Joyce was almost exclusively devoted to literary pursuits, but there was time to champion several artists. The first cause was that of the Irish poet James Clarence Mangan* (1803–1849), who Joyce claimed never achieved the fame he deserved because of the narrow attitudes of the Irish nationalists. The second and more prolonged *cause célèbre* was that of John Sullivan, whom Joyce thought the leading tenor of Europe, though one who had never received his just fame or rewards. Joyce was a tenor himself, who might have won the Feis Ceoil had he been able to sight read. When he was asked to read a piece, he strode indignantly from the stage and the gold medal was given to another. Although Joyce gave up the idea of a professional singing career, his works were to be sprinkled liberally with musical allusions, and his last work, *Finnegans Wake,* drew its name and theme from a ballad.

The influences on Joyce were as catholic as his reading. Besides his preoccupation with Ibsen, Joyce was undoubtedly influenced by his reading of W. B. Yeats. Many of Joyce's ideas came from the nineteenth-century aesthetes' movement, but his sources cover the whole range of European and classical literature. The theory of aesthetics advanced by Stephen Dedalus in *Portrait* has its origins in Plato and Aristotle. The influence of Joyce's heavily theological indoctrination also plays a paramount role in his literature, as do the realistic-naturalistic strains of Flaubert, Maupassant, Balzac, Ibsen, and Zola and the surrealism of Strindberg and others.

To begin to enumerate Joyce's sources is as frustrating as to attempt to identify all of the authors whose works in whole or part bear heavy strains of his influence. While writers like Woolf and Dos Passos are obviously indebted to Joyce, and most other major writers since have paid him homage, there is little in modern literature which does not reflect either directly or indirectly his innovation or stamp, from the surrealism of his literary nightmares to his refinements of the stream-of-consciousness technique.

Although all of Joyce's works were derived in large measure from his personal experience and so are heavily autobiographical, they have the distance and integrity of art. Readers must be wary of trying to extrapolate anything of Joyce's own life or his own philosophy from his fiction. Above all, Joyce was the consummate artist, creating distanced works of art with their own individual integrity.

INTRODUCTION TO THE WORKS

The measure of Joyce's literary achievement is reflected in his stature as one of the greatest writers of Western civilization. His major published works became increasingly complex and erudite as his career progressed, while his experimentation with the possibilities of the written word became more profound and at the same time more fundamental.

In his earlier works, Joyce's characters operate on the naturalistic level but do not always function symbolically. By the Circe episode of *Ulysses,* however, character and symbol have merged, and in his last work, *Finnegans Wake,* verisimilitude in language, plot, and action has been abandoned and replaced by archetype, innuendo, and impression. His erudition is evidenced in the abundance of allusions to untold numbers of literary works both classical and contemporary, Eastern and Western. In *Finnegans Wake* in particular, his handling of language reflects an acquaintance with scores of foreign tongues, and his parodies of previous literary styles, particularly in the Oxen of the Sun episode of *Ulysses,* suggest an intimacy with the major prose stylists of the English language from its beginnings through the nineteenth century. His use of contemporary dialects in the same episode also reveals a linguistic preciosity with the contemporary idiom, while his whole canon contains a broad sampling of common speech and a variety of language which has yet to be equaled by any other modern author.

Joyce's themes are at the same time as simple and as complex as life itself. *A Portrait of the Artist* is on one level a straightforward *bildungsroman,* but one which investigates, in both traditional and innovative ways, the relationship of life to art and the nature of truth. In *Ulysses,* Joyce sets up, through the contrast between the archetypal figure of Odysseus and the contemporary man, Leopold Bloom, the fundamental similarities to be found in people and situations of all ages. In his last work, *Finnegans Wake,* Joyce attempts a unique task in literature—the depiction of the macrocosm—all of everything—which is then related to the microcosm of H. C. Earwicker and his family. The universality of *Finnegans Wake* is reflected in the plethora of languages in the text which act with their English counterpart to produce multiple layers of meaning.

Joyce's works grew increasingly comic in both tone and language. In addition, throughout his work he retained aspects of pure realism even as his style of writing became more ingenious and difficult to comprehend. While he steadfastly denied any indebtedness to Freud or Jung, their influence is especially evident in his later works. Thus, Joyce is a symbolist, mythmaker, comic writer, naturalistic writer, satirist, linguistic innovator, and psychoanalytic novelist.

Chamber Music

Chamber Music, his slightest and simplest work, consists of thirty-six lyric poems about love and its failure. The original sequence of the poems differed from the final printed arrangement, which Joyce's brother Stanislaus ordered in such a way to comprise a story in which the persona of the poems meets a girl, falls in love, enjoys a period of relative bliss, but later experiences the dissolution of the relationship. The last poems recall the relationship, now passed, and the final poem, perhaps the best of the lot, is emotionally charged and yet poetically distant. Other structural progressions in the poetry are the evolution of the seasons and the light/darkness motif.

One interesting aspect of the poems is their lyrical quality. Joyce himself provided music for several of them, and most of the thirty-six have been set to music by various composers, especially Geoffrey Molyneux Palmer, whose *Chamber Music* songs Joyce tried repeatedly to convince Palmer to publish.

The poems most resemble Elizabethan, principally Jonsonian, lyrics, but they are heavily indebted to the lyrics of Yeats. Joyce also drew heavily upon the "Song of Solomon" for theme, diction, and symbol. Thus, the woman of the

poems is a universal figure, representing multiple aspects of the female archetype, the Great Mother, the temptress, and the Church, as well as the aspects of
the Virgin and Beatrice. Many of the themes that Joyce was to use prominently
in later works can be seen first in *Chamber Music,* especially the motifs of
betrayal, jealousy, and masochism.

The best critical treatment of the poems is by William York Tindall in his
introduction to the 1954 edition. Tindall's splendid explication is marred only
by an occasional overinsistence on Freudian and Jungian interpretation, cham-
berpots, and earthy allusions. Such ingredients were cornerstones of Joyce's later
work but are more difficult to see in *Chamber Music.* In 1993 Myra Russell did
a history of Palmer's songs, which took up the scholarship where Tindall left
off.

In summary, the poetry of *Chamber Music* is imitative, often naive, but occasionally striking. It is a product of youth, most of it written when Joyce was
eighteen or nineteen. All poems were composed by the time he was twenty-one.
Doubtless, it would never have received notice at all if it had to stand alone.

Pomes Penyeach

The eleven poems contained in *Pomes Penyeach* are mostly reflections of a
much maturer man. They are less lyrical than *Chamber Music,* though still
heavily metered. The themes are diverse. Some, like ''Bahnhofstrasse,'' deal
with age, while others, like ''A Flower Given to My Daughter,'' are concerned
with family. Many themes reappear in later works: the situation and the cadences
of ''She Weeps Over Rahoon'' can be found again in the conclusion of ''The
Dead,'' and the lost love motif of ''Tutto È Sciolto'' is seen later in the Sirens
chapter of *Ulysses.*

A final poem ''Ecce Puer,'' published separately, is of special interest because
it treats the theme of the relationship among the generations and life cycles—a
concern that grew more important in Joyce's later work, until in *Finnegans Wake*
it became paramount.

The poetry, then, taken in its entirety, is a very small segment of the Joyce
canon, in both volume and importance. While it has its enthusiasts among Joyce
critics, it is so far overshadowed by the major prose works that it becomes
ancillary in any overview of Joyce.

Exiles

Joyce's single play, *Exiles,* likewise contains a number of flaws, especially
when it is considered beside his novels and short stories. The structure of the
work is laid out in a series of confessions in which the four principal characters,
all overburdened with guilt, admit their relations with each other. The principal
character, Richard Rowan, like the later heroes Stephen Dedalus and Shem the
Penman, bears a striking resemblance to Joyce himself, in terms of both personal
history and temperament. However, readers can make a serious mistake by identifying his protagonists wholly with Joyce.

Part of the problem of *Exiles* is that the domestic situation is too close to Joyce's own. Joyce's notes on the play, provided at the end of the Viking edition, indicate the heavy emotional involvement Joyce had in the action. Consequently, the artistic potentialities are not completely realized. Nevertheless, the play deals interestingly with the freedom and restraints of the marital situation. Richard, the protagonist, and Bertha have tried to live a monogamous life unfettered by the formal ceremonies of marriage. Then, in an effort to attain an idealized kind of freedom, Richard places his mate in circumstances which could compromise her fidelity.

The play, like Joyce's later work, operates on an archetypal and symbolic level as well as a realistic one. The characters are classic representations of the major figures that dominate all of Joyce's work. Beatrice is the frail, intelligent, inspirational figure with intellectual pretensions; Bertha is the earth mother, a fertility-temptress figure who takes on characteristics of Ireland itself; Robert Hand is the classic antithesis of the artist, the successful public man who is extroverted, occasionally hypocritical, opportunistic, and charming, a figure later represented in *Ulysses* as Buck Mulligan and in *Finnegans Wake* as Shaun. His counterpart, Richard Rowan, is an artist in the mold of Stephen Dedalus and Shem, an introverted, egotistical, self-sacrificing pursuer of art and truth. At the same time he is self-centered, giving no quarter in the battle for artistic integrity and freedom.

All of the characters revolve around Richard and are in various states of emotional crisis in inverse proportion to their distance from him and in direct proportion to their commitment to and love for him. He is in effect the artist trying to manipulate those about him as if he were manipulating characters in fictive events. In a way, the complexities of Richard's mind and his motivation form the essence of the play's meaning. First, his feelings are much like that of a cuckold pretending he will overcome his wife's infidelity and his concurrent feelings of inadequacy by precipitating her liaison with Robert. His action strongly suggests masochism. But Richard is also sadistic when he insists upon telling his wife all the details of his own infidelities. At least part of Richard's action is motivated by love and a genuine concern for his wife's happiness with another man, but he is also motivated in part by pride and abhors the righteousness of her fidelity in the face of his own indiscretion. However, he gets an emotional kick out of thinking his wife desirable to other men, and the affair enhances his own Byronic self-image. Whether or not he does this remains ambiguous, as does the question of whether Bertha actually commits adultery with Robert Hand. In the end, the characters are at least as miserable as they were in the beginning, and the problem has been merely stated rather than resolved.

A final ambiguity is the character of Archie, the son of Richard and Bertha. Obviously some projection of the future, Archie is last seen being led off by Robert to hear a fairy story. The ultimate meaning of his role remains obscure, however, since he is both the product of the bond between Richard and Bertha, and the embodiment of the sort of faultless freedom Richard so desires.

While the tone of the play is almost unrelieved seriousness, there are classically comic situations—almost burlesque—such as Robert's preparations of the room for his prospective liaison and Richard's standing in the rain spying on the amorous couple. There is also some funny *double entendre* dialogue about where Robert will kiss Bertha.

The panorama of emotions from guilt to uncertainty to anguish, and the complicated responses of four intelligent and introspective characters, are simply too great for resolution or even complete development in the fairly brief confines of a three act play.

The range of complexities and the dilemmas represented in *Exiles* come into full flower in the larger forum of Joyce's novels, but encapsulated in this drama they lack the room to develop and thus form an artifice. The work is tantalizing and thought-provoking, but still not up to the high artistry of Joyce's fiction.

Dubliners

The first of Joyce's major works and his only volume of short stories, *Dubliners,* revealed for the first time the complexity of Joyce's artistic vision. The fifteen stories comprising the volume appear to be completely realistic and composed of commonplace situations of Dublin life. Many of the early reviewers and critics, in fact, saw little of great significance in them, and they were often characterized as plotless and trivial. Often one or another of the stories is anthologized, but at the expense of the meaning it draws from the others in overall tone and specific image. For instance, the reference to the former tenant of the boy's house in "Araby" as a priest, and the yellowing photograph of a priest in Eveline's room are both linked to the image of the priest in "The Sisters." The escape role of the opera *The Bohemian Girl* in "Eveline" is reinforced in "Clay," where Maria closes the story with a rendition of a song from the opera, leading us to assume that Maria is a sort of older Eveline, who, unable to escape, still cherishes the romantic notions of her younger counterpart from the earlier story. The coin extracted from the slavey in "Two Gallants" is returned to the servant Lily by Gabriel in "The Dead" as the stories merge in theme and symbol.

The structure of *Dubliners* follows a basic life-cycle pattern, with the first three stories covering early life; the next four, young adulthood; the following four, mature life from middle to advanced age; the next three, public life in Dublin politics, arts, and religion; and finally a summary story, "The Dead," with its sisters who bring us back full circle to the first story. "The Dead" also incorporates and summarizes most of the major themes and formulas in this collection of entrapment narratives.

The first three stories are all narrated by their youthful protagonists. These stories are in the *bildungsroman* tradition, with the first, "The Sisters," serving as introduction to the entire collection in its emphasis on paralysis, entrapment, and death. The lesson of "The Sisters" is a good deal more ambiguous to the boy than the revelations of the second and third stories, each of which reveals to the protagonists some sort of inadequacy about his own self-image.

These moments of enlightenment assert themselves in a form later formularized in *Stephen Hero* as the epiphany. The nature and meaning of epiphanies has been a central point in critical debate over Joyce through seven decades of criticism. Briefly, in the broadest and most popular definition, the term *epiphany* refers to moments of self-revelation or illumination of truth in events. These enlightenments may be acquired by the protagonist, the readers, or both. It must be stressed here that epiphanies, with all their aura of unassailable veracity, are often really only what appear at the time to be truth to the protagonists who experience them. While epiphanies are experienced by many of the protagonists of *Dubliners,* the lessons are frozen with the end of each story, so that there is no opportunity to analyze them in the light of subsequent events, such as there is in *A Portrait of the Artist.*

The second group of stories, the young adulthood section, further develops actions and metaphors of entrapment, as the protagonists at this stage of life have the maturity to realize that they are locked into life patterns. Some of the characters such as Corley and Mrs. Mooney realize and exploit the entrapment, while others, like Eveline and Bob Doran, struggle against it. Marriage, fleeing Ireland, and remaining single are all offered as alternative means of liberation in "Eveline" and "The Boarding House," while business success in "After the Race" and sexual exploitation in "Two Gallants" are other escape routes which fail.

In the third group of stories, the more mature characters are locked in so completely that the possibility of ultimate freedom exists only in fantasy. Again the alternatives of escape from place, from occupation, from marriage, and from the single life are explored, but the increasingly unavoidable answers are only frustration, violence, self-deception, resignation and death.

Stories in the middle sections are often paired in different ways, exploring alternative responses to entrapment and alternative modes of living, such as the married state in "A Little Cloud" and spinsterhood and bachelorhood in "Clay" and "A Painful Case"; the violent and the passive responses in "Counterparts" and "A Little Cloud"; and exploitation and being exploited in "Two Gallants" and "After the Race."

The fourth group of stories explores the institutions themselves. In his accounts of political, artistic, and social life in Dublin, Joyce turns for the first time to satire and the deep vein of humor that would become increasingly apparent in his later works. At the same time, the greed, pettiness, meanness, and outright stupidity which for Joyce characterize the practice of those institutions in Dublin are uncompromisingly portrayed.

"The Dead," one of the great short story masterpieces in any language, proceeds from a specific set of circumstances to an all-encompassing metaphor of universality. The large cast of characters at the Morkan sisters' dinner party discusses such immediate topics as the newspapers for which Gabriel writes or the sleeping habits of monks. However, these are topics which lead naturally into the underlying universals: escape and, more importantly, life and death. The scope of the account broadens as the implications of the action assume for Gabriel more and more universality until he reformulates them into his final powerful metaphor of the ultimate connection between all the living and the dead.

In *Dubliners,* Joyce begins with a first person narrative in the first three stories and then proceeds to a third person narrator who closely approximates the mind of each protagonist. The realistic tenor and style of the description stem from these individualized perspectives, which provide corresponding changes in dominant tone and metaphoric pattern for each story. The range is enormous, from the fury in "Counterparts" to the saccharine in "Clay"; from the subjectivity of "A Little Cloud" to the stentorian sermon-like tones of "Grace"; and from the tentativeness and ambiguity of "The Sisters" to the finality of "The Dead." The collection subtly shifts focus and style through a range of individual problems, moods, and solutions, finally combining in an artistic vision of communality across time, sex, class, and occupation.

Joyce had no easy time finding a publisher for his collection. Refused by publisher after publisher, with unhonored agreements from Grant Richards and later George Roberts, the book was finally published nine years after Joyce's first attempt. Objections were made about the language (words like "bloody" were anathema); about its disrespect for God, the Crown, and local politicians; and about libel. The publication squabbles produced a broadside poem from Joyce, "Gas from a Burner," printed at the author's expense in 1912. In a letter, Joyce recounts the publication history of the collection:

The type of the abortive first English edition (1906) was broken up. The second edition (Dublin 1910) was burnt entire almost in my presence. The third edition (London 1914) is the text as I wrote it and as I obliged my publisher to publish it after 9 years. . . . *Dubliners* was refused by *forty* publishers in the intervals of the events recorded above. [Ellmann, p. 429]

No other book except *Ulysses* was beset by such publication difficulties. Early reviews were decidedly mixed but not vociferously unfavorable, with many of the stories classified as "cynical, pointless or both." Among the early critics, only Ezra Pound saw the genius of the collection and sensed its real significance.

A Portrait of the Artist as a Young Man

Many of the critical problems of *A Portrait of the Artist as a Young Man* grow out of the critics equating the protagonist, Stephen Dedalus, with Joyce himself. In writing this *bildungsroman,* Joyce while using the events of his own life as a basic design, nevertheless succeeded in distancing himself from his novel. Readers are often duped into equating Stephen's hopes, ideas, and experiences with Joyce's own in part because the narrative perspective of the novel is essentially that of Stephen, though it is related in the third person omniscient voice. The central conscience of the novel is, however, greatly distanced from Joyce's own, and the author, to repeat Stephen's words, ''remains within or beyond or above his handiwork, invisible, refined out of existence, indifferent, paring his fingernails.'' When the reader acknowledges that this distancing is also one of the hallmarks of Stephen's own aesthetic theory, he begins to grasp the complexities of this book, which is as much about composing a work of art as it is a novel of youthful experience or ritual passage.

Since the book begins with a protagonist of about the age of three and takes him through his graduation from University College, Dublin, the narrative line paralleling his thoughts undergoes a continual and dramatic shift in style, tone, and concerns. Yet, at the same time the opening pages encompass all of the major themes which will occupy the book and the mind of its hero. These will be restructured, refined, reshaped, and remolded by Stephen Dedalus time and time again into new revelations of himself and his role in life. Each of the five chapters encompasses a phase of Stephen's development and produces a new revelation, plateau, or stage of increasing awareness of his own position in the world. Concurrent with this is the developing motif of art and what it means in terms of the truths of existence. The novel is not only about how a boy grows up, but also about how the very process is in itself transformed into a work of art. Part of this process is a rationalization on Stephen's part for his own feelings of inadequacy, a means of protecting himself from the harsh derisions of childhood comrades, of coping with inconsistencies of fact and ideals in his early training, and of separating himself from other youngsters against whom he might be judged. Another aspect of artistic creation stems from Stephen's natural verbal inclination and his enormous talent and intellect. The developing consciousness of the young man is reflected in his initial linguistic preoccupation with sounds, words, and meaning.

The development of Stephen's intellect is partly revealed through a gradual evolution of the narrative line from the childish language of the first pages to an abstruse and often tortured and analogical prose heavily sprinkled with Latin and St. Thomas in Chapter Five. The implications of identifying the narrative perspective as Stephen's are enormous for the reader. First of all, symbols do not exist outside of Stephen's awareness of them, for he makes and later evolves the symbolic patterns of the book. Beginning, for instance, with his mother as the foundation of his eventually complex female principle, he adds the Blessed Virgin and later, as he reads more courtly love and romance, the figure of Mercedes from *The Count of Monte Cristo,* finally adding the temptress figure as he reaches pubescence. His earlier association with Eileen merges with his infatuation for E.C., and subsequently they both blend with their archetypal literary and religious counterparts, until at the end of the fourth chapter an inspiration figure emerges in the all-encompassing vision of the girl on the beach, both a herald and a symbol of Stephen's art. His final villanelle in Chapter Five extols and abstracts his relationship with this composite symbol-reality, turning his experiences into art at the same time he makes an art work out of his description of the process.

Stephen's evolving self-image also encompasses the political and religious influences upon him. Coupling his early fever-ridden reception of the news of Charles Stewart Parnell's death with the religious conflict of the subsequent Christmas dinner scene, Stephen begins to conceive of himself as a sort of Parnell figure, a savior for Ireland, who, like Christ, must bear the interrogations of youth and manhood, suffer, and from the body of his own experience mold the uncreated conscience of his race. His difficulties with the boys first at Clongowes, later at Belvedere, and finally at University College lead to a series of confrontations or ''admit'' scenes in which Stephen increasingly assumes the role of Christ-like savior, derided by those he would save by transforming his life into an art of salvation as the priest transforms the wafer and wine into the body and blood of Christ. Not being content to provide merely the sacrifice, Stephen will also assume the role of priest or agent of transformation. Invited by the director of studies to join the Jesuit Order, Stephen rejects the formal boundaries of Holy Orders but accepts the principle of himself in a priestly role, transubstantiating life into art instead of wine and wafer into the Holy Eucharist. As a defense against the Philistine demands and derision of Irish society and his peers, Stephen will lead them out of their bondage with his own sacrifice and the truth which evolves from its transformation into art.

Each chapter builds on Stephen's initial realistic external surroundings, while also elaborating the images and resolution of preceding chapters. By the end of the chapter, the result is a new mental stance for Stephen, a new epiphany or revelation of his position. With the exception of Chapter Two, the moment of enlightenment or structural climax of the episode is followed by a denouement or period of reflection in which Stephen glories in the certainty of his newly established image. With the beginning of the next chapter, however, he is returned into the mundane world of his external surroundings and forced once again to take stock, to reevaluate and reform his image.

In the final chapter, Stephen refines and divides into two parts his process of self-definition. He provides the theoretical background in his aesthetic theory, and his artistic expression of himself as sacrifice and priest in his poem, the villanelle. Having decided what he wants to do, he must detach himself from everything which inhibits the development of his art: his family, his home, his religion, and his country. The book closes with his decision to leave, carrying with him the raw materials of his experience to form into the artifacts of art.

Like *Dubliners, A Portrait* is an extremely compact book, with nothing in it extraneous or tangential to Stephen's development. *Portrait* is a much abridged version of a longer and earlier manuscript, a part of which was preserved and later provided enough material for a fair-sized book in its own right. *Stephen Hero,* the earlier work, is worth mentioning here because of the contrast between its technique and that of *Portrait*. Because the central narrative consciousness is not as close to Stephen's, *Stephen Hero* is a less impressionistic, more naturalistic book, with long dialogues and a good deal of description omitted from its successor. Scenes, thoughts, and ideas which are developed in explicit detail in *Stephen Hero* are hinted at, reduced, or merely suggested without editorial comment by the narrator in *Portrait*. The reader of *Stephen Hero* is told the significance of actions by the narrator, while readers are led to extrapolate from the action often just what is taking place in Stephen's mind. In *Portrait* the technique results in a closely crammed text which can be read over and over with new insights each time. The result is perhaps the greatest *bildungsroman* ever written.

ULYSSES

The greatest work in the Joycean canon of classics, *Ulysses,* operates simultaneously on many levels of realism, symbolism, comedy, tragedy, and satire. At once a great comic satire and a serious in-depth psychological novel, *Ulysses* casts the least of all men, a humble and largely unsuccessful advertising salesman, Leopold Bloom, as the modern day Odysseus, the primary heroic figure of Western civilization. His wife, a sensual adulteress, becomes the faithful Penelope, and the intellectually snobbish and disdainful Stephen Dedalus, who apparently has nothing at all in common with his surrogate father, and who before the end of the day rejects any offer of a permanent or even semi-permanent association, becomes his devoted and searching son, Telemachus.

Rather than an epic journey of ten years' duration, however, the action of the novel is contained in a span of less than twenty-four hours, and the scene, instead of the entire Hellenic world, is the city of Dublin. Operating through paradox and understatement on the parody level, through the direct literalness of Bloom's perspective, and through historical, literary, and theological analogy in the symbolic frame of reference of Stephen Dedalus, Joyce weaves his way through a complex pattern of relationships, finally culminating in a unity of thought, method, and plot which universalize the situations of the several principal characters into a mélange of themes often mind-boggling in their complexity, and at the same time unified in a synonymy of events and situations.

Seen in its broadest and simplest context, *The Odyssey* is a homecoming story, a tale of a man returning and reestablishing his rights and sovereignty in his home. He is aided in his struggle by his son, who has carried on his father's image and sense of values, even in the face of usurping suitors, and by his wife's faithfulness despite her husband's long wanderings. In a sense she is the sanction of his behavior; hers is the home and the establishment for which the suitors vie, and hers is the approbation which must be given for the recalcitrant wanderer to regain his place as head of his life and home.

Leopold Bloom's lost key renders him the momentarily homeless wanderer. The suitors in the present form of Blazes Boylan also threaten his position. Like Bloom, Stephen Dedalus also is keyless, having surrendered his to his fellow

tenant, Buck Mulligan. Bloom and Stephen begin parallel odysseys, ending for
Bloom back at Seven Eccles Street, his home. Bloom's day is filled with seeming trivia, as he tries to obtain an ad for his paper (from a firm by the name of
Keyes), attends a funeral, has lunch, stops to inquire about a friend in the ma-
ternity hospital, goes to several pubs and a brothel, and has a late night cup of
coffee with his new acquaintance, Stephen. Each one of the scenes is mirrored
in the epic journey of Odysseus, and the commonality of their lives gives both
characters greater stature because of the universality of the episodes and events.
For instance, Bloom's altercation with the Citizen in Barney Kiernan's pub is a
comic version of Ulysses' encounter with the Cyclops. The seeming disparity
of the two heroes provides some of the incongruity and comedy of Joyce's
novel, and at the same time much of its significance in identity.

The themes of the novel are themselves universal. Communality among all
people is not only a part of the structure of the novel, but is also a theme with
a number of apparently disparate but essentially similar variations. Stephen
considers several ecclesiastical models, such as consubstantiality (when father
and son or wine and wafer are at the same time separate entities and both the
same) and transubstantiation (the metamorphosis of one substance into another); while Bloom ponders such physical phenomena as parallax (when one
thing appears as two from different vantage points) and metempsychosis and
reincarnation (the return of one thing as another). All are manifestations of the
identity motif.

The father and son theme, on the other hand, blends with the *Hamlet,* Shakespeare, and artistry metaphors in both Bloom's and Stephen's thoughts. Bloom
and Stephen both quote lines from *Hamlet,* and the essential link between Hamlet senior and junior becomes a potential source of atonement. Stephen in the
Scylla and Charybdis episode develops the theory that Shakespeare, in creating
both Hamlets, senior and junior, was in a sense writing out his own sense of
identity. Like Leopold, Shakespeare has had difficulties with an unfaithful wife
and seeks identification with his son. The fictive reality of the play *Hamlet*
encompasses not only Shakespeare's own domestic difficulties but also the story
of Bloom and Stephen and their own identity crises and betrayal motifs. All of
the father and son couples in the novel play variations on the father-son motif:
God and Christ, Hamlet senior and junior, Patty Dignam and son, Reuban J.
Dodd and son, Stephen and Simon Dedalus, Bloom and Rudy, and Bloom and
Stephen, as well as other less prominently mentioned pairs.

The Odyssey and *Hamlet* are not Joyce's only structural metaphors of the
novel. The Mass plays a role in the beginning with Mulligan's opening incan-
tation and with Stephen's chanting of the Introit at the beginning of Circe. Like
the Mass, which ritually celebrates episodes in the life of Christ and is about
transubstantiation, *Ulysses* celebrates episodes in the lives of the modern-day
Christ figures, Bloom and Stephen. Bloom is, of course, a surrogate not only
for Christ but also for Elijah, Moses, Parnell, and other political-historical-
theological figures. All of this becomes objectified in the *walpurgis nacht* of the

Circe episode, when the subconscious minds of the two protagonists are objectified in drama form.

The novel is divided into eighteen episodes, each with a parody of some action, character, or scene from *The Odyssey* and named in Joyce's early drafts according to their appropriate Odyssean counterparts. The book is further divided into three sections, the first consisting of three episodes and 51 pages of the Random House edition; and the last, of 45 pages, comprising one episode. The great bulk of the book, the middle section of some 687 pages, deals principally with the major character, Leopold Bloom, while the introductory section, the Telemachea, concentrates on Stephen Dedalus, and the last episode, the Penelope chapter, is wholly a stream-of-consciousness monologue by Molly Bloom. The first section sets a theoretical framework for the novel and the last acts as a recapitulation, throwing the events into the relief of Molly Bloom's value system. The main section deals with the mind and life of Leopold Bloom on June 16, 1904, affectionately known to Joyce enthusiasts as Bloom's Day.

Stylistically, *Ulysses* is a *tour de force* with multiple shifts in narrative point of view, emphasis, and tone. The narrative is shared for much of the book among a third person omniscient narrator, dialogue, and stream-of-conscious thought. The character of Bloom is developed through other people's perceptions of him, through his own conscious thought processes, and eventually through the representation of his subconscious thoughts in the Circe episode. Throughout this vital episode, the day's events are filtered through a Freudian perspective and appear in dramatic form as the dialogue and stage directions of a play. Incidents reappear in grotesque pantomime and caricature, as manifestations of the id.

The narrative point of view remains consistent throughout the first ten chapters with the exceptions of the intrusion of newspaper headlines in the Aeolus episode and a brief dramatic presentation in Scylla and Charybdis. But there are major changes in tone and character in each succeeding episode beginning with Sirens, which makes heavy use of musical devices in the narration. One episode contains more than a score of shifts in narrative style, paralleling the evolution of the English language from medieval Latin tracts to contemporary dialects. Altogether the novel represents an ingeniously comic assortment of narrative parodies.

Nonetheless, the story remains basically realistic in presentation, with a plethora of mundane details of varying significance. *Ulysses* requires an attention to minutiae which is unequaled in any lengthy work of contemporary prose. On the one hand, the streets of Dublin are represented with amazing verisimilitude; the businesses, characters, addresses, and activities of the day are nearly exactly what they were on June 16, 1904. At the same time, this layer of realism on the parody of Odysseus creates a belief in the theme of history repeating itself and a background of contemporary realism against which the book displays its sometimes grotesque and surrealistic scenes. Antiquity and analogy give an archetypal sanctity to the contemporary Dublin scene at the same time that they provide a basis of incongruity for the comedy of the novel.

Through it all, the gigantic figure of ineffectuality, Leopold Bloom, emerges as one of the most sympathetic, heroic, and understandable literary characters of Western literature. This microcosm of all men is married to the sensual embodiment of all womanhood, Molly Bloom. An infertile fertility figure, a stultifying inspirational figure, faithful temptress, and adulteress, she emerges as the measure of all things, the final judge and commentator, the eternal affirmation and concomitant denial. The ambiguities of the novel are as large as the history of man and as small as a day in the life of a nobody. There is in the book the spirit of eternal affirmation for some and existential denial for others. The conclusions of *Ulysses* are as complex and varied as life itself.

The publication history of *Ulysses* is as tangled as that of *Dubliners* and a good deal more famous. After Sylvia Beach published the first edition under the imprint of Shakespeare and Company in 1922, thousands of copies were smuggled into the United States by tourists, and it achieved an early reputation as a modern classic. When in 1933 Bennett Cerf decided to attempt to break the United States Post Office's censorship stranglehold over literature, he arranged publication terms with Joyce, and a Random House representative dutifully asked a customs official to confiscate his copy so a court case could be initiated. The result was the epic decision of United States District Court Judge John M. Woolsey lifting the ban on *Ulysses* and setting the standards for defining pornography. Few texts since the Bible have inspired such debate over a long period of time. The internecine pedantry came to a head with Hans Gabler's "Corrected Text," which brought about a sort of catharsis, but with the recent expiration of the copyright the topic of what constitutes an accurate text seems to draw less scholarly attention.

FINNEGANS WAKE

Finnegans Wake, Joyce's last great work, had fewer publication difficulties than its predecessors. Joyce began serious work on the *Wake* in 1922, and, although it was not to be finished completely until 1939 and was known only as "Work in Progress" throughout most of the intervening seventeen years, much of it was published serially and in separate volumes such as *Anna Livia Plurabelle, Tales Told of Shem and Shaun,* and *Haveth Childers Everywhere.*

Finnegans Wake took the author a third of his life to compose. It was intended as the culmination of his work, the ultimate linguistic experiment, the answer to the multitude of themes in his other works, and a panorama of human existence both present and past. In short, it is about all of everything. It is an allegory of the fall and resurrection of mankind. Campbell and Robinson summarize its complexity:

It is a strange book, a compound of fable, symphony, and nightmare—a monstrous enigma beckoning imperiously from the shadowy pits of sleep. Its mechanics resemble those of a dream, a dream which has freed the author from the necessities of common logic and has enabled him to compress all periods of history, all phases of individual and racial development, into a circular design, of which every part is beginning, middle, and end. [*Skeleton Key,* p. 3]

Its hero, HCE, lives his own life as a pubkeeper in Chapelizod and at the same time lives through the lives of scores of other heroes of antiquity and literature. In *The Second Census of Finnegans Wake,* Adaline Glasheen deals entirely with identifying and cross-referencing the characters and their historical counterparts.

The universalization process exists also on the level of style and language. There are phrases, words, and expressions in scores of foreign languages interwoven with Joyce's pseudo-English double, triple, quadruple, and even quintuple entendres to produce paradoxes in meaning, and association of events and times which seem to be wholly incongruous, and at the same time fraught with meaning beyond the wildest imagination of the reader. The book thus produces a feeling of frustration, of impenetrability, which caused early and casual readers, and even many serious scholars, to shrug it off as not being worth the effort to attain even a rudimentary understanding of what it was all about.

Serious readers now have several first-rate guides and critical crutches upon which to lean as they try to make their way through the literary brambles of the *Wake.* One of the first and still the most useful is *A Skeleton Key to Finnegans Wake* by Joseph Campbell and Henry M. Robinson. William York Tindall's later *Reader's Guide to Finnegans Wake* also deals with line-by-line allusion and explication. While Campbell and Robinson's work contains a heavy accent on mythopoeic elements, Tindall's is often Freudian in its bias.

The novel is based in part upon the song that provides its title, "The Ballad of Finnegan's Wake." Tim Finnegan is a hod carrier who falls from a ladder to his death only to be revived again at his wake when some whiskey, the Irish "water of life," is spilled on his lips. From this action the whole death and resurrection motif stems, becoming universalized in ever-broadening historical cycles until everything is included. Finnegan's fall is, of course, symbolic as well as literal, the symbolic fall encompassing Adam and Lucifer on one level and Humpty Dumpty and Newton's apple on another. So the world goes through a four-phase cycle analogous to Giambattista Vico's cycles in *La Scienza Nuova.*

At the wake, the mourners tell Finnegan that his replacement is Humphrey Chimpden Earwicker, whose initials provide a clue to his counterparts in the novel, particularly Here Comes Everybody and Haveth Childers Everywhere. Dublin, again utilized as the locale of the novel, becomes a universal scene. The sleeping giant of Irish legend, Finn McCool, is the counterpart of Tim Finnegan, with his body the whole landscape of greater Dublin, "Howth Castle and Environs." The giant Finn, like his namesake in the ballad, also represents the great heroes of the past. HCE commits some nameless sin in Phoenix Park (which itself literally as well as figuratively fits the resurrection theme). We are led to suspect that he indecently exhibits himself to two girls in the park, but he is observed also by three drunken soldiers, who are really not quite sure of what they have seen. The vagueness of the sin allows its universal connotation, as it becomes a species of Original Sin from which springs the guilt and punishment theme motivating much of the action throughout the novel and providing the basis of the nightmare which forms the substance of the book. One ramification of the Sin is a host of old man-young girl situations and cuckoldry references which permeate the text.

Earwicker is both original hero and usurper to the populace and to his family. He becomes the brunt of a rumor which runs through the city and throughout history. There is a letter which would either convict or vindicate him, found on a dung heap by a hen. There are slogans, advertisements, and speeches ostensibly dealing with the subject. There are twelve drunken jurymen and four judges who hear various aspects of HCE's case. They have counterparts in practically everything with which the numbers twelve and four are historically associated, as well as with the mourners at Finnegan's funeral and the patrons of HCE's pub.

HCE's wife, Anna Livia Plurabelle, is the symbolic center of the book, assuming all the attributes of the women of Joyce's earlier works, in addition to other historical roles women have traditionally assumed. She is also a personification of the River Liffey, always changing and always the same. Her identification with the Liffey further expands to include other rivers from the Nile to the Mississippi. Their sons, Shem and Shaun, represent the dichotomies of ego and super ego, of introvert and extrovert, of artist and public man discussed earlier (as well as all pairs of opposites). In fact, the entire book can be seen as a manifestation of Bruno's theory that each thing contains its opposite. Characters frequently change identities in *Finnegans Wake,* and both character and objects continually merge into their opposites. In *Finnegans Wake,* however, Shem the Penman is ostensibly the author of the Book, *Finnegans Wake.* The boys represent extensions of their father just as Issy, their sister, is a manifestation of her mother.

The novel follows its course through letters and lectures that purport to explain; through trials, denials, accusations, vindications, and convictions; through rumor and evidence; through incest and reproduction; through the old and the new; through the cataclysms of history and the closing of the pub; through the observations of the washerwomen and the end of the world to rebirth and a new beginning for the novel until the last sentence of the book becomes the beginning of the first.

The language of the book opens up the multilayered nature of signification itself. Joyce's imposition of several foreign languages on English words that already contain a variety of possible meanings has been a major impetus in the development of whole new schools of thought regarding the interpretation of the relationship of language to meaning. Of note here are such critics as Jacques Derrida and Hélène Cixous, who drew heavily on Joyce's works for both incentive and example for their ideas. Similarly, Jacques Lacan used Joyce's work to exemplify his new ventures into psychological theory, and his followers, such as Sheldon Brivic, have firmly established themselves in Joyce scholarship.

The book is a series of paradoxes, with the most incredible complexities evolving into mundane simplicities, and the whole panorama of man reduced to its simplest comic form. Above all, *Finnegans Wake,* like the ballad from which it draws its name, is funny. The final line of the song, "lots of fun at Finnegans Wake," is the only way in which an intelligent reader can approach the novel. Its puns and situations, universal though they may be, are more ludicrous and comic than pathetic or tragic, and its pages riotously joyful even in their pain.

The magnitude of the book, while initially baffling all but the most avid Joyceans, has over the years spawned a library of critical and scholarly commentary, and every year the pages of *PMLA Bibliography* reveal still more studies of one aspect or the other of *Wake* criticism. An entire periodical devoted to *Wake* explication and commentary, *A Wake Newsletter,* is published quarterly. Other Joycean periodicals include the *James Joyce Quarterly,* the *James Joyce Annual,* and the *James Joyce Literary Supplement* in the United States, as well as several European publications devoted exclusively to Joyce.

The entire catalog of Joyce criticism encompasses too great a list even to begin to enumerate here.

ZACK BOWEN

WORKS: *Chamber Music.* London: Elkin Mathews, 1907; *Dubliners.* London: Grant Richards, 1914; *A Portrait of the Artist as a Young Man.* New York: B. W. Huebsch, 1916; *Exiles.* London: Grant Richards, 1918; *Ulysses.* Paris: Shakespeare & Co., 1922/New York: Random House, 1961/ *Ulysses: The Corrected Text.* Hans Gabler, ed. New York: Random House/London: Bodley Head/ Harmondsworth: Penguin, 1986; *Pomes Penyeach.* Paris: Shakespeare & Co., 1927; *Collected Poems.* New York: Black Sun, 1936; *Finnegans Wake.* London: Faber/New York: Viking, 1939; *Stephen Hero.* Theodore Spencer, ed. London: Jonathan Cape/New York: New Directions, 1944; *The Portable James Joyce.* New York: Viking, 1947. (Contains *Dubliners, A Portrait of the Artist as a Young Man, Exiles, Collected Poems,* and selections from *Ulysses* and *Finnegans Wake*); *Letters of James Joyce.* Stuart Gilbert, ed. New York: Viking, 1957; *The Critical Writings of James Joyce.* Ellsworth Mason & Richard Ellmann, eds. New York: Viking, 1959; *Letters of James Joyce.* Richard Ellmann, ed. Vols. 2 & 3. New York: Viking, 1966; *Giacomo Joyce.* New York: Viking, 1968; *Selected Letters.* Richard Ellmann, ed. New York: Viking, 1976. (Contains several previously unpublished letters from Joyce to his wife). REFERENCES: Bibliographies—Beebe, Maurice, Phillip F. Herring, & Walton Litz. "Criticism of James Joyce: A Selected Checklist." *Modern Fiction Studies* 15 (Spring 1969): 105–182; Deming, Robert. *A Bibliography of James Joyce Studies. Second Edition, Revised and Enlarged.* Boston: G. K. Hall, 1977; Slocum, John J. & Cahoon, Herbert. *A Bibliography of James Joyce.* New Haven: Conn.: Yale University Press, 1953; Staley, Thomas F. *An Annotated Critical Bibliography of James Joyce.* New York: St. Martin's, 1989. Each year Alan Cohen updates the checklist in the *James Joyce Quarterly.* Biography—Costello, Peter. *James Joyce, The Years of Growth, 1882–1915—A Biography.* Schull, Ireland: Robert Rinehart, 1992; Ellmann, Richard. *James Joyce: New and Revised Edition.* New York & London: Oxford University Press, 1982. Criticism—Adams, Robert Martin. *James Joyce: Common Sense and Beyond.* New York: Random House, 1966; Adams, Robert Martin. *Surface and Symbol: The Consistency of James Joyce's Ulysses.* New York: Oxford University Press, 1962; Anderson, Chester. *James Joyce and His World.* New York: Viking, 1968; Attridge, Derek. *The Cambridge Companion to James Joyce.* Cambridge: Cambridge University Press, 1990; Bauerle, Ruth. *Picking Up Airs: Hearing the Music in Joyce's Text.* Urbana: University of Illinois Press, 1993; Begnal, Michael H.

& Senn Fritz, eds. *A Conceptual Guide to Finnegans Wake.* University Park: Pennsylvania State University Press, 1974; Beja, Morris. *James Joyce: A Literary Life.* Columbus: Ohio State University Press, 1992; Bell, Robert. *Jocoserious Joyce: The Fate of Folly in Ulysses.* Ithaca, N.Y.: Cornell University Press, 1991; Benstock, Bernard. *Joyce-Again's Wake: An Analysis of Finnegans Wake.* Seattle: University of Washington Press, 1965; Benstock, Bernard. *Narrative Con/Texts in Ulysses.* Urbana: University of Illinois Press, 1991; Bishop, John. *Joyce's Book of the Dark: Finnegans Wake.* Madison: University of Wisconsin Press, 1986; Blamires, Harry. *The Bloomsday Book: A Guide through Joyce's Ulysses.* London: Methuen, 1966; Bowen, Zack. *Musical Allusions in the Works of James Joyce: Early Poetry through Ulysses.* Albany: State University of New York Press, 1974; Bowen, Zack. *Ulysses as Comedy.* Syracuse, N.Y.: Syracuse University Press, 1990; Bowen, Zack & Carens, James. *A Companion to Joyce Studies.* Westport, Conn.: Greenwood, 1984; Boyle, Robert. *James Joyce's Pauline Vision: A Catholic Exposition.* Carbondale: Southern Illinois University Press, 1978; Brivic, Sheldon. *The Veil of Signs: Joyce, Lacan, and Perception.* Urbana: University of Illinois Press, 1991; Budgen, Frank. *James Joyce and the Making of Ulysses and Other Writings.* Introduction, Clive Hart. London: Oxford University Press, 1972; Burgess, Anthony. *Here Comes Everybody: An Introduction to James Joyce for the Ordinary Reader.* London: Faber, 1965/published as *Re Joyce,* New York: Norton, 1965; Campbell, Joseph & Robinson, Henry Morton. *A Skeleton Key to Finnegans Wake.* New York: Harcourt Brace, 1944; Connolly, Thomas E. *Joyce's Portrait: Criticisms and Critiques.* New York: Appleton-Century-Crofts, 1962; Devlin, Kimberly. *Wandering and Return in Finnegans Wake: An Integrative Approach to Joyce's Fictions.* Princeton, N. J.: Princeton University Press, 1991; DiBernard, Barbara. *Alchemy and Finnegans Wake.* Albany: State University of New York Press, 1980; Ellmann, Richard. *Ulysses on the Liffey.* New York: Oxford University Pess, 1972; Fairhall, *Joyce and the Question of History.* Cambridge: Cambridge University Press, 1993; French, Marilyn. *The Book as World: James Joyce's Ulysses.* Cambridge: Harvard University Press, 1976; Gifford, Don & Seidman, Robert J. *Notes for Joyce: An Annotation of James Joyce's Ulysses.* New York: E. P. Dutton, 1974; Gifford, Don, with Robert J. Seidman. *Notes for Joyce: Dubliners and Portrait of the Artist as a Young Man.* London: Faber, 1959/New York: E. P. Dutton, 1967; Gilbert, Stuart. *James Joyce's Ulysses: A Study.* London: Faber, 1930; Glasheen, Adaline. *A Third Census of Finnegans Wake: An Index of Characters and Their Roles.* Berkeley: University of California Press, 1977; Harkness, Marguerite. *The Aesthetic of Dedalus and Bloom.* Lewisburg, Pa.: Bucknell University Press, 1984; Hart, Clive, ed. *James Joyce's Dubliners: Critical Essays.* New York: Viking, 1969; Hart, Clive. *Structure and Motif in Finnegans Wake.* Evanston, Ill.: Northwestern University Press, 1962; Hayman, David. *Ulysses: The Mechanics of Meaning.* Englewood, Cliffs, N.J.: Prentice-Hall, 1970; Hayman, David. *The "Wake" in Transit.* Ithaca, N.Y.: Cornell University Press, 1990; Henke, Suzette A. *James Joyce and the Politics of Desire.* New York: Routledge, 1990; Herr, Cheryl. *Joyce's Anatomy of Culture.* Urbana: University of Illinois Press, 1966; Herring, Phillip F. *Joyce's Uncertainty Principle.* Princeton, N.J.: Princeton University Press, 1987; Kain, Richard M. *Fabulous Voyager: James Joyce's Ulysses.* Chicago: University of Chicago Press, 1947; Kenner, Hugh. *Dublin's Joyce.* London: Chatto & Windus, 1955/ Bloomington: Indiana University Press, 1956; Kershner, R. B. *Joyce, Bakhtin, and Popular Literature: Chronicles of Disorder.* Chapel Hill: University of North Carolina Press, 1989; Klein, Scott W. *The Fictions of James Joyce and Wyndham Lewis.* Cambridge: Cambridge University Press, 1994; Lawrence, Karen. *The Odyssey of Style in Ulysses.* Princeton, N.J.: Princeton University Press, 1981; Leonard, Garry. *Reading Dubliners Again: A Lacanian Perspective.* Syracuse, N.Y.: Syracuse University Press, 1993; Lernout, Geert. *The French Joyce.* Ann Arbor: University of Michigan Press, 1990; Levin, Harry. *James Joyce: A Critical Introduction.* Norfolk, Conn.: New Directions, 1941; Litz, A. Walton. *The Art of James Joyce: Method and Design in Ulysses and Finnegans Wake.* London: Oxford University Press, 1961; Magalaner, Marvin & Kain, Richard M. *Joyce: The Man, The Work, The Reputation.* New York: New York University Press, 1956; Magee, Patrick. *Paperspace: Style as Ideology in Joyce's Ulysses.* Lincoln: University of Nebraska Press, 1988; Martin, Timothy. *Joyce and Wagner: A Study of Influence.* Cambridge: Cambridge University Press, 1991; McCarthy, Patrick A. *The Riddles of Finnegans Wake.* Morristown, N.J.: Fairleigh Dickinson Uni-

versity Press, 1980; McCarthy, Patrick A. *Ulysses: Portals of Discovery.* Boston: Twayne, 1990;
Morse, J. Mitchel. *The Sympathetic Alien.* New York: New York University Press, 1959; Nadel, Ira
B. *Joyce and the Jews: Culture and Texts.* Iowa City: University of Iowa Press, 1989; Nolan, Emer.
James Joyce and Nationalism. London: Routledge, 1994; Noon, William T. *Joyce and Aquinas.*
New Haven, Conn.: Yale University Press, 1957; Norris, Margot. *Joyce's Web: The Social Unrav-
elling of Modernism.* Austin: University of Texas Press, 1992; O'Shea, Michael. *James Joyce and
Heraldry.* Albany: State University of New York Press, 1986; Pearce, Richard, ed. *Molly Blooms:
A Polylogue on "Penelope" and Cultural Studies.* Madison: University of Wisconsin Press, 1994;
Prescott, Joseph. *Exploring James Joyce.* Carbondale: Southern Illinois University Press, 1964;
Restuccia, Frances J. *Joyce and the Law of the Fathers.* New Haven, Conn.: Yale University Press,
1989; Rose, Daniel. *The Textual Diaries.* Dublin: Lilliput, 1995; Roughley, Alan. *James Joyce and
Critical Theory: An Introduction.* Ann Arbor: University of Michigan Press, 1991; Russell, Myra
Teicher. *Chamber Music: The Lost Song Settings.* Bloomington: Indiana University Press, 1993;
Scholes, Robert J. & Kain, Richard M. *The Workshop of Dedalus: James Joyce and the Materials
for the Portrait of the Artist as a Young Man.* Evanston, Ill.: Northwestern University Press, 1965;
Segall, Jeffrey. *Joyce in America: Cultural Politics and the Trials of* Ulysses. Berkeley: University
of California Press, 1993; Senn, Fritz. *Inductive Scrutinies.* Dublin: Lilliput, 1995; Shechner, Mark.
Joyce in Nighttown. Berkeley: University of California Press, 1974; Shutte, William M. *Joyce and
Shakespeare: A Study in the Meaning of Ulysses.* New Haven, Conn.: Yale University Press, 1957;
Steinberg, Erwin. *The Stream of Consciousness and Beyond in Ulysses.* Pittsburgh: University of
Pittsburgh Press, 1973; Strong, L. A. G. *The Sacred River: An Approach to James Joyce.* London:
Methuen, 1949; Sullivan, Kevin. *Joyce among the Jesuits.* New York: Columbia University Press,
1958; Sultan, Stanley. *The Argument of Ulysses.* Columbus: Ohio State University Press, 1965;
Thornton, Weldon. *Allusions in Ulysses.* Chapel Hill: University of North Carolina Press, 1961;
Thornton, Weldon. *The Antimodernism of Joyce's "Portrait of the Artist as a Young Man."* Syr-
acuse, N.Y.: Syracuse University Press, 1994; Tindall, William York. *A Reader's Guide to Finne-
gans Wake.* New York: Farrar, Straus & Giroux/London: Thames & Hudson, 1969; Torchiana,
Donald. *Backgrounds for Joyce's Dubliners.* Boston: Allen & Unwin, 1986; Tucker, Lindsey. *Ste-
phen and Bloom at Life's Feast: Alimentary Symbolism and the Creative Process in James Joyce's
Ulysses.* Columbus: Ohio State University Press, 1984; von Caspel, Paul. *Bloomers on the Liffey:
Eisegetical Readings of Joyce's Ulysses.* Baltimore: Johns Hopkins University Press, 1986.

JOYCE, P. W. (1827–1914), scholar. Joyce, one of the most extraordinary Irish
scholars, was born in Ballyorgan, County Limerick, in 1827. He was educated
at private schools and then at Trinity College, Dublin, where he received a B.A.
in 1861, an M.A. in 1864, and an LL.D. in 1870. He entered the service of the
Commissioners of National Education in 1845 and held successive posts until
1874, when he was appointed professor and later principal of the Commissioners' Training College in Dublin, a position he held until his retirement in 1893.
Joyce is noted particularly for his work on Irish place names, for his anthology
of airs entitled *Ancient Irish Music* (1873), and for his excellent translations of
the ancient Bardic tales entitled *Old Celtic Romances* (1879), which was used
by Tennyson for his "The Voyage of Maeldune." However, the breadth and
the extent of Joyce's learning may be better measured by a glance at the only
partial bibliography below. Joyce died in Rathmines on January 7, 1914. He
was the brother of R. D. Joyce,* the poet.

WORKS: *A Handbook of School Management and Methods of Teaching.* Dublin: McGlashan &
Gill, 1863; *The Origin and History of Irish Names of Places.* 3 vols. Dublin: McGlashan & Gill,
1869–1870/Dublin: Gill, 1913; *Irish Local Names Explained.* Dublin: McGlashan & Gill, [1870];

Ancient Irish Music. Dublin: McGlashan & Gill, 1873; *A Grammar of the Irish Language.* Dublin: Gill, [1878]; *Old Celtic Romances.* London: C. Kegan Paul, 1879; *The Geography of the Counties of Ireland.* London: Philip, 1883; *A Concise History of Ireland from the Earliest Times to 1837.* Dublin: Gill, 1893; *A Child's History of Ireland.* London: Longmans, Green, 1897; *Atlas and Cyclopedia of Ireland.* New York: Murphy & McCarthy, ca. 1900. Part I by Joyce and Part II, the General History, by A. M. Sullivan and P. D. Nunan; *Ireland.* Philadelphia: J. D. Morris, ca. 1900; *A Reading Book in Irish History.* London: Longmans, Green, 1900; *A Social History of Ancient Ireland.* 2 vols. London: Longmans, Dublin: Gill, 1907; *English as We Speak It in Ireland.* London: Longmans/Dublin: Gill, 1910; *The Wonders of Ireland, and Other Papers on Irish Subjects.* London: Longmans/Dublin: Gill, 1911. Most of these books went through many editions.

JOYCE, ROBERT DWYER (1830–1883), poet. Joyce was born in Glenosheen, County Limerick, the younger brother of P. W. Joyce.* Primarily a poet, his *Deirdre* (1876) sold ten thousand copies on its first publication in Boston, and his *Blanid* (1879) was almost equally successful. Nevertheless, these works are rather uninteresting today, and Joyce's poorer, more public poetry is a good deal more fun. For instance, his swashbuckling ''The Blacksmith of Limerick,'' which reads in part:

> The blacksmith raised his hammer, and rushed into the street,
> His 'prentice boys behind him, the ruthless foe to meet—
> High on the breach of Limerick, with dauntless hearts they stood
> Where the bombshells burst and shot fell thick, and redly ran the blood. . . .
> The first that gained the rampart, he was a captain brave!
> A captain of the Grenadiers, with blood-stained dirk and glaive;
> He pointed and he parried, but it was all in vain,
> For fast through skull and helmet the hammer found his brain!
>
> The next that topped the rampart, he was a colonel bold,
> Bright through the murk of battle his helmet flashed with gold.
> ''Gold is no match for iron!'' the doughty blacksmith said,
> As with that ponderous hammer he cracked his foeman's head!

Joyce's song ''The Wind That Shakes the Barley'' is still heard today. After some years in America, Joyce returned to Ireland where he died in Dublin on October 24, 1883.

WORKS: *Ballads, Romances and Songs.* Dublin: Duffy, 1861; *Legends of the Wars in Ireland.* Boston: J. Campbell, 1868; *Irish Fireside Tales.* Boston: P. Donahoe, 1871; *Ballads of Irish Chivalry.* Dublin: Talbot, n.d./Boston: P. Donahoe, 1872/London: Longmans, Green, 1908/Dublin: Gill, 1908; *Deirdre.* Boston: Roberts Brothers, 1876; *Blanid.* Boston: Roberts Brothers, 1879. REFERENCE: Taylor, Geoffrey. ''A Neglected Irish Poet.'' *The Bell* 3 (1942):308–312.

JOYCE, TREVOR (1947–   ), poet. Joyce was born in Dublin and educated at Blackrock College. He was a cofounder of New Writers' Press* and with Michael Smith* edited its magazine, *The Lace Curtain.* As a poet, he appears utterly enchanted with language, and so quite frequently he writes the memorably, but unintentionally, funny line. He is also given to the strong and squalid image, and his work abounds in descriptions of mucous, swill, worms, dung, and rat droppings. His third volume, *Pentahedron* (1972) seems a little less frenetic but is described with rather too much portentousness as "an essay towards the description of an epistemology of poetic apprehension." It hardly seems that, but it does have some better lines in it than do the first two volumes. The verses in his reworking of *Buile Suibhne,* however, are terse and telling and stand up well to Seamus Heaney's* version.

WORKS: *Sole Glum Trek.* Dublin: New Writers', 1967; *Watches.* Dublin: New Writers', 1969; *Pentahedron.* Dublin: New Writers, 1972; *The Poems of Sweeney Peregrine: A Working of the Corrupt Irish Text.* Michael Smith, ed. Dublin: New Writers', 1976. (Translation of *Buile Suibhne*); *Stone Fields.* Dublin: New Writers', 1995.

JUDGE, MICHAEL (1921–   ), playwright. Judge was born in Dublin on July 26, 1921, and educated at Colaiste Mhuire, at which he later taught, and at University College, Dublin. His first stage work was an adaptation of his television play, *The Chair,* which uses dialogue as laconically and rather more comically than does Pinter. His later plays include *Death Is for Heroes* (Abbey,* 1966), *Please Smash the Glass Gently* (Eblana, 1967), *Saturday Night Women* (Eblana, 1971), *There's an Octopus in the Gentlemen* (Peacock, 1972), *A Matter of Grave Importance* (Project, 1973), and *Someone to Talk To* (Project, 1973). *Saturday Night Women,* the only published play of these, is a black, woman's liberation comedy with songs. Its long prologue is in his drollest satiric style. The body of the play, despite the clever songs, is less trenchant, but the ending is startling and theatrical. Like John O'Donovan,* whom he succeeded as chairman of the Society of Irish Playwrights, Judge brought a rare and much-needed wit to the drama of the 1960s and 1970s. Since retiring from teaching, he has written frequently for Irish radio and television.

WORKS: *Saturday Night Women.* Newark, Del.: Proscenium, 1978; "The Chair" in *4 Irish Plays* (called in Ireland *4 One-Act Plays*). [Newark, Del.]: Proscenium, [1982].

K

KAVANAGH, JOHN (1960–   ), poet. Kavanagh was born in Sligo and works as a laboratory technician at Sligo Regional Technical College as well as being presenter of the "Arts" program on Radio North West. In 1988, he won the Listowel Writers' Week Poetry Award. His volume *Etchings* (1991) is the freest of free verse and depends for its effects basically on its imagery. Sometimes it can be a trifle ludicrous, as when it compares mouths to unfurled sails or his hair to "tangled rain forests." But sometimes it can convey real power, as in the conclusion of "New Year's Day."

WORK: *Etchings*. [Galway: Salmon, 1991].

KAVANAGH, JULIA (1824–1877), novelist and biographer. Julia was the daughter of Morgan Peter Kavanagh (ca. 1800–1874), a philologist of questionable reputation and the occasional author of novels and poetry. Her mother was the former Bridget Fitzpatrick. She was born in Thurles, County Tipperary, and baptized there in the "Big Chapel" on January 9, 1824. The family moved briefly to England while she was still a child and then to France for an extended period during her youth. Julia and her invalid mother returned to London in 1844, where Julia pursued a literary career in order to support them. In 1857, her father attempted to capitalize on her growing literary reputation by claiming her coauthorship of a book he had written. She publicly disowned any participation in *The Hobbies,* a badly written novel, but the incident caused temporary damage to her literary reputation and her estrangement from her father. While living in Nice, Julia was herself a semi-invalid for several years before her death on October 28, 1877. Her mother outlived her by about a decade.

Kavanagh's novels were extremely popular, often appearing as serials in periodicals and published as reprints in the Tauchnitz series. The critical views of *Madeleine* (1848) and *Nathalie* (1850) stressed her ability to portray realistically and cleverly life in rural France. Eleanor Langstaff notes that Kavanagh "addressed herself consistently to the problems of women in an unreformed but reformable society." Her biographical works, portraying the lives of both French and English literary women, are well written and rewarding. Unfortunately, the acrimonious relationship between Julia and her father usually overshadows her own literary achievements.

ANNE COLMAN

WORKS: *The Montyon Prizes*. 1846; *The Three Paths: A Story for Young People*. London, 1848/ Boston: W. H. Hill, Jr., 1866; *Madeleine: A Tale of Auvergne*. London: R. Bentley, 1848/Philadelphia: Kilner, [1848]/New York: D. Appleton, 1852; *Nathalie: A Tale*. London: Hurst & Blackett, 1850/Leipzig: B. Tauchnitz, 1851; *Woman in France during the Eighteenth Century*. London: Smith, Elder, 1850/Philadelphia: Lea & Blanchard, 1850; *Women of Christianity Exemplary for Acts of Piety and Charity*. London: Smith, Elder, 1852/New York: D. Appleton, 1860; *Daisy Burns: A Tale*. 3 vols. London: R. Bentley, 1853/New York: Appleton, 1864; *Grace Lee: A Tale*. 3 vols. London, 1855/Leipzig: B. Tauchnitz, 1855/New York: Appleton, 1887; *Rachel Gray: A Tale Founded on Fact*. London, 1856/Leipzig: Tauchnitz, 1856/New York: Appleton, 1856; *Saint-Gildas; or, the Three Paths*. Boston: Whittemore, Niles & Hall, 1856; *Adele: A Tale*. 3 vols. London, 1858/Leipzig: B. Tauchnitz, 1858/New York: D. Appleton, 1858; *A Summer and Winter in the Two Sicilies*. Leipzig: Tauchnitz/London: Hurst & Blackett, 1858; *Seven Years and Other Tales*. London, 1859/ Boston: Ticknor & Fields, 1859/Leipzig: B. Tauchnitz, 1859; *French Women of Letters: Biographical Sketches*. Leipzig: Tauchnitz, 1862/London: Hurst & Blackett, 1862; *English Women of Letters: Biographical Sketches*. Leipzig, 1862/London: Hurst & Blackett, 1863; *Queen Mab: A Novel*. 3 vols. London: Hurst & Blackett, 1863–1864/New York: D. Appleton, 1864; *Beatrice: A Novel*. 2 vols. Leipzig: B. Tauchnitz, 1864/New York: D. Appleton, 1865; *Sybil's Second Love: A Novel*. London, 1867/Leipzig: B. Tauchnitz, 1967/New York: D. Appleton, 1867; *Dora: A Novel*. 3 vols. London: Hurst & Blackett, 1868/Leipzig: B. Tauchnitz, 1868/New York: D. Appleton, 186?; *Silvia*. London: Hurst & Blackett/New York: D. Appleton/Leipzig: B. Tauchnitz, 1870; *Bessie: A Novel*. London, 1872/New York: D. Appleton, 1872; *John Dorrien: A Novel*. 3 vols. London, 1875/ New York: D. Appleton, 1875; *The Pearl Fountain and Other Fairy Tales*. 1876; *Two Lilies: A Novel*. 3 vols. London: Hurst & Blackett/New York: Appleton/Leipzig: B. Tauchnitz, 1877; *Forget-me-not*. London: R. Bentley, 1878.   REFERENCES: Langstaff, Eleanor. "Julia Kavanagh." In *An Encyclopaedia of British Women Writers*. Paul & June Schlueter, eds. Chicago & London: St. James, 1988; Macquoid, K. S. "Julia Kavanagh." In *Women Novelists of Queen Victoria's Reign*. 1897.

KAVANAGH, PATRICK (1904–1967), poet and novelist. Kavanagh may well be the most controversial writer of the post-Celtic revival period. He has been dead for nearly thirty years, but his presence is still very much alive in Irish literary circles. His followers, a varied but vocal group, speak of him admiringly as an important force in Irish letters, second only to Yeats.* His detractors, fewer in number but every bit as vocal, dismiss him as a loud-mouthed, ill-mannered peasant who disrupted rather than advanced the development of modern literature. While there is no denying that Kavanagh had his eccentricities, a number of his poems, particularly "The Great Hunger," his novel *Tarry Flynn,* and his autobiography *The Green Fool,* rank among the finest portrayals of peasant life in Ireland.

Born October 21, 1904, Patrick Joseph Kavanagh was the fourth child (and first son) of James and Bridget (Quinn) Kavanagh. Like his father, Kavanagh worked as a part-time cobbler and small farmer in the townland of Mucker,

Inniskeen Parish, County Monaghan. The most complete account of his early years is contained in *The Green Fool* (1938). Flowers, stones, ditches, and trees, as well as such social commonplaces as cattle and hiring fairs, drew his attention and served as agencies for insight into the glories and complexities of rural life. Like most boys, Kavanagh was led to believe it was not manly to feel poetic emotion, let alone express it. Nonetheless, he began to write juvenile verses in his school notebook sometime after his twelfth birthday.

During the years when he wrote his notebook verse, Kavanagh's relationship with his family and his growing interest in literature combined to make him feel an outsider in his native community. This predilection for seeing himself apart from his family and, later in his life, society as a whole, was constant from his childhood to his last days in Dublin, and is reflected in much of his writing, from his sense of personal fault in the early poetry to his declaration of failure in *Self Portrait* (1964). While he treats this aspect of his personality with humor in *The Green Fool*—the very title of the book suggests his concern, however— *Tarry Flynn* (1948) is the most sustained, and perhaps the most serious, attempt to explain this facet of his personality.

Kavanagh discovered modern literature as a result of his trips to Dundalk in the late 1920s. Here he purchased a variety of magazines, ranging from popular periodicals like *John O'London's Weekly* to literary journals such as *Poetry* and *The Irish Statesman.** In every sense of the phrase Kavanagh was a self-made man. He left school after his twelfth birthday and was forced to educate himself. This lack of formal education occasionally was an embarrassment to Kavanagh, particularly during his early years in Dublin in the late 1930s, and may account in part for his pose as the blustery peasant poet.

The period 1928–1939 served as Kavanagh's apprenticeship to literature. It was during these years that he wrote many of his finest lyric poems, such as "Ploughman," "To a Blackbird," and "Inniskeen Road: July Evening." These and other verses were published in his first book, *Ploughman and Other Poems,* in 1936. Along with the autobiography *The Green Fool, Ploughman* is important because it contains many of the ideas Kavanagh would pursue throughout his career as a writer. His concern with the meaning and function of poetry, for example, which is common to so much of his creative and critical writing, is one of the themes that dominates his early period. Perhaps the most significant theme present in both of these books is the urge to speak about the nature of the poet and the meaning of art.

In 1939, Kavanagh moved from his small farm in Inniskeen to Dublin on a more-or-less permanent basis. He managed to scrape a living out of various journalistic pursuits while he made himself into a professional writer. He wrote a column, "City Commentary," for *The Irish Press* from late 1942 to early 1944; a film review for *The Standard* from February 1946 to July 1949; and a lively, thought-provoking monthly diary in *Envoy** from December 1949 to July 1951. These writings were in addition to dozens of signed and unsigned books reviews, human interest stories, and critical pieces. By the early 1940s and well into the 1950s, Kavanagh was a popular fellow on the literary scene. The publication of *The Great Hunger* (1942), *A Soul for Sale* (1947), and *Tarry Flynn* (1948) signaled his arrival as a major force in the development of Irish letters.

Kavanagh's most interesting venture during this period was his newspaper, *Kavanagh's Weekly,* which appeared from April 12 to July 5, 1952. Stating that his purpose "was to introduce the critical-constructive note into Irish thought," Kavanagh spared no one from his bombastic indictments. His investigations ranged from questioning the need for Irish embassies around the world to revealing the pathetic state to which gossip had sunk on Grafton Street. Church, government, films, drama, poetry, painting, and other topics relevant and irrelevant to Irish life came under Kavanagh's scrutiny. However, for all its bluster and dogmatism, *Kavanagh's Weekly* had a certain freshness and sense of wit that made it popular with some and abhorrent to others. The enterprise finally closed from lack of funds rather than lack of interest.

In October 1952, an unsigned "Profile" of Kavanagh was published in *The Leader,* a popular weekly of the period. It contained bittersweet (with the emphasis on bitter) appraisal of Kavanagh, his journalism, and his creative work; the appearance of this article brought Kavanagh back to Dublin from London, where he had gone after the close of *Kavanagh's Weekly.* What followed was the darkest period of Kavanagh's life. He sued *The Leader* for libel, spent thirteen hours in the witness box defending his ideas before a hostile jury, fell ill, lost his case, and was ordered to pay costs, appealed, had the case continued, was granted a new trial, and, before he could get *The Leader* back in court, entered the Rialto Hospital in Dublin suffering from cancer of the lung. Against great odds and to the surprise of nearly everyone, including himself, he made a heroic recovery and spent the summer of 1955 regaining his strength on the banks of the Grand Canal in Dublin. This period, from summer 1955 to late 1956, Kavanagh referred to as his "rebirth."

The poetry Kavanagh wrote after 1955 is marked by a return to his early lyric voice. These poems differ from his earlier works, however: they are characterized by a depth of wisdom and a sense of understanding not found in his previous writing. Kavanagh's health began to decline again in the late 1950s, and by the early 1960s he was often too ill to write. His last years were once again given over to journalism. When he did attempt to write poetry, his efforts frequently fell artistically short of his earlier work. On April 19, 1967, Kavanagh married Katherine Moloney, whom he had known for a number of years. In the autumn, Kavanagh's health declined rapidly, and he died on November 30 at the age of sixty-three.

While he wrote fiction, journalism, autobiography, and literary criticism, Kavanagh is best known for his poetry. The best of his early poems are featured in *Ploughman and Other Poems,* a collection of thirty-one poems written between 1930 and 1935. This book demonstrates Kavanagh's growth from a schoolboy poet of the late 1920s to an accomplished literary artist. One of the central themes which unifies the collection is the vision of nature as explicator.

Here the poet sees various truths revealed through such natural phenomena as the twisted furrows of fields, birds in song, or late blooming trees. Most of the poems are short. Many, such as "The Intangible," "The Chase," and "After May," give in to sentiment too easily or suffer from clumsy rhymes. Yet, the bulk of these lyrics demonstrate a real talent, a talent that in six years was to produce one of the best long poems in modern literature.

Various commentators on Irish poetry have called *The Great Hunger* Kavanagh's best creative effort. Some of these critics, such as Liam Miller* ("The Future of Irish Poetry," *The Irish Times*, February 5, 1970), have hailed the poem as a watershed for future Irish poets. The poem is fashioned from Kavanagh's own personal observations of how life on the land could restrict and demean human development. Paddy Maguire, the poem's central figure, is sensitive to the possibilities of life, perceiving the powerful beauty and mystery of nature. He lacks the poet's insight, however, and fails to learn the lessons nature teaches until it is too late. Maguire's world is a web of personal and social entanglements where a man can easily become caught between social custom and personal desire. The Church, his mother, and the land itself combine to seal his fate, proving to be paralyzing forces against which he has no defense. The details of Maguire's slow discernment of his predicament, as well as the circumstances and nature of his paralysis, are presented through a series of descriptive and reflective passages that are among the best in Irish poetry. Though Kavanagh rejected this poem late in his life (see *Self Portrait*), it stands as one of his most significant achievements.

Kavanagh's other realistic portrait of rural life written during the 1940s is his novel, *Tarry Flynn*, which he liked to call "not only the best but the only authentic account of life as it was lived in Ireland in this century" (*Self Portrait*). Lighter in tone and atmosphere than *The Great Hunger*, and more accurate in its presentation of literal detail than *The Green Fool*, this novel lacks the vitality, verve, and power of the two earlier works. For all of its authenticity, and despite the fact that it illuminates Kavanagh's youthful struggle with his talent and his environment, *Tarry Flynn* is flawed by a lapse into artificial romanticism in its conclusion. Pressured between a need for security and the reassurance familiarity provides on the one hand, and a desire to escape the confines of rural Ireland to pursue adventure and a literary career on the other, the hero Tarry Flynn (whom Kavanagh would have us believe is himself at age twenty-eight) flees the townland of Drumnay with a vagabond uncle, produced out of nowhere, to find fortune and fame in the world beyond. Whatever shortcomings the novel may have, it is a valuable portrait of rural Ireland and, with *The Green Fool* and *The Great Hunger*, demonstrates the skillful use Kavanagh could make of his country background.

Kavanagh was less successful in writing about Dublin. During the period 1944–1952, he wrote a number of verse satires about the Dublin literary scene. Perhaps the most successful piece among such works as "Bardic Dust," "The Wake of the Books," "The Paddiad," and "Who Killed James Joyce?" is "A

Wreath for Tom Moore's Statue." Here Kavanagh attacks the attitudes and intentions of the insensitive and artless souls who wreathe statues rather than honor living poets. From the poem's opening lines, Kavanagh establishes and then sustains the attack without wandering into side issues or sinking into an emotional harangue against the philistines, his term for those Irishmen who valued artifice over art. The poem also attacks those writers who waste their energies treating mere appearances instead of the realities of life. In other poems, such as "Adventures in the Bohemian Jungle" and "House Party to Celebrate the Destruction of the Roman Catholic Church in Ireland," Kavanagh's satiric thrusts were less successful because of lapses in craft or a tendency to preach instead of parody.

Most of the poetry Kavanagh wrote during the 1940s and 1950s was neither satiric nor about Dublin. In *A Soul for Sale* (1947), for example, the majority of the poems deal with private rather than public themes. These poems continue his investigation of the self that began in *Ploughman and Other Poems.* The central subject of the book is failure. While it may be incorrect to say that Kavanagh was suffering a loss of confidence in his talent during the mid- and late 1940s, he was very conscious of not achieving the success he had hoped his move to Dublin would bring him. The title of his second book thus seems to underscore the degree to which failure was involved in his self-examination. It is one of the ironies of Kavanagh's literary development that while the public, satiric voice was so strong and confident in its outcries against the philistines, the private, lyric voice was often subdued in its utterances about the state of Kavanagh's own poetic soul.

Kavanagh seemed to be aware of this distinction when he noted in "The Gallivanting Poet" (*Irish Writing,* * November, 1947) that the essential difference between a public and a private speaker is that the former merely reports circumstances while the latter lives them. The extent of Kavanagh's creative failure is clearly revealed in "Pegasus," where the poet's soul is likened to an old horse being put up for sale at a fair. Finding no takers among the church, the state, or business, the soul grows wings, and the poet rides off to visit the lands of his imagination. Wallowing in sentimentality, the poem accurately summarizes the sources of Kavanagh's frustration and documents his overly romantic response to failure.

Perhaps to compensate for his failure to achieve a greater degree of financial and literary success, Kavanagh struck out at many of his contemporaries through his journalism and his critical articles. In addition to many of his *Envoy* "Diary" pieces and the bulk of *Kavanagh's Weekly,* he delivered his attacks upon friends, foes, and bystanders through such essays as "The Gallivanting Poet" (*Irish Writing,* * November 1947) and "Coloured Balloons" (*The Bell,* * December 1947). While these pieces often contained interesting insights and apt judgments, they suffered on the whole from an inconsistent critical approach.

Kavanagh's final three books of poems were *Recent Poems* (1958), *Come Dance with Kitty Stobling and Other Poems* (1960), and *Collected Poems*

(1964). The best of his later poems were the sonnets he wrote during his "rebirth" during the mid-1950s. In "Canal Bank Walk," "Lines Written on a Seat on the Grand Canal," "Dear Folks," "The Hospital," "Yellow Vestment," and others, Kavanagh emphasized the visible rather than the ideological. By depicting the excitement of the habitual, the ordinary, Kavanagh vitalized the self and articulated his doctrine of "not caring." The basis of this doctrine was a belief in the comic muse. To Kavanagh, comedy was the natural outgrowth of detachment—of not caring—while tragedy was occasioned by involvement. The ultimate truth of art, of life, Kavanagh preached in his last prose pieces (see *Self Portrait* in particular) was not to take the self too seriously. This same message was at the heart of his best poetry.

By the early 1960s, with his health in decline, Kavanagh's creative output declined in both quantity and quality. His literary energy was used up to fuel columns in *The Irish Farmers' Journal* (from June 1958 to March 1963) and in the *RTV Guide* (from January 1964 to October 1966). On the whole, his most successful poems include a half dozen lyrics from *Ploughman and Other Poems*, the sonnets from *Come Dance with Kitty Stobling and Other Poems*, and *The Great Hunger*. However one chooses to view him, the vitality that he brought to Irish literature, his lyrically articulated vision of rural Ireland, and his final affirmation of life combine to ensure his continued reputation as one of Ireland's great literary artists. He died in Dublin on November 30, 1967.

JOHN NEMO

WORKS: *Ploughman and Other Poems*. London: Macmillan, 1936; *The Green Fool*. London: Michael Joseph, 1938. (Novel); *The Great Hunger*. Dublin: Cuala, 1942; *A Soul for Sale*. London: Macmillan, 1947; *Tarry Flynn*. London: Pilot, 1948. (Novel); *Come Dance with Kitty Stobling*. London: Longmans, Green, 1960; *Self-Portrait*. Dublin: Dolmen, 1964; *Collected Poems*. London: MacGibbon & Kee, 1964; *Collected Pruse*. London: MacGibbon & Kee, 1967. (Essays); *Lapped Furrows*. New York: Peter Kavanagh Hand, 1969. (Correspondence with his brother); *Complete Poems*. Peter Kavanagh, ed. New York: Peter Kavanagh Hand, 1972/rpt. Newbridge, Co. Kildare: Goldsmith, [1984]; *Lough Derg*. The Curragh, Co. Kildare: Goldsmith, 1978/London: Martin Brian & O'Keeffe, 1979; *By Night Unstarred*. Peter Kavanagh, ed. The Curragh, Co. Kildare: Goldsmith, 1978. (Novel); *Kavanagh's Weekly*. [The Curragh, Co. Kildare]: Goldsmith, [1981]. (Facsimile reprint); and Tom MacIntyre. *The Great Hunger. Poem into Play*. Mullingar: Lilliput, 1988. REFERENCES: Cronin, Anthony. *Dead as Doornails*. Dublin: Dolmen, 1975, in association with Talbot, Dublin, and with Calder & Boyars, London. (Literary reminiscences); Heaney, Seamus. "The Poetry of Patrick Kavanagh: From Monaghan to the Grand Canal." In *Two Decades of Irish Writing*. Douglas Dunn, ed. Cheadle Hulme: Carcanet, 1975, pp. 105–117; Heaney, Seamus. "The Placeless Heaven: Another Look at Kavanagh." In *The Government of the Tongue*. London: Faber, 1988, pp. 3–14; Kavanagh, Peter. *Sacred Keeper: A Biography of Patrick Kavanagh*. Newbridge, Co. Kildare: Goldsmith, 1980/Orono, Maine: National Poetry Foundation, University of Maine, 1986; Kavanagh, Peter, ed. *Patrick Kavanagh: Man and Poet*. Orono, Maine: National Poetry Foundation, University of Maine, 1986/Newbridge, Co. Kildare: Goldsmith, 1987; Kennelly, Brendan. "Patrick Kavanagh." In *Irish Poems in English*. Sean Lucy, ed. Cork & Dublin: Mercier, 1972, pp. 159–184; Nemo, John. *Patrick Kavanagh*. Boston: Twayne, 1979; O'Brien, Darcy. *Patrick Kavanagh*. Lewisburg, Pa.: Bucknell University Press, 1975; O'Loughlin, Michael. *After Kavanagh*. Dublin: Raven Arts, 1985; Quinn, Antoinette. *Patrick Kavanagh: A Critical Study*. Syracuse, N.Y.: Syracuse University Press, 1991/as *Patrick Kavanagh: Born-Again Romantic*. Dublin: Gill & Macmillan, 1992; Ryan, John. *Remembering How We Stood: Bohemian Dublin at the Mid-Century*. Dublin: Gill & Macmillan, [1975]; Warner, Alan. *Clay Is the Word, Patrick Kavanagh 1904–1967.* Dublin: Dolmen, 1974.

KAVANAGH, ROSE (1859–1891), poet. Rose Kavanagh was born on June 24, 1859, on the Clougher side of the Avonban River, in Killadroy, County Tyrone. When she was eleven, the family moved near Augher, by the Blackwater, which was to feature in her poetry. Knockmany, another local landmark, was the focus of her first poem published in *The Irish Monthly.* She was initially educated at home, then sent to the Loreto Convent, Omagh, before deciding to pursue a career as an artist. At age twenty, she went to study at the Metropolitan School of Art in Dublin. About this time, she also began writing verses and eventually decided to forsake art for poetry. She was a staunch friend of Charles Kickham,* tending him through physical decline and mental depression. It was rumored that Kickham fell in love with her, although his feelings were not reciprocated beyond friendship. Her memorial poem to Kickham is a testimony to her feelings:

> Rare loyal heart, and stately head of grey,
> Wise with the wisdom wrested out of pain!
> We miss the slender hand, the brave bright brain,
> All faith and hope to point and light the way
> Our land should go. Oh! surely not in vain
> That beacon burned for us, for we can lay
> Fast hold of the fair life without a stain
> And mould our own upon it. . . .

Kavanagh was considered one of the most promising young women poets of her generation, until she died of consumption on February 16, 1891, in County Tyrone, at age thirty-two. Her small, posthumous volume offers a variety of poetic topics: nature, commemorative, Celtic legends, and nationalistic politics. She is at her best in the longer poems like "Dearvorgill, a Monologue" or "Christmas Eve in the Suspects' Home," where the length of the poem and of the line itself allows her highly descriptive style the room to maneuver:

> Ah! the daylight I dread, and the sun is my shame,
> But the night time is hardest to bear. I can claim
> No reprieve from the past, while I crouch in the dark,
> With ears opened wide, but to hold and to hark
> The fierce taunts of my deeds and the anguish that beats
> Through my brain when the shape of my infamy meets
> The dull pain of these eyes. . . .

Her commemorative poetry is less successful; although flashes of her emotions are conveyed, the formality of these memorial poems borders on the overpowering.

Until shortly before her death she wrote a children's section for *The Irish Fireside* and subsequently for the Dublin *Weekly Freeman,* under the pseudonym

of Uncle Remus. Her close friend Hester Sigerson assumed the column following her death. Kavanagh also published verse using the name Ruby. In addition
to Hester Sigerson, Rose was a close friend of Hester's sister Dora Sigerson
Shorter,* Katharine Tynan,* Anna Johnston (Ethna Carbery),* and Alice Milligan.* Her death occasioned commemorative verses by several poets, Ellen
O'Leary* and Tynan among them. Magdalen Rock, the pseudonym of a
Northern poet, referred to her as "the white Rose of green Tyrone." Indeed,
references to a rose in poetry written by Irish women poets of the 1890s are apt
to refer to Kavanagh. She seems to have epitomized the tragedy of a promising
talent that was not allowed the time to mature. W. B. Yeats* wrote an obituary
of her that appeared in the April 11, 1891, issue of the *Boston Pilot.* She frequently contributed to various American papers and to such Irish publications
as *Dublin University Review, The Nation,* Shamrock,* and *Young Ireland.*

ANNE COLMAN

WORK: *Rose Kavanagh and Her Verses.* Rev. Matthew Russell, ed. Dublin & Waterford: M. H.
Gill, 1909.   REFERENCE: Russell, Matthew. "Rose Kavanagh; Some Scraps from Her Life and
Letters." *Irish Monthly* 19 (October & November 1891): 512–521 & 601–607.

KEANE, JOHN B. (1928–   ), playwright and fiction writer. John B[rendan]
Keane was born on July 21, 1928, in Listowel, County Kerry. Save for two
years as a laborer in England, he has stayed close to Listowel where he owns
a much-frequented public house. Keane's first play, *Sive,* presented by the Listowel Drama Group, won the All-Ireland Amateur Drama Festival in 1959, and
its enormous impact immediately made Keane's reputation. *Sive,* as well as
Keane's 1960 plays, *The Highest House on the Mountain* and *Sharon's Grave,*
seemed to give a vital new impetus to the presumably worn-out genre of the
peasant play. However, Keane's fidelity to life in Kerry as well as his strong
eye for the theatrical made these plays intensely gripping theatre. *Sive,* for instance, treats the extremely traditional theme of the made marriage and does not
differ in content from many other Irish plays on the same subject, particularly
Louis D'Alton's* *Lovers Meeting.* However, a rousing song done by a chorus
of two wandering tinkers lifts the play with a startling theatricality.

Nevertheless, the rich rural life that Keane wrote about in these plays, and
which is reflected in the plays of Listowel's other notable dramatists George
Fitzmaurice* and Bryan MacMahon,* was even in Keane's own youth something of an anachronism. His next plays turned away somewhat from the folk
past of North Kerry and attempted, with varying success, to depict some of the
elements of change in modern rural Ireland. *Many Young Men of Twenty* (1961),
presented by Southern Theatre Group of Cork, is a musical about emigration.
Its milieu did reflect the fading past, but the lack of jobs in the present was
forcing the people of Keane's small Irish town to leave for the modern world
of England. Nearly as rich as *Sive* or *Sharon's Grave,* the play was enlivened
by the haunting title tune which memorably underscored the play's blend of
jaunty comedy and mournful nostalgia.

Keane's subsequent plays dealt more overtly, but rather less successfully, with the modern world. The unpublished *No More in Dust* (1961) relates the misfortunes of two country girls forced to make a living in the city. *The Man from Clare* (1962) is about the Irishman's childish obsession with sport, which for many years was a kind of national sublimation. Quiet and well-drawn, the play is probably too specifically Irish to work well outside of the country. Most of Keane's plays at this time were presented by the Southern Theatre Group, but *Hut 42* (1962) was originally done by the Abbey.* It is a melancholy play about the longing of Irish workers in England to return to Ireland. Better than these plays is *The Year of the Hiker* (1963), an understated but moving study of a modern farm family whose father had taken to the roads and now, years later, returns. As traditional in subject as Colum's* *The Fiddler's House,* the play is probably one of Keane's more underrated works; it is a successful contrast of the values of the old and the modern generations.

A similar theme, but stronger plot and characterization, make *The Field* (1965) one of Keane's best plays. In it the leasing of a field to an outsider results in murder, and the local inhabitants conspire to shield the culprit, despite pleas from both priest and police. In this powerful fable, Keane shows how deeply ingrained values, even pernicious ones, linger on.

The Rain at the End of Summer (1967) is an ineffectual attempt to deal with the urban middle class, but *Big Maggie* (1969) is more successful, treating a familiar Irish phenomenon, the domineering mother. Although somewhat arbitrary in the arrangement of its plot, the play creates a strong central character and a superb role for an actress. The main character in *The Change in Mame Fadden* (1971) is also a woman, and certainly this marks the first Irish play which attempts to treat deeply the psychological problems of menopause. Mame Fadden is not as convincing a character as Big Maggie, however, and the play remains more well-intentioned than successful. *Moll* (1971) is another woman's play, the main character being a canny and domineering housekeeper of the local parish priest. A pleasantly sardonic comedy, the play attempts less than the previous two, but more successfully achieves its goal.

Keane's 1973 plays represent his weakest work to date. *The Crazy Wall* has an engaging first act and then simply goes off the tracks of its plot. Of the three one-act plays in *Values,* two are so trivial that they should never have been published. *The Good Thing* (1978) is considerably better. Although some of its dialogue is unpolished and one character is a too easy theatrical joke, the play seriously addresses itself to the problem of sexuality after ten years of marriage, a topic not often investigated in Irish drama. Keane has published only two other plays, *The Buds of Ballybunion* (1979), a play with music about an anachronistic annual gathering of farm laborers, and *The Chastitute* (1981), a sad comedy about sexual deprivation in rural Ireland. When played initially as a contemporary drama, its frustrated hero seemed a man out of his time. Revived in the 1990s as a play set years earlier, it was much more effective. Although Keane has ceased to write plays, his pieces are constantly revived, and their almost annual appearance in the Gaiety in recent summers has been so popular that one of the theater's bars has been named after the author.

Throughout his career, Keane has worked prolifically in various genres. However, in 1968 with *Letters of a Successful T. D.,* Keane began a series of epistolary novellas about rural types such as a Parish Priest, a Love-Hungry Farmer, a Matchmaker, and a Civic Guard. The most successful was the first volume in which his Tull MacAdoo is an eminently droll and only faintly exaggerated satiric portrait of a highly usual character in Irish politics. The later volumes are uneven, as Keane seemed increasingly to play for the easy laugh and the broad caricature. However, the final volume, *Letters of an Irish Minister of State* (1978), returns delightfully and tellingly to the later career of Tull MacAdoo.

Keane's most important recent work has been a series of full-length novels. Except for *The Contractors* (1993), which deals with Irish building contractors and laborers in London, they are set in the rural Ireland with which Keane is most at home. *Durango* is probably the best of them because its cattle drive, which is opposed by drovers with vicious dogs, provides a solid spine of conventional Aristotelian plot, with its exposition, its rising conflict, and its exciting climax. Onto this spine, Keane grafts a broad diversity of well-caught characters and subplots. Particularly effective are the stories of the little runaway soldier hounded by a remorseless sergeant and of the dying American monsignor who joins forces with a drunken Protestant rector to aid the cattle drive. These two plots, one with its grim, and the other with its sad, conclusion, add an emotional fullness to the book and make it more than an entertaining read with a happy ending. Indeed, Keane's large cast in a complex tale lends itself to a considerable range of effect, from the farcical to even the harrowing, as in the drover Mooley's remark, "If a dog isn't obedient it should be hanged or drowned. I prefer hanging. It's a lesson to the others."

Although Keane seems most at ease with the rural Ireland of forty years ago, his latest novel at this writing, *A High Meadow* (1994), depicts a modern country town, its shopkeepers, publicans, and surrounding farmers. The large cast is, as usual, well characterized, and the book is a study of greed and sex set against virtue and honesty. If there is a main character, it is Edward Drannaghy, called the Ram of God, because as a young clerical student he had been seduced by an older Irish-American woman who was determined to have a child. Now, years later, he hopes to complete his clerical studies in America and to leave the farm to his younger twin brothers. There is much scheming by the wife of the local supermarket owner to marry her daughters to the twins and then, after their deaths, to two neighboring brothers. The motives are not greatly different from those of *The Field,* although sexual passion is as important as greed for land. Keane's modern rural Ireland is far from Maurice Walsh's romanticized little bit of heaven that fell from out the sky one day. A local pub, for instance, is called the Load of S and shows pornographic videos to young teenagers.

The cliché about Keane is that he produces too much too quickly and with too little consideration and revision, and certainly he has produced an uneven body of work. The poorest of it gives evidence of such hasty plotting and such trite dialogue that it seems penned by quite another writer than the eloquent author of *Sive* or the mordant author of *The Field*. Even the best of Keane has a tendency to rely on melodrama rather than drama and on caricature rather than character. There is a sameness to his work, in the sense that there was a sameness to that of Maurice Walsh or John Buchan; but perhaps that stricture could also be applied to the novels of Graham Greene or the plays of Tennessee Williams. The content of his plays and novels has often been strong and even tragic, but it has never been suffused with the pervading gloom of a McGahern* or a Trevor.* Technically, he has never been innovative and so will never claim, like Friel* or Thomas Murphy,* the highest esteem of academe. Nevertheless, in the tight form of the traditional play he found—and perhaps even more in the traditional structure of the long novel, he is finding—the scope for his rich and probing examination of Irish country people. What is certain is that his integrity of vision, warm feeling, gentle melancholy, and humorous observation, always presented in conventional form, have won him a greater popularity than most of his contemporaries, from the ordinary playgoer and the common reader.

Keane is a member of Aosdána,* and among his many awards and honors is a D. Litt. from Trinity College.

WORKS: *Sive*. Dublin: Progress House, [1959]. (Play); *Sharon's Grave*. Dublin: Progress House, [1960]/reprinted in *Seven Irish Plays 1946–1964*. Robert Hogan, ed. Minneapolis: University of Minnesota Press, [1967]. (Play); *The Highest House on the Mountain*. Dublin: Progress House, [1961]. (Play); *Many Young Men of Twenty*. Dublin: Progress House, [1961]/reprinted in *Seven Irish Plays*. (Play); *The Street and Other Poems*. Dublin: Progress House, [1961]; *The Man from Clare*. Cork: Mercier, 1962. (Play); *Strong Tea*. Cork: Mercier, [1963]. (Essays); *The Year of the Hiker*. Cork: Mercier, [1963]. (Play); *Self-Portrait*. Cork: Mercier, [1964]. (Autobiography); *The Field*. Cork: Mercier, [1966]. (Play); *Letters of a Successful T. D.* Cork: Mercier, [1967]. (Fiction); *Hut 42*. Dixon, Calif.: Proscenium, [1968]. (Play); *The Rain at the End of Summer*. Dublin: Progress House, [1968]. (Play); *Big Maggie*. Cork: Mercier, [1969]. (Play); *Moll*. Cork: Mercier, [1971]. (Play); *Letters of an Irish Parish Priest*. Cork: Mercier, [1972]. (Fiction); *The One-Way Ticket*. Barrington, Ill.: Performance, 1972. (One-act play); *The Change in Mame Fadden*. Cork & Dublin: Mercier, [1973]. (Play); *The Gentle Art of Matchmaking and Other Important Things*. Cork: Mercier, [1973]. (Essays); *Values*. Dublin & Cork: Mercier, [1973]. (One-act plays: "The Spraying of John O'Dorey," "Backwater," and "The Pure of Heart"); *The Crazy Wall*. Dublin & Cork: Mercier, [1974]. (Play); *Letters of an Irish Publican*. Dublin & Cork: Mercier, [1974]. (Fiction); *Letters of a Love-Hungry Farmer*. Dublin & Cork: Mercier, [1974]. (Fiction); *Letters of a Matchmaker*. Dublin & Cork: Mercier, [1975]. (Fiction); *Death Be Not Proud*. Dublin & Cork: Mercier, [1976]. (Fiction); *Letters of a Civic Guard*. Dublin & Cork: Mercier, [1976]. (Fiction); *Is the Holy Ghost Really a Kerryman? and Other Items of Interest*. Dublin & Cork: Mercier, [1976]. (Essays); *Dan Pheaidi Aindi*. Baile Atha Cliath & Corcaigh: Clo Mercier, 1977/English version, *Man of the Triple Name*. Dingle: Brandon, 1984. (Biography); *Letters of a Country Postman*. Dublin & Cork: Mercier, [1977]. (Fiction); *Unlawful Sex and Other Testy Matters*. Dublin & Cork: Mercier, [1978]. (Essays); *Letters of an Irish Minister of State*. Dublin & Cork: Mercier, [1978]. (Fiction); *The Good Thing*. Newark, Del.: Proscenium, [1978]. (Play); *The Buds of Ballybunion*. Dublin & Cork: Mercier, [1979]. (Play); *Stories from a Kerry Fireside*. Dublin & Cork: Mercier, [1980]. (Essays); *The Chastitute*. Dublin & Cork: Mercier, [1981]. (Play); *More Irish Short Stories*. Dublin & Cork: Mercier, [1981]. (Fiction); *Unusual Irish Careers*. Dublin & Cork: Mercier, [1982]. (Essays); *Owl Sandwiches*. [Dingle]: Brandon, [1985]. (Essays); *The Bodhran Makers*. [Dingle]: Brandon, [1986]. (Novel); *The Poser of the Word.* [Dingle]: Brandon, [1990]. (Collection of quotations); *Three Plays: Sive, The Field, Big Maggie.* [Cork]: Mercier, [1990]. (Revised two-act versions); *Love Bites.* Cork & Dublin: Mercier, [1991]. (Essays); *The Ram of God.* Cork & Dublin: Mercier, [1992]. (Essays); *Durango.* [Cork & Dublin]: Mercier, [1992]. (Novel); *The Contractors.* [Cork & Dublin]: Mercier, [1993]. (Novel); *Christmas Tales.* [Cork & Dublin]: Mercier, [1993]. (Short stories); *A High Meadow.* [Cork & Dublin]: Mercier, [1994]. (Novel); *Inlaws and Outlaws.* [Cork]: Mercier, [1995]. (Short stories); *The Voice of an Angel.* [Cork]: Mercier, [1995]. (Short stories).   REFERENCES: Feehan, John M., ed. *Fifty Years Young, A Tribute to John B. Keane.* Dublin & Cork: Mercier, [1979]; Kealy, Sister Marie Hubert. *Kerry Playwright.* Selinsgrove, Pa.: Susquehanna University Press/London & Toronto: Associated University Presses, [1993]; Smith, Gus & Des Hickey. *John B: The Real Keane.* Cork & Dublin: Mercier, [1992].

KEANE, KATHERINE (1904–1987), novelist. Keane was born Katherine Boylan in Drogheda, County Louth, where she was also educated. In the 1940s and 1950s, she wrote many plays for Radio Éireann, and she also published two very readable novels. *Who Goes Home?* (1947) is set in the years of Parnell's rise and fall, and he figures as a character in the book. Rather more important than the political story are the intertangled love stories of the four Donnellan children. The well-structured incidents are so plentiful and the style is so lucid, that the book is a compulsive page-turner. If not a work of art, this historical romance is a worthy and serious entertainment.

WORKS: *Who Goes Home?* Dublin: Talbot, 1947/[Dublin]: Arlen House, [1987]; *So Ends My Dream.* Dublin: Talbot, 1950.

KEANE, MOLLY (1904–1996), novelist and playwright. Molly Keane was born Mary Nesta Skrine in County Kildare on July 4, 1904, to a "rather serious Hunting and Fishing and Church-going family." Her mother, under the pen name of Moira O'Neill,* wrote the popular *Songs of the Glens of Antrim.* Keane, too, adopted a pen name, M. J. Farrell, in order to hide her intellectual side from her sporting friends, and she used her royalties to supplement her clothing allowance. Between 1928 and 1952, Keane composed ten novels; between 1938 and 1952, she composed three rather successful plays, particularly *Spring Meeting,* and in 1961 a play called *Dazzling Prospect,* which failed. Finally, after a lengthy hiatus occasioned by the death of her husband at the age of thirty-six, she composed between 1981 and 1988 three more novels and a cookbook. Her talent as a dramatist has been compared to that of Noel Coward, and her light comedies have been produced by John Gielgud, but it is as a novelist that she is most significant. Keane died on April 22, 1996.

Molly Keane wrote her first novel when she was only seventeen, and it was eventually published by Mills & Boon, the publishers of popular romances. Her earliest serious novels, *Young Entry* (1928), *Taking Chances* (1929), *Mad Puppetstown* (1931), and *Conversation Piece* (1932), may also be dismissed as juvenilia because of their contrived and highly forgettable plots, but in them the rebellious young writer lays the groundwork for many controversial issues she will treat in later works. In her fictitious Irish County WestCommon, Keane's

Anglo-Irish characters preserve the treasures, titles, and personality traits that define who they are in a changing Ireland. In *Taking Chances,* third baronet Sir Ralph Sorrier impregnates peasant Lizzie Conroy, who attempts an abortion and dies as a result. His weaker brother, Jer, who stutters and fears horses, ironically survives at the novel's end, to remain in the Big House with his sister and the family dogs. Physical and mental handicaps, perversions, and the darker side of human nature are portrayed by Keane in quasi-comical situations in her earliest writing.

Alternatives, such as abortions and nonheterosexual lifestyles, are frequently handled by Keane as well, both through allusions and direct references. In *Devoted Ladies* (1934), which is aptly called an art deco novel, she paints a portrait of the lives and surroundings of Jane Barker, whose exquisite bath seems devoid of pipes or fixtures, and also of her companion/lover, Jessica Houpe-Boswell, a jealous watchdog afflicted with alcoholic poisoning, who fiercely keeps surveillance over Barker. Their friend, Sylvester Browne, clearly averse to heterosexual romance, reappears in *The Rising Tide* (1937), a novel in which Keane largely sublimates the issue of nontraditional liaisons to take up the concerns of Home Rule, the First World War, and the ruling of Garonlea, another Anglo-Irish bastion of tradition. Lady Charlotte, despotic ruler of the manor house, ultimately cedes control to a scheming daughter-in-law, who, in turn, relinquishes her power over Garonlea, a symbolic reference to the tide of change that will eventually engulf and alter the social structure of Anglo-Ireland.

But such change does not occur quickly, and Keane presents the class struggle, the dilemma of the aristocrats' social and sexual intercourse with the peasants, and the stirrings of the Irish Republican Army in *Two Days in Aragon* (1941), a novel set in 1920 but rooted in the land-grant era of James I. Keane deals realistically with the crone who terminates servants' pregnancies one way or another and with the awkward problem of the heroine, Grania Fox's, infatuation with a social inferior. Although the novel explores more deeply the life of the peasants, unfortunately, a forced ending with accidental death and miscarriage and a decimating fire calls to mind earlier novels, in which sudden mishaps either create irony or exact poetic justice.

Keane's later writings, which maintain her trademark reversal of fortune, allow for fuller character development, detailing of the grotesque, and exposés of the cruelty of revelations to the uninitiated and naive. In *Good Behaviour* (1981), which redirected attention to the almost forgotten Keane, which was filmed for television, and which is considered her masterpiece, the author reveals the pitfalls of dissolute living and the tenacious adherence of the Anglo-Irish to social strictures. Miss Iris Aroon St. Charles of Castle Temple, like Faulkner's dispossessed gentry of Yoknapatawpha County, would remain a wallflower and die, a tall, chubby, "massive statue," before entertaining the notion of trafficking with the common people. Her philandering but doting alcoholic father and her neurotic, negligent mother strive to maintain a facade of integrity for Castle Temple through persistence and denial.

The pampered and cosseted dogs of earlier writing, symbols of the fox-hunting tribe's devotion to tradition, are gradually replaced by plants and flowers in later works. As costly horses and prized hounds are sold off, a certain absorption in, and fascination with, gardening fills the gap; and so Mrs. St. Clair clips roses while her world crumbles around her. Miss Aroon's attachment to a beloved homosexual brother, Hubert, and his friend Richard, whom she fantasizes to be her actual lover, shields her somewhat from reality; and her eventual inheritance of the estate enables her to control her self-created world of "normalcy."

Deformed or handicapped characters people the novel *Time after Time* (1983), which has been dubbed both comic and pathetic at once. The Swift siblings of Durraghglass, like Miss Aroon, deny realities: Jasper, a one-eyed homosexual, busies himself with his garden and his cooking; April, the deaf widow, smokes grass; May, a light-fingered spinster with a withered hand, flatters herself that the "flower ladies" live for her lectures; and Baby June, a dyslexic who has a mild crush on a young stable hand, prides herself on her physical strength and prowess at animal husbandry. It takes an intruder, the vengeful, blind Cousin Leda, alleged prisoner of a concentration camp but actually a collaborator and conniver, to force confrontations. But Keane's irony sees this defiler of the Swifts' peaceful existence (and literal defiler of "Mummie's" clothes) punished in the confines of a convent with health food fanatic Cousin April.

Keane leaves no transgressor unpunished, not even Nicandra Forrestor of *Loving and Giving* or *Queen Lear* (1988), whose childhood perverted cruelty toward a simple-minded servant's child is remembered forty years later. "Nico" of Deer Forest, product of a dysfunctional family, loses her mother to adultery, her best friend to deceit, and her husband to her best friend. The neglected eight-year-old turns into a woman capable of inducing an abortion to placate a gold-digging husband, yet incapable of recognizing his designs on her. Nicandra's epiphanies come too late, and, like the estates in many of Keane's works, her house falls into the hands of an outsider.

Molly Keane's focus on the stewardship of Anglo-Irish houses reflects her general interest in the decay of the families that once flourished in them. Her too tidy endings and obsession with characters' defects sometimes weaken her novels. Keane's real strength lies in her ability to paint a detailed picture of an Edwardian drawing room, to describe minutely seasonal changes in the garden or alterations on a dress for the Hunt Ball. With a woman's intuition, Keane properly demonstrates how a usurping female may enter a household and upset the balance of its members' lives.

MARGUERITE QUINTELLI-NEARY

WORKS: *As M. J. Farrell:* The *Knight of Cheerful Countenance.* London: Mills & Boon, 1926/ rpt., London: Virago, 1993; *Young Entry.* London: Mathews & Marrot, 1928/New York: H. Holt, [1929]. (Novel); *Taking Chances.* London: Mathews & Marrot, 1929/Philadelphia: J. B. Lippincott, 1930. (Novel); *Mad Puppetstown.* London: Collins, [1931]/New York: Farrar & Rinehart, [1932]. (Novel); *Conversation Piece.* London: Collins, 1932. (Novel); *Red Letter Days,* with Snaffles. London: Collins, [1933]/published as *Point-to-Point.* New York: Farrar & Rinehart, [1933]/redone with new introduction by Molly Keane, London: Andre Deutsch, 1987. (Hunting reminiscences); *Devoted Ladies.* London: Collins/Boston: Little, Brown, [1934]. (Novel); *Full House.* London: Collins/Boston: Little, Brown, 1935. (Novel); *The Rising Tide.* London: Collins, 1937/New York: Macmillan, 1938. (Novel); *Spring Meeting,* with John Perry. London: Collins, 1938. (Play); *Two Days in Aragon.* London: Collins, 1941. (Novel); *Ducks and Drakes.* London: Collins, 1942. (Play); *Treasure Hunt,* with John Perry. London: Collins, 1950. (Play); *Loving without Tears.* London: Collins, 1951. (Novel)/also published as *The Enchanting Witch.* New York: Crowell, [1951]; *Treasure Hunt.* London: Collins, 1951. (Novel based on the play written with Perry); *Dazzling Prospect,* with John Perry. London: Samuel French, 1961 (Play). *As Molly Keane: Good Behaviour.* London: Andre Deutsch/New York: Knopf, 1981. (Novel); *Time after Time.* London: Andre Deutsch, 1983/New York: Knopf, 1984. (Novel); *Molly Keane's Nursery Cooking.* London: Macdonald/New York: HarperCollins, 1985. (Cookbook); *Loving and Giving.* London: Andre Deutsch, 1988/also published as *Queen Lear.* London: Penguin, 1988/New York: Dutton, 1989; *Molly Keane's Ireland,* with Sally Phipps. London: HarperCollins, 1993. (Anthology). Most of Molly Keane's early novels have been republished in recent years by Virago. REFERENCES: Adams, Alice. "Coming Apart at the Seams: *Good Behaviour* as an Anti-Comedy of Manners." *Journal of Irish Literature* 20 (September 1991): 27–35; Imhof, Rüdiger. "Molly Keane: *Good Behaviour, Time after Time,* and *Loving and Giving.*" In *Ancestral Voices: The Big House in Anglo-Irish Literature.* Otto Rauchbauer, ed. Hildesheim: Georg Olms, 1992, pp. 195–203; Kreilkamp, Vera. "The Persistent Pattern: Molly Keane's Recent Big House Fiction." *Massachusetts Review* 28 (Autumn 1987): 453–460; O'Toole, Bridget. "Three Writers of the Big House: Elizabeth Bowen, Molly Keane, and Jennifer Johnston." In *Across a Roaring Hill: The Protestant Imagination in Modern Ireland.* G. Dawe & E. Longley, eds. Belfast: Blackstaff, 1985, pp. 124–138.

KEARNEY, COLBERT (1945–   ), novelist and critic. Kearney was born in Dublin on July 25, 1945. He was educated at Cambridge and is professor of English at University College, Cork. He is the grandson of Peadar Kearney,* who wrote the Irish national anthem, "The Soldier's Song," and his father was first cousin to Brendan Behan* and Seamus de Burca.* His novel, *The Consequence* (1993), tells of Fintan Kearney, a professor at University College, Cork, who finds out that his novel, *Gone the Time,* has been accepted for publication. The problem is that he cannot remember having written the book. Most of *The Consequence* concerns three figures in Kearney's life: his uncle Pearse, his teacher Eugene Watters* (Eoghan Ó Tuairisc), and Brendan Behan. Uncle Pearse and Behan get most of the comedy, while Watters is shown as a man with a loving feel for the classics, a man who jumps at the chance to share that interest with his students. In all three characters, the reader can find both the oddball relatives and the wise mentors who are a part of almost everyone's life. The book is rather like Flann O'Brien's* *At Swim-Two-Birds,* which Kearney mentions at one point, in that it seems to be a story taking place within a story, each one separate but crisscrossing at various points. Kearney sets the stage early when he recounts a story from his youth of looking at a sack with a picture of a man sitting next to a sack with a picture of a man sitting next to a sack, and so on. When he looks very closely, the lad sees nothing but the fibers that go into making up the sack. Just as from a distance those fibers make up a bag, so do the fibers of Kearney's recollections make up a story.

Kearney's chief critical work is *The Writings of Brendan Behan* (1977), and he also scripted an RTÉ program about Joyce, "Is There Anyone Who Understands Me?", which won an Emmy.

DONALD McNAMARA

WORKS: *The Writings of Brendan Behan.* Dublin: Gill & Macmillan, 1977; *The Consequence.* Belfast: Blackstaff, 1993. (Novel).

KEARNEY, PEADAR (1883–1942), song writer. Kearney, author of the Irish national anthem "The Soldier's Song," was born on December 12, 1883, and was educated by the Christian Brothers, the Capel Street Library, the theatre, and the music hall. After his father died (when Peader was just thirteen), he went to work at various blind-alley jobs to help his mother, sisters, and brothers. He joined the Irish Republican Brotherhood, the revolutionary organization, when he was twenty and began writing patriotic songs. In 1907, he wrote "The Soldier's Song," set to music by his friend Patrick Heeney. The first man to sing the song was P. J. Bourke* (1883–1932), the playwright, who was married to his sister Margaret; the song was first printed by Bulmer Hobson in 1912 in *Irish Freedom.* On the formation of the Irish Volunteers in 1914, it became their marching song. It was sung by the Republican soldiers in the Rebellion of 1916, and it became the official national anthem of the Irish Free State in 1926. Kearney was associated with the Abbey Theatre* from its first performance on December 27, 1904, first as property man and later as stage manager; he toured with the company in England in 1911 and 1916. Kearney was arrested in 1920 and interned in Ballykinlar Internment Camp, County Down, for more than a year. After the Civil War, he returned to civilian life. He had been a close friend of many of the national leaders, such as Tom Clarke and Sean McDermott who were executed in 1916, and Liam Mellowes and Michael Collins who died in the Civil War. He died on November 24, 1942, in Dublin, in comparative poverty. Apart from "The Soldier's Song," he is remembered for such songs as "The Three-Coloured Ribbon O!", "Down by the Glenside," and "Down by the Liffey Side." He was the uncle of Brendan Behan.*

SEAMUS de BURCA

WORK: *My Dear Eva: Letters Written from Ballykinlar Internment Camp (1921).* Dublin: P. J. Bourke, 1976. REFERENCE: De Burca, Seamus. *The Soldier's Song: The Story of Peadar Ó Cearnaigh.* Dublin: P. J. Bourke, 1957.

KEARNEY, RICHARD (1954–   ), critic, editor, novelist, and poet. Born in Cork, Kearney was educated at University College, Dublin, at McGill University, and at the Sorbonne. He was a cofounder and editor of *The Crane Bag** and of *The Irish Review.* He is associate professor in philosophy at University College, Dublin. In addition to his works on philosophy, Kearney has published a volume of verse, but his chief literary work is the intriguing novel *Sam's Fall* (1995). The story is largely told by a dead monk's journal, which is read by his twin brother after the funeral. The account of the boys' growing up and of the monk's growing attraction for his brother's sweetheart is quite absorbing. However, the story is equally concerned with the monk's work on a new edition of a ninth-century grammar thought to be the key to a universal language. Doubtless, the search for this elusive language is meant to parallel the difficulty of the main characters in understanding each other. Nevertheless, the twenty-five pages of appendixes about the manuscript are likely to be found a pedantic tedium by most readers.

WORKS: ed., *The Black Book: An Analysis of Third Level Education.* Dublin: Denam, 1975; ed., *Heidegger et la Question de Dieu.* Paris: Grasset, 1981; ed., *The Crane Bag Book of Irish Studies 1977–81.* Dublin: Blackwater, 1982; *Dialogues with Contemporary Continental Thinkers.* Manchester: Manchester University Press/New York: St. Martin's, 1984; *Poetique du Possible.* Paris: Beauchesnes, 1984; *Myth and Motherland.* Derry: Field Day, 1984. (Pamphlet); ed., *The Irish Mind: Exploring Intellectual Traditions.* Dublin: Wolfhound/Atlantic Highlands, N.J.: Humanities, 1985; *Modern Movements in European Philosophy.* Manchester: Manchester University Press/New York: St. Martin's, 1986; ed., *The Crane Bag Book of Irish Studies 1982–1985.* Dublin: Wolfhound/St. Paul, Minn.: Irish Books & Media, 1987; *The Wake of Imagination.* London: Hutchinson/Minneapolis: University of Minnesota Press, 1987; *Transitions: Narratives in Modern Irish Culture.* Dublin: Wolfhound/New York: St. Martin's, 1988; ed., *Across the Frontiers: Ireland in the 1990s.* Dublin: Wolfhound, 1988; *Angle of Patrick's Hill.* Dublin: Raven Arts, 1991. (Poetry) *Sam's Fall.* [London]: Sceptre, [1995]. (Novel).

KEARY, ANNIE (1825–1879), novelist. Keary was born at Bilton Rectory, near Wetherby in Yorkshire, where her father, an Irishman from Galway, was the rector. Keary wrote children's stories and adult novels. With her sister Eliza, she wrote *The Heroes of Asgard. Tales from Scandinavian Mythology* (1857). She also wrote such nonfictional works as *Early Egyptian History* (1861) and *The Nations Around* (1870), a study of the peoples bordering Israel. Her one Irish novel, *Castle Daly* (1875), was probably her best and most popular work, but actually she visited Ireland for the first time only when she was writing the book. The main action begins about 1840 and continues through the Famine and the uprising of 1848, and much of it is a perceptive study of the contrasts between the Irish and the English character. Her sister remarked that the book gave her little pleasure in its composition, but Robert Lee Wolff finds that "[n]either Victorian sentimentality . . . nor patriotic rant upsets the even-handed humanitarian view." Keary died in Eastbourne on March 3, 1879.

IRISH WORK: *Castle Daly: The Story of an Irish Home Thirty Years Ago.* 3 vols. London: Macmillan, 1875/New York & London: Garland, 1979. REFERENCES: Keary, Eliza. *Memoir of Annie Keary.* London: Macmillan, 1882/2d ed., 1883; Wolff, Robert Lee. Introduction to the Garland edition.

KEEGAN, JOHN (1809–1849), poet. Keegan was born at Laois in 1809 and was educated at a hedge-school. He wrote a great many poems for Irish periodicals such as *The Nation** and *Dolman's Magazine,* but his work was not collected until 1907. It is extremely simple public poetry, often written in the voice of a peasant speaker, but some few pieces—such as "Caoch the Piper" and "Bouchalleen Bawn"—are so simple that they escape many defects. He died of cholera in 1849 and was buried as a pauper in Glasnevin.

WORK: *Legends and Poems.* Canon O'Hanlon, ed. With a memoir by D. J. O'Donoghue. Dublin: Sealy, Bryers, & Walker, 1907.

KEERY, SAM (1930–   ), novelist. Keery was born in Belfast and emigrated to Australia in 1951 and then to England, where he now lives as a computer programmer.

WORKS: *The Last Romantic Out of Belfast.* [Belfast]: Blackstaff, [1984]; *The Streets of Laredo.* London: Jonathan Cape, [1986].

KEIGHTLEY, SIR SAMUEL ROBERT (1859–1949), novelist. Keightley was born in Belfast on January 13, 1859. He was educated privately and at Queen's College, Belfast, where he studied classics and law. He was admitted to the Irish bar in 1883 and knighted in 1912. He wrote eight historical novels, which, despite some tendency to long-windedness, have a lot of incident and some good characterization. He died in Dublin on August 14, 1949.

WORKS: *A King's Daughter and Other Poems.* Belfast: M'Caw, Stevenson, & Orr, 1888; *The Crimson Sign.* London: Hutchinson, 1894; *The Cavaliers.* London: Hutchinson, 1895; *The Last Recruit of Clare's.* New York: Harper/London: Hutchinson, 1897; *Heronford.* London: C. A. Pearson, 1899; *A Man of Millions.* London: Cassell, 1901; *The Pikemen.* London: Hutchinson, 1903; *Barnaby's Bridal.* London: John Long, 1906; *A Beggar on Horseback.* London: John Long, 1906.

KEILY, TONY

WORK: *The Shark Joke.* Dublin: Martello, 1995. (Novella).

KELL, RICHARD (1927–   ), poet. Kell was born in County Cork and, after an early childhood in India, was educated in Belfast and Dublin. In 1983, he retired from a senior lectureship in English literature to devote more time to writing. As a composer, he has had works performed by several orchestras, chamber groups, and soloists. A widower with two sons and two daughters, he lives in Newcastle upon Tyne.

Kell is among the most technically proficient of contemporary Irish poets. He is easily capable of writing the free verse that Irish poets nowadays inevitably use, but he is much more interesting for his wide variety of very controlled rhythms and rhyme patterns. His command of form and the effect he can get from it may be seen, for instance, in the superbly tight conclusion of "The Burning Crate." In other poems, his patterns are more complex. "Deficient Course," for instance, is in four, six-line stanzas with a rhyme scheme of ABCABC. The meter is iambic with the first, third, and fifth lines being five stress, the second four, and the fourth and sixth three. This is a difficult pattern to maintain; but, having established it, Kell, unlike many of his Irish colleagues, keeps to it. In some poems, he will use assonance, as in the six-stanza iambic trimeter "Nothing Left," which has the sound pattern of ABBA, or in "A Dream of Marriage," which is basically in iambic pentameter and has the assonantal sound pattern of ABAB. More playful and tricky is "The Butterfly

Effect,'' which has seven stanzas, the first being one line, the second two, and so on until the seven-line seventh. However, as the lines of each stanza increase, so also do the line lengths—from three syllables in the first line to an extraordinary twenty-four-syllable last one. Poem after poem is so formally successful in very different patterns that Kell appears utterly a virtuoso. He does not have to follow Yeats's* exordium to learn his trade; he knows it.

His diction is equally eclectic. ''Conversation in a City Pub'' successfully incorporates dialogue like:

''You're right, m'n! It's the same fuckin story every time y' gan t' the fuckin garage!''

''Star Quality'' uses, with a satirist's ear, that ubiquitous public speech of minimal vocabulary and vague content and begins, ''it's kinda like y know.'' At the other extreme, ''The Victims'' succeeds in actually incorporating stanzas from Herbert and Hopkins. Elsewhere, particularly in the sexual poems of an aging man, he finely combines an easy, fluent, contemporary conversational voice within a firmly established metrical pattern. His images are crisp and new. In ''The Neighbourhood,'' a terrace of houses is described as ''porridge brown,'' and in the same poem ''a chunky hedge'' is ''trim as a diplomat's moustache.''

In content and tone, the poems range from the witty to the sad, from the dramatic to the reflective to the epigrammatic. His more recent books, *In Praise of Warmth* (1987) and *Rock and Water* (1993), are, for a poet's slim volumes, quite fat, at ninety or so pages each. The perhaps 200 poems in them contain a surprising amount of solid successes, and many demand and repay a close re-reading. Much criticism of recent Irish poetry sounds as if it were written for a book blurb. In Kell's case, a critic's enthusiasm is hardly puffery. He is not in Aosdána* and was not even mentioned in *The Field Day Anthology,* but Kell is as good as any Irish poet writing today and considerably better than several with much bigger reputations.

WORKS: [*Poems*]. Swinford: Fantasy, 1957. (Poetry pamphlet); *Control Tower.* London: Chatto & Windus, Hogarth, 1962; *Differences.* London: Chatto & Windus, Hogarth, 1969; *Humours.* Sunderland: Ceolfrith, 1978. (Poetry pamphlet); *Heartwood.* Newcastle upon Tyne: Northern House, 1978. (Poetry pamphlet); *The Broken Circle.* Sunderland: Ceolfrith, 1981; *In Praise of Warmth: New and Selected Poems.* [Dublin]: Dedalus, [1987]; *Rock and Water.* [Dublin]: Dedalus, [1993].

KELLEHER, D[ANIEL] L[AURENCE] (1883–1958), travel writer and poet. Kelleher was born in Cork and educated by the Christian Brothers and at University College, Cork. His elder brother Stephen had a brilliant career as a mathematician, eventually becoming a fellow of Trinity, which cast a shadow over Kelleher's more modest aims. However, he edited the college paper, *Q.C.C.,* refounded the Philosophical and Literary Society, and graduated with distinction in 1905, after which he worked as a teacher in Liverpool and Dublin.

On March 11, 1909, his one-act play, *Stephen Grey,* was produced at the Abbey,* and in 1911 he published for himself a small volume of poems in

Liverpool. He also wrote travel articles and in 1913 was asked by George Lunn to write a book about Paris. He moved on to working as a tour guide for Lunn and also wrote guides to Continental resorts for him. He traveled extensively in France, Switzerland, and Italy, and his special love was for the small towns and villages. In 1944, asked about his finest holiday memory, he said that "holidays like every other day are memorable by trifles rather than by ponderosities." This was his philosophy in brief.

He created a series of distinctive books about aspects of Ireland that enjoyed great popularity between the wars. His forte was for the brief evocative essay, charmingly and vividly bringing alive a persona or moment of the past. He was a small man with a warm glint in his eyes, whose shyness hid from all but those who knew him well a keen sense of humor. He died, after a short illness, in a Dublin hospital on March 6, 1958.

PETER COSTELLO

WORKS: *Poems 12 a Penny*. Liverpool: Published by the Author, 1911; *Paris: Its Glamour and Life*. London: George Lunn Travel Books, 1914/rev. 1930; *Lake Geneva*. London: George Lunn Travel Books, 1914; *The Glamour of Dublin*. Dublin: Talbot, 1918/London: T. Fisher Unwin, 1919/ 3d ed., with etchings by Estella Solomons, 1928; *The Glamour of Cork*. Dublin & Cork: Talbot, 1919; *The Glamour of Manchester*. Manchester: Manchester National, 1920; *A Poet Passes*. London: Ernest Benn, 1922. (Shilling Books of New Verse, No. 2); *The Lovelight of Ireland*. Dublin: Talbot, 1922; *Round Italy—Milan, Florence, Naples, Rome, Venice*. London: George Lunn, 1923/2d ed. 1925; *Twelve Poems*. Cork: Privately printed, 1923; "Her Dowry." *Dublin Magazine* 1 (1924): 815–821. (One-act play); *Padna. The Story of a Corn-porter*. 1924; *The Environs of Lucerne and Lugano*. London: George Lunn, 1926; ed., *Christmas Carols*. London: Ernest Benn, 1927. (Augustan Books of English Poetry, No. 18); ed., *An Anthology of Christmas Prose & Verse*. London: Cresset, 1928; *The Glamour of the West—Bantry Bay to Lough Foyle*. Dublin: Talbot, 1928; *The Glamour of the South*. Dublin: Talbot, 1929; *Great Days with O'Connell*. Dublin: Talbot, 1929; *Ireland of the Welcomes*. Dublin: Irish Tourist Association, 1929/ed. ed., 1948; *Biarritz, the Basque Country and Lourdes*. London: George Lunn, 1930; *It's Ireland*. Dublin: Irish Tourist Association, 1932; *Padna, a Regional Love Story*. Dublin, 1938.

KELLY, HUGH (1739–1778), playwright and journalist. Born in Killarney in 1739, Hugh Kelly was raised and educated in Dublin, where his father became a publican following the loss of his estate. Kelly had no higher education, but, during his apprenticeship as a staymaker, he frequented the theatre and became friendly with actors. He moved to London when he was twenty-one, at first working as a staymaker and then as a scrivener to a lawyer. He soon became an industrious hack writer, editing in succession three magazines, *The Court Magazine, The Ladies' Museum,* and *The Public Ledger*. He contributed a regular column to *Owen's Weekly Chronicle* which he published anonymously as *The Babbler* in 1767. In 1766 and 1767, he established himself as a theatrical commentator with two long works, written in heroic couplets, called *Thespis: or, A Critical Examination into the Merits of All the Principal Performers Belonging to Drury Lane Theatre and Covent Garden Theatre*. In the first, he praised Garrick but attacked the other actors "with a ruffian cruelty," which he subsequently toned down. Neither of these forestalled the performers of both theatres from acting in his plays, and Kelly in several prefaces was effusive over the acting his plays received in what was evidently a series of well-mounted productions. In 1767, he also published a novel, *Memoirs of a Magdalen*, which is sentimental and reformist in tone.

In 1768, encouraged by Garrick, Kelly wrote *False Delicacy*, which Garrick wrote the prologue for and produced at Drury Lane in September. It was presented as competition to Goldsmith's* *The Good Natured Man*, which opened six nights later at Covent Garden. While everyone now prefers the Goldsmith play, *False Delicacy* ran for eight nights, was acted often throughout the season, became a standard in provincial repertories, and earned Kelly £700 from its first two editions. A comedy of intrigue and sentiment, it revolves around lovers who are too refined to express themselves directly and are thus trapped into arranged courtships. As Dr. Johnson said, it is ''totally devoid of character.'' Kelly was a sentimentalist and a moralist. The denouement depends on the unlikely reformation of the rake and on the candor of characters not too falsely delicate but not involved in the plot either. The success of the play led to an incident in which Kelly insulted Goldsmith; although the two never spoke again, Kelly was seen crying openly at Goldsmith's funeral.

Kelly's second play, *A Word to the Wise*, caused a theatrical furor at its production at Drury Lane on March 3, 1770. Kelly, a supporter of Lord North's ministry and a suspected hireling, attracted the scorn of the followers of John Wilkes. They catcalled and shouted loudly enough for two nights to prevent its performance, while Garrick tried vainly to quiet the house. Kelly defended his politics in a long preface to the printed version of *A Word to the Wise*, in which he bitterly described the fate of playwrights of his time, dependent on audience approval but condemned without a hearing. *A Word to the Wise* was produced after Kelly's death on a benefit night for his widow. For this production Dr. Johnson wrote a prologue that begins:

> This night presents a play, which public rage
> Or right or wrong, once hooted from the stage:
> From zeal or malice, now no more we dread,
> For English vengeance wars not with the dead.

The play itself is stronger in plot and comic situations than *False Delicacy*, although its besetting weaknesses, as in all of Kelly's plays, are sentimentality in language and an unlikely plot resolution.

Inspired by his friends' notion ''that his genius excelled in the sentimental and pathetic,'' Kelly next wrote a blank verse tragedy, *Clemantina* (produced at Covent Garden, 1771), that has all the earmarks of the sterile tragedy of the time: artificial situations and an implausible resolution of the plot, caused by adherence to the three unities, and operatically rhetorical language. He deals with two of his favorite themes: the tyrannical father who blindly misarranges a marriage for his daughter, and true lovers blighted by society from admitting their love. Kelly returned to comedy with *The School for Wives* in 1773, a play not derived from Molière. It is his most complicated play in its diversity of characters and situations, which take a very long fifth act to unravel.

Kelly wrote two more plays, the two-act farce *The Romance of an Hour* (1774) and *The Man of Reason* (1776). The last failed at Covent Garden, was never printed, and ended his theatrical career. He was called to the bar in 1774— with what success is disputed. He died on February 2, 1778, at the age of thirty-eight, as the result of excessive drinking (according to the *Dictionary of National Biography*) or an abscess (according to his anonymous biographer).

While Kelly, like Arthur Murphy,* immersed himself in English life, he openly defended the Irish, especially by attacking the Stage Irishman. He created the sympathetic, peacemaking character of Connolly, complete with a brogue, in *A School for Wives* ''to remove the imputation for barbarous ferocity'' which the Irish had gained. In his epilogue, which was intended to have been spoken by the character of Sir Callaghan O'Brallaghan in Macklin's farce *Love à la Mode*, he lectures the English audience for scorning the Irish, celebrates Irish accomplishments, and compares the Irish and the English as ''the equal heirs of liberty and fame.''

SVEN ERIC MOLIN

WORKS: *Thespis: or, A Critical Examination into the Merits of All the Principal Performers Belonging to Drury Lane Theatre*. 2 vols. London, 1766–1767. (Verse critique); *Memoirs of a Magdalen; or, The History of Louisa Mildmay*. 2 vols. 2d ed., London: W. Griffin/Dublin: P. Wilson, 1767. (Novel); *The Works of Hugh Kelly, to Which Is Prefixed the Life of the Author. . . .* London: Printed for the Author's Widow, 1778. Contains the plays *False Delicacy* (1768), *A Word to the Wise* (1770), *Clementina* (1771), *The School for Wives* (1774) and *The Romance of an Hour* (1774), as well as both parts of *Thespis* and various fugitive pieces. There is a modern reprinting of *False Delicacy* in *Plays of the Restoration and Eighteenth Century*. Dougald MacMillan & Howard Mumford Jones, eds. New York: Henry Holt, 1931, pp. 717–745. There is also a modern reprint edition, *The Plays of Hugh Kelly*. Larry Carver, ed. New York: Garland, 1980. REFERENCES: Short critical assessments may be found in Bernbaum, Ernest. *The Drama of Sensibility*. Gloucester, Mass.: Peter Smith, 1958, pp. 226–248; Kavanagh, Peter. *The Irish Theatre*. Tralee: Kerryman, 1946, pp. 329–336; Rawson, C. J. ''Some Remarks on Eighteenth Century 'Delicacy,' with a note on Hugh Kelly's *False Delicacy*.'' *JEGP* 61 (1962). See also Jean-Michel's *L'oeuvre de Hugh Kelly 1739–1777*. 2 vols. Lille: Atelier National de Reproduction de Thèses, 1984.

KELLY, JAMES PLUNKETT. *See* PLUNKETT, JAMES.

KELLY, JOHN (1965–   ), novelist. Born in Enniskillen.

WORK: *Grace Notes and Bad Thoughts*. Dublin: Martello, 1994.

KELLY, JOHN M. (1931–1991), novelist, authority on constitutional law, and politician. Kelly was born in Dublin in August 1931. He was educated at Glenstal Abbey, County Limerick, and later at University College, Dublin, where he received an M.A., Oxford where he received a B.Litt., an M.A., and a D.C.L., Heidelberg University, and King's Inns, Dublin. He practiced at the Irish bar from 1957 to 1962, was a fellow and lecturer in law at Trinity College, Dublin, from 1961 to 1965, and a professor of jurisprudence and Roman law at Uni-

versity College, Dublin, from 1965. His important legal publications included *Princeps Index* (Weimar, 1957), *Fundamental Rights in the Irish Law and Constitution* (Oxford, 1975), and *Studies in the Civil Judicature of the Roman Republic* (Oxford, 1976). He served in the Irish Senate from 1969 to 1973 and was elected to the Dail in 1973 as a Fine Gael T.D. He held many important posts in government, among them minister for industry, commerce and tourism, parliamentary secretary to the prime minister, attorney general, and, briefly, minister of foreign affairs. He was considered and able and sometimes acerbic political debater, calling Charles Haughey ''an economic Mussolini'' and Brian Lenihan ''the Bismarck of the lobster pots.'' A collection of his political speeches and articles was posthumously published under the title of *Belling the Cats* (1992). In April 1982, he retired from the Fine Gael front bench, deploring a further liaison with the Labour Party and arguing for a reconciliation with Fianna Fail. A Fine Gael description of his political stance remarks, ''John Kelly has been seen as an old-fashioned devotee of self-help and of small business enterprise. He was indeed wont to call for a renewal of the principles of Arthur Griffith* in Fine Gael.''

Kelly published his first novel, *Matters of Honour* (1964), under the pseudonym of John Brophy. The book is a cleanly written and excellently realized account of an Irish student's life in Heidelberg, where Kelly himself studied. It is mainly concerned with a love affair that breaks off when the girl asks if the student loves her and wants to marry her, and he is distinctly taken aback. The description of the giddiness of love and the anguish after the breakup will strike many readers with its authenticity. Much of the rest of the novel draws with clarity other students and colleagues at the university. The novel's chief weakness is the conclusion, in which Kelly attempts to get some tension out of twists of the plot—whether the student will desert the girlfriend again or take her to Ireland—but the climax is rather botched, if not avoided. *The Polling of the Dead* (1993) is a political thriller that Kelly wrote in the late 1960s and that was published only posthumously. It is thoroughly well crafted and readable.

PRINCIPAL WORKS: *Matters of Honour*. London: Hutchinson, [1964]. (Novel); *Belling the Cats: Selected Speeches and Articles of John Kelly*. John Fanagan, ed. Dublin: Moytura, [1992]; *The Polling of the Dead*. Dublin: Moytura, [1993]. (Novel); *The Irish Constitution*. 3d ed, revised by Gerard Hogan & Gerry Whyte. Dublin: Butterworth's, 1994.

KELLY, MAEVE (1930–   ), novelist, short story writer, and poet. Kelly was born in County Clare and educated in Dundalk, County Louth. She trained as a nurse in London, going on to Oxford to do postgraduate work. She now lives in Limerick and has been involved with various women's and social organizations. In 1972, she won the Hennessy Award for her short story ''A Life of Her Own,'' which was published in 1976 in a volume of short stories with that title. Many of these stories have been republished in *Orange Horses* of 1991.

Maeve Kelly writes mainly about women, often women caught in all kinds of deadening situations—those trapped and tyrannized by the land, by poverty, by conventional roles, by insensitive brothers, husbands, mothers, societies. Many of her characters are bitter and frustrated, having stored up years of repressed injustice, like the sisters in "The False God" or the old woman in "Amnesty." Those who get an involuntary glimpse of freedom, like Mary Murphy in "The Vain Woman," are overpowered by their own sense of guilt and the guilt that a conventional patriarchal society lays on them.

The novel *Necessary Treasons* (1985) follows the fortunes and, more importantly, the changes in consciousness of her young heroine, Eva Gleeson. When the story begins, Eva, just recently engaged to Hugh, some years her senior, is staying in County Clare with his unmarried sisters, women who have barricaded themselves against change. As the novel progresses, Eva undergoes a process of inner development that encourages her to question the roles she plays, or may be expected to play, and the values she holds.

Florrie's Girls (1991) refers to the life of a student nurse with all of its pain and satisfaction, while *Alice in Thunderland* (1993) is described as a "modern feminist fairytale."

Maeve Kelly writes with feeling and conviction. Her prose is strong and evocative. Her short stories, in particular, create their atmosphere through an economical use of description and telling detail. She writes with insight and compassion, sometimes with anger, and is at her best when she has put aside the didactic statement.

MARY BALL

WORKS: *A Life of Her Own.* Dublin: Poolbeg, 1976. (Short stories); *Necessary Treasons.* London: Michael Joseph, 1985. (Novel); *Resolution.* Belfast: Blackstaff, 1986. (Poetry); *Orange Horses.* Belfast: Blackstaff, 1991. (Short stories); *Florrie's Girls.* Belfast: Blackstaff, 1991. (Novel); *Alice in Thunderland.* Dublin: Attic, 1993. (Novel).

KELLY, MARY EVA (ca. 1825–1910), poet. Mary Eva (or sometimes Eva Mary) Kelly was born in Headford, County Galway. The Kellys were landed gentry and Unionist. She was educated at home by a series of governesses, one of whom encouraged her love of literature. An extended visit in 1849 to her nationalistic uncle, Martin O'Flaherty, established Kelly's own political beliefs, and she began writing patriotic verses for *The Nation.** She published under several pseudonyms before settling on "Eva." She, along with "Speranza" (Lady Wilde*), "Mary" (Ellen Mary Patrick Downing*), and "Brigid" (Katharine Murphy*), formed the female nucleus of *The Nation's* patriotic women poets. Her political verses are fervent and sincere, and she excelled at commemorative pieces.

Kelly was engaged to Kevin Izod O'Doherty when he was arrested for his connection with the 1848 Rising. O'Doherty was privately offered a pardon in return for a public confession, but the couple decided to refuse the offer. He was exiled to Van Diemen's Land, but they were married after his early release in 1854. His release stipulated that he live outside Ireland, so they settled in Paris and subsequently emigrated to Brisbane, Australia. There he was elected to the Legislative Assembly of Queensland. Returning to Ireland in 1886, he was elected a representative for County Meath. Due to O'Doherty's failing health, they returned to Brisbane, where he died in 1905. She died in May 1910 and is buried in Toowong Cemetery, Brisbane.

ANNE COLMAN

WORK: *Poems, by "Eva" of The Nation.* San Francisco: Thomas, 1877/Dublin: M. H. Gill, 1909. REFERENCES: Dillon, P. J. "Eva of the *Nation.*" *Capuchin Annual* (1933): 261–266; "Irish Literary Celebrities, No. 5: Mary Izod O'Doherty." *Nation* (December 8, 1888): 3; McCarthy, Justin. Biographical Sketch in *Poems.* Dublin edition; Obituary. *Irish Book Lover* 2 (July 1910): 163.

KELLY, MICHAEL (1764?–1826), memoirist, composer, and singer. Kelly was born in Dublin, studied music in Italy, and sang at the Vienna Opera. Mozart trained him for Basilio in the first performance of *Le Nozzi di Figaro*. In 1787, he returned to England, where he sang, acted, and wrote songs and also airs and overtures to many plays. His *Reminiscences* (1826), although ghostwritten by Theodore Hook, offers fascinating glimpses of the theater of the day. As he served as musical director for Drury Lane, he is particularly interesting about the vagaries of its manager, Richard Brinsley Sheridan.* He died on October 9, 1826.

LITERARY WORK: *Reminiscences of Michael Kelly . . .* 2d ed. 2 vols. London: Henry Colburn, 1826.

KELLY, RITA (1953–   ), poet and short story writer. A writer in English and Irish, Kelly was born in Galway and educated in Ballinasloe, County Galway. In 1975, she won the Merriman Poetry Award; in 1980, she won the Sean O'Riordain Memorial Prize for Poetry; in 1985, she received an Arts Council Bursary. She has lived in Enniscorthy, County Wexford, where she worked in the forestry business, and in New York. She was married to the late Eoghan Ó Tuairisc (Eugene Watters*).

The Whispering Arch (1986) is a slim collection of distinctive stories and sketches with a wide range of central women characters—a postulant in a convent, a young wife and mother, two lesbian lovers. Among the better pieces are "Trousseau," about an insensitive mother superior helping a sensitive postulant to buy underwear, and the more dramatized "The Cobweb Curtain," about a meeting of two young women, once school friends, who now have little to say to each other. The shorter sketches have some rather pretentious writing:

She was so much in control of the process [of driving] that her eyes could be divorced from it for inordinate periods, float disjunct, and be the only real portent of her interiority.

In others, she verges on the precious with much static use of sentence fragments and expressive, rather than conventional, punctuation. For instance, one of many examples is this bit describing a station after the train has left:

The withdrawing rumble allowing the silence to settle back, swathing the station, the isolation, the pathetic insignificance—left like a toy in a field, suffering the child's forgetfulness, the dusk and the dewdrops, rusting a little, disturbing really, a persistent memory, unrecognized.

Her poems in English, including some translations of her Irish poems, were collected in *Fare Well: Beir Beannacht* (1990). They are generally written in a spare, unadorned style. Possibly her strongest piece is the long "The Patriarch," with its horrendous description about how the speaker's butcher father made her aid him in slaughtering animals and also about his own animal helplessness as he nears death. The piece has a simple descriptive power, but if the lines had been justified at the right-hand margin, they would be indistinguishable from prose.

WORKS: With Eoghan Ó Tuairisc, *Dialann sa Díseart.* Baile Atha Cliath: Coiscéim, 1981. (Poetry); *An Bealach Eadóigh.* Baile Atha Cliath: Coiscéim, 1984. (Poetry); *The Whispering Arch and Other Stories.* [Dublin]: Arlen House, [1986]; *Fare Well: Beir Beannacht.* [Dublin]: Attic, [1990]. (Poetry in English and Irish).

KENEALY, EDWARD VAUGHAN (1819–1880), politician, lawyer, journalist, and poet. Kenealy was born in Cork on July 2, 1819. He was educated at Trinity College, Dublin, and called to the Irish bar in 1840 and to the English bar in 1847. He was imprisoned for a month in 1850 for cruelty to his six-year-old natural son. He was the leading counsel for the Tichborne claimant in 1873 and conducted the defense so violently and lengthily that he was disbarred. He was MP for Stoke from 1875 to 1880. He was a prolific poet and translator from many languages, including Irish. He died in London on April 16, 1880.

PRINCIPAL WORKS: *Poems and Translations.* London: Reeves & Turner, 1864; *The Poetical Works of Edward Vaughan Kenealy.* 3 vols. London: *Englishman* Office, 1875–1879. REFERENCES: Anon. "Edward Vaughan Kenealy." *Irish Book Lover* 11 (1919): 3–6; Kenealy, Arabella. *Memoirs of Edward Vaughan Kenealy.* London: Long, 1908.

KENNEDY, ANNE poet. She has lived in Galway since 1977, but was born in America.

WORK: *The Dog Kubla Dreams My Life.* Galway: Salmon, 1994.

KENNEDY, PATRICK (1801–1873), folklorist. Kennedy was born in County Wexford and educated by the Carew family. In 1823, he became assistant in the Kildare Place training school in Dublin. Presently, he opened a bookshop and lending library in Anglesea Street, where he lived until his death on March 28, 1873. His retold tales are fluent, somewhat colloquial, and entertaining. Douglas Hyde,* however, thought that "many of the stories appear to be the detritus of genuine Gaelic folk stories filtered through an English idiom—and much impaired and stunted in the process." Patrick Rafroidi, on the other hand, thought that Kennedy shares pride of place among nineteenth-century Irish folklorists with T. Crofton Croker.*

WORKS: *Legends of Mount Leinster.* Dublin: Patrick Kennedy, 1855; *Fictions of Our Forefathers.* . . . Dublin: McGlashan & Gill, 1859; *Legendary Fictions of the Irish Celts.* London: Macmillan, 1866; *The Banks of the Boro: A Chronicle of the County of Wexford.* Dublin: McGlashan & Gill, 1867; *Evenings in the Duffrey.* Dublin: McGlashan & Gill, 1869; *The Fireside Stories of Ireland.* Dublin: McGlashan & Gill, 1870; *The Bardic Stories of Ireland.* Dublin: McGlashan & Gill, 1871; *The Book of Modern Irish Anecdotes.* London: Routledge, ca. 1872. REFERENCE: Delaney, James. "Patrick Kennedy." *Past* 7 (1964): 9–87.

KENNELLY, [TIMOTHY] BRENDAN (1936–   ), poet and critic. Kennelly, professor of modern literature at Trinity College, Dublin, since 1973, was born in Ballylongford, County Kerry, on April 17, 1936 (his parents being a publican and a nurse), and educated at St. Ita's in Tarbert, at Trinity College, Dublin, and at Leeds University, obtaining a Ph.D. in 1966 for a dissertation on "Modern Irish Poetry and the Irish Epic." He is one of the foremost contemporary Irish poets, with a firmly based international reputation, and has become respected as a vigorous and perceptive critic, an energetic playwright, and a prolific broadcaster.

Kennelly has been consistently focused as a poet on the way the past continually reemerges in the modern world, through language, events, and affections. Committed to the craft of writing, which he sees as a vocation of self-discovery, he believes that "we should have the courage to be faithful to our relatively few moments of intensity." Kennelly has always courted the danger of over-expression and oversimplification, seeing poetry as a continual reflection on phenomena with which his imagination must engage.

> Though we live in a world that dreams of ending
> That always seems about to give in,
> Something that will not acknowledge conclusion
> Insists that we for ever begin. ("Begin")

The plethora and unevenness of his early work, the immense scale of conception and execution of his largest and most recent work, *The Book of Judas* (1991), and the verbal torrent of the writing in his plays such as *The Trojan Women* belie the fact that his twin claims to serious attention, by both critics and his fellow poets, rest chiefly on his mastery—and subversion—of the sonnet form, which he has placed at the service of his characteristic humor, compassion, and rage for justice and on his personal style, in which his work is informed by the rhythms, syntax, and vocabularies of his native townland: "[B]ehind everything I write is the story/ballad culture of my youth."

If we disregard a hesitant and unconvincing start as a novelist with *The Crooked Cross* (1963), a series of vignettes of village life, and the less well conceived *The Florentines* (1967), where an Irish adolescent encounters the English university, Kennelly first commanded attention with *My Dark Fathers* (1964), of which the title poem has become his best-known and perhaps most effective single piece. (He was awarded the AE* Memorial Prize for Poetry in 1967.) As a lyricist, he has progressed steadily with collections such as *Love*

Cry (1972), *A Kind of Trust* (1975), and *Islandman* (1977), mapping out a personal and communal terrain of the affections. Poems such as "Love Cry" and "The Swimmer" celebrate the congruence of nature and sexuality, while others like "The Stammer" and "The Blind Man" testify to his sense of pathos. His work is increasingly populated by living presences urgent to be voiced; recently, these have become more monstrous and dismaying, as Kennelly has explored the inequity, mendacity, and deviousness that reside in history and in the individual psyche. This achievement he calls "being-at-home-in-strangeness."

Moloney Up and At It (1965/1985) established the irreverence in the face of ancient pieties necessary for the poet to address the nightmares of history and conscience in *Cromwell* (1983–1987) and *The Book of Judas,* where he immersed himself in the most hated and reviled figures in the Irish and Christian calendars. *Cromwell* (which takes place entirely in the head of the Irishman Buffún) in particular unleashed a heated debate about the poet's view of Irish history, which tended to overshadow the larger issues of truthfulness to self and respect of, and for, others:

> I hate and fear you like the thought of hell.
> The murderous syllables of your name
> Are the foundations of my nightmare.
> I can never hate you enough. That is my shame.

Meanwhile, the sequence *A Girl* (commissioned in 1978 by RTÉ to be set to music by Seoirse Bodley) focused his energies on Irish womanhood, an impulse that has subsequently been channeled into four plays, *Antigone* produced in 1986, *Medea* in 1988, *Blood Wedding* (written in 1990 but as of yet unperformed), and *The Trojan Women* produced in 1993, all of which give voice to the "rage for a new order" and to the need of Irish men and women to engage imaginatively and psychically with one another:

> what man
> Knows anything of women?
> If he did
> He would change from being a man
> As men recognise a man. (*Antigone*)

Recently, Kennelly has participated in translation projects, which have seen his imagination coming full circle, as expressed in the opening stanza of "Santorini":

> In this volcanic, dreaming place
> Six Greek poets
> Resurrect my mother's face
> And set my father dancing again
> As if death had never happened.

As a critic, Kennelly has entered into debate about the status and purpose of poetry, which he sees as having a defining role in the modern world. Urging a sense of responsibility, he has condemned the "pedestellisation of mindlessness" and "thoughtless reaction." His trenchant essays, including the lecture "Poetry and Violence" and a revelatory view of Yeats,* "An Experiment in Living," are contained in his selected prose, *Journey into Joy* (1994).

RICHARD PINE

WORKS: *Cast a Cold Eye,* with Rudi Holzapfel. [Dublin]: Dolmen, [1959]; *The Rain, the Moon,* with Rudi Holzapfel. [Dublin]: Dolmen, 1961; *The Dark about Our Loves,* with Rudi Holzapfel. Dublin: Printed by John Augustine, [1962]; *Green Townlands,* with Rudi Holzapfel. Leeds: University Bibliographical, 1963; *Let Fall No Burning Leaf.* Dublin: New Square, 1963; *The Crooked Cross.* Dublin: Figgis, 1963/Dublin: Moytura, 1989. (Novel); *My Dark Fathers.* Dublin: New Square, 1964; *Up and At It.* Dublin: New Square, 1965/revised as *Moloney Up and At It.* Cork: Mercier, 1984; *Collection One: Getting Up Early.* Dublin: Figgis, 1966; *The Florentines.* Dublin: Figgis, 1967. (Novel); *Good Souls to Survive.* Dublin: Figgis, 1967; *Dream of a Black Fox.* Dublin: Figgis, 1968; *Selected Poems.* Dublin: Figgis, 1969/enlarged edition. New York: Dutton, 1971; *A Drinking Cup: Poems from the Irish.* Dublin: Figgis, 1970; ed., *The Penguin Book of Irish Verse.* [Harmondsworth, Middlesex]: Penguin, [1970]/2d ed. [London]: Penguin, [1981]; *Bread.* Dublin: Tara Telephone, 1971; *Love Cry.* Dublin: Figgis, 1972; *Salvation, the Stranger.* Dublin: Tara Telephone, 1972; *The Voices.* Dublin: Gallery, 1973; *Shelley in Dublin.* [Dun Laoire]: Anna Livia, [1974]/rpt. Dublin: Egotist, 1977/revised. Dublin: Beaver Row, 1982; *A Kind of Trust.* [Dublin]: Gallery, [1975]; *New and Selected Poems.* Peter Fallon, ed. Dublin: Gallery, 1976; *Islandman.* [Clondalkin, Co. Dublin]: Profile, [1977]; *The Visitor.* [Portmarnock, Co. Dublin]: St. Bueno's Handprinted Limited Editions, [1978]; *A Girl.* RTÉ commission, 1978/recording published. Dublin: Gael-Linn, 1981; *A Small Light.* Dublin: Gallery, 1979; *In Spite of the Wise.* Dublin: Trinity Closet, 1979. (Also entitled *Evasions*); *The Boats Are Home.* Dublin: Gallery, 1980; *The House That Jack Didn't Build.* Dublin: Beaver Row, 1982; *Cromwell: A Poem.* Dublin: Beaver Row, 1983/corrected ed. Newcastle upon Tyne: Bloodaxe, 1987; *Real Ireland.* Belfast: Appletree, 1984. (Text accompanied by photographs by Liam Blake); *Selected Poems.* Kevin Byrne, ed. Dublin: Kerrymount, 1985; ed. *Ireland Past and Present.* London: Multimedia, 1985; *Mary: From the Irish.* Dublin: Aisling, 1987; ed. *Landmarks of Irish Drama.* London: Methuen, 1988; *Love of Ireland: Poems from the Irish.* Cork: Mercier, 1989; *A Time for Voices: Selected Poems 1960–1990.* Newcastle upon Tyne: Bloodaxe, 1990; *Medea.* Newcastle upon Tyne: Bloodaxe, 1991. (Play); *The Book of Judas: A Poem.* Newcastle upon Tyne: Bloodaxe, 1991; *Breathing Spaces: Early Poems.* Newcastle upon Tyne: Bloodaxe, 1992; ed., with A. Norman Jeffares. *Joycechoice: The Poems in Verse and Prose of James Joyce.* Schull: Roberts Rinehart, 1992; ed., with Terence Brown. *Irish Prose Writings: Swift to the Literary Renaissance.* Tokyo: Hon-No Tomasha, 1992; ed. *Between Innocence and Peace: Favourite Poems of Ireland.* Cork: Mercier, 1993; *The Trojan Women.* [Newcastle upon Tyne]: Bloodaxe, [1993]. (Play); ed., with Katie Donovan. *Dublines.* [Newcastle upon Tyne]: Bloodaxe, [1996]; ed., with Katie Donovan & A. Norman Jeffares. *Ireland's Women: Writings Past and Present.* Dublin: Gill & Macmillan, 1994; *Journey into Joy: Selected Prose.* Åke Persson, ed. [Newcastle upon Tyne]: Bloodaxe, 1994; *Poetry My Arse.* [Newcastle upon Tyne]: Bloodaxe, [1995]; *Antigone* [Newcastle upon Tyne]: Bloodaxe (1996); *Blood Wedding* [Newcastle upon Tyne]: Bloodaxe (1996). REFERENCES: "Brendan Kennelly: Q&A with Richard Pine." *Irish Literary Supplement* 9 (1990); "Writer in Profile." RTE Television, transmitted May 26, 1993; Richard Pine, ed. *Dark Fathers into Light: Brendan Kennelly.* [Newcastle upon Tyne]: Bloodaxe, [1994].

ÅKE PERSSON

KENNEY, JAMES (1780–1849), playwright. Kenney's family moved from Ireland about 1800, and in 1803 he made a great success when his farce *Raising the Wind* was staged at Covent Garden. A long succession of farces, burlettas, comedies, and musical dramas followed, and Allardyce Nicoll credits him with more than fifty pieces. His work has proved ephemeral, although Byron was a trifle harsh in remarking in *English Bards and Scotch Reviewers:*

> Kenney's "World"—Ah, where is Kenney's wit?
> Tires the sad gallery, lulls the listless pit.

Kenney assuredly had some wit, for he was a frequent guest at Samuel Rogers' breakfasts and dinners. His only piece of Irish interest was the comedy *The Irish Ambassador* with a production date of 1831, but it would require a production of some brilliance to make it work today. He died in Brompton on July 25, 1849.

Kenney's witty son, Charles Lamb Kenney, was a schoolmate of Boucicault* and collaborated with him on the one-act farce *Up the Flue* (1846).

WORK: *The Irish Ambassador.* New York: Samuel French, [1860?]/London, [1888?]. Dick's Standard Plays, No. 733. (Two-act comedy).

KENNY, ADRIAN (1945–   ), fiction writer and travel writer. Kenny was born in Dublin, where his prosperous family ran a prominent chain of shoe shops. He was educated by the Jesuits at Gonzaga College, a school with a strong literary aspect, and at University College, Dublin. Though he trained as a tax-idermist, he has worked largely as a teacher, both in Ireland and abroad, especially in Turkey. A slow and careful writer, artistically (though not commercially) ambitious, his inspiration is largely autobiographical with an edge of the mysterious and philosophical. An interesting writer of the same generation as Neil Jordan* and Ronan Sheehan,* he has yet to achieve his full potential. His collection, *Arcady* (1983), however, does contain a fine comic story, "Bend Sinister," which makes good use of the childish eccentricities of some teachers in a boys' school.

PETER COSTELLO

WORKS: *The Feast of Michaelmas.* [Dublin]: Co-Op Books, [1979]; *Arcady and Other Stories.* Dublin: Co-Op Books, 1983; *Before the Wax Hardened.* Dublin: Odell & Adair, 1991; *Istanbul Diary.* Dublin: Poolbeg, 1994; tr., *An Caisideach Ban: The Songs and Adventures of Tomas Ó Caiside.* Ballyhaunis, Co. Mayo: Greenprint, 1994. (Pamphlet).

KENNY, LOUISE M. STACPOOLE (ca. 1885–1933), novelist. Louise M. Dunne was born about 1885 in Dublin. She was the daughter of James R. Dunne, and his wife, May, the daughter of Mathias Stacpoole of Moymore House, Ennistymon, County Clare. Louise Dunne married Thomas Hugh Kenny and lived most of her life at Indiaville, in Limerick. She continued to give Moymore House as one of her addresses, even after her marriage, which suggests that she may have inherited her maternal home. She died in 1933, in Bray, County Wicklow.

Confusion exists between her and another writer, Louise Kenny, of Freagh

Castle, Miltown Malbay, County Clare, who wrote *The Red-Haired Woman*, an autobiographical novel. They were, however, two different women.

Louise M. Stacpoole Kenny wrote mainly romance or historical romance novels, and she was very popular. Most of her novels were set in Ireland, or the scene shifts to Ireland at some point during the story. She was particularly fond of West of Ireland settings, including the County Clare areas with which she was so familiar. Her most successful novels were *Love Is Life* (1910) and *Carrow of Carrowduff* (1911), both of which generated sequels. *The King's Kiss* (1912) continues the historical romance begun in *Love Is Life,* and the story of Iseult Dymphna Macnamara at the court of Louis XIV. *Our Own Country* (1913) expands the tale begun in *Carrow of Carrowduff.* Kenny had an energetic writing style and a penchant for interweaving multiple love stories within a single text.

ANNE COLMAN

WORKS: *Jacquetta.* London: Washbourne, 1910; *Love Is Life.* London: Greening, 1910; *Carrow of Carrowduff.* London: Greening, 1911; *The King's Kiss.* London: Digby, Long, 1912; *Our Own Country.* London: Duffy, 1913; *Daffodil's Love Affairs.* London: Holden & Hardingham, 1913; *Heart of the Scarlet Fire.* London: Heath, Cranton, [ca. 1913); *Mary: A Romance of the West Country.* London: Washbourne, 1915.

KENNY, MARY (1944–   ), journalist and nonfiction and fiction writer. Kenny was born in Dublin and educated in convent schools. Later she became involved in the feminist movement and radical politics and renounced Catholicism. After her marriage and the birth of her two children, she reconsidered her position and returned to the Catholic Church. She is now on the staff of the *Sunday Telegraph* in London.

Kenny's first book, *Woman X Two* (1978), is essentially a self-help book that offers solutions to dilemmas faced by working women as wives and mothers, including family support structures, well-paid help, and supportive husbands. *Why Christianity Works* (1981) has been called by *The Economist* a work of Christian apologetics in the tradition of G. K. Chesterton. In it, Kenny admits to strict adherence to the tenets of Catholicism, including daily prayer and weekly mass attendance. She also renounces abortion as disrespectful of individuality and faults the birth control pill for its expeditious release of men from reproductive responsibility, views developed further in her *Abortion: The Whole Story* (1986).

Kenny's most recent work, a collection of short stories called *A Mood for Love* (1989), incorporates the themes of an angry feminist who has recognized the ongoing exploitation of women as a by-product of the women's movement. Her characters, confronted with the literal realities of sexual liberation, are often uncomfortable with the choices society offers them. In "A Change of Life," Margaret, who at forty-six must deal with glaucoma and eventual blindness, confronts a callow young married woman who frivolously considers the pros and cons of terminating her pregnancy. In "The European Spirit," a promiscuous Helene Greene, who has undergone five abortions and is considering a sixth, decides to bear and adopt out her unwanted child to a barren couple. "The Charm of Gerry Anderson" offers some ideas on the complications that result from easily established and noncommittal liaisons, as a feminist magazine editor reveals her penchant for sadomasochism and her ease with the idea of abortion to a bewildered and disillusioned protagonist. Sexual liberation is shown, ultimately, not to liberate. In the title story, the brash young American, Susy, pays for this "emancipation" through anxiety over continuing an affair with a married man. The final tale, "Election Night: The Road to Margaret Thatcher," depicts four faithful friends gathering on election nights from 1964 to 1987 and demonstrates how the idealism of young adults, based on theory, gives way to the realism of age, based on experience. The innocence-to-experience journey of Mary Kenny indicates disillusionment with Utopia, but at least the persistence of healthy anger at the aftermath of the feminist movement.

MARGUERITE QUINTELLI-NEARY

WORKS: *Woman X Two: How to Cope with a Double Life.* London: Sidgwick & Jackson, 1978; *Why Christianity Works.* London: Michael Joseph, 1981; *Abortion: The Whole Story.* London: Quartet Books, 1986; *A Mood for Love.* London: Quartet Books, 1989. (Short stories).

KENNY, SEAN

WORK: *The Hungry Earth.* Dublin: Wolfhound, 1995. (Novel).

KETTLE, THOMAS [MICHAEL] (1880–1916), economist, politician, and man of letters. Born in Artane, County Dublin, on February 2, 1880, Kettle was the son of the Land League advocate Andrew Kettle. He was educated at the Christian Brothers school in Richmond Street, Dublin, at Clongowes Wood College, and at University College, where he was auditor of the Literary and Historical Society and editor of *St. Stephen's.* After graduation, he had an active life in nationalist politics, often using his oratory to reconcile disagreeing factions. He became the first president of the Young Ireland Branch of the United Irish League in 1904, edited the short-lived *The Nationalist* in 1905, and received his little-used law degree in that same year. Kettle held the East Tyrone seat in Parliament from 1906 until he resigned in 1910. He was appointed the first professor of national economics in the National University in 1909. Kettle was chairman of the Peace Committee for the Dublin Lockout of 1913, served on the Education Commission, and helped found the National Volunteers. The Easter Rebellion of 1916 was not in accord with his vision of "a free united Ireland in a free Europe," and Kettle was killed on September 9, 1916, in the Battle of the Somme, while serving in the British army. The essays in *The Ways of War* (1917) describe the ideals that sent Kettle to Belgium and report his early experiences there.

Kettle was well grounded in economic literature and the philosophies of Aquinas, Schopenhauer, Guyau, Nietzsche, Heine, and Hegel. His political and economic writing is strongly humanistic and enlivened with witty images and aphorisms. Important works in the group are *Home Rule Finance: An Experiment in Justice* (1911), "The Economics of Nationalism," contained in *The Day's Burden* (1918, reprint 1968), and his "Introduction" to his translation of Louis Paul-Dubois' *Contemporary Ireland.* His poetry contained in *Poems and Parodies* (1912) is an interesting footnote to his oratory and prose. The subject is usually patriotic or martial, and the imagery often resembles the Celtic Twilight school of AE.* Occasionally there is a memorable metaphysical conceit, but his appealing philosophical side is under-represented.

Kettle was a critic of Irish literature throughout his life. He was among the protestors who disrupted Yeats'* *The Countess Cathleen,* and in an essay which appeared in the *United Irishman* he argued that Yeats had reversed the true image of the Irish Catholic's faith and "historical definiteness" in order to make the countess' white soul shine forth. Kettle had a sustained literary friendship with James Joyce.* Together in University College papers, they defended the literature of the 1890s and criticized the emphasis on folklore in the literature of the Celtic Revival. In the essays "On Saying Goodbye" and "Crossing the Irish Sea," both in *The Day's Burden,* Kettle detects the paralysis and tendency toward betrayal that Joyce ascribes to his *Dubliners.* Often a pessimist, Kettle used his natural curiosity to reinvigorate himself and his writing. Other works are *The Open Secret of Ireland* (1912), his editions *Battle Songs for the Irish Brigades* (1915) and *Irish Orators and Oratory* (1916), and his translation of Kneller's *Christianity and the Leaders of Modern Science.*

BONNIE KIME SCOTT

WORKS: *The Day's Burden.* Dublin: Maunsel, 1910; *Home Rule Finance.* Dublin: Maunsel, 1911; *The Open Secret of Ireland.* London: W. J. Ham-Smith, 1912; ed., *Irish Orators and Oratory.* London: Unwin, [1916]; *Poems and Parodies.* London: Duckworth, 1916; *The Ways of War.* London: Constable, 1917; *An Irishman's Calendar. A Quotation from the Works of T. M. Kettle for Every Day in the Year,* Compiled by Mary S. Kettle. Dublin: Brown & Nolan, [1938]. REFERENCES: Lyons, J. B. *The Enigma of Tom Kettle: Irish Patriot, Essayist, Poet, British Soldier, 1880–1916.* Dublin: Glendale, 1983; Lyons, J. B. *What Did I Die Of?: The Deaths of Parnell, Wilde, Synge, and Other Literary Pathologies.* Dublin: Lilliput, 1991.

KIBERD, DECLAN (1951–   ), critic. Born in Dublin, Kiberd was educated at St. Paul's College, Raheny, at Trinity College, Dublin, and at Oxford. He has been lecturer in English and American literature at the University of Kent from 1976 to 1977, lecturer in Irish at Trinity College, Dublin, from 1977 to 1979, and lecturer in English at University College, Dublin, since 1979.

WORKS: *Synge and the Irish Language.* London: Macmillan/Totowa, N.J.: Barnes & Noble, 1979; *Anglo-Irish Attitudes.* Derry: Field Day, 1984. (Pamphlet); *Men and Feminism in Modern Literature.* London: Macmillan/New York: St. Martin's, 1985; coed., *Omnium Gatherum. Essays for Richard Ellmann.* Gerrards Cross: Colin Smythe/Montreal: McGill University Press, 1989; coed., *An Crann Faoi Bhlath: The Flowering Tree—Gaelic Poetry and Translations 1940–1989.* Dublin: Wolfhound, 1990/1995; *History of Literature in the Irish Language.* London & Basingstoke: Macmillan, 1995; *Inventing Ireland: The Literature of the Modern Nation.* London: Jonathan Cape, [1995].

KICKHAM, CHARLES J. (1828–1882), novelist and Fenian. Charles Joseph Kickham was born on May 9, 1828, at Cnoceenagow near Mullinahone, County Tipperary, the son of a prosperous shopkeeper and farmer. Kickham became deaf after an accident with gunpowder when he was thirteen. As a young man he took part in the Young Ireland movement, and he became a Fenian in about 1860. In 1865, James Stephens, the Fenian leader, appointed Kickham to the supreme executive of his Irish Republic, and Kickham became one of the editors of the Fenian newspaper *The Irish People.* When the Fenian insurrection was suppressed, Kickham was arrested on November 11, 1865, and sentenced to fourteen years' penal servitude. He served four years of the sentence at Woking and at Portland prisons before he was released, broken in health. In prison, however, he did manage to write his novel *Sally Cavanagh.* He died in Blackrock, a suburb of Dublin, on August 22, 1882.

One or two of Kickham's poems, such as "Rory of the Hill," have retained some popularity, but today he is remembered mainly for his long novel *Knocknagow; or, The Homes of Tipperary* (1879), which has gone through many editions and is still in print. By purely literary standards, *Knocknagow* is inconsequential. It is overly sentimental and overly farcical, its characters are caught in unchanging Dickensian molds, and it is not very well written. Nevertheless, the book still has considerable appeal. Its complicated plot is engrossing. Its large cast contains some character types, such as Barney Broderick, Phil Lahy the tailor and, the stalwart Mat the Thresher, that cling in the memory. The death scene of Nora Lahy is reminiscent of some of the death scenes in Dickens or even in Mrs. Henry Wood, but is moving for all that. Its emotions, although simple, are never mawkish; and its deeply felt nostalgia still has charm. It has been effectively adapted for the stage by Seamus de Burca.*

WORKS: *Sally Cavanagh; or, The Untenanted Graves.* Dublin: W. B. Kelly/London: Simpkin, Marshal, 1869; *Knocknagow; or, The Homes of Tipperary.* Dublin: Duffy, 1873, 1879); *For the Old Land: A Tale of Twenty Years Ago.* Dublin: Gill, 1886; *The Eagle of Garryroe.* Dublin: Martin Lester, [1920]; Dublin: Talbot, 1963; *Tales of Tipperary.* Dublin: Talbot, [1926]; *Poems of Charles Joseph Kickham.* H. L. Doak, ed. Dublin: Educational, [1931]; *The Valley near Slievenamon: A Kickham Anthology.* James Maher, ed. [Kilkenny: Kilkenny People, 1942]. (Contains poems, memoirs, diary excerpts, letters, essays, and so on); *Sing a Song of Kickham: Songs of Charles J. Kickham. With Gaelic Versions and Musical Notation.* James Maher, ed. Dublin: Duffy, 1965. (Includes essays by Maher, Benedict Kiely, Katharine Tynan, & W. B. Yeats). REFERENCES: Comerford, R. V. *Charles J. Kickham: A Study in Irish Nationalism and Literature.* Portmarnock: Wolfhound, 1979; Healy, James J. *Life and Times of Charles J. Kickham.* Dublin: Duffy, 1915; Kelly, Richard J. *Charles Joseph Kickham: Patriot and Poet.* Dublin: Duffy, 1914.

KIELY, BENEDICT (1919–   ), novelist, short story writer, and critic. Like James Joyce* and Flann O'Brien (Brian O'Nolan),* Benedict Kiely is heir to the archaic Irish comic tradition characterized by linguistic verve, inventiveness of plot (to the extent of fantasy on occasions), and a satiric impulse. Like them, too, he is learnedly aware of his forebears, proven in Kiely's case by the range of reading demonstrated in his pioneering critical survey *Modern Irish Fiction—*

A Critique (1950). One predecessor who has influenced Kiely's fiction is William Carleton,* of whom Kiely wrote a critical biography entitled *Poor Scholar* (1947). In the manner of his fellow Tyroneman, Kiely has written short stories, novelle, and novels that seem to bridle in their narrative and anecdotal energies against the constraints and shapeliness of form. In both writers, the speaking voice of the storyteller is paramount, which perhaps is why Frank O'Connor,* who sought to preserve that voice in his own fiction, highly praised the stories of Kiely.

Benedict Kiely was born near Dromore on August 15, 1919, and was educated by the Christian Brothers in Omagh. In 1937, he entered the Jesuit novitiate in County Laois, but during a lengthy convalescence from a tubercular spinal ailment the following year, he decided not to answer the call to clerical life. Instead, he enrolled at the National University in Dublin from which he graduated with a B.A. in 1943. The abortive religious vocation and the severe illness and long convalescence have provided Kiely with material for several otherwise dissimilar novels, including *Honey Seems Bitter* (1952), *There Was an Ancient House* (1955), and *Dogs Enjoy the Morning* (1968). From 1945 until 1964, Kiely was a Dublin journalist with, successively, *The Standard, The Irish Independent,* and *The Irish Press,* following which he became a professor of creative writing at universities in Virginia, Oregon, and Georgia. Kiely returned to Dublin in 1968 and has since lectured at University College, written newspaper features and reviews, and made radio and television broadcasts.

Between 1946 and 1955, Kiely published six novels, ranging in subject matter and style from a psychological murder mystery, *Honey Seems Bitter,* to a modernized folktale, *The Cards of the Gambler* (1953). Three themes recur: crime or sin, clericalism, and initiation into manhood. These novels are eminently readable, but rarely are the central characters conveyed with sufficient penetration to ensure artistic triumph. As if in realization that his true strength lay with the short story, with which he has had successess in *The New Yorker, The Kenyon Review,* and other American magazines, Kiely published only three novels between 1955 and 1977, including *Proxopera* (1977), which is really a novella. But *The Captain with the Whiskers* (1960), a brooding mock-romance, and *Dogs Enjoy the Morning,* a comic extravaganaza drawing on Celtic mythology, are in fact more richly textured than the earlier novels and are in every way larger books.

It is as a short story writer that Kiely is likely to be remembered, for the form allows him to turn his archaic storytelling ability to artistic advantage. He is at his best when his plots, comedy, and pathos must be honed to fulfill the formal demands of the short story. The stories in his two volumes to date, *A Journey to the Seven Streams* (1963) and *A Ball of Malt and Madame Butterfly* (1973), are packed with memorable Irish figures, comic anecdotes, and blunt ironies. These weave a kind of tapestry around a scarcely satiric love of humanity and its foibles, a humanity whose symbolic residence is for Kiely the Ireland of living memory in which, despite their wide range of historical and geographic reference and allusion, all his stories are set. Few writers have known Ireland better than Kiely. Although he is most familiar with Ulster, especially the country west of the Bann, the settings of his stories and novels range freely throughout the thirty-two counties. In their artistic achievement, the stories prove that as a short story writer, he is within hailing distance of O'Connor* and Sean O'Faolain.*

Proxopera (1977) is a fictional departure for Kiely insofar as this attack on Republican terrorism in Northern Ireland is unwontedly bitter and outspoken. The irony of this work coming from the pen of the man who thirty-two years earlier had attacked partition in *Counties of Contention* (1945) is a capsulized object-lesson in Irish history during the 1970s. Formally, however, *Proxopera* exhibits the author's increasing fondness for the longer than conventional short story which he clearly feels can more satisfactorily accommodate his ample talent.

JOHN WILSON FOSTER

Benedict Kiely has continued to write prolifically and ever more distinctively. Indeed, his style is probably the most immediately recognizable of any modern Irish writer's. Whether it be short story, novella, novel, travel book, or memoir, one may expect to find a wealth of anecdote, allusion, and quotation, particularly from the popular poetry of the past, with which his mind is encyclopedically stocked. What you are really buying when you purchase a Kiely book are its author's character and personality; and, whatever the list price, you have gotten a bargain.

His novels are not so much plotted as ramblingly narrated, and even his short stories, where he is at his individual best, often give the impression of maundering around here and there. For instance, his 1985 novel, *Nothing Happens in Carmincross,* charts the return from America of an aging Irishman to his native village for the wedding of a favorite niece. Much of it is a leisurely ramble through the countryside, interspersed with pub conversations, memories, retellings of legends, and, above all, grim reflections on the Northern Troubles. The climax, in which the niece and other villagers are killed by Irish Republican Army bombs, is not so much dramatized as essayistically celebrated. It is one of Kiely's most brilliant, telling, and moving passages, but it is told at one remove from the actual action. Indeed, the entire book is not so much a narrative, but an essay posing as one. Consequently, it is not a book whose pace impels one to devour it at one sitting, but a book to be savored in small doses. As a journey, it is ambling, but the company and the craic are grand. To cite one rich passage among many, the section on the aged patriot living in the past is devastating.

The short story form is much more suited to Kiely's genius, particularly when there is a situation rather than the need for a development. Then the richness of the authorial voice may be relished as the piece's greatest virtue. Kiely has much in common with the Irish shanachie, and the rich personal voice not only borrows song by its constant quotation but even erupts into song. For instance, the story "Eton Crop" in *A Letter to Peachtree* (1987) has many paragraphs in loose, rollicking meter. The paragraphs are usually in three sentences of about the same length, and they rhyme. For example:

I read, but little understood, the words upon that book. For with a sidelong glance I marked my uncle's fearful look. And saw how all his quivering frame in strong convulsions shook.

A silent terror o'er me stole, a strange, unusual dread. His lips were white as bone, his eyes sunk far down in his head. He gazed on me, but 'twas the gaze of the unconscious dead.

One might be reading "The Rime of the Ancient Mariner," and, indeed, Kiely as both writer and raconteur has some common characteristics with Coleridge's worthy.

In his memoir *Drink to the Bird* (1991), Kiely acknowledges some notable characteristics as a writer:

The meticulous reader may detect digressions.

But the mind, such as it is, may surely, in this business of remembering, be allowed to meander. . . .

It could also be that the same meticulous reader will herein find repetitions.

Then he genially shrugs such faults off as the right of "a septuagenarian with eight grandchildren." What he has, in effect, done is create his own distinct style. But if a Kiely book is going nowhere in a hurry, the many stops along the way are often memorable. For instance:

Frank O'Connor* used to say quite frequently: "Yeats* said to me." Once, and in my presence, Thomas Flanagan* said to Frank O'Connor: "Michael, what did you say to Yeats?" With vast, all-embracing good humour, and no man had more of it, Frank O'Connor or Michael Donovan said: "Tom Flanagan, I said: 'Yes, Mr. Yeats.' "

Few writers since Laurence Sterne* have been so amazingly and worthily digressive. If that be a fault, Kiely has transformed it into a virtue.

WORKS: *Counties of Contention: A Study of the Origins and Implications of the Partition of Ireland.* Cork: Mercier, 1945; *Land Without Stars.* London: Christopher Johnson, 1946; *Poor Scholar: A Study of the Works and Days of William Carleton.* London & New York: Sheed & Ward, 1947; *In a Harbour Green.* London: Jonathan Cape, 1949; *Call for a Miracle.* London: Jonathan Cape, 1950; *Modern Irish Fiction—A Critique.* Dublin: Golden Eagle Books, 1950; *Honey Seems Bitter.* New York: E. P. Dutton, 1952/London: Methuen, 1954/reprinted as *The Evil Men Do,* New York: Dell, 1954; *The Cards of the Gambler.* London: Methuen, 1953; *There Was an Ancient House.* London: Methuen, 1955; *The Captain with the Whiskers.* London: Methuen, 1960; *A Journey to the Seven Streams: Seventeen Stories.* London: Methuen, 1963; *Dogs Enjoy the Morning.* London: Gollancz, 1968; *A Ball of Malt and Madame Butterfly: A Dozen Stories.* London: Gollancz, 1973; *Proxopera.* London: Gollancz, 1977; *All the Way to Bantry Bay—and Other Irish Journeys.* London: Gollancz, 1978. (Travel); *A Cow in the House and Other Stories.* London: Gollancz, 1978; *Nothing Happens in Carmincross.* London: Gollancz/New York: D. R. Godine, 1985. (Novel); *A Letter to Peachtree.* London: Gollancz, 1987. (Short stories); *Yeats's Ireland: An Illustrated Anthology.* London: Aurum Press, 1989; *Drink to the Bird.* London: Methuen, 1991. (Memoir); *God's Own Country: Selected Stories, 1963–1993.* [London]: Minerva, [1993]. REFERENCES: Cahill, Christopher, ed. "A Tribute to Benedict Kiely." *The Recorder: A Journal of the American Irish Historical Society* 7 (Summer 1994); Casey, Daniel J. *Benedict Kiely.* Lewisburg, Pa.: Bucknell University Press, 1974; Casey, Daniel J. "Benedict Kiely" in *Contemporary Irish Novelists.* Rüdiger Imhof, ed. Tübingen: Narr, 1990, pp. 25–29; Clarke, Jennifer. "An Interview with Benedict Kiely." *Irish Literary Supplement* (Spring 1987): 10–12; Eckley, Grace. *Benedict Kiely.* New York: Twayne, 1975; Foster, John Wilson. *Forces and Themes in Ulster Fiction.* Dublin: Gill & Macmillan/Totowa, N. J.: Rowman & Littlefield, 1974, pp. 72–81, 91–100.

KIELY, DAVID M. (1949–   ), short story writer and biographer. Kiely was born in Dublin, has worked in advertising on the Continent, and now lives in County Wicklow. His *A Night in the Catacombs* (1995) is an engaging collection of ten short stories, each featuring an Irish writer—Joyce,* Synge,* Behan,* Lady Gregory,* Goldsmith,* O'Casey,* Maria Edgeworth,* Edith Somerville,* George Moore,* and Swift.* There is some attempt to fit the style to the figure. The Lady Gregory story, for instance, is written as a dramatic dialogue in a bedroom between her and Wilfrid Scawen Blunt; the Synge makes a good stab at the English equivalent of Irish phrasing; the Goldsmith is eighteenth-centuryish. Not all of the pieces are of equal merit, but the book is a clever, knowledgeable, and entertaining debut, and the Goldsmith story has a plot worthy of the Stevenson of "The Sire de Malétroit's Door."

WORK: *John Millington Synge, a Biography.* [Dublin]: Gill & Macmillan, [1994]; *A Night in the Catacombs.* [Dublin]: Lilliput, [1995].

KIELY, JEROME (1925–   ), novelist and poet. Kiely was born in Kinsale, County Cork, attended Maynooth, and was ordained a Catholic priest in 1950. He has traveled widely in Africa, America, and the Near East. In 1953, he won the Adam Prize for Poetry, the adjudicator being C. Day-Lewis.*

WORKS: *The Griffin Sings. Poems.* London & Dublin: Geoffrey Chapman, 1966; *Seven Year Island.* London: Geoffrey Chapman, 1969. (Novel); *Yesterdays of the Heart.* Dublin: Dedalus, 1989. (Poetry); *Isle of the Blest.* Cork & Dublin: Mercier, 1993. (Nonfiction).

KIELY, KEVIN K. (1953–   ), novelist and poet. Kiely was born in Warrenpoint, County Down, on June 2, 1953. He was educated at Cistercian Abbey, Roscrea, and Blackrock College, Dublin, and at University College, Dublin (UCD). He attended the National Writers' Workshop at University College, Galway (UCG), and was reader at the National Library of Ireland and Trinity College Library. He traveled in England, France, and Germany and settled in Spain for a year from 1979 to 1980, lecturing at the British Council in Barcelona on Ezra Pound's poems. He worked as a translator and wrote criticism after coediting *The Belle,* a radical pamphlet on literature that had only two issues. In 1980, he married Mary Therese Timmons. He was Honorary Fellow in Writing at the University of Iowa in 1983, which was also the year of his American travels. He was the recipient of Arts Council Writer's Bursary Awards in 1980, 1989, and 1990.

Kiely's poems have been published in *Edinburgh Review, Adrift, The Salmon,*

Poetry Ireland Review, Crystal, Criterion (UCG), *Anvil* (UCD), *The Democrat, The Mayo News,* and *Foolscap.* At the time of writing, Kiely is putting together a collection of poems, with the working title *My Last Madness,* for a small press in England. He has three novels seeking publication in addition to the two that have appeared: *Quintesse* (1982) and *Mere Mortals* (1989). The published novels share a delight in narrative experimenting that is not altogether devoid of whimsy, as this specimen of word juggling from *Quintesse* may demonstrate: "It was Wednesday afternoon and dry, it was a dry after noon and Wednesday, it was a dryday afternoon and wednesdaying." Here as elsewhere in the two published narratives, Kiely appears to be mimicking Joycean* strategies and aiming at Beckettian* innovation (much is made of the fact that one character in *Quintesse* lives in Foxrock, "Beckett country") but without Joyce's and Beckett's artistic mastery.

In the form of a confessional conversation, *Quintesse* has the eponymous hero tell a French au pair girl, named Mime Matisse, about the two women he had been in love with before he fell for her. The first was called Nani Neary; he met her at a dance, went out with her a couple of times, and spent a night with her at Mrs. Neary's, and then she told him that she no longer wanted to see him. The second woman was Lila Langione from Spain. He had been working as a clown in a circus at Ely, Cambridgeshire, and met her, after leaving the circus, in a canning factory. They go to spend a few days in Stratford-upon-Avon. All the while, nothing of real import happens. Then she leaves him for Spain, and he meets Mime Matisse. Again after a drawn-out series of anything but striking occurrences, they separate; and in the last part, entitled "Of Consequences," Quintesse nurses his wounds.

The greater part of *Mere Mortals* reads like a not especially edifying effort at learned wit. Some sections look experimental, but unfortunately it is often difficult to discern what the stylistic and narrative antics are intended to signify. The account falls into two parts, the first one idiosyncratically describing a day in the life of the Rangans of Archmill and the second relating the fate of one Justin Howlin, whose studies in mathematics provide the raison d'être for numerous forays into eclectic erudition. The book starts off in telegram style, very much reminiscent of the way in which Joyce renders Bloom's interior monologues. There are occasional passages of wry humor, but these contribute little toward mitigating the tedium generated by the rest, which includes a series of Peacockian conversations. At the end of Part I, the narrative tries to evoke feelings and emotions in a manner reminiscent of the end of "The Dead." In Part II, Kiely takes the opportunity to flaunt his knowledge of mathematics, astronomy, and related sciences, from Hippocrates of Chios to Gauss and others. There is, furthermore, a great variety of different styles, including biblical language and Elizabethan language. At one point, someone tells Howlin, "You're a bunch of unpractical theories." That is also what Part II boils down to, its connection with Part I being that Howlin is Kitty Rangan's grandson.

RÜDIGER IMHOF

WORKS: *Quintesse*. Dublin: Co-op Books, 1982/New York: St. Martin's, 1985; *Mere Mortals*. Swords, Co. Dublin: Poolbeg, & Dublin: Odell & Adair, 1989. REFERENCE: Imhof, Rüdiger. "How It Is on the Fringes of Irish Fiction." *Irish University Review* 22 (Spring–Summer 1992): 151–167.

KILROY, THOMAS (1934–   ), playwright and novelist. Kilroy was born on September 23, 1934, in Callan, County Kilkenny. He was educated by the Christian Brothers in Callan and at Saint Kieran's College in Kilkenny and ultimately took three diplomas from University College, Cork: a B.A. in 1956, a Higher Diploma in Education in 1957, and an M.A. in English in 1959. He was headmaster of Stratford College in Dublin from 1959 to 1964, visiting professor at the University of Notre Dame in 1962–1963 and at Vanderbilt University in 1964–1965, assistant lecturer in the Department of Modern English and American Literature at University College, Dublin, from 1965 to 1973, lecturer at the School of Irish Studies in Dublin in 1972–1973, and visiting professor at Sir George Williams University and McGill University in 1973; he held posts at Dartmouth College in 1976, at University College, Dublin, in 1977–1978, at Thomond College in Limerick in 1983, and at Bamburg University in 1984; and he was professor of English at University College, Galway, in 1975–1976 and from 1977 to 1989. Kilroy has made his reputation not only as a teacher but also as a critic, playwright, director, and novelist. His awards for his literary achievements include the BBC prizewinning radio play in 1967, the *Guardian* Prize for fiction in 1971, the Royal Society of Literature's Heinemann Award for Fiction in 1972, the Irish Academy Prize in 1972, the Irish-American Foundation Award in 1974, an Arts Council of Ireland bursary in 1976, a Bellagio Study Centre Grant in 1986, and a Rockefeller Grant in 1986. In addition, Kilroy is a member of the Royal Society of Literature, the Irish Academy of Letters,* and Aosdána.*

Outside the theater, Kilroy has written two novels. *The Big Chapel* (1971) explores issues of religious zealotry and anticlericalism through events in County Kilkenny in the late nineteenth century. *Quirke* is scheduled to be published in 1996.

Kilroy's career in the theater includes directing plays for the Field Day Company* in Derry and the post as play editor for the Abbey Theatre* in Dublin. However, his reputation is based on his written works, including *The Death and Resurrection of Mr. Roche, The O'Neill, Tea and Sex and Shakespeare, Talbot's Box, The Seagull, Double Cross, Ghosts,* and *The Madam MacAdam Travelling Theatre*. For radio, he has written *The Door* and *That Man, Bracken*. For television, he has written *Farmers, Gold in the Streets,* and *The Black Joker*.

The Death and Resurrection of Mr. Roche, first produced at the Olympia Theatre in Dublin in 1968 and later in London (1969) and New York (1978), addresses themes of the banality of urban life and of homosexuality. The central action occurs in the apartment of a civil servant who invites his male drinking partners to come to his home after a wake for a dead friend. The men discuss their lives and experiences and reveal a cultural and spiritual vacuum in all their lives since they emigrated from rural Ireland to the city. All are seemingly happy, seemingly have good jobs, are seemingly conventional. However, the dialogue reveals a deep sense of discontent and dissatisfaction with the conventions and demands of urban life and its attendant loneliness and desperation. In addition, the group torments and seemingly kills Mr. Roche, an open homosexual, by forcing him into a cellar. Roche comes back to life in the end only after one of the other characters admits homosexual contact with him, and others admit dissatisfaction with their lives. The metaphor is clear: homosexuality or uniqueness is suppressed, even killed off, in the hope that normality and contentment will result. However, the act of suppression is that act that leads to desperation and discontent; and the act of conformity, of seeming happiness, drives individuals to suppress their desires.

Talbot's Box, first performed at the Abbey's* Peacock Theatre on October 13, 1977, stages the temptations of the Dublin mystic Matt Talbot. Talbot, played by the same actor throughout the play, is tormented by a variety of other characters, played interchangeably by four actors who refer to themselves as actors on the stage. The play reveals the spiritual integrity of Talbot in his actions and sufferings. The shallowness of his tormentors reveals itself in their lack of integrity as characters in a play, their self-reverential staging. Talbot, like Roche, is tormented but maintains an inner discipline, while his tormentors lack any coherent vision save cruelty and are essentially discontented.

Double Cross, first performed by Derry's Field Day Company* in 1986 and then taken to the Royal Court Theatre in London, explores the lives of two Irishmen on opposite sides in World War II. Brendan Bracken was minister of information for Winston Churchill, and William Joyce broadcast propaganda for the Nazis. Both roles are played by the same actor, Stephen Rea in the original production, with the first act devoted to Bracken and the second to Joyce. The play explores the intricacies of the meaning of treason, to England and to Ireland, and explores the motives and similarities of each character. In the end, the double meaning of the title reveals the double meaning of the play. It is about doubles crossing one another's lives and the intersection of their motives.

The Madam MacAdam Travelling Theatre, first performed in Derry by the Field Day Company in September 1991 and later at the Dublin Theatre Festival in October 1991, details the comic adventures of an English touring company trapped by circumstance in a rural Southern Irish town during the Second World War. The company becomes involved in a variety of activities in the town—a dog race, the search for a missing child, and the seduction of a teenager by a member of the company. Simultaneous with these activities, Kilroy integrates the seeking after vocation by the players; in essence, they are artists longing for expression. Like the characters of Roche and Talbot, the integrity of vocation, in this case the healing and transforming power of the theater, is played out on the stage.

Kilroy's *The Seagull* was first produced at London's Royal Court Theatre in

April 1981. Kilroy adopts the themes of the Chekhov text to the Irish West of the late nineteenth century, intersecting the motifs of doomed love and creative aspirations of the original with the politics of Ireland—the decline of the Anglo-Irish Big House society, the Land War, colonization.

Of his unpublished plays, *Tea and Sex and Shakespeare,* first performed by the Abbey at the Dublin Theatre festival in October 1976, is a comedy centering around a frustrated writer who plays out his fantasies regarding his family and neighbors in the attic of his Dublin home. The characters interact with improvised scenes and dialogue from Shakespeare. *Ghosts,* first performed by the Peacock in October 1989, transfers Ibsen's play to a 1980s provincial Irish town. In addition, Kilroy transfers several of Ibsen's characters into modern circumstances. Oswald Alving, now Oliver Aylward, comes home to die, experiencing the final stages of AIDS. Ibsen's Helene, in Kilroy Helen, is now more of an independent woman who is likely to take a direct role in alleviating her brother's suffering. Reviews praised Kilroy's ability to translate the themes of the original to modern Ireland while reinvigorating the characters and plot. *The O'Neill,* first produced in May 1969 at the Peacock, details the years before and after the Battle of the Yellow Ford in the sixteenth century among Hugh O'Neill, the earl of Tyrone, and the English forces.

BERNARD McKENNA

WORKS: *The Death and Resurrection of Mr. Roche.* London: Faber/New York: Grove, 1968; *The Big Chapel.* London: Faber, 1971. (Novel); *Talbot's Box.* Dublin: Gallery/Newark, Del.: Proscenium, 1979; *Double Cross.* London: Faber, 1986; *The Madam MacAdam Travelling Theatre.* London: Methuen, 1992; *The Seagull.* [Oldcastle, Co. Meath]: Gallery, [1993]; *The O'Neill.* [Oldcastle, Co. Meath]: Gallery, [1995]. Critical Writings: "Mervyn Wall: The Demands of Satire." *Studies* 47 (Spring 1958): 83–89; Review of *Plays of the Year,* chosen by J. C. Trewin, and of *The Hostage* by Brendan Behan. *Studies* 48 (Spring 1959): 111–113; "Groundwork for an Irish Theatre." *Studies* 48 (Summer 1959): 192–198; Review of *Reilly,* poems by Desmond O'Grady. *Studies* 51 (Spring 1962): 184–186; Review of *W. B. Yeats and the Theatre of Desolate Reality* by D. R. Clark, and *In Defense of Lady Gregory* by Ann Saddlemyer. *Studies* 55 (Winter 1966): 441–443; Review of *Like Any Other Man* by Patrick Boyle. *University Review* 4 (Spring 1967): 91–92; "Reading and Teaching the Novel." *Studies* 56 (Winter 1967): 356–367; "Fiction 1967." *University Review* 5 (Spring 1968): 112–117; Review of *Sean O'Faolain: A Critical Introduction* by Maurice Harmon. *Dublin Magazine* 7 (Autumn–Winter 1968): 98–100; "Tellers of Tales." *The Times Literary Supplement* 17 (March 1972): 301–302; "Synge and Modernism." In *J. M. Synge Centenary Papers, 1971.* Maurice Harmon, ed. Dublin: Dolmen, 1972, pp. 167–179; ed., *Sean O'Casey: A Collection of Critical Essays.* Teaneck, N.J.: Prentice-Hall, 1975; "Two Playwrights: Yeats and Beckett." In *Myth and Reality in Irish Literature.* Joseph Ronsley, ed. Toronto: Wilfrid Laurier University Press, 1977, pp. 183–195; "Anglo-Irish Playwrights and the Comic Tradition." *The Crane Bag* 3 (1979): 19–17; "The Moon in the Yellow River: Denis Johnston's Shavianism." In *Denis Johnston: A Retrospective.* Joseph Ronsley, ed. Gerrards Cross: Colin Smythe, 1981, pp. 49–58; "The Irish Writer: Self and Society, 1950–1980." In *Literature and the Changing Ireland.* Peter Connolly, ed. Gerrards Cross: Colin Smythe, pp. 175–187; "Brecht, Beckett, and Williams." *Sagetrieb: A Journal to Poets in the Pound–H. D.–Williams Tradition* 3 (Fall 1984): 81–87; "Goldsmith the Playwright." In *Goldsmith: The Gentle Master.* Sean Lucy, ed. Cork: Cork University Press, 1984, pp. 66–77; "The Autobiographical Novel." In *The Genius of Irish Prose.* Augustine Martin, ed. Dublin: Mercier, 1985, pp. 67–75; "A Generation of Playwrights." *Irish University Review* 22 (Spring 1992): 135–141; "Theatrical Text and Literary Text." In *The Achievement of*

Brian Friel. Alan Peacock, ed. Gerrards Cross: Colin Smythe, 1993, pp. 91–102. REFERENCES: Burke, Patrick. "Thomas Kilroy's Latest and Rough Magic." *Irish Literary Supplement* 7 (Fall 1988): 15; Comisky, Ray. "Searching for a Meaning on Treason." *Irish Times* (January 31, 1986): 12; Dawe, Gerald. "Thomas Kilroy." *Theatre Ireland* 3 (1983): 117–118; Etherton, Michael. *Contemporary Irish Dramatists*. London: Macmillan, 1989; Harmon, Maurice. "By Memory Inspired: Themes and Forces in Recent Irish Writing." *Éire-Ireland* 8 (Summer 1973): 3–19; Hayley, Barbara. "Self-Denial and Self-Assertion in Some Plays of Thomas Kilroy: *The Madam MacAdam Travelling Theatre*." in *Studies on the Contemporary Irish Theatre: Actes du Colloque de Caen*. Jacqueline Genet & Elisabeth Hellegourarc, eds. Caen: PU de Caen, 1991; Maxwell, D.E.S. *A Critical History of Modern Irish Drama 1891–1980*. Cambridge: Cambridge University Press, 1984; McGuinness, Frank. "A Voice from the Trees: Thomas Kilroy's Version of Chekhov's *The Seagull*." *Irish University Review* 21 (Spring–Summer 1991): 3–14; Roche, Anthony. "Two Plays by Thomas Kilroy." In *The Irish Writer and the City*. Maurice Harmon, ed. Gerrards Cross: Colin Smythe, 1984, pp. 159–168; Witiszek, Nina. *The Theatre of Recollection: A Cultural Study of the Modern Dramatic Tradition in Ireland and Poland*. Stockholm: University of Stockholm Press, 1988.

KINAHAN, CORALIE (1924–), novelist and artist. Kinahan was born in Surrey and educated in England. Married to Sir Robin Kinahan, she has exhibited widely in England and Ireland. In 1956, she was lady mayoress of Belfast.

WORKS: *You Can't Shoot the English!* Belfast: Pretani, 1982; *After the War Came . . . Peace?* Belfast: Pretani, 1988.

KING, RICHARD ASHE (1839–1932), novelist. King was born in County Clare on November 9, 1839, the son of the headmaster of Ennis College. He was educated there and at Trinity College, Dublin, from which he received an M.A. He was ordained in the Church of England and became vicar of Low Moor, Bradford. About 1880, he retired from the church and began publishing novels, at first under the pseudonym of Basil. Some of his books, such as "*The Wearing of the Green*" (1884), had an Irish background, and the Irish point of view was put with sympathy and intelligence. Indeed, one of the main characters of that novel is a lovable and eccentric priest. The difficulty of King's narratives is that they are less dramatic than talky, essayistic, and authorially intrusive. He was president of the Irish Literary Society in London, and he published nonfictional works on Swift* and Goldsmith.* He died on May 27, 1932.

WORKS: As Basil: *Love the Debt*. 3 vols. London: Chatto & Windus, 1882; *A Drawn Game*. 3 vols. London: Chatto & Windus, Windus, 1884; "*The Wearing of the Green*." 3 vols. London: Chatto & Windus, 1884; *A Coquette's Conquest*. London: R. Bentley, 1885. As King: *A Shadowed Life*. 3 vols. London: Ward & Downey, 1886; *A Leal Lass*. 2 vols. London: Ward & Downey, 1888; *Passion's Slave*. 3 vols. London: Chatto & Windus, 1889; *Love's Legacy*. 3 vols. London: Ward & Downey, 1890; *Bell Barry*. 2 vols. London: Chatto & Windus, 1891; *A Geraldine*. 2 vols. London: Ward & Downey, 1893; *Swift in Ireland*. London: T. Fisher Unwin, 1895. (Vol. 9 of the New Irish Library); *Oliver Goldsmith*. London: Methuen, 1910.

KINSELLA, THOMAS (1928–), poet. Born on May 4, 1928, in Dublin, Thomas Kinsella emerged in the 1950s as one of Ireland's most original and stimulating poets. Although his well-received translations from the early Irish, particularly the translation of the eighth-century prose epic *The Tain* (1969), might type him as an obvious Irish poet, the real matrix of his poetic creativity is not the Irish experience but the more profound human experience. This he manages to examine with all the emotional and intellectual scrupulosity that the most intricate interior terrain requires.

Kinsella abandoned a science scholarship while he was attending University College, Dublin, in order to enter the Irish civil service. In the civil service he eventually rose to the post of assistant principal officer in the Department of Finance. In 1965, after his election to the Irish Academy of Letters, he left the Department of Finance to accept an artist-in-residency at Southern Illinois University. In 1970, he joined the English Department at Temple University in Philadelphia as a professor. During his civil and academic career, he also served as a director of the Dolmen and Cuala Presses and founded Peppercanister, a small publishing company in Dublin.

Almost from the very beginning, Kinsella's poetry won public honor and acclaim. *Another September* (1958) was the Poetry Book Society choice, an award received also by *Downstream* (1962). "Thinking of Mr. D," a haunting, meditative poem in *Another September,* was the winner of the Guinness Poetry Award in 1958, and *Poems and Translations* (1961) was selected for the Irish Arts Council Triennial Book Award. Two volumes of poetry, *Wormwood* (1966) and *Nightwalker and Other Poems* (1968), were selected for the Denis Devlin Memorial Award. Kinsella himself was awarded Guggenheim fellowships in 1968–1969 and 1971–1972.

Kinsella's versatility might be accounted for by the fact that prose, not poetry, dominated the Irish literary scene when he began writing, encouraging a tendency, as Maurice Harmon points out in *The Poetry of Thomas Kinsella* (1974), "to search for models outside Ireland." Indeed, Kinsella's early poems are not obviously Irish nor do they particularly reflect his Catholic upbringing. They do, however, reveal a variety of debts to Auden, Pound, Eliot, and other American influences. The driving force of his themes, however—love, marriage, risk, the view of life as "ordeal," the necessity to strive for order, the threat of time and extinction—fashions a densely thicketed, deeply subjective style that is, finally, derivative of Kinsella's anguished experience alone. Typical of the subjectively directed, yet objectively controlled, poem is "First Light," where the minute details of a landscape, illuminated by the rising sun, provide the setting for an upstairs "whimper or sigh" which "lengthens to an ugly wail...." Kinsella describes the poems up to *Nightwalker and Other Poems* (1968) as "almost entirely lyrical," dealing with "love, death and the artistic act; with persons and relationships, places and objects seen against the world's processes of growth, maturing and extinction." The love poems in *Another September,* for example, are suffused with a sense of threat, as in "In the Ringwood." The organic development of this theme can be seen in the intensely subjective *Wormwood* (1966), a series of eight poems dealing with the risks and ordeals of marriage in which lovers "renew each other" but with a "savage smile."

Kinsella becomes more concerned with "questions of value and order" in *Nightwalker and Other Poems,* and deriving order from experience. Many of the poems in this collection show a conscious social revulsion to the mediocrity and materialism of modern Ireland, but even here the brave celebration of marriage in "Phoenix Park" and the touching farewell to Dublin it accomplishes show the deeper organic growth of Kinsella still in process: the enduring quality of life and marriage "ordered" by "ordeal" and healthy against extinction.

After 1968, according to Kinsella, his poetry "turned downward into the psyche toward origin and myth, and is set toward some kind of individuation." *Notes from the Land of the Dead and Other Poems* (1972), for example, demonstrates this direction and has caused some Kinsella admirers to suppose with Calvin Bedient in *The New York Times Book Review* that "Ireland's best living poet has brooded himself to pieces." That "brooding" could, of course, be seen as merely another form of "eliciting order from experience"—here, the experience enlarging into a mythically accessible order embedded perhaps in some sense of the collective unconscious. At any rate, Kinsella's myth-employing and mythmaking talents transform the commonplaces of experience into vivid, sometimes hair-raising spectaculars: a newly laid egg slips from an old lady's hand and is reconstituted into sheer Being which falls through "vast indifferent spaces" only to smash (having become a real egg again) into a suddenly appearing iron grating. What saves such mythic acrobatics from surrealistic excess, and even sentimentality, is the objective control that Kinsella always manages to sustain—not only the clear, precise language he uses, but the objectivist's eye for the telling image. The deeply psychological thrust of the poetry's intent in *Notes from the Land of the Dead,* ballasted by objective precision, conspires to produce reasonably authentic myth.

Some of the power of Kinsella's public poetry can be seen in works such as "Butcher's Dozen," a poignant longer poem which responds movingly to the Widgery tribunals into the British Army's fatal shooting of thirteen civil rights demonstrators in January 1972, and *The Good Fight* (1973), a poem commemorating the tenth anniversary of the death of John F. Kennedy. In the latter, Kinsella achieves historical and philosophical scope through extensive quotations from Plato, selected for their ironic pertinence, but it is the evocation of the memorable moment at the Kennedy Inauguration when Robert Frost stood blinded by the sun and snow which validates the effort here—an objective image enlivened and ordered by a vibrant contextual, even mythic, past.

In 1976 Kinsella established the Temple University School of Irish Tradition in Dublin, which afforded him the opportunity to divide his academic year between Philadelphia and Dublin and to continue his interest in Irish affairs and his own Peppercanister Press. His more recent volumes reflect his enduring commitment to Irish themes, but increasingly he exploits those themes in order to explore his personal consciousness or, as in the case of *St. Catherine's Clock* (1987) and *Poems from Centre City* (1990), to explore the consciousness of a specific place. While many of these explorations may seem enigmatically private or gnomically mystical to some, a few are quite touching in their simplicity. In *Personal Places* (1990), for example, there are simple pieces that do little more than record such homely domestic events as an automobile departure where "the children seen to and strapped in, / [are] speechless and taking us by surprise / with their tears." More typical, however, are the more ambitious efforts in *Madonna and Other Poems* (1991), where simple occasions such as "Morning Coffee" or hospital "Visiting Hours" are teased into, one is tempted to say, metaphysical labyrinths.

Now retired from teaching, he lives in County Wicklow.

THOMAS F. MERRILL

WORKS: *The Starlit Eye.* Dublin: Dolmen, 1952; *Three Legendary Sonnets.* Dublin: Dolmen, 1952; trans., *The Breastplate of St. Patrick.* Dublin: Dolmen, 1954/as *Faeth Fiadha: The Breastplate of St. Patrick,* 1957; trans., *The Exile and Death of the Sons of Usnech,* by Longes Mac n-Usnig. Dublin: Dolmen, 1954; trans., *Thirty Three Triads, Translated from the XII Century Irish.* Dublin: Dolmen, 1955; *The Death of a Queen.* Dublin: Dolmen, 1956; *Poems.* Dublin: Dolmen, 1956; *Another September.* Dublin: Dolmen/Philadelphia: Dufour, 1958/revised Dublin: Dolmen, and London: Oxford University Press, 1962; *Moralities.* Dublin: Dolmen, 1960; *Poems and Translations.* New York: Atheneum, 1961; *Downstream.* Dublin: Dolmen, 1962; *Six Irish Poets,* with others. Robin Skelton, ed. London & New York: Oxford University Press, 1962; *Nightwalker.* Dublin: Dolmen, 1966; *Wormwood.* Dublin: Dolmen, 1967; *Nightwalker and Other Poems.* Dublin: Dolmen/London: Oxford University Press/New York: Alfred A. Knopf, 1968; *Poems,* with David Livingstone & Anne Sexton. London & New York: Oxford University Press, 1968; *Tear.* Cambridge, Mass.: Pym Randall, 1969; trans., *The Tain.* Dublin: Dolmen, 1969/London & New York: Oxford University Press, 1970; *Butcher's Dozen.* Dublin: Peppercanister, 1972; *Finistere.* Dublin: Dolmen, 1972; *Notes from the Land of the Dead and Other Poems.* Dublin: Cuala, 1972/New York: Alfred A. Knopf, 1973; *A Selected Life.* Dublin: Peppercanister, 1972; *The Good Fight.* Dublin: Peppercanister, 1973; *New Poems,* 1973. Dublin: Dolmen, 1973; *Selected Poems, 1956–1968.* Dublin: Dolmen/London: Oxford University Press, 1973; *Vertical Man.* Dublin: Peppercanister, 1973; *One.* Dublin: Peppercanister, 1974; *A Technical Supplement.* Dublin: Dolmen/Peppercanister, 1976; *Song of the Night and Other Poems.* Dublin: Dolmen/Peppercanister, 1978; *The Messenger.* Dublin: Peppercanister, 1978; *Fifteen Dead.* Dublin: Peppercanister, 1979; *One and Other Poems.* Oxford & New York: Oxford University Press, 1979; *Peppercanister Poems.* Dublin: Peppercanister, 1979; *Poems 1956–1973.* Winston-Salem, N.C.: Wake Forest University Press, 1980; *One Fond Embrace.* Deerfield, Mass.: Deerfield, 1981; trans., *An Duanaire: Poetry of the Dispossessed 1600–1900.* Selected by Sean O Tuama. Dublin: Dolmen, 1981; *Songs of the Psyche.* Dublin: Peppercanister, 1985; *Her Vertical Smile.* Dublin: Peppercanister, 1985; *Out of Ireland.* Dublin: Peppercanister, 1987; *St. Catherine's Clock.* Dublin: Peppercanister, 1987; *Blood and Family.* Oxford & New York: Oxford University Press, 1988; *Poems from Centre City.* Dublin: Peppercanister, 1990; *Personal Places.* Dublin: Peppercanister, 1990; *Open Court.* Dublin: Peppercanister, 1991; *Madonna and Other Poems.* Dublin: Peppercanister, 1991; *The Dual Tradition: An Essay on Poetry and Politics in Ireland.* [Manchester]: Carcanet, [1995]. REFERENCES: Bedient, Calvin. *Eight Contemporary Poets.* London: Oxford University Press, 1974, pp. 119–138; Harmon, Maurice. *The Poetry of Thomas Kinsella.* Dublin: Wolfhound, 1974; Jackson, Thomas H. *The Poetic Evolution of Thomas Kinsella.* Dublin: Lilliput, 1995.

KIRKPATRICK, THOMAS PERCY CLAUDE (1869–1954), essayist, bibliographer, and medical historian. The second son of Professor John R. Kirkpatrick, an obstetrician, and his wife, Catherine Drury, Kirkpatrick was born at 4 Upper Merrion Street, Dublin, on September 10, 1869, and educated at Foyle

College, Derry, and at Trinity College, Dublin. Before reading medicine, he took a first in history. His earliest publications dealt with medical matters, but his *History of the Medical Teaching in Trinity College Dublin* (1912) was followed by *The Book of the Rotunda* (1913), *History of Dr. Steevens' Hospital, 1720–1920* (1924), and many biographical and literary essays, including "Goldsmith* in Trinity College and His Connection with Medicine" and "Michael Clancy, MD" in the *Irish Journal of Medical Science*. He was awarded the honorary degree of doctor of literature by both Dublin University and the National University, and a personal chair in the history of medicine was created for him at Trinity College in 1936.

A colleague used a phrase of Lucian to describe him: "He indulged in no Socratic irony, but his discourse was full of Attic grace." A bibliophile and book collector, he is remembered as a medical humanist, though he was physician for half a century to Dr. Steevens' Hospital. He was, indeed, an anesthetist early in his career and is honored still in the faculty's "Kirkpatrick Lecture."

He was a gregarious, clubable man and remained a bachelor. His writings are an invaluable source for Irish medical history and bibliography; he was an immediate influence on a generation of colleagues, including men such as William Doolin (editor of *Irish Journal of Medical Science*) and T. G. Wilson (Sir William Wilde's* biographer). Doolin pictured "Kirk" in his declining years: "a wise and kindly scholar sunk deep in the big chair in his own library, his face wreathed in smiles as he greeted his visitor, his figure framed against the loaded bookshelves that reached to the ceiling." He died in Dr. Steevens' Hospital on July 9, 1954.

J. B. LYONS

PRINCIPAL WORKS: *Notes on the Printers of Dublin during the Seventeenth Century.* Dublin: University Press, 1929; *Bartholomew Mosse—the Founder of a Great Hospital.* Dublin: Parkside, 1947; "The Life and Writings of Paul Hiffernan, MD." *Irish Book Lover* 19 (1931): 11–21; "Typefounding in Dublin, 1703–1719." *Irish Book Lover* 20 (1932): 39–41.

KNIGHT, SUSAN (1947–   ), novelist. Knight was born near London on April 7, 1947, and has lived in Dublin with her family since 1977. She has written several radio plays and in 1986 won the P. J. O'Connor Award. Her novel. *The Invisible Woman* (1993), about a woman abandoned in childhood and remembering her past, is an undramatized interior monologue and would probably work better as a radio play. There is little present action in this novella. *Grimaldi's Garden* (1995) has some well-rounded and memorable characters: Francis, the disappointed father; his uptight, DIY wife, Marion; their two sad children; Liam, their mother-ridden friend; Ruth, an artist, and her child, Starveling; Sonia, the hospitable Bohemian. All of these lives are linked by a pattern rather than a plot. Other characters, like the mysterious Moral Guardian who defaces library books, seem to just be there with no discernible purpose. Nevertheless, the book is well written, and there are genuinely comic and sad moments. The book has a dreamlike quality, reminiscent of Fournier's *Le Grand Meulnes,* and ends in a garden that is brightened by artificial flowers in winter, hence the title. Knight is concerned with the haphazardness of fate: you turn down one road and lead this life; you turn down another and lead that one. The book perhaps reflects this view, but the trouble is that, even if life is haphazard, art is highly organized.

MARY ROSE CALLAGHAN

WORK: *The Invisible Woman.* [Swords, Co. Dublin]: Poolbeg, [1993]. (Novella); *Grimaldi's Garden.* [Dublin]: Marino, [1995]. (Novel).

KNOWLES, JAMES SHERIDAN (1784–1862), playwright and actor. Knowles was born in Cork city on May 12, 1784, and was the second cousin of Richard Brinsley Sheridan.* His only Irish play was the early piece of fustian *Brian Boroihme* (1812); his great successes were *Virginius* (1820), *William Tell* (1825), and the powerful and confused *The Hunchback* (1832). He was a friend of Hazlitt, Lamb, Coleridge, Kean, Dickens, and Macready. In his day, if acted by Macready or by himself, some of Knowles's plays made an extraordinary impact. An early editor, R. Shelton MacKenzie, remarked of him: "The public had to learn that a genius like that of Knowles, soars, as on eagle pinions, taking a higher flight at each effort it makes. . . . His body may be resolved to dust, but his name will be immortal. He is inferior only to Shakespeare." The modern reader, however, would have to agree with Allardyce Nicoll's opinion: "If only Knowles could have escaped from melodrama on the one hand and from Elizabethanism on the other, he might have done something notable on the stage. As it is, many of his plays are but glorified tales of black evil and white innocence." He died in Torquay on December 1, 1862.

PRINCIPAL WORKS: *Brian Boroihme, or, The Maid of Erin.* New York: E. M. Murden, 1828; Select *Dramatic Works of James Sheridan Knowles,* with a memoir by R. Shelton Mackenzie. Baltimore: Edward J. Coale, 1835; *Fortescue.* New York: Harper, 1846. (Novel); *George Lovell.* London: Moxon/New York: Burgess, Stringer, 1847. (Novel); *The Dramatic Works of James Sheridan Knowles.* 2 vols. London: G. Routledge, 1856. REFERENCES: Knowles, Richard Brinsley. *The Life of James Sheridan Knowles.* London: Privately printed for James McHenry, 1872; Meeks, Leslie Howard. *Sheridan Knowles and the Theatre of his Time.* Bloomington, Ind.: Principia, 1933; Murray, Christopher. "James Sheridan Knowles: The Victorian Shakespeare?" In *Shakespeare and the Victorian Stage.* Cambridge: Cambridge University Press, 1986, pp. 164–179; Sweeney, St. John (Robert Hogan). "The Nineteenth Century Shakespeare." *Journal of Irish Literature* 13 (September 1984): 3–53.

L

LAMB, HILDA (ca. 1920–   ), historical novelist. Lamb was born Hilda Hawes in England of Irish descent. When very young, she was moved to Ireland and later became friends with various leaders of the nationalist movement and worked for many years on her first novel, *The Willing Heart* (1958), which was based on fifteenth- and sixteenth-century family papers.

WORKS: *The Willing Heart*. London: Hodder & Stoughton, [1958]; *Daughter of Aragon*. London: Robert Hale, 1965; *The Queen's Affair*. London: Robert Hale, 1968.

LANE, TEMPLE (1899–1978), novelist and poet. Temple Lane was the pseudonym of Mary Isabel Leslie, novelist, poet, and doctor of philosophy. She was born in Dublin in April, 1899, but spent most of her childhood in Tipperary. She was educated in England and later in Trinity College, Dublin, where she won the Large Gold Medal in 1922 and from which she received a Ph.D. As her father had a high position in the church as the dean of Lismore, she wrote under a pseudonym, which she chose at random—the name, in fact, of a street near her publishers. In 1932, she won Tailteann Gold Medal for her novel *The Little Wood*. She was a friend of Lady Gregory,* Elizabeth Bowen,* and Austin Clarke,* who encouraged her writing of verse. She died in Ballybrack, County Dublin, in February 1978.

She was a prolific and popular writer of what could be termed "female fiction before the Liberation." Her *Watch the Wall* (1927) is a formula romantic novel set in England during the Napoleonic Wars, and it uses the old trick of disguised identity rather unbelievably. Did the spirited young heroine really not recognize that her idle, laconic suitor and the heroic, daring smuggler were one and the same? A reader who was only half asleep would spot it on page two, but, if he continued ploughing through the turgid and stilted prose, he would find the whole effort a rather bad mixture of Georgette Heyer and Baroness Orczy, with neither the charm of the former nor the excitement of the latter.

Full Tide (1923) deals with the complex subject of snobbery and the break-down of class barriers between the wars in England. Although lucidly written and well observed and plotted, the novel is imbued with an irritating simplicity and nursery morality. A young widow whose husband was afflicted with "the vice of Drink" turns her hand to running a boarding house and manages a public school education and Cambridge for her son. But she neglects to spank him, so he turns out a snob and ashamed of her. All is forgiven when he acts the honorable gentleman in accordance with his education. After a spell in South America, no doubt he will come back and be the pillar of the family. This novel unwittingly upholds the system it aims to condemn. Virtue equals money: if you are brilliant and work hard to make enough, it does not matter if your father was only a chauffeur or your mother runs a boarding house. Money is honorable, or at least it covers a multitude of sins.

Friday's Well (1943), set in Ireland during World War II, suggests the danger of falling for the first good-looking American airman who drops from the sky. This is the fate of two sisters on a rural farm, but the airman is not what he seems, and they pay dearly. One sister is accidentally killed, but the other, after suffering, learns the true nature of love and marries the local bank manager. While the novel would be much better if edited to half its length, it does reflect the author's authentic knowledge of rural life and her ability to create fairly believable characters.

On the whole, however, Temple Lane writes to formula. There is little indi-viduality in her novels and much simplicity and humorless earnestness. Her poetry is not much better. It draws heavily on nature and expresses a sentimental hankering for the simple peasant life. Although she is sometimes remembered for "The Fairy Tree," set to music by Dr. Vincent O'Brien, her verses are little more than skillful rhyming and merry tinkles.

Brady and Cleeve remark that she also used the pseudonym of "Jean Her-bert"; Weekes remarks that she used the pseudonym of "Jane Herbert." A "Jean Herbert" did write a number of Mills & Boon romances in the 1940s and 1950s.

MARY ROSE CALLAGHAN

WORKS: *Burnt Bridges.* London: John Long, 1925; *No Just Cause.* London: John Long, 1925; *Defiance.* London: John Long, 1926; *Second Sight.* London: John Long, 1926; *Watch the Wall.* London: John Long, 1927; *The Bands of Orion.* London: Jarrolds, [1928]; *The Little Wood.* London: Jarrolds, [1930]; *Blind Wedding.* London: Jarrolds, [1931]; *Full Tide.* London: J. Heritage, [1932]; *Sinner Anthony.* London: Jarrolds, 1933; *The Trains Go South.* London: Jarrolds, [1938]; *Battle of the Warrior.* London: Jarrolds, [1940]; *Fisherman's Wake.* London: Longmans, [1940]. (Poems); *House of My Pilgrimage.* Dublin: Talbot/London: Frederick Muller, 1941; *Friday's Well.* Dublin: Talbot, 1943; *Come Back!* Dublin: Talbot, 1945; *Curlews.* Dublin: Talbot, 1946. (Poems); *My Bonny's Away.* Dublin: Talbot, 1947.

LANGBRIDGE, ROSAMUND (1880–?), novelist, journalist, and poet. Lang-bridge was born in Glenalla, County Donegal. She was the daughter of Reverend Frederick Langbridge, rector of St. John's, Limerick, chaplain of the district asylum, and a successful writer. Rosamund Langbridge was reared and privately educated in Limerick.

Langbridge was primarily a journalist and secondly a novelist. Her only volume of poetry, *The White Moth,* was published in 1932 when she was about fifty-two. Her first novel, *The Flame and the Flood* (1902), has a story line similar to that in one of her father's novels, *The Calling of the Weir.* Both books explore the results of marriages based on circumstances, rather than on love. Her father's treatment assumes a high moral tone and showcases his firmly Protestant convictions. Her novel takes a more ambiguous view of the couple's relationship and introduces a child as the welding agent in a marriage of convenience. Rosamund Langbridge's novels follow less orthodox paths than those of her father, with religion generally being downplayed. The only exception is *The Stars Beyond* (1907), in which the plot revolves around the heroine's religious indecision and her ultimate rejection of both the Catholic and the Protestant folds.

Perhaps her most interesting work, *Imperial Richenda* (1908), relates the life of a young waitress at a small hotel near Dublin. Stephen J. Brown in 1919 found the heroine "so equivocal that the book cannot be recommended for general reading." *Imperial Richenda* was slightly vulgar by early twentieth-century standards, but the humor and well-written dialogue are praiseworthy.

ANNE COLMAN

WORKS: *The Flame and the Flood.* London: Fisher, Unwin, 1902; *The Third Experiment.* London: Fisher, Unwin, 1904; *Ambush of Young Days.* London: Duckworth, 1906; *The Stars Beyond.* London: Nash, 1907; *Imperial Richenda.* London: Alston Rivers, 1908; *Land of the Ever Young.* London: S.P.C.K., 1920; *The Single Eye.* London: Hutchinson, ca. 1924; *The Golden Egg.* London: John Long, 1927; *Charlotte Brontë, A Psychological Study.* London: Heinemann, 1929; *The Green Banks of Shannon.* London: Collins, ca. 1929; *The White Moth.* London: G. G. Harrap, 1932. (Poetry).   REFERENCE: Brown, Stephen J. *Ireland in Fiction.* Dublin & London: Maunsel, 1919.

LANYON, CARLA LANYON (ca. 1905–?), poet. Lanyon was born in County Down and may have been related to Helen Lanyon.* At the age of nineteen, her first approach to a publisher was successful, and *The Wanderer and Other Poems* was published. She married Brigadier E. S. Hacker, and they had two sons and one daughter. She lived most of her life in England after her marriage. She published extensively, but her work has been undeservedly neglected. She was a judge for the Crabbe poetry competition in 1962 and served on the editorial panel of the magazine *Envoi.*

ANNE COLMAN

WORKS: *The Wanderer and Other Poems.* London: Sidgwick & Jackson, [ca. 1925]; *The Second Voyage.* London: Sidgwick & Jackson, 1928; *Far Country.* London: Sidgwick & Jackson, n.d. (Novel); *The Crag.* Oxford: Shakespeare Head, 1935; *Full Circle.* Oxford: Shakespeare Head, 1938.

LANYON, HELEN (ca. 1887–?), poet. Lanyon was the daughter of Elizabeth Helen Owens Lanyon and Sir Charles Lanyon, a well-known architect, former mayor of Belfast, and MP. The Lanyons lived at the Abbey, Whiteabbey, County

Antrim. Her brother, Sir William Owen Lanyon, was a colonial administrator, and she may have been related to Carla Lanyon Lanyon.* She was closely associated with the Belfast writers Ruth, Celia, and Emma Duffin, and Emma Duffin illustrated her *Fairy-Led and Other Verses* (1915). Lanyon's use of dialect is a bit clumsy, more so in the *Fairy-Led* volume than in her earlier *Hill o' Dreams* (1909), which is a better showcase for her talent. "The Girl Without a Dower" and "The House of Padraig" are particularly fine pieces, showing Lanyon's talented use of either the male or female persona in approaching the love between social unequals.

ANNE COLMAN

WORKS: *The Hill o' Dreams and Other Verses.* Dublin: Sealy, Bryers & Walker, 1909/New York: J. Lane, 1910; *Fairy-Led and Other Verses.* Belfast: W. & G. Baird, 1915.

LARGE, DOROTHY M[ABEL] (1891–?), fiction writer.

Large was born Dorothy Lumley in Tullamore, County Offaly. She was educated at Dr. Williams's School at Dolgelly in North Wales and at the Royal Irish Academy of Music in Dublin, which awarded her a teacher's certificate. She wrote humorous novels and tales and sketches of country life that tend to be sentimental and broadly brogued. She is pleasant enough, but hardly in the same class as Somerville and Ross* or George A. Birmingham* or even Lynn Doyle.*

WORKS: *Songs of Slieve Bloom.* Dublin: Talbot, 1926. (Poetry); *Cloonagh.* London: Constable, 1932; *Irish Airs.* London: Constable, 1932; *The Open Arms.* London: Constable, 1933; *An Irish Medley.* Belfast: Quota, [1934]; *The Cloney Carol, and Other Verses.* Belfast: Quota, 1934; *The Kind Companion.* Dublin & Cork: Talbot/London: Butterworth, 1936/New York: Frederick A. Stokes, 1937; *Talk in the Townlands.* Dublin & Cork: Talbot, 1937; *The Glen of the Sheep.* Dublin & Cork: Talbot, [1938]; *Man of the House.* Dublin: Browne & Nolan, 1939; *The Onlooker.* London: Methuen, 1940; *The Quiet Place.* London: Methuen, 1941.

LARKIN, MARY

WORK: *The Wasted Years.* London: Warner, 1993. (Novel).

LARMINIE, WILLIAM (1849?–1900), folklorist, poet, and critic.

Larminie was born in Castlebar, County Mayo, in 1849 or 1850 and graduated from Trinity College. Toward the end of his life, he published some carefully collected and charmingly told folktales as well as two volumes of verse. He is critically interesting because he advocated the use of the assonance of Gaelic poetry in English verse. His influence was not immediately apparent, perhaps partly because he was not as able a practitioner of poetry as he was a critic. It remained for Austin Clarke* several decades later to adapt assonance into English poetry in a more thoroughgoing and satisfying manner. AE* remarked of Larminie's poetry that "he is much more concerned with the subject of his thought than with the expression. . . . I might describe him as a poet by saying that the spirit is indeed kingly, but without the purple robe which would be the outer token of his lofty rank." Phillip L. Marcus justly points to his poem

"Consolation" as his finest achievement. Larminie also made an unpublished translation of Johannes Scotus Eriugena which has been described as superb. He died in Bray on January 19, 1900.

WORKS: *Fand and Other Poems*. Dublin: Hodges, Figgis, 1892; *West Irish Folk-Tales and Romances*. London: Elliot Stock, 1893; "The Development of English Metres." *Contemporary Review* 66 (November 1894): 717–736; "Joannes Scotus Eriugena." *Contemporary Review* 71 (April 1897): 557–572; *Glanlua and Other Poems*. London: Kegan Paul, 1899. REFERENCES: Eglinton, John. "William Larminie." *Dublin Magazine,* New Series XIX (April–June 1944): 12–16; Marcus, Phillip L. *Yeats and the Beginning of the Irish Renaissance*. Ithaca & London: Cornell University Press, [1970], pp. 207–221.

LAVELLE, PATRICIA (1898–1963), novelist and biographer. Lavelle was born on July 23, 1898, and died on May 5, 1963. She spent her childhood mainly in London as the eldest daughter of James O'Mara, a Westminster MP for Kilkenny, who resigned his seat to form the first Dail in the Mansion House. She married Richard Lavelle, a dispensary doctor, in 1924 and lived in Connemara, Ballinasloe, and Castleknock, moving as her children needed to be educated. She had five children, one of whom is the artist Colm Lavelle.

Her novel, *Crumbling Castle* (1949), is an enjoyable read and a valuable portrait of Irish society from the Famine to the Black and Tan War of Independence. It interweaves the story of several County Cork families, both peasant and Big House, and shows that in Ireland the borders between them were not so clearly defined. It is a pity that Lavelle did not write more novels in the same John Galsworthyish vein. There is, however, one unpublished novel.

In 1961, Lavelle published a biography of her father, who played a major role in raising the Dollar Loan in America. The book is also a valuable portrait of Irish society in that it traces the origins of an Irish Catholic merchant family, the O'Maras of Limerick, from the time of the Famine. Except for the novels of Kate O'Brien,* the Catholic middle classes were not much portrayed in Irish literature; and it is a fascinating literary footnote that the young protagonist of O'Brien's *Without My Cloak* was a keen gardener, as was the young James O'Mara. Indeed, Kate O'Brien's sister was married to another O'Mara, and *Without My Cloak* is supposed to be based on that family.

MARY ROSE CALLAGHAN

WORKS: *Crumbling Castle*. Dublin: Clonmore & Reynolds, [1949]; *James O'Mara, A Staunch Sinn Féiner, 1873–1948*. Dublin: Clonmore & Reynolds, [1961].

LAVERTY, MAURA [KELLY] (1907–1966), novelist, playwright, and author of cookbooks. Laverty was born and raised in Rathangan, a small village in County Kildare, a milieu which she vividly describes in her first novel, *Never No More* (1942). Following the death of the beloved grandmother who had provided her a home at "Derrymore House," she studied school teaching at the Brigadine Convent in County Carlow. In 1925, she went to Madrid as a governess. The need for a young girl to set her own values in a foreign culture is described in a second autobiographical novel, *No More than Human* (1944). In

Spain, she became a secretary to Princess Bibesco, a foreign correspondent in the Banco Calamarte, and finally a journalist for the paper *El Debate*. She returned to Ireland as a journalist and broadcaster in 1928. She was, for a time, in charge of women's and children's programs on Radio Éireann. She died unexpectedly of a heart attack on July 26, 1966, at her home in Rathfarnham.

Laverty's most noteworthy work is *Lift Up Your Gates* (1946; also published under the title, *Liffey Lane,* 1947). This well-structured, naturalistic novel follows Chrissie Doyle, a fourteen-year-old, fatherless girl of the Dublin slums, through her evening paper route. As she visits at the shops and mews-flats on the better side of Liffey Lane, we experience the backgrounds and present concerns of each of her customers. With all but one, there is an exchange of feeling and an attempt at mutual understanding. Chrissie's love of her small cousin, Kevin, and her need to make reparation to Sister Martha, a nun who believes in and fosters Chrissie, provide continuity and direction. Telefis Éireann's popular serial "Tolka Row" was based on this novel.

Sean O'Faolain* wrote an enthusiastic preface for *Never No More,* finding its innocent heroine, its garrulous, meandering narrative, and its mixture of village hyperbole and candor irresistible. Memories of her grandmother's cookery prompted Laverty to compose this first novel, and she tends to include recipes in all her rural books. She has written several cookbooks as well: *Flour Economy* (1941), *Kind Cooking* (1946), and *Full and Plenty* (1960).

Touched by Thorn (1943; also published as *Alone We Embark*) received an Irish Women Writers' Award and was banned in Ireland, probably because one of its heroines was guilty of marital infidelity. The novel has several memorable village characters and a typically strong, mature woman who provides guidance and culinary delicacies for village young people. The work is seriously marred, however, by a melodramatic conclusion that solves everyone's problems.

Laverty has also published several children's works, including *Gold of Glanaree* (1945), which combines a charming depiction of the daily lives of village children with an intriguing treasure hunt.

Laverty focuses on the sensitive, innocent point of view of girls and women. She represents Irish hospitality and rural life with spirit, feeling and candor, but sometimes has difficulty resolving plots and holding sentimentality in check.

BONNIE KIME SCOTT

WORKS: *Flour Economy.* Dublin: Browne & Nolan, [1941]; *Never No More.* London & New York: Longmans, 1942; *Alone We Embark.* London: Longmans, 1943/ in the United States as *Touched by the Thorn.* New York: Longmans, Green, 1943; *No More Than Human.* London: Longmans, 1944; *Gold of Glanaree.* New York: Longmans, Green, 1945; *The Cottage in the Bog.* Dublin: Browne & Nolan, 1946; *Lift Up Your Gates.* London: Longmans, Green, 1946/in the United States as *Liffey Lane,* New York: Longmans, Green, 1947; *Maura Laverty's Cook Book.* London: Longmans, Green, 1946/New York & Toronto: Longmans, Green, 1947; *The Green Orchard.* London: Longmans, Green, [1949]; *Kind Cooking.* Dublin: Electricity Supply Board, [1955]; *The Queen of Aran's Daughters.* [Dublin]: Poolbeg, [1995]. (Fairy stories).

LAVIN, MARY (1912–1996), short story writer and novelist. Lavin was born on June 11, 1912, in East Walpole, Massachusetts, the only child of Thomas and Nora (Mahon) Lavin. Nora, finding that she "loathed and detested" life in the United States, left her husband in America and returned with the nine-year-old Mary to the family home in Athenry, County Galway. After eight months, they purchased a house in Dublin, at Tom Lavin's expense and insistence. He reunited with his family there for several years before assuming the management of an estate in Bective, County Meath, that had been purchased by his American employer.

Mary Lavin attended the Loreto Convent school and University College, Dublin, where she won first honors in English and wrote an M.A. thesis on Jane Austen. She discovered her gift for fiction writing halfway through a dissertation on Virginia Woolf, which she promptly abandoned; and she says, since then "I have never written a single paragraph that has not had its source in the imagination." She taught French at her old convent school for two years before marrying William Walsh, a school friend and Dublin lawyer. When her beloved father died in 1945, Lavin and her young family used her inheritance to buy the Abbey Farm in Bective, close to where he had worked. The Walshes had three daughters, Valentine, Elizabeth, and Caroline, born in 1943, 1945, and 1953, respectively. Walsh himself died in 1954, leaving Lavin a young widow with three small children, a situation similar to that in "Happiness," one of her most popular stories. The widow in that story takes some comfort from Father Hugh, a priest, as did Lavin. She married Michael MacDonald Scott, a laicized Jesuit and old friend, in 1969.

Her first short story, "Miss Holland," was published in 1938. Though she has written two novels and some poetry, she is primarily committed to the genre of the short story, saying that "it is in the short story that a writer distills the essence of his thought." Part of her motivation was also the time constraints placed on her as a mother, farmer, and wife. Her later work has tended toward longer stories or novellas.

Though she does not consider herself an Irish writer per se, Lavin shares with her compatriots a tragicomic sense of the world, of humor within pain. Some critical ink has been spilled debating the issue of whether her vision is more tragic than comic or vice versa, but that very debate points up the fine ambiguity of her writing. Her awareness of the always doubled meaning of events, no matter how mundane, gives her often deceptively simple stories a depth and universality rare in modern fiction.

In her writing, Lavin is not driven by any political concerns. Her vision is profoundly personal, her style introspective. She writes compellingly of domestic situations in which passions are contained by religion, social mores, or just the sheer bulk of shared pain that separates couples or families instead of bringing them together. This is not to imply, however, that her characters are, in any radical way, disconnected from society. Indeed, they suffer from external constraints as much as internal ones. The themes for her stories are taken from quotidian reality: marriages good and bad, the struggles of children, loneliness, poverty, and the all-pervasive topic of social-class order. These situations, particularly the last, lead to the theme of freedom and escape that runs through much of her work. Another theme she often considers is death and mourning. Death is sometimes a punishment for illicit passion, as in her novel *The House in Clewe Street,* in which the servant girl Onny Soraghan is killed by a botched abortion. But it can also be a consummation devoutly to be wished, by the dying if not the survivors, as is Robert's death in "A Happy Death." Many of Lavin's characters seek peace in death; though suicide in these Roman Catholic stories never presents a legitimate alternative, most of Lavin's characters expect to achieve some sort of heavenly reward after life's struggle. While few of her characters do escape their difficult existences, the rest generally manage to cope, to rationalize, and to make the best of their lot.

One of the distinguishing characteristics of Lavin's fiction and one that marks it as distinctly female fiction is the concentration on relationships between and among women. Some of her most widely known stories are focused on this theme, including "The Becker Wives," "Lilacs," and "The Small Bequest," to name but a few. These relationships are as often marked by dedication and love as pettiness and snobbery; for every "Small Bequest" there is a "Happiness." In this, as in her treatment of comedy and tragedy, Lavin takes an admirably parallactic view. Some of her best stories deal intensely with some of the issues of widowhood she faced in her own life, including "In a Cafe," "The Cuckoo-Spit," and "Happiness." The last of these, especially, is a gracefully drawn vignette of a woman at once mourning her loss and rejoicing in her life.

Recognized with various prizes, such as the Katherine Mansfield Award, the Ella Lynan Cabot Award, and two Guggenheim fellowships, and in 1992 elected Saoi by members of Aosdána,* Lavin's work is now acquiring serious scholarly notice. The understated nature of her prose and her prominence as a female writer in the overwhelmingly male tradition of Irish letters make her a fine candidate for contemporary critical study. She died on March 25, 1996.

MARY E. DONNELLY

WORKS: *Tales from Bective Bridge.* Boston: Little, Brown, 1942/London: Michael Joseph, 1943/ reprint, Dublin: Poolbeg, 1978; *The Long Ago and Other Stories.* London: Michael Joseph, 1944; *The House in Clewe Street.* Boston: Little, Brown/London: Michael Joseph, 1945. (Novel); *The Becker Wives and Other Stories.* London: Michael Joseph, 1946; *At Sallygap and Other Stories.* Boston: Little, Brown, 1947; *Mary O'Grady.* Boston: Little, Brown/London: Michael Joseph, 1950. (Novel); *A Single Lady and Other Stories.* London: Michael Joseph, 1951; *The Patriot Son and Other Stories.* London: Michael Joseph, 1956; *A Likely Story.* New York: Macmillan/Dublin: Dolmen, 1957; *Selected Stories.* New York: Macmillan, 1959; *The Great Wave and Other Stories.* London & New York: Macmillan, 1961; *The Stories of Mary Lavin.* Vol. 1. London: Constable, 1964/Vol. 2, 1974; *In the Middle of the Fields and Other Stories.* London: Constable, 1967/New York: Macmillan, 1969; *Happiness and Other Stories.* London: Constable, 1969; *Collected Stories.* Boston: Houghton Mifflin, 1971; *The Second Best Children in the World.* Boston: Houghton Mifflin, 1972: *A Memory and Other Stories.* London: Constable, 1972/Boston: Houghton Mifflin, 1973; *The Shrine and Other Stories.* London: Constable, 1977; *A Family Likeness and Other Stories.* London: Constable, 1985. REFERENCES: Bowen, Zack. *Mary Lavin.* Lewisburg, Pa.: Bucknell University Press/London: Associated University Presses, 1975; Deane, Seamus. "Mary Lavin." In *The Irish*

Short Story. Patrick Rafroidi & Terence Brown, eds. Gerrards Cross: Colin Smythe/Atlantic Highlands, N.J.: Humanities, 1979; Dunleavy, Janet Egleson. "Mary Lavin, Elizabeth Bowen, and a New Generation: The Irish Short Story at Midcentury." In *The Irish Short Story.* James Kilroy, ed. [Boston]: Twayne, [1984]; *Irish University Review,* Mary Lavin Special Issue 9 (Autumn 1979); Kelly, A. A. *Mary Lavin: Quiet Rebel.* Dublin: Wolfhound, 1978/New York: Barnes & Noble, 1980; Peterson, Richard. *Mary Lavin.* Boston: Twayne, 1978

LAWLESS, EMILY (1845–1913), novelist and poet. Lawless, known in her day as the Honorable Emily Lawless, was born on June 17, 1845, the eldest daughter of the third Baron Cloncurry, a wealthy Anglo-Irish nobleman whose family rose to prominence in the late eighteenth century. Her mother, Elizabeth Kirwan, was a noted beauty and society woman from County Galway. The family was star-crossed, however, and Emily's father and two of her sisters committed suicide. She herself was noted for eccentricity and led a somewhat unhappy, if full, life. During her final years, in poor mental and physical health, she retreated into seclusion, but in her heyday she was one of the foremost Irish writers of both poetry and fiction. Her third novel, *Hurrish* (1886), appeared at a time when the question of Home Rule dominated politics in Ireland and England; the book examines the relationship of the Irish tenant farmer to the English law. Although sentimental and melodramatic, it won the praise of Gladstone, who felt that it shed much light on the Irish problem. Subsequently, Gladstone became Lawless's friend and occasional correspondent. Indeed, her ties with important figures in the political world, especially Sir Horace Plunkett, played a large part in her emotional and intellectual life until the very end. Always, however, she remained a Loyalist. Although she spent her final years in Surrey for reasons of health, her disenchantment with the turn that she discerned in Irish politics was equally important in her decision to leave Ireland.

Lawless wrote ten novels, four books of verse, a popular general history of Ireland, a biography of Maria Edgeworth,* and numerous short stories and historical essays. She was also a naturalist and published monographs in entomology. The best of her works are *Grania* (1892), *Maelcho* (1894), and *With the Wild Geese* (1902). *Grania* is a romantic depiction of life on the Aran Islands; the heroine dies tragically, her fiancé failing to come to her aid when she attempts to cross the rough seas in search of a priest for her dying sister. Sentimentality predominates, but the evocation of the landscape and day-to-day life of the Aran peasants is detailed and realistic. Lawless preceded Synge* in realizing the artistic possibilities of the barren islands. Swinburne hailed this novel as "one of the most exquisite and perfect works of genius in the language." *Maelcho* is an historical novel set in the Desmond Rebellion; it is panoramic, overlong, and sometimes disjointed in plot. The author's grasp of the political and economic causes of the war as well as her re-creation of the suffering and persecution endured by the Gaels give the work enduring value. In general, Lawless's historical fiction is superior to her other work. Mention should also be made of *With Essex in Ireland* (1890), which was originally published as an authentic sixteenth-century document but which Lawless later admitted having written herself. The work is noteworthy for its poetic rendering of a war-torn land and the antique richness of its language. *With the Wild Geese* contains the best of the author's verse. These are ballads and lyrics, many based on historical themes. Early in the century, this verse—especially "After Aughrim," "Clare Coast," and "Dirge of the Munster Forest"—was highly praised by both sides in the Home Rule controversy.

Rather than a member of the literary renaissance per se, Emily Lawless should be regarded as one of its forerunners. Her best work, verse or prose, both laments and celebrates Ireland's history. Some correspondence is contained in Marsh's Library in Dublin. She died in Gomshall, Surrey, on October 19, 1913.

WILLIAM J. LINN

WORKS: *A Chelsea Householder.* 3 vols. London: Sampson Low, 1882/New York: Holt, 1883. (Novel); *A Millionaire's Cousin.* London: Macmillan/New York: Holt, 1885. (Novel); *Hurrish: A Study.* 2 vols. Edinburgh: W. Blackwood/New York: Harper, 1886. (Novel); *Major Lawrence, F.L.S.* 3 vols. London: John Murray/New York: Holt, 1887. (Novel); *Ireland.* London & New York: T. Fisher Unwin, 1887/revised 1912 and 1923; *Plain Frances Mowbray and Other Tales.* London: John Murray, 1889; *With Essex in Ireland.* London: Smith, Elder/New York: J. W. Lovell, 1890/ new edition, London: Methuen, 1902. (Historical novel); *Grania: The Story of an Island.* 2 vols. London: Smith, Elder/New York: Macmillan, 1892. (Novel); *Maelcho: A Sixteenth-Century Narrative.* 2 vols. London: Smith, Elder/New York: D. Appleton, 1894; *A Colonel of the Empire.* New York: D. Appleton, 1895; *Traits and Confidences.* London: Methuen, 1897. (Stories); *Atlantic Rhymes and Rhythms.* Privately printed, 1898; *A Garden Diary. September 1899–September 1900.* London: Methuen, 1901; *With the Wild Geese.* London: Isbister, 1902. (Poems); *Maria Edgeworth.* London & New York: Macmillan, 1904; *The Book of Gilly: Four Months Out of a Life.* London: Smith, Elder, 1906; *The Point of View: Some Talks and Disquisitions.* London & Bungay: Richard Clay, 1909; with Shan F. Bullock, *The Race of Castlebar.* London: John Murray, 1913; *The Inalienable Heritage and Other Poems.* London: Privately printed, 1914; *The Poems of Emily Lawless.* Edited and introduced by Padraic Fallon. Dublin: Dolmen, 1965. REFERENCES: Brewer, Betty Webb. "She Was a Part of It": Emily Lawless (1845–1913)." *Éire-Ireland* 18 (Winter 1983): 119–131; Brewer Betty Webb. "Emily Lawless: An Irish Writer above All Else." Diss., University of North Carolina, 1982; Cahalan, James M. "Forging a Tradition: Emily Lawless and the Irish Literary Canon." *Colby Quarterly* 27 (March 1991): 27–39; Grubgeld, Elizabeth. "The Poems of Emily Lawless and the Life of the West." *Turn-of-the-Century Women* 3 (Winter 1986): 35–41; Grubgeld, Elizabeth. "Emily Lawless's *Grania: The Story of an Island.*" *Éire-Ireland* 22 (Fall 1987): 115–129; Linn, William J. "The Life and Works of the Hon. Emily Lawless, First Novelist of the Irish Literary Revival." Diss., New York University, 1971.

LAWRENCE, W[ILLIAM] J. (1862–1940), historian and critic of the drama. Lawrence was born in Belfast on October 29, 1862. His formal academic training ended in his middle teens, and his formidable learning and scholarship are owing only to his own prodigious industry and capacity for grubbing through innumerable dusty manuscripts and journals. He became best known as an historian of the Elizabethan stage. Critics as prestigious as T. S. Eliot admired such books as *Pre-Restoration Stage Studies* (1927), *The Physical Conditions of the Elizabethan Public Playhouse* (1927), *Shakespeare's Workshop* (1928), *Those Nut-Cracking Elizabethans* (1935), *Old Theatre Days and Ways* (1935), and *Speeding up Shakespeare* (1937). Lawrence's fascination with the stage led him into almost equally significant work on the eighteenth- and nineteenth-century theatre.

Lawrence's importance for Irish literature lies in his influence as a drama critic, largely for the London journal *The Stage*. From the time of Synge* to the time of O'Casey,* he wrote the most thoughtful, knowledgeable critiques of Irish plays and productions. His strength as a critic was, nevertheless, diminished by a strong Ulster puritanism and by a violent dislike of W. B. Yeats.* Thus, Lawrence often found himself in untenable but never relinquished critical positions, such as his vitriolic condemnations of Synge's *Playboy of the Western World*. Despite his deficiencies, Lawrence was the most engaged Irish theatre critic of the first quarter of this century. Even his most arrant prejudices brought to the drama an embattled and probably healthy vigor. He died in August 1940.

WORK: "Reviews of the Irish Theatre," ed. and with an Introduction by Peter Drewniany. *Journal of Irish Literature* 18 (May & September 1989): 1–60 & 11–39. REFERENCE: Hogan, Robert. "Yeats Creates a Critic." In *'Since O'Casey!' and Other Essays on Irish Drama*. Gerrards Cross: Colin Smythe, 1983, pp. 11–24.

LEADBEATER, MARY (1758–1826), writer of sketches. Leadbeater née Shackleton was born of a Quaker family in Ballitore, County Kildare, in December 1758. She became a friend of Maria Edgeworth* who helped her circulate her *Cottage Dialogues*. Her *Annals of Ballitore* and her posthumous *Leadbeater Papers* retell with clarity and energy anecdotes of life in her Irish Quaker village. In her account of the effect of the Insurrection of 1798 on her village, her direct style well captures the confusion and terror. She died in Ballitore on June 27, 1826. Her daughter, Mrs. Lydia Fisher, was the friend and inspiration of Gerald Griffin* and preserved many of his poems.

WORKS: *Extracts and Original Anecdotes for the Improvement of Youth*. Dublin: Jackson, 1794; *Poems*. . . . Dublin: Keene, 1808; *Cottage Dialogues among the Irish Peasantry*. London: Johnson, 1811; *The Landlord's Friend*. Dublin: Cumming, 1813; with Elizabeth Shackleton, *Tales for Cottagers, Accomodated to the Present Condition of the Irish Peasantry*. Dublin: Cumming, 1814; *Cottage Biography*. Dublin: C. Bentham, 1822; *Memoirs and Letters of Richard and Elizabeth Shackleton*. . . . London: Harvey & Darton, 1822; *Biographical Notices of Members of the Society of Friends, Who Were Resident in Ireland*. London: Harvey & Darton, 1823; *The Pedlars*. Dublin: Bentham & Harvey, 1826; *The Leadbeater Papers*. 2 vols. London: Bell & Daldy, 1862. REFERENCE: Young, Margaret Ferrier. "Ballitore and Its Institutions." *Journal of the County Kildare Archaeological Society* 8 (1916): 167–179. Contains some Leadbeater letters.

LEAMY, EDMUND (1848–1904), politician and writer of fairy tales. Leamy was born in Waterford on December 25, 1848. He became MP for Waterford and remained a staunch supporter of Parnell. In the fight for leadership of the Irish Party in Committee Room Fifteen, he and John Redmond rushed forward to restrain Parnell, who was apparently going to strike the inoffensive Justin McCarthy.* He was there when Parnell smashed the door of the *United Ireland* office with a crowbar. Much less violent were his popular Irish fairy stories, although they are perhaps a bit pretty in style and saccharine in tone for modern taste. He died in Pau on December 10, 1904.

WORKS: *Irish Fairy Tales.* Dublin: M. H. Gill, [1890]; *The Fairy Minstrel of Glenmalure, and Other Stories for Children.* Dublin: J. Duffy, [1899]; *By the Barrow River, and Other Stories.* Dublin: Sealy, Bryers, 1907; *The Golden Spears, and Other Fairy Tales.* New York: D. FitzGerald, [ca. 1911]. Stephen J. Brown attributes to Leamy the volume *Leandro; or, The Sign of the Cross. A Catholic Tale.* Philadelphia: P. F. Cunningham, 1870.

LECKY, W[ILLIAM] E[DWARD] H[ARTPOLE] (1838–1903), historian. Lecky was born on March 26, 1838, at Newtown Park, County Dublin. He attended Trinity College where he also taught and which he represented in the Westminster Parliament from 1895 to 1903. His formidable learning is apparent in his *Leaders of Public Opinion in Ireland* (1861), his two-volume *History of the Rise and Influence of Rationalism in Europe* (1865), and his two-volume *History of European Morals from Augustus to Charlemagne* (1869). His magnum opus is the twelve-volume *History of England in the Eighteenth Century* (1892). Five of the twelve volumes are devoted to a history of Ireland. This imbalance occurred because Lecky wanted to refute what he considered the calumnies of the historian Froude against the Irish people. Nevertheless, although a fair historian, Lecky was not a conventional nationalist; as a member of Parliament he opposed Home Rule. He died on October 22, 1903, in Dublin.

WORKS: *Leaders of Public Opinion in Ireland.* London: Saunders, 1861/rev. ed., London: Longmans, Green, 1871; *History of the Rise and Influence of Rationalism in Europe.* 2 vols. London: Longmans, Green, 1865; *History of European Morals from Augustus to Charlemagne.* 2 vols. London: Longmans, 1869; *A History of England in the Eighteenth Century.* 8 vols. London: Longmans, Green, 1878–1890; *A History of Ireland in the Eighteenth Century.* 4 vols. London: Longmans, 1892–1896, 1902–1903; *The Political History of Value.* London: E. Arnold, 1892; *Democracy and Liberty.* 2 vols. London: Longmans, 1896; *The Map of Life: Conduct and Character.* London: Longmans, 1899; *Historical and Political Essays,* ed. E. Lecky. London: Longmans, 1908; *A Victorian Historian,* ed. H. Montgomery Hyde. London: Home & Van Thal, 1947. (Letters). REFERENCES: Auchmuty, James Johnston. *Lecky.* Dublin: Hodges, Figgis/London: Longmans, Green, 1945; Lecky, Mrs. Elisabeth. *A Memoir of the Right Hon. William Edward Hartpole Lecky.* London: Longmans, 1909; McCartney, Donal. *W.E.H. Lecky: Historian and Politician 1838–1903.* Dublin: Lilliput, 1994.

LEDWIDGE, FRANCIS (1887–1917), poet. Born on August 19, 1887, in Slane, County Meath, and largely self-educated, Francis Ledwidge became a grocer's assistant, miner, laborer, and foreman with the County Council. His first poems, in *Songs of the Fields* (1915), published with an introduction by his patron, Lord Dunsany,* betray many unassimilated influences of Gray, Goldsmith,* and Keats. Edward Marsh's *Georgian Poetry II* (1913–1915) fairly accommodated some of Ledwidge's conventional, decorative, vapid escapism. But with access to Dunsany's advice and castle library, he began to control his self-consciousness and partiality to trite allusions and archaisms and to develop his genuine sympathies for landscape and local history.

After his introduction to Yeats'* Dublin circle, a number of poems with mythological themes appeared. These are set in the Boyne Valley and reflect fresh rural scenes, discriminating changes of light and season, rain showers, birdsongs, fox-hunts, and folk customs. He began to write in the Irish mode: after Douglas Hyde's* *Love Songs of Connacht* and Thomas MacDonagh's* translations, dialect poems following Lady Gregory's* example, and many showing the influences of AE* and Yeats (*Songs of Peace,* 1917).

Like thousands of nationalists of his generation, Ledwidge joined the British Army in World War I and served with the Royal Inniskilling Fusiliers at Gallipoli, in Serbia, and on the Western Front. This was a cruelly ironic predicament for one who had been a founding member of the labor movement in Meath, an organizer of the Irish Volunteers in Slane, and the lone defender of the Sinn Féin party against the predominantly Redmondite elected officialdom. His decision to join the Royal Inniskilling Fusiliers was not primarily political, however. A love affair with a landowner's daughter—Ellie Vaughey—had ended abruptly in the summer of 1913, and as a large proportion of his work over the subsequent two years shows, he brooded long over this rejection. The protracted horrors of the Gallipoli episode, the shock at the news of Ellie's sudden death in 1915, and, some months later, the news of the execution of Thomas Mac-Donagh and Joseph Plunkett,* produced in Ledwidge deeper moods of doubt and despair, leading to recurring premonitions of his own imminent death. His gentle nature seems to have responded to the events of Easter Week principally because of the participation of other poets. And unlike the war poets, he wrote nothing—jingoist or pacifist—that springs directly from the experience of that conflict. Francis Ledwidge remained a regional and pastoral poet, whose single source of constant wonder is the local landmarks and vistas "where even the fields have their names and traditions." His work in some ways foreshadows that of Patrick Kavanagh* and Seamus Heaney.*

The news of Easter Week affected Ledwidge deeply. His elegies for the poets of the Rising grieve for personal and national losses: the leaders, Ledwidge's flock of blackbirds, were reincarnations of "The Dead Kings" of Tara. The natural aristocracy of Ireland had revealed itself in his generation. The figure of Cathleen Ni Houlihan superseded that of Ellie Vaughey in his poems, and in the apparent futility of the deaths of MacDonagh and Plunkett he saw harbingers of his own fate. The poetry of his last year turns to religious meditations and combines a sparer use of nature imagery, a wider range of Irish literary and historical allusion, a less artificial invocation of Celtic myth, and more experimentation in the Irish mode. This work contains most of his best achievements, though no poem in the collection is wholly successful. On July 31, 1917, at Boesinghe, near Ypres, Belgium, a bomb put an end to his growing. Ledwidge's lament for Thomas MacDonagh, set into Slane Bridge, is appropriately his own:

> He shall not hear the bittern cry
> In the wild sky where he is lain,
> Nor voices of the sweeter birds
> Above the wailing of the rain.

CÓILÍN OWENS

WORK: *The Complete Poems of Francis Ledwidge.* Alice Curtayne, ed. London: Martin Brian
& O'Keefe, 1974. REFERENCE: Curtayne, Alice. *Francis Ledwidge: A Life of the Poet.* London:
Martin Brian & O'Keefe, 1972.

LEE, J[OSEPH] J. (1942–   ), historian. The son of a policeman, J. J. Lee was
born in County Kerry. Thanks, in part, to the sacrifices of his mother, he was
educated at a boarding school, the Franciscan College in Gormanstown, County
Meath. He attended University College, Dublin, with great success and worked
for a spell in the Department of Finance before going in the mid-1960s to the
Institute of European History in Mainz, Germany. He then spent several years
at Peterhouse, Cambridge, as a fellow, lecturing mainly in German history. In
1973, he took the Chair of Modern History at University College, Cork, and
published his stimulating, albeit over-Weberian work, *The Modernisation of
Irish Society 1848–1918.* Lee has moved his interests into the twentieth century
and edited a Thomas Davis collection of lectures, *Ireland 1945–70* (1979). This
included much new material on innovative Irish premier Sean Lemass and the
modernization of Irish society. Lee was to bring these themes to a triumphant
conclusion in his *Ireland 1912–1985* (1989).

Media comment tended to place Lee in the "antirevisionist" camp. In one
sense, this was true: in public interventions, he explicitly adopted a patriotic
tone; and his *Ireland 1912–1985,* the first really major general work to appear
in the aftermath of R. F. Foster's* *Modern Ireland,* inevitably was perceived by
some as a kind of riposte. This impression was fueled perhaps by Lee's *Times
Literary Supplement* review of Foster's work, a review that was less enthusiastic
than many others. In fact, Joseph Lee's relationship to the mainstream nationalist
tradition was rather more complex. Without much argument on the point, Lee
assumes that the objections of the national revolution—saving the Irish language, an end to emigration, and a successful economy supporting a much larger
population—were entirely attainable. The mystery then becomes, Why has independent Ireland never looked remotely like achieving any of these objectives?
The answer, of course, lies in the quality of those chosen to guide the fortunes
of the new Irish state. These unimaginative politicians are mercilessly flayed
throughout Lee's text, a text that was, however, based on the soundest scholarship. The possibility that the whole project was flawed in the first place is
never discussed—for which piety (à la Trotsky in the *Revolution Betrayed*)
nationalist readers owe him much thanks. He is also brutal in his discussion of
Ulster Unionist ideology. On the basis of a rather skimpy presentation of texts,
he does not scruple to make striking (though hardly developed) analogy with
Nazi Germany and the apartheid regime in South Africa. These tonal felicities—
for a nationalist audience, at any rate—explain, in part, the great popular success
of *Ireland 1912–1985.* In fact, Lee was *not,* as some believed, the D. P. Moran
de ses jours; he was simply too generous in his sympathies and too quick-witted
to be open to that charge: where Moran saw the problem as Jews, Protestant

"sourfaces," and "West Britains," Lee saw it simply as the absence of "quality of mind." Indeed, he was regularly to bemoan its absence in many quarters of Irish life.

A serious practitioner in the field of modern German history as well, Lee is intellectually the most gifted of the professional historians working in Ireland in his generation. No one was quicker, wittier, or more incisive—qualities that gave great pleasure to his readers. In the Senate in the mid-1990s, no one made more thoughtful contributions to Irish public debate. By his midfifties, Lee had established himself as one of the most distinctive and authoritative voices of modern Ireland; it was good to recall also that he was still capable of making further major contributions to Irish and European historiography.

PAUL BEW

PRINCIPAL IRISH WORKS: *The Modernisation of Modern Irish Society 1848–1918.* Dublin: Gill & Macmillan, 1973; ed., *Ireland 1945–70.* Dublin: Gill & Macmillan, 1979. (Thomas Davis Lectures); *Ireland 1912–1985: Politics and Society.* Cambridge: Cambridge University Press, [1989].

LeFANU, ALICIA [SHERIDAN] (1754–1817), playwright. LeFanu was the third surviving child of Thomas Sheridan the younger* and Frances Chamberlaine Sheridan.* As a child, she was educated for a brief period with her brother Richard Brinsley* at Samuel Whyte's* school in Grafton Street, but when the children rejoined the family in England, her mother described them as "impenetrable dunces." After that, Alicia and her younger sister Betsy (Elizabeth*) were educated at home. She married the equally stagestruck Joseph LeFanu* on October 11, 1781. Earlier in the year, a two-act farce that has not survived, *The Ambitious Lover,* was performed in Dublin at Crowe Street. Her only play to be produced in London was *The Sons of Erin; or, Modern Sentiment,* which appeared at the Lyceum in 1812, her nephew Tom overseeing rehearsals and making "some judicious curtailments and alterations." Those curtailments were hardly judicious enough, for the five-act comedy ran for only one night. Part of the reason was its excessive length, and part was a seriousness of purpose that dissipated her comic effect. Her father's Irishman in *The Brave Irishman* and her brother's Sir Lucius O'Trigger in *The Rivals* had been little more than stage Irishmen. Alicia attempted to present an "Irish Gentleman," but her comedy is a very sober one, even though it was later produced in Dublin and Boston. There are references in her letters to several other plays, and she is said to have had a dramatization of one of her mother's novels produced in Dublin. According to Lady Morgan, her house in Dublin was something of a literary salon, and she herself was "charming." She died on September 4, 1817. One of her grandsons was the novelist Joseph Sheridan LeFanu.*

WORK: *The Sons of Erin; or, Modern Sentiment.* London: J. Ridgeway, 1812.

LeFANU, ALICIA (THE YOUNGER) (1791–1844 or later), novelist and poet. Alicia LeFanu was born in December 1791, the daughter of Henry LeFanu and

Betsy Sheridan (Elizabeth*). When Tom Moore* was interviewing her mother in 1818, he described Alicia as "a lively, mincing & precious little Blue Stocking." She published two volumes of verse, the first when she was eighteen, as well as a series of three- and four-volume novels and a biography of her grandmother, Frances Sheridan.* Her prolific pace of writing ceased in 1826, but she was still living in 1844, when Caroline Norton* succeeded in getting £150 for her from the Royal Bounty Fund. A remark in one of Caroline Norton's letters suggests that her cousin had grown into a difficult, somewhat intractable old maid. When and where she died are unknown.

Alicia LeFanu's poetry is worth little notice. It tends to be saccharine, metrically slovenly, oppressively poetic in diction, and always trite, except in a few quaint instances such as "liliaceous," which may mean lilylike. The *Dictionary of National Biography* describes her novels as "long-winded historical romances," and there is considerable justice to the charge. Although inestimably better than her insipid poems, they are much too long; but among some appallingly dismal passages are others of merit and individuality. *Strathallan,* her four-volume novel of 1816, for instance, reflects in its 300,000 words all of her worst faults as well as her occasionally surprising strengths. Her several plot strands are variously told: one romantically melodramatic, one distinctly Gothic, and one a social comedy of manners with a good deal of effective satire. The serious sections are full of fustian such as "Cast thine eyes on that withered plant: 'tis thus those bright locks must inglorious kiss the dust." The comedy, however, has some good lines, such as "a pair of blue eyes (which possessed every charm but meaning)." There is also a Mrs. Malaprop-like character who defines wrongdoing as "moral turpentine" but also borrows some of her uncle, Richard Brinsley Sheridan's,* best lines. However, as Alicia blandly remarks, "I am of the opinion of Charles in The School for Scandal, that it is very hard if one may not make free with one's own relations." This is fair enough, as Sheridan himself had borrowed some of his mother's best lines for Mrs. Malaprop.

Alicia's biography of Frances Sheridan is the source of much of what we know about her grandmother, and we may assume that her information came largely from her mother, Betsy.

WORKS: *The Flowers; or, The Sylphid Queen.* London: J. J. Harris, 1809. (Poetry); *Rosara's Chain; or, The Choice of Life.* London: M. J. Godwin, 1812. (Poetry); *Strathallan.* 4 vols. London: Sherwood, Neely & Jones, 1816. (Novel); *Helen Monteagle.* 3 vols. London: Sherwood, Neely & Jones, 1818. (Novel); *Leolin Abbey.* 3 vols. London, 1819. (Novel); *Don Juan de las Sierras, or, El Empecinado.* 3 vols. London: A. K. Newman, 1823. (Novel); *Tales of a Tourist.* 4 vols. London: A. K. Newman, 1823. (Containing *The Outlaw* and *Fashionable Connexions.* Fiction); *Memoirs of the Life and Writings of Mrs. Frances Sheridan.* . . . London: G. & W. Whittaker, 1824. (Biography); *Henry the Fourth of France.* 4 vols. London: A. K. Newman, 1826.

LeFANU, ELIZABETH ("BETSY") SHERIDAN (1758–1837), diarist and novelist. Betsy Sheridan was born in London in 1758, the last child of Thomas Sheridan the younger* and Frances Chamberlaine Sheridan.* She was educated at home, but after her mother's death her actor father, who was often traveling, put her under the care of her "overbearing and penurious" older brother Charles. After three miserable years with him in Dublin, she joined her now elderly father in London. After her father died, she lived with her brother Richard Brinsley Sheridan* and his wife, and her frequent accounts to her sister Alicia LeFanu* of her experiences form the basis of her posthumously published *Journal.* In it she gives a lively and valuable record of high society and of such tense public events as the Regency Crisis and the trial of Warren Hastings, in which Richard Brinsley so prominently figured. On July 4, 1789, she married Henry, the younger brother of Joseph LeFanu,* who had married her sister. They lived in rather straitened circumstances in Bath and in Dublin, and in 1804 she brought out a two-volume epistolary novel, *The India Voyage.* It is a pleasant moral entertainment, although the heroine is, like her mother's Sidney Bidulph, something of an overscrupulous prude. Her real ability is shown in her *Journal.* She died in England on January 4, 1837. Her daughter Alicia* was a novelist and poet.

WORKS: *The India Voyage.* 2 vols. London: G. & J. Robinson, 1804. (Novel); *Betsy Sheridan's Journal,* ed. William LeFanu. London: Eyre & Spottiswoode, 1960.

LeFANU, JOSEPH (1743–1825), playwright. Joseph LeFanu belonged to a Huguenot family that had settled in Dublin about 1730. His second wife was Richard Brinsley Sheridan's* sister, Alicia,* and their grandson was Joseph Sheridan LeFanu,* the novelist. Joseph LeFanu's younger brother Henry married Sheridan's younger sister, Betsy.* Both LeFanu and his wife were stagestruck and often took part in elaborate private theatricals in Dublin. LeFanu himself was a rather prolific and rather good playwright who gamely attempted every popular dramatic genre of the day in order to get a play produced—farce, sentimental comedy, burlesque, verse tragedy, adaptation, and translation. But, despite being the brother-in-law of Sheridan, who managed Drury Lane, and a good friend of George Colman, who managed Covent Garden, he had practically no success. His one London play, *The Hour before Marriage,* based on Molière's *Le Mariage Forcé,* was hissed off the stage about halfway through and never revived. It was published with mild success as by "a Gentleman of Dublin," but a contemporary reviewer ascribed the work to Colman, a mistake reiterated as late as 1962 by George Winchester Stone, Jr., in *The London Stage.* That did not keep the assiduous LeFanu from writing and submitting his plays to Colman, but he never had another production. He died in Dublin in December 1825.

WORKS: *The Hour before Marriage.* London: W. Johnston, 1772 (Two-act comedy); "The Lover's Plot." *Journal of Irish Literature* 20 (May 1991): 25–56. (Two-act farce). REFERENCE: Eldemann, Theo (Robert Hogan). "The Unlucky Joseph LeFanu." *Journal of Irish Literature* 20 (May 1991): 3–24. The holograph manuscripts of LeFanu's plays are housed in the library of Cambridge University. The LeFanu papers also contain many of Colman's letters to Joseph LeFanu.

LE FANU, JOSEPH SHERIDAN (1814–1873), novelist and short story writer. A generation younger than C. R. Maturin,* whom he resembles in many ways,

Le Fanu's stories and novels convey less of the melodramatic effects of Gothic fiction in favor of deeper psychological investigation. His novels rely on elaborate plot contrivances, but they play with intellectual themes, and his explorations of subconscious impulses are often startling.

Born in Dublin on August 28, 1814, Le Fanu was related on his mother's side to the playwright Richard Brinsley Sheridan.* He was educated at Trinity College and was called to the bar in 1839 before turning to a career as a journalist. Many of his stories appeared in the *Dublin University Magazine,* which he edited from 1861 to 1869. His output as a fiction writer is impressive: fourteen novels and a great number of short stories. After his wife's death in 1858, he withdrew from society, remaining a recluse until his death in Dublin on February 7, 1873.

Le Fanu's narrative techniques, particularly in the short stories, were often experimental. The five long stories that make up *In a Glass Darkly* (1872) employ complex narrative schemes with the effect that the undercurrents of sexual frustration and self-destruction are amplified. These are the best of his stories. In his later stories, the psychological effects are less dominant, and the characters are often representations of pure evil.

The greater scope of the novel form better suited Le Fanu's interests, allowing for a greater use of setting and more complex twists of plot. *The Cock and Anchor* (1845) is set in eighteenth-century Dublin and records a tale of gradual and horrifying corruption. *The House by the Churchyard* (1863), set in Chapelizod, presents a more familiar mystery plot. His masterpiece is *Uncle Silas* (1864), which is narrated by a young girl who was the victim of the title character. Her mounting horror as she discovers the plot to control and ultimately to destroy her is conveyed with subtlety so that the final effect is strong indeed. The art is in the technique rather than the message in the best of his works. The narrators are so well developed, and their confusion and sense of vulnerability so evocative, that the novels sustain a mood of terror.

JAMES KILROY

WORKS: *The Cock and Anchor, Being A Chronicle of Old Dublin.* 3 vols. Dublin: W. Curry, 1845; *The Fortunes of Colonel Torlogh O'Brien: A Tale of the Wars of King James.* Dublin: M'Glashan/London: Orr, 1847; *Ghost Stories and Tales of Mystery.* Dublin: M'Glashan/London: Orr, 1851; *The House by the Churchyard.* 3 vols. London: Tinsley, 1863; *Wylder's Hand.* 3 vols. London: Richard Bentley, 1864; *Uncle Silas: A Tale of Bartram-Haugh.* 3 vols. London: Richard Bentley, 1864; *The Prelude, Being a Contribution towards a History of the Election for the University* [of Dublin] by John Figwood, Esq. [Pseud]. Dublin: G. Herbert, 1865. (Pamphlet); *Guy Deverell.* 3 vols. London: Richard Bentley, 1865; *All in the Dark.* 2 vols. London: Richard Bentley, 1866; *The Tenants of Malory.* 3 vols. London: Tinsley/New York: Harpers, 1867; *A Lost Name.* 3 vols. London: Richard Bentley, 1868; *Haunted Lives.* 3 vols. London: Tinsley, 1868; *The Wyvern Mystery.* 3 vols. London: Hurst & Blackett, 1869; *Checkmate.* London: Hurst & Blackett, 1871; *The Rose and the Key.* London: Chapman & Hall, 1871; *Chronicles of Golden Friars.* London: Richard Bentley, 1871; *In a Glass Darkly.* London: Richard Bentley, 1872; *Morley Court.* London: Chapman & Hall, 1873; *Willing to Die.* London: Downey. [1873?]/London: Hurst & Blackett, 1873; *The Bird of Passage.* New York: D. Appleton, 1878; *The Purcell Papers.* 3 vols. London: Richard Bentley, 1880; *The Evil Guest.* London: Ward & Downey, [1894]; *The Watcher and Other Weird Stories.*

London: Downey, [1894]; *A Chronicle of Golden Friars and Other Stories.* London: Downey, 1896; *The Poems of Joseph Sheridan Le Fanu.* London: Downey, 1896; *Shamus O'Brien* (Comic Opera founded on a Poem by LeFanu, Book by G. H. Jessop). London: Boosey, 1896; *Madam Crowl's Ghost, and Other Tales of Mystery.* Collected & edited by M. R. James. London: G. Bell, 1923; *Best Ghost Stories.* E. F. Bleiler, ed. New York: Dover, 1964; *Ghost Stories and Mysteries.* E. F. Bleiler, ed. New York: Dover, 1975. (The Bleiler volumes contain some previously uncollected material); *Borrhomeo the Astrologer.* W. J. McCormack, ed. Edinburgh: Tragara, 1985. REFERENCES: Begnal, Michael. *Joseph Sheridan Le Fanu.* Lewisburg, Pa.: Bucknell University Press, 1971; Browne, Nelson. *Sheridan Le Fanu.* London: Arthur Barker, 1951; Coughlin, Patricia. "Doubles, Shadows, Sedan-Chairs and the Past: The 'Ghost Stories' of Joseph Sheridan Le Fanu." In *Critical Approaches to Anglo-Irish Literature.* Michael Allen & Angela Wilcox, eds. Gerrards Cross: Colin Smythe, 1989, pp. 17–39; Hall, Wayne. "Le Fanu's House by the Marketplace." *Éire-Ireland* 21 (Spring 1986): 55–72; Le Fanu, William. *Seventy Years of Irish Life.* London: Arnold, 1893; Le Fanu, T. P. *Memoir of the Le Fanu Family.* Manchester: Privately printed by Sheratt & Hughes, [1924?]; McCormack, W. J. *Sheridan Le Fanu and Victorian Ireland.* Oxford: Clarendon, 1980; Meloda, Ivan. *Sheridan Le Fanu.* Boston: Twayne, 1987; Millbank, Alison. *Daughters of the House: Modes of Gothic in Victorian Fiction.* New York: St. Martin's, 1992; Stoddart, Helen. " 'The Precautions of Nervous People Are Infectious': Sheridan Le Fanu's Symptomatic Gothic." *Modern Language Review* 86 (January 1991): 19–34; Sweeney, St. John. "Sheridan LeFanu, the Irish Poe." *Journal of Irish Literature* 15 (January 1986): 3–32.

LEITCH, MAURICE (1933–   ), novelist. Leitch was born in Muckamore, County Antrim, on July 5, 1933. He was educated in Belfast and was a schoolteacher before becoming a features producer for the BBC in Northern Ireland. He now works for the BBC in England.

The most striking feature of Leitch's novels is their dark and angry vision of Ulster, be it the Belfast of *The Liberty Lad* (1965), the County Antrim of that same novel and of *Stamping Ground* (1975), or the south Armagh of *Poor Lazarus* (1969), which won the *Guardian* annual fiction prize. His characters are held in the stranglehold of an inhibitive environment, a post-World War II Ulster that is shabby and unpleasant and whose beauties are largely unsung by the author. In part, this is because his Ulster is mainly planter Protestant, cut off (as Leitch is himself) from any nationalist dream of a beautiful past or beautiful future, but in part because his Ulster is a portion of twentieth-century Ireland, pseudo-Americanized and myopically expedient. The one leader in the novels, Bradley the Unionist member of Parliament in *The Liberty Lad* (the author's *bildungsroman*), is a corrupt homosexual. Uneasy bonds between men underlie, in varying degrees of explicitness, the male camaraderie of Leitch's "hell-raisers" whose desperate antics conceal their loneliness and misogyny. When "hell-raising" becomes violent, as in *Poor Lazarus* and *Stamping Ground,* Leitch's fiction approaches the grotesquerie and even diabolism of the Irish comic tradition. Sectarianism is, of course, a constant source of violence and hatred. Leitch courageously explores the uneasy, peacetime concealment of sectarianism in *Poor Lazarus,* a fine and troubling story of a brief relationship between a local Protestant and a Catholic Irish-Canadian.

Leitch creates his world through his story lines but also through his prose style, the appropriateness of which is a two-edged sword, since he has cultivated a rather costive and flairless way of writing in order to create a social world equally devoid of flair and fluency. *Stamping Ground* is his densest work to date. It supports more characters than his two earlier novels (including Minnie Maitland, the spinster inhabitant of the local Protestant "Big House" and an almost Faulkerian creation), and it consists entirely of foreground, the characters' thoughts and musings, which are sometimes trivial. For density of texture, Leitch pays the price of a certain narrative and perspective and interest.

Northern Ireland did not maintain an unbreakable grip on Leitch, except perhaps in that psychic way familiar to exiled Irish authors. After some years as a schoolteacher—an experience he exploits in *The Liberty Lad*—he joined BBC Northern Ireland, and soon after that left for London where he is the Head of BBC Radio's drama features.

                                                      JOHN WILSON FOSTER

Silver's City won the Whitbread Prize for Fiction in 1981. It is a novel of the Northern Troubles and tells of a man, Silver, who had become something of a patriotic icon for killing a man in the early days. After ten years in prison and terminally ill, he is abducted from his hospital bed and plunged into a Belfast quite different from the one he had known and much more ruthless and vicious. The plot has its excitements, with Silver's accidental escape from his captors and some subsequent hide-and-seek. The tone, as is usual with Leitch, is glumly depressed and depressing.

Sonny in *Burning Bridges* (1989) is a forty-year-old exile from Ulster who lives in London, adores Hank Williams, dresses in cowboy clothes, and sings country and western songs. He leads an aimless life of drink and drugs until he meets Hazel, also from Ulster, at the funeral of a casual friend. Her life in England has been similarly unhappy, its sordid high point having been, years earlier, a friendship with the once-notorious Christine Keeler and Mandy Rice-Davis. He buys a van, and they head for Stonehenge and points west, meeting on the way New Age travelers and pitiful middle-aged country and western aficionados. Their relationship is warm and sensual and breaks up only because of Hazel's need to reclaim her punk teenage daughter. Sonny returns, sad and battered, to Ulster. There are more warmth and humanity in this picaresque journey than are usual in Leitch's sordid and pointless world, and it is one of his best works.

The Hands of Cheryl Boyd (1989) is a collection of stories, several of which are also about journeys in a bleak and tawdry world. "Black Is the Colour" is an account of a married man's seduction of a young black woman. "The Temperate House" tells of a pointless Sunday afternoon journey to Kew Gardens made by an Irishman and an elderly actor he has met in a pub. "Monkey Nuts" tells of a woman's journey from Northern Ireland to Towanda, Pennsylvania, to discover the father whom she had never known. She discovers, but does not speak to, a seedy old man. "Where Are You Taking Us Today, Daddy?" is about a man, separated from his wife, taking his children on an unfortunate outing to the scenes of his youth. "Green Roads" is about a small patrol of

British soldiers whose Landrover becomes mired down is some back country Irish road. The point of the stories seems to be the Beckettian* one that there is not much point.

Gilchrist (1995) is an uneven novel about a hellfire preacher who has absconded with church funds to run away with a teenage nymphet. The present plot, which occurs at a cheap resort on the Spanish coast after the girl has left Gilchrist, is an ambling affair, involving a dubious sort of doppelgänger of the hero and culminating in the hero's suicide. Some past incidents, however, are more dramatized, particularly the time the hero spent in his late teens as a mind reader with a ratty theatrical company.

Leitch has continued to produce, generally every three or four years, a serious and able work of fiction. His view of the world is an unrelievedly somber one. The lives of his characters seem tawdry and futile and usually end in death or failure. The world that he creates, however, is depressingly plausible.

WORKS: *The Liberty Lady.* London: MacGibbon & Kee, 1965; *Poor Lazarus.* London: MacGibbon & Kee, 1969; *Stamping Ground.* London: Secker & Warburg, 1975; *Silver's City.* London: Secker & Warburg, 1981; *Chinese Whispers.* London: Hutchinson, 1987; *The Hands of Cheryl Boyd and Other Stories.* London: Hutchinson, [1989]; *Burning Bridges.* London: Hutchinson, 1989; *Gilchrist.* London: Secker & Warburg, [1995].

LELAND, JEREMY (1932–   ), novelist and short story writer. Leland's ancestors were Huguenots who fled to Ireland in the sixteenth century, and he is a descendant of the eighteenth-century Thomas Leland, who wrote the three-volume *History of Ireland* (1773). Leland studied painting at the Slade School in London, and then, from 1955 to 1965, he farmed near Drogheda and began to write. He then moved to Norwich and worked as a textile designer and then in a Citizens' Advice Bureau.

A River Decrees (1969) is a very leisurely novel about a couple boating on the Shannon after the young wife recently had a miscarriage. They go to a party, and the vulnerable young wife, thinking her husband is being unfaithful, goes to bed with a chubby, balding, sympathetic middle-aged ex-priest who works in the Third World. In an uncharacteristically dramatic late scene in this talky book, the young couple fail to save him from drowning. Despite its pace, this is an absorbing and moving tale, but one wonders at the dramatic necessity for such intrusions in the plot as four successive dream sequences the heroine has.

The Last Sandcastle (1983) is a short but excellent collection of stories with precisely observed details. The interior of an old-fashioned shop is caught succinctly: "It was pillared with Victorian slender iron poles with lotus capitals which held up a tracery of light iron trusses and herringbone patterns of white-painted timber." The interior of a tiny kitchen in a poor house is described as having "a table in the centre, and as you squeezed round you dragged your buttocks against cooker-switches, drawer-knobs and the inevitably protruding sticky knife or gravy-smeared plate." Some of the pieces are little more than arresting sketches with a notable central idea. The longest, most dramatized story has perhaps the most engaging idea. "In a Suburban Sitting-Room" depicts a young painter whose husband has left her but who remains so absorbed in painting a mural on her sitting-room walls that she is able to persuade the milkman, two policemen, and a police inspector to strip and pose for her.

Bluff (1987) is a serious extravaganza of a novel. The serious portions are the hero's guilt about a plane crash that he survived but in which his girlfriend and others were killed. It concerns also his uneasy relations with various women, the horrendous torture and death of one of them, politics and the Irish Republican Army, and the daily business of running a farm. The extravagant portions concern the reappearance of one young woman in various guises and his uncertainty about who she really is. It also concerns the hero's invention of wings that allow him to fly. This is not, nevertheless, a frivolous novel. Much of it is rooted in the realistic details of farm life and somber matters of conscience. It is a most interesting example of how realism can be seriously wed to the fantastic. Leland is not quite a quirky, but certainly both an individual and an original, talent.

He has also written a couple of advice guides, *Breaking Up: Separation and Divorce* (1987) and *Tenants' Rights* (1987).

WORKS: *A River Decrees.* London: Victor Gollancz, 1969; *The Last Sandcastle.* Dublin: O'Brien, [1983]. (Short stories); *Bluff.* London: Victor Gollancz, 1987; *A Marked Woman.* Norwich: Rampant Horse, 1994. (Novel); *Voices.* Norwich: Rampant Horse, 1994. (Novel).

LELAND, MARY (1941–   ), novelist, short story writer, and journalist. Mary Leland was born and raised in Cork. She received her journalistic training on the *Cork Examiner,* and her feature articles often appear in the Dublin press. Her first story was published on the "New Irish Writing" page of the *Irish Press,* and in 1980 she won the Listowel Writers Short Story Award for the story "Displaced Persons." She has been awarded two Arts Council bursaries.

Her first novel, *The Killeen* (1985), was journalistic in its brevity but masterly in plot weaving, as a mosaic of telling incidents carries forward the action. The poverty and isolation of rural Ireland in the early twentieth century are concisely evoked, alongside the political and religious fervor brewing in urban Dublin and Cork. Character development sheds interior light on the characters of Margaret, Julia, and Michael and even on some minor characters. Margaret is a naive country girl who has no knowledge of the political intrigue in which her lover is involved. She bears a child out of matrimony, in great shame and sorrow. The child is sent to a Catholic orphanage for adoption, and Margaret is sent to the house of Julia, the wealthy young widow of a republican "martyr," as a domestic servant. Julia, however, has no sympathy for the cause to which her husband has given his life and becomes a great influence on Margaret. Eventually, Julia leaves Ireland to raise her son away from the political conflict, and Margaret leaves also to marry and live in England. Before she leaves, however, she removes her son from the orphanage and gives him to the care of her brother,

Michael. What happens to that child forms the tragic conclusion of this unforgettable book.

Curiously, the same light of understanding does not illuminate some of the other characters: Earnon, Margaret's lover, or Maurice Mulcahy, Julia's husband, or the mother of Margaret and Michael. The reader knows them only by their actions. The author seems to have taken a judgmental position on these characters, but that is the only flaw in this gem of writing.

Leland's second novel, *Approaching Priests* (1991), is written with something like a stream-of-consciousness approach. The central character, Claire Mackey, is a journalist living in Cork, and the book details twenty years in her life. She is affected by the social, political, and economic changes of those years, in some cases tragically so, as she tries to find a way to live serenely in the midst of the chaos of the twentieth century. The "Priests" in the title would seem to be a metaphor for "Truth," as she finds no answer to her questions in the church.

JEAN FRANKS

WORKS: *The Killeen.* London: Hamish Hamilton, 1985/London: Black Swan, 1986/New York: Atheneum, 1986. (Novel); *The Little Galloway Girls.* London: Hamish Hamilton, 1987. (Short stories); *Approaching Priests.* London: Sinclair Stevenson, 1991. (Novel).

LENDENNIE, JESSIE (fl. 1980s–1990s), poet and publisher. Born in America, Lendennie established Salmon Press* in Galway.

WORK: *Daughter.* Galway: Salmon, 1988.

LENNON, TOM (fl. 1990s), novelist. Lennon is a pseudonym; his novel is about homosexuality.

WORK: *When Love Comes to Town.* Dublin: O'Brien, 1993.

LENTIN, RONIT (1944–   ), novelist. Lentin was born in Haifa, Israel, and has studed at the Hebrew University in Jerusalem and at Trinity College, Dublin. She has written in both Hebrew and English and is married to the television producer Louis Lentin. Her novella *Tea with Mrs. Klein* (1986), is an effectively understated study of the life of an old Jewish woman in Ireland.

WORKS: *Stone of Claims.* Tel Aviv: Siman Kria, 1975. (Novel); *Like a Blindman.* Tel Aviv: Siman Kria, 1977. (Novel); *Who Is Minding the Children?* Dublin: Arlen, 1981. (Reference); *Conversations with Palestinian Women.* Jerusalem: Mifras, 1982. (Interviews); *Tea with Mrs. Klein.* In *Triad: Modern Irish Fiction.* [Dublin]: Wolfhound, [1986]. (Novella); *Night Train to Mother.* Dublin: Attic, 1989/Pittsburgh: Cleis, 1990. (Novel).

LEONARD, HUGH (1926–   ), playwright and prose writer. Although on the face of it a writer transparently comic and uncomplicated, Leonard is extraordinarily complex and protean. His pseudonym, Hugh Leonard, is taken from a character in a play rejected by the Abbey* in the mid-1950s and used for the next play he submitted and had accepted, *The Big Birthday* (1956); his "real" name, John Keyes Byrne, includes those of his adoptive father and actual mother, but not of his natural father. Hugh Leonard is an author who invented himself. Taken as a whole, his output—which includes autobiographical narrative, popular history, film scripts, journalism, theater and book reviews, television plays and adaptations, and, at this point, a total of sixteen published and fifteen unpublished plays—indicates a remarkable range unmatched by any of his contemporaries. His popularity and commercial success have exposed Leonard to negative criticism from academic critics, which has resulted in a neglect of his considerable artistry. But Leonard's own pretense that he is no more than an entertainer has colluded in this unfair assessment of his work. In truth, while refusing to participate in modernist, not to mention postmodernist, debates on language, text, and society, Leonard has so shrewdly immersed himself in questions of identity, personality, and time that his work can be said to embody issues he patently disavows. One must not take Hugh Leonard at face value.

Born in Dublin on November 9, 1926, Leonard was brought up in the suburb of Dalkey, whose bard and chronicler he has become. Educated locally, he entered the civil service in 1945 as a temporary clerk in the Land Commission, a position he retained until his resignation in 1959. He was attracted to the theater when he saw a production of O'Casey's* *The Plough and the Stars* at the Abbey, but it was an amateur group, Lancos, for which he wrote his earliest plays. These remain unpublished, but one of them, *Nightingale in the Branches,* was subsequently accepted by the Abbey under the title of *The Big Birthday* (1956). He gave one more play to the Abbey, *A Leap in the Dark* (1957), before breaking away to make his independent style as a dramatist.

This style is first seen, characteristically, in an adaptation. *Stephen D,* based on Joyce's* *A Portrait of the Artist as a Young Man* and *Stephen Hero,* traveled successfully to the West End following its premiere in the 1962 Dublin Theatre Festival and established Leonard's reputation internationally. In his production note to this play, Leonard said his objective was "to show the influences under which the mind of Stephen Dedalus (or Joyce, if you like) rebelled against and finally rejected the four great 'F's' of Ireland: faith, fatherland, family and friendship." This statement of artistic rebellion was an important one for the Irish theater at this time. In form (which was experimental) and in content (defiance of various manifestations of authority), *Stephen D* was part of the revolution in Irish drama that began in the 1960s some years after John Osborne and the Royal Court initiated a revolution in British drama. Leonard settled in London around this time, having spent a few years in Manchester writing television plays. From London, he participated annually in the Dublin Theatre Festival, an important outlet and artistic determinant for his work. In 1970, however, he returned to live in Ireland, settled in Dalkey, and began to produce the plays and prose works on which his reputation principally rests.

It is possible to divide these works into three categories: the satirical, the autobiographical, and the playful or fantastic. The satirical may be exemplified by *The Patrick Pearse Motel* (1971), *Suburb of Babylon* (or *Irishmen,* as these three one-acts were collectively called when first staged in 1975), and *Kill*

(1982). Leonard's targets include the nouveaux riches who suddenly appeared in Irish society in the affluent 1960s and the political corruption masquerading as patriotism that resurfaced following the notorious Arms Trial in 1970. While making expert use of the mechanics of farce, especially of Feydeau, Leonard managed to provide stinging criticisms of Irish life. One could include in this group also a more ambitious play, *The Au Pair Man* which was produced in 1968 and transferred to London and New York. Set in London, this is a political allegory concerning the relations between Ireland and England, viewed as both mutually dependent and exploitative. *Kill,* on the other hand, focused on Irish politics and in particular on a bête noire of Leonard's, Prime Minister Charles J. Haughey, and his artistic interests intermingled with ambition.

The autobiographical note is heard as early as *Madigan's Lock* (1958), in which a civil servant is seduced into a world of fantasy and escapism, but is more fully articulated in *Summer* (1974), written when Leonard suddenly became aware of his own mortality. *Summer* is a fine play in the Chekhovian mode, well crafted and sweetly melancholy. It is outshone, however, by *Da* (produced in 1973), which is Leonard's best play. Here he explores his relationships with his adoptive parents, placing center stage his uneducated, rough, but loving "Da," brought to life retrospectively after his funeral. It is a wonderful, warm, and funny representation that, in its fullness, exposes the inadequacies of the critical narrator, a version of Leonard himself. *Da* is a brave and beautiful achievement. In 1978, it was seen on Broadway, where it won a Tony Award and Drama Critics Circle Award for best play of the year. Although a hard act to follow, *Da* was, in fact, followed to Broadway by *A Life* (produced in 1979), where Leonard's portrait of Mr. Drumm, the cantankerous, retired civil servant who appears also in *Da,* did not have as much success as it deserved. The autobiographical details of both plays are borne out by Leonard's two prose accounts of his childhood, *Home before Night* (1979) and *Out after Dark* (1989), which contain as much wit and humor as local color and home truths. Leonard's transformation of his own history into drama and prose was taken one step further with the filming of *Da* in 1988, in which he himself appeared briefly as a pallbearer.

Finally, *Time Was* (produced in 1976), *Pizzazz* (produced in 1983), *The Mask of Moriarty* (produced in 1985), and *Moving* (produced in 1992) illustrate Leonard's skill in fantasy and pure play. In each play, a farcical idea is expanded for purely theatrical purposes, although *Moving* should probably be regarded as more serious in what it has to say about time, change, and social attitudes. The other plays in this group exist in a realm of uninhibited entertainment. This, indeed, is the realm where Leonard seems happiest. Yet to neglect the wider, more ambitious reaches of his work is to deny him his rightful place among Ireland's major writers.

CHRISTOPHER MURRAY

WORKS: *Stephen D.* London & New York: Evans, [1964]; *The Poker Session.* London: Evans, 1964; *Mick and Mick.* London: Samuel French, 1966; *The Late Arrival of the Incoming Aircraft.*

London: Evans/French, 1968; *The Patrick Pearse Motel.* London: Samuel French, [1971]; *The Au Pair Man.* New York: Samuel French, [1974]; *Da.* Newark, Del.: Proscenium, 1975/revised ed. New York: Atheneum/London: Samuel French, 1978; *Leonard's Last Book.* Enniskerry: Egotist, 1978. (Essays); *A Peculiar People and Other Foibles.* [Enniskerry: Tansy Books, 1979]. (Essays); *Summer.* London: Samuel French, 1979/Dublin & London: Brophy, 1988; *Home before Night.* London: Andre Deutsch, 1979. (Autobiography); *Time Was.* London: Samuel French, 1980; *A Life.* London: Samuel French, 1980/New York: Atheneum, 1981; *Da, Time Was, A Life.* [Harmondsworth, Middlesex]: Penguin, [1981]; *Suburb of Babylon.* London: Samuel French, 1983. (Three one-act plays: *A Time of Wolves and Tigers, Nothing Personal* & *The Last of the Mohicans*); *Leonard's Year.* Dublin: Canavaun Books & Brophy Educational, 1985. (Essays); *Pizzazz: A View from the Obelisk, Roman Fever, Pizzazz.* London: Samuel French, 1986. (Three one-act plays); *Leonard's Log.* Dublin & London: Brophy, 1987. (Essays); *Madigan's Lock and Pizzazz.* Dublin & London: Brophy, 1987; *The Mask of Moriarty.* With a ''Playwright's Diary'' by Hugh Leonard. Dublin & London: Brophy, 1987; *Leonard's Log—Again.* Dublin & London: Brophy, 1988. (Essays); *Out after Dark.* London: Andre Deutsch, 1989. (Autobiography); *Parnell and the Englishwoman.* [London]: Andre Deutsch, [1991]. (Novel); *Selected Plays of Hugh Leonard.* S. F. Gallagher, ed. Gerrards Cross: Colin Smythe, 1992. (Contains first publication of *Kill*); *Rover and Other Cats.* London: Andre Deutsch, 1992. (Nonfiction); *Moving: A Play.* London: Samuel French, 1994. REFERENCES: Billington, Michael. ''Hugh Leonard.'' In *Contemporary Dramatists.* James Vinson, ed. London: St. James/New York: St. Martin's, 1973, pp. 468–471; Chaillet, Ned. ''Hugh Leonard.'' In *Contemporary Dramatists.* 4th ed. D. L. Kirkpatrick, ed. Chicago & London: St. James, 1988, pp. 320–322; Cushman, Keith. ''Stand-Up Poker in Hugh Leonard's *The Poker Session.''* *Journal of Irish Literature* 8 (May 1979): 194–202; Etherton, Michael. *Contemporary Irish Dramatists.* [Houndmills, Baskingstoke & London]: M[acmillan], 1989, pp. 5–15; Gallagher, S. F. ''Q. & A. with Hugh Leonard.'' *Irish Literary Supplement* (Spring 1900): 13–14; Gallagher, S. F. ''Introduction.'' *Selected Plays of Hugh Leonard.* Gerrards Cross: Colin Smythe/Washington D.C.: Catholic University Press of America, 1992, pp. 1–12; Hickey, Des & Smith, Gus, eds. ''Leonard: Difficult to Say 'No.' '' In *A Paler Shade of Green.* London: Leslie Frewin, 1972, pp. 191–001/published in United States as *Flight from the Celtic Twilight.* Indianapolis: Bobbs Merrill, 1973; Hogan, Robert. *After the Irish Renaissance.* Minneapolis: University of Minnesota Press, 1967/London: Macmillan, 1968, pp. 186–189; Hogan, Robert. *''Since O'Casey'' and Other Essays on Irish Drama.* Gerrards Cross: Colin Smythe/Totowa, N.J.: Barnes & Noble, 1983, pp. 132–136; Kosok, Heinz. ''Hugh Leonard.'' In *Dictionary of Literary Biography 13: British Dramatists since World War II: Part 1: A–L.* Stanley Weintraub, ed. Detroit: Bruccoli Clark & Gale Research, 1982, pp. 284–291; Maxwell, D.E.S. *A Critical History of Modern Irish Drama 1891–1980.* Cambridge: Cambridge University Press, 1984, pp. 175–177; Moritz, Charles, ed. ''Hugh Leonard.'' *Current Biography* 44 (April 1983): 12–15; Murray, Christopher. ''Hugh Leonard.'' In *Post-War Literatures in English: A Lexicon of Contemporary Authors.* Joris Duytschaever, ed. Groningen: Wolters-Noordhoff (June 1990): 1–14; O'Grady, Thomas B. ''Insubstantial Fathers and Consubstantial Sons: A Note on Patrimony and Patricide in Friel and Leonard.'' *Canadian Journal of Irish Studies* 15 (1989): 71–79; Rollins, Ronald. ''Leonard and Friel: Fathers and Sons.'' In *Divided Ireland: Bifocal Vision in Modern Irish Drama.* Lanham, Md.: University Press of America, 1985, pp. 47–58.

LESLIE, ANITA [ANNE THEODOSIA MOIRA] (1914–   ), biographer. Leslie, the daughter of Sir Shane Leslie* and elder sister of Desmond Leslie,* was born on November 21, 1914. In 1937, she married Colonel Paul Rodzianko, the son of General Paul Rodzianko and the Princess Galitzine. From 1940 to 1942, she was in the South African army, and from 1944 to 1945 she was an ambulance driver in the Armored Division of the Free French Army, with which she served in Syria, Italy, and France and with which she entered Berlin. She was awarded the Croix de Guerre in February 1945. Though she had published a biography of Rodin before the war, her volume of war experiences, *Train to Nowhere* (1948), was regarded as one of the best books about the war by a woman and made her name. Her marriage was annulled in 1948, and the following year she married Commander William Donald Aelian King of Oranmore Castle, County Galway, now Bill Leslie-King, the solo sailor and nautical writer. *Love in a Nutshell* (1952) is an account of sailing in the West Indies with her second husband. Leslie has also written very informed and readable biographies, particularly about some of her notable relatives, such as the American entrepreneur Leonard Jerome, her aunt Lady Randolph Churchill, her cousin Randolph Churchill, her cousin Clare Sheridan,* and Clare's father, the perennially unsuccessful Moreton Frewen.

PETER COSTELLO

WORKS: *Rodin, Immortal Peasant.* New York: Prentice-Hall, 1937/London: Herbert Joseph, 1939; *Train to Nowhere.* London: Hutchinson, [1948]. (War experiences); *Love in a Nutshell.* London: Hutchinson/New York: Greenburg, 1952. (Travel); *The Fabulous Leonard Jerome.* London: Hutchinson, 1954/as *The Remarkable Mr. Jerome.* New York: Holt, 1954; *Mrs. Fitzherbert.* London: Hutchinson/New York: Scribner, 1960; *Mr. Frewen of England: A Victorian Adventurer.* London: Hutchinson, 1966; *Lady Randolph Churchill; The Story of Jennie Jerome.* New York: Scribner, 1969/as *Jennie: The Life of Lady Randolph Churchill.* London: Hutchinson, 1969; *Edwardians in Love.* London: Hutchinson, 1972; *The Marlborough House Set.* New York: Doubleday, 1973; *Francis Chichester.* London: Hutchinson, Hodder & Stoughton/New York: Walker, 1975; *Cousin Clare: The Tempestuous Career of Clare Sheridan.* London: Hutchinson, 1976/as *Clare Sheridan.* Garden City, N.Y.: Doubleday, 1977; *Madame Tussaud: Waxworker Extraordinary.* With Pauline Chapman. London: Hutchinson, 1978; *The Gilt and the Gingerbread: An Autobiography.* London: Hutchinson, 1981; *A Story Half Told: A Wartime Autobiography.* London: Hutchinson, 1983; *Cousin Randolph.* London: Hutchinson, 1985.

LESLIE, DESMOND [PETER ARTHUR] (1921–   ), novelist and nonfiction writer. Leslie, a son of Sir Shane* and brother of Anita Leslie,* was born on June 29, 1921. He was educated at Ampleforth and Trinity College, Dublin. During World War II, he served in the Royal Air Force as a pilot. In 1945, he married Agnes Bernauer (now Agnes Bernelle), the only daughter of Rudolf Bernauer, the Hungarian dramatist and producer. They had two sons and a daughter before separating. He now lives at the family seat, Castle Leslie, Glaslough.

His first novel drew on his flying experience; his second, *Pardon My Return* (1946), is a satirical view of life around Glaslough after the war, in which one of the characters is called Eucharistica Congressa. He formerly listed his recreation as "inventing." This and his flying experience mingled with his family background when he wrote the introduction and reedited George Adamski's celebrated book, *Flying Saucers Have Landed.* Though the subject was outlandish, this proved an influential volume in the rise of the modern mythology of flying saucers. (Adamski's claim was that he had met and communicated with a voluptuous, golden-haired Venusian, and the book contains photographs of this creature and of flying saucers). Leslie remains a leading figure in this field and claimed to have observed anomalous flying objects over the family home at Glaslough. His most recent book, *The Jesus File* (1975), deals with the career of Christ, as it might have been recorded by the apparatus of the bureaucratic state if it had existed 2,000 years ago. Imaginative and eccentric, Leslie belongs to a distinct tendency in Anglo-Irish literature towards the weird (with echoes of Sheridan Le Fanu* and Lord Dunsany*). His uncle, the explorer and author Lionel Leslie, was involved in investigations of lake monsters in Scotland.

PETER COSTELLO

WORKS: *Careless Lives.* London: Macdonald, [1945]; *Pardon My Return.* London: Macdonald, [1946]; *Angels Weep.* London: T. Werner Laurie, [1948]; with George Adamski, *Flying Saucers Have Landed.* London: W. Laurie/New York: British Book Centre, [1953]. (Nonfiction); *Hold Back the Night.* London: Peter Owen, 1956; *The Amazing Mr. Lutterworth.* London: Allan Wingate, 1958; with Patrick Moore, *How Britain Won the Space Race.* London: Mitchell Beazley, 1972. (Nonfiction); *The Jesus File.* London: Sidgwick & Jackson, 1975.

LESLIE, MARY ISABEL. *See* LANE, TEMPLE

LESLIE, SIR SHANE (1885–1971), man of letters.

Sir Shane Leslie, third baronet of Glaslough, was born John Randolph Leslie on September 24, 1885, at Castle Leslie in County Monaghan. He was educated at Eton and at King's College, Cambridge, where he became a Roman Catholic and assumed the name of Shane, an Irish version of John. After graduating in 1907, he journeyed to Russia where he met Tolstoy and became influenced by his social theories. In 1910, he stood as nationalist candidate for Derry, an incident portrayed in his autobiographical novel *Doomsland* (1923). In the remainder of his long and busy life, he published some forty volumes which included poetry, novels, short stories, memoirs, biographies, and nonfiction of various kinds. He was an extremely fluent writer and a member of the Irish Academy of Letters, but his major contribution to Irish literature is *Doomsland,* a *bildungsroman* of exceptional interest which has been most unfairly neglected. Much of his life was spent in England where he died on August 31, 1971, at Hove.

In her 1926 novel *Make Believe,* his cousin Clare Sheridan* uses him for the heroine's cousin, an unpleasant depiction of religious fanaticism; however, her Henry James character in the same book does not come off very well either.

WORKS: *The Landlords of Ireland at the Cross-Roads.* Dublin: Duffy, 1908. (Pamphlet); *Songs of Oriel.* Dublin: Maunsel, 1908. (Poems); *Isle of Columbcille.* Dublin: Catholic Truth Society of Ireland, 1909; *Lough Derg in Ulster.* Dublin: Maunsel, 1909; *A Sketch of the Oxford Movement.* Dublin: Catholic Truth Society of Ireland, 1909; *The End of a Chapter.* London: Constable, 1916/ revised, London: Constable, 1917/revised & rewritten, London: Heinemann, 1929. (Autobiography); *Verses in Peace and War.* London: Burns & Oates, 1916; *The Irish Issue in Its American Aspect.* New York: Scribner's, 1917/London: T. Fisher Unwin, 1918; *The Story of St. Patrick's Purgatory.* St. Louis, Mo., & London: B. Herder, 1917; *Henry Edward Manning, His Life and Labours. . . .* London: Burns, Oates, 1921; *The Oppidan.* London: Chatto & Windus, 1922. (Novel); *Doomsland.* London: Chatto & Windus, 1923. (Novel); *Mark Sykes: His Life and Letters.* London: Cassell, 1923; *Masquerades.* London: John Long, 1924; ed., *An Anthology of Catholic Poetry.* London: Burns, Oates, 1925/revised, London: Burns, Oates, 1952; *The Cantab.* 2d ed., revised, London: Chatto & Windus, 1926; *George the Fourth.* London: Ernest Benn, 1926; *The Delightful, Diverting, and Devotional Play of Mrs. Fitzherbert.* London: Ernest Benn, 1928; *The Poems of Shane Leslie.*

London: Cayme, 1928; *The Skull of Swift.* Indianapolis: Bobbs-Merrill/London: Chatto & Windus, 1928; *The Anglo-Catholic.* London: Chatto & Windus, 1929. (Novel); *A Ghost in the Isle of Wight.* London: E. Mathews & Marot, 1929. (Short story); *Lines Written in the Month's Mind of Mona Dunn. Dec. 19, 1928–Jan. 19, 1929.* [London: C. H. St. J. Hornby at the Ashendene Press, 1929]; *The Hyde Park Pageant.* [London]: Fortune, 1930. (Verse pamphlet); *Jutland, a Fragment of Epic.* London: Ernest Benn, 1930. (Poem); *Memoirs of John Edward Courtenay Bodley.* London, Toronto: Jonathan Cape, 1930; ed., *St. Patrick's Purgatory, a Record from History and Literature.* London: Burns, Oates, 1932; *Studies in Sublime Failure.* London: Ernest Benn, 1932. (Biographies); *The Oxford Movement, 1833 to 1933.* London: Burns, Oates, 1933; *Poems and Ballads.* London: Ernest Benn, 1933; *The Passing Chapter.* London: Cassell, 1934. (Autobiography); *Fifteen Odd Stories.* London: Hutchinson, [1935]; *The Script of Jonathan Swift, and Other Essays.* Philadelphia: University of Pennsylvania Press, 1935; *American Wonderland.* London: Michael Joseph, 1936. (Travel); *Men Were Different . . . Five Studies in Victorian Biography.* London: Michael Joseph, 1937; *The Film of Memory.* London: Michael Joseph, 1938; *Sir Evelyn Ruggles-Brise.* London: John Murray, 1938. (Biography); *Mrs. Fitzherbert.* London: Burns, Oates, 1939. (Biography); *Poems from the North.* Dublin, 1945. (Pamphlet); *The Irish Tangle for English Readers.* London: Mac-Donald, [1946]; *Salutation to Five.* London: Hollis & Carter, 1951. (Biographies); *Cardinal Gasquet, a Memoir.* London: Burns Oates, 1953; *Lord Mulroy's Ghost.* Dublin: At the Sign of the Three Candles, [1954]. (Play); *Shane Leslie's Ghost Book.* London: Hollis & Carter, 1955; ed., *Edward Tennyson Reed, 1860–1933.* London: Heinemann, 1957. (Biography); *Long Shadows.* London: Murray, 1966. (Autobiographical).

LETTS, WINIFRED M[ABEL] (1882–1972), poet, playwright, and fiction writer. Letts was born in 1882, the daughter of Rev. Ernest F. Letts, rector of Newton Heath, Manchester. She was educated at St. Anne's Abbots, Bromley, and at Alexandra College, Dublin. She was a masseuse, and she married W.H.F. Verschoyle. In her later years, she lived in Faversham, Kent, and she died on June 7, 1972.

Letts wrote mostly of rural Leinster and, with less devotion, of its urban center, Dublin. Occasionally sentimental but never stridently political, she created poetry, fiction, stories for children, hagiography, a book of reminiscences titled *Knockmaroon* (1933), two one-act plays for the Abbey,* and a three-act play, *Hamilton and Jones* (1941) for the Gate.* In her Abbey play *The Eyes of the Blind* (1907), a murderer gives himself up when a blind man claims knowledge of the covert crime. *The Challenge* (1909) tells of a duel between elderly men over a long-remembered insult. Her plays are of interest as artifacts of Abbey history. If she is remembered, it will be for her poetry and the wistful charm of *Knockmaroon.* It would be unrealistic to make any great claims for her poetry, although many of her pieces are rather better than the usual dialect poems about the peasant. Her ear seems more authentic; there are fewer clichés; there are touches of humor in the slum poems; and there are occasional touches of individuality, as in "For Sixpence," where she expresses her delight in the productions of the early Abbey Theatre. "Synge's Grave" is her wish that Synge had been buried in lonely Glenmalure rather than in a city cemetery.

WILLIAM J. FEENEY

WORKS: *The Story-Spinner.* London & Edinburgh: T. C. & E. C. Jack, 1907/London: Nelson, [1920]. (Tales); *Waste Castle* London & Edinburgh: T. C. & E. C. Jack, 1907/London: Nelson, [1916], [1920]. (Girls' book); *Bridget of All Work.* London: Henry Frowde/Hodder & Stoughton,

1909. (Novel); *Diana Dethroned.* London & New York: John Lane, 1909. (Novel); *The Quest of the Blue Rose.* London: Henry Frowde/Hodder & Stoughton, 1910 [1909]. (Novel); *The Mighty Army.* London: Wells Gardner/New York: F. A. Stokes, 1912. (Lives of saints); *Naughty Sophia.* London: Grant Richards, 1912. (Novel); *The Rough Way.* London: Wells Gardner, [1912]. (Novel); "The Company of Saints and Angels." *Irish Review* 1 (January 1912): 537–544. (Short story); "The Challenge." *Irish Review* 2 (April 1912): 87–96. (Short story adaptation of her play of the same title); *Songs from Leinster.* London: J. Murray, 1913/Dundalk: Dundalgan, 1947. (Poems); with M.F.S., *Helmet & Cowl. Stories of Monastic and Military Orders.* London: Wells Gardner, 1913. (Children's book); "The Man Who Burnt His Crucifix." *Irish Review* 4 (May 1914): 143–167. (Reprinted in *Knockmaroon*); *Christmas Son.* London: Wells Gardner, 1915. (Novel); *Hallow-e'en and Poems of the War.* London: Smith, Elder, 1916/reprinted as *The Spires of Oxford and Other Poems.* New York: E. P. Dutton, 1917; *Corporal's Corner.* London: Wells Gardner, 1919. (Novel); *What Happened Then.* London: Wells Gardner, [1921]. (Novel); More *Songs from Leinster.* London: J. Murray/New York: E. P. Dutton, 1926; *St. Patrick the Travelling Man.* London: J. Nicholson & Watson, 1932; *Knockmaroon.* London: J. Murray, 1933. (Memoirs); *Pomona and Co.* London: Nelson, [1934]. (Children's book); *Pomona's Island.* London: Nelson, [1935]. (Children's book); *The Gentle Mountain.* Dublin: Talbot, [1938]/London: R.T.S., [1939].

LEVER, CHARLES JAMES (1806–1872), novelist. Lever was born in Dublin on August 31, 1806, the son of an English architect and builder. He studied medicine at Trinity College and practiced that profession. After he achieved fame as a novelist, and he was a prolific and highly popular writer of his time, he spent most of life on the Continent. He died in Trieste on June 1, 1872.

The scope of Lever's collected works—thirty-seven volumes—indicates both his achievement and his limitations as a writer. His first novel, *The Confessions of Harry Lorrequer* (1839), brought him instant fame when it first appeared in the *Dublin University Magazine.* So elevated was his reputation that he exploited the audience with novels that often show evidence of haste and superficial attention. He knew what his audience wanted, and he seemed willing to adapt his attitudes to the fairly low denominator of the mass reading public. Add to that his personal weaknesses: he loved gambling and the high life and so was always under pressure to write merely to pay off debts. Late in his life he admitted: "You ask me how I write. My reply is, just as I live—from hand to mouth."

As a result, only a few of his novels earn critical acceptance from modern readers. In addition to his first novel, which has an appealing humor and liveliness, *Charles O'Malley* (1841) and *The Martins of Cro' Martin* (1856) deserve comment for their similar qualities. Both feature colorful characters, employ dialect that is itself appealing, and read quickly. Occasionally, both novels contain political commentary that is astute. The later novel investigates the social consequences of the Emancipation Bill and describes the political intrigue with rare perception. Like his friend Trollope,* Lever was interested in politics, and his accounts read like political analysis as told from the inside. His interests are as likely to be Continental political concerns as specifically English or Irish ones. But he knew and capitalized on the contemporary taste for comic Irish characters, and he gave his readers what they wanted. The title characters of many of his novels are little more than stage Irishmen, occasionally amusing, but finally annoying.

Lever was a sophisticated writer in many respects, and his novels reveal a breadth of reading and an intimate knowledge of social behavior. At his best, in parts of his novels, he even merits comparison with Trollope or Thackeray,* two of his close friends. But clearly, he lacked the professional discipline of those two master writers. The syntax of some of his novels is confused, the plots tenuous, and the characterization superficial. Recent critics have found his social and political commentary to be a valuable indicator of the period. In fact, as examples of popular literature, the novels no doubt contain useful data. But their literary merit is limited by their unrelieved superficiality.

JAMES KILROY

WORKS: *The Confessions of Harry Lorrequer.* Dublin: W. Curry, June & Co./Edinburgh: Fraser & Crawford, 1839; *Charles O'Malley, the Irish Dragoon.* 2 vols. Dublin: W. Curry, 1841; *Our Mess; Jack Hinton, the Guardsman.* Dublin: W. Curry, 1843; *Arthur O'Leary.* 2 vols. London: Colburn, 1844; *Tom Burke of "Ours."* 2 vols. Dublin: W. Curry, 1844; *Nuts and Nutcrackers.* London: Orr/Dublin: Curry, 1845, *The O'Donoghue.* Dublin: W. Curry, 1845; *St. Patrick's Eve.* London: Chapman & Hall, 1845; *Tales of the Trains.* London: W. S. Orr/Dublin: W. Curry, 1845; *The Knight of Gwynne.* London: Chapman & Hall, 1847; *Diary and Notes of Horace Templeton, Esq.* 2 vols. London: Chapman & Hall, 1848; *Confessions of Con Cregan, the Irish Gil Blas.* London: W. S. Orr, ca. 1850; *Maurice Tiernay, the Soldier of Fortune.* London: Hodgson, ca. 1850; *Roland Cashel.* London: Chapman & Hall, 1850; *The Daltons.* 2 vols. London: Chapman & Hall, 1852; *The Dodd Family Abroad.* London: Chapman & Hall, 1854; *Sir Jasper Carew.* London: T. Hodgson, ca. 1854; *The Martins of Cro' Martin.* London: Chapman & Hall, 1856; *The Fortunes of Glencore.* 3 vols. London: Chapman & Hall, 1857; *Davenport Dunn.* London: Chapman & Hall, 1859; *Gerald Fitzgerald.* New York: Harper, ca. 1859; *One of Them.* London: Chapman & Hall, 1861; *A Day's Ride.* London: Chapman & Hall, 1862; *Barrington.* London: Chapman & Hall, 1863; *Luttrell of Aran.* London: Chapman & Hall, 1865; *Tony Butler.* London & Edinburgh: Blackwood, 1865; *Cornelius O'Dowd.* 3 vols. Edinburgh & London: Blackwood, 1864–1865; *Sir Brook Fossbrooke.* 3 vols. Edinburgh & London: Blackwood, 1866; *The Bramleighs of Bishop's Folly.* 3 vols. London: Smith, Elder, 1868; *Paul Goslett's Confessions.* London: Virtue, 1868; *A Rent in a Cloud.* London: Chapman & Hall, 1869; *That Boy of Norcott's.* London: Smith, Elder, 1869; *Lord Kilgoblin.* 3 vols. London: Smith, Elder, 1872; *The Novels of Charles Lever,* ed. by his daughter, Julia Kate Neville. 37 vols. London: Downey, 1897–1899. REFERENCES: Bareham, Tony, ed. *Charles Lever: New Evaluations.* Gerrards Cross: Colin Smythe/Savage, Md.: Barnes & Noble, [1991]; Downey, Edmund. *Charles Lever: His Life in His Letters.* 2 vols. London: Blackwood, 1906; Fitzpatrick, William J. *The Life of Charles Lever.* 2 vols. London: Chapman & Hall, 1879/new ed. London: Ward, Lock, 1884; Lytton, Robert B. "Works of Charles Lever." *Blackwood's Magazine* 91 (1862): 452–472; O'Keefe, Thomas P. "Charles Lever: A Study of Nineteenth Century Anglo-Irish Fiction." Ph.D. thesis, National University of Ireland, 1972; Stevenson, Lionel. *Dr. Quicksilver: The Life of Charles Lever.* London: Chapman & Hall/New York: Russell & Russell, 1939.

LEVINE, JUNE (ca. 1940s–   ), novelist and journalist. Levine has worked as a journalist and as a researcher on RTÉ's *Late Late Show.* Her first book, *Sisters* (1982) is a somewhat autobiographical novel about a marriage breakdown and the early days of the modern feminist movement in Ireland. Her best book, *Lyn* (1987), is a telling, nonfictional account of the life of a Dublin prostitute. *A Season of Weddings* (1992) is a longish novel about a middle-aged Irishwoman whose marriage has broken down and who visits India for several weeks, during which the assassination of Indira Ghandi occurs. There is quite a lot of plot in the book, but the overall impression is of nothing happening for many pages while the heroine soaks up Indian impressions, and the reader is introduced to a multitude of sketchily drawn characters. On one half-page, Ashoke, Maya, Basai, Thangamani, Uma, Kumari, Dadiji, and Nirmal are all mentioned but remain pretty indistinct. The tumult after the Ghandi assassination is very well done.

WORKS: *Sisters.* Dublin: Ward River, 1982. (Novel); with Lynn Madden. *Lyn.* Dublin: Attic, 1987. (Nonfiction); *A Season of Weddings.* Dublin: New Island, 1992. (Novel).

LEYDEN, BRIAN (1960–   ), short story writer and broadcaster. Born on July 28, 1960, in County Roscommon, Leyden was reared on a small farm in Arigna, a coal-mining village on the Roscommon/Leitrim border. He left Sligo Regional Technical School with a diploma in art and design and a certificate in education.

After having spent over two years teaching, Leyden quit his job to devote all his time to writing. His efforts first met with success in 1988, when his "The Last Mining Village" won the RTÉ Francis MacManus* Short Story Award. This gave him a foot in the door of broadcasting. He has since had stories on BBC Radio 4 and on RTÉ. In 1991, RTÉ produced an award-winning radio broadcast based on Leyden's short stories. Under the title of *No Meadows in Manhattan,* it focused on emigration draining a small Leitrim community.

Leyden now lives in a remote part of County Leitrim and portrays with tender precision pictures of rural life as he knows it. This life is on the verge of disappearing, with emigration, rationalization, and European union-induced alterations taking their toll. *Departures* is the title of his collection of short stories, all of which are seen through the eyes of a young migrant. Although some aspects of rural life are mockingly observed, a gentle mourning for the irretrievable loss of this world hangs over all his stories. But Leyden's style never descends to sentimentality.

BARBARA FREITAG

WORK: *Departures.* [Dingle]: Brandon, [1991].

LIDDY, JAMES (1934–   ), poet. Liddy's grandfather, Daniel Reeves, immigrated to America, where he started the first chain of grocery stores in New York before dying at age thirty-six in 1910. Liddy's mother was born in New York but returned to Ireland, where James was born on July 1, 1934. He was raised in County Clare, trained as a barrister, and practiced law in Ireland until the mid-1960s, when he decided to devote himself to writing. Since 1982, he has taught at the University of Wisconsin–Milwaukee, where he is professor and coordinator of Irish studies.

At the heart of Liddy's poetry is an uncompromising commitment to love, but it is love in opposition to traditional attitudes. The kind of love Liddy acknowledges in his work is paradoxical and contradictory. It includes a recognition of anguish, pain, and evil, as well as an unapologetic delight in sexual pleasure. The work of William Blake, particularly *The Marriage of Heaven and Hell* (which Liddy parodies in *Corca Bascinn*, 1977), seems to have had a real impact on Liddy's imagination. Throughout *Baudelaire's Bar Flowers* (a book of translations and reworkings of Baudelaire), Liddy associates love and sex with Hell and Satan. He writes that "evil redeems good" (p. 17), echoing Blake's beliefs that "Evil is the active springing from Energy" and the "true Poet" is "of the Devil's party."

With Blake, and with his friend and mentor Patrick Kavanagh,* Liddy also shares an unswerving hostility to bourgeois values. From his earliest publication, *Esau, My Kingdom for a Drink* (1962), Liddy began attacking the "phoneyness and lies" (p. 10) around him. The world is "... a prison / Run by elderly bores ..." (*Blue Mountain,* 1968, p. 9) and bureaucrats who stand in the way of "the revolution we imagine / in which each of us will love / the other ..." (*In a Blue Smoke,* 1964, p. 13).

Liddy's relationship with Kavanagh illustrates his attraction to an intensified kind of friendship in which his taste for "[c]onversation, unusual people, a casual life" (*Blue Mountain,* p. 23) is honored. He rejects the standards of "straight" society in favor of homosexuality. In *A Munster Song of Love and War,* his "gay" sensibility started to emerge more openly in his poems. By *Corca Bascinn* he calls himself a "wandering pervert" (p. 45). He has steadfastly focused on "the possibilities of drink-life" and "the observance of the sexual life" (*A White Thought in a White Shade,* 1987, pp. 26–27).

Liddy's poems rely a great deal on humor. In his later work, he satirizes both Yeats's* elevated language (referring in one poem to "the Celtic Twilight zone" [*White Thought,* p. 24]) and Seamus Heaney's* carefully wrought hymns to the natural, mundane world (e.g., see p. 21 in *White Thought*). America and Ireland are increasingly synthesized to form his literary landscape, a place where Yeats and Jack Kerouac are equally likely to make an appearance.

In *A Life of Stephen Dedalus,* Liddy bids "Irish poets" to leave "the paraphernalia" of "literature" out of their work. He is not comfortable with what he calls elsewhere the "beautiful and decorative" language of Yeats ("Open Letter to the Young about Patrick Kavanagh," *The Lace Curtain* 1, n.d: 55) and has nothing but contempt for "those dogs on art grants" (*White Thought,* p. 36). In Yeats's work, "[t]here are flourishes brilliantly rhymed and stanza'd," but Liddy finds the work impersonal and "evasive" ("Open Letter"). He is drawn to poems of "emotional intelligence" in which the "language and imagery are clear and evocative yet mysterious" ("Open Letter," p. 56). Liddy's poems are written in a language of heightened conversation. They are often flat, stark poems. He rejects the idea of "the poem waiting there to be put together by the Department of English grammatical kit" in favor of "responsibility to the poem," in which the poem is founded on its allegiance to the imagination (*Baudelaire's Bar Flowers,* p. 23).

TERENCE WINCH

WORKS: *Esau, My Kingdom for a Drink.* Dublin: Dolmen, [1962]; *In a Blue Smoke.* Dublin: Dolmen, Philadelphia: Dufour, [1964]; *Blue Mountain.* Dublin: Dolmen, Chester Springs, Pa.: Dufour, 1968; with Jim Chapson & Thomas Hill, *Blue House: Poems in the Chinese Manner.* Honolulu: Nine Beasts Press, [ca. 1968]; *A Life of Stephen Dedalus.* San Francisco: White Rabbit Press, 1969; *A Munster Song of Love and War.* San Francisco: White Rabbit Press, 1971; *Homage to Patrick Kavanagh.* Dublin: New Writers', 1971. (Poetry pamphlet); *Corca Bascinn.* Dublin: Dolmen, 1977; *Comyn's Lay.* Berkeley, Calif.: Hit and Run, 1979. (Pamphlet of poems and translations); *Moon and Star Moments.* New York: At-Swim, 1982. (Nine-page chapbook of poems); *At the Grave of Fr. Sweetman.* Dublin: Malton, 1984. (Poetry pamphlet); *You Can't Jog for Jesus: Jack Kerouac as a Religious Writer.* Milwaukee, Wis.: Blue Canary, 1985. (Twelve-page monograph); "Young Men Go Walking." In *Triad: Modern Irish Fiction.* [Dublin]: Wolfhound, [1986]. (Novella); *A White Thought in a White Shade: New and Selected Poems.* Dublin: Kerr's Pinks, 1987; *In the Slovak Bowling Alley.* Milwaukee, Wis.: Blue Canary/Dublin: Kerr's Pinks, 1990. (Poetry pamphlet); *Art Is Not for Grownups.* Milwaukee, Wis.: Blue Canary/Dublin: Kerr's Pinks, 1990. (Poetry pamphlet); *Trees Warmer Than Green: Notes towards a Video of Avondale House.* Laois: International University Press, 1991. (Poetry pamphlet); *Collected Poems.* Omaha, Nebr.: Creighton University Press, [1994].

LILLIPUT PRESS (1984–   ), publishing house. The name Lilliput (deriving from an eponymous townland fringing Lough Ennell in County Westmeath, where Dean Swift* summered in 1721 reading Lucretius as a guest of his friend George Rochfort of Gaulstown), is emblematic of all the press denotes. Its founding by Antony Farrell at his home in Gigginstown, County Westmeath, was marked by the publication in May 1984 of "Setting Foot on the Shores of Connemara," a pamphlet-essay by Tim Robinson, and on September 14, 1984, of *The Rock Garden,* a novel set in the Aran Islands by Mullingar Joycean and local historian Leo Daly,* launched appropriately at Belvedere overlooking Lough Ennell by Benedict Kiely.* Both titles were designed and laid out by Jarlath Hayes, who became instrumental in setting a high typographic standard for Lilliput's subsequent work.

The initial years saw the establishment of three of the press's major writers and spheres of interest: the Kilkenny essayist Hubert Butler* (*Escape from the Anthill,* 1985), the West of Ireland cartographer Tim Robinson (*Stones of Aran,* 1986), and the United States-based, Lismore-born autobiographer George O'Brien* (*The Village of Longing,* 1987). Over the next eleven years some 120 titles appeared under the imprint, encompassing fiction, memoir and autobiography, essays, history, ecology, natural history and environment, literary criticism, and current affairs, with occasional forays into drama and poetry, all broadly focusing on Irish themes.

One emergent aim of the press, enlarging upon the publisher's experience as an editor in London during the 1970s, was to publish work of an international quality that could be "sold on" in the form of coeditions to publishing houses abroad. This found early fulfillment with Butler, Robinson, and O'Brien, all copublished with Viking Penguin in London and New York. In a survey of publishing in a 1989 issue of the *Times Literary Supplement,* historian Roy Foster* wrote, "Lilliput is, in its way, a small but decisive reversal of cultural imperialism.'' Recent copublications have included *Austin Clarke: Selected Poems* and Francis Stuart's* *Black List, Section H,* both licensed to Penguin Modern Classics. There has also been a steady exchange of authors with scholarly presses in the United States: John Wilson Foster and John Montague* to Syracuse University Press, David Lloyd to Duke University Press, Fritz Senn to Johns Hopkins University Press. Some others have been ''brought in'': literary critic Denis Sampson from Catholic University Press, anthropologist Lawrence Taylor from University of Pennsylvania Press.

In its first five years, Lilliput authors won the following awards: Hubert Butler, the 1986 American-Irish Foundation Literary Award, the 1987 Ewart-Biggs Memorial special citation, and the 1989 Irish Book Award for Literature; Tim Robinson, the 1987 Irish Book Award for Literature and the Rooney Prize special citation; George O'Brien, the 1988 Irish Book Award for Literature and the 1990 *Sunday Times* John Edryn Hughes Prize for Literature. Kilkenny Design Awards were given to the press in 1987, 1988, 1989, and 1990, when, sadly, the prize lapsed.

In 1989, the press moved from its rural base in Westmeath to Arbour Hill in Dublin. Among the highlights of eleven years' publishing are four volumes of essays by Hubert Butler (published in France with an introduction by Joseph Brodsky in 1995, and by Penguin in London and Farrar, Straus & Giroux in New York); the magisterial two volumes of *Stones of Aran* (1986, 1995) by Tim Robinson, which was welcomed by Coleridge scholar J.C.C. Mays as ''one of the most significant pieces of prose, from a literary view, written in Ireland in the past quarter-century''; *In the Prison of His Days* (1988), the first literary tribute in English to Nelson Mandala; radical economist Richard Douthwaite's *The Growth Illusion* (1992); the sumptuously illustrated *Trees of Ireland* by Wendy Walsh and Charles Nelson (1993); philosopher and poet John Moriarty's *Dreamtime* (1994); and an audio recording of James Joyce's* *Finnegans Wake* by Patrick Healy. In 1992, the press brought out an edition of *Dubliners* illustrated by Louis le Brocquy and announced a yet-to-be-finished edition of *Ulysses* by John Kidd.

ANTONY FARRELL

LINEHAN, FERGUS (1934–   ), author of review sketches and dramatic adaptations, novelist, and journalist. Linehan was born on June 4, 1934. He had a long connection with the *Irish Times* and has written many review sketches and a number of musical dramatizations of novels and plays, ranging from an unfortunate *Fursey* after Mervyn Wall,* to a mildly pleasant adaptation of Lennox Robinson's* *The Whiteheaded Boy,* to a superb version of James Stephens's* *The Charwoman's Daughter,* in which the music was by his wife, the excellent actress Rosalind Linehan, who also played the charwoman. His novel, *Under the Durian Tree* (1995), is not really about Ireland but is able and solid work.

WORK: *Under the Durian Tree.* Dublin: Town House/London: Macmillan, 1995. (Novel). REFERENCE: "Out of the East." *Books Ireland,* No. 187 (Summer 1995): 143–144.

LINGARD, JOAN (1932–   ), novelist and children's writer. Although born in Edinburgh, Scotland, Joan Lingard spent her formative years in World War II Belfast, and that experience has provided material for much of her writing. Her mother was a Christian Scientist, but at her death in 1948, Lingard began to reject that religious belief. Known primarily as a children's author, with multiple prestigious awards, she has also published a number of adult novels on themes of personal relationships, frequently against a background of friction, both religious and political. An insightful observer of human behavior and motivation, she exhibits the greatest strength in development of plot by natural interaction of the characters. Although most of her subjects are women, they represent all classes and walks of life. Her prose style is economic, and action evolves into a natural yet compelling inevitability.

Sisters by Rite (1984) makes use of her knowledge of the troubled conditions of Belfast, as a background for the lives and loves of three girls, one Catholic, one Protestant, and one Christian Scientist. They make a friendship pact as girls and, despite bigotry, rivalry in love, jealousy and betrayal, violence, and separation, are brought together again by a tragic murder and reaffirm their basic kinship.

Cora, the narrator of the novel and the Christian Scientist, is the most memorable character, as her motivations and conflicts are revealed firsthand. Her action propels the plot, and her jealousy sets up a chain that will eventually end in murder. Deeply saddened by the tragedy, she seeks absolution by confession to her friends. Rosie, the Protestant, and Teresa, the Catholic, although well delineated, are not as finely drawn as is Gerard, the doctor brother of Teresa, whose whole life is devoted to caring for his people in the bleak confines of troubled Belfast.

The Second Flowering of Emily Mountjoy (1979) and *The Women's House* (1989), as well as her other novels, reveal markedly different characters and situations, but in each case the author's genius for interaction of personality in the natural yet inevitable development of plot does much to enhance the structure of the novels. She uses her skill at characterization to give luster to prosaic lives. Prosaic lives in Joan Lingard's novels, as in real life, are often touched by violence, shootings, bombings, fire, murder—a sad symptom of the twentieth century. Yet her stories are related in a gentle prose, contrasting starkly with the incidents described, in a voice that recognizes and is resigned to the presence of evil in the human makeup but is quietly and realistically determined to find joy in life.

JEAN FRANKS

WORKS FOR ADULTS: *Liam's Daughter.* [London]: Hodder & Stoughton, [1963]; *The Prevailing Wind.* [London]: Hodder & Stoughton, [1964]; *The Tide Comes In.* London: Hodder & Stoughton, [1966]; *The Headmaster.* London: Hodder & Stoughton, [1967]; *The Lord on Our Side.*

London: Hodder & Stoughton, 1970; *The Second Flowering of Emily Mountjoy.* Edinburgh: Harris/
New York: St. Martin's, 1979; *Sisters by Rite.* London: Hamish Hamilton, 1984; *Reasonable Doubts.*
London: Hamish Hamilton, 1986; *The Women's House.* London: Hamish Hamilton/New York: St.
Martin's, 1989; *After Colette.* London: Sinclair Stevenson, 1993; *Night Fires.* London: Hamish
Hamilton, 1993.

LITTLE, PHILIP FRANCIS (1866–1926), poet, artist, and religious mystic.
One of the most curious characters in the Dublin literary world at the turn of
the nineteenth century, Little was born on May 31, 1866, in St. John's, Newfoundland, the second son of the Hon. Philip Francis Little, first prime minister
of Newfoundland under Home Rule and later Supreme Court justice there. On
Justice Little's resignation from the bench in 1867, the family came to live
permanently in Ireland, and the eight sons and two daughters were reared in
Dundrum and later in Monkstown.

In 1877, Philip Francis Little was sent to the Jesuit College at Tullabeg, later
incorporated with Clongowes, which he attended from 1881 to 1884. In 1884,
he entered University College, where he was a contemporary of Gerard Manly
Hopkins, then on the staff. He entered the Jesuit novitiate on October 25, 1886,
but only for fifteen months. Though he was deeply religious, his temperament
was not easily bent to the order. He went on to study at the Metropolitan School
of Art, where he was a contemporary and friend of George Russell (AE*). He
drew and painted for the rest of his life, but few of his works seem to survive
outside private hands, and no exhibitions of them have been traced.

He met Russell one evening while both were walking on a country road near
Dublin, and Little suggested they establish themselves in a wrecked van on the
East Pier at Kingstown and establish a mystical hermitage there. But writing in
1887, Russell realized that his friend's lack of worldly wisdom would isolate
him from people, preventing them from hearing his religious message.

Essentially a restless soul, he and his brothers went on a walking trip through
Germany in the summer of 1892, which left many impressions that would later
surface directly as images in his poems. He tramped all over Ireland in poverty,
staying with simple country people, sharing their food, and imparting his views
on the gospel. He also made several voyages. In October 1893, he sailed from
Gravesend for Melbourne, where he arrived in January 1894. He also lived for
a time in Egypt and in the South of France. From his family he had enough
money to be comfortable, if that is what he had wanted, but he preferred an
eccentric lifestyle that became increasingly strange as the years went on.

Having heard of him through Russell, W. B. Yeats* made use of Little's
character for the hero of his story "Where There Is Nothing," published in *The
Secret Rose* in 1896. The title came from a remark of Little's about his own
wanderings among the poor, "Where there is Nothing, there is God." In 1902,
Yeats and Russell related Little's story to George Moore,* who suggested they
turn it into a play. But then Moore decided to use the scenario for a novel and
forbade Yeats to use it. Yeats rushed out his drama *Where There Is Nothing* in

1902. Later he regretted this, as he realized that Moore might well have made Little the basis of a novel to set beside *The Lake.* Relations between Moore and Years never recovered from this breach.

Little returned to Ireland in 1911 and began two campaigns that were to last him his lifetime: street preaching and warning women and children against immodesty of dress. But this weird public figure was only the outer form of a remarkable poet. He was a frequent contributor of verse to the *New Island Review.* He began publishing there in 1897 and last appeared in 1906. He published a single volume of his poetry, *Thermopylae and Other Poems,* in 1915.

But as a singular public figure he most impressed his contemporaries. He would wander the streets of Rathgar and Rathmines warning women, girls, and small boys about the immodest dangers of bare bosoms, shoulders, and legs. In the habit of writing warnings to girls who went out with British soldiers from Portobello barracks, he was pursued from his house by a gang with blackened faces. Preaching at Portobello Bridge, he impressed many Dubliners as one of the city's quaintest characters. Austin Clarke,* in his memoir *A Penny in the Clouds,* gives a vivid impression of him at this time in his black sombrero and sackcloth apron.

His poetry always had admirers. Clarke admits the quality of some of it, and from time to time friends and relatives attempted to revive his reputation. He has faded, however, from neglect to oblivion. As late as 1924, he still read over his unpublished poems to Russell. For the last years of his life, he lived under the care of a landlady, Mrs. Cleary, at 30 Rathmines Road, where he died on November 21, 1926. He was buried without fanfare the next day in Dean's Grange Cemetery with other members of his family.

PETER COSTELLO

WORK: *Thermopylae and Other Poems.* London: John Long, 1915. REFERENCES: AE (George Russell). "The Poetry of Philip Francis Little." *Irish Statesman* (December 18, 1926): 355–356; AE. "The Sunset of Fancy." *Dublin Magazine* 13 (January 1938): 6–11; Campbell, J. J. "A Neglected Irish Poet." *Capuchin Annual* (1944): 304–306; [Finlay, Thomas A.]. "Philip Francis Little." *Clongownian* (1927): 102; Little, Patrick J. "Foreword to the Poems of Philip Francis Little." *Capuchin Annual* (1944): 165–303. (With the poems); O'Neill, George. "Philip Francis Little: The Man and the Poet." *Studies* (1927).

LLYWELYN, MORGAN (1937–   ), novelist. Llywelyn was born on December 3, 1937, in New York, the daughter of attorney Joseph John Snyder and his wife, Henri Price Llywelyn Synyder. She graduated from high school in Dallas, Texas, and was married on New Year's Day, 1957, to Charles Winter, a pilot. Her early career activities included modeling, dance instruction, and equestrian competition. In 1974, she turned to writing; and her first book, an outgrowth of her interest in the genealogy of her own family, was *The Wind from Hastings.* Her interest in Celtic life led to research in Ireland and on the Continent and resulted in a succession of books that chronicle the legendary and historical figures of Ireland's past, from the pre-Christian era to A.D. 1600. In 1981, her name was legally changed to Llywelyn. Her novel *The Horse Goddess* was named the best novel of 1983 by the National League of American Pen Women. Research led to increasing time spent in Ireland, and, since her husband's death in 1985, she has lived there.

Great imagination and copious detail in her books bring alive to the modern reader the legends of Cuchulain and Finn MacCool, and the days of Brian Boru, Grace O'Malley, Hugh O'Neill, and others. Wide distribution of her novels in the United States has made Celtic life known to the descendants of the Irish diaspora. Easily readable, her books appeal to a wide audience.

JEAN FRANKS

WORKS: *The Wind from Hastings*. Boston: Houghton Mifflin, 1978/London: Hale, 1980; *Lion of Ireland*. Boston: Houghton Mifflin/London: Bodley Head, 1980; *The Horse Goddess*. Boston: Houghton Mifflin, 1982/London: Macdonald, 1983; *Bard, The Odyssey of the Irish*. Boston: Houghton Mifflin, 1984/London: Century, 1985; *Grania: She-King of the Irish Seas*. New York: Crown, 1986/London: Sphere, 1987; *Xerxes*. New York: Chelsea House, 1987. (Children's book); *Red Branch*. New York: William Morrow, 1989; *On Raven's Wing*. London: Heinemann, 1990; *Brian Boru, Emperor of the Irish*. Dublin: O'Brien, 1990. (Children's book); *Druids*. New York: William Morrow/London: Heinemann, 1991; *The Last Prince of Ireland*. New York: William Morrow, 1992; *O'Sullivan's March*. London: Heinemann, 1993/new ed., London: Mandarin, 1993; *Strongbow: The Story of Richard and Aoife*. Dublin: O'Brien, 1992. (Children's book); *The Elementals*. New York: Tom Doherty, 1993/London: Pan, 1994. (Science fiction); *Star Dancer*. Dublin: O'Brien, 1993. (Children's book); *Finn Mac Cool*. New York: St. Martin's/London: Heinemann, 1994; *Pride of Lions*. New York: Tom Doherty, 1995.

LOBO, GEORGE EDMUND (1894–1971), poet and novelist. Lobo was born and died in Dublin, and in 1927 and 1928 he edited the short-lived *Dublin Art Monthly*.

WORKS: *In Memoriam Francis Sheehy Skeffington . . . A Poem*. [Dublin, 1917]; *The Sacrifice of Love, and Other Poems*. Dublin: Author, 1917; *Golden Dreams*. London: C. W. Daniels, 1926. (Novel); as Oliver Sheehy. *Mandrake*. London: Jarrolds, [1929]. (Novel); *Clay Speaks of the Fire*. London: Williams & Norgate, [1946]. (Poetry); *There Came Past. Episode of a Poet*. Dublin: Wolf's Head, [1952]. (Poetry pamphlet).

LOMBARD, CARL

WORKS: *The Disappearance of Rory Brophy*. London: Fourth Estate, 1992. (Novel); *Mortal Beings*. London: Fourth Estate, 1993. (Novel).

LONGFORD, LADY (1900–1980), playwright and woman of letters. Lady Longford's reputation has never been great outside her adopted Ireland, but she was a sophisticated and accomplished novelist as well as an able and prolific playwright.

She was born Christine Patti Trew on September 6, 1900, in Chedder, Somerset. She attended Somerset College, Oxford, and received an M.A. She married Edward Pakenham, the sixth earl of Longford,* and subsequently resided in Ireland. Her husband became the principal financial backer of the Gate Theatre* and then in 1936 founded his own company, which lasted until his death in 1961. For the Gate and then for Longford Productions, Lady Longford wrote many plays, including translations of the Greek classics, adaptations of English and Irish novels, original Irish historical plays, and contemporary comedies of Irish life. Of these more than twenty plays, only some of the histories and comedies have been published. The histories are generally less interesting. *Lord Edward* (Longford Productions, 1941) is merely competent, but *The United Brothers* (Longford Productions, 1942) has been called "as vivid and accomplished a historical play as any dramatist has written in modern Ireland."

Lady Longford's dramatic forte, however, is in genially satiric comedies of contemporary life, of which the best may be *Mr. Jiggins of Jigginstown* (Gate, 1933), a witty fantasy adapted from her own novel, and *The Hill of Quirke* (Longford Productions, 1953), which is about the efforts to plan for a civic festival in a small town.

Of her novels, which appear to be more substantial and lasting work, two might be singled out as indicating her range. *Making Conversation* (1931) is a sensitive and subtle exercise in the vein of Virginia Woolf, and *Country Places* (1932) seems almost an Irish version of Evelyn Waugh. Her close involvement with the running of a theater may have prevented her from developing her bent toward fiction as well as a more individual voice, but her intelligence and craft are noteworthy. She died in Dublin on May 14, 1980.

WORKS: *Vespasian and Some of His Contemporaries.* Dublin: Hodges, Figgis, 1928. (Nonfiction); *Making Conversation.* London: Stein & Gollancz, 1931. (Novel); *Country Places.* London: Gollancz, 1932. (Novel); *Mr. Jiggins of Jigginstown.* London: V. Gollancz, 1933. (Novel); *Printed Cotton.* London: Methuen, 1935. (Novel); *A Biography of Dublin.* London: Methuen, 1936. (Nonfiction); *Mr. Jiggins of Jigginstown* in *Plays of Changing Ireland.* Curtins Canfield, ed. New York Macmillan, 1936. (Play); *Lord Edward.* Dublin: Hodges, Figgis, 1941. (Play); *The United Brothers.* Dublin: Hodges, Figgis, 1942. (Play); *Patrick Sarsfield.* Dublin: Hodges, Figgis, 1943. (Play); *The Earl of Straw.* Dublin: Hodges, Figgis, 1945. (Play); *The Hill of Quirke.* Dublin: P. J. Bourke, 1958. (Play); *Mr. Supple, or Time Will Tell.* Dublin: P. J. Bourke, n.d. (Play); *Tankardstown.* Dublin: P. J. Bourke, n.d. (Play); "The Longford Memoirs I." *Irish Times* (March 7, 1981): 9; "The Longford Memoirs II." *Irish Times* (March 14, 1981): 9; "The Longford Memoirs III." *Irish Times* (March 21, 1981): 9; "The Longford Memoirs IV." *Irish Times* (March 28, 1981): 8. REFERENCES: Cowell, John. *No Profit but the Name: The Longfords and the Gate Theatre.* Dublin: O'Brien, 1988; Hogan, Robert. *After the Irish Renaissance.* Minneapolis: University of Minnesota Press, 1967, pp. 126–132.

LONGFORD, LORD (1902–1961), playwright and translator. The sixth Earl of Longford was a theatrical producer, a playwright, and a translator from the Irish. He was born Edward Arthur Henry Pakenham on December 29, 1902, into a family which had been in Ireland from the middle of the seventeenth century. He was educated at Eton and then at Christ Church, Oxford, where he received an M.A. in 1925. In 1931, he became closely involved with the Gate Theatre* which produced a number of his original plays and translations. In 1936, he formed his own independent production company, Longford Productions, whose repertoire for many years consisted primarily of classic plays staged at the Gate Theatre. He served in the Irish Senate from 1946 to 1948; he was a member of the Irish Academy of Letters; and he received a D. Litt. from Dublin University in 1954. He died on February 4, 1961, in Dublin.

Longford translated a good deal from the Irish, including a version of Brian Merriman's *The Midnight Court.* His work for the theatre included *The Melians* (1931), *Yahoo* (1933), *Ascendancy* (1935), *The Armlet of Jade* (1936), *Carmilla, after Le Fanu** (1937), and *The Vineyard* (1943). With Lady Longford* he translated *The Oresteia;* alone he translated Sophocles, Euripides, Calderon, Molière, and Beaumarchais. Longford's great contribution to the theatre was his own worthy production company, which existed until his death. His own work for the stage will not for the most part bear revival. One possible exception is his version of the Swift* story, *Yahoo,* which has an effective expressionistic conclusion.

WORKS: *A Book of Poems.* London: Privately printed by Bumpus, 1920; *The Oresteia of Aischylos,* with Christine Longford. Dublin: Hodges, Figgis, 1933; *Yahoo.* Dublin: Hodges, Figgis, 1934/reprinted in Curtis Canfield's *Plays of Changing Ireland,* New York: Macmillan, 1936; *Armlet of Jade.* Dublin: Hodges, Figgis, 1935. (Play); *Ascendancy.* Dublin: Hodges, Figgis, 1935. (Play); *The Vineyard.* Dublin: Hodges, Figgis, 1943. (Play); *Poems from the Irish.* Dublin: Hodges, Figgis, 1944; *More Poems from the Irish.* Dublin: Hodges, Figgis, 1945; *The Dove in the Castle.* Dublin: Hodges, Figgis, 1946. (Translations from the Irish); *The School for Wives,* by Molière. Dublin: Hodges, Figgis, 1948; *The Midnight Court,* by Brian Merriman in *Poetry Ireland,* No. 6 (July 1949). REFERENCES: Cowell, John. *No Profit but the Name: The Longfords and the Gate Theatre.* Dublin: O'Brien, 1988; *Longford Productions: Dublin Gate Souvenir, 1949.* Dublin: Corrigan & Wilson, 1949.

LONGLEY, EDNA (1940–), critic and teacher. Longley was born in Cork on December 24, 1940. Her father was T. S. Broderick, lecturer and professor of pure mathematics at Trinity College, Dublin, from 1944 to 1962. Longley has written of her father's close relation to Eamon de Valera, who sought his advice on mathematics. In Longley's childhood, her father left the Catholic Church. "Since my mother, also a mathematician, came from a Scottish Presbyterian family," writes Longley in *The Living Stream,* "my sister and I, though baptised Catholics, were brought up within the Anglican compromise (the Church of Ireland)." Longley entered Trinity in 1958. Soon after receiving her B.A., she married Michael Longley,* and they have three children. The Longleys began attending Philip Hobsbaum's group in Belfast in 1964. Her editions of Edward Thomas's poetry and prose appeared, respectively, in 1973 and 1981, and between 1986 and 1994 she published three books of criticism. She has served as reader and professor at the School of English at the Queen's University, Belfast, where she teaches English and Irish literature. She has been an organizer of the John Hewitt Summer School, an editor of *The Irish Review,* and a member of the Arts Council of Northern Ireland. Her articles, reviews, and letters have appeared regularly in the *Times Literary Supplement,* the *Irish Times, Notes and Queries,* and other periodicals. She has, for some time, been the most prominent literary critic working in Northern Ireland and one of the most noted commentators on Irish literature.

She may also be the most distinctive in her methods. "Most critics of contemporary poetry neglect form," she writes in *Poetry in the Wars* (1986). Her scrutiny of the formal characteristics of Irish poetry (as well as of American and English poetry, such as the work of Robert Frost and Thomas) often leads her to complex figurings. In *Poetry in the Wars,* she speculates that "there might be many explanations, including the obvious factor of individual talents, why Northern Irish poetry displays . . . notable formal concentration"; she notes, for instance, that "Northern Irish poetry of the sixties in certain respects assimilated and transmuted the Movement's formality," with the result that "the special hybridisations of Northern Irish poetry can escape both the Southern Irish Europeanism which ignores England and the English Atlanticism which ignores Ireland." Longley's first book maps stylistic connections that link Yeats* to Philip Larkin and Heaney* to Wilfred Owen.

But it is a misreading of Longley's formalism to see her, as Mark Patrick Hederman did, as "attempting to cordon [art] off into an anodyne, detached and insulated cocoon where it loses all its essential meaning and force and becomes," in words Hederman took from Heidegger, "a 'routine cultural phenomenon.' " There is nothing routine in the exacting labors Longley sees in the poems she admires. She explains the title of her first book as suggesting "that poetry is fought over, that in some sense it fights, and that these arenas overlap." But Longley does wish to "give the lie to the notion that language can operate politically in Irish poetry only by declaring firm allegiances." Though she believes that "good poems are exciting enough in themselves, while bad politics should remain unexciting," she has made a continuous argument for the way poets contribute through their linguistic care "in a country of unscrupulous rhetoricians, where names break bones, where careless talk costs lives."

Both the most subtle and the most sustained embodiment of Longley's faith in poetry's importance is her 1988 book on Louis MacNeice.* Her introductory comment on MacNeice might serve well to describe Longley's own priorities: "In a curious way MacNeice did more than other twentieth-century poets to test poetry against the century. He tested it against the claims of politics and philosophy, against the pressures of cities and war. And he did not take the outcome of these tests, or of anything else, for granted." Indeed, even the titles of the essays in her next book, *The Living Stream: Literature and Revisionism in Ireland* (1994), suggest her involvement in those very tests, for example, "The Writer and Belfast," "The Rising, the Somme, and Irish Memory," "Poetic Forms and Social Malformations." *The Living Stream* is most impressive for the complexities it attaches to matters of poetic lineage, such as Derek Mahon's* and Paul Muldoon's* very different inheritances from MacNeice: it shows literary tradition to be troubled and dynamic. At its best, *The Living Stream* might serve as a strong check against the invoking of Irish literary tradition on behalf of any singular allegiance.

Elsewhere, Longley has contributed to collections that have been designed to reclaim a plurality of Irish traditions (such as two *Cultural Traditions in Northern Ireland* volumes, edited by Maurna Crozier) or to make a case for the complexities of the Protestant tradition (such as the 1985 book she and Gerald

Dawe* edited, *Across a Roaring Hill: The Protestant Imagination in Modern Ireland*). "As a literary critic who sometimes notices distinctive elements in Northern writing," she says in *The Living Stream,* "I have been suspected equally of partisanship and partitionism." But her procedures should guard against any simple political advocacy's being ascribed to her. A critic in the fullest sense of the word, Longley can be hardest on the politics and the poetics of writers she admires. Though her essays are often undisciplined in both tone and structure, they are "striking," in George O'Brien's* words, for "their extraordinary commitment, tenacity and drive."

VICTOR LUFTIG

WORKS: Ed., Edward Thomas, *Poems and Last Poems.* Plymouth: Macdonald & Evans, 1973; ed., *The Selected James Simmons.* Belfast: Blackstaff, 1978; ed., *A Language Not to Be Betrayed: Selected Prose of Edward Thomas.* Manchester: Carcanet/New York: Persea, 1981; ed., *The Selected Paul Durcan.* Belfast: Blackstaff, 1982 & 1985; ed., with Gerald Dawe, *Across a Roaring Hill: The Protestant Imagination in Modern Ireland, Essays in Honour of John Hewitt.* Belfast: Blackstaff, 1985; *Poetry in the Wars.* Newcastle upon Tyne: Bloodaxe, 1986/Newark: University of Delaware Press, 1987; *Louis MacNeice: A Study.* London: Faber, 1988; ed., Dorothy Hewett, *Alice in Wormland: Selected Poems.* Newcastle upon Tyne: Bloodaxe, 1990; *From Cathleen to Anorexia: The Breakdown of Ireland.* Dublin: Attic, 1990; *The Living Stream: Literature and Revisionism in Ireland.* Newcastle upon Tyne: Bloodaxe, 1994.

LONGLEY, MICHAEL (1939–   ), poet. Born in Belfast on July 27, 1939, Longley was educated at the Royal Belfast Academical Institution and Trinity College, Dublin, where he took an honours degree in classics. After teaching for several years, he began working for the Arts Council of Northern Ireland and served as its director of literature and traditional arts until retiring in 1991 in order to devote himself more fully to writing. Often considered part of the Ulster or Northern school of poets who came to prominence in the 1960s and who include Derek Mahon* and Seamus Heaney,* Longley has published five major collections of verse as well as numerous poetry pamphlets and limited editions. He has edited *Causeway* (1971), a guide to the arts in Northern Ireland; *Under the Moon: Over the Stars* (1971), a collection of children's verse; *Selected Poems of Louis MacNeice* (1990); and *Poems: W. R. Rodgers* (1993). Among the awards he has received are the Eric Gregory Award and the Whitbread Award. He is married to the critic Edna Longley.*

The poem "The Ornithological Section," from his first major book, *No Continuing City* (1969), has the poet finding parallels between the suspended animation of taxidermically preserved birds and the human desire to have actions defined "[b]y that repose." The poised artificiality of the birds and the impulse to locate objectively and distill the essence of the self are apt images for Longely's concerns in *No Continuing City* and, to a lesser extent, in his subsequent work. Indeed, the most evident characteristic of this first volume is its carefully wrought formality. Longley himself has commented that he has a preoccupation with the possibilities of stanzaic form. While Longley's skills are evident throughout, there are times in poems like "Epithalamion" and "Personal Statement'' when extended metaphor and elaborate conceit strain under the weight of their self-conscious artifice. Tendencies like these have prompted critics to see in this volume an "over-cautious, elaborate formality" and to say that it is difficult "to capture any easily distinguishable poetic timbre in his voice."

Perhaps the strongest poem in *No Continuing City,* one that avoids these criticisms and anticipates the strengths in Longley's future development, is "In Memoriam." Though written in intricately rhymed, ten-lined stanzas, the direct, conversational language of this elegy to his father and his experiences in the First World War mutes what elsewhere appears as overly insistent formalism. Besides demonstrating Longley's strength as an elegist, the poem draws on two other tendencies that continue throughout his work. The role of the poet as self-conscious maker and commentator is evident when he writes in the first stanza, "Let yours / And other heartbreaks play into my hands." Moreover, Longley exhibits another emerging characteristic with his weaving of the domestic and intensely personal into the fabric of larger events.

In *An Exploded View* (1973), with its dedication to fellow Ulster poets James Simmons,* Derek Mahon, and Seamus Heaney and with its epigraph that begins, "We are trying to make ourselves heard," Longley further (and again self-consciously) explores the poet's role as he attempts to define himself for himself and for others. While there is a self-mocking tone to much of this volume, especially in poems like "Alibis" and "Options," the poet's place in society receives more serious scrutiny in the sequence "Letters," where it takes shape against the backdrop of sectarian violence in Ulster. In these letters to Simmons, Mahon, and Heaney, Longley attempts to place himself, to "[c]laim this my country," while cognizant of the complexities of that stance. The opening of his letter to fellow Protestant Mahon forthrightly exposes the difficulties:

Did we come into our own
When, minus muse and lexicon,
We traced in August sixty-nine
Our imaginary Peace Line
Around the burnt-out houses of
The Catholics we'd scarcely loved,
Two Sisyphuses come to budge
The sticks and stones of an old grudge . . . ?

In general, Longley's approach to the Troubles has been indirect, and he has spoken about the feeling of presumptuousness that comes with trying to address the subject. When he does write about it, however, it is in the context of personal, mundane details. In "Wounds" he evokes his English father's reminiscences about the "Ulster Division at the Somme" and juxtaposes his father's death many years after ("a belated casualty / . . . dying for King and Country, slowly") with victims of the more recent conflict: "Three teenage soldiers, bellies full of / Bullets and Irish beer" and a bus conductor

. . . shot through the head
By a shivering boy who wandered in

Before they could turn the television down
Or tidy away the supper dishes.

Again, the particularity of detail and directness of language in such verse support Neil Corcoran's contention that the "elegy is the mode in which [Longley] has done his best work so far" and makes *An Exploded View* an impressive advancement over Longley's first volume.

By comparison, *Man Lying on a Wall* (1976), which Longley has described as being a much more personal book, does not offer any new departures. Poems like "Landscape," "Weather," and "Fleadh" are delicately realized sketches, though they seem to repeat earlier approaches. Other poems, "Ars Poetica" and "Last Rites," for example, offer yet again self-mocking explorations of the poet as persona and, at times, appear to try too hard to develop and sustain Longley's tropes. On the other hand, *The Echo Gate* (1979) shows him exploring new territory. The same self-conscious self-objectification is there, as are the short, haikulike sketches that recall some of Longley's earlier work. But the four poems that make up the "Mayo Monologues" are refreshing departures. In each of the four portraits, the wounded or displaced psyche of the speaker defines itself by its keen sensitivity to place and landscape. In "Self-Heal," as the title implies, a girl sexually molested by a retarded boy gingerly revisits the event by musing on her attempt to teach the boy the names of wildflowers.

Another series of poems in *The Echo Gate,* "Wreathes," similarly plays to Longley's strengths. Here his precise selection of mundane detail intensifies the senseless, yet almost routine, nature of sectarian murders where a civil servant is shot while preparing breakfast or a greengrocer is found by his assassins working in his shop. Even the third section in the triptych, "The Linen Workers," which begins with the surrealistic image of "Christ's teeth ascend[ing] with him into heaven," quickly returns to the things of this world: Longley's opening dissolves into an image of his father's dentures and then into that of a set of dentures found at the site where ten linen workers were massacred. Unflinchingly objective, these poems seethe with complex emotion.

The advances made in *The Echo Gate* are continued in *Gorse Fires* (1991). There is a diversity of poems, some characteristic—lyrics in which the absences that impinge upon the speaker are absorbed into the familiar distances of landscape—and some not so characteristic, like the sequence "Ghetto" with its treatment of the Nazi extermination camps in Poland during the Second World War. Yet for all its variety, *Gorse Fires* has the greatest sense of cohesion and solidity of any of Longley's books. Longley accomplishes this with seven poems derived from Homer's *Odyssey* in which he "combin[es] free translation . . . with original lines." The way these poems resonate through, and unify, the volume is sometimes quite apparent as, for instance, in the pairing of "Northern Lights," in which Longley recalls his father's "tobacco-y breath / and the solar wind that ruffled . . . [his] thinning hair," and "Laertes," in which Odysseus "cradle[s] like driftwood . . . his dwindling father." Other times the connection is less pronounced, though no less effective. Thus the horrors of the Holocaust or of sectarian murders as well as Longley's personal sense of estrangement and homecoming are all modulated by the indirect commentary of Homer's epic.

Gorse Fires is a thin volume, but, like the best of Longley's work, it is not slight. Satisfying in its reverberations and construction, it shows that Longley is a poet of continuing promise and reaffirms him as an important voice in contemporary Irish poetry.

CHRISTOPHER PENNA

WORKS: *No Continuing City.* London: Macmillan/Chester Springs, Pa.: Dufour, 1969; ed., *Causeway.* Belfast: Arts Council of Northern Ireland, 1971; ed., *Under the Moon: Over the Stars.* Belfast: Arts Council of Northern Ireland, 1971; *An Exploded View.* London: Gollancz, 1973; *Man Lying on a Wall.* London: Gollancz, 1976; *The Echo Gate.* London: Secker & Warburg, 1979; *Selected Poems, 1963–1980.* Winston-Salem, N.C.: Wake Forest University Press, 1981; *Poems, 1963–1983.* Edinburgh: Salamander/Dublin: Gallery, 1985/London: Secker & Warburg, 1991. (Contains most of the poems from the previous four collections as well as new poems); ed., *Selected Poems of Louis MacNeice.* Winston-Salem, N.C.: Wake Forest University Press, 1990; *Gorse Fires.* London: Secker & Warburg/Winston-Salem, N.C.: Wake Forest University Press, 1991; ed., *Poems: W. R. Rodgers.* [Oldcastle, Co. Meath]: Gallery, [1993]; *The Ghost Orchard.* London: Cape, 1995. REFERENCES: Boran, Pat. "The Future Is behind Us." *Books Ireland,* No. 187 (Summer 1995): 147; Brown, Terence. "Four New Voices." In *Northern Voices.* Totowa, N.J.: Rowman & Littlefield, 1975, pp. 175–213; Corcoran, Neil. "Last Words: Michael Longley's Elegies." *Poetry Wales* 24, 2 (1989): 16–18; Dawe, Gerald. " 'Icon' and 'Lares': Derek Mahon and Michael Longley." In *Across a Roaring Hill.* Gerald Dawe & Edna Longley, eds. Belfast & Dover, N.H.: Blackstaff, 1985, pp. 218–235; Maxwell, D.E.S. "Contemporary Poetry in the North of Ireland." In *Two Decades of Irish Writing.* Douglas Dunn, ed. Cheadle Hulme, Cheshire: Carcanet/Chester Springs, Pa.: Dufour, 1975, pp. 166–185; McDonald, Peter. "Michael Longley's Homes." In *The Chosen Ground.* Neil Corcoran, ed. Bridgend, Mid Glamorgan: Seren Books/Chester Springs, Pa.: Dufour, 1992, pp. 65–83.

LOVER, SAMUEL (1797–1868), novelist, dramatist, song-writer, and painter. Lover was born on February 24, 1797, in Dublin, the eldest son of a Dublin stockbroker. He was a precocious child who was educated privately and who quite early demonstrated considerable talent both in music and in art. At the age of seventeen, he began to earn his living as a painter and was extremely successful, particularly as a miniaturist. The third string to his bow was literature, and he was equally at ease in several genres. For instance, he transformed his popular ballad "Rory O'More" (1826) into a popular novel and then into an equally popular play.

He was one of the founders of *The Dublin University Magazine* in 1833. After he removed to London in 1835, he became well known in literary and artistic circles, and with Dickens and others he founded *Bentley's Miscellany.*

His plays, especially *Rory O'More* (1837), *The White Horse of the Peppers* (1838), *The Happy Man* (1839) as well as his musical dramas and burlesque operas were popular fare in their day but have not held the stage.

After 1844, failing eyesight caused him to abandon painting, and he took to public recitals of his work in the manner of Dickens. His "Irish Evenings," as he called them, were as successful in the United States and Canada as they were in England.

Despite his fluency in all he attempted, Lover is most remembered for his fiction. His *Legends and Stories of Ireland* (1831), *Rory O'More* (1837), and, above all, *Handy Andy* (1842) are his most enduring productions. His Handy Andy is the great, amiable, awkward, moronic lout of Irish literature. But if he is exaggerated beyond the probabilities of reality, so it might also be said are Mr. Micawber and Mrs. Gamp. Despite its broadness, the book is genial, unforced good fun.

He died at St. Heliers, Jersey, on July 6, 1868.

WORKS: *Legends and Stories of Ireland*. 1st Series. Dublin: Wakeman, 1831; *The Parson's Horn Book*. Dublin: Printed & sold at the office of *The Comet*, 1831. (Illustrations & probably some of the satiric poems were by Lover); *Legends and Stories of Ireland*. 2d Series. London: Baldwin, 1834; *Popular Tales and Legends of the Irish Peasantry*. Dublin: Wakeman, 1834; *Rory O'More, a National Romance*. 3 vols. London: Bentley & Sons, 1837; *Rory O'More*. London: Dick's Standard Plays, 1837. (Adaptation in three acts of the novel); *The White Horse of the Peppers*. London: Acting National Drama, 1838. (Comic drama in 2 acts); *The Hall Porter*. London: Acting National Drama, 1839. (Comic drama in 2 acts); *The Happy Man*. London: Acting National Drama, 1839. (Extravaganza in 1 act); *Songs and Ballads*. London: Chapman & Hall, 1839; *English Bijou Almanack for 1840*. London: A. Schloss, 1840; *The Greek Boy*. London: Acting National Drama, 1840. (Musical drama in 2 acts); *Il Paddy Whack in Italia*. London: Duncombe's British Theatre, 1841. (Operetta in 1 act); *Handy Andy*. London: F. Lover, 1842/London: Dent, 1954; *Mr. Lover's Irish Evenings: The Irish Brigade*. London: Johnson, 1844. (Poem); *Treasure Trove*. London: F. Lover, 1844; *Characteristic Sketches of Ireland and the Irish*. Dublin: P. D. Hardy, 1845; *Barney the Baron*. London: Dick's Standard Plays, 1850. (Farce in 1 act); ed., *The Lyrics of Ireland*. London: Houlston & Wright, 1858; *Metrical Tales and Other Poems*. London: Houlston & Wright, 1860; *Mac Carthy More*. London: Lacy, 1861. (Comic drama in 2 acts); with Charles Mackay & Thomas Miller, *Original Songs for the Rifle Volunteers*. London: C. H. Clarke, 1861; *The Poetical Works of Samuel Lover*. REFERENCES: Bernard, W. B. *The Life of S. Lover, R. H. A., Artistic, Literary and Musical*. 2 vols. London: H. S. King, 1874; Sigwalt, Colette. "Samuel Lover; A Study in the Irish Picturesque." Diss., Strasbourg, 1969; Symington, A. J. *Samuel Lover*. London: Blackie, 1880.

LUCY, SEAN (1931–   ), poet and critic. Lucy was born in Bombay, India, and brought to Ireland in 1935. He received a B.A. in history and an M.A. in English from University College, Cork (UCC), and after teaching for eight years in England, returned to UCC, where he became professor of modern English in 1967. His poems are straightforward and strong in diction but irregularly rhythmic. He often plays with rhymes or off-rhymes, although not always in any consistent pattern. His "Donal Ogue" after an anonymous eighteenth-century Irish poem is quite moving. His often reprinted "Longshore Intellectual" is equally effective, and his short "The New Invasions," despite rather weak last lines to its two stanzas, is tellingly mordant.

WORKS: *T. S. Eliot and the Idea of Tradition*. London: Cohen & West, 1960; ed., *Love Poems of the Irish*. Cork: Mercier, 1967; ed., *Five Irish Poets*. Cork: Mercier, [1970]. (Contains about thirty pages of Lucy's work); ed., *Irish Poets in English: The Thomas Davis Lectures on Anglo-Irish Poetry*. Cork & Dublin: Mercier, 1973; *Unfinished Sequence and Other Poems*. Portmarnock,

Co. Dublin: Wolfhound, 1979; ed., *Goldsmith, the Gentle Master.* Cork: Cork University Press, 1984. (Thomas Davis Lectures).

LUSBY, JIM, novelist and Hennessy winner.

WORK: *Making the Cut.* London: Gollancz, 1995. (Thriller).

LUTTRELL, HENRY (1765?–1851), poet. Luttrell was born in Dublin, the natural son of Lord Carhampton. A member of the Irish Parliament in 1798, he removed to London after the Act of Union. There he was admired for his wit by Campbell, Macaulay, Samuel Rogers, Sydney Smith, Lord Byron, and Thomas Moore.* Byron thought him the ''most epigrammatic conversationalist'' he had ever met, and Moore consulted Luttrell before destroying Byron's memoirs. Moore particularly admired his letter in rhyme, *Advice to Julia* (1820), thinking it ''full of well-bred facetiousness and sparkle of the very first water.'' On another occasion, Moore thought Luttrell's parody of the Latin poem ''Quis multa gracilis'' was ''done with admirable ease & fun—but not publishable.'' The poem was about the king and syphilis and had the king holding ''the noseless tenor of his way.'' Luttrell's witty verses have been unfortunately overlooked in recent years. He died in London on December 19, 1851.

WORKS: *Lines Written at Ampthill Park in the Autumn of 1818.* London: J. Murray, 1819; *Advice to Julia.* London: J. Murray, 1820; *Crockford House.* London: J. Murray, 1827.   REFERENCES: Crosse, A. ''An Old Society Wit.'' *Temple Bar.* 104 (1895); Dobson, Austin. ''A Forgotten Poet of Society.'' *St. James's Magazine* 33 (1878).

LYNAM, WILLIAM FRANCIS (ca. 1845–1894), humorist and soldier. Born in County Galway, Lynam became a lieutenant colonel in the Royal Lancashire militia. He wrote serials for periodicals, including the vastly popular and broadly humorous ones about the scheming Mick McQuaid, who gave his name to a still-sold brand of pipe tobacco. Lynam died in Clontarf.

PRINCIPAL WORKS: *The Adventures of Mick McQuaid.* Dublin: Shamrock Office, 1875; *Darby the Dodger.* Dublin: Gerrard, 1877. (Comedy in four acts).   REFERENCE: O'Donoghue, D. J. ''The Author of 'Mick McQuaid.' '' *Irish Book Lover* 3 (1911): 4–7, 29.

LYNCH, BRIAN (1945–   ), poet. Lynch was born on February 2, 1945, in Glasnevin. He has been a teacher, civil servant, and journalist.

WORKS: With Paul Durcan. *Endsville.* Dublin: New Writers', 1967; *No Die Cast.* Dublin: New Writers', 1969; *Outside the Pheasantry.* Gorey: Gorey Arts Centre, 1975; *Perpetual Star.* [Dublin: Raven Arts, 1980]; *Voices from the Nettle Way.* Dublin: Raven Arts, 1990.

LYNCH, HANNAH (1862–1904), novelist, playwright, and historian. Born in Dublin, Lynch was well traveled and spent lengthy periods in Spain, Greece, and France. She was a friend of Anna Parnell, became an early member of the Ladies' Land League, and was solidly nationalist in her politics. She played a key role in the *United Ireland* periodical and, when it was suppressed, went to

France and printed the periodical from there. She became the Paris correspondent of *Academy* and a regular contributor to periodicals in both England and France. In *Macmillan's Magazine,* she published under the pseudonym of E. Enticknappe. She died in Paris on January 9, 1904.

Her most important work, *The Autobiography of a Child* (1899), is clearly her own autobiography. In *The Cabinet of Irish Literature,* Katharine Tynan* recalls that Lynch's book "excited great interest when it ran in *Blackwood* in serial form." *The Autobiography* recounts the unhappy childhood of a girl from Kildare. Her family moves to Dublin when she is about five years old, but her childhood proves to be troubled, particularly by the bullying of her sisters and mother. Her removal to a convent school near Birmingham does not alleviate her situation. Overall it is a troubled life, but a well-written volume.

ANNE COLMAN

WORKS: *Defeated.* London: Beeton's Christmas Annual, [1885]; *Through Troubled Waters.* London: Ward, Lock, [1885]; *George Meredith, A Study.* London: Methuen, 1891; *The Prince of the Glades.* 2 vols. London: Methuen, 1891; *Rosni Harvey.* 3 vols. London: Chapman & Hall, 1892; tr., *The History of Florence.* By F. T. Perrens. London: Methuen, 1892; tr., *The Great Galeoto. Folly or Saintliness.* London: John Lane, 1895. (Two prose versions of verse plays by J.M.W. Echegaray); *Clare Munro, The Story of a Mother and Daughter.* London: Milne, [1896]; *Denys d'Auvrillac, A Story of French Life.* London: J. Macqueen, 1896; *Dr. Vermont's Fantasy.* London: J. M. Dent, 1896; *Jimmy Blake.* London: J. M. Dent, 1897; *An Odd Experiment.* London: Methuen, 1897; *Toledo: The Story of an Old Spanish Capital.* London: J. M. Dent, 1898; *The Autobiography of a Child.* Dublin: Blackwood, 1899; *French Life in Town and Country.* London: George Newnes, 1901. REFERENCE: Brown, Stephen J. *Ireland in Fiction.* Dublin & London: Maunsel, 1919.

LYNCH, LIAM (1937–   ), novelist and playwright. Lynch was born in Dublin and has had several plays produced: *Do Thrushes Sing in Birmingham?* (Abbey, 1963), *Soldier* (Peacock, 1969), *Strange Dreams Unending* (RTÉ, 1973), *Krieg* (Project, 1982), and *Voids* (Dublin Theatre Festival, 1982). He has also published three novels, of which *Tenebrae* (1985) is usually considered the best. It is set in an Irish country town in the 1940s and concerns an Anglican priest's battle with loss of faith, insanity, and uncontrollable depression. The priest seems an allegorical figure for the death of the old Anglo-Irish order. Lynch also offers an alternative of vitality in the country life of Catholic rural communities.

BERNARD McKENNA

WORKS: *Shell, Sea Shell.* Dublin: Wolfhound, 1982. (Novel); *Tenebrae: A Passion.* Dublin: Wolfhound, 1985. (Novel); *Pale Moon of Morning.* Dublin: Wolfhound, 1991. (Novel).
REFERENCES: Quilligan, Blanaid. "Pulling Back the Stops: Liam Lynch Talks to Blanaid Quilligan." *New Hibernia* 11 (6) (1985): 21.

LYNCH, MARTIN (1950–   ), playwright. Lynch was born in Belfast, into a working-class Catholic family. He grew up in the Turf Lodge estate, left school at fifteen, but eventually attended the College of Business Studies, taking O Levels when he was twenty-seven. After he initially left school, Lynch began work as a cloth cutter, holding this position until the outbreak of the Unity Flat riots. After that, he began to organize for the Republican Clubs, which were, at various times, known as the Workers Party and the Sinn Féin Workers Party. In 1975, he saw the Lyric Players' Theatre's* production of Patrick Galvin's* *We Do It for Love.* This experience profoundly affected him, and he began to write for the Turf Lodge Fellowship Drama Group, composing *We Want Work, We Want Bread, A Roof under Our Heads,* and *Is There Life before Death?* In 1980, he began writing plays for the Lyric Theatre, including *Dockers* in 1981, *The Interrogation of Ambrose Fogarty* in 1982, *Castles in the Air* in 1983, *My Minstrel Boy* in 1985, and *Pictures of Tomorrow* in 1994. In 1984, the Peacock Theatre staged *The Interrogation of Ambrose Fogarty.* Lynch's plays reflect the plight of workers in conflict with themselves and with management and of people in the context of the Northern violence. Lynch witnessed the explosion of the first Loyalist "murder bomb" and recalls the sight of a man shot by the Provisional Irish Republican Army and others shot by the British army. Because his works address themes common to the working class, they have appealed to a broad-based audience.

Set in 1960, *Dockers* staged the efforts of one man, John Graham, to confront issues facing dockworkers by trying to have his union fulfill its stated mission. In *The Interrogation of Ambrose Fogarty,* a young socialist, suspected of terrorism, is arrested under Section 11 of the Northern Ireland Emergency Provisions Act of 1978. This act allowed for search, arrest, and internment without trial. The play focuses on the mental and physical trauma of the innocent protagonist during his three days of custody and on the motives and behavior of the authorities who carry out the torture. Lynch based the play on his own experiences of arrest and torture in the 1970s. He was taken in for questioning, for three- or four-hour screenings, over thirty times. However, on at least five occasions, he was held for as long as three days. During most of these detainments, Lynch was held at Castlereagh, the prison cited by Amnesty International for repeated instances of torture. *Castles in the Air,* a reworking of *A Roof under Our Heads,* ends with the suicide of Mary Fullerton after enduring physical and psychological abuse from her husband, facing the reality of loneliness because her eldest daughter prepares to leave the home for marriage, and seeing the trap of a lifetime of poverty and debt. In fact, the family is permanently trapped in substandard housing because they cannot afford to pay the rent; and, because they have not, the housing executive will not relocate them. *My Minstrel Boy,* set during the hunger strikes and staged during the signing of the Anglo-Irish Agreement at Hillsborough, explores the sense of commonality and Irishness of Protestants and Catholics while away from home and of their divisiveness and differing national identities while in Northern Ireland.

Lynch's lesser-known but, in many ways, most impressive work has been in organizing community drama and smaller-scale theater in Northern Ireland. In this field, he is perhaps best known for his work with Marie Jones* and the founders of the Charabanc Theatre. Equally impressive is his work for the Ulster Youth Theatre & Youth Drama Workshop, for which he wrote *Ricochets* (1982); for the Dock Ward Community Drama Project; for Stone Chair, for which he wrote *Stone Chair* (1990); for the Point Fields Theatre Company, for which he wrote *Rinty* (1990); for City-Wide, for which he wrote *Moths* (1992); and for the Saint Patrick's Training School, for which he wrote *Bunjour Mucker* (1993). Lynch sees his work with local theater companies as part of the effort of working-class communities to define themselves away from their stereotypical roles.

BERNARD McKENNA

WORKS: *Dockers.* Holywood, Co. Down: Farset Co-Operative Press, 1982; *The Interrogation of Ambrose Fogarty.* Dundonald, Co. Down: Blackstaff, 1982; *Three Plays.* Belfast: Lagan, 1995. REFERENCES: Bleike, Werner. *Prods, Taigs and Brits: Der Ulster-Krise als Theme im nordirischen und britischen Gegenwartsdrama.* Frankfurt am Main: Verlag Peter Lang, 1990; Etherton, Michael. *Contemporary Irish Dramatists.* London: Macmillan, 1989; Grant, David. *Playing the Wild Card.* Belfast: Community Relations Council, 1993; Klein, Michael. "Life and Theatre in Northern Ireland: Interview with Martin Lynch." *Red Letters* 16 (Spring/Summer 1984): 26–31; McAughtry, Sam. "Workers' Writers." *Irish Times* (March 5, 1981); McGuinness, Frank. "Beyond O'Casey: Working-Class Dramatists." *Irish Literary Supplement* 3 (Spring 1984): 35; Mengel, Hagal. " 'What Is the Point of Livin'—On Some Early Plays by Martin Lynch." *Études Irlandaises* 8 (1983): 145–163; Osmond, John. "Clash of Identities: The Ulster Theatre of Graham Reid and Martin Lynch." In *"Standing in Their Shifts Itself . . ." Irish Drama from Farquhar to Friel.* Eberhard Bort, ed. Bremen: European Society for Irish Studies, 1993; Triesman, Susan. "Caught by the Goolies—Susan Triesman Talks with Playwright Martin Lynch." *Theatre Ireland* 4 (1983): 2–5; Zach, Wolfgang. " 'The Troubles' as Reflected in Contemporary Irish Drama." In *Irland: Gesellschaft und Kultur.* Halle: Salle, 1987, pp. 137–149.

LYNCH, PATRICIA [NORA] (1900–1972), writer of children's books. Lynch was born in Cork on June 7, 1900, and was educated in convent schools in Ireland, England, and Belgium. On October 31, 1922, she married R[ichard] M[ichael] Fox, the journalist and historian. Her first book for children, *The Cobbler's Apprentice,* was published in 1932, and she was to publish about fifty more similar volumes. Her books have been greatly popular, translated into many languages, and won a number of awards. The pleasantest among them, perhaps, are the Turf-Cutter's Donkey series of books, the Brogeen the leprechaun series, *Orla of Burren,* and *The Bookshop on the Quay.* However, Lynch preserved such a constant standard of quality, that any such listing is bound to seem arbitrary and personal. She possessed such a supple and lucid prose style, such a keen ability to tell a swiftly moving story, and such a cosy and delightful sense of the pleasures of the home, the hearth, and the table that many of her books have given as much pleasure to adults as they have to children. Her *Storyteller's Holiday* (1947), a somewhat fictionalized recreation of her own girlhood, is perhaps an adult's best general introduction to her work. The first hundred pages before Patricia Nora leaves Ireland are a droll, vivid, almost enchanting recollection of childhood. If one has any reservation about Lynch's underplayed, minor, but genuine talent, it would only be the mild surprise about the extraordinary amount of eating in her books. With Maura Laverty,* she must be one of the most food-obsessed writers in all of Irish literature. She died on September 1, 1972, in Dublin.

JANE CUNNINGHAM

WORKS: *The Green Dragon.* London: Harrap, [1925]; *The Turf-cutter's Donkey.* London & Toronto: Dent/New York: E. P. Dutton, 1935; *The Turf-cutter's Donkey Goes Visiting.* London: Dent, 1935/published in the United States as *The Donkey Goes Visiting.* New York: E. P. Dutton, [1936]. *King of the Tinkers.* London: Dent, 1938; *The Grey Goose of Kilnevin.* London: Dent, [1939]; *Fiddler's Quest.* London: Dent, 1941; *Long Ears.* London: Dent, 1943; *Strangers at the Fair, and Other Stories.* Dublin: Browne & Nolan, [1945]; *Knights of God.* London: Hollis & Carter, [1946]/Chicago: H. Regnery, 1955/London & Sydney: Bodley Head, 1967/New York: Holt, Rinehart & Winston, [1969]; *The Turf-cutter's Donkey Kicks Up His Heels.* Dublin: Browne & Nolan, 1946; *Brogeen of the Stepping Stones.* London: Kerr-Cross, 1947; *The Cobbler's Apprentice.* London: Hollis & Carter, 1947; *A Storyteller's Childhood.* London: Dent, [1947]. (Autobiography); *The Mad O'Haras.* London: Dent, [1948]; *Lisheen at the Valley Farm, and Other Stories.* [Dublin: Gayfield, 1949]; *The Seventh Pig, and Other Irish Fairy Tales.* London: Dent, [1950]. *The Dark Sailor of Youghal.* London: Dent, [1951]; *The Boy at the Swinging Lantern.* London: Dent, [1952]; *Brogeen Follows the Magic Tune.* London: Burke, [1952]; *Grania of Castle O'Hara.* Boston: L. C. Page, [1952]; *Tales of Irish Enchantment.* Dublin: Clonmore & Reynolds, [1952]; *Brogeen and the Green Shoes.* London: Burke, [1953]; *Delia Daly of Galloping Green.* London: Dent, [1953]; *Brogeen and the Bronze Lizard.* London: Burke, [1954]/New York: Macmillan, [1970]; *Orla of Burren.* London: Dent, [1954]; *Brogeen and the Princess of Sheen.* London: Burke, [1955]; *Tinker Boy.* London: Dent, [1955]; *The Bookshop on the Quay.* London: Dent, [1956]; *Brogeen and the Lost Castle.* [London]: Burke, [1956]; *Cobbler's Luck.* London: Burke, [1957]; *Fiona Leaps the Bonfire.* London: Dent, [1957]; *Brogeen and the Black Enchanter.* London: Burke, [1958]; *The Old Black Sea Chest.* London: Dent, [1958]; *Shane Comes to Dublin.* New York: Criterion Books, [1958]; *The Black Goat of Slievemore, and Other Irish Fairy Tales.* London: Dent, [1959]; *Jimmy and the Changeling.* London: Dent, [1959]; *The Runaways.* Oxford: Blackwell, 1959; *The Stone House at Kilgobbin.* [London]: Burke, [1959]; *The Lost Fisherman of Carrigmore.* London: Burke, 1960; *Sally from Cork.* London: Dent. [1960]; *The Longest Way Round.* London: Burke, 1961; *Ryan's Fort.* London: Dent, 1961; *The Golden Caddy.* London: Dent, [1962]; *Brogeen and the Little Wind.* New York: Roy Publishers, [1963]; *Brogeen and the Red Fez.* London: Burke, 1963; *The House by Lough Neagh.* London: Dent, 1963; *Guests at the Beach Tree.* London: Burke, 1964; *Holiday at Rosquin.* London: Dent, [1964]; *The Twisted Key, and Other Stories.* London: Harrap, 1964; *Mona of the Isle.* London: Dent, 1965; *The Kerry Caravan.* London: Dent, 1967.

LYND, ROBERT [WILSON] (1879–1949), essayist and journalist. Lynd, born in Belfast on April 20, 1879, was the son of a Presbyterian minister. He graduated from Queen's College in 1899 (and also received a D.Litt. from there in 1946). In 1901, he went to England and worked on *The Daily Dispatch* in Manchester. Then as a free-lance journalist in London, he shared a studio for a while in Kensington with Paul Henry, the artist. In 1908, he joined the *London Daily News,* became literary editor in 1912, and remained in that position until near the end of his life. His best work was done under the pseudonym of "Y. Y." which he used in *The New Statesman* for a long series of light essays. His popularity in this decreasingly popular genre was immense, and, although he lacked Chesterton's wit and individuality, he wrote with charm, urbanity, and good sense. He was a fervent Irish nationalist and a sound, if unacademic, guide to literature. He published about thirty-five books and collections of his fugitive material, and he died in Hampstead on October 6, 1949.

WORKS: *Irish and English.* London: Francis Griffiths, 1908; *Home Life in Ireland.* London: Mills & Boon, 1909; *Rambles in Ireland.* London: Mills & Boon, 1912; *The Book of This and That.*

London: Mills & Boon, 1915; *If the Germans Conquered England.* Dublin & London: Maunsel, 1917; *Ireland a Nation.* London: Grant Richards, 1919; *The Art of Letters.* London: Unwin, 1920; *The Passion of Labour.* London: G. Bell, 1920; *Books and Authors.* London: Richard Dobden-Sanderson, [1922]/London: Jonathan Cape, 1929; *Solomon in All His Glory.* London: Grant Richards, 1922; *The Sporting Life and Other Trifles.* London: Grant Richards, 1922; *The Blue Lion, and Other Essays.* London: Methuen, 1923; *The Peal of Bells.* London: Methuen, 1924; *The Pleasures of Ignorance.* London: Methuen, 1924; *The Money Box.* London: Methuen, 1925; *The Little Angel.* London: Methuen, 1926; *The Orange Tree.* London: Methuen, 1926; *The Goldfish.* London: Methuen, 1927; *The Green Man.* London: Methuen, 1928; *It's a Fine World.* London: Methuen, 1930; *Rain, Rain, Go to Spain.* London: Methuen, 1931; *An Anthology of Essays,* under the pseudonym of "Y. Y." London: Methuen, 1933; *The Cockleshell.* London: Methuen, 1933; *Both Sides of the Road.* London: Methuen, 1934; *I Tremble to Think.* London: Dent, 1936; *Searchlights and Nightingales.* London: Dent, 1939; *Life's Little Oddities.* London: Dent, 1941; *Things One Hears.* London: Dent, 1945; *Essays on Life and Literature.* London: Dent/New York: E. P. Dutton, 1951; *Books and Writers.* London: Dent, 1952; *Galway of the Races: Selected Essays.* Sean McMahon, ed. Dublin: Lilliput, 1990. REFERENCE: Trager, Hildegard. "Der moderne englische literarische Essay: eine Studie zur Geschichte und Theorie der Gattung." Diss., Wurzburg, 1982.

LYONS, GENEVIEVE (twentieth century–), novelist. Born and educated in Dublin, Lyons became a successful actress and was a founder member of the Globe Theatre. Leaving acting to raise a family, she turned to writing and has published a number of popular novels. Several of them center around a fictional estate in Wicklow, Slievelea, where the lives of four generations of an Irish family are drawn. The multigenerational novel was also the format for *The Palucci Vendetta* (1991). The Palucci family originated in Italy and spread to America. After encounters with both the American and Italian Mafia, they returned to Europe and Britain, as family members married into wealth and aristocracy. Essentially a romance novelist, Lyons is a master of the genre, as the sales of her books affirm.

JEAN FRANKS

WORKS: *Slievelea.* London: Macdonald, 1986; *Green Years.* London: Macdonald, 1987; *The Last Inheritor.* New York: Doubleday, 1987; *Dark Rosaleen.* London: Macdonald, 1988; *House Divided.* London: Macdonald, 1989; *Zara.* London: Macdonald, 1991; *The Palucci Vendetta.* London: Macdonald, 1991; *Summer in Dramore.* London: Little, Brown, 1992; *Foul Appetite.* [London]: Little, Brown, [1994].

LYONS, J[OHN] B[ENINGNUS] (1922–), biographer, critic, and novelist. Lyons was born on July 22, 1922, in Kilkelly, County Mayo. A doctor of medicine, he attended the Medical School of University College, Dublin, and did postgraduate work in London and Manchester. From 1955 to 1987, he was consultant physician at St. Michael's Hospital in Dun Laoghaire, and since 1975 he has been professor of the history of medicine to the Royal College of Surgeons in Ireland. After three pseudonymous early novels, he has written prolifically on Irish medical history and on medicine and literature. His most significant literary books are sound and searching biographies of Oliver St. John Gogarty* and Thomas Kettle,* but he has made, from his physician's point of view, important contributions to James Joyce* studies.

PRINCIPAL LITERARY WORKS: *James Joyce and Medicine.* Dublin: Dolmen, [1973]; *Oliver St. John Gogarty.* Lewisburg, Pa.: Bucknell University Press, 1976; *The Mystery of Oliver Goldsmith's Medical Degree.* Blackrock, Co. Dublin: Carraig Books, 1978. (Pamphlet); *Oliver St. John Gogarty: The Man of Many Talents.* Dublin: Blackwater, [1980]; *The Enigma of Tom Kettle: Irish Patriot, Essayist, Poet, British Soldier, 1880–1916.* Dublin: Glendale, 1983; *Scholar and Sceptic: The Career of James Henry M. D., 1798–1976.* Dublin: Glendale, 1985. (Monograph); *Thrust Syphilis down to Hell and Other Rejoyceana: Studies in the Border-lands of Literature and Medicine.* Dun Laoghaire, Co. Dublin: Glendale, 1987; *What Did I Die Of?: The Deaths of Parnell, Wilde, Synge, and Other Literary Pathologies.* Dublin: Lilliput, 1991; *William Henry Drummond: Poet in Patois.* [Markham, Ontario]: Fitzhenry & Whiteside, 1994. Novels, as Michael Fitzwillian: *A Question of Surgery.* London: Jarrolds, 1960; *South Downs General Hospital.* London: Jarrolds, 1961; *When Doctors Differ.* London: Jarrolds, 1963/republished as *A Matter of Medicine.* London: Arrow, 1965.

LYRIC PLAYERS THEATRE, THE (1951–   ). Belfast's Lyric Players Theatre was inaugurated in 1951 in the drawing room of Mary O'Malley and her husband Dr. Pearse O'Malley in Lisburn Road. The initial productions were three poetic plays by Yeats,* Robert Farren,* and Austin Clarke.* For the first sixteen years or so of its existence, the theatre produced mainly plays which were either in verse or at least rich in language. In 1952, the O'Malleys moved to Derryvolgie Avenue and erected a tiny stage at the back of their house. There, for the next sixteen years, was presented an astonishing repertoire of about 180 plays, including all of Yeats' plays, as well as Irish work by Synge,* Shaw,* O'Casey,* Lady Gregory,* Denis Johnston,* Donagh MacDonagh,* Valentin Iremonger,* Samuel Beckett,* Brian Friel,* Eugene McCabe,* and others. These Irish pieces were intermingled with plays from world drama by Aristophanes, Euripides, Shakespeare, Schiller, Ibsen, Chekhov, Lorca, O'Neill, Eliot, Fry, Brecht, and others. Meticulous attention was paid to staging; Yeats himself would have approved of Mrs. O'Malley's principle that "Scenery and costumes are simple and nonrealistic, and each play is designed to a narrow colour-scheme . . . expressive of its particular atmosphere." At the same time, the theatre branched out into other areas of the arts: it held art exhibitions and sponsored lectures, recitals, and even a drama school.

One of the finest byproducts of the theatre was its literary magazine, *Threshold,* which began as a quarterly on February 1957 and was edited by Mrs. O'Malley until 1961. Thereafter, it has appeared much more intermittently under the changing editorship of various writers such as Roy McFadden,* Seamus Heaney,* John Montague,* John Boyd,* and Patrick Galvin.* The magazine has published many of the significant contemporary Irish writers, both North and South, and is particularly notable for its twenty-first number, which was a fine collection of Ulster writing. Also of special interest were its twenty-seventh number, which was devoted to three new plays by Patrick Galvin, and its twenty-eighth number, which focused on Forrest Reid.*

In 1960, the group became a nonprofit association and opened a drive for funds to build a real theatre. The cornerstone was laid for that theatre in 1965, and the theatre, seating three hundred, opened on October 26, 1968. Despite the

Northern Troubles and Mrs. O'Malley's withdrawal in 1976, the theater has continued to function and now receives a substantial subsidy from the Northern Arts Council. The theater's accomplishments and problems were well summed up by Conor O'Malley:

For the best part of thirty years this movement prospered and brought to life dozens of classic plays—a breadth and consistency of activity perhaps unrivalled in this island. Astonishing too was the fact that this movement occurred in a community constricted at every turn by one of the most restrictive social and political environments in Western Europe. The other intriguing aspect was the relative failure of this movement to find written expression. The virtual absence of new plays of quality appears incongruous in the light of other successes.

Nevertheless, the theater was particularly successful with its 1975 production of Patrick Galvin's* *We Do It for Love,* which was seen by over 20,000 people. More recently, the theater has staged new work by John Boyd, Martin Boylan,* Wilson John Haire,* Martin Lynch,* Graham Reid,* and Christina Reid.* Other productions, such as *Annie, Hello Dolly,* and *Jesus Christ Superstar,* were mounted simply to fill seats.

REFERENCES: Bell, Sam Hanna. *The Theatre in Ulster.* Dublin: Gill & Macmillan, 1972; O'Malley, Conor. *A Poets' Theatre.* [Dublin: Elo, 1988]; O'Malley, Mary. *Never Shake Hands with the Devil.* Dublin: [Elo], 1990.

LYSAGHT, EDWARD (1763–ca. 1810), poet. Lysaght was born at Brickhill, County Clare, on December 21, 1763, and was educated at Trinity College, Dublin, and at Oxford. He practiced law without much success in London, but then returned to Dublin where he was for a while quite successful at law and where he spent the last thirteen years of his life. He was engaged in Irish politics and strongly opposed the Act of Union, but was even better known as a wit and *bon vivant* than as a barrister and politician. He died impoverished, but was so popular that a subscription of more than £2000 was collected for his wife and family. In 1909, a Dublin newspaper gave the date of his death as February 28, 1809, but it seems more likely that he died in 1810 or even 1811.

Lysaght was a rhymester rather than a poet, and much of his work seems dashed off to delight a drawing room rather than to impress posterity. As such, his poor work is always better than vile, and his good work is so extremely deft that he was credited with writing a number of popular pieces that he probably did not—such as "The Rakes of Mallow," "Donnybrook Fair," and "Kitty of Coleraine." The last stanza of his "My Ambition" is nicely droll; his satiric "A Prospect" on the Act of Union contains one verse worthy of Swift*; and his poem on Grattan,* "The Man Who Led the Van of Irish Volunteers," is a rousing good public piece with a rattling meter and a complex and charming pattern of internal rhyme and rhyme. Perhaps the first stanza of his "Sweet Chloe" might stand as an example of how deft a technician he was:

Sweet Chloe advised me, in accents divine,
   The joys of the bowl to surrender;
Nor lose, in the turbid excesses of wine,
   Delights more ecstatic and tender;
She bade me no longer in vineyards to bask,
Or stagger, at orgies, the dupe of a flask,
For the sigh of a sot's but the scent of the cask,
   And a bubble the bliss of the bottle.

He was the godfather of Sydney Owenson, Lady Morgan.*

WORK: *Poems.* Dublin: Gilbert & Hodges, 1811.

LYSAGHT, S[IDNEY] R[OYSE] (ca. 1860–1941), novelist and man of letters. Lysaght was born near Mallow, County Cork, probably in the early 1860s. A good deal of his early life can be inferred from his autobiographical novel, *My Tower in Desmond* (1925). Like the novel's hero, Lysaght went into business and devoted the greater part of his life to the South Wales iron firm of John Lysaght, Ltd. Despite his apparent success in business, Lysaght's real interest was letters, and he managed to write a good deal, most of it with considerable fluency. His finest work is *My Tower in Desmond,* which has some effective evocation of place, particularly in the early sections. A somewhat romantic novel, nevertheless it is absorbing for its story and interesting for its rather dissociated view of the Irish Troubles. Lysaght's poetry is conventional and Edwardian without being memorable or striking, and his sympathies were thoroughly antimodern. In one uncharacteristically irascible passage in his poetic testament, "A Reading of Poetry," he roasts Pound, Eliot, the Sitwells, and Gertrude Stein ("a pure humbug"), and then concludes, "God help those who mistake the eruptive cacophony of Mr. James Joyce* for poetry." That essay appears in a collection called *A Reading of Life* (1936), in which much gracefully expressed love of beauty and faith in God walk hand in hand with the most appallingly reactionary remarks about racial inequality. Lysaght's other interesting volume is an unstageable 320-page play, entitled *The Immortal Jew* (1931). The interior monologues are written in bland verse, but the prose dialogues rise to some passages of real power. Lysaght died at Hazlewood, Mallow, County Cork, on August 20, 1941.

WORKS: *A Modern Ideal, a Dramatic Poem.* London: Kegan Paul, Trench, 1886; *The Marplot.* New York & London: Macmillan, 1893. (Novel); *One of the Grenvilles.* London: Macmillan, 1899. (Novel); *Poems of the Unknown Way.* London: Macmillan, 1901. *Her Majesty's Rebels.* London & New York: Macmillan, 1907. (Novel); *Horizons and Landmarks.* London: Macmillan, 1911. (Poems); *My Tower in Desmond.* New York: Macmillan, 1925. *The Immortal Jew.* London: Macmillan, 1931. (Closet drama); *A Reading of Poetry; an Essay.* London: Macmillan, 1934. *A Reading of Life.* London & New York: Macmillan, 1936.

LYSAGHT, SEAN

WORK: *The Clare Island Survey.* [Oldcastle, Co. Meath]: Gallery, [1991]. (Poetry).

ISBN 0-313-30175-1

90000>

EAN

9 780313 301759

HARDCOVER BAR CODE